新疆维吾尔自治区统计局·编
Compiled by Statistics Bureau of Xinjiang Uygur Autonomous Region

新疆统计年鉴

XINJIANG STATISTICAL YEARBOOK

2011

U0913580

中国统计出版社
China Statistics Press

(京)新登字 041 号

© 中国统计出版社。

版权所有。未经许可,本书的任何部分不得以任何方式在世界任何地区以任何文字翻印、拷贝、仿制或转载。

Copyright © CHINA STATISTICS PRESS

All rights reserved. No part of the publication may be reproduced or transmitted in any form or by any means, electronic or mechanical, including photocopying, recording, or by any information storage and retrieval system, without written permission from the publisher.

图书在版编目(CIP)数据

新疆统计年鉴. 2011:汉英对照 / 新疆维吾尔自治区统计局编.—北京:中国统计出版社, 2011.8

ISBN 978-7-5037-6317-5

Ⅰ.①新… Ⅱ.①新… Ⅲ.①统计资料—新疆—2011—年鉴—汉、英 Ⅳ.①C832.45-54

中国版本图书馆 CIP 数据核字(2011)第 164257 号

新疆统计年鉴—2011

作　　者 / 新疆维吾尔自治区统计局
责任编辑 / 佘竞雄　王立群
执行编辑 / 仲　玲
封面设计 / 黄永中
出版发行 / 中国统计出版社
通信地址 / 北京市西城区月坛南街 57 号
邮　　编 / 100826
办公地址 / 北京市丰台区西三环南路甲 6 号
电　　话 / (010)63376907
E-mail　 / yearbook@gj.stats.cn
印　　刷 / 新疆统计印刷厂
经　　销 / 新华书店
开　　本 / 890 × 1240 毫米　1/16
字　　数 / 1600 千字
印　　张 / 42.5
版　　别 / 2011 年 8 月第 1 版
版　　次 / 2011 年 8 月第 1 次印刷
书　　号 / ISBN 978-7-5037-6317-5/C·2537
定　　价 / 360.00 元(含光盘)

中国统计版图书,版权所有,侵权必究。
中国统计版图书,如有印装错误,本社发行部负责调换。

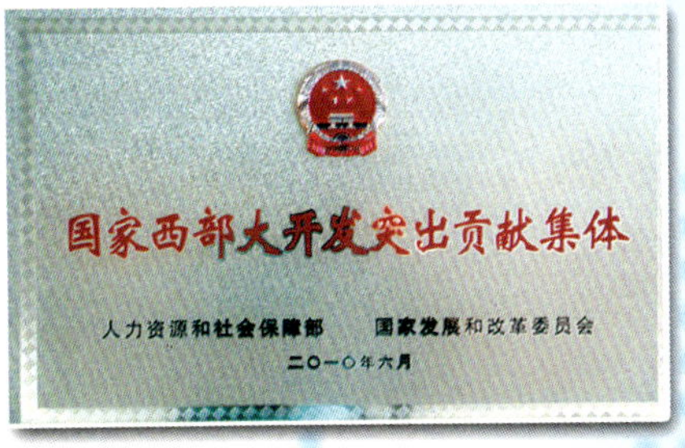

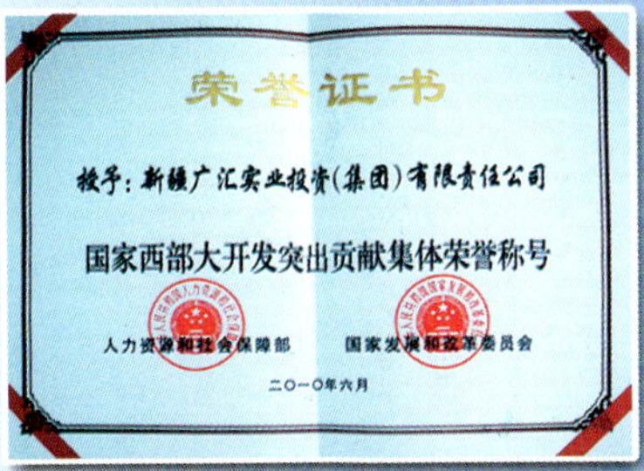

广汇米东汽车城奠基仪式

广汇时代广场项目全景

广汇飞虎男篮多次刷新新疆篮球历史记录，为新疆人民争得了荣誉，并受到自治区、乌鲁木齐市党政领导的亲切接见和表彰

广汇汽车股份公司代表队勇夺 2010 年度奥迪专业双杯竞赛全球总决赛服务杯第一名，为中国汽车服务业争得了荣誉

孙广信获得“领跑 LEAD2010 第四届风尚之巅年度十大风云人物奖”“领跑 LEAD2010 第四届风尚之巅年度十大区域经济贡献卓越企业家”

广汇房产置业在新疆乌鲁木齐的地标建筑，西北第一高楼广汇中天广场

西南地区最具影响力的综合汽车销售和售后服务市场——广汇中汽西南汽博中心

《新疆统计年鉴—2011》特邀编委

（排名不分先后）

新疆维吾尔自治区人民检察院	杨肇季　哈木斯·马木提
新疆维吾尔自治区经济和信息化委员会	贺晓江
新疆维吾尔自治区文化厅	阿不力孜·阿不都热依木
新疆维吾尔自治区国土资源厅	田建荣　马傲·赛依提哈木扎
新疆维吾尔自治区交通运输厅	王新华
新疆维吾尔自治区民委(宗教局)	刘振强　吐尔干·皮大
新疆维吾尔自治区信息中心	赵若平
新疆维吾尔自治区道路运输管理局	任存新
新疆维吾尔自治区金融工作办公室	王会民
新疆维吾尔自治区奶业办公室	齐新林
乌鲁木齐市水磨沟区委员会宣传部	韩惠敏
新疆维吾尔自治区塔里木河流域和田管理局	阿地里江·奴尔买买提
伊犁哈萨克自治州人民政府	毛肯·赛提哈木扎
伊犁哈萨克自治州伊宁市人民政府	李宁平
伊犁哈萨克自治州霍城县人民政府	扎克·左尔东
伊犁哈萨克自治州特克斯县人民政府	克孜尔开勒迪·阿布迪腊合曼
伊犁哈萨克自治州昭苏县人民政府	叶力夏提·吐尔逊拜
伊犁哈萨克自治州察布查尔锡伯自治县人民政府	王春光
塔城地区和布克赛尔蒙古自治县人民政府办公室	薛俊强　拉格瓦·才布格加甫
博尔塔拉蒙古自治州精河县人民政府	陈洪　艾斯尔江
博尔塔拉蒙古自治州温泉委员会	刘　强　阿　里
巴音郭楞蒙古自治州轮台县委员会	张正荣　吐逊·肉孜
克拉玛依市乌尔禾区委员会	魏天峰
新疆油田公司社会保险管理中心	贺　保
阿克苏地区行政公署	鲁晓忠
阿克苏地区库车县委员会	高克平　玉素甫江·买买提
哈密地区伊吾县委员会、人民政府	王跃兵　艾尼瓦尔·阿不列孜
哈密地区巴里坤县人民政府	陈毅士　叶尔江·胡斯满
喀什地区麦盖提县委员会	王胜平　阿布都艾尼·居买
喀什地区叶城县人民政府	李国平　司马义·阿都色力木
喀什地区莎车县人民政府	何利民　艾海提·沙依提
喀什地区伽师县人民政府	朱雪冰　尼亚孜·阿西木
喀什地区发展和改革委员会	李　阳
克孜勒苏柯尔克孜自治州阿图什市人民政府	刘军海　库尔班江·艾山
克孜勒苏柯尔克孜自治州乌什县人民政府	申海涛　吐尔洪·阿布拉
和田地区皮山县委员会	何成钢　艾斯喀尔·卡斯木
和田地区洛浦县人民政府	杨渭锋　阿力甫·阿不都力米提
新疆生产建设兵团农一师幸福城农场	武琳琳　王天昊
新疆生产建设兵团农十三师黄田农场	张世全
新疆维吾尔自治区塔里木大学	王合理
新疆维吾尔自治区伊斯兰教经学院	吾甫尔·热西提
新疆维吾尔自治区幼儿师范学院	罗　峰
巴音郭楞蒙古自治州第二中学	邢耀华
阿克苏地区第一中学	曹尔慧　阿不都克热木·伊迪热斯
新疆博乐农五师医院	苏怡茜
新疆广汇实业投资(集团)有限责任公司	孙广信
中国石油独山子石化公司	麦麦提·伊力
中国银联股份有限公司新疆分公司	苏长雄
中国移动通信集团新疆有限公司	白志刚
新疆金特钢铁股份有限公司	程爱民
新疆大明矿业集团股份有限公司	许　明
新疆好家乡超市有限公司	许　平
伊犁肖尔布拉克酒业公司	王天兵
喀什冠维房地产开发有限公司	杨光玉

《新疆统计年鉴—2011》编辑委员会

名誉主任　努尔·白克力

名誉副主任　黄　卫

主　　任　王忠山　余晓明

副 主 任　阿不拉·玉素甫　郜存峰　王　跃　冯　力
李仁玮　鲁协平

编　　委　（按姓氏笔划为序）
王　绚　王玉仓　边东风　刘莉萍　吕　乐　阿里木
张　凡　张德欢　李　进　陈振军　陈　强　金建新
胡晓燕　热孜万　郝俊清　蒋岳衡　韩永贵　廖　琳

主　　编　金建新

副 主 编　周　迎　吴　伟　王　瑛　仲　玲

责任编辑　佘竞雄　王立群

编　　辑　（按姓氏笔划为序）
马晓东　王　焱　王红艳　古丽娜孜　布海丽且木　叶钟玲
石雪梅　吉　岩　刘　镭　刘子淇　吐尔逊古丽　米合拉依
李　红　杨淑芳　杨　磊　肖开提　肖热提　阿依早热
阿达来提　孟　凯　易　滨　贺晓敏　热比古丽　袁　英
高卫红　盛玮玲　褚黎君　雷　敏

英文翻译　孟晓娴

光盘开发　王立群　仲　玲

排　　版　白云风

发行总监　赵玉西

编　　务　比利克孜·依麻木　刘　峻　孙亚婷　包银花

XINJIANG STATISTICAL YEARBOOK-2011
NAME LIST OF EDITORIAL BOARD

Honorary Director: *Nuer Baikeli*

Honorary Vice: *Huang Wei*

Director: *Wang Zhongshan Yu Xiaoming*

Vice-directors: *Abla Yusuf Gao Cunfeng Wang Yue Feng Li*
Li Renwei Lu Xiepin

Members of Editorial Board: (*Sequence is based on Chinese surname stroke*)
Wang Xuan Wang Yucang Bian Dongfeng Liu Lipin Lu Le
Alimu Zhang Fan Zhang Dehuan Li Jin Chen Zhenjun
Chen Qiang Jin Jianxin Hu Xiaoyan Rziwan Hao Junqing
Jiang Yueheng Han Yonggui Liao Lin

Liao LinChief-Editor: *Jin Jianxin*

Deputy Chief-Editors: *Zhou Ying Wu Wei Wang Ying Zhong Ling*

Responsible Editor: *She Jingxiong Wang Liqun*

Editors: (*Sequence is based on Chinese surname character stroke*)
Ma Xiaodong Wang Yan Wang Hongyan Gulinazi Buhailiqiemu
Ye Zhonglin Shi Xuemei Ji Yan Liu Lei Liu Ziqi Tuerxunguli
Mihelayi Li Hong Yang Shufang Yang Lei Xiaokaiti Xiaoreti
Ayizaore Adalaiti Meng Kai Yi Bin He Xiaomin Rebiguli
Yuan Ying Gao Weihong Sheng Weiling Chu Lijun Lei Min

English Proofreader and preface translator: *Meng Xiaoxian*

Developer of CD-ROM Software: *Wang Liqun Zhong Ling*

Typesetters: *Bai Yunfeng*

Supervisor of Publication: *Zhao Yuxi*

Members of Editing Affair: *Bilikiz Imam Liu Jun Sun Yating Bao Yinhua*

编者说明

一、《新疆统计年鉴—2011》(中英文对照)，是一部信息高度密集的统计资料书。本书收录了2010年新疆经济、社会等各方面的统计数据，以及重要历史年份和改革开放三十多年来的主要统计数据，是一部全面反映新疆经济和社会发展情况的资料性年刊。

二、全书内容分为：特载（新疆维吾尔自治区2010年国民经济和社会发展统计公报）；综合；国民经济核算；人口与就业；固定资产投资；对外经济贸易和旅游；能源生产和消费；财政、金融和保险；物价指数；人民生活和社会保障；城市概况；自然资源和环境保护；农业；工业；建筑业；运输和邮电；批发和零售、住宿和餐饮业；教育、科技和文化；体育、卫生及其他；各地州、市主要经济指标排序；附录（各省、市、区主要经济指标排序）等，各篇末均附有《主要统计指标解释》。

三、与2010年版《新疆统计年鉴》相比较，在统计内容和编辑上主要做了如下修订：

1、章节顺序进行了调整。

2、2010 年进行全国第六次人口普查，人口数据目前国家还未全部反馈，为此人口与就业卷中的人口部分仅保留了国家已反馈数据的表格。

四、资料中所使用的计算单位均采用国家法定计量单位。

五、本《年鉴》总量指标计算所采用的价格均为现行价格。

六、本《年鉴》伊犁哈萨克自治州的数据包括伊犁州直属县（市）、塔城地区和阿勒泰地区。

七、本《年鉴》使用符号说明：

“#”表示其中项；

“...”表示不足小数位的数据；

“空”表示没有或未掌握该指标数据。

八、本《年鉴》在编辑过程中得到自治区内外许多单位和同志们的大力支持，在此深表谢意。限于我们的水平，加之时间仓促，不足之处，敬请各级领导、各界人士和统计战线的同仁批评指正。

Editor’s Explanatory Notes

Ⅰ. *Xinjiang Statistical Yearbook-2011* (in both Chinese and English) is an annual statistic publication of comprehensive information with highly density. The yearbook covers very comprehensive data in 2010 and some selected data series in important years and the data since reform and opening of Xinjiang,reflects various aspects of Xinjiang’s social and economic development.

Ⅱ. The yearbook comprises such sections as: Special Article (Statistical Communique on National Economy and Social Development of Xinjiang Uygur Autonomous Region in the year 2010); general survey; national accounts; population and employment; investment in fixed assets; government finance,financial intermediation and insurance;price indices;people’s livelihood and social security;general survey of cities;natural resources and environment protection; agriculture; industry; construction; transport, post and telecommunication services; wholesale & retail trades, hotels and catering services; production and consumption of energy;foreign trade & economic cooperation and tourism;education,science & technology and culture;sports,public health and others; ranking of main economic indicators by region of Xinjiang; appendix (ranking of main economic indicators by region),etc.Each section is equipped with Explanatory Notes on Main Statistical Indicators at the end.

Ⅲ. Compared with the *Xinjiang Statistical Yearbook 2010*,some changes are made in contents and in editing mode, including the following:

1) The section pertaining were adjusted.

2) 2010 in the sixth all-china population census, according to the present state it is not all the feedback, population and employment in only part of the population of the country has feedback form.

Ⅳ.The units of measurement used in this yearbook are internationally standard measurement units.

Ⅴ. The computation of all the indicators in the yearbook is equipped with current prices.

Ⅵ. The data about Ili Kazak Autonomous Prefecture in the present Xinjiang Statistical Yearbook covers counties (cities) direct under Ili Prefecture, Tacheng Prefecture and Altay Prefecture.

Ⅶ. Description of signs or symbols in the yearbook:

“#”stands for interim item; “...” for data with insufficient decimal place; “blank” for absence of data indicators or ignorance of them.

Ⅷ. In the course of complication, the yearbook has received great support from many units and comrades in and out of Autonomous Region, we acknowledge their help to the book. Mistakes and faults are inevitable to take place for inadequate proficiency and limited time. Leaders, personnel from all walks of life and colleagues from statistical sector are welcome to make their critical comments and suggestions.

目 录 CONTENTS

第一篇 综 合

CHAPTER 1 GENERAL SURVEY

第 二 篇 国民经济核算

CHAPTER 2 NATIONAL ACCOUNTS

第三篇 人口与就业

CHAPTER 3 POPULATION AND EMPLOYMENT

第 四 篇 固定资产投资

CHAPTER 4 INVESTMENT IN FIXED ASSETS

第 五 篇 对外经济贸易和旅游

CHAPTER 5 FOREIGN TRADE & ECONOMIC COOPERATION AND TOURISM

第 六 篇 能源生产和消费

CHAPTER 6 PRODUCTION AND CONSUMPTION OF ENERGY

第 七 篇 财政、金融、保险

CHAPTER 7 GOVERNMENT FINANCE, FINANCIAL INTERMEDIATION AND INSURANCE

第 八 篇　物价指数

CHAPTER 8 PRICE INDICES

第 九 篇 人民生活和社会保障

CHAPTER 9 PEOPLE'S LIVELIHOOD AND SOCIAL SECURITY

第 十 篇 城市概况

CHAPTER 10 GENERAL SURVEY OF CITIES

第 十一 篇 自然资源和环境保护

CHAPTER 11 NATURAL RESOURCES AND ENVIRONMENT PROTECTION

第十二篇 农业

CHAPTER 12 AGRICULTURE

第十三篇 工 业

CHAPTER 13 INDUSTRY

第十四篇 建筑业

CHAPTER 14 CONSTRUCTION

第十五篇 运输和邮电

CHAPTER 15 TRANSPORT, POSTAL AND TELECOMMUNICATION SERVICES

第十六篇 批发和零售业、住宿和餐饮业

CHAPTER 16 WHOLESALE & RETAIL TRADES, HOTELS AND CATERING SERVICES

第 十七 篇　教育、科技和文化

CHAPTER 17 EDUCATION, SCIENCE & TECHNOLOGY AND CULTURE

第十八篇 体育、卫生及其他

CHAPTER 18 SPORTS, PUBLIC HEALTH AND OTHERS

第 十九 篇　各地州市主要经济指标排序

CHAPTER 19 RANKING OF MAIN ECONOMIC INDICATORS BY REGION OF XINJIANG

附录：各省市区主要经济指标排序

APPENDIX: RANKING OF MAIN ECONOMIC INDICATORS BY REGION

特　载

Special Article

新疆统计年鉴

XINJIANG STATISTICAL YEARBOOK 2011

新疆维吾尔自治区
2010年国民经济和社会发展
统 计 公 报

2010年，自治区党委、人民政府带领全区各族人民，以科学发展观为统领，认真贯彻落实中央新疆工作座谈会和自治区党委七届九次、十次全委（扩大）会议精神，解放思想，凝聚力量，抢抓机遇，扎实工作，综合经济实力迈上新台阶，发展质量进一步提升，民生得到持续改善，各项社会事业全面进步。

一、综　合

初步核算，全年实现生产总值（GDP）5437.47亿元，比上年增加1160.42亿元，首次突破5000亿元大关。按可比价格计算，比上年增长10.6%，其中，第一产业增加值1078.63亿元，增长4.5%；第二产业增加值2592.15亿元，增长12.6%；第三产业增加值1766.69亿元，增长10.8%。三次产业比例为19.8∶47.7∶32.5。

人均生产总值25057元，按可比价格计算，增长9.3%，以当年平均汇率折算，人均3702美元，首次突破人均3000美元大关。

居民消费价格比上年上涨4.3%，其中，食品价格上涨10.7%，居住价格上涨2.7%。服务项目价格上涨1.5%。

表1　2010年居民消费价格比上年涨跌幅度

指　　标	涨跌幅度（%）
居民消费价格	4.3
城　市	3.6
农　村	5.8
食　品	10.7
#粮　食	8.9
肉禽及其制品	13.0
油　脂	7.6
蛋　类	12.3
水产品	7.4
烟酒及用品	2.0
衣　着	-0.8
家庭设备用品及服务	1.2
医疗保健和个人用品	2.0
交通和通信	持平
娱乐教育文化用品及服务	1.2
居　住	2.7
水、电、燃料	2.5
租　房	3.3
建房及装饰材料	3.5

工业品出厂价格上涨25.3%，其中，轻工业上涨8.9%，重工业上涨28.7%。原材料、燃料、动力购进价格上涨23.9%。农业生产资料价格上涨3.1%。固定资产投资价格上涨4.6%。

二、农　业

农林牧渔业总产值1846.18亿元，按可比价格计算，比上年增长4.9%，其中，农业产值1376.89亿元，增长4.7%；林业产值35.27亿元，增长6.4%；畜牧业产值375.79亿元，增长5.1%；渔业产值12.67亿元，增长5.5%；农林牧渔服务业产值45.57亿元，增长6.1%。

农作物播种面积475.86万公顷，增长1.0%，其中，粮食播种面积199.16万公顷，下降0.1%；棉花播种面积146.06万公顷，增长3.6%；油料播种面积27.34万公顷，增长1.2%；甜菜播种面积7.53万公顷，增长18.1%；蔬菜播种面积30.36万公顷，增长15.8%。

全年粮食产量1150.20万吨，下降0.2%。棉花产量247.90万吨，下降1.8%。油料产量66.62万吨，增长4.2%。甜菜产量486.97万吨，增长16.4%。蔬菜产量1734.40万吨，增长25.4%。水果（含果用瓜）产量1028.85万吨，下降2.6%，其中，园林水果593.85万吨，增长5.1%。

年末牲畜存栏3722.12万头(只)，下降3.2%；全年牲畜出栏3498.52万头（只），增长25.9%。肉类总产量121.74万吨，增长5.6%，其中，羊肉产量46.95万吨，增长7.3%；牛肉产量35.47万吨，增长4.7%；猪肉产量23.05万吨，增长4.6%。牛奶产量128.60万吨，增长6.4%。绵羊毛产量8.40万吨，增长17.3%。水产品产量10.11万吨，增长11.4%。

年末农业机械总动力1642.93万千瓦，增长9.3%。拥有大中型拖拉机25.38万台，增长16.5%。小型拖拉机36.12万台，下降2.7%。化肥施用量（折纯）167.57万吨，增长7.2%。农村用电量64.29亿千瓦时，增长9.0%。

三、工业和建筑业

全部工业增加值2161.39亿元，按可比价格计算，比上年增长13.5%。

表2　2010年工业主要产品产量及增速

产品名称	单　位	产　量	比上年增长%
原　煤	万吨	9935.73	12.7
原　油	万吨	2558.16	1.8
天然气	亿立方米	249.91	1.8
原油加工量	万吨	2190.37	17.5
乙　烯	万吨	119.33	1.4倍
发电量	亿千瓦时	679.33	18.9
成品糖	万吨	45.10	10.6
卷　烟	亿支	150.00	11.1
罐　头	万吨	110.63	-8.1
纱	万吨	41.58	7.7
布	亿米	1.51	-0.5
机制纸及纸板	万吨	37.10	4.3
化肥(折100%)	万吨	159.10	持平
粗　钢	万吨	825.54	26.4
钢　材	万吨	892.04	29.1
生　铁	万吨	941.12	23.1
水　泥	万吨	2400.96	17.1
变压器	万千伏安	3582.94	37.2

规模以上工业增加值增长13.6%，其中，轻工业增长14.9%，重工业增长13.0%。在自治区重点监测的十大产业中，煤炭工业增长11.1%；石油工业增长6.7%；钢铁工业增长30.7%，有色工业增长10.4%；纺织工业增长6.5%；化学工业增长43.4%；电力工业增长18.8%；汽车工业增长38.3%；装备制造工业增长31.0%；农副食品加工工业增长16.2%。

规模以上工业产品销售率97.9%，比上年提高2.3个百分点，其中，轻工业94.3%，比上年提高1.4个百分点；重工业98.4%，比上年提高2.5个百分点。出口交货值54.19亿元，增长37.2%。实现利润总额852.43亿元，增长75.9%。亏损企业亏损额60.42亿元，增长3.5%。

全社会建筑业增加值430.76亿元，按可比价格计算，比上年增长7.9%。具有资质等级的总承包和专业承包建筑企业总产值969.47亿元，增长12.7%。

四、固定资产投资

全社会固定资产投资3539.69亿元，比上年增长25.2%。按城乡划分，城镇投资3181.58亿元，增长25.5%；农村投资358.11亿元，增长22.9%。

按三次产业划分，第一产业投资211.43亿元，增长22.7%；第二产业投资1667.06亿元，增长28.7%；第三产业投资1661.20亿元，增长22.2%。在第二产业中，工业投资1625.79亿元，增长28.4%，其中，制造业投资620.37亿元，增长37.5%。

房地产开发投资347.72亿元，增长47.4%。房屋施工面积3980.80万平方米，增长29.9%；竣工面积1012.90万平方米，下降1.9%。商品房销售面积1564.90万平方米，增长11.3%；销售额483.04亿元，增长31.9%。

五、国内贸易

社会消费品零售总额1324.48亿元，比上年增长17.1%，扣除物价上涨因素，实际增长12.0%。

按城乡划分，城镇零售额1181.26亿元，增长17.4%；乡村零售额143.21亿元，增长14.9%。按行业划分，批发和零售业零售额1156.62亿元，增长16.7%；住宿和餐饮业零售额167.85亿元，增长20.5%。

六、对外经济

全年货物进出口总额171.28亿美元，比上年增长23.9%，其中，出口129.70亿美元，增长19.8%；进口41.59亿美元，增长38.4%。

新批准设立外商直接投资企业51个，比上年增长18.6%。合同使用外商直接投资项目59个，增长7.3%；实际利用外商直接投资2.37亿美元，增长10.1%。

表3　2010年货物进出口总额及增速

单位：亿美元

指　标	绝对数	比上年增长（%）
货物进出口总额	171.28	23.9
货物出口额	129.70	19.8
其中：一般贸易	20.89	24.3
加工贸易	3.04	-5.6
边境小额贸易	76.75	1.8
其中：机电产品	22.20	24.9
高新技术产品	1.07	21.1
货物进口额	41.59	38.4
其中：一般贸易	15.46	20.1
加工贸易	0.23	-8.0
边境小额贸易	23.67	50.4
其中：机电产品	7.00	-3.3
高新技术产品	2.95	8.9

七、交通、邮电和旅游

铁路完成货运量6853.00万吨，比上年增长6.9%；公路50448万吨，增长7.8%；民航3.7万吨，下降2.6%。铁路完成客运量1523万人，增长11.1%；公路44333万人，增长6.6%；民航490万人，增长12.6%。

年末铁路营业里程4393公里，增长14.5%；民航通航里程17.70万公里，增长16.1%；公路里程15.28万公里，增长1.4%。

年末民用汽车保有量135.9万辆（包括三轮车和低速货车），增长22.8%，其中，私人汽车85.8万辆，增长31.6%。

邮电业务总量582.05亿元，比上年增长21.3%，其中，邮政业务总量16.58亿元，增长24.2%；电信业务总量565.47亿元，增长21.3%。固定电话用户547.50万户，下降4.5%，固定电话普及率每百人25.4部；移动电话用户1359.80万户，增长21.5%，移动电话普及率每百人63.0部；互联网用户161.10万户，增长20.5%。

全年接待国际旅游人数101.03万人次，比上年增长43.2%；国际旅游外汇收入3.68亿美元，增长40.8%。接待国内旅游人数3038万人次，增长44.8%；国内旅游收入281.13亿元，增长59.1%。

八、财政和金融

地方财政收入693.27亿元，增长40.6%。地方财政一般预算收入500.58亿元，增长28.8%，其中，各项税收收入416.23亿元，增长38.2%。在税收收入中，国内增值税75.31亿元，增长30.7%；营业税151.27亿元，增长34.6%；资源税32.47亿元，增长1.6倍。

地方财政支出1885.56亿元，增长27.9% 。地方财政一般预算支出1698.91亿元，增长26.1%，其中，教育支出313.84亿元，增长30.8%；医疗卫生支出103.56亿元，增长22.1%；社会保障和就业支出166.40亿元，增长19.7%。

年末金融机构（含外资）人民币各项存款余额8870.72亿元，比年初增加2025.65亿元，比上年增长29.6%。其中，企业存款余额2791.72亿元，增长36.3%；储蓄存款余额3713.47亿元，增长21.8%。

金融机构（含外资）人民币各项贷款余额4973.16亿元，比年初增加1190.24亿元，增长31.5%，其中，短期贷款1845.60亿元，增长20.9 %；中长期贷款2924.31亿元，增长43.5%。个人消费贷款457.76亿元，增长46.7%。

年末共有上市公司37家，比上年增加3家。股票总股本205.40亿股，比上年增长20.9%；股票总市值3703.07亿元，增长22.6%。全年通过IPO（首发融资上市）、增发、配股、公司债等方式共筹集资金213.52亿元人民币，增长3.9倍。其中，A股筹集资金143.13亿元，增长2.3倍。

全年保险公司各项保费收入190.92亿元，比上年增长21.9%，其中，寿险108.60亿元，增长22.7%；财产险63亿元，增长21.6%；健康险14.39亿元，增长17.6%；意外险4.93亿元，增长20.2%。各类保险赔款及给付支出49.33亿元，增长2.5%，其中，财产险赔款29.21亿元，增长9.8%；寿险赔付13.13亿元，下降14.3%；健康险赔付5.84亿元，增长10.7%；意外险赔付1.16亿元，增长25.9%。

九、教育和科学技术

年末共有普通高等学校32所。全年研究生教育招生4595人，比上年增长9.7%；在校研究生12675人，增长8.9%；毕业生3360人，增长11.2%。本专科招生7.46万人，增长7.0%；在校生25.12万人，增长3.9%；毕业生6.35万人，增长11.3%。

各类中等职业教育招生10.83万人，增长4.7%；在校生23.33万人，增长7.2%；毕业生6.64万人，增长11.7%。普通高中招生15.32万人，增长2.9%；在校生41.91万人，增长0.5%；毕业生13.57万人，下降1.2%。初中招生33.61万人，下降1.4%；在校生100.33万人，下降2.4%；毕业生33.75万人，下降4.9%。小学招生31.19万人，下降2.1%；在校生193.58万人，下降1.9%；毕业生33.44万人，下降1.6%；幼儿园在园幼儿57.90万人，增长18.0%。

小学学龄儿童入学率99.8%，其中，农村99.7%。初中阶段适龄少年入学率100.5%，其中，农村96.3%。初中毕业升入普通高中升学率45.4%。

全年安排自治区级科技计划项目1106项，承担国家级科技计划项目（课题）484项。获得省部级以上科技成果229项。拥有县以上部门属研究与技术开发机构106个。重点实验室23个，工程技术研究中心20个，其中国家级4个。自治区级科技成果转化基地45个。截至2010年底，按新办法认定的高新技术企业113个，国家级高新技术产业开发区2个，自治区级高新技术工业园区5个，国家大学科技园1个。生产力促进中心24家，其中，国家级示范中心9家。国家级创新型企业4个，国家级创新型试点企业6个。

受理专利申请3560项，其中，受理发明专利申请914项，占25.7%；获得专利授权2562项，其中，获得发明专利授权189项，占7.4%。签订技术合同1701项，技术合同成交金额4.64亿元，其中，技术交易额4.31亿元。

十、文化、卫生和体育

年末拥有群众艺术馆15个，文化馆、艺术馆112个，公共图书馆103个，博物馆71个。拥有广播电台6座，广播综合人口覆盖率94.9%。电视台8座，电视人口综合覆盖率95.3%。有线电视用户192.00万户，增长6.1%，其中，有线数字电视用户131.00万户，增长27.3%。拍摄故事片 2部，译制少数民族语故事片161部，增长37.6。出版各类期刊0.10亿册，各类图书1.12亿册（张）。

全区共有卫生机构7650个，拥有床位11.62万张，卫生技术人员12.29万人。其中，医院、卫生院1712个，床位10.99万张；疾病预防控制中心221个；妇幼保健机构90个。乡镇卫生院901个，床位1.99万张，卫生技术人员1.67万人。

成功举办2010年跆拳道世界杯比赛。我区运动健儿参加国际、国内比赛共获得21枚金牌、17枚银牌、15枚铜牌，在第十六届亚运会上，我区运动员参加团体和个人比赛获得1枚金牌、1枚银牌、1枚铜牌。

十一、人民生活

城镇居民人均可支配收入13644元，比上年增长11.3%。其中，工资性收入11328元，增长10.7%。人均消费性支出10197元，比上年增长9.3%，其中，人均食品支出3694元，增长9.1%。城镇居民家庭恩格尔系数36.2，比上年降低0.1个百分点。

农村居民人均纯收入4643元，增长19.6%。其中，工资性收入556元，增长20.5%；家庭经营纯收入3650元，增长18.9%；转移性纯收入310元，增长34.3%；财产性纯收入127元，增长4.3%。人均生活消费支出3458元，增长17.2%。农村居民家庭恩格尔系数40.3，比上年降低1.3个百分点。

十二、劳动就业和社会保障

年末就业人员889.35万人，比上年净增21.99万人，增长2.7%。通过各种途径实现城镇就业再就业51.68万人，其中，下岗职工再就业9.70万人。21902户“零就业”家庭中24414人实现就业。城镇登记失业率3.2%，比上年降低0.6个百分点。

年末全区参加失业保险180.29万人，领取失业保险金5.88万人。参加基本养老保险259.67万人，增加27.59万人，其中，参保职工193.07万人，增加15.49万人；参保离退休人员66.60万人，增加12.10万人。企业参加基本养老保险离退休人员64.83万人，增加12.10万人。城镇职工参加基本医疗保险296.72万人，增加17.63万人，其中，参保职工224.78万人，增加13.93万人；参保退休人员71.94万人，增加3.7万人。参加工伤保险184.13万人，增加16.43万人。参加生育保险188.23万人，增加12.16万人。

城镇居民中有85.13万人得到政府最低生活保障救济，比上年增加20.58万人。年末各类收养性社会福利单位拥有床位3万张；收养各类人员2.50万人。城镇各种社区服务设施1236个。销售社会福利彩票19.30亿元，增长21.9%；筹集社会福利资金5.66亿元，增长14.8%。直接接受社会捐赠1794.70万元。

开展新型农村合作医疗工作的县（市）89个，覆盖农牧业人口1033.70万人，比上年增加12.06万人.实际参加新型农牧区合作医疗的农牧民1019.03万人，增加25.45万人，参合率98.6%。

新型农村养老保险试点扩大到56个县(市)，参保人员357.93万人，已领取养老保险待遇58.03万人。

十三、资源、环境和安全生产

新发现大中型非油气矿产地22处，其中，能源矿产地19处，均为煤矿；金属矿产地3处，其中，铁矿1处、菱镁矿1处、铅锌矿1处。

全年共完成废气污染物二氧化硫减排项目57个，新增二氧化硫削减量2.10万吨；完成废水污染物化学需氧量减排项目37个，新增化学需氧量削减量1.62万吨。

在监测的19个城市中，有12个城市空气质量达到国家Ⅱ级以上标准，比去年增加2个；城市空气质量好于Ⅱ级的优良天数占84.0%。首府乌鲁木齐市空气质量好于Ⅱ级的优良天数占72.9%，比上年提高1.1个百分点。

在监测的64条河流160个断面中，Ⅰ～Ⅲ类优良水质断面比例为91.2%，提高2.9个百分点；Ⅳ～Ⅴ类轻中度污染水质断面比例为5.0%，下降1.5个百分点；劣Ⅴ类重度污染水质断面比例为3.8%，下降1.4个百分点。

在监测的30座湖库中，Ⅰ～Ⅲ类优良水质湖库占50.0%，比上年提高6.7个百分点；Ⅳ～Ⅴ类轻中度污染水质湖库占20%，下降3.4个百分点；劣Ⅴ类重度污染水质湖库占30.0%，下降3.3个百分点。

各类国家和自治区级自然保护区34个，保护区总面积2257.60万公顷，占辖区面积比重的13.6%，其中，国家级自然保护区9个。

全年共发生各类生产安全事故10602起，比上年上升0.4%。死亡2507人，下降3.2%。亿元GDP安全生产事故死亡率0.5，下降16.7%；道路交通万车死亡率7.58，下降2.9%；煤矿百万吨死亡率1.02，下降19.7%；工矿商贸十万从业人员事故死亡率8.1，上升6.4%。

说明：

1、规模以上工业指年销售收入500万元以上的工业企业。

2、自2010年起，社会消费品零售总额口径及统计分组有所调整，社会消费品零售总额中不包括除批发和零售业、住宿和餐饮业以外的其他行业零售额；统计分组由城市、农村分组改为城镇和乡村分组。基期数做同口径调整。

3、国际旅游人数增加了口岸旅游购物人数，基期数做同口径调整。

4、地区生产总值（GDP）、三次产业增加值及各行业增加值指标绝对数按现价计算，增长速度按可比价格计算。

Statistical Communique on the 2010 National Economic & Social Development of the Xinjiang Uygur Autonomous Region

In 2010, under the correct leadership of the Autonomous Region Party Committee and the People's Government, the people in different nationalities of the Autonomous Region fully implemented the view Scientific Developments Stratgy, fully implemented the spirit of the central committee of Xinjiang, the Autonomous Region Party Committee of the ninth and the tenth plenary session of the seventh committee of the Xinjiang autonomous region,emancipating our minds, targeting of socialist strenth,seizing the opportunity of development,working studily,general economic strengh stood a new stage in the increasing polar,development quality prevent further,the people's livelihood continulously improvement and allround progress in the social undertakings.

I. General Outlook

According to the Preliminary statistics, the gross domestic product (GDP) of Xinjiang was 543.747 billion yuan, an increase of 116.042 billion yuan over the previous year, up by 10.6% over the previous year, of which,the added value of the primary industry was 107.863 billion yuan,up by 12.6%;that of the secondary industry was 259.215 billion yuan,up by 12.6%;and that of the tertiary industry was 176.669 billion yuan,up by 10.8% over the previous year.The composition of three industries was 19.8:47.7:32.5.

The permanent-population-based per-capita GDP reached 25057 yuan, up by9.3% over the previous year, equivalent to US$3 702 at current exchange rate. First breakthrough exceeding $3000.

The total consumer price index of the year was up by 4.3% over the previous year, of which, the price of food was up by 10.7%.The price of housing was up by 2.7%,The price for service up by 1.5%.

Table 1: Span of rise and decrease on the consumer price indices

unit: %

Items	2010
Consumer price index	4.3
rural	3.6
urban	5.8
Food	10.7
# Grain	8.9
Meal poultry and processed products	13.0
Oil and Fat	7.6
Eggs	12.3
Aquatic products	7.4
Tobacco,Liquor and Articles	2.0
Clothing	-0.8
Household Facilities, Articles and Services	1.2
Health Care and Personal Articles	equ
Transportation and Communication	2.0
Recreation, Education and Culture Articles	1.2
Residence	2.7
Water Electric and fuel	2.5
Renting	3.3
Building and building decoration materials	3.5

The ex-Factory price index of industrial product was up by 25.3%.,of which,light industry was up by 8.9%,heavy industry was up by 28.7%.The purchasing price of raw material, fuel and power was down by 23.9%.The production price of agriculture products up by 3.1%. The price of fixed asset investment was up by4.6%.

II. Agriculture

Gross output value of agriculture,forestry, animal husbandry and fishery was 184.618 billion yuan,up by 4.9% over the previous year, of which,Gross output of agriculture was 137.689 billion yuan,up by 4.7%;Gross output of forestry was 3.527 billion yuan,up by 6.4%;Gross output of animal husbandry was 37.579 billion yuan,up by 5.1%; Gross output of fishery was 1.267 billion yuan,up by 5.5%;Gross output of services of griculture,forestry, animal husbandry husbandry was 4.557 billion yuan,up by 6.1%.

The total sown areas of farm crops was 4.7586 million hectares, up by 1.0% over the previous year; of which ,The sown area of grain crops was 1.9916 million hectares,down by 0.1%; The sown area of cotton crops was 1.4606 million hectares,up by 3.6%;The sown area of oil bearing crops was 27.34 ten thousand hectares, up by 1.2%; The sown area of sugar crops was 7.53 ten thousand acres, up by 18.1% over the previous year. The area of vegetable crops was 30.36 ten thousand hectares, up by 15.8% over the previous year.

The total output of grain was 1150.20 ten thousand tons, down by 0.2% over the previous year; The output of cotton was247.90 ten thousand tons, down by 16.3% over the previous year; The output of oil-bearing crops was 666.2 thousand tons, an increase of 4.2%; The output of sugar was 486.97 ten thousand tons, up by 16.4%. The output of vegetable was 17.344 million tons, an increase of 25.4% over the previous year; The output of fruit was 1028.85 ten thousand tons, down by 2.6%, of which, the output of fruit was 593.85 ten thousand, an increase of 5.1%.

The year-end domesticated animals in stock numbered 37.2212 million heads, down by 3.2% over the previous year; the domesticated animal out of stock 34.9852 million heads, up by 25.9% ;the total output of meat reached 1.2174 million tons, up by 5.6%; of which, the output of pork reached 46.95 ten thousand tons, up by 7.3%, the output of poultry reached 35.47 ten thousand tons, up by 4.7%; the output of mutton reached 23.05 ten thousand, up by 4.6%, the output of milk reached 128.60 ten thousand tons, up by 6.4%.the output of sheep wool was 8.40 ten thousand tons,up by 17.3%.the output of aquatic product reached 10.11 ten thousand tons, up by 11.4%.

Total agricultural machinery power was 16.4293 million kilowatt, up by 9.3% over the previous year. There were 25.38 ten thousand large and medium-size tractors, up by 16.5% ; and 36.12 ten thousand small-size tractors, down by 2.7%. The consumption of chemical fertilizer was 167.57 ten thousand tons(100% equivalent), up by 7.2%. Electricity consumed in rural areas was6.429 billion kwh, up by 9.0%.

III. Industry and Construction

The total value-added of the industrial sector was 216.139 billion yuan, up by 13.5% over the previous year.

Table2: Output of Major Industrial Products 2010

Item	Unit	Output	Increase over 2009(%)
Coal	10 000 tons	9935	12.7
Crude oil	10 000 tons	2558	1.8
Natural gas	100 million cubic meters	249.9	1.8
Processed oil	10 000 tons	2190.37	17.5
Ethylene	10 000 tons	119.33	1.4times
Electricity	100 million kilowatt-hours	679.33	18.9
Refind sugar	10 000 tons	45.10	10.6
Cigarettes	100 million pieces	150.00	11.1
Can	10 000 tons	110.6	-8.1
Chemical Fiber	10 000 tons	14.00	11.8
Yarn	10 000 tons	41.58	7.7
Cloth	10 000 meters	1.21	-0.5
Machine-made paper and paperbord	10 000 tons	37.10	4.3
Chemical fertilizers (100% equivalent)	10 000 tons	159.10	Equal
Crude steel	10 000 tons	825.54	26.4
Rolled steel	10 000 tons	829.04	29.1
Pig Iron	10 000 tons	941.12	23.1
Cement	10 000 tons	2400.96	17.1
Transformer	10 000 kilovolt-ampere	3582.94	37.2

The added value of industrial enterprises above designated size was up by 13.6%. Of which, The added value of light industry was up by 14.9%; the added value of heavy industry was up by 13.0% over the previous year. Among the ten proportion of industrial enterprises above designated, Minging of coal was up by 11.1%;Extraction of petroleum was up by 6.7%; Minging and processing of non-ferrous metal ores was up by 10.4%;Manufacture of textilw was up by 6.5%;Manufacture of chemical products was up by 43.4%; production of electric power was up by 18.8%;Manufacture of cars was up by 38.3%;Processing of food from agriculture products was up by 16.2%

The proportion of products sold of above designated size was 97.9%,.an increase of 2.3 percentage points.Of which, the proportion of light industry of products sold was 94.3%, an increase of 1.4 percentage points. The proportion of heavy industry of products sold was 98.4%,an increase of 2.5 percentage points. The value of delivered exported goods creat by industrial enterprises above designated size was 5.149billion yuan, down by 37.2%. The profits achieved to 85.243 billion yuan, up by 37.8%.

The added value of the construction sector was 43.076 billion yuan, up by 7.9% over the previous year, General contracting and special contracting construction enterprises with qualification grade reaped profits of 96.947 billion yuan, up by 12.7%.

IV. Investment in Fixed Asset

The completed investment in fixed assets was 353.969 billion yuan, up by 25.2% over the previous year. In terms of urban and rural areas, that in urban areas was 318.158 billion yuan, up by 25.5%; that in rural areas was 35.811 billion yuan, up by 22.9%.

In terms of three industries,the investment in the primary industry was 21.143 billion yuan, up by 22.7%; the investment in the secondary industry was 166.706 billion yuan, up by 28.7%, The third industry investment was 166.120 billion yuan, up by22.2%. Among the investment in the secondary industry,the investment in industry was 162.579 billion yuan,up by 28.4%,of which ,the investment in manufature was 62.037 billion yuan ,up by 37.5%.

The investment in real estate development was 34.772 billion yuan, up by 47.7% over the previous year. The floor space of buildings under construction was 39.8080 million square meters, up by 29.9%. The floor space of building completed was 10.1290 million square meters, down by 1.9%. The total sales area of commercial buildings for the whole year reached 15.6490 million square meters, up by 11.3%. The total sales of commercial building was 48.304 billion yuan, up by 31.9%.

V. Domestic Trade

The total retail sales of consumer goods reached 132.448 billion yuan, up by 17.1% over the previous year. Really up by 12.0%.

In terms of urban and rural areas, the retail sales of consumer goods in urban areas reached118.126 billion yuan, up by17.4%; and the retail sales of consumer goods in rural areas reached 14.321 billion yuan, up by 14.9%. In terms of different sectors, the sales of the wholesale and retail trade reached 115.662 billion yuan, up by 16.7%; the sales of the accommoda-

tion and catering service was 16.785 billion yuan, up by 20.5%.

VI. Foreign Trade

The total value of import and export reached US$ 17.128billion, up by 23.9% over the previous year. Of which, the value of export was US$ 12.970 billion, up by 19.8% ;and the value of import was US$ 4.159 billion, up by 38.4%.

The number of newly estabishied foeign directly investment enterprises was 51,up by 18.6% over the previous year. Foreign directly investment actually utilized this year stood at US$ 237 million, up by10.1%.

Table3: Total Value of Imports and Exports and Growth Rates

unit: US$ 100 million

Item	2010	Increase over 2009(%)
Total value of imports and exports	171.28	23.9
Total exports	129.70	19.8
#Ordinary trade	20.89	24.3
Processing trade	3.04	-5.6
Frontier small trade	76.75	1.8
#mechanical and electrical products	22.20	24.9
New and high-tech products	1.07	21.1
Total imports	41.59	38.4
# Ordinary trade	15.46	20.1
Processing trade	0.23	-8.0
Frontier small trade	23.67	50.4
#mechanical and electrical products	7.00	-3.3
New and high-tech products	2.95	8.9

VII. Transportation, Postal & Telecommunication and Tourism

The freight turnover by railways was68.53 million tons, up by6.9%; that by highways 504.48 million tons, up by 7.8%; that by civil aviation 3.70 ten thousands tons, down by 2.6%; Passenger traffic by railways was 15.23 million passengers,up by 11.1%; that by highways44.333 million passengers, up by 6.6%; that by civil aviation 4.90 million passengers, up by 12.6%.

At the end of the year,railway in operation reached 4393 kilometers,up by 14.5%;Total civil aviation routes reached 17.7ten thousand kilometers,up by 16.1%;Length of highways was 15.28 ten thousand kilometers,up by 1.4%.

At the end of the year, there were 135.90 ten thousand civilian automobiles, up by 22.8%, of which, there were 85.8 ten thousand private automobiles, up by31.6%.

The total volume of post and telecommunication was 58.205 billion yuan, up by 21.3% over the previous year. Of which, the volume of post stood at 1658 million yuan, up by 24.2%. the volume of telecommunication stood at 56.547 billion yuan, up by 21.3%; Number of fixed phone users 5.4750 million, down by 4.5%. Number of mobile phone users 13.5980 million, up by 21.5%. Year-end Internet customer 1.6110 million, up by 20.5%.

Tourists through customs to Xinjiang numbered 101.03ten thousand, up by 43.2%.Forien exchange income from tourism amounted to US$368 million, up by40.8%. In the year, Xinjiang recevied 3038 ten thousand forien tourists, up by 44.8% over the previous year.Income from foreign tourists amounted 28.113 billion yuan,up by 59.1%.

VIII. Finance, Banking and Insurance

The Local government revenue was 69.327billion yuan, up by 40.6%. the general budgetary revenue was 50.058 billion yuan, up by 28.8%. Of which, total taxes were 41.623 billion yuan, up by 38.2% over the previous year.In categories of taxes, income of deed tax were 7.531 billion yuan,up by 30.7%; Income of business tax were 15.127 billion yuan, up by 34.6%.

Income of resource tax were 3.247 billion yuan ,up by 1.6times.

Local government expenditure reached 188.56 billion yuan, up by 27.9%, the general budgetary expenditure was 169.891 billion yuan, up by26.1%,of which,expenditure of education were 31.384 billion yuan,up by 30.8%; expenditure of medical and health care were 10.356 billion yuan,up by22.1%; expenditure of social safety and employment were 16.64 0 billion yuan ,up by19.7%.

By the end of 2009, savings deposits of all kinds in financial institutions reached 887.072 billion yuan, increase by 202.565 billion yuan over the beginning, up by 29.6% over the previous year. Of which, enterprise savings deposits were 279.172 billion yuan, up by 36.3%;Savings deposits were 371.347 billion yuan, up by 21.8%.

Loans of all kinds in financial institutions were 497.31 6billion yuan, increase by 119.024 billion yuan over the beginning, up by 31.5%; of which, Loans of short-term were 184.560 billion yuan,up by 20.9%; loan of medium-and long-term were 292.413 billion yuan,up by 43.5%.individual consumption loans were 45.776 billion yuan, up by 46.7%.

At the end of 2009,there were 37 listed companies, increased by 3 units;total volume issred were 20.540 billion shares,up by 20.9%;Total market capitalization were 370.307 billion yuan,up by 22.6%.The transaction volume of vareous securities on the securities market totaled 4.360 billion yuan ,of which, IPO raise money 12.352 billion yuan;l up by 3.9 times. Of which,A shares raise money were14.313 billion yuan,up by 2.3 times.

The total premium of insurance companies reached 19.092billion yuan, up by 21.9% over the previous year. Of the total, life insurance premium was 10.860billion yuan, up by 22.7%; property insurance premium 6.3 billion yuan,up by 21.6%. health and casualty insurance premium were 1.439 billion yuan, up by17.6%; that against health and accidental injury were 493 million yuan,up by 20.2%; Insurance companies paid an indemnity of 4.933 billion yuan as reparation for various property and life insurance programs,up by 2.5%,of which, and that against property was 2.921billion yuan,up by 9.8%.the indemnity against life insurance was 1.313 billion yuan, down by14.3%; that against health were 584million yuan, up by10.7%, and accidental injury were 116million yuan,up by 25.9%.

IX. Education

By the end of 2010,there were totally 32 general colleges and universities.The enrollment of postgraduate students were 4595 new entrants, up by9.7%; the enrollment of postgraduate students was12675, up by 8.9%,graduates students were 3360,up by 11.2%.The enrollment of regular undergraduates and college student were7.46 ten thousand ,up by 7.0%; the enrollment of students was 25.12 ten thousand, up by 3.9%, graduates students were 6.35 ten thousand,up by 11.3%.

The enrollment of vocational secondary education was 10.83 ten thousand,up by 4.7%; enrollment were 23.33 ten thousand,up by 7.2%, graduates students were 6.64ten thousand,up by11.7%.

The enrollment of general senior high schools were 153.2 thousand,up by 2.9%; enrollment were 419.1 thousand,up by 0.5%; with135.7thousand graduates,down by 1.2%. Students enrolled in junior secondary schools totaled 336.1 ten thousand,down by 1.4%; enrollment were 100.33 ten thousand,down by 2.4%; with 337.5 thousand ,down by 4.9%.Regular primary schools had an enrollment of 31.19 ten thousand, down by 2.1%; enrollment were 1.9358 million, down by 1.9%,with 334.4 thousand graduates,down by 1.6%.There were 579.0 thousand pre-school children in kindergartens,up by 18.0%.

The enrollment rate of school-age children reached 99.8%, of which,rural were 99.7%. Enrollment rate of junior secondary school-age youth was 100.5%,of which,rural were 96.3%.Promotion rate from junior sendary school to senior secondary school was 45.4%.

X. Culture,Public Health and Sports

At the end of 2010, there were 15 mass art centers,112 cutural centers and art centers,103 public library,71 museums.there were 6 radio broadcasting stations, Radio broadcasting coverage rate was 94.9%, 8 television stations. television coverage rate was 95.3%. Number of users of cable television was 192.00 ten thousand,up by 6.1%, of which, number of Users of digital TV was 131 ten thousand,up by 27.3%. The Autonomous Region shot 2 feature movie, translated and edited 161 feature movies of minority language, up by 37.6%.There were 10 million magazine publications and 112 million book publications.

There were 7650 institutions of public health in all,the total number of beds was 11.62 ten thousand,the medical technical personnel totaled 12.29 ten thousands.of which, there were 1712 hospitals and public health centers,the total number beds was 10.99 ten thousands; ,the medical technical personnel totaled 12.29 ten thousands. ,the medical technical personnel totaled 1.67 ten thousands.

The autonomous region hosted 2010 kickboxing world cup sucessly.Athletes from the Autonomous Region in international matches won 21 gold medals,17 silver medals,15 bronze medals.in the 16th Asian Games, Athletes from the Autonomous Region won 1 gold medal,1 silver medal,1 bronze medal.

XI. People's Life

By the end of 2010, the per capital disposable income of urban residents reached 13644 yuan, up by 11.3% over the previous year.Of which,income of salary and wage was 11328 yuan,up by 10.7%,per capital annual expenditure was 10197 yuan,up by 9.3%,of which,the per capital annual food expenditure was 3694yuan ,up by 9.1%. Engle coefficient of urban households was 36.2%,down by 0.1 percentage.

The per capital auunal net income of rural households was 4643 yuan, up by19.6%,of which,income of salaries and wages was 556 yuan ,up by 20.5%;income from household operations was 3650 yuan ,up by 18.9%;Income from transfers was 310yuan ,up by 34.3%,Income from properties was 127 yuan,up by 4.3%,Per capita consumption expenditure of rural households was 3458 yuan,up by 17.2%.Engle coefficient of rural households was 40.3,down by 1.3 points over the previous year.

XII.Employment and Social Security

Number of employed person was 8.8935 million at year-end, net increase of 21.99 ten thousand as compared with the previous year. up by 2.7%,of which, number of urban employed persons were 51.68 ten thousand,of which,the reemployment of lady-off workers was 9.70 ten thousand. Registered unemployment rate in urban areas was 3.2%,down by 0.6 percentage points.

A total of 1.8029 million people participated in unemployment insurance programs, Receive unemployment insurance compensation was 5.88 ten thousand. 2.5967 million people participated in the basic retirement security programs, or an increase of 27.59ten thousand people as compared with the previous year. Among them, 1.9307 million were employees, an increase of 15.49ten thousand people; 66.60 ten thousand were retirees, an increase of 12.10 ten thousand people ; The population covered by basic medical insurance programs was 64.38 ten thousand, an increase of 12.10 ten thousand people, Among them, 2.9672 million were employees, an increase of 13.93 ten thousand people;71.94 ten thousand were retirees, an increase of 3.7 ten thousand people; 184.13ten thousand people participated in the basic retirement security programs were retirees, an increase of 2.55 ten thousand people; 6.34 ten thousand recevied unemployment insurance allowances,a increase of 16.43 ten thousand.There were 1.8823million people in participating in the industrial injury insruance program, an increase of 12.16 ten thousand.

85.13 ten thousand people recevied basic welfare for urban residents.increase of 20.58 ten thousand, Number of beds were 3.0 ten thousand in social welfare institutions at the end of year;Number of inmates were 2.50 ten thousand.Revenue from social welfare lottery tickets were 1.930 billion yuan ,up by 21.9%; Social welfare fund were 566 million yuan, up by 14.8%.Received 17.9470 million yuan of donatioas from the general public.

There are 89 countries(cities) which participated in the new rural cooperative medical service,covered total rural population was 10.3370 million, increased by 12.06 ten thousand over previous year.;10.1903million people participated acturally in the new rural cooperative medical service, incraese by 25.45 ten thousand.the rate of participation was 98.6%.

XIII. Resources Environment and Safe production

22mineral products were founded in non-oil mineral exploration of new mineral, of which, energy resouses mines were19, all were metal mine were3,of which,`non-metal mine were 1, vapor mine were1, zinc mine was 1.

Reduction of pollutant emissions of sulphur dioxide were 2.10ten thousand tons and pollutant emissions of waste water were 1.62ten thousand tons.

In the 19 monitored cities, 12 cities had their air quality reach national standard Grade II ,increase of 2 cities. In the Autonomous Region about 84.0% of the year the air quality was better than Grade II. And 72.9% of the year in Urmqi the air quality was better than Grade II, up by 1.1% over the previous year.

Monitoring of water quality on 160 sections of the 64rivers showed that good quality water of standard Grade I ~III accounted for 91.2%,up by2.9 percentage points. Quality water of standard Grade I ~III accounted for 5.0%, down by 1.5%, Quality water of standard Grade V accounted for 3.8%,down by 1.4%.

There were34 national and regional of nature reserves. Area of nature reserves were 2257.60ten thousand sqkm, proportion of nature reserves in total area of territory was 13.6%, of which, there were 9 national nature reserves.

There were 10602 safety accidents occurred, up by 0.4%, with 2507 person died, decrease of 3.2%;The 100-million-GDP-based death rate in production safety accidents was0.5, down by 16.7% over the previous year; among every 100 000 employees in trade sectors, 7.58persons died, down by 2.9%; for every 10 000 vehicles, for every one million tons output of coal mines, 1.02 persons died, down by 19.7%.

Notes to the Communique:

1.Industry above designated size are those with annual revenue from principal business over 5 million yuan.

2.Since 2010,Data in retail sales of commodities were adjusted,data in retail sale of consumer goods didn't included other sector of retail,except for wholesale and retail trades,hotels and catering servicess;Statistical grouping were adjusted,at present statistical grouping were rual and urban.

3.The number of foreigner tourists increased port to the shopping.

4.Data in region GDP and the tertiary industry GDP and every sector of GDP are caculated at current prices,while that of indices are at constant prices.

第一篇
综　合

CHAPTER 1
General Survey

简要说明
Brief Introduction

本篇资料的主要内容及来源

综合篇资料包括行政区划、部门机构数、国民经济和社会发展综合资料及企业景气指数四部分。

行政区划划分资料由新疆维吾尔自治区民政厅提供。部门机构数、国民经济和社会发展综合资料由新疆维吾尔自治区统计局国民经济综合统计处根据各篇主要指标加工整理而成。企业景气指数由国家统计局新疆调查总队统计监测处提供。

Main Content and Source of Data

This chapter mainly covers four parts: the data of division of administrative areas, grass-roots units,summary data on the national economy and social development and prosperity index on enterprises .

Data on division of administrative areas are provided by the Bureau of Civil Affairs of Xinjiang Uygur Autonomous Region。Data on grass-roots units and the national economy and social development are compiled and processed by the Department of Comprehensive statistics of the Xinjiang Bureau of Statistics using relevant. enterprises business climate index are provided by the Department of Monitoring Statistics , NBS Survey Office in Xinjiang.

1-1 行 政 区 划

Divisions of Administrative Areas in Xinjiang Uygur Autonomous Region

单位：个 (2010 年) (unit)

区划名称	Region	地级区划数 Number of Regions at Prefecture Level	地级市 Cities at Prefec-ture Level	地区 Admin-istrative Offices	自治州 Autono-mous Prefectu-res	县级区划数 Number of Regions at County level	自治区直辖市 Cities under the Autonom-ous Region	地州辖市 Cities under the Prefectu-res
总　计	**Total**	**14**	**2**	**7**	**5**	**98**	**4**	**15**
乌鲁木齐市	Urumqi City	1	1			8		
克拉玛依市	Karamay City	1	1			4		
吐鲁番地区	Turpan Administrative Offices	1		1		3		1
哈密地区	Hami [Kumul] Administrative Offices	1		1		3		1
昌吉回族自治州	Changji Hui Autonomous Prefecture	1			1	7		2
伊犁哈萨克自治州	Ili Kazak Autonomous Prefecture	3		2	1	24		5
伊犁州直属县(市)	Counties (Cities) Direct Under Ili Prefecture	1			1	10		2
塔城地区	Tacheng [Tarbagatai] Administrative Offices	1		1		7		2
阿勒泰地区	Altay Administrative Offices	1		1		7		1
博尔塔拉自治州	Bortala Mongol Autonomous Prefecture	1			1	3		1
巴音郭楞自治州	Bayangol Mongol Autonomous Prefecture	1			1	9		1
阿克苏地区	Aksu Administrative Offices	1		1		9		1
克孜勒苏自治州	Kizilsu Kirgiz Autonomous Prefecture	1			1	4		1
喀什地区	Kashgar [Kaxgar] Administrative Offices	1		1		12		1
和田地区	Hotan Administrative Offices	1		1		8		1
石河子市	Shihezi City					1	1	
阿拉尔市	Aral City					1	1	
图木舒克市	Tumxuk City					1	1	
五家渠市	Wujiaqu City					1	1	

区划名称	Region	县级区划数 Number of Counties: 市辖区 Districts under the Jurisdiction of Cities	县 Coun-ties	自治县 Autono-mous Counti-es	乡镇级区划数 Number of Regions at Town-ships Level	镇 Town	乡 Town-ship	民族乡 Natio-nal Town-ship	街道办事处 Street Com-munities
总　计	**Total**	**11**	**62**	**6**	**1020**	**237**	**578**	**43**	**162**
乌鲁木齐市	Urumqi City	7	1		87	8	13	1	65
克拉玛依市	Karamay City	4			14		2		12
吐鲁番地区	Turpan Administrative Offices		2		30	11	15	1	3
哈密地区	Hami [Kumul] Administrative Offices		1	1	42	10	24	3	5
昌吉回族自治州	Changji Hui Autonomous Prefecture		4	1	80	38	21	12	9
伊犁哈萨克自治州	Ili Kazak Autonomous Prefecture		17	2	241	61	139	17	24
伊犁州直属县(市)	Counties (Cities) Direct Under Ili Prefecture		7	1	110	20	67	10	13
塔城地区	Tacheng [Tarbagatai] Administrative Offices		4	1	74	27	34	5	8
阿勒泰地区	Altay Administrative Offices		6		57	14	38	2	3
博尔塔拉自治州	Bortala Mongol Autonomous Prefecture		2		20	7	9		4
巴音郭楞自治州	Bayangol Mongol Autonomous Prefecture		7	1	90	24	60	1	5
阿克苏地区	Aksu Administrative Offices		8		94	30	52	2	10
克孜勒苏自治州	Kizilsu Kirgiz Autonomous Prefecture		3		39	5	31	1	2
喀什地区	Kashgar [Kaxgar] Administrative Offices		10	1	172	30	135	3	4
和田地区	Hotan Administrative Offices		7		93	12	75	2	4
石河子市	Shihezi City				7	1	1		5
阿拉尔市	Aral City				5		1		4
图木舒克市	Tumxuk City				3				3
五家渠市	Wujiaqu City				3				3

1-2 县级以上行政区划

Divisions of Administrative Areas at and above County Level

(2010 年)

地、州、市名称 Name of Administrative Offices, Autonomous Prefectures, Cities		市 县 (市辖区)名称 Names of Cities and Counties (Districts under Cities)
乌鲁木齐市 Urumqi City		天山区、沙依巴克区、新市区、水磨沟区、头屯河区、达坂城区、米东区、乌鲁木齐县 Tianshan District, Shayibak District, Xinshi District, Shui Mogou District, Tou Tunhe District, Da Bancheng District, Midong District, Urumqi County
克拉玛依市 Karamay City		克拉玛依区、独山子区、白碱滩区、乌尔禾区 Karamay District, Dushanzi District, Bai Jiantan District, Urhe District
吐鲁番地区 Turpan Administrative Offices		吐鲁番市、鄯善县、托克逊县 Turpan City, Shanshan [Piqan] County, Toksun County
哈密地区 Hami [Kumul] Administrative Offices		哈密市、巴里坤哈萨克自治县、伊吾县 Hami [Kumul] City, Barkol Kazak Autonomous County, Yiwu[Araturuk] County
昌吉回族自治州 Changji Hui Autonomous Prefecture		昌吉市、阜康市、呼图壁县、玛纳斯县、奇台县、吉木萨尔县、木垒哈萨克自治县 Changji City, Fukang City, Hutubi County, Manas County, Qitai County, Jimsar County, Mori Kazak Autonomous County
伊犁哈萨克自治州 Ili Kazak Autonomous Prefecture	伊犁州直属县(市) Counties (Cities) Direct Under Ili Prefecture	伊宁市、奎屯市、伊宁县、察布查尔锡伯自治县、霍城县、巩留县、新源县、昭苏县、特克斯县、尼勒克县 Yining [Gulja] City, Kuytun City , Yining [Gulja] County, Qapqal Xibe AutonomousCounty, Huocheng [Korgas] County, Gongliu [Tokkuzlara] County, Xinyuan [Kunes] County, Zhaosu [Mongolkure] County, Tekes County, Nilka County
	塔城地区 Tacheng [Tarbagatai] Administrative Offices	塔城市、乌苏市、额敏县、沙湾县、托里县、裕民县、和布克赛尔蒙古自治县 Tacheng [Qoqek] City, Usu City, Emin [Dorbiljin] County, Shawan County, Toli County, Yumin [Qagantokay] County, Hoboksar Mongol Autonomous County
	阿勒泰地区 Altay Administrative Offices	阿勒泰市、布尔津县、富蕴县、福海县、哈巴河县、青河县、吉木乃县 Altay City, Burqin County, Fuyun [Koktokay] County, Fuhai [Burultokay] County, Habahe [Kaba] County, Qinghe [Qinggil] County, Jeminay county
博尔塔拉蒙古自治州 Bortala Mongol Autonomous Prefecture		博乐市、精河县、温泉县 Bole [Bortala] City, Jinghe [Jing] County, Wenquan [Arxang] County
巴音郭楞蒙古自治州 Bayangol Mongol Autonomous Prefecture		库尔勒市、轮台县、尉犁县、若羌县、且末县、焉耆回族自治县、和静县、和硕县、博湖县 Korla City, Luntai [Bugur] County, Yuli [Lopnur] County, Ruoqiang [Qarkilik] County, Qiemo [Qarqan] County, Yanqi Hui Autonomous County, Hejing County, Bohu [Bagrax] County
阿克苏地区 Aksu Administrative Offices		阿克苏市、温宿县、库车县、沙雅县、新和县、拜城县、乌什县、阿瓦提县、柯坪县 Aksu City, Wensu [Onsu] County, Kuqa County, Xayar County, Xinhe [Toksu] County, Baicheng [Bay] County, Wushi [Uqturpan] County, Awat County, Kalpin County
克孜勒苏柯尔克孜自治州 Kizilsu Kirgiz Autonomous Prefecture		阿图什市、阿克陶县、阿合奇县、乌恰县 Artux City, Akto County, Akqi County, Wuqia [Ulugqat] County
喀什地区 Kashgar [Kaxgar] Administrative Offices		喀什市、疏附县、疏勒县、英吉沙县、泽普县、莎车县、叶城县、麦盖提县、岳普湖县、伽师县、巴楚县、塔什库尔干塔吉克自治县 Kashgar [Kaxgar] City, Shufu County, Shule County, Yengisar County, Zepu [Poskam] County, Shache [Yarkant] County, Yecheng [Kagilik] County, Makit County, Yopurga County, Jiashi [Payzawat] County, Bachu [Maralbexi] County, Taxkorgan Tajik Aotonomous County
和田地区 Hotan Administrative Offices		和田市、和田县、墨玉县、皮山县、洛浦县、策勒县、于田县、民丰县 Hotan City, Hotan County, Moyu [Karakax] County, Pishan [Guma] County, Lop County, Qira County, Yutian [Keriya] County, Minfeng [niya] County
自治区直辖县级市 Municpality Country-Level City directly under the Central Government	石河子市 Shihezi City	
	阿拉尔市 Aral City	
	图木舒克市 Tumxuk City	
	五家渠市 Wujiaqu City	

1-3 各部门机构数
Grass-roots Units in Various Sectors

单位：个 (unit)

部门	Sector	机构数 Grass-roots Units 2009	机构数 Grass-roots Units 2010	2010年比上年增长(%) Increase Rate % in 2010 over 2009
农村基层单位	**Rural Grass-root Units**			
基层组织	Grass-roots Organization			
乡政府	Township Governments	622	618	-0.6
镇政府	Town Governments	176	183	4.0
村民委员会	Village Committees	8799	8796	...
乡村户数(万户)	Numbers of Rural Households (10 000 households)	245.68	255.15	3.8
乡镇企业	Township Enterprises	378983	383653	1.2
国营农场	State-owned Farms	474	540	13.9
规模以上工业企业	**Industrial Enterprises above Designated Size**	**2018**	**2465**	**22.2**
内资企业	Domestic Funded Enterprises	1938	2380	22.8
#国有企业	State-owned Enterprises	147	170	15.6
集体企业	Collective-owned Enterprises	29	26	-10.3
股份合作企业	Cooperative Enterprises	5	19	2.8 倍
联营企业	Joint Ownership Enterprises	8	10	25.0
有限责任公司	Limited Liability Corporations	831	1002	20.6
股份有限公司	Share Holding Corporation Ltd.	74	90	21.6
私营企业	Private Enterprises	843	1057	25.4
港澳台商投资企业	Enterprises with Funds from Hong Kong, Macao and Taiwan	26	33	26.9
外商投资企业	Foreign Funded Enterprises	54	52	-3.7
建筑业企业	**Construction Enterprises and Units**	**993**	**1004**	**1.1**
#国有企业	State-owned Enterprises	90	81	-10.0
城镇集体企业	Urban Collective-owned Enterprises	28	28	持平
邮电业	**Postal and Telecommunication Services**			
邮政局营业网点	Business Outlets of Post-office	1877	1276	-32
卫生事业	**Health Care**	**7288**	**7650**	**5.0**
#医院、卫生院	Hospitals and Health Centers	1669	1712	2.6
疗养院	Sanatoriums	5	4	-20.0
门诊部	Clinics	221	259	17.2
专科防治所、站	Specialized Prevention & Treatment Stations	5	4	-20.0
疾病防控中心	Epidemic Prevention Stations	214	221	3.3
妇幼保健所、站	Maternity and Child Care Centers	90	90	持平
社会福利事业	**Social Welfare Establishments**			
社会福利企事业单位	Social Welfare Institutions	1079	1212	12.3
#收养性福利事业单位	Adopting Social Welfare Institutions	530	546	3.0
社会福利企业	Social Welfare Enterprises	164	40	-75.6
社区服务中心	Community Services Units	133	260	95.5

1-3 续表 Continued

部门	Sector	机构数 Grass-roots Units 2009	机构数 Grass-roots Units 2010	2010年比上年增长(%) Increase Rate % in 2010 Over 2009
教育事业(所)	**Education (unit)**			
普通高等学校	Regular Institutions of Higher Education	32	32	持平
中等学校	Secondary Schools	1832	1772	-3.3
#中等专业学校	Specialized Schools	80	81	1.3
普通中学	Regular Secondary Schools	1610	1545	-4.0
职业中学	Vocational Secondary Schools	82	83	1.2
小学	Primary Schools	3651	3598	-1.5
特殊教育学校	Special Schools	10	13	30.0
艺术事业	**Art Institutions**	**158**	**148**	**-6.3**
艺术表演团体	Art Performance Troupes	136	132	-2.9
艺术表演场所	Art Show Centers	21	15	-28.6
#剧场、影剧院	Theaters	20	13	-35.0
艺术创作机构	Art Creation Institutions	1	1	持平
公共图书馆	**Public Libraries**	**94**	**103**	**9.6**
群众文化事业	**Mass Cultural Establishments**	**1181**	**1209**	**2.4**
群众艺术馆	Mass Art Centers	15	15	持平
文化馆	Cultural Centers	94	97	3.2
文化站	Cultural Stations	1072	1097	2.3
#乡镇文化站	Township Cultural Centers	953	977	2.5
艺术教育事业	**Arts Education Establishments**	**3**	**2**	**-33.3**
艺术研究机构	**Art Research Institutions**	**2**	**2**	**持平**
文化市场经营单位	**Entertainment Operators**	**7770**	**7577**	**-2.5**
文物事业	**Cultural Relic Establishments**	**161**	**171**	**6.2**
博物馆	Museums	63	71	12.7
文物机构	Cultural Relic Agencies	97	99	2.1
文物商店	Cultural Relic Shops	1	1	持平
广播电视台站（座）	**Broadcasting and Television Stations (unit)**			
广播电台	Radio Stations	6	6	持平
电视台	Television Stations	8	8	持平
广播电视台	Radio and TV Stations	83	88	6.0
#县级广播电视台	Number of Wire Broadcasting and Television Stations in County Level	75	80	6.7
金融、保险业	**Banking and Insurance**	**4582**	**4751**	**3.7**
金融机构合计	Sub-total of Banking System	3136	3282	4.7
保险机构合计	Sub-total of Insurance System	1446	1469	1.6

1-4 主要年份平均每天主要社会经济活动

Selected Indicators on Average Daily Social and Economic Activities in Main Years

指　　标	Item	1978	1990	2000	2009	2010
每天创造的财富	**Daily Production**					
新疆生产总值(万元)	Gross Domestic Product (10 000 yuan)	1070.4	7162.7	37357.8	117179.5	148971.8
第一产业	Primary Industry	382.7	2851.8	7895.3	20814.8	29551.5
第二产业	Secondary Industry	502.7	2278.9	14728.2	52865.5	71017.8
工　业	Industry	396.7	1958.9	11469.3	42625.8	59216.2
建筑业	Construction	106.0	320.0	3258.9	10239.7	11801.6
第三产业	Tertiary Industry	184.9	2032.0	14734.3	43499.2	48402.5
#交通运输仓储和邮政业	Transport, Storage and Post	32.6	400.8	4072.1	5728.8	6095.1
批发和零售业	Wholesale and Retail Trades	56.7	561.1	3016.4	6947.9	7569.3
地方财政一般预算收入(万元)	General Budgetary Revenue in Local Finance (10 000 yuan)	195.6	596.7	2166.4	10651.5	13714.4
地方财政一般预算支出(万元)	General Budgetary Expenditure in Local Finance (10 000 yuan)	466.3	1304.7	5231.6	36901.6	46545.6
粮食(吨)	Grain (ton)	10137.3	18544.9	22153.4	31561.6	31512.3
棉花(吨)	Cotton (ton)	150.7	1284.4	4109.6	6915.1	6791.8
油料(吨)	Oil-bearing Crops (ton)	283.0	1067.4	1647.7	1751.0	1825.2
肉类(吨)	Meat (ton)	264.4	834.5	2465.8	3159.2	3335.3
水产品(吨)	Aquatic Products (ton)	15.6	63.6	164.6	265.8	277.0
布(万米)	Cloth (10 000 m)	76.7	82.2	76.9	41.4	41.4
原煤(吨)	Coal (ton)	29561.9	57534.3	76682.1	241439.7	271965.2
发电量(万千瓦小时)	Electricity (10 000 kwh)	580.0	1912.1	5013.2	15652.3	18611.5
原油(吨)	Crude Oil (ton)	9672.6	19041.1	50641.9	68845.5	70086.6
粗钢(吨)	Crude Steel (ton)	231.8	999.7	3005.4	17899.2	22617.5
钢材(吨)	Steel Products (ton)	187.1	780.3	3596.1	18926.3	24430.1
水泥(吨)	Cement (ton)	2141.1	7808.2	24538.9	56153.4	65780.8
每天消费量	**Daily National Consumption**					
最终消费(万元)	Final Consumption Expenditure (10 000 yuan)	757.2	4569.1	20827.4	62087.6	78508.6
居民消费	Resident Consumption	619.3	3318.4	13488.1	35196.0	43258.4
农村居民	Rural Household	330.9	1251.1	4382.8	10566.1	12501.7
城镇居民	Urban Household	288.4	2067.3	9105.3	24629.9	30756.7
政府消费	Government Consumption Expenditure	137.9	1250.7	7339.3	26891.5	35250.2
能源消费量(万吨标准煤)	Energy Consumption (10 000 tons of SCE)		5.4	9.1	20.6	
社会消费品零售总额(万元)	Total Retail Sales of Consumer Goods (10 000 yuan)	599.7	2857.7	10260.3	32261.1	36287.1
每天其他经济活动	**Other Daily Economic Activities**					
资本形成总额(万元)	Gross Capital Formation (10 000 yuan)	504.9	3867.6	16934.9	69856.1	92362.1
固定资产形成	Fixed Capital Formation	363.0	2506.7	17756.8	67760.1	88575.3
存货增加	Increase in Stock	141.9	1360.9	-821.9	2096.0	3786.9
全社会固定资产投资总额	Total investment in Fixed Assets	35.6	2432.3	16722.7	77458.6	96977.8
城　镇	Urban	35.6	2168.8	15256.2	69475.9	87166.6
农　村	Rural		263.6	1466.6	7982.7	98112.6
能源生产总量(万吨标准煤)	Total Energy Production	3.9	7.7	14.8	37.1	
货运量(万吨)	Freight Traffic (10 000 tons)	16.6	38.1	90.7	164.8	177.0
客运量(万人)	Passenger Traffic (10 000 persons)	2.6	26.3	63.5	118.9	127.0
邮电业务总量(万元)	Business Volume of Post and Telecommunication Services (10 000 yuan)	13.0	47.6	1295.9	13141.1	15946.5
进出口总额(万美元)	Total Value of Imports and Exports (USD 10 000)	6.4	112.4	620.3	3788.4	4692.7
出口额	Exports	2.6	91.9	329.9	2965.3	3479.4
进口额	Imports	3.8	20.5	290.4	823.1	1139.3
实际利用外资额(万美元)	Foreign Capital Actually Used (USD 10 000)		20.9	5.3	59.1	65.0
国际旅游外汇收入(万美元)	Number of Tourists from Abroad (person)	…	3.3	26.0	37.4	100.9
每天婚姻变动	**Daily Marriages Changes**					
结　婚(对)	Marriages (couple)		434	445	727	723
离　婚(对)	Divorces (couple)		155	162	242	268

1-5 主要年份国民经济和社会发展总量与速度指标

指　　标	Item	1978
人口与就业	Population and Employment	
人口(万人)	Population (10 000 persons)	
年末总人口	Population at the Year-end	1233.01
男　性	Male	630.18
女　性	Female	602.83
就业(万人)	Employment (10 000 persons)	
就业人员数	Employment	491.25
#在岗职工人数	Staff and Workers	226.69
城镇登记失业人数	Urban Registeration Unemployment	
宏观经济	Macro Economy	
国民经济核算(亿元)	National Accounting (100 million yuan)	
新疆生产总值	Gross Domestic Product	39.07
第一产业	Primary Industry	13.97
第二产业	Secondary Industry	18.35
第三产业	Tertiary Industry	6.75
支出法新疆生产总值	Gross Domestic Product by Expenditure Approach	
#最终消费	Final Consumption Expenditure	27.64
居民消费	Houshold Consumption Expenditure	22.61
政府消费	Government Consumption Expenditure	5.03
资本形成总额	Gross Capital Formation	18.43
固定资本形成	Gross Fixed Capital Formation	13.25
存货增加	Changes in Inventories	5.18
货物和服务净出口	Net Export of Goods and Services	-7.00
固定资产投资(亿元)	Investment in Fixed Assets (100 million yuan)	
全社会固定资产投资总额	Total Investment in Fixed Assets	13.00
城　镇	Urban	13.00
#房地产	Real Estate Development	
农　村	Rural	
财政(亿元)	Public Finance (100 million yuan)	
地方财政一般预算收入	Local Financial Governments Intrabudgetary Ordinary Revenue	7.14
#税收收入	Various Taxes	4.34
地方财政一般预算支出	Local Financial Governments Intrabudgetary Ordinary Expenditures	17.02
#一般公共服务	General Common Service	
教育与科学技术	Operating Expenses for Education and Operating Expenses for Science and Technology	
社会保障和就业	Operating Expenses for Medical Treatment and Sanitation	
环境保护	Operating Expenses for Environmental Conservation	
城乡社区事务	Expenses of Community	
农林水事务	Expenses of Agriculture, Forest and Irrigation	
物价总指数(上年=100)	Price Indices (preceding year=100)	
居民消费价格总指数	Consumer Price Index	101.2
商品零售价格总指数	Retail Price Index	101.4
工业品出厂价格指数`	Producer Price Indices for Manufacture Goods	
原材料、燃料、动力购进价格指数	Purchasing Price Indices of Raw Material ,Fuel and Power	
固定资产投资价格指数	Investment in Fixed Assets Price Indices	
利用外资(万美元)	Utilization of Foreign Capital (USD 10 000)	
签订利用外资协议额	Amount of Foreign Capital for Utilization through Signed Contracts or Agreements	
实际利用外资额	Amount of Foreign Capital Actually Utilized	
能源生产与消费(万吨标准煤)	Production and Consumption of Energy (10 000 tons of SCE)	
能源生产总量	Total Energy Production	1410.75
能源消费总量	Total Energy Consumption	979.27

Principal Aggregate Indicators on National Economic and Social Development and Growth Rates in Main Years

总量指标 Aggregate Data				速度指标(%) Indices and Growth Rates						
				指数(2010 年比以下各年) Index (2010 as percentuage of the following years)				平均增长速度 Average Annual Growth Rate		
1990	2000	2009	2010	1978	1990	2000	2009	1979-2010	1991-2010	2001-2010
1529.16	1849.41	2158.63	2181.33	176.9	142.7	118.0	101.1	1.8	1.8	1.7
785.06	957.07	1098.31	1119.02	177.6	142.5	116.9	101.9	1.8	1.8	1.6
744.10	892.34	1060.32	1062.31	176.2	142.8	119.1	100.2	1.8	1.8	1.8
617.70	672.50	866.15	894.65	182.1	144.8	133.0	103.3	1.9	1.9	2.9
300.53	255.75	239.54	245.48	108.3	81.7	96.0	102.5	0.3	-1.0	-0.4
9.60	11.00	11.86	10.99		114.5	99.9	92.7		0.7	...
261.44	1363.56	4277.05	5437.47	2343.5	674.2	266.8	110.6	10.4	10.0	10.3
104.09	288.18	759.74	1078.63	992.2	316.6	172.9	104.5	7.4	5.9	5.6
83.18	537.58	1929.59	2592.15	2160.3	799.5	295.7	112.6	10.1	11.0	11.5
74.17	537.80	1587.72	1766.69	6023.1	957.7	290.8	110.8	13.7	12.0	11.3
166.77	760.20	2266.20	2865.56							
121.12	492.31	1284.66	1578.93							
45.65	267.88	981.54	1286.63							
141.17	618.12	2549.75	3371.22							
91.50	648.12	2473.24	3233.00							
49.67	-30.00	76.51	138.22							
-46.50	-14.76	-538.90	-799.31							
88.78	610.38	2827.24	3539.69	27228.4	3987.0	579.9	125.2	19.2	20.2	19.2
79.16	556.85	2535.87	3181.58	24473.7	4019.2	571.4	125.5	18.8	20.3	19.0
0.95	57.43	235.88	347.72		36602.1	605.5	147.4		34.3	19.7
9.62	53.53	291.37	358.11		3722.6	669.0	122.9		19.8	20.9
21.78	79.07	388.78	500.58	7010.9	2298.3	633.1	128.8	14.2	17.0	20.3
20.45	64.53	301.13	416.23	9590.6	2035.4	645.0	138.2	15.3	16.3	20.5
47.62	190.95	1346.91	1698.91	9981.8	3567.6	889.7	126.1	15.5	19.6	24.4
		195.64	195.57				100.0			
		256.29	334.02				130.3			
		177.49	166.40				93.8			
		36.42	51.02				140.1			
		79.03	95.28				120.6			
		196.78	220.50				112.1			
105.0	99.4	100.7	104.3							
104.1	98.3	100.4	104.6							
	129.4	85.5	125.3							
	115.2	90.6	123.9							
	103.6	98.0	104.6							
4463	9212	47000	30091		674.2	326.7	64.0		10.0	12.6
7629	1923	21570	23742		311.2	1234.6	110.1		5.8	28.6
2801.57	5419.77	13542.33								
1924.45	3316.03	7525.56								

1-5 续表 1

指　　标	Item	1978
产　业	**Industry**	
农　业	**Agriculture**	
农林牧渔业总产值(亿元)	Gross Output Value of Farming, Forestry, Animal Husbandry and Fishery (100 million yuan)	19.12
主要农产品产量(万吨)	Output of Major Farm Products (10 000 tons)	
粮　食	Grain	370.01
棉　花	Cotton	5.50
油　料	Oil-bearing Crops	10.33
甜　菜	Beet Roots	16.37
水　果	Fruits	13.98
肉　类	Meat	9.65
奶　类	Milk	5.25
水产品	Aquatic Products	0.57
工　业	**Industry**	
主要工业产品产量	Output of Major Industrial Products	
纱(万吨)	Yarn (10 000 tons)	2.80
布(亿米)	Cloth (100 million meter)	1.56
绒线(吨)	Knitting Wool (ton)	1239
呢绒(万米)	Woolen Goods (10 000 meter)	189
原盐(万吨)	Crude Salt (10 000 tons)	51.71
机制纸及纸板(万吨)	Machine-Made Paper and Paperboards (10 000 tons)	1.99
成品糖(万吨)	Refined Sugar (10 000 tons)	2.08
原煤(万吨)	Natural Crude Petroleum Coal (10 000 tons)	1079.01
原油(万吨)	Crude Oil (10 000 tons)	353.05
天然气(亿立方米)	Natural Gas (100 million cu.m)	2.51
发电量(亿千瓦小时)	ElectriCity (100 million kwh)	21.17
粗钢(万吨)	Crude Steel (10 000 tons)	8.46
钢材(万吨)	Steel Products (10 000 tons)	6.83
水泥(万吨)	Cement (10 000 tons)	78.15
全部工业总产值(亿元)	Gross industrial Output Value (100 million yuan)	33.91
规模以上工业企业主要经济指标	Principal Financial Indicators of Industrial Enterprises Above Designated Size	
固定资产原值(亿元)	Original Value of Fixed Assets (100 million yuan)	45.92
利润总额(亿元)	Profits (100 million yuan)	4.28
建筑业	**Construction**	
建筑业企业从业人员(万人)	Number of Employed Persons (10 000 persons)	
建筑业企业总产值(亿元)	Gross Output Value (100 million yuan)	
施工房屋面积(万平方米)	Floor Space of Buildings under Construction (10 000 sq.m)	
竣工房屋面积(万平方米)	Floor Space of Buildings Completed (10 000 sq.m)	
交通运输	**Transportation**	
货运量(万吨)	Freight Traffic (10 000 tons)	6065
铁　路	Railways	923
公　路	Highways	4843
管　道	Pipelines	298
航　空	Civil Aviation	0.12
客运量(万人)	Passenger Traffic Volume (10 000 persons)	941
铁　路	Railways	148
公　路	Highways	786
航　空	Civil Aviation	7

Continued

总量指标 Aggregate Data				速度指标(%) Indices and Growth Rates						
				指数(2010 年比以下各年) Index (2010 as percentage of the following years)				平均增长速度 Average Annual Growth Rate		
1990	2000	2009	2010	1978	1990	2000	2009	1979-2010	1991-2010	2001-2010
144.65	487.20	1297.61	1846.18							
676.89	808.60	1152.00	1150.20	310.9	169.9	142.2	99.8	3.6	2.7	3.6
46.88	150.00	252.40	247.90	4507.3	528.8	165.3	98.2	12.6	8.7	5.2
38.96	60.14	63.91	66.62	644.9	171.0	110.8	104.2	6.0	2.7	1.0
224.37	292.65	418.41	486.97	2974.8	217.0	166.4	116.4	11.2	4.0	5.2
79.88	151.87	565.15	593.85	4247.9	743.4	391.0	105.1	12.4	10.6	14.6
30.46	90.00	115.31	121.74	1261.6	399.7	135.3	105.6	8.2	7.2	3.1
35.64	78.23	125.15	132.82	2529.9	372.7	169.8	106.1	10.6	6.8	5.4
2.32	6.01	9.70	10.11	1773.7	435.8	168.2	104.2	9.4	7.6	5.3
10.19	33.43	38.61	41.58	1485.0	408.0	124.4	107.7	8.8	7.3	2.2
3.00	2.81	1.51	1.51	96.8	50.3	53.7	100.0	-0.1	-3.4	-6.0
2179	1184	533	741	59.8	34.0	62.6	139.0	-1.6	-5.3	-4.6
1230	754	376	326	172.5	26.5	43.2	86.7	1.7	-6.4	-8.0
159.00	31.78	129.36	174.67	337.8	109.9	549.6	135.0	3.9	0.5	18.6
9.09	17.65	35.58	37.10	1864.3	408.1	210.2	104.3	9.6	7.3	7.7
16.84	30.76	40.77	45.10	2168.3	267.8	146.6	110.6	10.1	5.0	3.9
2100.00	2798.90	8812.55	9926.73	920.0	472.7	354.7	112.6	7.2	8.1	13.5
695.00	1848.43	2512.86	2558.16	724.6	368.1	138.4	101.8	6.4	6.7	3.3
5.02	35.39	245.39	249.91	9956.6	4978.3	706.2	101.8	15.5	21.6	21.6
69.79	182.98	571.31	679.32	3208.9	973.4	371.3	118.9	11.4	12.1	14.0
36.49	109.70	653.32	825.54	9758.2	2262.4	752.5	126.4	15.4	16.9	22.4
28.48	131.26	690.81	891.70	13055.6	3131.0	679.3	129.1	16.4	18.8	21.1
285.00	895.67	2049.60	2401.00	3072.3	842.5	268.1	117.1	11.3	11.2	10.4
219.92	1061.29	4184.5	5766.51							
233.86	1387.56	5154.56	6111.28	13308.5	2613.2	440.4	118.6	16.5	17.7	16.0
3.13	90.49	484.58	852.43	19916.6	27234.2	942.0	175.9	18.0	32.4	25.1
22.86	26.16	48.18	56.48		247.1	215.9	117.2		4.6	8.0
27.39	234.95	791.38	969.47		3539.5	412.6	122.5		19.5	15.2
578.05	2241.48	5151.60	6620.14		1145.3	295.3	128.5		13.0	11.4
282.88	1261.42	2517.79	2891.44		1022.1	229.2	114.8		12.3	8.6
13920	33091	60163	64597	1065.1	464.1	195.2	107.4	7.7	8.0	6.9
1691	4199	6413	6854	742.6	405.3	163.2	106.9	6.5	7.2	5.0
11551	27048	46787	50447	1041.6	436.7	186.5	107.8	7.6	7.6	6.4
677	1840	6959	7293	2447.3	1077.3	396.4	104.8	10.5	12.6	14.8
0.87	3.50	3.80	3.70	3083.3	425.3	105.7	97.4	11.3	7.5	0.6
9602	23191	43410	46346	4925.2	482.7	199.8	106.8	13.0	8.2	7.2
388	1147	1371	1523	1029.1	392.5	132.8	111.1	7.6	7.1	2.9
9161	21877	41604	44333	5640.3	483.9	202.6	106.6	13.4	8.2	7.3
53	167	435	435	6214.3	820.8	260.5	100.0	13.8	11.1	10.0

1-5 续表 2

指　　标	Item	1978
邮电通信业	**Postal and Telecommunication Services**	
邮电业务总量(亿元)	Business Volunce of Postal and Telecommunication Services (100 million yuan)	0.21
函　件(万件)	Number of Letters Delivered (10 000 pieces)	4843
报刊期发数(万份)	Number of Newspapers and Magazines Distributed (10 000 copies)	224
局用交换机容量(万门)	CapaCity of Office Telephone Exchanges (10 000 lines)	
固定电话年末用户(万部)	Local Telephone Subscribers at Year-end (10 000 subscribers)	2.90
移动电话用户(万户)	Number of Mobile Telephone Subscribers (10 000 subscribers)	
国内商业	**Domestic Trades**	
社会消费品零售总额(亿元)	Total Retail Sales of Consumer Goods (100 million yuan)	21.89
对外经济贸易	**Foreign Trades**	
进出口总额(万美元)	Total Value of Exports and Imports (USD 10 000)	2346
出口额	Exports	937
进口额	Imports	1409
国际旅游	**International Tourism**	
入境旅游人数(万人)	Number of Tourists from Abroad (10 000 persons)	0.01
国际旅游收入(万美元)	Earnings from International Tourism (USD 10 000)	5
金　融	**Finance and Insurance**	
金融机构各项存款(亿元)	Deposits of National Banking System (100 million yuan)	32.07
金融机构各项贷款(亿元)	Loans of National Banking System (100 million yuan)	18.26
教育、科技、文化	**Education, Science & Technology and Culture**	
教　育	**Education**	
专任教师数(人)	Full-time Teachers (person)	
普通高等学校	Regular Institutions of Higher Education	2458
中等学校	Regular Secondary Schools	44417
小　学	Regular Primary Schools	82616
在校学生数(万人)	Students Enrollment (10 000 persons)	
普通高等学校	Regular Institutions of Higher Education	1.02
中等学校	Regular Secondary Schools	83.86
小　学	Regular Primary Schools	202.88
科　技	**Science and Technology**	
科学家、工程师数(人)	Number of Scientists and Engineers (person)	
研究与发展经费支出(万元)	Expenditures on Research and Development (10 000 yuan)	
技术市场成交额(万元)	Volume of Transaction in Technical Markets (10 000 yuan)	
文　化	**Culture**	
电视节目制作时间(小时)	Time for TV Programs Production (hour)	

Continued

总量指标 Aggregate Data				速度指标(%) Indices and Growth Rates						
				指数(2010 年比以下各年) Index (2010as percentage of the following years)				平均增长速度 Average Annual Growth Rate		
1990	2000	2009	2010	1978	1990	2000	2009	1979-2010	1991-2010	2001-2010
1.74	47.3	479.65	582.05	277166.7	33451.1	1230.5	121.3	28.1	33.7	28.5
7381	7148	2800	2926	60.4	39.6	40.9	104.5	-1.6	-4.5	-8.5
806	535	296	307	137.1	38.1	57.4	103.7	1.0	-4.7	-5.4
	241.67	930.00	928.20			384.1	99.8			14.4
8.94	191.03	573.10	547.50	18879.3	6124.2	286.6	95.5	17.8	22.8	11.1
	78.00	1119.60	1359.80			1743.3	121.5			33.1
104.30	374.50	1177.53	1324.48	6050.6	1269.9	353.7	112.5	13.7	13.6	13.5
41025	226399	1382771	1712834	73010.8	4175.1	756.6	123.9	22.9	20.5	22.4
33530	120408	1082325	1296981	138418.5	3868.1	1077.2	119.8	25.4	20.1	26.8
7495	105991	300446	415853	29514.1	5548.4	392.3	138.4	19.5	22.2	14.6
7.98	25.61	35.49	101.03	1010300.0	1266.0	394.5	284.7	33.4	13.5	14.7
1212	9494	13663	36844	736880.0	3039.9	388.1	269.7	32.1	18.6	14.5
221.80	1863.48	6845.07	8870.02	27658.3	3999.1	476.0	129.6	19.2	20.3	16.9
233.72	1403.13	3782.92	4973.16	27235.3	2127.8	354.4	131.5	19.2	16.5	13.5
7002	7924	16234	16506	671.5	235.7	208.3	101.7	6.1	4.4	7.6
78596	89211	125152	128306	288.9	163.2	143.8	102.5	3.4	2.5	3.7
95060	131259	134263	133963	162.2	140.9	102.1	99.8	1.5	1.7	0.2
3.13	7.41	25.33	26.38	2586.3	842.8	356.0	104.1	10.7	11.2	13.5
101.52	131.18	169.60	168.40	200.8	165.9	128.4	99.3	2.2	2.6	2.5
185.72	247.74	197.39	193.58	95.4	104.2	78.1	98.1	-0.1	0.2	-2.4
	16018	11111	9063			56.6	81.6			-5.5
	32381	8666	15644			48.3	180.5			-7.0
	66168	46418								
3699	29261	66321	76467		2067.2	261.3	115.3		16.4	10.1

1-5 续表 3

指　　标	Item	1978
家庭、生活、环境	**Family, People's Livelihood and Environment**	
家　庭	**Family**	
家庭总户数(万户)	Total Number of Households (10 000 households)	
婚　姻	**Marriages and Divorces**	
结婚数(万对)	Number of Marriages (10 000 couples)	
离婚数(万对)	Number of Divorces (10 000 couples)	
居　住	**Housing**	
城镇居民人均使用面积(平方米)	Per capita Gross Floor Space of Urban Residents (sq.m)	
城镇居民人均建筑面积(平方米)	Per capita Gross Living Space in Urban Areas (sq.m)	
农村居民人均居住面积(平方米)	Per capita Net Floor Space of Rural Residents (sq.m)	
生　活	**People's Livelihood**	
城镇居民人均可支配收入(元)	Per Capita Annual Disposable Income of Urban Households (yuan)	319
农村居民人均纯收入(元)	Per Capita Net Income of Rural Residents (yuan)	119
城乡居民储蓄存款余额(亿元)	Outstanding Amount of Saving Deposits in Urban and Rural Areas (100 million yuan)	6.42
工　资	**Wages and Welfare**	
工资总额(亿元)	Total Wages (100 million yuan)	15.94
在岗职工平均工资(元)	Average Wage of Staff and Workers (yuan)	717
卫　生	**Health Care**	
医院、卫生院(个)	Number of Hospitals (unit)	806
医生(人)	Number of Doctors (person)	16898
医院、卫生院床位数(张)	Number of Hospital Beds (unit)	39179
市政建设	**Municipal Works**	
自来水供应量(亿立方米)	Volume of Tapping Water Supply(100 million cu.m)	
下水道长度(公里)	Length of Sewer Pipelines (km)	
铺装道路长度(公里)	Length of Paved Roads (km)	
环境、灾害	**Environment and Disaster**	
工业污染治理项目年完成投资额(万元)	Investment Completed in Pollution Treatment Projects (10 000 yuan)	
火灾发生数(起)	Number of Fire Disasters (times)	
火灾损失(万元)	Fire Loss (10 000 yuan)	
交通事故发生数(起)	Number of Traffic Accidents (times)	
交通事故损失(万元)	Loss of Traffic Accidents (10 000 yuan)	

Continued

总量指标 Aggregate Data				速度指标(%) Indices and Growth Rates						
				指数(2010 年比以下各年) Index (2010 as percentage of the following years)				平均增长速度 Average Annual Growth Rate		
1990	2000	2009	2010	1978	1990	2000	2009	1979-2010	1991-2010	2001-2010
356.67	481.91	640.36	639.86		179.4	132.8	99.9		3.0	…
15.84	16.25	26.55	26.40		166.7	162.5	99.4		2.6	5.0
5.65	5.90	8.83	9.78		173.1	165.8	110.8		2.8	5.2
13.55	20.06	20.42	20.49		151.2	102.1	100.3		2.1	0.2
18.07	26.75	27.16	27.25		150.8	101.9	100.3		2.1	0.2
14.04	17.25	23.45	24.00		170.9	139.1	102.3		2.7	3.4
1314	5645	12258	13644	4277.1	1038.4	241.7	111.3	12.5	12.4	9.2
684	1618	3883	4643	3901.7	678.8	287.0	119.6	12.1	10.0	11.1
128.42	908.55	3050.81	3713.47	57842.2	2891.7	408.7	121.7	22.0	18.3	15.1
66.88	234.47	691.21	828.69	5198.8	1239.1	353.4	119.9	13.1	13.4	13.5
2272	8717	27753	32361	4513.4	1424.3	371.2	116.6	12.6	14.2	14.0
1049	1352	1669	1712	212.4	163.2	126.6	102.6	2.4	2.5	2.4
33683	45402	45616	48166	285.0	143.0	106.1	105.6	3.3	1.8	0.6
60707	65916	107193	109851	280.4	181.0	166.7	102.5	3.3	3.0	5.2
1.57	5.00	7.52	7.73		492.4	154.6	102.8		8.3	4.5
533	2008	4081	4372		820.3	217.7	107.1		11.1	8.1
970	2809	4940	5178		533.8	184.3	104.8		8.7	6.3
5138	22311	143495	66813		1300.4	299.5	46.6		13.7	11.6
	3050	4963	5209			170.8	105.0			5.5
	2329	2127	3041			130.6	143.0			2.7
	10048	5041	4949			49.3	98.2			-6.8
	4443	897	864			19.4	96.3			-15.1

1-6 主要年份国民经济和社会发展结构指标
Composition Indicators on National Economic and Social Development in Main Years

单位: % (%)

指　标	Item	1978	1990	2000	2009	2010
人口与就业	**Population and Employment**					
人　口	**Population**					
性别结构	Sexual Composition					
男	Male	51.1	51.3	51.8	50.9	51.3
女	Female	48.9	48.7	48.2	49.1	48.7
就　业	**Employment**					
产业结构	Industrial Composition					
第一产业	Primary Industry	72.1	61.3	57.7	49.4	49.0
第二产业	Secondary Industry	14.3	17.4	13.8	14.7	14.8
第三产业	Tertiary Industry	13.6	21.3	28.5	35.9	36.2
宏观经济	**Macro Economy**					
国民核算	**National Accounting**					
新疆生产总值产业结构	Industrial Composition					
第一产业	Primary Industry	35.8	39.8	21.1	17.8	19.8
第二产业	Secondary Industry	47.0	31.8	39.4	45.1	47.7
#工　业	Industry	37.1	27.3	30.7	36.4	39.8
第三产业	Tertiary Industry	17.2	28.4	39.5	37.1	32.5
固定资产投资	**Investment**					
全社会固定资产投资结构	Composition of Total Investment in Fixed Assets					
城　镇	Urban	100	89.2	91.2	89.7	89.9
#房地产	Real Estate Development		1.2	10.3	8.3	9.8
农　村	Rural		10.8	8.8	10.3	10.1
资金来源结构	Composition of Funded Sources					
国家预算内资金	State Budgetary Appropriation	79.0	11.9	8.3	19.2	16.8
国内贷款	Domestic Loans		33.2	22.1	17.3	15.2
利用外资	Foreign Investment		4.6	1.6	0.3	0.3
自筹和其他投资	Fundraising and Other Investment	21.0	50.3	68	63.2	67.7
对外经济贸易	**Foreign Economic Trade**					
进出口总额结构	Composition of total Value of Exports and Imports					
出口额	Exports	39.9	81.7	53.2	78.3	75.7
进口额	Imports	60.1	18.3	46.8	21.7	24.3
财　政	**Government Finance**					
地方财政一般预算收入结构	Composition of Government Revenue					
税收收入	Various Taxes	60.8	93.9	81.6	77.5	83.2
非税收入	Nontax Revenues	39.2	6.1	18.4	22.5	16.8
地方财政一般预算支出结构	Composition of Government Expenditures					
一般公共服务	General Common Service				14.5	11.5
教育与科学技术	Operating Expenses for Education and Operating Expenses for				19.0	19.7
社会保障和就业	Operating Expenses for Medical Treatment and Sanitation				13.2	9.8
环境保护	Operating Expenses for Environmental Conservation				2.7	3.0
城乡社区事务	Expenses of Community				5.9	5.6
农林水事务	Expenses of Agriculture, Forest and Irrigation				14.6	13.0
其他各项支出	Other Expense				30.1	37.4
能源生产与消费	**Energy Production and Consumption**					
能源生产总量结构	Composition of Total Energy Production					
原　煤	Coal	60.0	58.8	40.6	46.5	
原　油	Petroleum Crude Oil	35.8	35.8	48.7	26.5	
天然气	Natural Gas	2.4	2.4	7.9	24.1	
水风电	Water, Wind and Electricity	1.8	3.0	2.8	2.9	
能源消费总量结构	Composition of Total Energy Consumption					
煤　炭	Coal	72.5	69.6	63.6	65.9	
石　油	Petroleum Oil	21.5	22.5	23.3	16.9	
天然气	Natural Gas	3.4	3.5	8.6	12.0	
水电、风电	Hydro-power, Wind Power	2.6	4.4	4.5	5.2	

1-6 续表 1 Continued

单位: % (%)

指　标	Item	1978	1990	2000	2009	2010
产　业	**Industrial**					
农 业	**Agriculture**					
农林牧渔业产值结构	Composition of Gross Output Value of AgricultureForestry,Animal Husbandry, Fishery					
农 业	Farming	74.5	76.4	74.0	69.2	74.6
林 业	Forestry	1.8	2.6	1.7	2.1	1.9
牧 业	Animal Husbandry	23.5	20.4	23.5	24.5	20.4
渔 业	Fishery	0.2	0.6	0.8	0.9	0.7
农林牧渔服务业	Agricultural, Forestry, Animal Husbandry, Fishery and Their Services				3.3	2.4
工 业	**Industry**					
工业总产值规模结构	Composition of Gross Output Value of Industry					
大型企业	Large Enterprises		27.5	53.7	56.5	55.2
中型企业	Medium-sized Enterprises		17.4	10.1	23.1	24.4
小型企业	Small Enterprises		55.1	36.2	20.4	20.4
建筑业	**Construction**					
建筑业总产值结构	Composition of Gross Output Value of Construction Industry					
建筑工程	Construction Projects		88.2	88.3	87.5	87.2
安装工程	Installation Projects		10.3	9.1	11	11.4
其 他	Others		1.5	2.6	1.5	1.4
交通运输业	**Transportation**					
货运量结构按运输方式分	By Means of Transportation					
铁 路	Railways	15.2	12.1	12.7	10.6	10.6
公 路	Highways	79.9	83	81.7	77.8	78.1
民用航空	Civil Aviation	…	…	…	...	...
管道输油(气)	Pipelines	4.9	4.9	5.6	11.6	11.3
旅游业	**International Tourism**					
来华旅游人数结构	Composition of Tourists					
外国人	Foreigners	100.0	80.4	81.4	89.7	94.8
港澳台同胞	Compatriots form Hong Kong, Macao and Taiwan		19.6	18.6	10.3	5.2
金 融	**Finance**					
金融机构资金来源结构	Composition of Sources of Funds in State Banks					
各项存款	Various Deposits			122.8	110.5	110.1
应付及暂收款	Payable and Temporary Collection			…	1.7	1.5
所有者权益	Owner's Right and Interest			0.1	2.8	3.6
其 他	Others			-22.9	-15.0	-15.3
金融机构资金运用结构	Composition of Fund Uses in State Banks					
各项贷款	Loans			92.5	61.1	61.8
有价证券及投资	Securities and Investment			4.4	3.2	5.6
行内资金往来	Funds Tranfer inward Banks			1.6	32.8	29.1
库存现金	Cash in Stock			1.1	0.7	0.7
其 他	Others			0.4	2.2	2.8

1-6 续表 2 Continued

单位: % (%)

指 标	Item	1978	1990	2000	2009	2010
教育、科技	**Education and Science**					
教 育	**Education**					
在校学生结构	Composition of Student Enrollment					
大学生	College and University Students	0.4	1.1	2.0	6.5	6.8
中学生	Secondary School Students	29.1	31.4	30.8	43.2	43.4
小学生	Primary School Students	70.5	67.5	67.2	50.3	49.8
专任教师结构	Full-time Teachers by Type					
大 学	Colleges and Universities	1.9	3.9	3.5	5.9	5.9
中 学	Secondary Schools	34.3	43.5	39.1	45.4	46.0
小 学	Primary Schools	63.8	52.6	57.4	48.7	48.1
科 技	**Science and Technology**					
科学研究与试验发展经费支出结构	Composition of Expenditure on Research and Development					
基础研究	Basic Research			4.7	4.8	
应用研究	Supplied Research			27.4	35.6	
实验发展	Experimental Development			67.9	59.6	
生活、环境	**People's Livelihood and Environment**					
生 活	**People's Livelihood**					
城镇居民消费结构	Consumption Composition of Urban Residents					
食品类	Food		47.8	36.4	36.3	36.2
衣着类	Clothing		15.6	13.1	14.5	14.8
家庭设备、用品及服务	Articles for Daily Use and Others		11.0	7.6	5.9	6.6
医疗保健	Health Care and Medical Services		2.5	7.5	7.3	6.9
交通通讯	Transport and Communication		1.6	7.5	12.9	12.3
教育文化娱乐服务	Education ,Culture and Recreation Services		11.2	15.1	9.2	9.9
居 住	Residence		4.6	9.4	9.2	8.8
杂项商品和服务	Miscellaneous Goods and Services		5.7	3.4	4.7	4.5
农村居民消费结构	Consumption Composition of Rural Residents					
食品类	Food		53.7	50.0	41.6	40.3
衣着类	Clothing		15.3	9.2	8.9	8.8
家庭设备、用品及其他	Articles for Daily Use and Others		17.4	3.7	3.6	4.0
医疗保健	Health Care and Medical Services		7.0	6.0	10.7	9.1
交通通讯	Transport and Communication		1.1	4.9	10.8	11.1
教育文化娱乐服务	Education ,Culture and Recreation Services		5.3	8.6	5.4	4.9
居 住	Residence		13.5	13.8	17.4	20.1
其他商品和服务	Other Goods and Services		0.7	3.8	1.6	1.7
卫 生	**Health Care**					
卫生技术人员结构	Doctors by Types					
执业医师(西医师)	(Doctors of Western Medicine)	14.4	31.3	76.9	32.5	32.0
执业助理医师(西医士)	(Paramedics of Western Medicine)	18.7	10.9	23.1	7.3	7.2
注册护士	Registered Nurses	21.1	29.3		35.3	36.0
药剂人员	Pharmacist		7.9		5.2	5.2
技师(士)	Laboratory Technician				6.3	6.3
其他	Others				13.4	13.3
环境、灾害	**Environment and Disasters**					
治理工业污染资金使用结构	Uses of Funds Inindustrial Pollution Treatment					
治理废水	Waste Water Treatment		55.3	38.2	21.4	29.5
治理废气	Waste Gas Treatment		32.4	40.9	76.2	69.3
治理固体废物	Solid Wastes Treatment		10.6	1.6	0.4	1.2
治理噪声	Noise Abatement		0.9	18.4	0.1	
其 他	Others		0.8	0.9	1.9	…
火灾事故损失额结构	Composition of Fire Losses Converted into Cash					
特 大	Extraordinarily Serious Fires			15.7		
重 大	Serious Fires			14.3		...
较 大	Big Fires				0.1	0.1
一 般	Ordinary Fires			70	99.9	99.9

1-7 主要年份国民经济和社会发展比例和效益指标

Indicators on Proportions and Efficiency in National Economic and Social Development in Main Years

指标	Item	1978	1990	2000	2009	2010
就业	**Employment**					
城镇登记失业率(%)	Unemployment Rate in Urban Areas (%)		3.8	3.8	3.8	3.2
国民经济核算	**National Accounting**					
人均生产总值(元/人)	Per capita GDP (yuan/person)	313	1713	7372	19942	25057
固定资产投资	**Investment in Fixed Assets**					
全社会固定资产投资相当于新疆生产总值比例(%)	Proportion of Investment in Fixed Assets to GDP of Xinjiang (%)	33.3	34.0	44.8	66.1	65.1
全社会房屋建筑面积竣工率(%)	Rate of Total Floor Space of Buildings Completed in Construction (%)		76.8	58.7	48.4	40.9
消费	**Consumption**					
人均社会消费品零售额(元)	Per Capita Retail Sales of Consumer Goods(yuan)	179	699	2066	5490	6104
对外贸易	**Foreign Trade**					
进出口总额相当于新疆生产总值比例(%)	Proportion of Total Value of Imports & Exports to GDP	1.01	7.52	13.74	22.08	21.32
财政	**Finance**					
地方财政一般预算收入相当于新疆生产总值比例(%)	Proportion of Local Financial Revenue to GDP of Xinjiang (%)	18.3	8.3	5.8	9.1	9.2
地方财政一般预算支出相当于新疆生产总值比例(%)	Proportion of Local Financial Expenditure to GDP of Xinjiang (%)	43.6	18.2	14.0	31.5	31.2
利用外资	**Utilization of Foreign Capital**					
实际利用外资额相当于签订利用外资额比例(%)	Proportion of Actually Foreign Direct Investment for Foreign Direct Investment (%)		80.94	20.87	45.89	78.90
能源	**Energy**					
能源生产弹性系数	Elasticity Ratio of Energy Production	1.20	0.50	0.40	0.85	
电力生产弹性系数	Elasticity Ratio of Electricety Production		0.92	0.99	1.77	
能源消费弹性系数	Elasticity Ratio of Energy Consumption	0.74	0.79	0.38	0.80	
电力消费弹性系数	Elasticity Ratio of Electricity Consumption		0.92	0.99	1.77	
单位新疆生产总值能耗（吨标准煤/万元）	Energy Consumption per unit of GDP		7.37	2.43	1.93	

1-7 续表 1 Continued

指　　标	Item	1978	1990	2000	2009	2010
农　业	**Agriculture**					
每公顷播种面积农产品产量（公斤）	Output of Farm Crops per Hectare of Sown Area (kg)					
粮　食	Grain	1650	3705	5595	5779	5771
棉　花	Cotton	375	1080	1485	1791	1697
油　料	Oil-bearing Crops	510	1440	1935	2367	2437
工业（规模以上）	**Industry(Aboue Designated Size)**					
总资产贡献率（%）	Rate of Total Assets to Industrial Output Value (%)			11.2	15.1	18.2
资产负债率（%）	Assets-Liability Ratio (%)			62.7	54.1	50.8
成本费用利润率（%）	Rate of Profits to Industrial Cost (%)		2.6	12.8	14.3	19.3
流动资产周转次数（次/年）	Number of Times of Annual of Turnover Circulating Funds (times/year)		1.5	1.6	2.0	2.2
建筑业	**Construction**					
技术装备率（元/人）	Value of Machinery per Laborer (yuan/person)		2511	8582	9136	7145
动力装备率（千瓦/人）	Power of Machines Per Laborer (kw/person)		5	7	5	4
全员劳动生产率(按总产值计算)(元/人)	Overall Labor Productivity (yuan/person) (in terms of gross output value per employee)		12014	74994	173714	176404
交通运输业	**Transportation**					
铁路网密度（公里/万平方公里）	Railway Density (km/10 000 sq.km)	6.19	9.48	18.08	23.05	26.39
公路网密度（公里/万平方公里）	Highway Density (km/10 000 sq.km)	143	153	208	905	918
邮电通信业	**Post and Communications**					
固定电话普及率(部/百人)	PopularizationRate of Telephones (set/100 persons)		0.6	15.0	26.9	25.4
移动电话普及率(部/百人)	Popularization Rate of Mobile Telephone (set/100 persons)				52.6	63.0
国际旅游	**International Tourism**					
每一来华游客花费(美元)	Expenditure per International Tourist in China (USD)		152	371	385	346

1-7 续表 2 Continued

指　　标	Item	1978	1990	2000	2009	2010
金　融	**Finance**					
金融机构存款相当于新疆生产总值比例(%)	Bank Deposits as Percentage of GDP in Xinjiang (%)	82.08	84.98	136.62	160.04	163.13
金融机构贷款相当于新疆生产总值比例(%)	Bank Loans as Percentage of GDP in Xinjiang (%)	46.74	89.55	102.87	88.45	91.46
金融机构现金支出相当于收入比例(%)	Proportion of Cash Outlay to Cash Receipt in Bank (%)		105.71	101.65	101.49	101.73
教　育	**Education**					
学龄儿童入学率(%)	Rate of School-age Children Enrollment (%)	96.00	97.50	97.03	99.41	99.78
小学升学率(%)	Rate of Graduates of Primary Schools Entering Junior Secondary Schools (%)	88.67	82.17	92.01	100.33	100.53
初中升学率(%)	Rate of Graduates of Junior Secondary Schools Entering Senior Secondary Schools (%)	48.22	39.12	30.30	41.94	45.40
学校教师负担系数(%)	Student-teacher Ratio (in percentage) (%)					
高等学校	Colleges and Universities	4.16	4.47	9.34	14.88	15.22
普通中等	Secondary Schools	19.36	13.12	14.92	13.04	12.48
小学学校	Primary Schools	24.56	19.54	18.87	14.70	14.45
科　技	**Science and Technology**					
研究与开发经费支出相当于新疆生产总值比例(%)	R&D Expenditures as Percentage of GDP (%)			0.38	0.52	
文　化	**Culture**					
每百万人有艺术表演团体(个)	Number of Troupes per Million Persons(unit)	5.24	6.21	4.76	6.30	6.08
每百万人有公共图书馆(个)	Number of Public Libraries per Million Persons(unit)	0.41	4.05	4.33	4.35	4.75
每百万人有博物馆(个)	Number of Museums per Million Persons(unit)	0.08	0.52	1.24	2.92	3.27
卫　生	**Health Care**					
每万人医院、卫生院数(个)	Number of Hospitals and Health Centers per 10 000 Persons (unit)	0.66	0.69	0.73	0.77	0.79
每万人医生数(人)	Number of Doctors per 10 000 Persons (person)	13.70	22.03	24.59	21.13	22.25
每万人医院、卫生院床位数(张)	Number of Hospital and Health Centers Beds per 10 000 Persons (unit)	31.80	40.50	35.70	47.50	50.36
医院病床使用率(%)	Utilization Rate of Hospital Beds (%)		77.20	66.31	81.08	83.81
市政建设	**City Construction**					
城市自来水普及率(%)	Percentage of Households with Access to Tap Water (%)	59.0	80.9	98.8	99.0	99.2
城市燃气普及率(%)	Percentage of Households with Access to Tap Gas (%)	11.0	49.8	92.8	89.3	95.8
建成区绿化覆盖率(%)	Green Covrage Rate in Completed Area(%)		26.0	29.1	36.3	36.4
灾　害	**Disasters**					
平均每起火灾损失(元)	Average Loss of per Fire Disaster (yuan)			7635	4287	5422
平均每起交通事故损失(元)	Average Loss of per Traffic Accident (yuan)			4775	1779	1746

1-8 主要年份人均主要工农业产品产量

Per capita Output of Major Industrial and Agricultural Products in Main Years

年份 Year	粮食(公斤) Grain (kg)	棉花(公斤) Cotton (kg)	油料(公斤) Oil-bearing Crops (kg)	甜菜(公斤) Sugar Crops (kg)	水果(公斤) Fruits (kg)	猪牛羊肉(公斤) Pork, Beef and Mutton (kg)	水产品(公斤) Aquatic Products (kg)
1978	303.0	4.5	8.5	13.4	11.4	7.9	0.5
1980	304.1	6.2	13.9	30.3	12.3	9.4	0.5
1985	367.2	13.9	25.3	30.1	36.4	12.8	0.7
1990	453.8	31.4	26.1	150.4	53.6	18.6	1.6
1995	443.3	56.8	30.0	174.9	69.4	27.9	2.7
2000	446.2	82.8	33.2	161.5	83.8	42.4	3.3
2001	427.3	84.3	22.9	244.3	82.8	44.5	3.3
2002	463.3	79.3	23.5	246.9	104.8	46.9	3.4
2003	417.6	83.4	26.1	198.8	113.7	50.4	3.5
2004	425.2	89.9	22.9	176.7	135.6	55.2	3.8
2005	441.5	98.5	19.6	211.0	146.6	60.5	4.0
2006	441.0	131.8	16.2	273.6	169.0	66.5	4.1
2007	418.3	139.9	19.4	283.2	214.7	67.1	4.3
2008	430.2	142.7	26.9	207.7	213.4	47.4	4.4
2009	537.1	117.7	29.8	195.1	263.5	46.5	4.5
2010	530.1	114.2	30.7	224.4	275.1	48.6	4.7

年份 Year	布(米) Cloth (m)	机制纸及纸板(公斤) Machine-made Paper and Paperboard (kg)	纱(公斤) Yarn (kg)	原煤(公斤) Coal (kg)	原油(公斤) Crude Oil (kg)	发电量(千瓦小时) Electricity (kwh)	粗钢(公斤) Steel (kg)	水泥(公斤) Cement (kg)
1978	13.0	1.6	2.3	884	289	173	7	64
1980	13.0	1.9	2.5	895	308	186	8	72
1985	16.0	3.1	2.9	1183	369	282	15	149
1990	20.0	6.1	6.8	1408	466	468	23	191
1995	18.0	11.0	14.9	1652	770	731	43	297
2000	15.0	9.7	18.5	1546	1021	1011	61	495
2001	14.0	10.4	16.3	1514	1045	1061	72	527
2002	11.0	12.0	16.7	1639	1077	1123	93	545
2003	8.0	12.2	15.3	1814	1116	1222	106	588
2004	7.0	13.5	15.0	1924	1156	1367	128	623
2005	7.0	14.6	17.2	1962	1212	1545	154	625
2006	8.0	14.5	17.6	2226	1219	1759	194	657
2007	8.0	12.2	19.7	2421	1257	2011	216	742
2008	7.2	14.3	18.8	3201	1285	2315	254	792
2009	7.1	16.6	18.0	4108	1171	2664	305	956
2010	7.0	17.1	19.2	4575	1179	3131	380	1106

1-9 主要年份人均国民经济主要指标
Per Capita Main Indicators on National Economy in Main Years

指标	Item	1978	1990	2000	2009	2010
新疆生产总值(元)	Gross Domestic Product of Xinjiang (yuan)	313	1713	7372	19942	25057
工农业总产值(元)	Gross Output Value of Industry and Agriculture (yuan)	450	2444	8544	25557	35082
工业总产值	Gross Industrial Output Value	278	1474	5856	19508	26574
农林牧渔业总产值	Gross Output Value of Agriculture, Forestry, Animal Husbandry and Fishery	172	970	2688	6049	8508
固定资产投资总额(元)	Total Investment in Fixed Assets (yuan)	106	595	3368	13181	16312
地方财政一般预算收入(元)	General Budgetary Revenue in Local Finance (yuan)	58	146	436	1812	2307
地方财政一般预算支出(元)	General Budgetary Expenditure in Local Finance (yuan)	139	319	1054	6279	7829
耕地面积(公顷)	Cultivated Area (hectare)	0.26	0.20	0.18		
主要工农业产品产量	Output of Major Industrial and Agriculturd Produts					
粮食(公斤)	Grain Yield (kg)	303.0	453.8	446.2	537.1	530.1
棉花(公斤)	Cotton Yield (kg)	4.5	31.4	82.8	117.7	114.2
油料(公斤)	Oil-bearing Crops Yield (kg)	8.5	26.1	33.2	29.8	30.7
甜菜(公斤)	Beet Roots Yield (kg)	13.4	150.4	161.5	195.1	224.4
猪牛羊肉(公斤)	Pork, Beef and Mutton Yield (kg)	7.9	18.6	42.4	46.5	48.6
水产品(公斤)	Aquatic Products Yield (kg)	0.5	1.6	3.3	4.5	4.7
水果(公斤)	Fruits Yield (kg)	11.4	53.6	83.8	263.5	275.1
果用瓜(公斤)	Fruit Melon Yield (kg)	36.1	62.6	83.3	229.0	200.5
布(米)	Cloth (m)	12.8	20.0	15.0	7.1	7.0
机制纸和纸板(公斤)	Machine-made Paper and Paperboard (kg)	1.6	6.1	9.7	16.6	17.1
纱(公斤)	Yarn (kg)	2.3	6.8	18.5	18.0	19.2
原煤(公斤)	Coal Output (kg)	884	1408	1546	4108	4575
原油(公斤)	Crude Oil Output (kg)	289	466	1021	1171	1179
发电量(千瓦小时)	Electric Power (kwh)	173	468	1011	2664	3131
水泥(公斤)	Cement (kg)	64	191	495	956	1106
社会消费品零售总额(元)	Total Retail Sales of Consumer Goods (yuan)	179	699	2066	5490	6104
海关出口总额(美元)	Value of Exports (USD)	0.8	23.2	66.5	644.6	789.3
高等学校在校学生数(人/万人)	Students Enrollment in Institions of Higher Education (person/10 000 persons)	8.3	20.5	41.1	111.9	115.1
中等专业学校在校学生数(人/万人)	Students Enrollment in Specialized Secondary Schools (person/10 000 persons)	19.2	30.0	56.9	69.2	69.8
普通中学在校学生数(人/万人)	Students Enrollment in Regular Secondary Schools (person/10 000 persons)	654.0	564.0	638.0	669.3	652.1
医院、卫生院床位数(张/万人)	Beds of Medical and Health Centers (unit/10 000 persons)	31.8	40.5	35.7	47.5	50.4
卫生技术人员数(人/万人)	Medical Technical Personnel (person/10 000 persons)	41.4	52.2	53.0	53.1	56.3
#医　生	Doctors	13.7	22.0	24.6	21.1	22.3
城乡居民储蓄存款余额(元)	Urban and Rural Savings Deposits (yuan)	57	746	4913	14129	17113

1-10 新疆建区以来主要年份国民经济主要指标

年份 Year	年末总人口（万人） Year-end Population (10 000 persons)	就业人员（万人） Employed Persons (10 000 persons)	新疆生产总值（亿元） Gross Domestic Product of Xinjiang (100 million yuan)	第一产业 Primary Industry	第二产业 Secondary Industry	#工业 Industry	第三产业 Tertiary Industry	人均新疆生产总值（元） Per Capita GDP (yuan)
1955	511.78	254.58	12.31	6.69	3.22	2.10	2.40	241
1960	686.33	338.32	25.20	9.27	11.06	8.12	4.87	374
1965	789.10	350.25	24.20	12.48	7.32	5.03	4.40	312
1970	976.58	410.33	23.08	10.35	8.67	6.19	4.06	236
1975	1154.53	466.43	28.12	11.21	12.20	8.86	4.71	240
1978	1233.01	491.25	39.07	13.97	18.35	14.48	6.75	313
1980	1283.24	506.35	53.24	21.53	21.44	17.48	10.27	410
1985	1361.14	565.81	112.24	42.89	40.50	32.14	28.85	820
1990	1529.16	617.70	261.44	104.09	83.18	71.50	74.17	1713
1991	1554.57	638.49	335.91	111.86	107.99	84.07	116.06	2101
1992	1580.63	646.94	402.31	114.50	147.64	106.29	140.17	2477
1993	1605.26	655.98	495.25	126.85	205.07	155.92	163.33	2964
1994	1632.70	657.54	662.32	187.69	249.11	190.00	225.52	3888
1995	1661.35	676.00	814.85	240.71	283.97	219.01	290.17	4701
1996	1689.29	684.00	900.93	249.31	313.70	239.07	337.92	5102
1997	1718.08	715.40	1039.85	279.73	385.37	302.50	374.75	5848
1998	1747.35	680.92	1106.95	291.05	395.75	298.53	420.15	6174
1999	1775.00	694.34	1163.17	268.51	420.48	315.86	474.18	6443
2000	1849.41	672.50	1363.56	288.18	537.58	418.63	537.80	7372
2001	1876.19	685.38	1491.60	288.12	573.91	445.60	629.57	7945
2002	1905.19	701.49	1612.65	305.00	603.15	463.59	704.50	8457
2003	1933.95	721.27	1886.35	412.90	719.54	563.57	753.91	9828
2004	1963.11	744.49	2209.09	446.13	914.47	734.10	848.49	11337
2005	2010.35	791.62	2604.14	510.00	1164.80	961.62	929.34	13108
2006	2050.00	811.75	3045.26	527.80	1459.30	1241.33	1058.16	15000
2007	2095.19	830.42	3523.16	628.72	1647.55	1405.11	1246.89	16999
2008	2130.81	847.58	4183.21	691.07	2070.76	1755.35	1421.38	19797
2009	2158.63	866.15	4277.05	759.74	1929.59	1555.84	1587.72	19942
2010	2181.33	894.65	5437.47	1078.63	2592.15	2161.39	1766.69	25057
			平均增长速度(%)					
1956-2010	2.7	2.3	8.2	5.8	9.2	9.6	9.5	5.2
1979-2010	1.8	1.9	10.4	7.4	10.1	9.8	13.7	8.4
2001-2010	1.7	2.9	10.3	5.6	11.5	11.7	11.3	8.6

Main Indicators of National Economic since Xinjing Established in Main Years

全社会固定资产投资总额(亿元) Total Investment in Fixed Assets (100 million yuan)	社会消费品零售总额(亿元) Total Retail Sales of Consumer Goods (100 million yuan)	地方财政一般预算收入(亿元) General Budgetary Revenue in Local Finance (100 million yuan)	地方财政一般预算支出(亿元) General Budgetary Expenditure in Local Finance (100 million yuan)	金融机构存款余额(亿元) Deposits of National Banking System (100 million yuan)	金融机构贷款款余额(亿元) Loans of National Banking System (100 million yuan)	进出口总额(亿美元) Total Imports And Exports (USD 100 million)	#出口额 Exports	农村居民人均纯收入(元) Annual Per capita Net Income of Rural Residents (yuan)	城镇居民人均可支配收入(元) Annual Per capita Disposable Income of Urban Residents (yuan)
2.62	6.14	1.73	1.83	2.72	3.41	0.51	0.20		
10.59	11.91	6.36	9.58	6.89	15.50	0.73	0.48		
4.03	11.30	4.53	4.89	11.52	9.70	0.14	0.13		
4.50	13.23	3.57	6.05	17.25	14.35	0.02	...		
6.11	16.85	1.01	8.85	26.88	14.71	0.09	0.04		
13.00	21.89	7.14	17.02	32.07	18.26	0.23	0.09	119	319
20.47	29.36	4.03	16.22	38.56	24.74	0.32	0.17	201	427
44.48	57.38	8.47	28.60	82.96	72.68	2.92	1.80	394	735
88.78	104.30	21.78	47.62	221.80	233.72	4.10	3.35	684	1314
124.93	121.52	26.47	50.34	282.21	299.59	4.59	3.63	703	1476
170.03	138.25	26.07	56.09	336.58	380.26	7.50	4.54	740	1952
248.44	168.37	35.13	64.71	397.39	467.81	9.22	4.95	778	2423
285.48	197.11	28.70	71.10	634.44	632.32	10.41	5.76	936	3170
333.34	253.65	38.28	96.40	838.42	843.38	14.28	7.69	1137	4163
387.85	295.36	48.31	114.88	1012.47	1016.20	14.04	5.50	1290	4650
446.81	310.42	54.52	123.35	1180.78	1215.39	14.47	6.65	1500	4845
519.77	327.52	65.39	145.99	1336.58	1318.41	15.32	8.08	1600	5001
534.65	347.40	71.31	166.28	1548.72	1386.78	17.65	10.27	1473	5320
610.38	374.50	79.07	190.95	1863.48	1403.13	22.64	12.04	1618	5645
706.00	406.35	95.09	263.32	1972.55	1584.73	17.71	6.68	1710	6215
813.02	442.88	116.47	361.17	2225.31	1801.15	26.92	13.08	1863	6554
1002.13	421.16	128.22	368.47	2661.65	2099.09	47.72	25.42	2106	7006
1161.52	563.41	155.70	421.04	2959.78	2214.66	56.36	30.47	2245	7503
1352.27	637.78	180.32	519.02	3427.48	2272.08	79.42	50.40	2482	7990
1567.05	727.59	219.46	678.47	4040.78	2412.69	91.03	71.39	2737	8871
1850.84	847.70	285.86	795.15	4614.62	2685.00	137.16	115.03	3183	10313
2259.97	1025.72	361.06	1059.36	5399.34	2826.53	222.17	192.99	3503	11432
2827.24	1177.53	388.78	1346.91	6845.07	3782.92	138.28	108.23	3883	12258
3539.69	1324.48	500.58	1698.91	8870.02	4973.16	171.28	129.70	4643	13644
Average Annual Growth Rate (%)									
14.00	10.3	10.9	13.2	15.8	14.2	11.2	12.5		
19.2	13.7	14.2	15.5	19.2	19.2	22.9	25.4	11.9	12.3
19.2	13.5	20.3	24.4	16.9	13.5	22.4	26.8	11.1	10.0

1-10 续表

年 份 Year	主要农产品产量（万吨） Output of Major Farm(10 000 tons)					年末牲畜存栏数（万头（只）） The Year-end Domesticated Animals in Stock (10 000 heads)	
	粮食 Grain	棉花 Cotton	油料 Oil-bearing Crops	甜菜 Beet	水果 Fruit		#羊 Sheep and Goats
1955	147.02	2.51	6.84	0.10	12.33	1640.07	1224.33
1960	197.98	3.19	5.88	7.09	16.10	1911.59	1529.89
1965	261.74	7.59	6.97	15.97	22.35	2697.53	2192.31
1970	303.21	6.46	6.84	21.06	13.70	2431.32	1949.67
1975	310.96	4.67	9.04	15.12	14.25	2436.08	1916.15
1978	370.01	5.50	10.33	16.37	13.98	2476.98	1927.54
1980	386.13	7.92	17.59	38.52	15.62	2672.60	2105.43
1985	496.65	18.78	34.25	40.69	49.25	3016.04	2431.91
1990	676.89	46.88	38.96	224.37	79.88	3496.40	2830.81
1991	672.52	63.95	40.49	256.85	81.10	3494.00	2830.65
1992	706.27	66.76	35.62	329.07	91.89	3495.41	2830.36
1993	720.37	68.00	37.02	236.91	99.82	3514.72	2842.83
1994	666.17	88.21	50.76	299.24	107.52	3599.01	2905.80
1995	730.16	93.50	49.41	288.14	114.43	3724.32	3009.02
1996	818.20	94.04	30.95	354.52	115.99	3863.80	3136.21
1997	825.34	115.00	29.95	388.71	123.67	4007.66	3261.81
1998	830.00	140.00	37.52	513.12	121.48	4223.99	3447.38
1999	838.78	140.75	60.46	354.24	136.42	4396.54	3592.29
2000	808.60	150.00	60.14	292.65	151.87	4524.67	3690.21
2001	796.00	157.00	42.64	455.12	154.25	4603.78	3764.88
2002	875.87	150.00	44.37	466.81	198.20	4781.77	3908.23
2003	801.64	160.00	50.13	381.65	218.34	5026.54	4104.30
2004	828.53	175.25	44.54	344.21	264.22	5206.37	4266.73
2005	877.21	195.70	38.94	419.12	291.26	5333.60	4355.50
2006	895.22	267.53	32.82	555.53	343.14	5339.71	4359.50
2007	867.04	290.00	40.30	586.93	411.98	5023.37	4083.44
2008	909.00	301.55	56.85	438.88	450.87	3746.11	3025.70
2009	1152.00	252.40	63.91	418.41	565.15	3844.75	3127.50
2010	1150.20	247.90	66.62	486.97	593.85	3722.15	3013.37
			平均增长速度(%)				
1956-2010	3.8	8.7	4.2	16.7	7.3	1.5	1.7
1979-2010	3.6	12.6	6.0	11.2	12.4	1.4	1.4
2001-2010	3.6	5.2	1.0	5.2	14.6	-1.9	-2.0

Continued

主要畜产品产量（万吨）Output of Major Livestock Products(10 000 tons)			水产品产量（万吨）	主要工业产品产量 Output of Major Industrial Products				
肉类 Meat	羊毛 Wool	奶类 Milk	Output of Aquatic Products (10 000 tons)	原煤（万吨）Crude Coal (10 000 tons)	原油（万吨）Crude Oil (10 000 tons)	天然气（亿立方米）Natural Gas (100 million cu.m)	发电量（亿千瓦时）Volume of Electric Generation (100 million kwh)	钢材（万吨）Steel Rolled (10 000 tons)
6.69			0.07	64.55	3.29	0.01	0.55	0.66
6.08			0.57	473.85	166.23	0.06	3.44	3.63
9.17			0.46	387.00	97.31	0.01	4.46	3.94
8.84		8.53	0.65	558.82	153.60	0.66	7.95	4.21
9.16	3.16	6.35	0.50	716.25	300.19	3.76	13.23	2.20
9.65	3.08	5.25	0.57	1079.01	353.05	2.51	21.17	6.83
12.70	3.31	7.28	0.66	1136.84	390.58	3.53	23.58	8.59
18.37	7.07	19.70	0.90	1600.22	499.00	5.46	38.11	16.73
30.46	5.09	35.64	2.32	2100.00	695.00	5.02	69.79	28.48
32.94	5.19	37.49	2.52	2111.00	762.00	5.54	78.04	33.80
36.02	5.20	39.79	2.66	2204.46	831.66	6.75	86.80	40.30
38.30	5.28	40.85	2.88	2392.29	1065.50	8.43	95.78	45.98
42.81	5.46	44.83	3.53	2633.29	1156.62	9.06	106.17	57.71
52.38	5.66	49.81	4.44	2720.74	1267.83	11.48	120.43	66.55
60.31	5.99	54.22	4.79	2986.00	1457.10	14.06	136.03	86.70
64.40	6.25	58.78	5.24	3021.37	1629.25	21.30	150.58	99.89
75.19	6.48	65.02	5.34	2926.91	1628.38	23.78	157.76	116.19
81.36	6.76	70.43	5.58	2778.15	1739.65	31.06	169.30	117.30
90.00	6.98	78.23	6.01	2798.90	1848.43	35.39	182.98	131.25
97.00	7.30	87.85	6.09	2819.61	1946.95	41.74	197.62	134.42
105.44	7.78	100.71	6.39	3098.67	2036.19	48.52	212.24	173.07
115.00	8.21	119.21	6.73	3482.90	2141.40	50.29	234.62	203.10
128.13	8.91	139.73	7.33	3749.40	2253.02	57.48	266.30	238.52
141.46	9.38	157.84	7.93	3898.81	2408.32	106.64	306.92	326.96
158.21	9.62	185.41	8.45	4518.52	2474.74	164.21	357.15	411.45
160.58	9.34	201.77	8.89	5018.64	2604.31	210.33	416.87	470.94
114.74	9.03	137.40	9.26	6763.41	2715.13	235.89	489.17	576.62
115.31	7.60	125.15	9.70	8812.55	2512.86	245.39	571.31	690.81
121.74	8.69	132.82	10.11	9926.73	2558.16	249.91	679.32	891.70
Average Annual Growth Rate (%)								
5.4			9.5	9.6	12.9	20.2	13.8	14.0
8.2	3.3	10.6	9.4	7.2	6.4	15.5	11.4	16.4
3.1	2.2	5.4	5.3	13.5	3.3	21.6	14.0	21.1

1-11 各时期社会经济主要指标

Major Social and Economic Indicators of Each Period

时期	Period	新疆生产总值(亿元) Gross Domestic Product of Xinjiang (100 million yuan)	第一产业 Primary Industry	第二产业 Secondary Industry	#工业 Industry	第三产业 Tertiary Industry	全社会固定资产投资总额(亿元) Total Investment in Fixed Assets (100 million yuan)
"一五"时期	"First Five-year Plan" Period	60.35	33.86	15.54	8.82	10.95	
"二五"时期	"Second Five-year Plan" Period	102.65	43.27	39.48	28.37	19.90	31.42
	1963—1965	64.76	33.56	19.27	13.64	11.93	10.43
"三五"时期	"Third Five-year Plan" Period	111.94	53.53	38.02	27.84	20.39	18.82
"四五"时期	"Fourth Five-year Plan" Period	128.37	54.38	50.55	36.84	23.44	24.72
"五五"时期	"Fifth Five-year Plan" Period	205.39	77.27	91.75	72.34	36.37	69.12
"六五"时期	"Sixth Five-year Plan" Period	405.19	165.70	146.99	117.51	92.50	149.13
"七五"时期	"Seventh Five-year Plan" Period	948.99	356.55	318.96	263.20	273.48	331.97
"八五"时期	"Eighth Five-year Plan" Period	2710.64	781.61	993.78	755.30	935.25	1162.22
"九五"时期	"Ninth Five-year Plan" Period	5574.46	1376.78	2052.88	1574.58	2144.80	2499.46
"十五"时期	"Tenth Five-year Plan" Period	9803.83	1962.15	3975.87	3168.48	3865.81	5034.95
"十一五"时期	"Eleventh Five-year Plan " Period	20466.15	3685.96	9699.35	8119.02	7080.84	12044.80

时期	Period	住宅竣工建筑面积(万平方米) Floor Space of Building Completed (10 000 sq.m)	地方财政一般预算收入(亿元) General Budgetary Revenue in Local Finance (100 million yuan)	地方财政一般预算支出(亿元) General Budgetary Expenditure in Local Finance (100 million yuan)	进出口总额(万美元) Total Imports And Exports (USD 10 000)	#出口额 Exports	社会消费品零售总额(亿元) Total Retail Sales of Consumer Goods (100 million yuan)
"一五"时期	"First Five-year Plan" Period		8.65	9.50	20819	10945	31.38
"二五"时期	"Second Five-year Plan" Period		21.39	27.16	26197	17976	53.43
	1963—1965		12.20	11.61	4806	4632	31.92
"三五"时期	"Third Five-year Plan" Period		15.38	21.78	1243	633	63.75
"四五"时期	"Fourth Five-year Plan" Period		11.11	39.78	2922	1217	76.26
"五五"时期	"Fifth Five-year Plan" Period		18.24	54.80	10255	4310	113.51
"六五"时期	"Sixth Five-year Plan" Period	3279.57	27.35	100.30	81536	57445	215.35
"七五"时期	"Seventh Five-year Plan" Period	4175.39	75.48	197.04	190173	142124	323.14
"八五"时期	"Eighth Five-year Plan" Period	4928.74	155.63	338.64	460033	265704	878.89
"九五"时期	"Ninth Five-year Plan" Period	8341.78	318.60	741.45	841181	425462	1655.20
"十五"时期	"Tenth Five-year Plan" Period	12466.98	675.80	1933.02	2281284	1260601	2471.83
"十一五"时期	"Eleventh Five-year Plan " Period	19074.22	1755.75	5578.82	7599235	6173465	5134.21

1-12 各时期社会经济主要指标平均增长率

Growth Rate of Major Social and Economic Indicators of Each Period

单位：% (%)

时 期	Period	新疆生产总值 Gross Domestic Product of Xinjiang	第一产业 Primary Industry	第二产业 Secondary Industry	#工 业 Industry	第三产业 Tertiary Industry	全社会固定资产投资总额 Total Investment in Fixed Assets
"一五" 时期	"First Five-year Plan" Period	9.0	5.1	12.6	8.8	18.8	
"二五" 时期	"Second Five-year Plan" Period	4.5	2.8	11.0	24.5	-1.3	-14.8
	1963—1965	12.9	17.9	8.4	3.3	5.4	28.4
"三五" 时期	"Third Five-year Plan" Period	0.3	-3.1	3.8	4.3	4.8	2.2
"四五" 时期	"Fourth Five-year Plan" Period	2.9	…	7.2	7.3	-0.5	6.3
"五五" 时期	"Fifth Five-year Plan" Period	10.5	7.4	11.6	14.3	14.5	34.1
"六五" 时期	"Sixth Five-year Plan" Period	12.5	13.0	9.2	9.3	17.6	10.9
"七五" 时期	"Seventh Five-year Plan" Period	9.8	7.9	8.2	9.2	14.7	14.8
"八五" 时期	"Eighth Five-year Plan" Period	11.8	6.7	14.2	13.5	15.0	30.3
"九五" 时期	"Ninth Five-year Plan" Period	7.7	5.8	6.8	5.9	10.3	12.9
"十五" 时期	"Tenth Five-year Plan" Period	10.0	5.6	10.6	11.3	11.2	17.2
"十一五"时期	"Eleventh Five-year Plan " Period	10.6	5.6	11.8	12.1	11.4	21.2

时 期	Period	住宅竣工建筑面积 Floor Space of Building Completed	地方财政一般预算收入 General Budgetary Revenue in Local Finance	地方财政一般预算支出 General Budgetary Expenditure in Local Finance	进出口总 额 Total Imports And Exports	#出口额 Exports	社会消费品零售总额 Total Retail Sales of Consumer Goods
"一五" 时期	"First Five-year Plan" Period		25.0	30.7	17.8	17.8	18.5
"二五" 时期	"Second Five-year Plan" Period		4.7	-0.4	-12.5	-9.6	4.3
	1963—1965		16.8	30.5	-20.4	-13.8	2.3
"三五" 时期	"Third Five-year Plan" Period		-4.7	4.3	-34.4	-50.3	3.2
"四五" 时期	"Fourth Five-year Plan" Period		-22.3	7.9	40.6	58.0	5.0
"五五" 时期	"Fifth Five-year Plan" Period		31.9	12.9	28.4	35.5	11.7
"六五" 时期	"Sixth Five-year Plan" Period		16.0	12.0	56.0	60.2	14.3
"七五" 时期	"Seventh Five-year Plan" Period	2.3	20.8	10.7	7.0	13.2	12.7
"八五" 时期	"Eighth Five-year Plan" Period	3.1	11.9	15.1	28.3	18.1	19.4
"九五" 时期	"Ninth Five-year Plan" Period	12.1	15.6	14.6	9.7	9.4	8.1
"十五" 时期	"Tenth Five-year Plan" Period	14.0	17.9	22.1	28.5	33.2	11.2
"十一五"时期	"Eleventh Five-year Plan " Period	-1.9	22.7	26.8	16.6	20.8	15.7

1-13 天山北坡经济带主要经济指标

(2010 年)

指标	Item	全区合计 Total of the whole region	北坡经济带合计 Total of the economic belt	北坡经济带占全区比重(%) ratio of the economic belt (%)	乌昌合计 Total of Urmqi and Changji	乌昌占全区比重(%) Pencent-age of Urmqi and Changji to total(%)	乌鲁木齐市 Urumqi City
综　合	**General**						
新疆生产总值(亿元)	Gross Domestic Produc in Xinjiang (100 million yuan)	5437.47	2903.18	53.4	1896.51	34.9	1338.52
第一产业	First Industry	1078.63	246.22	22.8	186.21	17.3	19.94
第二产业	Second Industry	2592.15	1609.94	62.1	834.55	32.2	600.41
工　业	Industry	2161.39	1432.67	66.3	701.37	32.4	514.76
建筑业	Building Sector	430.76	177.27	41.2	133.18	30.9	85.65
第三产业	Tertiary Industry	1766.69	1047.03	59.3	875.75	49.6	718.17
#交通运输、仓储和邮政业	Communication, Storage and Telecom	222.47	184.92	83.1	157.68	70.9	134.24
批发和零售贸易业	Wholesale &Retail and Catering Sectoring	276.28	176.74	64.0	151.16	54.7	127.07
新疆生产总值构成(%)	Composition of Gross Domestic Produc in Xinjiang (%)						
第一产业	First Industry	19.8	8.5		9.8		1.5
第二产业	Second Industry	47.7	55.5		44.0		44.9
工　业	Industry	39.8	49.4		37.0		38.5
建筑业	Construction	7.9	6.1		7.0		6.4
第三产业	Tertiary Industry	32.5	36.0		46.2		53.6
#交通运输、仓储和邮政业	Communication, Storage and Telecom	4.1	6.4		8.3		10.0
批发和零售贸易业	Wholesale &Retail and Catering Sectoring	5.1	6.1		8.0		9.5
财政收入占新疆生产总值比重(%)	Ratio of GDP covered by financial Expenditure (%)	9.2	8.4		9.5		11.1
财政支出占新疆生产总值比重(%)	Ratio of GDP covered by financial Expenditure (%)	31.2	10.8		13.0		11.9
固定资产投资(亿元)	**Fixed Asset Investment (100 million yuan)**						
#城镇固定资产投资总额	Fixed Asset Value of the town	2833.86	888.75	31.4	571.43	20.2	392.57
财政、金融(亿元)	**Finance and Public Money(100 million yuan)**						
地方财政一般预算收入	Local Financial Income	500.58	242.91	48.5	180.72	36.1	147.99
#各项税收	Various Tax Incomes	416.23	219.85	52.8	164.43	39.5	135.37
地方财政一般预算支出	Expenditure of Local Finance	1698.91	312.37	18.4	247.48	14.6	159.61
#一般公共服务	General Common Service	195.57	39.19	20.0	29.92	15.3	19.89
教　育	Operating Expenses for Education	313.84	56.38	18.0	42.53	13.6	26.55
社保和就业	Operating Expenses for Medical Treatment and Sanitation	166.40	25.48	15.3	22.78	13.7	17.87
金融机构年末存款余额	Year-end Loan Balance of Finance	8870.02	5299.19	59.7	4158.80	46.9	3596.43
金融机构年末贷款余额	Year-end Deposit Balance of Finance	4973.16	2746.86	55.2	2421.79	48.7	2074.74
物价(上年=100)	**Commodity Price (Preceding year=100)**						
商品零售价格指数	Index of Commodity Retail Price	104.6					103.4
居民消费价格指数	Index of Price for Residents' Consumption	104.3					102.7
人民生活	**People's life**						
职工平均货币工资(元)	Average Staff''s Money Wage (yuan)	32361					41529
农村居民家庭人均纯收入(元)	Annual Per capita Net Income of Rural Residents (yuan)	4643					7466
城乡居民储蓄存款余额(亿元)	Balance of Both Urban and Rural Deposit(100 million yuan)	3713.47	1937.98	52.2	1535.96	41.4	1242.85
建成区绿化覆盖率(%)	Ratio of Green Coverage in Completed Areas(%)	36.42					34.80

Main Economic Indicators for Economic Belt on the Northern Slope of the Tianshan Mountains

克拉玛依市 Karamay City	石河子市 Shihezi City	奎屯市 Kuitun City	乌苏市 Usu City	沙湾县 Shawan County	昌吉市 Changji City	阜康市 Fukang City	呼图壁县 Hu Tubi County	玛纳斯县 Manas County	农六师 XJPCC No.6 Division	农七师 XJPCC No.7 Division	农八师 XJPCC No.8 Division	农十二师 XJPCC No.12 Division	建工师 XJPCC architectural engineer Division
711.35	135.00	72.38	96.17	108.57	178.63	80.72	79.89	101.95					
3.52	9.18	4.39	35.54	56.08	25.08	14.15	32.76	45.58					
638.41	68.62	40.14	41.62	28.61	78.41	50.27	26.98	36.46					
623.47	55.10	33.29	28.17	21.25	64.21	45.54	16.42	30.46					
14.95	13.52	6.85	13.45	7.36	14.20	4.73	10.56	6.00					
69.42	57.20	27.85	19.01	23.88	75.14	16.30	20.15	19.91					
12.13	5.89	5.07	2.53	3.21	14.54	2.12	3.03	2.16					
9.88	5.96	2.73	4.98	6.44	7.89	2.89	5.04	3.86					
0.5	6.8	6.1	37.0	51.6	14.0	17.5	41.0	44.7					
89.7	50.8	55.5	43.3	26.4	43.9	62.3	33.8	35.8					
87.6	40.8	46.0	29.3	19.6	36.0	56.4	20.6	29.9					
2.1	10.0	9.5	14.0	6.8	7.9	5.9	13.2	5.9					
9.8	42.4	38.4	19.7	22.0	42.1	20.2	25.2	19.5					
1.7	4.4	7.0	2.6	3.0	8.1	2.6	3.8	2.1					
1.4	4.4	3.8	5.2	5.9	4.4	3.6	6.3	3.8					
6.0	10.2	10.8	4.3	3.1	6.7	7.0	3.6	2.9					
7.7	12.8	16.8	12.7	9.4	10.5	12.3	10.8	8.8					
171.42	86.69	42.29	33.59	29.13	45.00	35.00	18.05	35.01					
42.43	13.75	7.82	4.09	3.34	11.96	5.68	2.86	2.99					
38.13	12.26	6.64	3.08	2.59	11.22	5.23	2.53	2.80					
54.77	17.24	12.14	12.19	10.25	18.70	9.90	8.62	8.95					
6.76	1.63	1.18	2.94	1.59	2.52	1.16	0.70	0.82					
11.53	2.67	2.47	2.48	2.56	3.07	1.48	1.93	1.64					
2.76	0.94	0.78	0.66	0.55	0.49	0.47	0.60	0.36					
792.49	296.27	138.14	52.27	44.87	227.38	55.15	51.62	44.57					
150.64	182.47	54.60	19.20	34.68	134.73	42.12	22.37	31.31					
104.2	103.9	103.8	104.9		104.0								
104.5	103.7	103.3	105.5		103.6								
42767	32221	30453	19866	26785	34653	31106	26245	33119					
10296	8508	7000	10149	11255	9408	9206	10036	11316					
195.60	183.51	56.25	32.65	34.10	102.46	27.29	34.04	29.23					
42.90	42.92	40.15	30.00	33.87	38.81	33.42	38.29	32.30					

1-13 续表

指标	Item	全区合计 Total of the whole region	北坡经济带合计 Total of the economic belt	北坡经济带占全区比重(%) ratio of the economic belt (%)	乌昌合计 Total of Urmqi and Changji	乌昌占全区比重(%) Pencent-age of Urmqi and Changji to total(%)	乌鲁木齐市 Urumqi City
农业	**Agriculture**						
农林牧渔业总产值(亿元)	Value of Farm, Forestry, Herding and Fishery (100 million yuan)	1846.18	509.27	27.6	237.69	12.9	27.31
农业	Farming	1376.88	338.54	24.6	110.17	8.0	13.04
林业	Forestry	35.27	5.44	15.4	2.55	7.2	0.29
牧业	Animal Husbandry	375.79	142.78	38.0	120.28	32.0	13.02
渔业	Fishery	12.67	3.71	29.3	2.04	16.1	0.58
农林牧渔服务业	Services for Farming, Forestry, Animal Husbandary and Fishery	45.57	18.82	41.3	2.65	5.8	0.38
主要农产品产量(万吨)	Main Rural Products Output (10 000 tons)						
粮食	Grain	1150.20	271.90	23.6	219.51	19.1	17.61
棉花	Cotton	247.90	86.09	34.7	14.00	5.6	0.11
油料	Oil-bearing Crops	66.62	13.85	20.8	6.54	9.8	0.85
甜菜	Beet	486.97	47.99	9.9	41.54	8.5	0.11
水果	Fruit	593.85	41.11	6.9	17.55	3.0	1.01
肉类	Meat	121.74	57.81	47.5	50.63	41.6	5.38
工业	**Industry**						
工业总产值(规模以上)(亿元)	Total Value of Industrial Products (100 million yuan)	5341.90	3723.08	69.7	2077.99	38.9	1674.76
轻工业	Light Industry	729.87	402.70	55.2	252.03	34.5	102.19
重工业	Heavy Industry	4612.04	3320.39	72.0	1825.96	39.6	1572.57
国有工业	State-owned Industry	3770.33	2785.38	73.9	1290.74	34.2	1246.69
集体工业	Collective-owned industry	84.30	56.47	67.0	28.92	34.3	21.68
其他工业	Other Industrial Sectors	1487.28	881.23	59.3	758.33	51.0	406.39
主要工业产品产量(全口径)	Output of Main Industrial Products						
纱(万吨)	Cotton Yarn (10 000 tons)	41.58	26.80	64.5	8.56	20.6	5.89
布(万米)	Cloth (10 000 m)	15069.11	11221.71	74.5	4027.53	26.7	2063.93
绒线(吨)	Woolen knitting wool (ton)	741.49	413.33	55.7	412.20	55.6	359.00
呢绒(万米)	Woolen Goods (10 000 m)	325.53	325.53	100.0	154.00	47.3	
原盐(万吨)	Crude Salt (10 000 tons)	174.67	13.39	7.7	13.22	7.6	13.22
成品糖(万吨)	Sugar (10 000 tons)	45.10	3.46	7.7	5.15	11.4	
原煤(万吨)	Crude Coal (10 000 tons)	9935.73	4058.71	40.8	5218.97	52.5	2424.20
原油(万吨)	Crude Oil (10 000 tons)	2558.16	1841.03	72.0	700.02	27.4	700.02
发电量(亿千瓦小时)	Volume of Electric Generation (100 million kwh)	679.33	453.06	66.7	286.84	42.2	181.19
粗钢(万吨)	Grude steel (10 000 tons)	825.54	710.31	86.0	685.03	83.0	685.03
钢材(万吨)	Steel Rolled (10 000 tons)	892.04	778.22	87.2	753.69	84.5	753.68
水泥(万吨)	Cement (10 000 tons)	2400.96	927.72	38.6	680.10	28.3	476.16
运输邮电业	**Traffic and Telecommunication Sector**						
公路客运量(万人)	Highway Passenger Volume (10 000 persons)	44333	10167	22.9	8139	18.4	2676
公路货运量(万吨)	Highway Cargo Volume (10 000 tons)	50448	25309	50.2	20046	39.7	13140
公路货物周转量(亿吨公里)	Turnover of Highway Cargo (100million tons-km)	767.14	321.20	41.9	281.22	36.7	184.21
邮电业务总量(亿元)	Volume of Postal-Telecommunication (100 million yuan)	582.05	59.32	10.2	55.93	9.6	45.11
国内商业	**Domestic Trades**						
社会消费品零售总额(亿元)	Retail Volume of Social Commodities (100 million yuan)	1324.48	803.33	60.7	627.03	47.3	514.24
教育、文化、卫生	**Education, Culture and Health**						
在校学生数(人)	Number of Registered Students (person)						
高等学校	Institutions of Higher Education	251160	197039	78.5	167195	66.6	154797
中等专业学校	Specialized Secondary School	233319	126526	54.2	100181	42.9	87823
普通中学	Ordinary Middle School	1422419	369787	26.0	229134	16.1	148720
小学	Elementary School	1935798	396821	20.5	259211	13.4	178206
毕业生数(人)	Number of Graduates (person)						
高等学校	Institutions of Higher Education	63543	49379	77.7	42761	67.3	39375
中等专业学校	Specialized Secondary School	66383	43526	65.6	34267	51.6	30499
普通中学	Ordinary Middle School	473216	115578	24.4	71911	15.2	46154
小学	Elementary School	334362	72635	21.7	45565	13.6	29891
医院床位数(张)	Number of Sick Beds (unit)	109851	48384	44.0	33849	30.8	24942
卫生技术人员数(人)	Number of Hygiene Technicians (person)	122860	56619	46.1	39621	32.2	29912

Continued

克拉玛依市 Karamay City	石河子市 Shihezi City	奎屯市 Kuitun City	乌苏市 Usu City	沙湾县 Shawan County	昌吉市 Changji City	阜康市 Fukang City	呼图壁县 Hu Tubi County	玛纳斯县 Manas County	农六师 XJPCC No.6 Division	农七师 XJPCC No.7 Division	农八师 XJPCC No.8 Division	建工师 XJPCC architectural engineer Division	农十二师 XJPCC No.12 Division
8.06	18.64	0.98	34.15	42.84	31.53	21.43	39.16	42.85	66.88	55.08	110.10	0.04	10.22
2.72	13.61	0.55	25.54	30.32	13.69	9.73	16.15	24.59	48.64	42.47	90.50	0.04	6.95
1.34	0.08	0.02	0.51	0.22	0.30	0.20	0.30	0.19	0.50	0.52	0.90		0.07
2.68	3.99	0.32	7.68	11.59	16.33	11.36	21.46	17.16	12.51	8.82	13.11		2.75
0.06	0.43		0.08	0.13	0.90	0.03	0.28	0.16	0.21	0.20	0.46		0.19
1.26	0.53	0.09	0.34	0.58	0.31	0.11	0.97	0.75	5.02	3.08	5.14		0.26
0.55	5.69	0.61	31.51	26.36	33.51	19.49	25.44	23.74	47.37	23.73	13.38	0.03	2.88
1.11	3.05	0.15	7.13	7.64	3.78	0.03	4.27	5.81	10.58	9.65	32.71	0.01	0.06
0.04	0.09	0.03	1.04	2.81	0.88	1.28	0.29	0.77	2.51	2.78	0.20	0.02	0.26
0.01	0.09		3.19	1.85	5.03		3.21	0.34	6.66	25.54	1.07		0.89
	3.34		0.27	1.12	5.23	1.41	1.19	7.65	3.68	2.27	7.28		6.66
0.99	1.92	0.29	2.88	4.09	8.06	6.27	7.01	5.98	6.00	2.95	5.19		0.80
1330.85	200.23	79.22	40.68	41.69	160.55	80.07	43.38	71.65					
2.35	71.56	45.86	17.21	31.07	60.39	1.57	22.99	47.51					
1328.50	128.67	33.36	23.47	10.62	100.16	78.51	20.39	24.14					
1268.89	138.31	55.39	27.23	9.25	4.38	21.04	3.43	10.77					
12.46	1.75	0.20		13.15		7.23							
49.50	60.17	23.63	13.45	19.29	156.16	51.80	39.95	60.89					
	14.06	2.35		1.82	0.45		1.35	0.87					
	4353.48	2556.00	52.00	232.70			1747.60	216.00					
	1.13						53.20						
	171.53				154.00								
0.17													
		1.71			1.74								
	9.00	18.21	258.54	93.28	529.97	423.68	262.63	39.20					
1089.01			52.00										
44.77	99.60	20.24	0.76	1.46	15.79	24.20		65.06					
			17.51	7.77									
0.02	3.05			21.46				0.01					
	142.82		2.95	101.85	152.35	51.59							
558	892	638	1162	1000	2130	505	606						
2324	1888	423	329	871	2654	3579	101						
49.79	31.15	8.46	5.88	6.50	33.68	0.58	0.95						
0.61	5.90	3.96	0.98	0.44	0.42	0.58	1.21	0.11					
34.79	43.45	13.59	8.69	9.43	46.86	15.57	13.24	14,55	27.90	15.56	36.26	0.55	8.65
3732	5149				33361								
1064	20077	907			6050	1874	631	506	1524	613	2353	2560	544
25175	18996	19575	15051	16674	32014	10274	9148	7536	19134	11510	25156	5588	5236
24256	11288	13697	17117	16542	27700	8100	11046	9633	21874	13405	30707	7062	6188
1528	807				7669								
346	6621	612			1396	1068	239	74	462	325	768	1001	115
7882	6291	5598	4909	5037	10447	2539	2686	2473	6159	3991	8018	1796	1598
4705	3173	2569	3270	2897	5011	1695	2062	1800	4103	2808	6223	1226	1202
1830	4116	2007	961	702	3150	550	946	620	1724	2410	4116	80	230
2759	4944	2108	1011	831	4167	643	808	767	2195	2006	3958	176	334

1-14 企业家信心指数
Entrepreneur Confidence Index

(2010 年)

经济类型及行业	Ownership and Sector	一季度 First Quarter		二季度 Second Quarter	
		本期实际 Index	比上年同期增减 as±of Last Same Period Index	本期实际 Index	比上年同期增减 as±of Last Same Period Index
企业家信心指数	**Entrepreneur Confidence Index**	**129.9**	**20.8**	**132.8**	**16.5**
按企业登记注册类型分	**Grouped by Status of Registration**				
国有企业	State-owned Enterprises	138.9	21.0	138.7	17.9
集体企业	Collective-owned Enterprises	101.0	23.5	86.8	-7.3
股份合作企业	Cooperative Enterprises	200.0	33.3	200.0	33.3
有限责任公司	Limited-Liability Corporations	128.0	19.9	127.9	14.1
股份有限公司	Share Holding Corporations Ltd.	146.2	36.4	146.2	12.0
私营企业	Private Enterprises	116.1	22.4	124.7	20.9
按行业分	**Grouped by Sector**				
工　业	Industry	126.8	20.5	133.4	19.2
建筑业	Construction	133.8	16.9	132.3	12.2
交通运输、仓储和邮政业	Transportation, Storage,Post and Telecommunications	124.5	3.9	124.7	2.6
批发和零售业	Wholesale and Retail Trades	140.0	32.7	132.6	18.1
房地产业	Real Estate	145.0	58.5	129.0	13.9
社会服务业	Social Services	112.8	18.7	128.2	37.0
信息传输、计算机服务和软件业	Information Transmission, Computer Servcie and Software Industries	165.2	8.5	163.6	9.2
住宿和餐饮业	Accommodation and Catering Services	112.7	14.6	118.2	12.4
按企业规模分	**Grouped by Size of Enterprises**				
大　型	Large	153.4	41.1	152.6	13.8
中　型	Medium	134.9	24.9	136.8	16.1
小　型	Small	124.6	15.8	125.3	15.0
按特殊群体分	**Grouped by Special Group**				
上市公司	Listed Companies	156.8	51.0	156.6	12.4
国有控股企业	State-owned and State-holding Enterprises	140.0	23.6	140.4	16.0

1-14 续表 Continued

经济类型及行业	Ownership and Sector	三季度 Third Quarter 本期实际 Index	三季度 Third Quarter 比上年同期增减 as±of Last Same Period Index	四季度 Fourth Quarter 本期实际 Index	四季度 Fourth Quarter 比上年同期增减 as±of Last Same Period Index
企业家信心指数	**Entrepreneur Confidence Index**	**138.4**	**23.2**	**135.9**	**12.0**
按企业登记注册类型分	**Grouped by Status of Registration**				
国有企业	State-owned Enterprises	139.1	25.8	138.1	9.8
集体企业	Collective-owned Enterprises	72.5	-5.0	86.8	-2.4
股份合作企业	Cooperative Enterprises	200.0	100.0	200.0	33.3
有限责任公司	Limited-Liability Corporations	138.8	26.8	135.1	11.3
股份有限公司	Share Holding Corporations Ltd.	151.1	23.5	152.8	19.4
私营企业	Private Enterprises	130.0	27.5	131.3	22.4
按行业分	**Grouped by Sector**				
工　业	Industry	137.4	21.9	134.2	11.4
建筑业	Construction	142.2	10.9	141.3	14.6
交通运输、仓储和邮政业	Transportation, Storage,Post and Telecommunications	128.4	25.6	120.8	6.2
批发和零售业	Wholesale and Retail Trades	137.6	24.0	146.7	18.7
房地产业	Real Estate	137.7	4.0	133.1	-23.2
社会服务业	Social Services	151.3	66.0	141.0	43.9
信息传输、计算机服务和软件业	Information Transmission, Computer Servcie and Software Industries	157.6	23.7	159.1	3.7
住宿和餐饮业	Accommodation and Catering Services	150.9	100.9	140.0	61.1
按企业规模分	**Grouped by Size of Enterprises**				
大　型	Large	150.7	26.1	155.4	22.7
中　型	Medium	142.0	19.7	141.3	9.7
小　型	Small	135.5	32.0	131.9	15.3
按特殊群体分	**Grouped by Special Group**				
上市公司	Listed Companies	158.0	21.7	159.5	26.3
国有控股企业	State-owned and State-holding Enterprises	145.2	26.9	145.7	16.6

1-15 企业景气指数
Prosperity Index on Enterprises

(2010 年)

经济类型及行业	Ownership and Sector	一季度 First Quarter		二季度 Second Quarter	
		本期实际 Index	比上年同期增减 as±of Last Same Period Index	本期实际 Index	比上年同期增减 as±of Last Same Period Index
企业景气指数	**Enterprises Business Climate Index**	**125.1**	**16.1**	**132.1**	**16.7**
按企业登记注册类型分	**Grouped by Status of Registration**				
国有企业	State-owned Enterprises	132.8	15.6	139.9	20.9
集体企业	Collective-owned Enterprises	92.9	4.7	101.0	7.9
股份合作企业	Cooperative Enterprises	100.0		200.0	100.0
有限责任公司	Limited-Liability Corporations	119.4	10.8	123.8	8.9
股份有限公司	Share Holding Corporations Ltd.	145.5	29.0	153.0	25.6
私营企业	Private Enterprises	108.7	3.7	116.1	20.0
按行业分	**Grouped by Sector**				
工　业	Industry	125.8	21.4	132.3	19.7
建筑业	Construction	103.7	-6.4	128.8	6.1
交通运输、仓储和邮政业	Transportation, Storage, Posts and Telecommunications	124.3	-1.5	129.6	16.4
批发和零售业	Wholesale and Retail Trades	140.9	17.7	132.5	10.1
房地产业	Real Estate	132.1	41.5	131.0	21.6
社会服务业	Social Services	100.0	2.9	120.5	17.6
信息传输、计算机服务和软件业	Information Transmission, Computer Servcie and Software Industries	159.1	5.0	163.6	13.6
住宿和餐饮业	Accommodation and Catering Services	107.3	7.3	114.6	5.0
按企业规模分	**Grouped by Size of Enterprises**				
大　型	Large	167.6	43.3	168.1	47.1
中　型	Medium	132.3	22.7	139.8	13.1
小　型	Small	113.6	4.8	119.1	11.6
按特殊群体分	**Grouped by Special Group**				
上市公司	Listed Companies	161.8	48.2	167.1	53.1
国有控股企业	State-owned and State-holding Enterprises	138.0	21.6	141.4	19.1
按观察指标分	**Grouped by Indicator Observed**				
生产总量	Production (Operation)	93.2	14.9	130.0	9.1
盈利(亏损)变化	Changes of Profit(Loss)	101.5	17.3	118.3	10.4
流动资金	Liquid Capital	94.5	16.1	92.3	14.3
货款拖欠	Payment Arrears for Goods	114.8	10.2	104.0	1.0
劳动力需求	Demand on Labors	103.7	14.7	125.5	14.8
固定资产投资	Investment in Fixed Assets	101.2	9.4	123.8	5.2
产品订货	Ordering of Productions	100.0	15.2	122.4	12.9
企业融资	Financing of Enterprises	83.7	11.0	82.8	5.0

1-15 续表 Continued

经济类型及行业	Ownership and Sector	三季度 Third Quarter		四季度 Fourth Quarter	
		本期实际 Index	比上年同期增减 as±of Last Same Period Index	本期实际 Index	比上年同期增减 as±of Last Same Period Index
企业景气指数	**Enterprises Business Climate Index**	**138.8**	**17.7**	**135.6**	**11.7**
按企业登记注册类型分	**Grouped by Status of Registration**				
国有企业	State-owned Enterprises	140.5	25.1	134.9	7.7
集体企业	Collective-owned Enterprises	115.3	32.9	100.0	17.6
股份合作企业	Cooperative Enterprises	100.0	33.3	200.0	100.0
有限责任公司	Limited-Liability Corporations	138.1	21.7	134.2	9.6
股份有限公司	Share Holding Corporations Ltd.	155.6	17.6	148.9	10.5
私营企业	Private Enterprises	125.0	27.6	122.5	15.0
按行业分	**Grouped by Sector**				
工　业	Industry	137.8	14.0	135.2	12.6
建筑业	Construction	143.8	5.8	135.2	1.1
交通运输、仓储和邮政业	Transportation, Storage, Posts and Telecommunications	128.1	27.8	129.3	16.1
批发和零售业	Wholesale and Retail Trades	138.7	22.0	144.8	14.3
房地产业	Real Estate	138.5	15.9	133.1	-2.8
社会服务业	Social Services	148.7	75.2	128.2	34.0
信息传输、计算机服务和软件业	Information Transmission, Computer Servcie and Software Industries	163.6	19.8	156.1	16.3
住宿和餐饮业	Accommodation and Catering Services	138.2	80.5	120.0	18.1
按企业规模分	**Grouped by Size of Enterprises**				
大　型	Large	168.6	22.0	160.8	22.0
中　型	Medium	143.5	22.7	143.9	15.3
小　型	Small	131.2	23.7	125.2	8.1
按特殊群体分	**Grouped by Special Group**				
上市公司	Listed Companies	167.8	23.7	155.2	10.0
国有控股企业	State-owned and State-holding Enterprises	146.3	19.5	144.6	12.6
按观察指标分	**Grouped by Indicator Observed**				
生产总量	Production (Operation)	135.0	18.4	110.6	5.0
盈利(亏损)变化	Changes of Profit(Loss)	122.2	15.0	119.5	3.9
流动资金	Liquid Capital	92.0	11.4	92.2	8.5
货款拖欠	Payment Arrears for Goods	102.8	-0.9	110.2	1.1
劳动力需求	Demand on Labors	127.5	16.4	105.6	7.7
固定资产投资	Investment in Fixed Assets	122.8	9.2	109.4	5.3
产品订货	Ordering of Productions	123.5	18.5	103.0	1.7
企业融资	Financing of Enterprises	82.3	5.0	86.2	6.6

主要统计指标解释

行政区划 指国家对行政区域的划分.根据宪法规定,我国的行政区域划分如下：(1)全国分为省、自治区、直辖市；(2)省、自治区分为自治州、县、自治县、市；(3)自治州分为县、自治县、市；(4)县、自治县分为乡、民族乡、镇；(5)直辖市和较大的市分为区、县；(6)国家在必要时设立的特别行政区。

平均增长速度 我国计算平均增长速度有两种方法：一种是习惯上经常使用的“水平法”，又称几何平均法，是以间隔期最后一年的水平同基期水平对比来计算平均每年增长(或下降)速度；另一种是“累计法”，又称代数平均法或方程法，是以间隔期内各年水平的总和同基期水平对比来计算平均每年增长(或下降)速度。在一般正常情况下，两种方法计算的平均每年增长速度比较接近；但在经济发展不平衡、出现大起大落时，两种方法计算的结果差别较大。

本《年鉴》内所列的平均增长速度，均用“水平法”计算。从某年到某年平均增长速度的年份，均不包括基期年在内。如建国四十三年的平均增长速度是以1949年为基期计算的，则写为1950-1992年平均增长速度，其余类推。

国民经济行业分类 自2003年定期报表开始使用新的《国民经济行业分类》(GB/T4754-2002)，该分类是由国家统计局组织修订，经国家质量监督检验检疫总局批准，于2002年5月10日发布实施。这次修订是在1994年分类标准的基础上，参照联合国《全部经济活动的国际标准产业分类》(ISIC/Rev.3)进行的。修订后的《国民经济行业分类》(GB/T4754-2002)共有门类20个，大类95个，中类396个，小类913个。新增门类4个，大类增加3个，中类增加28个，小类增加67个。

企业(单位)登记注册类型 是以在工商行政管理机关登记注册的各类企业为划分对象，以工商行政管理部门对企业登记注册的类型为依据，将企业登记注册类型分为内资企业、港澳台商投资企业和外商投资企业三大类。内资企业包括国有企业、集体企业、股份合作企业、联营企业、有限责任公司、股份有限公司、私营公司和其他企业；港澳台商投资企业和外商投资企业分别包括合资经营企业、合作经营企业、独资经营企业和股份有限公司。对不在工商行政管理部门进行登记注册的行政机关、事业单位和社会团体，主要按其经费来源和管理方式进行划分。

国有企业 指企业全部资产归国家所有，并按《中华人民共和国企业法人登记管理条例》规定登记注册的非公司制的经济组织。不包括有限责任公司中的国有独资公司。

集体企业 指企业资产归集体所有，并按《中华人民共和国企业法人登记管理条例》规定登记注册的经济组织。

股份合作企业 指以合作制为基础，由企业职工共同出资入股，吸收一定比例的社会资产投资组建，实行自主经营，自负盈亏，共同劳动，民主管理，按劳分配与按股分红相结合的一种集体经济组织。

联营企业 指两个及两个以上相同或不同所有制性质的企业法人或事业单位法人，按自愿、平等、互利的原则，共同投资组成的经济组织。联营企业包括国有联营企业、集体联营企业、国有与集体联营企业和其他联营企业。

有限责任公司 指根据《中华人民共和国公司登记管理条例》规定登记注册，由两个以上、五十个以下的股东共同出资，每个股东以其所认缴的出资额对公司承担有限责任，公司以其全部资产对其债务承担责任的经济组织。有限责任公司包括国有独资公司以及其他有限责任公司。

股份有限公司 指根据《中华人民共和国公司登记管理条例》规定登记注册，其全部注册资本由等额股份构成并通过发行股票筹集资本，股东以其认购的股份对公司承担有限责任，公司以其全部资产对其债务承担责任的经济组织。

私营企业 指由自然人投资设立或由自然人控股，以雇佣劳动为基础的营利性经济组织。包括按照《公司法》、《合伙企业法》、《私营企业暂行条例》规定登记注册的私营有限责任公司、私营股份有限公司、私营合伙企业和私营独资企业。

其他企业 指上述企业之外的其他内资经济组织。

与港澳台商合资经营企业 指港澳台地区投资者与内地企业依照《中华人民共和国中外合资经营企业法》及有关法律的规定，按合同规定的比例投资设立、分享利润和分担风险的企业。

与港澳台商合作经营企业 指港澳台地区投资者与内地企业依照《中华人民共和国中外合作经营企业法》及有关法律的规定，依照合作合同的约定进行投资或提供条件设立、分配利润和分担风险的企业。

港澳台商独资经营企业 指依照《中华人民共和国外资企业法》及有关法律的规定，在内地由港澳台地区投资者全额投资设立的企业。

港澳台商投资股份有限公司 指根据国家有关规定，经外经贸部依法批准设立，其中港、澳、台商的股本占公司注册资本的比例达25%以上的股份有限公司。凡其中港、澳、台商的股本占公司注册资本的比例小于25%的，属于内资企业中的股份有限公司。

中外合资经营企业 指外国企业或外国人与中国内地企业依照《中华人民共和国中外合资经营企业法》及有关法律的规定，按合同规定的比例投资设立、分享利润和分担风险的企业。

中外合作经营企业 指外国企业或外国人与中国内地

企业依照《中华人民共和国中外合作经营企业法》及有关法律的规定，依照合作合同的约定进行投资或提供条件设立、分配利润和分担风险的企业。

外资企业 指依照《中华人民共和国外资企业法》及有关法律的规定，在中国内地由外国投资者全额投资设立的企业。

外商投资股份有限公司 指根据国家有关规定，经外经贸部依法批准设立，其中外资的股本占公司注册资本的比例达 25% 以上的股份有限公司。凡其中外资股本占公司注册资本的比例小于 25%的，属于内资企业中的股份有限公司。

行政机关、事业单位和社会团体 参照企业登记注册类型，主要按其经费来源和管理方式划分。具体规定如下：

⑴行政机关：包括国家机关和政党机关，原则上均列为“国有”。但有特殊规定的，如供销社等，则列为“集体”。

⑵事业单位：包括经国家机构编制部门和有关业务主管部门批准成立的各类事业单位，不包括实行企业化管理的事业单位。事业单位的划分办法如下：

①由国家财政预算拨款或列入财政预算外资金管理以及经费主要来源于国有主管部门或国有上级单位的事业单位，列为“国有”。

②经费主要来源于集体单位的事业单位，列为“集体”。

③公民个人(或个人合伙)开办的事业单位，列为“私营”。

④上述以外的其他事业单位，如果其经费来源不明确，按管理方式进行归类。

⑶社会团体：包括经民政部门批准成立以及未纳入社会团体管理条例范围的工会、妇联等各类社会团体。社会团体的划分办法如下：

①未纳入民政部社会团体管理条例范围的工会、妇联、共青团、青联、工商联、科协、侨联等社会团体，国家拨款设立的基金会或基金管理组织以及经费主要来源于国有业务主管部门或国有上级单位的社会团体，列为“国有”。

②经费主要来源于集体单位的社会团体，列为“集体”。

③公民个人(或个人合伙)开办的社会团体，划为“私营”。

④上述以外的其他社会团体，如果其经费来源不明确，改按管理方式进行归类。

各个计划时期 表内所用各个“时期”代表的年份如下：恢复时期为 1950 到 1952 年；第一个五年计划时期(简称“一五”时期)为 1953 到 1957 年；第二个五年计划时期(简称“二五”时期)为 1958 到 1962 年；第三个五年计划时期(简称“三五”时期)为 1966 到 1970 年；第四个五年计划时期(简称“四五”时期)为 1971 到 1975 年；第五个五年计划时期(简称“五五”时期)为 1976 到 1980 年；第六个五年计划时期(简称“六五”时期)为 1981 到 1985 年；第七个五年计划时期(简称“七五”时期)为 1986 到 1990 年；第八个五年计划时期(简称“八五”时期)为 1991 到 1995 年；第九个五年计划时期(简称“九五”时期)为 1996 到 2000 年；第十个五年计划时期(简称“十五”时期)为 2001 到 2005 年；第十一个五年计划时期(简称“十一五”时期)为 2006 到 2010 年。第十二个五年计划时期（简称“十二五”时期）为 2011 到 2015 年。

企业景气调查 是通过对部分企业家定期进行问卷调查，并根据企业家对企业经营状况及宏观经济形势的判断和预期来编制景气指数，从而对现实经济运行状况及其发展趋势进行分析和预测的一种统计调查方法。

景气指数 又称为景气度，它是对企业景气调查中的定性指标通过定量方法加工汇总，综合反映某一特定调查群体或某一社会经济现象所处的状态或发展趋势的一种指标。通过其上升和下降的动态变化，反映经济发展状态及其变化过程。景气指数取值于 0--200 之间，100 为景气指数的临界值；当景气指数大于 100 时，表明经济状况趋于上升或改善，处于景气状态；当景气指数小于 100 时，表明经济状况趋于下降或恶化，处于不景气状态。

企业家信心指数 也称宏观经济景气指数，是根据企业家对企业外部市场经济环境与宏观政策的认识、看法、判断与预期而编制的指数，用以综合反映企业家对宏观经济环境的感受与信心。

企业景气指数 也称企业综合生产经营景气指数，是根据企业家对本企业综合生产经营情况的判断与预期而编制的指数，用以反映企业的综合生产经营状况。

Explanatory Notes on Main Statistical Indicators

Administrative Division refers to the division of administrative areas by the state. The Constitution of the People's Republic of China stipulates that the administrative areas in China are divided as: 1) The whole Country is divided into provinces, autonomous regions and municipalities directly under the central government; 2) Provinces and autonomous regions are divided into autonomous prefectures, counties, autonomous counties and cities; 3) Autonomous prefectures are divided into counties, autonomous counties and cities; 4) Counties and autonomous counties are divided into townships, nationality townships and towns; 5) Municipalities and large cities are divided into districts and counties, 6) The state shall, when necessary, establish special administrative regions.

Average Annual Growth Rate Two methods for calculating average annual growth rate are applied in China,one is often called level approachor the method of calculating geometric average,which is derived by comparing the level of the last year of the interval with that of the beginning year;the other is calledaccumulative approach or algebraic average or equation method,which is derived by the summation of the actual figure of each year in the interval divided by the figure in the base year.Usually the results calculated by the two methods are fairly close, but they differed sharply when uneven economic development occurred with striking fluctuations in growth.

The average annual growth rates listed in this statistical yearbook are calculated by level approach except for the growth rate of investment in fixed assets. The base years are not listed when the years are listed for average annual growth rates. For instance,the average annual growth rate of 43 years since 1949 is listed as average annual growth rate of 1950-1992 without listing the base year 1949.And the analogy of this is also the same for the rest of the years.

Industrial Classification of the National Economy The new Industrial Classification of the National Economy (GB/T 4754-2002) is introduced starting from the compilation of 2003 annual statistics. The new revision was based on the 1994 classification and organized by the National Bureau of Statistics taking into consideration of the International Standards of the Industrial Classification of All Economic Activities (ISIC/Rev.3) of the United Nations, and the new Classification was promulgated by the National Administration of Quality Supervision, Inspection and Quarantine on May 10, 2002. The revised version of the Industrial Classification of the National Economy (GB/T 4754-2002) is composed of 20 major divisions, 95 divisions, 396 major groups and 913 groups, including 4 new major divisions, 3 new divisions, 28 major groups and 67 groups.

Registration Status of Enterprises Enterprises are classified into 3 categories, namely domestic-funded enterprises, enterprises with investment from Hong Kong, Macau and Taiwan, and enterprises with foreign investment, in the light of the registration status of an enterprise in industrial and commercial administration agencies. Domestic-funded enterprises include state-owned enterprises, collective-owned enterprises, cooperative enterprises, jȯint ownership enterprises, limited liability corporations, share-holding corporations Ltd., private enterprises and other enterprises. Included in the enterprises with investment from Hong Kong, Macau and Taiwan and enterprises with foreign investment are joint-venture enterprises, cooperative enterprises, sole investment enterprises and share-holding corporations Ltd. For government agencies, institutions and social organizations which are not requested to be registered in industrial and commercial administration agencies, they are classified mainly by their sources of funds and way of management.

State-owned Enterprises refer to non-corporation economic units where the entire assets are owned by the state and which have registered in accordance with the Regulation of the Peoples Republic of China on the Management of Registration of Corporate Enterprises. Excluded from this category are sole state-funded corporations in the limited liability corporations.

Collective-owned Enterprises refer to economic units where the assets are owned collectively and which have registered in accordance with the Regulation of the Peoples Republic of China on the Management of Registration of Corporate Enterprises.

Cooperative Enterprises refer to a form of collective economic units (enterprises) where capitals come mainly from employees as their shares, with certain proportion of capital from the outside, where production is organized on the basis of independent operation, independent accounting for profits and losses, joint work, democratic management, and a distribution system that integrates remuneration according to work with dividend according to capital share.

Joint Ownership Enterprises refer to economic units established by two or more corporate enterprises or corporate institutions of the same or different ownership, through joint investment on the basis of equality, voluntary participation and mutual benefits. They include state joint ownership enterprises, collective joint ownership enterprises, joint state-collective enterprises, other joint ownership enterprises.

Limited Liability Corporations refer to economic units established with investment from 2-50 investors and registered in accordance with the Regulation of the Peoples Republic of China on the Management of Registration of Corporations, each investor bearing limited liability to the corporation depending on its share of investment, and the corporation bearing liability to its debt to the maximum of its total assets. Limited liability corporations include exclusive state-funded limited liability corporations and other limited liability corporations.

Share-holding Corporations Ltd. refer to economic units registered in accordance with the Regulation of the Peoples Republic of China on the Management of Registration of Corporations, with total registered capitals divided into equal shares and raised through issuing stocks. Each investor bears limited liability to the corporation depending on the holding of shares, and the corporation bears liability to its debt to the maximum of its total assets.

Private Enterprises refer to profit-making economic units invested and established by natural persons, or controlled by natural persons using employed labour. Included in this category are private limited liability corporations, private share-holding corporations Ltd., private partnership enterprises and private-funded enterprises registered in accordance with the Corporation Law, Partnership Enterprises Law and Interim Regulations on Private Enterprises .

Other Domestic-funded Enterprises refer to domesticfunded economic units other than those mentioned above.

Joint-venture Enterprises with Funds from Hong Kong, Macau and Taiwan refer to enterprises jointly established by investors from Hong Kong, Macau and Taiwan with enterprises in the mainland of China in accordance with the Law of the Peoples Republic of China on Sino-foreign Joint Venture Enterprises and other relevant laws, where the share of investment, profits and risks is stipulated in the contract.

Cooperative Enterprises with Funds from Hong Kong Macau and Taiwan established by investors from Hong Kong, Macau and Taiwan with enterprises in the mainland of China in accordance with the Law of the Peoples Republic of China on Sino-foreign Cooperative Enterprises and other relevant laws, where the investment or provision of facilities, and the share of profits and risks is stipulated in the cooperative contract.

Enterprises with Sole (exclusive) Investment from Hong Kong, Macau and Taiwan refer to enterprises established in the mainland of China with exclusive investment from investors from Hong Kong, Macau and Taiwan in accordance with the Law of the Peoples Republic of China on Foreign-Funded Enterprises and other relevant laws.

Share-holding Corporations Ltd. with Investment from Hong Kong, Macau and Taiwan refer to share-holding corporations Ltd. established with the approval from the Ministry of Foreign Trades and Economic Relations in line with relevant state regulations, where the share of investment from Hong Kong, Macau or Taiwan businessmen exceeds 25% of the total registered capital of the corporation. In case the share of investment from Hong Kong, Macau or Taiwan is less than 25% of the total registered capital, the enterprise is to be classified as domestic-funded share-holding corporation Ltd.

Joint-venture Enterprises with Foreign Investment refer to enterprises jointly established by foreign enterprises or foreigners with enterprises in the mainland of China in accordance with the Law of the Peoples Republic of China on Sino-foreign Joint Venture Enterprises and other relevant laws, where the share of investment, profits and risks is stipulated in the contract.

Cooperation Enterprises with Foreign Investment refer to enterprises jointly established by foreign enterprises or foreigners with enterprises in the mainland of China in accordance with the Law of the Peoples Republic of China on Sino-foreign Cooperative Enterprises and other relevant laws, where the investment or provision of facilities, and the share of profits and risks is stipulated in the cooperative contract.

Enterprises with Sole (exclusive) Foreign Investment refer to enterprises established in the mainland of China with exclusive investment from foreign investors in accordance with the Law of the Peoples Republic of China on Foreign-Funded Enterprises and other relevant laws.

Shareholding Corporations Ltd. with Foreign Investment refer to share-holding corporations Ltd. established with the approval from the Ministry of Foreign Trades and Economic Relations in line with relevant state regulations, where the share of investment from foreign investors exceeds 25% of the total registered capital of the corporation. In case the share of foreign investment is less than 25% of the total registered capital, the enterprise is to be classified as domestic-funded share-holding corporation Ltd.

Government Agencies, Institutions and Social Organizations are classified into following categories by source of funds and way of management taking reference of the registration status of enterprises:

(1) Government agencies: include state and party agencies, classified in principle as "state-owned". There are exceptions, such as supply and marketing cooperatives which are classified as

"collective".

(2) Institutions: include institutions of various types established with the approval by organization and staffing departments of the government, but exclude institutions where enterprise management system is introduced. Institutions are further classified as follows:

(a) Institutions whose main budget is listed in the government budget appropriations or extra-budget funds, or allocated from the budget of their competent government agencies. Such institutions are classified as "state-owned".

(b) Institutions whose budget mainly comes from collective units. Such institutions are classified as "collective".

(c) Institutions other than those mentioned above whose source of budget is not clear. Such institutions are classified by way of management.

(3) Social organizations: include social organizations established with the approval from the Ministry of Civil Affairs, and organizations that are not covered by social organization management regulations such as Trades unions, women's federations etc. Social organizations are further classified as follows:

(a) Social organizations that are not covered by social organization management regulations of the Ministry of Civil Affairs such as Trades unions, women's federations, communist youth leagues, youth associations, industrial and commerce associations, scientists associations, overseas Chinese associations, etc.foundations and fund management organizations established with funds from the state, and social organizations whose funds mainly come from the budget of their competent government agencies. Such institutions are classified as "state-owned".

(b) Social organizations whose budget mainly comes from collective units. Such institutions are classified as "collective".

(c) Social organizations established by individual or a group of citizens, which are classified as "private".

(d) Social organizations other than those mentioned above whose source of budget is not clear. Such organizations are classified by way of management.

Each Plan Period recovery period refer to 1950-1952;the first five-year plan refer to 1953-1957;the second five-year plan refer to 1958-1962;the third five-year plan refer to 1966-1970;the fourth five-year plan refer to 1971-1975;the fifth five-yaer plan refer to 1976-1980;the sixth five-year plan refer to 1980-1985;the seventh five-yaer plan refer to 1986-1990;the eighth five-yaer plan refer to 1991-1995;the ninth five-year plan refer to 1996-2000;the tenth five-year plan refer to 2001-2005;the eleventh five-year plan refer to 2006-2010the twelvth five-yaer plan refer to 2011-2015.

nterprises Climate Survey It is a statistics survey, which compile the climate index by regular paper survey to a section of entrepreneurs, based on entrepreneur's judgement and forecast to the production situation of their own enterprises and the macro-economy situation, and thus we can analyse and predict the current situation and future trend of the economic performance.

Business climate index It is the quantitative disposition and compilation of the qualitative economic indicators of the business climate survey, which can improve a comprehensive description of the real situation or the future trend of a special survey group or a social and economic phenomenon. The business climate index is ranging from 0 to 200. 100 is the critical value, when the climate index is larger than 100, it shows that the economic performance is picking up or improving. When it is lower than 100, it shows that the economic performance is declining or worsening.

Entrepreneur confidence index also called as the macro-economy climate index. It is a index based on entrepreneur's recognition, opinion, judgement and forecast to the market circumstances and macro-policies, It is a comprehensive desc-ryption of the entrepreneur's impression and confidents of the macro-economy circumstances .

Business climate index also called as the comprehensive production and management climate index of enterprises. It is compiled basing on entrepreneur's judgement on production situation of their own expectation for the future performance. It is the description of the comprehensive production and management situation of the enterprises.

第二篇
国民经济核算

CHAPTER 2
National Accounts

简要说明
Brief Introduction

本篇资料的主要内容及来源

国民经济核算篇资料主要包括新疆维吾尔自治区主要年份生产总值的绝对值、构成和指数,居民消费水平,各地、州、市、县生产总值、构成和指数等资料。以上资料是由新疆维吾尔自治区统计局国民经济核算处根据不同产业部门、不同支出构成的特点和资料来源,严格按照国家国民经济核算制度计算的。

关于数据使用的说明。本篇表 2-1、表 2-4 中三次产业数据使用的是国家 1994 年国民经济行业分类标准;2-5、2-6 表使用的是国家 2002 年国民经济行业分类标准。若做历史数据分析比较请使用表 2-1 表中公布的数据资料;若只使用当年数据,请用表 2-5 表或 2-6 表中公布的数据。

本章所列分地、州(市)、县的数据来自各地、州(市)、县统计局的国民经济核算资料。由于采用分级核算,各地区数据相加不等于全疆总计,地区所辖县、市数据相加不等于地区合计。

Main content and sources of data

Statistics on national accounts include mainly gross domestic product of Xinjiang Bureau of Statistics, it´s composition and indices of gross domestic product, household consumption level, composition and indices of gross domestic product by prefecture, autonomous prefecture, city and county. Data on GDP are calculated by the Department of National Accounts Statistics of the Xinjiang Bureau of Statistics with various approaches in the light of the features of various sectors, various expenditure structures and the data sources and National Accounts system.

Data on the table 2-1 and 2-4 use the Industrial Classification of National Economy of 1994;The table 2-5 and 2-6 use the Industrial Classification of National Economy of 2002.If analyze the historical data ,you could use the data of table 2-1.If use the present data, you use the data of 2-5 or 2-6.

Regional data in this chapter are prepared form the national accounts data provided by the statistical bureaus of the prefecture,autonomous prefecture,city and county.The sum of the regional data is not equal to the national total due to the decentralized accounting approach.

2-1 1978-2010 年历年新疆生产总值
Gross Domestic Product in Xinjiang(1978-2010)

单位：亿元 (100 million yuan)

年 份 Year	新疆生产总值 Gross Domestic Product	第一产业 Primary Industry	第二产业 Secondary Industry	工 业 Industry	建筑业 Construction	第三产业 Tertiary Industry	#交通运输仓储和邮政业 Transport, Storage and Post	#批发和零售业 Wholesale, and Retail Trades	人均新疆生产总值(元) Per Capita GDP (yuan)
1978	39.07	13.97	18.35	14.48	3.87	6.75	1.19	2.07	313
1979	45.63	16.32	21.43	17.16	4.27	7.88	1.52	2.34	359
1980	53.24	21.53	21.44	17.48	3.96	10.27	1.91	2.91	410
1981	59.41	25.18	22.39	17.93	4.46	11.84	2.25	3.41	450
1982	65.24	28.11	23.35	18.66	4.69	13.78	2.53	3.84	488
1983	78.55	32.84	29.10	23.33	5.77	16.61	3.01	4.75	583
1984	89.75	36.68	31.65	25.45	6.20	21.42	4.01	6.29	661
1985	112.24	42.89	40.50	32.14	8.36	28.85	4.59	8.97	820
1986	129.04	46.00	45.63	36.79	8.84	37.41	5.98	10.48	924
1987	148.50	56.18	50.30	41.16	9.14	42.02	7.73	12.45	1053
1988	192.72	72.27	66.02	53.53	12.49	54.43	11.60	16.11	1347
1989	217.29	78.01	73.83	60.21	13.62	65.45	12.90	17.59	1493
1990	261.44	104.09	83.18	71.50	11.68	74.17	14.63	20.48	1713
1991	335.91	111.86	107.99	84.07	23.92	116.06	22.63	36.88	2101
1992	402.31	114.50	147.64	106.29	41.35	140.17	28.32	39.85	2477
1993	495.25	126.85	205.07	155.92	49.15	163.33	32.58	43.46	2964
1994	662.32	187.69	249.11	190.00	59.11	225.52	44.40	57.67	3888
1995	814.85	240.71	283.97	219.01	64.96	290.17	59.63	73.78	4701
1996	900.93	249.31	313.70	239.07	74.63	337.92	73.74	87.25	5102
1997	1039.85	279.73	385.37	302.50	82.87	374.75	85.70	94.23	5848
1998	1106.95	291.05	395.75	298.53	97.22	420.15	106.87	98.06	6174
1999	1163.17	268.51	420.48	315.86	104.62	474.18	129.60	102.26	6443
2000	1363.56	288.18	537.58	418.63	118.95	537.80	148.63	110.10	7372
2001	1491.60	288.12	573.91	445.60	128.31	629.57	148.38	118.45	7945
2002	1612.65	305.00	603.15	463.59	139.56	704.50	168.58	123.88	8457
2003	1886.35	412.90	719.54	563.57	155.97	753.91	159.43	141.32	9828
2004	2209.09	446.13	914.47	734.10	180.37	848.49	186.70	160.30	11337
2005	2604.14	510.00	1164.80	961.62	203.18	929.34	149.61	145.10	13108
2006	3045.26	527.80	1459.30	1241.33	217.97	1058.16	165.60	163.15	15000
2007	3523.16	628.72	1647.55	1405.11	242.44	1246.89	177.28	187.10	16999
2008	4183.21	691.07	2070.76	1755.35	315.41	1421.38	191.84	222.74	19797
2009	4277.05	759.74	1929.59	1555.84	373.75	1587.72	209.10	253.60	19942
2010	5437.47	1078.63	2592.15	2161.39	430.76	1766.69	222.47	276.28	25057

注：1.本表绝对数按当年价格计算。2.2005年以后数据根据经济普查资料采用趋势离差法（国际上通用的调整历史数据的方法）修订。3. 2004年及以前年份第一产业不包括农林牧渔服务业，交通运输和邮政业包括电信业，但不包括城市公共交通业，批发和零售业包括餐饮业。（下表同）

Note: a) Data in value terms in this table are calculated at current prices. b) The data since 2005 were revised by trend deviation approach accordance with the economic census.c) In 2004 and preceding years the primary industry did not include service of farming, forestry,animal husbandry and fishery; transport, storage and post include telecommunication services, but did not include urban public transport; wholesale and retail Trades include catering servites.(The same as in the following table)

2-2 1978-2010 年历年新疆生产总值构成

Composition of Gross Domestic Product in Xinjiang(1978-2010)

单位：% (%)

年 份 Year	新疆生产总值构成 Composition of Gross Domestic Product	第一产业 Primary Industry	第二产业 Secondary Industry	工 业 Industry	建筑业 Construction	第三产业 Tertiary Industry	#交通运输仓储和邮政业 Transport, Storage and Post	#批发和零售业 Wholesale, and Retail Trades
1978	100	35.8	47.0	37.1	9.9	17.2	3.0	5.3
1979	100	35.7	47.0	37.6	9.4	17.3	3.3	5.1
1980	100	40.4	40.3	32.9	7.4	19.3	3.6	5.5
1981	100	42.4	37.7	30.2	7.5	19.9	3.8	5.7
1982	100	43.1	35.8	28.6	7.2	21.1	3.9	5.9
1983	100	41.8	37.1	29.8	7.3	21.1	3.8	6.0
1984	100	40.9	35.2	28.3	6.9	23.9	4.5	7.0
1985	100	38.2	36.1	28.7	7.4	25.7	4.1	8.0
1986	100	35.6	35.4	28.5	6.9	29.0	4.6	8.1
1987	100	37.8	33.9	27.7	6.2	28.3	5.2	8.4
1988	100	37.5	34.3	27.8	6.5	28.2	6.0	8.4
1989	100	35.9	34.0	27.7	6.3	30.1	5.9	8.1
1990	100	39.8	31.8	27.3	4.5	28.4	5.6	7.8
1991	100	33.3	32.1	25.0	7.1	34.6	6.7	11.0
1992	100	28.5	36.7	26.4	10.3	34.8	7.0	9.9
1993	100	25.6	41.4	31.5	9.9	33.0	6.6	8.8
1994	100	28.3	37.6	28.7	8.9	34.1	6.7	8.7
1995	100	29.5	34.9	26.9	8.0	35.6	7.3	9.1
1996	100	27.7	34.8	26.5	8.3	37.5	8.2	9.7
1997	100	26.9	37.1	29.1	8.0	36.0	8.2	9.1
1998	100	26.3	35.7	27.0	8.7	38.0	9.7	8.9
1999	100	23.1	36.1	27.1	9.0	40.8	11.1	8.8
2000	100	21.1	39.4	30.7	8.7	39.5	10.9	8.1
2001	100	19.3	38.5	29.9	8.6	42.2	9.9	7.9
2002	100	18.9	37.4	28.7	8.7	43.7	10.5	7.7
2003	100	21.9	38.1	29.8	8.3	40.0	8.5	7.5
2004	100	20.2	41.4	33.2	8.2	38.4	8.5	7.3
2005	100	19.6	44.7	36.9	7.8	35.7	5.7	5.6
2006	100	17.3	47.9	40.7	7.2	34.8	5.4	5.4
2007	100	17.8	46.8	39.9	6.9	35.4	5.0	5.3
2008	100	16.5	49.5	42.0	7.5	34.0	4.6	5.3
2009	100	17.8	45.1	36.4	8.7	37.1	4.9	5.9
2010	100	19.8	47.7	39.8	7.9	32.5	4.1	5.1

注：本表按当年价格计算。
Note: Data in value terms in this table are calculated at current prices.

2-3 1978-2010 年历年新疆生产总值指数

Indices of Gross Domestic Product in Xinjiang(1978-2010)

(上年=100) (preceding year=100)

年 份 Year	新疆生产总值 Gross Domestic Product	第一产业 Primary Industry	第二产业 Secondary Industry	工 业 Industry	建筑业 Construction	第三产业 Tertiary Industry	#交通运输仓储和邮政业 Transport, Storage and Post	#批发和零售业 Wholesale, and Retail Trades	人均新疆生产总值 Per Capita GDP
1978	109.8	110.2	110.3	112.8	101.8	107.2	102.1	109.3	106.9
1979	112.4	109.8	111.5	111.2	112.6	120.8	121.6	117.5	110.2
1980	107.3	106.0	105.2	108.5	93.1	116.6	115.6	125.5	105.0
1981	108.5	115.2	99.3	99.1	100.3	113.4	119.4	117.9	106.6
1982	109.9	111.2	104.3	104.6	102.8	117.1	118.9	119.8	108.5
1983	113.5	112.1	111.9	112.4	109.8	118.7	113.3	108.8	112.5
1984	114.1	113.6	114.7	115.1	112.9	114.0	100.0	109.2	113.2
1985	116.9	112.9	116.6	116.1	119.0	125.0	100.3	126.6	115.9
1986	111.7	108.3	109.5	111.0	102.5	120.7	124.7	110.0	109.2
1987	110.0	110.7	105.6	108.5	91.4	114.7	119.3	111.0	108.7
1988	109.6	103.3	114.6	113.6	120.2	112.9	118.8	114.7	108.0
1989	106.1	101.8	105.0	106.9	94.5	113.5	112.7	107.5	104.1
1990	111.7	116.0	106.7	106.4	108.6	112.0	106.7	104.5	106.8
1991	114.4	111.2	117.0	113.1	140.6	115.7	128.8	101.6	109.0
1992	113.1	105.5	119.4	112.6	152.8	115.7	124.6	112.6	111.3
1993	110.2	101.1	113.3	111.4	120.3	117.7	118.3	121.3	106.9
1994	112.1	111.2	110.2	111.3	106.3	115.3	109.7	105.6	110.2
1995	109.1	104.9	111.5	113.3	105.0	110.9	119.5	108.9	107.4
1996	106.5	103.5	107.8	107.4	109.5	108.0	113.0	109.6	104.5
1997	108.4	110.8	105.2	103.4	112.0	109.7	119.6	105.8	107.6
1998	107.5	107.2	105.7	103.0	115.0	109.6	117.5	104.9	106.6
1999	107.4	102.7	106.8	106.5	107.7	112.3	114.7	107.9	106.6
2000	108.7	104.8	108.6	109.1	107.3	112.1	114.4	109.6	106.2
2001	108.6	102.8	108.1	107.8	109.0	112.1	109.5	105.0	107.0
2002	108.2	105.0	107.4	107.7	106.3	110.4	114.3	110.3	106.5
2003	111.2	108.2	111.6	111.2	112.8	112.3	115.1	110.9	110.5
2004	111.4	105.7	114.0	114.5	112.2	111.5	115.1	112.6	109.7
2005	110.9	106.5	114.4	115.7	109.7	109.4	109.0	111.9	108.8
2006	111.0	105.7	111.2	112.5	105.0	113.6	107.2	110.5	108.7
2007	112.2	107.1	112.7	114.1	105.4	114.3	106.1	109.1	109.9
2008	111.0	106.4	114.3	114.3	114.1	109.2	108.7	110.3	108.9
2009	108.1	104.5	108.5	106.2	120.9	109.2	107.0	113.4	106.5
2010	110.6	104.5	112.6	113.5	108.3	110.8	107.9	108.3	109.3

注：本表按可比价计算。
Note: Data in this table are calculated at constant prices.

2-4 1978-2010 年历年新疆生产总值指数

Indices of Gross Domestic Product in Xinjiang(1978-2010)

(1978 年=100)

年 份 Year	新疆生产总值 Gross Domestic Product	第一产业 Primary Industry	第二产业 Secondary Industry	工 业 Industry	建筑业 Construction	第三产业 Tertiary Industry	#交通运输仓储和邮政业 Transport, Storage and Post	#批发和零售业 Wholesale, and Retail Trades	人均新疆生产总值 Per Capita GDP
1978	100.0	100.0	100.0	100.0	100.0	100.0	100.0	100.0	100.0
1979	112.4	109.8	111.5	111.2	112.6	120.8	121.6	117.5	110.2
1980	120.6	116.4	117.3	120.7	104.8	140.9	140.6	147.5	115.7
1981	130.9	134.1	116.5	119.6	105.1	159.8	167.9	173.9	123.3
1982	143.9	149.1	121.5	125.1	108.0	187.1	199.6	208.3	133.8
1983	163.3	167.1	136.0	140.6	118.6	222.1	226.1	226.6	150.6
1984	186.3	189.8	156.0	161.8	133.9	253.2	226.1	247.4	170.4
1985	217.8	214.3	181.9	187.8	159.3	316.5	226.8	313.2	197.5
1986	243.3	232.1	199.2	208.5	163.3	382.0	282.8	344.5	215.7
1987	267.6	256.9	210.4	226.2	149.3	438.2	337.4	382.4	234.5
1988	293.3	265.4	241.1	257.0	179.5	494.7	400.8	438.6	253.2
1989	311.2	270.2	253.2	274.7	169.6	561.5	451.7	471.5	263.6
1990	347.6	313.4	270.2	292.3	184.2	628.9	482.0	492.7	281.5
1991	397.7	348.5	316.1	330.6	259.0	727.6	620.8	500.6	306.9
1992	449.8	367.7	377.4	372.3	395.8	841.8	773.5	563.7	341.6
1993	495.7	371.7	427.6	414.7	476.1	990.8	915.1	683.8	365.1
1994	555.7	413.3	471.2	461.6	506.1	1142.4	1003.9	722.1	402.4
1995	606.3	433.6	525.4	523.0	531.4	1266.9	1199.7	786.4	432.1
1996	645.7	448.8	566.4	561.7	581.9	1368.3	1355.7	861.9	451.6
1997	699.9	497.3	595.9	580.8	651.7	1501.0	1621.4	911.9	485.9
1998	752.4	533.1	629.9	598.2	749.5	1645.1	1905.1	956.6	518.0
1999	808.1	547.5	672.7	637.1	807.2	1847.4	2185.1	1032.2	552.2
2000	878.4	573.8	730.6	695.1	866.1	2070.9	2499.8	1131.3	586.4
2001	953.9	589.9	789.8	749.3	944.0	2321.5	2737.3	1187.9	627.4
2002	1032.1	619.4	848.2	807.0	1003.5	2562.9	3128.7	1310.3	668.2
2003	1147.7	670.2	946.6	897.4	1131.9	2878.1	3601.1	1453.1	738.4
2004	1278.5	708.4	1079.1	1027.5	1270.0	3209.1	4144.9	1636.2	810.0
2005	1417.9	754.4	1234.5	1188.8	1393.2	3510.8	4517.9	1830.9	881.3
2006	1573.9	797.4	1372.8	1337.4	1462.9	3988.3	4843.2	2023.1	958.0
2007	1765.9	854.0	1547.1	1526.0	1541.9	4558.6	5138.6	2207.2	1052.8
2008	1960.1	908.7	1768.3	1744.2	1759.3	4978.0	5585.7	2434.5	1146.5
2009	2118.9	949.5	1918.6	1852.4	2127.0	5436.0	5976.7	2760.8	1221.0
2010	2343.5	992.2	2160.3	2102.5	2303.5	6023.1	6448.9	2989.9	1334.6

注：本表按可比价计算。
Note: Data in this table are calculated at constant prices.

2-5 分行业新疆生产总值
Gross Domestic Product by Sector in Xinjiang

指 标	Item	增加值(亿元) Added Value (100 million yuan)		构 成(%) Composition (%)		指数(上年=100) Indices (preceding year=100)	
		2009	2010	2009	2010	2009	2010
新疆生产总值	**Gross Domestic Product**	**4277.05**	**5437.47**	**100.0**	**100.0**	**108.1**	**110.6**
第一产业	Primary Industry	759.74	1078.63	17.8	19.8	104.5	104.5
第二产业	Secondary Industry	1929.59	2592.15	45.1	47.7	108.5	112.6
工 业	Industry	1555.84	2161.39	36.4	39.8	106.2	113.5
建筑业	Construction	373.75	430.76	8.7	7.9	120.9	108.3
第三产业	Tertiary Industry	1587.72	1766.69	37.1	32.5	109.2	110.8
交通运输、仓储和邮政业	Transport, storage and Post	209.10	222.47	4.9	4.1	107.0	107.9
批发和零售业	Wholesale and Retail Trades	253.60	276.28	5.9	5.1	113.4	108.3
住宿和餐饮业	Hotels and Catering Services	62.25	68.06	1.5	1.3	85.1	105.8
金融业	Financial Intermediation	198.87	225.20	4.6	4.1	111.8	113.6
房地产业	Real Estate	115.23	143.44	2.7	2.6	123.3	119.0
其他服务业	Others	748.67	831.24	17.5	15.3	108.7	110.9

注：本表按当年价格计算，采用 GB/T4754-2002 国民经济行业分类标准。
Note: Data in value terms in this table are calculated at current prices and adopted the new Industrial Classification of National Economy (GB/T4754-2002).

2-6 新疆生产总值项目结构

Components of Gross Domestic Product in Xinjiang

(2010 年)

指　　标	Item	新疆生产总值 Gross Domestic Product	劳动者报酬 Compensation of Employees	生产税净额 Net Taxes on Production	固定资产折旧 Depreciation of Fixed Assets	营业盈余 Operating Surplus
新疆生产总值(亿元)	**Gross Domestic Product (100 million yuan)**	**5437.47**	**2829.07**	**791.23**	**676.21**	**1140.96**
第一产业	Primary Industry	1078.63	1050.68		27.95	
第二产业	Secondary Industry	2592.15	679.49	594.82	389.68	928.16
工　业	Industry	2161.39	400.25	512.97	355.48	892.69
建筑业	Construction	430.76	279.24	81.85	34.20	35.47
第三产业	Tertiary Industry	1766.69	1098.90	196.41	258.58	212.80
交通运输、仓储和邮政业	Transport, storage and Post	222.47	146.68	45.21	39.27	-8.69
信息传输、计算机服务和软件业	Information Transmission, Computer Service and Software	85.75	23.57	5.76	42.27	14.15
批发和零售业	Wholesale and Retail Trades	276.28	123.48	73.23	23.16	56.41
住宿和餐饮业	Hotels and Catering Services	68.06	59.68	4.85	5.19	-1.66
金融业	Financial Intermediation	225.20	80.02	21.49	10.65	113.04
房地产业	Real Estate	143.44	17.67	30.74	65.27	29.76
租赁和商务服务业	Leasing and Business Service	47.37	31.21	4.96	8.16	3.04
科学研究、技术服务和地质勘查业	Scientific Research, Technology Service and Geological Prospecting	49.00	33.82	3.58	4.86	6.74
水利、环境和公共设施管理业	Water Conservancy, Environment and Public Facility Management	29.87	17.71	0.86	11.04	0.26
居民服务和其他服务业	Community Service and Other Services	43.72	38.27	3.72	1.25	0.48
教　育	Education	183.49	168.30	0.73	14.41	0.05
卫生、社会保障和社会福利业	Health, Social Security and Social Welfare	83.18	74.91	0.26	7.94	0.07
文化、体育和娱乐业	Culture, Sports and Entertainment	20.92	18.39	0.78	2.19	-0.44
公共管理和社会组织	Public Management and Social Organizations	287.94	265.19	0.24	22.92	-0.41

注：本表按当年价格计算。
Note: Data in value terms in this table are calculated at current prices.

2-7 主要年份支出法新疆生产总值
Gross Domestic Product by Expenditure Approach in Xinjiang in Main Years

单位：万元 (10 000 yuan)

年份 Year	支出法新疆生产总值 Gross Domestic Product by Expenditure	最终消费 Final Consumption Expenditures	资本形成总额 Gross Capital Formation	货物和服务净出口 Net Export of Goods and Services	最终消费率（消费率）(%) Final Consumption Rate (%)	资本形成率（投资率）(%) Capital Formation Rate (%)
1978	390667	276393	184279	-70005	70.7	47.2
1980	532441	398217	231515	-97291	74.8	43.5
1985	1122379	780423	584289	-242333	69.5	52.1
1986	1290398	923792	602593	-235987	71.6	46.7
1987	1485104	1037723	699416	-252035	69.9	47.1
1988	1927224	1260879	983051	-316706	65.4	51.0
1989	2172907	1374960	1178441	-380494	63.3	54.2
1990	2614402	1667725	1411667	-464990	63.8	54.0
1991	3359147	1965753	1691482	-298088	58.5	50.4
1992	4023096	2215692	2492589	-685185	55.1	61.9
1993	4952509	2699236	3561561	-1308288	54.5	71.9
1994	6623239	3369417	4875542	-1621720	50.9	73.6
1995	8148512	4446226	4737079	-1034793	54.6	58.1
1996	9009288	5539010	4569575	-1099297	61.5	50.7
1997	10398462	6118128	5649193	-1368859	58.8	54.3
1998	11069485	6424751	6858461	-2213727	58.0	62.0
1999	11631711	6905712	5815889	-1089890	59.4	50.0
2000	13635631	7601990	6181229	-147588	55.8	45.3
2001	14916046	8590024	7714187	-1388165	57.6	51.7
2002	16126539	9637142	8642721	-2153324	59.8	53.6
2003	18863541	10272223	11192144	-2600826	54.5	59.3
2004	22090869	11251138	13504699	-2664968	50.9	61.1
2005	26041353	12665161	15059657	-1683465	48.6	57.8
2006	30452623	14645277	16547021	-739675	48.1	54.3
2007	35131620	17405634	19700620	-1974634	49.5	56.1
2008	41832092	20730498	23014965	-1913371	49.6	55.0
2009	42770472	22661961	25497484	-5388973	53.0	59.6
2010	54374704	28655627	33712184	-7993107	52.7	62.0

注：2005 年以后数据依据 2008 年经济普查资料已修订。
Note: Since 2005 the data has adjusted according to the economic census in 2008.

2-8 主要年份资本形成总额及其构成

Gross Capital Formation and Its Composition in Main Years

年 份	Year	资本形成总额(万元) Gross Capital Formation (10 000 yuan)	固定资本形成 Gross Fixed Capital Formation	存货增加 Change in Inventories	以资本形成总额为100 Gross Capital Formation=100 固定资本形成(%) Gross Fixed Capital Formation (%)	存货增加(%) Change in Inventories (%)
	1978	184279	132469	51810	71.9	28.1
	1980	231515	181385	50130	78.3	21.7
	1985	584289	467807	116482	80.1	19.9
	1990	1411667	914955	496712	64.8	35.2
	1991	1691482	1247717	443765	73.8	26.2
	1992	2492589	1811739	680850	72.7	27.3
	1993	3561561	2648981	912580	74.4	25.6
	1994	4875542	3769512	1106030	77.3	22.7
	1995	4737079	3779069	958010	79.8	20.2
	1996	4569575	4228684	340891	92.5	7.5
	1997	5649193	4614059	1035134	81.7	18.3
	1998	6858461	5437824	1420637	79.3	20.7
	1999	5815889	5517222	298667	94.9	5.1
	2000	6181229	6481229	-300000	104.9	-4.9
	2001	7714187	7201155	513032	93.3	6.7
	2002	8642721	8567008	75713	99.1	0.9
	2003	11192144	10792366	399778	96.4	3.6
	2004	13504699	12395034	1109666	91.8	8.2
	2005	15059657	13843340	1216317	91.9	8.1
	2006	16547021	15961576	585445	96.5	3.5
	2007	19700620	18852366	848254	95.7	4.3
	2008	23014965	22855971	158994	99.3	0.7
	2009	25497484	24732424	765060	97.0	3.0
	2010	33712184	32329979	1382205	95.9	4.1
"一五" 时期	"First Five-year Plan" Period	162638	143262	19376	88.1	11.9
"二五" 时期	"Second Five-year Plan" Period	363925	266883	97042	73.3	26.7
	1963—1965	193986	143430	50556	73.9	26.1
"三五" 时期	"Third Five-year Plan" Period	306461	209622	96839	68.4	31.6
"四五" 时期	"Fourth Five-year Plan" Period	516970	321276	195694	62.1	37.9
"五五" 时期	"Fifth Five-year Plan" Period	877599	624988	252611	71.2	28.8
"六五" 时期	"Sixth Five-year Plan" Period	1913818	1584755	329063	82.8	17.2
"七五" 时期	"Seventh Five-year Plan" Period	4875168	3616395	1258773	74.2	25.8
"八五" 时期	"Eighth Five-year Plan" Period	17358253	13257018	4101235	76.4	23.6
"九五" 时期	"Ninth Five-year Plan" Period	29074347	26279018	2795329	90.4	9.6
"十五" 时期	"Tenth Five-year Plan" Period	56113408	52798903	3314506	94.1	5.9
"十一五"时期	"Eleventh Five-year Plan " Period	118472274	114732316	3739958	96.8	3.2

注：本表按当年价格计算。
Note: Data in value terms in this table are calculated at current prices.

2-9 主要年份最终消费及其构成

Final Consumption Expenditure and Its Composition in Main Years

单位：%　　(%)

年 份	Year	最终消费(万元) Final Consumption Expenditures (10 000yuan)	居民消费 Household Consumption	农村居民 Rural Household	城镇居民 Urban Household	政府消费 Government Consumption	最终消费=100 Final Consumption Expenditure=100 居民消费 Household Consumption	政府消费 Government Consumption	居民消费=100 Houshold Consumption=100 农村居民 Rural Household	城镇居民 Urban Household
	1978	276393	226066	120791	105275	50327	81.8	18.2	53.4	46.6
	1980	398217	327835	161988	165847	70382	82.3	17.7	49.4	50.6
	1985	780423	585134	264111	321023	195289	75.0	25.0	45.1	54.9
	1990	1667725	1211211	456657	754554	456514	72.6	27.4	37.7	62.3
	1991	1965753	1455536	522958	932578	510217	74.0	26.0	35.9	64.1
	1992	2215692	1592023	551827	1040196	623669	71.9	28.1	34.7	65.3
	1993	2699236	1977837	639604	1338233	721399	73.3	26.7	32.3	67.7
	1994	3369417	2427922	830385	1597537	941495	72.1	27.9	34.2	65.8
	1995	4446226	3206963	1084307	2122656	1239263	72.1	27.9	33.8	66.2
	1996	5539010	3976132	1560749	2415383	1562878	71.8	28.2	39.3	60.7
	1997	6118128	4366716	1648365	2718351	1751412	71.4	28.6	37.7	62.3
	1998	6424751	4573797	1757168	2816629	1850954	71.2	28.8	38.4	61.6
	1999	6905712	4757427	1589784	3167643	2148285	68.9	31.1	33.4	66.6
	2000	7601990	4923159	1599716	3323443	2678831	64.8	35.2	32.5	67.5
	2001	8590024	5454878	1759959	3694919	3135146	63.5	36.5	32.3	67.7
	2002	9637142	6154672	1908516	4246156	3482470	63.9	36.1	31.0	69.0
	2003	10272223	6236144	2026744	4209400	4036079	60.7	39.3	32.5	67.5
	2004	11251138	6712767	2099911	4612856	4538371	59.7	40.3	31.3	68.7
	2005	12665161	7642601	2389831	5252770	5022560	60.3	39.7	31.3	68.7
	2006	14645277	8538825	2535773	6003052	6106452	58.3	41.7	29.7	70.3
	2007	17405634	10134750	2955193	7179557	7270884	58.2	41.8	29.2	70.8
	2008	20730498	11710537	3406899	8303638	9019961	56.5	43.5	29.1	70.9
	2009	22661961	12846554	3856630	8989924	9815407	56.7	43.3	30.0	70.0
	2010	28655627	15789322	4563118	11226204	12866305	55.1	44.9	28.9	71.1
"一五"时期	"First Five-year Plan" Period	429668	386161	238855	147306	43507	89.9	10.1	61.9	38.1
"二五"时期	"Second Five-year Plan" Period	713994	640202	393021	247181	73792	89.7	10.3	61.4	38.6
	1963—1965	470001	424240	309298	114942	45761	90.3	9.7	72.9	27.1
"三五"时期	"Third Five-year Plan" Period	800945	729723	491304	238419	71222	91.1	8.9	67.3	32.7
"四五"时期	"Forth Five-year Plan" Period	974596	837494	517784	319710	137102	85.9	14.1	61.8	38.2
"五五"时期	"Fifth Five-year Plan" Period	1497660	1231107	650165	580942	266553	82.2	17.8	52.8	47.2
"六五"时期	"Sixth Five-year Plan" Period	2892722	2269952	1079305	1190647	622770	78.5	21.5	47.5	52.5
"七五"时期	"Seventh Five-year Plan" Period	6265079	4641659	1864681	2776978	1623420	74.1	25.9	40.2	59.8
"八五"时期	"Eighth Five-year Plan" Period	14696324	10660281	3629081	7031200	4036043	72.5	27.5	34.0	66.0
"九五"时期	"Ninth Five-year Plan" Period	32589591	22597231	8155782	14441449	9992360	69.3	30.7	36.1	63.9
"十五"时期	"Tenth Five-year Plan" Period	52415688	32201062	10184961	22016101	20214626	61.4	38.6	31.6	68.4
"十一五"时期	"Eleventh Five-year Plan " Period	104098997	59019988	17317613	41702375	45079009	56.7	43.3	29.3	70.7

注：本表按当年价格计算。
Note: Data in value terms in this table are calculated at current prices.

2-10 各地、州、市、县(市)地区生产总值

单位：万元 (2010 年) (10000 Yuan)

地　区	Region	地区生产总值 Gross Regional Product	第一产业 Primary Industry
乌鲁木齐市	**Urumqi City**	**13385172**	**199424**
#乌鲁木齐县	Urumqi County	181166	64800
克拉玛依市	**Karamay City**	**7113532**	**35171**
石河子市	**Shihezi City**	**1349995**	**91825**
吐鲁番地区	**Turpan Administrative Offices**	**1827866**	**244123**
吐鲁番市	Turpan City	518412	98147
鄯善县	Shanshan [Piqan] County	1026610	92383
托克逊县	Toksun County	293659	53594
哈密地区	**Hami [Kumul] Administrative Offices**	**1673848**	**240308**
哈密市	Hami [Kumul] City	1345594	150930
巴里坤哈萨克自治县	Barkol Kazak Autonomous County	218905	62197
伊吾县	Yiwu [Araturuk] County	109525	27181
昌吉回族自治州	**Changji Hui Autonomous Prefecture**	**5579917**	**1662667**
昌吉市	Changji City	1786301	250775
阜康市	Fukang City	807225	141534
呼图壁县	Hutubi County	798933	327573
玛纳斯县	Manas County	1019468	455820
奇台县	Qitai County	569392	285486
吉木萨尔县	Jimsar County	312012	115772
木垒哈萨克自治县	Mori Kazak Autonomous County	138095	67182
伊犁哈萨克自治州	**Ili Kazak Autonomous Prefecture**	**8850339**	**2546132**
伊犁州直属县(市)	**Counties (Cities) Direct Under Ili Prefecture**	**4082648**	**986517**
伊宁市	Yining [Gulja] City	950356	45437
奎屯市	Kuytun City	723764	43880
伊宁县	Yining [Gulja] County	421679	171994
察布查尔锡伯自治县	Qapqal Xibe Autonomous County	220406	110040
霍城县	Huocheng [Korgas] County	492908	169071
巩留县	Gongliu [Tokkuztara] County	192082	76037
新源县	Xinyuan [Kunes] County	505205	153037
昭苏县	Zhaosu [Mongolkure] County	215339	94187
特克斯县	Tekes County	134235	58429
尼勒克县	Nilka County	226558	64405
塔城地区	**Tacheng [Tarbagatai] Administrative Offices**	**3419047**	**1263861**
塔城市	Tacheng [Qoqek] City	421951	98583
乌苏市	Usu City	961768	355405
额敏县	Emin [Dorbiljin] County	324745	103206
沙湾县	Shawan County	1085703	560758
托里县	Toli County	231376	28153
裕民县	Yumin [Qagantokay] County	87064	37582
和布克赛尔蒙古自治县	Hoboksar Mongol Autonomous County	216074	43301

Gross Regional Product by Prefecture, Autonomous Prefecture, City and County

(10 000 yuan)

第二产业 Secondary Industry	工业 Industry	建筑业 Construction	第三产业 Tertiary Industry	#交通运输、仓储和邮政业 Transport,storage And Post	#批发和零售业 Wholesale, and Retail Trades	人均地区生产总值(元) Per Capita GDP (yuan)
6004066	**5147566**	**856500**	**7181682**	**1342369**	**1270681**	**43039**
50949	48000	2949	65417	6226	7665	19314
6384205	**6234705**	**149500**	**694156**	**121257**	**98764**	**121387**
686175	**550975**	**135200**	**571995**	**58895**	**59615**	**42816**
1161343	**993243**	**168100**	**422400**	**133186**	**27042**	**29828**
200441	169941	30500	219824	65879	15648	19165
779888	673786	106102	154339	61617	8329	45607
180336	148836	31500	59729	7767	3892	25056
750045	**522945**	**227100**	**683495**	**200171**	**89182**	**29375**
604425	413052	191373	590239	187035	81032	30234
91676	73533	18143	65032	9610	6459	21357
53952	36368	17584	28392	3523	1692	49139
2341420	**1866121**	**475299**	**1575830**	**234425**	**240896**	**35554**
784131	642136	141995	751395	145403	78885	37686
502717	455402	47315	162974	21171	28902	49251
269802	164200	105602	201558	30349	50381	36184
364598	304611	59987	199050	21586	38615	39316
145576	104376	41200	138330	15755	28970	26973
112808	90587	22221	83432	5779	11671	24038
20591	13679	6912	50322	2705	6862	15534
3226720	**2394506**	**832214**	**3077487**	**330110**	**577295**	**19479**
1460472	**1106072**	**354400**	**1635659**	**165823**	**240997**	**15633**
272426	163452	108974	632493	52254	112253	20518
401381	332861	68520	278503	50746	27313	47554
145634	120724	24910	104051	11186	4781	10188
50908	34715	16193	59458	3579	3712	11485
98534	78540	19994	225303	23104	78003	12520
60327	38854	21473	55718	3907	746	10185
238381	192579	45802	113787	13301	5685	16795
49174	37544	11630	71978	4222	4061	12118
23981	16582	7399	51825	3143	1180	8364
113868	84364	29504	48285	1735	2979	12573
1180363	**852249**	**328114**	**974823**	**103799**	**293300**	**23562**
118990	70056	48934	204378	28066	55333	19586
416223	281741	134482	190140	25329	49798	27069
116194	81663	34531	105345	11463	22328	20170
286122	212491	73631	238823	32068	64421	27486
150079	122414	27665	53144	7454	6831	23371
18721	6015	12706	30761	1425	2883	13547
119091	79293	39798	53682	6537	7370	35349

2-10 续表

单位：万元

地　　区	Region	地区生产总值 Gross Regional Product	第一产业 Primary Industry
阿勒泰地区	**Altay Administrative Offices**	**1348644**	**295754**
阿勒泰市	Altay City	348547	61966
布尔津县	Burqin County	111585	24751
富蕴县	Fuyun [Koktokay] County	330609	57070
福海县	Fuhai [Burultokay] County	200634	79287
哈巴河县	Habahe [Kaba] County	267983	49184
青河县	Qinghe [Qinggil] County	103610	25000
吉木乃县	Jeminay County	40019	14888
博尔塔拉蒙古自治州	**Bortala Mongolian Autonomous Prefecture**	**1314500**	**494741**
博乐市	Bole [Bortala] City	852107	246898
精河县	Jinghe [Jing] County	348511	195823
温泉县	Wenquan [Araxang] County	111995	54611
巴音郭楞蒙古自治州	**Bayangol Mongol ian Autonomous Prefecture**	**6401378**	**1081543**
库尔勒市	Korla City	4392402	295943
轮台县	Luntai [Bugur] County	341889	116765
尉犁县	Yuli [Lopnur] County	312932	186825
若羌县	Ruoqiang [Qarkilik] County	223782	51763
且末县	Qiemo [Qarqan] County	109058	53420
焉耆回族自治县	Yanqi Hui Autonomous County	318991	91430
和静县	Hejing County	425189	137547
和硕县	Hoxud County	153937	90355
博湖县	Bohu [Bagrax] County	123790	60614
阿克苏地区	**Aksu Administrative Offices**	**3961175**	**1380325**
阿克苏市	Aksu City	1114162	232061
温宿县	Wensu [Onsu] County	310231	171898
库车县	Kuqa County	810556	138849
沙雅县	Xayar County	256549	98476
新和县	Xinhe [Toksu] County	169840	82064
拜城县	Baicheng [Bay] County	265478	64863
乌什县	Wushi [Uxturpan] County	138420	62429
阿瓦提县	Awat County	277668	154637
柯坪县	Kalpin County	39875	11858
阿拉尔市	Aral City	578330	363190
克孜勒苏柯尔克孜自治州	**Kizilsu Kirgiz Autonomous Prefecture**	**388757**	**78022**
阿图什市	Artux City	174289	34281
阿克陶县	Akto County	97000	32359
阿合奇县	Akqi County	63076	6934
乌恰县	Wuqia [Ulugqat] County	35174	5918
喀什地区	**Kashgar [Kaxgar] Administrative Offices**	**3599718**	**1517509**
喀什市	Kashgar [Kaxgar] City	774733	39038
疏附县	Shufu County	207154	126902
疏勒县	Shule County	281699	142718
英吉沙县	Yengisar County	138671	72700
泽普县	Zepu [Poskam] County	198249	75025
莎车县	Shache [Yarkant] County	409468	241161
叶城县	Yecheng [Kagilik] County	315537	183570
麦盖提县	Makit County	228005	134223
岳普湖县	Yopurga County	117644	56793
伽师县	Jiashi [Payzawat] County	306020	172683
巴楚县	Bachu [Maralbexi] County	333218	136852
塔什库尔干塔吉克自治县	Taxkorgan Tajik Autonomous County	38848	7914
图木舒克市	Tumxule City	149915	111182
和田地区	**Hotan Administrative Offices**	**1034972**	**363132**
和田市	Hotan City	264788	28983
和田县	Hotan County	136608	59587
墨玉县	Moyu [Karakax] County	182086	82148
皮山县	Pishan [Guma] County	105162	53810
洛浦县	Lop County	113040	39400
策勒县	Qira County	78941	34759
于田县	Yutian [Keriya] County	113021	45978
民丰县	Minfeng [Niya] County	41326	11243

Continued

(10 000 yuan)

第二产业 Secondary Industry	工　业 Industry	建筑业 Construction	第三产业 Tertiary Industry	#交通运输、仓储和邮政业 Transport,storage And Post	#批发和零售业 Wholesale, and Retail Trades	人均地区生产总值(元) Per Capita GDP (yuan)
585885	**436185**	**149700**	**467005**	**60488**	**42998**	**22406**
68203	47303	20900	218378	22848	25930	18689
37305	15605	21700	49529	4438	4667	16780
216213	183613	32600	57326	16414	5459	37655
60568	26468	34100	60779	7570	7083	26365
171711	151511	20200	47088	9726	3484	32309
45940	32240	13700	32670	1637	3240	16240
8534	2034	6500	16597	885	1229	10787
257796	**159796**	**98000**	**561963**	**106328**	**133638**	**27374**
189710	119942	69768	415499	78205	120250	32523
55151	36187	18964	97537	21458	13342	24371
17154	7886	9268	40230	2939	2848	15073
4131707	**3611493**	**520214**	**1188128**	**188946**	**131751**	**46955**
3439955	3029961	409994	656504	84705	99669	80340
128983	116425	12558	96141	19956	10353	29990
63830	45273	18557	62277	6961	8909	27699
142400	135900	6500	29619	3289	1116	39149
15614	7087	8527	40024	2434	287	17031
106658	77520	29139	120903	21025	11131	22501
161820	141238	20582	125822	42470	4797	22653
26053	17456	8597	37529	4493	3953	20955
23706	13066	10640	39470	4438	4623	20495
1222787	**871187**	**351600**	**1358063**	**170030**	**196714**	**15872**
327591	219953	107638	554510	65391	101386	23165
66274	35685	30589	72060	2796	8549	12774
457537	353010	104527	214170	58922	23794	17183
45231	26490	18741	112842	7559	20821	10596
28547	19855	8692	59230	10100	8163	10299
120563	100348	20216	80051	12526	5097	11583
13564	5640	7924	62427	2020	4631	6670
34858	15635	19224	88173	4526	6690	11534
6346	1262	5084	21672	1802	1075	8308
122595	93615	28980	92545	4093	17509	34238
91153	**45853**	**45300**	**219582**	**19011**	**12380**	**7202**
29890	15138	14752	110118	14079	6815	7128
23538	9180	14358	41103	1447	1275	4936
22617	13223	9394	33526	2570	2082	11085
6566	412	6154	22690	1281	1074	8476
650210	**329710**	**320500**	**1431999**	**125347**	**343510**	**8748**
196838	125287	71551	538857	70975	132755	14645
19252	6452	12800	61000	2789	3534	6258
68379	27230	41149	70602	2450	4851	8254
20096	6137	13959	45875	1218	4561	5210
35778	17379	18399	87446	4600	27191	9809
49159	21785	27374	119148	3740	9482	5303
38648	16622	22026	93319	6530	16123	7250
38773	18386	20387	55009	3858	11158	9334
16872	5014	11858	43979	2759	4552	7517
56410	32945	23465	76927	12489	12281	7925
48798	22217	26581	147568	5637	63729	10126
15399	2870	12529	15535	486	1112	10791
10500	9129	1371	28233	1051	6399	12047
175493	**59435**	**116058**	**496347**	**23306**	**33032**	**5181**
79753	30549	49204	156052	12082	15601	8327
28020	10648	17372	49001	829	517	5109
18256	5756	12500	81682	2339	7345	3599
10683	4189	6494	40669	849	1295	4140
15536	3936	11600	58104	1412	2204	4796
9762	744	9018	34420	745	1177	5221
11259	1286	9973	55784	1979	2266	4541
6089	2173	3916	23994	824	336	11197

2-11 各地、州、市、县(市)地区生产总值构成

单位：% (2010 年)

地 区	Region	地区生产总值 Gross Regional Product	第一产业 Primary Industry
乌鲁木齐市	**Urumqi City**	**100.0**	**1.5**
#乌鲁木齐县	Urumqi County	100.0	35.8
克拉玛依市	**Karamay City**	**100.0**	**0.5**
石河子市	**Shihezi City**	**100.0**	**6.8**
吐鲁番地区	**Turpan Administrative Offices**	**100.0**	**13.4**
吐鲁番市	Turpan City	100.0	18.9
鄯善县	Shanshan [Piqan] County	100.0	9.0
托克逊县	Toksun County	100.0	18.3
哈密地区	**Hami [Kumul] Administrative Offices**	**100.0**	**14.4**
哈密市	Hami [Kumul] City	100.0	11.2
巴里坤哈萨克自治县	Barkol Kazak Autonomous County	100.0	28.4
伊吾县	Yiwu [Araturuk] County	100.0	24.8
昌吉回族自治州	**Changji Hui Autonomous Prefecture**	**100.0**	**29.8**
昌吉市	Changji City	100.0	14.0
阜康市	Fukang City	100.0	17.5
呼图壁县	Hutubi County	100.0	41.0
玛纳斯县	Manas County	100.0	44.7
奇台县	Qitai County	100.0	50.1
吉木萨尔县	Jimsar County	100.0	37.1
木垒哈萨克自治县	Mori Kazak Autonomous County	100.0	48.7
伊犁哈萨克自治州	**Ili Kazak Autonomous Prefecture**	**100.0**	**28.8**
伊犁州直属县(市)	**Counties (Cities) Direct Under Ili Prefecture**	**100.0**	**24.2**
伊宁市	Yining [Gulja] City	100.0	4.8
奎屯市	Kuytun City	100.0	6.1
伊宁县	Yining [Gulja] County	100.0	40.8
察布查尔锡伯自治县	Qapqal Xibe Autonomous County	100.0	49.9
霍城县	Huocheng [Korgas] County	100.0	34.3
巩留县	Gongliu [Tokkuztara] County	100.0	39.6
新源县	Xinyuan [Kunes] County	100.0	30.3
昭苏县	Zhaosu [Mongolkure] County	100.0	43.8
特克斯县	Tekes County	100.0	43.5
尼勒克县	Nilka County	100.0	28.4
塔城地区	**Tacheng [Tarbagatai] Administrative Offices**	**100.0**	**37.0**
塔城市	Tacheng [Qoqek] City	100.0	23.4
乌苏市	Usu City	100.0	37.0
额敏县	Emin [Dorbiljin] County	100.0	31.8
沙湾县	Shawan County	100.0	51.6
托里县	Toli County	100.0	12.1
裕民县	Yumin [Qagantokay] County	100.0	43.2
和布克赛尔蒙古自治县	Hoboksar Mongol Autonomous County	100.0	20.0

Composition of Gross Domestic Product by Prefecture, Autonomous Prefecture, City and County

(%)

第二产业 Secondary Industry	工 业 Industry	建筑业 Construction	第三产业 Tertiary Industry	#交通运输、仓储和邮政业 Transport,storage And Post	#批发和零售业 Wholesale, and Retail Trades
44.9	**38.5**	**6.4**	**53.6**	**10.0**	**9.5**
28.1	26.5	1.6	36.1	3.4	4.2
89.7	**87.6**	**2.1**	**9.8**	**1.7**	**1.4**
50.8	**40.8**	**10.0**	**42.4**	**4.4**	**4.4**
63.5	**54.3**	**9.2**	**23.1**	**7.3**	**1.5**
38.7	32.8	5.9	42.4	12.7	3.0
76.0	65.7	10.3	15.0	6.0	0.8
61.4	50.7	10.7	20.3	2.6	1.3
44.8	**31.2**	**13.6**	**40.8**	**12.0**	**5.3**
44.9	30.7	14.2	43.9	13.9	6.0
41.9	33.6	8.3	29.7	4.4	3.0
49.3	33.2	16.1	25.9	3.2	1.5
42.0	**33.5**	**8.5**	**28.2**	**4.2**	**4.3**
43.9	36.0	7.9	42.1	8.1	4.4
62.3	56.4	5.9	20.2	2.6	3.6
33.8	20.6	13.2	25.2	3.8	6.3
35.8	29.9	5.9	19.5	2.1	3.8
25.6	18.4	7.2	24.3	2.8	5.1
36.2	29.1	7.1	26.7	1.9	3.7
14.9	9.9	5.0	36.4	2.0	5.0
36.5	**27.1**	**9.4**	**34.7**	**3.7**	**6.5**
35.8	**27.1**	**8.7**	**40.0**	**4.1**	**5.9**
28.7	17.2	11.5	66.5	5.5	11.8
55.5	46.0	9.5	38.4	7.0	3.8
34.5	28.6	5.9	24.7	2.7	1.1
23.1	15.8	7.3	27.0	1.6	1.7
20.0	15.9	4.1	45.7	4.7	15.8
31.4	20.2	11.2	29.0	2.0	0.4
47.2	38.1	9.1	22.5	2.6	1.1
22.8	17.4	5.4	33.4	2.0	1.9
17.9	12.4	5.5	38.6	2.3	0.9
50.3	37.3	13.0	21.3	0.8	1.3
34.5	**24.9**	**9.6**	**28.5**	**3.0**	**8.6**
28.2	16.6	11.6	48.4	6.7	13.1
43.3	29.3	14.0	19.7	2.6	5.2
35.8	25.2	10.6	32.4	3.5	6.9
26.4	19.6	6.8	22.0	3.0	5.9
64.9	52.9	12.0	23.0	3.2	3.0
21.5	6.9	14.6	35.3	1.6	3.3
55.1	36.7	18.4	24.9	3.0	3.4

2-11 续表

单位：%

地　　区	Region	地区生产总值 Gross Regional Product	第一产业 Primary Industry
阿勒泰地区	**Altay Administrative Offices**	**100.0**	**21.9**
阿勒泰市	Altay City	100.0	17.8
布尔津县	Burqin County	100.0	22.2
富蕴县	Fuyun [Koktokay] County	100.0	17.3
福海县	Fuhai [Burultokay] County	100.0	39.5
哈巴河县	Habahe [Kaba] County	100.0	18.4
青河县	Qinghe [Qinggil] County	100.0	24.1
吉木乃县	Jeminay County	100.0	37.2
博尔塔拉蒙古自治州	**Bortala Mongolian Autonomous Prefecture**	**100.0**	**37.6**
博乐市	Bole [Bortala] City	100.0	29.0
精河县	Jinghe [Jing] County	100.0	56.2
温泉县	Wenquan [Araxang] County	100.0	48.8
巴音郭楞蒙古自治州	**Bayangol Mongol ian Autonomous Prefecture**	**100.0**	**16.9**
库尔勒市	Korla City	100.0	6.7
轮台县	Luntai [Bugur] County	100.0	34.2
尉犁县	Yuli [Lopnur] County	100.0	59.7
若羌县	Ruoqiang [Qarkilik] County	100.0	23.1
且末县	Qiemo [Qarqan] County	100.0	49.0
焉耆回族自治县	Yanqi Hui Autonomous County	100.0	28.7
和静县	Hejing County	100.0	32.3
和硕县	Hoxud County	100.0	58.7
博湖县	Bohu [Bagrax] County	100.0	49.0
阿克苏地区	**Aksu Administrative Offices**	**100.0**	**34.8**
阿克苏市	Aksu City	100.0	20.8
温宿县	Wensu [Onsu] County	100.0	55.4
库车县	Kuqa County	100.0	17.1
沙雅县	Xayar County	100.0	38.4
新和县	Xinhe [Toksu] County	100.0	48.3
拜城县	Baicheng [Bay] County	100.0	24.4
乌什县	Wushi [Uxturpan] County	100.0	45.1
阿瓦提县	Awat County	100.0	55.7
柯坪县	Kalpin County	100.0	29.7
阿拉尔市	Aral City	100.0	62.8
克孜勒苏柯尔克孜自治州	**Kizilsu Kirgiz Autonomous Prefecture**	**100.0**	**20.1**
阿图什市	Artux City	100.0	19.7
阿克陶县	Akto County	100.0	33.4
阿合奇县	Akqi County	100.0	11.0
乌恰县	Wuqia [Ulugqat] County	100.0	16.8
喀什地区	**Kashgar [Kaxgar] Administrative Offices**	**100.0**	**42.2**
喀什市	Kashgar [Kaxgar] City	100.0	5.0
疏附县	Shufu County	100.0	61.3
疏勒县	Shule County	100.0	50.7
英吉沙县	Yengisar County	100.0	52.4
泽普县	Zepu [Poskam] County	100.0	37.8
莎车县	Shache [Yarkant] County	100.0	58.9
叶城县	Yecheng [Kagilik] County	100.0	58.1
麦盖提县	Makit County	100.0	58.9
岳普湖县	Yopurga County	100.0	48.3
伽师县	Jiashi [Payzawat] County	100.0	56.4
巴楚县	Bachu [Maralbexi] County	100.0	41.1
塔什库尔干县	Taxkorgan Tajik Autonomous County	100.0	20.4
图木舒克市	Tumxule City	100.0	74.2
和田地区	**Hotan Administrative Offices**	**100.0**	**35.1**
和田市	Hotan City	100.0	10.9
和田县	Hotan County	100.0	43.6
墨玉县	Moyu [Karakax] County	100.0	45.1
皮山县	Pishan [Guma] County	100.0	51.2
洛浦县	Lop County	100.0	34.9
策勒县	Qira County	100.0	44.0
于田县	Yutian [Keriya] County	100.0	40.7
民丰县	Minfeng [Niya] County	100.0	27.2

Continued

(%)

第二产业 Secondary Industry	工 业 Industry	建筑业 Construction	第三产业 Tertiary Industry	#交通运输、仓储和邮政业 Transport,storage And Post	#批发和零售业 Wholesale, and Retail Trades
43.4	**32.3**	**11.1**	**34.7**	**4.5**	**3.2**
19.6	13.6	6.0	62.6	6.6	7.4
33.4	14.0	19.4	44.4	4.0	4.2
65.4	55.5	9.9	17.3	5.0	1.7
30.2	13.2	17.0	30.3	3.8	3.5
64.0	56.5	7.5	17.6	3.6	1.3
44.3	31.1	13.2	31.5	1.6	3.1
21.3	5.1	16.2	41.5	2.2	3.1
19.6	**12.1**	**7.5**	**42.8**	**8.1**	**10.2**
22.3	14.1	8.2	48.7	9.2	14.1
15.8	10.4	5.4	28.0	6.2	3.8
15.3	7.0	8.3	35.9	2.6	2.5
64.5	**56.4**	**8.1**	**18.6**	**3.0**	**2.1**
78.3	69.0	9.3	14.9	1.9	2.3
37.7	34.1	3.7	28.1	5.8	3.0
20.4	14.5	5.9	19.9	2.2	2.8
63.6	60.7	2.9	13.3	1.5	0.5
14.3	6.5	7.8	36.7	2.2	0.3
33.4	24.3	9.1	37.9	6.6	3.5
38.1	33.3	4.8	29.6	10.0	1.1
16.9	11.3	5.6	24.4	2.9	2.6
19.2	10.6	8.6	31.8	3.6	3.7
30.9	**22.0**	**8.9**	**34.3**	**4.3**	**5.0**
29.4	19.7	9.7	49.8	5.9	9.1
21.4	11.5	9.9	23.2	0.9	2.8
56.5	43.6	12.9	26.4	7.3	2.9
17.6	10.3	7.3	44.0	2.9	8.1
16.8	11.7	5.1	34.9	5.9	4.8
45.4	37.8	7.6	30.2	4.7	1.9
9.8	4.1	5.7	45.1	1.5	3.3
12.5	5.6	6.9	31.8	1.6	2.4
15.9	3.2	12.7	54.4	4.5	2.7
21.2	16.2	5.0	16.0	0.7	3.0
23.4	**11.7**	**11.7**	**56.5**	**4.9**	**3.2**
17.1	8.6	8.5	63.2	8.1	3.9
24.3	9.5	14.8	42.3	1.5	1.3
35.9	21.0	14.9	53.1	4.1	3.3
18.7	1.2	17.5	64.5	3.6	3.1
18.1	**9.2**	**8.9**	**39.7**	**3.5**	**9.5**
25.4	16.2	9.2	69.6	9.2	17.1
9.3	3.1	6.2	29.4	1.3	1.7
24.3	9.7	14.6	25.0	0.9	1.7
14.5	4.4	10.1	33.1	0.9	3.3
18.1	8.8	9.3	44.1	2.3	13.7
12.0	5.3	6.7	29.1	0.9	2.3
12.3	5.3	7.0	29.6	2.1	5.1
17.0	8.1	8.9	24.1	1.7	4.9
14.3	4.3	10.0	37.4	2.3	3.9
18.5	10.8	7.7	25.1	4.1	4.0
14.7	6.7	8.0	44.2	1.7	19.1
39.6	7.4	32.2	40.0	1.3	2.9
7.0	6.1	0.9	18.8	0.7	4.3
16.9	**5.7**	**11.2**	**48.0**	**2.3**	**3.2**
30.1	11.5	18.6	59.0	4.6	5.9
20.5	7.8	12.7	35.9	0.6	0.4
10.0	3.2	6.8	44.9	1.3	4.0
10.2	4.0	6.2	38.6	0.8	1.2
13.7	3.5	10.2	51.4	1.2	1.9
12.4	0.9	11.5	43.6	0.9	1.5
9.9	1.1	8.8	49.4	1.8	2.0
14.7	5.3	9.4	58.1	2.0	0.8

2-12 各地、州、市、县(市)地区生产总值指数

(上年=100) (2010 年)

地区	Region	地区生产总值 Gross Regional Product	第一产业 Primary Industry
乌鲁木齐市	**Urumqi City**	**112.3**	**105.5**
#乌鲁木齐县	Urumqi County	115.3	108.9
克拉玛依市	**Karamay City**	**117.4**	**103.9**
石河子市	**Shihezi City**	**118.1**	**113.2**
吐鲁番地区	**Turpan Administrative Offices**	**104.3**	**105.9**
吐鲁番市	Turpan City	108.5	107.5
鄯善县	Shanshan [Piqan] County	103.3	105.4
托克逊县	Toksun County	102.1	103.7
哈密地区	**Hami [Kumul] Administrative Offices**	**120.5**	**109.8**
哈密市	Hami [Kumul] City	120.0	108.9
巴里坤哈萨克自治县	Barkol Kazak Autonomous County	125.4	112.7
伊吾县	Yiwu [Araturuk] County	112.0	110.0
昌吉回族自治州	**Changji Hui Autonomous Prefecture**	**115.9**	**107.4**
昌吉市	Changji City	115.7	109.7
阜康市	Fukang City	116.1	107.2
呼图壁县	Hutubi County	116.0	108.0
玛纳斯县	Manas County	116.4	106.6
奇台县	Qitai County	121.4	106.4
吉木萨尔县	Jimsar County	119.8	107.5
木垒哈萨克自治县	Mori Kazak Autonomous County	115.2	108.1
伊犁哈萨克自治州	**Ili Kazak Autonomous Prefecture**	**113.2**	**109.5**
伊犁州直属县(市)	**Counties (Cities) Direct Under Ili Prefecture**	**114.5**	**108.7**
伊宁市	Yining [Gulja] City	114.6	105.1
奎屯市	Kuytun City	117.8	110.0
伊宁县	Yining [Gulja] County	111.5	110.7
察布查尔锡伯自治县	Qapqal Xibe Autonomous County	109.5	106.5
霍城县	Huocheng [Korgas] County	110.8	107.3
巩留县	Gongliu [Tokkuztara] County	113.4	110.6
新源县	Xinyuan [Kunes] County	115.1	106.4
昭苏县	Zhaosu [Mongolkure] County	113.2	112.6
特克斯县	Tekes County	113.4	109.2
尼勒克县	Nilka County	116.6	109.4
塔城地区	**Tacheng [Tarbagatai] Administrative Offices**	**112.9**	**111.5**
塔城市	Tacheng [Qoqek] City	134.2	136.4
乌苏市	Usu City	123.4	112.0
额敏县	Emin [Dorbiljin] County	116.8	109.7
沙湾县	Shawan County	116.6	109.1
托里县	Toli County	127.6	109.3
裕民县	Yumin [Qagantokay] County	112.2	109.5
和布克赛尔蒙古自治县	Hoboksar Mongol Autonomous County	124.0	108.0

Indices of Gross Domestic Product by Prefecture, Autonomous Prefecture, City and County

(preceding year=100)

第二产业 Secondary Industry	工业 Industry	建筑业 Construction	第三产业 Tertiary Industry	#交通运输、仓储和邮政业 Transport,storage And Post	#批发和零售业 Wholesale, and Retail Trades
111.2	**112.2**	**106.0**	**113.3**	**121.8**	**114.5**
128.9	128.5	136.0	113.7	112.3	116.3
118.4	**118.6**	**108.5**	**110.0**	**103.5**	**116.7**
115.4	**115.7**	**114.3**	**122.1**	**124.5**	**117.7**
103.0	**103.1**	**102.3**	**107.1**	**109.2**	**112.8**
110.6	111.2	108.7	107.5	107.7	114.1
103.1	104.2	96.5	103.3	108.6	90.0
98.4	93.1	119.5	110.5	107.8	108.0
130.0	**125.3**	**146.9**	**114.2**	**110.8**	**125.5**
128.3	122.5	148.5	114.7	110.7	127.0
150.2	156.4	129.8	110.3	114.7	118.9
111.4	99.3	150.4	115.1	114.6	101.1
124.8	**126.5**	**118.1**	**112.3**	**110.7**	**108.7**
118.9	122.7	105.7	114.6	111.7	101.8
119.0	119.6	114.0	113.8	113.3	117.1
126.6	132.3	115.7	113.3	109.2	112.3
129.1	129.3	128.0	113.7	111.0	114.7
161.2	167.0	143.0	110.6	110.3	111.0
142.4	143.9	135.6	112.6	112.3	114.0
136.4	150.1	109.8	113.7	108.6	113.2
118.6	**118.7**	**118.1**	**111.0**	**107.9**	**110.0**
121.3	**119.9**	**126.2**	**111.7**	**107.7**	**112.3**
118.7	111.8	132.9	113.5	104.1	115.3
121.3	120.8	124.4	113.8	108.9	115.9
116.3	113.0	134.4	107.2	110.1	103.6
113.4	108.3	122.7	111.6	107.7	114.3
116.8	117.1	115.7	110.5	112.6	109.1
122.3	120.0	127.5	107.5	104.4	116.4
124.6	124.6	124.5	108.2	106.6	104.7
119.9	115.4	133.3	110.4	113.2	101.3
127.2	126.1	129.8	111.2	105.4	107.9
123.7	128.7	110.7	108.4	110.1	106.0
117.9	**118.3**	**116.6**	**109.4**	**106.3**	**108.5**
198.0	108.3	109.4	112.7	114.8	130.5
139.0	141.8	132.3	111.1	112.1	105.8
130.5	133.2	123.2	115.3	104.6	97.6
130.5	133.2	123.2	115.3	104.6	97.6
142.2	142.2	117.2	112.0	112.0	112.4
125.0	125.0	144.1	112.8	115.4	102.4
137.4	136.0	139.8	110.9	107.2	109.2

2-12 续表 1

(上年=100)

地　　区	Region	地区生产总值 Gross Regional Product	第一产业 Primary Industry
阿勒泰地区	**Altay Administrative Offices**	**110.1**	**103.9**
阿勒泰市	Altay City	110.1	104.9
布尔津县	Burqin County	108.6	102.5
富蕴县	Fuyun [Koktokay] County	105.1	102.5
福海县	Fuhai [Burultokay] County	111.7	107.0
哈巴河县	Habahe [Kaba] County	111.0	107.9
青河县	Qinghe [Qinggil] County	113.8	104.6
吉木乃县	Jeminay County	109.2	100.9
博尔塔拉蒙古自治州	**Bortala Mongolian Autonomous Prefecture**	**111.4**	**112.4**
博乐市	Bole [Bortala] City	109.6	112.2
精河县	Jinghe [Jing] County	113.8	109.0
温泉县	Wenquan [Araxang] County	113.6	109.3
巴音郭楞蒙古自治州	**Bayangol Mongol ian Autonomous Prefecture**	**107.0**	**107.2**
库尔勒市	Korla City	104.3	107.4
轮台县	Luntai [Bugur] County	108.0	105.4
尉犁县	Yuli [Lopnur] County	109.0	102.4
若羌县	Ruoqiang [Qarkilik] County	127.2	113.1
且末县	Qiemo [Qarqan] County	110.3	110.5
焉耆回族自治县	Yanqi Hui Autonomous County	112.2	109.7
和静县	Hejing County	112.3	100.8
和硕县	Hoxud County	113.0	112.9
博湖县	Bohu [Bagrax] County	112.5	111.9
阿克苏地区	**Aksu Administrative Offices**	**113.4**	**108.2**
阿克苏市	Aksu City	113.0	105.2
温宿县	Wensu [Onsu] County	115.2	108.0
库车县	Kuqa County	111.5	105.7
沙雅县	Xayar County	113.3	105.9
新和县	Xinhe [Toksu] County	110.3	105.7
拜城县	Baicheng [Bay] County	118.5	105.5
乌什县	Wushi [Uxturpan] County	112.1	104.6
阿瓦提县	Awat County	110.7	110.5
柯坪县	Kalpin County	114.5	108.7
阿拉尔市	Aral City	116.2	112.8
克孜勒苏柯尔克孜自治州	**Kizilsu Kirgiz Autonomous Prefecture**	**113.1**	**100.8**
阿图什市	Artux City	110.3	97.0
阿克陶县	Akto County	109.1	106.0
阿合奇县	Akqi County	118.2	104.2
乌恰县	Wuqia [Ulugqat] County	117.8	108.5
喀什地区	**Kashgar [Kaxgar] Administrative Offices**	**112.2**	**105.7**
喀什市	Kashgar [Kaxgar] City	120.0	92.5
疏附县	Shufu County	116.0	122.9
疏勒县	Shule County	108.1	110.7
英吉沙县	Yengisar County	102.5	94.0
泽普县	Zepu [Poskam] County	112.8	110.9
莎车县	Shache [Yarkant] County	112.6	115.0
叶城县	Yecheng [Kagilik] County	122.5	124.0
麦盖提县	Makit County	104.5	98.3
岳普湖县	Yopurga County	115.6	109.6
伽师县	Jiashi [Payzawat] County	112.2	102.2
巴楚县	Bachu [Maralbexi] County	97.1	80.1
塔什库尔干县	Taxkorgan Tajik Autonomous County	108.0	121.6
图木舒克市	Tumxule City	94.3	100.9
和田地区	**Hotan Administrative Offices**	**112.2**	**106.8**
和田市	Hotan City	116.4	104.5
和田县	Hotan County	111.9	106.9
墨玉县	Moyu [Karakax] County	110.3	107.1
皮山县	Pishan [Guma] County	113.7	119.2
洛浦县	Lop County	110.3	102.5
策勒县	Qira County	112.5	111.1
于田县	Yutian [Keriya] County	110.7	105.7
民丰县	Minfeng [Niya] County	111.8	106.0

Continued

(preceding year=100)

第二产业 Secondary Industry	工业 Industry	建筑业 Construction	第三产业 Tertiary Industry	#交通运输、仓储和邮政业 Transport,storage And Post	#批发和零售业 Wholesale, and Retail Trades
112.0	**115.4**	**105.4**	**111.8**	**111.2**	**109.3**
117.1	111.3	130.5	109.9	106.1	110.2
110.8	141.6	91.2	110.4	102.9	113.2
104.4	103.6	108.3	109.3	108.9	113.8
118.7	165.5	96.1	111.3	108.1	113.3
112.0	112.4	110.0	111.6	106.4	111.3
124.3	135.2	115.6	112.3	104.3	113.2
112.2	105.7	114.3	114.0	100.0	109.7
128.3	**135.7**	**117.8**	**105.1**	**110.3**	**84.8**
124.3	134.3	121.7	105.9	111.3	81.2
133.2	146.9	111.7	109.9	109.8	114.0
140.2	137.1	143.7	108.6	108.1	128.5
106.6	**107.2**	**102.6**	**107.9**	**106.9**	**107.8**
102.8	102.0	107.8	110.0	119.1	108.1
100.6	99.0	116.9	120.8	128.4	117.5
123.1	129.7	108.8	114.6	116.7	110.5
134.2	135.8	109.0	114.1	104.0	147.3
111.8	115.0	109.2	109.5	100.8	104.6
112.6	109.1	122.2	113.9	110.8	127.4
117.2	117.7	113.0	114.9	121.4	118.3
112.3	110.1	118.4	113.9	115.0	109.5
102.6	90.5	123.5	119.3	111.2	116.8
124.4	**128.6**	**115.6**	**110.9**	**106.0**	**119.9**
118.9	121.5	113.4	112.9	104.7	145.7
143.6	164.7	123.8	111.2	155.9	97.0
121.9	124.9	116.9	104.7	113.2	91.7
109.9	103.0	118.5	122.2	103.7	133.8
148.7	178.8	101.2	103.3	101.3	106.1
132.2	134.2	116.7	105.4	112.2	69.9
131.7	124.3	142.8	116.1	104.3	72.8
119.5	127.3	114.0	108.3	115.1	104.5
146.0	158.2	139.6	110.8	100.8	98.1
129.8	139.3	106.6	112.3	90.9	114.5
125.9	**135.2**	**118.8**	**113.5**	**107.8**	**114.1**
121.2	152.1	103.4	112.3	99.6	108.8
114.9	107.2	121.0	108.1	103.1	106.3
127.2	135.0	118.0	116.3	112.4	108.6
151.7	102.5	155.9	112.8	108.0	118.0
113.4	**112.7**	**114.4**	**118.0**	**114.0**	**118.9**
117.8	117.2	118.7	123.0	120.3	114.3
107.4	118.4	102.6	107.8	123.5	103.1
103.9	93.3	117.4	108.4	104.5	104.1
105.0	103.2	105.9	115.9	144.9	103.0
116.2	102.0	133.2	113.1	112.9	107.4
108.3	110.5	106.7	110.2	109.5	104.9
115.7	129.2	108.4	123.1	127.3	110.5
112.6	108.4	116.9	114.3	107.9	105.4
108.4	85.4	119.5	126.3	125.9	120.8
154.4	187.6	123.5	118.1	109.8	119.0
102.4	99.7	104.7	115.1	118.6	106.1
94.7	64.1	108.8	117.4	132.9	111.9
83.9	93.0	50.4	80.0	72.3	111.8
117.7	**103.9**	**127.4**	**113.9**	**108.5**	**119.3**
118.5	112.0	124.7	117.9	115.4	114.8
108.9	108.4	109.2	121.0	119.6	115.8
115.4	105.7	120.0	112.7	122.4	111.2
107.1	108.2	106.4	109.3	109.1	104.9
99.9	60.4	131.3	119.1	108.6	112.4
123.8	106.0	125.5	110.9	107.8	117.0
118.7	94.3	123.2	113.3	116.7	113.2
107.2	81.1	129.0	116.6	109.4	115.1

2-13 主要年份居民消费水平及指数

Household Consumption Expenditure and Its Indices in Main Years

年 份 Year	居民消费水平（元） Household Consumption (yuan)	农村居民 Rural Households	城镇居民 Urban Households	居民消费水平指数（1952 年=100） Index of Residents' Consumption Level (1952=100)	农村居民 Rural Households
1978	181	131	323	140.5	144.5
1980	252	180	417	182.4	184.4
1985	428	280	755	267.0	252.3
1990	796	447	1508	299.5	236.3
1995	1852	977	3414	344.1	246.5
1996	2266	1387	3836	377.1	312.6
1997	2455	1445	4261	384.6	313.9
1998	2539	1520	4364	396.1	339.3
1999	2606	1358	4841	413.1	319.3
2000	2662	1308	5131	415.2	299.2
2001	2905	1427	5743	434.3	307.6
2002	3228	1525	6483	484.7	325.4
2003	3249	1603	6427	488.6	338.1
2004	3445	1652	6808	502.3	339.8
2005	3847	1884	7311	556.0	385.7
2006	4206	2000	7875	598.9	400.7
2007	4890	2320	8986	663.5	432.8
2008	5542	2661	9975	696.7	447.9
2009	5990	2984	10546	752.5	495.4
2010	7276	3590	12486	868.4	571.7

年 份 Year	城镇居民 Urban Households	居民消费水平指数（上年=100） Index of Residents' Consumption Level (preceding year=100)	农村居民 Rural Households	城镇居民 Urban Households
1978	99.0	104.7	102.3	102.8
1980	119.3	111.9	107.6	113.1
1985	183.8	110.5	105.9	114.6
1990	226.4	103.8	98.8	105.0
1995	257.4	109.0	102.3	112.3
1996	260.7	109.6	126.8	101.3
1997	268.5	102.0	100.4	103.0
1998	268.5	103.0	108.1	100.0
1999	297.8	104.3	94.1	110.9
2000	315.7	100.5	93.7	106.0
2001	338.7	104.6	102.8	107.3
2002	386.8	111.6	105.8	114.2
2003	386.8	100.8	103.9	100.0
2004	396.1	102.8	100.5	102.4
2005	421.1	110.7	113.5	106.3
2006	448.0	107.7	103.9	106.4
2007	491.9	110.8	108.0	109.8
2008	511.1	105.0	103.5	103.9
2009	543.8	108.0	110.6	106.4
2010	608.5	115.4	115.4	111.9

2-14 居民消费支出
Household Consumption Expenditure

单位：万元 (10 000 yuan)

项　　目	Item	2009	2010
居民消费支出	**Household Consumption Expenditure**	**12846554**	**15789322**
食品类支出	Foods	4470862	5263333
衣着类支出	Clothes	1494418	1796019
居住类支出	Residence	789468	1226314
家庭设备、用品及服务类支出	Family Facilities and Servises	609602	799388
医疗保健类支出	Medical and Hygiencic Expenditure	992150	1318230
交通和通信类支出	Traffic and Telecommunications	1434504	1665389
文教娱乐用品及服务类支出	Teathing, Entertainment and Services	933632	1156968
金融中介服务虚拟支出	Imaginary Expenditure of Middle Finance Services	789934	954406
自由住房服务虚拟支出	Imaginary Expenditure of Freeform Resident Services	578301	671469
实物消费支出	Reality Consumption	109009	214657
其他商品和服务类支出	Other Goods and Services	644675	723149
按城乡分	**By Residence**		
农村居民支出	Agricaltural Households Expenditure	3856630	4563118
食品类支出	Foods	1584253	1875692
衣着类支出	Clothes	337628	408379
居住类支出	Residence	312670	402664
家庭设备、用品及服务类支出	Family Facilities and Servises	138635	185194
医疗保健类支出	Medical and Hygiencic Expenditure	409079	423300
交通和通信类支出	Traffic and Telecommunications	412739	513992
文教娱乐用品及服务类支出	Teathing, Entertainment and Services	204353	228794
金融中介服务虚拟支出	Imaginary Expenditure of Middle Finance Services	168502	236096
自由住房服务虚拟支出	Imaginary Expenditure of Freeform Resident Services	227552	184030
其他商品和服务类支出	Other Goods and Services	61221	104978
城镇居民支出	Non-agricaltural Households Expenditure	8989924	11226204
食品类支出	Foods	2886609	3387641
衣着类支出	Clothes	1156790	1387640
居住类支出	Residence	476798	823650
家庭设备、用品及服务类支出	Family Facilities and Servises	470968	614194
医疗保健类支出	Medical and Hygiencic Expenditure	583071	894930
交通和通信类支出	Traffic and Telecommunications	1021765	1151397
文教娱乐用品及服务类支出	Teathing, Entertainment and Services	729279	928174
金融中介服务虚拟支出	Imaginary Expenditure of Middle Finance Services	621432	718310
自由住房服务虚拟支出	Imaginary Expenditure of Freeform Resident Services	350749	487439
实物消费支出	Reality Consumption	109009	214657
其他商品和服务类支出	Other Goods and Services	583454	618171

主要统计指标解释

国内生产总值(GDP) 指按市场价格计算的一个国家(或地区)所有常住单位在一定时期内生产活动的最终成果。国内生产总值有三种表现形态，即价值形态、收入形态和产品形态。从价值形态看，它是所有常住单位在一定时期内生产的全部货物和服务价值超过同期投入的全部非固定资产货物和服务价值的差额，即所有常住单位的增加值之和；从收入形态看，它是所有常住单位在一定时期内创造并分配给常住单位和非常住单位的初次收入之和；从产品形态看，它是所有常住单位在一定时期内最终使用的货物和服务价值减去货物和服务进口价值。在实际核算中，国内生产总值有三种计算方法，即生产法、收入法和支出法。三种方法分别从不同的方面反映国内生产总值及其构成。

对于一个地区来说，称为地区生产总值或地区GDP.

三次产业 三产业的划分是世界上较为常用的产业结构分类，但各国的划分不尽一致。我国的三次产业划分是：

第一产业是指农、林、牧、渔业和农林牧渔服务业。。

第二产业是指采矿业，制造业，电力、煤气及水的生产和供应业，建筑业。

第三产业是指除第一、二产业以外的其他行业。

劳动者报酬 指劳动者因从事生产活动所获得的全部报酬。包括劳动者获得的各种形式的工资、奖金和津贴，既包括货币形式的，也包括实物形式的，还包括劳动者所享受的公费医疗和医药卫生费、上下班交通补贴、单位支付的社会保险费、住房公积金等。对于个体经济来说，其所有者所获得的劳动报酬和经营利润不易区分，这两部分统一作为劳动者报酬处理。

生产税净额 指生产税减生产补贴后的余额。生产税指政府对生产单位从事生产、销售和经营活动以及因从事生产活动使用某些生产要素(如固定资产、土地、劳动力)所征收的各种税、附加费和规费。生产补贴与生产税相反，指政府对生产单位的单方面转移支出，因此视为负生产税，包括政策亏损补贴、价格补贴等。

固定资产折旧 指一定时期内为弥补固定资产损耗按照规定的固定资产折旧率提取的固定资产折旧，或按国民经济核算统一规定的折旧率虚拟计算的固定资产折旧。它反映了固定资产在当期生产中的转移价值。各类企业和企业化管理的事业单位的固定资产折旧是指实际计提的折旧费；不计提折旧的政府机关、非企业化管理的事业单位和居民住房的固定资产折旧是按照统一规定的折旧率和固定资产原值计算的虚拟折旧。原则上，固定资产折旧应按固定资产当期的重置价值计算，但是目前我国尚不具备对全社会固定资产进行重估价的基础，所以暂时只能采用上述办法。

营业盈余 指常住单位创造的增加值扣除劳动者报酬、生产税净额和固定资产折旧后的余额。它相当于企业的营业利润加上生产补贴，但要扣除从利润中开支的工资和福利等。

支出法国内生产总值 是从最终使用的角度反映一个国家(或地区)一定时期内生产活动最终成果的一种方法，包括最终消费支出、资本形成总额及货物和服务净出口三部分。计算公式为：

支出法国内生产总值=最终消费支出+资本形成总额+货物和服务净出口

最终消费支出 指常住单位为满足物质、文化和精神生活的需要，从本国经济领土和国外购买的货物和服务的支出。它不包括非常住单位在本国经济领土内的消费支出。最终消费分为居民消费和政府消费。

居民消费支出 指常住住户在一定时期内对于货物和服务的全部最终消费支出。居民消费除了直接以货币形式购买的货物和服务的消费支出外，还包括以其他方式获得的货物和服务的消费支出，即所谓的虚拟消费支出。居民虚拟消费支出包括如下几种类型：单位以实物报酬及实物转移的形式提供给劳动者的货物和服务；住户生产并由本住户消费了的货物和服务，其中的服务仅指住户的自有住房服务和付酬的家庭雇员提供的家庭和个人服务；金融机构提供的金融媒介服务；保险公司提供的保险服务。

政府消费支出 指政府部门为全社会提供的公共服务的消费支出和免费或以较低的价格向居民住户提供的货物和服务的净支出，前者等于政府服务的产出价值减去政府单位所获得的经营收入的价值，后者等于政府部门免费或以较低价格向居民住户提供的货物和服务的市场价值减去向住户收取的价值。

资本形成总额 指常住单位在一定时期内获得减去处置的固定资产和存货的净额，包括固定资本形成总额和存货增加两部分。

固定资本形成总额 指生产者在一定时期内获得的固定资产减处置的固定资产的价值总额。固定资产是通过生产活动生产出来的，且其使用年限在一年以上、单位价值在规定标准以上的资产，不包括自然资产。可分为有形固定资本形成总额和无形固定资本形成总额。有形固定资本形成总额包括一定时期内完成的建筑工程、安装工程和设备工器具购置(减处置)价值，以及土地改良、新增役、种、奶、毛、娱乐用牲畜和新增经济林木价值。无形固定资本形成总额包括矿藏的勘探、计算机软件等获得减处置。

存货增加 指常住单位在一定时期内存货实物量变动的市场价值，即期末价值减期初价值的差额，再扣除当期由于价格变动而产生的持有收益。存货增加可以是正值，也可以是负值，正值表示存货上升，负值表示存货下降。存货包括生产单位购进的原材料、燃料和储备物资等存货，以及生产单位生产的产成品、在制品和半成品等存货。

货物和服务净出口 指货物和服务出口减货物和服务进口的差额。出口包括常住单位向非常住单位出售或无偿转让的各种货物和服务的价值；进口包括常住单位从非常住单位购买或无偿得到的各种货物和服务的价值。由于服务活动的提供与使用同时发生，一般把常住单位从非常住单位得到的服务作为进口，非常住单位从常住单位得到的服务作为出口。货物的出口和进口都按离岸价格计算。

Explanatory Notes on Main Statistical Indicators

Gross Domestic Product (GDP) refers to the final products at market prices produced by all resident units in a country (or a region) during a certain period of time. Gross domestic product is expressed in three different forms, i.e. value, income, and products respectively. GDP in its value form refers to the total value of all goods and services produced by all resident units during a certain period of time, minus the total value of input of goods and services of the nature of non-fixed assets; in other term, it is the sum of the value-added of all resident units. GDP in the form of income includes the income created by all resident units and distributed to resident and non-resident units. GDP in the form of products refers to the value of all goods and services for final consumption by all resident units minus the net exports of goods and services during a given period of time. In the practice of national accounting, gross domestic product is calculated with three approaches, i.e. production approach, income approach and expenditure approach, which reflect gross domestic product and its composition from different aspects.

Three Industries Classification of economic activities into three branches of industries is a common practice in the world, although the grouping varies to some extent form country to country. In China economic activities are categorized into following industries:

Primary industry: refers to agriculture, forestry, animal husbandry and fishery.

Secondary industry: refers to mining and quarrying, manufacturing, production and supply of electricity, water and gas, and construction.

Tertiary industry: refers to all other economic activities not included in primary or secondary industry.

Labourers Remuneration refers to the whole payment of various forms earned by the labourers from the productive activities they are engaged in. It includes wages, bonuses and allowances the labourers earned in monetary form and in kind. It also includes the free medical services provided to the labourers and the medicine expenses, traffic subsidies and social insurance, housing fund paid by the employers. As the individual economy is concerned, since the labourers remuneration is not easily distinguished from the operating profit, both are treated as labourers remuneration.

Net Taxes on Production refers to the difference of the taxes on production minus the subsidies on production. The taxes on production refers to the various taxes, extra charges and fees levied on the production units on their production, sale and business activities as well as on the use of some factors of production, such as fixed assets, land and labour force in the production activities they are engaged in. In contrast to the taxes on production, the subsidies on production refer to the unilateral government transfer to the production units and are therefore regarded as negative taxes on production. They include subsidies on the loss due to implementation of government policies, price subsidies, etc.

Depreciation of Fixed Assets refers to the depreciation of fixed assets of a given period, drawn in accordance with the stipulated depreciation rate for the purpose of compensating the wear loss of the fixed assets or the depreciation of fixed assets calculated in a fictitious way in accordance with the stipulated unified depreciation rate in the national economic accounting system. It reflects the value of transfer of the fixed assets in the production of the current period. The depreciation of fixed assets in various enterprises and institutions managed as enterprises refers to the depreciation expenses actually drawn. In government agencies and institutions not managed as enterprises which do not draw the depreciation expenses, as well as for the houses of residents, the depreciation of fixed assets is the imputed depreciation, which is calculated in accordance with the stipulated unified depreciation rate. In principle, the depreciation of fixed assets should be calculated on the basis of the re-purchased value of the fixed assets. However, there is no actual condition to re-evaluate all the fixed assets in China. Therefore, the above-mentioned methods are temporarily adopted at present.

Operating Surplus refers to the balance of the value added created by the resident units deducting the labourers remuneration, net taxes on production and the depreciation of fixed assets. It is equivalent to the business profit of the enterprises plus subsidies on production, but the wages and welfare expenses paid from the profits should be deducted.

GDP by Expenditure Approach refers to the method of measuring the final results of production activities of a country (region) during a given period from the perspective of final use. It includes final consumption, total capital formation and net export of goods and services, i.e.:

GDP by expenditure approach = final consumption + total capital formation + net export of goods and services

Final Consumption refers to the total expenditure of resident units for purchases of goods and services from domestic economic territory and abroad to meet the require-

ments of material, cultural and spiritual life. It excludes the expenditure of non-resident units on consumption in the economic territory of the country. The final consumption is broken down into household consumption and government consumption.

Households Consumption refers to the total expenditure of resident households on the final consumption of goods and services. In addition to the consumption of goods and services bought by the households directly with money, the households consumption also includes expenditure on goods and services obtained by the households in other ways, i.e. the so-called imputed consumption expenditure, which includes the following: (a) the goods and services provided to the households by the employer in the form of payment in kind and transfer in kind; (b) goods and services produced and consumed by the households themselves, in which the services refer only to the owner-occupied housing and domestic and individual services provided by the paid household workers; (c) financial intermediate services provided by financial institutions; (d) insurance services provided by insurance companies.

Government Consumption refers to the expenditure on the consumption of the public services provided by the government to the whole society and the net expenditure on the goods and services provided by the government to the households free of charge or at low prices. The former equals to the output value of the government services minus the value of operating income obtained by the government departments. The latter equals to the market value of the goods and services provided by the government free of charge or at low prices to the households minus the value received by the government from the households.

Total Capital Formation refers to the fixed assets acquired minus those disposed of and the net value of inventory, including the total fixed capital formation and the increase in inventory.

Total Fixed Capital Formation refers to the value of fixed assets acquired minus those disposed of during a given period. Fixed assets are the assets produced through production activities with specified unit value which could be used for over one year, excluding natural assets. Total fixed capital formation can be categorized into total tangible capital formation and total intangible capital formation. The total tangible capital formation include the value of the construction projects, installation projects completed and the equipment, apparatus and instruments purchased as well as the value of land improved, the value of draught animals, breeding stock, animals

for milk, wool and for recreational purpose, and the newly increased forest with economic value during a given period. The total intangible capital formation includes the prospecting of minerals, the acquisition of computer software minus the disposal of them.

Increase in Inventory refers to the market value of the change in inventory of resident units during a given period, i.e. the difference of value between the beginning and the end of the period minus the current gains due to the change in prices. The increase in inventory can be positive or negative. A positive value indicates the increase in inventory while a negative value indicates the decrease in stock. The inventory includes the raw materials, fuels and reserve materials purchased by the production units as well as the inventory of finished products, semi-finished products, work-in-progress, etc.

Net Export of Goods and Services refers to the difference of the exports of goods and services minus the imports of goods and services. The imports include the value of various goods and services sold or gratuitously transferred by the resident units to the non-resident units. The imports include the value of various goods and services purchased or gratuitously acquired by the resident units from the non-resident units. Because the provision of services and the use of them happen simultaneously, the acquisition of services by the resident units from abroad is usually treated as import while the acquisition of services by non-resident units in this country is usually treated as export. The export and import of goods are calculated at FOB..

第三篇
人口与就业

CHAPTER 3
Population and Employment

简要说明
Brief Introduction

本篇资料的主要内容及来源

本篇内容主要包括人口、计划生育、就业、工资等资料。

计划生育资料由新疆维吾尔自治区计划生育委员会提供；失业资料由新疆维吾尔自治区人力资源和社会保障厅提供；人口普查主要数据、就业和工资资料由新疆维吾尔自治区统计局人口与就业统计处提供。

Main content and sources of data

Data in this chapter show the basic condition of population, employment, wages of staff and workers, family planning.

Data on family planning come from Municipal Family Planning Commission. Data on unemployment are provided by Bureau of Labor and Social Security. The data of population census, employment and wages are provided by the Department of Population and Social Science and Technology Statistic of the Xinjiang Bureau of Statistics.

3-1 主要年份人口数及构成
Population and Its Composition in Main Years

单位：万人、%　　(10 000 persons,%)

年 份 Year	年末总人口 Total Population (Year-end)	按性别分 By Sex 男 Male 人口数 Population	比 重 Proportion	女 Female 人口数 Population	比 重 Proportion
1978	1233.01	630.18	51.11	602.83	48.89
1980	1283.24	654.90	51.03	628.34	48.97
1985	1361.14	696.81	51.19	664.33	48.81
1990	1529.16	785.06	51.34	744.10	48.66
1995	1661.35	848.12	51.05	813.23	48.95
2000	1849.41	957.07	51.75	892.34	48.25
2005	2010.35	1029.70	51.22	980.65	48.78
2006	2050.00	1050.01	51.22	999.99	48.78
2007	2095.19	1072.53	51.19	1022.66	48.81
2008	2130.81	1083.94	50.87	1046.87	49.13
2009	2158.63	1098.31	50.88	1060.32	49.12
2010	2181.33	1119.02	51.30	1062.31	48.70

3-2 新疆人口普查基本情况
Basic Statistics on National Population Census in Xinjiang

单位：万人　　(10 000 persons)

指 标	Items	第二次普查 (1964 年) 1964 Census	第三次普查 (1982 年) 1982 Census	第四次普查 (1990 年) 1990 Census	第五次普查 (2000 年) 2000 Census	第六次普查 (2010 年) 2010 Census
总人口	**Total Population**	**727.01**	**1308.15**	**1515.69**	**1845.95**	**2181.33**
男	Male	389.47	673.22	782.32	955.22	1119.02
女	Female	337.54	634.93	733.37	890.73	1062.31
民族人口	**Nationality Population**					
汉 族	Han Nationality	232.12	528.40	569.54	748.99	874.61
少数民族	Minority Nationalities	494.89	779.75	946.15	1096.96	1306.72
各种文化程度人口	**Population by Educational Level**					
大专及以上	College and Above	4.10	8.37	27.98	94.65	231.99
高中和中专	Senior Secondary School and Specialized Secondary School	15.51	84.28	157.42	224.79	252.64
初 中	Junior Secondary School	50.37	228.63	313.51	508.59	787.37
小 学	Primary School	197.34	442.57	552.55	699.78	656.04
不识字或识字很少	Illiterate and Semi-iliterate	249.03	265.39	198.11	103.68	51.58

注：不识字或识字很少除 1964 年包含 12-14 岁人口外，其他均为 15 岁及以上人口。
Note:Illiterate or semi-illiterate population refers to the population aged above 15 except for the population aged between 12 and 14 in 1964.

3-3 主要年份婚姻登记情况

Number of Marriages Registry in Main Years

指 标	Item	2000	2005	2010
登记结婚(对)	**Registered Marriages (couple)**	**162527**	**184714**	**264013**
初婚(人)	First Marriage (person)	250461	275752	389342
再婚(人)	Remarriage (person)	74593	93676	138684
#男	Male	38484	42576	73863
#再婚中恢复结婚(对)	Resumed Marriages (couple)	3954	6815	11108
登记离婚(对)	**Registered Divorces (couple)**	**59000**	**74342**	**97817**
民政部门批准	Approved by the Civil Administration	26003	47917	69137
法院调判	Mediated by the court	32997	26425	28680
涉外及华侨港澳台居民婚姻	**Marital status of OverseasChinese ,Foreigner and Hong Kong, Macao and Taiwan Compatriots**			
登记结婚(对)	Registered Marriages (couple)	172	223	235
国内公民(人)	Citizen (person)	172	223	235
港澳台居民(人)	Compatriots of Hong Kong, Macao and Taiwan (person)	78	57	31
华 侨(人)	Overseas Chinese (person)	34	12	13
外国人(人)	Foreigner (person)	60	154	191
登记离婚(对)	Registered Divorces (couple)	6	6	26

3-4 各地、州、市计划生育及领证情况

Family Planning and Certificate Receiving by Prefecture, Autonomous Prefecture and City

(2010 年)

地 区	Region	计划生育率 (%) Family Planning Rate (%)	领证率 (%) Coverage of One-child Certificate (%)	领取计划生育证人数 (人) Number of Persons Receiving Certificates of Honor (person)	领取独生子女证人数 (人) Number of Married Couples with One-child Certificate (person)
总 计	**Total**	**99.82**	**34.83**	**561084**	**771315**
城 镇	Urban	99.69	55.64	214726	537932
农 村	Rural	99.86	23.45	346358	233383
乌鲁木齐市	Urumqi City	99.73	50.17	49120	189315
克拉玛依市	Karamay City	99.83	75.87	10375	37444
石河子市	Shihezi City	99.40	60.32	2035	76160
吐鲁番地区	Turpan Administrative Offices	100.00	32.27	22404	16213
哈密地区	Hami [Kumul] Administrative Offices	99.93	64.76	12660	46927
昌吉回族自治州	Changji Hui Autonomous Prefecture	99.82	47.52	22745	108752
伊犁州直属县(市)	Counties (Cities) Direct Under Ili Prefecture	99.88	33.33	97340	72805
塔城地区	Tacheng [Tarbagatai] Administrative Offices	99.76	41.82	26363	50443
阿勒泰地区	Altay Administrative Offices	99.81	42.42	27371	21858
博尔塔拉蒙古自治州	Bortala Mongol Autonomous Prefecture	99.85	40.55	10863	20275
巴音郭楞蒙古自治州	Bayangol Mongol Autonomous Prefecture	99.29	37.94	41177	52687
阿克苏地区	Aksu Administrative Offices	99.82	20.43	55469	38018
克孜勒苏柯尔克孜自治州	Kizilsu Kirgiz Autonomous Prefecture	99.90	32.47	22459	8794
喀什地区	Kashgar [Kaxgar] Administrative Offices	99.85	22.58	101005	63530
和田地区	Hotan Administrative Offices	99.93	27.76	61733	44254

3-5 各地、州、市采取各种避孕措施情况

Condition of Adopting Various Contraceptions by Prefecture, Autonomous Prefecture, City and County

单位：%　　(2010 年)　　(%)

地　区	Region	男性绝育 Masculine Sterilization	女性绝育 Female Sterilization	宫内节育器 IUD Intrauterine Device	皮下埋植 Subdermal Implant
总　计	**Total**	**0.17**	**4.85**	**64.21**	**0.28**
城　镇	Urban	0.13	2.99	63.86	0.21
农　村	Rural	0.19	5.87	64.40	0.32
乌鲁木齐市	Urumqi City	0.13	2.62	49.01	0.19
克拉玛依市	Karamay City	0.30	3.14	51.73	0.61
石河子市	Shihezi City	0.40	7.29	37.03	0.37
吐鲁番地区	Turpan Administrative Offices	0.02	1.81	70.42	0.38
哈密地区	Hami [Kumul] Administrative Offices	0.05	3.48	64.69	0.52
昌吉回族自治州	Changji Hui Autonomous Prefecture	0.19	6.31	70.26	0.39
伊犁州直属县(市)	Counties (Cities) Direct Under Ili Prefecture	0.14	3.81	63.50	0.19
塔城地区	Tacheng [Tarbagatai] Administrative Offices	0.29	7.25	66.35	1.02
阿勒泰地区	Altay Administrative Offices	0.10	3.05	66.03	0.49
博尔塔拉蒙古自治州	Bortala Mongol Autonomous Prefecture	0.51	7.33	65.08	0.68
巴音郭楞蒙古自治州	Bayangol Mongol Autonomous Prefecture	0.77	6.29	69.51	0.13
阿克苏地区	Aksu Administrative Offices	0.21	6.55	66.58	0.47
克孜勒苏柯尔克孜自治州	Kizilsu Kirgiz Autonomous Prefecture	0.01	2.56	73.47	0.10
喀什地区	Kashgar [Kaxgar] Administrative Offices	0.05	3.58	66.75	0.12
和田地区	Hotan Administrative Offices	0.03	8.46	64.44	0.02

地　区	Region	口服药及注射针 Medicine and Entry Needle	避孕套 Contraceptives	外用药 Drug for Exterior Use	其　他 Other
总　计	**Total**	**0.56**	**10.52**	**0.65**	**0.08**
城　镇	Urban	0.60	15.40	0.34	0.12
农　村	Rural	0.54	7.86	0.82	0.06
乌鲁木齐市	Urumqi City	0.80	29.25	0.21	0.26
克拉玛依市	Karamay City	0.45	28.16	0.47	0.54
石河子市	Shihezi City	1.65	20.17	0.55	0.89
吐鲁番地区	Turpan Administrative Offices	0.74	7.30	0.36	0.00
哈密地区	Hami [Kumul] Administrative Offices	0.49	17.41	0.18	0.05
昌吉回族自治州	Changji Hui Autonomous Prefecture	0.41	12.69	0.15	0.09
伊犁州直属县(市)	Counties (Cities) Direct Under Ili Prefecture	0.39	12.14	0.19	0.13
塔城地区	Tacheng [Tarbagatai] Administrative Offices	0.39	12.13	0.06	0.00
阿勒泰地区	Altay Administrative Offices	0.31	15.47	0.11	0.01
博尔塔拉蒙古自治州	Bortala Mongol Autonomous Prefecture	0.54	13.76	0.28	0.00
巴音郭楞蒙古自治州	Bayangol Mongol Autonomous Prefecture	0.21	10.40	0.15	0.00
阿克苏地区	Aksu Administrative Offices	1.06	4.40	1.13	0.05
克孜勒苏柯尔克孜自治州	Kizilsu Kirgiz Autonomous Prefecture	2.07	3.87	1.91	0.38
喀什地区	Kashgar [Kaxgar] Administrative Offices	0.48	1.70	1.58	0.01
和田地区	Hotan Administrative Offices	0.15	2.95	0.62	0.00

3-6 主要年份就业基本情况
Employment in Main Years

项　　目	Item	1995	2000	2010
就业人员合计(万人)	**Total Number of Employed Persons (10 000 persons)**	**676.00**	**672.50**	**894.65**
第一产业	Primary Industry	388.16	387.90	438.13
第二产业	Secondary Industry	124.21	92.70	132.75
第三产业	Tertiary Industry	163.63	191.90	323.77
就业人员构成(合计=100)	**Composition of Employed Persons (total=100)**			
第一产业	Primary Industry	57.42	57.68	48.97
第二产业	Secondary Industry	18.37	13.78	14.84
第三产业	Tertiary Industry	24.21	28.54	36.19
按城乡分就业人员(万人)	**Number of Employed Persons by Urban and Rural Areas (10 000 persons)**		**672.50**	**894.65**
城镇就业人员	Urban Employed Persons		318.40	387.31
国有单位	State-owned Units		223.36	184.15
城镇集体单位	Urban Collective-owned Units		15.58	3.14
股份合作单位	Cooperatire Units		1.43	0.53
联营单位	Joint Ownership Units		0.33	0.23
有限责任公司	Limited Liability Corporations		12.32	41.27
股份有限公司	Share-holding Corporations Ltd.		5.87	21.88
私营企业	Private Enterprises		17.15	65.36
其　他	Others			1.04
港澳台商投资单位	Units With Funds From Hong Kong, Macao&Taiwan		0.92	1.41
外商投资单位	Foreign Funded Units		0.51	1.31
个　体	Self-employed Individuals		40.93	66.99
乡村就业人员	Rural Employed Persons		354.10	507.34
#乡镇企业	Township and Village Enterprises		80.64	116.75
私营企业	Private Enterprises		5.24	18.74
个　体	Self-employed Individuals		19.82	23.52
在岗职工人数(万人)	**Number of Staff and Workers (10 000 persons)**	**311.93**	**255.75**	**245.48**
国有单位	State-owned Units	278.49	219.41	178.40
城镇集体单位	Urban Collective-owned Units	29.95	15.28	3.00
其他单位	Units of Other Types of Ownership	3.49	21.06	64.08
城镇单位女性就业人员(万人)	**Number of Female Employment in Urban Units (10 000 persons)**		**107.89**	**105.91**
城镇登记失业人数(万人)	**Number of Registered Unemployed Persons in Urban Areas (10 000 persons)**	**10.24**	**11.00**	**10.99**
城镇登记失业率(%)	**Registered Unemployment Rate in Urban Areas (%)**	**3.9**	**3.8**	**3.2**

3-7 主要年份城镇登记失业人数及失业率
Number of Registered Unemployed Persons in Urban Areas and Unemployment Rate in Main Years

单位：万人 (10 000 persons)

年份 Year	城镇登记失业人数 Number of Registered Unemployment Persons in Urban Area	城镇登记失业率(%) Registered Unemployment Rate in Urban Areas (%)	年份 Year	城镇登记失业人数 Number of Registered Unemployment Persons in Urban Area	城镇登记失业率(%) Registered Unemployment Rate in Urban Areas (%)
1980	13.55	7.5	2000	11.00	3.8
1985	4.04	1.9	2001	12.07	3.7
1990	9.60	3.8	2002	12.68	3.6
1991	9.95	3.8	2003	12.75	3.8
1992	9.81	3.7	2004	10.87	3.8
1993	9.50	3.6	2005	11.13	3.9
1994	10.00	3.8	2006	11.98	3.9
1995	10.24	3.9	2007	11.70	3.9
1996	9.81	3.8	2008	11.77	3.7
1997	10.20	3.8	2009	11.86	3.8
1998	11.06	3.9	2010	10.99	3.2
1999	10.30	3.7			

3-8 各地、州、市城镇登记失业率
Registered Unemployment Rate in Urban Area by Prefecture, Autonomous Prefecture and City

单位：% (%)

地区	Region	2009	2010
总计	**Total**	**3.84**	**3.23**
乌鲁木齐市	Urumqi City	4.10	3.72
克拉玛依市	Karamay City	1.80	1.48
石河子市	Shihezi City	2.02	1.69
吐鲁番地区	Turpan Administrative Offices	3.16	2.86
哈密地区	Hami [Kumul] Administrative Offices	3.61	3.24
昌吉回族自治州	Changji Hui Autonomous Prefecture	3.75	3.37
伊犁州直属县(市)	Counties (Cities) Direct Under Ili Prefecture	3.04	3.97
塔城地区	Tacheng [Tarbagatai] Administrative Offices	3.23	1.96
阿勒泰地区	Altay Administrative Offices	2.65	2.95
博尔塔拉蒙古自治州	Bortala Mongol Autonomous Prefecture	3.75	3.64
巴音郭楞蒙古自治州	Bayangol Mongol Autonomous Prefecture	3.31	2.85
阿克苏地区	Aksu Administrative Offices	3.02	3.53
克孜勒苏柯尔克孜自治州	Kizilsu Kirgiz Autonomous Prefecture	3.93	4.07
喀什地区	Kashgar [Kaxgar] Administrative Offices	3.95	3.96
和田地区	Hotan Administrative Offices	4.00	3.20

3-9 主要年份按三次产业分的就业人员

Number of Employed Persons by Three Strata of Industry in Main Years

单位：万人 (10 000 persons)

年 份 Year	经济活动人口 Economically Active Population	就业人员合计 Total Number of Employed persons	第一产业 Primary Industry	第二产业 Secondary Industry
1978		491.25	353.99	70.42
1980	519.90	506.35	354.49	75.12
1985	569.85	565.81	363.24	89.64
1990	627.30	617.70	378.47	107.42
1995	686.24	676.00	388.16	124.21
1996	693.81	684.00	390.98	119.39
1997	725.60	715.40	421.30	105.40
1998	691.98	680.92	387.80	106.22
1999	704.64	694.34	385.57	104.51
2000	683.50	672.50	387.90	92.70
2001	697.45	685.38	388.19	92.19
2002	714.17	701.49	391.84	95.82
2003	734.02	721.27	397.20	95.69
2004	755.36	744.49	403.31	98.49
2005	802.75	791.62	408.00	122.81
2006	823.73	811.75	414.45	111.28
2007	842.12	830.42	417.73	118.34
2008	859.35	847.58	421.32	120.05
2009	878.01	866.15	427.48	127.28
2010	905.64	894.65	438.13	132.75

年 份 Year		构成(合计=100) (%) Composition in Percentage (total=100)(%)		
	第三产业 Tertiary Industry	第一产业 Primary Industry	第二产业 Secondary Industry	第三产业 Tertiary Industry
1978	66.84	72.06	14.33	13.61
1980	76.74	70.01	14.84	15.15
1985	112.93	64.20	15.84	19.96
1990	131.81	61.27	17.39	21.34
1995	163.63	57.42	18.37	24.21
1996	173.63	57.16	17.45	25.39
1997	188.70	58.89	14.73	26.38
1998	186.90	56.95	15.60	27.45
1999	204.26	55.53	15.05	29.42
2000	191.90	57.68	13.78	28.54
2001	205.00	56.64	13.45	29.91
2002	213.83	55.86	13.66	30.48
2003	228.38	55.07	13.27	31.66
2004	242.69	54.17	13.23	32.60
2005	260.81	51.54	15.51	32.95
2006	286.02	51.06	13.71	35.23
2007	294.35	50.30	14.25	35.45
2008	306.21	49.71	14.16	36.13
2009	311.39	49.35	14.70	35.95
2010	323.77	48.97	14.84	36.19

3-10 按城乡分的年底就业人员数

单位：万人

年 份 Year	地 区 Region	总 计 Total	城 镇 Urban Area	国有单位 State-owned Units	集体单位 Collective-owned Units	股份合作单位 Cooperative Units	联营单位 Joint Ownership Units
	2000	672.50	318.40	223.36	15.58	1.43	0.33
	2001	685.38	319.92	201.10	12.03	0.93	0.41
	2002	701.49	327.37	193.57	9.68	0.77	0.43
	2003	721.27	339.00	188.89	8.02	0.64	0.27
	2004	744.49	349.43	188.18	6.86	0.82	0.33
	2005	791.62	358.78	186.96	6.05	0.79	0.33
	2006	811.75	370.10	187.19	5.32	0.64	0.33
	2007	830.42	375.59	186.77	4.64	0.64	0.42
	2008	847.58	381.37	186.17	3.80	0.58	0.36
	2009	866.15	379.41	181.34	3.68	0.47	0.30
	2010	894.65	387.31	184.15	3.14	0.53	0.23
乌鲁木齐市	Urumqi City	114.26	94.85	31.50	0.83	0.13	0.15
克拉玛依市	Karamay City	22.76	22.62	5.07	0.20	0.01	0.04
石河子市	Shihezi City	15.71	13.70	4.86	0.02		
吐鲁番地区	Turpan Administrative Offices	38.09	10.98	3.76	0.08	0.03	0.01
哈密地区	Hami [Kumul] Administrative Offices	23.03	12.21	5.93	0.06		0.03
昌吉回族自治州	Changji Hui Autonomous Prefecture	74.03	31.11	15.01	0.31	0.01	
伊犁哈萨克自治州	Ili Kazak Autonomous Prefecture	200.65	79.72	50.05	0.47	0.10	
伊犁州直属县(市)	Counties (Cities) Direct Under Ili Prefecture	111.93	38.13	20.70	0.23	0.07	
塔城地区	Tacheng [Tarbagatai] Administrative Offices	59.21	26.47	19.71	0.16	0.02	
阿勒泰地区	Altay Administrative Offices	29.51	15.12	9.64	0.08	0.01	
博尔塔拉蒙古自治州	Bortala Mongol Autonomous Prefecture	22.44	12.21	8.20	0.07	0.01	
巴音郭楞蒙古自治州	Bayangol Mongol Autonomous Prefecture	55.40	28.92	13.5	0.23	0.03	
阿克苏地区	Aksu Administrative Offices	100.14	32.38	17.64	0.21	0.14	
克孜勒苏柯尔克孜自治州	Kizilsu Kirgiz Autonomous Prefecture	21.31	5.33	3.88	0.05	0.01	
喀什地区	Kashgar [Kaxgar] Administrative Offices	130.98	29.47	16.74	0.54	0.05	
和田地区	Hotan Administrative Offices	75.85	13.81	8.01	0.07	0.01	

Number of Employed Persons at Year-end by Urban and Rural Areas

(10 000 persons)

有限责任公司 Limited Liability Corporations	股份有限公司 Share Holding Corporations Ltd.	私营企业 Private Enterprises	其　他 Others	港澳台商投资单位 Units with Funds from Hong Kong Macao and Taiwan	外商投资单位 Foreign Funded Units	个　体 Self-employed Individuals	乡　村 Rural Area	#乡镇企业 Township and Village Enterprises	#私营企业 Private Enterprises	#个　体 Self-employed Individuals
12.32	5.87	17.15		0.92	0.51	40.93	354.10	80.64	5.24	19.82
26.54	9.01	23.16		0.96	0.55	45.23	365.46	82.44	4.93	19.10
33.35	7.81	34.44		1.06	0.65	45.61	373.41	86.67	4.26	20.01
34.26	10.09	42.35	1.13	0.64	0.73	51.98	382.98	88.09	6.82	18.68
34.96	9.70	50.75	1.16	0.66	0.84	55.17	395.06	93.35	6.50	19.01
35.37	12.01	58.55	1.59	0.71	0.89	57.12	431.25	95.44	8.55	18.77
34.92	12.85	66.36	1.99	0.77	1.14	58.59	441.65	99.04	8.88	19.16
36.46	14.40	68.79	1.95	1.32	1.23	58.97	454.83	103.70	9.64	19.93
36.41	16.40	71.67	1.78	1.32	1.35	61.53	466.21	106.30	9.98	20.79
38.58	21.12	65.15	1.12	1.57	1.24	64.84	486.74	111.57	15.47	21.45
41.27	21.88	65.36	1.04	1.41	1.31	66.99	507.34	116.75	18.74	23.52
10.69	4.14	26.91	0.02	1.06	0.61	18.81	19.41	6.39	5.07	0.83
3.72	7.61	2.33	0.01	0.01	0.01	3.61	0.14	0.15		
2.57	1.97	2.13	0.01	0.02	0.19	1.93	2.01	1.85	0.11	0.76
1.00	2.26	1.94	0.01	0.02	0.06	1.81	27.11	4.67	1.01	1.58
1.81	0.37	1.37	0.04	0.03	0.06	2.51	10.82	2.72	0.08	0.54
4.17	1.20	5.21	0.07	0.06	0.21	4.86	42.92	14.03	3.15	2.15
6.86	1.43	8.59	0.46	0.06	0.11	11.59	120.93	32.00	3.04	4.65
4.47	1.04	4.28	0.25	0.04	0.11	6.94	73.80	15.87	1.58	2.69
1.48	0.04	2.15		0.02		2.89	32.74	10.49	1.12	1.23
0.91	0.35	2.16	0.21			1.76	14.39	5.64	0.34	0.73
0.51	0.06	1.75		0.08		1.53	10.23	3.06	0.30	0.77
2.52	1.78	5.46	0.03	0.02	0.03	5.32	26.48	7.70	1.01	2.81
3.76	0.52	3.63	0.03	0.05	0.03	6.37	67.76	11.71	2.84	2.32
0.07	0.03	0.49	0.02			0.78	15.98	2.02	0.38	0.34
2.98	0.40	3.61				5.15	101.51	16.66	1.20	3.77
0.61	0.11	1.94	0.34			2.72	62.04	13.79	0.55	3.00

3-11 各地区按行业分城镇单位就业人员(年底数)

Number of Employed Persons in Urban Units at Year-end by Sectors and Region

单位：人 (2010 年) (person)

项　目	Item	合　计 Total	国有单位 State-owned Units	城镇集体 Urban Collective-Owned Units	其他单位 Units of Other Types Of Ownership
总　计	**Total**	**2549566**	**1841520**	**31387**	**676659**
按国民经济行业分组	**Grouped by Sectors**				
农林牧渔业	Agriculture, Forestry, Animal Husbandry and Fishery	583455	576694	259	6502
采矿业	Mining	175200	30584	784	143832
制造业	Manufacturing	259793	38665	3602	217526
电力、燃气及水的生产和供应业	Production and Supply of Electricity, Gas and Water	60548	25077	292	35179
建筑业	Construction	150092	33704	3752	112636
交通运输、仓储和邮政业	Traffic Transport, Storage and Post	111062	86554	691	23817
信息传输、计算机服务和软件业	Information Transmission, Computer Servcie and Software	18463	9550	4	8909
批发和零售业	Wholesale and Retail Trades	64019	20723	4825	38471
住宿和餐饮业	Hotels and Catering Services	23059	11895	1130	10034
金融业	Financial Intermediation	71346	32401	9129	29816
房地产业	Real Estate	22975	6299	582	16094
租赁和商务服务业	Leasing and Business Services	48344	23244	4428	20672
科学研究、技术服务和地质勘查业	Scientific Research, Technical Service and Geological Prospecting	47903	42689	60	5154
水利、环境和公共设施管理业	Management of Water Conservancy, Environment and PublicFacility	50980	48240		2740
居民服务和其他服务业	Services to households and Other Services	5776	3954	228	1594
教　育	Education	338625	336380	101	2144
卫生、社会保障和社会福利业	Health, Social Security and Social Welfare	138321	136013	1500	808
文化、体育和娱乐业	Culture, Sports and Entertainment	26580	25886	3	691
公共管理和社会组织	Public Management and Social Organizations	353025	352968	17	40
按地区分	**By Region**				
乌鲁木齐市	Urumqi City	491115	314912	8414	167789
克拉玛依市	Karamay City	166801	50703	2012	114086
吐鲁番地区	Turpan Administrative Offices	72301	37608	779	33914
哈密地区	Hami [Kumul] Administrative Offices	83318	59295	604	23419
昌吉回族自治州	Changji Hui Autonomous Prefecture	190852	134235	3068	53549
伊犁哈萨克自治州	Ili Kazak Autonomous Prefecture	595372	500486	4624	90262
伊犁州直属县(市)	Counties (Cities) Direct Under Ili Prefecture	269105	207006	2301	59798
塔城地区	Tacheng [Tarbagatai] Administrative Offices	214243	197068	1556	15619
阿勒泰地区	Altay Administrative Offices	112024	96412	767	14845
博尔塔拉蒙古自治州	Bortala Mongol Autonomous Prefecture	89290	82006	695	6589
巴音郭楞蒙古自治州	Bayangol Mongol Autonomous Prefecture	181410	135048	2311	44051
阿克苏地区	Aksu Administrative Offices	182139	138044	2103	41992
克孜勒苏柯尔克孜自治州	Kizilsu Kirgiz Autonomous Prefecture	40640	38789	488	1363
喀什地区	Kashgar [Kaxgar] Administrative Offices	191007	153003	5424	32580
和田地区	Hotan Administrative Offices	91536	80139	688	10709
石河子市	Shihezi City	96422	48616	177	47629
阿拉尔市	Aral City	41722	38417		3305
图木舒克市	Tumxuk City	16147	14344		1803
五家渠市	Wujiaqu City	19494	15875		3619

3-12 各地区年底单位在岗职工人数
Number of Staff and Workers at Year-end by Region

单位：万人 (10 000 persons)

年份 Year	地区 Region	合计 Total	国有单位 State-owned Units	城镇集体 Urban Collective-owned Units	其他单位 Units of Other Types of Ownership
	2002	242.26	189.26	9.31	43.69
	2003	237.94	184.02	7.55	46.37
	2004	235.97	182.80	6.43	46.74
	2005	237.84	181.92	5.96	49.96
	2006	238.95	182.91	5.19	50.85
	2007	239.45	181.46	4.58	53.41
	2008	239.16	180.29	3.64	55.23
	2009	239.54	175.90	3.54	60.10
	2010	245.48	178.40	3.00	64.08
乌鲁木齐市	Urumqi City	46.89	29.74	0.83	16.32
克拉玛依市	Karamay City	15.15	4.54	0.19	10.42
吐鲁番地区	Turpan Administrative Offices	7.09	3.67	0.08	3.34
哈密地区	Hami [Kumul] Administrative Offices	7.98	5.81	0.05	2.12
昌吉回族自治州	Chāngji Hui Autonomous Prefecture	18.63	13.27	0.30	5.06
伊犁哈萨克自治州	Ili Kazak Autonomous Prefecture	58.54	49.40	0.45	8.69
伊犁州直属县(市)	Counties (Cities) Direct Under Ili Prefecture	26.51	20.50	0.23	5.78
塔城地区	Tacheng [Tarbagatai] Administrative Offices	21.15	19.49	0.15	1.51
阿勒泰地区	Altay Administrative Offices	10.88	9.41	0.07	1.40
博尔塔拉蒙古自治州	Bortala Mongol Autonomous Prefecture	8.68	7.99	0.07	0.62
巴音郭楞蒙古自治州	Bayangol Mongol Autonomous Prefecture	17.21	12.85	0.23	4.13
阿克苏地区	Aksu Administrative Offices	18.01	13.64	0.21	4.16
克孜勒苏柯尔克孜自治州	Kizilsu Kirgiz Autonomous Prefecture	3.64	3.48	0.05	0.11
喀什地区	Kashgar [Kaxgar] Administrative Offices	17.60	14.64	0.47	2.49
和田地区	Hotan Administrative Offices	8.75	7.70	0.06	0.99
石河子市	Shihezi City	9.63	4.85	0.02	4.76
阿拉尔市	Aral City	4.17	3.84		0.33
图木舒克市	Tumxuk City	1.60	1.42		0.18
五家渠市	Wujiaqu City	1.93	1.57		0.36

3-13 分行业年底单位在岗职工人数
Number of Staff and Workers at Year-end by Sectors

单位：人 (2010 年) (person)

项　目	Item	合 计 Total	国有单位 State-owned Units	城镇集体 Urban Collective-owned Units	其他单位 Units of Other Types of Ownership
总　计	**Total**	**2454762**	**1783972**	**29987**	**640803**
农林牧渔业	**Agriculture, Forestry, Animal Husbandry and Fishery**	**576308**	**569953**	**259**	**6096**
农　业	Farming	457368	455644	79	1645
林　业	Forestry	8484	8005		479
畜牧业	Animal Husbandry	79376	76863	9	2504
渔　业	Fishery	236	186		50
农林牧渔服务业	Services in Support of Agriculture	30844	29255	171	1418
采矿业	**Mining**	**164719**	**28013**	**621**	**136085**
#煤炭开采和洗选业	Mining and Washing of Coal	44479	6405	566	37508
石油和天然气开采业	Extraction of Petroleum and Natural Gas	103269	17551	4	85714
制造业	**Manufacturing**	**251144**	**36990**	**3236**	**210918**
#农副食品加工业	Processing of Food from Agriculture Products	19019	1657	14	17348
食品制造业	Manufacture of Food	12432	1389	97	10946
饮料制造业	Manufacture of Beverage	10334	473	133	9728
纺织业	Manufacture of Textile	27086	5405	45	21636
造纸及纸制品业	Manufacture of Paper and Paper Products	5333	295	114	4924
印刷业和记录媒介的复制	Printing and Record Medium Reproduction	4720	3670	72	978
石油加工、炼焦及核燃料加工业	Oil processing, Refining and Nuclear-fuel processing	33236	11142	13	22081
化学原料及化学制品制造业	Raw Chemical Materials and Chemical Products	38067	1880	608	35579
塑料制品业	Plastic Products	8452	256	219	7977
非金属矿物制品业	Manufacture of Non-metal Mineral Products	27548	2879	661	24008
黑色金属冶炼及压延加工业	Smelting and Pressing of Ferrous Metals	24109	527	477	23105
有色金属冶炼及压延加工业	Smelting and Pressing of Nonferrous Metals	6235	1795	87	4353
通用设备制造业	Manufacturing of Equipment for General Purpose	2514	178	106	2230
电力、燃气及水的生产和供应业	**Production and Distribution of Electricity, Gas and Water**	**59330**	**24710**	**292**	**34328**
电力、热力的生产和供应业	Production and Distribution of Electric Power, Thermal Power	50189	20110	183	29896
燃气生产和供应业	Production and Distribution of Gas	2262	47		2215
水的生产和供应业	Production and Distribution of Water	6879	4553	109	2217
建筑业	**Construction**	**141310**	**32869**	**3563**	**104878**
房屋和土木工程建筑业	Construction of Buildings and Civil Engineering	122108	26155	2127	93826
建筑安装业	Building Installation	14743	2999	1294	10450
建筑装饰业	Building Decoration	671	213	142	316

3-13 续表 1 Continued

单位：人 (person)

项目	Item	合计 Total	国有单位 State-owned Units	城镇集体 Urban Collective-owned Units	其他单位 Units of Other Types of Ownership
其他建筑业	Other Construction	3788	3502		286
交通运输、仓储和邮政业	**Transport Storage and Post**	**99540**	**75310**	**672**	**23558**
铁路运输业	Railway Transport	34835	34835		
道路运输业	Road Transportat	27188	20445	244	6499
城市公共交通业	Urban Public Transport	12244	705	7	11532
航空运输业	Air Transportat	8883	4175		4708
管道运输业	Via Pipe Transportat	190			190
装卸搬运和其他运输服务业	Loading and Discharging; Other Transportation Service	2824	2140	414	270
仓储业	Storage	3243	2877	7	359
邮政业	Post	10133	10133		
信息传输、计算机服务和软件业	**Information Transmission, Computer Service and Software**	**17756**	**9150**	**4**	**8602**
电信和其他信息传输服务业	Telecommunication and Other I.T Transmission Service	16498	8710	4	7784
计算机服务业	Computer Service	354	267		87
软件业	Software	904	173		731
批发和零售业	**Wholesale and Retail Trades**	**62007**	**19980**	**4656**	**37371**
批发业	Wholesale Trades	42650	16009	4127	22514
零售业	Retail Trades	19357	3971	529	14857
住宿和餐饮业	**Hotels and Catering Services**	**21717**	**10656**	**1116**	**9945**
住宿业	Hotels	19506	9719	1030	8757
餐饮业	Catering Services	2211	937	86	1188
金 融 业	**Financial Intermediation**	**58290**	**28918**	**8891**	**20481**
银行业	Banking	43105	24239	8891	9975
证券业	Security Activities	603	53		550
保险业	Insurance	13333	4229		9104
其他金融活动	Other Finance Activities	1249	397		852
房地产业	**Real Estate**	**22261**	**5893**	**581**	**15787**
#房地产开发经营	Development and Management of Real Estate	8226	929	146	7151
物业管理	Real Estate Management	11647	3801	298	7548
房地产中介服务	Agency Service for Real Estate	609	273	5	331
租赁和商务服务业	**Leasing and Business Service**	**46749**	**22402**	**4200**	**20147**
租赁业	Leasing	327	115		212
商务服务业	Business Service	46422	22287	4200	19935

3-13 续表 2 Continued

单位：人 (person)

项　　目	Item	合 计 Total	国有单位 State-owned Units	城镇集体 Urban Collective-owned Units	其他单位 Units of Other Types of Ownership
科学研究、技术服务和地质勘查业	**Scientific Research, Technology Service and Geological Prospecting**	**46118**	**41305**	**60**	**4753**
研究与试验发展	Research and Experiment Development	5968	5899		69
专业技术服务业	Professional Technique Service	22021	17770	52	4199
科技交流和推广服务业	Services of Science and Technology Exchanges and Promotion	8926	8525	8	393
地质勘查业	Geologica Prospecting	9203	9111		92
水利、环境和公共设施管理业	**Management of Water Conservancy, Environment and Public Facility**	**48835**	**46121**		**2714**
水利管理业	Management of Water Conservance	21196	21196		
环境管理业	Environmental Management	15993	15664		329
公共设施管理业	Management of Public Facilities	11646	9261		2385
居民服务和其他服务业	**Service to Households and Other Services**	**5700**	**3879**	**227**	**1594**
居民服务业	Services to Households	3838	3572	143	123
其他服务业	Other Services	1862	307	84	1471
教　育	**Education**	**334469**	**332313**	**101**	**2055**
#初等教育	Junior Education	135668	135178		490
中等教育	Secondary Education	155151	154482	15	654
高等教育	Senior Education	27619	27619		
卫生、社会保障和社会福利业	**Health, Social Security and Social Welfare**	**131887**	**129630**	**1488**	**769**
卫　生	Health	126345	124196	1481	668
社会保障业	Social Security	2604	2604		
社会福利业	Social Welfare	2938	2830	7	101
文化、体育和娱乐业	**Culture, Sports and Entertainment**	**25927**	**25240**	**3**	**684**
新闻出版业	Journalism and Publishing Activities	4781	4252		529
广播、电影、电视和音像业	Broadcasting, Movies, Televisions and Audiovisual Activities	10184	10165	3	16
文化艺术业	Culture and Art Activities	9576	9546		30
体　育	Sports	1050	1050		
娱乐业	Entertainment	336	227		109
公共管理和社会组织	**Public Management and Social Organization**	**340695**	**340640**	**17**	**38**
#中国共产党机关	Organs of Communist Party of China	22269	22269		
国家机构	Government Agencies	312289	312289		
人民政协和民主党派	People's Political Consultative Conference and Democratic Parties	2319	2319		
群众团体、社会团体和宗教组织	Non-Governmental Organizations, Social Organizations and Religion Organizations	3818	3763	17	38

3-14 各地、州、市分行业年底单位在岗职工人数

Number of Staff and Workers at Year-end by Sector and Prefecture, Autonomous Prefecture and City

单位：人　　(2010 年)　　(person)

年 份 Year	地 区 Region	合 计 Total	农林牧渔业 Farming, Forestry, Animal Husbandry and Fishery	采矿业 Mining	制造业 Manufacturing	电力、燃气及水的生产和供应业 Production and Distribution of Power, Gas and Water
总 计	**Total**	**2454762**	**576308**	**164719**	**251144**	**59330**
乌鲁木齐市	Urumqi City	468883	12326	14973	78261	10761
克拉玛依市	Karamay City	151513	8699	66640	26631	56
吐鲁番地区	Turpan Administrative Offices	70913	3630	24656	4975	2228
哈密地区	Hami [Kumul] Administrative Offices	79778	19524	13876	5306	2283
昌吉回族自治州	Changji Hui Autonomous Prefecture	186326	58943	5513	25409	7181
伊犁哈萨克自治州	Ili Kazak Autonomous Prefecture	585328	249352	16483	37987	11928
伊犁州直属县(市)	Counties (Cities) Direct Under Ili Prefecture	265068	75526	2946	27924	6881
塔城地区	Tacheng [Tarbagatai] Administrative Offices	211484	127027	7546	7487	2522
阿勒泰地区	Altay Administrative Offices	108776	46799	5991	2576	2525
博尔塔拉蒙古自治州	Bortala Mongol Autonomous Prefecture	86785	42023	252	3953	2286
巴音郭楞蒙古自治州	Bayangol Mongol Autonomous Prefecture	172078	51031	13418	12520	3237
阿克苏地区	Aksu Administrative Offices	180133	36923	8113	15127	5707
克孜勒苏柯尔克孜自治州	Kizilsu Kirgiz Autonomous Prefecture	36375	2775	42	977	408
喀什地区	Kashgar [Kaxgar] Administrative Offices	175952	20433	122	6799	4735
和田地区	Hotan Administrative Offices	87455	12262	631	1806	2049
石河子市	Shihezi City	96287	12434		27173	5464
阿拉尔市	Aral City	41719	28897		1633	344
图木舒克市	Tumxuk City	15978	9436		523	411
五家渠市	Wujiaqu City	19259	7620		2064	252

年 份 Year	地 区 Region	建筑业 Construction	交通运输、仓储和邮政业 Transport Storage and Post	信息传输、计算机服务和软件业 Information Transmission, Computer Servcie and Software	批发和零售业 Wholesale and Retail Trades	住宿和餐饮业 Hotels and Catering Services
总 计	**Total**	**141310**	**99540**	**17756**	**62007**	**21717**
乌鲁木齐市	Urumqi City	56108	62277	5129	19686	9194
克拉玛依市	Karamay City	11986	2131	772	3183	1032
吐鲁番地区	Turpan Administrative Offices	849	1472	491	1778	503
哈密地区	Hami [Kumul] Administrative Offices	921	1062	729	1047	992
昌吉回族自治州	Changji Hui Autonomous Prefecture	5802	3271	1351	3001	362
伊犁哈萨克自治州	Ili Kazak Autonomous Prefecture	12169	11224	3651	11195	5181
伊犁州直属县(市)	Counties (Cities) Direct Under Ili Prefecture	7794	6902	1526	8132	2976
塔城地区	Tacheng [Tarbagatai] Administrative Offices	2555	2005	956	1937	603
阿勒泰地区	Altay Administrative Offices	1820	2317	1169	1126	1602
博尔塔拉蒙古自治州	Bortala Mongol Autonomous Prefecture	944	1442	412	1190	514
巴音郭楞蒙古自治州	Bayangol Mongol Autonomous Prefecture	5655	4220	965	3780	1400
阿克苏地区	Aksu Administrative Offices	9953	2994	1226	6169	586
克孜勒苏柯尔克孜自治州	Kizilsu Kirgiz Autonomous Prefecture	276	995	330	455	189
喀什地区	Kashgar [Kaxgar] Administrative Offices	8573	4770	1107	6843	846
和田地区	Hotan Administrative Offices	3656	2436	778	1548	189
石河子市	Shihezi City	20371	1054	770	728	729
阿拉尔市	Aral City	1762	28		1158	
图木舒克市	Tumxuk City	1738			24	
五家渠市	Wujiaqu City	547	164	45	222	

3-14 续表 Continued

单位：人 (person)

年 份 Year	地 区 Region	金融业 Financial Intermedia-tion	房地产业 Real Estate	租赁和商务服务业 Leasing and Business Services	科学研究、技术服务和地质勘查业 Scientific Research, Technology Service and Geological Prospecting	水利、环境和公共设施管理业 Management of Water Conservancy, Environment and Public Facility
总 计	**Total**	**58290**	**22261**	**46749**	**46118**	**48835**
乌鲁木齐市	Urumqi City	16949	7234	12284	18813	5216
克拉玛依市	Karamay City	2028	2973	7672	428	831
吐鲁番地区	Turpan Administrative Offices	1502	347	127	1515	1031
哈密地区	Hami [Kumul] Administrative Offices	1814	281	823	2284	3110
昌吉回族自治州	Changji Hui Autonomous Prefecture	4086	1716	5057	3979	5441
伊犁哈萨克自治州	Ili Kazak Autonomous Prefecture	10441	3472	5658	6831	9901
伊犁州直属县(市)	Counties (Cities) Direct Under Ili Prefecture	5533	3011	4713	3451	4558
塔城地区	Tacheng [Tarbagatai] Administrative Offices	3236	226	631	1289	3518
阿勒泰地区	Altay Administrative Offices	1672	235	314	2091	1825
博尔塔拉蒙古自治州	Bortala Mongol Autonomous Prefecture	1568	344	5403	949	1592
巴音郭楞蒙古自治州	Bayangol Mongol Autonomous Prefecture	4062	2273	4015	2800	4266
阿克苏地区	Aksu Administrative Offices	3584	1388	1613	2145	4818
克孜勒苏柯尔克孜自治州	Kizilsu Kirgiz Autonomous Prefecture	856	68	503	1662	573
喀什地区	Kashgar [Kaxgar] Administrative Offices	5123	1601	889	2079	4028
和田地区	Hotan Administrative Offices	1933	265	338	1167	2260
石河子市	Shihezi City	3513	204	2055	1034	1850
阿拉尔市	Aral City		56	107	97	2823
图木舒克市	Tumxuk City			77	19	296
五家渠市	Wujiaqu City	831	39	128	316	799

年 份 Year	地 区 Region	居民服务和其他服务业 Service to Households and Other Services	教 育 Education	卫生、社会保障和社会福利业 Health, Social Security and Social Welfare	文化、体育和娱乐业 Culture, Sports and Entertainment	公共管理和社会组织 Public Management and Social Organizations
总 计	**Total**	**5700**	**334469**	**131887**	**25927**	**340695**
乌鲁木齐市	Urumqi City	682	46628	28332	9948	54082
克拉玛依市	Karamay City	48	6185	2734	133	7351
吐鲁番地区	Turpan Administrative Offices	72	9645	3215	380	12497
哈密地区	Hami [Kumul] Administrative Offices	172	8828	4646	951	11129
昌吉回族自治州	Changji Hui Autonomous Prefecture	5	22046	9948	966	22249
伊犁哈萨克自治州	Ili Kazak Autonomous Prefecture	457	74736	28912	4914	80836
伊犁州直属县(市)	Counties (Cities) Direct Under Ili Prefecture	243	42563	16087	2503	41799
塔城地区	Tacheng [Tarbagatai] Administrative Offices	159	20044	8092	1143	20508
阿勒泰地区	Altay Administrative Offices	55	12129	4733	1268	18529
博尔塔拉蒙古自治州	Bortala Mongol Autonomous Prefecture	94	9171	3860	589	10199
巴音郭楞蒙古自治州	Bayangol Mongol Autonomous Prefecture	119	20461	9602	1117	27137
阿克苏地区	Aksu Administrative Offices	174	31140	11015	1449	36009
克孜勒苏柯尔克孜自治州	Kizilsu Kirgiz Autonomous Prefecture	1983	10187	2945	899	10252
喀什地区	Kashgar [Kaxgar] Administrative Offices	193	56158	13091	2620	35942
和田地区	Hotan Administrative Offices	201	25444	7385	1381	21726
石河子市	Shihezi City	1492	7435	3788	369	5824
阿拉尔市	Aral City	7	2911	1013	105	778
图木舒克市	Tumxuk City		1336	326		1792
五家渠市	Wujiaqu City	1	2158	1075	106	2892

3-15 分行业城镇单位年底女性就业人员

Number of Female Employed in Urban Units at Year-end by Sectors

单位：人 (2010 年) (person)

项　目	Item	合　计 Total	国有单位 State-owned Units	城镇集体 Urban Collective-owned Units	其他单位 Units of Other Types of Ownership
总　计	**Total**	**1059091**	**823055**	**11542**	**224494**
农林牧渔业	Agriculture, Forestry, Animal Husbandry and Fishery	257051	254507	66	2478
采矿业	Mining	47450	5211	75	42164
制造业	Manufacturing	90264	14345	1663	74256
电力、燃气及水的生产和供应业	Production and Distribution of Electricity, Gas and Water	19408	7662	78	11668
建筑业	Construction	27876	8106	544	19226
交通运输、仓储和邮政业	Transport, Storage and Post	36133	26771	373	8989
信息传输、计算机服务和软件业	Information Transmission, Computer Servcie and Software Industries	7514	4046		3468
批发和零售业	Wholesale and Retail Trades	26151	8516	1788	15847
住宿和餐饮业	Hotels and Catering Services	12843	6823	604	5416
金融业	Financial Intermediation	38593	16347	3888	18358
房地产业	Real Estate	9800	2609	215	6976
租赁和商务服务业	Leasing and Business Services	18414	7889	1018	9507
科学研究、技术服务和地质勘查业	Scientific Research, Technology Service and Geological Prospecting	16235	14789	14	1432
水利、环境和公共设施管理业	Management of Water Conservancy, Environment and Public Facility	21843	20327		1516
居民服务和其他服务业	Services to households and Other Services	3852	2705	73	1074
教　育	Education	204188	202902	62	1224
卫生、社会保障和社会福利业	Health, Social Security and Social Welfare	91885	90304	1075	506
文化、体育和娱乐业	Culture, Sports and Entertainment	11644	11278	1	365
公共管理和社会组织	Public Management and Social Organizations	117947	117918	5	24

3-16 单位在岗职工工资总额及构成
Total Wages of Staff and Workers and Its Composition

年份 Year	地区 Region	工资总额（万元） Total wage Bill(10 000 yuan) 合计 Total	国有单位 State-owned Units	城镇集体单位 Urban Collective-owned Units	其他单位 Units of Other Types of Ownership	构成(总计=100)(%) composition (total=100)(%) 国有单位 State-owned Units	城镇集体单位 Urban Collective-owned Units	其他单位 Units of Other Types of ownership
	1978	159409	148278	11131		93.0	7.0	
	1980	212446	196711	15735		92.6	7.4	
	1985	339110	304999	33789	322	89.9	10.0	0.1
	1990	668808	601300	65858	1650	90.0	9.8	0.2
	1995	1677257	1521670	135990	19597	90.7	8.1	1.2
	2000	2344694	2007823	125510	211361	85.6	5.4	9.0
	2001	2677431	2092155	105861	479415	78.1	4.0	17.9
	2002	2915398	2211411	93605	610382	75.9	3.2	20.9
	2003	3315399	2497369	77460	740570	75.3	2.3	22.4
	2004	3563312	2691462	78224	793626	75.5	2.2	22.3
	2005	3874068	2871542	75971	926555	74.1	2.0	23.9
	2006	4429959	3318694	77978	1033287	74.9	1.8	23.3
	2007	5332395	3951882	82215	1298298	74.1	1.5	24.4
	2008	6198976	4428784	84187	1686005	71.4	1.4	27.2
	2009	6912058	4796811	91488	2023759	69.4	1.3	29.3
	2010	8286857	5669760	105413	2511684	68.4	1.3	30.3
乌鲁木齐市	Urumqi City	2113978	1341249	26595	746134	63.4	1.3	35.3
克拉玛依市	Karamay City	632192	188529	4168	439495	29.8	0.7	69.5
吐鲁番地区	Turpan Administrative Offices	269723	116302	2505	150916	43.1	0.9	56.0
哈密地区	Hami [Kumul] Administrative Offices	260785	171798	1304	87683	65.9	0.5	33.6
昌吉回族自治州	Changji Hui Autonomous Prefecture	660406	454727	15028	190651	68.8	2.3	28.9
伊犁哈萨克自治州	Ili Kazak Autonomous Prefecture	1495426	1213617	19870	261939	81.2	1.3	17.5
伊犁州直属县(市)	Counties (Cities) Direct Under Ili Prefecture	709634	527796	9671	172167	74.3	1.4	24.3
塔城地区	Tacheng [Tarbagatai] Administrative Offices	512321	461713	5868	44740	90.1	1.2	8.7
阿勒泰地区	Altay Administrative Offices	273471	224108	4331	45032	81.9	1.6	16.5
博尔塔拉蒙古自治州	Bortala Mongol Autonomous Prefecture	224261	200673	7548	16040	89.5	3.4	7.1
巴音郭楞蒙古自治州	Bayangol Mongol Autonomous Prefecture	575670	363882	8595	203193	63.2	1.5	35.3
阿克苏地区	Aksu Administrative Offices	515495	388714	6535	120246	75.4	1.3	23.3
克孜勒苏柯尔克孜自治州	Kizilsu Kirgiz Autonomous Prefecture	113158	110158	896	2104	97.3	0.8	1.9
喀什地区	Kashgar [Kaxgar] Administrative Offices	551953	464260	9041	78652	84.1	1.6	14.3
和田地区	Hotan Administrative Offices	277426	249903	1972	25551	90.1	0.7	9.2
石河子市	Shihezi City	363814	204159	1356	158299	56.1	0.4	43.5
阿拉尔市	Aral City	129459	118520		10939	91.5		8.5
图木舒克市	Tumxuk City	43692	38895		4797	89.0		11.0
五家渠市	Wujiaqu City	59419	44374		15045	74.7		25.3

3-17 主要年份在岗职工工资总额指数

Indices of Total Wages of Staff and Workers in Main Years

年 份 Year	指数(上年=100) Indices (preceding year=100)				指数(1978 年=100) Indices (1978=100)			
	合 计 Total	国 有 单 位 State-owned Units	城镇集体单 位 Urban Collective-owned Units	其 他 单 位 Units of Other Types of Ownership	合 计 Total	国 有 单 位 State-owned Units	城镇集体单 位 Urban Collective-owned Units	其 他 单 位 Units of Other Types of Ownership
1978	114.2	114.5	109.6		100.0	100.0	100.0	
1980	120.5	120.1	125.2		133.3	132.7	141.4	
1985	117.4	117.5	116.0	167.5	212.7	205.7	303.6	100.0
1990	116.6	116.3	126.9	132.6	419.6	405.5	591.7	513.4
1995	126.3	126.8	119.3	146.6	1052.2	1026.2	1221.7	6097.7
2000	110.7	108.1	91.4	171.0	1470.9	1354.1	1127.6	65762.7
2001	114.2	104.2	84.3	226.8	1679.6	1411.0	951.0	149164.7
2002	108.9	105.7	88.4	127.3	1828.9	1491.4	840.9	189913.4
2003	113.7	112.9	82.8	121.3	2079.8	1684.2	695.9	230420.0
2004	107.5	107.8	101.0	107.2	2235.3	1815.1	702.8	246927.8
2005	108.7	106.7	97.1	116.7	2430.3	1936.6	682.5	288287.3
2006	114.3	115.6	102.6	111.5	2779.0	2238.2	700.5	321896.3
2007	120.4	119.1	105.4	125.6	3345.1	2665.2	738.6	403198.1
2008	116.3	112.1	102.4	129.9	3888.7	2986.8	756.3	523604.0
2009	111.5	108.3	108.7	120.0	4336.1	3235.0	821.9	628496.6
2010	119.9	118.2	115.2	124.1	5198.5	3823.7	947.0	780026.1

注：2000 年起职工工资总额指数由在岗职工工资总额计算而得。
Note: The indices of total wages of staff workers fom the year 2000 are calculated on the basis of on-the-job staff.

3-18 主要年份在岗职工工资情况

Wages of Full-Employed Staff and Workers in Main Years

年 份 Year	在岗职工工资总额(万元) Total Wages of staff and workers (10 000 yuan)	国有单位 State-owned Units	城镇单位 Urban Collective-owned Units	其他单位 Units of Other Types of Ownership	在岗职工平均工资(元) Average Wage of Staff and Workers (yuan)	国有单位 State-owned Units	城镇单位 Urban Collective-owned Units	其他单位 Units of Other Types of Ownership
1999	2118609	1857722	137261	123626	7611	7614	6815	8681
2000	2344694	2007823	125510	211361	8717	8731	7489	9498
2001	2677431	2092155	105861	479415	10278	10145	8197	11594
2002	2915398	2211411	93605	610382	11605	11435	9353	12767
2003	3315399	2497369	77460	740570	13255	13199	9966	13937
2004	3563312	2691462	78224	793626	14484	14477	11594	14870
2005	3874068	2871542	75971	926555	15558	15364	12738	16503
2006	4429959	3318694	77978	1033287	17819	17704	14209	18566
2007	5332395	3951882	82215	1298298	21434	21369	17780	21921
2008	6198976	4428784	84187	1686005	24687	24016	22060	26815
2009	6912058	4796811	91488	2023759	27753	26872	22862	30409
2010	8286857	5669760	105413	2511684	32361	31390	31997	34807

3-19 主要年份在岗职工平均货币工资
Average Money Wage of Staff and Workers in Main Years

单位：元 (yuan)

年 份 Year	全部职工 Full Staff and Workers	国有单位 State-owned Units	城镇集体单位 Urban Collective-owned Units	其他单位 Units of Other Types of Ownership
1978	717	726	614	
1980	882	904	676	
1985	1277	1310	1038	1707
1990	2272	2345	1765	2498
1995	5348	5431	4509	5973
2000	8717	8731	7489	9498
2001	10278	10145	8197	11594
2002	11605	11435	9353	12767
2003	13255	13199	9966	13937
2004	14484	14477	11594	14870
2005	15558	15364	12738	16503
2006	17819	17704	14209	18566
2007	21434	21369	17780	21921
2008	24687	24016	22060	26815
2009	27753	26872	22862	30409
2010	32361	31390	31997	34807

3-20 主要年份在岗职工平均工资指数
Indices of Average Wage of Staff and Workers in Main Years

(上年=100) (preceding year=100)

年 份 Year	货币工资 Money Wage				实际工资 Real Wage			
	合 计 Total	国有单位 State-owned Units	城镇集体单位 Urban Collective-owned Units	其他单位 Units of Other Types of Ownership	合 计 Total	国有单位 State-owned Units	城镇集体单位 Urban Collective-owned Units	其他单位 Units of Other Types of Ownership
1978		105.2				103.9		
1980	114.5	115.3	108.3		109.3	110.0	103.4	
1985	115.7	116.0	112.5	124.6	105.9	106.0	102.7	113.7
1990	113.2	113.3	113.6	96.5	108.3	108.4	108.7	92.3
1995	125.8	125.7	125.8	120.9	105.7	105.6	105.7	101.6
2000	114.5	114.7	109.9	109.4	115.2	115.4	110.6	110.1
2001	117.9	116.2	109.5	122.1	113.4	111.7	105.3	117.4
2002	112.9	112.7	114.1	110.1	113.6	113.4	114.8	110.8
2003	114.2	115.4	106.6	109.2	113.6	114.8	106.1	108.7
2004	109.3	109.7	116.3	106.7	107.0	107.4	113.9	104.5
2005	107.4	106.1	109.9	111.0	106.7	105.4	109.1	110.2
2006	114.5	115.2	111.5	112.5	113.7	114.4	110.7	111.7
2007	120.3	120.7	125.1	118.1	114.0	114.4	118.6	111.9
2008	115.2	112.4	124.1	122.3	106.6	104.0	114.8	113.1
2009	112.4	111.9	103.6	113.4	111.6	111.1	102.9	112.6
2010	116.6	116.8	140.0	114.5	111.8	112.0	134.2	109.7

3-21 各地、州、市分行业单位在岗职工平均货币工资

Average Money Wage of Staff and Workers by Sector and by Prefecture, Autonomous Prefecture and City

单位：元 (2010 年) (yuan)

年 份 Year	地 区 Region	合 计 Total	农林牧渔业 Agriculture, Forestry, Animal Husbandry and Fishery	采矿业 Mining	制造业 Manufacturing	电力、燃气及水的生产和供应业 Production and Distribution of Power, Gas and Water
总 计	**Total**	**32361**	**20174**	**48338**	**31666**	**44435**
乌鲁木齐市	Urumqi City	41529	21219	57819	37505	59512
克拉玛依市	Karamay City	42767	23027	48968	43310	46020
吐鲁番地区	Turpan Administrative Offices	37757	16594	51732	26027	54791
哈密地区	Hami [Kumul] Administrative Offices	33040	22125	48263	25207	56748
昌吉回族自治州	Changji Hui Autonomous Prefecture	32196	26350	36727	27551	47426
伊犁哈萨克自治州	Ili Kazak Autonomous Prefecture	24935	16939	29000	25200	41030
伊犁州直属县(市)	Counties (Cities) Direct Under Ili Prefecture	26438	17147	30473	26337	43412
塔城地区	Tacheng [Tarbagatai] Administrative Offices	23583	18742	28932	22453	39302
阿勒泰地区	Altay Administrative Offices	23976	11763	28351	20760	36446
博尔塔拉蒙古自治州	Bortala Mongol Autonomous Prefecture	25157	18558	21624	18934	32416
巴音郭楞蒙古自治州	Bayangol Mongol Autonomous Prefecture	31468	19174	64727	30884	33521
阿克苏地区	Aksu Administrative Offices	28421	19453	38985	29759	38083
克孜勒苏柯尔克孜自治州	Kizilsu Kirgiz Autonomous Prefecture	30957	25883	4619	22219	29852
喀什地区	Kashgar [Kaxgar] Administrative Offices	31108	22735	19213	17377	48242
和田地区	Hotan Administrative Offices	31743	17228	23485	16797	36866
石河子市	Shihezi City	32221	34953		27639	31614
阿拉尔市	Aral City	30066	28066		18720	36985
图木舒克市	Tumxuk City	26746	23263		22457	22687
五家渠市	Wujiaqu City	27564	22199		27757	28747

年 份 Year	地 区 Region	建筑业 Construction	交通运输、仓储和邮政业 Transport, Storage and Post	信息传输、计算机服务和软件业 Information Transmission, Computer Servcie and Software	批发和零售业 Wholesale and Retail Trades	住宿和餐饮业 Hotels and Catering Services
总 计	**Total**	**29339**	**47070**	**43777**	**32726**	**21599**
乌鲁木齐市	Urumqi City	30972	31533	53191	40981	25737
克拉玛依市	Karamay City	41632	34350	44062	51886	25099
吐鲁番地区	Turpan Administrative Offices	22833	22879	40526	33229	11651
哈密地区	Hami [Kumul] Administrative Offices	21578	35064	48834	35082	21604
昌吉回族自治州	Changji Hui Autonomous Prefecture	27365	26218	36754	34354	18930
伊犁哈萨克自治州	Ili Kazak Autonomous Prefecture	24645	27093	35694	23859	18312
伊犁州直属县(市)	Counties (Cities) Direct Under Ili Prefecture	29997	23309	40774	22050	17071
塔城地区	Tacheng [Tarbagatai] Administrative Offices	16503	34916	34221	25681	15771
阿勒泰地区	Altay Administrative Offices	23406	31497	30289	32836	21380
博尔塔拉蒙古自治州	Bortala Mongol Autonomous Prefecture	21631	37537	41085	34264	19664
巴音郭楞蒙古自治州	Bayangol Mongol Autonomous Prefecture	31058	27439	35894	32954	21429
阿克苏地区	Aksu Administrative Offices	28930	25059	38641	21813	19997
克孜勒苏柯尔克孜自治州	Kizilsu Kirgiz Autonomous Prefecture	22141	28072	25055	16147	13848
喀什地区	Kashgar [Kaxgar] Administrative Offices	27701	24591	55464	21722	15390
和田地区	Hotan Administrative Offices	25831	29932	31625	24467	15894
石河子市	Shihezi City	27389	37542	51286	51380	17283
阿拉尔市	Aral City	31749	17821		40154	
图木舒克市	Tumxuk City	27000			42083	
五家渠市	Wujiaqu City	22197	30287	34432	24089	

3-21 续表 Continued

单位：元 (yuan)

年 份 Year	地 区 Region	金融业 Financial Intermedition	房地产业 Real Estate	租赁和商务服务业 Leasing and Business Services	科学研究、技术服务和地质勘查业 Scientific Research, Technology Service and Geological Prospecting	水利、环境和公共设施管理业 Management of Water Conservancy, Environment and Public Facility
总 计	**Total**	**59082**	**23288**	**22531**	**38696**	**26220**
乌鲁木齐市	Urumqi City	84541	30327	30039	43198	35458
克拉玛依市	Karamay City	67311	19824	24340	39709	20806
吐鲁番地区	Turpan Administrative Offices	43275	18711	19023	30878	18205
哈密地区	Hami [Kumul] Administrative Offices	54017	17722	19488	32452	17407
昌吉回族自治州	Changji Hui Autonomous Prefecture	68702	27201	17087	36299	29167
伊犁哈萨克自治州	Ili Kazak Autonomous Prefecture	52460	20618	18871	36685	23768
伊犁州直属县(市)	Counties (Cities) Direct Under Ili Prefecture	54553	20492	19012	35715	21143
塔城地区	Tacheng [Tarbagatai] Administrative Offices	47024	22473	18392	38086	27276
阿勒泰地区	Altay Administrative Offices	56238	19734	17781	37416	24137
博尔塔拉蒙古自治州	Bortala Mongol Autonomous Prefecture	66137	19924	9658	42738	24062
巴音郭楞蒙古自治州	Bayangol Mongol Autonomous Prefecture	46913	12602	20342	38627	22302
阿克苏地区	Aksu Administrative Offices	39121	19764	20510	36772	24291
克孜勒苏柯尔克孜自治州	Kizilsu Kirgiz Autonomous Prefecture	31824	21900	14043	29396	33246
喀什地区	Kashgar [Kaxgar] Administrative Offices	30991	18013	21488	28345	26820
和田地区	Hotan Administrative Offices	39186	11537	30865	37765	27558
石河子市	Shihezi City	42176	59817	32726	40893	33602
阿拉尔市	Aral City		34679	17890	40317	29907
图木舒克市	Tumxuk City			28736	21000	30068
五家渠市	Wujiaqu City	52260	36886	47992	39167	17106

年 份 Year	地 区 Region	居民服务和其他服务业 Services to households and Other Services	教 育 Education	卫生、社会保障和社会福利业 Health, Social Security and Social Welfare	文化、体育和娱乐业 Culture, Sports and Entertainment	公共管理和社会组织 Public Administration and Social Organizations
总 计	**Total**	**18453**	**35256**	**33381**	**33014**	**36753**
乌鲁木齐市	Urumqi City	41529	36224	37925	35265	44113
克拉玛依市	Karamay City	28306	39754	37548	60351	41667
吐鲁番地区	Turpan Administrative Offices	12944	33777	27672	27450	32622
哈密地区	Hami [Kumul] Administrative Offices	26301	36741	28909	27068	34253
昌吉回族自治州	Changji Hui Autonomous Prefecture	10000	41019	36297	39435	39629
伊犁哈萨克自治州	Ili Kazak Autonomous Prefecture	20175	32885	30141	30284	33303
伊犁州直属县(市)	Counties (Cities) Direct Under Ili Prefecture	21277	31751	28957	29372	31636
塔城地区	Tacheng [Tarbagatai] Administrative Offices	18281	32939	30056	29269	34588
阿勒泰地区	Altay Administrative Offices	19143	36767	34221	33004	35686
博尔塔拉蒙古自治州	Bortala Mongol Autonomous Prefecture	20204	37111	34008	36206	37777
巴音郭楞蒙古自治州	Bayangol Mongol Autonomous Prefecture	21106	36760	33612	32869	36885
阿克苏地区	Aksu Administrative Offices	24070	31578	28479	29144	31424
克孜勒苏柯尔克孜自治州	Kizilsu Kirgiz Autonomous Prefecture	15181	34781	35326	29258	33961
喀什地区	Kashgar [Kaxgar] Administrative Offices	32052	34842	29483	30217	36091
和田地区	Hotan Administrative Offices	29867	35487	34373	34248	37365
石河子市	Shihezi City	12490	43428	45707	35206	48188
阿拉尔市	Aral City	31429	41320	39321	33424	36390
图木舒克市	Tumxuk City		31282	24199		44616
五家渠市	Wujiaqu City	32000	32484	34276	40457	34382

3-22 各地、州、市、县(市)在岗职工平均货币工资
Average Money Wages of Fully Employed Staff and Workers by Prefecture, Autonomous Prefecture, City and County

单位：元 (2010 年) (yuan)

地区	Region	合计 Total	国有单位 State-owned Units	城镇集体单位 Urban Collective-owned Units	其他单位 Units of Other Types of Ownership
总　计	**Total**	**32361**	**31390**	**31997**	**34807**
乌鲁木齐市	**Urumqi City**	**41529**	**44927**	**30831**	**36961**
天山区	Tianshan District	43402	45084	30690	40307
沙依巴克区	Shayibak District	33761	35278	26269	32177
新市区	Xinshi District	38998	38213	44991	39577
水磨沟区	Shui Mogou District	33692	40284	16145	27504
头屯河区	Tou Tunhe District	33010	27016	31590	39013
达坂城区	Da Bancheng District	46146	38399	38049	48634
米东区	Midong District	43919	50622	31776	36530
乌鲁木齐县	Urumqi County	40794	40794		
克拉玛依市	**Karamay City**	**42767**	**41403**	**22850**	**43746**
独山子区	Dushanzi District	45333	41744	20202	47177
克拉玛依区	Karamay District	42732	42351	24175	43127
乌尔河区	Urhe District	40327	42055	23000	39779
白碱滩区	Bai Jiantan District	27777	22091	44340	64127
吐鲁番地区	**Turpan Administrative Offices**	**37757**	**31762**	**32037**	**44336**
吐鲁番市	Turpan City	30132	30761	30278	28562
鄯善县	Shanshan [Piqan] County	45517	32414	58458	51393
托克逊县	Toksun County	33243	33687	20125	33109
哈密地区	**Hami [Kumul] Administrative Offices**	**33040**	**30061**	**27393**	**41158**
哈密市	Hami [Kumul] City	34441	31095	20869	41260
巴里坤哈萨克自治县	Barkol Kazak Autonomous County	26460	26184	45573	33932
伊吾县	Yiwu [Araturuk] County	31021	31088	31350	17950
昌吉回族自治州	**Changji Hui Autonomous Prefecture**	**32196**	**32792**	**49745**	**30058**
昌吉市	Changji City	34653	38729	52631	29880
阜康市	Fukang City	31106	29931	53840	32314
呼图壁县	Hutubi County	26245	25872	107804	24635
玛纳斯县	Manas County	33119	32631	17302	38086

3-22 续表 1 Continued

单位：元 (yuan)

地　　区	Region	合　计 Total	国有单位 State-owned Units	城镇集体单位 Urban Collective-owned Units	其他单位 Units of Other Types of Ownership
奇台县	Qitai County	29455	30241	52990	25447
吉木萨尔县	Jimsar County	36189	36219	135703	17459
木垒哈萨克自治县	Mori Kazak Autonomous County	34513	36538	39658	19470
伊犁哈萨克自治州	**Ili Kazak Autonomous Prefecture**	**24935**	**24462**	**39060**	**26592**
伊犁州直属县(市)	**Counties (Cities) Direct Under Ili Prefecture**	**26438**	**25890**	**33615**	**27916**
伊宁市	Yining [Gulja] City	29155	28969	27536	29503
奎屯市	Kuytun City	30453	30754	13701	29376
伊宁县	Yining [Gulja] County	20799	20222	22619	23581
察布查尔锡伯自治县	Qapqal Xibe Autonomous County	25644	25526	33582	25578
霍城县	Huocheng [Korgas] County	22175	21922	25472	24732
巩留县	Gongliu [Tokkuztara] County	28426	28915	74738	
新源县	Xinyuan [Kunes] County	25426	24620	37484	26492
昭苏县	Zhaosu [Mongolkure] County	24747	24673	35475	23699
特克斯县	Tekes County	31907	31912	112578	26677
尼勒克县	Nilka County	28600	27066	58612	35470
塔城地区	**Tacheng [Tarbagatai] Administrative Offices**	**23583**	**23574**	**38682**	**22509**
塔城市	Tacheng [Qoqek] City	27444	26723	19609	32328
乌苏市	Usu City	19866	19293	40077	23650
额敏县	Emin [Dorbiljin] County	18181	17417	53748	25290
沙湾县	Shawan County	26785	28069	47041	11754
托里县	Toli County	32852	32897	50473	12125
裕民县	Yumin [Qagantokay] County	22230	22231	26390	18017
和布克赛尔蒙古自治县	Hoboksar Mongol Autonomous County	23751	22796	48981	29085
阿勒泰地区	**Altay Administrative Offices**	**23976**	**23245**	**62491**	**26560**
阿勒泰市	Altay City	25499	24859	118598	26828
布尔津县	Burqin County	24932	24499	29377	26410
富蕴县	Fuyun [Koktokay] County	18832	16363	48144	26342
福海县	Fuhai [Burultokay] County	21658	21944	42392	16869
哈巴河县	Habahe [Kaba] County	26892	26079	46451	28952

3-22 续表 2 Continued

单位：元 (yuan)

地　区	Region	合　计 Total	国　有 单　位 State-owned Units	城镇集体 单　位 Urban Collective-owned Units	其　他 单　位 Units of Other Types of Ownership
青河县	Qinghe [Qinggil] County	28000	26937	56764	35929
吉木乃县	Jeminay County	24325	24116	46000	24571
博尔塔拉蒙古自治州	**Bortala Mongol Autonomous Prefecture**	**25157**	**25172**	**27487**	**24030**
博乐市	Bole [Bortala] City	27396	27547	34142	25576
精河县	Jinghe [Jing] County	22944	22946	24938	20164
温泉县	Wenquan [Araxang] County	20015	19569	102371	20142
巴音郭楞蒙古自治州	**Bayangol Mongol Autonomous Prefecture**	**31468**	**28346**	**36512**	**38916**
库尔勒市	Korla City	34628	30458	21196	40085
轮台县	Luntai [Bugur] County	31588	30166	99194	38481
尉犁县	Yuli [Lopnur] County	27304	27603	30303	12133
若羌县	Ruoqiang [Qarkilik] County	33859	29755	74256	40181
且末县	Qiemo [Qarqan] County	30229	29936	49777	19349
焉耆回族自治县	Yanji Hui Autonomous County	29237	27976	83075	34967
和静县	Hejing County	25456	25271	22179	27847
和硕县	Hoxud County	22698	22425	67963	19789
博湖县	Bohu [Bagrax] County	25252	25019	64797	19361
阿克苏地区	**Aksu Administrative Offices**	**28421**	**28113**	**31510**	**29302**
阿克苏市	Aksu City	30716	30388	36213	31627
温宿县	Wensu [Onsu] County	19813	19338	25763	25453
库车县	Kuqa County	33226	32837	31860	34010
沙雅县	Xayar County	23686	27334	18843	16565
新和县	Xinhe [Toksu] County	29878	31055	71329	22609
拜城县	Baicheng [Bay] County	31588	29342	49982	34736
乌什县	Wushi [Uxturpan] County	29403	29757	28076	24631
阿瓦提县	Awat County	26775	29459	15626	18173
柯坪县	Kalpin County	26320	26434	16558	
克孜勒苏柯尔克孜自治州	**Kizilsu Kirgiz Autonomous Prefecture**	**30957**	**31442**	**19699**	**19793**
阿图什市	Artux City	28473	29044	14081	21094
阿克陶县	Akto County	35594	36250	24241	8648

3-22 续表 3 Continued

单位：元 (yuan)

地　区	Region	合计 Total	国有单位 State-owned Units	城镇集体单位 Urban Collective-owned Units	其他单位 Units of Other Types of Ownership
阿合奇县	Akqi County	34485	34580	23038	
乌恰县	Wuqia [Ulugqat] County	30671	30699	27750	15571
喀什地区	**Kashgar [Kaxgar] Administrative Offices**	**31108**	**32029**	**19215**	**28318**
喀什市	Kashgar [Kaxgar] City	31895	33542	16392	30135
疏附县	Shufu County	33980	34666	26183	13198
疏勒县	Shule County	27731	29045	22653	17015
英吉沙县	Yengisar County	28785	29067	29539	22151
泽普县	Zepu [Poskam] County	28796	30799	17907	8333
莎车县	Shache [Yarkant] County	33658	34693	17837	13559
叶城县	Yecheng [Kagilik] County	33077	35290	14431	21974
麦盖提县	Makit County	25147	25261	22338	23762
岳普湖县	Yopurga County	32522	32583	28806	
伽师县	Jiashi [Payzawat] County	29512	29714	21538	18788
巴楚县	Bachu [Maralbexi] County	30265	30894	20090	19366
塔什库尔干塔吉克自治县	Taxkorgan Tajik Autonomous County	48317	48317		
和田地区	**Hotan Administrative Offices**	**31743**	**32503**	**31492**	**25846**
和田市	Hotan City	34701	36523	30838	28313
和田县	Hotan County	38237	38667		23168
墨玉县	Moyu [Karakax] County	26060	26274	28936	21198
皮山县	Pishan [Guma] County	27950	28260	37029	22904
洛浦县	Lop County	28724	30435	33478	19045
策勒县	Qira County	34647	35875	31711	25032
于田县	Yutian [Keriya] County	36304	36765		27746
民丰县	Minfeng [Niya] County	36689	36886	24200	36878
自治区直辖县级市	**Municpality Country-LevelCity Directly under the Central Government**	**30763**	**31143**	**80254**	**29849**
石河子市	Shihezi City	32221	34032	80254	30008
阿拉尔市	Aral City	30066	30145		29234
图木舒克市	Tumxuk City	26746	26747		26740
五家渠市	Wujiaqu City	27564	26894		29750

主要统计指标解释

人口数　指一定时点、一定地区范围内的有生命的个人的总和。

年度统计的年末人口数指每年12月31日24时的人口数。

市、镇、县人口　其定义有两种口径：

第一种口径(按行政建制)

市人口：市管辖区域内的全部人口(含市辖镇，不含市辖区县)；

镇人口：县辖镇的全部人口(不含市辖镇)；

县人口：县辖乡人口。

第二种口径(按常住人口划分)

市人口：设区的市的区人口和不设区的市所辖的街道人口；

镇人口：不设区的市所辖镇的居民委员会人口和县辖镇的居民委员会人口；

县人口：除上述两种人口以外的全部人口。

出生率(又称粗出生率)　指在一定时期内(通常为一年)平均每千人所出生的人数的比率，一般用千分率表示。计算公式为：

出生率＝年出生人数／年平均人数×1000‰

式中：出生人数指活产婴儿，即胎儿脱离母体时(不管怀孕月数)，有过呼吸或其他生命现象。年平均人数指年初、年底人口数的平均数，也可用年中人口数代替。

死亡率(又称粗死亡率)　指在一定时期内(通常为一年)一定地区的死亡人数与同期平均人数(或期中人数)之比，一般用千分率表示。计算公式为：

死亡率＝年死亡人数／年平均人数×1000‰

人口自然增长率　指在一定时期内(通常为一年)人口自然增加数(出生人数减死亡人数)与该时期内平均人数(或期中人数)之比，一般用千分率表示。计算公式为：

人口自然增长率＝(本年出生人数－本年死亡人数)／年平均人数×1000‰＝人口出生率－人口死亡率

经济活动人口　指在16岁以上，有劳动能力，参加或要求参加社会经济活动的人口；包括就业人员和失业人员。

就业人口　指16周岁及以上从事一定的社会劳动并取得劳动报酬或经营收入的人员。这一指标反应了一定时期内全部劳动力资源的实际利用情况，是研究我国基本国情国力的重要指标。

单位就业人员　指在各级国家机关、政党机关、社会团体及企业、事业单位中工作，取得工资或其他形式的劳动报酬的全部人员。包括在岗职工、再就业的离退休人员、民办教师以及在各单位中工作的外方人员和港澳台方人员、兼职人员、借用的外单位人员和第二职业者。不包括离开本单位仍保留劳动关系的职工。各单位的从业人员反映了各单位实际参加生产或工作的全部劳动力。

国有单位　指资产归国家所有的经济组织。包括按《中华人民共和国企业法人登记管理条例》规定登记注册的非公司制的经济组织，以及中央、地方各级国家机关、事业单位和社会团体。

集体单位　指生产资料归集体所有，并按《中华人民共和国企业法人登记管理条例》规定登记注册的经济组织。

其他单位　包括股份合作单位、联营单位、有限责任公司、股份有限公司、港澳台商投资单位以及外商投资单位等其他登记注册类型单位。

城镇私营和个体就业人员　城镇私营就业人员指在工商管理部门注册登记，其经营地址设在县城关镇(含城关镇)以上的私营企业从业人员；包括私营企业投资者和雇工。城镇个体就业人员指在工商管理部门注册登记，并持有城镇户口或在城镇长期居住，经批准从事个体工商经营的从业人员；包括个体经营者和在个体工商户劳动的家庭帮工和雇工。

在岗职工　指在本单位工作并由单位支付工资的人员，以及有工作岗位，但由于学习、病伤产假等原因暂未工作，仍由单位支付工资的人员。

工资总额　指各单位在一定时期内直接支付给本单位全部职工的劳动报酬总额。工资总额的计算原则应以直接支付给职工的全部劳动报酬为根据。各单位支付给职工的劳动报酬以及其他根据有关规定支付的工资，不论是计入成本的还是不计入成本的，不论是按国家规定列入计征奖金税项目的，还是未列入计征奖金税项目的，不论是以货币形式支付的还是以实物形式支付的，均包括在工资总额内。

平均工资　指企业、事业、机关单位的职工在一定时期内平均每人所得的货币工资额。它表明一定时期职工工资收入的高低程度，是反映职工工资水平的主要指标。计算公式为：

平均工资＝报告期实际支付的全部职工工资总额／报告期全部职工平均人数

平均工资指数　指报告期职工平均工资与基期职工平均工资的比率，是反映不同时期职工货币工资水平变动情况的相对数。计算公式为：

平均工资指数＝报告期职工平均工资／基期职工平均工资

平均实际工资指数　职工平均实际工资指扣除物价变动因素后的职工平均工资。职工平均实际工资指数是反映实际工资变动情况的相对数，表明职工实际工资水平提高或降低的程度。计算公式为：

平均实际工资指数＝报告期职工平均工资指数／报告期城镇居民消费价格指数×100%

城镇登记失业人员　指有非农业户口，在一定的劳动年龄内（16周岁至退休年龄），有劳动能力，无业而要求就业，并在当地就业服务机构进行求职登记的人员。

城镇登记失业率　指城镇登记失业人数同城镇单位就业人数（扣除使用的农村劳动力、聘用的离退休人员、港澳台及外方人员）、城镇单位中不在岗职工、城镇私营业主、个体户主、城镇私营企业和个体就业人员与城镇登记失业人数之和的比。计算公式为：

城镇登记失业率=城镇登记失业人数／{(城镇就业从业人数-使用的农村劳动力-聘用的离退休人员-港澳台及外方人员)+ 不在岗职工+城镇私营业主+个体户主+城镇私营企业和个体就业人员+城镇登记失业人数)}×100%

Explanatory Notes on Main Statistical Indicators

Total Population refers to the total number of people alive at a certain point of time within a given area.

The annual statistics on total population is taken at midnight, the 3lst of December.

City,Town and County Population Urban Population and Rural Population.

There are two definitions.The first definition (according to the administrative organizational system):

City Population Total population under the jurisdiction of City (including population of the town under the jurisdiction of City. excluding the population of counties under the jurisdiction of City).

Town Population Total population of town under the jurisdiction of County (excluding the population of town under the jurisdiction of City).

County Population Total population of country under the jurisdiction of County).

The second definition (classified by the permanent population):

City Population Total population of districts under the jurisdiction of City with district establishment and the population of street under the jurisdiction of City without district establishment.

Town Population Total resident-committees population of towns under the jurisdiction of City without district establishment and the resident-committees population of towns under the jurisdiction of County.

County Population Total population except City population and town population.

Birth Rate(or Crude Birth Rate) refers to the ratio of the number of births to the average population during a certain period of time(usually a year) which is often expressed in‰. The following formula is used:

Brith Rate= Number of Births/Annual Average Number of Population

Number of births refers to live births i.e. the births when babies had showed any vital phenomena regardless of the length of pregnancy.

Annual average number of population is the average of the number of population at the beginning of the year and that at the end of the year. Sometimes it is substituted for with the mid year population.

Death Rate(or Crude Death Rate) refers to the ratio of the number of deaths to the average population (or mid year population) during a certain period of time (usually a year) which is often expressed in‰. The following formula is used:

Death Rate =Number of Deaths/ Annual Average Number of Population

Natural Growth Rate of Population refers to the ratio of natural increase in population(number of births minus number of deaths)in a certain period of time(usually a year)to the average population(or mid year population)of the same period which is often expressed in‰. The following formula is applied:

Natural Growth Rate of Population= Number of Births-Number of Deaths / Average Number of Population

Natural Growth Rate of Population=Birth Rate-Death Rate

Economically Active Population refers to the population aged 16 and over who are capable to work, are participating in or willing to participate in economic activities, including employed persons and unemployed persons.

Employed Population refers to population aged 15 or over engaging in social labour which generates income.

Persons Employed in Various Units refer to all the persons working in government agencies of various levels, political and party organizations, social organizations, enterprises and institutions, and receiving wages or other forms of payment. They include fully-employed staff and workers, re-employed retirees, teachers in schools run by the local people, foreigners and Chinese compatriots from Hong Kong, Macao, and Taiwan working in various units, part-time employees, employees of other units working temporarily at current posts, and employees holding the second job, but exclude staff and workers who have left their working units while keeping their labour contract (employment relation) unchanged. This indicator reflects the total number of laborers actually engaged in production or other operations in various units.

State-owned Units refer to economic units whose assets are owned by the state.Included are non-corporation units registered according to Regulation of the People's Republic of China on the Registration of Enterprises and Corporation ,state argans,institutions and social organizations at the central and local levels.

Collective-owned Units refer to economic units registered according to Regulation of the People's Republic of China on the Registration of Enterprises and Corporations where the means of production are collectively owned.

Units of Other Types of Ownership refer to units registered with other types of ownership,including cooperative units,joint ownership units,limited companies,share holding corporation,units invested by entrepreneurs from Hong Kong,

Macao,and Taiwan,and foreign-invested units.

Persons Employed in Private Enterprises and Self-Employed Individuals in Urban Areas Persons employed in private enterprises refer to the persons employed in the private enterprises which have been registered at the departments of industrial and commercial administration and are situated at a County town (i.e. a town where the County government is located) for business operation or at urban areas with the level higher than a County town. The self-employed individuals in urban areas refer to persons who hold the certificates of residence in urban areas or have resided in the urban areas for a long time and have been registered at the departments of industrial and commercial administration and approved to be engaged in individual industrial or commercial business, including self-employed persons as well as helpers and hired labourers who work in the individual households engaged in industrial or commercial business.

Staff and Workers refer to the persons who work in(and receive payment therefrom)enterprises and institutions of state ownership, collective ownership, joint ownership, share holding, foreign ownership, and ownership by entrepreneurs from Hong Kong, Macao, and Taiwan, and other types of ownership and their affiliated units, excluding the retired persons invited to work in the units again, teachers in the schools run by the local people and foreigners and persons coming from Hong Kong, Macao and Taiwan and working in the state-owned economic units. (Number of staff and workers in this yearbook include only fully employed staff and workers, excluding those who have left their working units while keeping their labour contract/employment relation unchanged).

Total Wages refer to the total remuneration payment to staff and workers in various units during a certain period of time. The calculation of total wages is based on the total remuneration payment to the staff and workers. Therefore, all the wages and salaries and other payments to staff and workers are included in the total wages regardless of their sources, category, and forms (in kind or cash). (Total wages of staff and workers in this yearbook include only total wages of fully employed staff and workers, excluding the living allowances distributed to those who have left their working units while keeping their labour contract/employment relation unchanged).

Average Wage refers to the average wage in money terms per person during a certain period of time for staff and workers in enterprises, institutions, and government agencies, which reflects the general level of wage income during a certain period of time and is calculated as follows:

Average Wage of Staff and Workers =Total Wages of Staff and Workers in Reference Period/Average Number of Staff and Workers in Reference Period

Index of Average Wage refers to the ratio of average wage of staff and workers at the report time to that at the reference time. It reflects the relative changing degree of average wage in money terms at the various of time, which is calculated as following:

Index of Average Wage of Staff and Worker = average wage of staff and workers at the report time/average wage of staff and workers at the reference time

Index of Average Real Wage refers to the average wage which has removed the factor of price change. Index of average real wage of staff and worker reflects the relative changing degree of average real wage, and indicates the degree of the rising or declining degree of real wage of staff and worker, which is calculated as following:

Index of Average Real Wage of Staff and Worker = Index of Average Wage of Staff and Worker at the Report Time/Urban Consumer Prices Index at the Report Time

Registered Unemployed Persons in Urban Areas refer to the persons with non-agricultural household registration at certain working ages (16 years old to retirement age), who are capable of working, unemployed and willing to work, and have been registered at the local employment service agencies to apply for a job.

Registered Unemployment Rate in Urban Areas refers to the ratio of the number of the registered unemployed persons to the sum of the number of persons employed in various units (minus the employed rural labour force, re-employed retirees, and Hong Kong, Macao, Taiwan or foreign employees), laid-off staff and workers in urban units, owners of private enterprises in urban areas, owners of self-employed individuals in urban areas, employees of private enterprises in urban areas, employyee of self-employed individuals in urban areas, and the registered unemployed persons in urban areas. The formula is as follows:

$$\text{Registered unemployment rate in urban areas} = \frac{\text{number of registered urban unemployed persons}}{\begin{array}{c}\text{number of persons employed in urban units - employed rural labour force}\\ \text{re - employed retirees - Hong Kong, Macao, Taiwan or foreign employees}\\ \text{+ laid - off staff and workers + owners of urban private enterprises + owners of}\\ \text{urban self - employed individuals + employees of urban private enterprises + employees of}\\ \text{urban self - employed individuals + registered unemployed persons in urban areas}\end{array}} \times 100\%$$

第四篇
固定资产投资

CHAPTER 4
Investment in Fixed Assets

简要说明
Brief Introduction

本篇资料的主要内容及来源

本篇资料包括主要年份全社会固定资产投资及其主要分组;2010 年及同期的全区固定资产投资及其细化分组;2010 年自治区新增主要产品生产能力(或效益);房地产开发企业基本情况;农村非农户及农户固定资产投资情况。

农村固定资产投资来自国家统计局新疆调查总队商业和投资建筑业调查处;其余资料均来自新疆维吾尔自治区统计局固定资产投资统计处。

本篇的统计调查方法除农户固定资产投资统计采用抽样调查方法外,其他均为全面调查。

Main content and sources of data

Statistics in this chapter cover the total investment in fixed assets of the whole society and its composition, total investment in fixed assets and its refining grouping by region in 2010; newly increased production capacity of major production in 2010; basic condition of enterprises for real estate development, basic condition of individual investment in fixed assets of farm households and non–farm households.

The data of individual investment in fixed assets in rural areas come from the Trade and Fixed Assets and Construction Census Division of NBS Survey Office in Xinjiang; Others data come from the Division of Investment in Fixed Assets, Xinjiang Bureau of Statistics.

Method of data collection: All data on the investment in fixed assets are collected by the statistical reporting system with complete enumeration, except data on the investment in fixed assets in rural areas which are collected through sample surveys.

4-1 1978-2010 年历年全社会固定资产投资

Total Investment in Fixed Assets in the Whole Country by Period(1978-2009)

单位：万元 (10 000 yuan)

年 份 Year	合 计 Total	城 镇 Urban Area	#房地产 Real Estate Development	农 村 Rural Area	非农户 Non-Farm Households	农村个人 Farm Individuals
1978	129999	129999				
1979	138253	138253				
1980	204652	203489		1163		1163
1981	183986	171706		12280	10000	2280
1982	247382	233668		13714	9693	4021
1983	277923	262027		15896	8804	7092
1984	337250	305713		31537	11089	20448
1985	444758	408435		36323	11528	24795
1986	484658	443631		41027	13934	27093
1987	512479	469898		42581	14714	27867
1988	684119	622041		62078	16848	45230
1989	750698	664243		86455	18841	67614
1990	887775	791555	9456	96220	20578	75642
1991	1249325	1130155	16886	119170	26946	92224
1992	1700326	1571456	23941	128870	33202	95668
1993	2484352	2336810	53616	147542	40738	106804
1994	2854786	2614211	86244	240575	70349	170226
1995	3333404	3035386	171238	298018	92118	205900
1996	3878472	3495942	156232	382530	111936	270594
1997	4468148	3987127	169906	481021	131063	349958
1998	5197673	4709794	148577	487879	136402	351477
1999	5346468	4847597	234481	498871	150744	348127
2000	6103843	5568492	574347	535351	171862	363489
2001	7059970	6469753	979184	590217	210040	380177
2002	8130223	7474024	877060	656199	252891	403308
2003	10021256	9213289	1024908	807967	327137	480830
2004	11615245	10608048	1125577	1007197	463358	543839
2005	13522757	12232255	1016618	1290502	573585	716917
2006	15670521	14180110	1208786	1490411	699084	791327
2007	18508415	16591894	1683160	1916521	1080611	835910
2008	22599746	20256393	2286267	2343353	1412796	930557
2009	28272359	25358648	2358805	2913711	1874325	1039386
2010	35396941	31815829	3477185	3581112	2395698	1185414

4-2 全社会固定资产投资
Total Investment in Fixed Assets in the Whole Country

单位：万元 (2010 年) (10 000 yuan)

项 目	Item	合 计 Total	城 镇 Urban	#房地产 Real Estate Development
投资总额	**Total Investment**	**35396941**	**31815829**	**3477185**
#住 宅	Residential Buildings	5612891	4819395	2815620
#国有经济控股	State-holding	22910921	21269697	473427
按构成分	**Grouped by Use of Funds**			
建筑工程	Construction	22224487	20018924	2742491
安装工程	Installation	1943535	1859044	161703
设备工器具购置	Purchase of Equipment and Instruments	7960420	6990194	51777
其他费用	Other Expenses	3268499	2947667	521214
按三次产业分	**Grouped by Three Strata of Industry**			
第一产业	Primary Industry	2114275	992872	
第二产业	Secondary Industry	16670631	15834532	
第三产业	Tertiary Industry	16612035	14988425	3477185
按登记注册类型分	**Grouped by Types of Registration**			
内 资	Domestic Fund	35020686	31444072	3469759
国 有	State-owned	15378029	13840464	116115
集 体	Collective-owned	108054	82057	80
股份合作	Share-holding Cooperative	41713	41713	30
国有联营	State Joint Ownership	26550	26550	
其他联营	Others	3210	508	
国有独资公司	State-funded Corporations	926996	911393	91575
其他有限责任公司	Other Limited Liability Corporations	6430202	6080241	1231596
股份有限公司	Share-holding Corporations Ltd	5855892	5816666	50628
私营个体	Private	5829306	4299712	1976399
#个体户	Self-employed Individual	214332	144170	
个体合伙	Individual Partenership	10657	3469	
其 他	Others	420734	344768	3336
港澳台商投资	Enterprises With Funds from Hong Kong, Macao and Taiwan	162998	161600	7426
外商投资	Foreign Funded	213257	210157	
按隶属关系分	**By Administrative Relationship**			
中 央	Central Government	11085399	10517562	175564
地 方	Local	24311542	21298267	3301621
资金来源小计	**All Sources**	**37844438**	**34221886**	**5380739**
国家预算内资金	State Budget Funds	6347565	5567658	
国内贷款	Domestic Loans	5750361	5407269	684191
债 券	Bonds	11544	11544	
利用外资	Foreign Investment	120367	119073	
自筹资金	Self-raising Funds	19771509	17577945	1397982
其他资金来源	Others	5843092	5538397	3298566
本年新增固定资产	**Newly Increased Fixed Assets**	**20069081**	**16842817**	**1800214**
房屋施工面积(万平方米)	**Floor Space of Buildings (10 000 sq.m)**	**11361.96**	**9380.96**	**3980.80**
#住 宅	Residential Buildings	7640.58	6035.02	3317.68
房屋竣工面积(万平方米)	**Floor Space of Buildings Completed (10 000 sq.m)**	**4649.89**	**3160.74**	**1012.90**
#住 宅	Residential Buildings	3291.89	2028.26	859.92

4-2 续表 Continued

单位：万元 (10 000 yuan)

项 目	Item	农 村 Rural	非农户 Non-Rural Households	农村个人 Rural Individuals
投资总额	**Total Investment**	**3581112**	**2395698**	**1185414**
#住 宅	Residential Buildings	793496	326715	466781
#国有经济控股	State-holding	1641224	1641224	
按构成分	**Grouped by Use of Funds**			
建筑工程	Construction	2205563	1680923	524640
安装工程	Installation	84491	84491	
设备工器具购置	Purchase of Equipment and Instruments	970226	441866	528360
其他费用	Other Expenses	320832	188418	132414
按三次产业分	**Grouped by Three Strata of Industry**			
第一产业	Primary Industry	1121403	625516	495887
第二产业	Secondary Industry	836099	748335	87764
第三产业	Tertiary Industry	1623610	1021847	601763
按登记注册类型分	**Grouped by Types of Registration**			
内 资	Domestic Fund	3576614	2391200	1185414
国 有	State-owned	1537565	1537565	
集 体	Collective-owned	25997	25997	
其他联营	Others	2702	2702	
国有独资公司	State-funded Corporations	15603	15603	
其他有限责任公司	Other Limited Liability Corporations	349961	349961	
股份有限公司	Share-holding Corporations Ltd	39226	39226	
私营个体	Private	1529594	344180	1185414
#个体户	Self-employed Individual	70162	70162	
个体合伙	Individual Partenership	7188	7188	
其 他	Others	75966	75966	
港澳台商投资	Enterprises With Funds from Hong Kong, Macao and Taiwan	1398	1398	
外商投资	Foreign Funded Enterprises	3100	3100	
按隶属关系分	**By Administrative Relationship**			
中 央	Central Government	567837	567837	
地 方	Local	3013275	1827861	1185414
资金来源小计	**All Sources**	**3622552**	**2437138**	**1185414**
国家预算内资金	State Budget Funds	779907	779907	
国内贷款	Domestic Loans	343092	140959	202133
债 券	Bonds			
利用外资	Foreign Investment	1294	1294	
自筹资金	Self-raising Funds	2193564	1246453	947111
其他资金来源	Others	304695	268525	36170
本年新增固定资产	**Newly Increased Fixed Assets**	**3226264**	**2040850**	**1185414**
房屋施工面积(万平方米)	**Floor Space of Buildings (10 000 sq.m)**	**1981.00**	**856.62**	**1124.38**
#住 宅	Residential Buildings	1605.56	526.44	1079.12
房屋竣工面积(万平方米)	**Floor Space of Buildings Completed (10 000 sq.m)**	**1489.15**	**450.52**	**1038.63**
#住 宅	Residential Buildings	1263.63	269.21	994.42

4-3 按构成分全社会固定资产投资

Structure of Total Investment in Fixed Assets in the whole Country

单位：万元 (10 000 yuan)

年份 Year	地区 Region	合计 Total	建筑工程 Construction Works	安装工程 Installation Works	设备工具器具购置 Purchase of Equipment and Instruments	其他费用 Others
1978		129999	86667		35686	7646
1985		444758	323395		93254	28109
1990		887775	571461		274647	41667
1995		3333404	2145762		810995	376647
1996		3878472	2245924	278445	929463	424640
1997		4468148	2725428	310687	988070	443963
1998		5197673	3435120	278895	920992	562666
1999		5346468	3245779	344130	1039617	716942
2000		6103843	3833328	416759	1254077	599679
2001		7059970	4232768	454765	1616907	755530
2002		8130223	4815707	593242	1787899	933375
2003		10021256	6075091	690459	2030335	1225371
2004		11615245	7133323	806705	2304931	1370286
2005		13522757	8499303	993311	2637777	1392366
2006		15670521	9776613	1014851	3166617	1712440
2007		18508415	10667717	1517359	4312525	2010814
2008		22599746	13071829	1773200	5488261	2266456
2009		28272359	17511739	1938944	5855684	2965992
2010		35396941	22224487	1943535	7960420	3268499
乌鲁木齐市	Urumqi City	5478633	3110042	398945	1361660	607986
克拉玛依市	Karamay City	1810368	1413097	191231	116401	89639
吐鲁番地区	Turpan Administrative Offices	923933	499540	78630	204558	141205
哈密地区	Hami [Kumul] Administrative Offices	1564777	751523	117204	540451	155599
昌吉回族自治州	Changji Hui Autonomous Prefecture	2646599	1510326	110941	797221	228111
伊犁哈萨克自治州	Ili Kazak Autonomous Prefecture	5535821	3443204	284089	1258662	549866
伊犁州直属县(市)	Counties (Cities) Direct Under Ili Prefecture	2798952	1778577	177750	594235	248390
塔城地区	Tacheng [Tarbagatai] Administrative Offices	1588108	1029370	58713	388930	111095
阿勒泰地区	Altay Administrative Offices	1148761	635257	47626	275497	190381
博尔塔拉蒙古自治州	Bortala Mongol Autonomous Prefecture	664152	364226	50617	198765	50544
巴音郭楞蒙古自治州	Bayangol Mongol Autonomous Prefecture	3159785	2140498	189759	586971	242557
阿克苏地区	Aksu Administrative Offices	1618337	864144	126255	523030	104908
克孜勒苏柯尔克孜自治州	Kizilsu Kirgiz Autonomous Prefecture	314130	263748	5270	24895	20217
喀什地区	Kashgar [Kaxgar] Administrative Offices	2781169	2113442	135764	346073	185890
和田地区	Hotan Administrative Offices	820779	665279	36214	47484	71802
石河子市	Shihezi City	994023	366404	69396	472120	86103
阿拉尔市	Aral City	300553	189462	18968	73654	18469
图木舒克市	Tumxuk City	125303	69283	8522	35081	12417
五家渠市	Wujiaqu City	755475	342564	59869	318622	34420
跨地区投资	Trans-regional Investment	4717690	3593065	61861	526412	536352

注：各地区投资中不包括农村个人投资。
Note: Investment classified in different regions does not include rural individual investment.

4-4 全社会固定资产投资资金来源情况

Sources of Funds for Total Investment in Fixed Assets in the Whole Country

单位：万元 (10 000 yuan)

年份 Year	地区 Region	合计 Total	国家预算内资金 State Budget	国内贷款 Domestic Loans	债券 Bonds	利用外资 Foreign Investment	自筹及其他资金 Self-raising Fund And Others
1978		129999	102693				27306
1985		444758	117439	72227		7708	247384
1990		887775	105423	294985		40927	446440
1995		3333404	98004	818914		307619	2108867
1996		3878472	128725	756412		324532	2668803
1997		4468148	269106	749345		109629	3340068
1998		5197673	384195	1116497		133936	3563045
1999		5346468	512364	1097949	12376	93895	3629884
2000		6103843	506867	1346175	19429	99942	4131430
2001		7059970	545176	1321317	8340	64834	5120303
2002		8130223	1323660	1607535	30504	62992	5105532
2003		10021256	1626261	1896104	21586	95287	6382018
2004		11490824	1799593	1555105	46095	87388	8002643
2005		13543432	2093022	1677020	15428	109968	9647994
2006		15773966	2119253	1854512	8193	88675	11703333
2007		19070184	2258779	2480410	5526	110034	14215435
2008		22725814	3388141	3020001	3410	90233	16224029
2009		30345365	5813486	5246186	54636	94000	19137057
2010		37844438	6347565	5750361	11544	120367	25614601
乌鲁木齐市	Urumqi City	6900569	208352	1553494		2635	5136088
克拉玛依市	Karamay City	1934056	313716	50558			1569782
吐鲁番地区	Turpan Administrative Offices	943186	60021	349994	301	14496	518374
哈密地区	Hami [Kumul] Administrative Offices	1492069	162971	252282	281	2100	1074435
昌吉回族自治州	Changji Hui Autonomous Prefecture	2988210	465991	312720		11848	2197651
伊犁哈萨克自治州	Ili Kazak Autonomous Prefecture	6020137	906849	643955	3230	35520	4430583
伊犁州直属县(市)	Counties (Cities) Direct Under Ili Prefecture	3018184	433536	357051	2351	7990	2217256
塔城地区	Tacheng [Tarbagatai] Administrative Offices	1878818	287534	79415		23375	1488494
阿勒泰地区	Altay Administrative Offices	1123135	185779	207489	879	4155	724833
博尔塔拉蒙古自治州	Bortala Mongol Autonomous Prefecture	679162	192445	48579		7537	430601
巴音郭楞蒙古自治州	Bayangol Mongol Autonomous Prefecture	3102994	259753	171275	3934		2668032
阿克苏地区	Aksu Administrative Offices	1816968	292560	180991	3569	300	1339548
克孜勒苏柯尔克孜自治州	Kizilsu Kirgiz Autonomous Prefecture	318417	115193	55970		5750	141504
喀什地区	Kashgar [Kaxgar] Administrative Offices	3017657	1106341	22930	229	238	1887919
和田地区	Hotan Administrative Offices	843432	385677	4495			453260
石河子市	Shihezi City	1023823	30840	453368		3933	535682
阿拉尔市	Aral City	309367	37097	7645		1729	262896
图木舒克市	Tumxuk City	123916	45381	13449		1120	63966
五家渠市	Wujiaqu City	747052	20976	22669			703407
跨地区投资	Trans-regional Investment	4398009	1743402	1403854		33161	1217592

注：1.自 2004 年起资金来源为本年实际到位资金。2.各地区资金来源中不包括农村个人资金。

Note: a) Sources of capital caculated on actual arrived investment from 2004. b) Sources of Capital from different regions excludes rural individdual fund.

4-5 按行业分全社会固定资产投资

Total Investment in Fixed Assets in the Whole Country by Sector

单位：万元 (10 000 yuan)

行 业	Sector	2009	2010
总 计	**Total**	**28272359**	**35396941**
农、林、牧、渔业	**Agriculture, Forestry, Animal Husbandry and Fishery**	**1722559**	**2114275**
农 业	Agriculture	278112	450471
林 业	Forestry	180975	151687
畜牧业	Animal Husbandry	152025	189623
渔 业	Fishing	1097	1007
农、林、牧、渔服务业	Services in Support of Agriculture	669881	825600
采矿业	**Mining**	**5092564**	**6103290**
#煤炭开采和洗选业	Mining and Washing of Coal	1108500	1457434
石油和天然气开采业	Extraction of Petroleum and Natural Gas	3250115	3898628
#天然原油和天然气开采	Extraction of Ores Crude Oil and Natural Gas Extraction	3080244	3814989
黑色金属矿采选业	Mining and Processing of Ferrous Metals Ores	286816	289312
#铁矿采选	Mining and Processing of Iron Ore	261466	240194
有色金属矿采选业	Mining and Processing of Non-ferrous Metals Ores	335513	345735
#常用有色金属矿采选	Mining and Processing of Common Non-ferrous Metal	264843	269480
非金属矿采选业	Mining and Processing of Nonmetal Ores	107030	112181
#土砂石开采	Mining of Earth and Gravel	15657	53726
化学矿采选	Extracting of Chemical Ore	72877	42826
采 盐	Extracting of Salt	5000	780
制造业	**Manufacturing**	**4511815**	**6203672**
#农副食品加工业	Processing of Food from Agricultural Products	317698	407465
#制 糖	Sugar Making	14295	6922
食品制造业	Manufacture of Food	246238	272215
#液体乳及乳制品制造	Manufacture of Liquid Milk and Dairy Products	29105	18060
饮料制造业	Manufacture of Beverage	87037	143675
烟草加工业	Manufacture of Tobacco	2917	2885
纺织业	Manufacture of Textile	204547	248669
#棉、化纤纺织及印染精加工	Cotton, Chemical Fiber, Dying, Printing and Processing	190389	216760
毛纺织和染整精加工	Dyeing and Printing of Wool Textile	5268	6200
麻纺织	Manufacture of Flax Textile	2500	780
纺织服装、鞋、帽制造业	Textile Wearing Apparel,Footware and Caps Manufacturing	5155	3239
皮革、毛皮、羽绒及其制品业	Leather, Fur, Feather and Related Products Manufacturing	950	1241
木材加工及竹、藤、棕、草制品业	Processing of Timber, Wood, Bamboo, Cane, Grass Products	21115	35088
家具制造业	Furniture Manufacturing	3003	28944
造纸及纸制品业	Paper and Paper Products Manufacturing	35090	71405
印刷业、记录媒介的复制	Printing and Copying of Medium for Record	21775	21925
石油加工及炼焦业	Oil Processing, Coking and Nuclear Fuel Processing	1090729	1113217
#精炼石油产品的制造	Manufacture of Oil Products	736612	527028
炼 焦	Coking	354117	586189
化学原料及化学制品制造业	Raw Chemical Material and Chemical Products	899506	1258730
#基础化学原料制造	Basic Chemical Material	388903	486289
肥料制造	Fertilizer Making	158329	332691
医药制造业	Medicine Manufacturing	10484	31019
#中药饮片加工	Processing of Chinese Herbs and Tablet	850	11081
中成药制造	Manufacture of Chinese Herbs and Patent Medicine	933	16036
化学纤维制造业	Chemical Fiber Manufacturing	98352	98801

注：该表大类包括农村个人投资，中类未包括。
Note: The major category contains rural individual investment while sub-category excludes it.

4-5 续表 1 Continued

单位：万元 (10 000 yuan)

行　业	Sector	2009	2010
橡胶制品业	Manufacture of Rubber	6838	25630
塑料制品业	Manufacture of Plastic	123962	145562
非金属矿物制品业	Manufacture of Non-metallic Mineral Products	571575	1010184
＃水泥、石灰和石膏的制造	Cement Manufacturing	354530	536239
黑色金属冶炼及压延加工业	Smelting and Pressing of Non-Ferrous Metals	311809	428391
＃钢压延加工	Steel Rolling	66961	82301
有色金属冶炼及压延加工业	Smelting and Pressing of Nonferrous Metals	93515	366537
＃常用有色金属冶炼	Smeltering of Common Non-ferrous Metal	76126	342064
金属制品业	Manufacture of Metal Products	76501	122182
通用设备制造业	Manufacture of General Purpose Machinery	38084	86164
专用设备制造业	Manufacture of Special Purpose Machinery	154296	143701
交通运输设备制造业	Manufacture of Transport Equipment	11135	15609
＃汽车制造	Manufacture of Car	10995	11835
电气机械及器材制造业	Manufacture of Electricial Equipment and Machinery	44269	50934
工艺品及其他制造业	Manufouture of Art work and Other Manufacturing	6793	7478
电力、燃气及水的生产和供应业	**Production and Supply of Electricity Gas and Water**	**3058582**	**3950975**
电力、热力的生产和供应业	Production and Supply of Electric Power and Heat Power	2618825	3485983
电力生产	Production of Electric Power	1586113	2469999
电力供应	Distribution of Electric Power	881957	817756
热力生产和供应	Production and Supply of Heat Power	150755	198228
燃气生产和供应业	Production and Supply of Gas	116759	254207
水的生产和供应业	Production and Supply of Water	322998	210785
＃自来水的生产和供应	Production and Distribution of Running Water	219049	146352
污水处理及其再生利用	Treatment and Recycle of Waste Water	103949	64433
建筑业	**Construction**	**289225**	**412694**
＃房屋和土木工程建筑业	Construction of Buildings and Givil Engineering	175915	291129
建筑安装业	Building Installation	19671	23675
交通运输、仓储和邮政业	**Transport, Storage and Post**	**4415243**	**5320635**
铁路运输业	Railway Transport	1864735	2272319
道路运输业	Road Transport	2183331	2451150
城市公共交通业	Urban Public Transport	12746	2618
航空运输业	Air Transport	92720	100143
管道运输业	Via Pipeline Transport	11872	20438
装卸搬运和其他运输服务业	Loading, Unloading and Other Transport Services	6106	24775
仓储业	Storage	84510	234921
邮政业	Post	549	1275
信息传输、计算机服务和软件业	**Information Transmission, Computer Services and Software**	**460143**	**420315**
＃电信和其他信息传输服务业	Telecommunication and Other Information Transmission Services	460142	416935
＃电　信	Telecommunication	420583	385146
批发和零售业	**Wholesal and Retail Trades**	**280849**	**283876**
批发业	Wholesale Trade	185490	190923
零售业	Retail Trade	93179	92953
住宿和餐饮业	**Hotels and Catering Services**	**131714**	**138710**
住宿业	Hotels	101856	124232
＃旅游饭店	Tourist Restaurant	69247	91078
餐饮业	Catering Service	29858	13914
金融业	**Financial Intermediation**	**52318**	**71712**
银行业	Banks	51695	62576

4-5 续表 2 Continued

单位：万元 (10 000 yuan)

行　业	Sector	2009	2010
保险业	Insurance	623	9021
其他金融活动	Other Financial Activities		115
房地产业	**Real Estate**	**4128120**	**6251295**
#房地产开发与经营业	Real Estate Development and Operation	2486388	3758227
物业管理	Real Estate Management	17887	2210
租赁和商务服务业	**Leasing and Business Services**	**121764**	**113650**
租赁业	Leasing	10275	11315
商务服务业	Business Service	111489	102335
#旅行社	Travel Agencies	115	
科学研究、技术服务和地质勘查业	**Scientific Research, Technical Services and Geological Prospecting**	**136523**	**172180**
研究与试验发展	Research and Experimental Development	23146	3694
专业技术服务业	Professional Technical Service	19792	14292
科技交流和推广服务业	Services of Science and Technology Exchanges and Promotion	7834	31510
地质勘查业	Geologic Prospecting	85751	122684
水利、环境和公共设施管理业	**Management of Water Conservancy, Environment and Public Facilities**	**1878919**	**1957772**
水利管理业	Management of Water Conservancy	681910	673343
环境管理业	Management of Environmental	107313	109044
公共设施管理业	Management of Public Facilities	1089696	1175385
市政公共设施管理	Management of Public Facilities	970442	1047890
城市绿化管理	Urban Greening Management	43515	44854
游览景区管理	Scenic-Spot Management	75739	82641
居民服务和其他服务业	**Services to Households and Other Services**	**36915**	**38130**
教　育	**Education**	**684132**	**568427**
#初等教育	Junion Education	218632	107592
中等教育	Secondary Education	307442	260587
高等教育	Senior Education	76298	77415
卫生、社会保障和社会福利业	**Health, Social Security and Social Welfare**	**283329**	**314415**
卫　生	Health Care	243859	278867
#医　院	Hospital	168011	200665
专科疾病防治活动	Control Over Special Diseases	466	2578
疾病预防控制及防疫活动	Prevention and Control of Diseases	849	835
社会保障业	Social Security	3155	10034
社会福利业	Social Welfare	36315	25514
文化、体育和娱乐业	**Culture, Sports and Entertainment**	**130086**	**172127**
新闻出版业	Journalism and Publishing Activities	5958	7302
广播、电视、电影和音像业	Broadcasting,Movies,Televisions and Audiovisual Activites	11254	19689
文化艺术业	Culture and Art Activities	81377	103963
体　育	Sports	15477	32991
娱乐业	Entertainment	16020	8182
公共管理和社会组织	**Public Management and Social Organization**	**857559**	**788791**
中国共产党机关	Orgars of Communist Party of China	8889	20470
国家机构	Govemment Agencies	821522	752701
人民政协和民主党派	People's Political Consultative Conference and Democratic Parties	2046	819
群众团体、社会团体和宗教组织	Non-Govemmental Institutions,Social Organizations and Religion Organizations	10064	6774
基层群众自治组织	Grass Roots Self-governing Organizations	15038	8027

4-6 全社会房屋施工面积、竣工面积

Floor Space of Buildings under Construction and Completed in Whole Country

单位：万平方米 (10 000 sq.m)

年 份 Year	地 区 Region	施工面积 Floor Space of Buildings under Construction	#住 宅 Residential Buildings	竣工面积 Floor Space of Buildings Completed	#住 宅 Residential Buildings	房屋建筑面积竣工率 (%) Rate of Floor Space of Building Completed (%)	#住 宅 Residential Buildings
	1985	1670.30	945.76	1327.69	816.26	79.5	86.3
	1990	1740.94	1074.98	1337.06	912.57	76.8	84.9
	1995	2420.38	1368.84	1634.33	1064.14	67.5	77.7
	1996	2952.02	1901.01	2095.58	1441.22	71.0	75.8
	1997	2574.79	1732.19	1903.96	1393.11	73.9	80.4
	1998	2946.76	2057.08	2148.75	1604.68	72.9	78.0
	1999	3439.11	2470.41	2618.98	2020.89	76.2	81.8
	2000	4485.77	2509.17	2633.23	1881.88	58.7	75.0
	2001	4940.70	3282.51	3386.60	2411.78	68.5	73.5
	2002	3986.81	2358.04	2706.44	1790.82	67.9	75.9
	2003	5004.13	2863.92	3599.74	2347.04	71.9	82.0
	2004	5290.77	2999.85	4273.02	2298.56	80.8	76.6
	2005	6677.06	4522.20	4705.07	3618.78	70.5	80.0
	2006	7854.43	5694.75	4773.93	3785.46	60.8	66.5
	2007	8028.32	5915.83	5441.23	4458.77	67.8	75.4
	2008	8317.15	5938.78	5184.01	4125.67	62.3	69.5
	2009	9511.02	6344.39	4598.79	3412.43	48.4	53.8
	2010	11361.96	7640.58	4649.89	3291.89	40.9	43.1
乌鲁木齐市	Urumqi City	2346.07	1541.82	532.88	323.19	22.7	21.0
克拉玛依市	Karamay City	180.18	110.81	28.95	23.64	16.1	21.3
吐鲁番地区	Turpan Administrative Offices	93.16	58.91	16.68	9.05	17.9	15.4
哈密地区	Hami [Kumul] Administrative Offices	396.46	314.38	118.66	87.00	29.9	27.7
昌吉回族自治州	Changji Hui Autonomous Prefecture	562.89	410.67	162.66	106.55	28.9	25.9
伊犁哈萨克自治州	Ili Kazak Autonomous Prefecture	1753.69	1249.36	736.57	564.92	42.0	45.2
伊犁州直属县(市)	Counties (Cities) Direct Under Ili Prefecture	1018.20	733.84	353.23	284.32	34.7	38.7
塔城地区	Tacheng [Tarbagatai] Administrative Offices	460.64	328.71	258.76	191.38	56.2	58.2
阿勒泰地区	Altay Administrative Offices	274.85	186.81	124.58	89.22	45.3	47.8
博尔塔拉蒙古自治州	Bortala Mongol Autonomous Prefecture	264.24	202.34	56.06	47.91	21.2	23.7
巴音郭楞蒙古自治州	Bayangol Mongol Autonomous Prefecture	812.78	555.27	348.75	265.06	42.9	47.7
阿克苏地区	Aksu Administrative Offices	550.08	292.36	192.91	94.38	35.1	32.3
克孜勒苏柯尔克孜自治州	Kizilsu Kirgiz Autonomous Prefecture	245.92	107.83	145.01	29.26	59.0	27.1
喀什地区	Kashgar [Kaxgar] Administrative Offices	1772.19	978.36	658.99	317.20	37.2	32.4
和田地区	Hotan Administrative Offices	585.19	424.02	302.18	229.44	51.6	54.1
石河子市	Shihezi City	356.21	158.35	121.78	81.23	34.2	51.3
阿拉尔市	Aral City	80.15	46.43	61.52	44.48	76.8	95.8
图木舒克市	Tumxuk City	66.90	43.96	53.57	37.83	80.1	86.1
五家渠市	Wujiaqu City	123.71	48.09	56.15	18.71	45.4	38.9
跨地区投资	Trans-regional Investment	28.90					

注：分地区房屋施工面积、竣工面积未包括农村个人。
Note: Floor space under construction and completed floor space by sectors exclude those in rural areas.

4-7 按构成及建设性质分城镇固定资产投资

Investment in Fixed Assets in Urban Area by Composition of Funds and Type of Construction

单位：万元 (10 000 yuan)

年份 Year	地区 Region	合计 Total	按构成分 By Composition of Funds			
			建筑安装工程 Construction and Installation	设备工具器具购置 Purchase of Equipment and Instruments	#用于更新的设备 Update Equipmeng	其他费用 Others
1978		129999	86667	35686		7646
1985		408435	314651	67295	5499	26489
1990		782099	516443	224673	25153	40983
1995		2864148	1817364	754369	64612	292415
1996		3339710	2167304	825067	66119	347339
1997		3817221	2600884	858958	61094	357379
1998		4561217	3333948	792449	71986	434820
1999		4613116	3294346	831951	82363	486819
2000		4994145	3531280	1103399	104850	359466
2001		5490569	3638754	1392920	186605	458895
2002		6596964	4379556	1558818	181920	658590
2003		8188381	5599787	1718853	105728	869741
2004		9482471	6451184	2047000	232343	984287
2005		11215637	7926905	2230165	145514	1058567
2006		12971324	8943879	2686125	188170	1341320
2007		14908734	9646247	3746476	177062	1516011
2008		17970126	11542024	4772937	311014	1655165
2009		22999843	15632380	5026513	552733	2340950
2010		28338644	18973774	6938417	346525	2426453
乌鲁木齐市	Urumqi City	3925724	2215407	1316701	85698	393616
克拉玛依市	Karamay City	1714244	1516456	115186	16775	82602
吐鲁番地区	Turpan Administrative Offices	846630	533550	181531	2745	131549
哈密地区	Hami [Kumul] Administrative Offices	1368488	700497	537693	6549	130298
昌吉回族自治州	Changji Hui Autonomous Prefecture	1788633	1016164	624140	28449	148329
伊犁哈萨克自治州	Ili Kazak Autonomous Prefecture	4359655	2799948	1159214	44069	400493
伊犁州直属县(市)	Counties (Cities) Direct Under Ili Prefecture	2055345	1344608	554666	36833	156071
塔城地区	Tacheng [Tarbagatai] Administrative Offices	1246407	850867	329721	5500	65819
阿勒泰地区	Altay Administrative Offices	1057903	604473	274827	1736	178603
博尔塔拉蒙古自治州	Bortala Mongol Autonomous Prefecture	543689	329591	176541	6650	37557
巴音郭楞蒙古自治州	Bayangol Mongol Autonomous Prefecture	2759088	2017030	566194	80482	175864
阿克苏地区	Aksu Administrative Offices	1271297	712784	484656	33780	73857
克孜勒苏柯尔克孜自治州	Kizilsu Kirgiz Autonomous Prefecture	262380	232661	14977		14742
喀什地区	Kashgar [Kaxgar] Administrative Offices	2102107	1684928	307534	29788	109645
和田地区	Hotan Administrative Offices	788964	675047	45566	1320	68351
石河子市	Shihezi City	866979	322080	471617	500	73282
阿拉尔市	Aral City	202656	127283	62582	291	12791
图木舒克市	Tumxuk City	92483	53967	31338		7178
五家渠市	Wujiaqu City	727937	381455	316535		29947
跨地区投资	Trans-regional Investment	4717690	3654926	526412	9429	536352

注：城镇投资额未含房地产投资，以下同。
Note: Urban Investment exclude real estate, the following the same as follows.

4-7 续表 Continued

单位：万元 (10 000 yuan)

年份 Year	地区 Region	按建设性质分 By Type of Construction 新建 New Construction	扩建 Expansion	改建 Reconstruction	其他 Others
	1978	93462	34399		2138
	1985	110236	160639	116006	21554
	1990	299356	148222	277007	57514
	1995	1067281	886882	646081	263904
	1996	1240585	820966	967022	311137
	1997	1405259	911902	1155121	344939
	1998	1648622	1017786	1338994	555815
	1999	1381764	1226797	1326775	677780
	2000	1410065	1424339	1558514	601227
	2001	891146	2373927	1614961	610535
	2002	1429874	2687996	1984657	494437
	2003	2207269	3128374	2237752	614986
	2004	2358662	3595847	2781101	746861
	2005	3397472	3657464	3063457	1097244
	2006	3633284	5436397	2430373	1471270
	2007	3759028	7439715	2386806	1323185
	2008	5350574	8078708	2759536	1781308
	2009	9465044	7634515	4113649	1786635
	2010	13612835	8408038	4177527	2140244
乌鲁木齐市	Urumqi City	901961	2154211	501875	367677
克拉玛依市	Karamay City	1497220	9397	160959	46668
吐鲁番地区	Turpan Administrative Offices	418195	326146	69258	33031
哈密地区	Hami [Kumul] Administrative Offices	357686	899096	74336	37370
昌吉回族自治州	Changji Hui Autonomous Prefecture	560558	390183	652614	185278
伊犁哈萨克自治州	Ili Kazak Autonomous Prefecture	2122561	1179835	624182	433077
伊犁州直属县(市)	Counties (Cities) Direct Under Ili Prefecture	1177734	367383	308178	202050
塔城地区	Tacheng [Tarbagatai] Administrative Offices	550185	340640	222162	133420
阿勒泰地区	Altay Administrative Offices	394642	471812	93842	97607
博尔塔拉蒙古自治州	Bortala Mongol Autonomous Prefecture	227924	145150	85108	85507
巴音郭楞蒙古自治州	Bayangol Mongol Autonomous Prefecture	1836962	560045	251362	110719
阿克苏地区	Aksu Administrative Offices	815265	266213	154689	35130
克孜勒苏柯尔克孜自治州	Kizilsu Kirgiz Autonomous Prefecture	238358	8633	8224	7165
喀什地区	Kashgar [Kaxgar] Administrative Offices	1424378	350961	90951	235817
和田地区	Hotan Administrative Offices	15412	590985	86075	96492
石河子市	Shihezi City	585685	171290	65544	44460
阿拉尔市	Aral City	115945	19950	32137	34624
图木舒克市	Tumxuk City	32865	27708	10736	21174
五家渠市	Wujiaqu City	469273	158716	83893	16055
跨地区投资	Trans-regional Investment	1992587	1149519	1225584	350000

4-8 分行业城镇固定资产投资主要指标

Main Indicators of Investment in Fixed Assets in Urban Area by Sector

(2010 年)

行业	Sector	投资额(万元) Total Investment (10 000 yuan)	#地方 Local	施工项目个数(个) Number of Projects under Construction (unit)	竣工项目个数(个) Number of Projects Completed (unit)	本年新增固定资产(万元) Newly Increased Fixed Assets (10 000 yuan)
总计	**Total**	**28338644**	**17996646**	**8179**	**5369**	**15042603**
农、林、牧、渔业	**Agriculture, Forestry, Animal Husbandry and Fishery**	**992872**	**909098**	**835**	**635**	**843795**
农业	Agriculture	244945	231385	105	74	203856
林业	Forestry	112426	109286	156	132	108530
畜牧业	Animal Husbandry	119354	106054	124	90	89294
渔业	Fishing	312	312	2	1	212
农、林、牧、渔服务业	Service in Support of Agriculture	515835	462061	448	338	441903
采矿业	**Mining**	**5954933**	**1944271**	**443**	**231**	**2728370**
#煤炭开采和洗选业	Mining and Washing of Coal	1351131	1259207	153	76	563954
石油和天然气开采业	Extraction of Petroleum and Natural Gas	3879328	41319	30	13	1760332
#天然原油和天然气开采	Extraction of Ores Crude Oil and Natural Gas Extraction	3810689	21570	18	6	1736492
黑色金属矿采选业	Mining and Processing of Ferrous Metals Ores	287912	287912	98	58	153324
#铁矿采选	Mining and Processing of Iron Ore	238994	238994	86	50	112984
有色金属矿采选业	Mining and Processing of Non-ferrous Metals Ores	329851	285417	99	41	201042
#常用有色金属矿采选	Mining and Processing of Common Non-ferrous Metal	254994	210696	59	27	159886
非金属矿采选业	Mining and Processing of Nonmetal Ores	106711	70416	63	43	49718
#土砂石开采	Mining of Earth and Gravel	50756	49867	48	33	34791
化学矿采选	Extracting of Chemical Ore	42826	7420	6	2	2420
采盐	Extraction of Salt	780	780	1	1	780
制造业	**Manufacturing**	**5825204**	**4761043**	**1290**	**727**	**3039197**
#农副食品加工业	Processing of Food from Agricultural Products	347096	275193	232	145	240904
食品制造业	Manufacture of Foods	241308	216942	94	56	169567
#液体乳及乳制品制造	Manufacture of Liquid Milk and Dairy Products	18060	16948	9	4	5110
饮料制造业	Manufacture of Beverages	119240	108294	51	29	77749
纺织业	Manufacture of Textile	242129	194136	57	33	245710
#棉、化纤纺织及印染精加工	Cotton, Chemical Fiber Dyeing, Printing and Processing	213800	168257	38	19	224279
麻纺织	Manufacture of Flax Textile					
皮革、毛皮、羽绒及其制品业	Manufacture of Leather, Fur, Feather and Related Products	1241	1241	1		
木材加工及竹、藤、棕、草制品业	Processing of Timber, Wood, Bamboo, Cane, Grass Products	29565	29565	19	17	36897
家具制造业	Manufacture of Furniture	28394	28394	17	15	27684
造纸及纸制品业	Manufacture of Paper and Paper Products	67765	66665	28	14	42387
印刷业、记录媒介的复制	Printing,Reproduction,of Recording Media	21925	19537	12	7	11760
石油加工及炼焦业	Processing of Petroleum,Coking	1068467	679371	59	23	193742
#精炼石油产品的制造	Manufacture of Oil Products	512628	157690	30	12	89828
炼焦	Coking	555839	521681	29	11	103914

4-8 续表 1 Continued

行业	Sector	投资额(万元) Total Investment (10 000 yuan)	#地方 Local	施工项目个数(个) Number of Projects under Construction (unit)	竣工项目个数(个) Number of Projects Completed (unit)	本年新增固定资产(万元) Newly Increased Fixed Assets (10 000 yuan)
化学原料及化学制品制造业	Manufacture of Raw Chemical Material and Chemical Products	1215046	883475	113	59	625330
#基础化学原料制造	Manufacture of Basic Chemical Material	465889	401494	28	8	45329
肥料制造	Fertilizer Making	328061	195885	35	21	148024
医药制造业	Manufacture of Medicine	31019	30869	21	14	24848
#中药饮片加工	Manufacture and Processing of Chinese Herbs and Tablet	11081	10931	9	7	9005
橡胶制品业	Manufacture of Rubber Products	25630	25630	6	2	5818
塑料制品业	Manufacture of Plastic Products	129696	119792	80	45	64950
非金属矿物制品业	Manufacture of Non-metallic Mineral Products	904469	783287	227	128	531148
#水泥、石灰和石膏的制造	Cement Manufacturing	487216	371322	59	28	251390
黑色金属冶炼及压延加工业	Smelting and Pressing of Ferrous Metals	425931	425671	43	22	250424
#钢压延加工	Steel Rolling	79841	79841	15	10	49303
有色金属冶炼及压延加工业	Smelting and Pressing of Nonferrous Metals	350137	335057	30	14	208393
#常用有色金属冶炼	Smeltering of Common Non-ferrous Metal	325664	316096	22	12	201894
金属制品业	Manufacture of Metal Products	116282	116026	71	46	85791
通用设备制造业	Manufacture of General Purpose Machinery	81864	81864	29	13	31017
专用设备制造业	Manufacture of Special Purpose Machinery	142701	133701	27	9	66359
交通运输设备制造业	Manufacture of Transport Equipment	15009	14877	13	7	10163
#汽车制造	Manufacture of Car	11235	11103	10	5	8389
电气机械及器材制造业	Manufacture of Electric Equipment and Machinery	48610	46360	17	6	9425
电力、燃气及水的生产和供应业	**Production and Supply of Electricity,Gas and Water**	**3784710**	**2465702**	**625**	**359**	**2006958**
电力、热力的生产和供应业	Production and Supply of Electricity Power and Heat Power	3333385	2038534	416	252	1807157
电力生产	Production of Electric Power	2362832	1628389	123	39	690847
电力供应	Supply of Electric Power	776093	236462	197	143	1026677
热力生产和供应	Production and Supply of Heat Power	194460	173683	96	70	89633
燃气生产和供应业	Production and Supply of Gas	250364	242218	71	38	64875
水的生产和供应业	Production and Supply of Water	200961	184950	138	69	134926
#自来水的生产和供应	Production and Distribution of Running Water	136528	123201	102	58	84895
污水处理及其再生利用	Treatment and Recycle of Waste Water	64433	61749	36	11	50031
建筑业	**Construction**	**269685**	**211540**	**167**	**110**	**177083**
#房屋和土木工程建筑业	Buildings and Givil Engineering Construction	235550	181721	144	94	152885
建筑安装业	Building Installation	23604	19438	10	7	15672

4-8 续表 2 Continued

行　业	Sector	投资额（万元）Total Investment (10 000 yuan)	#地方 Local	施工项目个数（个）Number of Projects under Construction (unit)	竣工项目个数（个）Number of Projects Completed (unit)	本年新增固定资产（万元）Newly Increased Fixed Assets (10 000 yuan)
交通运输、仓储和邮政业	**Transport Storage and Post**	**4853566**	**2336012**	**531**	**315**	**1245879**
#铁路运输业	Railway Transport	2272319	21149	28	3	63145
道路运输业	Road Transport	2218600	2016698	399	255	989936
城市公共交通业	Urban Public Transport	2618	1300			2118
航空运输业	Air Transportation	100143	78184	9	5	76231
管道运输业	Via Pipelines Transport	20438	993	2	1	19795
仓储业	Storage	213398	191888	82	47	81659
邮政业	Post	1275	1025	4	3	1125
信息传输、计算机服务和软件业	**Information Transmission, Computer Services and Software**	**413540**	**185485**	**107**	**74**	**294753**
#电信和其他信息传输服务业	Telecommunication and Other Information Transmission Services	410270	182215	107	74	291483
#电　信	Telecommunication	381546	162773	76	47	214227
批发和零售业	**Wholesale&Retail Trades**	**260273**	**209328**	**195**	**129**	**218181**
批发业	Wholesale Trades	175517	139977	98	61	136782
零售业	Retail Trades	84756	69351	97	68	81399
住宿和餐饮业	**Hotels and Catering Services**	**133121**	**105945**	**85**	**54**	**95254**
#住宿业	Hotels	119857	93308	66	41	78664
#旅游饭店	Tourist Restaurant	86923	65705	32	16	47835
金融业	**Financial Intermediation**	**70783**	**16671**	**39**	**25**	**64285**
银行业	Bank	61762	16071	34	22	61598
保险业	Insurance	9021	600	5	3	2687
房地产业	**Real Estate**	**2058684**	**1495946**	**844**	**573**	**1519286**
#房地产开发与经营业	Real Estate Development and Operation	271414	271414	138	82	204192
物业管理	Management of Real Estate	1500	1213	3	3	1500
租赁和商务服务业	**Leasing and Business Services**	**102288**	**101616**	**46**	**27**	**35529**
租赁业	Leasing	988	988	1	1	988
商务服务业	Business Service	101300	100628	45	26	34541
#旅行社	Travel Service					
科学研究、技术服务和地质勘查业	**Scientific Research, Technical Service and Geological Prospecting**	**164415**	**143581**	**109**	**76**	**131128**
研究与试验发展	Research and Experiment Development	3694	3264	4	3	4100
专业技术服务业	Professional Technical Service	13546	11197	31	18	11026
科技交流和推广服务业	Services of Science and Technology Exchanges and Difussion	30453	23846	30	24	22346

4-8 续表 3 Continued

行　业	Sector	投资额(万元) Total Investment (10 000 yuan)	#地 方 Local	施工项目个数(个) Number of Projects under Construction (unit)	竣工项目个数(个) Number of Projects Completed (unit)	本年新增固定资产(万元) Newly Increased Fixed Assets (10 000 yuan)
地质勘查业	Geologic Prospection	116722	105274	44	31	93656
水利、环境和公共设施管理业	**Management of Water Conservancy, Environment and Public Facilities**	**1762038**	**1595642**	**874**	**606**	**1257036**
水利管理业	Management of Water Conservancy	494964	419076	289	196	390204
环境管理业	Environmental Management	103371	101384	87	60	70954
公共设施管理业	Management of Public Facilities	1163703	1075182	498	350	795878
市政公共设施管理	Management of Public Facilities	1040177	957011	369	260	684287
城市绿化管理	Management of Urban Greening	44675	40856	62	49	42303
游览景区管理	Scenic-Spot Management	78851	77315	67	41	69288
居民服务和其他服务业	**Resident Service and Other Services**	**35592**	**33814**	**43**	**38**	**36977**
教　育	**Education**	**536821**	**436456**	**791**	**575**	**430502**
#初等教育	Elementary Education	99751	72885	208	159	79948
中等教育	Secondary Education	257863	205301	310	242	216380
高等教育	Higher Education	77415	68515	26	16	61576
卫生、社会保障和社会福利业	**Health, Social Security and Social Welfare**	**287882**	**257499**	**335**	**234**	**244129**
卫　生	Health Care	269255	241602	289	200	231380
#医　院	Hospital	199176	177153	136	76	168066
专科疾病防治活动	Prerention and Control of Special Diseases	2578	2578	2	2	2700
疾病预防控制及防疫活动	Prevention and Control of Diseases	835	835	5	3	883
社会保障业	Social Security	1134	1124	4	4	1974
社会福利业	Social Welfare	17493	14773	42	30	10775
文化、体育和娱乐业	**Culture, Sports and Entertainment**	**160899**	**144013**	**176**	**129**	**163302**
新闻出版业	Journalism and Publishing Activities	7302	7252	3	2	4840
广播、电视、电影和音像业	Broadcasting,Movies,Televisions and Audiovisual Activites	18335	18335	18	13	19193
文化艺术业	Cultural and Art Activities	95387	78731	118	84	95243
体　育	Sports	32793	32793	22	17	39566
娱乐业	Entertainment	7082	6902	15	13	4460
公共管理和社会组织	**Public Management and Social Organization**	**671338**	**642984**	**644**	**452**	**510959**
中国共产党机关	Orgars of Communist Party of China	19240	17903	24	12	11186
国家机构	Govemment Agencies	638778	612770	582	408	485176
人民政协和民主党派	People's Political Consultative Conference and Democratic Parties	819	819	2	1	619
群众团体、社会团体和宗教组织	Non-Govemmental Institutions,Social Organizations and Religion Organizations	6624	5615	15	13	8101
基层群众自治组织	Grass Roots Self-governing Organizations	5877	5877	21	18	5877

4-9 分行业城镇固定资产投资资金来源情况

单位：万元 (2010 年)

行　业	Sector	本年资金来源小计 Sub-total Funds This Year
总　计	**Total**	**28841147**
农、林、牧、渔业	**Agriculture, Forestry, Animal Husbandry and Fishery**	**1007664**
农　业	Agriculture	242171
林　业	Forestry	115894
畜牧业	Animal Husbandry	125694
渔　业	Fishing	20
农、林、牧、渔服务业	Activities for Agriculture, Forestry, Animal Husbandry and Fishing	523885
采矿业	**Mining and Quarrying**	**6008979**
#煤炭开采和洗选业	Mining and Washing of Coal	1375358
石油和天然气开采业	Extraction of Petroleum and Natural Gas	3916543
#天然原油和天然气开采	Extraction of Ores Crude Oil and Natural Gas Extraction	3847716
黑色金属矿采选业	Mining and Processing of Ferrous Metals Ores	273038
#铁矿采选	Mining and Processing of Iron Ore	224088
有色金属矿采选业	Mining and Processing of Non-ferrous Metals Ores	337275
#常用有色金属矿采选	Mining and Processing of Common Non-ferrous Metal	262115
非金属矿采选业	Processing of Nonmetal Ores	106765
#土砂石开采	Mining of Earth and Gravel	50060
化学矿采选	Extracting of Chemical Ore	43544
采　盐	Extraction of Salt	780
制造业	**Manufacturing**	**6163267**
#农副食品加工业	Processing of Food from Agricultural Products	363091
食品制造业	Manufacture of Foods	235542
#液体乳及乳制品制造	Manufacture of Liquid Milk and Dairy Products	17130
饮料制造业	Manufacture of Beverages	135791
纺织业	Manufacture of Textile	240597
#棉、化纤纺织及印染精加工	Cotton, Chemical Fiber Dyeing, Printing and Processing	212648
麻纺织	Manufacture of Flax Textile	
皮革、毛皮、羽绒及其制品业	Manufacture of Leather, Fur, Feather and Related Products	1241
木材加工及竹、藤、棕、草制品业	Processing of Timber, Manufacture of Cane, Grass Products	31808
家具制造业	Manufacture of Furniture	28442
造纸及纸制品业	Manufacture of Paper and Paper Products	70069
印刷业、记录媒介的复制	Printing, Reproduction of Recording Media	23104
石油加工及炼焦业	Processing of Petroleum, Coking	1167668
#精炼石油产品的制造	Manufacture of Oil Products	554601
炼　焦	Coking	613067

Sources of Funds of Investment in Fixed Assets in Urban Area by Sector

(10 000 yuan)

国家预算内资金 State Budget	国内贷款 Domestic Loans	债券 Bonds	利用外资 Foreign Investment	自筹资金 Self-raising Funds	其他资金来源 Others
5567658	**4723078**	**11544**	**119073**	**16179963**	**2239831**
351286	**142017**	**3114**	**602**	**373845**	**136800**
44824	108900			71862	16585
46726			602	56555	12011
48997	5072	606		54993	16026
20					
210719	28045	2508		190435	92178
47333	**772192**		**11009**	**4737549**	**440896**
1478	139483		11009	1191483	31905
38595	543097			2994406	340445
38595	539523			2929153	340445
6700	67009			168389	30940
4700	67009			150779	1600
300	21292			281257	34426
300	15492			221932	24391
260	1311			102014	3180
	1050			48760	250
				42344	1200
				780	
333922	**863684**		**31987**	**4779455**	**154219**
5840	14389		1026	316292	25544
359	22880		22365	167220	22718
250	500			16280	100
190	4700		682	129268	951
	61382			166841	12374
	61282			149892	1474
				1241	
				29958	1850
282				26760	1400
380	3683			58701	7305
	300			21518	1286
180600	7573			979380	115
180000	723			373763	115
600	6850			605617	

4-9 续表 1

单位：万元

行　　业	Sector	本年资金来源小计 Sub-total Funds This Year
化学原料及化学制品制造业	Manufacture of Raw Chemical Material and Chemical Products	1344134
#基础化学原料制造	Manufacture of Basic Chemical Material	601305
肥料制造	Making of Fertilizer	297763
医药制造业	Manufacture of Medicine	35530
#中药饮片加工	Manufacture of Chinese Herbs and Tablet	10822
橡胶制品业	Manufacture of Rubber Products	61946
塑料制品业	Manufacture of Plastic Products	142528
非金属矿物制品业	Manufacture of Non-metallic Mineral Products	908474
#水泥、石灰和石膏的制造	Manufacture of Cement	487205
黑色金属冶炼及压延加工业	Smelting and Pressing of Ferrous Metals	437133
#钢压延加工	Steel Rolling	86830
有色金属冶炼及压延加工业	Smelting and Pressing of Non-ferrous Metals	384990
#常用有色金属冶炼	Smeltering of Common Non-ferrous Metal	356777
金属制品业	Manufacture of Metal Products	123589
通用设备制造业	Manufacture of General Purpose Machinery	74092
专用设备制造业	Manufacture of Special Purpose Machinery	125848
交通运输设备制造业	Manufacture of Transport Equipment	15895
#汽车制造	Manufacture of Car	11621
电气机械及器材制造业	Manufacture of Electrical Equipment and Machinery	51519
电力、燃气及水的生产和供应业	**Production and Supply of Electricity, Gas and Water**	**4022138**
电力、热力的生产和供应业	Production and Supply of Electric Power and Heat Power	3579647
电力生产	Production of Electric Power	2638965
电力供应	Supply of Electric Power	791072
热力生产和供应	Production and Supply of Heat Power	149610
燃气生产和供应业	Production and Supply of Gas	241478
水的生产和供应业	Production and Supply of Water	201013
#自来水的生产和供应	Production and Distribution of Running Water	135824
污水处理及其再生利用	Treatment and Recycle of Waste Water	65189
建筑业	**Construction**	**289072**
#房屋和土木工程建筑业	Buildings and Givil Engineering Construction	254465
建筑安装业	Building Installation	24074

Continued

(10 000 yuan)

国家预算内资金 State Budget	国内贷款 Domestic Loans	债券 Bonds	利用外资 Foreign Investment	自筹资金 Self-raising Funds	其他资金来源 Others
140096	411716		1010	785134	6178
140000	98586			359296	3423
96	90000		1010	205837	820
180	1500			31850	2000
				8822	2000
	22000			39946	
	5600			127830	9098
290	118673		3672	741808	44031
	96318			363937	26950
	74832			348199	14102
	9000			77179	651
	15453			367887	1650
	12953			343374	450
	32608			90551	430
				73342	750
	34300			91548	
			1200	13138	1557
			1200	8864	1557
5160	4865			41114	380
269889	**1380567**	**200**	**11655**	**2138208**	**221619**
205240	1345999	200		1917332	110876
86735	830119			1621101	101010
98534	467572			220866	4100
19971	48308	200		75365	5766
4196	28250			166091	42941
60453	6318		11655	54785	67802
41783	2173		6438	29930	55500
18670	4145		5217	24855	12302
72172	**1022**		**2617**	**174061**	**39200**
68191	1022		2617	144088	38547
2071				21693	310

4-9 续表 2

单位：万元

行　业	Sector	本年资金来源小计 Sub-total Funds This Year
交通运输、仓储和邮政业	**Transport,Storage and Post**	**4519865**
#铁路运输业	Railway Transport	2249760
道路运输业	Road Transport	1901273
城市公共交通业	City Public Transport	2618
航空运输业	Air Transportation	101689
管道运输业	Via Pipeline Transport	20993
仓储业	Storage	214708
邮政业	Post	1275
信息传输、计算机服务和软件业	**Information Transmission, Computer Services and Software**	**360328**
#电信和其他信息传输服务业	Telecommunications and Other Information Transmission Services	357058
#电　信	Telecommunication	329172
批发和零售业	**Wholesale&Retail Trades**	**260468**
批发业	Wholesale Trades	173260
零售业	Retail Trades	87208
住宿和餐饮业	**Hotels and Catering Services**	**130262**
#住宿业	Hotels	118576
#旅游饭店	Tourist Restaurant	82614
金融业	**Financial Intermediation**	**69168**
银行业	Banks	59979
保险业	Insurance	9189
其他金融活动	Others	
房地产业	**Real Estate**	**2145165**
#房地产开发与经营业	Real Estate Development and Operation	293793
物业管理	Real Estate Management	1500
租赁和商务服务业	**Leasing and Business Services**	**94456**
租赁业	Leasing	988
商务服务业	Business Service	93468
#旅行社	Travel Service	
科学研究、技术服务和地质勘查业	**Scientific Research, Technical Service and Geological Prospecting**	**179764**
研究与试验发展	Research and Experiment Development	3594
专业技术服务业	Professional Technical Service	14097
科技交流和推广服务业	Services of Science and Technology Exchanges and Difussion	34012

Continued

(10 000 yuan)

国家预算内资金 State Budget	国内贷款 Domestic Loans	债券 Bonds	利用外资 Foreign Investment	自筹资金 Self-raising Funds	其他资金来源 Others
2143287	**1077405**		**33297**	**1056498**	**209378**
1398301	554831			181928	114700
682740	506966		33297	626304	51966
				2618	
37120	5300			38957	20312
20000				993	
4876	10308			184950	14574
250				895	130
16378	**1280**			**325994**	**16676**
13378	1280			325724	16676
8849	600			307428	12295
12618	**23923**			**208982**	**14945**
6643	23688			137972	4957
5975	235			71010	9988
10529	**1000**		**3251**	**105203**	**10279**
10529	1000		3251	94137	9659
8900	1000		3251	65013	4450
3425				**58828**	**6915**
2825				51839	5315
600				6989	1600
548703	**42345**	**3951**	**839**	**847135**	**702192**
46593	5700	1772		204276	35452
1117				383	
9407	**48650**			**34943**	**1456**
88				900	
9319	48650			34043	1456
49688			**300**	**125855**	**3921**
1870				1724	
6481				6891	725
30972				2834	206

4-9 续表 3

单位：万元

行业	Sector	本年资金来源小计 Sub-total Funds This Year
地质勘查业	Geologic Prospecting	128061
水利、环境和公共设施管理业	**Management of Water Conservancy, Environment and Public Facilities**	**1851456**
水利管理业	Management of Water Conservancy	641654
环境管理业	Environmental Management	106993
公共设施管理业	Management of Public Facilities	1102809
市政公共设施管理	Management of Public Facilities	972270
城市绿化管理	Management of Urban Greening	43983
游览景区管理	Scenic-Spot Management	86556
居民服务和其他服务业	**Services to Households and Other Services**	**39951**
教 育	**Education**	**556573**
#初等教育	Elementary Education	101272
中等教育	Secondary Education	267144
高等教育	Higher Education	81672
卫生、社会保障和社会福利业	**Health, Social Security and Social Welfare**	**312745**
卫 生	Health Care	294147
#医 院	Hospital	212887
专科疾病防治活动	Prerention and Control of Special Diseases	2619
疾病预防控制及防疫活动	Prevention and Control of Diseases	1060
社会保障业	Social Security	645
社会福利业	Social Welfare	17953
文化、体育和娱乐业	**Culture, Sport and Entertainment**	**161260**
新闻出版业	Journalism and Publishing Activities	6928
广播、电视、电影和音像业	Broadcasting,Movies,Televisions and Audiovisual Activites	16517
文化艺术业	Culture and Art Activities	99485
体 育	Sports Activities	30130
娱乐业	Entertainment	8200
公共管理和社会组织	**Public Management and Social Organization**	**668566**
中国共产党机关	Orgars of Communist Party of China	19058
国家机构	Government Agencies	636145
人民政协和民主党派	People's Political Consultative Conference and Democratic Parties	819
群众团体、社会团体和宗教组织	Non-Governmental Organizations,Social Organizations and Religion Organizations	6689
基层群众自治组织	Grass Root Self-governing Organizations	5855

Continued

(10 000 yuan)

国家预算内资金 State Budget	国内贷款 Domestic Loans	债券 Bonds	利用外资 Foreign Investment	自筹资金 Self-raising Funds	其他资金来源 Others
10365			300	114406	2990
743876	**310854**		**22396**	**687636**	**86694**
431439	28410		1238	142783	37784
44693	30568		972	26639	4121
267744	251876		20186	518214	44789
217322	249936		19726	445312	39974
23142	90			19368	1383
27280	1850		460	53534	3432
13358	**2000**			**22285**	**2308**
360018	**30609**	**1242**		**110404**	**54300**
68546	3643	210		15524	13349
181873	9225	1032		53062	21952
24465	17741			23556	15910
111093	**19579**	**1009**	**1120**	**150096**	**29848**
98096	19579	1009	1120	146469	27874
58904	16421	64	1120	119063	17315
				2619	
789				271	
635				10	
12362				3617	1974
91972	**72**			**48191**	**21025**
1327				5601	
10095				5615	807
55576	72			25111	18726
22035				6963	1132
2939				4901	360
378704	**5879**	**2028**		**194795**	**87160**
9977				1662	7419
358058	5879	2028		190811	79369
200				619	
5000				1435	254
5469				268	118

4-10 各地、州、市、县(市)城镇固定资产投资和新增固定资产

Total Investment and Newly Increased Fixed Assets in Urban Area by Prefecture, Autonomous Prefecture, City and County

单位：万元 (2010 年) (10 000 yuan)

地区 Region	投资总额 Total Investment	第一产业 Primary Industry	第二产业 Secondary Industry	第三产业 Tertiary Industry	新增固定资产 Newly Increased Fixed Assets	房屋建筑面积(万平方米) Floor Space of Buildings (10 000 sq.m) 施工面积 Floor Space Under Construction	竣工面积 Floor Space Completed
总计 Total	**28338644**	**992872**	**15834532**	**11511240**	**15042603**	**5400.16**	**2147.84**
按隶属关系分 By Administrative Relationship							
中央 Central Government	10341998	83774	6451976	3806248	4477930	973.51	507.35
地方 Local	17996646	909098	9382556	7704992	10564673	4426.66	1640.49
按区域分 Grouped by Region							
乌鲁木齐市 Urumqi City	**3925724**	**41270**	**2210375**	**1674079**	**3230243**	**697.26**	**245.94**
#乌鲁木齐县 Urumqi County	99181	20342	18653	60186	70524	4.47	
克拉玛依市 Karamay City	**1714244**	**5209**	**1561793**	**147242**	**213614**	**55.47**	**7.58**
吐鲁番地区 Turpan Administrative Offices	**846630**	**140354**	**603522**	**102754**	**576229**	**37.43**	**12.31**
吐鲁番市 Turpan City	181490	77463	53364	50663	155584	16.31	8.52
鄯善县 Shanshan [Piqan] County	490142	59898	400216	30028	364158	7.24	1.92
托克逊县 Toksun County	174998	2993	149942	22063	56487	13.88	1.87
哈密地区 Hami [Kumul] Administrative Offices	**1368488**	**50382**	**970396**	**347710**	**416633**	**189.68**	**30.24**
哈密市 Hami [Kumul] City	789090	36800	491645	260645	291100	154.51	29.10
巴里坤哈萨克自治县 Barkol Kazak Autonomous County	180915	4941	140132	35842	65092	26.35	0.71
伊吾县 Yiwu [Araturuk] County	398483	8641	338619	51223	60441	8.82	0.43
昌吉回族自治州 Changji Hui Autonomous Prefecture	**1788633**	**60723**	**1252026**	**475884**	**1489984**	**275.54**	**105.30**
昌吉市 Changji City	450028	13613	279247	157168	237882	93.70	14.60
阜康市 Fukang City	349988	4177	302610	43201	407816	16.52	8.10
呼图壁县 Hutubi County	180528	16822	93767	69939	149337	52.12	33.43
玛纳斯县 Manas County	350050	20011	234412	95627	318964	51.12	32.75
奇台县 Qitai County	221353	1196	144943	75214	158404	26.57	5.11
吉木萨尔县 Jimsar County	232342	4788	194247	33307	215475	34.15	11.30
木垒哈萨克自治县 Mori Kazak Autonomous County	4344	116	2800	1428	2106	1.36	
伊犁哈萨克自治州 Ili Kazak Autonomous Prefecture	**4359655**	**240011**	**2665184**	**1454460**	**2088987**	**908.26**	**448.65**
伊犁州直属县(市) Counties (Cities) Direct Under Ili Prefecture	**2055345**	**54753**	**1324554**	**676038**	**761077**	**419.34**	**169.56**
伊宁市 Yining [Gulja] City	354608		206076	148532	121572	107.52	30.32

4-10 续表 1 Continued

单位：万元 (10 000 yuan)

地区 Region	投资总额 Total Investment	第一产业 Primary Industry	第二产业 Secondary Industry	第三产业 Tertiary Industry	新增固定资产 Newly Increased Fixed Assets	房屋建筑面积(万平方米) Floor Space of Buildings (10 000 sq.m) 施工面积 Floor Space Under Construction	竣工面积 Floor Space Completed
奎屯市 Kuytun City	422934		250111	172823	163314	115.02	10.75
伊宁县 Yining [Gulja] County	383887	113	349308	34466	41104	4.57	1.30
察布查尔锡伯自治县 Qapqal Xibe Autonomous County	107809	7049	52786	47974	75315	30.67	24.75
霍城县 Huocheng [Korgas] County	179313	5533	102116	71664	86958	59.52	39.70
巩留县 Gongliu [Tokkuztara] County	68067	24768	15175	28124	35813	15.72	7.29
新源县 Xinyuan [Kunes] County	197122	7001	85170	104951	172257	43.59	38.72
昭苏县 Zhaosu [Mongolkure] County	28897	4497	9415	14985	16409	12.47	1.35
特克斯县 Tekes County	81606	4711	41117	35778	41227	21.19	13.94
尼勒克县 Nilka County	231102	1081	213280	16741	7108	9.08	1.44
塔城地区 Tacheng [Tarbagatai] Administrative Offices	**1246407**	**64551**	**772942**	**408914**	**729792**	**329.96**	**191.19**
塔城市 Tacheng [Qoqek] City	75848	7646	17061	51141	69881	49.81	16.17
乌苏市 Usu City	335900	6872	279407	49621	134333	32.75	19.21
额敏县 Emin Ciunty	211458	22414	105206	83838	170044	51.91	40.89
沙湾县 Shawan County	291331	14186	158437	118708	232681	112.58	66.18
托里县 Toli County	92202	4557	50830	36815	39834	29.98	22.64
裕民县 Yumin [Qagantokay] County	24760	2037	4208	18515	23078	19.49	14.52
和布克赛尔蒙古自治县 Hoboksar Mongol Autonomous County	214908	6839	157793	50276	59941	33.45	11.58
阿勒泰地区 Altay Administrative Offices	**1057903**	**120707**	**567688**	**369508**	**598118**	**158.96**	**87.90**
阿勒泰市 Altay City	184863	23221	51020	110622	92508	47.89	27.81
布尔津县 Burqin County	155192	10351	94986	49855	120371	22.78	9.22
富蕴县 Fuyun [Koktokay] County	255222	6905	194414	53903	47105	9.39	4.04
福海县 Fuhai [Burultokay] County	133328	33337	38233	61758	59380	23.99	19.47
哈巴河县 Habahe [Kaba] County	142929	26317	74684	41928	165439	28.80	16.22
青河县 Qinghe [Qinggil] County	106233	14780	56345	35108	94720	13.12	7.35
吉木乃县 Jeminay County	80136	5796	58006	16334	18595	12.99	3.79
博尔塔拉蒙古自治州 Bortala Mongol Autonomous Prefecture	**543689**	**42599**	**222652**	**278438**	**349634**	**197.29**	**29.37**
博乐市 Bole [Bortala] City	408630	17847	176986	213797	235078	123.85	16.37

4-10 续表 2 Continued

单位：万元 (10 000 yuan)

地　区 Region	投资总额 Total Investment	第一产业 Primary Industry	第二产业 Secondary Industry	第三产业 Tertiary Industry	新增固定资产 Newly Increased Fixed Assets	房屋建筑面积(万平方米) Floor Space of Buildings (10 000 sq.m) 施工面积 Floor Space Under Construction	竣工面积 Floor Space Completed
精河县 Jinghe [Jing] County	95241	17025	40674	37542	85654	54.79	5.79
温泉县 Wenquan [Araxang] County	39818	7727	4992	27099	28902	18.65	7.20
巴音郭楞蒙古自治州 Bayangol Mongol Autonomous Prefecture	**2759088**	**111464**	**2076556**	**571068**	**1736775**	**352.22**	**155.16**
库尔勒市 Korla City	1844970	5215	1586987	252768	1129404	127.90	74.27
轮台县 Luntai [Bugur] County	166763	18860	100669	47234	133574	14.31	6.72
尉犁县 Yuli [Lopnur] County	56872	8607	12165	36100	39105	17.68	5.23
若羌县 Ruoqiang [Qarkilik] County	199905	18040	129702	52163	123505	64.50	14.39
且末县 Qiemo [Qarqan] County	61190	11497	8998	40695	63760	26.27	10.30
焉耆回族自治县 Yanqi Hui Autonomous County	112632	18052	27476	67104	69129	56.00	23.45
和静县 Hejing County	236389	16813	184444	35132	109945	19.56	13.12
和硕县 Hoxud County	51404	11566	20677	19161	46279	12.14	5.98
博湖县 Bohu [Bagrax] County	28963	2814	5438	20711	22074	13.86	1.68
阿克苏地区 Aksu Administrative Offices	**1271297**	**79028**	**844945**	**347324**	**418662**	**269.71**	**80.17**
阿克苏市 Aksu City	348196	38906	205232	104058	168938	82.21	39.42
温宿县 Wensu [Onsu] County	161532	6089	84473	70970	32711	21.59	2.03
库车县 Kuqa County	371229	4838	287333	79058	53116	22.30	0.26
沙雅县 Xayar County	104825	419	90071	14335	32121	18.42	6.87
新和县 Xinhe [Toksu] County	47194	12446	22255	12493	36352	31.29	11.97
拜城县 Baicheng [Bay] County	132125	3800	88639	39686	21166	39.02	0.46
乌什县 Wushi [Uxturpan] County	34789	1851	21038	11900	24110	23.55	8.05
阿瓦提县 Awat County	53027	8943	30879	13205	42013	27.55	11.12
柯坪县 Kalpin County	18380	1736	15025	1619	8135	3.78	
克孜勒苏柯尔克孜自治州 Kizilsu Kirgiz Autonomous Prefecture	**262380**	**28422**	**127843**	**106115**	**107365**	**145.02**	**60.73**
阿图什市 Artux City	56154		29653	26501	24379	50.45	16.57
阿克陶县 Akto County	99852	20670	38501	40681	45093	50.54	33.62
阿合奇县 Akqi County	62842	6947	54196	1699	3976	16.68	1.56
乌恰县 Wuqia [Ulugqat] County	43532	805	5493	37234	33917	27.35	8.99

4-10 续表 3 Continued

单位：万元 (10 000 yuan)

地区 Region	投资总额 Total Investment	第一产业 Primary Industry	第二产业 Secondary Industry	第三产业 Tertiary Industry	新增固定资产 Newly Increased Fixed Assets	房屋建筑面积(万平方米) Floor Space of Buildings (10 000 sq.m) 施工面积 Floor Space Under Construction	竣工面积 Floor Space Completed
喀什地区 Kashgar [Kaxgar] Administrative Offices	**2102107**	**106457**	**710646**	**1285004**	**1720809**	**1291.42**	**539.17**
喀什市 Kashgar [Kaxgar] City	432356	111	82425	349820	178809	226.06	6.75
疏附县 Shufu County	89026	28583	18623	41820	104290	56.84	24.79
疏勒县 Shule County	332169	9183	107550	215436	310218	166.07	1.12
英吉沙县 Yengisar County	103374	5647	60581	37146	61919	247.64	225.44
泽普县 Zepu [Poskam] County	144771	9800	64158	70813	115803	113.63	37.32
莎车县 Shache [Yarkant] County	204664	22142	50265	132257	222745	188.81	151.94
叶城县 Yecheng [Kagilik] County	146191	442	74441	71308	152113	46.45	1.02
麦盖提县 Makit County	109776	17893	36404	55479	102030	9.44	6.92
岳普湖县 Yopurga County	62243	384	39166	22693	51889	18.18	1.12
伽师县 Jiashi [Payzawat] County	170358	10067	55744	104547	149274	48.63	
巴楚县 Bachu [Maralbexi] County	210717		92739	117978	175357	157.17	82.43
塔什库尔干塔吉克自治县 Taxkorgan Tajik Autonomous County	96462	2205	28550	65707	96362	12.51	0.33
和田地区 Hotan Administrative Offices	**788964**	**58657**	**147899**	**582408**	**696025**	**547.25**	**278.41**
和田市 Hotan City	248133	17139	45024	185970	217096	199.22	87.47
和田县 Hotan County	128029	3525	61201	63303	83314	59.16	46.58
墨玉县 Moyu [Karakax] County	135502	12279	15694	107529	146901	108.43	60.45
皮山县 Pishan [Guma] County	67224	2383	2823	62018	85055	42.81	31.97
洛浦县 Lop County	66023	6329	12633	47061	39507	45.00	4.26
策勒县 Qira County	59570	8524	5569	45477	61023	52.23	35.38
于田县 Yutian [Keriya] County	61999	6107	4615	51277	48479	22.64	7.26
民丰县 Minfeng [Niya] County	22484	2371	340	19773	14650	17.76	5.04
自治区直辖县级市 Municpality Country-LevelCity directly under the Central Government	**1890055**	**28296**	**1499499**	**362260**	**943711**	**404.71**	**154.81**
石河子市 Shihezi City	866979	11389	725985	129605	372705	217.07	38.89
阿拉尔市 Aral City	202656	7683	113999	80974	162474	52.12	37.99
图木舒克市 Tumxuk City	92483	250	44089	48144	116084	46.82	35.51
五家渠市 Wujiaqu City	727937	8974	615426	103537	292448	88.69	42.41
跨地区投资 Trans-regional Investment	**4717690**		**941196**	**3776494**	**1053932**	**28.90**	

4-11 各地、州、市分行业城镇固定资产投资

单位：万元 (2010 年)

行业 Sector	合计 Total	乌鲁木齐市 Urumqi City	克拉玛依市 Karamay City	吐鲁番地区 Turpan Administrative Offices	哈密地区 Hami [Kumul] Administrative Offices	昌吉回族自治州 Changji Hui Autonomous Prefecture	伊犁哈萨克自治州 Ili Kazak Autonomous Prefecture	伊犁州直属县(市) Counties (Cities) Direct Under Ili Prefecture
总计 Total	**28338644**	**3925724**	**1714244**	**846630**	**1368488**	**1788633**	**4359655**	**2055345**
农、林、牧、渔业 Farming, Forestry, Animal Husbandry and Fishery	992872	41270	5209	140354	50382	60723	240011	54753
采矿业 Mining	5954933	166224	1238638	373602	625060	434133	389357	140391
制造业 Manufacturing	5825204	1030648	290228	203264	72870	570027	1243318	839741
电力、燃气及水的生产和供应业 Production and Supply of Electricity, Gas and Water	3784710	961421	8141	26656	272275	247164	1010984	325790
建筑业 Construction	269685	52082	24786		191	702	21525	18632
交通运输、仓储及邮政业 Transport, Storage, Postal and Telecommunications Services	4853566	243738	12482	20742	54471	48637	253432	150209
信息传输、计算机服务和软件业 Information Transmission, Computer Services and Software	413540	250426	6467		2925	9063	27009	7645
批发和零售业 Wholesale&Retail Trades	260273	92711	3528	2680	9980	11573	30112	7638
住宿和餐饮业 Hotels and Catering Services	133121	11313	298	4993	757	8240	26305	15175
金融业 Financial Intermediation	70783	46494		2579	497	3100	2259	1261
房地产业 Real Estate	2058684	224202	11064	4407	124395	180513	424041	185822
租赁和商务服务业 Leasing and Business Services	102288	53442	215			1788	11591	10713
科学研究、技术服务和地质勘查业 Scientific Research, Technical Service and Geological Prospection	164415	12648	614		420	1115	94333	18347
水利、环境和公共设施管理业 Management of Water Conservancy, Environment and Public Facilities	1762038	503178	12795	37850	119895	142772	309235	125570
居民服务和其他服务业 Service to Households and Others Services	35592	8230	3329	400	83	170	3599	1464
教育 Education	536821	97317	36412	8170	9534	28289	83302	35040
卫生、社会保障和社会福利业 Health, Social Securities and Social Welfare	287882	67363	12807	1884	6674	8879	53062	26553
文化、体育和娱乐业 Culture, Sports and Entertainment	160899	21707	35848	745	5581	13717	12452	4977
公共管理和社会组织 Public Management and Social Organization	671338	41310	11383	18304	12498	18028	123728	85624

Investment in Fixed Assets in Urban Area by Sectors in Prefecture, Autonomous Prefecture and City

(10 000 yuan)

塔城地区 Tacheng [Tarbagatai] Administrative Offices	阿勒泰地区 Altay Administrative Offices	博尔塔拉蒙古自治州 Bortala Mongol Autonomous Prefecture	巴音郭楞蒙古自治州 Bayangol Mongol Autonomous Prefecture	阿克苏地区 Aksu Administrative Offices	克孜勒苏柯尔克孜自治州 Kizilsu Kirgiz Autonomous Prefecture	喀什地区 Kashgar [Kaxgar] Administrative Offices	和田地区 Hotan Administrative Offices	石河子市 Shihezi City	阿拉尔市 Aral City	图木舒克市 Tumxuk City	五家渠市 Wujiaqu City	跨地区投资 Trans-regional Investment
1246407	**1057903**	**543689**	**2759088**	**1271297**	**262380**	**2102107**	**788964**	**866979**	**202656**	**92483**	**727937**	**4717690**
64551	120707	42599	111464	79028	28422	106457	58657	11389	7683	250	8974	
92216	156750	20671	1474683	110120	6002	141233	28310		2180	3524		941196
304641	98936	53399	544647	413926	12196	369633	37698	552444	51045	23768	356093	
373192	312002	143044	56555	242472	100699	124890	81551	172041	60774	16710	259333	
2893		5538	671	78427	8946	74890	340	1500		87		
56782	46441	63367	92216	81061	5287	85083	68093	25473	24270	250	33470	3741494
11986	7378	14899	9586	13235	2070	52228	21086	3464		1082		
11412	11062	1722	15296	14528	5283	51925	14544	1015	953	4353	70	
2899	8231	8411	5440	5240		43622	5880	12472		150		
600	398	600	1778	1189	728	6357	3520	1682				
179910	58309	91273	137662	61242	23894	489211	173746	36988	38979	19572	17495	
878		800	7895	3259	1493	17768	3546		491			
2238	73748	2831	6252	4223	20150	6348	13664		993	768	56	
68825	114840	29782	180373	73237	4017	144172	80733	25265	11908	5642	46184	35000
689	1446	480		1537	2180	6356	5203	3205	820			
30027	18235	14450	31504	48382	12787	99626	40657	15658	1908	7044	1781	
16821	9688	1610	20667	20579	9335	53567	26076	3209		2170		
3696	3779	5747	6950	4581	3343	24756	17711	1174	152	2241	4194	
22151	15953	42466	55449	15031	15548	203985	107949		500	4872	287	

4-12 城镇固定资产投资效果指标

Investment Result of Urban Investment

指　标	Item	2009	2010
建设周期(年)	Construction Cycle (year)	3	3
计划总投资(万元)	Total Planned Investment (10 000 yuan)	67958324	80276938
本年完成投资(万元)	Completed Invetsment for the Current Year (10 000 yuan)	22999843	28338644
本年新增固定资产(万元)	Newly Increased Fixed Assets for the Current Year (10 000 yuan)	17063103	15042603
固定资产交付使用率(%)	Rate of Projects of Fixed Assets Completed and Put into Operation (%)	74.2	53.1
施工项目个数(个)	Number of Projects under Construction (unit)	8200	8179
竣工项目个数(个)	Number of Projects Completed (unit)	5469	5369
建设项目投产率(%)	Rate of Projects Completed&Put into Use (%)	66.7	65.6
施工面积(万平方米)	Construction Area (10 000 sq.m)	4430.23	5400.16
#住　宅	Residential Buildings	2112.05	2717.34
竣工面积(万平方米)	Completed Area (10 000 sq.m)	1968.75	2147.84
#住　宅	Residential Buildings	1093.41	1168.34
房屋面积竣工率(%)	Rate of Floor Space of Buildings Completed (%)	44.4	39.8
#住　宅	Residential Buildings	51.8	43.0

4-13 主要年份房地产开发企业基本情况

Basic Condition of Enterprises for Real Estate Development in Main Years

指　标	Item	2005	2009	2010
企业单位数(个)	**Number of Enterprises (unit)**	**756**	**1159**	**1233**
#亏损企业	Loss- Suffering Enterprises	410	592	606
从业人员数(人)	**Number of Employed Persons (person)**	**15558**	**20548**	**22855**
从业人员劳动报酬(万元)	**Work Pay for Employees (10 000 yuan)**	**27184**	**53853**	**72530**
主要财务指标（万元)	**Main Financial Indices (10 000 yuan)**			
年末资产负债情况	Situation of Year-end Liabilities			
资产总计	Total Assets	4861415	8879986	12591584
固定资产累计折旧	Accumulated Depreciation of Fixed Assets	81096	136850	156739
#本年折旧	Depreciation for the Current Year	17981	30420	34814
负债总计	Total Liabilities	2932694	6409943	9422446
所有者权益合计	Total of Owner's Right and Interest	1928721	2470043	3169138
实收资本合计	Total of Actual Capital	970103	1738165	2109245
#国家资本	State-owned Capital	59976	147195	162505
损益情况	Situation of Profit and Loss			
主营业务收入	Total Income of Business	1084796	2995468	4119413
土地转让收入	Income of Land Transfer	11295	12355	19029
商品房销售收入	Sales Income of Commercial Flat	1047965	2914370	4022490
房屋出租收入	Income of Renting House	15773	16533	39343
其他收入	Others	9763	52211	38550
主营业务成本	Cost of Business	871320	2243191	3040741
主营业务税金及附加	Tax and Extra Charges on Business	63562	204086	295011
销售费用	Expenses of sales	27319	77073	100896
其他业务利润	Other Business Profits	9161	16480	28592
管理费用及财务费用	Expenses of Both Management and Finance	80949	213617	257405
投资收益及营业外收入	Income of Investment earnings and Extra-business	7829	14809	14881
营业外支出	Expenditure of Extra-business	3456	13419	14909
利润总额	Total Profits	34320	270638	454814

4-14 主要年份房地产投资主要指标
Main Indicators of Real Estate Investment in Main Years

指 标	Item	2005	2009	2010
本年购置土地面积(万平方米)	**Land Area Purchased for the Current Year (10 000 sq. m)**	**447.30**	**429.35**	**557.69**
完成开发土地面积(万平方米)	**Land Area Completed for Development (10 000 sq. m)**	**478.54**	**675.40**	
房地产开发投资额(万元)	**Total Investment of Real-Estate Development (10 000 yuan)**	**1016618**	**2358805**	**3477185**
土地开发投资	Investment in Land Development	50588	112950	
按中央和地方分	Classified by Central and Local			
中央企业	Central Enterprises	54128	163412	175564
地方企业	Local Enterprises	962490	2195393	3301621
按投资构成分	Classified by Use of Funds			
建筑工程	Construction Works	810003	1890270	2742491
安装工程	Works of Installation	49559	102635	161703
设备工器具购置	Purchase of Equipment and Instruments	14135	17931	51777
其他费用	Other Expenses	142921	347969	521214
#土地购置费	Expenses of Land Purchase	94230	202045	313568
按工程用途分	Classified by Purpose of Projects			
住 宅	Residential buildings	679521	1882530	2815620
办公楼	Office Building	40977	81926	102895
商业营业用房	Houses for Commercial and Business Purpose	247033	281946	380275
其 他	Others	49087	112403	178395
本年资金来源小计(万元)	**Sub-total of Capital Sources for the Current Year (10 000 yuan)**	**1137693**	**3683795**	**5380739**
国内贷款	Domestic Loans	113887	453692	684191
利用外资	Foreign Investment	160	50	
自筹资金	Self-raising Funds	479948	915219	1397982
其它资金	Others	543698	2314834	3298566

4-15 按用途分房地产开发企业（单位）投资完成额

Investment Actually Completed by Enterprises for Real Estate Development by Use

单位：万元 (10 000 yuan)

年 份 Year	地 区 Region	企业个数 (个) Number of Enterprises (unit)	本年完成投资 Investment Completed This Year	住 宅 Residential Buildings	#别墅、高档公寓 Villas, High-grade Apartments	#经 济适用房 Economically Affordable Housing
1996		139	156232	80728		4489
1997			169906	81886	1668	21474
1998			148577	95225	1000	27388
1999		165	234481	174446	2994	55345
2000		209	574347	500381	2390	236923
2001		293	979184	757490	3126	350362
2002		335	877060	570643	11001	236731
2003		492	1024908	547770	20212	243651
2004		709	1125577	599276	29585	207447
2005		756	1016618	679521	26634	245022
2006		824	1208786	899482	48542	304890
2007		909	1683160	1390360	57776	164429
2008		1130	2286267	1937460	94256	164559
2009		1159	2358805	1882530	148916	160840
2010		1233	3477185	2815620	194136	99339
乌鲁木齐市	Urumqi City	365	1501919	1201234	81006	20531
克拉玛依市	Karamay City	41	91929	67175	9020	16064
吐鲁番地区	Turpan Administrative Offices	15	28515	19838	2971	535
哈密地区	Hami [Kumul] Administrative Offices	80	147280	117011	1058	6405
昌吉回族自治州	Changji Hui Autonomous Prefecture	98	305173	283662	3536	26828
伊犁哈萨克自治州	Ili Kazak Autonomous Prefecture	222	484315	396868	4692	12767
伊犁州直属县(市)	Counties (Cities) Direct Under Ili Prefecture	122	326098	267214	4292	4568
塔城地区	Tacheng [Tarbagatai] Administrative Offices	46	81511	74076	400	464
阿勒泰地区	Altay Administrative Offices	54	76706	55578		7735
博尔塔拉蒙古自治州	Bortala Mongol Autonomous Prefecture	44	44002	32297	290	332
巴音郭楞蒙古自治州	Bayangol Mongol Autonomous Prefecture	126	314995	265022	90499	
阿克苏地区	Aksu Administrative Offices	99	203507	145611	244	6139
克孜勒苏柯尔克孜自治州	Kizilsu Kirgiz Autonomous Prefecture	7	7000	1460	700	
喀什地区	Kashgar [Kaxgar] Administrative Offices	66	200775	162063		
和田地区	Hotan Administrative Offices	2	4292	2700		
石河子市	Shihezi City	45	97019	87474	120	1291
阿拉尔市	Aral City	8	21646	10413		6239
图木舒克市	Tumxuk City	2	1550	860		200
五家渠市	Wujiaqu City	13	23268	21932		2008

4-15 续表 Continued

单位：万元 (10 000 yuan)

年 份 Year	地 区 Region	办公楼 Office buildings	商业营业用房 Houses for Business Use	其 他 Other
	1996	18108	42562	14834
	1997	25347	41935	20738
	1998	17394	22027	13931
	1999	9133	27068	23834
	2000	13171	42601	18194
	2001	41911	111028	68755
	2002	81119	153498	71800
	2003	81497	286896	108745
	2004	77843	390566	57892
	2005	40977	247033	49087
	2006	28233	236945	44126
	2007	27629	205590	59581
	2008	56358	221418	71031
	2009	81926	281946	112403
	2010	102895	380275	178395
乌鲁木齐市	Urumqi City	79567	117343	103775
克拉玛依市	Karamay City	4756	11564	8434
吐鲁番地区	Turpan Administrative Offices	2170	5093	1414
哈密地区	Hami [Kumul] Administrative Offices	3174	23107	3988
昌吉回族自治州	Changji Hui Autonomous Prefecture	545	15179	5787
伊犁哈萨克自治州	Ili Kazak Autonomous Prefecture	3402	72597	11448
伊犁州直属县(市)	Counties (Cities) Direct Under Ili Prefecture	2077	49802	7005
塔城地区	Tacheng [Tarbagatai] Administrative Offices	834	3021	3580
阿勒泰地区	Altay Administrative Offices	491	19774	863
博尔塔拉蒙古自治州	Bortala Mongol Autonomous Prefecture	174	9350	2181
巴音郭楞蒙古自治州	Bayangol Mongol Autonomous Prefecture	1378	37120	11475
阿克苏地区	Aksu Administrative Offices	3670	32727	21499
克孜勒苏柯尔克孜自治州	Kizilsu Kirgiz Autonomous Prefecture		4330	1210
喀什地区	Kashgar [Kaxgar] Administrative Offices	3342	30141	5229
和田地区	Hotan Administrative Offices	63	1479	50
石河子市	Shihezi City	479	7942	1124
阿拉尔市	Aral City		11233	
图木舒克市	Tumxuk City		690	
五家渠市	Wujiaqu City	175	380	781

4-16 房地产开发企业（单位）资金来源
Sources of Funds of Enterprises for Real Estate Development

单位：万元 (10 000 yuan)

年 份 Year	地 区 Region	合 计 Total	国内贷款 Domestic Loans	利用外资 Foreign Investment	自筹资金 Self-raising Funds	其他资金来源 Others
	1996	154995	51048	742	45104	58101
	1997	161399	51443	500	60573	48883
	1998	151094	22419	500	49427	78748
	1999	244252	29665	5770	73899	134918
	2000	701332	113823	600	232768	354141
	2001	890102	106794	1278	303975	478055
	2002	1064031	158511		455707	449813
	2003	1117659	208348		448441	460870
	2004	1215850	125553		546282	544015
	2005	1137693	113887	160	479948	543698
	2006	1446593	145340		478871	822382
	2007	2243755	217380		766344	1260031
	2008	2427323	253427		961343	1212553
	2009	3683795	453692	50	915219	2314834
	2010	5380739	684191		1397982	3298566
乌鲁木齐市	Urumqi City	2886408	443023		579367	1864018
克拉玛依市	Karamay City	129857	7974		49826	72057
吐鲁番地区	Turpan Administrative Offices	24706	500		16951	7255
哈密地区	Hami [Kumul] Administrative Offices	171434	16534		37944	116956
昌吉回族自治州	Changji Hui Autonomous Prefecture	435899	64310		128501	243088
伊犁哈萨克自治州	Ili Kazak Autonomous Prefecture	686860	67566		214933	404361
伊犁州直属县(市)	Counties (Cities) Direct Under Ili Prefecture	525691	57654		105367	362670
塔城地区	Tacheng [Tarbagatai] Administrative Offices	86060	1180		60161	24719
阿勒泰地区	Altay Administrative Offices	75109	8732		49405	16972
博尔塔拉蒙古自治州	Bortala Mongol Autonomous Prefecture	45328	300		26089	18939
巴音郭楞蒙古自治州	Bayangol Mongol Autonomous Prefecture	361342	33416		108439	219487
阿克苏地区	Aksu Administrative Offices	215534	20700		97699	97135
克孜勒苏柯尔克孜自治州	Kizilsu Kirgiz Autonomous Prefecture	7928	5300		626	2002
喀什地区	Kashgar [Kaxgar] Administrative Offices	260151	14025		105587	140539
和田地区	Hotan Administrative Offices	4333			3900	433
石河子市	Shihezi City	102309	8000		7467	86842
阿拉尔市	Aral City	21713			17763	3950
图木舒克市	Tumxuk City	1150	200		950	
五家渠市	Wujiaqu City	25787	2343		1940	21504

4-17 房地产开发企业（单位）施工、销售和空置情况

单位：万平方米

年 份 Year	地 区 Region	本年施工房屋面积 Floor Space of Building under Construction This Year	#住宅 Residential Buildings	#商业营业用房 Houses for Business Use	本年新开工房屋面积 Floor Space Started This Year	#住宅 Residential Buildings	#商业营业用房 Houses for Business Use
	1996	224.90	150.80	41.67	103.87	69.84	19.52
	1997	222.20	144.50	47.68	90.24	70.08	12.81
	1998	252.61	188.38	40.72	133.26	120.95	6.35
	1999	343.38	295.62	34.33	212.73	194.77	12.48
	2000	771.86	665.30	74.20	453.63	397.77	43.00
	2001	1433.54	1207.89	150.63	912.06	778.55	97.24
	2002	1246.89	946.11	204.52	577.04	433.57	98.13
	2003	1382.14	962.89	298.51	782.78	557.28	175.73
	2004	1333.03	863.19	357.53	771.47	550.66	178.43
	2005	1371.15	941.58	340.63	793.55	639.98	130.90
	2006	1567.70	1188.61	307.19	1035.59	875.99	131.90
	2007	2053.76	1715.00	271.52	1347.11	1216.39	101.82
	2008	2639.06	2247.80	259.78	1703.86	1500.75	129.11
	2009	3064.41	2560.67	305.81	1718.17	1482.86	158.07
	2010	3980.80	3317.68	410.96	2177.24	1852.88	214.50
乌鲁木齐市	Urumqi City	1636.46	1323.80	146.25	799.65	677.73	56.26
克拉玛依市	Karamay City	124.30	101.77	10.71	25.08	23.39	0.42
吐鲁番地区	Turpan Administrative Offices	54.53	42.86	7.26	24.53	20.79	3.19
哈密地区	Hami [Kumul] Administrative Offices	205.99	164.31	31.81	110.22	91.22	14.58
昌吉回族自治州	Changji Hui Autonomous Prefecture	235.93	216.67	16.36	199.18	181.84	14.45
伊犁哈萨克自治州	Ili Kazak Autonomous Prefecture	552.70	483.00	59.49	367.92	321.05	37.75
伊犁州直属县(市)	Counties (Cities) Direct Under Ili Prefecture	364.56	326.96	31.77	230.73	202.20	22.90
塔城地区	Tacheng [Tarbagatai] Administrative Offices	78.91	71.23	4.84	66.81	61.46	2.77
阿勒泰地区	Altay Administrative Offices	109.23	84.81	22.88	70.38	57.39	12.08
博尔塔拉蒙古自治州	Bortala Mongol Autonomous Prefecture	57.51	46.72	10.14	31.83	27.72	3.74
巴音郭楞蒙古自治州	Bayangol Mongol Autonomous Prefecture	441.57	389.01	36.53	219.57	194.37	19.75
阿克苏地区	Aksu Administrative Offices	222.91	179.12	28.60	149.23	117.84	21.20
克孜勒苏柯尔克孜自治州	Kizilsu Kirgiz Autonomous Prefecture	8.64	5.37	3.27	6.62	3.42	3.20
喀什地区	Kashgar [Kaxgar] Administrative Offices	229.85	185.62	35.49	130.29	103.57	21.92
和田地区	Hotan Administrative Offices	6.98	6.65	0.33	1.53	1.45	0.08
石河子市	Shihezi City	127.48	105.74	16.24	60.83	45.74	10.37
阿拉尔市	Aral City	20.37	13.21	7.16	11.08	3.92	7.16
图木舒克市	Tumxuk City	1.90	1.26	0.64	1.02	0.97	0.05
五家渠市	Wujiaqu City	34.82	34.06	0.38	22.03	21.27	0.38

Condition of Under Construction, Sale and Idle of Enterprises for Real Estate Development

(10 000 sq.m)

本年竣工房屋面积 Floor Space of Buindings Completed This Year	#住宅 Residential Buildings	#商业营业用房 Houses for Business Use	本年房屋销售面积 Floor Space of Building Sold This Year	#住宅 Residential Buildings	#商业营业用房 Houses for Business Use	房屋销售额(万元) Sales Value of Buildings (10 000 yuan)	#住宅 Residential Buildings	#商业营业用房 Houses for Business Use
81.19	64.51	8.14	45.60	41.29	2.91	67514	57024	5883
93.56	73.32	6.93	55.43	52.48	0.98	75110	67585	1569
94.28	79.92	6.23	83.29	75.97	3.46	118386	98803	8544
159.99	143.93	13.52	127.48	120.44	4.67	177683	158304	12599
330.11	298.79	23.07	262.52	250.95	9.82	373801	333166	35153
633.25	559.91	57.01	419.87	381.67	31.77	643814	537818	90441
727.21	616.12	85.03	506.66	455.68	46.34	879287	658157	208821
791.14	626.50	126.42	587.02	516.48	53.44	1066640	768012	224579
704.25	511.61	156.54	635.53	538.33	81.27	1106143	784408	281856
717.43	553.48	121.37	687.20	606.48	68.16	1235410	915191	288747
679.06	551.63	104.13	892.41	806.46	73.96	1658176	1358136	265450
890.55	798.12	72.07	1144.34	1078.28	51.57	2381520	2113425	211508
1049.29	943.40	67.30	954.35	886.35	51.22	2137859	1861169	212861
1032.72	900.87	76.28	1406.55	1326.67	65.81	3662638	3271682	317310
1012.90	859.92	98.40	1564.90	1450.02	94.42	4830392	4164140	523153
278.75	217.92	28.29	473.73	433.49	23.68	2115924	1824357	164651
20.97	16.48	3.68	57.64	53.79	3.20	152237	130402	20758
3.17	2.74	0.44	19.54	17.63	1.91	39360	31533	7827
87.77	69.85	15.96	69.76	66.74	2.93	197104	169147	27673
29.61	26.45	3.16	162.71	154.61	7.99	436504	401044	34502
131.71	122.03	8.72	263.87	248.63	14.68	613172	551495	60352
81.07	76.43	4.30	185.89	177.78	7.64	440262	402742	36340
20.62	18.77	1.57	37.40	35.51	1.89	90115	85416	4699
30.02	26.83	2.84	40.59	35.34	5.15	82795	63337	19313
23.73	22.57	0.95	23.48	19.78	3.57	53877	38406	15278
187.09	163.05	14.59	179.14	172.68	6.17	422081	389612	32037
74.30	60.18	7.11	109.03	93.80	14.21	265724	195870	67145
2.02	1.95	0.07	4.17	2.25	1.92	31872	3289	28583
52.63	47.37	3.92	98.15	89.91	7.42	247580	202105	37023
0.30	0.30		2.95	2.91	0.05	7075	6846	229
72.23	64.63	7.32	52.55	48.29	4.04	153351	133450	19148
15.87	12.61	3.26	16.27	14.51	1.76	26666	20902	5764
1.28	0.64	0.64	1.63	1.24	0.39	2477	1570	907
13.54	13.54		18.24	18.06	0.18	45573	45166	407

4-17 续表 Continued

单位：万平方米 (10 000 sq.m)

年 份 Year	地 区 Region	房屋待售面积 Floor Space At Idle	#住宅 Residential Buildings	#商业营业用房 Houses for Business Use
	1996	33.20	27.41	4.44
	1997	36.33	25.58	3.76
	1998	27.20	20.33	2.78
	1999	63.01	49.00	8.91
	2000	69.75	58.92	6.35
	2001	200.46	169.78	20.26
	2002	353.23	285.87	51.33
	2003	422.11	313.93	84.81
	2004	400.40	248.38	125.31
	2005	460.99	269.07	151.02
	2006	406.25	208.02	157.83
	2007	289.22	115.39	150.68
	2008	389.70	245.81	119.10
	2009	419.83	254.36	121.41
	2010	348.98	195.47	106.55
乌鲁木齐市	Urumqi City	141.43	58.98	41.87
克拉玛依市	Karamay City	6.24	0.10	3.98
吐鲁番地区	Turpan Administrative Offices	5.00	3.62	1.38
哈密地区	Hami [Kumul] Administrative Offices	2.22	1.45	0.71
昌吉回族自治州	Changji Hui Autonomous Prefecture	21.28	15.55	4.82
伊犁哈萨克自治州	Ili Kazak Autonomous Prefecture	36.90	23.59	11.86
伊犁州直属县(市)	Counties (Cities) Direct Under Ili Prefecture	25.93	14.33	10.38
塔城地区	Tacheng [Tarbagatai] Administrative Offices	7.33	6.83	0.46
阿勒泰地区	Altay Administrative Offices	3.64	2.43	1.02
博尔塔拉蒙古自治州	Bortala Mongol Autonomous Prefecture	7.88	5.60	2.29
巴音郭楞蒙古自治州	Bayangol Mongol Autonomous Prefecture	47.70	31.95	14.58
阿克苏地区	Aksu Administrative Offices	27.35	20.18	6.68
克孜勒苏柯尔克孜自治州	Kizilsu Kirgiz Autonomous Prefecture	5.83	2.36	3.47
喀什地区	Kashgar [Kaxgar] Administrative Offices	18.50	15.58	2.82
和田地区	Hotan Administrative Offices	0.80		0.80
石河子市	Shihezi City	10.34	5.81	4.51
阿拉尔市	Aral City	7.41	1.79	5.61
图木舒克市	Tumxuk City	0.27	0.02	0.25
五家渠市	Wujiaqu City	3.34	2.41	0.94

4-18 新增主要产品生产能力

Newly Increased Production Capacity of Major Products

项　目	Item	2009	2010
原煤开采(万吨/年)	Coal Mining (10 000 tons/year)	3019.10	4874.90
焦炭(万吨/年)	Coke (10 000 tons/year)	669.50	564.00
天然原油开采(万吨/年)	Petroleum Extractin (10 000 tons/year)	155.30	330.55
天然气开采(亿立方米/年)	Natural Gas Extraction (100 million cu.m/year)	11.72	20.00
铁矿石开采(原矿) (万吨/年)	Iron-Ore Mining (10 000 tons/year)	9300.95	486.70
铁矿选矿处理原矿量(万吨/年)	Iron-ore Dressing (10 000 tons/year)	520.00	62.00
铁矿石成品矿(万吨/年)	Eed Products of Iron Ore Mine(10 000 tons/year)	231.20	58.00
生铁(万吨/年)	Pig Iron(10 000 tons/year)	342.40	88.50
粗钢(万吨/年)	Crude Steel(10 000 tons/year)	540.00	160.00
热轧钢材(万吨/年)	Hot-rolled Steel(10 000 tons/year)	120.00	60.00
铜采矿(原矿)(万吨/年)	Copper Ore Mining (10 000 tons/year)	49.05	627.00
铜选矿	Copper Ore Dressing		
处理原矿(万吨/年)	Raw Ore Treatment (10 000 tons/year)	192.10	686.25
铅锌采矿(原矿) (万吨/年)	Plumbum/Zinc Ore Mining (10 000 tons/year)	20.30	3.03
铝加工(吨/年)	Aluminium Processing (ton/year)	20500	29500
黄金(公斤/年)	Gold (kg/year)	3027	475
发电机组容量(万千瓦)	Capacity of Generating Setes (10 000 kw/year)		
水力发电	Hydropower	109.76	39.42
火力发电	Thermal Power	147.35	97.10
其他发电	Others	9.10	29.75
输电线路长度(11 万伏及以上)(公里)	Transmission Line (110 000V)(km)	5743.00	6967.70
水泥(万吨/年)	Cement (10 000 tons/year)	598.00	863.00

4-18 续表 Continued

项 目	Item	2009	2010
石墨及炭素制品(吨/年)	Graphite and Carbon Products(ton/year)	10	450050
电石(吨/年)	Calcium Carbide (ton/year)	300000	780000
农用氮、磷、钾化学肥料(吨/年)	Farm-use Nitrogen, Phosphorus and Potassium Fertilizer (ton/year)		
氮肥	Nitrogen Fertilizer	237000	316500
磷肥	Phoshate Fertilizer	2800	4150
钾肥	Potash Fertilizer	763097	850453
塑料树脂及共聚物(吨/年)	Plastic Colophony and Polymer (ton/year)	75000	368000
化学纤维(吨/年)	Chemical Fiber (ton/year)	180000	10199
粘胶纤维(吨/年)	Viscose Fiber(ton/year)	90000	100
棉纺锭(锭)	Cotton Spindle (spindle)	417160	430560
酒(万吨/年)	Liquors (10 000 tons/year)	0.85	14.74
其他酒	Others	0.85	5.62
程控交换机安装能力(万线/年)	Program-Controlled Telephone Exchange (10 000 lines/year)	122.42	3.00
新建公路(公里)	Length of New Highways (km)	1632	2915
二级公路	Second Class highway	241	252
改建公路(公里)	Length of Reconstructed Highways(km)	9622	10490
二级公路	Second Class highway	1250	1412
新建独立公路桥梁(延长米)	New-Built Separate Highway and Bridge (Extended Length m)	1345	5159
(座)	(unit)	5	12
新(扩)建客、货运站(个)	Number of newly-Built or Expanded Passenger and Freight Stations (unit)	13	11
(平方米)	(sq.m)	12859	11171
民航机场跑道(条)	Length of runway(unit)	1	1
(米)	(m)	3200	2600
城市自来水供水能力(万吨/日)	Capacity of City Tap Water Supply (10 000 tons/day)	36.70	4.21
城市公共交通车辆购置(辆)	Purchase of City Communiting Vehicles (unit)	213	107
城市污水处理能力(万吨/日)	Disposal Capacity of Sewer (10 000 tons/day)	37.72	26.70

4-19 农村非农户固定资产投资情况
Investment in Fixed Assets of Non-Rural Households in Rural Areas

单位：万元 (10 000 yuan)

指 标	Item	2009	2010
新增固定资产	**Newly Increased Investment in Fixed Assets**	**1508222**	**2040850**
固定资产投资完成额	**Completed Investment in Fixed Assets**	**1874325**	**2395698**
按投资构成分	By Use of Funds		
建筑工程	Construction Works	1222339	1680923
安装工程	Installation Works	94285	84491
设备工器具购置	Purchase of Equipment and Instruments	393237	441866
#用于更新的设备	Renew of Equipment and Instruments	45337	24961
其 他	Others	164464	188418
按投资方向分	By Sector of Investment		
农、林、牧、渔业	Agriculture, Forestry, Animal Husbandry and Fishing	544723	625516
采矿业	Mining	109824	148357
制造业	Manufacturing	248010	377963
电力、燃气及水的生产及供应业	Production and Supply of Electricity Gas and Water	143534	166265
建筑业	Construction	26914	55750
交通运输、仓储和邮政业	Transport, Storage and Post	200812	254073
信息传输、计算机服务和软件业	Information Transmission, Computer Servcies and Software	27633	6775
批发和零售业	Wholesale and Retail Trades	15529	23603
住宿和餐饮业	Hotel and Catering Service	6563	5025
金融业	Financial Intermediation	150	929
房地产业	Real Estate	146571	327223
租赁和商务服务业	Leasing and Business Service Industries	18757	11362
科学研究、技术服务和地质勘查业	Scientific Research, Technology Service and Geological Prospecting	15050	7765
水利、环境和公共设施管理业	Water Conservancy, Environment and Public Facility Management	188592	195734
居民服务和其他服务业	Community Service and Other Services	6782	2538
教 育	Education	42804	31606
卫生、社会保障和社会福利业	Health, Social Security and Social Welfare	28058	26533
文化、体育和娱乐业	Culture, Sports and Entertainment	14377	11228
公共管理和社会组织	Public Management and Social Organizations	89642	117453
资金来源小计	**Sub-total Funds**	**1993076**	**2437138**
国家预算内资金	State Budgetary Funds	666258	779907
国内贷款	Domestic Loans	139994	140959
债 券	Bonds	1519	
利用外资	Foreign Investment	10291	1294
自筹资金	Self-raising Funds	982155	1246453
其他资金	Others	192859	268525
本年施工房屋面积(万平方米)	**Floor Space of Buildings Under Construction (10 000 sq.m)**	**600.02**	**856.62**
#住 宅	Residential Building	308.29	526.44
本年竣工房屋面积(万平方米)	**Floor Space of Completed Building (10 000 sq.m)**	**257.54**	**450.52**
#住 宅	Residential Building	130.96	269.21

4-20 农户固定资产投资情况
Investment in Fixed Assets of Rural Households in Rural Areas

单位:万元　　(抽样调查 Sampled Survey)　　(10 000 yuan)

指　　标	Item	2009	2010
新增固定资产原值	**Newly Increased Investment in Fixed Assets**	**1039386**	**1185414**
固定资产投资完成额	**Complete Investment in Fixed Assets**	**1039386**	**1185414**
按投资来源分	By Source of Fund		
国内贷款	Domestic Loans	110434	202133
自筹资金	Self-raising Funds	893236	947111
其他资金	Others	35716	36170
按投资构成分	By Use of Funds		
建筑工程	Construction	508774	524640
#水　利	Water Conservancy	33421	34805
房　屋	Building	473156	485835
#住　宅	Residential Building	463297	466781
设备工、器具购置	Purchase of Equipment And Instruments	418003	528360
#生产设备	Production of Equipment	383669	424014
其　它	Others	112609	132414
按投资方向分	By Sector of Funds		
第一产业	Primary	440469	495887
第二产业	Secondary	85803	87764
第三产业	Tertiary	513114	601763
按具体投资项目分	By Project of Investment		
房　屋	Building	473156	485835
#住　宅	Residential Building	463297	466781
设　备	Equipment	418003	528360
水　利	Water Conservancy	33421	34805
其　他	Others	114806	136414
本年施工房屋面积(万平方米)	**Floor Space of Buildings Under Construction (10 000 sq.m)**	**1416.36**	**1124.38**
#住 宅	Residential Building	1363.38	1079.12
本年竣工房屋面积(万平方米)	**Floor Space of Completed Building (10 000 sq.m)**	**1339.78**	**1038.63**
#住 宅	Residential Building	1287.19	994.42
调查户总人口(人)	**Total Number of Households (person)**	**7183**	**7169**

主要统计指标解释

全社会固定资产投资 以货币形式表现的在一定时期内全社会建造和购置固定资产的工作量以及与此有关的费用的总称。该指标是反映固定资产投资规模、结构和发展速度的综合性指标,又是观察工程进度和考核投资效果的重要依据。全社会固定资产投资按登记注册类型可分为国有、集体、个体、联营、股份制、外商、港澳台商、其他等。

城镇固定资产投资 指城镇各种登记注册类型的企业、事业、行政单位及个体户进行的计划总投资(或实际需要总投资)50 万元及 50 万元以上的建设项目投资、房地产开发投资。县城及以上区域内发生的投资，县及县以上各级政府及主管部门直接领导、管理的建设项目和企业事业单位的投资均为城镇固定资产投资。

房地产开发投资 指各种登记注册类型的房地产开发公司、商品房建设公司及其他房地产开发法人单位和附属于其他法人单位实际从事房地产开发或经营活动的单位统一开发的包括统代建、拆迁还建的住宅、厂房、仓库、饭店、宾馆、度假村、写字楼、办公楼等房屋建筑物和配套的服务设施，土地开发工程(如道路、给水、排水、供电、供热、通讯、平整场地等基础设施工程)的投资;不包括单纯的土地交易活动。

农村投资 包括在农村区域范围内进行固定资产投资活动的企业、事业、行政单位及农户投资。

建设总规模 是指在报告期内所有施工项目的计划总投资。这个指标和施工项目相对应。

在建总规模 是指在报告期末所有在建项目的计划总投资。

在建净规模 是指报告期末所有在建项目建成投产尚需的投资总量。在建净规模＝在建总规模－累计完成投资。

固定资产投资的资金来源 根据固定资产投资的资金来源不同，分为国家预算内资金、国内贷款、利用外资、自筹资金和其他资金来源。

(1)国家预算内资金:分为财政拨款和财政安排的贷款两部分。包括中央财政的基本建设基金(分经营性基金和非经营性基金两部分)、专项支出(如煤代油专项等)、收回再贷、贴息资金，财政安排的挖潜改造和新产品试制支出、城建支出、商业部门简易建筑支出、不发达地区发展基金等资金中用于固定资产投资的资金;地方财政中由国家统筹安排的资金等。

(2)国内贷款:指报告期固定资产投资单位向银行及非银行金融机构借入的用于固定资产投资的各种国内借款，包括银行利用自有资金及吸收的存款发放的贷款、上级主管部门拨入的国内贷款、国家专项贷款(包括煤代油贷款、劳改煤矿专项贷款等)、地方财政专项资金安排的贷款、国内储备贷款、周转贷款等。

(3)利用外资:指报告期收到的用于固定资产建造和购置的国外资金(包括设备、材料、技术在内)。包括对外借款(外国政府、国际金融组织贷款、出口信贷、外国银行商业贷款、对外发行债券和股票)、外商直接投资及外商其他投资。不包括我国自有外汇资金(国家外汇、地方外汇、留成外汇、调剂外汇和中国银行自有资金发行的外汇贷款等)。计算利用外资时，需要折算成人民币，折算中所使用的外汇汇率按现汇计算，即按使用外汇时的汇率计算。

(4)自筹资金:指固定资产投资单位报告期收到的，由各地区、各部门及企、事业单位筹集用于固定资产投资的预算外资金，包括中央各部门、各级地方和企、事业单位的自筹资金。

(5)其他资金:指在报告期收到的除以上各种资金之外其他用于固定资产投资的资金，包括企业或金融机构通过发行各种债券筹集到的资金、群众集资、个人资金、无偿捐赠的资金及其他单位拨入的资金等。

固定资产投资按国民经济行业分 根据建设项目建成投产后的主要产品或主要用途及社会经济活动性质来确定国民经济行业。一般情况下，一个建设项目或一个企业、事业单位只能属于一种国民经济行业。为了更准确地反映国民经济各行业之间的比例关系，联合企业(总厂)所属分厂属于不同行业的，原则上按分厂划分行业。

固定资产投资按建设性质分 根据建设项目情况来确定。 建设项目的性质一般分为新建、扩建、改建、迁建、恢复。房地产开发单位、农村投资、城镇工矿区私人建房投资不划分建设性质。

(1)新建:一般指从无到有“平地起家”开始建设的企业、事业和行政单位或建设项目。有的单位原有基础很小，经过建设后新增的固定资产价值超过该企、事业、行政单位原有固定资产价值(原值)三倍以上的也应作为新建。

(2)扩建:指在厂内或其他地点，为扩大原有产品的生产能力(或效益)或增加新的产品生产能力，而增建主要的生产车间(或主要工程)、分厂、独立的生产线。行政、事业单位在原单位增建业务用房(如学校增建教学用房、医院增建门诊部、病房等)也作为扩建。

现有企、事业单位为扩大原有主要产品生产能力或增加新的产品生产能力，增建一个或几个主要生产车间(或主要工程)、分厂，同时进行一些更新改造工程的，也应作为扩建。

(3)改建和技术改造:指现有企业、事业单位，对原有设施进行技术改造或更新(包括相应配套的辅助性生产、生活福利设施)的建设项目。现有企业、事业单位为适应市场变化的需要，而改变企业的主要产品种类(如军工企业转产民品等) 的建设项目，应作为改建。原有产品生产作业线由于各工序(车间)之间能力不平衡，为填平补齐充分发挥原有生产能力而增建不增加本企业主要产品设计能力的车间，也应作为改建。技术改造是指企业、事业单位在现有基础上，用先进的技术代替落后的技术，用先进的工艺和装备代替落后的工艺和装备，以改变企业落后的技术经济面貌，实现以内涵为主的扩大再生产，达到提高产品质量、促进产品更新换代、节约能源、降低消耗、扩大生产规模、全面提高社会经济效益的目的。技术改造具体包括以下内容：机器设备和工具的更新改造；生产工艺改革、节约能源和原材料的改造；厂房建筑和公共设施的改造；劳动条件和生产环境的改造。

固定资产投资按构成分　固定资产投资活动按其工作内容和实现方式分为建筑安装工程，设备、工具、器具购置，其他费用三个部分。

(1)建筑安装工程(建筑安装工作量):指各种房屋、建筑物的建造工程和各种设备、装置的安装工程。包括各种房屋建造工程，各种用途设备基础和各种工业窑炉的砌筑工程及金属结构工程;为施工而进行的各种准备工作和临时工程以及完工后的清理工作等;铁路、道路的铺设，矿井的开凿及石油管道的架设等;水利工程;防空地下建筑等特殊工程;列入房屋工程预算内的暖气、卫生、通风、照明、煤气等设备的价值及装设油饰工程;列入建筑工程预算内的各种管道(蒸汽、压缩空气、石油、给排水等管道)、电力、电讯电缆导线等的敷设工程;以及各种机械设备的安装工程;为测定安装工程质量，对设备进行的试运工作;房地产开发单位进行的商品房屋开发建设工程、土地开发工程。

在安装工程中，不包括被安装设备本身的价值。

(2)设备、工具、器具购置:指建设单位或企、事业单位购置或自制的，达到固定资产标准的设备、工具、器具的价值。新建单位及扩建单位的新建车间，按照设计或计划要求购置或自制的全部设备、工具、器具，不论是否达到固定资产标准均计入“设备、工具、器具购置”中。

(3)其他费用:指在固定资产建造和购置过程中发生的，除上述几项内容以外的各种应分摊计入固定资产的费用。

施工项目　指报告期内进行过建筑或安装施工活动的项目。凡是报告期内施过工的建设项目，不论施工时间长短，均作为施工项目统计。施工项目个数可以反映一定时期固定资产投资的实际规模，与同期建成投产的建设项目个数相比，可以从建设速度的角度反映固定资产投资的效果。根据建设项目施工活动的不同性质，施工项目又分为:本年正式施工项目、本年收尾项目和以前年度全部停缓建项目。

全部建成投产项目　工业项目指设计文件规定形成生产能力的主体工程及其相应配套的辅助设施全部建成，经负荷试运转，证明具备生产设计规定合格产品的条件，并经过验收鉴定合格或达到竣工验收标准，与生产性工程配套的生活福利设施可以满足近期正常生产的需要，正式移交生产的建设项目。非工业项目指设计文件规定的主体工程和相应的配套工程全部建成，能够发挥设计规定的全部效益，经验收鉴定合格或达到竣工验收标准，正式移交使用的建设项目。

新增生产能力(或工程效益)　指通过固定资产投资活动而增加的设计能力(或工程效益)，该指标是以实物形态表现的反映固定资产投资成果的指标，也是考核投资经济效果的重要依据之一。

新增生产能力(或工程效益)一般有以下几种表现形式:

(1)用产品数量表示，以工程在单位时间内(一般是一年)所能生产的产品数量(即年产量)表示。如原煤开采用万吨／年表示，化学农药用吨／年表示，拖拉机制造用台／年表示等。某些化工产品由于含量差别较大，按其设计含量计算折合量表示，如硫酸、纯碱、烧碱等。

(2)用单位时间内所能处理的原料数量表示，以工程每天(或小时)所能处理原料的数量表示。如机制糖工程日处理原料吨，食用植物油日处理原料吨，城市污水处理能力用万吨／日表示等。

(3)用新增加的主要设备的数量或容量表示，如新增棉布织机、丝织机等台数，毛纺锭等锭数，发电厂新增发电机组容量用千瓦表示等。

(4)用建筑物容积、容量、面积、长度表示，是非工业项目或工程新增效益的一种表现形式。如铁路投产里程、新建公路、水库容量、粮食仓库、学校学生席位、医院病床、有效灌溉面积等。

根据工程的特点，有时需要用两种或两种以上的复合计量单位表示新增生产能力(或工程效益)，如新增内燃机生产能力同时用年产台数、千瓦数表示等。

为了规范新增生产能力(或工程效益)的名称和计算单位，国家统计局制订了《新增生产能力(或工程效益)目录及代码》。各固定资产投资单位在统计新增生产能力(或工程效益)时，必须按目录中规定的名称、计量单位和代码填报。

房屋建筑面积　指房屋建筑物勒脚以上外墙外围的水平截面面积，包括房屋建筑物的有效面积和结构面积。该指标是从实物形态上反映建设规模和建设成果的重要指标之一，也是检查工程形象进度、计算工程造价、分析投资效果、研究施工任务和建筑材料之间平衡情况的重要依据。

住宅建筑面积　指施工和竣工房屋建筑面积中供居住用的房屋建筑面积。

施工面积　指报告期内施工的全部房屋建筑面积。包括本期新开工的面积和上期开工跨入本期继续施工的房屋面积，以及上期已停建在本期恢复施工的房屋面积。本期竣工和本期施工后又停缓建的房屋，其建筑面积仍计入本期房屋施工面积中。

竣工面积 指在报告期内房屋建筑按照设计要求已经全部完工，达到住人和使用条件，经验收鉴定合格(或达到竣工验收标准)，正式移交使用单位的各栋房屋建筑面积的总和。

房屋建筑面积竣工率 指一定时期内房屋竣工面积占同期房屋施工面积的比率。该指标从房屋建筑施工速度的角度反映投资效果的指标。

新增固定资产 指报告期内已经完成建造和购置过程，并已交付生产或使用单位的固定资产价值。该指标是表示固定资产投资成果的价值指标，也是反映建设进度，计算固定资产投资效果的重要指标。

建设项目投产率 指一定时期内全部建成投产项目个数与同期施工项目个数的比率。该指标是从建设单位建设速度的角度反映投资效果的指标。

固定资产交付使用率 指一定时期新增固定资产与同期完成投资额的比率。该指标是反映固定资产动用速度，衡量建设过程中宏观投资效果的综合指标。由于新增固定资产是较长时期内形成的结果，而投资额则是当年完成的，因此，该指标一般适宜于反映较长时期内固定资产的动用情况。

商品房销售面积 指报告期内出售商品房屋的合同总面积（即双方签署的正式买卖合同中所确定的建筑面积）。由现房销售建筑面积和期房销售建筑面积两部分组成。

商品房销售额 指报告期内出售商品房屋的合同总价款（即双方签署的正式买卖合同中所确定的合同总价）。该指标与商品房销售面积同口径，由现房销售建筑面积和期房销售建筑面积两部分组成。

经济适用房 指根据国家经济适用房计划安排建设的政策性住宅。经济是指房屋建筑造价和销售价格低于一般商品住宅;适用是指适合中低收入家庭购买使用。经济适用房主要是由国家统一下达投资计划，房地产公司开发，对外销售;用地一般采用行政划拨或招标投标方式，免收土地出让金;对各种经批准的收费减半征收，开发利润不超过3%;销售价格实行政府指导价。该指标可以分析房地产投资结构，反映中低收入家庭商品住宅的供求平衡情况。

Explanatory Notes on Main Statistical Indicators

Total Investment in Fixed Assets in the Whole Country refers to the volume of activities in construction and purchases of fixed assets and related fees, expressed in monetary terms. It is a comprehensive indicatorwhich shows the size, structure and growth of the investment in fixed assets, providing basis for observing the progress of construction projects and evaluating results of investment. Total investment in fixed assets in the whole country includes, by type of ownership, the investment by the state-owned units, collective units, individuals, joint ownership units, share-holding units, as well as investment by businessmen from foreign countries and from Hong Kong, Macau and Taiwan, and by other units.

Urban Investment in Fixed Assets refer to construction projects involving a total planned (or required) investment of 500,000 yuan and over by urban enterprises and institutions of various types of ownership, by administrative units and by individuals, investment in real estate development, and housing investment by individuals in urban areas and in industrial and mining areas. In other words, all investments that take place in county towns and urban areas, investment in construction projects under the direct leadership and management of government agencies at and above county levels and investments by enterprises and institutions at and above county levels are covered in urban investment in fixed assets.

Investment in Real Estate Development refers to the investment by the real estate development companies, commercial buildings construction companies and other real estate development units of various types of ownership in the construction of house buildings, such as residential buildings, factory buildings, warehouses, hotels, guesthouses, holiday villages, office buildings, and the complementary service facilities and land development projects, such as roads, water supply, water drainage, power supply, heating, telecommunications, land leveling and other projects of infrastructure. It excludes the activities in pure land transactions.

Investment in Rural Areas refers to investment in fixed assets by enterprises, institutions and individuals in rural areas.

Total Size of Construction refers to the planned total investment for all construction projects during the reference period.

Total Size of Investment in Projects under Construction refers to the planned total investment of all projects under construction at the end of the reference period.

Net Size of Investment in Projects under Construction refers to the required investment of all projects under construction at the end of the reference period.

Net Size of Investment = Total Size of Investment – accumulated completed investment

Sources of Funds for Investment in Fixed Assets include fund from state budget, domestic loans, foreign investment, self-raised funds, and others depending on the source of investment. (1) Fund from state budget consists of budgetary appropriation and loans from state budget. More specifically, it includes, from the budget of the central government, capital construction fund (operation fund and non-operational fund), special expenses (e.g. expenses on substituting petroleum with coal), loans from repayment, discount fund, expenses on innovation and trial production of new products, expenses on urban construction, expenses on temporary construction by Trades departments, development fund for less developed areas, as well as local budgetary fund transferred from the central budget. (2) Domestic loans refer to loans of various forms borrowed by investing units from banks and non-bank financial institutions during the reference period for the purpose of investment in fixed assets, including loans issued by banks from their self-owned funds and deposit, loans appropriated by higher responsible authorities, special loans by government (including loan for substituting petroleum with coal, special loan for reform-through-labour coal mines), loans arranged by local government from special funds, domestic reserve loan, and working loan, etc. (3) Foreign Investment refers to foreign funds received during the reference period for the construction and purchase of investment in fixed assets (covering equipment, materials and technology), including foreign borrowings (loans from foreign governments and international financial institutions, export credit, commercial loans from foreign banks, issue of bonds and stocks overseas), foreign direct investment and other foreign investment. Excluded in this category are capitals in foreign exchanges owned by China (foreign exchanges owned by the central and local governments, foreign exchanges retained by enterprises, foreign exchanges by enterprises through regulating mechanism, loans in foreign exchanges issued by the Bank of China with its own fund, etc.). In calculating the utilization of foreign capitals, foreign currencies are converted into Chinese Renminbi applying the current exchange rate when the foreign capitals are actually used. (4) Self-raised funds refer to extra-budgetary funds for investment in fixed assets received by investing units from central government ministries, local governments, enterprises and institutions, including their self-raised funds. (5) Others refer to funds for investment in fixed assets received from the sources other than those listed above, including capitals raised through issuing bonds by enterprises or financial institutions, funds raised from individuals and through donations, and funds transferred from other units.

Investment in Fixed Assets by Sector The classification of construction projects by sector is determined by the major products or the purpose of the projects when they are put into production or use, and by the nature of their social economic activities. In general, one project or one enterprise or institution can only be classified into one sector.

Investment in Fixed Assets by Type of Construction The construction projects in general can be classified, by the type of construction, into new construction, expansion, reconstruction and technical transformation, moving and restoration. However, investment by type of construction is not applied to investment by real-estate development units, investment in rural areas and investment in housing by urban individuals. (1) New construction in general refers to newly constructed enterprises, institutions, administrative agencies or independent projects from scratch. Construction in the existing enterprises, institutions or agencies is not considered as new construction. In case the assets of the existing unit is quite small, and the value of newly added fixed assets exceeds the original value of assets by three times, the expansion will be considered as new construction.(2) Expansion refers to construction of new major production workshop, branch factory or independent production line within a factory or in other locations, for the purpose of increasing the production capacity (or improving efficiency) of the original products. Newly constructed houses for the operation of institutions and administrative organizations (such as the newly constructed buildings for teaching in schools, buildings for clinics or wards in hospitals, etc.) are also classified as expansion.Also included in the expansion are investments by existing enterprises or institutions in building major production line(s) or branch factory(ies) along with some work on innovation, for the purpose of expending the production capacity of original products or producing new products. (3) Reconstruction refers to construction projects by existing enterprises or institutions in innovation or technical transformation of the old facilities (including auxiliary production equipment and welfare facilities). Also considered as reconstruction is the construction of new workshops by the existing enterprises or institutions to change the variety of products to meet the market demand (such as the production of civil products by defence industries), or to bring the designed production capacity into full play through a more balanced production process on production lines. Technical transformation refers to replacement of old technology or equipment by new technology or equipment, in order to expand the reproduction through improvement of technology contents in production, to improve product quality, to promote new products, to save energy and reduce consumption and to improve overall social-economic efficiency. Contents of technical transformation include: updating of machinery, equipment and tools; reforming production process by using energy or materials saving technology; construction of factory workshops and transformation of public facilities; improvement of working conditions and environment, etc.

Investment in Fixed Assets by Structure By their contents, investment activities are classified into 3 categories, i.e. construction and installation, purchase of equipment and instrument, and other expenses.(1) Construction and installation (work volume of construction and installation) refers to the construction of various houses and buildings and installation of various kinds of equipment and instruments. They include construction of various houses; equipment foundations, industrial kilns and stoves, and metal structure work; preparation works for project construction, and clearing up works post project construction; pavement of railways and roads, drilling of mines and putting up of oil pipes; construction of projects of water conservancy; construction of underground air-raid shelters and construction of other special projects; value of equipment for heating, sanitation, ventilation, lighting, gas, painting, etc. that are covered by the budget of housing projects; laying out of various pipelines (for steam, compressed air, petroleum, tap water and sewage) and lines for electric power and for communications; installation of various machinery equipment, testing operation for pre-testing the quality of installation projects, and land and other development work conducted by real estate developers for commercial housing. The value of equipment installed is not included in the value of installation projects.(2) Purchase of equipment and instruments refers to the total value of equipment, tools, and instruments purchased or self-produced which come up to standards for fixed assets by the construction units or investing enterprises or institutions. Equipment, tools and instruments purchased or self-produced for new workshops by newly established or expanded units are categorized as "purchase of equipment and instruments" no matter whether they come up to the standards for fixed assets.(3) Other expenses refer to expenses occurring during the construction or purchase of fixed assets other than those mentioned above.

Projects under Construction refer to projects with construction and installation activities undertaken in the reference period. All projects that have construction activities undertaken during the reference period are reported as projects under construction irrespective of the length of construction work. The number of projects under construction can reflect the actual size of investment in fixed assets during a given period, and when compared with the number of projects completed and put into use during the same period, it demonstrates the results of investment in fixed assets. Depending on the nature of const ruction activities, projects under construction can also be classified into projects under construct ion in current y ear, winding-up projects in current year and stopped or suspended projects in previous years (with preservation work in current year).

Projects Completed and Put into Use Industrial projects refer to the major projects and accessory facilities completed which result in forming production capaCity and have been checked and accepted while the living and welfare facilities have been completed and can ensure normal production and formally put into production. Non-industrial projects refer to the major project s and accessory facilities completed which possess the designed capaCity and have been checked, accepted and formally put into production.

Newly Increased Production Capacity (or Project Efficiency) refers to the increase of designed capaCity (or project efficiency) through investment in fixed assets, which reflects the accomplishment of investment in fixed assets in kind and serves as important basis for evaluating the economic efficiency of in-vestment.

The newly increased product ion capaCity (project efficiency) are usually expressed in one of the following forms: (1) output of products, i.e. the output that the project can produce during a given period (usually a year). For instance, the capaCity in coal mining is expressed in 10, 000 tons/year , the capaCity in producing chemical pesticides expressed in ton/year, the capaCity in producing tractors in tractor/year, etc. For some chemical products where the effective contents differ significantly, the production capaCity is expressed as the designed effective content equivalent, such as in the case of sulphuric acid, soda ash, caustic soda, etc; (2) raw materials processing capaCity, i.e. the volume of raw materials that could be processed by the project per day (or per hour), such as tons of materials processed per day by a sugar refining project or edible vegetable oil project, or tons of urban sewage processed per day; (3) number or capaCity of major equipment increased, such as number of cotton or silk looms increased, wool spindles in-creased, or capaCity (in kilowatt s) of power generators increased; (4) saved raw materials, fuels or power, which are mainly used for the efficiency of innovation and transformation projects; and (5) physical measures (volume, capaCity, area, and length) of construction, which is typical for non industrial projects, for instance, the length of new railways or highways, the capaCity of reservoirs, the floor space of housing projects, capaCity f or new students in schools or beds in hospitals, areas under new irrigation project, etc. Features of projects sometimes call for combined use of two or more measurement to reflect the increased production capaCity (or project efficiency), for instance, the new capaCity for the production of internal combustion engines are expressed in set s per year and kilowatts per year simultaneously. To standardize the nomenclature and unit of measurement for new production capaCity (or project efficiency), the National Bureau of Statistics has developed Nomenclature for New Production CapaCity (Project Efficiency) and Nomenclature for Saving Raw Materials, Fuels and Power. All reporting units with investment activities are required to follow these two nomenclatures in reporting statistics on new production capaCity (project efficiency).

Floor Space of Buildings under Construction refers to total floor space of the horizontal section of outer walls above the plinth of the building, including the effective area and the area occupied by the structure. This indicator is one of the important indicators in physical terms to reflect the scale and accomplishment of the construction industry, and important basis for monitoring the pr ogress, calculating the cost, analyzing the efficiency and studying the sup ply of building materials in relation with the construction projects.

Floor Space of Residential Buildings refers to the floor space of the residential buildings among the total space of buildings under construction or completed.

Floor Space under Construction refers to total floor space of all buildings under construct ion during the reference period, including floor space of newly start ed buildings during the reference period, floor space of construction extended from the previous period to the current period, and floor space of construction suspended during the previous period and resumed in the current period. Floor space of const ruction completed in the current period, and floor space of const ruction started and then suspended in the current period are also included in the floor space under const ruction of the current year.

Floor Space of Buildings Completed refers to the floor space of all buildings completed in the reference period, which have been appraised and accepted (or come up to the designed standards) and have been transferred to the owners for use.

Completion Rate of Floor Space of Buildings refers to the ratio of the floor space of buildings completed in certain period of time to the floor space of buildings under const ruction in the same period. This indicator reflects the investment result from the perspective of t he speed of construction.

Newly Increased Fixed Assets refer to the newly in-creased value of fixed assets, constructed or purchased, that have been transfer red to the investors. This is an indicator that demonstrates the results of investment in fixed assets in monetary terms, and an important indicator to reflect the speed of construct ion and to calculate the efficiency of investment.

Rate of Construction Projects Completed and Put into Use refers to the ratio of the number of construction projects completed and put into use in certain period of time to the number of projects under construction in the same period. This reflects the investment efficiency from the perspective of the speed of projects construction.

Rate of Projects of Fixed Assets Completed and Put into Operation refers to the ratio of the newly increased fixed assets to the total investment made in the same period. This is a comprehensive indicator reflecting the speed of the employment of fixed assets and the investment efficiency at the macro-level. As the newly increase fixed assets is the result of a long period while the investment is completed in the current year, this indicator is expected to be used to reflect the employment of fixed assets over a long period of time.

Area of Commercialized Housing Sold refers to total contracted area of commercialized housing (i.e. area of floor space as designated in the formal contracts signed by both sides) during the reference time. It constitutes floor space of completed housing and floor space of future housing.

Value of Commercialized Housing Sold refers to the total contracted value (i.e. value of sales/purchase for selling/purchase of commercialized housing as designated in the contract signed by both sides) during the reference time. This indicator has the same coverage as the area of commercialized housing sold, which constitutes floor space of completed housing and floor space of housing yet to be completed.

Economically Affordable Housing refers to housing constructed according to the state plan for economically affordable housing. Houses of this category featured in low cost in construct ion and low prices, and therefore are affordable to mid-income or low-income households. Economically affordable housing projects are developed by real estate companies under the state investment plan, with the land provided through government allocation or tendering procedures. Developers are exempted from land utilization fees and enjoy another 50% exemption of all other legitimate fees, while their profits are limited to less than 3%, and the completed houses are sold under the government guided prices. This indicator helps to analyze the investment structure of the real estate industry and the demand and supply of housing for mid or low income households.

第五篇
对外经济贸易和旅游

CHAPTER 5
Foreign Trade & Economic Cooperation and Tourism

新疆统计年鉴

XINJIANG STATISTICAL YEARBOOK 2011

简要说明
Brief Introduction

本篇资料的主要内容及来源

本篇内容包括海关进出口额、主要进出口商品数量及金额、对外承包工程和劳务合作、利用外资、外国和港澳台地区在新疆直接投资情况、新疆在国外和港澳台地区直接投资、经济技术开发(合作)主要情况、旅游情况等。

海关进出口额、利用外资、旅游资料由新疆维吾尔自治区统计局贸易外经统计处分别根据乌鲁木齐海关、新疆维吾尔自治区对外经济贸易厅、新疆维吾尔自治区工商管理局和新疆维吾尔自治区旅游局的有关资料加工整理。

Main content and source of data

Data in this chapter cover mainly total imports and exports at customs, main imports and exports in volume and value, contracted projects and labor services cooperation, utilization of foreign capital, basic condition of direct investment in Xinjiang by foreign countries and compatriots from Hong Kong, Macao and Taiwan, main condition of economic and technological development and cooperation zones, condition of tourism.

Data on imports and exports, utilization of foreign capitals, tourism are collected and processed by the Department of Trade Statistics, the Xinjiang Bureau of Statistics in accordance with the data from custom of Urumqi, Foreign Economic and Trade Commission of Xinjiang,Xinjiang Administration for Industry and Commerce, Tourist Bureau of Xingjiang.

5-1 进出口贸易总额
Total Value of Imports and Exports

单位：万美元 (USD 10 000)

年份 Year	地区 Region	进出口总额 Total Imports and Exports	出口额 Exports	#一般贸易 Ordinary Trade	#边境贸易 Border Trade	进口额 Imports	#一般贸易 Ordinary Trade	#边境贸易 Border Trade
	1978	2346	937			1409		
	1985	29197	18020			11177		
	1990	41025	33530		3506	7495		3416
	1995	142798	76880	44550	27562	65918	17640	41888
	1996	140367	54975	30281	18647	85392	25982	54484
	1997	144667	66547	36061	22962	78120	24061	52031
	1998	153214	80789	32268	37599	72425	20972	49354
	1999	176534	102743	37120	57329	73791	25723	44976
	2000	226399	120408	55060	58020	105991	28020	73950
	2001	177148	66849	29523	18418	110299	24895	79661
	2002	269186	130849	54404	47218	138337	26028	107152
	2003	477198	254221	71115	160411	222977	72510	143504
	2004	563563	304658	50194	223782	258905	101540	147058
	2005	794189	504024	88036	386237	290165	108894	167648
	2006	910327	713923	158842	522038	196404	61915	126429
	2007	1371623	1150311	294000	806885	221312	75418	134778
	2008	2221680	1929925	290237	1576911	291755	92279	187279
	2009	1382771	1082325	168078	754206	300446	128702	157390
	2010	1712834	1296981	208909	767478	415853	154567	236745
乌鲁木齐市	Urumqi City	598533	443695			154838		
克拉玛依市	Karamay City	28008	25504			2504		
石河子市	Shihezi City	53666	43972			9694		
吐鲁番地区	Turpan Administrative Offices	931	652			279		
哈密地区	Hami [Kumul] Administrative Offices	2157	1770			387		
昌吉回族自治州	Changji Hui Autonomous Prefecture	207620	191685			15935		
伊犁哈萨克自治州	Ili Kazak Autonomous Prefecture	622142	421685			200457		
伊犁州直属县(市)	Counties (Cities) Direct Under Ili Prefecture	488391	300538			187853		
塔城地区	Tacheng [Tarbagatai] Administrative Offices	65155	53125			12030		
阿勒泰地区	Altay Administrative Offices	68596	68022			574		
博尔塔拉蒙古自治州	Bortala Mongol Autonomous Prefecture	61045	36103			24942		
巴音郭楞蒙古自治州	Bayangol Mongol Autonomous Prefecture	12078	10814			1264		
阿克苏地区	Aksu Administrative Offices	26215	25707			508		
克孜勒苏柯尔克孜自治州	Kizilsu Kirgiz Autonomous Prefecture	10277	5443			4834		
喀什地区	Kashgar [Kaxgar] Administrative Offices	89446	89248			198		
和田地区	Hotan Administrative Offices	716	703			13		

注：1998 年以前的资料由外经贸厅提供，1998 年以后资料由乌鲁木齐海关提供(5-2、5-3、5-4 表相同)。
Note: The data prior to 1998 is offered by the Bureau of Foreign Economic and Trades , data after 1998 is offered by Urumqi Customs (The same in the 5-2, 5-3, 5-4 tables).

5-2 主要进出口商品数量和金额
Main Imports and Exports in Volume and Value

项　目	Item	2009		2010	
		数量 Volume	金额(万美元) Value (USD 10 000)	数量 Volume	金额(万美元) Value (USD 10 000)
主要出口商品	**Main Export Commodities**				
棉花(吨)	Cotton (ton)	1487	388		
棉纱(吨)	Cotton Yarn (ton)	3374	1216	2925	1306
棉机织物(万米)	Cotton Woven Fabrics(10 000 m)	4659	4002	9734	9169
肠衣(吨)	Casings (ton)	613	2188	617	2073
番茄酱(万吨)	Tomato Jam (10 000 tons)	44	42006	60	41574
电视机(万台)	TV Sets (10 000 sets)	2	129	2	224
地毯(吨)	Carpets (ton)	16229	555	1904	722
药材(吨)	Medical Materials (ton)	186	75	250	126
鞋　类	Shoes		132352		155524
主要进口商品	**Main Import Commodities**				
羊毛及条(吨)	Wool and Wool Tops (ton)	5050	634	5425	719
钢材(万吨)	Rolled Steel (10 000 tons)	42	33146	20	17550
纸及纸板(未切成型的)(吨)	Paper and Paperboard in Rolls (ton)	270	159	35	7
原木(万立方米)	Logs (10 000 cu.m)	2	279	1	161
医疗仪器及器械	Medical Equipment and Apparatus		1970		3592
肥料(万吨)	Fertilizers (10 000 tons)	2	990	10	3159
原油(万吨)	Crude Oil (10 000 tons)	193	96928	296	166080
成品油(万吨)	Oil Product (10 000 tons)	15	4970	24	9552
牛皮革及马皮革(吨)	Cattle and Horse Leather (ton)	11323	1593	13840	1806

注：2009 年地毯的计量单位为百平方米。
Note:Carpets of the units of measurement is 100 Square meters in 2009.

5-3 新疆同各国(地区)海关进出口总额

Value of Xinjiang's Imports and Exports by Countries(Region) of Destination

单位：万美元 (USD 10 000)

国别(地区)	Country (Territory)	2009 进出口总额 Total Value Imports and Exports	2009 出口额 Exports	2009 进口额 Imports	2010 进出口总额 Total Value Imports and Exports	2010 出口额 Exports	2010 进口额 Imports
总　计	**Total**	**1382771**	**1082325**	**300446**	**1712834**	**1296981**	**415853**
亚　洲	**Asia**	**1203741**	**992462**	**211279**	**1482222**	**1162187**	**320035**
阿富汗	Afghanistan	294	289	5	441	438	3
巴　林	Bahrain	95	95		112	112	
孟加拉国	Bangladesh	81	81		275	274	1
文　莱	Brunei	23	23		67	67	
缅　甸	Myanmar	713	713		194	194	
柬埔寨	Cambodia	53	3	50	114	64	50
塞浦路斯	Cyprus	21	21		32	32	
朝　鲜	Korea DPR	2	2		7	7	
香港	Hong Kong, China	1647	1631	16	2511	1704	807
印　度	India	1247	1019	228	3488	1668	1820
印度尼西亚	Indonesia	2809	2725	84	4538	4354	184
伊　朗	Iran	1045	467	578	2497	2006	491
伊拉克	Iraq	14	14		574	517	57
以色列	Israel	518	166	352	604	402	202
日　本	Japan	13426	5397	8029	16951	6087	10864
约　旦	Jordan	210	210		151	151	
科威特	Kuwait	105	94	11	171	165	6
老　挝	Laos	2	2		14	14	
黎巴嫩	Lebanon	148	148		123	123	
马来西亚	Malaysia	5676	5543	133	6894	6767	127
蒙　古	Mongolia	5787	5217	570	27181	24908	2273
尼泊尔	Nepal	27	27		34	34	
阿　曼	Aman	181	181		171	171	
巴基斯坦	Pakistan	19192	19084	108	12728	12534	194
巴勒斯坦	Palestine				1	1	
菲律宾	Philppines	1687	1513	174	1650	1293	357
卡塔尔	Qatar	290	43	247	59	59	
沙特阿拉伯	Saudi Arbia	2757	2726	31	2306	2203	103
新加坡	Singapore	1542	439	1103	1339	308	1031
韩　国	Korea Rep.	14975	1797	13178	8277	1738	6539
斯里兰卡	Sri Lanka	128	122	6	123	117	6
叙利亚	Syria	150	71	79	356	125	231
泰　国	Thailand	1219	1136	83	2614	2372	242
土耳其	Turkey	1476	482	994	2007	1129	878
阿拉伯联合酋长国	Unitd Arab Emirates	1445	1416	29	3159	3146	13
也门共和国	Republic of Yemen	1385	1385		701	701	
越　南	Viet Nam	2288	2256	32	2961	2838	123
中华人民共和国	P.R.China	193		193	315		315
台湾省	Taiwan, China	1258	917	341	2237	1690	547
东帝汶	Timor Leste	4	4		5	5	
哈萨克斯坦	Kazakhstan	689751	524671	165080	925918	682821	243097
吉尔吉斯斯坦	Kirghizia	297259	292803	4456	265725	258836	6889
塔吉克斯坦	Tadzhikistan	86770	86281	489	107574	106057	1517

5-3 续表 1 Continued

单位：万美元 (USD 10 000)

国别（地区）	Country (Territory)	2009			2010		
		进出口总额 Total Value Imports and Exports	出口额 Exports	进口额 Imports	进出口总额 Total Value Imports and Exports	出口额 Exports	进口额 Imports
土库曼斯坦	Turkmenistan	7243	6122	1121	12883	10989	1894
乌兹别克斯坦	Uzbekistan	38605	25126	13479	62140	22966	39174
非　洲	**Africa**	**14034**	**13841**	**193**	**19581**	**17052**	**2529**
阿尔及利亚	Algeria	2017	2017		2334	2334	
安哥拉	Angola	9	9		47	47	
贝　宁	Benin	101	101		34	34	
喀麦隆	Cameroon	165	165		195	193	2
佛得角	Cape Verde				2	2	
中　非	Central Africa	115	115				
乍　得	Chad	2	2				
刚　果	Congo	26	26		11	11	
吉布提	Djibouti	8	8		31	31	1
埃　及	Egypt	195	193	2	317	286	31
埃塞俄比亚	Ethiopia	9	9		139	139	
加　纳	Ghana	890	890		831	825	6
冈比亚	Gambia	230	230		17	17	
加　蓬	Gabon	1	1		8	8	
几内亚	Guinea				14	14	
科特迪瓦共和国	Cote d'lvoire	72	72		45	45	
肯尼亚	Kenya	38	38		69	69	
利比里亚	Liberia	1	1				
利比亚	Libya	20	20		1213	1213	
马达加斯加	Madagascar	2	2		21	21	
马拉维	Malawi	12	12				
毛里塔尼亚	Mauritania	10	10		18	18	
毛里求斯	Mauritius	127	127		298	298	
摩洛哥	Morocco	214	214		221	221	
莫桑比克	Mozambique	86	86		22	22	
纳米比亚	Mozanmbique	184	184		171	171	
尼日尔	Niger	1526	1526				
尼日利亚	Nigeria				1043	1041	2
留尼汪	Reunion	4	4		1	1	
圣多美和普林西比	Monetary				2	2	
塞内加尔	Senegal	146	146		193	193	
塞拉利昂	SierraLeone	73	73		207	207	
南　非	South Africa	802	611	191	845	698	147
苏　丹	Sudan	6554	6554		8310	8310	
坦桑尼亚	Tanzania	166	166		109	109	
多　哥	Togo	178	178		66	66	
突尼斯	Tunisia	22	22		226	226	
乌干达	Uganda	5	5				
刚果（金）	Congo DR	6	6		42	42	
赞比亚	Zambia				2462	121	2341
莱索托	Lesotho				14	14	
厄立特里亚	Eritrea	3	3				
马约特岛	Mayotte	2	2		3	3	
非洲其他国家(地区)	Other Countries(Regions)in Africa	13	13				

5-3 续表 2 Continued

单位：万美元 (USD 10 000)

国 别 (地 区)	Country (Territory)	2009			2010		
		进出口总额 Total Value Imports and Exports	出口额 Exports	进口额 Imports	进出口总额 Total Value Imports and Exports	出口额 Exports	进口额 Imports
欧 洲	**Europe**	**126302**	**63425**	**62877**	**175167**	**103156**	**72011**
比利时	Belgium	793	237	556	1986	695	1291
丹 麦	Denmark	1323	81	1242	565	82	483
英 国	United Kingdom	2447	1529	918	3331	2118	1213
德 国	Germany	25584	4008	21576	24092	4846	19246
法 国	France	2898	1576	1322	3176	721	2455
爱尔兰	Ireland	502	261	241	306	172	134
意大利	Italy	13666	6678	6988	11534	7301	4233
卢森堡	Luxembourg	1		1			
荷 兰	Netherlands	1173	1015	158	1261	1023	238
希 腊	Greece	161	42	119	93	84	9
葡萄牙	Portugal	335	334	1	91	89	2
西班牙	Spain	470	381	89	707	479	228
阿尔巴尼亚	Albania	18	18		12	12	
奥地利	Austria	936	152	784	1127	215	912
保加利亚	Bulgaria	166	166		242	242	
芬 兰	Finland	12683	174	12509	15849	229	15620
匈牙利	Hungary	43	40	3	69	43	26
冰 岛	Iceland	1	1		5	5	
马耳他	Malta	54	54		67	67	
挪 威	Norway	660	519	141	541	474	67
波 兰	Poland	1251	1202	49	1745	1744	1
罗马尼亚	Romania	949	889	60	1628	1069	559
瑞 典	Sweden	1122	141	981	951	130	821
瑞 士	Switzerland	5108	787	4321	3617	965	2652
爱沙尼亚	Estonia	11	11		21	21	
拉脱维亚	Latvia	133	133		293	293	
立陶宛	Lithuania	291	291		272	272	
格鲁吉亚	Georgia	91	38	53	372	360	12
亚美尼亚	Argentina	5	1	4	1314	1314	
阿塞拜疆	Azerbajan	19771	19771		35494	35473	21
白俄罗斯	Belorussia	507	326	181	274	88	186
摩尔多瓦	Moldova				5	5	
俄罗斯	Russia	30911	20467	10444	56889	35348	21541
乌克兰	Ukraine	1699	1637	62	6796	6778	18
斯洛文尼亚	Slovenia	51	51		60	60	
克罗地亚	Croatia	84	84		96	96	
捷 克	Czecho	344	270	74	249	206	43
斯洛伐克	Slovak	1	1				
前南马其顿	Macedonia	8	8				
波黑	Bosnia				10	10	
塞尔维亚	Serbia	39	39		21	21	
黑 山	Montenegro	12	12		6	6	

5-3 续表 3 Continued

单位：万美元 (USD 10 000)

国 别 (地 区)	Country (Territory)	2009			2010		
		进出口总额 Total Value Imports and Exports	出口额 Exports	进口额 Imports	进出口总额 Total Value Imports and Exports	出口额 Exports	进口额 Imports
拉丁美洲	**Latin America**	**5616**	**2879**	**2737**	**5789**	**3791**	**1998**
安提瓜和巴布达	Antigua and Barbuda	1	1				
阿根廷	Argentina	290	65	225	723	418	305
巴哈马	Bahamas	4	4		3	3	
巴巴多斯	Barbados	2	2		3	3	
伯利兹	Belize				1	1	
巴 西	Brazil	2090	708	1382	2757	1450	1307
智 利	Chile	283	283		682	314	368
哥伦比亚	Colombia	244	244		180	180	
多米尼加	Dominica				12	12	
哥斯达黎加	Costarica	393	393		71	71	
古 巴	Cuba	7	7		14	14	
多米尼加共和国	Dominica Rep.	31	30	1	30	29	1
厄瓜多尔	Ecuador	79	79		116	116	
格林纳达	Granada	4	4				
危地马拉	Guatemala	93	93		128	128	
圭亚那	Guyana				2	2	
海 地	Hayti	220	220		175	175	
洪都拉斯	Honduras				39	39	
牙买加	Jamaica	76	76		82	82	
墨西哥	Mexico	143	89	54	160	143	17
尼加拉瓜	Nicaragua	22	22		1	1	
巴拿马	Panama	16	16		56	56	
巴拉圭	Paraguay	75	75		116	116	
秘 鲁	Peru	276	266	10	300	300	
波多黎各	Puerto Rico	60	60		25	25	
圣卢西亚	Saint Lucia	3	3		1	1	
圣文森特和格林纳丁斯	Saint Vincent and the Grenadines				1	1	
萨尔瓦多	El. Salvador	30	30		21	21	
苏里南	Surinam	1	1				
特立尼达和多巴哥	Trinidada and Tobago	7	7		27	27	
乌拉圭	Uruguay	37	37		39	39	
委内瑞拉	Venezuela	1102	37	1065	24	24	
拉美其他国家(地区)	Other countries(regions) in Latin America	27	27				
北美洲	**North America**	**29918**	**8324**	**21594**	**26107**	**9209**	**16898**
加拿大	Canada	3646	1062	2584	1680	1356	324
美 国	United States	26272	7262	19010	24427	7853	16574
大洋洲	**Oceania**	**3160**	**1394**	**1766**	**3968**	**1586**	**2382**
澳大利亚	Australia	2309	1018	1291	2799	1168	1631
斐 济	Fiji	30	30		35	35	
新喀里多尼亚	New Caledonia	11	11		11	11	
瓦努阿图	Vanuatu	2	2		5	5	
新西兰	New Zealand	452	280	172	688	331	357
巴布亚新几内亚	Papua New Guinea	326	23	303	430	36	394
所罗门群岛	Solomon Is.	2	2				
密克罗尼西亚联邦	Micronesia Commonwealth	28	28				

5-4 按贸易方式和登记注册类型分的海关进出口额

Total Value of Imports and Exports by Customs Regime and Registration (Customs Statiatics)

单位：万美元 (USD 10 000)

项　　目	Item	2009			2010		
		进出口总额 Total Imports and Exports	出口额 Exports	进口额 Imports	进出口总额 Total Imports and Exports	出口额 Exports	进口额 Imports
总　　计	**Total**	**1382771**	**1082325**	**300446**	**1712834**	**1296981**	**415853**
按贸易方式分	**By Customs Regime**						
一般贸易	Ordinary Trades	296780	168078	128702	363476	208909	154567
加工贸易	Processing Trades	34736	32194	2542	32690	30404	2286
边境小额贸易	Petty-volume Border Trades	911596	754206	157390	1004223	767478	236745
其它贸易	Other Trades	139659	127847	11812	312445	290190	22255
按登记注册类型分	**By Registration Status**						
国有经济	State-owned Units	394246	167591	226655	470176	170865	299311
集体经济	Collective-owned Units	32017	30831	1186	27094	22977	4117
私营经济	Private-owned Units	929157	868634	60523	1179989	1085210	94779
三资企业	Three Kinds of Ventures	27346	15267	12079	35518	17872	17646
其它经济	Other Types of Ownership	5	2	3	57	57	

5-5 主要年份人民币对主要外币年平均汇价(中间价)

Average Exchange Rate of RMB Yuan Against Main Convertible Currences in Main Years (Medium Rate)

单位：人民币元 (RMB yuan)

年 份 Year	100 美元 100 US Dollars	100 日元 100 JapaneseYen	100 港元 100 Hong Kong Dollars	100 欧元 100 Euros
1985	293.66	1.25	37.57	
1990	478.32	3.32	61.39	
1995	835.10	8.92	107.96	
1996	831.42	7.64	107.51	
1997	828.98	6.86	107.09	
1998	827.91	6.35	106.88	
1999	827.83	7.29	106.66	
2000	827.84	7.69	106.18	
2001	827.70	6.81	106.08	
2002	827.70	6.62	106.07	800.58
2003	827.70	7.15	106.24	936.13
2004	827.68	7.66	106.23	1029.00
2005	819.17	7.45	105.30	1019.53
2006	797.18	6.86	102.62	1001.90
2007	760.40	6.46	97.46	1041.75
2008	694.51	6.74	89.19	1022.27
2009	683.10	7.29	88.12	952.70
2010	676.95	7.73	87.13	897.25

5-6 对外承包工程和劳务合作
Contracted Projects in Foreign Countries or Territories

单位：个、万美元 (unit,USD 10 000)

项　目	Item	2009	2010
承包工程	**Contracted Projects**		
新签合同数	Number of Newly Signed Contracts	40	54
新签合同金额	Newly Signed Contracted Value	147000	46948
实际营业额	Actual Business Volume	44890	62945

5-7 外商直接投资
Direct Foreign Investments

单位：个、万美元 (unit, USD 10 000)

指　标	Item	2009			2010		
		项目 Number of Projects	合同金额 Contract Value	实际使用金额 Used Value	项目 Number of Projects	合同金额 Contract Value	实际使用金额 Used Value
总　计	**Total**	**55**	**47000**	**21570**	**59**	**30091**	**23742**
独资经营企业	Foreign Investment Enterprises	35	29918	14348	28	9070	14571
合资经营企业	Joint Ventures Enterprises	16	8869	3890	28	8988	7991
合作经营企业	Cooperative Operation Enterprises	4	6955	2440	3	2880	752
股份制企业	Share-holding Corporations Ltd.		1258	892		9153	428

5-8 外国和港澳台地区在华直接投资情况

Basic Conditions of Direct Investment in China by Foreign Countries and Compatriots from Hongkong，Macao and Taiwan

单位：个、万美元　　(2010 年)　　(unit, USD 10 000)

项　目	Item	签订协议情况 Signed Agreements 合同数 Number of Contracts	签订协议情况 Signed Agreements 客商投资额 Actually Used Amount of Region Investment	客商实际投资额 Used Amount of Foreign Investment	年末实有企业个数 Year-end Number of Enterprises
总　计	**Total**	**59**	**30091**	**23742**	**499**
按投资方式分	**Grouped by Investment Mode**				
独资经营企业	Foreign Investment Enterprises	28	9070	14571	227
合资经营企业	Joint Ventures Enterprises	28	8988	7991	227
合作经营企业	Cooperative Operation Enterprises	3	2880	752	36
外商投资股份制企业	Foreign Investment Share Enterprises		9153	428	9
按国民经济行业分	**Grouped by Economic Sector**				
农、林、牧、渔业	Farming, Forestry, Animal Husbandry and Fishery	3	2588	1236	30
采矿业	Mining and Quarrying	2	-3670	6294	28
制造业	Manufacturing	18	6664	7888	193
电力、煤气及水的生产和供应业	Production and Distribution of Electricity, Gas and Water	2	583		8
建筑业	Construction				6
交通运输、仓储及邮电通讯业	Transport, Storage, Post and Telecommunications	5	14535	4513	12
信息传输、计算机服务和软件业	Information Transmission, Computer Service and Software				5
批发和零售业	Wholesale and Retail Trades	19	4558	2714	120
住宿和餐饮业	Accommodation and Catering Service	4	24		25
金融业	Financial Intermediation				1
房地产业	Real Estate			1075	17
租赁和商务服务业	Leasing and Business Services	4	2875	22	20
科学研究、技术服务和地质勘察业	Scientific Research, Technical Service and Geological Prospecting	1	1927		18
水利、环境和公共设施管理业	Water Conservancy, Environment and Public Facility Management				5
居民服务和其他服务业	Services to Households and Other Services	1	7		4
教育	Education				2
文化、体育和娱乐业	Culture,Sports and Entertainment				3
其他行业	Others Sectors				2
按国别、地区分	**By Country or Territory**				
中国香港	Hong Kong，China	28	19091	12683	181
中国台湾	Taiwan，China	3	328	1010	22
日　本	Japan			215	11
美　国	United States	1	12	1	28
加拿大	Canada	1	-135	14	14
丹　麦	Denmark		1897		3
意大利	Italy				3
德　国	Federal Republic of Germany				6
土耳其	Turkey	2	129	11	10
英　国	United Kingdom			133	3
泰　国	Thailand		-8		2
新加坡	Singapore		608	609	14
澳大利亚	Australia	1	670	791	12
独联体	Commonwealth of Independent States	16	1256	4081	88
马来西亚	Malaysia	1	4		2
韩　国	Republic of Korea	4	30	12	19

5-9 各地、州、市利用外商直接投资情况

Conditions of Foreign Direct Investment Used by Prefecture, Autonomous Prefecture and City

单位：个、万美元 (unit, USD 10 000)

地区	Region	2009			2010		
		签订合同数 Number of Contracts	合同金额 Contract Value	实际利用投资 Amount of Foreingn Capital Actually Used	签订合同数 Number of Contracts	合同金额 Contract Value	实际利用投资 Amount of Foreign Capital Actually Used
总　计	**Total**	**55**	**47000**	**21570**	**59**	**30091**	**23742**
乌鲁木齐市	Urumqi City	32	16943	14019	28	15125	5038
克拉玛依市	Karamay City	1	1500				
石河子市	Shihezi City	4	2975	1497	9	2683	1171
吐鲁番地区	Turpan Administrative Offices		-150	57	1	18	
哈密地区	Hami [Kumul] Administrative Offices	2	1011	459	2	-453	2282
昌吉回族自治州	Changji Hui Autonomous Prefecture	5	4448	2934	6	4418	2471
伊犁哈萨克自治州	Ili Kazak Autonomous Prefecture	7	17018	2143	5	2781	9955
伊犁州直属县(市)	Counties (Cities) Direct Under Ili Prefecture	5	5701	1992	5	2781	5908
塔城地区	Tacheng [Tarbagatai] Administrative Offices			112			
阿勒泰地区	Altay Administrative Offices	2	11317	39			4047
博尔塔拉蒙古自治州	Bortala Mongol Autonomous Prefecture		-175	231			
巴音郭楞蒙古自治州	BayangolMongol Autonomous Prefecture	2	6516		2	733	1764
阿克苏地区	Aksu Administrative Offices	1	-2818		3	3848	
克孜勒苏柯尔克孜自治州	Kizilsu Kirgiz Autonomous Prefecture		71	230		661	876
喀什地区	Kashgar [Kaxgar] Administrative Offices	1	-339		1	13	185
和田地区	Hotan Administrative Offices				2	264	

5-10 新疆在外国和港澳台地区直接投资

Direct Investment in Foreign Countries and Hong Kong，Macao and Taiwan Made by Xinjiang Partner

单位：个、万美元 (unit, USD 10 000)

项目	Item	2009		2010	
		合同数 Number of Contracts	我方投资额 National Investment	合同数 Number of Contracts	我方投资额 National Investment
总　计	**Total**	**31**	**28619**	**46**	**47809**
独资经营企业	Foreign Investment Enterprises	25	27366	30	46521
合资经营企业	Joint Ventures Enterprises	6	1253	16	1288

5-11 主要年份旅游事业发展情况
Development of Tourism in Main Years

项　　目	Item	1995	2000	2010
旅行社总数（个）	**Total Number of Travel Agencies (unit)**	**79**	**130**	**462**
入境旅游人数（人）	**Total Number of International Tourists Inbound (person)**	**203579**	**256082**	**1065261**
外国人	Foreigners	185514	208374	1010294
#日　本	Japan	43983	51974	32629
新加坡	Singapore	2048	5137	6269
美　国	United States	5595	10231	27603
英　国	United Kingdom	2422	3702	18289
法　国	France	3062	5218	10818
德　国	Federal Republic of Germany	4892	6310	10540
独联体	Commonwealth of Independent States	93578	76966	689063
香港同胞	Compatriots from Hong Kong		12710	17111
澳门同胞	Compatriots from Macao		1387	5395
台湾同胞	Compatriots from Taiwan	8816	33611	32461
按地区分	**By Regions**			
乌鲁木齐市	Urumqi City	63275	144830	581624
克拉玛依市	Karamay City		505	1325
石河子市	Shihezi City		532	510
吐鲁番地区	Turpan Administrative Offices	27230	43641	71210
哈密地区	Hami [Kumul] Administrative Offices	1220	624	20145
昌吉回族自治州	Changji Hui Autonomous Prefecture	224	213	1120
伊犁哈萨克自治州	Ili Kazak Autonomous Prefecture	68948	18204	266934
伊犁州直属县(市)	Counties (Cities) Direct Under Ili Prefecture	67651	15356	217613
塔城地区	Tacheng [Tarbagatai] Administrative Offices	1297	298	13693
阿勒泰地区	Altay Administrative Offices		2550	35628
博尔塔拉蒙古自治州	Bortala Mongol Autonomous Prefecture	354	672	27105
巴音郭楞蒙古自治州	BayangolMongol Autonomous Prefecture	1738	7313	6012
阿克苏地区	Aksu Administrative Offices	5737	6028	3001
克孜勒苏柯尔克孜自治州	Kizilsu Kirgiz Autonomous Prefecture	2485	2100	20861
喀什地区	Kashgar [Kaxgar] Administrative Offices	31102	27510	43665
和田地区	Hotan Administrative Offices	1266	3910	21749
国内旅游人数（万人）	**Total Number of Domestic Tourist (10 000 persons)**	**514**	**758**	**3038**
疆内居民出境游（人）	**Total Number of Domestic Resident Outbound (person)**	**591**	**4535**	**12499**
旅游收入	**Income of Tourism**			
国际旅游收入(万美元)	Earnings from International Tourism (USD 10 000)	5268	9494	36844
国内旅游收入(亿元)	Earnings from Domestic Tourism (100 million yuan)	7.10	62.67	281.13

注：1.1998 年以后的旅游外汇收入根据抽样调查取得。
Note: The Foreign Exchange Earnings from Tourism after 1998 are obtained from Sampled Survey.
2.2010 年国际旅游人数统计口径有所变化增加了口岸旅游购物人数。.
Note:International tourist arrivals statistics have changed,increased the number of tourist in the custom offices to the shopping.

5-12 各地、州、市旅行社及旅游宾馆(酒店)基本情况

Accommodation of Travel Agencies and Tourist Hotels by Prefecture, Autonomous Prefecture and City

(2010 年)

地区	Region	旅行社总数 (个) Number of Travel Agencies (unit)	星级宾馆 (个) Number of Tourist Hotels (unit)	客房 (间) Number of Rooms (unit)	床位 (张) Number of Beds (unit)
总计	**Total**	**462**	**472**	**46585**	**86989**
乌鲁木齐市	Urumqi City	231	112	15374	26851
克拉玛依市	Karamay City	23	20	1721	2882
吐鲁番地区	Turpan Administrative Offices	8	25	2094	3908
哈密地区	Hami [Kumul] Administrative Offices	12	16	1690	3225
昌吉回族自治州	Changji Hui Autonomous Prefecture	10	31	1875	5309
伊犁哈萨克自治州	Ili Kazak Autonomous Prefecture	85	124	10157	19592
伊犁州直属县(市)	Counties (Cities) Direct Under Ili Prefecture	35	66	5250	9934
塔城地区	Tacheng [Tarbagatai] Administrative Offices	6	12	857	1547
阿勒泰地区	Altay Administrative Offices	44	46	4050	8111
博尔塔拉蒙古自治州	Bortala Mongol Autonomous Prefecture	11	10	842	1477
巴音郭楞蒙古自治州	Bayangol Mongol Autonomous Prefecture	21	45	4470	8353
阿克苏地区	Aksu Administrative Offices	10	30	2883	5434
克孜勒苏柯尔克孜自治州	Kizilsu Kirgiz Autonomous Prefecture	1	3	325	438
喀什地区	Kashgar [Kaxgar] Administrative Offices	31	36	3246	6143
和田地区	Hotan Administrative Offices	4	16	1303	2199
兵团	The xinjiang Production and Construction Corps	15	4	605	1178

5-13 各地、州、市旅游收入情况

Income of Tourism by Prefecture, Autonomous Prefecture and City

(2010 年)

地　区	Region	入境旅游收入 (万美元) Earnings International Tourism (USD 10 000)	国内旅游收入 (万元) Domestic Tourism (10 000 yuan)
总　计	**Total**	**36844**	**2811300**
乌鲁木齐市	Urumqi City	19547	1281058
克拉玛依市	Karamay City	44	68339
石河子市	Shihezi City	28	81295
吐鲁番地区	Turpan Administrative Offices	3883	302104
哈密地区	Hami [Kumul] Administrative Offices	912	87962
昌吉回族自治洲	Changji Hui Autonomous Prefecture	45	97418
伊犁哈萨克自治州	Ili Kazak Autonomous Prefecture	5716	366888
伊犁州直属县(市)	Counties (Cities) Direct Under Ili Prefecture	4454	138565
塔城地区	Tacheng [Tarbagatai] Administrative Offices	529	60148
阿勒泰地区	Altay Administrative Offices	733	168175
博尔塔拉蒙古自治州	Bortala Mongol Autonomous Prefecture	554	40471
巴音郭楞蒙古自治州	BayangolMongol Autonomous Prefecture	346	157364
阿克苏地区	Aksu Administrative Offices	381	107214
克孜勒苏柯尔克孜自治州	Kizilsu Kirgiz Autonomous Prefecture	1697	30125
喀什地区	Kashgar [Kaxgar] Administrative Offices	3108	145216
和田地区	Hotan Administrative Offices	583	45846

5-14 国际旅游外汇收入及构成
Foreign Exchange Earnings and Its Composition

单位：万美元、% (USD 10 000,%)

指标	Item	2009 金额 Value	2009 比重 Percentage	2010 金额 Value	2010 比重 Percentage
总计	**Total**	**26167**	**100**	**36844**	**100**
长途交通费	Long Distance Transportation	5783	22.1	9543	25.9
民航	Air	3585	13.7	6374	17.3
铁路	Railway	1439	5.5	1326	3.6
汽车	Highway	759	2.9	1843	5.0
游览	Visiting	1387	5.3	1769	4.8
住宿	Accommodation	2093	8.0	2984	8.1
餐饮	Catering	1596	6.1	2026	5.5
商品销售	Commodity Sales	12089	46.2	13374	36.3
娱乐	Entertainment	419	1.6	516	1.4
邮电通信	Post and Communication Services	680	2.6	1216	3.3
市内交通	Local Transportation	628	2.4	921	2.5
其他服务	Other Services	1492	5.7	4495	12.2

5-15 接待外国旅游人数(按国别分)
Number of Foreign Tourists Received by Country

单位：人 (person)

国别	Country	2009	2010	国别	Country	2009	2010
总计	**Total**	**705640**	**1010294**	法国	France	7654	10818
亚洲	**Asia**	**395433**	**576312**	意大利	Italy	3997	5599
印度	India	2969	4319	西班牙	Spain	2723	3709
印度尼西亚	Indonesia	1560	2194	瑞典	Sweden	4019	5573
日本	Japan	23342	32629	瑞士	Switzerland	4702	6505
马来西亚	Malaysia	2887	3950	独联体	Commonwealth of Independent States	210307	296076
蒙古	Mongolia	36365	59052	其他	Others	6385	8745
菲律宾	The Philppines	1026	1346	**北美洲**	**North America**	**31669**	**42543**
新加坡	Singapore	4288	6269	加拿大	Canada	6782	8394
韩国	Republic of Korea	9558	13613	美国	United States	19755	27603
泰国	Thailand	4219	4613	其他	Others	5132	6546
巴基斯坦	Pakistan	24019	35340	**大洋洲**	**Oceania**	**11829**	**15127**
其他	Others	285200	412987	澳大利亚	Australia	6387	7875
非洲	**Africa**	**782**	**1141**	新西兰	New Zealand	2474	3429
欧洲	**Europe**	**259976**	**365854**	其他	Others	2968	3823
英国	United Kingdom	12840	18289	**其他小计**	**Other sub-total**	**5951**	**9317**
德国	Federal Republic of Germany	7349	10540				

注：表中独联体仅指独联体在欧洲部分的国家。
Note:Commonwealth of Independent State in the table only refer to the part of the countries in Europe.

主要统计指标解释

进出口总额 指实际进出我国国境的货物总金额。包括对外贸易实际进出口货物，来料加工装配进出口货物，国家间、联合国及国际组织无偿援助物资和赠送品，华侨、港澳台同胞和外籍华人捐赠品，租赁期满归承租人所有的租赁货物，进料加工进出口货物，边境地方贸易及边境地区小额贸易进出口货物(边民互市贸易除外)，中外合资企业、中外合作经营企业、外商独资经营企业进出口货物和公用物品，到、离岸价格在规定限额以上的进出口货样和广告品(无商业价值、无使用价值和免费提供出口的除外)，从保税仓库提取在中国境内销售的进口货物，以及其他进出口货物。进出口总额用以观察一个国家在对外贸易方面的总规模。我国规定出口货物按离岸价格统计，进口货物按到岸价格统计。

利用外资 指我国各级政府、部门、企业和其他经济组织通过对外借款、吸收外商直接投资以及用其他方式筹措的境外现汇、设备、技术等。

外商直接投资 指外国企业和经济组织或个人(包括华侨、港澳台胞以及我国在境外注册的企业)按我国有关政策、法规，用现汇、实物、技术等在我国境内开办外商独资企业、与我国境内的企业或经济组织共同举办中外合资经营企业、合作经营企业或合作开发资源的投资(包括外商投资收益的再投资)，以及经政府有关部门批准的项目投资总额内企业从境外借入的资金。

对外承包工程 指各对外承包公司以招标议标承包方式承揽的下列业务：(1)承包国外工程建设项目，(2)承包我国对外经援项目，(3)承包我国驻外机构的工程建设项目，(4)承包我国境内利用外资进行建设的工程项目，(5)与外国承包公司合营或联合承包工程项目时我国公司分包部分，(6)对外承包兼营的房屋开发业务。对外承包工程的营业额是以货币表现的本期内完成的对外承包工程的工作量，包括以前年度签订的合同和本年度新签订的合同在报告期内完成的工作量。

对外劳务合作 指以收取工资的形式向业主或承包商提供技术和劳动服务的活动。我国对外承包公司在境外开办的合营企业，中国公司同时又提供劳务的，其劳务部分也纳入劳务合作统计。劳务合作营业额按报告期内向雇主提交的结算数(包括工资、加班费和奖金等)统计。

旅游人数 包括入境旅游人数、出境人数和国内旅游人数。

(1)入境旅游人数：指报告期内来我国观光、度假、探亲访友、就医疗养、购物、参加会议或从事经济、文化、体育、宗教活动的外国人、港澳台同胞等入境游客。统计时，外国人、港澳台同胞每入境一次统计1人次。

(2)出境人数：指中国（大陆）居民因公或因私出境前往其他国家、中国香港特别行政区、澳门特别行政区和台湾省观光、度假、探亲访友、就医疗养、购物、参加会议或从事经济、文化、体育、宗教活动的人数，即出境游客。统计时，按每出境一次统计1人次。

(3)国内旅游人数：指在报告期内在中国（大陆）观光游览、度假、探亲访友、就医疗养、购物、参加会议或从事经济、文化、体育、宗教活动的中国（大陆）居民人数，其出游的目的不是通过所从事的活动谋取报酬。统计时，国内游客按每出游一次统计1人次。

国际旅游(外汇)收入 指入境游客在中国（大陆）境内旅行、游览过程中用于交通、参观游览、住宿、餐饮、购物、娱乐等全部花费。

国内旅游收入 又称旅游总花费指国内游客在国内旅行、游览过程中用于交通、参观游览、住宿、餐饮、购物、娱乐等全部花费。

国际旅行社 指经营业务范围包括入境旅游业务、出境旅游业务和国内旅游业务的旅行社。

国内旅行社 指经营范围仅限于国内旅游业务的旅行社。

星级饭店 指设备、设施、服务符合《旅游饭店星级的划分与评定》（GB/T14308-2003），通过相关旅游管理部门评定，并取得星级饭店称号的饭店（含预备星级饭店）。

Explanatory Notes on Main Statistical Indicators

Total Imports and Exports at Customs refer to the real value of commodities imported and exported across the border of China. They include the actual imports and exports through foreign trade, imported and exported goods under the processing and assembling trades and materials, supplies and gifts as aid given gratis between governments and by the United Nations and other international organizations, and contributions donated by overseas Chinese, compatriots in Hong Kong and Macao and Chinese with foreign citizenship, leasing commodities owned by tenant at the expiration of leasing period, the imported and exported commodities processed with imported materials, commodities trading in border areas (excluding mutual exchange goods), the imported and exported commodities and articles for public use of the Sino-foreign joint ventures, cooperative enterprises and ventures with sole foreign investment. Also included is import or export of samples and advertising goods for which CIF or FOB value are beyond the permitted ceiling (excluding goods of no trading or use value and free commodities for export), imported goods sold in China from bonded warehouses and other imported or exported goods. The indicator of the total imports and exports at customs can be used to observe the total size of external trade in a country. In accordance with the stipulation of the Chinese government, imports are calculated at CIF, while exports are calculated at FOB.

Utilization of Foreign Capitals refers to remittance, equipment and technology financed from abroad, by loans, foreign direct investment and other forms undertaken by the Chinese governments at all levels, by various departments, enterprises and other economic units.

Foreign Direct Investment refers to the investments inside China by foreign enterprises and economic organizations or individuals (including overseas Chinese, compatriots from Hong Kong, Macao and Taiwan, and Chinese enterprises registered abroad), following the relevant policies and laws of China, for the establishment of ventures exclusively with foreign own investment, Sino-foreign joint ventures and cooperative enterprises or for co-operative exploration of resources with enterprises or economic organizations in China. It includes the re- investment of the foreign entrepreneurs with the profits gained from the investment and the funds that enterprises borrow from abroad in the total investment of projects which are approved by the relevant department of the government.

Overseas Contracted Project refers to projects undertaken by Chinese contractors (project contracting companies) through bidding process. They include: (1) overseas civil engineering construction projects financed by foreign investors; (2) overseas projects financed by the Chinese government through its foreign aid programs; (3) construction projects of Chinese diplomatic missions, trade offices and other institutions stationed abroad; (4) construction projects in China financed by foreign investment; (5) sub-contracted projects to be taken by Chinese contractors through a joint umbrella project with foreign contractor(s); (6) housing development projects. The business income from international contracted projects is the work volume of contracted projects completed during the reference period, expressed in monetary terms, including completed work on projects signed in previous years.

Overseas Labour Services refer to the activities of providing technology and labour services to employers or contractors in the forms of receiving salaries and wages. Labour services providing by contractual joint ventures of Chinese international contracting corporations should be included in the statistics of service co-operation with foreign countries. The business income of labour service cooperation is the income in the form of wages and salaries, overtime pay, bonuses and other remuneration received from the employers during the reference period.

Number of Tourists include international tourists entering into China, Chinese residents going abroad and domestic tourists.

(1) International tourists refer to foreigners, overseas Chinese, Chinese compatriots from Hong Kong, Macao and Taiwan coming to China for sightseeing, visits, tours, family reunions, vacations, study tours, conferences and other activities of a business, scientific and technological, cultural, educational and religious nature. It does not include representatives and employees of resident institutions of foreign countries in China such as embassies, consulates, news agencies and offices of foreign companies and organizations, nor does it include long-term foreign experts or students residing in China, or persons in transition without spending a night in China.

(2) Chinese residents going abroad refer to Chinese residents going abroad for short terms for either public business or private purposes. Chinese employees working on international transport carriers are included in those going abroad for public business purpose, not in those for private purpose.

(3) Domestic tourists refer to residents of the mainland of China who stay for one night at least but no more than 6 months at tourist facilities in other places than their permanent residence within the territory of the mainland China, including foreigners, overseas Chinese and Chinese compatriots from Hong Kong, Macao and Taiwan who have resided in China for over one year.

Foreign Exchange Earnings from International Tourism refer to the total expenditures of foreigners, overseas Chinese, Chinese compatriots from Hong Kong, Macao and Taiwan during their stay in the mainland of China, which are earnings of foreign exchange from international tourism from the point of view from China.

Earning from domestic travel refer to the domestic tourists during their stay in the mainland of China ,which are earnings of transportaion,inviting,hoteling,catering,shopping and entertainment

International Travel Agencies refer to travel agencies engaged in the promotion, solicitation, organization and reception of tours to the mainland of China by foreigners, overseas Chinese, Chinese compatriots from Hong Kong, Macao and Taiwan.

Domestic Travel Agencies refer to travel agencies engaged in the promotion, solicitation, organization and reception of domestic tourists, and in the reception of foreigners, overseas Chinese, Chinese compatriots from Hong Kong, Macao and Taiwan organized by international travel agencies or other departments concerned, without their own promotion and solicitation programmes.

Start-Hotels refer to hotels that are able, with the approval of departments concerned, to accommodate foreigners, overseas Chinese, Chinese compatriots from Hong Kong, Macao and Taiwan Province.

第六篇 能源生产和消费

CHAPTER 6 Production and Consumption of Energy

简要说明
Brief Introduction

本篇资料的主要内容及来源

本篇包括的主要内容有能源生产、消费总量及品种构成，综合能源平衡表和主要能源品种单项平衡表，分行业、分主要能源品种的消费量，能源生产和消费弹性系数，能源加工转换效率及生活用能源消费量等。

从 2006 年度开始，能源生产、消费等指标需经国家审定后方可公布，因国家审定、公布各省的这部分指标数据为每年的八月份，时间在年鉴出版时间之后，为此，这部分数据采取错年上，即 2010 年上 2009 年数据。

本篇资料由新疆维吾尔自治区统计局能源与资源统计处依据能源年报整理提供。

Main content and source of data

Data in this chapter cover mainly the energy production and consumption and their composition, the overall balance of energy and the balance by different types of energy, the consumption of energy by sector and by types of energy the elasticity ratio of energy production and consumption, efficiency of energy conversion and the consumption of energy for non-production uses.

Since 2006, data on production and consumption of energy are announced after NBS authorized. Time of publication is August every year. So the data on energy in 2010 Statistical Yearbook is data in 2009.

Data in this chapter are provided and processed in accordance with the statistical reporting scheme on energy by the Department of Industry and Transport of the Xinjiang Bureau of Statistics.

6-1 主要年份能源生产总量及构成

Total Production of Energy and Its Composition in Main Years

年 份 Year	能源生产总量 (万吨标准煤) Total Energy Production (10 000 tons of SCE)	占能源生产总量的比重(%) Percentage of Total Energy Production (%)			
		原 煤 Coal	原 油 Crude Oil	天然气 Natural Gas	水风电 Hydro- Power and Wind Power
1978	1410.75	60.0	35.8	2.4	1.8
1980	1527.72	58.4	36.5	3.1	2.0
1985	2092.47	60.0	34.1	3.5	2.4
1990	2801.57	58.8	35.8	2.4	3.0
1995	4266.06	50.1	43.5	3.6	2.8
2000	5419.77	40.6	48.7	7.9	2.8
2001	5720.04	38.7	48.6	9.7	3.0
2002	6156.05	39.5	47.3	10.5	2.7
2003	6657.43	41.1	46.0	10.2	2.7
2004	7112.95	41.4	45.3	10.7	2.6
2005	8175.74	37.9	42.1	17.3	2.7
2006	9528.72	37.3	37.1	22.9	2.7
2007	10735.84	36.7	34.7	26.0	2.6
2008	12669.13	41.9	30.6	24.8	2.7
2009	13542.33	46.5	26.5	24.1	2.9

注：电力折算标准煤的系数根据当年平均发电煤耗计算，并将历史资料做了调整，下表同。

Note: The coefficient for conversion of electric power into SCE (standard coal equivalent) is calculated on the basic of the data on the average coal consumption in generating electric power in the same year. The same is as in the following tables.

6-2 主要年份能源消费总量及构成

Total Consumption of Energy and Its Composition in Main Years

年 份 Year	能源消费总量 (万吨标准煤) Total Energy Consumption (10 000 tons of SCE)	占能源消费总量的比重(%) As percentage of Total Energy Consumption (%)			
		煤 炭 Coal	石 油 Crude Oil	天然气 Natural Gas	水风电 Hydro- Power and Wind Power
1978	979.27	72.5	21.5	3.4	2.6
1980	1026.45	71.3	21.1	4.6	3.0
1985	1410.84	72.0	19.3	5.1	3.6
1990	1924.38	69.6	22.5	3.5	4.4
1995	2733.04	66.2	23.8	5.6	4.4
2000	3316.03	63.6	23.3	8.6	4.5
2001	3496.44	60.4	21.6	13.2	4.8
2002	3622.40	62.2	20.5	12.7	4.6
2003	4064.43	60.3	21.7	13.1	4.9
2004	4784.83	61.0	20.1	15.0	3.9
2005	5506.49	56.1	26.2	13.7	4.0
2006	6047.27	56.7	24.7	14.3	4.3
2007	6575.92	57.8	23.9	14.1	4.2
2008	7069.39	61.7	20.3	13.1	4.9
2009	7525.56	65.9	16.9	12.0	5.2

6-3 主要年份综合能源平衡表

Overall Energy Balance Sheet in Main Years

单位:万吨标准煤 (10 000 tons of SCE)

项　　目	Item	1990	1995	2000	2005	2009
可供消费的能源总量	**Total Energy Available for Consumption**	**2045.32**	**2883.61**	**3430.05**	**5349.17**	**7603.74**
一次能源生产量	Primary Energy Output	2801.57	4266.06	5419.77	8175.74	13542.33
进口量	Imports			107.39	130.80	1127.24
外省调入量	Inflow from other Provinces (Autonomons Regions and Municipalities)	2.26	8.29	25.59	58.17	130.42
出口量(-)	Exports (-)	4.84	1.04	31.90	60.80	8.17
本区调出量(-)	Outflow (-)	694.89	1414.05	2144.79	3172.41	7270.95
年初年末库存差额	Stock Changes in the Year	-58.78	24.35	53.99	95.71	67.99
能源消费总量	**Total Energy Consumption**	**1924.45**	**2733.01**	**3316.03**	**5506.49**	**7525.56**
在总量中:	Consumption by Sector					
农、林、牧、渔、水利业	Farming, Forestry, Animal Husbandry, Fishery and Water Conservancy	134.91	189.13	274.97	314.25	414.76
工　业	Industry	1095.22	1571.88	1860.26	3440.83	5192.25
建筑业	Construction	41.16	63.01	81.73	43.22	66.63
交通运输和邮电通讯业	Transportation, Post and Telecommunications Services	99.72	152.77	189.76	413.77	620.17
商业、饮食、物资供销和仓储业	Commerce, Catering Services, Materials Supply, Marketing and Storage	26.28	51.37	93.83	138.39	172.85
其　他	Others	99.12	205.04	164.57	177.51	203.33
生活消费	Residential Consumption	428.04	499.84	650.91	978.54	855.56
在总量中:	Consumption by Usage					
终端消费	End-use Consumption	1825.44	2587.35	3148.77	5086.96	6875.93
#工　业	Industry	996.27	1426.22	1692.96	3021.27	4678.98
加工转换损失量	Losses During the Process of Energy Conversion	27.90	62.06	91.25	228.26	336.82
#炼　焦	Coking	13.00	27.56	72.05	77.60	205.76
炼　油	Petroleum Refining	13.16	33.49	75.99	62.18	99.56
损失量	Energy Losses	71.05	83.60	76.05	191.27	312.80
平衡差额	**Balance**	**120.87**	**150.60**	**114.02**	**-157.32**	**78.18**

注：1.村办工业包括在工业中(下同)。
2.电力、热力按等价热值折算，因此加工转换损失量中不包括发电、供热损失量。
3.进口量包括新疆飞机在国外加油量，出口量包括外国飞机在新疆的加油量。

Note: a) Data on industry includes the data of village-run industry. (The same is as in the following tables).
b) Electric power and heat are converted on the basic of equal caloric value. Therefore, losses in processing and transformation exclude losses in power generation and heating.
c) Data on imports include the petroleum consumed by the Xinjiang airplanes in refueling abroad. Data on exports include the petroleum consumed by the foreign airplanes in refueling in Xinjiang.

6-4 主要年份石油平衡表
Petroleum Balance Sheet in Main Years

单位:万吨 (10 000 tons)

项　　目	Item	1990	1995	2000	2005	2009
可供量	**Total Energy Available for Consumption**	**333.19**	**496.35**	**616.14**	**1021.31**	**839.25**
生产量	Output	701.26	1299.83	1848.43	2408.32	2512.86
进口量	Imports			75.16	91.54	788.96
外省调入量	Inflow from other Provinces (Autonomons Regions and Municipalities)	1.44	3.31	10.85	14.85	14.09
出口量(-)	Exports (-)	3.29	0.63	11.17	5.18	0.93
本区调出量(-)	Outflow (-)	353.59	849.63	1285.38	1525.72	2531.78
年初年末库存差额	Stock Changes in the Year	-12.63	43.47	-21.75	37.50	56.05
消费量	**Total Energy Consumption**	**300.16**	**451.26**	**527.71**	**1014.84**	**839.25**
在消费量中：	Consumption by Sector					
农、林、牧、渔、水利业	Farming, Forestry, Animal Husbandry, Fishery and Water Conservancy	42.46	44.56	63.65	70.68	74.91
工　业	Industry	171.96	269.79	273.95	611.18	279.34
建筑业	Construction	16.87	16.67	32.10	15.36	23.73
交通运输和邮电通讯业	Transportation, Post and Telecommunications Services	48.30	76.55	86.89	210.00	348.79
商业、饮食、物资供销和仓储业	Commerce, Catering Services, Materials Supply, Marketing and Storage	3.66	8.80	18.78	31.91	38.46
其　他	Others	8.48	20.25	32.70	46.20	43.29
生活消费	Residential Consumption	8.43	14.64	19.64	29.51	30.73
在消费量中：	Consumption by Sector					
终端消费	Final Consumption	257.06	411.94	457.99	936.88	689.02
#工　业	Industry	128.86	230.47	204.23	533.22	217.11
中间消费(用于加工转换)	Intermediate Consumption	15.69	10.01	17.34	47.37	62.23
#发　电	Power Generation	15.69	10.01	2.10	8.65	9.32
供　热	Heating			1.24	1.04	18.23
此外：当年炼油投入量	Petroleum Refining Input	464.29	692.40	1001.32	1531.68	1862.63
平衡差额	**Balance**	**33.03**	**45.09**	**88.43**	**6.47**	

注：1.生产量为原油产量。
2.进口量包括新疆飞机在国外加油量，出口量包括外国飞机在新疆的加油量。

Note: a) Data on output refer to the output of crude oil.
b) Data on imports include the petroleum consumed by the Xinjiang Airplanes in refueling abroad. Data on exports include the petroleum consumed by the foreign airplanes in refueling in Xinjiang.

6-5 主要年份煤炭平衡表
Coal Balance Sheet in Main Years

单位:万吨 (10 000 tons)

项　　目	Item	1990	1995	2000	2005	2009
可供量	**Total Energy Available for Consumption**	**1816.32**	**2444.21**	**2702.81**	**3702.32**	**7511.31**
生产量	Output	2100.20	2720.74	2798.90	3942.29	8812.55
外省调入量	Inflow from other Provinces (Autonomons Regions and Municipalities)		1.40	10.70	30.40	121.87
进口量	Imports				0.03	0.12
出口量(-)	Exports (-)	0.01	0.14	0.22	0.01	
本区调出量(-)	Outflow (-)	232.76	221.00	203.12	323.47	1370.00
年初年末库存差额	Stock Changes in the Year	-51.11	-56.79	96.55	53.08	-53.23
消费量	**Total Energy Consumption**	**1716.11**	**2327.52**	**2702.40**	**3859.91**	**7417.71**
在消费量中:	Consumption by Sector					
农、林、牧、渔、水利业	Farming, Forestry, Animal Husbandry, Fishery and Water Conservancy	23.96	80.44	100.00	103.30	107.00
工　业	Industry	1080.07	1452.19	1801.40	3110.44	6889.81
建筑业	Construction	11.67	26.02	26.00	17.00	19.90
交通运输和邮电通讯业	Transportation, Post and Telecommunications Services	25.42	32.56	55.00	56.60	52.00
商业、饮食、物资供销和仓储业	Commerce, Catering Services, Materials Supply, Marketing and Storage	20.50	33.00	40.00	31.78	48.00
其　他	Others	79.48	176.31	90.00	40.00	46.00
生活消费	Residential Consumption	479.37	527.00	590.00	500.79	255.00
在消费量中:	Consumption by Sector					
终端消费	Final Consumption	1163.46	1427.87	1502.63	1503.83	2445.89
#工　业	Industry	523.06	552.54	601.63	754.36	1917.99
中间消费(用于加工转换)	Intermediate Consumption	525.51	842.96	1199.77	2356.08	4971.82
#发　电	Power Generation	372.01	575.88	849.20	1363.96	2386.66
供　热	Heating	32.32	102.93	204.46	585.51	995.00
炼　焦	Coking	111.39	158.93	137.77	380.90	1507.35
平衡差额	**Balance**	**100.21**	**116.69**	**0.41**	**-157.59**	**93.60**

注：生产量为原煤产量。
Note: Data on output refer to the output of raw coal.

6-6 主要年份电力平衡表
Electricity Balance Sheet in Main Years

单位:亿千瓦小时 (100 million kwh)

项　　目	Item	1990	1995	2000	2005	2009
可供量	**Total Energy Available for Consumption**	**69.79**	**120.43**	**182.98**	**310.14**	**547.88**
生产量	Output	69.79	120.43	182.98	310.14	547.88
水　电	Hydropower	14.25	22.82	30.54	46.49	79.84
风　电	Wind Power	0.08	0.34	1.73	2.32	17.62
火　电	Thermal Power	55.46	97.27	150.71	261.33	450.42
消费量	**Total Energy Consumption**	**69.79**	**120.37**	**182.98**	**310.14**	**547.88**
在消费量中:	Consumption by Sector					
农、林、牧、渔、水利业	Farming, Forestry, Animal Husbandry, Fishery and Water Conservancy	9.16	11.50	22.30	28.72	56.59
工　业	Industry	48.86	83.53	118.85	221.67	398.23
建筑业	Construction	1.18	3.20	3.50	1.44	4.67
交通运输和邮电通讯业	Transportation, Post and Telecommunications Services	1.48	2.73	4.00	4.74	6.08
商业、饮食、物资供销和仓储业	Commerce, Catering Services, Materials Supply, Marketing and Storage	0.81	2.30	6.90	11.09	15.39
其　他	Others	4.08	7.00	9.83	15.38	24.30
生活消费	Residential Consumption	4.22	10.11	17.60	27.10	42.62
在消费量中:	Consumption by Sector					
终端消费	Final Consumption	65.74	112.87	170.86	282.42	504.23
#工　业	Industry	44.81	76.03	106.73	193.95	354.58
输配电损失量	Losses in Transmission	4.05	7.50	12.12	27.72	43.65

6-7 分行业能源消费总量和主要能源消费量

(2009 年)

行　业	Sector	能源消费总量(万吨标准煤) Total Energy Consumption (10 000 tons of SCE)	煤炭消费量(万吨) Coal Consumption (10 000 tons)	焦炭消费量(万吨) Coke Consumption (10 000 tons)
消费总量	**Total Consumption**	**7525.56**	**7417.71**	**528.24**
农、林、牧、渔业	**Farming, Forestry, Animal Husbandry, and Fishery**	**414.76**	**107.00**	
工　业	**Industry**	**5192.25**	**6889.81**	**528.24**
采 矿 业	**Mining and Quarrying**	**907.57**	**328.19**	**3.24**
煤炭开采和洗选业	Mining and Washing of Coal	128.12	210.27	0.17
石油和天然气开采业	Extraction of Petroleum and Natural Gas	698.86	78.55	
黑色金属矿采选业	Mining and Processing of Ferrous Metals Ores	44.15	20.02	0.90
有色金属矿采选业	Mining and Processing of Nonferrous Metals Ores	24.33	6.22	2.17
非金属矿采选业	Mining and Processing of Non-metal Ores	12.11	13.14	
制 造 业	**Manufacturing**	**3587.63**	**3697.75**	**525.00**
农副食品加工业	Processing of Food from Agricultural Products	105.11	116.28	2.23
食品制造业	Manufacture of Food	76.23	71.73	
饮料制造业	Manufacture of Beverage	20.20	14.53	
烟草制品业	Manufacture of Tobacco	1.45	1.28	
纺织业	Manufacture of Textile	71.78	25.53	
纺织服装、鞋、帽制造业	Manufacture of Textile Wearing Apparel,Footware and Caps	0.29	0.16	
皮革、毛皮、羽绒及其制品业	Manufacture of Leather, Fur, Feather and Related Products	0.29	0.26	
木材加工及木、竹、藤、棕、草制品业	Timber Production, Wood, Bamboo, Cane and Grass	7.16	8.28	
家具制造业	Manufacture of Furniture	1.64	0.80	
造纸及纸制品业	Manufacture of Paper and Paper Products	32.48	28.59	
印刷业和记录媒介的复制	Printing and Copying of Medium for Record	1.40	0.30	
石油加工、炼焦及核燃料加工业	Processing of Oil Processing, Coking and Nuclear Fuel	953.71	1636.27	

Consumption of Total Energy and Its Main Varieties by Sector

原油消费量 (万吨) Crude Oil Consumption (10 000 tons)	汽油消费量 (万吨) Gasoline Consumption (10 000 tons)	煤油消费量 (万吨) Kerosene Consumption (10 000 tons)	柴油消费量 (万吨) Diesel Oil Consumption (10 000 tons)	燃料油消费量 (万吨) Fuel Oil Consumption (10 000 tons)	天然气消费量 (亿立方米) Natural Gas Consumption (100 million cu.m)	电力消费量 (亿千瓦小时) Electricity Consumption (100 million kwh)
1997.90	**121.87**	**31.40**	**331.70**	**22.37**	**67.93**	**547.88**
	11.50	**0.40**	**62.00**			**56.59**
1909.90	**9.20**	**0.09**	**41.70**	**22.37**	**58.50**	**398.23**
86.30	**3.85**		**29.15**	**0.04**	**41.74**	**47.79**
	1.00		5.27			7.58
86.30	2.58		18.44	0.04	41.70	30.20
	0.16		4.24		0.04	5.46
	0.08		0.58			4.16
	0.03		0.62			0.39
1823.59	**3.96**	**0.09**	**11.20**	**22.30**	**16.60**	**250.54**
	0.35		0.37		0.02	5.45
	0.20		0.27		0.05	3.93
	0.12		0.03		0.04	1.20
	0.01					0.13
	0.13	0.01	0.06			11.70
	0.01					0.02
	0.01		0.01			0.02
	0.01		0.05			0.74
	0.03		0.01			0.15
	0.03		0.05	0.09		2.46
	0.06		0.01			0.15
1823.59	0.40	0.05	0.67	22.19	6.94	26.57

6-7 续表

行　　业	Sector	能源消费总量（万吨标准煤）Total Energy Consumption (10 000 tons of SCE)	煤炭消费量（万吨）Coal Consumption (10 000 tons)	焦炭消费量（万吨）Coke Consumption (10 000 tons)
化学原料及化学制品制造业	Manufacture of Raw Chemical Material and Chemical Products	808.21	518.98	97.61
医药制造业	Manufacture of Medicine	6.05	6.21	
化学纤维制造业	Manufacture of Chemical Fiber	95.32	83.86	
橡胶制品业	Manufacture of Rubber Products	4.26	4.09	
塑料制品业	Manufacture of Plastic Products	10.90	0.97	
非金属矿物制品业	Manufacture of Non-metallic Mineral Products	497.52	491.23	7.04
黑色金属冶炼及压延加工业	Smelting and Pressing of Ferrous Metals	778.60	583.24	410.2
有色金属冶炼及压延加工业	Smelting and Pressing of Non-ferrous Metals	50.82	46.47	2.40
金属制品业	Metal Products Manufacturing	13.22	2.94	5.42
通用设备制造业	Manufacture of General Purpose Machinery	2.57	0.81	0.03
专用设备制造业	Manufacture of Special Purpose Machinery	3.61	4.67	0.03
交通运输设备制造业	Manufacture of Transport Equipment	2.37	0.45	0.04
电气机械及器材制造业	Manufacture of Electric Equipment and Machinery	5.22	2.54	
通信设备、计算机及其他电子设备制造业	Communication Equipment, Computer and Other Electronic Equipment	36.48	47.26	
仪器仪表及文化办公用机械制造业	Manufacture of Equipment, Meter, Culture and Office Machinery	0.11		
工艺品及其他制造业	Manufacture of Artwork and Other Manufacturing Sector	0.59	0.04	
电力、燃气及水的生产和供应业	**Electric Power, Gas and Water Production and Supply**	**697.05**	**2863.86**	
电力、热力的生产和供应业	Production and Distribution of Power, Steam and Hot Water	688.28	2862.46	
燃气生产和供应业	Production and Supply of Gas	2.23	0.03	
水的生产和供应业	Production and Supply of Water	6.54	1.36	
建筑业	**Construction**	**66.63**	**19.90**	
交通运输、仓储及邮电通信业	**Transportation, Storage, Post & Telecommunications Services**	**620.17**	**52.00**	
批发和零售贸易业、餐饮业	**Wholesale, Retail Trades and Catering Services**	**172.85**	**48.00**	
其他行业	**Others**	**203.33**	**46.00**	
生活消费	**Household Consumption**	**855.56**	**255.00**	

Continued

原油消费量 (万吨) Crude Oil Consumption (10 000 tons)	汽油消费量 (万吨) Gasoline Consumption (10 000 tons)	煤油消费量 (万吨) Kerosene Consumption (10 000 tons)	柴油消费量 (万吨) Diesel Oil Consumption (10 000 tons)	燃料油消费量 (万吨) Fuel Oil Consumption (10 000 tons)	天然气消费量 (亿立方米) Natural Gas Consumption (100 million cu.m)	电力消费量 (亿千瓦小时) Electricity Consumption (100 million kwh)
	0.45	0.02	2.14		9.19	97.66
	0.05		0.04		0.01	0.18
	0.05		0.05			4.84
	0.01		0.01			0.31
	0.11		0.04		0.01	2.20
	1.02	0.01	4.75		0.19	33.73
	0.29		1.95		0.07	42.14
	0.08		0.32	0.02	0.01	6.85
	0.13		0.12		0.04	1.13
	0.15		0.06			0.29
	0.08		0.03			0.34
	0.04		0.02		0.02	0.13
	0.09		0.06		0.01	0.69
	0.02		0.04			7.44
	0.02					0.01
	0.01		0.04			0.08
0.01	**1.39**		**1.35**	**0.03**	**0.16**	**99.90**
0.01	1.26		1.24	0.03	0.10	98.12
	0.04		0.08		0.04	0.44
	0.09		0.03		0.02	1.34
	3.00	**0.17**	**12.50**			**4.67**
88.00	**59.00**	**30.00**	**162.00**		**3.90**	**6.08**
	10.50	**0.06**	**24.00**		**1.15**	**15.39**
	18.37	**0.33**	**23.00**		**0.48**	**24.30**
	10.30	**0.35**	**6.50**		**3.90**	**42.62**

6-8 主要年份能源生产弹性系数

Elasticity Ration of Energy Production in Main Years

年 份 Year	能源生产比上年增长(%) Growth Rate of Energy Production Over Preceding Year(%)	电力生产比上年增长(%) Growth Rate of Electricity Production over Preceding Year(%)	新疆生产总值比上年增长(%) Growth Rate of Gross Domestic Product (GDP) Over Preceding Year(%)	能源生产弹性系数 Elasticity Cofficient of Energy Production	电力生产弹性系数 Elasticity Ratio of Electricity Production
1980	7.8	3.6	7.2	1.08	0.50
1985	11.6	11.5	16.9	0.69	0.68
1990	5.8	10.8	11.7	0.50	0.92
1995	7.8	13.4	9.0	0.87	1.49
2000	3.3	8.1	8.2	0.40	0.99
2001	5.5	8.0	8.1	0.68	0.99
2002	7.6	7.4	8.1	0.94	0.91
2003	8.1	10.5	10.8	0.75	0.97
2004	6.8	13.3	11.1	0.61	1.20
2005	14.9	16.6	10.9	1.37	1.52
2006	16.6	15.2	11.0	1.51	1.38
2007	12.7	16.7	12.2	1.04	1.37
2008	18.0	16.0	11.0	1.64	1.45
2009	6.9	14.3	8.1	0.85	1.77

注：新疆生产总值增速按可比价格计算，下表同。
Note: The growth rate of GDP in Xinjiang is calculated at comparable prices and the same as in the following tables.

6-9 主要年份能源消费弹性系数

Elasticity Ration of Energy Consumption in Main Years

年 份 Year	能源消费比上年增长(%) Growth Rate of Energy Consumption Over Preceding Year(%)	电力消费比上年增长(%) Growth Rate of Electricity Consumption over Preceding Year(%)	新疆生产总值比上年增长(%) Growth Rate of Gross Domestic Product (GDP) Over Preceding Year(%)	能源消费弹性系数 Elasticity Ration of Energy Consumption	电力消费弹性系数 Elasticity Ration of Electricity Consumption
1980	4.5	3.6	7.2	0.63	0.50
1985	13.6	11.5	16.9	0.80	0.68
1990	9.3	10.8	11.7	0.79	0.92
1995	4.9	13.4	9.0	0.54	1.49
2000	3.1	8.1	8.2	0.38	0.99
2001	5.4	8.0	8.1	0.67	0.99
2002	3.6	7.4	8.1	0.44	0.91
2003	12.2	10.5	10.8	1.13	0.97
2004	17.7	13.3	11.1	1.59	1.20
2005	15.1	16.6	10.9	1.39	1.52
2006	9.8	14.8	11.0	0.89	1.35
2007	8.7	16.0	12.2	0.71	1.31
2008	7.5	16.0	11.0	0.68	1.45
2009	6.5	14.3	8.1	0.80	1.77

6-10 主要年份能源加工转换效率
Efficiency of Energy Procession and Conversion in Main Years

单位：%　　(%)

年 份 Year	总效率 Total Efficiency	发 电 Electricity Generation	供 热 Heating	炼 焦 Coking	炼 油 Petroleum Refining
1980	73.9	21.2		72.0	96.9
1985	74.9	21.1		75.5	98.1
1990	73.9	20.9	69.4	85.5	98.0
1995	72.7	23.6	71.2	78.6	96.6
2000	73.6	26.6	75.0	89.4	94.7
2001	73.7	26.1	74.6	78.2	97.4
2002	73.6	26.8	73.5	83.4	96.8
2003	73.8	26.0	78.0	92.0	97.9
2004	70.2	25.9	70.3	78.8	96.2
2005	72.3	27.0	77.7	75.7	97.1
2006	74.8	27.8	76.7	85.0	97.6
2007	73.3	28.6	73.5	86.3	96.4
2008	73.8	30.0	76.6	84.8	96.6
2009	73.5	30.4	77.4	82.2	96.3

6-11 主要年份平均每天各种能源消费量
Average Daily Energy Consumption by Type of Energy in Main Years

能源品种	Variey of Energy	1990	1995	2000	2005	2009
总计(万吨标准煤)	**Total (10 000 tons of SCE)**	**5.41**	**7.60**	**9.09**	**15.09**	**20.62**
煤炭(万吨)	Coal (10 000 tons)	5.04	6.67	7.48	10.58	20.32
焦炭(万吨)	Coke (10 000 tons)	0.16	0.20	0.20	0.50	1.45
原油(万吨)	Crude Oil (10 000 tons)	1.33	1.99	2.94	4.46	5.47
燃料油(万吨)	Fuel Oil (10 000 tons)	0.25	0.32	0.16	0.50	0.06
汽油(万吨)	Gasoline (10 000 tons)	0.20	0.28	0.28	0.29	0.33
煤油(万吨)	Kerosene (10 000 tons)	0.01	0.04	0.06	0.07	0.09
柴油(万吨)	Diesel Oil (10 000 tons)	0.24	0.33	0.43	0.83	0.91
天然气(万立方米)	Natural Gas (10 000 cu.m)	137.53	314.52	642.19	1546.85	1861.10
电力(亿千瓦时)	Electricity (100 million kwh)	0.19	0.33	0.50	0.85	1.50

6-12 主要年份分品种生活能源年消费总量

Average Annual Energy Consumption for Household by Variety in Main Years

年 份 Year	合 计 (万吨标准煤) Total (10 000 tons of SCE)	煤 炭 (万吨) Coal (10 000 tons)	煤 油 (万吨) Kerosene (10 000 tons)	液化石油气 (万吨) Liquefied Petroleum Gas (10 000 tons)	天然气 (亿立方米) Natural Gas (100 million cu.m)	热 力 (万百万千焦) Heat (10 billion kilo-joule)	电 力 (亿千瓦小时) Electricity (100 million kwh)
1980	330.44	404.10					1.70
1985	355.65	421.72	0.71	3.00			2.38
1990	428.04	479.37	0.58	5.35		160.02	4.22
1995	499.84	527.00	0.50	8.94		177.29	10.11
2000	650.91	590.00	0.75	10.89	0.13	1611.81	17.60
2001	703.97	600.00	0.67	12.31	0.46	2209.66	19.50
2002	752.10	610.00	0.10	14.22	0.32	3112.58	19.20
2003	782.21	625.04		16.62	0.60	3191.14	20.37
2004	901.88	605.00		17.00	1.00	3363.45	24.26
2005	978.54	500.79	0.55	12.96	1.92	6219.00	27.10
2006	612.66	211.00	0.55	14.10	2.60	5008.00	31.90
2007	652.36	213.00	0.42	14.53	2.70	5097.43	33.52
2008	752.73	232.20	0.35	11.60	2.89	7371.00	38.55
2009	855.56	255.00	0.35	13.50	3.90	9073.84	42.62

注：表 6-12 和 6-13 中，除 2006 年，其余年份数据未按新口径进行调整。
Note: Figures in table6-12 and6-13 did not adjusted at new coverage, except for figures in 2006.

6-13 主要年份每人年平均生活用能源

Annual Average Per-Capital Energy Consumption for Non-Production Purpose in Main Years

年 份 Year	平均每人生活消费能源 (公斤标准煤/人) Annual Per Capita Consumption for Household (kg of SCE/person)	煤 炭 (公斤) Coal (kg)	电 力 (千瓦小时) Electricity (kwh)	煤 油 (公斤) Kerosene (kg)	液化石油气 (公斤) Liquefied Petroleum Gas (kg)	天然气 (立方米) Natural Gas (cu.m)
1980	258	315	13.25			
1985	261	310	17.49	0.52	2.20	
1990	268	313	27.60	0.38	3.50	
1995	301	317	65.60	0.30	5.33	
2000	353	320	95.33	0.41	5.90	0.70
2001	375	320	103.93	0.36	6.56	2.45
2002	395	320	100.78	0.05	7.46	1.68
2003	404	323	105.33		8.59	3.10
2004	459	308	123.58		8.66	5.09
2005	487	249	134.80	0.27	6.45	9.55
2006	302	104	157.13	0.27	6.95	12.81
2007	311	102	159.99	0.20	6.93	12.89
2008	352	109	180.92	0.16	5.44	13.56
2009	396	118	197.44	0.16	6.25	18.07

6-14 各地、州、市规模以上工业企业能源消费量

Energy Consumption of Industry above Designated Size by Prefecture, Autonomous Prefecture and City

(2009 年)

能源品种	Item	合 计 Total	乌鲁木齐市 Urumqi City	克拉玛依市 Karamay City	吐鲁番地区 Turpan Administrative Offices
原煤(吨)	Coal (ton)	55299523	14204646	2222097	2151790
洗精煤(吨)	Washed Coal(ton)	4449759	3274116		
其他洗煤(吨)	Other Washed Coal (ton)	122589	66556		
焦炭(吨)	Coke (ton)	5282446	2618878		612640
焦炉煤气(万立方米)	Coke Oven Gas (10 000 cu.m)	67176	59180		
高炉煤气(万立方米)	High Oven Gas (10 000 cu.m)	839520	839520		
天然气(万立方米)	Natural Gas (10 000 cu.m)	595004	83114	246717	47539
原油(吨)	Coal (ton)	19186935	5547027	10644236	51134
汽油(吨)	Gasoline (ton)	43403	13002	9240	521
煤油(吨)	Kerosene (ton)	147	113		
柴油(吨)	Diesel Oil (ton)	349707	43648	150491	17863
燃料油(吨)	Fuel Oil (ton)	248635	246571	777	
液化石油气(吨)	Liquefied Petroleum Gas (ton)	52802	505	52271	
炼厂干气(吨)	Refinary Dry Gas (ton)	756047	175279	475105	
其他石油制品(吨)	Other Oil Product (ton)	364616	185820		
热力(百万千焦)	Heat (million KJ)	55814882	16223269	15796723	1730890
电力(万千瓦时)	Electricity (10 000 kwh)	3624793	1078960	334608	112531
其他燃料(吨标准煤)	Other (ton of SCE)	126584	28869		5378
能源合计(吨标准煤)	Energy Total (ton of SCE)	94696574	28974232	22095014	3253570

能源品种	Item	哈密地区 Hami [kumul] Administrative Offices	昌吉回族自治州 Changji Hui Autonomous Prefecture	博尔塔拉蒙古自治州 Bortala Mongol Autonomous Prefecture	伊犁州直属县(市) Counties (Cities) Direct Under Ili Prefecture
原煤(吨)	Coal (ton)	3227290	12433621	480862	3598797
洗精煤(吨)	Washed Coal (ton)		800		436784
其他洗煤(吨)	Other Washed Coal (ton)				
焦炭(吨)	Coke (ton)	62949	25276	135291	485184
焦炉煤气(万立方米)	Coke Oven Gas (10 000 cu.m)		780		6916
高炉煤气(万立方米)	High Oven Gas (10 000 cu.m)				
天然气(万立方米)	Natural Gas (10 000 cu.m)		2112		71
原油(吨)	Coal (ton)		37879		
汽油(吨)	Gasoline (ton)	4592	3171	349	2454
煤油(吨)	Kerosene (ton)	2			7
柴油(吨)	Diesel Oil (ton)	22171	26828	2009	9271
燃料油(吨)	Fuel Oil (ton)				
液化石油气(吨)	Liquefied Petroleum Gas (ton)				
炼厂干气(吨)	Refinary Dry Gas (ton)				
其他石油制品(吨)	Other Oil Product (ton)		3951	59	17485
热力(百万千焦)	Heat (million KJ)		2632370	156243	426561
电力(万千瓦时)	Electricity (10 000 kwh)	90179	346227	21224	286311
其他燃料(吨标准煤)	Other (ton of SCE)		26147		276
能源合计(吨标准煤)	Energy Total (ton of SCE)	2515388	9657953	509831	3805994

注：各地区数含兵团工业在内。
Note:Figures in different prefectures include data of XPCG enterprises.

6-14 续表 Continued

名　称	Variey of Energy	塔城地区 Tacheng [Tarbagatai] Administrative Office	阿勒泰地区 Altay Administrative Offices	巴音郭楞蒙古自治州 Bayangol Mongol Autonomous Prefecture	阿克苏地区 Aksu Administrative Offices
原煤(吨)	Coal (ton)	1424317	562291	2572122	4153115
洗精煤(吨)	Washed Coal (ton)			92476	493953
其他洗煤(吨)	Other Washed Coal (ton)			25551	30482
焦炭(吨)	Coke (ton)	10096	56318	464348	2554
焦炉煤气(万立方米)	Coke Oven Gas (10 000 cu.m)				299
高炉煤气(万立方米)	High Oven Gas (10 000 cu.m)				
天然气(万立方米)	Natural Gas (10 000 cu.m)			153847	57893
原油(吨)	Coal (ton)			843357	2063302
汽油(吨)	Gasoline (ton)	1156	588	4834	1492
煤油(吨)	Kerosene (ton)			24	
柴油(吨)	Diesel Oil (ton)	4477	25783	24023	10974
燃料油(吨)	Fuel Oil (ton)			975	
液化石油气(吨)	Liquefied Petroleum Gas (ton)			16	
炼厂干气(吨)	Refinary Dry Gas (ton)			33409	72254
其他石油制品(吨)	Other Oil Product (ton)	190		22261	134590
热力(百万千焦)	Heat (million KJ)	695949		8729739	1501849
电力(万千瓦时)	Electricity (10 000 kwh)	102450	69825	254030	147491
其他燃料(吨标准煤)	Other (ton of SCE)	240		18060	43643
能源合计(吨标准煤)	Energy Total (ton of SCE)	1201440	583227	6253449	7856225

名　称	Variey of Energy	克孜勒苏柯尔克孜自治州 Kizilsu Kirgiz Autonomous Prefecture	喀什地区 Kashgar [kaxgar] Administrative Offices	和田地区 Hotan Administrative Offices	石河子市 Shihezi City
原煤(吨)	Coal (ton)	18976	1268605	270168	6710826
洗精煤(吨)	Washed Coal (ton)				151629
其他洗煤(吨)	Other Washed Coal (ton)				
焦炭(吨)	Coke (ton)		85942		722971
焦炉煤气(万立方米)	Coke Oven Gas (10 000 cu.m)				
高炉煤气(万立方米)	High Oven Gas (10 000 cu.m)				
天然气(万立方米)	Natural Gas (10 000 cu.m)	687	971	27	2026
原油(吨)	Coal (ton)				
汽油(吨)	Gasoline (ton)	100	672	480	752
煤油(吨)	Kerosene (ton)				1
柴油(吨)	Diesel Oil (ton)	1832	2512	1743	6084
燃料油(吨)	Fuel Oil (ton)			1	310
液化石油气(吨)	Liquefied Petroleum Gas (ton)				
炼厂干气(吨)	Refinary Dry Gas (ton)				
其他石油制品(吨)	Other Oil Product (ton)	198			62
热力(百万千焦)	Heat (million KJ)				7921288
电力(万千瓦时)	Electricity (10 000 kwh)	4788	47802	25248	703122
其他燃料(吨标准煤)	Other (ton of SCE)		1618	2354	
能源合计(吨标准煤)	Energy Total (ton of SCE)	31610	1067572	205306	6685764

主要统计指标解释

能源生产总量 指一定时期内，一个地区一次能源生产量的总和。该指标是观察一个地区能源生产水平、规模、构成和发展速度的总量指标。一次能源生产量包括原煤、原油、天然气、水电、核能及其他动力能(如风能、地热能等)发电量，不包括低热值燃料生产量、生物质能、太阳能等的利用和由一次能源加工转换而成的二次能源产量。

能源消费总量 指一定时期内，一个地区和居民生活消费的各种能源的总和，该指标是观察能源消费水平、构成和增长速度的总量指标。能源消费总量包括原煤和原油及其制品、天然气、电力，不包括低热值燃料、生物质能和太阳能等的利用。能源消费总量分为终端能源消费量、能源加工转换损失量和损失量三部分。

(1)终端能源消费量：指一定时期内，一个地区生产和生活消费的各种能源在扣除了用于加工转换二次能源消费量和损失量以后的数量。

(2)能源加工转换损失量：指一定时期内，一个地区投入加工转换的各种能源数量之和与产出各种能源产品之和的差额，该指标是观察能源在加工转换过程中损失量变化的指标。

(3)能源损失量：指一定时期内，能源在输送、分配、储存过程中发生的损失和由客观原因造成的各种损失量，不包括各种气体能源放空、放散量。

能源生产弹性系数 是研究能源生产增长速度与国民经济增长速度之间关系的指标。计算公式为：

能源生产弹性系数＝能源生产总量年平均增长速度／国民经济年平均增长速度

国民经济年平均增长速度，可根据不同的目的或需要，用国民生产总值、国内生产总值等指标来计算，本年鉴是采用国内生产总值指标计算的。

电力生产弹性系数 是研究电力生产增长速度与国民经济增长速度之间关系的指标。一般来说，电力的发展应当快于国民经济的发展，也就是说电力应超前发展。计算公式为：

电力生产弹性系数＝电力生产量年平均增长速度／国民经济年平均增长速度

能源消费弹性系数 是反映能源消费增长速度与国民经济增长速度之间比例关系的指标。计算公式为：

能源消费弹性系数＝能源消费量年平均增长速度／国民经济年平均增长速度

电力消费弹性系数 反映电力消费增长速度与国民经济增长速度之间比例关系的指标。计算公式为：

电力消费弹性系数＝电力消费量年平均增长速度／国民经济年平均增长速度

能源加工转换效率 指一定时期内，能源经过加工、转换后，产出的各种能源产品的数量与同期内投入加工转换的各种能源数量的比率。该指标是观察能源加工转换装置和生产工艺先进与落后、管理水平高低等的重要指标。计算公式为：

能源加工转换效率＝能源加工、转换产出量／能源加工、转换投入量×100%

单位国内生产总值能耗 指一定时期内，一个国家或地区每生产一个单位的国内生产总值所消耗的能源。计算公式为：

单位国内生产总值能耗=能源消费总量/国内生产总值

单位国内生产总值电耗 指一定时期内，一个国家或地区每生产一个单位的国内生产总值所消耗的电力。计算公式为：

单位国内生产总值电耗=全社会用电量/国内生产总值

单位工业增加值能耗 指一定时期内，一个国家或地区每生产一个单位的工业增加值所消耗的能源。计算公式为：

单位工业增加值能耗=工业能源消费量/工业增加值

Explanatory Notes on Main Statistical Indicators

Total Energy Production refers to the total production of primary energy by all energy producing enterprises in the country in a given period of time. It is a comprehensive indicator to show the level, scale, composition and pace of development of energy production of the country. The production of primary energy includes that of coal, crude oil, natural gas, hydro-power and electricity generated by nuclear energy and other means such as wind power and geothermal power. However, it does not include the production of fuels of low calorific value, bio-energy, solar energy and secondary energy converted from primary energy.

Total Energy Consumption refers to the total consumption of energy of various kinds by the production sectors and the households in the country in a given period of time. It is a comprehensive indicator to show the scale, composition and pace of increase of energy consumption. Total energy consumption includes that of coal, crude oil and their products, natural gas and electricity. However, it does not include the consumption of fuel of low calorific value, bio-energy and solar energy. Total energy consumption can be divided into three parts: end-use energy consumption; loss during the process of energy conversion; and energy loss.

(1)End-use Energy Consumption: It refers to the total energy consumption by the production sectors and the households in the country (region) in a given period of time. It does not include the consumption during the conversion of primary energy into secondary energy and the loss in the process of energy conversion.

(2)Loss During the Process of Energy Conversion: It refers to the total input of various kinds of energy for conversion, minus the total output of various kinds of energy in the country in a given period of time. It is an indicator to show the loss that occurs during the process of energy conversion.

(3)Energy Loss: It refers to the total of the loss of energy during the course of energy transport, distribution and storage and the loss caused by any objective reason in a given period of time. The loss of various kinds of gas due to gas discharges and stocktaking is not included.

Elasticity Ratio of Energy Production is an indicator to show the relationship between the growth rate of energy production and the growth rate of the national economy. The formula is:

$$\text{Elasticity Ratio of Energy Production} = \frac{\text{Average Annual Growth Rate of Energy Production}}{\text{Average Annual Growth Rate of National Economy}}$$

The average annual growth rate of the national economy can be measured by indicators such as the Gross National Product and the Gross Domestic Product, depending on the purposes or needs. The Gross Domestic Product has been used in the calculation of the ratio in this Yearbook.

Elasticity Ratio of Electricity Production is an indicator to show the relationship between the growth rate of electricity production and the growth rate of the national economy. Generally speaking, the growth rate of electricity production should be higher than that of the national economy.

Its formula is:

$$\text{Elasticity Ratio of Electricity Production} = \frac{\text{Average Annual Growth Rate of Electricity Production}}{\text{Average Annual Growth Rate of National Economy}}$$

Elasticity Ratio of Energy Consumption is an indicator to show the relationship between the growth rate of energy consumption and the growth rate of the national economy. The formula is:

$$\text{Elasticity Ratio of Energy Consumption} = \frac{\text{Average Annual Growth Rate of Energy Consumption}}{\text{Average Annual Growth Rate of National Economy}}$$

Elasticity Ratio of Electricity Consumption is an indicator to show the relationship between the growth rate of electricity consumption and the growth rate of the national economy. The formula is:

$$\text{Elasticity Ratio of Electricity Consumption} = \frac{\text{Average Annual Growth Rate of Electricity Consumption}}{\text{Average Annual Growth Rate of National Economy}}$$

Efficiency of Energy Processing and Conversion refers to the ratio of the total output of energy products of various kinds after processing and conversion to the total input of energy of various kinds for processing and conversion in the same reference period. It is an important indicator to show the current conditions of energy processing and conversion equipment, production technique and management. The formula is:

$$\text{Efficiency of Energy Processing \& Conversion} = \frac{\text{Output of Energy After Processing \& Conversion}}{\text{Input of Energy for Processing \& Conversion}} \times 100\%$$

Energy Consumption per Unit of GDP refers to the energy consumption per unit of Gross Domestic Product in a country or the Gross Regional Product in a region in the same reference period. The formula is:

$$\text{Energy Consumption per Unit of GDP} = \frac{\text{Total Energy Consumption}}{\text{Gross Domestic Product}}$$

Electricity Consumption per Unit of GDP refers to the electricity consumption per unit of Gross Domestic Product in a country or the Gross Regional Product in a region in the same reference period. The formula is:

$$\text{Electricity Consumption per Unit of GDP} = \frac{\text{Total Electricity Consumption}}{\text{Gross Domestic Product}}$$

Energy Consumption per Unit of Industrial Value-added refers to the energy consumption per unit of industrial value-added in a country or region in the same reference period. The formula is:

$$\text{Energy Consumption per Unit of Industrial Value - added} = \frac{\text{energy consumption of industry}}{\text{Industrial Value - added}}$$

第七篇
财政、金融、保险

CHAPTER 7
Government Finance, Financial Intermediation and Insurance

简要说明

Brief Introduction

本篇资料的主要内容及来源

本篇反映自治区财政、金融、证券和保险业发展情况,有以下四个部分:一是地方财政预算收支情况;二是金融机构存贷及现金收支等活动情况;三是保险业务情况;四是证券上市情况。

地方财政预算收支情况取自新疆维吾尔自治区财政厅年度决算;金融资料来自中国人民银行乌鲁木齐中心支行金融机构信贷统计月报;保险业务情况资料取自中国保险监督管理委员会新疆监管局编制的保险统计资料;证券及上市公司情况来自新疆证监会。

本篇章数据由新疆维吾尔自治区统计局国民经济综合统计处根据上述部门所提供的资料整理。

Main content and source of data

The data in this chapter show the development of Xinjiang Uygur Autonomous region government finance, banking, securities and insurance, in the following 4 aspects(1)The government revenue and expenditure;(2)The financial activities of banking institutions;(3) The business of insurance;(4)The condition of listed securities.

Data on the government revenue and expenditure come from the final state financial accounts, Data on financial intermediation come from the credit funds sheet of financial institutions of Urumqi municipal sub –branches, People´s Bank of China; Data on insurance come from Xinjiang Insurance Regulatory Bureau of CIRC. Data on listed securities are from Xinjiang Security Regulatory Bureau of CSRC.

Data in this chapter are compiled and collected by the Division of comprehensive of the Xinjing Bureau of Statistics on the basis of data from the relative departments.

7-1 主要年份地方财政一般预算收支及增长速度
The General Budgetary Revenue & Expenses and Growth Rate of Local Finance in Main Years

单位：万元 (10 000 yuan)

年份 Year	地方财政一般预算收入 General Budgetary Revenue in Local Finance	地方财政一般预算支出 General Budgetary Expenditure in Local Finance	收支差额 Balance	指数(上年=100) Indices (precding year=100)	
				地方财政一般预算收入 General Budgetary Revenue in Local Finance	地方财政一般预算支出 General Budgetary Expenditure in Local Finance
1978	71416	170169	-98753	196.5	153.3
1980	40309	162159	-121850	73.4	95.4
1985	84663	286031	-201368	117.2	122.6
1990	217784	476210	-258426	118.9	114.2
1995	382818	964021	-581203	133.4	135.6
2000	790724	1909529	-1118805	110.9	114.8
2001	950933	2633232	-1682299	120.3	137.9
2002	1164724	3611729	-2447005	122.5	137.2
2003	1282218	3684676	-2402458	110.1	102.0
2004	1557040	4210446	-2653406	121.4	114.3
2005	1803184	5190179	-3386995	115.8	123.3
2006	2194628	6784723	-4590095	121.7	130.7
2007	2858600	7951540	-5092940	130.3	117.2
2008	3610616	10593638	-6983022	126.3	133.2
2009	3887848	13469125	-9581277	107.7	127.1
2010	5005759	16989126	-11983367	128.8	126.1

7-2 主要年份地方财政一般预算收入占新疆生产总值的比重
Ration of the General Budgetary Revenue in Local Finance to GDP of Xinjiang in Main Years

单位：亿元 (100 million yuan)

年份 Year	地方财政一般预算收入 General Budgetary Revenue in Local Finance	新疆生产总值 Gross Domestic Product in Xinjiang	地方财政一般预算收入占新疆生产总值的比重(%) Ration of Budgetary Revenue to Xinjiang GDP (%)
1978	7.14	39.07	18.27
1980	4.03	53.24	7.57
1985	8.47	112.24	7.56
1990	21.78	261.44	8.34
1995	38.28	814.85	4.70
2000	79.07	1363.56	5.80
2001	95.09	1491.60	6.37
2002	116.47	1612.65	7.22
2003	128.22	1886.35	6.79
2004	155.70	2209.09	7.05
2005	180.32	2604.14	6.92
2006	219.46	3045.26	7.21
2007	285.86	3523.16	8.11
2008	361.06	4183.21	8.63
2009	388.78	4277.05	9.09
2010	500.58	5437.47	9.21

7-3 地方财政收支情况

Statistics on Total Government Revenue and Expenditures in Local Finance

单位：万元 (10 000 yuan)

项　　目	Item	2009	2010
收入合计	**Total Revenue**	**4930685**	**6932683**
地方财政一般预算收入	General Budgetary Revenue in Local Finance	3887848	5005759
税收收入	Taxes Revenue	3011283	4162343
增值税	Value-added Tax	576267	753113
营业税	Business Tax	1123708	1512668
企业所得税（含退税）	Corporate Income Tax	280564	400152
个人所得税	Individual Income Tax	202029	273834
资源税	Resources Tax	122793	324678
城市维护建设税	City Maintenance and Construction Tax	230415	318406
房产税	House Property Tax	102494	123506
契　税	Contract Tax	111762	152583
其他税收收入	Other Revenues	261251	303403
非税收入	Non-tax Revenues	876565	843416
专项收入	Special Program Receipts	287021	324350
行政性收费收入	Charge of Administrative and Institutional Units	151994	196106
罚没收入	Penalty Receipts	121243	123790
其他收入	Other Revenues	316307	199170
基金预算收入	Fund Budgetary Revenues	1042837	1926924
支出合计	**Total Expenditures**	**14741064**	**18855622**
地方财政一般预算支出	General Budgetary Expenditure in Local Finance	13469125	16989126
一般公共服务	Expenditure for General Public Services	1956383	1955676
教　育	Expenditure for Education	2401460	3138356
科学技术	Expenditure for Science and Technology	161414	201869
文化体育与传媒	Expenditure for Culture Sports and Media	333355	339222
社会保障和就业	Expenditure for Social Safety Net and Employment Effort	1774879	1664041
医疗卫生	Expenditure for Medical and Health Care	849380	1035599
环境保护	Expenditure for Environmental Protection	364226	510155
城乡社区事务	Expenditure for Urban and Rural Community Affairs	790336	952755
农林水事务	Expenditure for Agriculture, Forestry and Water Conservancy	1967828	2204962
交通运输	Expenditure for Transportation	659074	915385
资源勘探电力信息等事务	Expenditure for Miming and Quarrying,Electriaty and Information Technology	283035	385301
其他各项支出	Other Expenditures	1927755	3685805
基金预算支出	Fund Budgetary Expenditure	1271939	1866496

7-4 各地、州、市、县(市)地方财政一般预算收支

Government Revenue and Expenditures by Prefecture, Autonomous Prefecture, City and County

单位：万元　　(2010 年)　　(10 000 yuan)

地　区	Region	收入 Revenue	支出 Expenditures
总　计	**Total**	**5005759**	**16989126**
自治区本级	Autonomous regional Level	516058	4748575
乌鲁木齐市昌吉州	**Urumqi City and Changji Prefecture**	**1807175**	**2474779**
乌昌本级	Urumqi and Changji Level	889523	1029452
天山区	Tianshan District	125379	127304
沙依巴克区	Shayibak District	91136	103690
新市区	Xinshi District	87403	95713
水磨沟区	Shui Mogou District	90101	99355
头屯河区	Tou Tunhe District	47169	59047
达坂城区	Da Bancheng District	34480	36531
米东区	Midong District	114758	144513
乌鲁木齐县	Urumqi County	22802	46948
昌吉市	Changji City	119565	187024
阜康市	Fukang City	56756	99047
呼图壁县	Hutubi County	28644	86153
玛纳斯县	Manas County	29851	89531
奇台县	Qitai County	30277	119837
吉木萨尔县	Jimsar County	28911	84347
木垒哈萨克自治县	Mori Kazak Autonomous County	10420	66287
克拉玛依市	**Karamay City**	**424303**	**547711**
市本级	City Level	257711	303568
克拉玛依区	Karamay District	94585	114228
独山子区	Dushanzi District	52046	83565
白碱滩区	Bai Jiantan District	15933	36963
乌尔河区	Urhe District	4028	9387
吐鲁番地区	**Turpan Administrative Offices**	**145963**	**332106**
地区本级	Prefecture Level	21166	49742
吐鲁番市	Turpan City	34905	97225
鄯善县	Shanshan [Piqan] County	61942	104712
托克逊县	Toksun County	27950	80427
哈密地区	**Hami [Kumul] Administrative Offices**	**150435**	**386270**
地区本级	Prefecture Level	4591	100156
哈密市	Hami [Kumul] City	122381	172566
巴里坤哈萨克自治县	Barkol Kazak Autonomous County	11866	71274
伊吾县	Yiwu [Araturuk] County	11597	42274
伊犁哈萨克自治州	**Ili Kazak Autonomous Prefecture**	**648482**	**2646054**
伊犁州直属县(市)	**Counties (Cities) Direct Under Ili Prefecture**	**312194**	**1282002**
州本级	Autonomous Prefecture Level	18332	144005
伊宁市	Yining [Gulja] City	95181	200553
奎屯市	Kuytun City	78216	121445
伊宁县	Yining [Gulja] County	21183	145098
察布查尔锡伯自治县	Qapqal Xibe Autonomous County	13106	94153
霍城县	Huocheng [Korgas] County	17498	109073

7-4 续表 1 Continued

单位：万元 (10 000 yuan)

地　区	Region	收入 Revenue	支出 Expenditures
巩留县	Gongliu [Tokkuztara] County	8516	83323
新源县	Xinyuan [Kunes] County	29165	112793
昭苏县	Zhaosu [Mongolkure] County	5965	92268
特克斯县	Tekes County	6354	85157
尼勒克县	Nilka County	18678	94134
塔城地区	**Tacheng [Tarbagatai] Administrative Office**	**183366**	**685169**
地区本级	Prefecture Level	3616	51937
塔城市	Tacheng [Qoqek] City	17122	88479
乌苏市	Usu City	40854	121871
额敏县	Emin [Dorbiljin] County	13139	89753
沙湾县	Shawan County	33358	102529
托里县	Toli County	15385	73090
裕民县	Yumin [Qagantokay] County	2606	57368
和布克赛尔蒙古自治县	Hoboksar Mongol Autonomous County	57286	100142
阿勒泰地区	**Altay Administrative Offices**	**152922**	**678883**
地区本级	Prefecture Level	17657	111858
阿勒泰市	Altay City	18683	118944
布尔津县	Burqin County	9319	63856
富蕴县	Fuyun [Koktokay] County	57685	114954
福海县	Fuhai [Burultokay] County	13048	69488
哈巴河县	Habahe [Kaba] County	27647	91090
青河县	Qinghe [Qinggil] County	6648	59180
吉木乃县	Jeminay County	2235	49513
博尔塔拉蒙古自治州	**Bortala Mongol Autonomous Prefecture**	**63038**	**315170**
州本级	Autonomous Prefecture Level	19402	85715
博乐市	Bole [Bortala] City	30211	97287
精河县	Jinghe [Jing] County	10003	73404
温泉县	Wenquan [Araxang] County	3422	58764
巴音郭楞蒙古自治州	**Bayangol Mongol Autonomous Prefecture**	**351807**	**880084**
州本级	Autonomous Prefecture Level	31630	152339
库尔勒市	Korla City	156342	208617
轮台县	Luntai [Bugur] County	53532	75453
尉犁县	Yuli [Lopnur] County	10593	57109
若羌县	Ruoqiang [Qarkilik] County	26285	62308
且末县	Qiemo [Qarqan] County	17524	63122
焉耆回族自治县	Yanqi Hui Autonomous County	14233	64700
和静县	Hejing County	27759	101482
和硕县	Hoxud County	8806	52134
博湖县	Bohu [Bagrax] County	5103	42820
阿克苏地区	**Aksu Administrative Offices**	**427314**	**1143958**
地区本级	Prefecture Level	16502	128440
阿克苏市	Aksu City	81544	151980
温宿县	Wensu [Onsu] County	17678	99331

7-4 续表 2 Continued

单位：万元 (10 000 yuan)

地　　区	Region	收 入 Revenue	支 出 Expenditure
库车县	Kuqa County	166020	224018
沙雅县	Xayar County	47606	104270
新和县	Xinhe [Toksu] County	28560	95334
拜城县	Baicheng [Bay] County	57164	119456
乌什县	Wushi [Uxturpan] County	4106	84216
阿瓦提县	Awat County	7170	92885
柯坪县	Kalpin County	964	44028
克孜勒苏柯尔克孜自治州	**Kizilsu Kirgiz Autonomous Prefecture**	**32581**	**419683**
州本级	Autonomous Prefecture Level	3013	80848
阿图什市	Artux City	9962	106286
阿克陶县	Akto County	8284	112015
阿合奇县	Akqi County	2844	56546
乌恰县	Wuqia [Ulugqat] County	8478	63988
喀什地区	**Kashgar [Kaxgar] Administrative Offices**	**196421**	**1880404**
地区本级	Prefecture Level	3933	119132
喀什市	Kashgar [Kaxgar] City	77326	315308
疏附县	Shufu County	5426	127999
疏勒县	Shule County	13016	116085
英吉沙县	Yengisar County	6269	112251
泽普县	Zepu [Poskam] County	14519	88963
莎车县	Shache [Yarkant] County	17579	277992
叶城县	Yecheng [Kagilik] County	16095	194680
麦盖提县	Makit County	9216	104506
岳普湖县	Yopurga County	4515	91196
伽师县	Jiashi [Payzawat] County	11971	146318
巴楚县	Bachu [Maralbexi] County	12009	127286
塔什库尔干塔吉克自治县	Taxkorgan Tajik Autonomous County	4547	58688
和田地区	**Hotan Administrative Offices**	**63142**	**976442**
地区本级	Prefecture Level	2849	92872
和田市	Hotan City	25575	126110
和田县	Hotan County	5540	112745
墨玉县	Moyu [Karakax] County	8166	182215
皮山县	Pishan [Guma] County	6803	106289
洛浦县	Lop County	4685	101440
策勒县	Qira County	2980	89704
于田县	Yutian [Keriya] County	4423	119964
民丰县	Minfeng [Niya] County	2121	45103
自治区直辖县级市	**Municpality Country-LevelCity directly under the Central Govern-ment**	**179040**	**237890**
石河子市	Shihezi City	137555	172440
阿拉尔市	Aral City	13103	20915
图木舒克市	Tumxuk City	5500	15111
五家渠市	Wujiaqu City	22882	29424

7-5 1978-2010 年历年金融机构各项存款和各项贷款余额

Banlance of Deposits and Loans of National Banking System (1978-2010)

单位：亿元 (100 million yuan)

年份 Year	各项存款合计 Total Deposits	#企业存款 Deposits by Enterprises	#储蓄存款 Savings Deposit	各项贷款合计 Total Loans
1978	32.07	6.86	6.42	18.26
1979	33.44	7.03	7.21	21.19
1980	38.56	9.60	9.52	24.74
1981	45.59	12.21	12.29	28.84
1982	53.47	15.23	15.30	32.86
1983	61.94	17.95	19.01	38.85
1984	73.63	23.35	24.31	52.02
1985	82.96	29.87	29.55	72.68
1986	102.75	38.15	40.37	93.18
1987	124.93	44.13	53.25	111.14
1988	141.10	47.41	66.25	139.43
1989	167.03	52.76	83.33	173.02
1990	221.80	71.23	114.13	233.72
1991	282.21	92.78	145.01	299.59
1992	336.58	119.51	175.62	380.26
1993	397.39	129.98	220.45	467.81
1994	634.44	214.13	347.71	632.32
1995	838.42	274.24	477.18	843.38
1996	1012.47	364.51	575.79	1016.20
1997	1180.78	442.76	676.13	1215.39
1998	1336.58	461.02	759.14	1318.41
1999	1548.72	544.22	824.68	1386.78
2000	1863.48	702.21	908.55	1403.13
2001	1972.55	691.74	994.00	1584.73
2002	2225.31	705.82	1137.87	1801.15
2003	2661.65	763.49	1371.59	2099.09
2004	2959.78	832.50	1534.67	2214.66
2005	3427.48	909.45	1816.38	2272.08
2006	4040.78	1106.42	2035.63	2412.69
2007	4614.62	1452.25	2054.91	2685.00
2008	5399.34	1473.24	2550.95	2826.53
2009	6845.07	2043.54	3049.91	3782.92
2010	8870.72	2791.72	3713.47	4973.16

7-6 金融机构和人员数

Number of Financial Institutions and Staff

单位：个、人 (2010 年) (unit, person)

项　目	Item	合　计 Total		自治区级 Level of Autonomous Region		地区级 Prefectural Level	
		机 构 Institutions	人 员 Employees	机 构 Institutions	人 员 Employees	机 构 Institutions	人 员 Employees
总　计	**Total**	**3282**	**57297**	**20**	**4948**	**141**	**14764**
人民银行	**The People's Bank of China**	**68**	**3571**	**1**	**436**	**14**	**1816**
银监会新疆监管局	**China Banking Regulatory Commission Xingjiang Bureau**	**56**	**938**	**1**	**137**	**14**	**655**
中资全国性大型银行	**Large National Bank of Chinese Investment**	**1875**	**35051**	**9**	**3182**	**78**	**10249**
工商银行	Industrial and Commercial Bank	295	8774	2	528	15	3246
农业银行	Agricultural Bank	365	8368	1	411	15	2508
农业银行兵团分行	Agricultural Bank, XPCG Branch	248	3903	1	266	3	462
中国银行	Bank of China	164	3661	1	707	14	1126
建设银行	Bank of Construction	188	5469	1	719	14	2095
国家开发银行	State Development Bank	1	130	1	130		
交通银行	Bank of Communication	28	797	1	324		
邮政储蓄银行	Postal Savings Bank	586	3949	1	97	17	812
中资全国性中小银行	**Small and Medium-sized National Bank of Chinese Investment**	**141**	**3920**	**3**	**440**	**25**	**1431**
农业发展银行	Agricultural Development Bank	90	2249	1	169	17	647
中信银行`	China Citic Bank	1	95			1	95
华夏银行	Hua Xia Bank	6	210			1	135
招商银行	Merchants Bank	11	413			1	210
浦发银行	Shanghai PuDong Development Bank	8	226	1	137	1	16
兴业银行	XinYe Bank	7	230	1	134		
昆仑银行	KunLun Bank	18	497			4	328
中资区域性中小银行	**Small and Medium-sized Regional Bank of Chinese Investment**	**143**	**2308**	**1**	**475**	**6**	**279**
城市商业银行	City Commercial Bank	117	1943	1	475	5	258
农村商业银行	Rural Commercila Bank	3	42				
村镇银行	County Bank	6	115			1	21
农村合作银行	Rural Cooperation Bank	17	208				
外资银行	**Foreign Bank**	**2**	**45**	**1**	**38**		
农村信用社	**Rural Credit Cooperative**	**991**	**11168**	**1**	**125**	**1**	**153**
财务公司	**Finance Company**	**1**	**12**			**1**	**12**
信托投资公司	**Trust and Investment Company**	**1**	**101**			**1**	**101**
金融租赁公司	**Financial Leasing Company**	**1**	**68**			**1**	**68**
资产管理公司	**Assets Management Company**	**3**	**115**	**3**	**115**		
信达公司	Xinda Firm	1	29	1	29		
华融公司	Huarong Firm	1	37	1	37		
长城公司	Great Wall Firm	1	49	1	49		

7-6 续表 Continued

单位：个、人 (unit, person)

项　目	Item	县　级 County Level		营业网点 Business Outlets	
		机 构 Institutions	人 员 Employees	机 构 Institutions	人 员 Employees
总　计	**Total**	**805**	**19422**	**2316**	**18163**
人民银行	**The People's Bank of China**	**53**	**1319**		
银监会新疆监管局	**China Banking Regulatory Commission Xingjiang Bureau**	**41**	**146**		
中资全国性大型银行	**Large National Bank of Chinese Investment**	**533**	**12160**	**1255**	**9460**
工商银行	Industrial and Commercial Bank	200	4146	78	854
农业银行	Agricultural Bank	102	3108	247	2341
农业银行兵团分行	Agricultural Bank, XPCG Branch	24	1192	220	1983
中国银行	Bank of China	22	639	127	1189
建设银行	Bank of Construction	69	1462	104	1193
国家开发银行	State Development Bank				
交通银行	Bank of Communication	1	21	26	452
邮政储蓄银行	Postal Savings Bank	115	1592	453	1448
中资全国性中小银行	**Small and Medium-sized National Bank of Chinese Investment**	**88**	**1629**	**25**	**420**
农业发展银行	Agricultural Development Bank	72	1433		
中信银行`	China Citic Bank				
华夏银行	Hua Xia Bank			5	75
招商银行	Merchants Bank			10	203
浦发银行	Shanghai PuDong Development Bank	1	15	5	58
兴业银行	XinYe Bank	1	12	5	84
昆仑银行	KunLun Bank	14	169		
中资区域性中小银行	**Small and Medium-sized Regional Bank of Chinese Investment**	**8**	**215**	**128**	**1339**
城市商业银行	City Commercial Bank	2	21	109	1189
农村商业银行	Rural Commercila Bank	3	42		
村镇银行	County Bank	2	63	3	31
农村合作银行	Rural Cooperation Bank	1	89	16	119
外资银行	**Foreign Bank**			**1**	**7**
农村信用社	**Rural Credit Cooperative**	**82**	**3953**	**907**	**6937**
财务公司	**Finance Company**				
信托投资公司	**Trust and Investment Company**				
金融租赁公司	**Financial Leasing Company**				
资产管理公司	**Assets Management Company**				
信达公司	Xinda Firm				
华融公司	Huarong Firm				
长城公司	Great Wall Firm				

7-7 金融机构信贷资金平衡表
Balance Sheet of Credit Funds of Financial Institutions

单位：亿元 (100 million yuan)

项　　目	Item	2010
资金来源合计	**All Sources**	**8052.77**
各项存款	Total Deposits	8870.02
企业存款	Deposits by Enterprises	2791.72
活期存款	Current Deposits	2020.30
定期存款	Time Deposits	771.41
财政存款	Fiscal Deposits	349.98
机关团体存款	Deposits of Government Agencies and Organizations	1167.27
储蓄存款	Savings Deposits	3713.47
活期存款	Current Deposits	1799.77
定期存款	Time Deposits	1913.70
农业存款	Agricultural Deposits	410.28
委托存款	Commission Deposits	8.87
其他存款	Others	428.43
应付及暂收款	Payable and Temporary Collection	123.54
各项准备金	Various Preparations	92.45
所有者权益	Owner's Right and Interest	286.04
其　他	Others	-1319.28
资金运用合计	**All Uses**	**8052.77**
各项贷款	Total Loans	4973.16
#境内贷款	Domestic Loans	4973.02
短期贷款	Short-term Loans	1845.60
个人贷款及透支	Personal loans and overdrafts	317.75
#个人消费贷款	Personal Consumption Loans	17.37
单位贷款及透支	Unit loans and overdrafts	1425.85
#经营贷款	Loans to Business	1357.32
固定资产贷款	Loans to fixed Assets	67.71
银团贷款	Syndicated Loans	54.51
贸易融资	Trade finance	47.49
中长期贷款	Medium & Long-term Loans	2924.31
个人贷款	Personal loans	617.42
#个人消费贷款	Personal Consumption Loans	440.40
单位贷款	Units Loans	1984.62
#经营贷款	Loans to Business	616.30
固定资产贷款	Loans to fixed Assets	1361.33
普通并购贷款	Ordinary Loans	4.30
银团贷款	Syndicated Loans	317.98
融资租赁	Finance leasing	58.72
票据融资	Bills financing	143.47
各项垫付	The various funds	0.92
境外贷款	Foreign Loans	0.14
有价证券及投资	Portfolio Investment	449.19
行内资金往来(运用方)	Bank financial dealings	2341.58
固定资产	Fixed assets	108.02
其他	Others	180.82

7-8 金融机构现金收支表

Cash Income and Expenditure of Financial Institutions

单位：亿元 (100 million yuan)

项　目	Item	2009	2010
收入合计	**Total Income**	**13012.50**	**15414.28**
商品销售收入	Income from Commodity Sales	915.91	1038.71
服务业收入	Income from Service Trades	590.42	648.06
行政税款收入	Income from Taxes	62.27	66.71
城乡个体经营收入	Income from Urban and Rural Individual Business	178.02	189.31
储蓄存款收入	Income from Savings Deposits	9108.45	11217.22
居民归还贷款收入	Income from Repayment of Loans by Residents	249.89	307.04
汇兑收入	Income from Remittances	77.69	75.19
有价证券及其他投资性收入	Income from Securities	30.44	26.49
其他金融性公司收入	Income from Other Financial Company	35.12	41.28
其他收入	Other Income	1764.29	1804.27
支出合计	**Total Expenditure**	**13206.56**	**15681.29**
工资性支出	Wages	578.42	573.96
农副产品采购支出	Purchases of Agricultural and Sideline Products	450.08	599.36
工矿及其他产品采购支出	Expenditure for Purchases of Industrial and Mineral Products	31.61	36.68
行政事业管理和经营费支出	Government and Enterprises Overhead	411.88	401.34
城乡个体经营支出	Expenditure for Individual Business	180.11	183.61
储蓄存款支出	Expenditure for Savings Deposits	9777.18	12189.35
其他金融性公司支出	Expenditure for Other Financial Company	28.44	40.23
居民提取贷款支出	Expenditure for Loans withdrawn by Residents	115.92	79.65
汇兑支出	Expenditure for Remittances	25.31	33.70
有价证券及其他投资性支出	Expenditure for Securities	78.01	16.52
其他支出	Other Expenditures	1529.60	1526.89
投放(+)、回笼(-)	**Monetary Issues (+) Cash Withdrawn (-)**	**194.06**	**267.01**

7-9 个人消费贷款情况

Basic Conditons of Personal Consumption Loans

单位：亿元 (100 million yuan)

项　　目	Item	2009	2010
个人消费贷款	**Personal Consumption Loans**	**312.01**	**457.76**
短期个人消费贷款	Short-term Loans for Personal Consumption	14.04	17.36
住房贷款	Housing Loans	0.67	0.56
汽车贷款	Auto Loans	0.26	0.20
其他贷款	Other Loans	12.01	11.64
个人卡透支	Personalized Card is Overdrawn	1.10	4.96
长期个人消费贷款	Long-term Loans for Personal Consumption	297.97	440.40
住房贷款	Housing Loans	255.03	376.58
汽车贷款	Auto Loans	6.96	14.08
助学贷款	Student Loans	1.06	0.88
其他贷款	Other Loans	34.92	48.86

7-10 主要年份国内保险业务情况

Conditions of Domestic Insurance Service in Main Years

单位：亿元 (100 million yuan)

年　份 Year	承保额 Amount Insured		保　费 Premium		赔款及给付 Claim and Payment	
	财产险 Property Insurance	人身险 Life Insurance	财产险 Property Insurance	人身险 Life Insurance	财产险 Property Insurance	人身险 Life Insurance
1980	4		0.01			
1985	70	2	0.40	0.01	0.15	…
1990	241	41	1.04	0.53	0.47	0.08
1995	613	168	4.59	2.06	2.38	0.41
2000	1612	1711	12.49	15.72	5.99	3.72
2001	2112	1371	14.17	19.98	7.43	4.37
2002	2283	3524	16.48	35.25	7.84	5.02
2003	5588	1362	19.12	43.06	10.36	7.10
2004	6401	1735	20.04	48.09	10.65	7.70
2005	8949	9418	20.93	51.57	12.60	7.65
2006	8333	27028	24.61	60.79	12.92	10.34
2007	12188	13081	34.67	70.95	18.78	18.64
2008	13641	17555	44.25	108.26	23.61	20.79
2009	16296	19819	51.82	104.87	26.60	21.51
2010	17431	18129	63.00	127.92	29.21	20.12

7-11 保险机构
Number of Insurance Institutions

单位：个 (2010 年) (unit)

项目	Item	机构数 Number of Institution	自治区分公司 Xinjiang Branch Company
总 计	**Total**	**1469**	**21**
中国人民财产保险公司新疆分公司	The People's Insurance Corporation of China	441	1
中华联合财产保险公司	The Property Insurance Corporation, XPCG	234	
中国平安财产保险公司	The Ping An Insurance Corporation, Property Insurance Company	40	1
中国太平洋财产保险公司	The Pacific Insurance Corporation, Property Insurance Company	16	1
永安财产保险公司	Yong An Property Insurance Corporation	58	1
天安财产保险公司	Tian An Property Insurance Corporation	14	1
安邦财产保险公司	An Bang Property Insurance Corporation	23	1
大地财产保险公司	Da Di Property Insurance Corporation	17	1
阳光财产保险公司	Sunshine Property Insurance Corporation	21	1
都邦财产保险股份有限公司	Du-bang Property Insurance Corporation Ltd.	1	1
渤海财产保险股份有限公司	Bohai Property Insurance Corporation Ltd.	4	1
永诚财产保险股份有限公司	Yong chen Insurance Corporation Ltd.	1	1
中国人寿保险公司新疆分公司	The Life Insurance Corporation of China	377	1
中国平安人寿保险公司	The Ping An Insurance Corporation, Life Insurance Company	62	1
中国太平洋人寿保险公司	The Pacific Insurance Corporation, Life Insurance Company	27	1
新华人寿保险公司	Xin Hua Life Insurance Corporation	41	1
泰康人寿保险公司	Tai Kang Life Insurance Corporation	57	1
中国平安养老保险公司	Ping An Endowment Insurance Corporation	1	1
中国人民人寿保险公司	PICC Life Insurance Corporation	19	1
太平人寿保险股份有限公司	Taiping Life Insurance Corporation Ltd.	5	1
中国人民健康保险股份有限公司	PICC Health Insurance Corporation Ltd.	2	1
合众人寿保险股份有限公司	Union Life Insurance Corporation Ltd.	8	1

项目	Item	地区级中心支公司 Branch Company at Prefecture Level	县级支公司 Branch Company at County Level	营销服务部 Marke-Ting Depart-ment
总 计	**Total**	**158**	**365**	**925**
中国人民财产保险公司新疆分公司	The People's Insurance Corporation of China	15	85	340
中华联合财产保险公司	The Property Insurance Corporation, XPCG	14	145	75
中国平安财产保险公司	The Ping An Insurance Corporation, Property Insurance Company	14	4	21
中国太平洋财产保险公司	The Pacific Insurance Corporation, Property Insurance Company	7	8	
永安财产保险公司	Yong An Property Insurance Corporation	14	2	41
天安财产保险公司	Tian An Property Insurance Corporation	6		7
安邦财产保险公司	An Bang Property Insurance Corporation	8	1	13
大地财产保险公司	Da Di Property Insurance Corporation			16
阳光财产保险公司	Sunshine Property Insurance Corporation	5	6	9
都邦财产保险股份有限公司	Du-bang Property Insurance Corporation Ltd.			
渤海财产保险股份有限公司	Bohai Property Insurance Corporation Ltd.	3		
永诚财产保险股份有限公司	Yong chen Insurance Corporation Ltd.			
中国人寿保险公司新疆分公司	The Life Insurance Corporation of China	15	68	293
中国平安人寿保险公司	The Ping An Insurance Corporation, Life Insurance Company	12	9	40
中国太平洋人寿保险公司	The Pacific Insurance Corporation, Life Insurance Company	8	15	3
新华人寿保险公司	Xin Hua Life Insurance Corporation	8	5	27
泰康人寿保险公司	Tai Kang Life Insurance Corporation	11	6	39
中国平安养老保险公司	Ping An Endowment Insurance Corporation			
中国人民人寿保险公司	PICC Life Insurance Corporation	10	8	
太平人寿保险股份有限公司	Taiping Life Insurance Corporation Ltd.	4		
中国人民健康保险股份有限公司	PICC Health Insurance Corporation Ltd.			1
合众人寿保险股份有限公司	Union Life Insurance Corporation Ltd.	4	3	

7-12 保险事业发展情况
Statistics on Development of Insurance

单位：万元　　(2010 年)　　(10 000 yuan)

项　目	Item	承保额(亿元) Amount Insured (100 million yuan)	保 费 Premium	赔款及给付 Claim and Payment
总　计	**Total**	**35560.03**	**190.92**	**49.34**
产险公司小计	Sub-total	19096.38	68.04	31.63
中国人民财产保险股份有限公司新疆分公司	The People's Insurance Corporation of China	8014.78	36.63	16.49
中华联合财产保险股份有限公司	The Property Insurance Corporation, XPCG	5671.26	14.49	7.58
中国平安财产保险股份有限公司新疆分公司	The Ping An Insurance Corporation, Property Insurance Company	2161.76	5.66	2.26
中国太平洋财产保险股份有限公司新疆分公司	The Pacific Insurance Corporation, Property Insurance Company	1195.32	5.02	2.39
永安财产保险股份有限公司新疆分公司	Yong An Property Insurance Corporation	498.02	1.67	0.91
天安保险股份有限公司新疆分公司	Tian An Property Insurance Corporation	176.11	0.70	0.53
安邦财产保险股份有限公司新疆分公司	An Bang Property Insurance Corporation	52.10	0.47	0.26
中国大地财产保险股份有限公司新疆分公司	Da Di Property Insurance Corporation	374.28	0.84	0.30
阳光财产保险股份有限公司新疆分公司	Sunshine Property Insurance Corporation	727.14	1.96	0.72
都邦财产保险股份有限公司新疆分公司	Du-bang Property Insurance Corporation Ltd.	72.39	0.26	0.11
渤海财产保险股份有限公司新疆分公司	Bohai Property Insurance Corporation Ltd.	12.66	0.07	0.05
永诚财产保险股份有限公司新疆分公司	Yongcheng Property Insurance Corporation Ltd	140.56	0.25	0.03
寿险公司小计	Sub-total	16463.65	122.89	17.71
中国人寿保险股份有限公司新疆分公司	The Life Insurance Corporation of China	11012.85	50.27	12.20
中国平安人寿保险股份有限公司新疆分公司	The Ping An Insurance Corporation, Life Insurance Company	2805.97	20.20	2.29
中国太平洋人寿保险股份有限公司新疆分公司	The Pacific Insurance Corporation, Life Insurance Company	580.00	17.53	1.77
新华人寿保险股份有限公司新疆分公司	Xin Hua Life Insurance Corporation	220.15	12.42	0.41
泰康人寿保险股份有限公司新疆分公司	Tai Kang Life Insurance Corporation	416.51	9.57	0.37
中国人民人寿保险股份有限公司新疆分公司	PICC Life Insurance Corporation	154.29	6.79	0.11
太平人寿保险有限公司新疆分公司	Taiping Life Insurance Corporation Ltd.	31.58	2.46	0.08
中国人民健康保险股份有限公司新疆分公司	PICC Health Insurance Corporation Ltd.	442.96	1.95	0.32
合众人寿保险股份有限公司新疆分公司	Union Life Insurance Corporation Ltd.	44.11	1.31	0.02
平安养老保险股份有限公司新疆分公司	The Pingan Old-age Pension Insurance Company	755.23	0.38	0.14

7-13 各地区保险业务情况
Conditions of Insurance Service by Region

单位：万元　　　　(2010 年)　　　　(10 000 yuan)

地　　区	Region	全部业务 All Insurance Business 保费收入 Premium Income	全部业务 比上年增长(%) Increase Rate Over preceding year(%)	财产保险公司业务 Property Insurance Business 保费收入 Premium Income	财产保险公司业务 比上年增长(%) Increase Rate Over preceding year(%)
总　计	**Total**	**1909238.66**	**21.84**	**680352.05**	**20.78**
乌鲁木齐市	Urumqi City	637895.21	26.77	163935.22	31.31
克拉玛依市	Karamay City	118718.14	19.84	37293.37	38.22
石河子市	Shihezi City	94354.99	0.82	31089.82	-17.86
吐鲁番地区	Turpan Administrative Offices	44191.38	18.29	17619.38	19.76
哈密地区	Hami [Kumul] Administrative Offices	76338.80	30.99	22653.60	34.18
昌吉回族自治州	Changji Hui Autonomous Prefecture	177693.73	24.44	68801.38	32.44
伊犁州直属县(市)	Counties (Cities) Direct Under Ili Prefecture	122495.06	25.23	51543.20	27.49
塔城地区	Tacheng [Tarbagatai] Administrative Offices	68590.13	22.08	23218.15	20.26
阿勒泰地区	Altay Administrative Offices	45190.42	22.59	18425.09	30.80
博尔塔拉蒙古自治州	Bortala Mongol Autonomous Prefecture	49643.98	19.00	21846.58	19.72
巴音郭楞蒙古自治州	Bayangol Mongol Autonomous Prefecture	153174.05	15.41	62350.12	8.19
阿克苏地区	Aksu Administrative Offices	130803.40	23.46	60828.95	17.59
克孜勒苏柯尔克孜自治州	Kizilsu Kirgiz Autonomous Prefecture	7881.80	34.35	5167.61	61.57
喀什地区	Kashgar [Kaxgar] Administrative Offices	109005.16	12.69	60560.81	14.79
和田地区	Hotan Administrative Offices	25892.82	35.51	15607.92	44.83
奎屯市	Kuytun City	46113.17	19.92	18154.54	-12.13

地　　区	Region	人寿保险公司业务 Life Insurance Business 保费收入 Premium Income	人寿保险公司业务 比上年增长(%) Increase Rate Over preceding year(%)	保险密度(元) Insurance Density (yuan)	保险深度(%) Insurance Depth(%)
总　计	**Total**	**1228886.61**	**22.44**	**875**	**3.51**
乌鲁木齐市	Urumqi City	473960.00	25.27	2051	4.77
克拉玛依市	Karamay City	81424.77	12.96	3036	1.67
石河子市	Shihezi City	63265.17	13.50		6.99
吐鲁番地区	Turpan Administrative Offices	26571.99	17.33	710	2.42
哈密地区	Hami [Kumul] Administrative Offices	53685.21	29.69	1334	4.56
昌吉回族自治州	Changji Hui Autonomous Prefecture	108892.36	19.86	1244	3.18
伊犁州直属县(市)	Counties (Cities) Direct Under Ili Prefecture	70951.86	23.64	493	3.00
塔城地区	Tacheng [Tarbagatai] Administrative Offices	45371.98	23.03	563	2.01
阿勒泰地区	Altay Administrative Offices	26765.33	17.51	749	3.35
博尔塔拉蒙古自治州	Bortala Mongol Autonomous Prefecture	27797.41	18.44	1119	3.78
巴音郭楞蒙古自治州	Bayangol Mongol Autonomous Prefecture	90823.94	20.95	1198	2.39
阿克苏地区	Aksu Administrative Offices	69974.44	29.07	552	3.30
克孜勒苏柯尔克孜自治州	Kizilsu Kirgiz Autonomous Prefecture	2714.19	1.72	150	2.03
喀什地区	Kashgar [Kaxgar] Administrative Offices	48444.35	10.18	274	3.03
和田地区	Hotan Administrative Offices	10284.91	23.46	129	2.50
奎屯市	Kuytun City	27958.63	57.15		6.37

7-14 保险业务经济技术指标
Economic and Technical Indicators of Insurance Company

单位：万元 (10 000 yuan)

项目	Item	保费 Premium 2009	保费 Premium 2010	赔款及给付 Claim and Payment 2009	赔款及给付 Claim and Payment 2010
财产保险业务	**Property Insurance Companies**	**518242**	**630010**	**266006**	**292149**
企业财产险	Insurance of Enterprise Property	32750	43282	15736	14045
家庭财产险	Insurance of Family Property	4009	5018	1266	1278
机动车辆险	Insurance of Mobile Vehicles	296678	390415	146137	178104
工程保险	Engineering Insurance	6227	9861	1503	3291
责任保险	Insurance of Liability	17821	22343	6894	7223
信用保险	Insurance of Credit	3	-3	12	13
保证保险	Insurance of Guaranty	8944	11715	1577	1061
船舶险	Insurance of Snip		3		
货物运输险	Insurance of Cargo Transportation	5955	7747	1747	1408
特殊风险保险	Special insurance against risk	2881	980	3400	467
农业保险	Insurance of Agriculture	142971	138642	87735	85257
其他险	Other Insurance	3	6	-1	
人身保险业务	**Life Insurance Companies**	**1048699**	**1279229**	**215144**	**201203**
寿　险	Life Insurance	885277	1086009	153232	131278
健康险	Health Insurance	122374	143927	52723	58355
人身意外伤害险	Unforeseen Human Injury Insurance	41048	49292	9189	11569

7-15 新疆辖区证券、期货经营机构和人员数
Operators and Staff of Securities and Futures in Xinjiang

单位：个、人 (2010 年) (unit, person)

公司名称	Name of Enterprise	机构数 Number of Institution	人员 Staff	营业部数量 Number of Business Department	人员 Staff
总　计	**Total**	**3**	**3486**	**85**	**1952**
新疆辖区证券机构	**Stock Instituions in the Territory of Xinjiang**	**1**	**3356**	**57**	**1172**
宏源证券股份有限公司	Hongyuan Securities Stock Limited Company	1	3356	38	491
异地证券公司营业部	**Business Department, Non-local Stock Company**			**19**	**681**
长江证券股份有限公司	Dapeng Securities Liability Corporation Ltd.			2	91
光大证券股份有限公司	Everbright Securities Liability Corporation Ltd.			1	30
广发证券股份有限公司	Guangfa Securities Liability Corporation Ltd.			1	99
国泰君安证券股份有限公司	Jun'an Securities Stock Corporation Ltd.			1	26
海通证券股份有限公司	Haitong Securities Company			1	58
平安证券有限责任公司	Pin'An Securities Liability Corporation Ltd.			1	53
申银万国股份有限公司	Shenyin Universal Stock Corporation Ltd.			1	30
湘财证券有限责任公司	Xiangcai Securities Liability Corporation Ltd.			2	63
中国银河证券股份有限公司	China Yinhe Securities Liability Corporation Ltd.			1	42
中国民族证券有限责任公司	Nationality Securities Company			1	35
金元证券股份有限公司	Jinyuan Securities Company			1	29
华融证券股份有限公司	Huarong Securities Company			4	64
华龙证券股份有限公司	Hualong Securities Compang			1	44
齐鲁证券有限责任公司	QiLU Securities Liability Corporation Ltd.			1	17
新疆辖区期货经纪公司	**Xinjiang Futures Broker's Company**	**2**	**130**	**9**	**99**
新疆天利期货经纪有限公司	Xinjiang Tianli Futures Broker's Company	1	33	3	18
新疆金石期货经纪有限公司	Xinjiang Jingshi Futures Broker's Company	1	97	4	34
万达期货经纪有限公司	Henan Wanda Futures Broker's Company			1	20
宏源期货有限公司	Hongyuan Futures Broker's Company			1	27

7-16 上市公司基本情况表
Basic Condition of Listed Companies

公司简称 Names of Businesses		上市时间 Listed Time	上市交易所 Listing Stock Exchange	发行时股本(万股) Total Capital Stock (10 000 share) 总股本 Total Stock Capital	流通股本 Circulating Capital Stock	发行募集资金(万元) Floated Raised Funds (10 000 yuan)	2010年末股本(万股) Stock Capital by 2010 (10 000 share) 总股本 Total Stock Capital	流通股本 Circulating Stock Capital	2010年累计募集资金(万元) Capital Raised by 2010 (10 000 yuan)
总　计	**Total**			**557884**	**155975**	**1250008**	**2054007**	**1722901**	**4178243**
宏源证券	Hongyuan Trust	1994	深交所 SZSE	17500	4500	10550	146120	146117	320952
新疆众和	Xijiang Zhonghe	1996	上交所 SHSE	7953	2025	9690	35206	34206	114990
ST 百花	Bai Huacun	1996	上交所 SHSE	6128	2700	11800	26885	8714	112043
*ST 汇通	Huitong Water Conservancy	1996	深交所 SZSE	5000	1250	7062	30034	30028	17262
友好集团	Youhao Group	1996	上交所 SHSE	10700	2700	10607	31149	30884	61238
中粮屯河	Zhongliang Tunhe	1997	上交所 SHSE	7000	1750	9400	100560	80560	167200
啤酒花	Hop	1997	上交所 SHSE	8000	3000	11523	36792	36792	11523
新疆天业	Xinjiang Tianye	1997	上交所 SHSE	6300	2430	16896	43859	43859	63900
特变电工	Toban Electric Engineering	1997	上交所 SHSE	8168	3000	14820	202735	202735	612250
*ST 中葡	Suntime International	1997	上交所 SHSE	8600	2700	24071	80992	46446	76858
天山纺织	Tianshan Textile	1998	深交所 SZSE	18782	4230	20783	36346	36346	40459
天山股份	Tianshan Stock	1999	上交所 SHSE	12946	4500	26394	38895	30872	197944
新农开发	Xinnong Development	1999	上交所 SHSE	29400	9000	32905	32100	32100	32905
伊力特	Yilite	1999	上交所 SHSE	22050	7500	45375	44100	44100	45375
新中基	Xin Zhongji	2000	上交所 SHSE	12459	4500	21011	48205	41907	119096
广汇股份	Guanghui Stock	2000	上交所 SHSE	35378	5000	31652	123847	71917	31652
国际实业	Industry International	2000	深交所 SZSE	17179	7000	39837	48114	48114	39837
美克股份	Markor Stock	2000	上交所 SHSE	9208	4000	50923	63268	51060	288686
天利高科	Tianli High-Tech	2000	上交所 SHSE	17000	6000	42653	52560	45681	93113
ST 天宏	Xinjinag Tianhong	2001	上交所 SHSE	8016	3000	16633	8016	8016	16633
*ST 香梨	Fragrant Pear Stock	2001	上交所 SHSE	16050	5000	23141	14771	14771	23141
天富热电	Tianfu Thermoelectricity	2002	上交所 SHSE	16909	6000	42000	65570	65570	153331
八一钢铁	August 1st Steel	2002	上交所 SHSE	40943	13000	92254	76645	76645	92254
冠农股份	Guannong Stock	2003	上交所 SHSE	12000	4000	21610	36210	36210	64530
青松建化	Qubgsibg Cement	2003	上交所 SHSE	18493	6000	24265	47870	47870	165482
新疆城建	Xinjiang Urban Construction	2003	上交所 SHSE	16054	6000	33546	67579	49631	104965
新赛股份	Xinsai Stock	2003	上交所 SHSE	15000	5000	31441	23285	23285	62307
中泰化学	Zhongtai Chemical	2006	深交所 SZSE	23600	8000	66000	115434	80488	546208
天康生物	TianKang Animal	2006	深交所 SZSE	6400	1280	15868	22674	19469	56811
金风科技	Goldwind	2007	深交所 SZSE	50000	5000	180000	269459	208867	180000
国统股份	Guotong Stock	2008	深交所 SZSE	8000	2000	15380	10000	3928	15380
准油股份	Zhunyou Stock	2008	深交所 SZSE	9946	2500	19625	9946	2500	19625
北新路桥	Beixin Road&Bridge	2009	深交所 SZSE	18945	3800	37635	18945	7810	37635
西部建设	West Construction	2009	深交所 SZSE	14000	2800	48473	21000	9745	48473
西部牧业	Xinjiang Western Animal Husbandry	2010	深交所 SZSE	11700	3000	35700	11700	3000	35700
光正钢构	Guangzheng Steel Structure	2010	深交所 SZSE	9038	1810	34307	9038	1810	34307
科研股份	Research Shares Corporation	2010	深交所 SZSE	3040		74179	4100	850	74179

主要统计指标解释

财政收入　指国家财政参与社会产品分配所取得的收入，是实现国家职能的财力保证。主要包括：

（1）**各项税收**：包括国内增值税、国内消费税、进口货物增值税和消费税、出口货物退增值税和消费税、营业税、企业所得税、个人所得税、资源税、城市维护建设税、房产税、印花税、城镇土地使用税、土地增值税、车船税、船舶吨税、车辆购置税、关税、耕地占用税、契税、烟叶税等。

（2）**非税收入**：包括专项收入、行政事业性收费、罚没收入和其他收入。

地方财政收入　属于地方财政的收入包括营业税，地方企业所得税，个人所得税，城镇土地使用税，固定资产投资方向调节税，城镇维护建设税，房产税，车船使用税，印花税，屠宰税，农牧业税，农业特产税，耕地占用税，契税，增值税25%部分，证券交易税(印花税)50%部分和除海洋石油资源税以外的其他资源税。

地方财政支出　地方财政支出主要包括地方行政管理和各项事业费，地方统筹的基本建设、技术改造支出，支援农村生产支出，城市维护和建设经费，价格补贴支出等。

信贷资金　指金融机构以信用方式积聚和分配的货币资金。金融机构信贷资金的来源有各项存款、金融债券、对国际金融机构负债、流通中现金、其他项目等；信贷资金的运用有各项贷款、有价证券及投资、金银占款、外汇占款、财政借款及在国际金融机构中的资产等。

存款　指企业、机关、团体或居民根据资金必须收回的原则，把货币资金存入银行或其他信贷机构保管并取得一定利息的一种信用活动形式。根据存款对象或性质的不同可划分为企业存款、财政存款、机关团体存款、城乡储蓄存款、农业存款、信托及委托类存款、其他存款等科目。它是银行信贷资金的主要来源。

贷款　指银行或其他信用机构根据资金必须归还的原则，按一定利率，为企业、个人等提供资金的一种信用活动形式。我国银行贷款分为短期贷款、委托及信托类贷款、其他类贷款等

保险金额　指保险人承担赔偿或者给付保险金责任的最高限额。

保费　指投保人为取得保险人在约定范围内所承担赔偿责任而支付给保险人的费用。

赔款　指保险人根据保险合同的规定，向被保险人支付的赔偿保险责任损失的金额。

给付　包括死伤医疗给付和满期给付。死伤医疗给付是指保险人根据人寿保险及长期健康保险合同的规定，因被保险人在保险期内发生保险责任范围内的保险事故支付给被保险人(或受益人)的金额。满期给付是指被保险人生存期满，保险人按人寿保险合同规定支付给被保险人的满期保险金额。

Explanatory Notes on Main Statistical Indicators

Government Revenue refer to the revenue of the government finance by means of participating in the distribution of the social products,which is the financial resources for ensuring the government to function,The contents of government revenue have been changed several times.Now it includes the following main items:

(1)Various tax revenue including value added tax,business tax,consumption tax,land value added tax,tax on city maintenance and construction,resources tax,tax on use of urban land,enterprise income tax,personal income tax,tariff,stamp tax on security transactions,tax on purchase of motor vehicles,tax on agriculture and animal husbandary and tax on occupancy of cultivated land,etc.

(2)Non-tax revenue including Special income, Administrative fees, Incomes from imposition and oter incomes.

Revenue of the Local Governments The revenue of the local governments includes business tax, income tax of the enterprises subordinate to the local government, personal income tax, tax on the use of urban land, tax on the adjustment of the investment in fixed assets, tax on town maintenance and construction, tax on real estates, tax on the use of vehicles and ships, stamp tax, slaughter tax, tax on agriculture and animal husbandry, tax on special agricultural products, tax on the occupancy of cultivated land, contract tax, 25% of the value added tax, 50% of the tax on stock dealing (stamp tax) and tax on resources other than the ocean petroleum resources.

Expenditure of the Local Governments The expenditure of the local governments includes mainly the administrative expenses and various operating expenses at the vel of local governments, the expenditure for capital construction and technological innovation with the funds raised by the local government, expenditure for supporting rural production, expenditure for City maintenance and construction and expenditure for price subsidies, etc.

Credit Funds refer to the funds issued as loans by banking institutions. The sources of credit funds of the banking institutions included deposits, liabilities to international financial institutions, currency in circulation, self-owned funds and current retained profits, etc. The credit funds can be used in forms of loans, gold, foreign exchange, government debt and assets in the international financial institutions.

Deposit is a form of credit by which enterprises, institutions, organizations or households can put money into banks and other credit institutions for safekeeping and interest earning under the principle of free withdrawal. According to different depositors, deposits are divided into enterprise deposits,treasury deposits, deposits of government agencies and organizations,capital construction deposits, urban savings deposits, rural deposits and other deposits. Deposits are major sources of the credit funds of banks.

Loan is a form of credit by which banks and other credit institutions provide funds at certain interest rate to enterprises and individuals in the light of the principle of unconditional repayment. Loans from Chinese banks include circulating capital loans, fixed assets loans, loans to urban and rural individuals engaged in industrial and commercial business and agricultural loans.

Amount Insured refers to the maximum that the insurant will get for the claim of the case insured.

Premium is the fee paid by the insurant to the insurer to obtain the obligation of compensation from the insurance within the agreed terms.

Settled Claim is the compensation paid by the insurer to the insurant in accordance with the insurance contract.

Payment includes payment for death, injury or medical treatment and mature payment. Payment for death, injury or medical treatment refers to the money paid to the insurant (or the beneficiary) in accordance with the life or health insurance contract when the insurant encounters accidents within the insured period covered in the contract. Mature payment refers to the mature payment to the insurant in accordance with the life insurance contract at the end of the insured period.

第八篇
价格指数

CHAPTER 8
Price Indices

简要说明
Brief Introduction

本篇资料的主要内容及来源

本篇价格指数资料反映生产、流通、消费与投资环节的价格变动趋势和变动幅度，主要包括居民消费价格指数、商品零售价格指数、农业生产资料价格指数、工业品出厂价格指数（生产价格指数）、原材料、燃料、动力购进价格指数、固定资产投资价格指数、房屋销售价格指数。

居民消费价格指数、商品零售价格指数和农业生产资料价格指数出自出国家统计局新疆调查总队消费价格调查处；工业品出厂价格指数（生产价格指数）、原材料、燃料、动力购进价格指数、固定资产投资价格指数、房屋销售价格指数出自国家统计局新疆调查总队生产投资价格调查处。

Main content and source of data

Data on the price indices in this chapter show the changing trend and the change rates in production, circulation, consumption and investment, including mainly consumer price indices of residents, retail price indices, price indices of agricultural means of production, purchasing price indices of farm products, producers´ price indices of industrial products, purchasing price indices of raw materials, fuels and power, price indices of investment in fixed assets, and real estate price indices.

Data on the consumer price index, retail price index and price indices of agriculture production come from Division of Consumer Price of NBS Survey Office in Xinjiang; Data on the price indices of industrial products, indices of purchasing price of raw materials, fuels and power, price indices of investment in fixed assets, price indices for real estate come from Division of Consumer Price of NBS Survey Office in Xinjiang.

8-1 主要年份各种物价指数

Price Indices in Main Years

年份 Year	居民消费价格指数 Consumer Price Index	城市居民消费价格指数 Urban Household	农村居民消费价格指数 Rural Household	商品零售价格指数 Retail Price Index
上年=100 Preceding year=100				
1978	101.2	101.4	100.3	101.4
1980	102.8	104.1	102.0	104.2
1985	107.8	109.5	106.4	108.1
1990	105.0	104.5	105.9	104.1
1995	119.7	118.4	122.5	116.7
1996	110.5	110.4	110.6	108.8
1997	103.7	103.5	103.9	101.8
1998	100.2	99.9	100.8	99.7
1999	97.4	97.7	96.8	96.2
2000	99.4	100.1	97.6	98.3
2001	104.0	104.0	103.8	102.5
2002	99.4	98.9	100.9	97.9
2003	100.4	100.5	100.2	99.2
2004	102.7	102.1	104.5	100.7
2005	100.7	100.6	101.2	99.4
2006	101.3	101.0	102.0	101.8
2007	105.5	104.6	107.2	105.1
2008	108.1	107.3	109.5	108.5
2009	100.7	100.2	102.0	100.4
2010	104.3	103.6	105.8	104.6
1978 年=100 Year 1978 =100				
1978	100.0	100.0	100.0	100.0
1980	105.1	106.6	103.8	107.8
1985	120.9	125.6	117.9	124.2
1990	194.3	206.0	184.0	197.6
1995	392.7	422.7	364.2	381.0
1996	433.9	466.7	402.9	414.6
1997	450.0	483.0	418.6	422.0
1998	450.9	482.5	421.9	420.8
1999	439.2	471.4	408.4	404.8
2000	436.5	471.9	398.6	397.9
2001	454.0	490.8	413.8	407.8
2002	451.3	485.4	417.5	399.3
2003	453.1	487.8	418.3	396.1
2004	465.3	498.1	437.1	398.9
2005	468.6	501.1	442.3	396.5
2006	474.7	506.1	451.1	403.6
2007	500.8	529.4	483.6	424.2
2008	541.4	568.0	529.5	460.3
2009	545.2	569.1	540.1	462.1
2010	568.6	589.6	571.4	483.4

8-2 居民消费价格分类指数
Consumer Price Indices by Category

(上年=100) (2010 年) (preceding year=100)

项目	Item	全区 Autonomous Region	城市 Urban Indices	农村 Rural Indices
居民消费价格总指数	**Consumer Price Index**	**104.3**	**103.6**	**105.8**
食品	**Food**	**110.7**	**109.5**	**113.1**
粮食	Grain	108.9	108.5	109.4
大米	Rice	129.6	129.6	129.6
面粉	Flour	95.7	96.4	94.9
粮食制品	Grain Products	100.9	100.8	101.7
其它	Others	116.6	116.8	116.6
淀粉	Starches and Tubers	105.7	104.5	107.6
干豆类及豆制品	Bean and Its Products	109.6	109.7	109.4
油脂	Oil or Fat	107.6	104.3	112.9
肉禽及其制品	Meat, Poultry and Processed Products	113.0	111.9	115.0
蛋	Eggs	112.3	110.7	115.1
水产品	Aquatic Products	107.4	108.0	106.4
菜	Vegetables	120.0	117.5	124.9
鲜菜	Fresh Vegetables	120.0	117.3	125.6
干菜及菜制品	Dried Vegetables and Vegetable Products	108.1	108.5	107.3
薯类	Tubers	130.9	133.0	124.6
调味品	Flavoring	105.4	107.1	102.7
糖	Carbohydrate	108.1	106.7	109.8
食糖	Sugar	118.5	114.6	122.8
糖果	Candy	102.2	101.7	103.5
巧克力制品	Chocolate Goods	105.5	108.3	101.5
糖类小食品	Carbohydrate Products	103.8	103.6	104.0
茶及饮料	Tea and Beverages	101.7	101.4	102.2
干鲜瓜果	Dried and Fresh Melons and Fruits	114.1	112.1	118.3
鲜瓜果	Fresh Fruits	112.7	109.8	118.1
干(坚)果	Drie (nut) Fruits	117.6	117.0	119.2
糕点饼干	Cake and Biscuit	101.9	102.4	100.9
液体乳及乳制品	Milk and Its Products	108.7	107.7	111.4
在外用膳食品	Dining Out	105.8	105.4	107.3
主食	Staple Food	103.4	103.0	104.7
炒菜	Fried Dishes	105.9	105.5	107.2
地方小吃	Local Snack	110.6	109.9	113.0
其他食品	Other Foods	101.8	102.4	100.5
烟酒及用品	**Tobacco, Liquor and Articles**	**102.0**	**102.6**	**100.8**
烟草	Tobacco	98.7	98.9	98.2
酒	Liquor	105.3	106.4	103.3
吸烟饮酒用品	Articles for Smoking and Drinking	103.8	104.5	101.5
衣着	**Clothing**	**99.2**	**98.2**	**101.8**
服装	Garments	99.3	98.2	102.0
衣着材料	Clothing Material	102.7	103.2	102.2
棉布	Cotton Cloth	103.8	104.8	102.8

8-2 续表 Continued

(上年=100) (preceding year=100)

项　目	Item	全　区 Autonomous Region	城　市 Urban Areas	农　村 Rural Areas
棉混纺布	Blend Cloth	102.3	103.2	101.6
化纤布	Chemical Fiber Cloth	101.1	101.2	101.0
毛　线	Wool	103.7	103.9	103.6
鞋袜帽	Footwear and Hats	98.4	97.2	101.4
鞋	Shoes	98.0	96.5	101.9
袜　子	Socks and Stockings	100.3	100.5	99.9
帽　子	Hats	99.9	100.0	99.8
衣着加工服务费	Clothing Processing	102.4	105.1	99.4
家庭设备用品及维修服务	**Household Facilities,Articles and Services**	**101.2**	**100.9**	**101.9**
耐用消费品	Durable Consumer Goods	100.0	99.6	100.6
家　具	Furniture	101.3	101.0	101.9
家庭设备	Household Facilities	99.1	98.7	99.8
室内装饰品	Interior Decorations	100.3	100.5	99.8
床上用品	Bed Articles	101.1	101.7	99.8
家庭日用杂品	Daily Use Household Articles	100.5	100.5	100.7
家庭服务及加工维修服务	Household Service	110.2	107.4	116.9
医疗保健和个人用品	**Health Care and Personal Articles**	**102.0**	**102.0**	**101.9**
医疗保健	Health Cares	101.7	101.8	101.3
医疗器具及用品	Medical Instruments and Articles	103.2	103.1	103.3
中药材及中成药	Traditional Chinese Medicine	107.2	107.7	106.2
西　药	Western Medicine	100.4	100.7	99.8
保健器具及用品	Constitutional Appliances and Articles	100.4	100.4	100.6
医疗保健服务	Medical and Health Service	100.1	100.1	100.2
个人用品及服务	Personal Articles and Services	102.5	102.3	103.0
交通和通信	**Transportation and Communication**	**100.0**	**99.7**	**100.5**
交　通	Transportation	101.7	101.1	102.9
通　信	Communication	98.4	98.5	98.0
娱乐教育文化用品及服务	**Recreation, Education, Culture Articles**	**101.2**	**101.4**	**100.7**
文娱用耐用消费品及服务	Durable Consumer Goods for Cultural and Recreationl Use and Services	97.5	96.4	100.1
教　育	Education	101.9	102.3	101.0
文化娱乐	Culture and Recreation Articles	100.9	100.8	101.0
文化娱乐用品	Cultural and Recreational Articles	100.4	99.7	102.0
书报杂志	Newspapers and Magazines	101.0	101.2	100.6
文娱费	Expenditure on Culture and Recreation	101.3	101.6	100.3
旅　游	Touring and Outing	105.2	107.5	100.2
居　住	**Housing**	**102.7**	**101.7**	**104.7**
建房及装修材料	Building and Building Decoration Materials	103.5	101.3	108.1
租　房	Rent	103.3	102.3	105.1
自有住房	Private Housing	101.6	101.8	101.5
水、电、燃料	Water, Electricity and Fuels	102.5	101.9	103.7
服务项目价格指数	**Services**	**101.5**	**101.6**	**101.3**

8-3 各市县居民消费价格分类指数

(上年=100) (2010 年)

项目	Item	乌鲁木齐市 Urumqi City	喀什市 Kashgar [Kaxgar] City	伊宁市 Yining [Gulja] City	和田市 Hotan City	克拉玛依市 Karamay City	哈密市 Hami [Kumul] City
居民消费价格总指数	**Consumer Price Index**	**102.7**	**104.8**	**106.2**	**104.4**	**104.5**	**105.0**
食品	**Food**	**108.5**	**111.7**	**112.0**	**110.4**	**111.3**	**113.3**
粮食	Grain	108.8	106.4	107.4	105.1	123.6	106.9
大米	Rice	131.3	123.6	127.5	123.8	167.5	121.7
面粉	Flour	95.1	94.6	94.4	94.7	100.2	95.1
粮食制品	Grain Products	100.3	101.4	98.5	102.7	102.0	100.8
其它	Others	116.7	119.6	116.0	105.7	114.5	114.5
淀粉	Starches and Tubers	99.8	109.7	112.3	117.6	99.0	96.6
干豆类及豆制品	Bean and Its Products	108.2	120.5	129.0	117.1	109.9	115.7
油脂	Oil or Fat	101.6	110.0	106.6	107.2	106.1	100.4
肉禽及其制品	Meat, Poultry and Their Products	109.9	116.5	114.8	112.1	109.1	111.7
蛋	Eggs	110.4	115.2	116.0	104.2	111.1	105.8
水产品	Aquatic Products	111.2	112.7	97.6	109.0	104.1	111.8
菜	Vegetables	110.8	119.3	130.4	126.8	126.2	133.2
鲜菜	Fresh Vegetables	110.1	119.9	132.1	128.1	126.7	132.3
干菜及菜制品	Dried Vegetables and Vegetable Products	105.8	100.3	113.9	109.1	113.1	124.5
薯类	Tubers	132.2	113.7	126.4	115.4	133.9	162.3
调味品	Flavoring	106.3	102.3	102.7	103.7	103.8	107.2
糖	Carbohydrate Products	101.7	113.0	113.8	107.2	104.0	114.5
食糖	Sugar	102.3	124.2	121.7	118.1	107.0	133.2
糖果	Candy	100.3	100.0	111.8	100.0	104.7	103.7
巧克力制品	Chocolate Goods	105.5	136.2	122.5	112.3	100.0	120.1
糖类小食品	Carbohydrate	103.5	109.2	100.0	104.0	104.2	101.3
茶及饮料	Tea and Beverages	99.5	101.9	105.6	100.2	100.3	103.4
干鲜瓜果	Dried and Fresh Melons and Fruits	111.7	113.8	109.7	121.0	104.9	122.8
鲜瓜果	Fresh Fruits	107.4	114.7	106.9	122.3	105.3	126.6
干(坚)果	Dried(nut)Fruits	123.6	109.5	117.4	115.7	101.1	114.9
糕点饼干	Cake, Cookie	103.6	101.2	102.9	101.0	100.2	100.7
液体乳及乳制品	Milk and Its Products	108.5	104.1	103.9	98.5	104.9	103.7
在外用膳食品	Dining Out	106.0	107.3	101.9	105.5	102.9	103.2
主食	Staple Food	103.4	101.6	100.6	103.5	100.2	102.5
炒菜	Fried Dishes	105.4	103.1	103.4	108.4	100.5	103.9
地方小吃	Local Snack	114.3	125.7	100.9	100.0	108.1	103.2
其他食品	Other Foods	101.2	100.4	100.3	101.1	107.5	98.7
烟酒及用品	**Tobacco, Liquor and Articles**	**101.6**	**100.6**	**105.2**	**102.9**	**101.8**	**98.9**
烟草	Tobacco	98.4	99.1	97.0	98.3	101.2	96.6
酒	Liquor	104.8	102.2	112.6	107.7	102.5	101.4
吸烟饮酒用品	Articles for Smoking and Drinking	105.6	101.1	102.7	100.0	100.4	97.3
衣着	**Clothing**	**94.7**	**99.4**	**105.0**	**100.1**	**101.6**	**95.1**
服装	Garments	95.8	99.1	105.1	100.1	101.1	89.5
衣着材料	Clothing Material	100.5	102.1	109.2	101.4	104.5	106.3
棉布	Cotton Cloth	101.1	103.3	103.1	102.7	109.9	108.1

Consumer Price Indices by Category in Cities and Counties

(preceding year=100)

昌吉市 Changji City	库尔勒市 Korla City	阿克苏市 Aksu City	焉耆回族自治县 Yanqi Hui Autonomous County	塔城市 Tacheng [Qoqek] City	阿勒泰市 Altay City	乌苏市 Usu City	博乐市 Bole [Bortala] City	吐鲁番市 Turpan City	库车县 Kuqa County	阿图什市 Artux City	莎车县 Shache [Yarkant] County	奎屯市 Kuytun City	石河子市 Shihezi City
103.6	**104.5**	**106.1**	**104.7**	**105.2**	**104.6**	**105.5**	**105.7**	**104.6**	**105.2**	**104.3**	**107.3**	**103.3**	**103.7**
108.7	**111.1**	**110.4**	**111.5**	**113.1**	**112.0**	**112.6**	**111.5**	**110.9**	**111.7**	**111.2**	**114.9**	**108.0**	**107.0**
102.4	105.4	109.6	107.6	106.4	106.2	109.3	113.8	106.2	110.6	106.0	110.9	100.2	105.4
113.3	112.4	123.7	118.7	122.7	118.9	124.8	130.8	120.3	142.9	124.4	129.8	105.0	111.9
97.0	100.7	98.4	96.1	94.8	96.0	91.5	105.2	94.6	83.3	94.0	93.5	98.0	98.5
99.2	100.2	102.0	101.6	100.0	100.9	107.5	100.8	106.6	106.3	100.2	102.7	98.0	101.3
115.2	128.6	132.2	122.8	110.7	113.1	147.5	105.4	108.4	116.9	109.4	125.8	101.7	114.3
129.4	101.6	109.4	110.7	100.0	100.0	97.1	115.5	133.3	101.1	100.0	110.6	100.0	100.6
112.2	108.2	103.7	116.1	109.9	118.3	114.0	104.9	109.8	125.4	101.4	111.3	123.0	116.6
104.9	107.9	102.6	109.8	121.3	117.9	102.4	106.8	103.8	123.3	116.2	109.3	113.7	111.1
114.4	116.2	112.6	112.0	112.2	115.4	113.2	112.3	112.7	107.3	115.3	119.9	105.5	104.6
104.9	114.4	115.2	108.1	109.5	108.9	110.0	104.2	116.2	107.7	113.4	132.4	108.8	105.0
107.5	106.5	105.9	105.3	101.8	101.4	105.0	104.8	106.2	104.7	114.5	111.1	104.9	108.1
108.6	123.0	111.4	122.7	126.2	123.3	127.9	125.2	126.4	126.5	123.8	108.8	122.6	113.7
109.3	125.0	110.3	120.6	128.3	124.9	128.5	133.8	126.3	132.1	124.7	109.2	123.0	115.7
100.2	98.5	119.8	118.4	100.0	111.9	114.9	102.8	102.2	104.7	104.0	106.7	100.7	105.3
96.9	142.1	118.8	147.7	98.2	125.7	144.1	93.4	134.2	100.0	122.9	103.7	133.6	96.3
106.9	100.5	113.4	100.8	105.8	113.8	102.1	104.3	100.4	103.8	101.4	100.0	100.0	103.0
105.8	104.2	106.6	111.6	110.9	105.5	108.5	112.8	106.8	109.2	104.7	110.6	104.7	110.4
114.9	111.5	125.8	131.5	121.5	118.7	131.3	121.1	118.2	121.2	113.1	126.5	112.7	117.9
102.6	103.3	98.9	98.1	100.0	100.0	100.5	113.0	100.7	103.4	100.0	107.0	100.0	108.4
100.0	100.5	100.0	108.0	103.4	101.5	100.0	106.4	100.0	102.2	100.0	97.5	103.4	99.3
100.3	100.7	105.9	103.5	120.6	100.0	102.1	100.0	100.0	100.7	100.0	102.7	100.0	114.3
105.1	101.3	109.8	100.2	98.3	100.9	99.9	100.7	104.0	99.5	106.3	106.0	100.0	101.6
104.4	119.4	105.7	119.5	118.0	122.1	119.7	116.3	116.3	120.2	107.2	120.3	113.2	105.7
104.0	119.1	98.8	120.0	122.4	128.2	122.5	115.1	110.0	130.6	107.0	117.0	119.5	100.4
105.5	121.1	121.9	118.7	102.1	100.0	112.1	118.7	122.0	104.0	108.7	130.7	100.0	124.6
100.0	101.9	103.7	102.8	100.0	100.0	100.9	100.0	102.7	100.4	100.0	101.4	105.7	101.7
118.7	102.5	107.3	103.4	125.3	108.6	107.7	104.5	101.6	101.3	100.6	111.3	101.0	113.7
105.9	101.5	113.1	107.4	104.6	102.0	108.3	103.7	101.1	109.3	103.0	113.2	100.3	103.9
102.8	103.5	107.4	103.7	106.6	103.8	100.0	101.9	101.1	107.0	100.0	107.5	101.9	104.2
110.6	100.4	116.9	109.0	100.0	101.1	107.9	101.2	100.0	106.7	103.2	118.2	100.0	104.1
105.2	100.0	113.3	109.6	116.5	100.0	114.2	111.8	103.1	117.6	110.0	115.0	101.9	102.7
100.4	100.0	113.3	100.3	103.2	100.0	100.0	100.0	100.0	100.0	100.0	100.0	101.4	101.0
105.4	**101.5**	**106.4**	**101.2**	**100.1**	**100.3**	**100.4**	**103.5**	**98.4**	**100.6**	**100.3**	**100.6**	**104.1**	**101.3**
100.8	100.0	99.2	97.8	100.0	99.6	95.6	101.1	93.0	97.7	97.9	98.8	103.9	99.7
110.1	103.4	111.5	105.8	100.5	101.3	105.0	105.4	104.9	105.5	103.2	102.7	104.5	102.5
99.8	100.8	114.4	100.0	97.8	100.0	100.0	111.9	100.0	100.0	100.0	101.5	100.6	105.6
99.4	**99.1**	**106.1**	**99.8**	**99.1**	**100.7**	**101.7**	**101.5**	**100.9**	**100.9**	**100.3**	**103.8**	**100.6**	**101.9**
99.0	98.2	103.6	98.8	98.6	102.5	100.3	102.2	99.7	100.8	100.4	104.9	100.7	100.4
101.5	100.2	104.8	101.9	108.6	100.4	100.0	102.2	102.9	100.5	100.6	106.7	101.8	103.4
108.9	101.2	107.2	103.4	113.3	100.0	100.0	103.3	113.3	100.0	100.0	106.3	100.0	106.4

8-3 续表

(上年=100)

项目	Item	乌鲁木齐市 Urumqi City	喀什市 Kashgar [Kaxgar] City	伊宁市 Yining [Gulja] City	和田市 Hotan City	克拉玛依市 Karamay City	哈密市 Hami [Kumul] City
棉混纺布	Blend Cloth	101.5	104.2	103.3	101.0	107.8	103.9
化纤布	Chemical Fiber Cloth	100.0	101.4	101.4	101.5	100.0	111.4
毛　线	Wool	100.8	100.0	124.6	100.0	101.8	100.0
鞋袜帽	Footgear and Hats	90.9	98.6	104.1	100.0	100.6	100.8
鞋	Shoes	90.0	100.0	104.4	100.1	101.0	101.1
袜　子	Socks and Stockings	100.0	92.5	102.7	100.0	97.3	100.0
帽　子	Hats	97.1	101.0	100.9	100.0	100.4	100.0
衣着加工服务费	Clothing Manufacturing Services	100.7	106.4	103.5	100.0	113.6	108.7
家庭设备用品及维修服务	**Household Facilities and Articles and Services**	**100.7**	**99.2**	**101.3**	**101.8**	**100.8**	**98.3**
耐用消费品	Durable Consumer Goods	99.3	96.9	100.0	99.9	99.8	96.8
家　具	Furniture	101.4	95.8	101.3	100.0	99.7	99.2
家庭设备	Household Facilities	97.9	97.7	99.4	99.8	99.9	95.8
室内装饰品	Interior Decorations	101.0	98.7	103.0	101.4	99.6	100.0
床上用品	Bed Articles	106.1	99.4	100.0	96.6	100.0	91.2
家庭日用杂品	Daily Use Household Articles	99.6	101.8	99.9	108.4	100.0	101.5
家庭服务及加工维修服务	Household Services and Maintenance and Renovation	113.9	102.3	111.8	100.0	110.2	103.2
医疗保健和个人用品	**Health Care and Personal Articles**	**101.4**	**102.9**	**100.9**	**101.2**	**100.7**	**105.6**
医疗保健	Health Cares	101.8	101.1	100.2	101.1	99.8	106.7
医疗器具及用品	Medical Appliances and Articles	97.7	117.2	111.1	100.0	104.9	112.9
中药材及中成药	Traditional Chinese Medicine	105.5	104.8	96.5	104.0	96.3	119.7
西　药	Western Medicine	100.8	98.9	102.4	100.6	101.4	100.7
保健器具及用品	Constitutional Appliances and Articles	100.0	100.3	99.9	99.8	99.2	102.7
医疗保健服务	Medical and Health Service	100.0	100.5	98.7	100.0	100.0	100.0
个人用品及服务	Personal Articles and Services	100.4	105.8	102.0	101.4	101.8	103.8
交通和通信	**Transportation and Communication**	**99.3**	**100.3**	**100.5**	**100.9**	**101.0**	**99.3**
交　通	Transportation	100.8	102.3	101.3	102.7	102.7	101.1
通　信	Communication	97.8	97.9	99.9	99.7	99.1	97.2
娱乐教育文化用品及服务	**Recreation, Education and Culture Articles and Services**	**101.9**	**99.6**	**103.4**	**100.6**	**101.1**	**102.2**
文娱用耐用消费品及服务	Durable Consumer Goods for Cultural and Recreationl Use and Services	92.1	92.0	99.5	99.5	99.4	96.3
教　育	Education	102.2	100.0	101.6	100.0	102.7	102.3
文化娱乐	Culture and Recreation Articles	99.9	104.3	99.5	101.1	102.1	100.9
文化娱乐用品	Cultural and Recreational Articles	98.9	100.5	98.8	99.7	100.0	98.7
书报杂志	Newspapers and Magazines	100.3	110.7	99.8	102.5	104.8	100.0
文娱费	Expenditure on Culture and Recreation	100.8	103.0	100.0	102.3	103.0	106.4
旅　游	Touring and Outing	108.5	106.8	114.4	114.4	100.6	115.2
居　住	**Residence**	**99.9**	**104.1**	**105.1**	**102.5**	**101.3**	**103.3**
建房及装修材料	Building and Building Decoration Materials	99.2	101.6	101.3	101.0	102.9	102.1
租　房	Renting	102.6	100.0	100.0	100.0	100.0	104.8
自有住房	Private Housing	100.3	105.7	102.0	100.7	103.1	100.6
水、电、燃料	Water, Electricity and Fuels	100.0	105.9	107.3	104.8	100.0	104.8
服务项目价格指数	**Services**	**101.7**	**102.0**	**102.5**	**100.7**	**102.2**	**102.7**

Continued

(preceding year=100)

昌吉市 Changji City	库尔勒市 Korla City	阿克苏市 Aksu City	焉耆回族自治县 Yanqi Hui Autonomous County	塔城市 Tacheng [Qoqek] City	阿勒泰市 Altay City	乌苏市 Usu City	博乐市 Bole [Bortala] City	吐鲁番市 Turpan City	库车县 Kuqa County	阿图什市 Artux City	莎车县 Shache [Yarkant] County	奎屯市 Kuytun City	石河子市 Shihezi City
105.3	100.0	102.7	103.3	101.3	101.6	100.0	101.6	100.0	100.0	102.2	102.6	105.8	101.0
98.6	100.0	100.0	100.0	106.9	100.0	100.0	102.8	100.0	100.0	100.0	106.2	100.6	108.0
100.0	100.0	111.6	102.0	100.8	100.0	100.0	100.0	100.7	102.2	100.0	111.6	100.0	99.0
99.8	100.6	110.8	100.9	100.0	100.0	105.4	100.1	103.2	102.2	100.0	99.6	100.0	105.3
100.1	100.5	108.7	101.5	100.0	100.0	109.1	100.2	103.9	102.6	100.0	99.5	98.4	107.3
97.9	101.9	119.6	97.7	100.0	100.0	100.0	100.0	100.0	100.0	100.0	100.0	102.1	100.1
99.4	100.0	106.6	97.7	100.0	100.0	100.0	100.0	100.0	100.0	100.0	99.5	104.8	99.9
100.4	100.0	119.0	101.1	101.2	84.5	100.0	100.3	100.0	100.0	100.0	106.7	100.0	100.3
101.0	**100.6**	**102.7**	**102.3**	**102.7**	**99.8**	**100.9**	**100.4**	**101.1**	**105.1**	**99.9**	**104.2**	**100.2**	**100.9**
100.8	100.2	100.4	104.3	98.5	99.2	100.0	100.3	99.9	101.1	100.0	102.8	98.3	97.5
100.2	101.2	102.6	110.9	100.0	100.5	100.0	100.0	100.0	100.3	100.0	104.1	98.2	97.0
100.9	99.8	98.7	100.5	97.8	98.2	100.0	100.5	99.9	101.8	100.0	102.0	98.3	97.7
97.1	101.2	99.7	100.0	100.0	100.0	100.0	100.4	100.2	100.0	100.0	100.0	99.8	107.5
101.9	103.0	101.7	100.0	100.0	100.0	100.0	100.0	102.6	100.0	100.0	100.9	98.4	100.1
101.4	100.3	106.5	97.6	99.9	100.0	100.3	100.8	103.3	98.5	99.3	102.4	104.1	102.1
103.9	100.8	109.4	110.6	147.5	101.2	108.7	100.0	101.6	140.8	100.0	120.3	102.0	107.7
101.8	**101.1**	**102.7**	**101.1**	**102.8**	**104.9**	**98.0**	**104.3**	**101.7**	**101.0**	**100.9**	**101.0**	**100.7**	**104.7**
101.5	100.7	101.2	100.1	103.1	106.8	94.3	103.9	101.0	100.4	101.8	100.3	100.3	104.4
100.0	101.9	110.6	97.1	100.9	100.0	100.0	100.2	124.9	106.4	100.0	100.0	100.0	115.0
108.5	102.3	101.7	102.6	110.5	123.9	91.6	119.2	101.8	97.1	105.6	102.2	101.4	116.0
98.5	99.9	101.0	99.7	105.1	101.0	91.4	98.6	100.2	101.5	99.7	99.3	99.9	101.7
102.8	100.0	100.6	100.2	102.3	100.1	100.0	103.5	99.9	98.9	105.5	100.2	99.4	101.6
100.3	100.0	101.2	98.0	100.0	100.0	100.0	100.0	100.0	102.0	101.6	100.2	100.0	100.0
102.3	101.7	105.0	102.6	102.2	101.5	102.9	104.9	102.7	101.9	99.5	102.0	101.3	105.2
99.4	**101.5**	**101.2**	**99.6**	**100.6**	**99.6**	**100.9**	**101.7**	**100.5**	**99.3**	**98.3**	**102.2**	**98.6**	**101.2**
101.2	102.9	103.1	101.1	101.0	102.1	101.9	104.3	102.9	101.8	101.9	106.2	100.3	102.9
97.8	99.5	98.6	98.5	100.0	96.7	100.0	99.3	99.1	95.4	94.4	97.8	96.9	99.2
100.9	**102.5**	**101.6**	**102.3**	**99.9**	**100.0**	**101.0**	**102.1**	**101.0**	**101.6**	**100.2**	**100.4**	**100.0**	**99.3**
99.0	99.3	96.8	103.2	98.7	99.4	100.3	99.2	99.2	99.2	100.0	101.6	98.2	92.6
102.4	105.0	103.8	102.6	100.4	100.0	100.0	106.8	100.6	101.1	100.0	100.0	100.6	101.1
100.5	101.2	102.0	100.5	99.9	100.8	104.4	101.5	103.6	101.4	101.2	100.1	100.8	100.4
100.7	101.1	99.4	100.0	99.9	100.0	109.1	103.3	100.0	100.1	103.2	100.2	101.9	99.9
100.6	102.1	100.0	100.0	99.4	102.3	100.0	100.0	102.6	102.9	100.0	100.0	100.0	101.6
100.0	100.0	106.9	101.7	100.0	100.0	100.0	100.0	110.5	101.6	100.0	100.0	100.0	100.0
99.4	101.8	99.1	100.0	100.0	100.0	100.0	93.6	104.8	106.4	100.0	100.0	100.3	102.2
101.9	**101.6**	**106.4**	**101.7**	**103.7**	**100.8**	**106.8**	**104.1**	**102.7**	**104.5**	**101.2**	**108.2**	**103.6**	**103.7**
104.2	101.4	104.5	102.7	105.6	101.4	104.1	106.2	104.8	108.5	98.6	117.6	103.0	104.3
107.8	100.0	111.1	105.0	100.2	100.0	104.2	106.6	100.0	100.0	100.0	116.4	100.0	107.1
100.4	105.1	100.0	102.3	100.0	100.7	116.1	100.0	100.3	100.7	100.3	102.0	100.6	100.2
100.6	100.7	108.9	100.8	103.9	100.7	106.5	104.1	102.9	104.0	103.6	102.7	105.2	104.0
101.4	**102.2**	**103.3**	**101.3**	**102.0**	**99.5**	**102.4**	**102.5**	**101.1**	**103.2**	**100.2**	**101.2**	**100.3**	**101.5**

8-4 商品零售价格分类指数
Retail Price Indices by Category

(上年=100) (2010 年) (preceding year=100)

项 目	Item	全 区 Autonomous Region	城 市 Urban Areas	农 村 Rural Areas
商品零售价格总指数	**Retail Price Index**	**104.6**	**103.9**	**106.4**
食 品	**Food**	**110.6**	**109.4**	**113.4**
粮 食	Grain	109.7	109.3	110.3
油 脂	Oil or Fat	107.8	104.1	113.7
肉禽及其制品	Meat, Poultry and Processed Products	111.6	110.7	113.6
猪 肉	Pork	104.3	103.5	106.1
牛 肉	Beef	111.0	109.4	114.1
羊 肉	Mutton	118.0	116.3	122.1
鸡	Chicken	113.9	113.7	114.1
鲜 蛋	Fresh Eggs	112.5	111.2	115.1
水产品	Aquatic Products	108.1	109.2	105.3
鲜瓜果	Fresh Fruits	111.3	108.2	117.8
糕点、饼干、面包	Cake、Biscuit and Bread	102.5	103.1	100.9
饮料、烟酒	**Beverages, Tobacco and Liquor**	**101.7**	**101.8**	**101.2**
茶及饮料	Tea and Beverages	101.9	101.6	102.3
#饮 料	Beverages	101.0	101.4	100.2
烟 草	Tobacco	98.6	98.7	98.3
酒	Liquor	104.9	105.5	103.4
服装鞋帽	**Garments, Shoes and Hats**	**98.0**	**96.4**	**101.6**
服 装	Garments	98.2	96.8	101.7
鞋袜帽	Footgear and Hats	97.3	95.4	101.6
#鞋	Shoes	96.6	94.3	102.1
纺织品	**Textiles**	**103.5**	**104.0**	**101.4**
棉 布	Cotton Cloth	104.2	103.9	104.6
棉混纺布	Blend Cloth	102.4	102.6	101.7
化纤布	Chemical Fiber Cloth	100.7	100.3	101.8
毛 线	Wool	103.4	102.9	104.4
家用电器及音响器材	**Household Appliances,Music and Video Equipment**	**97.8**	**97.0**	**99.7**
家庭设备	Household Facilities	98.6	98.3	99.2
文娱用耐用消费品	Durable Consuming Goods for Entertainment	96.8	95.1	100.1
音响器材	Sound Apparatus	99.5	99.2	100.1

8-4 续表 Continued

(上年=100) (preceding year=100)

项　　目	Item	全　区 Autonomous Region	城　市 Urban Indices	农　村 Rural Indices
文化办公用品	**Cultural and Office Goods**	**99.2**	**98.3**	**101.1**
日用品	**Articles for Daily Use**	**100.7**	**100.7**	**100.6**
日用百货	General Merchandise for Daily Use	100.7	100.9	100.1
日用杂品	Miscellaneous for Daily Use	100.6	100.4	101.1
洗涤用品	Washing and Cleaning Goods	101.6	101.8	100.8
其他日用品	Other Daily-use Goods	99.1	98.5	100.4
体育娱乐用品	**Sports and Entertainment Goods**	**97.5**	**96.5**	**100.1**
体育用品	Sports Articles	99.8	99.6	100.2
娱乐用品	Recreational Articles	95.6	94.1	100.0
交通、通信用品	**Traffic and Telecommunication Goods**	**96.8**	**95.8**	**98.6**
交通运输机械	Traffic and Transport Machinery	99.3	98.6	100.8
通信器材	Telecommunication Apparatus	93.7	92.2	96.3
家　具	**Furniture**	**101.3**	**101.2**	**101.4**
化妆品	**Cosmetics**	**99.5**	**99.6**	**99.3**
金银珠宝	**Gold and Silver Jewelry**	**110.7**	**108.0**	**118.1**
中西药品及医疗保健用品	**Chinese and Western Medicine, Medical-care and Healthy Goods**	**102.6**	**102.3**	**103.4**
医疗器具及用品	Medical-care Apparatus and Goods	102.0	100.1	105.3
中药材及中成药	Chinese Herbs and Patent Medicine	107.5	107.0	108.3
西　药	Western Medicine	100.6	100.8	100.0
保健品及器具	Healthy Devices and Goods	100.4	100.2	101.4
书报杂志及电子出版物	**Books, Magazines and Electronic Publications**	**103.0**	**103.9**	**100.6**
教材及参考书	Texts and Reference Books	106.9	109.6	101.1
书报杂志	Newspapers and Magazines	100.9	101.0	100.6
电子音像制品	Electronic Audio and Video Products	101.2	101.6	100.0
燃　料	**Fuels**	**107.7**	**107.1**	**109.2**
煤炭及制品	Coal and Its Products	102.0	99.9	104.1
石油及制品	Oil and Its Products	110.3	109.2	114.3
建筑材料及五金电料	**Building Apparatus, Hardwares and Electrical Apparatus**	**103.0**	**101.4**	**105.9**
建筑装璜材料	Building Decoration Materials	104.2	102.3	108.1
五金电料	Hardwares and Electrical Apparatus	99.6	99.0	100.6

8-5 各市县商品零售价格分类指数

(上年=100)　　(2010 年)

项　　目	Item	乌鲁木齐市 Urumqi City	喀什市 Kashgar [Kaxgar] City	伊宁市 Yining [Gulja] City	和田市 Hotan City	克拉玛依市 Karamay City	哈密市 Hami [Kumul] City
商品零售价格总指数	**General Retail Price Index**	**103.4**	**105.1**	**106.5**	**105.2**	**104.2**	**105.1**
食　品	**Food**	**108.6**	**112.0**	**111.8**	**111.3**	**111.5**	**114.0**
粮　食	Grain	109.4	106.0	107.4	107.0	123.6	106.6
油　脂	Oil or Fat	102.1	110.8	106.7	107.2	106.1	101.1
肉禽及其制品	Meat, Poultry and Their Products	109.7	116.3	114.8	112.5	108.7	112.8
猪　肉	Pork	102.2	113.7	103.2	119.7	105.5	108.5
牛　肉	Beef	106.8	113.8	113.6	113.9	109.2	109.6
羊　肉	Mutton	114.2	117.1	128.9	110.5	118.8	122.5
鸡	Chicken	115.0	118.1	104.5	111.3	103.9	104.2
鲜　蛋	Fresh Egg	111.4	115.6	117.5	104.5	115.0	105.6
水产品	Aquatic Products	111.1	110.9	97.9	109.0	104.1	112.2
鲜瓜果	Fresh Fruits	107.4	114.7	106.9	122.3	105.3	126.6
糕点、饼干、面包	Cake、Biscuit and Bread	104.0	101.1	102.8	101.0	100.2	100.8
饮料、烟酒	**Beverages, Tobacco and Liquor**	**101.2**	**100.3**	**105.1**	**103.1**	**101.3**	**99.9**
茶及饮料	Tea and Beverages	99.5	102.1	105.0	99.6	100.2	103.2
#饮 料	Beverages	99.5	101.3	104.8	100.7	99.2	99.2
烟　草	Tobacco	98.4	99.1	97.1	98.3	101.2	96.9
酒	Liquor	105.0	102.1	110.5	107.7	102.5	101.4
服装鞋帽	**Garments, Shoes and Hats**	**94.4**	**99.2**	**104.7**	**100.0**	**100.9**	**94.2**
服　装	Garments	96.0	99.3	105.1	100.1	101.1	89.3
鞋袜帽	Footgear and Hats	90.9	99.1	104.1	100.0	100.6	100.8
#鞋	Shoes	89.9	100.0	104.4	100.0	101.0	101.0
纺织品	**Textiles**	**104.6**	**101.1**	**104.9**	**99.3**	**101.4**	**99.1**
棉　布	Cotton Cloth	101.1	103.3	103.1	102.7	109.9	108.1
棉混纺布	Blend Cloth	101.5	104.2	103.3	101.0	107.8	103.9
化纤布	Chemical Fiber Cloth	100.0	101.4	101.4	101.5	100.0	111.4
毛　线	Wool	100.8	100.0	124.6	100.0	101.8	100.0
家用电器及音响器材	**Household Appliances, Music and Sound Apparatus**	**96.2**	**95.4**	**99.4**	**99.7**	**99.7**	**96.2**
家庭设备	Household Facilities	97.9	98.1	99.4	99.8	99.9	95.7
文娱用耐用消费品	Durable Consuming Goods for Entertainment	93.6	91.9	99.5	99.3	99.3	96.0
音响器材	Sound Apparatus	99.8	95.6	97.9	100.0	100.0	100.0

Retail Price Indices by Category in Cities and Counties

(receding year=100)

昌吉市 Changji City	库尔勒市 Korla City	阿克苏市 Aksu City	焉耆回族自治县 Yanqi Hui Autonomous County	塔城市 Tacheng [Qoqek] City	阿勒泰市 Altay City	乌苏市 Usu City	博乐市 Bole [Bortala] City	吐鲁番市 Turpan City	库车县 Kuqa County	阿图什市 Artux City	莎车县 Shache [Yarkant] County	奎屯市 Kuytun City	石河子市 Shihezi City
104.0	**104.5**	**106.2**	**104.7**	**105.7**	**106.1**	**104.9**	**105.7**	**105.5**	**103.7**	**105.1**	**107.9**	**103.8**	**103.9**
108.3	**110.7**	**110.6**	**111.2**	**112.4**	**113.4**	**111.3**	**111.0**	**111.4**	**110.0**	**111.6**	**113.9**	**109.1**	**107.0**
102.5	105.6	109.0	107.8	106.4	106.8	108.6	112.5	106.2	109.8	106.8	112.5	100.3	105.5
105.1	110.9	102.6	109.6	121.3	122.1	102.1	106.9	103.8	116.0	118.0	109.4	117.0	109.2
113.0	111.9	112.6	110.6	112.2	116.5	111.7	111.3	112.5	108.3	115.2	118.4	106.4	104.9
102.9	108.9	103.8	97.6	105.4	109.5	107.8	110.1	101.8	99.3	101.2	113.5	97.9	102.5
109.0	119.8	118.6	114.4	110.0	111.6	112.6	107.4	114.6	108.4	114.2	121.4	113.5	107.9
123.9	123.0	124.2	123.7	124.3	125.5	126.9	120.7	118.9	113.4	122.6	122.2	125.0	115.2
116.5	113.5	109.3	110.3	108.4	123.4	110.4	117.8	110.8	117.3	110.4	117.0	107.7	102.7
104.6	115.0	115.2	108.6	111.0	109.8	109.8	105.3	117.1	111.1	113.7	134.5	109.8	104.6
107.7	105.8	105.2	105.4	101.8	101.7	104.5	105.4	106.2	104.0	115.2	110.8	102.2	108.5
104.0	119.1	98.8	120.0	122.4	128.2	122.5	115.1	110.0	130.6	107.0	117.0	119.5	100.4
100.0	102.2	103.7	102.6	100.0	100.0	100.9	100.0	102.7	100.8	100.0	101.8	107.0	101.2
104.0	**101.0**	**105.6**	**101.2**	**99.7**	**100.2**	**100.3**	**102.4**	**100.0**	**101.3**	**102.4**	**101.8**	**103.3**	**101.9**
104.1	101.2	108.1	100.2	98.3	101.0	99.9	100.5	104.0	99.7	106.5	104.6	100.0	104.6
106.2	102.0	106.0	100.3	100.0	99.2	99.8	100.8	103.0	99.5	98.7	99.2	100.0	108.0
101.0	100.0	99.3	97.7	100.0	98.9	95.8	102.6	92.9	98.2	98.0	99.1	104.7	99.7
108.3	102.0	111.5	106.0	100.5	101.2	104.8	103.7	104.9	105.6	102.5	103.2	103.5	102.2
99.3	**99.1**	**105.9**	**99.0**	**99.0**	**101.4**	**102.4**	**101.3**	**100.8**	**101.3**	**100.1**	**104.0**	**101.4**	**102.7**
99.0	98.2	102.8	98.5	98.6	102.3	100.4	101.6	99.7	101.3	100.1	105.0	101.4	101.8
99.8	100.5	111.2	100.1	100.0	100.0	105.5	101.0	103.2	101.4	100.0	99.8	99.4	104.7
100.1	100.4	108.7	101.3	100.0	100.0	108.4	101.6	103.9	102.6	100.0	99.6	98.3	107.2
103.0	**101.7**	**104.3**	**101.2**	**102.5**	**100.2**	**100.0**	**101.1**	**102.8**	**100.3**	**100.3**	**104.8**	**100.2**	**101.3**
108.9	101.2	107.2	103.4	113.3	100.0	100.0	103.3	113.3	100.0	100.0	106.3	100.0	106.4
105.3	100.0	102.7	103.3	101.3	101.6	100.0	101.6	100.0	100.0	102.2	102.6	105.8	101.0
98.6	100.0	100.0	100.0	106.9	100.0	100.0	102.8	100.0	100.0	100.0	106.2	100.6	108.0
100.0	100.0	111.6	102.0	100.8	100.0	100.0	100.0	100.7	102.2	100.0	111.6	100.0	99.0
101.0	**99.5**	**97.2**	**101.4**	**98.8**	**98.5**	**100.0**	**99.8**	**99.6**	**101.3**	**100.0**	**102.1**	**98.3**	**95.6**
101.2	99.8	98.7	100.5	97.8	98.0	100.0	100.4	99.9	102.3	100.0	102.1	98.4	98.0
100.9	99.0	95.3	103.0	99.7	98.9	100.0	99.2	99.1	99.6	100.0	102.1	97.8	91.9
93.8	100.0	99.9	100.0	100.0	100.0	100.0	100.0	100.0	100.0	100.0	101.3	100.0	100.0

8-5 续表

(上年=100)

项　　目	Item	乌鲁木齐市 Urumqi City	喀什市 Kashgar [Kaxgar] City	伊宁市 Yining [Gulja] City	和田市 Hotan City	克拉玛依市 Karamay City	哈密市 Hami [Kumul] City
文化办公用品	**Cultural and Office Appliances**	**97.1**	**100.7**	**99.3**	**99.8**	**100.0**	**97.4**
日用品	**Articles for Daily Use**	**100.7**	**99.5**	**100.9**	**102.4**	**100.3**	**101.6**
日用百货	General Merchandise for Daily Use	101.2	95.6	101.2	99.7	100.4	102.0
日用杂品	Miscellaneous for Daily Use	100.0	100.5	100.0	109.3	100.0	101.2
洗涤用品	Washing and Cleaning Goods	101.9	102.0	101.2	100.3	100.4	101.9
其他日用品	Other Daily-use Goods	97.4	98.7	101.0	100.0	100.3	100.4
体育娱乐用品	**Sports and Entertainment Goods**	**94.0**	**99.4**	**98.5**	**100.0**	**100.3**	**98.6**
体育用品	Sports Articles	99.6	99.0	99.2	100.1	100.5	97.6
娱乐用品	Recreational Articles	89.3	99.9	97.9	100.0	100.0	99.8
交通、通信用品	**Traffic and Telecommunication Goods**	**94.8**	**94.5**	**100.3**	**99.1**	**99.0**	**95.2**
交通运输机械	Traffic and Transport Machinery	98.3	97.1	101.4	99.2	99.9	97.3
通信器材	Telecommunication Apparatus	90.2	90.5	99.4	99.0	97.9	92.1
家　具	**Furniture**	**101.9**	**95.5**	**101.3**	**100.0**	**99.7**	**99.1**
化妆品	**Cosmetics**	**99.3**	**101.0**	**102.4**	**101.9**	**99.9**	**101.9**
金银珠宝	**Gold and Silver Jewelry**	**107.6**	**112.0**	**112.9**	**115.3**	**105.7**	**106.5**
中西药品及医疗保健用品	**Chinese and Western Medicine, Medical-care and Healthy Goods**	**102.6**	**101.6**	**100.1**	**101.4**	**100.1**	**108.7**
医疗器具及用品	Medical-care Apparatus and Goods	97.7	117.2	111.1	100.0	104.9	112.9
中药材及中成药	Chinese Herbs and Patent Medicine	109.0	104.8	96.5	104.0	96.3	119.7
西　药	Western Medicine	100.8	99.4	102.4	100.8	101.4	100.7
保健品及器具	Healthy Devices and Goods	100.0	100.2	99.9	99.9	99.2	103.1
书报杂志及电子出版物	**Books, Magazines and Electronic Publications**	**104.9**	**103.9**	**101.1**	**100.8**	**101.4**	**102.3**
教材及参考书	Texts and Reference Books	115.9	100.5	102.7	100.0	101.0	107.3
书报杂志	Newspapers and Magazines	100.3	111.1	99.8	102.3	104.8	100.0
电子音像制品	Electronic Audio and Video Products	103.2	97.6	100.0	100.0	97.5	94.0
燃　料	**Fuels**	**106.8**	**118.2**	**115.2**	**110.4**	**106.6**	**105.3**
煤炭及制品	Coal and Its Products	100.0	106.5	94.3	105.8	100.7	96.2
石油及制品	Oil and Its Products	107.3	123.7	118.5	111.4	110.0	110.6
建筑材料及五金电料	**Building Apparatus, Hardwares and Electrical Apparatus**	**100.0**	**102.6**	**101.3**	**100.9**	**102.9**	**102.8**
建筑装璜材料	Building Decoration Materials	100.8	103.1	102.8	101.3	104.3	102.5
五金电料	Hardwares and Electrical Apparatus	97.3	100.4	96.1	100.0	100.4	103.6

Continued

(preceding year=100)

昌吉市 Changji City	库尔勒市 Korla City	阿克苏市 Aksu City	焉耆回族自治县 Yanqi Hui Autonomous County	塔城市 Tacheng [Qoqek] City	阿勒泰市 Altay City	乌苏市 Usu City	博乐市 Bole [Bortala] City	吐鲁番市 Turpan City	库车县 Kuqa County	阿图什市 Artux City	莎车县 Shache [Yarkant] County	奎屯市 Kuytun City	石河子市 Shihezi City
96.9	**101.1**	**100.0**	**99.1**	**93.5**	**100.0**	**107.3**	**103.2**	**100.0**	**98.1**	**103.2**	**99.9**	**100.0**	**94.6**
100.3	**100.4**	**103.8**	**101.2**	**100.4**	**99.8**	**102.0**	**101.3**	**100.7**	**100.6**	**100.5**	**100.9**	**101.0**	**102.2**
99.4	100.7	104.2	98.1	100.3	99.4	104.3	99.4	100.3	101.0	99.8	101.0	100.2	102.5
98.4	100.0	104.8	97.2	100.0	100.0	100.0	104.1	100.0	100.0	100.0	105.2	103.3	101.5
102.2	100.4	104.6	106.0	102.1	99.7	101.8	102.4	101.8	100.0	101.2	99.6	100.0	103.9
98.7	100.0	102.5	100.0	100.0	100.0	100.4	100.0	100.0	101.4	100.3	100.8	101.0	98.4
97.8	**100.0**	**104.4**	**100.5**	**99.8**	**100.0**	**100.0**	**100.0**	**100.0**	**100.0**	**100.2**	**100.3**	**100.4**	**99.1**
99.5	100.0	100.0	101.3	100.0	100.0	100.0	100.0	100.0	100.0	100.3	100.5	100.1	102.9
96.1	100.0	106.3	99.5	99.6	100.0	100.0	100.0	100.0	100.0	100.0	100.0	100.7	94.9
95.7	**99.5**	**97.7**	**96.4**	**99.5**	**96.2**	**100.0**	**99.2**	**98.1**	**92.3**	**93.2**	**102.7**	**96.2**	**96.6**
96.2	99.9	100.0	100.0	99.5	99.9	100.0	100.0	100.5	95.8	100.3	106.6	100.0	98.5
95.2	98.6	94.6	94.9	99.6	93.0	100.0	98.2	96.7	88.6	87.0	100.0	93.5	93.9
99.9	**101.6**	**102.6**	**110.8**	**100.0**	**100.6**	**100.0**	**100.0**	**100.0**	**100.3**	**100.0**	**104.2**	**98.2**	**96.4**
98.5	**100.3**	**100.8**	**102.1**	**100.0**	**102.4**	**100.0**	**100.4**	**100.0**	**97.0**	**99.4**	**100.3**	**100.4**	**103.0**
108.6	**107.4**	**113.0**	**112.2**	**109.3**	**114.6**	**118.1**	**118.2**	**114.0**	**136.9**	**113.9**	**125.6**	**101.7**	**111.6**
103.2	**100.9**	**101.6**	**100.4**	**107.3**	**107.4**	**91.4**	**105.7**	**102.8**	**100.1**	**102.3**	**100.2**	**100.0**	**106.7**
100.0	101.9	110.6	97.1	100.9	100.0	100.0	100.2	124.9	106.4	100.0	100.0	100.0	115.0
109.1	102.6	101.7	102.7	110.5	120.2	91.6	116.1	101.6	96.8	106.2	102.5	101.3	116.0
99.9	99.8	101.0	99.3	105.1	100.6	89.1	100.0	100.2	101.8	99.6	99.2	99.9	101.7
103.1	100.0	100.6	100.2	102.3	100.1	100.0	105.1	99.9	99.2	106.0	100.2	97.8	101.4
100.5	**103.6**	**100.3**	**102.1**	**99.7**	**100.9**	**100.0**	**99.8**	**101.0**	**105.1**	**100.0**	**100.0**	**100.3**	**101.4**
100.6	108.0	100.9	103.6	100.0	100.0	100.0	99.5	100.0	112.4	100.0	100.0	101.1	101.3
100.7	103.2	100.0	100.0	99.4	102.2	100.0	100.0	102.6	102.9	100.0	100.0	100.0	101.5
100.0	100.0	100.0	100.0	99.5	100.0	100.0	100.0	100.0	100.0	100.0	100.0	100.0	101.2
105.8	**107.2**	**123.3**	**105.5**	**110.4**	**108.3**	**106.8**	**109.7**	**112.1**	**102.2**	**111.9**	**110.6**	**115.1**	**110.2**
94.7	99.6	114.9	100.9	98.5	102.8	94.1	96.0	116.2	98.9	96.1	108.6	100.0	99.0
108.7	110.1	126.1	108.5	115.0	112.2	118.3	116.4	108.2	106.9	116.0	111.6	124.3	113.8
104.4	**102.6**	**105.3**	**102.6**	**104.5**	**101.1**	**104.0**	**103.9**	**103.5**	**106.0**	**99.3**	**112.5**	**102.2**	**102.5**
106.0	103.0	105.3	103.1	105.8	100.9	107.1	105.3	105.2	112.7	98.8	115.5	102.3	102.8
99.3	101.8	105.1	101.1	89.8	101.8	100.0	101.1	100.0	99.2	100.0	102.8	101.6	102.0

8-6 主要年份农业生产资料价格分类指数
Price Indices for Means of Agricultural Production by Category in Main Years

(上年=100) (preceding year=100)

项　目	Item	2000	2005	2010
农业生产资料价格指数	**Price Indices for Means of Agricultural Production**	**97.9**	**105.3**	**103.1**
农用手工工具	Farm Handtools	99.1	104.9	101.0
饲料类	Forage	93.5	101.3	114.0
产品畜	Commodity Animals	94.4	89.4	127.1
半机械化农具	Semi-mechanized Farm Tools	97.8	100.9	101.7
机械化农具	Mechanized Farm Machinery	97.7	102.5	100.1
化学肥料	Chemical Fertilizer	92.8	110.2	95.3
农药及农药械	Pesticide and Its Appliances	98.5	102.8	101.7
农用机油	Oil for Farm Machinery	110.3	111.0	110.1
其他农业生产资料	Other Means of Agricultural Production	98.4	105.5	100.7
农业生产服务	Service for Agriculture Production			102.0

8-7 各市县农业生产资料价格指数
Price Indices for Means of Agricultural Production in Cities and Counties

(上年=100) (2010 年) (preceding year=100)

项　目	Item	塔城市 Kashgar [Kaxgar] City	阿勒泰市 Altay City	乌苏市 Usu City	博乐市 Bole [Bortala] City	吐鲁番市 Turpan City	库车县 Kuqa County	阿图什市 Artux City	莎车县 Shache [Yarkant] County	焉耆回族自治县 Yanqi Hui Autonomous County
农业生产资料价格指数	**Price Indices for Means of Agricultural Production**	**98.0**	**101.4**	**101.5**	**103.4**	**100.8**	**101.8**	**104.4**	**104.3**	**104.8**
农用手工工具	Farm Handtools	100.0	100.0	100.0	108.0	100.0	100.0	100.0	100.0	99.2
饲料类	Forage	109.3	106.3	112.0	118.0	92.9	136.7	111.5	113.0	117.1
产品畜	Commodity Animals	127.2	103.8	101.4	113.3	110.2	88.5	119.3	152.7	108.2
半机械化农具	Semi-mechanized Farm Tools	99.4	100.0	100.0	100.0	100.0	100.0	100.0	102.9	100.0
机械化农具	Mechanized Farm Machinery	89.6	100.5	100.0	100.0	100.0	100.0	105.1	104.7	100.0
化学肥料	Chemical Fertilizer	95.9	98.3	94.5	100.5	100.5	91.1	99.5	86.5	103.9
农药及农药械	Pesticide and Its Appliances	94.9	103.2	102.3	100.4	100.0	100.0	100.0	102.6	105.7
农用机油	Oil for Farm Machinery	92.3	109.7	115.7	105.4	108.7	116.1	118.0	115.3	114.4
其他农业生产资料	Other Means of Agricultural Production	94.7	100.2	98.0	98.8	99.8	90.8	101.5	104.7	100.1
农业生产服务	Service for Agriculture Production	106.2	100.0	101.9	100.2	100.0	101.9	104.2	104.5	102.7

8-8 2007-2010 年历年房屋销售价格指数
Selling Price Indices of Houses by Period(2007-2010)

(上年=100) (preceding year=100)

项 目	Item	2007	2008	2009	2010
房屋销售价格指数	**Selling Price Indices of Houses**	**109.0**	**115.5**	**102.4**	**107.5**
新建房	Newly-built Buildings	109.9	116.1	102.9	108.0
住 宅	Residential Buildings	111.1	116.2	102.8	107.8
经济适用房	Economically Affordable Housing	110.1	112.3	99.4	99.9
普通住宅	General Residential Buildings	112.4	116.5	103.2	108.3
高档住宅	Luxury Residential Buildings	110.3	121.5	102.5	107.2
非住宅	Non-Residential Buildings	105.1	110.5	104.2	111.1

8-9 房屋销售价格指数
Selling Price Indices of Houses

(上年=100) (2010 年) (preceding year=100)

项 目	Item	一季度 First Quarter	二季度 Second Quarter	三季度 Third Quarter	四季度 Fourth Quarter
房屋销售价格指数	**Selling Price Indices of Houses**	**106.8**	**107.5**	**107.4**	**108.3**
新建房	Newly-built Buildings	107.0	108.2	108.2	108.6
住 宅	Residential Buildings	106.9	107.9	108.0	108.5
经济适用房	Economically Affordable Housing	99.5	100.0	100.0	100.0
普通住宅	General Residential Buildings	107.5	108.4	108.5	108.8
多层住宅	Multi-storey Buildings	106.5	108.5	109.9	110.8
高层住宅	High-layer Buildings	108.5	108.8	108.1	107.9
高档住宅	Luxury Residential Buildings	98.9	105.2	106.5	118.0
非住宅	Non-Residential Buildings	108.5	113.8	111.7	110.4
办公楼	Office Buildings	111.1	127.4	124.3	122.0
商业营业用房	Houses for Business Use	110.1	113.8	111.6	110.3

8-10 主要年份工业品出厂价格分类指数

Producer Price Indices for Manufactured Goods by Category in Main Years

(上年=100) (preceding year=100)

项　目	Item	2000	2005	2010
全部工业品	**Total Industrial Products**	**129.4**	**116.6**	**125.3**
轻工业	Light Industry	97.3	99.6	108.9
以农产品为原料	Using Farm Produces as Raw Materials	97.1	98.4	111.2
以非农产品为原料	Using Non-farm Produces as Raw Materials	103.5	101.9	104.6
重工业	Heavy Industry	141.8	122.5	128.7
采　掘	Mining and Quarrying	164.2	136.2	153.1
原　料	Raw Materials	114.3	114.2	114.0
加　工	Processing	98.6	104.1	105.6
生产资料	Means of Production	138.0	118.4	127.1
采　掘	Mining and Quarrying	164.0	136.0	151.9
原　料	Raw Materials	113.7	114.3	115.1
加　工	Processing	97.7	100.4	107.3
生活资料	Consumer Goods	96.6	101.3	104.1
食　品	Food	93.0	101.7	104.4
衣　着	Clothing	100.3	96.4	101.5
一般日用品	Articles for Daily Use	98.1	101.1	101.4
耐用消费品	Durable Consumer Goods	99.7	99.2	102.3
按工业部门分	**Division of Industrial Setors**			
冶金工业	Metallurgical Industry	103.9	101.9	114.4
电力工业	Power Industry	104.8	100.9	100.7
煤炭及炼焦工业	Coal and Coking Industry	98.2	109.4	104.0
石油工业	Petroleum Industry	162.2	130.5	141.6
化学工业	Chemical Industry	102.6	106.1	112.1
机械工业	Machine Manufacturing Industry	97.4	112.4	97.4
建筑材料工业	Building Materials Industry	98.4	99.4	101.1
森林工业	Timber Industry	99.7	99.9	101.7
食品工业	Food Industry	92.2	101.1	104.9
纺织工业	Textile Industry	101.8	92.1	122.8
缝纫工业	Tailoring Industry	101.7	96.3	101.5
皮革工业	Leather Industry	95.7	100.0	101.1
造纸工业	Paper Industry	98.4	102.6	127.8
文教艺术用品工业	Cultural, Educational and Handicrafts Articles	98.2	99.7	101.1
其他工业	Other Industry	98.8	104.0	107.7

8-11 主要年份原材料、燃料、动力购进价格分类指数
Purchasing Prices Indices for Raw Material, Fuels and Power by Category in Main Years

(上年=100) (preceding year=100)

项　　目	Iterm	2000	2005	2010
全部原材料价格指数	**Total of Raw Material**	**115.2**	**110.7**	**123.9**
燃料、动力类	Fuel and Power	137.9	132.0	137.6
黑色金属材料类	Ferrous Metals	100.5	113.8	105.0
#钢　材	Rolled Steel	104.8	112.9	102.5
其　他	Others	95.5	114.9	112.3
有色金属材料和电线类	Nonferrous Metals and Wire Type	112.2	108.5	139.6
化工原料类	Raw Chemistry Material	104.4	113.0	106.8
木材及纸浆类	Timber and Paper Pulp	100.5	102.0	104.0
建筑材料及非金属矿类	Building Material and Non-metal Ore	100.4	103.9	103.0
其他工业原材料及半成品类	Other Industrial Raw Material and Semi-finished Category	111.4	105.5	101.1
农副产品类	Agricultural Products	97.2	91.9	118.7
纺织原料类	Textile Raw Materials	95.2	93.0	144.2

8-12 主要年份固定资产投资价格指数
Price Indices for Investment in Fixed Assets in Main Years

(上年=100) (preceding year=100)

项　　目	Item	2000	2005	2010
固定资产投资价格指数	**Investment in Fixed Assets**	**103.6**	**102.8**	**104.6**
建筑安装工程	**Construction and Installtion**	**105.5**	**102.7**	**105.9**
人工费	Manpower Expenses	108.2	103.8	110.6
材料费	Material Expenses	104.9	102.3	104.8
#钢　材	Rolled Steel	108.3	101.7	104.4
木　材	Timber	102.2	102.5	104.8
水　泥	Cement	100.6	100.1	104.7
地方材料	Local Material	102.8	102.0	104.6
化工材料	Chemical Material	107.4	109.1	104.9
电　料	Electrical Wire	99.2	104.0	105.1
其他材料	Other Material	102.9	99.9	101.7
机械使用费	Expenses of Machine Use	104.4	102.3	103.3
设备工器具	**Purchase of Equipment,Tools and Instruments**	**97.4**	**104.8**	**100.4**
其他费用	**Others**	**103.2**	**100.0**	**105.2**

主要统计指标解释

居民消费价格指数 是反映一定时期内城乡居民所购买的生活消费品价格和服务项目价格变动趋势和程度的相对数，是对城市居民消费价格指数和农村居民消费价格指数进行综合汇总计算的结果。该指数可以观察和分析消费品的零售价格和服务价格变动对城乡居民实际生活费支出的影响程度。

商品零售价格指数 是反映一定时期内城乡商品零售价格变动趋势和程度的相对数。商品零售物价的变动直接影响到城乡居民的生活支出和国家的财政收入，影响居民购买力和市场供需的平衡，影响到消费与积累的比例关系。因此，该指数可以从一个侧面对上述经济活动进行观察和分析。

农业生产资料价格指数 指反映一定时期内农业生产资料价格变动趋势和程度的相对数。其编制目的是了解农业生产中物质资料投入价格的变动状况，服务于国民经济核算。1994年以前，农业生产资料价格指数仅仅是商品零售价格指数的一个类别，此后，从商品零售价格指数中分离出来，单独编制。

工业品出厂价格指数 是反映一定时期内全部工业产品出厂价格总水平的变动趋势和程度的相对数，包括工业企业售给本企业以外所有单位的各种产品和直接售给居民用于生活消费的产品。该指数可以观察出厂价格变动对工业总产值及增加值的影响。

原材料、燃料和动力购进价格指数 是反映工业企业作为生产投入，而从物资交易市场和能源、原材料生产企业购买原材料、燃料和动力产品时，所支付的价格水平变动趋势和程度的统计指标，是扣除工业企业物质消耗成本中的价格变动影响的重要依据

固定资产投资价格指数 是反映一定时期内固定资产投资品及费用项目的价格变动趋势和程度的相对数。固定资产投资额是由建筑安装工程投资完成额、设备工器具购置投资完成额和其他费用投资完成额三部分组成的。编制固定资产投资价格指数应首先分别编制上述三部分投资的价格指数，然后采用加权算术平均法求出固定资产投资价格总指数。

该指数可以准确地反映固定资产投资中涉及的各类投资品和取费项目价格变动趋势和变动幅度，消除按现价计算的固定资产投资指标中的价格变动因素，真实地反映固定资产投资的规模、速度、结构和效益，为国家科学地制定、检查固定资产投资计划并提高宏观调控水平，为完善国民经济核算体系提供科学的、可靠的依据。

房地产价格指数 是反映一定时期内房地产价格变动趋势和程度的相对数,包括房屋价格指数、房屋租赁价格指数、土地交易价格指数和物业管理价格指数。这四套指数的计算方法相似,均采用由下到上逐级汇总的方法。

Explanatory Notes on Main Statistical Indicators

Consumer Price Indices reflect the trend and degree of changes in prices of consumer goods and services purchased by urban households during a given period,and is a composite index derived from the urban consumer price index and the rural consumer price index. Consumer price index can be used to analyze the impact of consumer price change on actual expenditure for living cost of urban and rural residents.

Retail Price Indices reflect the trend and degree of change in retail prices of commodities during a given period. The change in retail prices of commodities directly affect the living expenses of urban and rural residents, government revenue, purchasing power of residents and the equilibrium of market supply and demand, and the ratio of consumption to accumulation. Therefore, the retail price indices are useful from an oblique perspective for observing and analyzing the changes of the above economic activities.

Price Indices for Means of Agricultural Production reflect the trend and degree of changes in the prices of the means of agricultural production during a given period. Compilation of these indices helps to understand the changes in prices of input into agricultural production and facilitate the compilation of national accounts statistics. Before 1994, price indices for means of agricultural production were a sub-category in the retail price indices for commodities, and it has been compiled separately since 1994.

Producer Price Indices for Manufactured Goods reflect the trend and degree of changes in general ex-factory prices of all manufactured goods during a given period, including sales of manufactured goods by an industrial enterprise to all units outside the enterprise, as well as sales of consumer goods to residents. It can be used to analyze the impact of ex-factory prices on gross output value and value-added of the industrial sector.

Indices of Purchasing Prices of Raw Materials,Fuels and Power reflect changes in the levels and degree of prices paid by industrial enterprises when they purchase production input such as raw materials ,fuels and power from the market or from other energy or raw materials producing enterprises,These indices provide important basis for measuring the material consumption of industrial enterprises afer removing influence of price changes.

Price Indices for Investment in Fixed Assets reflect the trend and degree of changes in prices of investment goods and projects in fixed assets during a given period. The investment in fixed assets consists of three components, namely the investment in construction and installation, the investment in purchases of equipment and instrument, and the investment in other items. Price indices for investment in fixed assets are calculated as the weighted arithmetic mean of the price indices for the three components of investment in fixed assets.

Removing the factor of price change in the aggregates of investment at current prices, this indicator shows the changes in the prices of commodities and fees involved in the investment of fixed assets, and can be used to observe the actual size, growth, structure, and efficiency of investment in fixed assets and provides reliable and scientific data for government planning, management, decisionmaking, and further improving the current national accounting system.

Price Indices for Real Estate reflect the trend and degree of changes in prices of real estate during a given period, including sale price indices for houses, price indices for renting houses, price indices for land transactions and price indices for management of properties. The methods for the compilation of these four sets of indices are similar in that they all use the bottom-up approach under which data are reported from lower level to higher level

第九篇
人民生活和社会保障

CHAPTER 9
People's Living Conditions and Social Security

简要说明
Brief Introduction

本篇资料的主要内容及来源

本篇资料反映新疆城乡人民生活现状及变化以及城镇居民社会保障情况，分为城镇居民生活和农村居民生活两部分，主要包括居民家庭基本情况、家庭收入、支出情况、主要商品购买数量及支出金额、居住状况和耐用消费品的拥有量等。

城镇居民生活状况的数据来源于国家统计局新疆调查总队城镇住户调查处。

农村居民生活状况的数据来源于国家统计局新疆调查总队农村住户调查处。

城镇居民社会保障情况数据来源于新疆维吾尔自治区人力资源和社会保障厅。

Main content and source of data

Data in this chapter show the condition of people´s livelihood in Xinjiang and social security in urban and rural, consisting of two parts on the life of urban and rural households respectively, including mainly basic condition of people´s household, income of households, income and expenditure of the household, the quantity and the expenditure on major commodities purchased, the housing condition and the possession of the durable consumer goods, etc.

Data on the livelihood of the urban residents are from the Department of Urban households Survey , NBS Survey office in Xinjiang.

Data on the livelihood of the rural residents are from the Department of Rural households Surveys, NBS Survey Office in Xinjiang

Data on social security in urban and rural are from Bureau of Human Resources and Social Security of Xinjiang Uygur Autonomous Region.

9-1 主要年份人民物质文化生活情况

People's Material and Cultural Living Conditions in Main Years

项　目	Item	1990	2000	2005	2009	2010
就 业	**Employment**					
每一农村劳动力负担人数(人)	Number of Dependents Per Laborer of Rural Household(person)	1.94	1.74	1.62	1.49	1.47
每一城镇就业者负担人数(人)	Number of Dependents Per Employee of Urban Household(person)	2.11	2.03	2.04	1.93	1.94
城镇登记失业率(%)	Registered Urban Unemployment Rate (%)	3.8	3.8	3.9	3.8	3.2
收 入	**Income of Rural and Urban Residents**					
农村居民家庭人均纯收入(元)	Annual Per capita Net Income of Rural Household (yuan)	684	1618	2482	3883	4643
农村居民家庭人均纯收入指数(1978 年=100)	Index of Annual Per capita Net Income of Rural Residents (1978=100)	574.8	1359.3	2084.0	3263.0	3901.7
城镇居民家庭人均可支配收入(元)	Annual Per capita Disposable Income of Urban Household Residents (yuan)	1314	5645	7990	12258	13644
城镇居民家庭人均可支配收入指数(1978 年=100)	Index of Annual Per capita Disposable Income of Urban Residents (1978=100)	411.8	1589.4	2483.0	3701.8	4120.0
在岗职工年平均工资(元)	Annual Average Wages of Staff and Workers (yuan)	2272	8717	15558	27753	32361
消费水平 (元)	**Annual Per capita Consumption (yuan)**					
全区居民	All Residents	796	2662	3847	5990	7276
农村居民	Rural Residents	447	1308	1884	2984	3590
城镇居民	Urban Residents	1508	5131	7311	10546	12486
储 蓄	**Savings**					
城乡居民年底储蓄存款余额(亿元)	Balance of Savings Deposit of Rural and Urban Residents (Year-end) (100 million yuan)	114.13	908.55	1816.38	3050.81	3713.47
平均每人储蓄存款余额(元)	Per capita Balance of Saving Deposit (yuan)	746	4913	9035	14129	17113
住房面积 (平方米)	**Per Capita Floor Space of Residential Buildings (sq.m)**					
农村居民人均住房面积	Per-capital Living Space in Rural Areas	14.04	17.25	21.23	23.45	24.00
城镇居民人均使用面积	Per-capital Using Space in Urban Areas	13.55	20.06	20.15	20.42	20.49
交 通	**Traffic**					
城镇每百户拥有摩托车(辆)	Number of Motorcycle per 100 Households in Urban Areas (unit)	3.22	8.53	16.04	17.31	18.53
城镇公用事业	**Public Utilities in Urban Areas**					
自来水普及率 (%)	Coverage Rate of Population with Access to Tap Water (%)	80.9	98.8	97.9	99.0	99.2
燃气普及率 (%)	Coverage Rate of Population with Access to Gas(%)	49.8	92.8	89.3	89.3	95.8
文 化	**Culture**					
城镇每百户拥有彩色电视机(台)	Number of Color TV per 100 Households in Urban Areas (set)	67.80	102.57	105.70	104.64	105.61
农村每百户拥有电视机(台)	Number of TV per 100 Households in Rural Areas (set)	33.95	91.20	96.97	101.48	101.48
广播综合人口覆盖率 (%)	Radio Coverage Rate of Population (%)	70.00	89.77	93.14	94.40	94.90
电视综合人口覆盖率 (%)	TV Coverage Rate of Population (%)	65.00	92.15	92.78	94.78	95.28
教 育	**Education**					
学龄儿童入学率(%)	Enrollment Ratio of School-Age Children (%)	97.50	97.03	98.70	99.41	99.78
每万人口中在校大学生数(人)	Number of University Students per 10 000 Population (person)	20.45	41.05	90.40	111.94	115.14
卫 生	**Public Health**					
每万人有医院、卫生院床位(张)	Number of Hospital Beds per 10 000 Population (unit)	40.5	35.7	39.7	47.5	50.4
每万人有医生数(人)	Number of Doctors per 10 000 Population (person)	22.0	24.6	21.0	21.1	22.3

注：2002 年以后的城镇人均拥有指标按城镇人口计算，以前按非农业人口计算。
Note: Per Capita Ownership is calculated on the population in cities since 2002, it was based on non-agricultural Population before 2002.

9-2 主要年份城乡居民储蓄存款年底余额和年增加额

Savings Deposit of Urban and Rural Households at Year-end in Main Years

单位: 亿元 (100 million yuan)

年份 Year	年底余额 Blance at Year-end			年增加额 Year-on-year Increase		
	总计 Total	定期 Time Deposits	活期 Demand Deposits	总计 Total	定期 Time Deposits	活期 Demand Deposits
1978	6.42					
1980	9.52	8.26	1.26	2.31		
1985	29.55	24.76	4.79	5.24	4.60	0.64
1990	114.13	98.04	16.09	35.68	28.72	6.96
1995	477.18	382.61	94.57	129.47	107.90	21.57
2000	908.55	653.58	254.97	83.86	22.50	61.36
2001	994.00	722.85	271.15	85.46	39.32	48.59
2002	1137.87	760.32	377.55	143.85	68.39	75.46
2003	1371.59	879.93	491.66	233.81	119.59	114.23
2004	1534.67	991.62	543.05	162.85	111.61	51.24
2005	1816.38	1170.89	645.49	281.71	179.27	102.44
2006	2035.63	1270.16	765.47	219.25	99.27	119.98
2007	2054.91	1153.18	901.73	19.29	-116.97	136.26
2008	2550.95	1047.58	1503.37	499.45	352.79	146.66
2009	3049.91	1705.40	1344.50	498.79	201.80	296.99
2010	3713.47	1913.70	1799.77	662.61	207.52	455.09

9-3 主要年份城乡居民家庭人均收入及指数

Per Capita Annual Income of Urban and Rural Households and the Related Index in Main Years

年份 Year	农村居民家庭人均纯收入 Per capita Annual Net Income of Rural Households		城镇居民家庭人均年可支配收入 Per capita Annual Disposable Income of Urban Households		农村居民家庭恩格尔系数(%) Engel's Coefficient of Rural Households (%)	城镇居民家庭恩格尔系数(%) Engel's Coefficient of Urban Households (%)
	绝对数(元) Value (yuan)	指数(1978=100) Index	绝对数(元) Value (yuan)	指数(1978=100) Index		
1978	119	100.0	319	100.0		
1980	201	168.9	427	133.9	60.8	57.3
1985	394	331.1	735	230.4	57.9	46.8
1990	684	574.8	1314	411.8	53.7	47.8
1995	1137	955.5	4163	1172.3	50.1	44.8
2000	1618	1359.3	5645	1589.4	50.0	36.4
2001	1710	1437.0	6215	1749.9	50.4	34.8
2002	1863	1564.9	6554	1979.1	49.0	33.9
2003	2106	1768.3	7006	2115.7	45.5	35.9
2004	2245	1885.0	7503	2265.9	45.2	36.1
2005	2482	2084.0	7990	2412.9	41.8	36.4
2006	2737	2300.0	8871	2679.0	39.9	35.5
2007	3183	2674.8	10313	3114.5	39.9	35.1
2008	3503	2943.7	11432	3452.4	42.5	37.3
2009	3883	3263.0	12258	3701.8	41.6	36.3
2010	4643	3901.7	13644	4120.0	40.3	36.2

注: 1992 年以前城镇居民人均年可支配收入为人均年生活费收入。

Note: Per capita disposal income of urban households before the year 1992 is Per capita annual income as life expense.

9-4 主要年份城镇居民家庭生活基本情况
Basic Living Conditions of Urban Households in Main Years

(抽样调查 Sampled Survey)

项　　目	Item	1990	2000	2005	2009	2010
调查户数（户）	**Number of Households Surveyed (household)**	**590**	**790**	**1380**	**1560**	**1560**
平均每户家庭人口(人)	**Average Household Size (person)**	**3.92**	**3.15**	**3.02**	**2.99**	**2.98**
平均每户就业人口(人)	**Average Number of Employed Persons Per Household (person)**	**1.86**	**1.55**	**1.48**	**1.55**	**1.54**
平均每户就业面（%）	**Proportion of Employment per Household (%)**	**47.45**	**49.21**	**49.01**	**51.84**	**51.68**
平均每一就业者负担人数（包括就业者本人)(人)	**Number of Dependents Per Employee (including the employee himself or herself) (person)**	**2.11**	**2.03**	**2.04**	**1.93**	**1.94**
平均每人全部年收入(元)	**Per Capita Annual Income (yuan)**	**1432.38**	**5686.52**	**8693.67**	**13602.18**	**15421.59**
#可支配收入	Disposable Income	1313.54	5644.86	7990.15	12257.52	13643.77
工资性收入	Income from Wages and Salaries	1166.64	4128.29	6553.47	10232.91	11327.91
工资及补贴收入	Salary & Subsidy	1146.15	4027.36	6331.74	10139.46	11208.19
其他劳动收入	Part-time Income	20.49	100.93	221.73	93.45	119.72
经营净收入	Net Business Income	21.75	230.29	522.14	974.62	1131.78
财产性收入	Income from Porperties	8.81	38.03	54.51	115.77	151.94
转移性收入	Income from Transfer	235.18	1243.55	1563.54	2278.88	2809.96
平均每人消费性支出(元)	**Per Capita Annual Consumption Expenditures (yuan)**	**1104.42**	**4422.92**	**6207.52**	**9327.55**	**10197.09**
平均每人消费性支出构成(%)（人均消费支出=100)	**Composition of Per Capita Annual Consumption (%)**	**100**	**100**	**100**	**100**	**100**
食　品	Food	47.78	36.38	36.37	36.30	36.23
衣　着	Clothing	15.59	13.05	13.31	14.55	14.84
家庭设备用品及服务	Household Facilities,Articles and Service	11.01	9.29	4.99	5.92	6.57
医疗保健	Health Care and Medical Service	2.48	7.48	8.04	7.34	6.94
交通通讯	Transport and Communication	1.62	7.48	12.20	12.85	12.32
教育文化娱乐服务	Education , Cultural and Recreation Services	11.22	13.58	11.94	9.17	9.93
居　住	Residence	4.64	7.76	9.21	9.19	8.81
其他商品和服务	Miscellaneous Goods and Services	5.66	4.98	3.94	4.68	4.36

9-5 城镇居民家庭基本情况
Basic Conditions of Urban Households

(2010 年) (抽样调查 Sampled Survey)

项 目	Item	全 区 Whole Region	最低收入户 Lowest Income Households	#困难户 Poor Households	低收入户 Low Income Households
调查户数(户)	Number of Households Surveyed (household)	1560	156	78	156
比重(%)	Proportion (%)	100	10	5	10
平均每户家庭人口(人)	Average Household Size (person)	2.98	3.70	4.01	3.21
平均每户就业人口(人)	Average Number of Employees per Household (person)	1.54	1.23	1.16	1.43
平均每户就业面(%)	Proportion of Employment per Household (%)	51.68	33.24	28.93	44.55
平均每一就业者负担人数(包括就业者本人)(人)	Number of Dependents per Employee (Including the employee himself or herself) (person)	1.93	3.01	3.46	2.24
平均每人全部年收入(元)	Per Capita Annual Income (yuan)	15421.59	4658.33	3644.5	8350.93
平均每人可支配收入(元)	Per Capita Disposable Income (yuan)	13643.77	3922.06	3090.54	7159.58
平均每人消费性支出(元)	Per Capita Annual Consumption Expenditure (yuan)	10197.09	4243.09	3534.74	6408.72

项 目	Item	中等偏下户 Lower Middle Income Households	中等收入户 Middle Income Households	中等偏上户 Upper Middle Income Households	高收入户 High Income Households	最高收入户 Highest Income Households
调查户数(户)	Number of Households Surveyed (household)	312	312	312	156	156
比重(%)	Proportion (%)	20	20	20	10	10
平均每户家庭人口(人)	Average Household Size (person)	3.13	3.05	2.81	2.53	2.22
平均每户就业人口(人)	Average Number of Employees per Household (person)	1.58	1.74	1.71	1.32	1.41
平均每户就业面(%)	Proportion of Employed Persons per Household (%)	50.48	57.05	60.85	52.17	63.51
平均每一就业者负担人数(包括就业者本人)(人)	Number of Dependents per Employee (Including the employee himself or herself) (person)	1.98	1.75	1.64	1.92	1.57
平均每人全部年收入(元)	Per Capita Annual Income (yuan)	11444.68	15472.47	19931.63	25697.86	36943.26
平均每人可支配收入(元)	Per Capita Disposable Income (yuan)	9931.05	13593.46	17727.84	23008.35	33810.81
平均每人消费性支出(元)	Per Capita Annual Consumption Expenditure (yuan)	8069.31	10395.39	13155.58	15106.19	20738.02

9-6 城镇居民家庭平均每人全年消费性支出

Per Capita Annual Living Expenditure of Urban Households

单位：元　　(2010 年) (抽样调查　Sampled Survey)　　(yuan)

项目	Item	总平均 Total Average	最低收入户 Lowest Income Households	#困难户 Poor Households	低收入户 Low Income Households
消费性支出	**Consumption Expenditures**	**10197.09**	**4243.09**	**3534.74**	**6408.72**
食品	Food	3694.81	1948.69	1793.19	3048.27
#粮食	Grain	362.74	369.57	373.22	390.91
肉禽及其制品	Meat, Poultry and Processed Products	972.04	611.04	604.04	885.41
蛋类	Eggs	68.38	49.84	46.63	68.68
水产品	Aquatic Products	87.82	36.28	20.36	68.32
奶及奶制品	Milk and Processed Products	164.52	72.01	62.39	133.93
衣着	Clothing	1513.42	454.96	377.26	790.72
#服装	Garments	1073.12	287.33	235.69	521.37
家庭设备用品及服务	Household Appliances and Services	669.87	229.19	171.84	314.99
#耐用消费品	Durable Consumer Goods	259.25	50.08	30.54	73.92
医疗保健	Health Care and Medical Services	708.16	308.46	218.55	467.51
交通通讯	Transport and Communication Services	1255.87	320.94	249.14	544.07
教育文化娱乐服务	Education , Cultural and Recreation Services	1012.37	358.18	241.57	487.49
#文化娱乐用品	Recreation Articles	305.39	85.67	50.13	163.29
居住	Residence	898.38	543.85	426.63	615.48
#住房	Housing	256.17	153.27	82.48	101.18
其他商品和服务	Miscellaneous Goods and Services	444.20	78.82	56.56	140.18

项目	Item	中等偏下户 Lower Middle Income Households	中等收入户 Middle Income Households	中等偏上户 Upper Middle Income Households	高收入户 High Income Households	最高收入户 Highest Income Households
消费性支出	**Consumption Expenditures**	**8069.31**	**10395.39**	**13155.58**	**15106.19**	**20738.02**
食品	Food	3294.08	3696.18	4399.67	4839.96	6238.29
#粮食	Grain	355.75	341.25	344.27	410.74	383.83
肉禽及其制品	Meat, Poultry and Processed Products	888.54	1007.52	1087.85	1217.14	1386.27
蛋类	Eggs	63.92	68.48	70.91	85.99	91.02
水产品	Aquatic Products	77.19	80.27	115.75	124.22	159.39
奶及奶制品	Milk and Processed Products	141.71	184.40	195.01	210.50	274.70
衣着	Clothing	1094.27	1766.33	2002.99	2194.73	3274.65
#服装	Garments	753.91	1248.33	1431.90	1610.44	2447.29
家庭设备用品及服务	Household Appliances and Services	542.02	673.71	893.00	1108.91	1414.03
#耐用消费品	Durable Consumer Goods	229.90	253.80	379.89	414.55	583.17
医疗保健	Health Care and Medical Services	567.74	655.87	755.07	1420.71	1560.04
交通通讯	Transport and Communication Services	861.54	1419.08	1733.06	1933.80	2983.01
教育文化娱乐服务	Education , Cultural and Recreation Services	834.70	852.64	1478.59	1625.94	2239.04
#文化娱乐用品	Recreation Articles	220.23	294.49	490.63	456.95	594.13
居住	Residence	623.23	890.28	1204.67	1328.33	1635.67
#住房	Housing	122.00	221.28	482.90	374.81	487.65
其他商品和服务	Miscellaneous Goods and Services	251.73	441.31	688.53	653.82	1393.30

9-7 城镇居民家庭平均每人全年消费性支出构成

Composition of Per Capita Living Expenditure of Urban Households

单位：% (2010 年) (抽样调查 Sampled Survey) (%)

项目	Item	总平均 Total Average	最低收入户 Lowest Income Households	#困难户 Poor Households	低收入户 Low Income Households
消费性支出	**Consumption Expenditures**	**100**	**100**	**100**	**100**
食品	Food	36.23	45.93	50.73	47.56
衣着	Clothing	14.84	10.72	10.67	12.34
家庭设备用品及服务	Household Facilities, Articles and Services	6.57	5.40	4.86	4.92
医疗保健	Health Care and Medical Services	6.94	7.27	6.18	7.29
交通通讯	Transport and Communication Services	12.32	7.56	7.05	8.49
教育文化娱乐服务	Education , Cultural and Recreation Services	9.93	8.44	6.83	7.61
居住	Residence	8.81	12.82	12.07	9.60
其他商品和服务	Miscellaneous Goods and Services	4.36	1.86	1.60	2.19

项目	Item	中等偏下户 Lower Middle Income Households	中等收入户 Middle Income Households	中等偏上户 Upper Middle Income Households	高收入户 High Income Households	最高收入户 Highest Income Households
消费性支出	**Consumption Expenditures**	**100**	**100**	**100**	**100**	**100**
食品	Food	40.82	35.56	33.44	32.04	30.08
衣着	Clothing	13.56	16.99	15.23	14.53	15.79
家庭设备用品及服务	Household Facilities, Articles and Services	6.72	6.48	6.79	7.34	6.82
医疗保健	Health Care and Medical Services	7.04	6.31	5.74	9.40	7.52
交通通讯	Transport and Communication Services	10.68	13.65	13.17	12.80	14.38
教育文化娱乐服务	Education , Cultural and Recreation Services	10.34	8.20	11.24	10.76	10.80
居住	Residence	7.72	8.56	9.16	8.79	7.89
其他商品和服务	Miscellaneous Goods and Services	3.12	4.25	5.23	4.33	6.72

9-8 主要年份城镇居民家庭年人均购买的主要商品数量

Per Capita Annual Purchases of Major Commodities of Urban Households in Main Years

(抽样调查 Sampled Survey)

项 目	Item	1990	2000	2005	2009	2010
粮食(千克)	Grain (kg)	139.73	81.91	88.38	59.83	89.76
鲜菜(千克)	Fresh Vegetables (kg)	132.96	90.56	109.45	100.44	96.15
食用植物油(千克)	Edible Vegetable Oil (kg)	10.09	9.69	11.01	11.35	10.94
猪肉(千克)	Pork (kg)	5.56	5.17	6.37	7.19	7.33
牛肉(千克)	Beef (kg)	13.51	3.62	3.51	3.56	3.86
羊肉(千克)	Mutton(kg)		13.06	11.99	11.28	9.87
家禽(千克)	Poultry (kg)	2.12	6.11	6.71	5.88	8.14
鲜蛋(千克)	Fresh Eggs (kg)	4.46	7.39	7.44	7.61	7.91
水产品(千克)	Aquatic Products (kg)	3.73	4.35	4.98	4.83	5.27
鲜乳品(千克)	Fresh Dairy Products (kg)	12.70	18.44	26.26	24.19	21.80
鲜瓜果(千克)	Fresh Fruits & Melons(kg)	59.47	64.31	66.99	62.84	57.36
服装(件)	Clothes(piece)	2.12	6.36	7.51	8.10	8.60
罐装液化石油气(千克)	Liquefied Petrolum Gas (kg)	11.40	24.77	15.62	9.37	10.03
管道天然气(立方米)	Natural Gas (cu.m)		1.93	22.12	38.27	39.68
煤炭(千克)	Coal (kg)	90.10	123.78	133.57	84.11	84.07

注: 2009 年粮食购买量仅指面粉和大米，不包括其他粮食及制品。
Note: In 2009 purchase of grain only refer to flour and rice, does not include miscellaneous grain and processed products.

9-9 主要年份城镇居民家庭平均每百户年底耐用消费品拥有量

Number of Major Durable Consumer Goods Owned Per-100 Urban Households at Year-end in Main Years

项 目	Item	1990	2000	2005	2009	2010
摩托车(辆)	Motorcycle (unit)	3.22	8.53	16.04	17.31	18.53
家用汽车(辆)	Automobil (unit)		0.82	2.81	7.61	8.63
家用电脑(台)	Household Computer (set)		5.68	23.86	45.19	47.68
组合音响(套)	Hi-Fi Stereo Component System (set)	0.51	17.53	16.10	14.97	15.06
摄相机(架)	Pickug Camera (set)		1.02	3.12	4.28	4.57
钢琴(架)	Piano (set)		1.38	2.23	2.23	2.04
其他中高档乐器(件)	Other Medium and High Grade Musical Instrument (piece)	11.53	9.09	5.97	6.63	6.54
微波炉(台)	Oven (unit)		5.39	19.68	33.76	34.84
空调器(台)	Air Conditioner (unit)	0.17	2.78	7.02	11.22	12.42
淋浴热水器(台)	Shower (unit)		47.91	59.58	72.55	74.27
消毒碗柜(台)	Disinfectant Machine (unit)			4.56	4.05	3.80
健身器材(台)	Healthy Equipment (unit)		2.35	3.89	2.44	2.65
固定电话(部)	Telephone (unit)		71.69	87.23	82.80	82.42
移动电话(部)	Mobile phone (unit)		4.81	108.61	154.47	159.79
洗衣机(台)	Washing Machine (unit)	79.66	95.48	88.53	93.57	93.43
电冰箱(台)	Refrigerator (unit)	32.20	81.76	79.72	89.75	90.20
彩色电视机(台)	Color TV Set (set)	67.80	102.57	105.70	104.64	105.61
照相机(架)	Camera (set)	20.00	33.71	37.42	26.29	26.83

9-10 按收入等级分城镇居民家庭平均每人全年购买商品数量
Per Capita Annual Purchases of Major Commodities of Urban Households by Level of Income

(2010 年) (抽样调查 Sampled Survey)

项目	Item	总平均 Total Average	最低收入户 Lowest Income Households	#困难户 Poor Households	低收入户 Low Income Households
粮 食(千克)	Grain (kg)	89.76	106.06	114.73	99.17
食用植物油(千克)	Edible Vegetable Oil (kg)	10.94	11.17	12.04	11.74
猪 肉(千克)	Pork (kg)	7.33	3.75	2.62	6.90
牛 肉(千克)	Beef (kg)	3.86	1.91	1.16	3.50
羊 肉(千克)	Mutton (kg)	9.87	8.98	11.15	9.86
家 禽(千克)	Poultry (kg)	8.14	3.64	2.82	6.88
鲜 蛋(千克)	Fresh Eggs (kg)	7.91	6.25	5.91	8.28
鱼 (千克)	Fish (kg)	4.17	2.07	1.15	3.76
虾 (千克)	Shrimp (kg)	0.42	0.13	0.07	0.34
鲜 菜(千克)	Fresh Vegetables (kg)	96.15	80.35	71.61	97.27
白 酒(千克)	Liquor (kg)	1.12	0.37	0.16	0.98
果 酒(千克)	Fruit Wine (kg)	0.20	0.05	0.04	0.19
啤 酒(千克)	Beer (kg)	2.05	0.69	0.24	1.91
鲜瓜果(千克)	Fresh Melons & Fruits (kg)	57.36	32.47	27.39	55.18
糕 点(千克)	Cake (kg)	4.01	1.91	1.74	2.77
鲜乳品(千克)	Fresh Dairy Products (kg)	21.80	11.56	10.57	21.59
奶 粉(千克)	Milk Powder (kg)	0.23	0.08	0.07	0.10
酸 奶(千克)	Yogurt (kg)	3.38	1.37	1.26	2.54
服 装(件)	Clothing (piece)	8.60	4.25	3.81	6.30

项目	Item	中等偏下户 Lower Middle Income Households	中等收入户 Middle Income Households	中等偏上户 Upper Middle Income Households	高收入户 High Income Households	最高收入户 Highest Income Households
粮 食(千克)	Grain (kg)	85.79	84.87	82.29	94.32	84.49
食用植物油(千克)	Edible Vegetable Oil (kg)	10.92	11.05	10.15	11.77	10.07
猪 肉(千克)	Pork (kg)	8.39	6.21	8.82	8.93	9.09
牛 肉(千克)	Beef (kg)	3.46	3.77	4.85	5.29	5.49
羊 肉(千克)	Mutton (kg)	8.12	12.14	8.48	10.96	13.13
家 禽(千克)	Poultry (kg)	7.52	7.53	11.74	10.02	10.71
鲜 蛋(千克)	Fresh Eggs (kg)	7.62	8.06	7.93	9.00	9.80
鱼 (千克)	Fish (kg)	4.01	3.97	5.21	5.16	6.01
虾 (千克)	Shrimp (kg)	0.33	0.40	0.56	0.62	0.79
鲜 菜(千克)	Fresh Vegetables (kg)	97.2	87.27	98.47	117.95	116.78
白 酒(千克)	Liquor (kg)	0.91	1.13	1.54	1.76	1.67
果 酒(千克)	Fruit Wine (kg)	0.07	0.21	0.25	0.37	0.56
啤 酒(千克)	Beer (kg)	1.76	2.60	2.34	2.20	3.21
鲜瓜果(千克)	Fresh Melons & Fruits (kg)	54.33	69.57	66.85	68.98	81.41
糕 点(千克)	Cake (kg)	3.55	4.33	4.97	5.71	6.06
鲜乳品(千克)	Fresh Dairy Products (kg)	20.89	21.49	23.19	28.13	35.09
奶 粉(千克)	Milk Powder (kg)	0.10	0.49	0.30	0.21	0.22
酸 奶(千克)	Yogurt (kg)	2.73	3.71	4.53	4.22	5.72
服 装(件)	Clothing (piece)	7.06	10.24	10.53	10.81	13.20

9-11 按收入等级分城镇居民家庭平均每百户年底耐用消费品拥有量

Ownership of Durable Consumer Goods Per100 Urban Households at Year-end by Level of Income

(2010 年)(抽样调查 Sampled Survey)

项目	Item	总平均 Total Average	最低收入户 Lowest Income Households	#困难户 Poor Households	低收入户 Low Income Households
摩托车(辆)	Motorcycle(unit)	18.53	14.42	21.33	14.68
家用汽车(辆)	Automobile(unit)	8.63	2.90	5.54	2.45
洗衣机(台)	Washing Machine (unit)	93.43	78.69	74.33	88.80
电冰箱(台)	Refrigerator (unit)	90.20	59.18	50.40	85.71
彩色电视机(台)	Color TV (set)	105.61	99.56	97.34	103.65
家用电脑(台)	Household Computer (set)	47.68	16.78	13.68	21.12
组合音响(套)	Hi-Fi Stereo Sound System (set)	15.06	5.54	7.23	7.32
摄像机(架)	Pickup Camera (set)	4.57	1.56	1.49	1.01
照相机(架)	Camera (set)	26.83	7.96	8.53	14.57
钢　琴(架)	Piano (set)	2.04			0.78
中高档乐器(件)	Other Medium and High Grade Musical Instrument (piece)	6.54	0.97		3.18
微波炉(台)	Microwave Oven (unit)	34.84	5.44	4.06	15.96
空调器(台)	Air Conditioner (unit)	12.42	2.06	1.79	1.62
淋浴热水器(台)	Water Heater for Shower (unit)	74.27	29.97	23.49	54.08
健身器材(件)	Health Equipment (unit)	2.65	0.19		
固定电话(部)	Fixed Telephone (unit)	82.42	73.98	74.76	80.29
移动电话(部)	Mobile Telephone (unit)	159.79	77.77	58.38	123.48

项目	Item	中等偏下户 Lower Middle Income Households	中等收入户 Middle Income Households	中等偏上户 Upper Middle Income Households	高收入户 High Income Households	最高收入户 Highest Income Households
摩托车(辆)	Motorcycle(unit)	17.08	27.02	21.58	14.25	10.12
家用汽车(辆)	Automobile(unit)	6.24	11.14	8.30	12.15	19.91
洗衣机(台)	Washing Machine (unit)	93.23	94.21	96.46	98.33	103.35
电冰箱(台)	Refrigerator (unit)	89.06	92.32	94.54	102.68	107.73
彩色电视机(台)	Color TV (set)	106.37	106.43	103.09	110.50	112.14
家用电脑(台)	Household Computer (set)	44.74	50.42	61.41	61.60	71.80
组合音响(套)	Hi-Fi Stereo Sound System (set)	14.34	16.44	16.03	23.51	23.30
摄相机(架)	Pickup Camera (set)	5.11	4.98	5.63	4.18	8.26
照相机(架)	Camera (set)	22.83	25.44	31.8	46.29	44.84
钢　琴(架)	Piano (set)	1.66	1.61	2.00	4.57	5.32
中高档乐器(件)	Other Medium and High Grade Musical Instrument (piece)	5.76	7.16	8.47	7.92	11.88
微波炉(台)	Microwave Oven (unit)	31.82	33.77	44.09	50.19	65.20
空调器(台)	Air Conditioner (unit)	11.06	8.77	13.44	29.71	28.60
淋浴热水器(台)	Water Heater for Shower (unit)	74.53	81.24	89.00	85.13	90.77
健身器材(件)	Health Equipment (unit)	1.11	0.65	2.92	6.34	12.33
固定电话(部)	Fixed Telephone (unit)	84.36	79.65	83.07	91.42	85.85
移动电话(部)	Mobile Telephone (unit)	162.30	182.98	176.54	172.91	192.51

9-12 主要年份农村居民家庭基本情况
Basic Conditions of Rural Households in Main Years

(抽样调查 Sampled Survey)

项 目	Item	1990	2000	2005	2010
调查户数(户)	**Number of Households Surveyed(household)**	**1240**	**1500**	**1550**	**1550**
调查户人口(人)	**Number of Residents Surveyed (person)**	**6659**	**7999**	**7315**	**7169**
平均每户常住人口	Average Number of Permanent Residents per Household	5.37	5.33	4.72	4.63
平均每户整半劳动力	Average Number of Full/semi Labour Fource per Household	2.76	3.06	2.92	3.14
平均每个劳动力负担人口(含本人)	Average Number of Dependents per Labour Force (Including the laborer himself and herself)	1.94	1.74	1.62	1.47
户均经营耕地面积(亩)	Per Household Area of Cultivated Land Managed(mu)	21.80	22.39	19.16	22.02
平均每人经营耕地面积(亩)	Per Capita Area of Cultivated Land Managed(mu)	4.06	4.20	4.11	4.76
年内每户新建房屋面积(平方米)	Space of Rooms per Household Newly Built Within the Year (sq.m)	4.18	2.03	6.45	3.68
年底人均居住面积(平方米)	Per Capita Net Living Rooms Space in Rural Area (sq.m)	14.04	17.25	21.13	24.00
平均每人年收入(元)	**Per Capita Annual Income(yuan)**				
总收入	Total Income	1112.01	3129.35	4604.9	8806.87
工资性收入	Income from Wages and Salaries	56.53	104.58	195.51	556.26
家庭经营收入	Income from Household Operations	1034.69	2926.75	4252.96	7795.26
财产性收入	Income from Properties		40.42	33.87	126.53
转移性收入	Income from Transfers	20.79	57.60	122.56	328.82
现金收入	Cash Income	830.88	2444.30	3921.17	7517.22
工资性收入	Income from Wages and Salaries	55.50	104.46	195.51	556.26
家庭经营收入	Income from Household Operations	750.34	2245.31	3580.44	6525.27
财产性收入	Income from Properties		37.87	22.84	106.87
转移性收入	Income from Transfers	25.04	56.66	122.38	328.82
平均每人年支出(元)	**Per Capita Annual Expenditures(yuan)**				
总支出	Total Expenditure	971.46	2819.77	4302.26	8241.28
家庭经营费用支出	Expenditure for Household Operations	325.97	1198.23	1928.63	3800.24
购置生产性固定资产	Purchase of Productive Fixed Assets	57.71	115.19	258.79	568.14
税费支出	Taxes and Fees	62.07	177.24	14.36	7.83
生活消费支出	Expenditure on Household Consumption	506.82	1236.45	1924.41	3458.14
转移性和财产性支出	Expenditure for Transfer and Property	18.89	92.66	176.07	406.93
现金支出	Cash Expenditure	716.73	2353.45	3855.34	7464.48
家庭经营费用支出	Expenditure for Household Operations	236.36	1100.43	1823.95	3643.29
购置生产性固定资产	Purchase of Productive Fixed Assets	57.71	115.19	258.79	568.14
税费支出	Taxes and Fees	58.19	177.22	14.36	7.83
生活消费支出	Expenditure on Household Consumption	333.88	871.37	1582.17	2838.29
转移性和财产性支出	Expenditure for Transfer and Property	30.59	89.24	176.07	406.93
平均每人年纯收入(元)	**Per Capita Annual Net Income (yuan)**	**683.47**	**1618.08**	**2482.15**	**4642.67**
工资性收入	Income from Wages and Salaries	56.53	104.58	195.51	556.26
家庭经营纯收入	Income from Household Business	612.70	1451.33	2140.76	3649.98
财产性收入	Income from Properties		40.43	33.87	126.52
转移性收入	Income from Transfers	14.24	21.74	112.01	309.91

9-13 农村居民家庭人均年总收入、纯收入和构成

Per Capita Annual Gross and Net Income and Its Composition of Rural Households

单位：元　　(抽样调查 Sampled Survey)　　(yuan)

项　目	Item	2009	2010	构成(%) Composition 2009	构成(%) Composition 2010
全年总收入	**Annual Gross Income**	**7269.49**	**8806.87**	**100**	**100**
工资性收入	Income from Wages and Salaries	461.49	556.26	6.35	6.32
家庭经营收入	Income from Household Operations	6444.07	7795.26	88.64	88.51
财产性收入	Income from Transfers	121.26	126.53	1.67	1.44
转移性收入	Income from Properties	242.67	328.82	3.34	3.73
全年总支出	**Annual Gross Expenditure**	**6847.48**	**8241.28**	**100**	**100**
#家庭经营费用支出	Expenditure for Household Business	3100.89	3800.24	45.29	46.11
生活消费支出	Expenditure for Consumption	2950.63	3458.14	43.09	41.96
全年纯收入	**Annual Net Income**	**3883.1**	**4642.67**	**100**	**100**
基本纯收入	Basic Net Income	3531.06	4206.24	90.94	90.60
转移性纯收入	Income from Transfers	230.78	309.91	5.94	6.68
财产性纯收入	Income from Properties	121.26	126.52	3.12	2.73

9-14 主要年份农村居民家庭平均每人总收入和纯收入

Per Capita Annual Gross and Net Income of Rural Households in Main Years

单位：元　　(抽样调查 Sampled Survey)　　(yuan)

项　目	Item	1990	2000	2009	2010
总 收 入	**Gross Income**	**1112.01**	**3129.35**	**7269.49**	**8806.87**
基本收入	Basic Income	1091.22	3031.33	6905.56	8351.52
工资性收入	Income from Wages and Salaries	56.53	104.58	461.49	556.26
家庭经营收入	Income from Household Operations	1034.69	2926.75	6444.07	7795.26
转移性和财产性收入	Income from Transfers and Properties	20.79	98.02	363.93	455.35
纯收入	**Net Income**	**683.47**	**1618.08**	**3883.10**	**4642.67**
基本收入	Basic Income	669.23	1555.91	3531.06	4206.24
工资性收入	Income from Wages and Salaries	56.53	104.58	461.49	556.26
家庭经营纯收入	Income from Household Operations	612.70	1451.33	3069.57	3649.98
农业收入	Farming	541.84	1109.39	2141.05	2670.60
林业收入	Forestry	8.80	22.51	132.01	172.01
牧业收入	Animal Husbandry	25.39	171.18	517.83	469.08
工业收入	Industry	1.05	6.35	22.42	34.65
建筑业收入	Construction	2.51	4.31	18.12	22.71
交通、运输和邮电业收入	Transportation, Post and Telecommunications Services	12.29	26.48	69.33	94.88
批发和零售贸易业、饮食业收入	Wholesale, Retail Trades and Catering Services	14.13	23.80	101.14	128.47
社会服务业收入	Services Trades	4.17	15.01	17.33	22.70
文教卫生业收入	Cultural, Education, Medicines and Medical Services			10.19	10.53
其他行业收入	Others	2.52	72.30	40.15	24.36
转移性和财产性收入	Income from Transfers and Properties	14.24	62.17	352.04	436.43

9-15 主要年份农村居民家庭人均主要消费品消费量

Per Capita Consumption of Major Consumer Goods of Rural Households in Main Years

单位:公斤 (抽样调查 Sampled Survey) (kg)

项　目	Item	1990	1995	2000	2005	2010
粮食(原粮)	Grain(Unprocessed)	249.71	206.68	244.83	235.66	236.10
#小 麦	Wheat	201.37	162.52	199.83	188.38	191.28
稻 谷	Rice	13.39	8.44	15.19	19.93	23.20
豆类及豆制品	Soybeans and Processed Products		0.10	0.50	0.60	0.56
蔬　菜	Fresh Vegetable	121.56	64.02	89.24	67.89	77.72
食　油	Edible Oil	7.87	6.38	9.64	10.90	10.74
#植物油	Vegetable Oil	7.41	6.14	9.56	10.79	10.69
肉禽及制品	Meats,Poultry and Processed Products	9.02	8.11	12.41	14.31	15.38
#猪 肉	Pork	2.25	1.58	1.95	0.67	1.04
牛 肉	Beef	6.77	2.09	1.95	2.56	2.32
羊 肉	Mutton		3.22	7.03	8.99	9.18
家 禽	Poultry	0.90	1.00	1.36	1.70	2.27
蛋及制品	Eggs and Processed Products	1.77	0.80	1.20	1.00	1.92
食　糖	Sugar	0.63	0.51	0.42	0.45	0.49
酒	Liquor	1.04	0.92	1.12	1.27	1.06
水果及制品	Fruits and Processed Products	41.94	21.78	46.89	34.81	25.30
茶　叶	Tea	5.96	0.56	0.37	0.45	0.43

9-16 主要年份农村居民家庭平均每百户耐用消费品拥有量

Number of Durable Consumer Goods Owned by Per100 Rural Households in Main Years

(抽样调查 Sampled Survey)

项　目	Item	1990	1995	2000	2005	2010
洗衣机(台)	Washing Machine (unit)	12.58	16.39	20.87	28.26	47.94
电冰箱(台)	Refrigerator (unit)	0.40	2.26	9.93	20.13	43.48
空调机(台)	Air Conditioner (unit)				0.39	0.65
抽油烟机(台)	Exhaust Fan(unit)		0.13	1.13	1.23	2.77
自行车(辆)	Bicycle (unit)	111.21	151.29	136.60	80.97	78.52
摩托车(辆)	Motorcycle (unit)	1.37	4.90	18.33	45.42	62.84
电话机(部)	Telephone(unit)			15.07	36.26	38.97
移动电话(部)	Mobile phone (unit)			0.33	21.29	84.32
黑白电视机(台)	Black and White TV (set)	28.79	55.03	59.33	35.16	11.61
彩色电视机(台)	Color TV (set)	5.16	14.39	31.87	61.81	89.87
照像机(架)	Camera (set)	0.73	1.16	2.20	3.23	3.29
影碟机(台)	Video Disc Player (set)			3.60		31.94
微波炉(台)	Microwave Oven (unit)					1.81

9-17 农村居民人均生活消费支出及构成
Composition of Per Capita Living Expendture of Rural Households

单位：元 (抽样调查 Sampled Survey) (yuan)

项目	Item	2009	2010	构成(%) Composition(%) 2009	构成(%) Composition(%) 2010
生活消费支出	**Expenditure for Consumption**	**2950.63**	**3458.14**	**100**	**100**
食　品	Food	1225.93	1394.65	41.55	40.33
#主　食	Staple Food	407.32	432.02	13.80	12.49
副食及其他食品	Non-staple Food and others	697.42	830.25	23.64	24.01
衣　着	Clothing	261.26	303.66	8.85	8.78
居　住	Residence	514.72	695.17	17.44	20.10
家庭设备、用品及服务	Household Facilities,Articles and Services	107.28	137.69	3.64	3.98
医疗保健	Health Care and Medical Services	316.55	314.73	10.73	9.10
交通和通讯	Transport and Communications	319.39	382.14	10.82	11.05
文教娱乐用品及服务	Cultural, Education ,Recreation and Services	158.13	170.15	5.36	4.92
其他商品和服务	Other Commodities and Services	47.37	59.94	1.61	1.73

9-18 农村居民家庭平均每百户耐用消费品拥有量
Number of Durable Consumer Goods Owned by Per100 Rural Households

(抽样调查 Sampled Survey)

项目	Item	2009	2010
自行车(辆)	Bicycle (unit)	80.39	78.52
黑白电视机(台)	Black and White TV (set)	17.87	11.61
彩色电视机(台)	Color TV (set)	83.61	89.87
抽油烟机(台)	Exhaust Fan(unit)	1.55	2.77
照像机(架)	Camera (set)	3.94	3.29
移动电话(部)	Mobile phone (unit)	73.35	84.32
洗衣机(台)	Washing Machine (unit)	42.71	47.94
电冰箱(台)	Refrigerator (unit)	36.26	43.48
摩托车(辆)	Motorcycle (unit)	56.32	62.84
影碟机(台)	Video Disc Player (set)	27.10	31.94
微波炉(台)	Microwave Oven (unit)	1.74	1.81

9-19 农村居民家庭人均商品性和自给性生活消费品支出

Per Capita Self-Sufficiency and Consumption on Commodity Goods of Living Expenditure in Rural Households

(抽样调查 Sampled Survey)

项目	Item	2009			2010		
		合计 Total	货币性 In Money	实物性 In Kind	合计 Total	货币性 In Money	实物性 In Kind
生活消费支出合计(元/人)	**Expenditure for Consumption (yuan/person)**	**2950.63**	**2459.08**	**491.55**	**3458.14**	**2838.29**	**619.85**
食品	Food	1225.93	759.88	466.05	1394.65	850.35	544.30
衣着	Clothing	261.26	257.25	4.01	303.66	301.17	2.49
居住	Residence	514.72	495.79	18.93	695.17	625.91	69.26
家庭设备、用品及服务	Household Appliances and Services	107.28	104.72	2.56	137.69	133.90	3.79
医疗保健	Health Care and Medical Services	316.55	316.55		314.73	314.73	
交通和通讯	Transportation and Communications	319.39	319.39		382.14	382.14	
文教娱乐用品及服务	Cultural, Education and Recreational Articles and Services	158.13	158.13		170.15	170.15	
其他商品和服务	Other Commodities and Services	47.37	47.37		59.94	59.94	
生活消费支出构成(%)	**Composition of Living Expenditures (%)**	**100**	**100**	**100**	**100**	**100**	**100**
食品	Food	41.55	30.90	94.81	40.33	29.96	87.81
衣着	Clothing	8.85	10.46	0.82	8.78	10.61	0.40
居住	Residence	17.44	20.16	3.85	20.10	22.05	11.17
家庭设备、用品及服务	Household Facilities,Articles and Services	3.64	4.26	0.52	3.98	4.72	0.61
医疗保健	Health Care and Medical Services	10.73	12.87		9.10	11.09	
交通和通讯	Transportation and Communications	10.82	12.99		11.05	13.46	
文教娱乐用品及服务	Cultural, Education and Recreational Articles and Services	5.36	6.43		4.92	5.99	
其他商品和服务	Other Commodities and Services	1.61	1.93		1.73	2.11	
生活消费支出中货币性和实物性比重(%)	**Percentage of Expenditure for Consumption in Money and Kind (%)**	**100**	**83.34**	**16.66**	**100**	**82.08**	**17.92**
食品	Food	100	61.98	38.02	100	60.97	39.03
衣着	Clothing	100	98.47	1.53	100	99.18	0.82
居住	Residence	100	96.32	3.68	100	90.04	9.96
家庭设备、用品及服务	Household Facilities,Articles and Services	100	97.61	2.39	100	97.25	2.75
医疗保健	Health Care and Medical Services	100	100		100	100	
交通和通讯	Transportation and Communications	100	100		100	100	
文教娱乐用品及服务	Cultural, Education and Recreational Articles and Services	100	100		100	100	
其他商品和服务	Other Commodities and Services	100	100		100	100	

9-20 农村居民家庭人均纯收入分组
Rural Households Grouped by Per Capita Annual Net Income

(2010 年) (抽样调查 Sampled Survey)

项 目	Item	合 计 Total	0-400 元 0-400 yuan	400-600 元 400-600 yuan	600-800 元 600-800 yuan	800-1000 元 800-1000 yuan	1000-1200 元 1000-1200 yuan
调查户数(户)	**Number of Households Surveyed (household)**	**1550**	**24**	**8**	**19**	**19**	**39**
构成(%)	Percentage (%)	100	1.55	0.52	1.23	1.23	2.52
常住人口(人)	**Number of Permanent Residents in the Households Surveyed (person)**	**7169**	**106**	**36**	**117**	**111**	**210**
构成(%)	Percentage (%)	100	1.48	0.50	1.63	1.55	2.93
人均纯收入(元)	**Per Capita Net Income (yuan)**	**4642.67**	**-1099.26**	**510.24**	**697.87**	**906.62**	**1090.95**

项 目	Item	1200-1500 元 1200-1500 yuan	1500-1700 元 1500-1700 yuan	1700-2000 元 1700-2000 yuan	2000-2500 元 2000-2500 yuan	2500-3000 元 2500-3000 yuan
调查户数(户)	**Number of Households Surveyed (household)**	**70**	**57**	**96**	**144**	**113**
构成(%)	Percentage (%)	4.52	3.68	6.19	9.29	7.29
常住人口(人)	**Number of Permanent Residents in the Households Surveyed (person)**	**367**	**294**	**502**	**733**	**558**
构成(%)	Percentage (%)	5.12	4.10	7.00	10.22	7.78
人均纯收入(元)	**Per Capita Net Income (yuan)**	**1335.52**	**1597.46**	**1858.73**	**2234.60**	**2757.43**

项 目	Item	3000-3500 元 3000-3500 yuan	3500-4000 元 3500-4000 yuan	4000-4500 元 4000-4500 yuan	4500-5000 元 4500-5000 yuan	5000 元以上 over 5000 yuan
调查户数(户)	**Number of Households Surveyed (household)**	**107**	**110**	**83**	**76**	**585**
构成(%)	Percentage (%)	6.90	7.10	5.35	4.90	37.74
常住人口(人)	**Number of Permanent Residents in the Households Surveyed (person)**	**528**	**559**	**383**	**361**	**2304**
构成(%)	Percentage (%)	7.37	7.80	5.34	5.04	32.14
人均纯收入(元)	**Per Capita Net Income (yuan)**	**3246.15**	**3737.73**	**4239.74**	**4725.73**	**9013.66**

9-21 分地区农村居民家庭人均总收入和纯收入

Per Capita Annual Gross and Net Income of Rural Households by Region

单位：元 (2010 年) (抽样调查 Sampled Survey) (yuan)

项 目 Item	自治区 Autonomous Region	昌吉回族自治州 Changji Hui Autonomous Prefecture	伊犁州直属县(市) Counties (Cities) Direct Under Ili Prefecture	塔城地区 Tacheng [Tarbagatai] Administrative Offices
调查县、市(个) Number of Counties and Cities Surveyed (unit)	**30**	**4**	**5**	**4**
调查户数(户) Number of Households Surveyed (household)	**1550**	**160**	**260**	**145**
常住人口(人) Number of Permanent Residents In the Households Surveyed (person)	**7169**	**541**	**1215**	**632**
总收入 Annual Gross Income	**8806.87**	**21699.02**	**8996.59**	**16061.08**
工资性收入 Income from Wages and Salaries	556.26	1142.11	933.29	280.75
在非企业组织中劳动得到的 From Non-enterprise Organization	126.22	191.05	254.75	75.70
在本地企业中劳动得到的 From Local Enterprise	236.75	568.09	501.80	205.05
常住人口外出从业得到的 Out of Migrant Workers	193.29	382.97	176.75	
家庭经营收入 Income From Household Business	7795.26	20005.99	7208.28	15364.44
农业收入 Farming	5636.32	15071.05	4512.45	11390.06
林业收入 Forestry	192.22	31.15	35.39	7.71
牧业收入 Animal Husbandry	1415.96	3601.97	1802.87	3890.00
渔业收入 Fishery		420.62		
工业收入 Industry	42.90		42.15	38.71
建筑业收入 Construction	32.31		85.19	
交通、运输和邮电业收入 Transportation, Post and Telecommunications Services	220.95	730.05	308.38	11.46
批发和零售贸易、餐饮业收入 Wholesale, Retail Trades and Catering Services	177.11	51.41	278.56	26.49
社会服务业收入 Social Services	23.91	7.67	60.59	
文教卫生业收入 Cultural, Education, Medicines and Medical Services	19.06		70.91	
其他家庭经营收入 Others	34.52	92.07	11.80	
财产性收入 Income from Properties	126.53	215.08	482.80	155.86
#利 息 Interest	3.21	11.64	4.34	2.55
租 金 Rent	5.73	24.55	2.39	3.06
转移性收入 Income from Transfer	328.82	335.83	372.22	260.03
全年家庭人均纯收入 Annual Net Income	**4642.67**	**8554.68**	**5325.64**	**7371.29**
可支配收入 Disposable Income	**4254.66**	**6491.68**	**4957.04**	**6790.99**

9-21 续表 Continued

单位：元 (yuan)

项 目 Item	阿勒泰地区 Altay Administrative Offices	巴音郭楞蒙古自治州 Bayangol Mongol Autonomous Prefecture	阿克苏地区 Aksu Administrative Offices	喀什地区 Kashgar [Kaxgar] Administrative Offices	和田地区 Hotan Administrative Offices
调查县、市(个) Number of Counties and Cities Surveyed (unit)	**4**	**6**	**5**	**6**	**4**
调查户数(户) Number of Households Surveyed (household)	**130**	**235**	**235**	**325**	**235**
常住人口(人) Number of Permanent Residents In the Households Surveyed (person)	**640**	**1024**	**1096**	**1550**	**1138**
总收入 Annual Gross Income	**6688.97**	**13238.19**	**9389.51**	**5181.59**	**3828.28**
工资性收入 Income from Wages and Salaries	599.47	581.64	304.09	434.57	586.81
在非企业组织中劳动得到的 From Non-enterprise Organization	233.42	231.51	109.56	37.07	83.03
在本地企业中劳动得到的 From Local Enterprise	163.59	288.87	190.70	100.77	145.59
常住人口外出从业得到的 Out of Migrant Workers	202.45	61.27	3.83	296.72	358.19
家庭经营收入 Income From Household Business	5884.26	11773.52	8856.56	4425.53	3019.96
农业收入 Farming	2718.67	9180.01	7309.09	2912.45	1453.20
林业收入 Forestry		50.46	224.76	285.34	419.74
牧业收入 Animal Husbandry	2699.22	1989.11	976.05	935.41	748.30
渔业收入 Fishery					
工业收入 Industry		14.40	17.61	0.10	180.34
建筑业收入 Construction	37.94	18.96	30.74	20.39	30.38
交通、运输和邮电业收入 Transportation, Post and Telecommunications Services	94.84	209.30	110.09	52.03	49.61
批发和零售贸易、餐饮业收入 Wholesale, Retail Trades and Catering Services	171.88	229.85	95.95	157.50	90.10
社会服务业收入 Social Services	19.53	73.43	14.84	9.46	12.34
文教卫生业收入 Cultural, Education, Medicines and Medical Services					
其他家庭经营收入 Others	142.19	8.01	77.44	52.86	35.95
财产性收入 Income from Properties	19.64	635.88	107.25	72.27	3.88
#利 息 Interest	7.02	0.20	0.33		
租 金 Rent		10.74	0.18		
转移性收入 Income from Transfer	185.60	247.15	121.60	249.22	217.63
全年家庭人均纯收入 Annual Net Income	**4915.82**	**7431.76**	**5554.37**	**3269.58**	**2753.74**
可支配收入 Disposable Income	**4832.65**	**7063.91**	**5371.34**	**3196.71**	**2633.07**

9-22 分地区农村居民家庭平均每人总支出

Per Capita Total Expenditure of Rural Household by Region

单位：元　　(2010 年)(抽样调查 Sampled Survey)　　(yuan)

项目 Item	自治区 Autonomous Region	昌吉回族自治州 Changji Hui Autonomous Prefecture	伊犁州直属县(市) Counties (Cities) Direct Under Ili Prefecture	塔城地区 Tacheng [Tarbagatai] Administrative Offices
全年总支出 Annual Total Expenditure	**8241.28**	**21737.10**	**7923.98**	**15547.89**
家庭经营费用支出 Expenditure for Household Business	**3800.24**	**12514.74**	**3231.26**	**8326.55**
农业生产 Farming	2782.53	10004.00	1912.91	6589.39
林业生产 Forestry	20.17	4.46	17.08	5.86
牧业生产 Animal Husbandry	821.54	1725.50	938.70	1720.57
渔业生产 Fishery		369.32		
工业生产 Industry	7.28		19.13	2.45
建筑业生产 Construction	9.10		32.63	
交通、运输和邮电业支出 Transportation, Post and Telecommunications Services	97.42	327.47	202.65	8.29
批发和零售贸易、餐饮业支出 Wholesale, Retail Trades and Catering Services	46.27	56.88	67.23	
社会服务业支出 Social Services	1.20	2.56	4.72	
文教卫生业支出 Cultural, Education, Medicines and Medical Services	7.13	5.37	35.58	
其他经营支出 Others	7.60	19.18	0.63	
购置生产用固定资产支出 Expenditure for Productive Fixed Assets	**568.14**	**732.93**	**744.37**	**710.94**
税费支出 Taxes and Fee	**7.83**	**5.12**		
生活消费支出 Expenditure for Consumption	**3458.14**	**6358.06**	**3542.83**	**5913.41**
食品 Food	1394.65	2280.37	1215.36	2454.19
#主食 Staple Food	432.02	406.73	259.16	333.57
副食 Non-staple Food	830.25	1700.18	844.71	1751.42
衣着 Clothing	303.66	482.49	332.48	539.93
居住 Residence	695.17	643.82	841.37	1497.00
家庭设备、用品及服务 Household Facilities, Articles and Services	137.69	306.15	159.03	131.39
医疗保健 Health Care and Medical Services	314.73	519.80	395.66	370.88
交通和通讯 Transportation and Communications	382.14	635.34	345.81	435.63
文化教育娱乐用品及服务 Cultural, Education and Recreational Articles and Services	170.15	1298.04	195.82	421.22
其他商品和服务 Other Commodities and Services	59.94	192.05	57.31	63.17
附：生产用固定资产折旧 Depreciation Charge for Productive Fixed Assets	337.20	677.52	402.77	346.54

9-22 续表 Continued

单位：元 (yuan)

项目 Item	阿勒泰地区 Altay Administrative Offices	巴音郭楞蒙古自治州 Bayangol Mongol Autonomous Prefecture	阿克苏地区 Aksu Administrative Offices	喀什地区 Kashgar [Kaxgar] Administrative Offices	和田地区 Hotan Administrative Offices
全年总支出 Annual Total Expenditure	**4472.35**	**10398.21**	**7422.73**	**4397.41**	**3240.36**
家庭经营费用支出 Expenditure for Household Business	**1625.90**	**5375.86**	**3394.17**	**1803.83**	**1004.44**
农业生产 Farming	870.63	4353.39	2638.09	1313.64	501.99
林业生产 Forestry		12.55	38.03	15.25	10.83
牧业生产 Animal Husbandry	657.30	869.98	657.40	466.06	435.97
渔业生产 Fishery					
工业生产 Industry		3.40			21.17
建筑业生产 Construction	0.69	35.63	17.36	0.24	3.33
交通、运输和邮电业支出 Transportation, Post and Telecommunications Services	33.91	86.93	9.79	2.53	8.92
批发和零售贸易、餐饮业支出 Wholesale, Retail Trades and Catering Services	39.16	11.65	7.41	4.41	20.40
社会服务业支出 Social Services		1.10	0.23	0.58	
文教卫生业支出 Cultural, Education, Medicines and Medical Services		0.71	1.19		0.05
其他经营支出 Others	24.22	0.52	24.66	1.11	1.78
购置生产用固定资产支出 Expenditure for Productive Fixed Assets	**119.22**	**456.68**	**460.49**	**306.30**	**118.27**
税费支出 Taxes and Fee	**37.82**	**1.02**	**36.31**	**0.29**	**1.85**
生活消费支出 Expenditure for Consumption	**2592.32**	**4155.77**	**3346.27**	**2213.99**	**1989.48**
食品 Food	1529.39	1669.32	1310.60	1116.11	1115.21
#主食 Staple Food	357.67	361.97	515.00	477.17	399.34
副食 Non-staple Food	1151.18	1175.17	706.51	551.60	644.29
衣着 Clothing	323.01	348.87	342.09	270.61	186.15
居住 Residence	303.98	599.91	631.91	374.74	321.33
家庭设备、用品及服务 Household Facilities, Articles and Services	80.46	166.14	108.10	94.86	90.40
医疗保健 Health Care and Medical Services	97.84	394.99	316.56	146.71	110.44
交通和通讯 Transportation and Communications	165.58	612.19	486.56	168.83	124.24
文化教育娱乐用品及服务 Cultural, Education and Recreational Articles and Services	73.19	326.89	40.36	31.29	7.13
其他商品和服务 Other Commodities and Services	18.87	37.48	110.11	10.83	34.59
附：生产用固定资产折旧 Depreciation Charge for Productive Fixed Assets	301.54	388.53	402.21	107.76	62.60

9-23 分地区农村居民家庭人均现金收支

Per Capita Income and Expenditure in Cash of Rural Household by Region

单位：元 (2010 年)(抽样调查 Sampled Survey) (yuan)

项目	Item	自治区 Autonomous Region	昌吉回族自治州 Changji Hui Autonomous Prefecture	伊犁州直属县(市) Counties (Cities) Direct Under Ili Prefecture	塔城地区 Tacheng [Tarbagatai] Administrative Offices
期内现金收入	**Annual Total Income In Cash**	**7517.22**	**19933.65**	**9053.28**	**15503.47**
工资性收入	Income from Wages and Salaries	556.26	1142.11	933.29	280.75
在非企业组织中劳动得到的	From Non-enterprise Organization	126.22	191.05	254.75	75.70
在本地企业中劳动得到的	From Local Enterprises	236.75	568.09	501.80	205.05
常住人口外出从业得到的	Out of Migrant Workers	193.29	382.97	176.75	
家庭经营收入	Income of Household Operation	6525.27	18269.12	7480.11	14833.04
农业现金收入	Cash Income from Farming	4517.45	13778.70	4750.89	11262.22
#出售农产品收入	Sale of Agricultural Products	4312.76	13320.72	4435.22	11037.04
林业现金收入	Cash Income from Forestry	172.18	31.15	35.02	7.71
#出售林业产品收入	Sale of Forestry Products	166.82	31.15	15.14	7.71
牧业现金收入	Cash Income from Animal Husbandry	1284.88	3157.45	1836.63	3486.45
#出售牧业产品收入	Sale of Animal Husbandry Products	1275.50	3130.90	1797.55	3486.45
渔业现金收入	Cash Income from Fishery		420.62		
#出售渔业产品收入	Sale of Fishery Products		420.62		
工业收入	Income from Industry	42.90		42.15	38.71
#出售工业产品收入	Sale of Industrial Products	24.77		2.47	
工业服务性收入	Income from Industrial services	18.13		39.68	38.71
建筑业收入	Income from Construction	32.31		85.19	
#出售建筑业产品收入	Sale of Constructive Products				
建筑业服务性收入	Income from Constructive services	32.31		85.19	
交通、运输、邮电业收入	Income from Transport,Post and Telecommunication Servies	220.95	730.05	308.38	11.46
批零贸易业、饮食业收入	Income from Wholesale and Retail Trades and Catering Servies	177.11	51.41	278.56	26.49
社会服务业收入	Income from Social Services	23.91	7.67	60.59	
文教卫生业收入	Income from Culture,Edcuation and Health Care	19.06		70.91	
其他行业收入	Others	34.52	92.07	11.80	
财产性收入	Property Income	106.87	186.59	267.66	129.65
#利 息	Interest	3.21	11.64	4.34	2.55
租 金	Rent	5.73	24.55	2.39	3.06
转移性收入	Transfer Income	328.82	335.83	372.22	260.03
非收入所得	**Non-income Gain**	**2247.95**	**5131.95**	**1466.57**	**6789.28**
#从银行信用社得到的贷款	Credit	1245.65	2838.87	919.26	3448.94
借入款	Borrowed Money	292.07	587.03	123.91	415.18
收回借出款	Recall Loaned Money	78.85	86.70	24.32	577.94
从银行信用社取回存款	Take Deposit back	339.16	1282.16	178.39	2120.42
出售财产所得款	Sold Property	126.96	178.39	78.63	69.45
期内现金支出	**Annual Expenditure in Cash**	**7464.48**	**20518.90**	**7486.53**	**14778.36**
生产费用支出	Producing Expenditure	4211.42	12897.00	3927.16	8964.37
家庭经营费用支出	Expenditure for Household Business	3643.29	12164.07	3182.79	8253.43
农业生产支出	Farming	2727.24	9816.57	1912.91	6589.39
林业生产支出	Forestry	20.17	4.46	17.08	5.86
牧业生产支出	Animal Husbandry	719.88	1562.26	890.24	1647.44

9-23 续表 1Continued

单位：元 (yuan)

项　　目	Item	自治区 Autonomous Region	昌吉回族自治州 Changji Hui Autonomous Prefecture	伊犁州直属县(市) Counties (Cities) Direct Under Ili Prefecture	塔城地区 Tacheng [Tarbagatai] Administrative Offices
渔业生产支出	Fishery		369.32		
工业生产支出	Industry	7.28		19.13	2.45
建筑业生产支出	Construction	9.10		32.63	
交通运输支出	Transportation	97.42	327.47	202.65	8.29
批发和零售贸易、餐饮业	Wholesale Retail Trades and Catering services	46.27	56.88	67.23	
社会服务业支出	Social Services	1.20	2.56	4.72	
文教卫生业	Cultural, Education, Medicines and Medical Services	7.13	5.37	35.58	
其他经营支出	Others	7.60	19.18	0.63	
购置生产性固定资产支出	Expenditure for Productive Fixed Assets	568.14	732.93	744.37	710.94
税费支出	Taxes and Fee	7.83	5.12		
生活消费支出	Expenditure for Consumption	2838.29	5490.53	3153.85	5217.00
财产性支出	Expenditure for Properties	182.52	1718.92	149.38	216.61
转移性支出	Expenditure for Transfers	224.40	407.33	256.14	380.38
非消费性现金付出	**Expenditure for Non-consumption**	**2027.17**	**4308.09**	**1886.53**	**6421.48**
#归还银行信用社贷款	Loan Returned to Bank	958.70	2278.01	628.16	2974.96
借出款	Lending Money	34.49	12.79	23.32	55.07
归还借款	Return Borrowed Money	232.43	583.47	247.77	453.74
存入银行信用社	Deposit	506.72	821.37	617.28	2598.46
期末金融资产余额	**Balance of Financial Assets in Year-end**	**2493.60**	**5643.35**	**2120.70**	**3445.14**
#银行存款	Deposit	1658.03	5130.43	1429.47	3076.35
手存现金	Cash	804.61	512.92	691.24	368.79
期末债务余额	**Balance of Debt in Year-end**	**1089.23**	**1953.96**	**876.05**	**1419.92**
#银行、信用社贷款	Loan from Bank and Credit Cooperatives	818.81	1595.91	786.01	1061.46
个人借(欠)款	Borrowed Money from Individual	246.92	230.18	90.04	358.46
生活消费支出的现金	**Expenditure for Consumption**	**2838.29**	**5490.53**	**3153.85**	**5217.00**
食　品	Food	850.35	1412.84	952.85	1763.12
#主　食	Staple Food	156.34	215.17	174.61	293.60
副　食	Non-staple Food	561.63	1024.21	666.75	1100.32
衣 着	Clothing	301.17	482.49	332.48	539.93
居 住	Residence	625.91	643.82	714.89	1491.66
家庭设备、用品及服务	Household Facilities，Articles and Services	133.90	306.15	159.03	131.39
医疗保健	Health Care and Medical Services	314.73	519.80	395.66	370.88
交通和通讯	Transportation and Communications	382.14	635.34	345.81	435.63
文化教育、娱乐用品及服务	Cultural，Education and Recreational Articles and Services	170.15	1298.04	195.82	421.22
#文化教育、娱乐用品	Cultural，Education and Recreational Articles	28.94	91.69	41.04	87.27
文化教育、娱乐服务	Cultural，Education and Recreational Services	122.78	1066.11	130.82	322.49
#学杂费	Tuition	73.69	558.37	101.40	301.78
技术培训费	Charge for Training	11.91	59.30	7.59	10.40
其他商品和服务	Other Commodities and Services	59.94	192.05	57.31	63.17
商品性支出	Commodities	33.61	63.97	31.14	32.07
服务支出	Services	26.34	128.08	26.17	31.10

9-23 续表 2 Continued

单位：元 (yuan)

项　目	Item	阿勒泰地区 Altay Adminis-trative Offices	巴音郭楞蒙古自治州 Bayangol Mongol Autono-mous Prefecture	阿克苏地区 Aksu Adminis-trative Offices	喀什地区 Kashgar [Kaxgar] Adminis-trative Offices	和田地区 Hotan Adminis-trative Offices
期内现金收入	**Annual Total Income In Cash**	**5579.54**	**12784.09**	**7670.22**	**3797.35**	**2713.76**
工资性收入	Income from Wages and Salaries	599.47	563.09	304.09	434.57	586.81
在非企业组织中劳动得到的	From Non-enterprise Organization	233.42	212.95	109.56	37.07	83.03
在本地企业中劳动得到的	From Local Enterprises	163.59	288.87	190.70	100.77	145.59
常住人口外出从业得到的	Out of Migrant Workers	202.45	61.27	3.83	296.72	358.19
家庭经营收入	Income of Household Operation	4780.89	11477.19	7189.54	3042.90	1906.30
农业现金收入	Cash Income from Farming	2165.03	8773.21	5776.15	1644.79	556.94
＃出售农产品收入	Sale of Agricultural Products	2084.96	8532.99	5556.23	1621.89	530.63
林业现金收入	Cash Income from Forestry		108.79	197.19	276.59	332.86
＃出售林业产品收入	Sale of Forestry Products		106.83	197.01	268.92	332.86
牧业现金收入	Cash Income from Animal Ausbandry	2149.48	2041.25	869.54	829.18	617.79
＃出售牧业产品收入	Sale of Animal Husbandry Products	2099.02	1946.77	865.61	826.90	617.35
渔业现金收入	Cash Income from Fishery					
＃出售渔业产品收入	Sale of Fishery Products					
工业收入	Income from Industry		14.40	17.61	0.10	180.34
＃出售工业产品收入	Sale of Industrial Products			16.42		137.59
工业服务性收入	Income from Industrial services		14.40	1.19	0.10	42.75
建筑业收入	Income from Construction	37.94	18.96	30.74	20.39	30.38
＃出售建筑业产品收入	Sale of Constructive Products					
建筑业服务性收入	Income from Constructive services	37.94	18.96	30.74	20.39	30.38
交通、运输、邮电业收入	Income from Transport,Post and Telecommunication Servies	94.84	209.30	110.09	52.03	49.61
批零贸易业、饮食业收入	Income from Wholesale and Retail Trades and Catering Servies	171.88	229.85	95.95	157.50	90.10
社会服务业收入	Income from Social Services	19.53	73.43	14.84	9.46	12.34
文教卫生业收入	Income from Culture,Edcuation and Health Care					
其他行业收入	Others	142.19	8.01	77.44	52.86	35.95
财产性收入	Property Income	13.58	496.66	54.99	70.67	3.01
＃利　息	Interest	7.02	0.20	0.33		
租　金	Rent		10.74	0.18		
转移性收入	Transfer Income	185.60	247.15	121.60	249.22	217.63
非收入所得	**Non-income Gain**	**173.78**	**1812.83**	**2125.58**	**668.32**	**227.70**
＃从银行信用社得到的贷款	Credit	132.81	973.14	1475.68	458.81	46.49
借入款	Borrowed Money		222.22	245.51	71.07	29.26
收回借出款	Recall Loaned Money		61.37	7.04	3.45	
从银行信用社取回存款	Take Deposit back	15.63	388.59	119.89	74.41	16.65
出售财产所得款	Sold Property		58.30	161.76	7.12	41.51
期内现金支出	**Annual Expenditure in Cash**	**3230.27**	**10082.35**	**6686.31**	**3390.84**	**2293.02**
生产费用支出	Producing Expenditure	1406.58	5820.84	3794.29	1847.96	927.09
家庭经营费用支出	Expenditure for Household Business	1287.37	5364.16	3333.79	1541.66	808.82
农业生产支出	Farming	779.69	4344.32	2635.54	1247.81	422.02
林业生产支出	Forestry		12.55	38.03	15.25	10.83
牧业生产支出	Animal Husbandry	409.70	867.35	599.58	269.72	320.32

9-23 续表 3 Continued

单位：元 (yuan)

项　目	Item	阿勒泰地　区 Altay Adminis-trative Offices	巴音郭楞蒙古自治州 Bayangol Mongol Autono-mous Prefecture	阿克苏地　区 Aksu Adminis-trative Offices	喀什地区 Kashgar [Kaxgar] Adminis-trative Offices	和田地区 Hotan Adminis-trative Offices
渔业生产支出	Fishery					
工业生产支出	Industry		3.40			21.17
建筑业生产支出	Construction	0.69	35.63	17.36	0.24	3.33
交通运输支出	Transportation	33.91	86.93	9.79	2.53	8.92
批发和零售贸易、餐饮业	Wholesale, Retail Trades and Catering services	39.16	11.65	7.41	4.41	20.40
社会服务业支出	Social Services		1.10	0.23	0.58	
文教卫生业	Cultural, Education, Medicines and Medical Services		0.71	1.19		0.05
其他经营支出	Others	24.22	0.52	24.66	1.11	1.78
购置生产性固定资产支出	Expenditure for Productive Fixed Assets	119.22	456.68	460.49	306.30	118.27
税费支出	Taxes and Fee	37.82	1.02	36.31	0.29	1.85
生活消费支出	Expenditure for Consumption	1688.79	3851.62	2670.23	1469.59	1237.77
财产性支出	Expenditure for Properties		81.54	138.11	27.37	23.08
转移性支出	Expenditure for Transfers	97.08	327.34	47.38	45.63	103.24
非消费性现金付出	**Expenditure for Non-consumption**	**1166.38**	**1629.09**	**1688.89**	**918.37**	**160.34**
#归还银行信用社贷款	Loan Returned to Bank	87.50	467.82	1002.40	377.28	23.36
借出款	Lending Money		62.81	12.14	2.41	4.39
归还借款	Return Borrowed Money	17.19	162.93	256.13	57.77	29.21
存入银行信用社	Deposit	1000.00	437.99	147.44	340.00	65.91
期末金融资产余额	**Balance of Financial Assets in Year-end**	**5848.63**	**6949.40**	**2120.18**	**1320.16**	**582.84**
#银行存款	Deposit	5285.31	5357.62	1195.26	755.17	102.05
手存现金	Cash	563.32	1591.78	913.97	564.99	480.79
期末债务余额	**Balance of Debt in Year-end**		**1627.00**	**420.67**	**235.85**	**71.61**
#银行、信用社贷款	Loan from Bank and Credit Cooperatives		1067.19	272.35	181.27	26.71
个人借(欠)款	Borrowed Money from Individual		530.52	116.38	54.59	44.89
生活消费支出的现金	**Expenditure for Consumption**	**1688.79**	**3851.62**	**2670.23**	**1469.59**	**1237.77**
食　品	Food	660.23	1366.79	710.60	510.09	412.86
#主　食	Staple Food	262.99	305.20	156.84	70.29	51.12
副　食	Non-staple Food	375.60	929.40	464.67	352.46	290.16
衣　着	Clothing	304.26	347.24	338.94	265.19	184.05
居　住	Residence	288.36	599.91	559.26	246.07	288.91
家庭设备、用品及服务	Household Facilities, Articles and Services	80.46	166.14	107.84	90.58	75.55
医疗保健	Health Care and Medical Services	97.84	394.99	316.56	146.71	110.44
交通和通讯	Transportation and Communications	165.58	612.19	486.56	168.83	124.24
文化教育、娱乐用品及服务	Cultural, Education and Recreational Articles and Services	73.19	326.89	40.36	31.29	7.13
#文化教育、娱乐用品	Cultural, Education and Recreational Articles	13.28	28.35	11.51	7.84	2.39
文化教育、娱乐服务	Cultural, Education and Recreational Services	59.91	282.44	23.68	21.11	3.41
#学杂费	Tuition	59.48	257.90	20.47	19.55	3.41
技术培训费	Charge for Training		7.97	3.07		
其他商品和服务	Other Commodities and Services	18.87	37.48	110.11	10.83	34.59
商品性支出	Commodities	12.04	21.61	100.47	3.94	30.19
服务支出	Services	6.83	15.86	9.64	6.89	4.40

9-24 主要年份农村居民家庭房屋使用情况
Housing Conditions of Rural Households in Main Years

(抽样调查 Sampled Survey)

项 目	Item	1990	2000	2005	2009	2010
本年新建房屋	**Houses Newly built This Year**					
面积(平方米/人)	Per Capita Floor Space of Houses (sq.m/person)	0.78	0.38	1.37	1.11	0.73
价值(元/平方米)	Value of Houses (yuan/sq.m)	51.25	169.37	225.20	390.33	442.00
住房结构(平方米/人)	Structure of Houses (sq.m/person)					
#钢筋混凝土结构	Reinforced Concrete Structure	0.08	0.03	0.08	0.15	0.22
砖木结构	Brick and Wood Structure	0.44	0.16	1.04	0.82	0.50
生活用房面积(平方米/人)	Per Capita Living Rooms Space (sq.m/person)	0.55	0.38	0.72	1.11	0.80
年末住房情况	**Houses at Year-end**					
住房面积(平方米/人)	Per Capita Floor Space of Houses (sq.m/person)	14.04	17.25	21.13	23.45	24.00
住房价值(元/平方米)	Value of Houses (yuan/sq.m)	22.16	120.86	160.99	226.49	252.79
住房结构(平方米/人)	Structure of House (sq.m/person)					
#钢筋混凝土结构	Reinforced Concrete Structure	0.29	0.53	0.98	1.51	1.83
砖木结构	Brick and Wood Structure	3.97	2.75	6.48	10.34	10.95

9-25 主要年份城乡新建住宅面积和居民住房情况
Floor Space of Newly Built Residential Buildings and Housing Conditions of Urban and Rural Residents in Main Years

年 份 Year	城镇新建住宅面积(万平方米) Floor Space of Newly Built Residential Buildings In Urban Areas (10 000 sq.m)	农村新建住宅面积(万平方米) Floor Space of Newly Built Residential Buildings in Rural Areas (10 000 sq.m)	城镇人均使用面积(平方米) Per Capita Gross Living Space in Urban Areas (sq.m)	城镇人均建筑面积(平方米) Per Capita Floor Space of Residential Building in Urban Areas (sq.m)	农村人均居住面积(平方米) Per Capita Floor Space of Residential Building in Rural Areas (sq.m)
1985	353.26	463.00	10.70	14.27	12.75
1990	381.61	593.96	13.55	18.07	14.04
1995	567.54	496.60	16.57	22.09	16.12
1996	683.51	757.71	17.61	23.48	16.12
1997	673.58	719.53	13.62	18.16	16.13
1998	874.97	729.71	18.95	25.27	16.20
1999	1315.89	705.00	19.76	26.35	16.90
2000	1327.29	554.59	20.06	26.75	17.25
2001	1517.22	894.56	20.60	27.47	18.04
2002	1256.72	534.10	18.17	23.78	18.56
2003	1546.23	800.81	17.91	23.36	18.62
2004	1565.72	732.84	18.82	24.44	19.10
2005	2226.97	1391.81	20.15	26.02	21.23
2006	2212.08	1573.38	20.33	26.31	21.96
2007	2491.60	1967.17	20.38	27.17	22.45
2008	2584.23	1541.44	20.47	27.29	22.79
2009	1994.28	1418.15	20.42	27.16	23.45
2010	2028.26	1263.63	20.49	27.25	24.00

9-26 分地区农村居民家庭平均每人粮食收支平衡表

Per Capita Grain Banlance of Debit and Credit by Region

单位：公斤 (2010 年)(抽样调查 Sampled Survey) (kg)

项 目	Item	自治区 Autonomous Region	昌吉回族自治州 Changji Hui Autonomous Prefecture	伊犁州直属县(市) Counties (Cities) Direct Under Ili Prefecture	塔城地区 Tacheng [Tarbagatai] Administrative Office
年初粮食结存	**Inventory of Grain at Beginning of Year**	**434.37**	**575.75**	**865.08**	**129.66**
粮食收入合计	**Total of Debit**	**1232.45**	**4112.98**	**1540.63**	**1957.97**
家庭经营生产的	From Household Business	1107.13	3530.61	1404.83	1724.08
购 入	Purchases	125.32	582.37	135.79	233.89
其他粮食收入	Others				
粮食支出合计	**Total of Expenditure**	**1030.76**	**3737.08**	**1579.35**	**1910.06**
主食用粮	Staple Food	236.10	209.01	133.15	155.10
出 售	Sales	636.61	2856.55	1357.03	1597.31
种 籽	Seeds	45.47	193.03	31.90	62.52
饲 料	Fodder	109.61	478.49	57.27	95.13
其他粮食支出	Others	2.96			
年末粮食结存(实际数)	**Inventory of Grain at Year-end**	**531.62**	**516.74**	**1128.00**	**162.56**

项 目	Item	阿勒泰地区 Altay Adminis-trative Offices	巴音郭楞蒙古自治州 Bayangol Mongol Autonomous Prefecture	阿克苏地区 Aksu Adminis-trative Offices	喀什地区 Kashgar [Kaxgar] Adminis-trative Offices	和田地区 Hotan Adminis-trative Offices
年初粮食结存	**Inventory of Grain at Beginning of Year**	**193.59**	**164.68**	**364.05**	**407.16**	**340.08**
粮食收入合计	**Total of Debit**	**853.54**	**675.42**	**968.66**	**937.99**	**645.06**
家庭经营生产的	From Household Business	722.93	504.69	873.33	888.66	613.87
购 入	Purchases	130.61	170.73	95.33	49.33	31.18
其他粮食收入	Others					
粮食支出合计	**Total of Expenditure**	**822.99**	**563.09**	**786.81**	**704.53**	**519.69**
主食用粮	Staple Food	114.01	163.72	279.56	276.62	241.72
出 售	Sales	585.62	349.80	433.97	254.29	131.58
种 籽	Seeds	7.29	21.28	18.34	44.62	21.75
饲 料	Fodder	116.07	28.30	54.95	116.71	121.67
其他粮食支出	Others				12.29	2.97
年末粮食结存(实际数)	**Inventory of Grain at Year-end**	**264.16**	**320.19**	**380.78**	**452.81**	**401.28**

9-27 主要年份农村居民家庭平均每户饲养畜禽、其他小动物生产情况
Output of Livestock, Poultry and Other Small Animals Per Rural Households in Main Years

单位：公斤 (抽样调查)(Sampled Surrey) (kg)

年 份 Year	出售自宰猪肉产量 Output of Pork Sold and Self-slaugutered	出售自宰羊肉产量 Output of Mutton Sold and Self-slaughtered	羊毛产量 Output of Wool	牛羊奶产量 Output of Cow and Sheep Milk	出售自宰家禽产量 Output of Poultry Sold and Self-slaughtered	禽蛋产量 Output of Poultry and Eggs	蚕茧产量 Output of Silkworm
1985	16.76	47.54	10.51	51.53		13.95	0.26
1990	24.97	45.72	15.86	67.16		17.68	1.26
1995	23.42	61.41	14.86	66.16	28.86	23.14	1.69
1996	23.10	62.09	7.61	34.93	7.61	8.20	0.89
1997	12.46	73.78	7.37	33.57	9.87	7.97	1.08
1998	10.18	84.42	5.40	42.53	7.39	8.78	1.58
1999	12.91	100.45	4.06	34.92	7.65	13.90	1.38
2000	16.48	94.55	5.49	34.27	13.03	25.26	1.01
2001	13.24	91.54			16.92	35.71	
2002	11.01	110.97			16.09	41.07	
2003	13.16	86.23	4.51	91.91	12.48	37.10	0.66
2004	10.30	105.20	4.09	89.54	12.75	6.03	0.23
2005	8.29	107.11	6.28	134.36	14.95	49.14	0.23
2006	4.28	114.78	6.91	112.72	12.33	71.07	0.14
2007	2.70	112.08	7.05	144.28	12.25	40.59	0.02
2008	9.39	105.70	5.06	169.98	18.43	62.33	0.03
2009	9.64	102.68	5.19	136.18	25.58	67.18	
2010	11.64	108.72	4.05	145.32	19.16	36.26	

注：因调查户调整，部分指标数据与往年相比变动较大。
Note:Beceucse of Households Surveyed adjustment, Parts of Index sign data quite changed compared to last yesr.

9-28 主要年份农村居民家庭平均每户饲养畜禽、其他小动物出售量
Quantities of Livestock, Poultry and Other Small Animals Sold Per Rural Households in Main Years

(抽样调查) (Sampled Surrey)

年 份 Year	猪(头) Pork (head)	牛(头) Cattle (head)	羊(只) Sheep (head)	家禽(只) Poultry (head)	蛋类(公斤) Eggs (kg)	羊毛(公斤) Wool (kg)	牛羊奶(公斤) Milk (kg)
1985	0.10		1.94	3.30	7.68	6.87	5.68
1990	0.22	0.11	1.50	4.15	8.25	9.63	17.47
1995	0.17	0.22	2.21	11.69	17.28	5.80	26.76
1996	0.24	0.14	2.14	1.98	3.08	3.13	12.43
1997	0.11	0.16	2.74	3.00	3.51	4.16	11.56
1998	0.07	0.15	3.47	2.14	4.30	2.23	18.04
1999	0.08	0.25	3.89	2.70	9.23	1.67	12.75
2000	0.14	0.39	3.81	4.89	21.27	1.82	21.30
2001	0.12	0.37	3.85	7.55	31.60	1.43	39.77
2002	0.11	0.35	4.61	6.64	34.55	1.95	55.33
2003	0.18	0.35	4.14	3.60	33.55	1.81	73.94
2004	0.12	0.32	4.55	4.28	3.01	1.86	77.30
2005	0.09	0.39	6.03	4.42	46.51	4.54	117.65
2006	0.06	0.59	7.21	4.12	68.19	5.19	91.42
2007	0.03	0.65	6.03	3.54	38.11	5.43	123.35
2008	0.11	0.56	4.92	6.35	59.54	3.28	148.16
2009	0.12	0.43	4.62	9.63	63.91	3.06	119.28
2010	0.12	0.39	4.32	6.12	33.01	2.88	129.76

9-29 社会保险基本情况
Basic Conditions on Social Insurance

单位：万元 (10 000 yuan)

指 标	Item	2009	2010
基本养老保险	**Basic Endowment Insurance**		
年末参保人数(万人)	Year-end Contributors (10 000 persons)	232.08	259.67
#参保职工	Staff and Workers	177.58	193.07
离退休人员	Number of Retirees	54.50	66.60
养老保险当年实际缴纳保险金	Actual Revenue of Urban Basic Endowment Insurance in Current Year	1101562	1260407
实发养老金额	Retirement Pension Actually Provided	876269	1176874
失业保险	**Unemployment Insurance**		
年末参保人数(万人)	Year-end Contributors (10 000 persons)	169.6	180.29
企 业	Enterprises	107.84	117.13
#国有企业	State-owned	58.65	59.47
集体企业	Collective-owned	3.33	3.56
事业单位	Institutions	59.30	60.84
其 他	Others	2.46	2.32
失业保险当年实际缴纳保险金	Actual Revenue of Unemployment Insurance in Current Year	126075	125870
领取失业保险金人数(万人)	Beneficiaries of Unemployment Insurance in Current Year (10 000 persons)	6.34	5.88
城镇基本医疗保险	**Basic Medical Insurance**		
年末参保人数(万人)	Year-end Contributors (10 000 persons)	535.99	571.32
#城镇职工	Staff and Workers	279.09	296.72
城镇居民	Urban Residents	256.90	274.60
工伤保险	Work Injury Insurance		
年末参保人数(万人)	Year-end Contributors (10 000 persons)	167.70	184.13
年末享受待遇人次数（万人次）	Beneficiaries at Year-end	1.20	1.48
生育保险	Maternity Insurance		
年末参保人数(万人)	Year-end Contributors (10 000 persons)	176.07	188.23
年末享受待遇人次数（万人次）	Beneficiaries at Year-end	4.21	4.67

9-30 各地、州、市社会保险年末参保人数

Number of Social Insured Persons at the Year-end by Prefecture, Autonomous Prefecture and City

单位：万人 (10 000 persons)

年 份 Year	地 区 Region	基本养老保险 Basic Endowment Insurance	失业保险 Unemployment Insurance	基本医疗保险 Basic Medical Insurance
	2000	140.34	122.10	88.20
	2001	148.08	126.47	116.17
	2002	152.07	131.29	148.04
	2003	160.04	135.12	176.37
	2004	173.76	138.58	195.97
	2005	181.87	140.84	211.85
	2006	191.97	145.27	227.15
	2007	205.00	151.55	244.78
	2008	222.17	162.75	438.61
	2009	232.08	169.60	535.99
	2010	259.67	180.20	571.32
乌鲁木齐市	Urumqi City	82.19	60.82	141.38
克拉玛依市	Karamay City	3.45	2.79	11.19
石河子市	Shihezi City		7.39	
吐鲁番地区	Turpan Administrative Offices	4.12	3.57	15.57
哈密地区	Hami [Kumul] Administrative Offices	8.49	5.48	19.07
昌吉回族自治州	Changji Hui Autonomous Prefecture	17.37	11.55	41.43
伊犁哈萨克自治州	Ili Kazak Autonomous Prefecture	39.28	24.01	103.29
伊犁州直属县(市)	Counties (Cities) Direct Under Ili Prefecture	21.92	13.16	56.67
塔城地区	Tacheng [Tarbagatai] Administrative Offices	10.37	5.80	23.01
阿勒泰地区	Altay Administrative Offices	7.00	5.05	23.61
博尔塔拉蒙古自治州	Bortala Mongol Autonomous Prefecture	4.71	3.20	13.28
巴音郭楞蒙古自治州	Bayangol Mongol Autonomous Prefecture	17.52	13.07	39.26
阿克苏地区	Aksu Administrative Offices	10.58	8.94	43.10
克孜勒苏柯尔克孜自治州	Kizilsu Kirgiz Autonomous Prefecture	2.47	2.85	12.22
喀什地区	Kashgar [Kaxgar] Administrative Offices	11.02	12.44	61.63
和田地区	Hotan Administrative Offices	4.20	5.76	27.23

主要统计指标解释

一、城镇住户

城镇家庭人口 指居住在一起,经济上合在一起共同生活的家庭成员。凡计算为家庭人口的成员其全部收入包括在家庭中。

城镇就业者负担人数 指家庭人口与就业人口之比。

城镇家庭总收入 指家庭成员得到的工薪收入、经营净收入、财产性收入、转移性收入之和，不包括出售财物收入和借贷收入。

城镇家庭可支配收入 指家庭成员得到可用于最终消费支出和其它非义务性支出以及储蓄的总和，即居民家庭可以用来自由支配的收入。它是家庭总收入扣除交纳的所得税、个人交纳的社会保障支出以及记账补贴后的收入。计算公式为：

可支配收入=家庭总收入-交纳个人所得税-个人交纳的社会保障支出-记帐补贴

城镇家庭消费性支出 指家庭用于日常生活的支出，包括食品、衣着、家庭设备用品及服务、医疗保健、交通和通信、娱乐教育文化服务、居住、其他商品和服务等八大类支出。

城镇家庭服务性消费支出 指家庭用于支付社会提供的各种非商品性服务费用。

城镇家庭收入分组方法 是将所有调查户依户人均可支配收入由低到高排队，按10%，10%，20%，20%，20%，10%，10%的比例依次分成：最低收入户、低收入户、中等偏下收入户、中等收入户、中等偏上收入户、高收入户、最高收入户等七组。总体中最低5%的户为困难户。

恩格尔系数 指食物支出金额在消费性总支出金额中所占的比例。计算公式为：

恩格尔系数=食品支出金额/消费性总支出金额×100%

二、农村住户

总收入 指调查期内农村住户和住户成员从各种来源渠道得到的收入总和。按收入的性质划分为工资性收入、家庭经营收入、财产性收入和转移性收入。

工资性收入 指农村住户成员受雇于单位或个人，靠出卖劳动所而获得的收入。

家庭经营收入 指农村住户以家庭为生产经营单位进行生产筹划和管理而获得的收入。农村住户家庭经营活动按行业划分为农业、林业、牧业、渔业、工业、建筑业、交通运输业邮电业、批发和零售贸易餐饮业、社会服务业、文教卫生业和其他家庭经营。

财产性收入 指金融资产或有形非生产性资产的所有者向其他机构单位提供资金或将有形非生产性资产供其支配，作为回报而从中获得的收入。

转移性收入 指农村住户和住户成员无须付出任何对应物而获得的货物、服务、资金或资产所有权等，不包括无偿提供的用于固定资本形成的资金。一般情况下，是指农村住户在二次分配中的所有收入。

现金收入 指农村住户和住户成员在调查期内得到以现金形态表现的收入。按来源分成工资性收入、家庭经营现金收入、财产性收入、转移性收入。

纯收入 指农村住户当年从各个来源得到的总收入相应地扣除所发生的费用后的收入总和。计算方法：

纯收入=总收入-税费支出-家庭经营费用支出-税费支出生产性固定资产折旧-赠送农村外部亲友支出

纯收入主要用于再生产投入和当年生活消费支出，也可用于储蓄和各种非义务性支出。“农民人均纯收入”按人口平均的纯收入水平，反映的是一个地区或一个农户农村居民的平均收入水平。

总支出 指农村住户用于生产、生活和再分配的全部支出。家庭经营费用支出、购置生产性固定资产支出、生产性固定资产折旧、税费支出、生活消费支出、财产性支出和转移性支出。

三、社会保险

基本养老保险

1.参加保险职工人数：指报告期末按照国家法律、法规和有关政策规定参加基本养老保险并在社保经办机构已建立缴费记录档案的职工人数。包括中断缴费但未终止养老关系的职工人数，不包括只登记未建立缴费记录档案的人数。

2.（参保）离退休人员人数 指报告期末参加基本养老保险的离休、退休和退职人员的人数。

3.基本养老保险基金收入：指根据国家有关规定，由纳入基本养老保险范围的单位和个人按照国家规定的缴费基数和缴费比例缴纳的养老保险基金，以及通过其他方式取得的形成基金来源的收入，包括单位和职工个人缴纳的基本养老保险费、基本养老基金利息收入、上级补助收入、下级上解收入、转移收入、财政补贴和其他收入。

4. 基本养老保险基金支出：指按照国家政策规定的开支范围和开支标准从基本养老保险基金中支付给参加基本养老保险的个人的养老金、丧葬抚恤补助，以及由于保险关系转移、上下级之间调剂资金等原因而发生的支出。包括：离休金、退休金、退职金、各种补贴、医疗费、死亡丧葬补助费、抚恤救济费、社会保险经办机构管理费、补助下级支出、上解上级支出、转移支出、其他支出等。

4. 基本养老保险基金结余：指截止报告期末基本养老

基金收支相抵后的累计余额。

基本医疗保险

1.参保人数：指报告期末按国家有关规定参加基本医疗保险的人数。包括参加保险的职工人数和退休人员人数。

2.基金收入：指根据国家有关规定，由纳入基本医疗保险范围的缴费单位和个人，按国家规定的缴费基数和缴费比例缴纳的基金，以及通过其他方式取得的形成基金来源的款项，包括：单位缴纳的社会统筹基金收入、个人缴纳的个人账户基金收入、财政补贴收入、利息收入、其他收入。

3.基金支出：指按照国家政策规定的开支范围和开支标准从社会统筹基金中支付给参加基本医疗保险的职工和退休人员的医疗保险待遇支出，和从个人帐户基金中支付给参加基本医疗保险的职工和退休人员的医疗费用支出，以及其他支出。包括：住院医疗费用支出、门急诊医疗费用支出、个人账户基金支出、其他支出。

4.基金累计结余：指截止报告期末基本医疗保险的社会统筹和个人帐户基金累计结余金额。包括银行存款、财政专户、债券投资和其他。

失业保险

1.参加保险人数：指报告期末按照国家法律、法规和有关政策规定参加了失业保险的城镇企业事业单位的职工及地方政府规定参加失业保险的其他人员的人数。

2.失业保险基金收入：指按照规定从企业、事业及其他单位筹集的失业保险费及其他并入失业保险基金收入的总额。包括单位和个人缴纳的失业保险费、失业保险基金利息收入、上级补助收入、下级上解收入、转移收入、财政补贴和其他收入。

3.失业保险基金支出：指报告期内为保障失业人员和下岗职工基本生活、促进其再就业等支出的基金总额。包括失业救济金、医疗费、死亡丧葬补助费、抚恤救济费、转业训练费支出、失业保险经办机构管理费、补助下级支出、上解上级支出、转移支出、其他支出。

4.基金累计结余：指截止报告期末失业保险基金收支相抵后的累计余额。

工伤保险

1.参加保险人数：指报告期末依据国家有关规定参加工伤保险的职工人数。

2.享受保险待遇人数：指劳动者因工负伤致残、死亡或因患职业病致残，根据有关规定享受工伤保险待遇职工或供养直系亲属人数。包括伤残人数、职业病人数、因工死亡人数、供养直系亲属人数。

3.基金收入：指根据国家有关规定，由参加工伤保险的单位按国家规定的缴费基数和缴费比例缴纳的工伤保险基金，以及通过其他形式取得的形成基金来源的款项。包括：单位缴纳的社会统筹基金收入、财政补贴收入、利息收入、其他收入。

4.基金支出：指按照国家政策规定的开支范围和开支标准从工伤保险基金中支付给参加工伤保险的人员及供养直系亲属工伤保险待遇支出及其他支出。包括工伤医疗费、伤残补助金、工亡补助金、护理费、丧葬补助费、工伤预防费用、职业康复费用和其他支出。

5.基金累计结余：指截止报告期末工伤保险基金累计结余金额。包括银行存款、财政专户、债券投资和其他。

生育保险

1.参保人数：指报告期末依据有关规定参加生育保险的职工人数。

2.基金收入：指根据国家有关规定，由参加生育保险的单位按照国家规定的缴费基数和缴费比例缴纳的生育保险基金，以及通过其他方式取得的形成基金来源的款项，包括：单位缴纳的基金收入、利息收入和其他收入。

3.基金支出：指按照国家政策规定的开支范围和开支标准，从生育保险基金中支付给参加生育保险的职工，因妊娠、分娩和计划生育手术而享受的待遇及其他支出。包括：生育津贴、医疗费用支出及其他支出。

4.基金累计结余：指截止报告期末生育保险基金累计结余金额。包括银行存款、财政专户、债券投资和其他。

Explanatory Notes on Main Statistical Indicators

I. Urban Households

Population of Urban Households refer to members of households living and sharing economically together in the urban areas. All the income and expenditure of all the members of such households are included in the income and expenditure of the household.

Number of Dependents per Urban Employee refers to the ratio between number of persons in an urban household and the number of employed persons.

Total Income of Urban Households refers to the sum of wage and salary; net business income; income from properties; and income from transfers of members of the households. Income from selling of properties and income from borrowing are not included.

Disposable Income of Urban Households refers to the actual income at the disposal of members of the households which can be used for final consumption, other non-compulsory expenditure and savings. This equals to total income minus income tax, personal contribution to social security and subsidy for keeping diaries in being a sample household. The following formula is used:

Disposable income = total household income - income tax - personal contribution to social security - subsidy for keeping diaries for a sampled household.

Consumption Expenditure of Urban Households refers to total expenditure of households for consumption in daily life, including expenditure on the eight categories of food; clothing; housing; household appliances and services; health care and medical services; transport and communications; recreation, education and cultural services; and miscellaneous goods and services.

Expenditure of Urban Households on Consumption of Services refers to expenditure of households on various kinds of non-commercial services provided by society.

Urban Households by Income Group All households in the sample are grouped, by per capita disposable income of the household, into groups of lowest income, low income, lower middle income, middle income, upper middle income, high income and highest income, each group consisting of 10%, 10%, 20%, 20%, 20%, 10% and 10% of all households respectively. The lowest 5% of households are also referred to as poor households.

Engel's Coefficient refers to the percentage of expenditure on food in the total consumption expenditure, using the following formula:

$$\text{Engel's Coefficient} = \frac{\text{expenditure on food}}{\text{total consumption expenditure}} \times 100\%$$

II. Rural Household

Total Income refers to the sum of income earned from various sources by the rural households and their members during the reference period, and is classified as income from wages and salaries, income from household operations, income from properties and income from transfers.

Income from Wages and Salaries refers to income from labour earned by the members of rural households employed by other units or individuals.

Income from Household Operations refers to income by the rural households as units of production and operation. Operations by rural households are classified according to their economic activities namely agriculture, forestry, animal husbandry, fishery, manufacturing, construction, transportation, post and telecommunications, wholesale, retail and catering, social service, culture, education, health, and other household operations.

Income from Properties refers to the income received as returns by owners of financial assets or tangible non-productive assets by providing capitals or tangible non-productive assets to other institutional units.

Income from Transfers refers to the receipt by rural households and their members of goods, services, capital or rights of assets without giving or repaying accordingly, excluding capital provided to them for the formation of fixed assets. In general, it refers to all income received by rural households through redistribution.

Cash Income refers to income received by rural households and their members in the form of cash during the reference period. It is classified, by source of income, into income from wages and salaries, cash income from household operations, income from properties and income from transfers.

Net Income refers to the total income of rural households from all sources minus all corresponding expenses. The formula for calculation is as follows:

Net income = total income - taxes and fees paid - household operation expenses - taxes and fees depreciation of fixed assets for production - gifts to non-rural relatives

Net income is mainly used as input for reinvestment in production and as consumption expenditure of the year, and also used for savings and non-compulsory expenses of various forms. "Per capita net income of farmers" is the level of net income averaged by population, reflecting the average income level of rural households in a given area.

Total Expenditure refers to total expenses of rural households on production, consumption and redistribution, including expenditure on household operations; purchase of productive fixed assets; depreciation of productive fixed assets; taxes and fees; expenses on household consumption; expenses on properties; and expenses on transfers.

Ⅲ.Social Insurance

Basic Pension Insurance

1. Number of staff and workers covered refer to staff and workers participating in the basic pension insurance programme according to national laws, regulations and related policies at the end of the reference period, who have already had payment records in social security management agencies, including those who have interrupt payment without terminating the insurance programme. Those who have registered in the programme but with no payment records are not included.

2. **Number of retirees participating in basisc pension insurance programme** refer to number retirees participating in basic pension insurance programme by the end of reference period.

3. Revenue of the basic pension insurance programme refers to payments made by employers and individuals participating in the pension insurance programme in accordance with the basis and proportion stipulated in State regulations, and income from other sources that become source of pension insurance fund, including the premium paid by employers and staff and workers, interest income, subsidies from higher level agencies, income as transfer from subordinate agencies, transferred income, government financial subsidies and other income.

4. Expenditure of basic pension insurance programme refers to payment made on pensions and funeral subsidies to those retired and resigned people covered in pension insurance programmes according to related national policies on scopeand standard of expenditure. Also included are expenditure which arises due to shift of the insurance relationship or adjustment of funds among agencies. More specifically, included are pensions for resigned people, pensions for retired people, pension for people quitting jobs, various subsidies, medical fees, funeral subsidies, compensation payments, management fees for social security agencies, expenses on subsidies to lower subordinates, expenses as transfer to agencies at higher level, transferred expenditure and other expenditures on properties; and expenses on transfers.

5. Balance of basic pension insurance programme refers to the balance of basic pension insurance funds at the end of the reference period after deducting expenses from revenue.

Basic Medical Care Insurance

1. Number of people participating in the insurance programme refers to people participating in the basic medical care insurance programme according to related regulations as at the end of reference period, including number of staff and workers and retirees participating in this insurance programme.

2. Revenue of the insurance programme refers to payments made by employers and individuals participating in the medical care insurance programme in accordance with the basis and proportion stipulated in State regulations, and income from other sources that become source of medical insurance fund, including income of social comprehensive funds paid by employers, income from individual accounts, government financial subsidies, interest income and other income.

3. Expenditure of the insurance programme refers to payment made from social comprehensive funds to those retired and resigned people covered in basic medical care insurance within the scope and standards of expenditure according to related national policies, and medical care payment made from individual accounts to staff and workers and retirees, and other expenses, including medical expenses of hospital inpatients, medical expenses for outpatients and emergency patients, payment from individual accounts and other expenditure.

4. Balance of the basic medical care insurance programme refer to the balance of medical care insurance of social comprehensive funds and individual accounts at the end of the reference period, including bank savings, special fiscal accounts, investment in bonds and others.

Unemployment Insurance

1. Number of people covered refers to staff and workers in urban enterprises or institutions who have participated in the unemployment insurance programme according to relevant policies and regulations, and other people who have participated according to local government regulations, as at the end of reference period.

2. Revenue of the unemployment insurance programme refers to payments made by employers and individuals participating in unemployment insurance programme in accordance with relevant regulations and other income contributed to this programme, including unemployment insurance premium made by employers and individuals, interest income, subsidies from higher level agencies, income as transfer from subordinate agencies, transferred income, government financial subsidies and other income.

3. Expenditure of the unemployment insurance programme refers to total expenses during the reference period to guarantee the basic livelihood of unemployed people and laid-off staff and workers and to encourage their re-employment. Included are unemployment relief, medical fees, funeral subsidies, compensation payments, training expenses, management fees for unemployment insurance agencies, subsidies to lower level agencies, expenses as transfer to higher level agencies, transferred expenditure and other expenditure.

4. Balance of the unemployment insurance programme refers to the balance of revenue of the programme after deducting expenses at the end of the reference period.

Work Injury Insurance

1. Number of people covered refers to staff and workers who have participated in the work injury insurance programme according to relevant national regulations.

2. Number of beneficiaries refers to staff and workers and their direct dependents who can, in accordance with relevant regulations, benefit from work injury insurance, as a result of work injury leading to disability or death of the staff/worker, or occupational disease leading to disability. Included in this category are number of injured and disabled people, number of people with occupational diseases, number of deaths at work places, and number of direct dependents.

3. Revenue of the work injury insurance programme refers to payments made by employers participating in the work injury insurance programme in accordance with the basis and proportion stipulated in State regulations, and income from other sources that become source of work injury insurance fund, including income of social comprehensive funds paid by employers, government financial subsidies, interest income and other income.

4. Expenditure of the work injury insurance programme refers to payments made from work injury insurance funds to those who participated in the work injury insurance programme and their direct dependents within the scope and standards of expenditure according to related national policies, and other expenditure, including medical fees for work injury, injury and disability subsidies, death subsidies, nursing fees, funeral subsidies, injury prevention fees, occupational rehabilitation fees and other expenditure.

5. Balance of the work injury insurance programme refers to the balance of the work injury funds at the end of the reference period, including bank savings, special fiscal account, investment in bonds and others.

Maternity Insurance

1. Number of people covered refers to staff and workers who have participated in the maternity insurance programme according to relevant regulation at the end of the reporting period.

2. Revenue of maternity insurance refers to payments made by employers participating in the maternity insurance programme in accordance with the basis and proportion stipulated in State regulations, and income from other sources that become source of maternity insurance fund, including income of funds paid by employers, interest income and other income.

3. Expenditure of the maternity insurance programme refers to payments made from maternity insurance funds to staff and workers who participate in the maternity insurance programme within the scope and standards of expenditure in accordance with related national policies, expenses paid for pregnancy, child delivery or surgeries related to family planning, and other expenditure, including allowance for child bearing, medical fees and other expenditure.

4. Balance of the maternity programme refers to the balance of the maternity insurance funds at the end of reference period, including bank savings, special fiscal account, investment in funds and others.

第十篇 城市概况

CHAPTER 10 General Survey of Cities

简要说明
Brief Introduction

本篇资料的主要内容及来源

本篇资料反映新疆城市社会、经济发展和城市建设的基本情况。

城市概况资料主要包括城市公用事业基本情况、主要经济指标、市政设施、园林绿化、环境卫生、供水供气等。

本篇资料由新疆维吾尔自治区统计局国民经济综合统计处根据新疆维吾尔自治区建设厅和新疆维吾尔自治区统计局相关处室提供的年度数据整理。

Main content and source of data

Data in this chapter show the social and economic development and the urban construction of Xinjiang.

Data on the general survey cities include the basic condition of urban public facilities, main economic indicators, civil facilities, urban greenery, environment and sanitation, supply of gas and heating, public transportation, etc.

Data on this chapter are compiled by the Department of National Accounts of the Xinjiang Bureau of Statistics according to the data of yearly statistics, which are provided by the Construction Bureau of Xinjiang Uygur Autonomous Region and related departments of Statistics Bureau of Xinjiang Uygur Autonomous Region.

10-1 城市公用事业基本情况
Basic Statistics on City Public Utilities

项　　目	Item	2009	2010
城市及建筑物面积	**City Areas and Floor Space of Buildings**		
建成区面积(平方公里)	Area of Built Districts(sq.km)	800	838
征用土地面积(平方公里)	Land Put in Requisition for State Construction Projects (sq. km)	7.8	17.7
城市人口密度(人/平方公里)	Population Density of City Districts(persons/sq.km)	4922	4977
供水、供气及供热	**Water Supply, Gas Supply and Heating**		
自来水年供水量(万立方米)	Annual Volume of Tap Water Supply (10 000 cu.m)	75215	77263
＃生活用水量	Water Consumption for Residential use	25241	26078
平均每人日生活用水量(升)	Per -Capita Water Consumption for Residential Use (litre)	148.7	150.8
用水普及率(%)	Coverage Rate of Population with Access to Tap Water (%)	99.0	99.2
人工煤气供气量(万立方米)	Gaswork Gas Supply (10 000 cu.m)	931300	1752
＃家庭用量	Consumption of Gaswork Gas for Residential Use	1800	1752
天然气供气量(万立方米)	Natural Gas Supply (10 000 cu.m)	104498	134711
＃家庭用量	Consumption of Coal Gas for Residential Use	30615	40067
液化石油气供气量(吨)	Liquefied Petroleum Gas (ton)	81999	79617
＃家庭用量	Consumption of Liquefied Gas for Residential Use	65831	61050
天然气、煤气管道长度(公里)	Length of Gas Pipelines (km)	6214	7298
燃气普及率(%)	Goverage Rate of Urban Population with Access to Gas (%)	89.3	95.8
集中供热面积(万平方米)	Area of Centralized Heating (10 000 sq.m)	17073	19162
＃住　宅	Residential Buildings	12190	13298
市政工程	**Municipal Engineering**		
铺装道路长度(公里)	Length of Paved Roads (km)	4940	5178
平均每万人拥有 (公里)	Length of Paved Roads per 10 000 Population (km)	5.8	6.1
铺装道路面积(万平方米)	Area of Paved Roads (10 000 sq.m)	7715	8323
平均每人拥有(平方米)	Area of Paved Roads per Population (sq.m)	9.1	9.7
下水道长度(公里)	Length of Sewer Pipelines (km)	4081	4372
平均每万人拥有 (公里)	Length of Sewer Pipelines per 10 000 Population (km)	4.8	5.1
城市绿化	**City Greening**		
建成区绿化覆盖面积(公顷)	Green Areas of Completed Area (hectare)	29055	30530
每万人建成区绿地面积(公顷)	Green Areas of Completed Area per 10 000 Population (hectare)	34.1	35.7
公园数(个)	Number of Parks and Zoos(unit)	129	131
公园面积(公顷)	Area of Parks (hectare)	3146	3156
环境卫生	**Environmental Sanitation**		
清运生活垃圾(万吨)	Volume of Garbage Disposal (10 000 tons)	298	317
清运粪便(万吨)	Volume of Disposal of Excrement and Urine (10 000 tons)	4.8	4.1
每万人拥有公共厕所(座)	Number of Public Lavatories per 10 000 Population (unit)	2.2	2.5

10-2 各城市主要经济指标
Major Economic Indicators by Cities

单位: 万元 (2010 年) (10 000 yuan)

城市名称	City	地区生产总值(当年价格) Gross Region Production (current-year price)	第一产业 Primary Industry	第二产业 Secondary Industry	#工业 Industry
乌鲁木齐市	Urumqi City	13385172	199424	6004066	5147566
克拉玛依市	Karamay City	7113532	35171	6384205	6234705
吐鲁番市	Turpan City	518412	98147	200441	169941
哈 密 市	Hami [Kumul] City	1345594	150930	604425	413052
昌 吉 市	Changji City	1786301	250775	784131	642136
阜 康 市	Fukang City	807225	141534	502717	455402
伊 宁 市	Yining [Gulja] City	950356	45437	272426	163452
奎 屯 市	Kuytun City	723764	43880	401381	332861
塔 城 市	Tacheng [Qoqek] City	421951	98583	118990	70056
乌 苏 市	Usu City	961768	355405	416223	281741
阿勒泰市	Altay City	348547	61966	68203	47303
博 乐 市	Bole [Bortala] City	852107	246898	189710	119942
库尔勒市	Korla City	4392402	295943	3439955	3029961
阿克苏市	Aksu City	1114162	232061	327591	219953
阿图什市	Artux City	174289	34281	29890	15138
喀 什 市	Kashgar [Kaxgar] City	774733	39038	196838	125287
和 田 市	Hotan City	264788	28983	79753	30549
石河子市	Shi Hezi City	1349995	91825	686175	550975
阿拉尔市	Aral City	578330	363190	122595	93615
图木舒克市	Tumxuk City	149915	111182	10500	9129
五家渠市	Wujiaqu City				

城市名称	City	第三产业 Tertiary Industry	#交通运输、仓储和邮政业 Transport, Storage and Post	人均地区生产总值(元) Per Capita GDP (yuan)
乌鲁木齐市	Urumqi City	7181682	1342369	43039
克拉玛依市	Karamay City	694156	121257	121387
吐鲁番市	Turpan City	219824	65879	19165
哈 密 市	Hami [Kumul] City	590239	187035	30234
昌 吉 市	Changji City	751395	145403	37686
阜 康 市	Fukang City	162974	21171	49251
伊 宁 市	Yining [Gulja] City	632493	52254	20518
奎 屯 市	Kuytun City	278503	50746	47554
塔 城 市	Tacheng [Qoqek] City	204378	28066	19586
乌 苏 市	Usu City	190140	25329	27069
阿勒泰市	Altay City	218378	22848	18689
博 乐 市	Bole [Bortala] City	415499	78205	32523
库尔勒市	Korla City	656504	84705	80340
阿克苏市	Aksu City	554510	65391	23165
阿图什市	Artux City	110118	14079	7128
喀 什 市	Kashgar [Kaxgar] City	538857	70975	14645
和 田 市	Hotan City	156052	12082	8327
石河子市	Shi Hezi City	571995	58895	42816
阿拉尔市	Aral City	92545	4093	34238
图木舒克市	Tumxuk City	28233	1051	12047
五家渠市	Wujiaqu City			

10-2 续表 Continued

单位：万元 (10 000 yuan)

城市名称	City	固定资产投资总额 Investment in Fixed Assets	规模以上工业总产值（当年价格） Gross Industrial Output Value above Designated Size (At Current Prices)	地方财政一般预算收入 General Budgetary Revenue in Local Finance	地方财政一般预算支出 General Budgetary Expenditure in Local Finance
乌鲁木齐市	Urumqi City	3925724	16747592		
克拉玛依市	Karamay City	1714244	13308538	424303	547711
吐鲁番市	Turpan City	181490	376009	34905	97225
哈密市	Hami [Kumul] City	789090	947893	122381	172566
昌吉市	Changji City	450028	1605465	119565	187024
阜康市	Fukang City	349988	800734	56756	99047
伊宁市	Yining [Gulja] City	354608	284519	95181	200553
奎屯市	Kuytun City	422934	792199	78216	121445
塔城市	Tacheng [Qoqek] City	75848	96218	17122	88479
乌苏市	Usu City	335900	406839	40854	121871
阿勒泰市	Altay City	184863	103466	18683	118944
博乐市	Bole [Bortala] City	408630	266458	30211	97287
库尔勒市	Korla City	1844970	4423329	156342	208617
阿克苏市	Aksu City	348196	607806	81544	151980
阿图什市	Artux City	56154	47261	9962	106286
喀什市	Kashgar [Kaxgar] City	432356	292362	77326	315308
和田市	Hotan City	248133	62305	25575	126110
石河子市	Shi Hezi City	866979	2002302	137555	172440
阿拉尔市	Aral City	202656	337606	13103	20915
图木舒克市	Tumxuk City	92483	68879	5500	15111
五家渠市	Wujiaqu City	727937	438361	22882	29424

城市名称	City	居民消费价格指数(上年=100) Consumer Price Index (preceding year=100)	社会消费品零售总额 Total Retail Sales of Consumer Goods	在岗职工人数(万人) Number of Fully-employed Staff and Workers (10 000 persons)	在岗职工平均货币工资(元) Average Money Wage of Staff and Workers (yuan)
乌鲁木齐市	Urumqi City	102.7	5142359	46.89	41529
克拉玛依市	Karamay City	104.5	347872	15.15	42767
吐鲁番市	Turpan City	104.6	148335	2.81	30132
哈密市	Hami [Kumul] City	105.0	346704	6.37	34441
昌吉市	Changji City	103.6	468594	6.08	34653
阜康市	Fukang City		155691	2.35	31106
伊宁市	Yining [Gulja] City	106.2	364339	7.12	29155
奎屯市	Kuytun City	103.3	135857	2.89	30453
塔城市	Tacheng [Qoqek] City	105.2	91809	2.74	27444
乌苏市	Usu City	105.5	86907	5.40	19866
阿勒泰市	Altay City	104.6	113004	4.05	25499
博乐市	Bole [Bortala] City	105.7	134811	5.18	27396
库尔勒市	Korla City	104.5	425335	9.08	34628
阿克苏市	Aksu City	106.1	328201	6.19	30716
阿图什市	Artux City	104.3	55554	1.86	28473
喀什市	Kashgar [Kaxgar] City	104.8	345560	5.27	31895
和田市	Hotan City	104.4	99934	2.68	34701
石河子市	Shi Hezi City	103.7	434506	9.63	32221
阿拉尔市	Aral City			4.17	30066
图木舒克市	Tumxuk City			1.60	26746
五家渠市	Wujiaqu City			1.93	27564

10-3 各城市市区设施水平

Level of Urban Public Facilities in Cities

(2010 年)

城市名称	City	城市用水普及率(%) Coverage Rate of Urban Population with Access to Tap Water (%)	城市燃气普及率(%) Coverage Rate of Population with Access to Gas (%)	人均铺装道路面积(平方米) Per Capital Area of Paved Roads (sq.m)	人均公园绿地面积(平方米) Per Capital Area of Parks and Green Land (sq.m)	排水管道密度(公里/平方公里) Density of Sewage Pipelines (km/sq.km)
总　计	**Total**	99.17	95.80	13.19	8.61	5.22
乌鲁木齐市	Urumqi City	99.93	99.60	7.18	7.39	3.42
克拉玛依市	Karamay City	100.00	100.00	23.60	9.04	7.09
吐鲁番市	Turpan City	100.00	92.31	17.50	10.19	3.97
哈密市	Hami [Kumul] City	100.00	99.92	15.73	8.71	10.09
昌吉市	Changji City	100.00	100.00	9.37	8.69	3.35
阜康市	Fukang City	100.00	91.75	12.95	7.92	7.11
伊宁市	Yining [Gulja] City	99.19	92.52	17.09	8.51	11.20
奎屯市	Kuytun City	100.00	90.69	13.80	9.01	8.31
塔城市	Tacheng [Qoqek] City	91.96	77.66	15.80	13.76	6.67
乌苏市	Usu City	89.44	67.78	26.11	6.89	6.00
阿勒泰市	Altay City	95.17	77.13	8.76	19.46	5.93
博乐市	Bole [Bortala] City	94.96	49.26	9.79	11.57	5.01
库尔勒市	Korla City	100.00	100.00	27.38	10.90	4.43
阿克苏市	Aksu City	100.00	99.80	12.18	6.96	6.41
阿图什市	Artux City	100.00	94.29	16.00	1.86	5.90
喀什市	Kashgar [Kaxgar] City	100.00	94.16	17.54	10.63	3.44
和田市	Hotan City	96.54	97.38	16.54	9.23	4.19
石河子市	Shihezi City	100.00	97.12	22.56	10.40	10.68
阿拉尔市	Aral City	96.77	96.77	23.00	12.26	7.51
图木舒克市	Tumxuk City	57.36	54.72	30.57	30.57	4.80
五家渠市	Wujiaqu City	96.49	83.45	39.31	7.99	6.57

10-4 主要年份城市自来水情况

Basic Statistics on Tap Water Supply in Cities in Main Years

指　标	Item	2000	2005	2010
年末水厂生产能力(万吨/日)	Production Capacity of TapWater Supply (10 000 tons/day)	292	360	373
年末供水管道总长度(公里)	Length of Water Supply Piplines (km)	4448	4586	6507
全年供水总量(亿立方米)	Total Annual Volume of Water supply (100 millon cu.m)	5.0	5.4	7.7
＃生活用水	For Residential Use	2.5	2.3	2.6
生产用水	For Productive Use	2.0	1.8	2.1
平均每人日生活用水量(升)	Per-Capitall Daily Consumption of Tap Water for Residential Use (litre)	165.1	163.2	150.8
用水人口(万人)	Number of Residents with Access to Tap Water (10 000 persons)	418	510	626

10-5 主要年份城市市政建设情况
Statistics on City Construction in Cities in Main Years

指　　标	Item	2000	2005	2010
实有道路长度(公里)	Length of Paved Roads (km)	2809	3849	5178
实有道路面积(万平方米)	Area of Paved Roads (10 000 sq.m)	3654	5984	8323
城市桥梁(座)	Number of City Bridges (unit)	253	315	384
防洪堤长度(公里)	Length of Dyke for Control of Flood (km)	130	203	262
城市下水道总长度(公里)	Length of Sewer Pipelines (km)	2008	2960	4372
城市污水日处理能力(万立方米)	Daily Disposal Capacity of Sewage (10 000 cu.m)	46	125	157
城市路灯盏数(千盏)	Number of Street Light (1 000 units)	72.9	250.3	400.1

注：城市污水日处理能力指污水处理厂处理能力，不包括其他污水处理设施处理量。
Note: The daily treatment capacity in urban area refers to the treatment capacity of a waste- water treatment plant, excluding the volume handled by other polluted-water treatment facility.

10-6 主要年份城市园林绿化情况
Basic Statistics on Parks and Green Areas in Cities in Main Years

指　　标	Item	2000	2005	2010
城市园林绿地面积(公顷)	Area of Park and Green Land (hectare)	19124	22466	37686
#建成区绿地面积	Green Land of Completed Area			27773
每万人建成区绿地面积(公顷)	Green Areas of Completed Area Per 10 000 Population (hectare)	53.4	43.1	35.7
建成区绿化覆盖率(%)	Green Covrage Rate of Completed Area (%)	29.1	31.8	36.4
平均每人公园绿地面积(平方米)	Per Capita Parks Green Areas (sq.m)	6.4	6.4	8.6
公园数(个)	Number of Parks and Zoos (unit)	84	112	131
公园面积(公顷)	Area of Parks (hectare)	1568	2211	3156

10-7 主要年份城市环境卫生情况
Basic Statistics on Urban Environment in Cities in Main Years

指　　标	Item	2000	2005	2010
环卫专用车辆设备数量(辆)	Number of Special Vehicles for Environmental Sanitation (unit)	767	1094	1690
公共厕所(座)	Number of Public Lavatories (unit)	1684	1905	2119
每万人拥有公共厕所(座)	Number of Public Lavatories Per 10 000 Population (unit)	4.7	3.7	2.5
道路清扫面积(万平方米)	Area under Cleaning Program (10 000 sq.m)	3224	5671	8080
#机械化	Mechanization			3163
清运生活垃圾(万吨)	Volum of Garbage Disposal (10 000 tons)	259	344	317
清运粪便 (万吨)	Volum of Excrement and Urine Disposal (10 000 tons)	16	4	4

10-8 主要年份城市煤气、液化石油气、天然气情况
Basic Statistics on Supply of Gas, Liquefied Petroleum Gas and Natural Gas in Cities in Main Years

指　　标	Item	2000	2005	2010
人工煤气生产能力(万立方米/日)	Production Capacity of Gaswork Gas (10 000 cu.m/day)		1526	49
管道长度(公里)	Length of Gas Pipelines (km)	385	2327	7298
人工煤气	Coal Gas		80	71
液化石油气	Liquefied Petroleum Gas		60	82
天然气	Natural Gas	385	2187	7145
全年供气总量(万立方米)	Volume of Gas Supply (10 000 cu.m)			
人工煤气	Coal Gas		232340	1752
液化石油气(吨)	Liquefied Petroleum Gas (ton)	244018	147314	79617
天然气	Natural Gas	5385	45665	134711
用气人口(万人)	Population with Access to Gas (10 000 persons)		465.55	604.37
人工煤气	Coal Gas		5.00	8.75
液化石油气	Liquefied Petroleum Gas	305.70	240.18	150.64
天然气	Natural Gas	27.00	220.37	444.98

10-9 主要年份城市集中供热情况
Basic Statistics on Heating in Cities in Main Years

指　　标	Item	2000	2005	2010
供应能力	**Heating Capacity**			
蒸汽(吨/小时)	Steam (ton/hour)	1638	1441	1376
热水(兆瓦)	Hot Water (1 billion kw)	6145	12309	18897
供热总量(万吉焦)	**Quantity of Heating Supplied (10 000 gigajoules)**			
蒸 汽	Steam		1095	1242
热 水	Hot Water		8187	16866
管道长度(公里)	**Length of Heating Pipelines (km)**			
蒸 汽	Steam	250	137	207
热 水	Hot Water	2064	2818	5912
供热面积(万平方米)	**Area of Centralized Heating (10 000 sq.m)**	**5170**	**10964**	**19162**
#住 宅	Residential Buildings		7567	13298

主要统计指标解释

供水综合生产能力 指按供水设施取水、净化、送水、出厂输水干管等环节设计能力计算的综合生产能力。包括在原设计能力的基础上，经挖、革、改增加的生产能力。计算时，以四个环节中最薄弱的环节为主确定能力。

年末供水管道长度 指从送水泵到用户水表之间所有管道的长度。不包括新安装尚未使用、水厂内以及用户建筑物内的管道。

全年供水总量 指报告期供水企业(单位)供出的全部水量。包括有效供水量和漏损水量。

生活用水量 包括公共服务用水和居民家庭用水。公共服务用水指为城市社会公共生活服务的用水。包括行政事业单位、部队营区和公共设施服务、社会服务业、批发零售贸易业、旅馆饮食业以及其他公共服务业等单位的用水。居民家庭用水指城市范围内所有居民家庭的日常生活用水。包括城市居民、农民家庭、公共供水站用水。

用水普及率 指城市用水人口数与城市人口总数的比率。计算公式为：

用水普及率＝城市用水人口数／城市人口总数×100%

人工煤气生产能力 指报告期末人工煤气生产厂制气、净化、输送等环节的综合生产能力，不包括备用设备能力。一般按设计能力计算，如果实际生产能力大于设计能力时应按实际测定的生产能力计算。

供气管道长度 指报告期末从气源厂压缩机的出口或门站出口至各类用户引入管之间的全部已经通气投入使用的管道长度。不包括煤气生产厂、输配站、液化气储存站、灌瓶站、储配站、气化站、混气站、供应站等厂(站)内的管道。

全年供气总量 指全年燃气企业(单位)向用户供应的燃气数量。包括销售量和损失量。

燃气普及率 指报告期末使用煤气的城市人口数)与城市人口总数的比率。计算公式为：

燃气普及率＝城市用气人口数／城市人口总数×100%

城市供热能力 指供热企业（单位）向城市热用户输送热源的设计能力。

城市供热总量 指在报告期供热企业（单位）向城市热用户输送全部蒸汽和热水的总热量。

城市供热管道长度 指从各种热源到热用户建筑物接入口之间的全部蒸汽和热水的管道长度。不包括各类热源厂内部的管道长度。

年末道路长度 指年末道路长度和与道路相通的桥梁、隧道的长度，按车行道中心线计算。在统计时只统计路面宽度在3.5米（含3.5米）以上的各种铺装道路，包括开放型工业区和住宅区道路在内。

城市桥梁 指为跨越天然或人工障碍物而修建的构筑物。包括跨河桥、立交桥、人行天桥以及人行地下通道等。按使用年限分为永久性桥和半永久性桥。

城市排水道总长度 指所有排水总管、干管、支管、检查井及连接井进出口等长度之和。

城市污水日处理能力 指污水处理厂（污水处理处理装置）每昼夜处理污水量的设计能力。

城市绿地面积 指报告期末用作园林和绿化的各种绿地面积。包括园林绿地、公共绿地、防护绿地、附属绿地和其他绿地面积。

公园绿地 城市中向公众开放的以游憩为主要功能，有一定的游憩设施和服务设施，同时兼有健全生态、美化景观，防灾减灾等综合作用的绿化用地。包括综合公园、社区公园、专类公园、带状公园和街旁绿地。其中综合公园、专类公园和带状公园面积之和为公园面积。

清扫保洁面积 指报告期末对城市道路和公共场所（主要包括城市行车道、人行道、车行隧道、人行过街地下通道、道路附属绿地、地铁站、高架路、人行过街天桥、立交桥、广场、停车场及其他设施等）进行清扫保洁的面积。一天清扫多次的，按清扫保洁面积最大的一次计算。

市容环卫专用车辆 指用于环境卫生作业、监察的专用车辆和设备，包括用于道路清扫、冲洗、洒水、除雪、垃圾粪便清运、市容监察以及与其配套使用的车辆和设备。

Explanatory Notes on Main Statistical Indicators

Production Capacity of Water Supply refers to the designed overall production capacity of water facilities, covering the four segments of water collection, purification, conveyance, and outflow through trunk pipelines. Increased capacity through transformation and innovation projects is included as well. The capacity is determined mainly on the weakest of the above-mentioned four segments.

Length of Water Supply Pipelines at Year-end refers to the total length of all the pipelines between the water pumps and the user water meters, excluding pipelines newly installed but not used yet, pipeline in the water factory,and pipeline in the user's buildings.

Annual Volume of Water Supply refers to the total volume of water supplied by water-works (units) during the reference period, including both the effective water supply and loss during the water supply.

Consumption of Water for Residential Use refers to water consumption of households for daily life and water consumption of public service facilities. The latter refers to water consumption for urban public services, including the consumption of government agencies and public institutions, military barracks, public facilities, wholesale and retail outlets, restaurants, hotels, and other units providing public services. Household water consumption refers to consumption of water for daily life of all households within the boundary of cities, including households of urban residents and farmers, and public water supply stations.

Coverage Rate of Urban Population with Access to Tap Water refers to the ratio of the urban population with access to tap water to the total urban population. The formula is:

$$\text{Coverage of urban population with access to tap water} = \frac{\text{Urban population with access to tap water}}{\text{Urban population}} \times 100\%$$

Production Capacity of Gaswork Gas refers to the overall production capacity of the urban gasworks in gas generation, purification and delivery at the end of the reference period, excluding capacity of the reserved facilities. In general, it is determined by the designed capacity, and when actual production capacity is larger than the designed capacity, the capacity is determined by the actual measurement on the weakest segment in the production, purification and delivery.

Length of Gas Pipelines refers to the total length of pipelines in use between the outlet of the compressor of gas-work or outlet of gas stations and the leading pipe of users, excluding pipelines within gasworks, delivery stations, LPG storage stations, refilling stations, gas-mixing stations and supply stations.

Volume of Gas Supply refers to the total volume of gas provided to users by gas-producing enterprises (units) in a year, including the volume sold and the volume lost.

Coverage Rate of Urban Population with Access to Gas refers to the ratio of the urban population with access to gas to the total urban population at the end of the reference period. The formula is:

$$\text{Coverage rate of urban population with access to gas} = \frac{\text{Urban population with access to gas}}{\text{Urban population}} \times 100\% .$$

Heating Capacity in Urban Areas refers to the designed capacity of heating enterprises (units) in supplying heating energy to urban users during the reference period.

Quantity of Heat Supplied in Urban Areas refers to the total quantity of heat from steam and hot water supplied to urban users by heating enterprises (units) during the reference period.

Length of Urban Heating Pipelines refers to the total length of steam or hot water pipelines for sources of heat to the leading pipelines of the buildings of the users, excluding internal pipelines in heat generating enterprises.

Length of Paved Roads at Year-end refers to the length of roads with paved surface including bridges and tunnels connected with roads by the end of the year. Length of the roads is measured by the central lines for vehicles for paved roads with a width of 3.5 meters and over, including roads in open-ended factory compounds and residential quarters.

Urban Bridges refer to bridges built to cross over natural or man-made barriers, including bridges over rivers, overpasses for traffic and for pedestrians, underpasses for pedestrians, etc. Both permanent and semi-permanent bridges are included.

Length of Urban Sewage Pipes refers to the total length of general drainage, trunks, branch and inspection wells, connection wells, inlets and outlets, etc.

Daily Disposal Capacity of Urban Sewage refers to the designed 24-hour capacity of sewage disposal by the sewage treatment works or facilities.

Area of Urban Green Areas refers to the total area occupied for green projects at the end of the reference period, including park green land, production green land, protection green land, green land attached to institutions, and other green areas.

Park Green Area refers to green areas open to the public for amusement and rest with the facilities of amusement, rest and services. Its function includes perfecting ecology, beautifying landscape, and preventing and reducing disaster. Park green areas include comprehensive park, community park, topic park, belt-shaped park and green area nearby street. Total areas of comprehensive park, topic park and belt-shaped is the area of park.

Area Cleaned refers to the area which are regularly cleaned, as at the end of the reference period, at urban roads and public places (mainly including urban roadways, pedestrian walkways, vehicular tunnels, pedestrian underpasses, underground railway stations, lifted roads, pedestrians walk bridges, overpasses, plazas, carparks and other facilities). If there are several times of cleaning in a day at a location, the area of that time of cleaning with the largest area cleaned will be taken.

Vehicles Dedicated to Urban Cleanliness and Environmental Sanitation refer to vehicles and facilities dedicated for use in the operation, management and monitoring of environmental hygiene work. They include vehicles for road cleaning, washing, showering, ice removal, disposal of garbage and human wastes, cleanliness monitoring and related activities.

第十一篇
自然资源和环境保护

CHAPTER 11
Natural Resources and Environment Protection

简要说明
Brief Introduction

本篇资料的主要内容及来源

本篇主要反映新疆维吾尔自治区自然资源、自然状况及环境保护事业发展情况等资料。主要内容包括自然资源储量和自然状况及水环境、大气环境、固体废物、声环境、生态环境、自然灾害和环境污染治理投资等内容。

水资源、城市生活垃圾清运及处理、地质灾害与防治、矿产资源资料、土地资源和土地利用情况、林木资源等资料分别由新疆维吾尔自治区水利厅、建设厅、地震局、国土资源厅、林业厅提供;气象资料由新疆维吾尔自治区气象局提供。环境污染与治理、声环境、工业污染治理投资等情况由新疆维吾尔自治区环境保护厅依据年报资料整理提供。

2009 年国家进行了第二次全国土地调查，我区调查数据目前国土资源部尚未反馈,为此,2011 年年鉴中涉及土地资源、矿产资源及相关内容表式仍然沿用 2008 年度数据。

Main Content and Source of Data

This chapter contain information that reflect the natural conditions and natural resources and data on development of environment protection in Xinjiang Uygur Autonomous Region, including natural resources and natural condition,total water resources, atmosphere environment, solid wastes, environmental noise, eco-environment protection, natural disaster and investments in the treatment of environmental pollution etc.

Data on water resource, collection and disposal of urban consumption wastes, geological disasters, land use, forest resource, etc. are provided respectively by Bureau of Water Conservancy, Bureau of Construction, Seismological Bureau, Bureau of Land and Resources, Forestry Bureau in Xinjiang Uygur Autonomous Region; Meteorological data are provided by the Xinjiang Uygur Autonomous Region Meteorological Bureau. Data on environment pollution and treatment, noise monitoring and on investment in the treatment of industrial pollution are provided by the Xinjiang Environmental Protection Bureau.

Because data of the second National land sruvey ni 2009 don´t feedback.So data on land ensured reserves of major minerai followed data in 2008.

11-1 自 然 资 源
Natural Resources

指　标	Item	2010
自然状况	**State of the Nature**	
经纬度	Longitude and Latitude	
东　经	East Longitude	73° 40′ ~96° 23′
北　纬	North Latitude	34° 25′ ~49° 10′
气　候	Climate	
年平均气温(摄氏度)	Annual Average Temperature (℃)	9.8
北　疆	North Xinjiang	7.4
南　疆	South Xinjiang	12.9
东　疆	East Xinjiang	13.1
年平均降水量(毫米)	Annual Average Precipitation (mm)	217.6
北　疆	North Xinjiang	299.7
南　疆	South Xinjiang	142.5
东　疆	East Xinjiang	36.0
平均日照时数(小时)	Average Sunny Hours (hour)	2751.4
北　疆	North Xinjiang	2703.3
南　疆	South Xinjiang	2689.9
东　疆	East Xinjiang	3121.5
自然资源	**Natural Resources**	
土地资源(万公顷)	Land Resources (10 000 hectares)	
土地总面积	Total Land Area	16648.97
农用地	Land for farm use	6308.48
耕地面积	Area of Cultivated Land	412.46
园地面积	Garden Area	36.42
林地面积	Woodland Area	676.48
牧草地面积	Pastureland Area	5111.38
其他农用地	Other Land for Agriculture	71.75
建设用地	Land for Construction	123.98
未利用地	Land yet to be Used	10216.51
土地利用率(%)	Land utilization rate (%)	38.64
林木资源	Forest resources	
活立木总蓄积量(万立方米)	Total Standing Stock Volume (10 000 cu.m)	33914.50
林地蓄积量(万立方米)	Woodland Stock Volume (10 000 cu.m)	30100.54

11-1 续表 Continued

指　标	Item	2010
有林地面积(万公顷)	Woodland Area (10 000 hectares)	201.62
灌木林地面积(万公顷)	Bush Woodland Area (10 000 hectares)	462.78
四旁树(万株)	Surrounding Woods (10 000 trees)	23696.00
森林覆盖率(%)	Forest coverage Rate (%)	4.02
水资源(亿立方米)	Water Resources (100 million cu.m)	
水资源总量	Total Water Resources Volume	754.29
地表水水资源量	Surface Water Volume	713.64
地下水水资源量	Underground Water Volume	470.47
重复计算量	Volume of Repeated Computation	429.82
主要矿产资源保有储量	**Reserve of Main Mineral Resources**	
铁矿(万吨)	Iron Ore (10 000 tons)	101875.89
铬矿(万吨)	Chromium Ore (10 000 tons)	170.88
铜矿(金属)(万吨)	Copper Ore (10 000 tons)	246.99
铅矿(金属)(万吨)	Lead Ore (10 000 tons)	98.91
锌矿(金属)(万吨)	Zinc Ore (10 000 tons)	205.69
铝土矿(万吨)	Bauxite(10 000 tons)	55.32
镍矿(金属)(万吨)	Nickel Ore (10 000 tons)	96.59
煤(亿吨)	Coal (100 million tons)	1977.25
耐火粘土(万吨)	Fire-proof Clay (10 000 tons)	709.50
钠硝石(万吨)	Nitratite (10 000 tons)	6164.70
芒硝(Na_2SO_4) (万吨)	Mirabilite(Na_2SO_4) (10 000 tons)	3777799.50
盐矿(NaCl) (万吨)	Solidum Salt(NaCI) (10 000 tons)	743420.20
钾盐(KCl) (万吨)	Potassium(KCI) (10 000 tons)	9186.90
石棉(万吨)	Asbest (10 000 tons)	830.60
云母(吨)	Mica (ton)	54416.87
蛭石(万吨)	Roseite (10 000 tons)	1335.60
水泥用灰岩(万吨)	Limestone Used for Cement (10 000 tons)	157905.48
膨润土(万吨)	Bentonite (10 000 tons)	36049.40
饰面用花岗岩(万立方米)	Granite as Veneer (10 000 cu.m)	12268.40

注：1.水资源为 2009 年数据。2.林木资源为 2006 年自治区森林资源第五次复查数据（2009 年公布）。3.因 2009 年第二次全国土地调查数据国家尚未反馈，土地资源及主要矿产资源保有储量仍沿用 2008 年度数据。

Note: a)Water-resources is based on the data in 2009.b)Figures of 2006 forest resources were form the fifth Autonomous Region Forest Survey(2009 announced).c)Because data of the Second National Land Survey in 2009 don't feedback, so data of land resources and ensured reserves of major mineral followed in 2008.

11-2 主要山脉基本情况
Main Mountain Ranges

山脉名称	Mountain Range	山峰高程 (米) Height of Mountain Peak (m)	雪线高程 (米) Height of Snow Line (m)	冰川面积 (平方公里) Glacier Area (sq.km)
合 计	**Total**			**23020**
天 山	Tianshan Mountains	7435	3600-4400	9548
阿尔泰山	Altay Mountains	4374	3000-3200	287
喀喇昆仑山及昆仑山	Karakorum Mountains and Kunlun Mountains	8611	5100-5400	3265
帕米尔	Pamirs	7579	5500-5700	2258

11-3 主要湖泊基本情况
Major Lakes

湖泊名称	Lake	湖水面积 (平方公里) Area of Lakes (sq. km)	湖面高程 (米) Height of Lake Surface (m)	水质类型 Water Type
博斯腾湖	The Bosten Lake [Bagrax]	972	1048	微咸 slight salty
乌伦古湖	The Ulunggur Lake	736	468	盐 salt
赛里木湖	The Sayram Lake	454	2073	咸 alkaline
艾比湖	The Aybi Lake [Eynur]	898	189	盐 salt

11-4 主要河流基本情况
Major Rivers

(2010 年)

河流名称	River	流域面积 (平方公里) Drainage Area (sq.km)	河长 (公里) Length (km)	年径流量 (亿立方米) Annual Flow (100 million cu.m)
玛纳斯河	Manas River	5156	190	16.57
开都河	Kaidu River	19022	530	43.36
渭干河	Ugan River	16660	256	34.32
克孜河	Kizil River	15710	233	33.48
乌伦古河	Ulunggur River	32040	821	25.87
塔里木河	Tarim River		2437	71.95

11-5 主要城市平均气温

Monthly Average Temperature of Major Cities

单位：摄氏度 (2010 年) (℃)

城　　市	City	一月 Jan.	二月 Feb.	三月 Mar.	四月 Apr.	五月 May	六月 June	七月 July
乌鲁木齐市	Urumqi City	-10.6	-12.3	-4.4	8.7	16.2	22.5	24.0
克拉玛依市	Karamay City	-13.1	-14.5	-4.0	10.4	19.4	25.9	26.8
石河子市	Shihezi City	-12.7	-13.8	-5.5	10.0	18.8	24.4	25.6
阜康市	Fukang City	-13.6	-14.4	-5.5	9.9	18.3	24.5	25.7
伊宁市	Yining [Gulja] City	-4.4	-5.6	4.9	13.5	17.3	22.6	23.6
塔城市	Tacheng [Qoqek] City	-8.6	-12.1	-3.3	8.9	15.5	22.5	23.8
阿勒泰市	Altay City	-16.2	-18.1	-9.6	2.2	13.7	21.3	21.9
博乐市	Bole [Bor tala] City	-13.3	-15.0	-4.5	9.2	17.9	23.2	24.1
库尔勒市	Korla City	-4.9	-0.7	7.2	14.0	19.3	26.8	27.9
阿克苏市	Aksu City	-4.8	-1.8	7.8	14.9	19.1	22.9	24.6
阿图什市	Artux City	-2.3	-0.7	10.0	16.9	20.2	23.0	26.3
喀什市	Kashgar [Kaxgar] City	-2.0	-0.4	10.4	16.7	19.5	22.5	25.8
和田市	Hotan City	-0.5	1.8	11.8	17.3	21.0	22.3	26.3
吐鲁番市	Turpan City	-4.4	1.8	9.1	18.2	25.1	32.3	33.3
哈密市	Hami [Kumul] City	-7.7	-3.3	2.9	11.9	19.7	26.8	28.3

城　　市	City	八月 Aug.	九月 Sept.	十月 Oct.	十一月 Nov.	十二月 Dec.	全年平均 Annual Average
乌鲁木齐市	Urumqi City	22.8	18.0	9.7	2.4	-8.2	7.4
克拉玛依市	Karamay City	25.7	20.3	11.0	2.2	-9.8	8.4
石河子市	Shi Hezi City	23.8	18.4	10.3	1.9	-10.3	7.6
阜康市	Fukang City	23.9	18.2	9.6	0.4	-10.8	7.2
伊宁市	Yining [Gulja] City	22.6	17.5	11.0	3.9	-2.9	10.3
塔城市	Tacheng [Qoqek] City	21.8	16.9	10.1	1.9	-8.6	7.4
阿勒泰市	Altay City	19.6	14.1	7.5	-2.1	-14.4	3.3
博乐市	Bole [Bor tala] City	22.7	17.7	9.6	1.6	-9.6	7.0
库尔勒市	Korla City	27.9	20.2	12.5	3.6	-5.7	12.3
阿克苏市	Aksu City	25.5	18.6	12.6	4.3	-5.0	11.6
阿图什市	Artux City	27.4	19.6	14.2	6.7	-2.5	13.2
喀什市	Kashgar [Kaxgar] City	26.5	18.8	13.9	7.0	-2.1	13.1
和田市	Hotan City	27.4	20.2	14.6	7.6	-0.7	14.1
吐鲁番市	Turpan City	31.2	24.2	16.2	5.9	-5.4	15.6
哈密市	Hami [Kumul] City	25.1	18.5	10.5	2.0	-9.2	10.5

11-6 主要城市降水量
Monthly Precipitation of Major Cities

单位：毫米 (2010 年) (millimeter)

城　　市	City	一月 Jan.	二月 Feb.	三月 Mar.	四月 Apr.	五月 May	六月 June	七月 July
乌鲁木齐市	Urumqi City	15.6	9.5	46.8	30.0	26.2	31.2	13.2
克拉玛依市	Karamay City	5.4	10.0	3.7	26.4	6.4	25.7	13.0
石河子市	Shi Hezi City	21.2	37.7	57.2	27.2	40.8	39.3	29.1
阜康市	Fukang City	19.3	6.3	26.5	14.4	15.2	25.7	10.7
伊宁市	Yining [Gulja] City	27.8	64.5	86.1	39.1	22.3	29.2	35.2
塔城市	Tacheng [Qoqek] City	82.5	21.2	55.0	48.3	42.5	18.2	26.1
阿勒泰市	Altay City	75.0	26.6	53.3	8.1	25.6	6.0	10.6
博乐市	Bole [Bortala] City	11.8	3.6	33.2	14.7	22.8	46.2	12.4
库尔勒市	Korla City		1.5	0.7	10.1	7.7	1.5	7.1
阿克苏市	Aksu City		7.2	4.6		6.2	35.9	38.7
阿图什市	Artux City		15.9	8.2	0.5	12.7	47.9	56.5
喀什市	Kashgar [Kaxgar] City		18.7	11.4	0.3	35.0	29.1	32.2
和田市	Hotan City		11.3	15.8		23.5	31.5	2.8
吐鲁番市	Turpan City					0.4	2.5	1.1
哈密市	Hami [Kumul] City	2.5		1.0	6.1	7.6	20.4	6.5

城　　市	City	八月 Aug.	九月 Sept.	十月 Oct.	十一月 Nov.	十二月 Dec.	全年合计 Annual Total
乌鲁木齐市	Urumqi City	12.5	5.1	32.5	28.3	31.5	282.4
克拉玛依市	Karamay City	3.4	4.3	19.3	0.6	8.7	126.9
石河子市	Shihezi City	24.3	8.7	33.9	23.3	24.4	367.1
阜康市	Fukang City	5.2	8.6	31.4	25.1	19.8	208.2
伊宁市	Yining [Gulja] City	10.6	13.2	85.8	25.6	26.0	465.4
塔城市	Tacheng [Qoqek] City	22.1	2.0	19.5	46.4	86.5	470.3
阿勒泰市	Altay City	19.2	3.6	26.3	41.3	42.9	338.5
博乐市	Bole [Bortala] City	7.0	8.5	24.2	15.1	2.9	202.4
库尔勒市	Korla City	2.4	2.2	6.3	2.8	2.5	44.8
阿克苏市	Aksu City	0.2	35.9	15.2	0.2		144.1
阿图什市	Artux City	0.3	62.5	15.4			219.9
喀什市	Kashgar [Kaxgar] City	0.8	49.1	15.0			191.6
和田市	Hotan City	0.3	13.3	13.4			111.9
吐鲁番市	Turpan City	0.1	0.4		1.1	1.4	7.0
哈密市	Hami [Kumul] City	4.4	8.3	1.2		6.9	64.9

11-7 主要城市日照时数
Monthly Sunshine Hours of Major Cities

单位：小时 (2010 年) (hour)

城 市	City	一月 Jan.	二月 Feb.	三月 Mar.	四月 Apr.	五月 May	六月 June	七月 July
乌鲁木齐市	Urumqi City	107.8	99.2	219.8	286.9	309.1	315.3	301.7
克拉玛依市	Karamay City	77.2	121.0	181.9	274.2	332.3	317.3	301.9
石河子市	Shi Hezi City	81.8	66.8	177.9	239.1	296.6	288.7	301.7
阜康市	Fukang City	64.7	88.9	203.5	266.9	298.6	313.1	290.7
伊宁市	Yining [Gulja] City	133.6	78.9	219.4	277.6	333.1	319.6	315.2
塔城市	Tacheng [Qoqek] City	103.9	143.5	200.3	275.7	334.3	342.3	325.0
阿勒泰市	Altay City	128.3	181.3	247.6	302.4	321.9	334.6	359.6
博乐市	Bole [Bortala] City	132.1	141.8	155.7	231.3	331.6	284.3	286.7
库尔勒市	Korla City	183.6	147.3	227.3	259.9	273.6	296.7	270.4
阿克苏市	Aksu City	184.2	173.7	203.4	250.8	270.8	243.6	268.4
阿图什市	Artux City	131.1	115.1	186.9	188.5	268.9	247.8	316.6
喀什市	Kashgar [Kaxgar] City	166.7	141.3	221.8	258.0	291.1	283.7	337.6
和田市	Hotan City	144.8	137.8	157.1	189.4	238.7	238.9	256.4
吐鲁番市	Turpan City	134.1	169.5	223.9	281.2	281.0	317.4	277.8
哈密市	Hami [Kumul] City	232.0	232.2	305.1	335.0	355.6	381.3	367.0

城 市	City	八月 Aug.	九月 Sept.	十月 Oct.	十一月 Nov.	十二月 Dec.	全年合计 Annual Total
乌鲁木齐市	Urumqi City	309.2	283.2	229.6	201.7	152.2	2815.7
克拉玛依市	Karamay City	335.9	279.0	215.3	165.1	121.9	2723.0
石河子市	Shi Hezi City	308.0	266.6	223.7	164.9	91.3	2507.1
阜康市	Fukang City	295.2	283.2	229.4	151.1	119.3	2604.6
伊宁市	Yining [Gulja] City	304.3	278.7	226.4	202.9	167.4	2857.1
塔城市	Tacheng [Qoqek] City	307.9	264.5	252.1	167.1	127.9	2844.5
阿勒泰市	Altay City	321.5	287.7	252.8	154.1	143.7	3035.5
博乐市	Bole [Bortala] City	296.3	234.8	167.1	112.6	136.6	2510.9
库尔勒市	Korla City	280.3	265.7	218.6	222.8	167.4	2813.6
阿克苏市	Aksu City	269.0	200.4	210.7	232.9	202.9	2710.8
阿图什市	Artux City	267.0	191.4	229.8	212.2	183.8	2539.1
喀什市	Kashgar [Kaxgar] City	286.5	211.2	243.0	235.4	209.7	2886.0
和田市	Hotan City	253.7	181.3	251.4	251.5	198.9	2499.9
吐鲁番市	Turpan City	302.4	268.4	227.8	125.8	40.8	2650.1
哈密市	Hami [Kumul] City	344.1	304.3	285.2	244.3	206.7	3592.8

11-8 环境保护基本情况

Basic Statistics on Environmental Protection

项　　目	Item	2009	2010
水环境	**Water**		
废水排放总量(亿吨)	Waste Water Discharge (100 million tons)	7.72	8.37
工业废水排放量	Industry	2.42	2.54
城镇生活废水排放量	Non-industrial	5.30	5.83
工业废水排放达标量(亿吨)	Industrial Waste Water Meeting Discharge Standards (100 million tons)	1.62	1.46
工业废水排放达标率(%)	Percentage of Industrial Waste Water Meeting Discharge Standards (%)	66.74	57.33
化学需氧量排放量(万吨)	Discharge Amount of COD (10 000 tons)	28.67	29.60
工业化学需氧量排放量	Industry	15.14	16.29
城镇生活化学需氧量排放量	Non-industrial	13.53	13.32
氨氮排放量(万吨)	Ammonia Nitrogen Discharge (10 000 tons)	2.55	2.66
工业氨氮排放量	Industry	0.58	0.63
城镇生活氨氮排放量	Non-industrial	1.97	2.04
大气环境	**Atmosphere Environment**		
工业废气排放量(亿标立方米)	Industrial Waste Air Emission (100 million cu.m)	6974.88	9309.61
燃料燃烧	Fuels Burning	4657.77	5711.23
生产工艺	Production Process	2317.11	3598.38
二氧化硫排放量(万吨)	Sulphur Dioxide Emission (10 000 tons)	58.99	58.85
工 业	Industry	51.54	51.84
生 活	Non-industrial	7.45	7.00
烟尘排放量(万吨)	Soot Emission (10 000 tons)	31.67	34.40
工 业	Industry	21.98	24.84
生 活	Non-industrial	9.69	9.56
工业粉尘排放量(万吨)	Industrial Dust Emission (10 000 tons)	18.47	18.46

11-8 续表 1 Continued

项　　目	Item	2009	2010
固体废物	**Solid Wastes**		
工业固体废物产生量(万吨)	Industrial Solid Wastes Produced (10 000 tons)	3206.08	3914.12
#危险废物	Hazardous Wastes	85.41	48.93
工业固体废物综合利用量(万吨)	Industrial Solid Wastes Utilized (10 000 tons)	1527.19	1876.86
工业固体废物综合利用率(%)	Ratio of Industrial Solid Wastes Utilized (%)	47.32	47.54
工业固体废物排放量(万吨)	Industrial Solid Wastes Discharged (10 000 tons)	105.20	62.79
"三废"综合利用产品产值(亿元)	Output Value of Products Made from Waste Gas, WasteWater & Solid Wastes (100 million yuan)	15.29	22.22
生态环境	**Eco-Environment Protection**		
当年造林面积(万公顷)	Area of Reforestation of the Year (10 000 hectares)	32.39	21.94
自然保护区数(个)	Number of Nature Reserves (unit)	34	34
#国家级	National Level	9	9
自然保护区面积(万公顷)	Area of Nature Reserves (10 000 hectares)	2257.60	2257.60
自然保护区面积占辖区面积比重(%)	Area of Nature Reserves in Regions (%)	13.56	13.56
生态示范区数(个)	Number of Demonstration Zones of Ecology (unit)	8	8
#国家级	National Level	8	8
自然灾害	**Natural Disaster**		
发生地质灾害起数(次)	Geological Disaster (case)	6	321
#滑　坡	Landslide	3	114
崩　塌	Collapse	1	16
泥石流	Mudflow	2	186
发生地震灾害次数(次)	Seismic Disaster (case)	6	2
#5.0 级以上	Magnitude above 5 Richter Scale	6	2
森林火灾次数(次)	Forest Fire (case)	51	34
森林火灾受灾面积 (公顷)	Fire-Affected Forest Area (hectare)	72.66	43.82
森林病虫害发生面积(万公顷)	Forest Area Affected by Disease and Pests (10 000 hectares)	99.06	105.11
森林病虫害防治面积(万公顷)	Forest Area Provented and Cured from Disease and Pests (10 000 hectares)	57.27	57.10
森林病虫害防治率(%)	Rate of Prevention and Cure (%)	57.8	54.3

11-8 续表 2 Continued

项　　目	Item	2009	2010
环境污染治理投资	**Investment in the Treaiment of Environmental Pollution**		
环境污染治理投资总额(万元)	Total Investment in Pollution Treatment (10 000 yuan)	735475	650247
城镇环境基础设施建设投资额	Investment in Urban Environment Infrastructure	419340	328690
#污水处理	Volume of Waste Water	18336	14999
垃圾处理	Volume of Garbage Disposal	6113	2229
燃　气	Gas Supply	72750	57891
集中供热	Central Heating	137429	144444
园林绿化	Landscape and Greening	183746	109127
工业污染治理项目年完成投资总额	Investment Completed in Industrial Pollution TreatmentProjects	143495	66813
治理废水	Waste Water	30740	19687
治理废气	Waste Gas	109356	46276
治理固体废物	Solid Wastes	600	800
治理噪声	Noise Pollution	170	
治理其他	Others	2629	50
实际执行"三同时"项目环保投资总额	Investment in "Three Simultaneity" Projects	190700	254744
环境污染治理投资总额占新疆生产总值比重(%)	Investment in Pollution Treatment Out of XJ GDP (%)	1.72	1.20
当年施工工业污染治理项目数(个)	Number of Projects in Industrial Pollution Treatment under Construction of The Year (unit)	109	56
当年竣工工业污染治理项目数(个)	Number of Projects Completed in Industrial Pollution Treatment of the Year Projects (unit)	100	48

11-9 水资源情况

Water Resource

年 份 Year	地 区 Region	水资源总量(亿立方米) Total Amount Of Water Resources (100 million cu.m)	地表水资源量 Surface Water Resources	地下水资源量 Ground Water Resources	地下水与地下水资源重复量 Duplicated Measurement Between surface Water and Groundwater	人均水资源量(立方米/人) Per Capita Water Resources (cu.m/person)
	2000	952.40	897.10	636.29	580.99	5255
	2001	1024.40	966.90	692.31	634.81	5500
	2002	1068.60	1006.00	724.85	662.25	5652
	2003	920.10	863.20	604.30	547.40	4793
	2004	855.40	809.20	502.60	456.40	4390
	2005	962.82	910.66	562.57	510.41	4789
	2006	953.12	903.84	554.13	504.85	4695
	2007	863.80	816.60	514.10	466.90	4168
	2008	802.60	759.50	518.50	475.36	3798
	2009	754.29	713.64	470.47	429.82	3517
乌鲁木齐市	Urumqi City	12.28	11.78	5.28	4.78	515
克拉玛依市	Karamay City	0.50	0.05	1.15	0.70	182
石河子市	Shihezi City	0.15	0.08	0.92	0.85	24
吐鲁番地区	Turpan Administrative Offices	7.31	5.65	6.86	5.20	1197
哈密地区	Hami [Kumul] Administrative Offices	10.47	8.63	6.99	5.15	1852
昌吉回族自治州	Changji Hui Autonomous Prefecture	34.63	30.51	21.23	17.11	2488
伊犁州直属县(市)	Counties (Cities) Direct Under Ili Prefecture	156.90	153.80	69.69	66.59	5694
塔城地区	Tacheng [Tarbagatai] Administrative Offices	55.16	51.04	35.24	31.12	5431
阿勒泰地区	Altay Administrative Offices	89.64	86.14	41.90	38.40	13691
博尔塔拉蒙古自治州	Bortala Mongol Autonomous Prefecture	23.55	21.70	13.67	11.82	4929
巴音郭楞蒙古自治州	Bayangol Mongol Autonomous Prefecture	107.28	103.00	56.58	52.30	8416
阿克苏地区	Aksu Administrative Offices	57.26	51.01	72.71	66.46	2512
克孜勒苏柯尔克孜自治州	Kizilsu Kirgiz Autonomous Prefecture	59.46	58.44	32.14	31.12	11383
喀什地区	Kashgar [Kaxgar] Administrative Offices	59.60	55.41	66.51	62.32	1559
和田地区	Hotan Administrative Offices	80.10	76.40	39.60	35.90	4144

11-10 供水和用水情况
Water Supply and Water Used

单位：亿立方米　　　　(2009 年)　　　　(100 million cu.m)

年 份 Year	地 区 Region	供水总量 Water Supply	地表水 Surface Water	地下水 Ground Water	其 他 Others	用水总量 Water Used	生 产 Production
总 计	**Total**	**530.91**	**440.25**	**89.96**	**0.70**	**530.91**	**506.12**
乌鲁木齐市	Urumqi City	12.13	7.47	4.19	0.47	12.13	10.39
克拉玛依市	Karamay City	3.43	3.01	0.28	0.14	3.43	2.76
石河子市	Shihezi City	15.56	12.81	2.75		15.56	14.90
吐鲁番地区	Turpan Administrative Offices	13.13	6.19	6.91	0.03	13.13	12.38
哈密地区	Hami [Kumul] Administrative Offices	12.08	5.84	6.23	0.01	12.08	11.35
昌吉回族自治州	Changji Hui Autonomous Prefecture	36.90	22.54	14.36		36.90	35.94
伊犁州直属县(市)	Counties (Cities) Direct Under Ili Prefecture	52.70	49.54	3.16		52.70	51.20
塔城地区	Tacheng [Tarbagatai] Administrative Offices	24.04	16.33	7.71		24.04	23.41
阿勒泰地区	Altay Administrative Offices	39.56	39.04	0.52		39.56	31.55
博尔塔拉蒙古自治州	Bortala Mongol Autonomous Prefecture	13.43	9.39	4.04		13.43	13.21
巴音郭楞蒙古自治州	Bayangol Mongol Autonomous Prefecture	41.89	33.55	8.29	0.05	41.89	40.01
阿克苏地区	Aksu Administrative Offices	103.77	97.35	6.42		103.77	102.66
克孜勒苏柯尔克孜自治州	Kizilsu Kirgiz Autonomous Prefecture	8.32	7.32	1.00		8.32	8.11
喀什地区	Kashgar [Kaxgar] Administrative Offices	108.15	87.45	20.70		108.15	105.51
和田地区	Hotan Administrative Offices	45.82	42.42	3.40		45.82	42.74

年 份 Year	地 区 Region	第一产业 Primary Industry	第二产业 Secondary Industry	第三产业 Tertiary Industry	居民生活 Consumption	生态环境 Ecological Protection	人均用水量(立方米/人) Per Capita Water Used (cu.m/person)
总 计	**Total**	**492.80**	**11.78**	**1.54**	**8.27**	**16.52**	**2112**
乌鲁木齐市	Urumqi City	7.90	2.14	0.35	1.46	0.28	408
克拉玛依市	Karamay City	1.87	0.84	0.05	0.21	0.46	1222
石河子市	Shihezi City	13.17	1.64	0.09	0.38	0.28	2156
吐鲁番地区	Turpan Administrative Offices	11.72	0.61	0.05	0.27	0.48	1492
哈密地区	Hami [Kumul] Administrative Offices	10.82	0.49	0.04	0.28	0.45	1648
昌吉回族自治州	Changji Hui Autonomous Prefecture	34.88	0.97	0.10	0.74	0.22	1972
伊犁州直属县(市)	Counties (Cities) Direct Under Ili Prefecture	49.45	1.58	0.17	1.00	0.50	1708
塔城地区	Tacheng [Tarbagatai] Administrative Offices	22.78	0.55	0.09	0.41	0.22	1952
阿勒泰地区	Altay Administrative Offices	31.28	0.23	0.04	0.22	7.79	5708
博尔塔拉蒙古自治州	Bortala Mongol Autonomous Prefecture	13.04	0.11	0.06	0.21	0.01	2227
巴音郭楞蒙古自治州	Bayangol Mongol Autonomous Prefecture	39.28	0.63	0.10	0.52	1.36	2520
阿克苏地区	Aksu Administrative Offices	101.32	1.16	0.18	0.71	0.40	3408
克孜勒苏柯尔克孜自治州	Kizilsu Kirgiz Autonomous Prefecture	7.96	0.11	0.04	0.17	0.04	1211
喀什地区	Kashgar [Kaxgar] Administrative Offices	104.78	0.58	0.15	1.18	1.46	2455
和田地区	Hotan Administrative Offices	42.55	0.14	0.05	0.51	2.57	2023

11-11 主要年份环保系统机构、人员数

Number of Environmental Protection Agencies and Persons Engaged in Main Years

年 份 Year	机构数 (个) Number of Agencies (unit)	人员数 (人) Total Number of Staff & Workers (person)	#科技人员 Scientific and Technical Personnel	#监测人员 Monitoring Personnel	#监察人员 Supervising and Administrative Personnel
2000	208	1965	110	654	416
2001	208	2096	109	636	420
2002	238	2386	99	692	523
2003	275	2588	107	766	671
2004	288	2694	107	763	701
2005	304	2796	120	758	790
2006	326	2968	125	777	923
2007	326	2962	77	786	955
2008	296	2962	100	812	993
2009	319	3197	103	857	998
2010	324	3237	109	936	1126

注：本表数据从 2009 年开始不包含兵团数据。(11-15、11-16、11-17 同)
Note: The date of this table don't cover the date of XJPCC from 2009.(the same as the table of 11-15,11-16,11-17)

11-12 分行业重点调查企业工业废水及污染物排放量

Discharge of Industrial Waste Water and Pollutants in Major Investigated Enterprises by Sector

(2010 年)

行业	Sector	工业废水排放量 (万吨) Volume Of Waste Water Discharged (10 000 tons)	工业废水中化学需氧量排放量 (吨) COD Discharge From Industral WasteWater (ton)	工业废水中氨氮排放量 (吨) Ammonia Nitrogen Discharge form Industrial Waste Water (ton)	工业废水排放达标量 (万吨) Industrial WasteWater Meeting Discharge Standards (10 000 tons)
合 计	**Total**	**22286.85**	**135028.52**	**5593.93**	**14138.07**
农副食品加工业	Processing of Food from Agricultural Products	1503.41	21214.53	454.34	589.04
食品制造业	Food Manufacturing	2205.74	13027.68	777.79	924.51
饮料制造业	Beverage Manufacturing	475.03	15423.64	154.13	208.92
纺织业	Textile Industry	952.10	6685.36	179.86	240.74
造纸及纸制品业	Paper and Paper Products Manufacturing	1593.68	5456.86	80.35	1156.61
石油加工、炼焦及核燃料加工业	Oil Processing, Coking and Nuclear Fuel Processing	2002.10	2039.83	473.51	1965.22
化学原料及化学制品制造业	Raw Chemical Material and Chemical Products	2399.87	2967.08	1969.46	1029.98
化学纤维制造业	Chemical Fiber Manufacturing	3380.20	61477.61	617.86	2345.51
黑色金属冶炼及压延加工业	Smelting and Pressing of Ferrous Metals	2188.58	1671.95	702.29	1727.28
电力、热力的生产和供应业	Electricity and Thermal Production and Supply	1703.39	934.13	38.14	1470.21
其他行业	Ohters	3882.75	4129.84	146.19	2480.06

11-13 分行业重点调查企业工业废气及污染物排放量

Emission of Industrial Waste Gas and Pollutants in Major Investigated Enterprises by Sector

单位：吨 (2010 年) (ton)

行业	Sector	工业废气排放总量(亿标立方米) Total Volume of Industrial Waste Gas Emission (100 million cu.m)	工业二氧化硫排放量 Volume of Sulphur Dioxide Emission by Industry	工业氮氧化物排放量 Volume of Nitrogen Dioxide Emission by Industry	工业烟尘排放量 Volume of Industrial Soot Emission	工业粉尘排放量 Volume of Industrial Dust Emission	工业废气污染物排放达标量 Industrial Waste Gas Meeting Discharge Standards
合计	**Total**	**9309.61**	**507965.07**	**368016.58**	**234909.79**	**161963.30**	**817461.19**
黑色金属矿采选业	Processing of Ferrous Metals Ores	378.50	13209.39	901.85	579.27	14246.83	19337.32
有色金属矿采选业	Processing of Nonferrous Metals Ores	4.77	25884.73	166.12	3514.65	664.31	3284.67
农副产品加工业	Processing of Food from Agricultural Products	98.02	10412.02	4869.48	5692.02	20.37	11665.76
造纸及纸制品业	Paper and Paper Products Manufacturing	44.51	4635.65	1236.20	2331.83	1500.00	7513.72
石油加工炼焦及核燃料加工业	Oil Processing, Coking and Nuclear Fuel Processing	1272.91	88722.00	46964.36	43401.25	21702.77	138551.30
化学原料及化学制品制造业	Raw Chemical Material and Chemical Products	799.75	24096.35	13371.02	22831.75	1398.92	36931.12
非金属矿物制品业	Nonmetal Mineral Products Manufacturing	1810.89	19944.65	33130.11	24349.88	42892.39	73155.82
黑色金属冶炼及压延加工业	Smelting and Pressing of Ferrous Metals	1176.36	27698.36	16697.44	9162.34	17273.35	57155.18
有色金属冶炼及压延加工业	Smelting and Pressing of Nonferrous Metals	56.56	31872.39	1635.96	4644.64	238.24	17790.78
电力、热力的生产和供应业	Electricity and Thermal Production and Supply	3072.68	234601.78	235878.93	108444.03		386275.37
其他行业	Ohters	594.65	26887.77	13165.12	9958.14	62026.12	65800.15

11-14 分行业重点调查企业固体废物产生量及处理利用

Production,Treatment and Utilization of Solid Wastes in Major Investigated Enterprises by Sector

单位：万吨 (2010 年) (10 000 tons)

行业	Sector	工业固体废物产生量 Volume of Industrial SolidWastes Produced	工业固体废物综合利用量 Volume of Industrial SolidWastes Utilized	工业固体废物贮存量 Volume of Industrial SolidWastes in Stocks	工业固体废物处置量 Volume of Industrial SolidWastes Treated	工业固体废物排放量 Volume of Industrial SolidWastes Discharged
合计	**Total**	**3846.77**	**1853.81**	**1721.16**	**253.77**	**57.70**
煤炭开采和洗选业	Mining and Washing of Coal	238.65	152.90	3.86	81.85	0.04
黑色金属矿采选业	Processing of Ferrous Metals Ores	1000.98	136.73	852.17	9.39	2.68
有色金属矿采选业	Processing of Nonferrous Metals Ores	474.75	26.70	378.27	48.87	37.08
农副产品加工业	Processing of Food from Agricultural Products	133.70	124.96	0.79	6.69	1.25
食品制造业	Food Manufacturing	36.43	35.03		1.29	0.11
纺织业	Textile Industry	11.91	8.39	0.02	3.50	
化学原料及化学制品制造业	Raw Chemical Material and Chemical Products	308.73	266.45	41.95	1.22	0.02
非金属矿物制品业	Nonmetal Mineral Products Manufacturing	138.35	133.97	0.01	2.92	1.45
黑色金属冶炼及压延加工业	Smelting and Pressing of Ferrous Metals	487.10	316.99	166.10	4.91	0.18
电力、热力的生产和供应业	Electricity and Thermal Production and Supply	538.93	449.27	77.67	30.68	2.43
其他行业	Ohters	477.24	202.40	200.32	62.44	12.46

11-15 环境污染治理投资

Investment in the Treatment of Environment Pollution

项　　目	Item	2009	2010
环境污染治理投资总额(亿元)	**Total Investment in the Treatment of Environment Pollution (100 million yuan)**	**73.55**	**65.02**
城镇环境基础设施建设投资	Investment in Urban Environment Infrastructure Facilities	41.93	32.87
#污水处理	Volume of Waste Water	1.83	1.50
垃圾处理	Volume of Garbage Disposal	0.61	0.22
燃　气	Gas Supply	7.28	5.79
集中供热	Centralized Heating	13.74	14.44
园林绿化	Gardening and Greening	18.37	10.91
工业污染源治理投资	Investment in the Treatment of Industrial Pollution	12.54	6.68
建设项目"三同时"环保投资	"Three Simultaneities" Environmental Investment for New Project	19.07	25.47
环境污染治理投资总额占新疆生产总值比重(%)	**Investment in the Treatment of Environmental Pollution as Percent of GDP (%)**	**1.72**	**1.20**

11-16 主要年份工业污染治理投资完成情况

Investment Completed in the Treatment of Industrial Pollution in Main Years

年 份 Year	汇总工业企业数(个) Number of Industrial Enterprises (unit)	污染治理项目本年完成投资(万元) Investment In the Treatment of Industrial Pollution (10 000 yuan)	治理废水 Treatment of Waste Water	治理废气 Treatment of Waste Gas	治理固体废物 Treatment of Solid Waste	治理噪声 Treatment of Noise Pollution	治理其他 Treatment of Other Pollution	本年施工项目数(个) Projects Under Construction (unit)	本年竣工项目数(个) Projects Completed (unit)
2000	154	22311	8528	9116	349	4109	209	203	198
2001	113	32009	25917	4886	723	66	416	113	106
2002	89	16952	5015	8241	2206	261	1229	129	85
2003	83	26509	9298	9514	4865	21	2811	104	94
2004	94	29622	12334	13114	2756	92	1327	146	110
2005	97	44008	23549	9656	371	321	10111	162	153
2006	92	45229	26876	12036	2582	32	3703	143	132
2007	90	60138	29958	23891	1676	219	4394	117	103
2008	72	68004	33123	31999	1964	270	648	120	120
2009	99	125435	22242	99849	600	170	2574	109	100
2010	66	66813	19687	46276	800		50	56	48

11-17 工业污染治理投资来源
Source of Investment in the Treatment of Industrial Pollution

单位：万元 (10 000 yuan)

项　　目	Item	2009	2010
施工项目本年投资来源	Source of Current Investment	125435	66813
排污费补助	Pollution Charges Subsidies	1865	270
政府其他补助	Other Government Subsidies	1248	1169
企业自筹	Self-raising Funds	122322	65374
#银行贷款	Bank Loans	11168	10

11-18 主要城市空气质量指标
Ambient Air Quality in Main Cities

单位:毫克/立方米 (2010 年) (milligram/cu.m)

城　市	City	可吸入颗粒物 (PM10) Paticulate Matters	二氧化硫 (SO_2)	二氧化氮 (NO_2)	空气质量达到及好于二级的天数(天) Days of Air Quality Equal to or Above Grade II (day)
乌鲁木齐市	Urumqi City	0.133	0.089	0.067	266
克拉玛依市	Karamay City	0.054	0.018	0.033	364
石河子市	Shihezi City	0.086	0.033	0.032	344
吐鲁番市	Turpan City	0.154	0.016	0.018	252
哈 密 市	Hami [Kumul] City	0.086	0.024	0.021	349
昌 吉 市	Changji City	0.106	0.045	0.044	320
阜 康 市	Fukang City	0.097	0.033	0.021	310
奎 屯 市	Kuytun City	0.077	0.012	0.020	340
伊 宁 市	Yining [Gulja] City	0.089	0.041	0.039	347
塔 城 市	Tacheng [Qoqek] City	0.036	0.020	0.025	365
乌 苏 市	Usu City	0.059	0.013	0.023	364
阿勒泰市	Altay City	0.046	0.010	0.014	364
博 乐 市	Bole [Bortala] City	0.052	0.016	0.018	364
库尔勒市	Korla City	0.137	0.013	0.028	254
阿克苏市	Aksu City	0.161	0.023	0.022	234
阿图什市	Artux City	0.176	0.013	0.014	230
喀 什 市	Kashgar [Kaxgar] City	0.277	0.030	0.015	130
和 田 市	Hotan City	0.299	0.021	0.022	96

11-19 主要城市道路交通噪声监测情况
Monitoring of Urban Road Traffic Noise in Major Cities

(2010 年)

城 市	City	路段总长度(米) Total Length of Roads (m)	超标路段(米) Roads with Excess Noise (m)	路段超标率(%) Percentage of Roads with Excess Noise (%)	路段平均宽度(米) Average Width of Roads (m)	平均车流量(辆/小时) AverageTraffic Volume (unit/hour)	噪声均值(LeqdBA) Average NoiseValue (LeqdBA)
乌鲁木齐市	Urumqi City	226280	47615	21.0	42.8	2907	68.2
克拉玛依市	Karamay City	452800	9800	2.2	17.7	717	64.2
石河子市	Shihezi City	45600	1000	2.2	16.5	1002	66.8
吐鲁番市	Turpan City	30214	2796	9.3	19.0	995	67.1
哈 密 市	Hami [Kumul] City	25300	12600	49.8	32.4	191	69.6
昌 吉 市	Changji City	45100	11800	26.2	18.0	1493	67.1
奎 屯 市	Kuytun City	7225	500	6.9	18.4	927	67.0
伊 宁 市	Yining [Gulja] City	73210	1550	2.1	17.3	1788	65.7
塔 城 市	Tacheng [Qoqek] City	10520			24.7	747	64.5
阿勒泰市	Altay City	21555	480	2.2	14.9	136	64.7
博 乐 市	Bole [Bortala] City	22090	150	0.7	17.1	762	62.6
库尔勒市	Korla City	33518	2000	6.0	43.6	2106	66.7
阿克苏市	Aksu City	27988			21.9	770	66.7
阿图什市	Artux City	8050			35.0	911	54.9
喀 什 市	Kashgar [Kaxgar] City	16000	3600	22.5	24.0	2295	68.3
和 田 市	Hotan City	27310	8450	30.9	40.5	994	68.5

11-20 国控主要城市区域环境噪声监测情况
Monitoring of Urban Environment Noise in Major Cities under National Control Programme

(2010 年)

城 市	City	网格长度(米) Grid Length (m)	网格宽度(米) Grid Width (m)	网格总数(个) Total number of Grids (unit)	等效声级(LeqdBA) Sound Level (LeqdBA)
乌鲁木齐市	Urumqi City	750	750	232	53.9
克拉玛依市	Karamay City	317	317	111	53.3
石河子市	Shihezi City	250	250	267	54.8
吐鲁番市	Turpan City	300	300	110	50.6
哈 密 市	Hami [Kumul] City	500	500	100	53.6
昌 吉 市	Changji City	400	400	194	53.0
奎 屯 市	Kuytun City	400	400	102	49.8
伊 宁 市	Yining [Gulja] City	500	500	108	54.5
塔 城 市	Tacheng [Qoqek] City	250	250	106	50.2
阿勒泰市	Altay City	250	250	123	52.7
博 乐 市	Bole [Bortala] City	250	250	141	49.1
库尔勒市	Korla City	500	500	281	51.3
阿克苏市	Aksu City	500	500	110	51.1
阿图什市	Artux City	250	250	110	52.7
喀 什 市	Kashgar [Kaxgar] City	250	250	105	51.6
和 田 市	Hotan City	250	250	134	55.4

11-21 主要年份自然保护区基本情况

Basic Situation of Natural Protection in Main Years

年 份 Year	自然保护区 Nature Reserves			国家级生态示范区 National-level Ecological Demonstration Zones		
	个 数 (个) Number (unit)	面 积 (万公顷) Area (10 000 hectares)	占辖区面积比重 (%) Percentage of Zone in the Region (%)	个 数 (个) Number (unit)	面 积 (万公顷) Area (10 000 hectares)	占辖区面积比重 (%) Percentage of Zone in the Region (%)
2000	23	1594.05	9.6	5	869.08	5.2
2001	26	2042.40	12.3	7	1105.50	6.6
2005	28	2183.49	13.1	8	1275.86	7.7
2006	28	2162.49	13.0	8	1275.86	7.7
2007	34	2257.60	13.6	8	1275.86	7.7
2008	34	2257.60	13.6	8	1275.86	7.7
2009	34	2257.60	13.6	8	1275.86	7.7
2010	34	2257.60	13.6	8	1275.86	7.7

注：2007 年起,自然保护区包括兵团及地县级保护区。
Note: Since 2007,natural reserves include reserves of Xinjiang prodution and construction Group and cities at country level.

11-22 各地区城市生活垃圾清运和处理情况

Collection, Transport and Disposal of Consumption Wastes in Cities by Region

(2010 年)

地 区	Region	生活垃圾清运量 (万吨) Consumption Wastes Collected and Transported (10 000 tons)	生活垃圾处理量 (万吨) Disposal of Consumption Wastes Treatment (10 000 tons)	无害化处理厂数 (座) Number of Factories for Wastes Treatment (unit)	无害化处理能力 (吨/日) Treatment Capacity (ton/day)	无害化处理量 (万吨) Volume of Wastes Disposed (10 000 tons)	生活垃圾处理率 (%) Treatment Rate of Consumption Wastes (%)
总 计	**Total**	**317.27**	**300.45**	**17**	**6295**	**214.04**	**94.70**
乌鲁木齐市	Urumqi City	104.36	101.49	2	2600	91.21	97.25
克拉玛依市	Karamay City	14.23	14.23	3	450	13.50	100.00
吐鲁番市	Turpan City	10.80	9.70	1	300	9.70	89.81
哈 密 市	Hami [Kumul] City	17.60	17.60				100.00
昌 吉 市	Changji City	12.75	12.75	1	450	12.75	100.00
阜 康 市	Fukang City	2.19	2.19	1	150	2.19	100.00
伊 宁 市	Yining [Gulja] City	19.80	19.70	1	600	19.70	99.49
奎 屯 市	Kuytun City	5.09	5.09	1	200	5.09	100.00
塔 城 市	Tacheng [Qoqek] City	6.30	6.10	1	190	6.10	96.83
乌 苏 市	Usu City	7.90	7.20	1	170	7.20	91.14
阿勒泰市	Altay City	3.80	3.70	1	140	3.70	97.37
博 乐 市	Bole [Bortala] City	8.39	4.54	1	150	4.54	54.11
库尔勒市	Korla City	24.12	24.12	1	500	24.12	100.00
阿克苏市	Aksu City	11.34	11.34	1	315	11.34	100.00
阿图什市	Artux City	3.00	2.90	1	80	2.90	96.67
喀 什 市	Kashgar [Kaxgar] City	19.00	17.00				89.47
和 田 市	Hotan City	12.22	10.50				85.92
石河子市	Shihezi City	28.00	28.00				100.00
阿拉尔市	Aral City	2.40	2.30				95.83
图木舒克市	Tumxuk City	0.70					
五家渠市	Wujiaqu City	3.28					

注：表中无害化处理数据均为二级以上无害化处理厂数据。
Note: Data on wastes disposed are provided by secondary and above factories for wastes treatment.

11-23 地质灾害及防治情况

Geological Disasters and Prevention and Cure

年 份 Year	地 区 Region	发生地质灾害起数(次) Geological Disasters (case)	滑 坡 Land-slide	崩 塌 Collapse	泥石流 Mud-rock Flow	地面塌陷 Land Subside
	2000	10	2	1	6	1
	2005	91	28	12	48	3
	2009	6	3	1	2	
	2010	321	114	16	186	5
乌鲁木齐市	Urumqi City					
克拉玛依市	Karamay City					
石河子市	Shihezi City					
吐鲁番地区	Turpan Administrative Offices					
哈密地区	Hami [Kumul] Administrative Offices					
昌吉回族自治州	Changji Hui Autonomous Prefecture					
伊犁州直属县(市)	Counties (Cities) Direct Under Ili Prefecture	101	80	2	14	5
塔城地区	Tacheng [Tarbagatai] Administrative Offices	1	1			
阿勒泰地区	Altay Administrative Offices	3	3			
博尔塔拉蒙古自治州	Bortala Mongol Autonomous Prefecture					
巴音郭楞蒙古自治州	Bayangol Mongol Autonomous Prefecture	25	13	7	5	
阿克苏地区	Aksu Administrative Offices	4	2	1	1	
克孜勒苏柯尔克孜自治州	Kizilsu Kirgiz Autonomous Prefecture	11		2	9	
喀什地区	Kashgar [Kaxgar] Administrative Offices	10		2	8	
和田地区	Hotan Administrative Offices	166	15	2	149	

年 份 Year	地 区 Region	人员伤亡(人) Casualties (person)	#死亡人数 Deaths	直接经济损失(万元) Direct Economic Loss (10 000 yuan)	地质灾害防治 Projects of Prevention of Geological Disasters	
					项目数(个) Projects (unit)	投资(万元) Investment (10 000 yuan)
	2000	8	8	1000.0		
	2005	5	2	384.0	12	238
	2009	1	1	101.3	16	2409
	2010	13	11	12107.5	14	2313
乌鲁木齐市	Urumqi City					
克拉玛依市	Karamay City					
石河子市	Shihezi City					
吐鲁番地区	Turpan Administrative Offices					
哈密地区	Hami [Kumul] Administrative Offices				1	51
昌吉回族自治州	Changji Hui Autonomous Prefecture				1	81
伊犁州直属县(市)	Counties (Cities) Direct Under Ili Prefecture	7	7	475.8	5	1057
塔城地区	Tacheng [Tarbagatai] Administrative Offices			15.7	1	31
阿勒泰地区	Altay Administrative Offices			1.6	4	643
博尔塔拉蒙古自治州	Bortala Mongol Autonomous Prefecture					
巴音郭楞蒙古自治州	Bayangol Mongol Autonomous Prefecture			30.0		
阿克苏地区	Aksu Administrative Offices			96.6		
克孜勒苏柯尔克孜自治州	Kizilsu Kirgiz Autonomous Prefecture			11.0		
喀什地区	Kashgar [Kaxgar] Administrative Offices	5	3	714.5	2	450
和田地区	Hotan Administrative Offices	1	1	10762.3		

11-24 各地区土地利用情况
Land Use by Region

单位:万公顷 (10 000 hectares)

年份 地区 Year Region	土地调查面积 Area under Land Survey	农用地 Land for Agriculture Use	#园地 Garden Land	#牧草地 Grazing and Pasture Land	建设用地 Land for Construction	居民点及工矿用地 Land for Living Quarters, Mining and Manufacturing Sites	交通用地 Land for Transport Facilities	水利设施用地 Land for Water Conservancy Facilities
2000	16648.97	6346.21	19.22	5136.05	154.38	88.69	22.30	43.39
2001	16648.97	6295.64	19.68	5135.35	112.11	88.88	5.25	17.98
2002	16648.97	6297.36	22.21	5135.75	118.20	94.63	5.49	18.08
2003	16648.97	6301.54	29.58	5131.49	119.96	96.12	5.76	18.08
2004	16648.97	6304.57	33.59	5121.58	121.05	97.02	5.89	18.14
2005	16648.97	6306.07	35.43	5116.07	122.07	97.62	6.12	18.33
2006	16648.97	6307.61	36.37	5112.47	122.66	98.15	6.16	18.35
2007	16648.97	6308.05	36.45	5111.92	123.43	98.86	6.21	18.36
2008	16648.97	6308.48	36.42	5111.38	123.98	99.33	6.27	18.38
乌鲁木齐市 Urumqi City	113.84	90.75	0.34	78.05	4.41	3.88	0.35	0.18
克拉玛依市 Karamay City	86.54	35.99	0.03	23.13	6.50	5.91	0.37	0.22
石河子市 Shihezi City	4.60	3.44	0.07	0.61	0.62	0.57	0.05	...
吐鲁番地区 Turpan Administrative Offices	675.63	84.37	2.19	72.97	2.95	2.49	0.35	0.11
哈密地区 Hami [Kumul] Administrative Offices	1420.95	443.06	1.34	374.21	18.57	17.94	0.51	0.12
昌吉回族自治州 Changji Hui Autonomous Prefecture	776.39	602.96	0.87	497.76	11.69	9.89	0.71	1.1
伊犁州直属县(市) Counties (Cities) Direct Under Ili Prefecture	563.81	476.23	2.14	360.56	9.15	8.31	0.51	0.33
塔城地区 Tacheng [Tarbagatai] Administrative Offices	946.98	765.34	0.57	643.19	9.86	8.13	0.52	1.22
阿勒泰地区 Altay Administrative Offices	1176.99	1069.72	0.03	962.91	4.43	3.08	0.31	1.03
博尔塔拉蒙古自治州 Bortala Mongol Autonomous Prefecture	249.34	192.61	0.36	159.74	2.22	1.92	0.17	0.13
巴音郭楞蒙古自治州 Bayangol Mongol Autonomous Prefecture	4709.54	970.86	7.43	824.19	11.37	8.89	0.84	1.64
阿克苏地区 Aksu Administrative Offices	1313.41	542.5	6.32	403.7	12.67	8.00	0.41	4.26
克孜勒苏柯尔克孜自治州 Kizilsu Kirgiz Autonomous Prefecture	724.68	324.82	0.63	298.14	1.55	1.20	0.16	0.19
喀什地区 Kashgar [Kaxgar] Administrative Offices	1394.80	302.46	10.55	160.61	18.61	13.08	0.53	5.00
和田地区 Hotan Administrative Offices	2491.47	403.37	3.55	251.61	9.38	6.04	0.48	2.85

11-25 造 林 面 积
Area of Afforestation

单位:公顷 (hectare)

年份 Year	地区 Region	造林总面积 Total Area of Afforestation	按造林方式分 By Approach: 人工造林 Manual Planting	飞机播种 Airplane Planting	无林地和疏林地新封 Woodless Area and Dispersive Woodland	按林种用途分 By Function of Forest: 用材林 Timber Forests	经济林 By-product Forests	防护林 Protection Forests	薪炭林 Fuel Forests	特种用途林 Forests for Special Purpose
2000		64173	63793	200		1605	44564	16512	1012	480
2001		106771	106771			2149	78203	24536	1424	459
2002		216924	216924			3034	78302	134723	706	159
2003		263781	253781	10000		10152	59777	191380	2390	82
2004		176540	176540			3897	73103	96897	2638	5
2005		136990	130323	6667		3226	40523	92449	738	54
2006		97424	97424			1780	38495	56548	588	13
2007		146632	124642		21990	2991	71667	71325	589	60
2008		239951	217429		22522	8744	136046	94820	341	
2009		301438	266301		35137	9387	155503	135584	954	10
2010		199629	156964		42665	1996	104527	90546	2298	262
	乌鲁木齐市 Urumqi City	2092	2092				91	2001		
	克拉玛依市 Karamay City	156	156					156		
	石河子市 Shihezi City	93	93					93		
	吐鲁番地区 Turpan Administrative Offices	5255	4522		733	21	2704	2463	67	
	哈密地区 Hami [Kumul] Administrative Offices	5946	3612		2334		2596	3350		
	昌吉回族自治州 Changji Hui Autonomous Prefecture	16248	11382		4866		4087	12161		
	伊犁州直属县(市) Counties (Cities) Direct Under Ili Prefecture	33993	31060		2933	1577	26990	5168		258
	塔城地区 Tacheng [Tarbagatai] Administrative Offices	10016	5083		4933		604	7699	1713	
	阿勒泰地区 Altay Administrative Offices	21882	7686		14196		875	21007		
	博尔塔拉蒙古自治州 Bortala Mongol Autonomous Prefecture	8979	2641		6338			8979		
	巴音郭楞蒙古自治州 Bayangol Mongol Autonomous Prefecture	8679	8546		133		5985	2694		
	阿克苏地区 Aksu Administrative Offices	29086	26754		2332		19534	9552		
	克孜勒苏柯尔克孜自治州 Kizilsu Kirgiz Autonomous Prefecture	8509	8243		266	394	1301	6717	97	
	喀什地区 Kashgar [Kaxgar] Administrative Offices	33963	31496		2467	4	29568	4386	1	4
	和田地区 Hotan Administrative Offices	14732	13598		1134		10192	4120	420	
	自治区林业厅 Xinjiang Forestry Bureau									

11-26 林业重点工程造林面积
Area of Key Afforestation Projects

单位:公顷 (hectare)

年份 Year	地区 Region	造林总面积 Total Area of Afforestation	退耕还林工程 Grain for Green Projects	三北及长江流域等防护林工程 Project on Protection Forests in North China and Yangtze River Basin
	2001	102317	13173	
	2002	199324	113010	
	2003	235924	175314	
	2004	152967	82838	70129
	2005	133778	62457	71321
	2006	88744	38160	50584
	2007	138700	32926	105774
	2008	187318	50977	136341
	2009	270997	48120	222877
	2010	177674	38034	139640
乌鲁木齐市	Urumqi City	2092	67	2025
克拉玛依市	Karamay City			
吐鲁番地区	Turpan Administrative Offices	5254	2067	3187
哈密地区	Hami [Kumul] Administrative Offices	5946	800	5146
昌吉回族自治州	Changji Hui Autonomous Prefecture	13870	3199	10671
伊犁州直属县(市)	Counties (Cities) Direct Under Ili Prefecture	33993	3666	30327
塔城地区	Tacheng [Tarbagatai] Administrative Offices	10016	4350	5666
阿勒泰地区	Altay Administrative Offices	21882	4631	17251
博尔塔拉蒙古自治州	Bortala Mongol Autonomous Prefecture	8174	3188	4986
巴音郭楞蒙古自治州	Bayangol Mongol Autonomous Prefecture	8679	2679	6000
阿克苏地区	Aksu Administrative Offices	29086	3998	25088
克孜勒苏柯尔克孜自治州	Kizilsu Kirgiz Autonomous Prefecture	8509	4179	4330
喀什地区	Kashgar [Kaxgar] Administrative Offices	15441	2678	12763
和田地区	Hotan Administrative Offices	14732	2532	12200
自治区林业厅	Xinjiang Forestry Bureau			

11-27 各地区天然湿地面积
Area of Wetlands by Region

单位:百公顷 (2008 年) (100 hectares)

地　区 Region	天然湿地面积 Area of Natural Wetlands	河流 Rivers	湖泊 Lakes	沼泽 Marshland	天然湿地面积占土地总面积比重(%) Proportion of Natural Wetlands in Total Area of Territory(%)
总　计 Total	**12673.56**	**4732.99**	**4763.91**	**3176.66**	**0.76**
乌鲁木齐市 Urumqi City	74.72	20.98	39.37	14.37	0.66
克拉玛依市 Karamay City	214.69	23.59	154.58	36.52	2.48
石河子市 Shihezi City	4.92	4.77		0.15	1.07
吐鲁番地区 Turpan Administrative Offices	127.84	5.99	0.18	121.67	0.19
哈密地区 Hami [Kumul] Administrative Offices	179	35.73	122.34	20.93	0.13
昌吉回族自治州 Changji Hui Autonomous Prefecture	264.46	50.27	2.58	211.61	0.34
伊犁州直属县(市) Counties (Cities) Direct Under Ili Prefecture	543.92	246.61	6.59	290.72	0.96
塔城地区 Tacheng [Tarbagatai] Administrative Offices	352.75	113.36	5.98	233.41	0.37
阿勒泰地区 Altay Administrative Offices	1353.84	353.78	845.49	154.57	1.15
博尔塔拉蒙古自治州 Bortala Mongol Autonomous Prefecture	1331.27	28.88	1176.41	125.98	5.34
巴音郭楞蒙古自治州 Bayangol Mongol Autonomous Prefecture	4034.7	979.74	2098.16	956.8	0.86
阿克苏地区 Aksu Administrative Offices	1018.86	709.19	68.68	240.99	0.78
克孜勒苏柯尔克孜自治州 Kizilsu Kirgiz Autonomous Prefecture	326.89	94.18	46.61	186.1	0.45
喀什地区 Kashgar [Kaxgar] Administrative Offices	1056.83	556.6	88.55	411.68	0.76
和田地区 Hotan Administrative Offices	1788.87	1509.32	108.39	171.16	0.72

11-28 森林火灾情况

Forest Fires

年份 Year	地区 Region	森林火灾次数(次) Forest Fires (case)	一般火灾 Ordinary Fires	较大火灾 Large Fires	重大火灾 Major Fires	特大火灾 Severe Fires
	2005	28	1			
	2006	35	5			
	2007	47	13			
	2008	67	19			
	2009	51	35	16		
	2010	34	27	7		
乌鲁木齐市	Urumqi City	7	7			
克拉玛依市	Karamay City	1	1			
石河子市	Shihezi City					
吐鲁番地区	Turpan Administrative Offices					
哈密地区	Hami [Kumul] Administrative Offices					
昌吉回族自治州	Changji Hui Autonomous Prefecture	2	2			
伊犁州直属县(市)	Counties (Cities) Direct Under Ili Prefecture	12	10	2		
塔城地区	Tacheng [Tarbagatai] Administrative Offices					
阿勒泰地区	Altay Administrative Offices	9	6	3		
博尔塔拉蒙古自治州	Bortala Mongol Autonomous Prefecture	2	1	1		
巴音郭楞蒙古自治州	Bayangol Mongol Autonomous Prefecture	1		1		
阿克苏地区	Aksu Administrative Offices					
克孜勒苏柯尔克孜自治州	Kizilsu Kirgiz Autonomous Prefecture					
喀什地区	Kashgar [Kaxgar] Administrative Offices					
和田地区	Hotan Administrative Offices					

年份 Year	地区 Region	火场总面积(公顷) Total Area of Fires (hectare)	受灾森林总面积(公顷) Destructed Forest Area (hectare)	#天然林 Natural Forest	#人工林 Man-made Forest	经济损失(万元) Economic Loss (10 000 yuan)
	2005	42.33	11.62	10.63	0.99	12.52
	2006	258.27	94.10	78.28	1.39	9.26
	2007	137.09	75.34	31.44	39.37	19.47
	2008	191.38	122.74	58.39	65.64	145.53
	2009	83.58	72.66	8.24	49.86	52.29
	2010	65.95	43.82	17.56	15.70	5.48
乌鲁木齐市	Urumqi City	0.277	0.277	0.021	0.256	
克拉玛依市	Karamay City	20.000	0.001		0.001	
石河子市	Shihezi City					
吐鲁番地区	Turpan Administrative Offices					
哈密地区	Hami [Kumul] Administrative Offices					
昌吉回族自治州	Changji Hui Autonomous Prefecture	0.005	0.005	0.005		
伊犁州直属县(市)	Counties (Cities) Direct Under Ili Prefecture	7.156	7.156	0.006	7.150	
塔城地区	Tacheng [Tarbagatai] Administrative Offices					
阿勒泰地区	Altay Administrative Offices	19.749	19.642	2.327	6.750	4.67
博尔塔拉蒙古自治州	Bortala Mongol Autonomous Prefecture	16.860	14.940	13.400	1.540	0.81
巴音郭楞蒙古自治州	Bayangol Mongol Autonomous Prefecture	1.900	1.800	1.800		
阿克苏地区	Aksu Administrative Offices					
克孜勒苏柯尔克孜自治州	Kizilsu Kirgiz Autonomous Prefecture					
喀什地区	Kashgar [Kaxgar] Administrative Offices					
和田地区	Hotan Administrative Offices					

11-29 森林病虫害防治情况
Prevention of Forest Diseases and Pests

单位：公顷 (hectare)

年份 Year	地区 Region	合计 Total 发生面积 Area of Occurrence	防治面积 Area of Prevention	防治率(%) Prevention Rate (%)	森林病害 Forest Diseases 发生面积 Area of Occurrence	防治面积 Area of Prevention	防治率(%) Prevention Rate (%)
	2005	241713	221720	91.7	4467	3440	77.0
	2006	400127	344146	86.0	21993	19273	87.6
	2007	787087	441533	56.1	30194	23393	77.5
	2008	1066659	609457	57.1	147035	92811	63.1
	2009	990580	572735	57.8	82273	68525	83.3
	2010	1051060	570973	54.3	80820	73573	91.0
乌鲁木齐市	Urumqi City	5926	5700	96.2			
吐鲁番地区	Turpan Administrative Offices	18000	17267	95.9			
哈密地区	Hami [Kumul] Administrative Offices	14220	12626	88.8	1333	1300	97.5
昌吉回族自治州	Changji Hui Autonomous Prefecture	429540	18501	4.3	1353	1327	98.1
伊犁州直属县(市)	Counties (Cities) Direct Under Ili Prefecture	24227	22300	92.0	1687	1181	70.0
塔城地区	Tacheng [Tarbagatai] Administrative Offices	2193	2146	97.9	200	200	100.0
阿勒泰地区	Altay Administrative Offices	44801	30224	67.5	3633	1825	50.2
博尔塔拉蒙古自治州	Bortala Mongol Autonomous Prefecture	14520	5933	40.9			
巴音郭楞蒙古自治州	Bayangol Mongol Autonomous Prefecture	22486	22101	98.3	213	207	97.2
阿克苏地区	Aksu Administrative Offices	162427	156620	96.4	15987	15893	99.4
克孜勒苏柯尔克孜自治州	Kizilsu Kirgiz Autonomous Prefecture	18127	14014	77.3	1627	1520	93.4
喀什地区	Kashgar [Kaxgar] Administrative Offices	173967	152607	87.7	21307	18753	88.0
和田地区	Hotan Administrative Offices	113893	104554	91.8	33400	31287	93.7
自治区林业厅	Xinjiang Forestry Bureau	6733	6380	94.8	80	80	100.0

年份 Year	地区 Region	森林虫害 Forest Diseases 发生面积 Area of Occurrence	防治面积 Area of Prevention	防治率(%) Prevention Rate (%)	森林鼠害 Forest Rat Plague 发生面积 Area of Occurrence	防治面积 Area of Prevention	防治率(%) Prevention Rate (%)
	2005	221500	199700	89.9	21747	18580	85.4
	2006	340320	290693	85.4	37813	34180	90.4
	2007	350592	331735	94.6	406301	86405	21.3
	2008	527465	446766	84.7	392159	69880	17.8
	2009	474213	431197	90.9	434093	73013	16.8
	2010	470961	432316	91.8	499279	65084	13.0
乌鲁木齐市	Urumqi City	4393	4167	94.9	1533	1533	100.0
吐鲁番地区	Turpan Administrative Offices	17267	17267	100.0	733		
哈密地区	Hami [Kumul] Administrative Offices	10720	9373	87.4	2167	1953	90.1
昌吉回族自治州	Changji Hui Autonomous Prefecture	3927	3867	98.5	424260	13307	3.1
伊犁州直属县(市)	Counties (Cities) Direct Under Ili Prefecture	20533	19253	93.8	2007	1866	93.0
塔城地区	Tacheng [Tarbagatai] Administrative Offices	1700	1666	98.0	293	280	95.6
阿勒泰地区	Altay Administrative Offices	6815	4528	66.4	34353	23871	69.5
博尔塔拉蒙古自治州	Bortala Mongol Autonomous Prefecture	7613	5920	77.8	6907	13	0.2
巴音郭楞蒙古自治州	Bayangol Mongol Autonomous Prefecture	20220	19847	98.2	2053	2047	99.7
阿克苏地区	Aksu Administrative Offices	146440	140727	96.1			
克孜勒苏柯尔克孜自治州	Kizilsu Kirgiz Autonomous Prefecture	12947	9927	76.7	3553	2567	72.2
喀什地区	Kashgar [Kaxgar] Administrative Offices	131393	116347	88.5	21267	17507	82.3
和田地区	Hotan Administrative Offices	80493	73267	91.0			
自治区林业厅	Xinjiang Forestry Bureau	6500	6160	94.8	153	140	91.5

注：自治区林业厅数据中包括石河子市和克拉玛依市的数据。
Note: The data on Bureau of Forestry include the data of Shihezi City and Karamay City.

11-30 地震灾害情况
Earthquake Disasters

年 份 Year	地 区	Region	地震次数(次) Number of Earthquakes (case)	5.0-5.9 级 5.0-5.9 Richterscale	6.0-6.9 级 6.0-6.9 Richterscale	7.0 级以上 Over 7.0 Richterscale
2005			**4**	**3**	**1**	
	乌什县	Wushi [Uxturpan] County	2	1	1	
	阿瓦提县	Awat County	1	1		
	墨玉县	Moyu [Karakax] County	1	1		
2006			**2**	**2**		
	和田县	Hotan County	1	1		
	乌苏市	Usu City	1	1		
2007			**1**	**1**		
	特克斯县	Tekes County	1	1		
2008			**4**	**2**	**1**	**1**
	于田县、策勒县	Yutian [Keriya] County, Qira County	1			1
	裕民县	Yumin [Qagantokay] County	1	1		
	和静县	Hejing County	1	1		
	乌恰县	Wuqia [Ulugqat] County	1		1	
2009			**6**	**6**		
	察布查尔县、昭苏县	Qapqai Xibe Autonomous County, Zhaosu[Mongolrure] County	1	1		
	柯坪县、阿合齐县	Kalpin County, Akqi County	1	1		
	阿合齐县、乌什县	Akqi County, Wushi[Uxtnrpan] County	1	1		
	阿图什市	Artux City	1	1		
	叶城县、皮山县	Yecheng[Kagilik] County, Pishan[Guma] County	1	1		
	哈密市	Hami[Kumul] City	1	1		
2010			**2**	**2**		
	乌恰县	Wuqia [Ulugqat] County	2	2		

年 份 Year	地 区	Region	人员伤亡(人) Casualties (person)	#死亡人数 Deaths	经济损失(万元) Economic Losses (10 000 yuan)	失去住所(户) Homeless (household)
2005					**16316**	**5823**
	乌什县	Wushi [Uxturpan] County			15758	5823
	阿瓦提县	Awat County				
	墨玉县	Moyu [Karakax] County			558	
2006					**126**	
	和田县	Hotan County				
	乌苏市	Usu City			126	
2007					**11060**	**5074**
	特克斯县	Tekes County			11060	5074
2008					**38437**	**5702**
	于田县、策勒县	Yutian [Keriya] County, Qira County			19480	3004
	裕民县	Yumin [Qagantokay] County			8585	2302
	和静县	Hejing County			3644	220
	乌恰县	Wuqia [Ulugqat] County			6728	176
2009					**20498**	**4393**
	察布查尔县、昭苏县	Qapqai Xibe Autonomous County, Zhaosu[Mongolrure] County			4612	1396
	柯坪县、阿合齐县	Kalpin County, Akqi County			9068	1706
	阿合齐县、乌什县	Akqi County, Wushi[Uxtnrpan] County			4636	708
	阿图什市	Artux City			2182	583
	叶城县、皮山县	Yecheng[Kagilik] County, Pishan[Guma] County				
	哈密市	Hami[Kumul] City				
2010					**2408**	**675**
	乌恰县	Wuqia [Ulugqat] County			2408	675

注：本表数据由自治区地震局提供。
Note: The data in this table is Provided by theBureau of Earthquake.

11-31 林业系统营林固定资产投资完成情况

Completed Investment in Fixed Assets for Afforestation in Forest System

单位：万元 (10 000 yuan)

年 份 Year	地 区 Region	本年完成投资 Investment Completed During the Year	#国家投资 State Investment	#国债资金 National Debt	本年新增固定资产 Newly Increased Fixed Assets
	2000	23582	11686	5170	4542
	2001	45890	23725	5433	12492
	2002	68861	35835	21369	
	2003	71277	40821	20448	27223
	2004	60631	43475	15748	23047
	2005	80150	57680	17224	24988
	2006	96062	82235	19937	31047
	2007	115523	94094	15698	33091
	2008	158416	129294	21054	55295
	2009	193818	153538	21312	52765
	2010	168930	142678	8667	28725
乌鲁木齐市	Urumqi City	7384	4623		
克拉玛依市	Karamay City	4247			4247
石河子市	Shihezi City	353			
吐鲁番地区	Turpan Administrative Offices	5434	5026	356	962
哈密地区	Hami [Kumul] Administrative Offices	4391	4180	439	4114
昌吉回族自治州	Changji Hui Autonomous Prefecture	12520	5102	1568	59
伊犁州直属县(市)	Counties (Cities) Direct Under Ili Prefecture	16778	15944	160	454
塔城地区	Tacheng [Tarbagatai] Administrative Offices	13688	12812		428
阿勒泰地区	Altay Administrative Offices	10633	8846	4420	41
博尔塔拉蒙古自治州	Bortala Mongol Autonomous Prefecture	4038	3807	191	4033
巴音郭楞蒙古自治州	Bayangol Mongol Autonomous Prefecture	9362	9362		561
阿克苏地区	Aksu Administrative Offices	20684	20604	836	8319
克孜勒苏柯尔克孜自治州	Kizilsu Kirgiz Autonomous Prefecture	5080	5080		96
喀什地区	Kashgar [Kaxgar] Administrative Offices	12394	12394	695	514
和田地区	Hotan Administrative Offices	13473	13473		116
自治区林业厅	Xinjiang Forestry Bureau	28471	21425	2	4781

主要统计指标解释

国土　指一个主权国家管辖下的领土、领海和领空。

气候　指地球与大气之间长期能量交换与质量交换所形成的一种自然环境状态，它是多种因素综合作用的结果。气候既是人类生活和生产的环境要素之一，又是供给人类生活和生产的重要资源。气温、降水、湿度等气象要素的多年平均值是用来描述一个地区气候状况的主要参数，而各种气象要素某年、某月的平均值(或总量)则可以反映出该时期天气气候状况的重要特征。

自然资源　指人类可以直接从自然界获得，并用于生产和生活的物质资源。自然资源一般可以分成可再生资源和非再生资源两大类。可再生资源指在较短时间内可以再生、可以循环利用的资源，包括土地资源、水资源、气候资源、生物资源和海洋资源等。非再生资源指在使用后不能再生的资源，包括矿产资源和地热能源。

土地资源　土地指陆地的表层部分，它主要由岩石、岩石的风化物和土壤构成。土地资源按利用类型可以分为农用地、建筑用地和未利用地。农用地包括耕地、园地、林地、牧草地和水面。建筑用地包括居民点及工矿用地、交通用地和水利设施用地。未利用地指农用地和建筑用地以外的土地，包括滩涂、荒漠、戈壁、冰川和石山等。

耕地面积　指经过开垦用以种植农作物并经常进行耕耘的土地面积。包括种有作物的土地面积、休闲地、新开荒地和抛荒未满三年的土地面积。

林业用地面积　指生长乔木、竹类、灌木、沿海红树林等林木的土地面积，包括有林地、灌木林、疏林地、未成林造林地、迹地、苗圃等。

草地面积　指牧区和农区用于放牧牲畜或割草，植被盖度在5%以上的草原、草坡、草山等面积。包括天然的和人工种植或改良的草地面积。

森林资源　指森林、林木、林地以及依托森林、林木、林地生存的野生动物、植物和微生物。林木指树木和竹子。森林指以乔木为主体的植物群落，是集生的乔木及与共同作用的植物、动物、微生物和土壤、气候等的总体。

活立木总蓄积量　指一定范围内土地上全部树木蓄积的总量，包括森林蓄积、疏林蓄积、散生木蓄积和四旁树蓄积。

森林面积　指由乔木树种构成，郁闭度0.2以上(含0.2)的林地或冠幅宽度10米以上的林带的面积，即有林地面积。森林面积包括天然起源和人工起源的针叶林面积、阔叶林面积、针阔混交林面积和竹林面积，不包括灌木林地面积和疏林地面积。

森林蓄积量　指一定森林面积上存在着的林木树干部分的总材积。它是反映一个国家或地区森林资源总规模和水平的基本指标之一，也是反映森林资源的丰富程度、衡量森林生态环境优劣的重要依据。

森林覆盖率　指一个国家或地区森林面积占土地面积的百分比。在计算森林覆盖率时，森林面积包括郁闭度0．2以上的乔木林地面积和竹林地面积，国家特别规定的灌木林地面积、农田林网以及四旁(村旁、路旁、水旁、宅旁)林木的覆盖面积。森林覆盖率是反映森林资源的丰富程度和生态平衡状况的重要指标。计算公式为：

森林覆盖率(%)=森林面积／土地总面积×100%

水资源　水在自然界中以固体、液体和气态三种聚集状态存在，分布于海洋、陆地(包括土壤)以及大气之中，通过水循环形成水资源。水资源包括经人类控制并直接可供灌溉、发电、给水、航运、养殖等用途的地表水和地下水，以及江河、湖泊、井、泉、潮汐、港湾和养殖水域等。水资源是发展国民经济不可缺少的重要自然资源。

地表水和地下水　陆地上的水因空间分布不同，可以分为地表水和地下水。地表水指分别存在于河流、湖泊、沼泽、冰川和冰盖等水体中水分的总称，又称陆地水。地下水指储存在地面以下饱和岩土孔隙、裂隙及溶洞中的水。

内陆水域总面积　指江、河、湖泊、池塘、塘堰、水库等各种流水或蓄水的水面占地面积。

径流量　指在一定时段内通过河流某一过水断面的水量，用以反映一个国家或地区水资源的丰歉程度。计算公式为：

径流量=降水量-蒸发量

矿产资源　矿产指由地质作用形成，富集于地壳中或出露于地表达到工农业利用要求的有用矿物。矿产是一种重要的自然资源，是社会发展的重要物质基础。从某种意义上讲，一个国家对矿产资源开发利用的广度和深度，可以作为这个国家经济发展水平的标志。

矿产保有储量　指探明的矿产储量(包括工业储量和远景储量)，扣除已开采部分和地下损失量后的年末实有储量，是反映国家矿产资源现状的重要指标。

气温　指空气的温度，我国一般以摄氏度(℃)为单位表示。气象观测的温度表是放在离地面约1.5米处通风良好的百叶箱里测量的，因此，通常说的气温指的是离地面1.5米处百叶箱中的温度。其统计计算方法为：

降水量　指从天空降落到地面的液态或固态(经融化后)水，未经蒸发、渗透、流失而在地面上积聚的深度。

月降水量　是将全月各日的降水量累加而得。

年降水量　是将12个月的月降水量累加而得。

日照时数　指太阳实际照射地面的时间。其统计方法与降水量相同。

水资源总量　指评价区内降水形成的地表和地下产水

总量，即地表产流量与降水入渗补给地下水量之和，不包括过境水量。

地表水资源量 指评价区内河流、湖泊、冰川等地表水体中可以逐年更新的动态水量，即当地天然河川径流量。

地下水资源量 指评价区内降水和地表水对饱水岩土层的补给量，包括降水入渗补给量和河道、湖库、渠系、渠灌田间等地表水体的入渗补给量。

地表水与地下水资源重复计算量 指地表水和地下水相互转化的部分，即天然河川径流量中的地下水排泄量和地下水补给量中来源于地表水的入渗量。

供水总量 指各种水源工程为用户提供的包括输水损失在内的毛供水量之和。

地表水源供水量 指地表水体工程的取水量，按蓄、引、提、调四种形式统计。从水库、塘坝中引水或提水，均属蓄水工程供水量；从河道或湖泊中自流引水的，无论有闸或无闸，均属引水工程供水量；利用扬水站从河道或湖泊中直接取水的，属提水工程供水量；跨流域调水指水资源一级区或独立流域之间的跨流域调配水量，不包括在蓄、引、提水量中。

地下水源供水量 指水井工程的开采量，按浅层谈水、深层承压水和微咸水分别统计。城市地下水源供水量包括自来水厂的开采量和工矿企业自备井的开采量。

用水总量 指分配给各类用户的包括输水损失在内的毛用水量之和。按用户特性分为农业、工业、生活和生态用水四大类。

农业用水 指农田灌溉用水、林果地灌溉用水、草地灌溉用水和鱼塘补水。

工业用水 指工矿企业在生产过程中用于制造、加工、冷却、空调、净化、洗涤等方面的用水，按新水取用量计，不包括企业内部的重复利用水量。

生活用水 包括城镇生活用水和农村生活用水。城镇生活用水由居民用水和公共用水(含第三产业及建筑业等用水)组成；农村生活用水除居民生活用水外，还包括畜用水在内。

生态补水 仅包括人为措施供给的城镇环境用水和部分河湖、湿地补水，而不包括降水、径流自然满足的水量。

工业废水排放量 指经过企业厂区所有排放口排到企业外部的工业废水量。包括生产废水、外排的直接冷却水、超标排放的矿井地下水和与工业废水混排的厂区生活污水，不包括外排的间接冷却水(清污不分流的间接冷却水应计算在内)。

工业废水排放达标量 指报告期内废水中各项污染物指标都达到国家或地方排放标准的外排工业废水量，包括未经处理外排达标的，经废水处理设施处理后达标排放的，以及经污水处理厂处理后达标排放的。

工业废水排放达标率 指工业废水排放达标量占工业废水排放量的百分率，计算公式为：

工业废水排放达标率=工业废水排放达标量/工业废水排放量×100%

化学需氧量(COD) 只指用化学氧化剂氧化水中有机污染物时所需要的氧量。COD 值越高，表示水中有机污染物污染越重。

工业废气排放量 指报告期内企业厂区内燃料燃烧和生产工艺过程中产生的各种排入大气的含有污染物的气体的总量，以标准状态(273K，101325Pa)计算。测算公式为：

工业废气排放量=燃料燃烧过程中废气排放量+生产工艺过程中废气排放量

工业烟尘排放量 指企业厂区内燃料燃烧过程中产生的烟气中夹带的颗粒物排放量。

工业粉尘排放量 指企业在生产工艺过程中排放的能在空气中悬浮一定时间的固体颗粒物排放量。如钢铁企业的耐火材料粉尘、焦化企业的筛焦系统粉尘、烧结机的粉尘、石灰窑的粉尘、建材企业的水泥粉尘等。不包括电厂排入大气的烟尘。

工业固体废物产生量 指报告期内企业在生产过程中产生的固体状、半固体状和高浓度液体状废弃物的总量，包括危险废物、冶炼废渣、粉煤灰、炉渣、煤矸石、尾矿、放射性废物和其他废物等；不包括矿山开采的剥离废石和掘进废石(煤矸石和呈酸性或碱性的废石除外)。酸性或碱性废石指采掘的废石其流经水、雨淋水的 pH 值小于 4 或 pH 值大于 10.5 者。

工业固体废物综合利用量 指报告期内企业通过回收、加工、循环、交换等方式，从固体废物中提取或者使其转化为可以利用的资源、能源和其他原材料的固体废物量(包括当年利用往年的工业固体废物贮存量)，如用作农业肥料、生产建筑材料、筑路等。综合利用量由原产生固体废物的单位统计。

工业固体废物综合利用率 指工业固体废物综合利用量占工业固体废物产生量(包括综合利用往年贮存量)的百分率。计算公式为：

工业固体废物综合利用率=工业固体废物综合利用量/(工业固体废物产生量+综合利用往年贮存量)×100%

工业固体废物贮存量 指报告期内企业以综合利用或处置为目的，将固体废物暂时贮存或堆存在专设的贮存设施或专设的集中堆存场所内的数量。专设的固体废物贮存场所或贮存设施必须有防扩散、防流失、防渗漏、防止污染大气、水体的措施。

工业固体废物处置量 指报告期内企业将固体废物焚烧或者最终置于符合环境保护规定要求的场所，并不再回取的工业固体废物量(包括当年处置往年的工业固体废物贮存量)。处置方式有填埋(其中危险废物应安全填埋)、焚烧、专业贮存场(库)封场处理、深层灌注、回填矿井及海洋处置(经海洋管理部门同意投海处置)等。

工业固体废物排放量 指报告期内企业将所产生的固体废物排到固体废物污染防治设施、场所以外的数量，不包括矿山开采的剥离废石和掘进废石(煤矸石和呈酸性或碱性的废石除外)。

生活垃圾清运量 指报告期内收集和运送到垃圾处理厂(场)的生活垃圾数量。生活垃圾指城市日常生活或为城市日常生活提供服务的活动中产生的固体废物以及法律行政规定的视为城市生活垃圾的固体废物。包括：居民生活垃圾、商业垃圾、集市贸易市场垃圾、街道清扫垃圾、公共场所垃圾和机关、学校、厂矿等单位的生活垃圾。

生活垃圾无害化处理率 指报告期生活垃圾无害化处理量与生活垃圾产生量比率。在统计上，由于生活垃圾产生量不易取得，可用清运量代替。计算公式为：

生活垃圾无害化处理率=生活垃圾无害化处理量/生活垃圾产生量×100%

农用地 指直接用于农业生产的土地，包括耕地、园地、林地、牧草地及其他农用地。

人工林面积 指由人工播种、植苗或扦插造林形成的生长稳定，(一般造林 3-5 年后或飞机播种 5-7 年后)每公顷保存株数大于或等于造林设计植树株数 80%或郁闭度 0.20 以上(含 02.0)的林分面积。

造林总面积 指在宜林荒山荒地、宜林沙荒地、无立木林地、疏林地和退耕地等其它宜林地上通过人工措施形成或恢复森林、林木、灌木林的过程。用材林 指以生产木材为主要目的的森林和林木，包括以生产竹材为主要目的的竹林。

经济林 指以生产果品，食用油料、饮料、调料，工业原料和药材为主要目的的林木。经济林是人们为了取得林木的果实、叶片、皮层、胶液等产品作为工业原料或者供食用所营造的林木，如油茶、油桐、核桃、樟树、花椒、茶、桑、果等。

防护林 指以防护为主要目的的森林、林木和灌木丛。包括水源涵养林，水土保持林，防风固沙林，农田、牧场防护林，护岸林，护路林等。

薪炭林 指以生产燃料为主要目的的林木。

天然林保护工程 是我国林业的“天”字号工程、一号工程,也是投资最大的生态工程。具体包括三个层次:全面停止长江上游、黄河上中游地区天然林采伐；大幅度调减东北、内蒙古等重点国有林区的木材产量；同时保护好其他地区的天然林资源。主要解决这些区域天然林资源的休养生息和恢复发展问题。

退耕还林还草工程 是我国林业建设上涉及面最广、政策性最强、工序最复杂、群众参与度最高的生态建设工程。主要解决重点地区的水土流失问题。

三北和长江流域等重点防护林体系建设工程 三北和长江中下游地区等重点防护林体系建设工程,是我国涵盖面最大、内容最丰富的防护林体系建设工程。具体包括三北防护林四期工程、长江中下游及淮河太湖流域防护林二期工程、沿海防护林二期工程、珠江防护林二期工程、太行山绿化二期工程和平原绿化二期工程。主要解决三北地区的防沙治沙问题和其他区域各不相同的生态问题。

野生动植物保护及自然保护区建设工程 野生动植物保护及自然保护区建设工程,是一个面向未来,着眼长远,具有多项战略意义的生态保护工程,也是呼应国际大气候、树立中国良好国际形象的“外交工程”。主要解决基因保存、生物多样性保护、自然保护、湿地保护等问题。

湿地 指天然或人工、长久或暂时性的沼泽地、泥炭地或水域地带，包括静止或流动、淡水、半咸水、咸水体，低潮时水深不超过6米的水域以及海岸地带地区的珊瑚滩和海草床、滩涂、红树林、河口、河流、淡水沼泽、沼泽森林、湖泊、盐沼及盐湖。

自然保护区 指为了保护自然环境和自然资源，促进国民经济的持续发展，将一定面积的陆地和水体划分出来，并经各级人民政府批准而进行特殊保护和管理的区域个数。根据保护对象，自然保护区分为自然生态系统类、野生生物类、自然遗迹类。风景名胜区、文物保护区不计在内。

生态示范区 指省级以上环境保护行政主管部门批准，以省、地、县政府为主按批准的生态示范区建设规划实施的行政区域。包括已经过国家或省级环境保护行政主管部门验收的和正在开展试点工作的。

滑坡 指斜坡上不稳定的岩土体在重力作用下沿一定软面(或滑动带)整体向下滑动的物理地质现象。地表水和地下水的作用以及人为的不合理工程活动对斜坡岩、土体稳定性的破坏，经常是促使滑坡发生的主要因素。在露天采矿、水利、铁路、公路等工程中，滑坡往往造成严重危害。

崩塌 指陡坡上大块的岩土体在重力作用下突然脱离母体崩落的物理地质现象。它可因多裂隙的岩体经强烈的物理风化、雨水渗入或地震而造成，往往毁坏建筑物，堵塞河道或交通路线。

泥石流 指山地突然爆发的包含大量泥沙、石块的特殊洪流，多见于半干旱山地高原地区。其形成条件是地形陡峻，松散堆积物丰富，有特大暴雨或大量冰融水的流出。

地面塌陷 指地表岩、土体在自然或人为因素作用下向下陷落，并在地面形成塌陷坑(洞)的一种动力地质现象。由于其发育的地质条件和作用因素的不同，地面塌陷可分为：岩溶塌陷、非岩溶塌陷。

环境污染与破坏事故 指由于违反环境保护法规的经济、社会活动与行为，以及意外因素的影响或不可抗拒的自然灾害等原因，致使环境受到污染，国家重点保护的野生动植物、自然保护区受到破坏，人体健康受到危害，社会经济和人民财产受到损失，造成不良社会影响的突发性事件。

环境污染治理投资 指在污染源治理和城市环境基础设施建设的资金投入中，用于形成固定资产的资金，其中污染源治理投资包括工业污染源治理投资和“三同时”项目环保投资两部分。环境污染治理投资为城市环境基础设施投资、工业污染源治理投资与“三同时”项目环保投资之和。

营林固定资产投资 指在报告期内进行的营林基本建设和营林更新改造活动投资。

Explanatory Notes on Main Statistical Indicators

Territory refers to territorial land, sea and air space under the administration of the People's Republic of China.

Climate refers to the natural environmental status formed by the long-term exchange of energy and mass between the earth and the atmosphere, and is the result of interaction of many factors. Climate is both one of the environment factors and also the important resources for living and production activities of the human being. The average values across several years of meteorological factors such as temperature, rainfall and humidity are used as important parameters to describe the climate of a region, while the average values (or total values) of a given year or month of meteorological factors reflect the key characteristics of climate for that period of time.

Natural Resources refer to material resources that could be obtained from the nature by human being and used for production and living. Natural resources in general can be classified as renewable resources and non-renewable resources. Renewable resources refer to resources that could be renewed and recycled during a relatively short period of time, including land resource, water resource, climate resource, biology resource and marine resource. Non-renewable resources include resources that could not be renewed, such as minerals and geothermal resource.

Land Resource Land refers to the surface of the earth, consisting of mainly rocks and its weathering and earth. Land resource can be classified, by its utilization, as land for agriculture, land for construction and unused land. Land for agriculture includes cultivated land, plantation land, forestland, grassland and waters. Land for construction includes land for residential purpose, for manufacturing and mining, for transportation and for water-conservancy projects. Unused land refers to land other than land for agriculture and construction, including beaches, deserts, Gobi, glaciers and rock mountains.

Area of Cultivated Land refers to area of land reclaimed for the regular cultivation of various farm crops, including crop-cover land, fallow, newly reclaimed land and land laid idle for less than 3 years.

Area of Afforested Land refers to area for land for trees bamboo, bushes and mangrove, including forest-covered land, bush-covered land, sparse forest land, land planned for afforestation and nurseries of young trees.

Area of Grassland refers to area of grassland, grass-slopes and grass-covered hills with a vegetation-covering rate of over 5% that are used for animal husbandry or harvesting of grass. It includes natural, cultivated and improved grassland areas.

Forest Resource refers to forests, trees, forestland and wild animals, plants and microorganism that live on forest and trees. Trees include trees and bamboo. Forest refers to the population of clusters of trees and other plants, animals and microorganism as well as the earth and climate that have interactions with the trees.

Total Standing Stock Volume refers to the total stock volume of trees growing in land, including trees in forest, trees in sparse forest, scattered trees and trees planted by the side of villages, farm houses and along roads and rivers.

Forest Area refers to the area of forest where trees and bamboo grow with canopy density above 0.2, including land of natural woods and planted woods, but excluding bush land and thin forest land. It reflects the total areas of afforestation.

Stock Volume of Forest refers to total stock volume of wood growing in forest area, which shows the total size and level of forest resources of a country or a region. It is also an important indicator illustrating the richness of forest resource and the status of forest ecological environment.

Forest Coverage Rate refers to the ratio of area of afforested land to total land area. It is a very important indicator that reflects the status of abundance of forest resource and balance of the ecosystem. Forest area includes the area of trees and bamboo grow with canopy density above 0.2, the area of shrubby tree according to regulations of the government, the area of forest land inside farm land and the area of trees planted by the side of villages, farm houses and along roads and rivers. The formula for calculating forest coverage rate is as follows:

$$\text{Forestry coverage rate (\%)} = \frac{\text{Area of Afforested Land}}{\text{Area of Total Land}} \times 100\,\%$$

Water Resource Water exists in the nature in solid, liquid and gaseous states, is distributed in the ocean, land (including earth) and air, and constitutes the water resource through the circulation of water. Water resource includes the surface water and underground water that is controlled by the human being for irrigation, power-generation, water supply, navigation and cultivation. It also includes rivers, lakes, wells, springs, tides, gulf and water area for cultivation. Water resource as an important natural resource is indispensable for the development of the national economy.

Surface Water and Underground Water Water on earth can be divided into surface water and underground water according to its distribution. Surface water refers to moisture exists in rivers, lakes, swamps, glaciers, icecaps and so on. It is also called land water. The underground water refers to water deposited underground in the cranny and the hole of saturated rock soil and in the water-eroded cave.

Inland Water Area refers to water area of rivers, lakes, ponds, reservoir, etc.

Volume of Runoff refers to the total volume of water running through a certain cross section of a river during a certain period of time, reflecting the water resource condition in a country or a region. The formula for calculating volume or runoff is as follows:

Runoff =Precipitation-Evaporation

Mineral Resources refer to useful minerals that can be used for industrial or agricultural purposes enriched in lithosphere or on earth due to the geological process.

Ensured Mineral Reserves refer to the actual mineral reserves, which equal to the proven mineral reserves (including industrial reserves and prospective reserves) minus extracted parts and underground losses. This indicator shows the current condition of the mineral resources of a Country.

Temperature refers to the air temperature. China uses centigrade as the unit. The thermometry used for weather observation is put in a breezy shutter, which is 1.5 meters high from the ground. Therefore, the commonly used temperature refers to the temperature in the breezy shutter 1.5 meters away from the ground. The calculation method is as follows:

Volume of Precipitation refers to the deepness of liquid state or solid state (thawed) water falling from the sky to the ground that has not been evaporated, infiltrated or run off. The calculation method is as follows:

Monthly precipitation is the summation of daily precipitation of a month.

Annual precipitation is the summation of 12 months precipitation of a year.

Sunshine Hours refer to the actual hours of sun irradiating the earth. The calculation method is the same as that of the precipitation.

Total Water Resources refers to total volume of water resources measured as run-off for surface water from rainfall and recharge for groundwater in a given area, excluding transit water.

Surface Water Resources refers to total renewable resources which exist in rivers, lakes, glaciers and other collectors from rainfall and are measured as run-off of rivers.

Groundwater Resources refers to replenishment of aquifers with rainfall and surface water.

Duplicated Measurement between Surface Water and Groundwater refers to mutual exchange between surface water and groundwater, i.e. run-off of rivers includes some depletion into groundwater while groundwater includes some replenishment from surface water.

Water Supply refers to gross water supply by supply systems from sources to consumers, including losses during distribution.

Surface Water Supply refers to withdrawals by surface water supply system, broken down with storage, flow, pumping and transfer. Supply from storage projects includes withdrawals from reservoirs; supply from flow includes withdrawals from rivers and lakes with natural flows no matter if there are locks or not; supply from pumping projects includes withdrawals from rivers or lakes with pumping stations; and supply from transfer refers to water supplies transferred from first-level regions of water resources or independent river drainage areas to others, and should not be covered under supplies of storage, flow and pumping.

Groundwater Supply refers to withdrawals from supplying wells, broken down with shallow layer freshwater, deep layer freshwater and slightly brackish water. Groundwater supply for urban areas includes water mining by both waterworks and own wells of enterprises.

Water Use refers to gross water use distributed to users, including loss during transportation, broken down into use by agriculture, industry, living consumption and ecological protection.

Water Use by Agriculture includes uses of water by irrigation of farming fields and by forestry, animal husbandry and fishing. Water use by forestry, animal husbandry and fishery includes irrigation of forestry and orchards, irrigation of grassland and replenishment of fishing farms.

Water Use by Industry refers to new withdrawals of water, excluding reuse of water within enterprises.

Water Use by Living Consumption includes use of water for living consumption in both urban and rural areas. Urban water use by living consumption is composed of household use and public use (including services, commerce, restaurants, cargo transportation, posts, telecommunications and construction). Rural water use by living consumption includes both households and animals.

Water Use by Ecological Protection includes replenishment of rivers and lakes and use for urban environment.

Waste Water Discharged by Industry refers to the volume of waste water discharged by industrial enterprises through all their outlets, including waste water from production process, directly cooled water, groundwater from mining wells which does not meet discharge standards and sewage from households mixed with waste water produced by industrial activities, but excluding indirectly cooled water discharged (It should be included if the discharge is not separated from waste water).

Industrial Waste Water Meeting Discharge Standards refers to volume of industrial waste water discharge which, with or without treatment, reaches national or local standards with regard to all pollutants.

Ratio of Industrial Waste Water Meeting Discharge Standards refers to percentage of industrial waste water meeting discharge standards over total industrial waste water discharge. It is calculated as:

$$\text{Ratio of industrial waste water meeting discharge standards} = \frac{\text{industrial waste water meeting discharge standards}}{\text{total industrial waste water discharge}}$$

Chemical Oxygen Demand (COD) refers to the amount of oxygen required when chemical oxidants are used to oxidize organic pollutants in water. A higher value of COD corresponds to more serious pollution by organic pollutants.

Industrial Waste Air Emission refers to discharge into atmosphere of waste air containing pollutants generated from fuel burning and production process in enterprises within a given period of time. It is converted into standard (273K, 101325Pa) with the following formula:

Emission=emission from fuel burning+ emission through production process

Industrial Soot Emission refers to the volume of soot in smoke emitted in the process of fuel burning in the premises of enterprises.

Industrial Dust Emission refers to volume of dust emitted by production process of enterprises and suspended in the air for a given period of time, including dust from refractory material of iron and steel works, dust from coke-screening systems and sintering machines of coke plants, dust from lime kilns and dust from cement production in building material enterprises, but excluding soot and dust emitted from power plants.

Industrial Solid Wastes Produced refers to total volume of solid, semi-solid and high concentration liquid residues produced by industrial enterprises from production process in a given period of time, including hazardous wastes, slag, coal ash, gangue, tailings, radioactive residues and other wastes, but excluding stones stripped or dug out in mining - gangue and acid or alkaline stones not included (a stone is acid or alkaline according to the pH value of the water being below 4 or above 10.5 when the stone is in, or soaked by water).

Industrial Solid Wastes Utilized refers to volume of solid wastes from which useful materials can be extracted or which can be converted into usable resources, energy or other materials by means of reclamation, processing, recycling and exchange (including utilizing in the year the stocks of industrial solid wastes of the previous year). Examples of such utilizations include fertilizers, building materials and road materials. The information shall be collected by the producing units of the wastes.

Rate of Utilization of Industrial Solid Wastes refers to the percentage of industrial solid wastes utilized over industrial solid wastes produced (including stocks of the previous years). It is calculated as:

$$\text{Rate of utilization of industrial solid wastes} = \frac{\text{volume of industrial solid wastes utilized}}{\text{industrial solid wastes produced} + \text{stock of previous years}} \times 100\%$$

Stock of Industrial Solid Wastes refers to the volume of solid wastes placed in special facilities or special sites for purposes of utilization or disposal. The sites or facilities should take measures against dispersion, loss, seepage, and air and water contamination.

Industrial Solid Wastes Disposed refers to the quantity of industrial solid wastes which are burnt or placed ultimately in the sites meeting the requirements for environmental protection and not salvaged or recycled (including disposition in the year of those wastes of previous years). The disposition includes landfill (Safe landfills should be conducted for hazardous wastes), incineration, containment spaces, deep underground disposal, backfill in mining pits and disposal at sea.

Industrial Solid Wastes Discharged refers to the volume of industrial solid wastes discharged by producing enterprises to disposal facilities or to other sites. The wastes exclude stones stripped or dug from mining (gangue and acid or alkaline waste stones not included).

Consumption Wastes Transported refers to volume of consumption wastes collected and transported to disposal factories or sites. Consumption wastes are solid wastes produced from urban households or from service activities for urban households, and solid wastes regarded by laws and regulations as urban consumption wastes, including those from households, commercial activities, markets, cleaning of streets, public sites, offices, schools, factories, mining units and other sources.

Ratio of Consumption Wastes Treated refers to consumption wastes treated over that produced. In practical statistics, as it is difficult to estimate, the volume of consumption wastes produced is replaced with that transported. It is calculated as:

$$\text{Ratio of consumption treated} = \frac{\text{consumption wastes treated}}{\text{consumption wastes produced}} \times 100\%$$

Land for Agriculture Use refers to land directly used for agriculture production, including land for cultivation, gardening, forests, herbage and other agriculture activities.

Area of Man-made Forests refer to the area of stable growing forests, planted manually or by airplanes, with a survival rate of 80% or higher of the designed number of trees per hectare, or with a canopy density of or above 0.20 after 3-5 years of manual planting or 5-7 years of airplane planting.

Total Area of Afforestation refers to the total area of land suitable for afforestation, including barren hills, idle land, sand dunes, "grain for green" land, on which acres of arbores or bushes are planted through manual planting, airplane planting, plant seedlings, etc. in accordance with the required density standards of the Technical Procedures of Afforestation, and with a survival rate of over 85% in line with the Implementing Rules of the Forest Law of the People's Republic of China (or a survival rate of 75% in areas with less that 400 mm of annual rainfall and without irrigation facilities). Included in the this category are trees planted alone the roadsides, riversides, or next to houses that occupy an area over 0.066 hectares, or where more than 4 lines of trees are planted. Total area of afforestation is further classified by ownership (state-owned, state-collective, collective or private), by approach of planting (manual, airplane), and by type of forests (timber, by-products, protection, fuel, special use, etc.).

By-product Forests refer to forests that mainly produce fruits, nuts, edible oil, beverages, indigents, raw materials and medicine materials. By-product forests are planted to harvest the fruits, leaves, bark or liquid of trees, and consume them as food or raw materials for the manufacturing industry, such as tea-oil trees, tung oil trees, walnut trees, camphor trees, tea bushes, mulberry trees, fruit trees, etc.

Protection Forests refer to forests, trees and bushes planted mainly for protection or preservation purpose, including water resource conservation forests, water and soil conservation forests, windbreak and dune-fixing forests, farmland and pasture protection forests, riverside protection forests, roadside protection forests, etc.

Fuel Forests refer to forests planted mainly for fuels.

Project on Preservation of Natural Forests is the Number One ecological project in China's forest industry that involves the largest investment. It consists of 3 components: 1) Complete halt of all cutting and logging activities in the natural forests at the upper stream of Yangtze River and the upper and middle streams of the Yellow River. 2) Significant reduction of timber production of key state forest zones in northeast provinces and in Inner Mongolia. 3) Better protection of natural forests in other regions through rehabilitation programmes.

Projects on Converting Cultivated Land to Forests and Grassland (Grain for Green Projects) aiming at preventing soil erosion in key regions, these projects are ecological construction projects in the development of forest industry that have the widest coverage and most sophisticated procedures, with strong policy implications and most active participation of the people.

Projects on Protection Forests in North China and Yangtze River Basin covering the widest areas in China with a rich variety of contents, these projects aim at solving the problem of sand and dust in northeastern China, northern China and northwestern China and the ecological issues in other areas. More specifically, they include phase IV of Project on North China protection forests, phase II of Project on protection forests at the middle and lower streams of Yangtze River and at the Huihe River and Taihu Lake valley, phase II of Project on coastal protection forests, phase II of Project on Pearl River protection forests, phase II Project on greenery of Taihang Mountain and phase II Projects on greenery of plains.

Projects on Preserving Wild Animals and Plants and on Construction of Natural Reserves aiming at gene preservation and protection of bio-diversity, nature and wetlands, these projects are forward-looking with strategic perspectives in line with international trends and practices.

Wetlands refer to marshland and peat bog, whether natural or man-made, permanent or temporary; water covered areas, whether stagnant or flowing, with fresh or semi-fresh or salty water that is less than 6 meters deep at low tide; as well as coral beach, weed beach, mud beach, mangrove, river outlet, rivers, fresh-water marshland, marshland forests, lakes, salty bog and salt lakes along the coastal areas.

Natural Reserves refer to certain areas of land, waters or sea demarked and approved by relevant governments at all levels to put under special protection and management in order to protect the natural environment and natural resources and to promote the sustainable development of the national economy. According to the objects be protected, the natural reserves are classified into classes of natural ecosystem, wild life and natural heritage. Scenic spots and cultural preservation zones are not included.

Ecological Demonstration Zones refer to administrative areas approved by the environment protection agencies of central and provincial governments and established by provincial, prefecture or county governments in line with the approved programme for ecological demonstration zones. They include those evaluated and accepted by the environment protection agencies of central and provincial governments and those under pilot development stage.

Landslides refer to the geological phenomenon of unstable rocks and earth on slopes sliding down along certain soft surface as a result of gravitational force. Role of surface water and underground water, and destruction of the stability of slopes by irrational construction work are usually main factors triggering the landslides. Several damages are often caused by landslides in open mining, in water conservancy projects, and in the construction of railways and highways.

Collapse refers to the geological phenomenon of large mass of rocks or earth suddenly collapsing from the mountain or cliff as a result of gravitational force. Usually caused by weathering of rocks, permeance of rain or earthquakes, collapse often destructs buildings and blocks river course or transport routes.

Mud-rock Flow refers to the sudden rush of flood torrents containing large amount of mud and rocks in mountainous areas. It is found mostly in semi-arid hills or plateaus. High and precipitous topographic features, loose soil mass, heavy rains or melting water contribute to the mud-rock flow.

Landslides refer to the geological phenomenon of unstable rocks and earth on slopes sliding down along certain soft surface as a result of gravitational force. Role of surface water and underground water, and destruction of the stability of slopes by irrational construction work are usually main factors triggering landslides. Severe damages are often caused by landslides in open mining, in water conservancy projects, and in the construction of railways and highways.

Land Subside refers to the geological phenomenon of surface rocks or earth subsiding into holes or pits as a result of natural or human factors. Land subside can be classified as karst subside and non-karst subside.

Environment Pollution and Destruction Accidents refer to sudden accidents, due to economic or social activities that are contrary to environment protection laws or due to unforeseen factors or natural disasters, that lead to environment pollution, destruction of protected wild animals, plants or nature reserves, damage to human health, economic and property losses, and other negative impacts on the society.

Investment in Environment Pollution Harnessing Projects refers to the proportion of investment in fixed assets in the total investment in harnessing pollution and in the construction of urban environment infrastructure facilities. The investment in harnessing pollution It includes investment in harnessing sources of industrial pollution and investment in environment protection facilities designed concurrently with construction projects. Investment in environment pollution harnessing is the total of investment in harnessing pollution and investment in urban environment infrastructure facilities.

Investment in Fixed Assets for Afforestation refers to the investment in capital construction and updating projects in afforestation during the reference period.

第十二篇
农　业

CHAPTER 12
Agriculture

简要说明
Brief Introduction

本篇资料的主要内容及来源

本篇资料反映新疆维吾尔自治区农业生产和农村经济基本情况，主要内容包括农村基层组织情况、乡村从业人员、国有农、林、牧、渔场情况、主要农业生产条件、耕地、农林牧渔业产值、主要农产品生产情况、特色农作物生产情况、乡镇企业情况等。

本篇资料除表 12-4 来自新疆维吾尔自治区国土资源厅，表 12-10、12-11、12-12 来自新疆维吾尔自治区水利厅，表 12-27 来自新疆维吾尔自治区民政厅，乡镇企业主要指标来自新疆维吾尔自治区乡镇企业局外，其余资料均由新疆维吾尔自治区统计局农村统计处提供。

Main content and source of data

The data in this chapter show the basic conditions of agricultural production and rural economy in Xinjiang Uygur Autonomous Region, including mainly rural grassroots units rural population, rural employed labor force, basic conditions of township enterprises, statistic on forest products, cultivated land, gross output value farming, forest, animal husbandry and fishery, output of major farm products,output of characteristic farm crops and condition on the township enterprises, ect.

Data on this chapter of table 12-4 are provided by the Xinjiang Bureau of Land Natural Resousce ,the data on table the 12-10,12-11,12-12 are provided by the Xinjiang Bureau of Water Resources , the data on table 12-27 are provided by the Xinjiang Bureau of Civil Affairs. the data on the township enterprises are from the Xinjiang Bureau of Township Enterprises. Others are provided by the Department of Rural statistics, Xinjiang Bureau of Statistics.

12-1 主要年份农村基层组织情况
Basic Conditions of Rural Grass-roots Unit in Main Years

指　　标	Item	2000	2005	2010
乡镇政府(个)	**Number of Township and Town Governments (unit)**	**794**	**796**	**801**
＃镇政府	Number of Township Governments	124	169	183
村民委员会(个)	Number of Villagers' Committees (unit)	9378	8953	8796
乡村户数(户)	Number of Rural Households (household)	2008794	2239238	2551479
乡村人口(人)	Rural Population (person)	9131922	9896017	10737179
乡村从业人员(人)	**Number of Rural Laborers (person)**	**3540789**	**4039199**	**4650560**
按性别分	Grouped by Gender			
男	Male	1950559	2242973	2558491
女	Female	1590230	1796226	2092069
按行业分	Grouped by Sector			
农林牧渔业	Agriculture, Forestry, Animal Husbandry & Fishery	3144461	3440500	3758972
工　业	Industry	84766	113912	161325
建筑业	Construction	49126	92921	162427
交通运输、仓储和邮政业	Transportation,Storage, Postal and Telecommunication Services		105390	145132
信息传输、计算机服务和软件业	Information Transmission, Computer Service and Software Sector		5244	13915
批发与零售业	Wholesale and Retail Trades	76727	115550	157457
住宿和餐饮业	Hotels and Catering Serives	109217	65092	106191
其　他	Others	76492	100590	145141

12-2 国有农林牧渔场基本情况
Basic Conditions of State Agriculture, Forestry, Animal Husbandry and Fishery

指　　标	Item	2009	2010
场数合计(个)	**Total (unit)**	**474**	**472**
农 场	Number of Farms	288	285
林 场	Number of Forest Farms	44	44
牧 场	Number of Ranch	126	130
渔 场	Number of Fishing Ground	16	13
场内户数(户)	**Number of Households on a Farm (household)**	**796325**	**803022**
＃牧业户数	Number of Stock-breeding Household	66720	68284
场内人口(人)	**Farm Population (person)**	**2529850**	**2538956**
＃牧业人口	Stock-breeding Population	249717	252044
场内实有从业人员(人)	**Persons Actually Engaged on a Farm (person)**	**1020662**	**1035763**
男	Male	569240	578631
女	Female	451422	457132
农　业	Employed Persons in Agriculture	756597	768773
工　业	Employed Persons in Industry	56120	56237
建筑业	Employed Persons in Construction	25322	25444
交通运输、仓储和邮政业	Transportation,Storage, Post and Telecommunications Services	30491	30382
信息传输、计算机服务和软件业	Information Transmission, Computer Service and Software Sector	907	910
批发与零售业	Wholesale and Retail Trades	48625	48775
住宿和餐饮业	Hotels and Catering Serives	20756	20767
其　他	Others	81844	84475

12-3 各地、州、市、县(市)农村基层组织情况

(2010 年)

地 区	Region	乡镇数(个) Number of Township and Town Govern-ments (unit)	#镇 town	村民委员会(个) Number of Villagers' Committees (unit)	乡村户数(户) Number of Rural House-Holds (household)	#牧业户数 Stock-breeding households
总 计	**Total**	**801**	**183**	**8796**	**2551479**	**327507**
一、地 方	**Local Regions**	**799**	**183**	**8767**	**2544401**	**327137**
乌鲁木齐市	**Urumqi City**	**22**	**8**	**176**	**60092**	**7776**
#乌鲁木齐县	Urumqi County	9	2	59	17648	4051
克拉玛依市	**Karamay City**	**2**		**6**	**591**	**45**
吐鲁番地区	**Turpan Administrative Offices**	**24**	**7**	**172**	**103333**	**3281**
吐鲁番市	Turpan City	9	1	60	41821	2144
鄯善县	Shanshan [piqan]County	9	4	65	38379	352
托克逊县	Toksun County	6	2	47	23133	785
哈密地区	**Hami [Kumul]Administrative Offices**	**31**	**5**	**170**	**52270**	**13028**
哈密市	Hami [Kumul]City	15	2	91	31622	6882
巴里坤哈萨克自治县	Barkol KazakAutonomous County	10	2	47	17902	5111
伊吾县	Yiwu [Araturuk]County	6	1	32	2746	1035
昌吉回族自治州	**Changji Hui Autonomous Prefecture**	**67**	**34**	**571**	**177819**	**28078**
昌吉市	Changji City	10	7	87	32989	5779
阜康市	Fukang City	6	3	106	17430	2824
呼图壁县	Hutubi County	6	5	49	20432	3828
玛纳斯县	Manas County	11	6	112	25928	3432
奇台县	Qitai County	15	6	102	35119	4441
吉木萨尔县	Jimsar County	9	5	55	26211	2516
木垒哈萨克自治县	Mori Kazak Autonomous County	10	2	60	19710	5258
伊犁哈萨克自治州	**Ili Kazak Autonomous Prefecture**	**212**	**53**	**1931**	**538780**	**84344**
伊犁州直属县(市)	**Counties (Cities) Direct Under Ili Prefecture**	**99**	**21**	**656**	**319835**	**43956**
伊宁市	Yining [Gulja]City	9	1	46	32097	982
奎屯市	Kuytun City	1		4	349	314
伊宁县	Yining [Gulja]County	18	2	130	67792	5867
察布查尔锡伯自治县	Qapqal Xibe Autonomous County	13	2	58	32324	2113
霍城县	Huocheng [korgas]County	10	5	75	47594	2075
巩留县	Gongliu [Tokkuzlara]County	8	1	53	25215	4063
新源县	Xinyuan [kunes]County	11	6	83	41893	7548
昭苏县	Zhaosu [mongolkure]County	10	1	73	23273	6205
特克斯县	Tekes County	8	2	59	21436	6910
尼勒克县	Nilka County	11	1	75	27862	7879
塔城地区	**Tacheng [Tarbagatai] Administrative Offices**	**62**	**21**	**781**	**141909**	**16116**
塔城市	Tacheng [Qoqek] City	6	1	115	20311	1819
乌苏市	Usu City	14	7	134	29155	386
额敏县	Emin [Dorbiljin] County	12		139	19546	1285
沙湾县	Shawan County	12	9	227	44684	1450
托里县	Toli County	7	3	66	15709	8161
裕民县	Yumin [Qagantokay] County	5		45	6945	1568
和布克赛尔蒙古自治县	Hoboksar Mongol Autonomous County	6	1	55	5559	1447
阿勒泰地区	**Altay Administrative Offices**	**51**	**11**	**494**	**77036**	**24272**
阿勒泰市	Altay City	10	2	96	15879	3247
布尔津县	Burqin County	7	2	63	11249	4189
富蕴县	Fuyun [Koktokay] County	9	3	68	11030	3937
福海县	Fuhai [Burultokay] County	5		61	9164	3271
哈巴河县	Habahe [Kaba] County	7	1	113	16043	4280
青河县	Qinghe [Qinggil] County	7	2	52	7510	4317
吉木乃县	Jeminay County	6	1	41	6161	1031

Basic Conditions of Rural Grass-roots Units by Prefecture, Autonomous Prefecture, City and County

乡村人口数(人) Rural Population (person)	#牧业人口数 Population Engaged in Livestocks	乡村从业人员(人) Number of Rural Laborers (person)	#男 Male	农林牧渔业 Agriculture, Forestry, Animal Husbandry & Fishery	工业 Industry	建筑业 Construction	交通仓储和邮政业 Transport, Storage, Post and Telecommunication Services	信息传输、计算机服务和软件业 Information Transmission, Computer Servcie and Software Industries	批发与零售业 Retail and Wholesale Trades	住宿和餐饮业 Hotels and Catering Serives	其他 Others
10737179	**1357099**	**4650560**	**2558491**	**3758972**	**161325**	**162427**	**145132**	**13915**	**157457**	**106191**	**145141**
10713003	**1355080**	**4639411**	**2553003**	**3749471**	**160890**	**162367**	**144950**	**13915**	**157078**	**106121**	**144619**
220813	**26433**	**135114**	**71710**	**83223**	**10742**	**1418**	**11167**	**264**	**8813**	**9487**	**10000**
66065	14854	40334	21418	32739	564	121	1361	50	936	998	3565
2034	**127**	**1341**	**752**	**1256**			**6**		**18**	**18**	**43**
432622	**16438**	**245232**	**133937**	**201422**	**6385**	**5046**	**10833**	**1041**	**10120**	**7574**	**2811**
177815	11780	98418	53194	76851	2238	2062	5096	176	5524	5066	1405
158478	1308	95932	52060	83476	1567	1435	2777	763	2830	1958	1126
96329	3350	50882	28683	41095	2580	1549	2960	102	1766	550	280
178673	**48728**	**102007**	**55658**	**76675**	**3673**	**3421**	**6983**	**748**	**3798**	**3041**	**3668**
110826	24632	63784	34053	50486	1738	1296	4135	198	2583	1536	1812
59857	19990	33626	19067	22181	1919	2101	2785	542	1081	1434	1583
7990	4106	4597	2538	4008	16	24	63	8	134	71	273
666085	**108910**	**376239**	**204079**	**308215**	**13747**	**6542**	**12897**	**544**	**11545**	**8131**	**14618**
114477	18669	66130	35689	52643	3051	1445	2288	59	2205	1595	2844
64861	11749	41470	22436	30881	2482	1481	1155	30	1254	1443	2744
81870	16317	43535	23349	37331	1030	110	1819	87	1313	799	1046
91106	12210	50147	27209	39244	4049	347	2330	87	1490	947	1653
150234	19447	81388	44943	66913	1133	1718	3096	204	2915	1980	3429
94072	9424	54424	29265	45625	1113	757	1737	36	1580	1027	2549
69465	21094	39145	21188	35578	889	684	472	41	788	340	353
2283099	**391348**	**1132428**	**642293**	**895682**	**50770**	**47825**	**36044**	**4775**	**39646**	**26854**	**30832**
1465517	**215685**	**695288**	**399159**	**534314**	**33081**	**35528**	**26205**	**3920**	**26826**	**17496**	**17918**
142306	4891	69452	38776	40287	5811	6417	5584	217	5593	2854	2689
1228	1130	750	410	710	3	22	5		10		
321292	23439	165532	96728	129222	8908	8618	4745	1451	5374	3771	3443
123321	9228	63881	37925	53604	2513	1927	1145	151	1749	1107	1685
207870	11005	121516	65062	97150	3189	4103	5832	898	3644	3940	2760
118152	21183	40740	24036	35421	1265	818	1326	22	1685	156	47
213489	39364	87856	51324	66051	5721	4050	3226	497	3554	2095	2662
107915	31791	39278	25509	30112	1762	2289	1432	196	1598	642	1247
108751	36734	54395	30209	42045	2178	4875	607	371	1458	1700	1161
121193	36920	51888	29180	39712	1731	2409	2303	117	2161	1231	2224
518394	**65896**	**303895**	**166135**	**259922**	**11171**	**6186**	**5654**	**619**	**7938**	**5178**	**7227**
64575	5779	41195	21780	33809	967	522	781	107	1517	610	2882
111819	636	63364	34198	53375	3567	1095	1122	62	1640	1668	835
83709	5094	48157	26486	42529	1099	649	1027	89	1495	503	766
147592	8176	91545	48156	79676	3921	1121	1463	162	2046	1728	1428
58518	33248	35012	22758	29070	1080	2586	805	152	650	329	340
33506	8215	17625	9013	15665	316	120	345	3	418	305	453
18675	4748	6997	3744	5798	221	93	111	44	172	35	523
299188	**109767**	**133245**	**76999**	**101446**	**6518**	**6111**	**4185**	**236**	**4882**	**4180**	**5687**
63092	15101	29304	17482	23296	2215	845	758	39	870	262	1019
46559	18055	21746	12648	16675	376	600	564		919	1262	1350
42649	16243	17323	9586	11436	1656	1157	560	74	520	369	1551
35773	16355	19074	10776	14654	698	1933	708	51	413	556	61
56022	17700	20869	11742	15958	766	756	759	37	1056	892	645
37799	22215	17512	9663	12964	789	820	817	35	980	717	390
17294	4098	7417	5102	6463	18		19		124	122	671

12-3 续表

地　　区	Region	乡镇数（个）Number of Township and Town Governments (unit)	#镇 town	村民委员会（个）Number of Villagers' Committees (unit)	乡村户数（户）Number of Rural Households (unit)	#牧业户数 Stock-Breeding households
博尔塔拉蒙古自治州	**Bortala Mongol Autonomous Prefecture**	**14**	**5**	**250**	**52190**	**6110**
博乐市	Bole [Bortala] City	5	3	130	19099	2192
精河县	Jinghe [Jing] County	4	1	55	20759	1861
温泉县	Wenquan [Araxang] County	5	1	65	12332	2057
巴音郭楞蒙古自治州	**Bayangol Mongol Autonomous Prefecture**	**73**	**12**	**407**	**120014**	**11355**
库尔勒市	Korla City	10	1	59	19288	355
轮台县	Luntai [Bugur] County	10	3	65	18450	878
尉犁县	Yuli [Lopnur] County	7		49	12656	1936
若羌县	Ruoqiang [Qarkilik] County	5		25	5636	185
且末县	Qiemo [Qarqan] County	11		53	8381	1141
焉耆回族自治县	Yanqi Hui Autonomous County	7	3	49	17937	572
和静县	Hejing County	11	4	55	19346	3851
和硕县	Hoxud County	6		26	10175	1976
博湖县	Bohu [Bagrax] County	6	1	26	8145	461
阿克苏地区	**Aksu Administrative Offices**	**75**	**22**	**1107**	**329267**	**26086**
阿克苏市	Aksu City	6	2	122	33634	6651
温宿县	Wensu [Onsu] County	9	4	104	35194	4198
库车县	Kuqa County	14	8	210	66442	3718
沙雅县	Xayar County	8	3	152	45108	1401
新和县	Xinhe [Toksu] County	7	1	110	31771	3920
拜城县	Baicheng [Bay] County	12	2	150	34394	2750
乌什县	Wushi [Uxturpan] County	8		107	39876	1467
阿瓦提县	Awat County	7	2	119	34894	1181
柯坪县	Kalpin County	4		33	7954	800
克孜勒苏柯尔克孜自治州	**Kizilsu Kirgiz Autonomous Prefecture**	**35**	**3**	**238**	**91539**	**24951**
阿图什市	Artux City	7		77	36883	6877
阿克陶县	Akto County	13	2	109	38627	8146
阿合奇县	Akqi County	6	1	18	7516	4509
乌恰县	Wuqia [Ulugqat] County	9		34	8513	5419
喀什地区	**Kashgar [Kaxgar] Administrative Offices**	**157**	**23**	**2353**	**616100**	**85876**
喀什市	Kashgar [Kaxgar] City	8	2	106	38741	2158
疏附县	Shufu County	12	1	165	61541	9300
疏勒县	Shule County	14	2	223	54913	2500
英吉沙县	Yengisar County	13		163	52415	4005
泽普县	Zepu [Poskam] County	11	1	138	25245	1485
莎车县	Shache [Yarkant] County	28	6	504	126782	27812
叶城县	Yecheng [Kagilik] County	19	2	309	67408	9647
麦盖提县	Makit County	9	1	128	30039	1672
岳普湖县	Yopurga County	8	2	87	27014	3284
伽师县	Jiashi [Payzawat] County	13	2	297	74350	7410
巴楚县	Bachu [Maralbexi] County	11	3	186	52135	11086
塔什库尔干塔吉克自治县	Taxkorgan Tajik Autonomous County	11	1	47	5517	5517
和田地区	**Hotan Administrative Offices**	**87**	**11**	**1386**	**402406**	**36207**
和田市	Hotan City	8	2	111	37766	3198
和田县	Hotan County	11	1	211	59398	3425
墨玉县	Moyu [Karakax] County	16	1	365	103198	6819
皮山县	Pishan [Guma] County	15	2	169	46449	2173
洛浦县	Lop County	8	1	207	54358	8777
策勒县	Qira County	8	1	123	38357	7254
于田县	Yutian [Keriya] County	15	2	170	56546	3102
民丰县	Minfeng [Niya] County	6	1	30	6334	1459
二、生产建设兵团	**Xinjiang Production and Construction Group**	**2**		**29**	**7078**	**370**

Continued

乡村人口数(人) Rural Population (person)	#牧业人口数 Population Engaged in Livestocks	乡村从业人员(人) Number of Rural Laborers (person)	#男 Male	农林牧渔业 Agriculture, Forestry, Animal Husbandry & Fishery	工业 Industry	建筑业 Construction	交通仓储和邮政业 Transport, Storage, Post and Telecommunication Services	信息传输、计算机服务和软件业 Information Transmission, Computer Servcie and Software Industries	批发与零售业 Retail and Wholesale Trades	住宿和餐饮业 Hotels and Catering Serives	其他 Others
194830	**22876**	**91611**	**50867**	**68232**	**3846**	**3367**	**2797**	**228**	**3861**	**3103**	**6177**
86172	10133	41718	23508	28713	2379	1863	1741	124	1833	1743	3322
68719	6136	28482	15462	21955	612	918	604	32	1354	974	2033
39939	6607	21411	11897	17564	855	586	452	72	674	386	822
479791	**44483**	**226623**	**130475**	**185918**	**12581**	**5165**	**6894**	**487**	**7427**	**3661**	**4490**
74102	1033	36374	20888	30925	206	369	1309	88	2549	668	260
72088	2878	32747	17860	29635	315	354	272	65	754	481	871
48310	7659	20816	12065	19051	55	229	387	84	446	226	338
23443	736	17872	13324	8521	6471	1230	1150	6	402	84	8
38909	4819	13385	7705	11336	209	631	615	45	311	155	83
72253	3462	28913	17348	20834	3102	986	1226	11	849	620	1285
79891	14789	42132	21982	35445	1715	958	1092	54	1052	910	906
37775	7147	17002	9691	14673	171	131	366	115	609	364	573
33020	1960	17382	9612	15498	337	277	477	19	455	153	166
1444386	**91402**	**625980**	**344934**	**539676**	**10773**	**17453**	**13158**	**1853**	**17953**	**11144**	**13970**
152536	20480	63939	36713	43007	1633	6146	3269	455	2924	3028	3477
146941	13737	46526	26333	42485	347	567	475	126	1290	650	586
309261	13222	157829	87445	130526	3176	6061	5399	649	4472	2881	4665
188835	7229	71401	40699	62592	1480	1090	321	125	3110	1157	1526
126411	8741	59350	32320	56044	318	560	635	112	1162	423	96
152641	12070	70843	39450	66463	350	485	655	45	1310	665	870
167974	6481	59640	30855	52160	1541	1037	962	149	1547	828	1416
163456	5441	79035	41679	70879	1488	1011	1142	176	1788	1267	1284
36331	4001	17417	9440	15520	440	496	300	16	350	245	50
405082	**119169**	**152622**	**86420**	**122675**	**5835**	**5585**	**4527**	**97**	**5566**	**3711**	**4626**
176985	31570	65271	37135	44911	4447	3006	3286	81	3634	3033	2873
163117	37166	67134	38561	59738	1146	2024	829		1100	658	1639
29881	22545	7050	3878	6345	67	159	84	16	245	20	114
35099	27888	13167	6846	11681	175	396	328		587		
2784725	**346217**	**965350**	**518147**	**803418**	**18257**	**37373**	**24779**	**2035**	**29581**	**19396**	**30511**
179324	8134	66714	38206	30602	1552	7300	3890		5360	6810	11200
272000	38200	91669	52000	69800	2640	5105	2580	120	5200	2010	4214
278668	6722	60930	37503	55600	1700	1300	1500	100	330	200	200
223215	20025	102727	53418	95827	763	1381	1087		1487	1331	851
102947	5016	32657	16560	28713	374	1097	698		1000	33	742
596015	122959	223322	116746	186203	4896	10683	5304	823	6091	1760	7562
313420	40644	105218	56864	87459	2753	4686	3635	347	1012	2668	2658
126144	6441	55400	29186	50915	430	483	591	137	1563	132	1149
119990	17612	49910	24524	43857	675	1493	1214	251	857	1523	40
341310	33345	96500	51627	84922	1444	2115	2896	188	2346	2488	101
205490	32500	70318	35418	60775	842	1399	1100	69	4107	306	1720
26202	14619	9985	6095	8745	188	331	284		228	135	74
1620863	**138949**	**584864**	**313731**	**463079**	**24281**	**29172**	**14865**	**1843**	**18750**	**10001**	**22873**
163657	12881	54023	31036	34503	5133	2593	2548	525	3395	2038	3288
249539	11355	89269	47821	71212	4401	3808	2033	88	2300	1444	3983
449671	24794	137936	74527	102742	7039	11025	4088	393	6389	3439	2821
188106	7002	68427	35704	56939	882	1297	1200		1023	482	6604
208543	38321	92768	48788	77832	3881	5045	1949	453	1706	400	1502
130492	26339	46844	25403	41290	951	1479	683	109	1187	686	459
208275	12642	88426	46429	73243	1858	3516	1880	254	2444	1249	3982
22580	5615	7171	4023	5318	136	409	484	21	306	263	234
24176	**2019**	**11149**	**5488**	**9501**	**435**	**60**	**182**		**379**	**70**	**522**

12-4 各地、州、市、县(市)耕地面积

Area of Cultivated land by Prefecture, Autonomous Prefecture, City and County

单位：公顷 (2008 年) (hectare)

地 区	Region	年末耕地面积 Cultivated Land at Year-end	#水浇地 # Irrigable Land	#旱 地 Arid Land
总 计	**Total**	**4124563.70**	**3812247.55**	**204501.81**
乌鲁木齐市	**Urumqi City**	**96950.66**	**78328.45**	**4035.06**
#乌鲁木齐县	Urumqi County	55412.44	48787.55	2206.13
克拉玛依市	**Karamay City**	**41926.31**	**41150.26**	**34.34**
石河子市	**Shihezi City**	**21886.21**	**21444.27**	
吐鲁番地区	**TurpanAdministrative Offices**	**48182.08**	**47560.93**	
吐鲁番市	Turpan City	17365.34	16883.43	
鄯善县	Shanshan [piqan]County	13707.94	13577.23	
托克逊县	Toksun County	17108.80	17100.27	
哈密地区	**Hami [Kumul]Administrative Offices**	**87087.69**	**83783.52**	**2617.09**
哈密市	Hami [Kumul]City	48101.16	47484.37	0.91
巴里坤哈萨克自治县	Barkol KazakAutonomous County	33793.67	31248.76	2494.56
伊吾县	Yiwu [Araturuk]County	5192.86	5050.39	121.62
昌吉回族自治州	**Changji Hui Autonomous Prefecture**	**629255.41**	**575551.19**	**48255.72**
昌吉市	Changji City	81216.70	79559.30	
阜康市	Fukang City	45008.84	43705.99	438.04
呼图壁县	Hutubi County	108240.93	107083.42	
玛纳斯县	Manas County	142651.23	140149.81	1646.14
奇台县	Qitai County	141463.80	125593.52	15405.67
吉木萨尔县	Jimsar County	59196.71	54743.95	4118.61
木垒哈萨克自治县	Mori Kazak Autonomous County	51477.20	24715.20	26647.26
伊犁哈萨克自治州	**Ili Kazak Autonomous Prefecture**	**1370619.63**	**1206934.23**	**147541.35**
伊犁州直属县(市)	**Counties (Cities) Direct Under Ili Prefecture**	**565724.94**	**462766.85**	**93380.19**
伊宁市	Yining [Gulja]City	13143.75	12397.65	157.73
奎屯市	Kuytun City	13830.81	13416.21	
伊宁县	Yining [Gulja]County	91060.36	87325.21	3074.98
察布查尔锡伯自治县	Qapqal Xibe Autonomous County	78010.92	67482.83	8691.95
霍城县	Huocheng [korgas]County	90103.57	86672.14	2627.72
巩留县	Gongliu [Tokkuzlara]County	42300.77	34067.58	5769.73
新源县	Xinyuan [kunes]County	69968.00	64130.84	3631.87
昭苏县	Zhaosu [mongolkure]County	89646.90	46655.06	42897.45
特克斯县	Tekes County	29857.44	23166.80	6399.81
尼勒克县	Nilka County	47802.42	27452.53	20128.95
塔城地区	**Tacheng [Tarbagatai] Administrative Offices**	**623638.56**	**574819.09**	**44346.27**
塔城市	Tacheng [Qoqek] City	116362.76	111668.61	4375.15
乌苏市	Usu City	90090.34	88675.34	
额敏县	Emin [Dorbiljin] County	147338.60	125362.73	21758.60
沙湾县	Shawan County	189499.02	186954.94	254.66
托里县	Toli County	24924.02	24791.30	70.37
裕民县	Yumin [Qagantokay] County	44247.45	26309.92	17887.49
和布克赛尔蒙古自治县	Hoboksar Mongol Autonomous County	11176.37	11056.25	
阿勒泰地区	**Altay Administrative Offices**	**181256.13**	**169348.29**	**9814.89**
阿勒泰市	Altay City	40931.04	40585.26	24.04
布尔津县	Burqin County	20584.37	16887.53	3469.38
富蕴县	Fuyun [Koktokay] County	14892.11	11654.88	2860.36
福海县	Fuhai [Burultokay] County	48402.20	47386.39	105.63
哈巴河县	Habahe [Kaba] County	31714.03	29103.31	2462.77
青河县	Qinghe [Qinggil] County	9825.27	8902.88	892.71
吉木乃县	Jeminay County	14907.11	14828.04	

12-4 续表 Continued

单位：公顷 (hectare)

地区	Region	年末耕地面积 Cultivated Land at Year-end	#水浇地 # Irrigable Land	#旱地 Arid Land
博尔塔拉蒙古自治州	**Bortala Mongol Autonomous Prefecture**	**135223.32**	**133774.95**	**23.79**
博乐市	Bole [Bortala] City	65574.44	64586.74	
精河县	Jinghe [Jing] County	36147.89	35728.97	23.79
温泉县	Wenquan [Araxang] County	33500.99	33459.24	
巴音郭楞蒙古自治州	**Bayangol Mongol Autonomous Prefecture**	**322556.95**	**312340.71**	
库尔勒市	Korla City	63399.62	55645.29	
轮台县	Luntai [Bugur] County	32947.41	32914.37	
尉犁县	Yuli [Lopnur] County	68263.86	67857.08	
若羌县	Ruoqiang [Qarkilik] County	7132.15	7070.05	
且末县	Qiemo [Qarqan] County	15088.73	15059.49	
焉耆回族自治县	Yanqi Hui Autonomous County	36128.76	35999.77	
和静县	Hejing County	45540.81	45088.93	
和硕县	Hoxud County	36168.43	35167.26	
博湖县	Bohu [Bagrax] County	17887.18	17538.47	
阿克苏地区	**Aksu Administrative Offices**	**614943.17**	**585562.62**	**1674.65**
阿克苏市	Aksu City	168847.83	161536.10	394.20
温宿县	Wensu [Onsu] County	78711.69	67549.42	831.61
库车县	Kuqa County	65204.00	63182.13	6.41
沙雅县	Xayar County	56653.34	56359.21	
新和县	Xinhe [Toksu] County	37933.16	34910.01	
拜城县	Baicheng [Bay] County	72601.88	71028.51	
乌什县	Wushi [Uxturpan] County	46465.29	43538.75	
阿瓦提县	Awat County	79372.13	78323.46	442.43
柯坪县	Kalpin County	9153.85	9135.03	
克孜勒苏柯尔克孜自治州	**Kizilsu Kirgiz Autonomous Prefecture**	**52859.60**	**50149.91**	**252.68**
阿图什市	Artux City	15715.38	15293.50	223.54
阿克陶县	Akto County	29250.53	27006.77	11.71
阿合奇县	Akqi County	6164.41	6140.43	
乌恰县	Wuqia [Ulugqat] County	1729.28	1709.21	17.43
喀什地区	**Kashgar [Kaxgar] Administrative Offices**	**530457.07**	**516515.12**	**66.56**
喀什市	Kashgar [Kaxgar] City	7165.97	6271.21	
疏附县	Shufu County	51747.77	48541.95	
疏勒县	Shule County	49364.21	47766.47	
英吉沙县	Yengisar County	5718.17	5537.15	60.69
泽普县	Zepu [Poskam] County	37625.15	36203.14	
莎车县	Shache [Yarkant] County	98935.41	95867.11	
叶城县	Yecheng [Kagilik] County	53928.82	52503.91	4.67
麦盖提县	Makit County	50533.09	50138.07	
岳普湖县	Yopurga County	22224.51	22149.50	
伽师县	Jiashi [Payzawat] County	52288.15	51455.31	0.54
巴楚县	Bachu [Maralbexi] County	96950.39	96108.71	0.66
塔什库尔干塔吉克自治县	Taxkorgan Tajik Autonomous County	3975.44	3972.59	
和田地区	**Hotan Administrative Offices**	**172615.60**	**159151.39**	**0.57**
和田市	Hotan City	5996.45	5300.40	
和田县	Hotan County	30130.79	27035.19	
墨玉县	Moyu [Karakax] County	34013.32	28767.52	
皮山县	Pishan [Guma] County	27499.96	27193.71	
洛浦县	Lop County	26977.43	26784.99	
策勒县	Qira County	16489.41	16046.82	0.57
于田县	Yutian [Keriya] County	27445.86	24235.45	
民丰县	Minfeng [Niya] County	4062.38	3787.31	

12-5 农、林、牧、渔业总产值

Gross Output Value of Agriculture, Forestry, Animal Husbandry and Fishery

单位：万元 (10 000 yuan)

年份 Year	地区 Region	农林牧渔业总产值 Total	农业产值 Farming	林业产值 Forestry	牧业产值 Animal Husbandry	渔业产值 Fishery	农林牧渔服务业产值 Output Value of Services for Farming, Forestry, Animal Husbandary and Fishery
1978		191184	142460	3397	44990	337	
1980		220135	164187	5394	50148	406	
1985		565699	429519	25906	108598	1676	
1990		1446535	1104742	38152	294963	8678	
1995		4057332	3150055	56381	823351	27545	
1996		4309617	3340735	61940	875560	31382	
1997		4764743	3738602	64913	925923	35305	
1998		4992355	3873616	74394	1008783	35562	
1999		4611503	3409380	75565	1092279	34279	
2000		4872005	3605405	83451	1145142	38007	
2001		4968125	3488409	100847	1340236	38633	
2002		5250446	3627669	110897	1480382	31498	
2003		6883187	4827597	136936	1619823	32065	266766
2004		7506792	5150018	138204	1874660	42985	300925
2005		8310614	5958464	152851	1835206	43405	320688
2006		8835409	6385954	171994	1890700	46945	339816
2007		10634648	7669468	208623	2315097	70149	371311
2008		11766907	7841922	231830	3182256	99097	411802
2009		12976109	8986167	266451	3183730	111403	428358
2010		18461828	13768852	352701	3757905	126663	455707
一、地　方	**Local Regions**	**13629134**	**8457017**	**613111**	**4168781**	**70736**	**319489**
乌鲁木齐市	Urumqi City	273161	130416	2904	130230	5801	3810
克拉玛依市	Karamay City	80604	27222	13399	26772	625	12586
吐鲁番地区	Turpan Administrative Offices	402992	318108	4642	72471	418	7353
哈密地区	Hami [Kumul] Administrative Offices	292973	152001	7936	127898	1410	3728
昌吉回族自治州	Changji Hui Autonomous Prefecture	2103836	971332	22587	1072622	14644	22651
伊犁哈萨克自治州	Ili Kazak Autonomous Prefecture	3163395	1859698	47015	1192553	16848	47281
伊犁州直属县(市)	Counties (Cities) Direct Under Ili Prefecture	1347896	715951	24409	575235	9344	22957
塔城地区	Tacheng [Tarbagatai] Administrative Offices	1348595	922117	11200	397610	2774	14894
阿勒泰地区	Altay Administrative Offices	466904	221630	11406	219708	4730	9430
博尔塔拉蒙古自治州	Bortala Mongol Autonomous Prefecture	544307	425549	6294	91197	256	21011
巴音郭楞蒙古自治州	Bayangol Mongol Autonomous Prefecture	1610513	1279383	20617	252865	10204	47444
阿克苏地区	Aksu Administrative Offices	1634693	1208014	109616	244288	7580	65195
克孜勒苏柯尔克孜自治州	Kizilsu Kirgiz Autonomous Prefecture	159098	88036	2936	57198	198	10730
喀什地区	Kashgar [Kaxgar] Administrative Offices	2599047	1535469	265036	722990	10398	65154
和田地区	Hotan Administrative Offices	764515	461789	110129	177697	2354	12546
二、生产建设兵团	**Xinjiang Production and Construction Group**	**5692849**	**4504210**	**54456**	**768463**	**30387**	**335333**

注：本表按当年价格计算；全区合计不等于地方和生产建设兵团汇总数。
Note：The number in this form is caculated by current price. Gross output value of autonomous region is not equal to the sum of output value of every prefecture.

12-6 主要年份农、林、牧、渔业总产值指数

Indices of Gross Output Value of Agriculture, Forestry, Animal Husbandry and Fishery in Main Years

年份 Year	农林牧渔业总产值 Total	#农业产值 Farming	#林业产值 Forestry	#牧业产值 Animal Husbandry	#渔业产值 Fishery
(上年=100) (preceding year=100)					
1978	113.0	118.6	108.8	105.4	106.7
1980	108.9	108.4	151.2	104.4	112.7
1985	110.9	111.5	131.3	104.6	135.1
1990	115.1	119.2	95.2	102.0	111.3
1995	107.1	107.0	88.5	109.0	127.0
1996	104.2	103.3	101.0	107.7	112.3
1997	109.5	109.6	100.5	110.2	108.6
1998	110.8	111.5	105.5	109.0	102.0
1999	104.8	103.9	100.9	108.1	106.3
2000	105.3	104.2	110.3	108.0	116.4
2001	104.5	103.9	116.1	105.8	104.2
2002	105.2	103.9	111.5	108.9	102.1
2003	106.3	105.2	120.7	108.7	101.7
2004	106.4	104.5	100.7	112.0	108.2
2005	107.4	107.0	105.8	109.0	105.3
2006	107.5	107.7	106.5	107.8	105.3
2007	108.2	108.9	108.6	106.0	115.2
2008	106.7	106.1	107.5	109.4	107.5
2009	105.1	107.8	106.5	98.5	106.9
2010	104.9	104.7	106.4	105.1	105.5
(1978 年=100) (1978=100)					
1978	100.0	100.0	100.0	100.0	100.0
1980	115.9	115.5	158.8	111.1	120.5
1985	188.4	194.3	245.4	160.0	140.9
1990	303.7	322.6	244.4	243.7	442.4
1995	420.7	453.3	247.4	325.5	863.7
1996	438.4	468.1	249.8	350.6	970.0
1997	480.2	512.8	251.1	386.4	1053.2
1998	531.8	571.7	265.1	421.1	1073.9
1999	557.1	593.8	267.5	455.3	1141.6
2000	586.3	618.8	295.0	491.9	1328.4
2001	612.9	642.8	342.5	520.6	1384.1
2002	644.8	668.1	381.9	566.9	1413.2
2003	685.4	702.6	460.9	616.0	1437.2
2004	729.3	734.2	464.1	689.9	1555.1
2005	783.3	785.6	491.0	752.0	1637.5
2006	842.0	846.1	522.9	810.7	1724.3
2007	911.0	921.4	567.9	859.3	1986.4
2008	972.0	977.6	610.5	940.1	2135.4
2009	1021.6	1053.9	650.2	926.0	2282.7
2010	1071.7	1103.4	691.8	973.2	2408.2

12-7 各地、州、市、县(市)农林牧渔业总产值
Gross Output Value of Agriculture, Forestry, Animal Husbandry and Fishery by Prefecture, Autonomous Prefecture, City and County

单位：万元　　(2010 年)　　(10 000 yuan)

地　　区	Region	农林牧渔业总产值 Total	农业产值 Farming	林业产值 Forestry	牧业产值 Animal Husbandry	渔业产值 Fishery	农林牧渔服务业产值 Output Value of Services for Farming, Forestry, Animal Husbandary and Fishery
总　计	**Total**	**18461828**	**13768852**	**352701**	**3757905**	**126663**	**455707**
一、地 方	**Local Regions**	**13629134**	**8457017**	**613111**	**4168781**	**70736**	**319489**
乌鲁木齐市	**Urumqi City**	**273161**	**130416**	**2904**	**130230**	**5801**	**3810**
#乌鲁木齐县	Urumqi County	110423	60385	1459	42776	2953	2850
克拉玛依市	**Karamay City**	**80604**	**27222**	**13399**	**26772**	**625**	**12586**
吐鲁番地区	**TurpanAdministrative Offices**	**402992**	**318108**	**4642**	**72471**	**418**	**7353**
吐鲁番市	Turpan City	162144	130706	1844	25312	250	4032
鄯善县	Shanshan [piqan]County	152317	124883	1922	24033	90	1389
托克逊县	Toksun County	88531	62519	876	23126	78	1932
哈密地区	**Hami [Kumul]Administrative Offices**	**292973**	**152001**	**7936**	**127898**	**1410**	**3728**
哈密市	Hami [Kumul]City	148749	100829	3195	41705	1189	1831
巴里坤哈萨克自治县	Barkol KazakAutonomous County	101496	34145	756	65497	208	890
伊吾县	Yiwu [Araturuk]County	42728	17027	3985	20696	13	1007
昌吉回族自治州	**Changji Hui Autonomous Prefecture**	**2103836**	**971332**	**22587**	**1072622**	**14644**	**22651**
昌吉市	Changji City	315268	136859	2955	163316	9026	3112
阜康市	Fukang City	214271	97252	2050	113620	276	1073
呼图壁县	Hutubi County	391589	161456	3034	214585	2823	9691
玛纳斯县	Manas County	428504	245949	1900	171585	1604	7466
奇台县	Qitai County	453453	195950	5218	252031		254
吉木萨尔县	Jimsar County	173045	79121	5275	86754	915	980
木垒哈萨克自治县	Mori Kazak Autonomous County	127706	54745	2155	70731		75
伊犁哈萨克自治州	**Ili Kazak Autonomous Prefecture**	**3163395**	**1859698**	**47015**	**1192553**	**16848**	**47281**
伊犁州直属县(市)	**Counties (Cities) Direct Under Ili Prefecture**	**1347896**	**715951**	**24409**	**575235**	**9344**	**22957**
伊宁市	Yining [Gulja]City	78716	51277	1311	22015	1837	2276
奎屯市	Kuytun City	9772	5454	153	3214		951
伊宁县	Yining [Gulja]County	289248	153126	6484	119009	5884	4745
察布查尔锡伯自治县	Qapqal Xibe Autonomous County	141716	98723	2183	37537	475	2798
霍城县	Huocheng [korgas]County	163858	84987	3646	72247	162	2816
巩留县	Gongliu [Tokkuzlara]County	131138	68011	2823	59682	349	273
新源县	Xinyuan [kunes]County	228419	130011	4421	90147	552	3288
昭苏县	Zhaosu [mongolkure]County	94263	41760	376	50819		1308
特克斯县	Tekes County	102513	47248	1420	52885	60	900
尼勒克县	Nilka County	108253	35354	1592	67680	25	3602

注：本表按当年价格计算。
Note: The number in this form is caculated by current price.

12-7 续表 1 Continued

单位：万元 (10 000 yuan)

地　区	Region	农林牧渔业总产值 Total	农业产值 Farming	林业产值 Forestry	牧业产值 Animal Husbandry	渔业产值 Fishery	农林牧渔服务业产值 Output Value of Services for Farming, Forestry, Animal Husbandary and Fishery
塔城地区	**Tacheng [Tarbagatai] Administrative Offices**	**1348595**	**922117**	**11200**	**397610**	**2774**	**14894**
塔城市	Tacheng [Qoqek] City	196475	151225	822	42449	649	1330
乌苏市	Usu City	341476	255418	5114	76788	794	3362
额敏县	Emin [Dorbiljin] County	205208	131522	878	72045		763
沙湾县	Shawan County	428408	303191	2241	115902	1284	5790
托里县	Toli County	55248	18051	817	34660		1720
裕民县	Yumin [Qagantokay] County	63735	37111	848	25021	35	720
和布克赛尔蒙古自治县	Hoboksar Mongol Autonomous County	58045	25599	480	30745	12	1209
阿勒泰地区	**Altay Administrative Offices**	**466904**	**221630**	**11406**	**219708**	**4730**	**9430**
阿勒泰市	Altay City	84760	43808	562	38456	521	1413
布尔津县	Burqin County	44724	18457	1883	22877	229	1278
富蕴县	Fuyun [Koktokay] County	92489	31871	1614	57619	130	1255
福海县	Fuhai [Burultokay] County	95411	53705	1763	33431	3590	2922
哈巴河县	Habahe [Kaba] County	80317	43449	3577	32225	173	893
青河县	Qinghe [Qinggil] County	42855	19033	1945	21012	57	808
吉木乃县	Jeminay County	26348	11307	62	14088	30	861
博尔塔拉蒙古自治州	**Bortala Mongol Autonomous Prefecture**	**544307**	**425549**	**6294**	**91197**	**256**	**21011**
博乐市	Bole [Bortala] City	212553	161374	2332	40694	256	7897
精河县	Jinghe [Jing] County	252438	217527	2480	23665		8766
温泉县	Wenquan [Araxang] County	79316	46648	1482	26838		4348
巴音郭楞蒙古自治州	**Bayangol Mongol Autonomous Prefecture**	**1610513**	**1279383**	**20617**	**252865**	**10204**	**47444**
库尔勒市	Korla City	408893	354943	2303	42552	884	8211
轮台县	Luntai [Bugur] County	208721	175983	1019	28968	245	2506
尉犁县	Yuli [Lopnur] County	212183	183462	1432	13458	6	13825
若羌县	Ruoqiang [Qarkilik] County	78717	68427	986	7977	2	1325
且末县	Qiemo [Qarqan] County	97390	69292	1297	20597	356	5848
焉耆回族自治县	Yanqi Hui Autonomous County	146968	101174	1759	37734	521	5780
和静县	Hejing County	172954	98496	2243	68009	210	3996
和硕县	Hoxud County	185347	154368	8887	17823	66	4203
博湖县	Bohu [Bagrax] County	99340	73238	691	15747	7914	1750
阿克苏地区	**Aksu Administrative Offices**	**1634693**	**1208014**	**109616**	**244288**	**7580**	**65195**
阿克苏市	Aksu City	253573	199872	7349	32650	2348	11354
温宿县	Wensu [Onsu] County	281945	186914	36079	38795	1610	18547
库车县	Kuqa County	280304	188794	18642	69375	439	3054

12-7 续表 2 Continued

单位：万元 (10 000 yuan)

地　区	Region	农林牧渔业总产值 Total	农业产值 Farming	林业产值 Forestry	牧业产值 Animal Husbandry	渔业产值 Fishery	农林牧渔服务业产值 Output Value of Services for Farming, Forestry, Animal Husbandary and Fishery
沙雅县	Xayar County	187715	161417	3346	18910	161	3881
新和县	Xinhe [Toksu] County	173863	129341	18689	13737	156	11940
拜城县	Baicheng [Bay] County	122775	83539	4205	30245	2686	2100
乌什县	Wushi [Uxturpan] County	96310	55391	17866	19665	88	3300
阿瓦提县	Awat County	209766	180494	3024	16406	92	9750
柯坪县	Kalpin County	28442	22252	416	4505		1269
克孜勒苏柯尔克孜自治州	**Kizilsu Kirgiz Autonomous Prefecture**	**159098**	**88036**	**2936**	**57198**	**198**	**10730**
阿图什市	Artux City	65938	36105	1180	23734	176	4743
阿克陶县	Akto County	69910	45829	1381	18566	22	4112
阿合奇县	Akqi County	11589	3005	188	7518		878
乌恰县	Wuqia [Ulugqat] County	11661	3097	187	7380		997
喀什地区	**Kashgar [Kaxgar] Administrative Offices**	**2599047**	**1535469**	**265036**	**722990**	**10398**	**65154**
喀什市	Kashgar [Kaxgar] City	114328	54837	4084	50727	680	4000
疏附县	Shufu County	267738	162659	14442	85537	600	4500
疏勒县	Shule County	252468	161024	8500	81960	624	360
英吉沙县	Yengisar County	156965	97524	8662	42978	50	7751
泽普县	Zepu [Poskam] County	169942	84308	31364	51080	3190	
莎车县	Shache [Yarkant] County	462931	290713	57365	93469	2884	18500
叶城县	Yecheng [Kagilik] County	336096	131065	111419	88972	941	3699
麦盖提县	Makit County	161664	113331	1903	38725	198	7507
岳普湖县	Yopurga County	96690	61576	3242	30754	172	946
伽师县	Jiashi [Payzawat] County	296483	201560	6305	79759	659	8200
巴楚县	Bachu [Maralbexi] County	268476	174441	17750	67385	400	8500
塔什库尔干塔吉克自治县	Taxkorgan Tajik Autonomous County	15266	2431		11644		1191
和田地区	**Hotan Administrative Offices**	**764515**	**461789**	**110129**	**177697**	**2354**	**12546**
和田市	Hotan City	70334	36711	9978	21364	844	1437
和田县	Hotan County	133229	65390	42513	23300	646	1380
墨玉县	Moyu [Karakax] County	165841	96704	22430	43924	378	2405
皮山县	Pishan [Guma] County	94889	59742	16093	16227	22	2805
洛浦县	Lop County	87298	59097	6922	19635	237	1407
策勒县	Qira County	76414	52824	6729	15906	29	926
于田县	Yutian [Keriya] County	114035	79040	4227	28840	147	1781
民丰县	Minfeng [Niya] County	22475	12281	1237	8501	51	405
二、生产建设兵团	**Xinjiang Production and ConstructionGroup**	**5692849**	**4504210**	**54456**	**768463**	**30387**	**335333**

12-8 各地、州、市、县(市)农业机械拥有量

Agricultural Machinery by Prefecture, Autonomous Prefecture, City and County

(2010 年)

地 区	Region	农业机械总动力(千瓦) Total Power of Agricultural Machinery (kw)	农用大中型拖拉机 Large and Medium Agricultural Tractors		小型拖拉机 Small Tractors	
			数量(台) Number (unit)	动力(千瓦) Capacity (kw)	数量(台) Number (unit)	动力(千瓦) Capacity (kw)
总 计	**Total**	**16429281**	**253839**	**7605282**	**361241**	**4438132**
一、地 方	**Local Regions**	**12735935**	**217020**	**5945120**	**323898**	**3972091**
乌鲁木齐市	**Urumqi City**	**277554**	**2537**	**73852**	**5635**	**67719**
#乌鲁木齐县	Urumqi County	135751	1817	42332	3687	46132
克拉玛依市	**Karamay City**	**31356**	**371**	**16454**	**396**	**6227**
吐鲁番地区	**TurpanAdministrative Offices**	**502947**	**1963**	**65866**	**10666**	**123207**
吐鲁番市	Turpan City	193576	512	14508	3704	41583
鄯善县	Shanshan [piqan]County	210585	714	26040	4418	53776
托克逊县	Toksun County	98786	737	25318	2544	27848
哈密地区	**Hami [Kumul]Administrative Offices**	**293284**	**2515**	**83595**	**10976**	**129831**
哈密市	Hami [Kumul]City	137966	1333	41598	4876	58706
巴里坤哈萨克自治县	Barkol KazakAutonomous County	127899	930	31944	5207	60286
伊吾县	Yiwu [Araturuk]County	27419	252	10053	893	10839
昌吉回族自治州	**Changji Hui Autonomous Prefecture**	**1759210**	**15602**	**612278**	**54645**	**655721**
昌吉市	Changji City	293814	1947	113066	9415	122323
阜康市	Fukang City	139263	1451	51947	3881	43037
呼图壁县	Hutubi County	301565	3807	128186	8201	102581
玛纳斯县	Manas County	292793	3652	117452	10049	122106
奇台县	Qitai County	413117	2424	121770	11504	126486
吉木萨尔县	Jimsar County	181452	1084	42065	6206	74168
木垒哈萨克自治县	Mori Kazak Autonomous County	137206	1237	37791	5389	65020
伊犁哈萨克自治州	**Ili Kazak Autonomous Prefecture**	**3482950**	**57635**	**1743179**	**78117**	**988906**
伊犁州直属县(市)	**Counties (Cities) Direct Under Ili Prefecture**	**1266104**	**20888**	**696770**	**27297**	**332339**
伊宁市	Yining [Gulja]City	67240	928	32492	1185	14233
奎屯市	Kuytun City	9163	250	9163		
伊宁县	Yining [Gulja]County	232552	3428	134337	5046	62699
察布查尔锡伯自治县	Qapqal Xibe Autonomous County	151234	2592	75755	2343	28753
霍城县	Huocheng [korgas]County	177802	4320	143111	5507	58390
巩留县	Gongliu [Tokkuzlara]County	144759	1756	54121	4767	60264
新源县	Xinyuan [kunes]County	199251	3918	116380	1915	22520
昭苏县	Zhaosu [mongolkure]County	108737	1027	45589	2847	37666
特克斯县	Tekes County	73996	1450	39571	1360	17563
尼勒克县	Nilka County	101370	1219	46251	2327	30251
塔城地区	**Tacheng [Tarbagatai] Administrative Offices**	**1668828**	**27657**	**794233**	**35084**	**449891**
塔城市	Tacheng [Qoqek] City	240461	3584	130066	4979	60143
乌苏市	Usu City	480880	8433	239415	11322	142586
额敏县	Emin [Dorbiljin] County	229889	2531	70987	4344	67332
沙湾县	Shawan County	492094	10296	275301	10502	127796
托里县	Toli County	73640	860	23319	1031	12952
裕民县	Yumin [Qagantokay] County	118362	1401	42427	2205	30365
和布克赛尔蒙古自治县	Hoboksar Mongol Autonomous County	33502	552	12718	701	8717
阿勒泰地区	**Altay Administrative Offices**	**548018**	**9090**	**252176**	**15736**	**206676**
阿勒泰市	Altay City	142628	2079	74594	4030	51583
布尔津县	Burqin County	70498	1048	22929	2668	34684
富蕴县	Fuyun [Koktokay] County	67741	1147	25626	2263	33492
福海县	Fuhai [Burultokay] County	103936	2570	65798	1678	20997
哈巴河县	Habahe [Kaba] County	97624	1105	32927	3456	44999
青河县	Qinghe [Qinggil] County	43424	699	18252	1164	15135
吉木乃县	Jeminay County	22167	442	12050	477	5786

12-8 续表 1 Continued

地　　区	Region	农业机械总动力(千瓦) Total Power of Agricultural Machinery (kw)	农用大中型拖拉机 Large and Medium Agricultural Tractors		小型拖拉机 Small Tractors	
			数量(台) Number (unit)	动力(千瓦) Capacity (kw)	数量(台) Number (unit)	动力(千瓦) Capacity (kw)
博尔塔拉蒙古自治州	**Bortala Mongol Autonomous Prefecture**	**463650**	**7451**	**206259**	**14132**	**170270**
博乐市	Bole [Bortala] City	200138	3371	93395	5259	64749
精河县	Jinghe [Jing] County	161027	2696	71314	6496	76788
温泉县	Wenquan [Araxang] County	102485	1384	41550	2377	28733
巴音郭楞蒙古自治州	**Bayangol Mongol Autonomous Prefecture**	**1264566**	**21435**	**637583**	**28139**	**366645**
库尔勒市	Korla City	322503	4958	171938	10050	140700
轮台县	Luntai [Bugur] County	119977	1943	50370	3802	46496
尉犁县	Yuli [Lopnur] County	199860	3916	124427	1220	16912
若羌县	Ruoqiang [Qarkilik] County	35624	966	20577	277	3529
且末县	Qiemo [Qarqan] County	73048	1570	38478	2096	29038
焉耆回族自治县	Yanqi Hui Autonomous County	145428	2053	69034	3697	45922
和静县	Hejing County	152223	3109	79033	2085	26625
和硕县	Hoxud County	91435	1140	32775	1417	17287
博湖县	Bohu [Bagrax] County	124468	1780	50951	3495	40136
阿克苏地区	**Aksu Administrative Offices**	**1887682**	**32082**	**861836**	**64047**	**771061**
阿克苏市	Aksu City	201605	3380	88452	7360	91158
温宿县	Wensu [Onsu] County	312584	6454	183936	7264	83681
库车县	Kuqa County	238174	3325	89391	8738	113594
沙雅县	Xayar County	216208	4035	113414	6625	74485
新和县	Xinhe [Toksu] County	133856	2231	37400	4672	56064
拜城县	Baicheng [Bay] County	254374	3354	84428	10730	134650
乌什县	Wushi [Uxturpan] County	169260	3799	76559	5842	74778
阿瓦提县	Awat County	324135	4813	167941	12229	134885
柯坪县	Kalpin County	37486	691	20315	587	7766
克孜勒苏柯尔克孜自治州	**Kizilsu Kirgiz Autonomous Prefecture**	**259571**	**6470**	**149327**	**5776**	**73494**
阿图什市	Artux City	92942	1853	49291	1676	21114
阿克陶县	Akto County	135259	3385	75570	3664	46553
阿合奇县	Akqi County	14150	564	11212	145	1986
乌恰县	Wuqia [Ulugqat] County	17220	668	13254	291	3841
喀什地区	**Kashgar [Kaxgar] Administrative Offices**	**1980405**	**57696**	**1226159**	**40784**	**485068**
喀什市	Kashgar [Kaxgar] City	56243	1441	27460	1270	15036
疏附县	Shufu County	237819	5296	108086	5964	72192
疏勒县	Shule County	210132	5503	115337	6080	73104
英吉沙县	Yengisar County	109302	3100	58069	3785	45988
泽普县	Zepu [Poskam] County	138196	4734	93580	2562	30688
莎车县	Shache [Yarkant] County	353223	8774	205142	8361	102315
叶城县	Yecheng [Kagilik] County	165700	6183	107974	2517	21239
麦盖提县	Makit County	161004	5039	114799	2120	26094
岳普湖县	Yopurga County	89971	3181	64000	1657	19546
伽师县	Jiashi [Payzawat] County	196590	5605	118332	4175	50636
巴楚县	Bachu [Maralbexi] County	244444	8180	202659	2126	26226
塔什库尔干塔吉克自治县	Taxkorgan Tajik Autonomous County	17781	660	10721	167	2004
和田地区	**Hotan Administrative Offices**	**532759**	**11263**	**268732**	**10585**	**133942**
和田市	Hotan City	54642	1320	39590	737	10833
和田县	Hotan County	70973	1204	22940	1699	21730
墨玉县	Moyu [Karakax] County	118033	2582	57171	1817	21842
皮山县	Pishan [Guma] County	60648	1532	33800	862	11400
洛浦县	Lop County	80214	1844	43706	1226	15790
策勒县	Qira County	47975	750	18746	1878	21931
于田县	Yutian [Keriya] County	79455	1590	41230	1920	24090
民丰县	Minfeng [Niya] County	20819	441	11549	446	6326
二、生产建设兵团	**Xinjiang Production and Construction Group**	**3693346**	**36819**	**1660162**	**37343**	**466041**

12-8 续表 2 Continued

地　区	Region	大中型拖拉机配套农具(部) Number of Large and Medium Tractor Towing Farm Machinery (unit)	小型拖拉机配套农具(部) Number of Small Tractor Towing Farm Machinery (unit)	农用排灌柴油机 Diesel Engines 数量(台) Number (unit)	农用排灌柴油机 Diesel Engines 动力(千瓦) Capacity (kw)
总　计	**Total**	**478983**	**625781**	**12517**	**188674**
一、地 方	**Local Regions**	**408111**	**592258**	**9341**	**124488**
乌鲁木齐市	**Urumqi City**	**2897**	**4689**	**5**	**33**
＃乌鲁木齐县	Urumqi County	1576	3344	5	33
克拉玛依市	**Karamay City**	**706**	**860**	**2**	**40**
吐鲁番地区	**TurpanAdministrative Offices**	**4127**	**18559**	**13**	**158**
吐鲁番市	Turpan City	709	4711		
鄯善县	Shanshan [piqan]County	1654	5874		
托克逊县	Toksun County	1764	7974	13	158
哈密地区	**Hami [Kumul]Administrative Offices**	**6646**	**19552**		
哈密市	Hami [Kumul]City	3890	6713		
巴里坤哈萨克自治县	Barkol KazakAutonomous County	2255	11011		
伊吾县	Yiwu [Araturuk]County	501	1828		
昌吉回族自治州	**Changji Hui Autonomous Prefecture**	**32561**	**62199**	**43**	**631**
昌吉市	Changji City	5164	11705		
阜康市	Fukang City	2937	3788		
呼图壁县	Hutubi County	9030	14787		
玛纳斯县	Manas County	5479	16721	15	183
奇台县	Qitai County	6484	7415		
吉木萨尔县	Jimsar County	2052	4729		
木垒哈萨克自治县	Mori Kazak Autonomous County	1415	3054	28	448
伊犁哈萨克自治州	**Ili Kazak Autonomous Prefecture**	**125697**	**127853**	**5022**	**67794**
伊犁州直属县(市)	**Counties (Cities) Direct Under Ili Prefecture**	**40763**	**23449**	**782**	**8244**
伊宁市	Yining [Gulja]City	2447	811	24	397
奎屯市	Kuytun City	602	54		
伊宁县	Yining [Gulja]County	5142	4765	215	2026
察布查尔锡伯自治县	Qapqal Xibe Autonomous County	6004	3542	45	793
霍城县	Huocheng [korgas]County	6000	6000	219	2084
巩留县	Gongliu [Tokkuzlara]County	2803	2357	51	937
新源县	Xinyuan [kunes]County	8099	2873	63	695
昭苏县	Zhaosu [mongolkure]County	2154	157	72	
特克斯县	Tekes County	4110	1590	8	382
尼勒克县	Nilka County	3402	1300	85	930
塔城地区	**Tacheng [Tarbagatai] Administrative Offices**	**74415**	**96634**	**2542**	**37123**
塔城市	Tacheng [Qoqek] City	9513	6535	34	633
乌苏市	Usu City	24449	39621	1050	12084
额敏县	Emin [Dorbiljin] County	10124	15204	1335	22073
沙湾县	Shawan County	25125	30432	30	330
托里县	Toli County	1280	981	75	1835
裕民县	Yumin [Qagantokay] County	3666	3781		
和布克赛尔蒙古自治县	Hoboksar Mongol Autonomous County	258	80	18	168
阿勒泰地区	**Altay Administrative Offices**	**10519**	**7770**	**1698**	**22427**
阿勒泰市	Altay City	3210	1565	51	601
布尔津县	Burqin County	880	1856	167	2171
富蕴县	Fuyun [Koktokay] County	2106	1028	600	7938
福海县	Fuhai [Burultokay] County	2612	627	333	3986
哈巴河县	Habahe [Kaba] County	445	1090	312	4001
青河县	Qinghe [Qinggil] County	786	868	217	3417
吉木乃县	Jeminay County	480	736	18	313

12-8 续表 3 Continued

地区	Region	大中型拖拉机配套农具(部) Number of Large and Medium Tractor Towing Farm Machinery (unit)	小型拖拉机配套农具(部) Number of Small Tractor Towing Farm Machinery (unit)	农用排灌柴油机 Diesel Engines	
				数量(台) Number (unit)	动力(千瓦) Capacity (kw)
博尔塔拉蒙古自治州	**Bortala Mongol Autonomous Prefecture**	**10558**	**11325**	**8**	**187**
博乐市	Bole [Bortala] City	4955	3434	3	33
精河县	Jinghe [Jing] County	3643	6942		
温泉县	Wenquan [Araxang] County	1960	949	5	154
巴音郭楞蒙古自治州	**Bayangol Mongol Autonomous Prefecture**	**40570**	**68291**	**2165**	**26315**
库尔勒市	Korla City	10871	26256	1268	13314
轮台县	Luntai [Bugur] County	3421	8091		
尉犁县	Yuli [Lopnur] County	4350	7080	675	8450
若羌县	Ruoqiang [Qarkilik] County	1487	1821	112	3399
且末县	Qiemo [Qarqan] County	2018	3527		
焉耆回族自治县	Yanqi Hui Autonomous County	6364	9297	4	92
和静县	Hejing County	7230	4572	46	700
和硕县	Hoxud County	2508	3188	60	360
博湖县	Bohu [Bagrax] County	2321	4459		
阿克苏地区	**Aksu Administrative Offices**	**72773**	**144953**	**837**	**9722**
阿克苏市	Aksu City	12685	19396	38	558
温宿县	Wensu [Onsu] County	7126	11104	49	606
库车县	Kuqa County	8313	18350	50	670
沙雅县	Xayar County	10586	15445	500	5170
新和县	Xinhe [Toksu] County	3417	10140	97	1069
拜城县	Baicheng [Bay] County	8490	27150		
乌什县	Wushi [Uxturpan] County	6213	11276	18	210
阿瓦提县	Awat County	15011	30361	46	721
柯坪县	Kalpin County	932	1731	39	719
克孜勒苏柯尔克孜自治州	**Kizilsu Kirgiz Autonomous Prefecture**	**8254**	**8863**	**31**	**560**
阿图什市	Artux City	3684	3324	30	556
阿克陶县	Akto County	3378	5064		
阿合奇县	Akqi County	1144	296		
乌恰县	Wuqia [Ulugqat] County	48	179	1	4
喀什地区	**Kashgar [Kaxgar] Administrative Offices**	**92234**	**108469**	**1163**	**17950**
喀什市	Kashgar [Kaxgar] City	948	2790		
疏附县	Shufu County	4161	31040		
疏勒县	Shule County	26364	14324	32	512
英吉沙县	Yengisar County	3450	8500		
泽普县	Zepu [Poskam] County	4216	7612		
莎车县	Shache [Yarkant] County	12580	12861	498	8717
叶城县	Yecheng [Kagilik] County	11350	13619		
麦盖提县	Makit County	4368	6325	306	4498
岳普湖县	Yopurga County	5129	3822	30	260
伽师县	Jiashi [Payzawat] County	10369	6262	212	2976
巴楚县	Bachu [Maralbexi] County	8449	754	85	987
塔什库尔干塔吉克自治县	Taxkorgan Tajik Autonomous County	850	560		
和田地区	**Hotan Administrative Offices**	**11088**	**16645**	**52**	**1097**
和田市	Hotan City	1432	503		
和田县	Hotan County	1426	1598	12	132
墨玉县	Moyu [Karakax] County	2590	1691	23	329
皮山县	Pishan [Guma] County	1530	3554	5	65
洛浦县	Lop County	1210	2570		
策勒县	Qira County	711	3347	8	424
于田县	Yutian [Keriya] County	1880	2900		
民丰县	Minfeng [Niya] County	309	482	4	147
二、生产建设兵团	**Xinjiang Production and Construction Group**	**70872**	**33523**	**3176**	**64186**

12-9 各地、州、市、县(市)农村电气化和农田水利情况
Statistics on Water Conservancy and Electrification in Rural Areas by Prefecture, Autonomous Prefecture, City and County

(2010 年)

地 区	Region	有效灌溉面积(千公顷) Irrigated Area (1000 hectares)	化肥施用量(吨)(折纯) Consumption of Chemical Fertilizer (ton) (100% Purity)	#氮肥 Nitrogenous Fertilizer	#磷肥 Phosphate Fertilizer	#钾肥 Potash Fertilizer
总 计	**Total**	**4065.30**	**1675652**	**786620**	**422615**	**102587**
一、地 方	**Local Regions**	**2992.63**	**1130201**	**534241**	**324235**	**62794**
乌鲁木齐市	**Urumqi City**	**44.75**	**10249**	**5092**	**2141**	**619**
#乌鲁木齐县	Urumqi County	18.37	4877	1615	1069	472
克拉玛依市	**Karamay City**	**10.09**	**4182**	**1270**	**793**	**234**
吐鲁番地区	**TurpanAdministrative Offices**	**35.25**	**16934**	**7278**	**2514**	**1627**
吐鲁番市	Turpan City	14.36	10596	4143	990	1269
鄯善县	Shanshan [piqan]County	10.07	4458	2565	604	315
托克逊县	Toksun County	10.82	1880	570	920	43
哈密地区	**Hami [Kumul]Administrative Offices**	**43.22**	**14057**	**6714**	**3645**	**1006**
哈密市	Hami [Kumul]City	20.61	8441	4565	1512	742
巴里坤哈萨克自治县	Barkol KazakAutonomous County	17.33	3494	1629	1521	124
伊吾县	Yiwu [Araturuk]County	5.28	2122	520	612	140
昌吉回族自治州	**Changji Hui Autonomous Prefecture**	**417.07**	**130992**	**66816**	**30575**	**7439**
昌吉市	Changji City	80.65	27233	12425	6526	2712
阜康市	Fukang City	40.02	8516	4865	1719	6
呼图壁县	Hutubi County	71.26	29691	16453	8547	1306
玛纳斯县	Manas County	66.15	29600	14447	7664	852
奇台县	Qitai County	100.00	19166	9876	3496	456
吉木萨尔县	Jimsar County	37.45	12310	7243	1237	1476
木垒哈萨克自治县	Mori Kazak Autonomous County	21.54	4476	1507	1386	631
伊犁哈萨克自治州	**Ili Kazak Autonomous Prefecture**	**820.52**	**246745**	**99985**	**52647**	**14828**
伊犁州直属县(市)	**Counties (Cities) Direct Under Ili Prefecture**	**294.44**	**97067**	**29133**	**14997**	**4864**
伊宁市	Yining [Gulja]City	14.75	3042	1638		
奎屯市	Kuytun City	3.36	2321	928	929	62
伊宁县	Yining [Gulja]County	70.83	25380	7970	3198	1180
察布查尔锡伯自治县	Qapqal Xibe Autonomous County	45.06	13035	4217	3811	1371
霍城县	Huocheng [korgas]County	40.10	11972	1731	2460	651
巩留县	Gongliu [Tokkuzlara]County	23.93	9014	3910		
新源县	Xinyuan [kunes]County	37.98	10815	3065	1389	491
昭苏县	Zhaosu [mongolkure]County	18.79	6173	2098	996	884
特克斯县	Tekes County	16.10	3640	855	842	
尼勒克县	Nilka County	23.54	11675	2721	1372	225
塔城地区	**Tacheng [Tarbagatai] Administrative Offices**	**380.12**	**128261**	**57310**	**31877**	**8904**
塔城市	Tacheng [Qoqek] City	80.74	23726	10560	8924	1689
乌苏市	Usu City	86.89	25720	15258	2894	1377
额敏县	Emin [Dorbiljin] County	71.27	21990	7217	6695	327
沙湾县	Shawan County	99.84	47206	20493	12100	5421
托里县	Toli County	21.66	850	420	250	
裕民县	Yumin [Qagantokay] County	18.77	5080	1942	757	8
和布克赛尔蒙古自治县	Hoboksar Mongol Autonomous County	0.95	3689	1420	257	82
阿勒泰地区	**Altay Administrative Offices**	**145.96**	**21417**	**13542**	**5773**	**1060**
阿勒泰市	Altay City	24.11	5015	3191	1700	67
布尔津县	Burqin County	13.78	2899	2211	688	
富蕴县	Fuyun [Koktokay] County	18.00	1169	838	294	14
福海县	Fuhai [Burultokay] County	39.70	7565	4301	1827	539
哈巴河县	Habahe [Kaba] County	27.73	2761	1659	630	426
青河县	Qinghe [Qinggil] County	12.67	1369	946	423	
吉木乃县	Jeminay County	9.97	639	396	211	14

12-9 续表 1 Continued

地　　区	Region	有效灌溉面积(千公顷) Irrigated Area(1000 hectares)	化肥施用量(吨)(折纯) Consumption of Chemical Fertilizer (ton) (100% Purity)	#氮肥 Nitrogenous Fertilizer	#磷肥 Phosphate Fertilizer	#钾肥 Potash Fertilizer
博尔塔拉蒙古自治州	**Bortala Mongol Autonomous Prefecture**	**118.72**	**40510**	**18695**	**12405**	**1978**
博乐市	Bole [Bortala] City	42.71	14768	6328	4206	905
精河县	Jinghe [Jing] County	43.81	13580	5710	4121	379
温泉县	Wenquan [Araxang] County	32.20	12162	6657	4078	694
巴音郭楞蒙古自治州	**Bayangol Mongol Autonomous Prefecture**	**235.59**	**115139**	**60489**	**32313**	**7127**
库尔勒市	Korla City	54.26	23554	13245	7347	1469
轮台县	Luntai [Bugur] County	29.85	17966	9783	3532	390
尉犁县	Yuli [Lopnur] County	36.67	20855	9027	7910	2356
若羌县	Ruoqiang [Qarkilik] County	7.25	4544	2864	498	232
且末县	Qiemo [Qarqan] County	14.95	7018	4798	470	
焉耆回族自治县	Yanqi Hui Autonomous County	24.78	11121	6228	1668	778
和静县	Hejing County	22.58	9723	4210	3783	1100
和硕县	Hoxud County	30.08	11528	6154	4621	189
博湖县	Bohu [Bagrax] County	15.17	8830	4180	2484	613
阿克苏地区	**Aksu Administrative Offices**	**489.25**	**214831**	**100998**	**78422**	**8404**
阿克苏市	Aksu City	57.31	44856	20531	20599	1812
温宿县	Wensu [Onsu] County	88.77	22346	10769	9219	1234
库车县	Kuqa County	68.87	40014	17076	12047	1163
沙雅县	Xayar County	75.00	36290	16673	15161	1590
新和县	Xinhe [Toksu] County	40.12	10937	3885	4764	478
拜城县	Baicheng [Bay] County	36.64	17229	6010	7629	1329
乌什县	Wushi [Uxturpan] County	31.21	11639	8287	771	
阿瓦提县	Awat County	82.00	28623	16270	6832	798
柯坪县	Kalpin County	9.33	2897	1497	1400	
克孜勒苏柯尔克孜自治州	**Kizilsu Kirgiz Autonomous Prefecture**	**34.55**	**16274**	**8566**	**5508**	**943**
阿图什市	Artux City	11.39	7808	4223	3585	
阿克陶县	Akto County	17.51	8321	4236	1885	943
阿合奇县	Akqi County	3.27	72	50	22	
乌恰县	Wuqia [Ulugqat] County	2.38	73	57	16	
喀什地区	**Kashgar [Kaxgar] Administrative Offices**	**578.21**	**256809**	**121951**	**85606**	**14552**
喀什市	Kashgar [Kaxgar] City	11.96	11462	5731	5731	
疏附县	Shufu County	40.00	24750	12925	11165	660
疏勒县	Shule County	49.29	22107	11200	8040	1700
英吉沙县	Yengisar County	27.56	16209	6569		
泽普县	Zepu [Poskam] County	25.68	13976	7696	5143	30
莎车县	Shache [Yarkant] County	115.16	40043	17322	10816	1975
叶城县	Yecheng [Kagilik] County	75.51	22871	9902	5060	4776
麦盖提县	Makit County	61.33	14817	10390	3945	42
岳普湖县	Yopurga County	32.73	30230	13817	8558	2719
伽师县	Jiashi [Payzawat] County	59.91	27539	15333	8656	800
巴楚县	Bachu [Maralbexi] County	74.67	32467	10944	18492	1850
塔什库尔干塔吉克自治县	Taxkorgan Tajik Autonomous County	4.41	338	122		
和田地区	**Hotan Administrative Offices**	**165.41**	**63479**	**36387**	**17666**	**4037**
和田市	Hotan City	10.30	4535	2667	1398	444
和田县	Hotan County	20.62	9497	5552	2845	892
墨玉县	Moyu [Karakax] County	35.30	12470	5345	2375	1187
皮山县	Pishan [Guma] County	29.64	10509	7406	2006	581
洛浦县	Lop County	21.24	9473	6353	3120	
策勒县	Qira County	16.17	4689	3225	1383	68
于田县	Yutian [Keriya] County	28.25	10069	4559	3624	834
民丰县	Minfeng [Niya] County	3.89	2237	1280	915	31
二、生产建设兵团	**Xinjiang Production and Construction Group**	**1072.67**	**545451**	**252379**	**98380**	**39793**

12-9 续表 2 Continued

地　　区	Region	乡村及村以下办水电站 Hydropower Station inVillage or Below		农村用电量(万千瓦小时) Electricity Consumed in Rural Areas (10 000 kwh)
		装机容量(万千瓦) Installed Capacity (10 000 kw)	发电量(万千瓦) Generating Capacity (10 000 kw)	
总　计	**Total**	**21**	**26304**	**642889**
一、地 方	**Local Regions**	**15**	**7433**	**362418**
乌鲁木齐市	**Urumqi City**			**17575**
#乌鲁木齐县	Urumqi County			5077
克拉玛依市	**Karamay City**			**500**
吐鲁番地区	**TurpanAdministrative Offices**	**1**	**4**	**35975**
吐鲁番市	Turpan City			11970
鄯善县	Shanshan [piqan]County			17353
托克逊县	Toksun County	1	4	6652
哈密地区	**Hami [Kumul]Administrative Offices**		**244**	**21979**
哈密市	Hami [Kumul]City			18350
巴里坤哈萨克自治县	Barkol KazakAutonomous County			2655
伊吾县	Yiwu [Araturuk]County		244	974
昌吉回族自治州	**Changji Hui Autonomous Prefecture**		**520**	**72639**
昌吉市	Changji City			17138
阜康市	Fukang City			5301
呼图壁县	Hutubi County			15138
玛纳斯县	Manas County			7263
奇台县	Qitai County			22226
吉木萨尔县	Jimsar County		520	2514
木垒哈萨克自治县	Mori Kazak Autonomous County			3059
伊犁哈萨克自治州	**Ili Kazak Autonomous Prefecture**	**2**	**3421**	**61031**
伊犁州直属县(市)	**Counties (Cities) Direct Under Ili Prefecture**	**1**	**2012**	**20112**
伊宁市	Yining [Gulja]City			1235
奎屯市	Kuytun City			1135
伊宁县	Yining [Gulja]County		72	2914
察布查尔锡伯自治县	Qapqal Xibe Autonomous County			1522
霍城县	Huocheng [korgas]County			5495
巩留县	Gongliu [Tokkuzlara]County		350	890
新源县	Xinyuan [kunes]County		1422	3580
昭苏县	Zhaosu [mongolkure]County		5	906
特克斯县	Tekes County		163	895
尼勒克县	Nilka County			1540
塔城地区	**Tacheng [Tarbagatai] Administrative Offices**			**27311**
塔城市	Tacheng [Qoqek] City			5583
乌苏市	Usu City			3312
额敏县	Emin [Dorbiljin] County			2389
沙湾县	Shawan County			9373
托里县	Toli County			1690
裕民县	Yumin [Qagantokay] County			3520
和布克赛尔蒙古自治县	Hoboksar Mongol Autonomous County			1444
阿勒泰地区	**Altay Administrative Offices**	**1**	**1409**	**13608**
阿勒泰市	Altay City	1	194	812
布尔津县	Burqin County		36	1120
富蕴县	Fuyun [Koktokay] County		64	3655
福海县	Fuhai [Burultokay] County			996
哈巴河县	Habahe [Kaba] County			839
青河县	Qinghe [Qinggil] County		1115	5687
吉木乃县	Jeminay County			499

12-9 续表 3 Continued

地　　区	Region	乡村及村以下办水电站 HydroPower Station inVillage or Below		农村用电量(万千瓦小时)
		装机容量(万千瓦) Installed Capacity (10 000 kw)	发电量(万千瓦) Generating Capacity (10 000 kw)	Electricity Consumed in Rural Areas (10 000 kwh)
博尔塔拉蒙古自治州	**Bortala Mongol Autonomous Prefecture**	**1**	**1702**	**13897**
博乐市	Bole [Bortala] City	…	710	7331
精河县	Jinghe [Jing] County	…	992	5781
温泉县	Wenquan [Araxang] County			785
巴音郭楞蒙古自治州	**Bayangol Mongol Autonomous Prefecture**			**45398**
库尔勒市	Korla City			12851
轮台县	Luntai [Bugur] County			7031
尉犁县	Yuli [Lopnur] County			5210
若羌县	Ruoqiang [Qarkilik] County			398
且末县	Qiemo [Qarqan] County			368
焉耆回族自治县	Yanqi Hui Autonomous County			2183
和静县	Hejing County			1220
和硕县	Hoxud County			13592
博湖县	Bohu [Bagrax] County			2545
阿克苏地区	**Aksu Administrative Offices**	**6**	**96**	**36797**
阿克苏市	Aksu City			3629
温宿县	Wensu [Onsu] County	6	96	2053
库车县	Kuqa County			8238
沙雅县	Xayar County			7092
新和县	Xinhe [Toksu] County			7014
拜城县	Baicheng [Bay] County			1590
乌什县	Wushi [Uxturpan] County			1758
阿瓦提县	Awat County			3981
柯坪县	Kalpin County			1442
克孜勒苏柯尔克孜自治州	**Kizilsu Kirgiz Autonomous Prefecture**		**253**	**4335**
阿图什市	Artux City		253	1412
阿克陶县	Akto County			1959
阿合奇县	Akqi County			826
乌恰县	Wuqia [Ulugqat] County			138
喀什地区	**Kashgar [Kaxgar] Administrative Offices**	**3**	**59**	**29360**
喀什市	Kashgar [Kaxgar] City			660
疏附县	Shufu County	3	23	1650
疏勒县	Shule County			1100
英吉沙县	Yengisar County		36	710
泽普县	Zepu [Poskam] County			878
莎车县	Shache [Yarkant] County			2453
叶城县	Yecheng [Kagilik] County			1106
麦盖提县	Makit County			4170
岳普湖县	Yopurga County			2198
伽师县	Jiashi [Payzawat] County			3344
巴楚县	Bachu [Maralbexi] County			11031
塔什库尔干塔吉克自治县	Taxkorgan Tajik Autonomous County			60
和田地区	**Hotan Administrative Offices**	**2**	**1134**	**22932**
和田市	Hotan City	1	350	4326
和田县	Hotan County			4339
墨玉县	Moyu [Karakax] County	1		4386
皮山县	Pishan [Guma] County			1335
洛浦县	Lop County		784	3568
策勒县	Qira County			1866
于田县	Yutian [Keriya] County			2218
民丰县	Minfeng [Niya] County			894
二、生产建设兵团	**Xinjiang Production and Construction Group**	**6**	**18871**	**280471**

12-10 灌溉、水库和除涝、治水情况

Irrigation, Reservoirs, Flood Prevention, Water and Soil Conservation

项　　目	Item	2008	2009
灌溉面积(千公顷)	Irrigated Areas (1000 hectares)	3793.72	3933.54
有效灌溉面积	Effective Irrigated Areas	2562.76	2666.46
林地灌溉面积	Irrigated Wooded-land Areas	445.30	458.57
果园灌溉面积	Irrigated Orchard Areas	366.44	407.37
牧草灌溉面积	Irrigated Pasture-land Areas	344.89	340.46
其他灌溉面积	Other Irrigated Areas	74.33	60.68
水库(座)	Number of Reservoirs (unit)	450	452
大型水库	Large Reservoir	13	13
中型水库	Medium-sized Reservoir	86	86
小型水库	Small Reservoir	351	353
水库库容量 (亿立方米)	Capacity of Reservoirs (100 million cu.m)	103.06	102.83
大型水库	Large Reservoir	70.19	70.17
中型水库	Medium-sized Reservoir	25.20	25.17
小型水库	Small Reservoir	7.67	7.49
节水灌溉面积 (千公顷)	Water-saving Irrigated Areas (1000 hectares)	1765.32	1995.11
除涝面积　(千公顷)	Areas wish Flood Prevention Measures (1000 hectares)	39.52	39.52
水土流失治理面积(千公顷)	Area of Soil Erosion under Control (1000 hectares)	319.32	336.91
堤防长度 (公里)	Total Length of Dikes (km)	6491.04	6717.55
堤防保护耕地面积 (千公顷)	Area of Land Protected by Dikes (1000 hectares)	1453.84	1531.97

注: 1.大型水库库容: 1 亿立方米以上; 中型水库库容: 1 千万至 1 亿立方米;小型水库库容: 10 万至 1 千万立方米。2.本表和 12-11，12-12 表资料由水利厅提供。

Note: a) The capacity of the large reservoirs is over 100 million cubic meters, while that of the medium ones is from 10 million to 100 million cubic meters, and that of the small ones is from 100 000 to 10 million cubic meters. b) The data in the table is offered by the Bureau of Water Conservancy, together with table 12-11,12-12.

12-11 各地、州、市水利设施和除涝面积

Water Conservancy Facilities and Area with Flood Prevention Measures by Prefecture, Autonomous Prefecture and City

(2009 年)

地 区	Region	水库数 (座) Number of Reservoirs (unit)	水库总库容量 (万立方米) Capacity of Reservoirs (10 000 cu.m)	除涝面积 (千公顷) Area with Flood Prevention Measures (1 000 hectares)	水土流失治理面积 (千公顷) Area of Soil Erosion under Control (1 000 hectares)
总 计	**Total**	**452**	**1028331**	**39.52**	**336.91**
乌鲁木齐市	Urumqi City	32	16536	3.00	18.18
克拉玛依市	Karamay City	7	28680		7.58
吐鲁番地区	Turpan Administrative Offices	15	10448		6.79
哈密地区	Hami [Kumul]Administrative Offices	37	10557		21.48
昌吉回族自治州	Changji HuiAutonomous Prefecture	80	35229		27.96
伊犁州直属县(市)	Counties (Cities) Direct Under Ili Prefecture	14	255535	16.95	55.32
塔城地区	Tacheng [Tarbagatai] Administrative Offices	58	25162		9.86
阿勒泰地区	Altay Administrative Offices	65	101333		11.30
博尔塔拉蒙古自治州	Bortala Mongol Autonomous Prefecture	4	6838		12.14
巴音郭楞蒙古自治州	Bayangol Mongol Autonomous Prefecture	16	20690		74.78
阿克苏地区	Aksu Administrative Offices	6	22829	19.04	33.47
克孜勒苏柯尔克孜自治州	Kizilsu Kirgiz Autonomous Prefecture	12	10525		1.63
喀什地区	Kashgar [Kaxgar] Administrative Offices	50	79598		13.25
和田地区	Hotan Administrative Offices	43	29147		31.34
其 他	Others	13	375224	0.53	11.83

12-12 各地、州、市农村饮水安全情况

Basic Statistics on Security of Drinking Water in Rural Area by Prefecture, Autonomous Prefecture and City

单位:万人 (2009 年) (10 000 persons)

地 区	Region	农村饮水安全达标人口 Reach the Standards in Security of Drinking Water of Rural Population	本年新增饮水安全达标人口 Increased in Security of Drinking Water of Rural Population This Year	农村饮水安全未达标人口 Not Reach the Standards in Security of Drinking Water of Rural Populaition
总 计	**Total**	**651.91**	**181.06**	**463.24**
乌鲁木齐市	Urumqi City	15.58	4.46	12.41
克拉玛依市	Karamay City	2.38		
吐鲁番地区	Turpan Administrative Offices	13.78	4.06	24.34
哈密地区	Hami [Kumul]Administrative Offices	12.15	1.65	9.94
昌吉回族自治州	Changji HuiAutonomous Prefecture	35.28	15.36	44.36
伊犁州直属县(市)	Counties (Cities) Direct Under Ili Prefecture	82.72	18.88	61.48
塔城地区	Tacheng [Tarbagatai] Administrative Offices	24.70	8.62	35.13
阿勒泰地区	Altay Administrative Offices	19.09	8.35	21.22
博尔塔拉蒙古自治州	Bortala Mongol Autonomous Prefecture	13.81	2.83	14.30
巴音郭楞蒙古自治州	Bayangol Mongol Autonomous Prefecture	22.29	8.60	34.30
阿克苏地区	Aksu Administrative Offices	79.55	16.35	58.06
克孜勒苏柯尔克孜自治州	Kizilsu Kirgiz Autonomous Prefecture	23.82	10.11	17.17
喀什地区	Kashgar [Kaxgar] Administrative Offices	194.21	51.95	71.97
和田地区	Hotan Administrative Offices	99.35	28.33	44.52
其 他	Others	13.20	1.51	14.04

12-13 主要年份农作物播种面积

Total Sown Areas of Farm Crops in Main Years

单位：千公顷 (1 000 hectares)

年份 Year	农作物播种面积 Total Sown Area	粮食作物播种面积 Sown Area of Grain Crops	谷物 Cereal	#水稻 Rice	#小麦 Wheat	#玉米 Corn	#大麦 Barley	豆类 Soybeans	薯类 Tubers	棉花 Cotton
1978	3021.67	2310.71	2297.44	105.59	1348.82	621.39	50.01	13.27	23.09	150.42
1980	2993.71	2162.37	2147.60	98.39	1354.83	555.79	23.24	14.77	17.55	181.22
1985	2846.63	1853.04	1844.47	74.50	1278.43	418.43	13.63	8.57	10.56	253.52
1990	2979.51	1826.61	1813.16	84.13	1180.11	442.40	42.92	13.45	10.67	435.22
1995	3051.44	1593.29	1528.62	73.38	952.58	439.16	41.58	64.67	10.34	742.90
2000	3388.76	1445.77	1353.99	78.15	838.99	382.45	33.50	91.78	22.59	1012.39
2001	3404.12	1394.96	1281.38	73.28	744.27	410.29	34.11	113.58	20.77	1129.72
2002	3478.37	1493.96	1386.81	74.96	749.74	501.93	36.45	107.15	20.65	943.97
2003	3470.28	1307.02	1202.61	67.16	626.09	454.14	38.25	104.41	23.89	1037.05
2004	3571.89	1378.61	1273.03	66.77	658.08	505.69	24.53	105.58	24.23	1127.55
2005	3728.11	1471.76	1371.89	69.07	761.84	497.64	27.42	99.87	20.51	1157.99
2006	4206.28	1465.82	1369.68	68.00	740.11	496.43	50.96	96.14	22.79	1664.43
2007	4394.25	1379.00	1300.58	70.95	634.02	528.91	55.86	78.42	33.15	1782.60
2008	4536.87	1649.97	1554.43	70.12	877.97	545.39	54.68	95.54	36.02	1668.01
2009	4710.26	1993.50	1867.77	73.49	1153.32	598.38	31.73	125.73	37.68	1409.31
2010	4758.64	1991.61	1879.36	66.93	1120.01	653.82	28.94	112.25	36.99	1460.60

年份 Year	#长绒棉 Long-Staple Cotton	油料 Oil Bearing Crops	#油菜 Rapeseeds	#胡麻 Flax	#葵花 Helianthus	甜菜 Beetroots	蔬菜 Vegetables	果用瓜 Melon	#甜瓜 Musk-melon	苜蓿 Lucerne
1978	29.05	202.13	90.90	65.49	23.68	17.67	55.12	41.95		174.90
1980	38.50	269.39	107.47	81.85	50.08	24.27	46.99	39.54		191.65
1985	26.28	294.78	89.82	81.12	111.39	15.51	54.91	53.69	27.95	132.07
1990	62.69	269.27	117.35	46.04	96.11	66.87	58.07	28.84	15.09	159.34
1995	8.35	306.70	130.11	26.75	140.10	71.10	71.54	25.15	9.72	120.25
2000	49.29	310.07	96.23	24.57	157.05	55.75	127.75	55.99	26.01	120.49
2001	67.69	217.64	72.85	17.10	99.76	85.54	125.96	58.19	26.55	165.06
2002	46.30	215.05	70.00	23.84	96.60	85.32	164.21	82.47	48.47	235.11
2003	70.13	226.38	74.48	22.30	100.07	67.31	163.84	62.45	32.82	294.13
2004	70.63	215.47	67.52	13.74	85.55	59.88	185.60	61.29	36.07	301.10
2005	73.38	185.49	59.92	17.37	84.62	69.90	176.66	70.57	36.02	275.91
2006	106.94	151.73	49.25	14.28	64.29	94.42	186.82	74.02	41.27	242.38
2007	142.53	176.47	59.48	12.32	96.41	94.02	234.88	103.40	62.81	231.36
2008	132.18	286.68	83.67	9.51	172.44	71.14	258.04	110.60	68.22	171.42
2009	82.60	270.05	76.95	12.43	155.74	63.74	262.17	143.47	86.70	165.34
2010	96.79	273.37	70.15	8.75	164.87	75.27	303.59	122.78	69.44	150.14

12-14 各地、州、市、县(市)农作物播种面积

单位：千公顷 (2010年)

地区	Region	农作物播种面积 Total Sown Area	粮食 Grain Crops	谷物 Cereal	#水稻 Rice	#小麦 Wheat	#玉米 Corn	豆类 Soy-beans
总 计	**Total**	**4758.64**	**1991.61**	**1879.36**	**66.93**	**1120.01**	**653.82**	**112.25**
一、地 方	**Local Regions**	**3815.37**	**1902.84**	**1784.19**	**49.08**	**1048.09**	**657.11**	**118.65**
乌鲁木齐市	**Urumqi City**	**54.85**	**28.02**	**27.27**	**7.05**	**13.30**	**3.49**	**0.75**
#乌鲁木齐县	Urumqi County	21.91	6.75	6.56	0.19	3.08	0.14	0.19
克拉玛依市	**Karamay City**	**10.11**	**0.64**	**0.64**		**0.05**	**0.59**	
吐鲁番地区	**TurpanAdministrative Offices**	**48.65**	**4.09**	**3.99**		**0.04**	**0.70**	**0.10**
吐鲁番市	Turpan City	13.14	1.99	1.99			0.14	
鄯善县	Shanshan [piqan]County	12.07	0.57	0.57		0.01	0.20	
托克逊县	Toksun County	23.44	1.54	1.44		0.03	0.36	0.10
哈密地区	**Hami [Kumul]Administrative Offices**	**57.77**	**24.89**	**24.62**		**16.46**	**2.80**	**0.27**
哈密市	Hami [Kumul]City	30.31	6.53	6.48		2.65	2.29	0.05
巴里坤哈萨克自治县	Barkol KazakAutonomous County	21.63	16.02	15.90		13.32	0.04	0.12
伊吾县	Yiwu [Araturuk]County	5.83	2.34	2:24		0.49	0.47	0.10
昌吉回族自治州	**Changji Hui Autonomous Prefecture**	**500.91**	**308.58**	**286.10**	**0.79**	**196.61**	**84.99**	**22.48**
昌吉市	Changji City	91.00	49.60	47.63	0.38	35.85	11.25	1.97
阜康市	Fukang City	43.14	28.40	26.39	0.15	19.13	7.11	2.01
呼图壁县	Hutubi County	85.80	41.57	39.41	0.17	27.65	11.58	2.16
玛纳斯县	Manas County	68.46	28.84	28.68	0.09	13.04	15.46	0.16
奇台县	Qitai County	123.89	92.05	84.07		54.97	27.11	7.98
吉木萨尔县	Jimsar County	41.33	27.75	27.03		19.54	7.06	0.72
木垒哈萨克自治县	Mori Kazak Autonomous County	47.28	40.37	32.89		26.42	5.41	7.48
伊犁哈萨克自治州	**Ili Kazak Autonomous Prefecture**	**1052.60**	**594.90**	**541.17**	**12.13**	**334.52**	**183.42**	**53.73**
伊犁州直属县(市)	**Counties (Cities) Direct Under Ili Prefecture**	**460.53**	**330.99**	**290.87**	**11.33**	**186.09**	**89.35**	**40.12**
伊宁市	Yining [Gulja]City	19.46	13.05	12.00		5.35	6.64	1.05
奎屯市	Kuytun City	3.36	1.22	1.22		0.85	0.37	
伊宁县	Yining [Gulja]County	89.78	73.77	61.51		23.77	37.71	12.26
察布查尔锡伯自治县	Qapqal Xibe Autonomous County	66.95	48.80	44.08	9.38	24.40	10.30	4.72
霍城县	Huocheng [korgas]County	45.03	26.80	25.68	0.02	12.23	13.43	1.12
巩留县	Gongliu [Tokkuzlara]County	52.81	42.94	29.46	0.24	22.51	6.72	13.48
新源县	Xinyuan [kunes]County	59.27	47.19	40.48	1.67	30.60	7.98	6.71
昭苏县	Zhaosu [mongolkure]County	52.65	27.50	27.50		26.72		
特克斯县	Tekes County	33.27	19.40	19.07		15.33	2.67	0.33
尼勒克县	Nilka County	37.95	30.32	29.87	0.02	24.33	3.53	0.45
塔城地区	**Tacheng [Tarbagatai] Administrative Offices**	**430.69**	**208.43**	**207.28**	**0.80**	**123.53**	**77.33**	**1.15**
塔城市	Tacheng [Qoqek] City	86.17	66.94	66.90		41.22	23.79	0.04
乌苏市	Usu City	81.30	28.24	28.10	0.80	9.85	17.13	0.14
额敏县	Emin [Dorbiljin] County	87.37	49.54	49.53		37.47	10.03	0.01
沙湾县	Shawan County	104.70	30.96	30.07		18.42	11.35	0.89
托里县	Toli County	21.66	14.12	14.05		7.41	5.59	0.07
裕民县	Yumin [Qagantokay] County	38.52	17.00	17.00		7.85	9.13	
和布克赛尔蒙古自治县	Hoboksar Mongol Autonomous County	10.97	1.63	1.63		1.31	0.31	
阿勒泰地区	**Altay Administrative Offices**	**161.38**	**55.48**	**43.02**		**24.90**	**16.73**	**12.46**
阿勒泰市	Altay City	24.11	9.39	6.23		2.70	3.53	3.16
布尔津县	Burqin County	20.93	6.16	2.22		1.03	1.20	3.94
富蕴县	Fuyun [Koktokay] County	23.37	9.81	8.25		5.16	2.15	1.56
福海县	Fuhai [Burultokay] County	37.58	3.56	3.55		1.21	2.34	0.01
哈巴河县	Habahe [Kaba] County	32.00	13.43	9.85		3.82	5.64	3.58
青河县	Qinghe [Qinggil] County	13.40	8.08	7.92		6.90	0.95	0.16
吉木乃县	Jeminay County	9.97	5.05	5.00		4.08	0.92	0.05

注:全区农作物播种面积及棉花面积合计不等于地方和生产建设兵团汇总数。

Sown Areas of Farm Crops by Prefecture, Autonomous Prefecture, City and County

(1 000 hectares)

薯类 Tubers	棉花 Cotton	#长绒棉 Longstaple Cotton	油料 Oil Bearing Crops	#油菜 Rapeseeds	#胡麻 Flax	#葵花 Helianthus	甜菜 Beetroots	蔬菜 Vegetables	果用瓜 Melon	#甜瓜 Muskmelon	苜蓿 Lucerne
36.99	**1460.60**	**96.79**	**273.37**	**70.15**	**8.75**	**164.87**	**75.27**	**303.59**	**122.78**	**69.44**	**150.14**
32.29	**947.35**	**77.01**	**205.60**	**48.20**	**8.74**	**123.86**	**49.62**	**223.92**	**112.00**	**62.42**	**110.17**
3.45	**0.92**		**4.69**	**0.34**	**0.01**	**3.71**	**0.02**	**11.42**	**0.23**		**2.35**
3.02			1.93	0.23		1.70	0.01	6.79	0.19		1.69
	7.27		**0.14**	**0.01**		**0.13**	**0.01**	**0.17**	**0.09**	**0.01**	**0.23**
	19.00		**0.53**			**0.05**		**6.29**	**8.35**	**5.74**	**0.34**
	3.83							2.87	3.58	2.14	0.25
	5.75							1.53	3.46	2.49	0.07
	9.42		0.53			0.05		1.89	1.31	1.11	0.02
0.97	**14.98**		**2.16**	**1.94**	**0.03**	**0.19**		**2.24**	**5.17**	**4.51**	**4.19**
0.03	14.80		1.65	1.46	0.01	0.18		1.66	2.73	2.07	0.79
0.93	0.16		0.33	0.33		0.01		0.56	0.17	0.17	2.40
0.01	0.02		0.18	0.15	0.02			0.02	2.27	2.27	1.00
8.04	**77.36**		**21.34**	**0.26**	**0.57**	**15.98**	**7.29**	**36.51**	**4.99**	**0.61**	**3.99**
0.02	23.49		2.88			2.10	0.69	8.58	2.96	0.17	0.06
0.26	0.24		3.76			3.76		4.25	0.37	0.14	0.20
0.37	25.15		1.64			1.43	0.41	7.50	0.60	0.11	1.70
0.38	28.48		1.65			1.46	0.04	5.92	0.24		0.41
3.10			7.75	0.16		5.12	6.02	4.17	0.33	0.01	0.01
3.33			2.33	0.01		1.45	0.06	5.88	0.41	0.15	0.36
0.56			1.32	0.09	0.57	0.66	0.07	0.22	0.08	0.03	1.24
7.25	**104.24**	**8.68**	**143.35**	**33.67**	**5.21**	**88.14**	**28.37**	**40.66**	**3.36**	**1.30**	**32.66**
3.81	**10.12**	**8.45**	**55.36**	**23.50**	**5.21**	**24.46**	**23.47**	**17.60**	**1.45**	**0.01**	**2.15**
0.07			1.17	0.06		1.11	0.45	3.62	0.19		0.02
	1.63		0.09			0.09		0.17			
0.49	0.04		4.84	1.06		3.20	5.23	3.89	0.58		0.05
0.01	7.74	7.74	2.90	0.05	1.06	1.62	1.57	2.41	0.40		0.67
0.16	0.71	0.71	6.78		0.01	5.46	5.97	2.83	0.14	0.01	
0.14			3.16	0.17	0.22	2.77	2.36	1.22	0.06		0.39
1.18			3.75	0.74	0.17	2.71	4.36	1.04	0.06		0.01
1.41			22.10	19.52	1.44	1.14	0.67	0.10			
0,07			7.33	1.53	0.27	5.53	1.33	1.61	0.01		
0.27			3.24	0.37	2.05	0.83	1.54	0.71	0.01		1.01
1.41	**94.12**	**0.23**	**43.06**	**10.17**		**18.75**	**4.44**	**21.25**	**0.63**	**0.39**	**9.50**
0.46			4.12	3.08		0.87	0.54	1.75	0.03	0.01	2.83
0.29	39.94		2.65			2.65	0.39	7.53	0.20	0.08	0.18
			13.48	5.23		7.57	3.17	1.64			2.05
0.37	47.38		7.77			5.95	0.31	10.26	0.40	0.31	0.62
0.06	0.23	0.23	3.50	1.69		1.00		0.04			2.50
0.19			10.85	0.16		0.01		0.01			1.06
0.04	6.57		0.70			0.70	0.03	0.03			0.26
2.03			**44.93**			**44.93**	**0.46**	**1.81**	**1.28**	**0.90**	**21.01**
0.15			5.78			5.78	0.12	0.20	0.70	0.67	2.72
0.07			7.98			7.98		0.17	0.03	0.03	1.80
0.38			6.58			6.58		0.41	0.08	0.02	3.39
0.04			18.13			18.13	0.34	0.07	0.12	0.09	4.88
0.86			4.30			4.30		0.55	0.35	0.09	3.27
0.35			0.37			0.37		0.33			3.88
0.18			1.79			1.79		0.08			1.07

Note:Total of sown areas of farm crops and cotton areas by region do not mean that summary number of local and Production&Construction Corps.

12-14 续表

单位：千公顷

地 区	Region	农作物播种面积 Total Sown Area	粮食 Grain Crops	谷物 Cereal	#水稻 Rice	#小麦 Wheat	#玉米 Corn	豆类 Soy-beans
博尔塔拉蒙古自治州	**Bortala Mongol Autonomous Prefecture**	**120.38**	**51.11**	**50.91**	**0.16**	**20.76**	**29.98**	**0.20**
博乐市	Bole [Bortala] City	43.83	22.33	22.24	0.16	5.60	16.48	0.09
精河县	Jinghe [Jing] County	44.35	7.43	7.42		3.61	3.80	0.01
温泉县	Wenquan [Araxang] County	32.20	21.35	21.25		11.55	9.70	0.10
巴音郭楞蒙古自治州	**Bayangol Mongol Autonomous Prefecture**	**278.95**	**58.86**	**58.20**	**0.17**	**38.76**	**18.99**	**0.66**
库尔勒市	Korla City	49.92	1.98	1.97		1.55	0.42	0.01
轮台县	Luntai [Bugur] County	45.05	13.82	13.82		8.04	5.77	
尉犁县	Yuli [Lopnur] County	37.21	0.23	0.23		0.19	0.04	
若羌县	Ruoqiang [Qarkilik] County	10.58	2.24	2.06		1.43	0.63	0.18
且末县	Qiemo [Qarqan] County	19.98	7.16	7.11		4.08	2.93	0.05
焉耆回族自治县	Yanqi Hui Autonomous County	33.40	13.25	12.91		10.24	2.68	0.34
和静县	Hejing County	30.66	10.45	10.37		6.34	3.85	0.08
和硕县	Hoxud County	30.16	5.50	5.50	0.04	3.83	1.62	
博湖县	Bohu [Bagrax] County	21.99	4.23	4.23	0.13	3.07	1.03	
阿克苏地区	**Aksu Administrative Offices**	**571.01**	**204.76**	**203.09**	**14.87**	**109.13**	**78.31**	**1.67**
阿克苏市	Aksu City	81.54	23.05	22.91	2.55	10.98	9.37	0.14
温宿县	Wensu [Onsu] County	76.41	32.39	31.42	10.00	15.00	6.31	0.97
库车县	Kuqa County	87.60	31.68	31.61		17.30	14.32	0.07
沙雅县	Xayar County	87.55	25.71	25.71		15.24	10.47	
新和县	Xinhe [Toksu] County	53.93	17.97	17.97		10.47	7.51	
拜城县	Baicheng [Bay] County	49.42	28.07	27.85	0.99	13.48	12.77	0.22
乌什县	Wushi [Uxturpan] County	32.90	21.24	21.05	1.33	12.91	6.74	0.19
阿瓦提县	Awat County	90.60	20.17	20.09		10.75	9.34	0.08
柯坪县	Kalpin County	11.05	4.48	4.48		3.00	1.48	
克孜勒苏柯尔克孜自治州	**Kizilsu Kirgiz Autonomous Prefecture**	**52.05**	**39.90**	**39.82**	**0.55**	**22.36**	**16.45**	**0.08**
阿图什市	Artux City	17.34	12.38	12.38	0.04	8.01	4.29	
阿克陶县	Akto County	28.63	23.21	23.21	0.51	11.87	10.72	
阿合奇县	Akqi County	3.27	2.31	2.31		1.20	0.83	
乌恰县	Wuqia [Ulugqat] County	2.81	2.00	1.92		1.27	0.61	0.08
喀什地区	**Kashgar [Kaxgar] Administrative Offices**	**833.01**	**428.17**	**390.75**	**5.60**	**216.97**	**166.96**	**37.42**
喀什市	Kashgar [Kaxgar] City	21.08	12.37	12.38	1.52	7.44	3.41	
疏附县	Shufu County	84.12	62.40	44.53	0.67	26.00	17.87	17.87
疏勒县	Shule County	71.98	36.27	35.86	0.15	20.70	15.01	0.41
英吉沙县	Yengisar County	50.42	31.52	30.05		15.73	14.31	1.47
泽普县	Zepu [Poskam] County	45.19	26.67	16.48	0.33	11.35	4.80	10.19
莎车县	Shache [Yarkant] County	168.81	89.63	87.03	2.33	46.67	38.00	2.60
叶城县	Yecheng [Kagilik] County	90.06	53.35	49.13	0.60	26.19	22.02	4.22
麦盖提县	Makit County	77.37	21.73	21.67		11.67	10.00	0.06
岳普湖县	Yopurga County	44.22	16.33	16.33		8.33	8.00	
伽师县	Jiashi [Payzawat] County	83.27	41.80	41.47		24.13	17.33	0.33
巴楚县	Bachu [Maralbexi] County	92.03	32.60	32.60		16.67	15.93	
塔什库尔干塔吉克自治县	Taxkorgan Tajik Autonomous County	4.45	3.50	3.23		2.09	0.27	0.27
和田地区	**Hotan Administrative Offices**	**235.09**	**158.91**	**157.61**	**7.77**	**79.12**	**70.45**	**1.30**
和田市	Hotan City	17.56	13.49	13.49	0.42	7.47	5.60	
和田县	Hotan County	33.17	25.53	25.53	2.40	12.73	10.39	
墨玉县	Moyu [Karakax] County	53.42	40.53	40.53	2.13	21.00	17.40	
皮山县	Pishan [Guma] County	31.57	18.28	17.56		8.75	8.79	0.72
洛浦县	Lop County	31.94	21.92	21.92	0.01	10.67	11.25	
策勒县	Qira County	25.67	14.40	13.93		6.92	6.79	0.47
于田县	Yutian [Keriya] County	36.92	21.95	21.84	2.80	9.97	9.04	0.11
民丰县	Minfeng [Niya] County	4.83	2.81	2.81		1.61	1.20	
二、生产建设兵团	**Xinjiang Production and Construction Group**	**1119.20**	**278.66**	**269.59**	**18.19**	**156.18**	**85.62**	**9.06**

Continued

(1 000 hectares)

薯类 Tubers	棉花 Cotton	#长绒棉 Longstaple Cotton	油料 Oil Bearing Crops	#油菜 Rapeseeds	#胡麻 Flax	#葵花 Helianthus	甜菜 Beetroots	蔬菜 Vegetables	果用瓜 Melon	#甜瓜 Muskmelon	苜蓿 Lucerne
0.04	**44.22**		**9.55**	**0.04**		**9.38**	**3.20**	**2.07**	**0.12**	**0.02**	**1.20**
	17.29		0.77	0.04		0.73	1.05	1.74	0.01		0.26
	26.93		0.36			0.23	1.16	0.31	0.07	0.02	
0.04			8.42			8.42	0.99	0.02	0.05		0.94
0.47	**150.46**		**5.32**	**1.95**	**0.02**	**3.35**	**3.99**	**36.76**	**6.43**	**5.69**	**0.99**
	46.47		0.01			0.01	0.01	1.01	0.15	0.06	
	29.95		0.01	0.01				0.51	0.77	0.60	
	36.70							0.07	0.13	0.04	0.09
	3.00							0.18	4.73	4.72	0.02
	10.92		0.01	0.01				0.24	0.18	0.15	0.68
	0.75		1.67	0.22		1.45	2.52	6.43	0.03	0.01	0.01
0.39	4.21		2.22	1.63	0.02	0.57	0.90	9.91	0.13	0.05	0.08
0.08	13.23		0.52	0.07		0.45	0.32	9.18	0.07		0.11
	5.23		0.88	0.01		0.87	0.24	9.23	0.24	0.06	
4.40	**300.00**	**68.33**	**5.93**	**4.45**	**0.84**	**0.62**	**6.74**	**20.51**	**12.15**	**5.65**	**10.15**
0.01	44.67	8.78					0.83	3.99	2.81	2.54	6.20
0.14	36.67		1.29	1.13	0.08	0.07	0.51	1.57	1.16	0.10	2.15
0.13	50.00		0.14	0.13			0.16	2.66	2.58	1.35	0.14
	56.67	2.58	1.29	1.27		0.01	1.35	0.85	0.94	0.59	0.10
	33.33		0.07	0.07				0.83	0.92	0.42	0.18
4.02			2.28	1.38	0.37	0.53	2.63	6.20	1.44	0.18	0.49
0.09	6.67		0.79	0.41	0.38		0.45	2.93	0.24	0.05	0.46
	66.67	56.97	0.06	0.06			0.17	1.06	1.91	0.28	0.43
	5.33		0.01			0.01	0.65	0.42	0.15	0.15	
0.06	**6.10**		**0.80**	**0.14**	**0.59**	**0.04**		**1.26**	**0.67**	**0.38**	**1.69**
0.01	2.07		0.11	0.05	0.01	0.04		0.50	0.27	0.25	0.62
	4.01		0.01			0.01		0.66	0.39	0.13	0.14
0.03			0.59		0.59			0.07			0.26
0.02	0.01		0.09	0.09				0.02	0.01		0.66
6.73	**197.81**		**6.71**	**3.26**	**0.57**	**1.72**		**51.09**	**65.63**	**36.23**	**32.26**
								6.55	0.65	0.13	1.51
0.67	3.33		0.33		0.13	0.20		8.52	8.41	3.94	0.47
	12.00							5.69	13.68	7.08	4.20
0.03	6.67		3.17	2.83		0.12		3.37	2.34	1.68	2.33
2.67	8.00		0.40		0.40			1.61	1.85	0.37	
0.73	43.33		1.21	0.42	0.04	0.20		8.07	12.93	8.19	4.67
2.17	6.67		1.40			1.00		9.18	1.53	0.93	5.59
	36.95							1.90	2.55	0.75	2.07
	13.33		0.20			0.20		0.33	3.95	2.62	4.07
	16.80							4.65	12.06	8.73	5.09
	50.67							1.09	5.68	1.81	2.00
0.47	0.07							0.14			0.27
0.88	**24.98**		**5.10**	**2.15**	**0.90**	**0.54**		**14.95**	**4.82**	**2.30**	**20.13**
	1.13		0.15					1.52	0.43	0.18	0.73
0.24	2.67		0.51	0.39	0.08	0.02		1.84	0.70	0.36	0.94
0.10	4.00		0.27					2.78	0.89	0.41	4.03
0.14	3.83		0.99	0.91	0.01	0.01		2.98	0.07	0.02	5.08
	3.53		0.92	0.03	0.14			1.39	0.65	0.29	3.01
0.06	3.29		1.30	0.08	0.64	0.37		1.73	0.76	0.21	2.77
0.34	6.53		0.92	0.74	0.04	0.14		2.49	0.71	0.32	2.40
			0.02					0.22	0.60	0.50	1.17
6.04	**497.98**	**19.78**	**67.78**	**21.96**	**0.01**	**41.01**	**25.65**	**79.68**	**10.78**	**7.02**	**39.97**

12-15 主要年份农作物种植结构
Planting Structure of Major Farm Crops in Main Years

单位：% (%)

项　　目	Item	1990	1995	2000	2010
农作物总播种面积	**Total Sown Areas of Farm Crops**	**100**	**100**	**100**	**100**
粮食作物	Grain Crops	61.30	52.21	42.66	41.85
谷　物	Cereal	60.85	50.10	39.95	39.49
稻　谷	Rice	2.82	2.40	2.31	1.41
小　麦	Wheat	39.61	31.22	24.75	23.54
玉　米	Corn	14.85	14.39	11.29	13.74
谷　子	Millet	0.02	0.02	0.04	0.02
高　粱	Jowar	0.72	0.47	0.39	0.12
其它谷物	Other Cereal	2.83	1.59	1.18	0.67
豆　类	Soybeans	0.45	2.12	2.71	2.36
#大　豆	Soja	0.45	0.94	1.85	1.56
杂　豆	Miscellaneous Beans		1.18	0.20	0.80
薯　类	Tubers	0.36	0.34	0.66	0.78
油　料	Oil-bearing Crops	9.04	10.05	9.15	5.74
#花　生	Peanuts	0.01		0.14	0.08
油菜籽	Rapeseeds	3.94	4.26	2.84	1.47
芝　麻	Sesame	0.05		0.02	0.03
胡麻籽	Benne	1.55	0.88	0.72	0.18
向日葵	Helianthus	3.23	4.59	4.63	3.46
棉　花	Cotton	14.61	24.35	29.87	30.69
麻　类	Fiber Crops	0.11	0.14	0.21	0.05
甜　菜	Beetroots	2.24	2.33	1.65	1.58
烟　叶	Tobacco	0.03	0.03	0.08	0.02
药　材	Medicinal Materials	0.04	0.22	0.38	0.42
蔬菜、瓜类	Vegetables and Melon	2.92	3.17	5.42	8.96
#蔬　菜	Vegetables	1.95	2.34	3.77	6.38
其他农作物	Other Farm Crops	9.35	7.16	9.92	9.91
#青饲料	Succulence	0.41	3.94	3.56	1.26

12-16　主要年份农作物产品产量
Output of Major Farm Crops in Main Years

单位：万吨　　(10 000 tons)

年 份 Year	粮 食 Grain Crops	谷 物 Cereal	#水 稻 Rice	#小 麦 Wheat	#玉 米 Corn	#大 麦 Barley	豆 类 Soybeans	薯 类 Tubers	棉 花 Cotton	#长绒棉 Long-staple Cotton
1978	370.01	367.71	27.39	180.02	134.45	5.01	2.30	22.91	5.50	1.19
1980	386.13	384.16	25.62	213.19	126.43	3.50	1.97	16.03	7.92	1.74
1985	496.65	495.16	30.63	314.52	139.38	1.93	1.49	15.14	18.78	1.40
1990	676.89	673.18	47.27	390.80	209.42	10.51	3.71	22.57	46.88	3.48
1995	730.16	716.83	48.25	381.21	266.74	12.82	13.33	26.43	93.50	1.13
1996	818.20	808.67	51.49	420.32	312.54	17.39	9.53	32.50	94.04	1.72
1997	825.34	813.07	55.27	437.60	294.31	17.92	12.27	26.73	115.00	3.10
1998	830.00	814.54	49.56	444.00	302.25	11.00	15.46	33.12	140.00	1.39
1999	838.78	821.70	54.14	423.29	323.06	8.00	17.08	46.06	140.75	1.67
2000	808.60	782.93	60.35	405.80	298.22	11.75	25.67	64.01	150.00	6.16
2001	796.00	767.53	56.79	374.14	318.41	11.86	28.47	60.02	157.00	9.71
2002	875.87	849.48	60.62	386.44	379.05	13.78	26.39	62.41	150.00	6.67
2003	801.64	774.62	50.73	335.67	366.25	14.33	27.02	71.80	160.00	10.10
2004	828.53	800.04	51.31	345.94	388.12	8.06	28.49	70.79	175.25	11.22
2005	877.21	852.00	54.18	400.71	380.36	10.23	25.22	65.86	195.70	11.87
2006	895.22	870.21	59.27	400.31	386.80	17.85	25.01	76.50	267.53	18.59
2007	867.04	846.35	62.52	359.22	396.00	24.26	20.69	101.36	290.00	25.02
2008	909.00	885.99	56.50	395.69	416.41	14.75	23.01	107.62	301.55	19.73
2009	1152.00	1119.77	58.30	630.70	439.38	14.30	32.23	126.06	252.40	11.04
2010	1150.20	1121.88	58.98	623.49	421.61	12.54	28.32	102.50	247.90	13.03

年 份 Year	油 料 Oil bearing Crops	#油 菜 Rapeseeds	#胡 麻 Flax	#葵 花 Helianthus	甜 菜 Beetroots	蔬 菜 Vegetables	果用瓜 Melons	#甜 瓜 Muskmelon	苜 蓿 Lucerne
1978	10.33	3.30	3.14	2.29	16.37	91.26	44.05		
1980	17.59	5.59	5.17	4.59	38.52	73.44	55.68		
1985	34.25	7.29	8.10	16.90	40.69	111.08	103.18	47.02	49.69
1990	38.96	12.17	6.32	18.17	224.37	187.42	93.38	37.75	89.29
1995	49.41	15.12	3.79	29.06	288.14	269.56	68.75	18.31	82.62
1996	30.95	10.15	3.12	16.91	354.52	301.94	67.16	17.33	75.42
1997	29.95	8.92	2.53	17.69	388.71	295.59	86.78	25.90	70.05
1998	37.52	12.32	2.53	20.82	513.12	321.79	88.32	29.45	67.56
1999	60.46	16.37	2.75	35.69	354.24	406.18	143.49	46.38	69.98
2000	60.14	14.75	3.60	35.47	292.65	527.84	151.03	51.22	76.32
2001	42.64	12.19	2.47	23.31	455.12	486.74	156.87	56.86	103.12
2002	44.37	12.90	3.69	23.26	466.81	674.96	233.40	107.49	149.93
2003	50.13	15.43	3.49	25.80	381.65	761.00	189.32	77.61	249.60
2004	44.54	12.16	2.10	21.90	344.21	919.13	186.06	92.54	273.04
2005	38.94	9.22	2.39	21.69	419.12	862.23	220.65	95.58	295.74
2006	32.82	9.73	2.52	16.17	555.53	958.04	237.28	109.98	240.15
2007	40.30	9.60	1.58	25.39	586.93	1173.99	338.67	192.63	205.47
2008	56.85	10.67	1.23	42.87	438.88	970.67	404.17	248.81	150.83
2009	63.91	15.72	1.89	41.40	418.41	1383.21	491.20	286.30	154.90
2010	66.62	15.14	1.32	44.11	486.97	1734.40	435.00	222.58	132.93

注：粮食总产量为国家审定数。
Note:Total grain output refers to the number of state approved.

12-17 各地、州、市、县(市)主要农产品产量

单位：吨 (2010 年)

地区	Region	粮食作物 Grain Crops	谷物 Cereal	#水稻 Rice	#小麦 Wheat	#玉米 Corn	豆类 Soybeans
总计	**Total**	**11502000**	**11218800**	**589800**	**6234900**	**4216100**	**283200**
一、地方	**Local Regions**	**13004819**	**12717122**	**434502**	**6092537**	**6069997**	**287697**
乌鲁木齐市	**Urumqi City**	**176082**	**173227**	**59801**	**67768**	**31830**	**2855**
#乌鲁木齐县	Urumqi County	31588	30945	2100	15632	896	643
克拉玛依市	**Karamay City**	**5463**	**5463**		**143**	**5320**	
吐鲁番地区	**TurpanAdministrative Offices**	**22223**	**22090**		**175**	**4399**	**133**
吐鲁番市	Turpan City	12210	12210			812	
鄯善县	Shanshan [piqan]County	2757	2757		32	1135	
托克逊县	Toksun County	7256	7123		143	2452	133
哈密地区	**Hami [Kumul]Administrative Offices**	**122211**	**121473**		**78765**	**22462**	**738**
哈密市	Hami [Kumul]City	37099	36876		12465	20145	223
巴里坤哈萨克自治县	Barkol KazakAutonomous County	76450	76159		63804	212	291
伊吾县	Yiwu [Araturuk]County	8662	8438		2496	2105	224
昌吉回族自治州	**Changji Hui Autonomous Prefecture**	**2018999**	**1986102**	**6778**	**1104210**	**858767**	**32897**
昌吉市	Changji City	335062	331135	3046	203849	123993	3927
阜康市	Fukang City	194916	190094	1316	116879	71899	4822
呼图壁县	Hutubi County	254392	251954	1450	166985	83471	2438
玛纳斯县	Manas County	237393	236808	966	82362	153300	585
奇台县	Qitai County	641417	632612		325710	296869	8805
吉木萨尔县	Jimsar County	187617	186532		112828	72460	1085
木垒哈萨克自治县	Mori Kazak Autonomous County	168202	156967		95597	56775	11235
伊犁哈萨克自治州	**Ili Kazak Autonomous Prefecture**	**4227384**	**4072559**	**112345**	**1794228**	**2121395**	**154825**
伊犁州直属县(市)	**Counties (Cities) Direct Under Ili Prefecture**	**2257043**	**2141887**	**104545**	**993662**	**1026951**	**115156**
伊宁市	Yining [Gulja]City	104456	101089		27946	73123	3367
奎屯市	Kuytun City	6112	6112		2787	3325	
伊宁县	Yining [Gulja]County	612019	576710		124899	451761	35309
察布查尔锡伯自治县	Qapqal Xibe Autonomous County	332218	317418	90058	124264	103096	14800
霍城县	Huocheng [korgas]County	226599	222637	160	69832	152645	3962
巩留县	Gongliu [Tokkuzlara]County	241817	207447	2051	131794	73602	34370
新源县	Xinyuan [kunes]County	329181	308949	12126	195209	99951	20232
昭苏县	Zhaosu [mongolkure]County	126308	126308		122931		
特克斯县	Tekes County	112312	110816		73600	32409	1496
尼勒克县	Nilka County	166021	164401	150	120400	37039	1620
塔城地区	**Tacheng [Tarbagatai] Administrative Offices**	**1669036**	**1665180**	**7800**	**683711**	**948924**	**3856**
塔城市	Tacheng [Qoqek] City	518560	518467		222571	286226	93
乌苏市	Usu City	315108	314636	7800	69432	236305	472
额敏县	Emin [Dorbiljin] County	342216	342192		207422	124335	24
沙湾县	Shawan County	263614	260567		113430	145759	3047
托里县	Toli County	85332	85112		30094	52918	220
裕民县	Yumin [Qagantokay] County	136551	136551		36527	99961	
和布克赛尔蒙古自治县	Hoboksar Mongol Autonomous County	7655	7655		4235	3420	
阿勒泰地区	**Altay Administrative Offices**	**301305**	**265492**		**116855**	**145520**	**35813**
阿勒泰市	Altay City	50208	39859		13348	26509	10349
布尔津县	Burqin County	26402	14758		3889	10869	11644
富蕴县	Fuyun [Koktokay] County	49705	46790		23078	21492	2915
福海县	Fuhai [Burultokay] County	29012	28999		5474	23525	13
哈巴河县	Habahe [Kaba] County	80423	69975		17751	51643	10448
青河县	Qinghe [Qinggil] County	40417	40037		33244	6479	380
吉木乃县	Jeminay County	25138	25074		20071	5003	64

注：1.地方与生产建设兵团粮食产量合计不等于全区总计数。2.全区总计数为国家统计局审定数。

Output of Major Farm Crops by Prefecture, Autonomous Prefecture, City and County

(ton)

薯类 Tubers	棉花 Cotton	#长绒棉 Longstaple Cotton	油料 Oil Bearing Crops	#油菜 Rapeseeds	#胡麻 Flax	#葵花 Helianthus	甜菜 Beetroots	蔬菜 Vegetables	果用瓜 Melon	#甜瓜 Muskmelon	苜蓿 Lucerne
1025000	2479000	130303	666236	151427	13229	441146	4869676	17343985	4349980	2225817	1329302
808640	1588505	94052	480003	94674	13210	321934	3052463	11527757	3921969	1989944	1045820
77575	1095		8503	630	19	7571	1107	548581	4088	152	19206
64265			3422	417		3005	750	315012	2347		10812
	11128		394	18		376	100	6200	3598	196	1225
	23372		2165			160		244479	234537	151872	8607
	4900							129400	102000	63160	3515
	7879							55762	93400	56100	4392
	10593		2165			160		59317	39137	32612	700
42770	24504		2704	2113	69	522		100341	155041	127293	31009
830	24196		1843	1313	17	513		74437	74704	46956	9699
39840	289		556	547		9		25036	1976	1976	16832
2100	19		305	253	52			868	78361	78361	4478
180795	138940		56912	453	789	46541	414271	2376908	252323	20569	34413
490	37812		8758			5698	50315	689438	159589	5376	817
5900	289		12802			12802		176440	14630	4270	2182
8385	42733		2919			2620	32134	516885	29976	4120	14975
8520	58103		7692			5457	3392	444917	16029		6223
69850			16683	323		14175	320675	203161	14108	560	88
74985	3		5566	5		4211	3905	339965	15140	5180	2426
12660			2492	125	789	1578	3850	6103	2851	1063	7702
212830	169395	10255	335095	71570	7293	224096	1730069	2206381	127009	35542	232664
124785	11380	9915	131621	54458	7293	57994	1419040	797760	60758	187	13634
2780			2779	123	5	2621	28387	240610	6737		358
	1465		268			268		13314			
16590	48	48	12847	2893		6514	322400	119674	28378		602
345	9057	9057	8781	115	1272	3710	91934	73985	16674		5729
5380	810	810	16282		36	12534	394170	120016	4871	187	
3360			7893	495	324	7074	153710	58882	1032		1802
39635			9317	1867	181	6259	238146	67036	2756		143
34225			48880	44367	1779	2734	40000	3379			
14000			17049	3448	321	13280	65957	71089	60		
8470			7525	1150	3375	3000	84336	29775	250		5000
30105	158015	340	92471	17112		55099	285052	1345803	23510	10802	68659
17300			6619	4674		1703	35891	94060	714	194	16086
860	71298		10374			10374	31878	572791	11276	3780	1261
			27886	9190		17817	197295	112980			16946
3245	76418		28142			21646	18461	564107	11520	6828	5592
830	340	340	6626	3044		2152		1279			18645
7795			11457	204		40		246			4339
75	9959		1367			1367	1527	340			5790
57940			111003			111003	25977	62818	42741	24553	150371
4510			17345			17345	8205	9664	15628	15459	25841
715			21893			21893		6225	1400	1232	11341
10140			14512			14512		13436	3679	837	17870
1345			39875			39875	17772	2827	3731	2450	36908
29850			12218			12218		16767	18303	4575	29684
8855			627			627		13026			23271
2525			4533			4533		873			5456

Note:a) The region total output of grain is not equal to the sum of local and Production and Construction Groups.b) The region total data of grain refer to approvable data by NBS.

12-17 续表

单位：吨

地区	Region	粮食作物 Grain Crops	谷物 Cereal	#水稻 Rice	#小麦 Wheat	#玉米 Corn	豆类 Soy-beans
博尔塔拉蒙古自治州	**Bortala Mongol Autonomous Prefecture**	**536533**	**535885**	**1556**	**125229**	**409087**	**648**
博乐市	Bole [Bortala] City	269546	269247	1556	35782	231909	299
精河县	Jinghe [Jing] County	63076	63054		21866	41188	22
温泉县	Wenquan [Araxang] County	203911	203584		67581	135990	327
巴音郭楞蒙古自治州	**Bayangol Mongol Autonomous Prefecture**	**387528**	**386392**	**948**	**236978**	**147787**	**1136**
库尔勒市	Korla City	8727	8713		6686	2027	14
轮台县	Luntai [Bugur] County	75098	75098		45312	29786	
尉犁县	Yuli [Lopnur] County	752	752		417	335	
若羌县	Ruoqiang [Qarkilik] County	10444	10217		7574	2643	227
且末县	Qiemo [Qarqan] County	40904	40790		25098	15381	114
焉耆回族自治县	Yanqi Hui Autonomous County	98476	97877		65759	32118	599
和静县	Hejing County	82044	81862		42773	38721	182
和硕县	Hoxud County	40794	40794	216	22559	18019	
博湖县	Bohu [Bagrax] County	30289	30289	732	20800	8757	
阿克苏地区	**Aksu Administrative Offices**	**1502129**	**1499415**	**148516**	**723318**	**625567**	**2714**
阿克苏市	Aksu City	171622	171242	26423	73651	71168	380
温宿县	Wensu [Onsu] County	245912	245150	102198	99063	43638	762
库车县	Kuqa County	210661	210641		116797	93842	20
沙雅县	Xayar County	183458	183458		104534	78924	
新和县	Xinhe [Toksu] County	116667	116667		70163	46504	
拜城县	Baicheng [Bay] County	252961	252322	8435	88190	154186	639
乌什县	Wushi [Uxturpan] County	158807	157928	11460	80705	65513	879
阿瓦提县	Awat County	134899	134865		71978	62887	34
柯坪县	Kalpin County	27142	27142		18237	8905	
克孜勒苏柯尔克孜自治州	**Kizilsu Kirgiz Autonomous Prefecture**	**236789**	**236594**	**4680**	**126727**	**104148**	**195**
阿图什市	Artux City	65833	65833	254	41644	23886	
阿克陶县	Akto County	153256	153256	4426	73946	74663	
阿合奇县	Akqi County	9045	9045		5004	3358	
乌恰县	Wuqia [Ulugqat] County	8655	8460		6133	2241	195
喀什地区	**Kashgar [Kaxgar] Administrative Offices**	**2699781**	**2612887**	**44588**	**1353176**	**1212064**	**86894**
喀什市	Kashgar [Kaxgar] City	82279	82279	15833	45102	21344	
疏附县	Shufu County	336941	296741	4700	163648	128393	40200
疏勒县	Shule County	238591	237669	1056	129510	107103	922
英吉沙县	Yengisar County	201869	199229		96949	102280	2640
泽普县	Zepu [Poskam] County	138699	111006	1925	76669	32412	27693
莎车县	Shache [Yarkant] County	559706	554831	17240	291690	245841	4875
叶城县	Yecheng [Kagilik] County	374159	364830	3834	163722	196218	9329
麦盖提县	Makit County	153281	153160		74498	78662	121
岳普湖县	Yopurga County	111869	111869		52188	59681	
伽师县	Jiashi [Payzawat] County	271152	270649		148673	121976	503
巴楚县	Bachu [Maralbexi] County	220722	220722		104025	116697	
塔什库尔干塔吉克自治县	Taxkorgan Tajik Autonomous County	10513	9902		6502	1457	611
和田地区	**Hotan Administrative Offices**	**1069697**	**1065035**	**55290**	**481820**	**527171**	**4662**
和田市	Hotan City	96068	96068	3355	46390	46323	
和田县	Hotan County	166234	166234	15756	79140	71338	
墨玉县	Moyu [Karakax] County	266260	266260	16246	128023	121991	
皮山县	Pishan [Guma] County	129151	126104		50934	75136	3047
洛浦县	Lop County	143983	143983	30	65440	78513	
策勒县	Qira County	99260	98019		41435	56003	1241
于田县	Yutian [Keriya] County	148985	148611	19903	61153	67416	374
民丰县	Minfeng [Niya] County	19756	19756		9305	10451	
二、生产建设兵团	**Xinjiang Production and Construction Group**	**2093062**	**2064212**	**181557**	**963275**	**857216**	**28850**

Continued

(ton)

薯 类 Tubers	棉 花 Cotton	#长绒棉 Longstaple Cotton	油 料 Oil Bearing Crops	#油 菜 Rapeseeds	#胡 麻 Flax	#葵 花 Helianthus	甜 菜 Beetroots	蔬 菜 Vegetables	果用瓜 Melon	#甜 瓜 Muskmelon	苜 蓿 Lucerne
900	**94400**		**27177**	**116**		**26891**	**187111**	**120774**	**4841**	**523**	**5662**
	36784		2466	116		2350	68291	106790	192		1382
	57616		742			572	58290	13482	2484	523	
900			23969			23969	60530	502	2165		4280
10650	**300680**		**10056**	**2239**	**25**	**7762**	**346549**	**2668538**	**124149**	**88374**	**10271**
	91430		16			16	277	93523	5184	1058	47
	57947		30	28		2		30078	13514	10677	
	81468							1863	5977	1052	500
	5325							3985	68253	68000	230
	21860		13	13				5798	3171	2710	7312
	910		3441	269		3172	226830	572449	2287	987	85
8795	7330		3755	1840	25	1890	81060	501947	8790	2625	842
1855	25518		1010	74		906	19925	811655	3440		1247
	8892		1791	15		1776	18457	647240	13533	1265	8
106385	**455186**	**83797**	**10505**	**7412**	**1210**	**1400**	**373256**	**754686**	**355820**	**161521**	**157567**
380	90457	13809					32224	255674	104051	94172	112483
2125	52261		2034	1786	125	117	22737	29421	25579	1877	16120
3030	69240		174	163	4		4230	67856	58996	30381	3572
	88511	3955	2129	2106		23	21509	11953	30366	10225	2121
	54060		86	86				21200	20815	7542	3600
98500			4817	2595	498	1254	232050	241455	61566	5944	4033
2350	8360		1244	661	583		30600	101000	7440	2400	9000
	83080	66033	15	15			10164	16934	44745	6780	6638
	9217		6			6	19742	9193	2262	2200	
895	**9100**		**936**	**262**	**583**	**59**		**28963**	**18749**	**10442**	**17171**
250	3086		163	79	11	41		13174	5567	5285	7250
	5994		18			18		14638	13139	5142	2492
410			572		572			918			2182
235	20		183	183				233	43	15	5247
151425	**314240**		**14122**	**5763**	**1240**	**4728**		**1995600**	**2475217**	**1316117**	**255750**
								268888	24628	2294	11300
15000	5220		475		190	285		331861	339538	167969	3500
	16338							255786	580185	283185	37800
600	9296		6043	5411		220		126716	91699	53739	21000
60000	7440		960		960			61319	73616	14617	
16500	53040		1844	352	90	452		276114	399192	249692	39000
48825	9300		4560			3531		355910	67747	41197	41900
	70938							89487	115088	33900	15550
	20003		240			240		13000	131960	91960	30500
	27158							167222	401979	301979	38200
	95457							44873	249585	75585	15000
10500	50							4424			2000
24415	**46465**		**11434**	**4098**	**1982**	**1828**		**476306**	**166597**	**77343**	**272275**
	1718		1357					68615	27791	9361	7678
6485	5108		737	580	71	30		58816	14444	7453	8408
2150	7590		338	2	6			57221	19336	9514	49310
3030	7293		2304	1891	15	281		102867	1799	603	48208
	6784		1292	35	200	4		48382	27437	10397	92482
1450	6231		3031	85	1580	783		59347	23389	4419	27441
11270	11741		2362	1505	110	728		76165	36106	21346	29540
30			13			2		4893	16295	14250	9208
216465	**1150137**	**36251**	**186233**	**56753**	**19**	**119212**	**1817213**	**5816228**	**428011**	**235873**	**283482**

12-18 各地、州、市、县(市)农作物单位面积产量

Output of Major Farm Products Per Hectare by Prefecture, Autonomous Prefecture, City and County

单位：公斤/公顷 (2010 年) (kg / hectare)

地 区	Region	粮 食 Grain	#谷 物 Cereal	#小 麦 Wheat	#玉 米 Corn	棉 花 Cotton	油 料 Oil-Bearing Crops	甜 菜 Beetroots
总 计	**Total**	**5771**	**5969**	**5567**	**6448**	**1697**	**2437**	**64692**
一、地 方	**Local Regions**	**6804**	**7128**	**5813**	**9237**	**1677**	**2335**	**61516**
乌鲁木齐市	**Urumqi City**	**6089**	**6352**	**5096**	**9129**	**1192**	**1815**	**68616**
#乌鲁木齐县	Urumqi County	4555	4720	5072	6254		1769	75000
克拉玛依市	**Karamay City**	**8551**	**8551**	**2996**	**9000**	**1530**	**2775**	**15000**
吐鲁番地区	**TurpanAdministrative Offices**	**5429**	**5537**	**4325**	**6303**	**1230**	**4080**	
吐鲁番市	Turpan City	6146	6146		5913	1278		
鄯善县	Shanshan [piqan]County	4878	4878	4486	5754	1370		
托克逊县	Toksun County	4707	4955	4290	6750	1125	4080	
哈密地区	**Hami [Kumul]Administrative Offices**	**5055**	**4933**	**4784**	**8030**	**1636**	**1253**	
哈密市	Hami [Kumul]City	5687	5696	4695	8790	1635	1119	
巴里坤哈萨克自治县	Barkol KazakAutonomous County	4978	4788	4790	5648	1802	1663	
伊吾县	Yiwu [Araturuk]County	3851	3759	5099	4500	1154	1730	
昌吉回族自治州	**Changji Hui Autonomous Prefecture**	**6491**	**6942**	**5616**	**10105**	**1796**	**2667**	**56812**
昌吉市	Changji City	6754	6952	5686	11026	1610	3044	72647
阜康市	Fukang City	6841	7203	6109	10107	1228	3405	
呼图壁县	Hutubi County	6106	6394	6039	7206	1699	1781	78992
玛纳斯县	Manas County	8185	8258	6315	9913	2040	4654	93016
奇台县	Qitai County	6887	7525	5925	10952		2152	53235
吉木萨尔县	Jimsar County	6518	6900	5775	10260	1250	2384	66186
木垒哈萨克自治县	Mori Kazak Autonomous County	4171	4772	3618	10488		1885	52500
伊犁哈萨克自治州	**Ili Kazak Autonomous Prefecture**	**7091**	**7525**	**5364**	**11566**	**1625**	**2338**	**60979**
伊犁州直属县(市)	**Counties (Cities) Direct Under Ili Prefecture**	**6816**	**7364**	**5340**	**11494**	**1124**	**2378**	**60455**
伊宁市	Yining [Gulja]City	8003	8422	5225	11006		2376	63430
奎屯市	Kuytun City	5015	5015	3281	8999	900	3000	
伊宁县	Yining [Gulja]County	8286	9376	5255	11980	1125	2657	61605
察布查尔锡伯自治县	Qapqal Xibe Autonomous County	6808	7201	5094	10008	1170	3028	58729
霍城县	Huocheng [korgas]County	8443	8670	5708	11370	1139	2403	66000
巩留县	Gongliu [Tokkuzlara]County	5628	7041	5856	10950		2497	65253
新源县	Xinyuan [kunes]County	6969	7632	6380	12522		2486	54632
昭苏县	Zhaosu [mongolkure]County	4606	4593	4600			2211	60000
特克斯县	Tekes County	5913	5811	4800	12150		2325	49500
尼勒克县	Nilka County	5483	5504	4949	10500		2323	54749
塔城地区	**Tacheng [Tarbagatai] Administrative Offices**	**7983**	**8034**	**5535**	**12270**	**1679**	**2147**	**64276**
塔城市	Tacheng [Qoqek] City	7745	7749	5400	12031		1607	66489
乌苏市	Usu City	11053	11197	7047	13794	1785	3922	82500
额敏县	Emin [Dorbiljin] County	6908	6910	5536	12391		2069	62250
沙湾县	Shawan County	8433	8665	6159	12845	1613	3622	60475
托里县	Toli County	6031	6058	4062	9468	1500	1895	
裕民县	Yumin [Qagantokay] County	8033	8032	4652	10950		1056	
和布克赛尔蒙古自治县	Hoboksar Mongol Autonomous County	4603	4709	3224	10950	1515	1950	45000
阿勒泰地区	**Altay Administrative Offices**	**5441**	**6171**	**4693**	**8697**		**2471**	**55961**
阿勒泰市	Altay City	5358	6396	4950	7500		3000	67512
布尔津县	Burqin County	4262	6634	3780	9090		2745	
富蕴县	Fuyun [Koktokay] County	5078	5674	4473	9979		2206	
福海县	Fuhai [Burultokay] County	8147	8177	4526	10066		2200	51864
哈巴河县	Habahe [Kaba] County	6043	7105	4650	9150		2840	
青河县	Qinghe [Qinggil] County	5002	5051	4815	6802		1703	
吉木乃县	Jeminay County	4899	5015	4914	5466		2531	

注：个别县(市)油料等作物种植在边角地头，未计面积，故单产偏高。

Note: The oil-bearing crop planted at the edge or margin of fields in small number of counties (cities), whose area is not calculated, thus per-unit output is relatively higher.

12-18 续表 Continued

单位：公斤/公顷 (kg/ hectare)

地　区	Region	粮　食 Grain	#谷 物 Cereal	#小 麦 Wheat	#玉 米 Corn	棉 花 Cotton	油 料 Oil-Bearing Crops	甜 菜 Beet-roots
博尔塔拉蒙古自治州	**Bortala Mongol Autonomous Prefecture**	**10495**	**10527**	**6031**	**13644**	**2135**	**2845**	**58391**
博乐市	Bole [Bortala] City	12071	12104	6385	14069	2127	3221	64994
精河县	Jinghe [Jing] County	8497	8502	6051	10831	2139	2066	50250
温泉县	Wenquan [Araxang] County	9544	9583	5853	14026		2844	60912
巴音郭楞蒙古自治州	**Bayangol Mongol Autonomous Prefecture**	**6566**	**6639**	**6114**	**7783**	**1998**	**1890**	**86956**
库尔勒市	Korla City	4411	4424	4326	4783	1967	2759	52595
轮台县	Luntai [Bugur] County	5436	5436	5633	5160	1935	3750	
尉犁县	Yuli [Lopnur] County	3269	3269	2248	7511	2220		
若羌县	Ruoqiang [Qarkilik] County	4653	4969	5304	4207	1776		
且末县	Qiemo [Qarqan] County	5714	5734	6151	5250	2002	1726	
焉耆回族自治县	Yanqi Hui Autonomous County	7430	7579	6425	11992	1215	2057	90000
和静县	Hejing County	7726	7891	6747	10050	1740	1688	90000
和硕县	Hoxud County	7377	7420	5884	11092	1929	1953	62697
博湖县	Bohu [Bagrax] County	7156	7156	6781	8475	1700	2027	76500
阿克苏地区	**Aksu Administrative Offices**	**7284**	**7383**	**6628**	**7989**	**1517**	**1773**	**55345**
阿克苏市	Aksu City	7446	7476	6706	7594	2025		38880
温宿县	Wensu [Onsu] County	7571	7803	6604	6911	1425	1575	45000
库车县	Kuqa County	6642	6663	6753	6555	1385	1271	27000
沙雅县	Xayar County	7136	7136	6859	7541	1562	1655	15952
新和县	Xinhe [Toksu] County	6491	6491	6703	6195	1622	1201	
拜城县	Baicheng [Bay] County	8497	9060	6540	12075		2110	88120
乌什县	Wushi [Uxturpan] County	7465	7503	6252	9720	1254	1568	67500
阿瓦提县	Awat County	6689	6713	6693	6735	1246	271	60000
柯坪县	Kalpin County	6053	6053	6079	6000	1728	750	30416
克孜勒苏柯尔克孜自治州	**Kizilsu Kirgiz Autonomous Prefecture**	**5931**	**5942**	**5668**	**6332**	**1492**	**1177**	
阿图什市	Artux City	5322	5321	5197	5572	1489	1449	
阿克陶县	Akto County	6602	6602	6229	6964	1493	2903	
阿合奇县	Akqi County	3897	3918	4170	4049		975	
乌恰县	Wuqia [Ulugqat] County	4312	4398	4810	3670	1463	2039	
喀什地区	**Kashgar [Kaxgar] Administrative Offices**	**6277**	**6687**	**6237**	**7260**	**1589**	**2106**	
喀什市	Kashgar [Kaxgar] City	6652	6652	6065	6253			
疏附县	Shufu County	5390	6663	6294	7186	1566	1425	
疏勒县	Shule County	6578	6628	6257	7134	1362		
英吉沙县	Yengisar County	6404	6631	6162	7146	1394	1908	
泽普县	Zepu [Poskam] County	5136	6733	6753	6753	930	2400	
莎车县	Shache [Yarkant] County	6231	6375	6251	6470	1224	1528	
叶城县	Yecheng [Kagilik] County	6915	7425	6251	8911	1395	3256	
麦盖提县	Makit County	7053	7069	6386	7866	1920		
岳普湖县	Yopurga County	6849	6849	6263	7460	1500	1200	
伽师县	Jiashi [Payzawat] County	6487	6527	6160	7037	1617		
巴楚县	Bachu [Maralbexi] County	6771	6771	6242	7324	1884		
塔什库尔干塔吉克自治县	Taxkorgan Tajik Autonomous County	3183	3066	3116	5464	750		
和田地区	**Hotan Administrative Offices**	**6725**	**6757**	**6090**	**7483**	**1860**	**2244**	
和田市	Hotan City	7120	7120	6213	8268	1524	8865	
和田县	Hotan County	6502	6512	6215	6866	1916	1437	
墨玉县	Moyu [Karakax] County	6563	6569	6096	7011	1898	1267	
皮山县	Pishan [Guma] County	7046	7181	5820	8550	1905	2326	
洛浦县	Lop County	6568	6568	6135	6981	1920	1401	
策勒县	Qira County	6885	7036	5984	8251	1891	2327	
于田县	Yutian [Keriya] County	6785	6805	6134	7460	1798	2555	
民丰县	Minfeng [Niya] County	7026	7031	5780	8709		567	
二、生产建设兵团	**Xinjiang Production and Construction Group**	**7504**	**7657**	**6168**	**10012**	**2310**	**2748**	**70835**

12-19 各地、州、市、县(市)特色农作物播种面积

Soun Areas of Characteristic Farm Crops by Prefecture,Autonomous Prefecture ,City and County

单位：千公顷 (2010 年) (1000 hectares)

地区	Region	番茄 Tomato	工业用番茄 Tonato in Industry	辣椒 Peppers	工业用辣椒 Capsicum	打瓜籽 Melon Seeds	啤酒花 Hop
总计	**Total**	**112.93**	**93.85**	**57.21**	**40.26**	**139.08**	**4.15**
一.地方	**Local Regions**	**65.28**	**48.37**	**37.15**	**22.41**	**89.34**	**1.09**
乌鲁木齐市	**Urumqi City**	**0.86**	**0.19**	**0.97**		**0.07**	
#市辖区	Municipal Districts	0.53	0.12	0.29		0.06	
乌鲁木齐县	Urumqi County	0.33	0.07	0.68		0.01	
克拉玛依市	**Karamay City**	**0.10**	**0.10**	**0.01**		**1.15**	
吐鲁番地区	**TurpanAdministrative Offices**	**0.94**		**0.22**			
吐鲁番市	Turpan City	0.32		0.09			
鄯善县	Shanshan [piqan]County	0.24		0.13			
托克逊县	Toksun County	0.38					
哈密地区	**Hami [Kumul]Administrative Offices**	**0.23**		**0.20**		**0.16**	
哈密市	Hami [Kumul]City	0.19		0.16		0.16	
巴里坤哈萨克自治县	Barkol KazakAutonomous County	0.04		0.04			
伊吾县	Yiwu [Araturuk]County						
昌吉回族自治州	**Changji Hui Autonomous Prefecture**	**19.74**	**18.25**	**3.40**	**1.42**	**15.19**	**0.34**
昌吉市	Changji City	6.54	6.43	0.12		0.48	0.06
阜康市	Fukang City	1.18	0.34	0.30		5.63	
呼图壁县	Hutubi County	4.26	4.17	1.33	1.23	0.73	0.24
玛纳斯县	Manas County	3.56	3.50	0.20	0.11	1.00	
奇台县	Qitai County	0.91	0.78	0.62		4.17	
吉木萨尔县	Jimsar County	3.26	3.03	0.83	0.08	0.46	0.04
木垒哈萨克自治县	Mori Kazak Autonomous County	0.03				2.72	
伊犁哈萨克自治州	**Ili Kazak Autonomous Prefecture**	**10.84**	**7.95**	**5.60**	**0.10**	**67.26**	**0.60**
伊犁州直属县(市)	**Counties (Cities) Direct Under Ili Prefecture**	**2.31**	**0.44**	**1.71**	**0.09**	**2.01**	
伊宁市	Yining [Gulja]City	0.62	0.02	0.60	0.03		
奎屯市	Kuytun City	0.14	0.14	0.03	0.03	0.25	
伊宁县	Yining [Gulja]County	0.61		0.53		0.11	
察布查尔锡伯自治县	Qapqal Xibe Autonomous County	0.33		0.23		0.17	
霍城县	Huocheng [korgas]County	0.46	0.28	0.14	0.03	0.78	
巩留县	Gongliu [Tokkuzlara]County	0.04		0.12			
新源县	Xinyuan [kunes]County	0.05		0.03		0.11	
昭苏县	Zhaosu [mongolkure]County						
特克斯县	Tekes County	0.04		0.01			
尼勒克县	Nilka County	0.02		0.02		0.59	

12-19 续表 1 Continued

单位：千公顷 (1000 hectares)

地　区	Region	番　茄 Tomato	工业用番　茄 Tonato in Industry	辣　椒 Peppers	工业用辣　椒 Capsicum	打瓜籽 Melon Seeds	啤酒花 Hop
塔城地区	**Tacheng[Tarbagatai] Administrative Officess**	**8.38**	**7.51**	**3.72**	**0.01**	**41.02**	**0.52**
塔城市	Tacheng [Qoqek] City	0.26	0.02	0.12		8.69	0.42
乌苏市	Usu City	3.94	3.70	0.11		0.77	
额敏县	Emin [Dorbiljin] County	1.27	0.98	0.01		17.49	
沙湾县	Shawan County	2.91	2.81	3.47		2.81	0.10
托里县	Toli County					1.23	
裕民县	Yumin [Qagantokay] County					9.35	
和布克赛尔蒙古自治县	Hoboksar Mongol Autonomous County			0.01	0.01	0.68	
阿勒泰地区	**Altay Administrative Offices**	**0.15**		**0.17**		**24.23**	**0.08**
阿勒泰市	Altay City	0.02		0.02		2.70	
布尔津县	Burqin County	0.01		0.01		3.88	
富蕴县	Fuyun [Koktokay] County	0.03		0.02		1.88	
福海县	Fuhai [Burultokay] County					7.77	0.08
哈巴河县	Habahe [Kaba] County	0.07		0.11		7.05	
青河县	Qinghe [Qinggil] County	0.02		0.01		0.18	
吉木乃县	Jeminay County					0.77	
博尔塔拉蒙古自治州	**Bortala Mongol Autonomous Prefecture**	**0.99**	**0.82**	**0.05**		**0.53**	
博乐市	Bole [Bortala] City	0.91	0.78	0.02		0.23	
精河县	Jinghe [Jing] County	0.08	0.04	0.03		0.05	
温泉县	Wenquan [Araxang] County					0.25	
巴音郭楞蒙古自治州	**Bayangol Mongol Autonomous Prefecture**	**15.08**	**14.39**	**14.26**	**13.38**	**3.51**	**0.05**
库尔勒市	Korla City	0.13		0.12		0.08	
轮台县	Luntai [Bugur] County	0.28	0.26				
尉犁县	Yuli [Lopnur] County	0.01					
若羌县	Ruoqiang [Qarkilik] County	0.01					
且末县	Qiemo [Qarqan] County	0.03		0.01			
焉耆回族自治县	Yanqi Hui Autonomous County	3.83	3.79	1.66	1.59	1.93	
和静县	Hejing County	2.89	2.72	6.52	6.14		
和硕县	Hoxud County	3.68	3.41	3.53	3.29	0.78	
博湖县	Bohu [Bagrax] County	4.22	4.21	2.42	2.36	0.72	0.05
阿克苏地区	**Aksu Administrative Offices**	**5.28**	**4.03**	**2.97**	**2.09**	**0.86**	**0.09**
阿克苏市	Aksu City	0.34		0.15			
温宿县	Wensu [Onsu] County	0.15		0.18			
库车县	Kuqa County	0.26	0.02	0.17			

12-19 续表 2 Continued

单位：千公顷 (1000 hectares)

地　区	Region	番　茄 Tomato	工业用番茄 Tonato in Industry	辣　椒 Peppers	工业用辣椒 Capsicum	打瓜籽 Melon Seeds	啤酒花 Hop
沙雅县	Xayar County	0.08		0.07			
新和县	Xinhe [Toksu] County	0.13		0.03		0.13	
拜城县	Baicheng [Bay] County	2.25	2.01	2.24	2.09	0.70	0.08
乌什县	Wushi [Uxturpan] County	2.00	2.00	0.08			0.01
阿瓦提县	Awat County	0.06		0.04		0.03	
柯坪县	Kalpin County	0.01		0.01			
克孜勒苏柯尔克孜自治州	**Kizilsu Kirgiz Autonomous Prefecture**	**0.18**		**0.18**			
阿图什市	Artux City	0.03		0.02			
阿克陶县	Akto County	0.14		0.16			
阿合奇县	Akqi County	0.01					
乌恰县	Wuqia [Ulugqat] County						
喀什地区	**Kashgar [Kaxgar] Administrative Offices**	**8.28**	**1.37**	**8.12**	**5.25**	**0.60**	
喀什市	Kashgar [Kaxgar] City	1.05		0.25			
疏附县	Shufu County	1.31		1.03			
疏勒县	Shule County	0.44		0.20			
英吉沙县	Yengisar County	0.47		0.51			
泽普县	Zepu [Poskam] County	0.09		0.41	0.41		
莎车县	Shache [Yarkant] County	0.80	0.67	3.47	3.47	0.60	
叶城县	Yecheng [Kagilik] County	0.89	0.67	1.38	1.21		
麦盖提县	Makit County	0.57	0.03	0.55	0.16		
岳普湖县	Yopurga County	0.03		0.01			
伽师县	Jiashi [Payzawat] County	2.44		0.31			
巴楚县	Bachu [Maralbexi] County	0.19					
塔什库尔干塔吉克自治县	Taxkorgan Tajik Autonomous County						
和田地区	**Hotan Administrative Offices**	**2.72**	**1.27**	**1.17**	**0.18**	**0.01**	
和田市	Hotan City	0.26		0.18			
和田县	Hotan County	0.08		0.25			
墨玉县	Moyu [Karakax] County	0.38		0.17			
皮山县	Pishan [Guma] County	1.30	1.27	0.17	0.06		
洛浦县	Lop County	0.12		0.04			
策勒县	Qira County	0.11		0.03		0.01	
于田县	Yutian [Keriya] County	0.43		0.32	0.12		
民丰县	Minfeng [Niya] County	0.04		0.01			
二.生产建设兵团	**Xinjiang Production and Construction Group**	**47.65**	**45.48**	**20.05**	**17.85**	**49.74**	**3.06**

12-20 各地、州、市、县(市)特色农作物产量

Output of Characteristic Farm Crops by Prefecture,Autonomous Prefectura,City and County

单位：吨 (ton)

地区	Region	番茄 Tomato	工业用番茄 Tonato in Industry	辣椒 Peppers	工业用辣椒 Capsicum	枸杞 Medlar	打瓜籽 Melon Seeds	啤酒花 Hop
总计	**Total**	**9704458**	**8641337**	**1845432**	**1186859**	**18736**	**221064**	**16815**
一.地方	**Local Regions**	**5098475**	**4228253**	**1242334**	**677700**	**15287**	**133564**	**8841**
乌鲁木齐市	**Urumqi City**	**62654**	**12314**	**48351**		**144**	**97**	
#市辖区	Municipal Districts	38844	8354	17433		144	91	
乌鲁木齐县	Urumqi County	23810	3960	30918			6	
克拉玛依市	**Karamay City**	**4623**	**4422**	**402**			**1293**	
吐鲁番地区	**TurpanAdministrative Offices**	**35279**		**3064**				
吐鲁番市	Turpan City	13823		1167				
鄯善县	Shanshan [piqan]County	10056		1897				
托克逊县	Toksun County	11400						
哈密地区	**Hami [Kumul]Administrative Offices**	**14106**		**7693**			**712**	
哈密市	Hami [Kumul]City	12161		6774			707	
巴里坤哈萨克自治县	Barkol KazakAutonomous County	1865		676			5	
伊吾县	Yiwu [Araturuk]County	80		243				
昌吉回族自治州	**Changji Hui Autonomous Prefecture**	**1646227**	**1564025**	**118919**	**41899**	**647**	**27491**	**2301**
昌吉市	Changji City	541506	523573	5981			1068	833
阜康市	Fukang City	66512	32997	11746			12426	
呼图壁县	Hutubi County	383381	376582	38148	34927		1053	1340
玛纳斯县	Manas County	335860	331105	5970	4837	647	2245	
奇台县	Qitai County	67256	54836	24615			6094	
吉木萨尔县	Jimsar County	250933	244932	32353	2135		957	128
木垒哈萨克自治县	Mori Kazak Autonomous County	779		106			3648	
伊犁哈萨克自治州	**Ili Kazak Autonomous Prefecture**	**925880**	**720435**	**206945**	**3013**	**2238**	**93078**	**5445**
伊犁州直属县(市)	**Counties (Cities) Direct Under Ili Prefecture**	**135906**	**31007**	**85529**	**2940**		**3651**	
伊宁市	Yining [Gulja]City	48873	1810	50790	1608			
奎屯市	Kuytun City	12714	12714	600	600		685	
伊宁县	Yining [Gulja]County	23479		18572			262	
察布查尔锡伯自治县	Qapqal Xibe Autonomous County	16656		7369			272	
霍城县	Huocheng [korgas]County	24843	16483	1411	732		1136	
巩留县	Gongliu [Tokkuzlara]County	2516		4821				
新源县	Xinyuan [kunes]County	4653		1005			201	
昭苏县	Zhaosu [mongolkure]County							
特克斯县	Tekes County	1220		260				
尼勒克县	Nilka County	952		701			1095	

12-20 续表 1 Continued

单位：吨 (ton)

地　区	Region	番　茄 Tomato	工业用番　茄 Tonato in Industr	辣　椒 Peppers	工业用辣　椒 Capsicum	枸　杞 Medlar	打瓜籽 Melon Seeds	啤酒花 Hop
塔城地区	**Tacheng[Tarbagatai] Administrative Officess**	**784976**	**689428**	**115607**	**73**	**1876**	**50929**	**4957**
塔城市	Tacheng [Qoqek] City	9755	1440	4310			12381	4225
乌苏市	Usu City	443408	389617	756		296	2182	
额敏县	Emin [Dorbiljin] County	97329	85347	306			21820	
沙湾县	Shawan County	234421	213024	110154		1580	4327	730
托里县	Toli County	12		8			1139	
裕民县	Yumin [Qagantokay] County						8418	
和布克赛尔蒙古自治县	Hoboksar Mongol Autonomous County	51		73	73		662	2
阿勒泰地区	**Altay Administrative Offices**	**4998**		**5809**		**362**	**38498**	**488**
阿勒泰市	Altay City	940		812			5061	
布尔津县	Burqin County	306		346			4892	
富蕴县	Fuyun [Koktokay] County	986		511			3039	
福海县	Fuhai [Burultokay] County	83		63		362	11510	488
哈巴河县	Habahe [Kaba] County	2012		3186			12684	
青河县	Qinghe [Qinggil] County	586		858			242	
吉木乃县	Jeminay County	85		33			1070	
博尔塔拉蒙古自治州	**Bortala Mongol Autonomous Prefecture**	**81932**	**73886**	**1444**	**29**	**12258**	**796**	
博乐市	Bole [Bortala] City	76483	69686	374	29	7	360	
精河县	Jinghe [Jing] County	5449	4200	1044		12247	120	
温泉县	Wenquan [Araxang] County			26		4	316	
巴音郭楞蒙古自治州	**Bayangol Mongol Autonomous Prefecture**	**1518546**	**1441366**	**548763**	**452755**		**7087**	**730**
库尔勒市	Korla City	10998		17482			125	
轮台县	Luntai [Bugur] County	18872	18556	215				
尉犁县	Yuli [Lopnur] County	260		140				
若羌县	Ruoqiang [Qarkilik] County	130		19				
且末县	Qiemo [Qarqan] County	704		265				
焉耆回族自治县	Yanqi Hui Autonomous County	410348	406970	66335	64287		4534	
和静县	Hejing County	305215	286015	177281	165767			
和硕县	Hoxud County	392225	351147	185196	123685		1298	
博湖县	Bohu [Bagrax] County	379794	378678	101830	99016		1130	730
阿克苏地区	**Aksu Administrative Offices**	**303950**	**255956**	**24641**	**9358**		**1794**	**365**
阿克苏市	Aksu City	24869		4049				
温宿县	Wensu [Onsu] County	2571		2365				
库车县	Kuqa County	7468	744	3184				

12-20 续表 2 Continued

单位：吨 (ton)

地　区	Region	番　茄 Tomato	工业用番　茄 Tonato in Industr	辣　椒 Peppers	工业用辣　椒 Capsicum	枸　杞 Medlar	打瓜籽 Melon Seeds	啤酒花 Hop
沙雅县	Xayar County	832		749				
新和县	Xinhe [Toksu] County	5550		774			240	
拜城县	Baicheng [Bay] County	191200	184782	12600	9358		1554	225
乌什县	Wushi [Uxturpan] County	70430	70430	305				140
阿瓦提县	Awat County	880		465				
柯坪县	Kalpin County	150		150				
克孜勒苏柯尔克孜自治州	**Kizilsu Kirgiz Autonomous Prefecture**	**4835**		**3533**				
阿图什市	Artux City	740		194				
阿克陶县	Akto County	3917		3327				
阿合奇县	Akqi County	150						
乌恰县	Wuqia [Ulugqat] County	28		12				
喀什地区	**Kashgar [Kaxgar] Administrative Offices**	**366620**	**84000**	**250904**	**169610**		**1200**	
喀什市	Kashgar [Kaxgar] City	55300		9400				
疏附县	Shufu County	59145		32361				
疏勒县	Shule County	18500		6500				
英吉沙县	Yengisar County	9860		7806				
泽普县	Zepu [Poskam] County	3507		15250	15250			
莎车县	Shache [Yarkant] County	47312	47000	95483	95000		1200	
叶城县	Yecheng [Kagilik] County	46900	35000	58717	50960			
麦盖提县	Makit County	28719	2000	15857	8400			
岳普湖县	Yopurga County	2100		330				
伽师县	Jiashi [Payzawat] County	91500		9200				
巴楚县	Bachu [Maralbexi] County	3777						
塔什库尔干塔吉克自治县	Taxkorgan Tajik Autonomous County							
和田地区	**Hotan Administrative Offices**	**133823**	**71849**	**27675**	**1036**	**3**	**16**	
和田市	Hotan City	15612		2887		3		
和田县	Hotan County	2737		6774				
墨玉县	Moyu [Karakax] County	8354		2474				
皮山县	Pishan [Guma] County	72763	71849	4246	638			
洛浦县	Lop County	4297		1011				
策勒县	Qira County	4902		1526			16	
于田县	Yutian [Keriya] County	24090		8583	398			
民丰县	Minfeng [Niya] County	1068		174				
二.生产建设兵团	**Xinjiang Production and Construction Group**	**4605983**	**4413084**	**603098**	**509159**	**3449**	**87500**	**7974**

12-21 各地、州、市林业生产情况

Condition on Forest Products by Prefecture, Autonomous Prefecture, City

单位:公顷 (2010 年) (hectare)

地 区	Region	当年造林面积 Planting Area in the Current Year	用材林 Timber Forest	经济林 Economic Forest	防护林 Windbreak	薪炭林 Firewood Forest	特种用途林 Forest for Special Purpose
总 计	**Total**	**219371**	**2019**	**105898**	**108894**	**2298**	**262**
一、地 方	**Local Regions**	**199629**	**1996**	**104527**	**90546**	**2298**	**262**
乌鲁木齐市	Urumqi City	2092		91	2001		
克拉玛依市	Karamay City	156			156		
吐鲁番地区	Turpan Administrative Offices	5255	21	2704	2463	67	
哈密地区	Hami [Kumul]Administrative Offices	5946		2596	3350		
昌吉回族自治州	Changji Hui Autonomous Prefecture	16248		4087	12161		
伊犁哈萨克自治州	Ili Kazak Administrative Prefecture	65891	1577	28469	33874	1713	258
伊犁州直属县(市)	Counties (Cities) Direct Under Ili Prefecture	33993	1577	26990	5168		258
塔城地区	Tacheng [Tarbagatai] Administrative Offices	10016		604	7699	1713	
阿勒泰地区	Altay Administrative Offices	21882		875	21007		
博尔塔拉蒙古自治州	Bortala Mongol Autonomous Prefecture	8979			8979		
巴音郭楞蒙古自治州	Bayangol Mongol Autonomous Prefecture	8679		5985	2694		
阿克苏地区	Aksu Administrative Offices	29086		19534	9552		
克孜勒苏柯尔克孜自治州	Kizilsu Kirgiz Autonomous Prefecture	8509	394	1301	6717	97	
喀什地区	Kashgar [Kaxgar] Administrative Offices	33963	4	29568	4386	1	4
和田地区	Hotan Administrative Offices	14732		10192	4120	420	
二、生产建设兵团	**Xinjiang Production and Construction Group**	**19742**	**23**	**1371**	**18348**		

地 区	Region	迹地更新面积 Renewing Area in Slash	当年零星植树(万株) Fragmentary Planting (10 000 trees)	年末实有育苗面积 Actual Sapling Breeding Area	幼林抚育作业面积 Tending Area of Young Growth	成林抚育面积 Tending Area of Full Growth	核桃产量(吨) Walnut Output (ton)	村及村以下木材采伐量(立方米) Timber Felling Output in Village or Below (cu.m)
总 计	**Total**	**4938**	**2245.24**	**11487**	**2111944**	**1251610**	**241514**	**280557**
一、地 方	**Local Regions**	**4326**	**1983.40**	**10114**	**1880407**	**1168786**	**185654**	**279840**
乌鲁木齐市	Urumqi City	1	40.00	704	933	3600		1259
克拉玛依市	Karamay City		140.00	200	2400	9162		
吐鲁番地区	Turpan Administrative Offices	20		146	17742	9380	432	1196
哈密地区	Hami[Kumul] Administrative Offices			102	93699	22637		1133
昌吉回族自治州	Changji Hui Autonomous Prefecture	1966	28.80	3302	63769	37193		41375
伊犁哈萨克自治州	Ili Kazak Administrative Prefecture	764	490.88	1099	265296	290778	609	61227
伊犁州直属县(市)	Counties (Cities) Direct Under Ili Prefecture	349	386.76	793	194945	80880	609	36016
塔城地区	Tacheng [Tarbagatai] Administrative Offices	415	29.12	166	26905	124054		18787
阿勒泰地区	Altay Administrative Offices		75.00	140	43446	85844		6424
博尔塔拉蒙古自治州	Bortala Mongol Autonomous Prefecture	82	25.30	78	13312	13239		12055
巴音郭楞蒙古自治州	Bayangol Mongol Autonomous Prefecture	15	50.25	510	100121	25322	199	40278
阿克苏地区	Aksu Administrative Offices	198	45.30	302	577632	302600	50745	41948
克孜勒苏柯尔克孜自治州	Kizilsu Kirgiz Autonomous Prefecture		11.70	726	43141	22956	125	8694
喀什地区	Kashgar [Kaxgar] Administrative Offices	706	758.07	1108	485796	238504	82982	48058
和田地区	Hotan Administrative Offices	574	393.10	1588	215126	161543	50562	22617
二、生产建设兵团	**Xinjiang Production and Construction Group**	**612**	**261.84**	**1373**	**231537**	**82824**	**55860**	**717**

12-22 各地、州、市水果种植面积
Planted Area of Fruits by Prefecture, Autonomous Prefecture, City

单位:公顷 (2010 年) (hectare)

地 区	Region	合 计 Total	苹 果 Apples	梨 Pears	葡 萄 Grapes	#无核葡萄 Seedless Grapes
总 计	**Total**	**991719**	**73346**	**68806**	**125272**	**42666**
一、地 方	**Local Regions**	**815275**	**58386**	**51527**	**91254**	**34716**
乌鲁木齐市	Urumqi City	899	87	2	576	
克拉玛依市	Karamay City					
吐鲁番地区	TurpanAdministrative Offices	36660	4	19	30933	29078
哈密地区	Hami [Kumul] Administrative Offices	28581	14	37	3702	2976
昌吉回族自治州	Changji Hui Autonomous Prefecture	15591	2406	14	8494	
伊犁哈萨克自治州	Ili Kazak Autonomous Prefecture	83834	37029	210	6264	
伊犁州直属县(市)	Counties (Cities) Direct Under Ili Prefecture	81978	36090	169	5690	
塔城地区	Tacheng [Tarbagatai] Administrative Offices	1714	925	41	455	
阿勒泰地区	Altay Administrative Offices	142	15		119	
博尔塔拉蒙古自治州	Bortala MongolAutonomous Prefecture	216	74	3	134	
巴音郭楞蒙古自治州	Bayangol Mongol Autonomous Prefecture	86706	756	36062	11983	455
阿克苏地区	Aksu Administrative Offices	180962	12918	13236	6155	
克孜勒苏柯尔克孜自治州	Kizilsu Kirgiz Autonomous Prefecture	27063	78	10	7017	
喀什地区	Kashgar [Kaxgar] Administrative Offices	292193	3865	1427	4412	33
和田地区	Hotan Administrative Offices	62570	1154	509	11585	2172
二、生产建设兵团	**Xinjiang Production and Construction Group**	**176444**	**14960**	**17279**	**34018**	**7950**

地 区	Region	桃 Peaches	杏 Apricots	红 枣 Jujubes	石 榴 Pomegraniate	其 它 Others
总 计	**Total**	**14568**	**211947**	**397491**	**13319**	**86970**
一、地 方	**Local Regions**	**12137**	**207001**	**295520**	**13269**	**86181**
乌鲁木齐市	Urumqi City	146	62	13		13
克拉玛依市	Karamay City					
吐鲁番地区	TurpanAdministrative Offices	3	1952	3213	451	83
哈密地区	Hami [Kumul] Administrative Offices	12	2326	20908		1581
昌吉回族自治州	Changji Hui Autonomous Prefecture	832	2146	60		1640
伊犁哈萨克自治州	Ili Kazak Autonomous Prefecture	2170	27111	2000	2	9048
伊犁州直属县(市)	Counties (Cities) Direct Under Ili Prefecture	2038	27100	1983	2	8906
塔城地区	Tacheng [Tarbagatai] Administrative Offices	126	11	17		140
阿勒泰地区	Altay Administrative Offices	6				2
博尔塔拉蒙古自治州	Bortala Mongol Autonomous Prefecture	6				
巴音郭楞蒙古自治州	Bayangol Mongol Autonomous Prefecture	165	17279	18165	4	2291
阿克苏地区	Aksu Administrative Offices	433	32015	113467	103	2636
克孜勒苏柯尔克孜自治州	Kizilsu Kirgiz Autonomous Prefecture	710	16531	1420	214	1083
喀什地区	Kashgar [Kaxgar] Administrative Offices	6459	88124	114397	8068	65442
和田地区	Hotan Administrative Offices	1200	19456	21876	4427	2364
二、生产建设兵团	**Xinjiang Production and Construction Group**	**2431**	**4946**	**101971**	**50**	**789**

12-23 各地、州、市水果产量

Output of Fruits by Prefecture, Autonomous Prefecture, City

单位：吨 (2010 年) (ton)

地 区	Region	合 计 Total	苹 果 Apples	梨 Pears	葡 萄 Grapes	#无核葡萄 Seedless Grapes
总 计	**Total**	**5938497**	**658728**	**1052854**	**1965695**	**986613**
一、地 方	**Local Regions**	**4713121**	**458278**	**699514**	**1596456**	**860842**
乌鲁木齐市	Urumqi City	10059	1095		7524	
克拉玛依市	Karamay City					
吐鲁番地区	TurpanAdministrative Offices	834490	75	155	819996	752445
哈密地区	Hami [Kumul] Administrative Offices	95426	156	365	79780	65464
昌吉回族自治州	Changji Hui Autonomous Prefecture	165384	8937	25	140913	6
伊犁哈萨克自治州	Ili Kazak Autonomous Prefecture	255228	117041	1701	73273	
伊犁州直属县(市)	Counties (Cities) Direct Under Ili Prefecture	234555	110475	991	61806	
塔城地区	Tacheng [Tarbagatai] Administrative Offices	19799	6090	710	11262	
阿勒泰地区	Altay Administrative Offices	874	476		205	
博尔塔拉蒙古自治州	Bortala MongolAutonomous Prefecture	3386	907		2349	
巴音郭楞蒙古自治州	Bayangol Mongol Autonomous Prefecture	596331	7903	434855	20250	1153
阿克苏地区	Aksu Administrative Offices	1136775	227688	243669	93837	
克孜勒苏柯尔克孜自治州	Kizilsu Kirgiz Autonomous Prefecture	194438	294	41	84241	
喀什地区	Kashgar [Kaxgar] Administrative Offices	1073089	82082	13808	85974	600
和田地区	Hotan Administrative Offices	348515	12100	4895	188319	41174
二、生产建设兵团	**Xinjiang Production and Construction Group**	**1225376**	**200450**	**353340**	**369239**	**125771**

地 区	Region	桃 Peachs	杏 Apricots	红 枣 Jujubes	石 榴 Pomegranate	其 它 Others
总 计	**Total**	**104713**	**1323425**	**627319**	**47318**	**158445**
一、地 方	**Local Regions**	**71945**	**1303865**	**381338**	**47235**	**154490**
乌鲁木齐市	Urumqi City	1137	239			64
克拉玛依市	Karamay City					
吐鲁番地区	TurpanAdministrative Offices	110	9154	3792	1183	25
哈密地区	Hami [Kumul] Administrative Offices	52	1646	13382		45
昌吉回族自治州	Changji Hui Autonomous Prefecture	10384	2255	112		2758
伊犁哈萨克自治州	Ili Kazak Autonomous Prefecture	18039	39399	636		5139
伊犁州直属县(市)	Counties (Cities) Direct Under Ili Prefecture	16638	39359	636		4650
塔城地区	Tacheng [Tarbagatai] Administrative Offices	1236	40			461
阿勒泰地区	Altay Administrative Offices	165				28
博尔塔拉蒙古自治州	Bortala MongolAutonomous Prefecture	130				
巴音郭楞蒙古自治州	Bayangol Mongol Autonomous Prefecture	682	84202	43978	2	4459
阿克苏地区	Aksu Administrative Offices	1165	366080	169460	853	34023
克孜勒苏柯尔克孜自治州	Kizilsu Kirgiz Autonomous Prefecture	491	105507	153	850	2861
喀什地区	Kashgar [Kaxgar] Administrative Offices	32164	599652	131044	27881	100484
和田地区	Hotan Administrative Offices	7591	95731	18781	16466	4632
二、生产建设兵团	**Xinjiang Production and Construction Group**	**32768**	**19560**	**245981**	**83**	**3955**

12-24 主要年份牲畜饲养情况

Number of Livestock in Main Years

单位：万头(只) (10 000 heads)

年 份 Year	大牲畜年底头数 Large Animals (year-end)	牛 Cattle and Buffaloes	马 Horses	驴 Donkeys	骡 Mules	骆 驼 Camels	在大牲畜中役畜 Draught Animals
1978	446.19	222.39	112.39	96.61	1.61	13.19	148.34
1980	482.55	250.65	106.89	108.88	1.72	14.41	154.86
1985	517.55	293.26	99.54	106.57	2.17	16.05	197.29
1990	575.88	338.22	104.58	112.96	2.69	17.43	209.95
1995	580.04	343.54	100.47	117.04	2.77	16.22	213.61
1996	589.41	349.78	101.16	119.36	2.76	16.34	215.05
1997	600.12	359.81	100.32	120.74	2.87	16.38	207.15
1998	606.79	364.29	100.26	123.45	2.80	15.99	205.31
1999	615.91	370.52	101.47	124.99	2.78	16.15	189.86
2000	632.93	384.98	102.57	125.94	2.74	16.70	173.37
2001	630.67	386.40	99.38	126.06	2.84	15.99	172.08
2002	654.46	414.13	99.71	122.22	2.59	15.81	169.51
2003	694.53	453.06	99.39	124.02	2.48	15.58	163.72
2004	716.56	482.30	95.78	120.82	2.36	15.30	151.49
2005	739.72	504.16	94.19	123.90	2.38	15.09	134.81
2006	736.33	502.86	92.09	124.94	2.14	14.30	145.97
2007	702.03	486.98	86.09	113.92	1.83	13.20	120.79
2008	543.41	336.00	83.85	109.25	1.45	12.86	96.56
2009	536.83	330.76	84.60	107.17	1.35	12.95	99.48
2010	536.82	330.47	85.29	106.96	1.19	12.91	108.93

年 份 Year	猪年底头数 Hogs (year-end)	羊年底只数 Sheep and Goats (year-end)	山 羊 Goats	绵 羊 Sheep	牲畜出栏头数 Slanghtered Fattened Animals withina Year	#猪 Pork Pig	#牛 Beef Cattle	#羊 Mutton Sheep
1978	103.25	1927.34	349.63	1577.91	460.41	50.75	18.75	382.76
1980	84.62	2105.43	388.89	1716.54	584.09	67.32	24.22	477.81
1985	66.58	2431.91	394.79	2037.12	836.39	49.07	42.33	723.51
1990	89.71	2830.81	449.43	2381.38	1242.89	78.93	70.10	1070.43
1995	135.26	3009.02	471.38	2537.64	1709.93	122.32	101.20	1448.72
1996	138.18	3136.21	498.10	2638.11	1859.28	153.75	116.25	1550.65
1997	145.73	3261.81	514.60	2747.21	2096.67	173.06	125.72	1753.88
1998	169.82	3447.38	528.05	2919.33	2222.27	197.39	140.82	1837.57
1999	188.34	3592.29	555.21	3037.08	2223.89	203.87	145.95	1820.71
2000	201.53	3690.21	586.70	3103.51	2455.99	224.46	154.53	2017.36
2001	208.23	3764.88	601.14	3163.74	2633.83	246.00	179.32	2147.31
2002	219.08	3908.23	626.42	3281.81	2878.39	259.05	188.65	2363.02
2003	227.71	4104.30	657.15	3447.15	3201.99	307.74	202.23	2626.94
2004	223.08	4266.73	669.47	3597.26	3437.59	352.83	220.80	2790.53
2005	238.38	4355.50	659.75	3695.75	3756.92	358.71	249.41	3081.88
2006	243.88	4359.50	654.26	3705.24	4063.52	390.82	278.69	3317.99
2007	237.90	4083.44	608.10	3475.34	4108.28	393.70	271.76	3361.99
2008	177.00	3025.70	453.85	2571.85	3388.09	265.50	207.30	2842.30
2009	180.42	3127.50	469.13	2658.37	3135.72	254.23	210.89	2604.48
2010	171.96	3013.37	528.73	2484.64	3498.52	262.72	216.69	2947.22

注：牲畜出栏数 1999 年以后计算口径与 1998 年以前不同。
Note: The calculating norm of cattles out of stock after 1999 was different from that prior to that in 1998.

12-25 各地、州、市、县(市)牲畜年底头数

Number of Livestock at the Year-end by Prefecture, Autonomous Prefecture, City and County

单位：万头(只) (2010 年) (10 000 heads)

地 区	Region	合 计 Total	#牛 Cattle and Buffaloes	#马 Horses	#驴 Donkeys	#猪 Hogs	#山羊 Goats	#绵羊 Sheep
总 计	**Total**	**3722.15**	**330.47**	**85.29**	**106.96**	**171.96**	**528.73**	**2484.64**
一、地 方	**Local Regions**	**4319.06**	**471.6**	**82.89**	**105.73**	**195.20**	**517.85**	**2932.10**
乌鲁木齐市	**Urumqi City**	**70.11**	**7.65**	**1.77**	**0.22**	**6.57**	**18.04**	**35.57**
#乌鲁木齐县	Urumqi County	26.31	3.13	1.32	0.12	1.27	3.19	17.22
克拉玛依市	**Karamay City**	**15.45**	**0.79**	**0.07**	**0.01**	**8.20**	**1.83**	**4.52**
吐鲁番地区	**TurpanAdministrative Offices**	**105.84**	**5.13**	**0.31**	**2.38**	**1.98**	**18.57**	**77.06**
吐鲁番市	Turpan City	35.11	1.76	0.03	0.79	0.95	7.59	23.96
鄯善县	Shanshan [piqan]County	34.20	0.84	0.08	0.71	0.98	4.12	27.31
托克逊县	Toksun County	36.53	2.53	0.20	0.88	0.05	6.86	25.79
哈密地区	**Hami [Kumul]Administrative Offices**	**114.48**	**7.04**	**1.25**	**0.99**	**13.1**	**19.64**	**71.32**
哈密市	Hami [Kumul]City	41.25	2.32	0.32	0.37	2.89	7.98	27.05
巴里坤哈萨克自治县	Barkol KazakAutonomous County	54.69	3.55	0.60	0.48	5.41	7.66	36.41
伊吾县	Yiwu [Araturuk]County	18.54	1.17	0.33	0.14	4.80	4.00	7.86
昌吉回族自治州	**Changji Hui Autonomous Prefecture**	**395.75**	**40.79**	**4.92**	**1.30**	**49.26**	**42.85**	**254.85**
昌吉市	Changji City	68.99	7.40	0.93	0.09	14.97	10.72	34.68
阜康市	Fukang City	27.67	3.49	0.42	0.04	2.87	6.01	14.71
呼图壁县	Hutubi County	57.82	8.46	1.20	0.04	6.26	5.36	36.25
玛纳斯县	Manas County	52.67	4.41	0.59	0.08	7.99	1.47	37.94
奇台县	Qitai County	84.23	9.44	0.62	0.43	9.11	7.87	56.42
吉木萨尔县	Jimsar County	51.95	5.06	0.53	0.24	5.46	4.00	36.58
木垒哈萨克自治县	Mori Kazak Autonomous County	52.42	2.53	0.63	0.38	2.60	7.42	38.27
伊犁哈萨克自治州	**Ili Kazak Autonomous Prefecture**	**1323.84**	**218.98**	**56.04**	**3.38**	**49.22**	**129.27**	**860.55**
伊犁州直属县(市)	**Counties (Cities) Direct Under Ili Prefecture**	**617.05**	**122.65**	**36.83**	**3.04**	**30.14**	**25.88**	**397.90**
伊宁市	Yining [Gulja]City	20.10	4.30	0.29	0.19	1.18	1.06	13.05
奎屯市	Kuytun City	3.22	0.09	0.01		2.49	0.11	0.52
伊宁县	Yining [Gulja]County	87.36	16.48	2.20	0.74	9.60	7.72	50.48
察布查尔锡伯自治县	Qapqal Xibe Autonomous County	41.24	6.58	1.36	0.92	3.02	3.29	26.07
霍城县	Huocheng [korgas]County	69.92	11.71	1.64	0.67	4.19	1.97	49.63
巩留县	Gongliu [Tokkuzlara]County	55.00	12.13	3.66	0.36	2.90	2.57	33.34
新源县	Xinyuan [kunes]County	100.03	21.56	7.69	0.05	2.06	2.07	66.59
昭苏县	Zhaosu [mongolkure]County	82.64	15.22	7.94	0.03	2.80	1.37	55.23
特克斯县	Tekes County	69.44	16.54	4.13	0.03	0.83	2.47	45.41
尼勒克县	Nilka County	88.10	18.04	7.91	0.05	1.07	3.25	57.58
塔城地区	**Tacheng [Tarbagatai] Administrative Offices**	**433.85**	**42.71**	**8.92**	**0.31**	**17.21**	**63.87**	**298.89**
塔城市	Tacheng [Qoqek] City	61.33	6.30	1.40	0.09	1.91	5.65	45.80
乌苏市	Usu City	70.11	4.50	0.81	0.13	3.65	12.24	48.47
额敏县	Emin [Dorbiljin] County	71.03	6.12	1.13		1.61	10.29	51.71
沙湾县	Shawan County	58.87	7.39	0.66	0.02	9.34	7.01	34.30
托里县	Toli County	65.62	8.24	1.89	0.05	0.20	11.14	43.64
裕民县	Yumin [Qagantokay] County	57.69	5.86	1.73		0.40	7.35	41.93
和布克赛尔蒙古自治县	Hoboksar Mongol Autonomous County	49.20	4.30	1.30	0.02	0.10	10.19	33.04
阿勒泰地区	**Altay Administrative Offices**	**272.94**	**53.62**	**10.29**	**0.03**	**1.87**	**39.52**	**163.76**
阿勒泰市	Altay City	50.24	11.65	1.97	0.01	0.38	3.34	32.24
布尔津县	Burqin County	30.03	11.59	1.68		0.23	3.23	12.87
富蕴县	Fuyun [Koktokay] County	61.24	6.87	2.60	0.01	0.08	8.69	41.77
福海县	Fuhai [Burultokay] County	40.56	7.01	0.78		0.88	4.54	26.73
哈巴河县	Habahe [Kaba] County	39.62	10.98	1.51		0.08	5.98	20.71
青河县	Qinghe [Qinggil] County	30.56	3.11	1.00		0.09	10.90	15.15
吉木乃县	Jeminay County	20.69	2.41	0.75	0.01	0.13	2.84	14.29

注: 1.全区总计不等于地方与生产建设兵团汇总数。2.全区总计数为国家统计局审定数。

Note:a)The region total data is not equal to the sum of local and Production and Construction Groups.b)The region total data refer to approvable data of NBS.

12-25 续表 Continued

单位：万头(只) (10 000 heads)

地　区	Region	合计 Total	#牛 Cattle and Buffaloes	#马 Horses	#驴 Donkeys	#猪 Hogs	#山羊 Goats	#绵羊 Sheep
博尔塔拉蒙古自治州	**Bortala Mongol Autonomous Prefecture**	**109.79**	**6.69**	**1.50**	**0.18**	**4.77**	**12.80**	**83.62**
博乐市	Bole [Bortala] City	38.12	2.51	0.32	0.11	2.46	2.75	29.86
精河县	Jinghe [Jing] County	36.64	1.69	0.39	0.02	1.16	6.76	26.58
温泉县	Wenquan [Araxang] County	35.03	2.49	0.79	0.05	1.15	3.29	27.18
巴音郭楞蒙古自治州	**Bayangol Mongol Autonomous Prefecture**	**298.69**	**15.19**	**3.80**	**3.11**	**26.23**	**57.81**	**191.93**
库尔勒市	Korla City	27.62	1.12	0.06	0.14	9.01	3.08	14.21
轮台县	Luntai [Bugur] County	35.90	1.31	0.04	0.78	1.55	8.56	23.64
尉犁县	Yuli [Lopnur] County	33.31	0.66	0.05	0.18	0.46	18.53	13.42
若羌县	Ruoqiang [Qarkilik] County	9.75	0.35	0.06	0.38	0.95	1.53	6.43
且末县	Qiemo [Qarqan] County	35.60	1.85	0.12	1.13	0.79	8.56	22.92
焉耆回族自治县	Yanqi Hui Autonomous County	24.86	1.87	0.08	0.07	1.45	0.69	20.7
和静县	Hejing County	94.62	6.77	3.01	0.32	3.66	10.11	70.63
和硕县	Hoxud County	21.30	0.73	0.23	0.03	2.90	5.70	11.53
博湖县	Bohu [Bagrax] County	15.73	0.53	0.15	0.08	5.46	1.05	8.45
阿克苏地区	**Aksu Administrative Offices**	**428.67**	**32.90**	**5.58**	**10.48**	**21.16**	**109.45**	**248.11**
阿克苏市	Aksu City	49.75	2.81	0.52	0.61	12.7	5.27	27.84
温宿县	Wensu [Onsu] County	57.47	4.27	1.01	0.77	2.08	14.97	34.33
库车县	Kuqa County	63.37	4.79	0.72	1.71	1.96	15.02	38.97
沙雅县	Xayar County	43.12	2.54	0.46	1.36	1.68	18.72	18.24
新和县	Xinhe [Toksu] County	22.59	2.96	0.56	1.22	0.36	1.55	15.88
拜城县	Baicheng [Bay] County	85.45	7.55	0.80	2.61	1.75	21.80	50.89
乌什县	Wushi [Uxturpan] County	52.02	5.20	1.23	1.49	0.13	18.31	25.49
阿瓦提县	Awat County	36.90	2.51	0.24	0.28	0.48	4.81	28.57
柯坪县	Kalpin County	18.00	0.27	0.04	0.43	0.02	9.00	7.90
克孜勒苏柯尔克孜自治州	**Kizilsu Kirgiz Autonomous Prefecture**	**161.37**	**16.34**	**2.39**	**3.46**	**0.42**	**37.35**	**100.61**
阿图什市	Artux City	47.00	4.57	0.36	1.00	0.28	11.71	28.83
阿克陶县	Akto County	51.72	9.27	0.21	1.88	0.07	8.23	31.93
阿合奇县	Akqi County	32.63	1.25	1.40	0.15	0.05	9.74	19.97
乌恰县	Wuqia [Ulugqat] County	30.02	1.25	0.42	0.43	0.02	7.67	19.88
喀什地区	**Kashgar [Kaxgar] Administrative Offices**	**809.62**	**90.91**	**3.87**	**45.94**	**12.07**	**41.9**	**614.55**
喀什市	Kashgar [Kaxgar] City	26.74	1.56		0.96	2.01	0.45	21.76
疏附县	Shufu County	104.55	10.56	0.11	3.94	1.61	3.49	84.79
疏勒县	Shule County	77.80	9.99	0.04	5.00	5.10	0.63	57.00
英吉沙县	Yengisar County	38.00	6.18	0.04	2.61	0.36	0.10	28.69
泽普县	Zepu [Poskam] County	39.68	5.80	0.18	2.28	0.92	1.42	29.08
莎车县	Shache [Yarkant] County	119.08	14.91	2.40	5.97	0.30	4.55	90.93
叶城县	Yecheng [Kagilik] County	119.70	16.16	0.30	6.89	0.36	6.58	89.29
麦盖提县	Makit County	56.69	6.89	0.22	2.11	0.47	4.65	42.34
岳普湖县	Yopurga County	37.00	4.90	0.11	7.50	0.12	3.00	21.36
伽师县	Jiashi [Payzawat] County	100.50	5.90	0.28	6.66	0.10	6.15	81.40
巴楚县	Bachu [Maralbexi] County	71.05	4.93	0.12	1.47	0.72	5.51	58.30
塔什库尔干塔吉克自治县	Taxkorgan Tajik Autonomous County	18.83	3.13	0.07	0.55		5.37	9.61
和田地区	**Hotan Administrative Offices**	**485.45**	**29.19**	**1.39**	**34.28**	**2.22**	**28.34**	**389.41**
和田市	Hotan City	32.24	2.47	0.06	1.38	1.46	0.59	26.27
和田县	Hotan County	75.41	5.86	0.18	5.49	0.08	1.99	61.72
墨玉县	Moyu [Karakax] County	113.89	8.87	0.26	8.95	0.12	1.97	93.71
皮山县	Pishan [Guma] County	49.20	1.12	0.14	3.49	0.07	2.60	41.69
洛浦县	Lop County	50.10	4.51	0.06	4.20	0.14	1.11	40.05
策勒县	Qira County	49.01	1.12	0.23	2.77	0.08	2.71	42.02
于田县	Yutian [Keriya] County	87.84	4.83	0.41	7.19	0.20	8.51	66.52
民丰县	Minfeng [Niya] County	27.76	0.41	0.05	0.81	0.07	8.86	17.43
二、生产建设兵团	**Xinjiang Production and Construction Group**	**624.06**	**36.84**	**2.40**	**1.23**	**155.42**	**40.21**	**387.55**

12-26 主要年份畜产品产量
Output of Livestock Products in Main Years

年份 Year	肉类产量(万吨) Output of meat (10 000 tons)	#牛 Beef	#马 Horse Meat	#骆驼 Camels	#猪 Pork	#羊 Mutton	#禽兔肉 Poultry and Rabbit Meat
1978	9.65	1.85			2.48	5.32	
1980	12.70	2.20	0.60	0.05	3.29	6.48	
1985	18.37	4.23	0.86	0.15	3.09	9.97	
1990	30.46	7.08	1.18	0.18	4.93	15.75	1.22
1995	52.38	13.14	2.05	0.40	8.37	24.48	3.61
1996	60.31	15.18	2.24	0.38	10.43	26.93	4.82
1997	64.40	16.40	2.55	0.38	11.52	27.72	5.38
1998	75.19	19.19	2.82	0.47	13.60	32.49	6.16
1999	81.36	20.61	2.93	0.62	16.02	33.57	6.94
2000	90.00	22.24	3.57	0.63	17.18	37.50	7.76
2001	97.00	23.99	3.55	0.72	18.36	40.48	8.66
2002	105.44	25.90	3.65	0.68	19.70	43.06	10.38
2003	115.00	28.77	3.88	0.69	22.41	45.54	11.46
2004	128.13	30.42	4.34	0.70	24.58	52.65	13.27
2005	141.46	34.22	4.67	0.77	26.18	59.89	13.46
2006	158.21	39.25	4.80	0.90	28.78	66.99	14.92
2007	160.58	42.25	5.09	0.94	31.73	65.02	13.74
2008	114.74	32.40	4.29	0.95	22.30	45.40	7.89
2009	115.31	33.88	4.33	0.73	22.03	43.77	8.52
2010	121.74	35.47	4.67	0.78	23.05	46.95	8.71

年份 Year	羊毛(万吨) Wool (10 000 tons)	#绵羊毛 Sheep Wool	山羊绒(吨) Cashmere (ton)	驼毛(吨) Camel Hair (ton)	牛奶(万吨) Cow Milk (10 000 tons)	羊奶(万吨) Sheep Milk (10 000 tons)	牛皮(万张) Oxhide (10 000 sheets)	羊皮(万张) Sheep Skin (10 000 sheets)	禽蛋(万吨) Poultry Eggs (10 000 tons)
1978	3.08	3.00	324	371	4.50	0.75	17.36	300.05	
1980	3.31	3.21	263	353	5.84	1.44	18.22	338.32	
1985	7.07	3.91	325	530	16.43	3.27	35.72	587.69	4.29
1990	5.09	4.93	607	656	30.81	4.83	56.76	839.69	6.30
1995	5.66	5.45	716	716	45.21	4.60	91.54	1125.72	9.51
1996	5.99	5.77	780	787	48.76	5.46	92.31	1178.39	10.33
1997	6.25	6.01	813	742	54.18	4.60	96.88	1326.69	12.16
1998	6.48	6.22	811	768	59.96	5.06	110.12	1391.77	13.34
1999	6.76	6.50	849	727	64.81	5.62	118.35	1569.50	16.68
2000	6.98	6.67	893	757	72.54	5.69	125.62	1686.03	18.53
2001	7.30	6.99	973	736	81.09	6.76	143.13	1689.24	20.37
2002	7.78	7.44	1034	824	94.87	5.84	139.87	1801.67	22.64
2003	8.21	7.84	1143	793	113.00	6.21	141.57	1692.35	23.62
2004	8.91	8.49	1228	770	133.32	6.41	150.15	1981.82	24.99
2005	9.38	8.98	1258	730	152.22	5.62	169.53	2022.61	24.99
2006	9.62	8.96	1263	746	179.81	5.60	196.97	2300.73	25.80
2007	9.34	8.92	1265	946	196.23	5.54	191.90	2409.84	28.37
2008	9.03	8.40	1157	1040	137.40	4.96	208.07	2441.52	28.92
2009	7.60	7.16	1261	578	120.88	4.27	193.52	2358.98	23.20
2010	8.69	8.40	1324	602	128.60	4.22	204.14	2403.25	24.35

12-27 各地、州、市、县(市)总产肉量

Total Output of Meat by Prefecture, Autonomous Prefecture, City and County

单位：吨 (2010 年) (ton)

地　　区	Region	合 计 Total	#牛 Beef	#马 Horse	#骆 驼 Camels	#猪 Pork	#山 羊 Goats	#绵 羊 Sheep	#禽 肉 Poultry Meat	#兔肉 Rabbit Meat
总　计	**Total**	**1217400**	**354700**	**46727**	**7761**	**230500**	**82400**	**387100**	**82900**	**4173**
一、地 方	**Local Regions**	**1763700**	**417381**	**45253**	**7427**	**346306**	**73958**	**544649**	**307178**	**2192**
乌鲁木齐市	**Urumqi City**	**53840**	**15306**	**1357**	**205**	**15764**	**3909**	**10524**	**6406**	**15**
#乌鲁木齐县	Urumqi County	13701	3438	990	123	2514	990	3610	1797	
克拉玛依市	**Karamay City**	**9944**	**468**	**75**		**8240**	**107**	**429**	**624**	**1**
吐鲁番地区	**TurpanAdministrative Offices**	**40259**	**10543**	**160**	**143**	**963**	**3912**	**23578**	**915**	**45**
吐鲁番市	Turpan City	22108	4663	34	13	143	2527	14598	130	
鄯善县	Shanshan [piqan]County	9416	1780	60	60	600	820	5680	410	6
托克逊县	Toksun County	8735	4100	66	70	220	565	3300	375	39
哈密地区	**Hami [Kumul]Administrative Offices**	**46639**	**7004**	**537**	**670**	**16446**	**2945**	**16746**	**1929**	**2**
哈密市	Hami [Kumul]City	20530	3969	94	129	3715	1585	9616	1307	1
巴里坤哈萨克自治县	Barkol KazakAutonomous County	18195	2562	240	414	7608	701	5924	539	1
伊吾县	Yiwu [Araturuk]County	7914	473	203	127	5123	659	1206	83	
昌吉回族自治州	**Changji Hui Autonomous Prefecture**	**452504**	**64015**	**4317**	**1527**	**158189**	**11208**	**84412**	**128107**	**244**
昌吉市	Changji City	80552	11657	1094	344	30197	2760	11960	22294	167
阜康市	Fukang City	62698	8709	467	103	13278	2157	10162	27812	
呼图壁县	Hutubi County	70130	11113	924	265	16376	457	12620	28317	42
玛纳斯县	Manas County	59828	5610	609	126	19033	1940	10642	21840	20
奇台县	Qitai County	105825	12484	148	96	63240	1501	17991	10230	11
吉木萨尔县	Jimsar County	43008	9205	204	48	8858	930	12082	11606	4
木垒哈萨克自治县	Mori Kazak Autonomous County	30463	5237	871	545	7207	1463	8955	6008	
伊犁哈萨克自治州	**Ili Kazak Autonomous Prefecture**	**438470**	**142326**	**31472**	**2987**	**71960**	**19041**	**130336**	**37750**	**1543**
伊犁州直属县(市)	**Counties (Cities) Direct Under Ili Prefecture**	**220844**	**78854**	**20355**	**189**	**37815**	**3665**	**55714**	**23249**	**118**
伊宁市	Yining [Gulja]City	10419	4002	460	14	2468	192	2291	900	2
奎屯市	Kuytun City	2941	60			2471	3	87	320	
伊宁县	Yining [Gulja]County	36030	17248	1290	32	4506	693	7578	4365	
察布查尔锡伯自治县	Qapqal Xibe Autonomous County	17478	5205	600		6195	416	3209	1571	40
霍城县	Huocheng [korgas]County	30266	5916	1860		7620	285	6842	7632	20
巩留县	Gongliu [Tokkuzlara]County	25941	10063	2820	15	4038	349	4496	4000	40
新源县	Xinyuan [kunes]County	33048	10745	4380		5303	292	10767	1546	8
昭苏县	Zhaosu [mongolkure]County	22387	8471	3240	32	1898	235	7850	650	3
特克斯县	Tekes County	16312	7400	1485		1272	429	5225	500	1
尼勒克县	Nilka County	26022	9744	4220	96	2044	771	7369	1765	4

注：同 12-25 表。
Note:The same applies to 12-25 table following.

12-27 续表 1 Continued

单位：吨 (ton)

地　区	Region	合计 Total	#牛 Beef	#马 Horse	#骆驼 Camels	#猪 Pork	#山羊 Goats	#绵羊 Sheep	#禽肉 Poultry Meat	#兔肉 Rabbit Meat
塔城地区	**Tacheng [Tarbagatai] Administrative Officess**	**145401**	**35571**	**8242**	**1442**	**29750**	**10742**	**48293**	**11155**	**49**
塔城市	Tacheng [Qoqek] City	15313	4300	883	123	1268	690	6980	1035	1
乌苏市	Usu City	28771	5392	1920	396	10110	2981	6468	1380	18
额敏县	Emin [Dorbiljin] County	22806	5274	2012	205	4898	1735	7880	802	
沙湾县	Shawan County	40891	9779	365	61	12079	1883	9153	7523	30
托里县	Toli County	17593	5508	1103	215	444	1529	8726	68	
裕民县	Yumin [Qagantokay] County	10953	3878	609	190	663	370	4946	297	
和布克赛尔蒙古自治县	Hoboksar Mongol Autonomous County	9074	1440	1350	252	288	1554	4140	50	
阿勒泰地区	**Altay Administrative Offices**	**72225**	**27901**	**2875**	**1356**	**4395**	**4634**	**26329**	**3346**	**1376**
阿勒泰市	Altay City	15339	6870	681	324	552	1526	5242	126	5
布尔津县	Burqin County	9896	3552	261	32	1020	445	3828	414	344
富蕴县	Fuyun [Koktokay] County	16117	5006	806	280	172	715	6326	1813	999
福海县	Fuhai [Burultokay] County	11651	3879	319	330	2189	559	4023	347	5
哈巴河县	Habahe [Kaba] County	8604	4789	171	64	112	576	2697	190	5
青河县	Qinghe [Qinggil] County	6406	2475	493	200	233	552	2208	232	13
吉木乃县	Jeminay County	4212	1330	144	126	117	261	2005	224	5
博尔塔拉蒙古自治州	**Bortala Mongol Autonomous Prefecture**	**20623**	**3530**	**478**	**78**	**5247**	**1142**	**8532**	**1579**	**8**
博乐市	Bole [Bortala] City	8483	1473	138	52	2599	308	2946	952	
精河县	Jinghe [Jing] County	5996	748	86	4	1036	569	3157	388	8
温泉县	Wenquan [Araxang] County	6144	1309	254	22	1612	265	2429	239	
巴音郭楞蒙古自治州	**Bayangol Mongol Autonomous Prefecture**	**83651**	**16447**	**1160**	**247**	**24754**	**5423**	**25531**	**9011**	**160**
库尔勒市	Korla City	18394	1935	3		5637	509	4126	6056	39
轮台县	Luntai [Bugur] County	8017	876	24		2199	1052	3358	465	4
尉犁县	Yuli [Lopnur] County	5107	978	14		671	1576	1457	341	10
若羌县	Ruoqiang [Qarkilik] County	2315	283	52	10	890	166	648	105	7
且末县	Qiemo [Qarqan] County	7517	1763	106	96	768	1041	3234	109	33
焉耆回族自治县	Yanqi Hui Autonomous County	9844	3454	99		1827	48	3513	745	58
和静县	Hejing County	22123	6125	793	38	6952	236	7517	392	6
和硕县	Hoxud County	5061	411	44	95	2010	710	1193	583	
博湖县	Bohu [Bagrax] County	5273	622	25	8	3800	85	485	215	3
阿克苏地区	**Aksu Administrative Offices**	**157310**	**43979**	**3406**	**779**	**23700**	**14563**	**41848**	**22133**	**12**
阿克苏市	Aksu City	40200	10700	246		11080	2258	6462	8838	1
温宿县	Wensu [Onsu] County	16430	4298	710	33	2340	1871	4724	2266	
库车县	Kuqa County	41586	13391	1050	320	3384	3834	13846	4257	

12-27 续表 2 Continued

单位：吨 (ton)

地区	Region	合计 Total	#牛 Beef	#马 Horse	#骆驼 Camels	#猪 Pork	#山羊 Goats	#绵羊 Sheep	#禽肉 Poultry Meat	#兔肉 Rabbit Meat
沙雅县	Xayar County	9303	1885	155		1745	1483	2280	1544	11
新和县	Xinhe [Toksu] County	5491	2057	108		266	187	1430	1323	
拜城县	Baicheng [Bay] County	17175	4925	260	60	3742	1622	4896	1000	
乌什县	Wushi [Uxturpan] County	14315	4795	810	198	336	1853	3386	2565	
阿瓦提县	Awat County	10510	1668	27		780	795	3897	226	
柯坪县	Kalpin County	2300	260	40	168	27	660	927	114	
克孜勒苏柯尔克孜自治州	**Kizilsu Kirgiz Autonomous Prefecture**	**34828**	**13713**	**1312**	**439**	**1000**	**3047**	**12589**	**2728**	
阿图什市	Artux City	13497	5472	128	27	864	1383	4873	750	
阿克陶县	Akto County	11817	5610	65	56	36	649	4066	1335	
阿合奇县	Akqi County	4864	1632	756	56	91	751	1485	93	
乌恰县	Wuqia [Ulugqat] County	4650	999	363	300	9	264	2165	550	
喀什地区	**Kashgar [Kaxgar] Administrative Offices**	**354185**	**85098**	**679**	**112**	**18546**	**6416**	**144775**	**89199**	**95**
喀什市	Kashgar [Kaxgar] City	23534	5320			3128	230	13381	1425	
疏附县	Shufu County	39896	11980	20	15	2216	501	17711	7063	
疏勒县	Shule County	37308	10220	10	15	4624	68	13700	7560	3
英吉沙县	Yengisar County	19317	7700			224	72	7166	3650	
泽普县	Zepu [Poskam] County	25903	3906	24		3100	154	7350	11143	
莎车县	Shache [Yarkant] County	47655	6900	180	30	2144	689	23261	12666	84
叶城县	Yecheng [Kagilik] County	49446	15484	101	45	563	1126	16472	14272	8
麦盖提县	Makit County	19249	3672	50		536	704	9342	4655	
岳普湖县	Yopurga County	13726	3400	12		128	396	5850	3415	
伽师县	Jiashi [Payzawat] County	40132	6200	150		200	1015	18017	11800	
巴楚县	Bachu [Maralbexi] County	32562	7260	80		1683	724	11020	11550	
塔什库尔干塔吉克自治县	Taxkorgan Tajik Autonomous County	5457	3056	52	7		737	1505		
和田地区	**Hotan Administrative Offices**	**71447**	**14952**	**300**	**240**	**1497**	**2245**	**45349**	**6797**	**67**
和田市	Hotan City	9839	2364			1099	41	5111	1224	
和田县	Hotan County	9510	2436	10	45	7	147	6096	751	18
墨玉县	Moyu [Karakax] County	17723	4680	40		169	169	11288	1370	7
皮山县	Pishan [Guma] County	6401	444	20	30	59	216	4366	1259	7
洛浦县	Lop County	7896	2232	10	30	46	66	4956	541	15
策勒县	Qira County	5768	480	40	60	39	183	4433	531	2
于田县	Yutian [Keriya] County	10966	2100	150	30	65	712	7293	598	18
民丰县	Minfeng [Niya] County	3344	216	30	45	13	711	1806	523	
二、生产建设兵团	**Xinjiang Production and Construction Group**	**319923**	**37231**	**1474**	**334**	**171065**	**9400**	**72294**	**24389**	**1981**

12-28 水产品产量和养殖面积

Output of Aquatic Products and Cultured Area

年 份 Year	地 区 Region	水产品产量（吨） Aquatic Products (ton)	#养殖产量 Cultured Output	养殖面积（公顷） Culture Area (hectare)
1985		8958	3403	32775
1990		23217	15401	68838
1995		44432	35341	72538
1996		47890	38876	79006
1997		52366	42656	75895
1998		53391	44557	67473
1999		55840	48068	70524
2000		60065	50974	69806
2001		60876	50902	63340
2002		63906	55159	62629
2003		67278	57244	67374
2004		73296	60405	74996
2005		79320	65571	76037
2006		84539	71440	76606
2007		88879	78639	77590
2008		92587	82040	73909
2009		97037	87863	73433
2010		101063	90913	73289
一、地　方	**Local Regions**	**75380**	**65075**	**39960**
乌鲁木齐市	Urumqi City	7778	7778	4065
克拉玛依市	Karamay City	606	512	60
吐鲁番地区	Turpan Administrative Offices	348	348	43
哈密地区	Hami [Kumul] Administrative Offices	1035	985	675
昌吉回族自治州	Changji Hui Autonomous Prefecture	15780	15780	2855
伊犁哈萨克自治州	Ili Kazak Autonomous Prefecture	18738	16514	16428
伊犁州直属县(市)	Counties (Cities) Direct Under Ili Prefecture	11405	11205	855
塔城地区	Tacheng [Tarbagatai] Administrative Offices	2350	1667	1176
阿勒泰地区	Altay Administrative Offices	4983	3642	14397
博尔塔拉蒙古自治州	Bortala Mongol Autonomous Prefecture	1559	828	894
巴音郭楞蒙古自治州	Bayangol Mongol Autonomous Prefecture	10438	3974	3083
阿克苏地区	Aksu Administrative Offices	8937	8623	1043
克孜勒苏柯尔克孜自治州	Kizilsu Kirgiz Autonomous Prefecture			
喀什地区	Kashgar [Kaxgar] Administrative Offices	8351	8043	8424
和田地区	Hotan Administrative Offices	1810	1690	2390
二、生产建设兵团	**Xinjiang Production and Construction Group**	**25683**	**25838**	**33329**

12-29 受灾面积情况
Areas Covered by Natural Disaster

单位：公顷 (hectare)

年份 Year	地区 Region	受灾面积 Areas Covered	#水灾 Flood	#旱灾 Drought
1990		282787	16900	87040
1991		530933	30733	256000
1992		511067	35333	72067
1993		378833	63538	55778
1994		568782	54413	139366
1995		665580	49812	210422
1996		558297	114905	83547
1997		372060	20200	165400
1998		535900	74990	22340
1999		1290799	145633	36696
2000		932545	49219	461136
2001		740888	82242	151703
2002		493400	128345	16634
2003		440982	80231	21291
2004		524402	35562	368935
2005		482066	93102	210796
2006		515289	35562	359823
2007		557411	68910	273312
2008		1286750	20150	840665
2009		137545	15165	122380
2010		4157411	134447	5934
乌鲁木齐市	Urumqi City	3489	1199	
克拉玛依市	Karamay City			
石河子市	Shihezi City			
吐鲁番地区	Turpan Administrative Offices	18560		4400
哈密地区	Hami [Kumul] Administrative Offices	226146	594	
昌吉回族自治州	Changji Hui Autonomous Prefecture	58843	5650	
伊犁州直属县(市)	Counties (Cities) Direct Under Ili Prefecture	436483	8037	
塔城地区	Tacheng [Tarbagatai] Administrative Offices	280179	4412	
阿勒泰地区	Altay Administrative Offices	284960	11849	
博尔塔拉蒙古自治州	Bortala Mongol Autonomous Prefecture	437032	2059	1534
巴音郭楞蒙古自治州	Bayangol Mongol Autonomous Prefecture	1124036	6503	
阿克苏地区	Aksu Administrative Offices	623855	11224	
克孜勒苏柯尔克孜自治州	Kizilsu Kirgiz Autonomous Prefecture	214822	21014	
喀什地区	Kashgar [Kaxgar] Administrative Offices	411777	31495	
和田地区	Hotan Administrative Offices	37229	30411	

12-30 乡镇企业主要指标

Main Indicators of Township Enterprises

单位：万元 (10 000 yuan)

年 份 Year	地 区 Region	企业个数（个）Number of Enterprises (unit)	从业人数（人）Employees of Enterprises (person)	总产值 Total Output Value
1985		98826	367753	75179
1990		144281	464027	222218
1991		145762	472332	314765
1992		155711	498132	402139
1993		202274	600687	553616
1994		250037	686425	924082
1995		281130	745291	1319217
1996		282733	781784	1622442
1997		43548	355585	1219032
1998		269048	712490	2457410
1999		297147	749205	2736766
2000		316524	806368	3022076
2001		334694	824499	3316049
2002		307963	866661	3629499
2003		354640	880874	4119555
2004		368553	933473	4562898
2005		366883	954411	4994156
2006		368724	990365	5574730
2007		377385	1037023	4265895
2008		378343	1063023	8629234
2009		378983	1115703	8486719
2010		383653	1167548	9574341
乌鲁木齐市	Urumqi City	19129	63930	965662
克拉玛依市	Karamay City	178	1509	12778
石河子市	Shihezi City	51413	18528	123604
吐鲁番地区	Turpan Administrative Offices	21049	46738	346302
哈密地区	Hami [Kumul] Administrative Offices	10100	27226	185404
昌吉回族自治州	Changji Hui Autonomous Prefecture	38798	140259	1850323
伊犁州直属县(市)	Counties (Cities) Direct Under Ili Prefecture	51413	158746	1584227
塔城地区	Tacheng [Tarbagatai] Administrative Offices	26065	104884	1452109
阿勒泰地区	Altay Administrative Offices	24653	56350	358445
博尔塔拉蒙古自治州	Bortala Mongol Autonomous Prefecture	8445	30622	286253
巴音郭楞蒙古自治州	Bayangol Mongol Autonomous Prefecture	25194	76951	1133113
阿克苏地区	Aksu Administrative Offices	39336	117115	456005
克孜勒苏柯尔克孜自治州	Kizilsu Kirgiz Autonomous Prefecture	9128	20225	32126
喀什地区	Kashgar [Kaxgar] Administrative Offices	62500	166580	509433
和田地区	Hotan Administrative Offices	44708	137885	278557

12-30 续表 Continued

单位：万元 (10 000 yuan)

年 份 Year	地 区 Region	营业收入 Business Income	利润总额 Total Profits	国家税金 National Tax	增加值 Added Value
	1985	105072	9357	3136	
	1990	249906	8614	5206	
	1991	299890	25974	13747	
	1992	374810	34644	16976	
	1993	584089	51880	27354	
	1994	957701	75439	69494	
	1995	1493924	110656	76479	
	1996	1927425	136410	76479	
	1997	1128271	43337	48945	
	1998	2455629	156578	82365	
	1999	2742029	164949	93490	
	2000	3071497	191764	100444	745728
	2001	3377589	211439	108864	807174
	2002	3739524	225723	126732	904892
	2003	4276322	264661	137880	1024772
	2004	4757808	304998	152243	1153561
	2005	5164593	294021	164604	1318134
	2006	5806803	332070	190833	1508846
	2007	6776709	318943	228386	1767506
	2008	7548573	563293	249122	1909350
	2009	8547580	671806	271759	2206982
	2010	9596967	756277	306105	2490324
乌鲁木齐市	Urumqi City	978403	50821	24862	272381
克拉玛依市	Karamay City	12240	1154	495	2957
石河子市	Shihezi City	163102	5003	2229	20599
吐鲁番地区	Turpan Administrative Offices	272968	27137	12148	72918
哈密地区	Hami [Kumul] Administrative Offices	164287	12412	9169	49462
昌吉回族自治州	Changji Hui Autonomous Prefecture	1967344	164883	72948	586351
伊犁州直属县(市)	Counties (Cities) Direct Under Ili Prefecture	1676366	75128	30138	273993
塔城地区	Tacheng [Tarbagatai] Administrative Offices	1406658	163295	34840	450651
阿勒泰地区	Altay Administrative Offices	411839	37272	13827	103124
博尔塔拉蒙古自治州	Bortala Mongol Autonomous Prefecture	279982	10461	7343	68044
巴音郭楞蒙古自治州	Bayangol Mongol Autonomous Prefecture	988853	93179	56167	269645
阿克苏地区	Aksu Administrative Offices	471083	36201	16190	120385
克孜勒苏柯尔克孜自治州	Kizilsu Kirgiz Autonomous Prefecture	31658	3264	857	6022
喀什地区	Kashgar [Kaxgar] Administrative Offices	503350	53312	13741	132150
和田地区	Hotan Administrative Offices	268834	22755	11151	61642

主要统计指标解释

农林牧渔业总产值 指以货币表现的农、林、牧、渔业全部产品和对农林牧渔业生产活动进行的各种支持性服务活动的价值总量，它反映一定时期内农林牧渔业生产总规模和总成果。1957年以前的农林牧渔业总产值中包括了厩肥和农民自给性手工业(如农民自制衣服、鞋、袜，自己从事粮食初步加工等)。1958年及以后，林业中增加了村及村以下竹木采伐产值；牧业中取消了厩肥产值；副业中取消了农民自给性手工业产值，增加了村及村以下办的工业产值； 渔业中增加了海洋捕捞水产品产值。1980年及以后，在副业中增加了农民家庭兼营工业商品部分的产值。从1984年起村及村以下工业产值划归工业。从1993年起取消副业，将野生动物的捕猎划入牧业，野生植物采集和农民家庭兼营商品性工业划归农业。从2003年起，执行新的国民经济行业分类标准，农林牧渔业总产值中包括了农林牧渔服务业产值。林业中增加了森林采运业产值。农业中取消了家庭兼营商品性工业产值，将野生林产品的采集划归林业。第一次农业普查以后，由于畜牧业产品年报数据与普查数据之间存在一定的差距，国家统计局农调总队对畜牧业年报数据与普查数据进行衔接，对畜牧业产值进行相应调整。

农林牧渔业总产值的计算方法通常是按农、林、牧、渔业产品及其副产品的产量分别乘以各自单位产品价格求得；少数生产周期较长，当年没有产品或产品产量不易统计的，则采用间接方法匡算其产值；然后将四业产品产值及农林牧渔服务业产值相加即为农林牧渔业总产值。

粮食产量 指全社会的产量。包括国有经济经营的、集体统一经营的和农民家庭经营的粮食产量，还包括工矿企业办的农场和其他生产单位的产量。粮食除包括稻谷、小麦、玉米、高粱、谷子及其他杂粮外，还包括薯类和豆类。其产量计算方法，豆类按去豆荚后的干豆计算；薯类(包括甘薯和马铃薯，不包括芋头和木薯)1963年以前按每4公斤鲜薯折1公斤粮食计算，从1964年开始改为按5公斤鲜薯折1公斤粮食计算。城市郊区作为蔬菜的薯类(如马铃薯等)按鲜品计算，并且不作粮食统计。其他粮食一律按脱粒后的原粮计算。1989年以前全国粮食产量数据主要靠全面报表取得，1989年开始使用抽样调查数据。

棉花产量 指全社会的产量。包括春播棉和夏播棉。产量按皮棉计算。不包括木棉。

油料产量 指全部油料作物的生产量。包括花生、油菜籽、芝麻、向日葵籽、胡麻籽(亚麻籽)和其他油料。不包括大豆、木本油料和野生油料。花生以带壳干花生计算。

水产品产量 指人工养殖的水产品和天然生长的水产品的捕捞量。包括海水的鱼类、虾蟹类、贝类和藻类以及内陆水域的鱼类、虾蟹类和贝类，不包括淡水生植物。水产品产量是通过各级水产和统计部门逐级上报取得数据。1995年及以前，贝类中牡蛎按鲜肉计算；蚶、蛤、蛙按 5 斤鲜品折1斤计算。1996 年以后则统一按鲜品计算。

猪、牛、羊肉产量 指当年出栏并已屠宰、除去头蹄下水后带骨肉(即胴体重)的重量。包括全社会范围内的产量。1996年前为各级逐级上报数据。1996年第一次农业普查以后，由于畜牧业产品年报数据与普查数据之间存在一定的差距，国家统计局农调总队对畜牧业年报数据与普查数据进行衔接。1999年以后，国家统计局在部分地区开展了猪、牛、羊、禽等主要畜禽品种的抽样调查，并用抽样数据作为国家定案数据使用。未开展抽样调查的地区和品种，仍使用各级统计部门逐级上报数据。

期初(末)畜禽存栏头(只)数 指报告期初(末)农村各种合作经济组织和国营农场、农民个人、机关、团体、学校、工矿企业、部队等单位以及城镇居民饲养的大牲畜、猪、羊、家禽等畜禽的存栏数。数据上报方式及数据调整情况同猪、牛、羊肉产量。

农作物播种面积 指实际播种或移植有农作物的面积。凡是实际种植农作物的面积，不论种植在耕地上还是种植在非耕地上，均包括在农作物播种面积中。在播种季节基本结束后，因遭灾而重新改种和补种的农作物面积，也包括在内。该指标可以反映我国耕地面积的利用情况。目前，农作物播种面积主要包括粮食、棉花、油料、糖料、麻类、烟叶、蔬菜和瓜类、药材和其它农作物九大类。

有效灌溉面积 指具有一定的水源，地块比较平整，灌溉工程或设备已经配套，在一般年景下，当年能够进行正常灌溉的耕地面积。在一般情况下，有效灌溉面积应等于灌溉工程或设备已经配备，能够进行正常灌溉的水田和水浇地面积之和。它是反映我国耕地抗旱能力的一个重要指标。

农用化肥施用量 指本年内实际用于农业生产的化肥数量，包括氮肥、磷肥、钾肥和复合肥。化肥施用量要求按折纯量计算数量。折纯量是指把氮肥、磷肥、钾肥分别按含氮、含五氧化二磷、含氧化钾的百分之百成份进行折算后的数量。复合肥按其所含主要成分折算。公式为:

折纯量= 实物量 × 某种化肥有效成份含量的百分比

农业机械总动力 指主要用于农、林、牧、渔业的各种动力机械的动力总和。包括耕作机械、排灌机械、收获机械、农用运输机械、植物保护机械、牧业机械、林业机械、渔业机械和其他农业机械〔内燃机按引擎马力折成瓦(特)计算、电动机按功率折成瓦(特)计算〕。不包括专门用于乡、镇、村、组办工业、基本建设、非农业运输、科学试验和教学等非农业生产方面用的动力机械与作业机械。这个指标的统计数据主要来源于农机部门。

Explanatory Notes on Main Statistical Indicators

Gross Output Value of Agriculture, Forestry, Animal Husbandry and Fishery refers to the total value of products of agriculture, forestry, animal husbandry and fishery, and total value of services in support of agriculture, forestry, animal husbandry and fishery activities. It reflects the total scale and results of agricultural production during a given period. Prior to 1957, China's gross agricultural output value included barnyard manure and handicraft products for self-consumption (clothes, shoes, stockings, and initial grain processing undertaken by peasants). Since 1958, cutting and felling of bamboo and trees by villages and other cooperative organizations under villages have been included in forestry; value of barnyard manure has been excluded from animal husbandry; self consumed handicrafts have not been included from sideline occupations, while the output value of industries run by villages and cooperative organizations under village has been included in sideline occupations; and the output value of fish catches by motor fishing boats has been added to fishery. Since 1980, the value of handicraft products made for sale by individuals in households has been added to sideline occupations. Since 1984, industries run by villages and under villages have been included in the sector of industry. Since 1993, the subdivision of sideline occupations has been cancelled, and the hunting of wild animals has been classified into animal husbandry, and the gathering of wild plants and commodity industry run by rural household have been included in farming. A new industrial classification of economic activities was introduced in 2003. Under the new classification, value of services to agriculture, forestry, animal husbandry and fishery is included in the gross output value of agriculture, value of wood felling and transport is included in forestry, value of industrial output by rural households is not included in agriculture, and the collection of wild forest products is taken from agriculture and included in forestry. The First Agriculture Census of China revealed some discrepancy between the production of animal products from the annual reports and that from the census. Efforts were made by the Rural Survey of NBS to adjust the output value of animal husbandry to make the figures from the annual reports consistent with the census data.

Gross output value of agriculture is obtained by multiplying the output of each product or by-product by its price, resulting in the output value of each single item. For a small number of products, annual output of which is not available or difficult to get due to the long production (growing) process involved, the output value is estimated through an indirect approach. The sum of output values of all products of agriculture, forestry, animal husbandry and fishery and services in support to those industries is then equal to the gross output value of agriculture.

Grain Output refers to the total output in the whole country including grains produced by State farms, collective units, rural households, as well as by farms affiliated to industrial and mining enterprises and other production units. Grain includes rice, wheat, corn, sorghum, millet and other miscellaneous grains as well as tubers and beans. Output of beans refers to dry beans without pods. The output of tubers (sweet potatoes and potatoes, not including taros and cassava) are converted into that of grain at the ratio 4:1, i.e. 4 kilograms of fresh tubers were equivalent to 1 kilogram of grain up to 1963. Since 1964 the ratio for conversion has been 5:1. Tubers supplied as vegetables (such as potatoes) in cities and suburbs are calculated as fresh vegetables and their output is not included in the output of grain. Output of all other grains refers to husked grain. Data on grain production before 1989 were obtained through the Comprehensive Statistical Reporting System. Since 1989, data from sample surveys are used.

Cotton Output refers to cotton production in the whole country including cotton planted in spring and in autumn. Output is measured as the weight of ginned cotton. Ceiba is not included.

Output of Oil-bearing Crops refers to the total Production of oil-bearing crops of various kinds, including peanuts (dry, in shell), rapeseeds, sesame, sunflower seeds, flax seeds, and other oil-bearing crops. Soybeans, oil-bearing woody plants, and wild oil-bearing crops are not included.

Output of Aquatic Products refers to catches of both artificially cultured and naturally grown aquatic products, including fish, shrimps, crabs and shellfish in sea and inland water as well as seaweed. Freshwater plants are not included. Data on output of aquatic products are reported by aquatic product and statistical agencies level by level. Before 1995, among the shellfish, oyster was counted as fresh meat; 5 kilograms of ark shell, clams and frogs are equivalent to 1 kilogram of fresh aquatic products; they have all been counted as fresh aquatic products since 1996.

Output of Pork, Beef, and Mutton refers to the meat of slaughtered hogs, cattle, sheep and goats with head, feet, and offal taken away. Data refers to the production of the whole country. The First Agricultural Census of China in 1996 revealed some discrepancy between the production of animal products from the annual reports and that from the census. Efforts were made by the Rural Survey Organization of the NBS to adjust the output value of animal husbandry to make the figures from the annual reports consistent with the census data. Since 1999, the NBS conducted sample surveys for the major animal husbandry products, such as hogs, cattle, sheep and goats and fowls, and the data from sample surveys are used as national finalized data. Those products, which are not covered by the sample survey, are still reported by statistical agencies level by level.

Number of Livestock or Poultry in Stock at Beginning (or End) of Period refers to the total number of large animals, pigs, sheep, fowls, etc. raised by rural cooperative organizations, State farms, rural individuals, government agencies, schools, industrial and mining enterprises, army, and urban residents at the beginning (or end) of the reference period. Data reporting system and data adjustment are the same as that in the output of pork, beef and mutton.

Sown Area of Crops refer to area of land sown or transplanted with crops regardless of being in cultivated area of noncultivated area, Area of land re-sown due to natural disaster is also included.This is an important indicator that can reflect the utilization comdition of the cultivated land in China,At present,the sown area of crops mainly include the following categories of crops:grain,cotton,oil-bearing crops ,sugar crops,fiber crops,Tobacco,Vegetables and melons,medical materials and other farm crops.

Irrigated Area refers to area of land that are effectively irrigated, i.e. relatively level land, where there are water sources or complete sets of irrigation facilities to lift and move adequate water for irrigation purpose under normal conditions. Under normal situations, irrigated area is the sum of watered fields and irrigated fields where irrigation systems or equipment have been installed for regular irrigation purpose. This important indicator reflects drought resistance capacity of the cultivated land in China.

Consumption of Chemical Fertilizers in Agriculture refers to the quantity of chemical fertilizers applied in agriculture in the year, including nitrogenous fertilizer, phosphate fertilizer, potash fertilizer, and compound fertilizer. The consumption of chemical fertilizers is calculated in terms of volume of effective components by means of converting the gross weight of the respective fertilizers into weight containing effective component (e.g. nitrogen content in nitrogenous fertilizer, phosphorous pentoxide contents in phosphate fertilizer, and potassium oxide contents in potash fertilizer). Compound fertilizer is converted in regard to its major components. The formula is:

Volume of effective component= physical quantity× effective component of certain chemical fertilizer (%)

Total Power of Agricultural Machinery refers to total mechanical power of machinery used in agriculture, forestry, animal husbandry and fishery, including machinery for ploughing, irrigation and drainage, harvesting, transport, plant protection, animal husbandry, forestry and fishery and other agricultural machineries. (For the power of internal combustion engines, it is converted from its horsepower into watts while for electric motors the output power is converted into watts.) Machinery employed for non-agricultural purposes, such as the machines used in township-run and village-run industry, construction, non-agricultural transport, scientific experiments and teaching, are not included. Data are mainly from agricultural machinery agencies.

第十三篇 工 业

CHAPTER 13 Industry

简要说明
Brief Introduction

本篇资料的主要内容及来源

本篇资料反映新疆维吾尔自治区工业经济方面的基本情况，包括所辖地（州、市）、县（市、区）的主要工业经济统计数据：

1、主要年份工业总产值及工业总产值指数。

2、全区规模以上工业企业主要经济指标，以及按企业登记注册类型、轻重工业、企业规模、工业行业大类和按地（州、市）、县（市、区）分组的主要经济指标和经济效益指标。

3、国有控股工业企业按工业行业大类和按地（州、市）、县（市、区）分组的主要经济指标和经济效益指标。

4、大中型工业企业按工业行业大类分组的主要经济指标和经济效益指标。

5、主要工业产品产量和生产能力。

6、国有控股和重点行业主要指标占全区规模以上工业比重。

主要年份工业总产值及工业总产值指数为全部工业企业；其他资料的统计范围均为年主营业务收入在500万元以上工业企业（即规模以上工业企业）。

本篇资料由新疆维吾尔自治区统计局工业交通统计处根据工业统计年度报表中有关资料整理汇总。

Main Content and Source of Data

Data in this chapter reflect the basic conditions of the industrial sector ,presenting main industrial economic indicators of the prefecture,Autonomous prefecture,city and county.

(1) the gross industrial output and indices of industrial enterprises in the main period;

(2) Main indicator on economic and economic benefit of industrial enterprises above designated size by status of registration, light & heavy industries, size of enterprises, industrial sector.

(3) Main economic indicators and efficiency indicators of state -owned industrial enterprises classified by branch of industry and prefecture,Autonomous prefecture,city and county.

(4) Main economic indicators and efficency indicators of large and medium-sized industrial enterprises classified bu branch of industry and by the prefecture,Autonomous prefecture,city and county.

(5) Output and production capacity of key industrial products.

(6) Main economic indicator of state -owned and non -state -owned industrial enterprises.

Statistical scope of data on output of major industrial products is all industrial enterprises.othes scope of data is industrial enterprises with revenue from principal business over 5 million yuan.

Data in this chapter are collected and compiled by the Department of Industry and transport, XBS in accordance with the annual report of industrial statistics.

13-1 主要年份工业总产值
Gross Industrial Output Value in Main Years

单位:亿元 (100 million yuan)

年 份 Year	工业总产值 Gross Industrial Output Value	国有工业 State-owned Enterprises	集体工业 Collective-owned Enterprises	其它经济类型工业 Enterprises of Other Types of Ownership
1978	33.91	30.22	3.69	
1980	40.71	36.20	4.50	0.01
1985	86.78	73.18	11.93	1.67
1990	219.92	176.52	36.72	6.68
1995	593.43	461.31	89.24	42.88
2000	1061.29	258.93	72.78	729.58
2001	1084.22	155.26	53.31	875.65
2002	1133.38	159.73	46.39	927.26
2003	1330.15	161.94	35.69	1132.52
2004	1756.18	224.63	19.14	1512.41
2005	2358.83	236.18	17.29	2105.36
2006	2894.88	272.06	16.14	2606.68
2007	3471.51	358.28	17.29	3095.94
2008	4639.02	387.53	15.70	4235.79
2009	4184.50	404.01	15.61	3764.88
2010	5766.51	382.00	25.54	5358.97

13-2 主要年份工业总产值指数
Indices of Gross Industrial Output Value in Main Years

(1978 年=100)

年 份 Year	工业总产值 Gross Industrial Output Value	国有工业 State-owned Enterprises	集体工业 Collective-owned Enterprises	其它经济类型工业 Enterprises of Other Types of Ownership
1978	100.0	100.0	100.0	
1980	117.7	118.0	113.2	(1981 年=100)
1985	220.6	199.5	428.2	851.7
1990	380.3	326.0	915.9	2096.1
1995	670.8	506.1	2104.5	7441.5
2000	1000.4	227.3	1763.6	66265.2
2001	1077.8	151.0	1311.5	87376.0
2002	1180.9	149.3	1123.1	99435.1
2003	1306.7	152.9	837.3	113823.3
2004	1567.8	210.4	442.4	135173.5
2005	1821.8	218.2	388.9	160072.4
2006	2057.1	246.3	344.8	180922.4
2007	2322.8	319.9	339.3	201240.8
2008	2707.5	336.5	272.4	237624.5
2009	2942.2	353.4	289.2	259031.4
2010	3331.8	325.7	431.9	298801.3

13-3 规模以上工业企业分行业、地区增加值

Value-added of Industrial Enterprises above Designated Size by Sector and Region

单位：万元

行　　业	Sector	2009	2010
总　　计	**Total**	**14982299.3**	**21201273.9**
煤炭开采和洗选业	Mining and Washing of Coal	772896.4	854612.8
石油和天然气开采业	Extraction of Petroleum and Natural Gas	6777661.4	9547499.8
黑色金属矿采选业	Mining and Processing of Ferrous Metals Ores	207373.6	404862.5
有色金属矿采选业	Mining and Processing of Nonferrous Metals Ores	203778.3	344571.3
非金属矿采选业	Mining and Processing of Nonmetal Ores	29702.3	54395.6
其他采矿业	Mining of Other Ores		811.2
农副食品加工业	Processing of Food from Agricultural Products	265639.0	398726.4
食品制造业	Manufacture of Food	230357.6	215907.7
饮料制造业	Manufacture of Beverage	178430.1	236289.2
烟草制品业	Manufacture of Tobacco	152468.2	188135.8
纺织业	Manufacture of Textile	162813.7	298197.7
纺织服装、鞋、帽制造业	Manufacture of Textile Wearing Apparel, Footware and Caps	6013.0	5936.0
皮革、毛皮、羽毛(绒)及其制品业	Leather, Fur, Feather and Related Products Manufacturing	3850.8	8360.8
木材加工及木、竹、藤、棕、草制品业	Processing of Timber, Wood, Bamboo, Cane, Grass Products	9252.3	19250.6
家具制造业	Manufacture of Furniture	19669.8	26886.8
造纸及纸制品业	Manufacture of Paper and Paper Products	40785.9	53418.8
印刷业和记录媒介的复制	Printing and Copying of Medium for Record	24716.7	25514.7
石油加工、炼焦及核燃料加工业	Oil Processing, Coking and Nuclear Fuel Processing	2531343.1	3270110.0
化学原料及化学制品制造业	Raw Chemical Material and Chemical Products	580089.1	962663.8
医药制造业	Manufacture of Medicine	30588.3	35160.2
化学纤维制造业	Manufacture of Chemical Fiber	166847.1	195765.0
橡胶制品业	Manufacture of Rubber Products	9749.6	12217.1
塑料制品业	Manufacture of Plastic Products	78464.4	121251.6
非金属矿物制品业	Manufacture of Nonmetal Mineral Products	453813.6	624397.7
黑色金属冶炼及压延加工业	Smelting and Pressing of Ferrous Metals	377590.6	759983.7
有色金属冶炼及压延加工业	Smelting and Pressing of Nonferrous Metals	99225.2	164119.0
金属制品业	Manufacture of Metal Products	67680.7	71533.0

13-3 续表 Continued

单位: 万元

行业	Sector	2009	2010
通用设备制造业	Manufacture of General Purpose Machinery	25590.9	36463.4
专用设备制造业	Manufacture of Special Purpose Machinery	40936.9	48982.8
交通运输设备制造业	Manufacture of Transport Equipment	6467.7	9509.5
电气机械及器材制造业	Manufacture of Electric Equipment and Machinery	240186.5	669609.5
通信设备、计算机及其他电子设备制造业	Telecom Equipment, Computer and Other Electronic Equipment	49208.3	53549.1
仪器仪表及文化、办公用机械制造业	Measuring Instruments and Machinery for Cultunal Activify and OfficeWork	2375.3	3371.9
工艺品及其他制造业	Manufacture of Art work and Other Manufacturing	977.3	3000.4
废弃资源和废旧材料回收加工业	Recycling and Disposal of Waste		4939.7
燃气生产和供应业	Production and Supply of Gas	43321.7	1379267.7
电力、热力的生产和供应业	Production and Supply of Electricity and Therma	1067340.6	59146.5
水的生产和供应业	Production and Supply of Water	25093.1	32854.7
按地区分	**Grouped by Region**		
乌鲁木齐市	Urumqi City	3656165.5	4969848.1
克拉玛依市	Karamay City	4185736.9	6420764.6
吐鲁番地区	Turpan Administrative Offices	735566.0	906892.6
哈密地区	Hami [Kumul] Administrative Offices	246152.4	371660.9
昌吉回族自治州	Changji Hui Autonomous Prefecture	693800.4	1009640.6
伊犁州直属县(市)	Counties (Cities) Direct Under Ili Prefecture	540907.5	746330.0
塔城地区	Tacheng [Tarbagatai] Administrative Offices	431886.2	482460.3
阿勒泰地区	Altay Administrative Offices	267890.1	433901.6
博尔塔拉蒙古自治州	Bortala Mongol Autonomous Prefecture	55716.0	79314.3
巴音郭楞蒙古自治州	Bayangol Mongol Autonomous Prefecture	2766259.0	3495396.5
阿克苏地区	Aksu Administrative Offices	420889.5	638457.1
克孜勒苏柯尔克孜自治州	Kizilsu Kirgiz Autonomous Prefecture	20482.4	40112.8
喀什地区	Kashgar [Kaxgar] Administrative Offices	88822.7	132080.6
和田地区	Hotan Administrative Offices	35310.3	43090.4
生产建设兵团	Xinjiang Production and Construction Group	836714.4	1431323.7

13-4 规模以上工业企业主要经济指标

单位：万元 (2010 年)

项目	Item	企业单位数（个）Number of Enterprises (unit)	#亏损企业 Loss- Suffering Enterprises	工业总产值（当年价格）Gross Industrial Output Value (At Current Prices)
总计	**Total**	**2465**	**552**	**53419038.4**
按登记注册类型分	**By Status of Registration**			
内资企业	Domestic Funded Enterprises	2380	526	52241549.2
国有企业	State-owned Enterprises	170	54	3669961.0
#中央企业	Central Enterprises	68	15	2737465.8
地方企业	Local Enterprises	102	39	932495.2
#自治区属企业	Autonomous	33	11	434810.3
地区(州、市)属企业	Prefecture or City	15	6	147865.3
县(市)属企业	County or City	46	21	156436.0
集体企业	Collective-owned Enterprises	26	1	211985.6
#自治区属企业	Autonomous	8		91093.0
地区(州、市)属企业	Prefecture or City	4		9826.9
县(市)属企业	County or City	7	1	33362.8
镇属企业	Town	2		7293.6
股份合作企业	Cooperative Enterprises	19	3	106823.6
联营企业	Joint Ownership Enterprises	10	4	34950.2
#国有联营企业	State Joint Ownership Enterprises	5	2	16844.2
国有与集体联营企业	Joint State-collective Enterprises	1	1	3575.5
其他联营企业	Other Joint Ownership Enterprises	4	1	14530.5
有限责任公司	Limited Liability Corporations	1002	215	14763803.0
#国有独资公司	State Sole funded Corporations	59	14	2493764.6
其他有限责任公司	Other Limited Liability Corporations	943	201	12270038.4
股份有限公司	Share-holding Corporations Ltd.	90	16	25676663.6
私营企业	Private Enterprises	1057	230	7769052.3
#私营独资企业	Private-funded Enterprises	82	14	279521.0
私营合伙企业	Private Partnership Enterprises	23	6	81459.3
私营有限责任公司	Private Limited Liability Corporations	922	204	4920039.2
私营股份有限公司	Private Share-holding Corporations Ltd.	30	6	2488032.8
港、澳、台商投资企业	Enterprises with Funds from Hong Kong, Macao and Taiwan	33	15	366746.2
外商投资企业	Foreign Funded Enterprises	52	11	810743.0
在总计中：国有控股企业	Of the Total : State-owned and State-holding Enterprises	574	132	37703302.8
在总计中：农村工业	Of the Total : Rural Industry	24	5	76489.8
按轻、重工业分	**Grouped by Light & Heavy Industry**			
轻工业	Light Industry	916	199	7298673.6
以农产品为原料	Using Farm Produces as Raw Materials	824	173	6987295.2
以非农产品为原料	Using Non-Farm Produces as Raw Materials	92	26	311378.4
重工业	Heavy Industry	1549	353	46120364.8
采掘工业	Mining and Quarrying	329	83	14432543.9
原料工业	Raw Material Industry	567	152	25695491.1
加工工业	Manufacturing Industry	653	118	5992329.8
按企业规模分	**Grouped by Size of Enterprises**			
大型企业	Large Enterprises	34	5	29464761.5
中型企业	Medium-sized Enterprises	296	49	13045857.5
小型企业	Small Enterprises	2135	498	10908419.4

Main Economic Indicators of Industrial Enterprises above Designated Size

(10 000 yuan)

增加值 Value-added	工业销售产值(当年价) Sales Value of Industry Products (At Current Prices)	出口交货值 Delivery Value of Industry Export	实收资本 Total Capital Hold	资产合计 Total Assets	流动资产合计 Total Working Capitals	#产成品 Finished Product	固定资产原价 Net Value of Fixed Assets
21201273.9	**52266596.1**	**541927.5**	**25400781.3**	**79119654.3**	**25406382.4**	**2704622.8**	**61112837.7**
20870785.5	51180838.5	497415.2	24923172.9	77577580.3	24627098.2	2590052.8	60285867.2
1489206.6	3643076.4	20866.0	1999491.6	7788652.6	1992375.2	113793.0	6178091.3
972833.7	2750054.1	11259.0	1257124.1	5167485.5	1235398.0	55948.4	4273911.0
362414.0	893022.3	9607.0	742367.5	2621167.1	756977.2	57844.6	1904180.3
197109.3	427768.9		540902.4	1559182.3	331376.7	14823.6	1192992.4
24408.4	141078.0		68716.0	284154.3	144701.1	11728.6	238592.5
66798.3	146688.7		94175.7	440407.8	109729.0	5154.4	359381.0
50189.7	206809.4		18500.9	123803.5	88467.1	15833.1	53602.5
21969.9	92743.4		3573.8	48237.8	39528.4	2244.4	12904.0
2118.3	9969.0		1025.7	6102.9	5560.2	768.9	1846.0
12670.4	31070.4		7761.9	33594.8	19418.5	3024.1	18772.4
6463.9	7444.4		461.0	3130.6	2208.1	346.6	1432.1
29429.3	99621.7		24175.4	114389.0	62494.8	8655.3	64795.2
15528.2	35704.0		13183.6	61648.2	25265.4	2231.3	24819.6
7551.2	16895.6		11070.0	36767.9	15213.2	974.4	18725.1
2373.2	3446.4		700.0	12360.7	2083.8		893.6
5603.9	15362.0		1413.6	12519.6	7968.4	1256.9	5200.9
4534669.3	14199303.3	190899.2	6614496.8	23791389.2	8547865.2	1076819.1	14676420.1
954839.0	2464115.2	765.0	1250510.3	4284174.5	1095682.5	86014.5	3374605.1
3579830.3	11735188.1	190134.2	5363986.5	19507214.7	7452182.7	990804.6	11301815.0
13074956.8	25685360.8	194836.7	14369046.9	35715434.7	8398917.9	859749.4	36373861.6
1829671.0	7302914.5	90813.3	1883627.7	9971315.8	5503620.8	512224.7	2910630.4
106395.8	239112.1	62.9	53924.7	300816.9	124021.1	22885.7	145880.6
17297.4	75413.6		19067.7	54136.6	28874.0	3985.1	26192.1
1062031.2	4638990.0	90601.4	1217915.5	5797726.4	2878606.4	443778.0	2314944.3
643946.5	2349398.8	149.0	592719.8	3818635.9	2472119.3	41575.9	423613.4
99185.8	322614.3	19493.7	180332.1	509342.9	276002.3	41644.7	293533.3
231302.6	763143.3	25018.6	297276.3	1032731.1	503281.9	72925.3	533437.2
17060539.5	37555639.7	328738.3	20311592.9	55947597.5	13677842.2	1497921.3	52854625.2
24814.8	72847.1		33396.3	110454.8	58590.5	4913.5	45498.4
1763065.7	6854624.3	301578.7	2427481.4	10243250.3	5340792.5	1092317.9	4834875.4
1665200.0	6559885.8	296531.0	2101885.9	9397754.1	5055515.2	1065664.1	4235288.3
97865.6	294738.5	5047.7	325595.5	845496.2	285277.3	26653.8	599587.1
19438208.2	45411971.8	240348.8	22973299.9	68876404.0	20065589.9	1612304.9	56277962.3
11206303.4	14245329.5	364.5	14263332.8	28124288.6	6356395.7	508541.1	29292541.3
6639461.3	25445114.2	144155.6	6889537.1	30720412.8	8099329.5	782025.2	24357809.0
1592443.5	5721528.1	95828.7	1820430.0	10031702.6	5609864.7	321738.6	2627612.0
14103317.9	29433499.3	59022.2	16054623.0	40454869.4	9272001.1	720933.0	41347535.3
4244061.8	12613002.8	250255.6	4683999.2	20906232.8	8974334.1	837544.6	10606023.7
2853894.2	10220094.0	232649.7	4662159.1	17758552.1	7160047.2	1146145.2	9159278.7

13-4 续表

单位：万元

项　　目	Item	流动负债合　计 Total Working Liabilities	长期负债合　计 Long-term Liabilities	所有者权益合计 Total Owners' Equities
总　　计	**Total**	**24836841.6**	**14749769.5**	**38884012.0**
按登记注册类型分	**By Status of Registration**			
内资企业	Domestic Funded Enterprises	24046535.8	14642575.9	38246063.1
国有企业	State-owned Enterprises	2516488.0	2350695.7	2817308.2
#中央企业	Central Enterprises	1936498.1	1345801.1	1799217.7
地方企业	Local Enterprises	579989.9	1004894.6	1018090.5
#自治区属企业	Autonomous	235832.0	607869.5	710512.8
地区(州、市)属企业	Prefecture or City	133804.9	97840.0	50950.3
县(市)属企业	County or City	115605.9	180714.4	133623.1
集体企业	Collective-owned Enterprises	63879.0	846.1	54484.8
#自治区属企业	Autonomous	23712.4	136.1	20505.9
地区(州、市)属企业	Prefecture or City	1580.5		4522.2
县(市)属企业	County or City	12204.4	710.0	19970.4
镇属企业	Town	2002.1		1128.5
股份合作企业	Cooperative Enterprises	70358.8	453.0	42207.0
联营企业	Joint Ownership Enterprises	33552.5	12679.3	11458.1
#国有联营企业	State Joint Ownership Enterprises	21712.5	1914.1	9183.0
国有与集体联营企业	Joint State-collective Enterprises	6575.3	5363.0	422.4
其他联营企业	Other Joint Ownership Enterprises	5264.7	5402.2	1852.7
有限责任公司	Limited Liability Corporations	9696984.4	4547812.6	9146154.8
#国有独资公司	State Sole funded Corporations	1475483.5	806651.9	1907143.2
其他有限责任公司	Other Limited Liability Corporations	8221500.9	3741160.7	7239011.6
股份有限公司	Share-holding Corporations Ltd.	7181047.8	6770011.4	21734350.7
私营企业	Private Enterprises	4472876.6	960077.8	4440500.9
#私营独资企业	Private-funded Enterprises	163708.9	13757.2	120137.2
私营合伙企业	Private Partnership Enterprises	22631.8	3300.9	27849.5
私营有限责任公司	Private Limited Liability Corporations	2777421.9	698665.3	2250557.0
私营股份有限公司	Private Share-holding Corporations Ltd.	1509114.0	244354.4	2041957.2
港、澳、台商投资企业	Enterprises with Funds from Hong Kong, Macao and Taiwan	257892.9	38461.6	212809.7
外商投资企业	Foreign Funded Enterprises	532412.9	68732.0	425139.2
在总计中：国有控股企业	Of the Total : State-owned and State-holding Enterprises	14661123.4	12003455.7	29007782.3
在总计中：农村工业	Of the Total : Rural Industry	34556.2	18618.8	54356.7
按轻、重工业分	**Grouped by Light & Heavy Industry**			
轻工业	Light Industry	5111540.8	1011590.0	3834728.2
以农产品为原料	Using Farm Produces as Raw Materials	4874286.7	817391.6	3439179.7
以非农产品为原料	Using Non-Farm Produces as Raw Materials	237254.1	194198.4	395548.5
重工业	Heavy Industry	19725300.8	13738179.5	35049283.8
采掘工业	Mining and Quarrying	5457844.6	6144962.9	16450625.8
原料工业	Raw Material Industry	10393057.6	6274838.5	13790982.9
加工工业	Manufacturing Industry	3874398.6	1318378.1	4807675.1
按企业规模分	**Grouped by Size of Enterprises**			
大型企业	Large Enterprises	8662235.6	8423896.8	23306169.0
中型企业	Medium-sized Enterprises	8174869.8	3528131.8	8936760.0
小型企业	Small Enterprises	7999736.2	2797740.9	6641083.0

Continued

(10 000 yuan)

主营业务收入 Revenue from Principal Business	#主营业务成本 Cost of Principal Business	主营业务税金及附加 Taxes and Other Charges on Principal Business	营业利润 Business Profit	利润总额 Total Profit	亏损企业亏损总额 Losses Value of Loss-Suffering Enterprises	利税总额 Total Profits and Taxes	本年应交增值税 Value-added Taxes Payable	全部从业人员年平均人数(人) Annual Average Employed Persons (person)
54926143.4	**39489633.0**	**2569233.6**	**8305982.5**	**8524251.8**	**604203.6**	**13708719.9**	**2615234.5**	**601818**
53709416.1	38551741.8	2560400.2	8188598.3	8408602.8	583619.4	13540406.4	2571403.4	584369
3598326.2	3214155.8	119965.2	12900.3	29425.0	201629.7	283622.1	134231.9	69555
2722197.8	2532158.7	112663.0	-53715.5	-34077.4	164727.4	169071.2	90485.6	49525
876128.4	681997.1	7302.2	66615.8	63502.4	36902.3	114550.9	43746.3	20030
421441.3	325778.0	2617.6	32846.1	33555.7	10691.8	59359.2	23185.9	10104
144064.5	137983.2	245.9	-5903.0	-11587.4	21518.1	-8436.4	2905.1	2443
131034.8	99642.7	1730.4	6569.9	7763.3	4415.9	15176.2	5682.5	5850
221468.1	190366.3	3207.0	11028.5	10592.1	138.7	21625.5	7826.4	3950
96712.8	84926.0	478.6	3635.8	3466.6		7915.2	3970.0	1262
9986.0	8623.2	39.4	431.8	440.4		851.9	372.1	309
32119.8	24190.4	1774.7	4271.3	4269.1	138.7	7673.5	1629.7	775
7654.4	4737.7	169.9	2039.3	1982.1		3280.7	1128.7	203
95997.6	75852.8	670.0	11360.6	11498.5	251.8	13981.9	1813.4	2211
37648.8	27260.2	681.0	3525.6	3682.9	364.0	7172.5	2808.6	1391
17122.0	11352.4	445.2	2839.6	3035.8	68.8	4819.6	1338.6	407
3566.6	2308.5	73.5	-263.6	-277.6	277.6	216.2	420.3	200
16960.2	13599.3	162.3	949.6	924.7	17.6	2136.7	1049.7	784
14445994.7	11492836.2	275703.4	1360947.7	1474800.5	162562.5	2357645.2	607141.3	232483
2554674.8	1962854.9	161177.5	227278.8	257252.0	22977.4	535071.3	116641.8	41715
11891319.9	9529981.3	114525.9	1133668.9	1217548.5	139585.1	1822573.9	490499.5	190768
27692434.4	17482211.8	2114566.3	5817424.9	5887514.2	170736.0	9596807.6	1594727.1	165167
7609437.4	6061261.5	45602.0	971478.3	991145.4	47456.5	1259492.5	222745.1	109312
252273.3	183997.6	2548.5	39011.7	37629.8	1819.4	51568.2	11389.9	7318
72923.1	62611.9	880.8	5321.4	5239.5	756.9	8332.3	2212.0	1409
4890562.1	4087573.7	31779.2	412583.0	430917.0	41835.3	592710.6	130014.4	88559
2393678.9	1727078.3	10393.5	514562.2	517359.1	3044.9	606881.4	79128.8	12026
352543.9	280090.3	588.3	28782.1	29561.6	5020.8	42624.1	12474.2	7351
864183.4	657800.9	8245.1	88602.1	86087.4	15563.4	125689.4	31356.9	10098
39430339.9	27244253.3	2436861.0	6500190.6	6647661.5	478264.9	11186422.4	2101899.9	353759
74770.9	59830.5	174.9	7923.5	7883.6	1040.0	11696.6	3638.1	2212
7216997.7	5858552.8	162909.9	432934.9	520167.0	119694.2	905138.9	222062.0	143145
6915360.4	5626325.5	161010.5	426478.4	515097.4	101728.8	886393.8	210285.9	132638
301637.3	232227.3	1899.4	6456.5	5069.6	17965.4	18745.1	11776.1	10507
47709145.7	33631080.2	2406323.7	7873047.6	8004084.8	484509.4	12803581.0	2393172.5	458673
15756643.1	7821785.2	766610.9	5209103.2	5273382.3	284368.6	7410541.6	1370548.4	190722
26001031.2	21303950.9	1600394.0	1685601.4	1714902.2	177675.3	4167327.3	852031.1	192394
5951471.4	4505344.1	39318.8	978343.0	1015800.3	22465.5	1225712.1	170593.0	75557
31112130.9	20784403.5	2136860.8	5840378.8	5925779.0	320673.5	9756540.8	1693901.0	218465
13164152.7	10068502.5	332432.5	1482235.2	1579069.0	125721.4	2487909.9	576408.4	196119
10649859.8	8636727.0	99940.3	983368.5	1019403.8	157808.7	1464269.2	344925.1	187234

13-5 按行业分规模以上工业企业主要经济指标

单位: 万元 (2010 年)

行 业	Sector	企业单位数(个) Number of Enterprises (unit)	#亏损企业 Loss- Suffering Enterprises	工业总产值(当年价格) Gross Industrial Output Value (At Current Prices)
煤炭开采和洗选业	Mining and Washing of Coal	148	47	1504627.9
石油和天然气开采业	Extraction of Petroleum and Natural Gas	31	2	11442905.6
#天然原油和天然气开采	Extraction of Ores Crude Oil and Natural Gas Extraction	6		10418332.7
黑色金属矿采选业	Mining and Processing of Ferrous Metals Ores	83	20	877567.9
有色金属矿采选业	Mining and Processing of Nonferrous Metals Ores	41	10	460091.1
非金属矿采选业	Mining and Processing of Nonmetal Ores	24	3	143433.3
#采 盐	Extraction of Salt	4		32728.4
农副食品加工业	Processing of Food from Agricultural Products	345	65	2371733.4
#谷物磨制	Grain Grinding	62	11	315192.8
饲料加工	Fodder Processing	34	5	344841.0
制 糖	Sugar Making	15		243686.0
食品制造业	Manufacture of Food	164	44	1103349.2
#罐头制造	Manufacture of can	73	26	480265.4
饮料制造业	Manufacture of Beverage	76	13	648051.4
#酒的制造	Manufacture of Wine	54	7	431891.8
烟草制品业	Manufacture of Tobacco	1		236475.5
纺织业	Manufacture of Textile	108	22	1204723.9
#棉、化纤纺织及印染精加工	Cotton, Chemical Fiber, Dyeing, Printing and Processing	81	11	1080312.2
毛纺织和染整精加工	Wool Textile, Dyeing and Printing	9	4	31697.4
纺织服装、鞋、帽制造业	Manufacture of Textile Wearing Apparel, Footware and Caps	6	1	13984.9
皮革、毛皮、羽毛(绒)及其制品业	Leather, Fur, Feather and Related Products Manufacturing	4	1	48228.8
#皮革鞣制加工	Leather Tanning and Processing	2		34318.0
皮革制品制造	Manufacture of Leather Products	1	1	737.0
木材加工及木、竹、藤、棕、草制品业	Processing of Timber, Wood, Bamboo, Cane, Grass Products	21	6	94474.3
家具制造业	Manufacture of Furniture	8	2	94738.8
造纸及纸制品业	Manufacture of Paper and Paper Products	52	16	195070.1
印刷业和记录媒介的复制	Printing and Copying of Medium for Record	33	4	65060.2
石油加工、炼焦及核燃料加工业	Oil Processing, Coking and Nuclear Fuel Processing	100	22	12450842.0
#炼 焦	Coking	62	17	714580.2
化学原料及化学制品制造业	Raw Chemical Material and Chemical Products	181	31	3166536.6
#基础化学原料制造	Basic Chemical Material	40	11	725507.7
肥料制造	Fertilizer Making	45	8	466278.3
医药制造业	Manufacture of Medicine	25	6	113384.1
化学纤维制造业	Manufacture of Chemical Fiber	17	2	952127.3
橡胶制品业	Manufacture of Rubber Products	6	1	67329.4
塑料制品业	Manufacture of Plastic Products	164	29	565844.8
非金属矿物制品业	Manufacture of Nonmetal Mineral Products	263	52	2051822.0
#水泥制造	Manufacture of Cement	66	12	961553.3
黑色金属冶炼及压延加工业	Smelting and Pressing of Ferrous Metals	57	18	5531476.4
有色金属冶炼及压延加工业	Smelting and Pressing of Nonferrous Metals	31	6	694500.8
金属制品业	Manufacture of Metal Products	75	12	489679.6
通用设备制造业	Manufacture of General Purpose Machinery	58	5	127956.4
专用设备制造业	Manufacture of Special Purpose Machinery	46	8	208709.4
交通运输设备制造业	Manufacture of Transport Equipment	14	8	94925.5
电气机械及器材制造业	Manufacture of Electric Equipment and Machinery	39	5	2604813.6
通信设备、计算机及其他电子设备制造业	Telecom Equipment, Computer and Other Electronic Equipment	3	1	156824.6
仪器仪表及文化、办公用机械制造业	Measuring Instruments and Machinery for Cultural Activify and Office Work	4	1	11324.6
工艺品及其他制造业	Art work and Other Manufacturing Sector	3	1	13548.0
电力、热力的生产和供应业	Electricity and Thermal Production and Supply	178	66	3385869.0
#电力生产和电力供应	Electricity Production and Supply	97	33	3163485.2
燃气生产和供应业	Gas Production and Supply	26	4	149656.8
水的生产和供应业	Water Production and Supply	27	17	66500.5

Main Economic Indicators of Industrial Enterprises above Designated Size by Sectors

(10 000 yuan)

增加值 Value-added	工业销售产值（当年价） Sales Value of Industry Products (At Current Prices)	出口交货值 Delivery Value of Industry Export	实收资本 Total Capital Hold	资产合计 Total Assets	流动资产合计 Total Working Capitals	#产成品 Finished Product	固定资产原价 Original Value of Fixed Assets
854683.9	1381438.4		1094707.2	4055999.4	1078231.8	108272.9	1642827.6
9546979.6	11429360.4	340.7	12620911.9	21293199.4	4147493.8	272130.9	26639712.3
9191532.2	10404946.1	17.0	11799259.8	20000936.2	3550669.4	267066.8	25768132.9
404838.2	854648.6		301363.2	1518655.5	735507.4	79450.9	562194.0
344572.6	446079.3		224906.0	1139402.7	334553.6	39065.5	394727.3
54414.2	129981.1	23.8	19444.6	109594.2	57342.0	9350.9	49903.5
16925.2	26471.0	23.8	3977.3	27458.6	14682.1	4017.4	12669.0
398731.8	2183155.4	44954.5	593490.0	2811592.7	1786276.2	463884.9	1008002.0
39185.6	308554.4		59185.5	247834.4	107893.9	6939.3	91221.9
50820.0	342238.2		50542.9	297602.6	162180.8	9952.3	90844.8
89172.8	234809.3	854.6	72480.9	325061.9	179493.6	100460.4	241797.1
215914.2	975718.9	200073.4	391308.2	1759112.4	870225.7	295916.3	920231.2
57587.9	366073.7	169999.3	185953.9	1085720.9	608095.6	259273.5	512769.0
236301.6	619568.8	1296.6	255123.1	898440.3	473495.8	50952.8	405269.1
180016.7	412631.8		196095.5	710590.7	401702.0	35450.0	277853.3
188122.6	235999.5		18741.7	217131.0	131090.0		127180.0
298142.2	1195560.1	31966.6	435591.5	1810392.1	974616.9	127011.8	887244.0
269395.6	1085496.2	15011.4	356018.3	1592783.1	860183.9	105916.6	772137.1
7698.1	33590.4	1335.6	11589.3	43005.0	21821.9	4118.0	24382.9
5930.3	12588.5	671.6	3691.2	23066.7	15852.0	319.6	6999.7
8375.2	46279.0		2860.2	16787.8	11577.9	2785.0	5777.3
6805.2	32721.8		2256.4	12625.4	8522.3	1596.2	4501.2
264.3	722.0		303.8	1543.9	1142.4	245.0	373.0
19260.9	83533.8		20889.3	91883.0	47256.3	13002.5	38559.0
26892.6	91641.2	14859.9	81074.0	349707.1	75009.2	878.9	72352.2
53440.9	183452.0		60012.6	312932.3	150022.2	26962.5	188063.4
25537.7	64568.0		29963.8	116417.4	55975.6	4642.7	89320.7
3270530.3	12392198.0	5697.0	1304125.0	7603188.0	1964720.1	275578.8	7340560.8
165841.1	651451.5	5697.0	254841.2	1071004.4	424623.5	64249.4	438994.0
962675.9	3076593.7	116695.4	1467517.6	6450479.6	1960222.6	155474.8	3487979.0
208327.1	718977.8	51984.0	448165.3	2345457.3	669468.7	36261.7	746659.2
222675.7	418746.6	1120.0	182540.4	958139.3	312899.3	22817.5	700737.0
35215.2	100704.7	4961.3	60519.7	188153.7	104164.6	22471.4	82614.3
195744.4	907416.9	840.5	210102.1	1023026.1	465226.9	77296.5	510098.6
12206.3	67392.6	2923.7	1986.5	35580.3	32574.0	4006.9	3459.0
121274.4	552516.6	7882.0	194863.6	687712.1	395519.1	82167.5	267745.0
624317.1	1978114.2	9607.0	935420.8	4295476.3	1583851.5	95087.4	1873476.6
361427.8	947911.2		510117.5	2473571.3	798268.7	30205.9	1273217.4
760012.0	5455418.7	24958.0	1020681.6	3570922.6	1592584.9	268316.4	2508081.0
164092.9	649906.5		477006.0	928924.3	468133.6	67642.2	399106.6
71468.1	510679.0	3733.3	139300.6	510203.8	300868.8	24861.9	130464.7
36453.3	126405.9	1894.3	45202.6	183714.9	129018.9	19690.2	60524.6
48960.0	204748.1	29609.6	66940.9	290793.8	198565.5	28641.1	91116.6
9519.7	89643.9	242.3	49204.8	148076.2	86627.3	14314.4	54137.8
669650.5	2452033.5	5198.8	544628.4	4471561.3	3024178.4	60147.2	267287.8
53547.8	159278.2	33497.2	41506.0	384410.0	175523.0	8191.5	152206.3
3371.2	11088.0		6500.0	31059.4	24468.9	1963.9	1568.6
3011.3	12163.4		2888.0	8464.2	4338.9	514.0	6179.4
1379323.0	3378539.6		2319442.6	10695433.3	1650627.8	2645.7	10051204.3
1294473.1	3156642.6		2125395.9	9861233.2	1362768.8	1605.2	9293281.8
59125.6	131655.3		81108.4	445408.8	162089.0	712.9	253928.0
32858.9	65772.0		270757.7	603369.9	123743.0		520102.8

13-5 续表

单位: 万元

行　　业	Sector	流动负债合　计 Total Working Liabilities	长期负债合　计 Long-term Liabilities	所有者权益合计 Total Owners' Equities
煤炭开采和洗选业	Mining and Washing of Coal	1439227.3	1038592.0	1535075.2
石油和天然气开采业	Extraction of Petroleum and Natural Gas	2798667.9	4833113.7	13644218.2
#天然原油和天然气开采	Extraction of Ores Crude Oil and Natural Gas Extraction	2228108.0	4639272.4	13133555.8
黑色金属矿采选业	Mining and Processing of Ferrous Metals Ores	754466.1	161749.6	599958.8
有色金属矿采选业	Mining and Processing of Nonferrous Metals Ores	409913.2	104741.6	617147.5
非金属矿采选业	Mining and Processing of Nonmetal Ores	52124.2	4766.0	52234.7
#采　盐	Extraction of Salt	7581.6	2492.7	17384.3
农副食品加工业	Processing of Food from Agricultural Products	1674689.0	156602.1	951131.3
#谷物磨制	Grain Grinding	111351.2	13433.7	121239.7
饲料加工	Fodder Processing	119681.1	27841.7	148644.1
制　糖	Sugar Making	187707.2	3462.3	131676.2
食品制造业	Manufacture of Food	1070004.0	106728.8	552452.9
#罐头制造	Manufacture of can	725308.8	80921.1	253731.7
饮料制造业	Manufacture of Beverage	374167.4	38855.0	318843.5
#酒的制造	Manufacture of Wine	284748.4	29019.6	230248.8
烟草制品业	Manufacture of Tobacco	97962.0		119169.0
纺织业	Manufacture of Textile	849513.9	259979.6	683841.3
#棉、化纤纺织及印染精加工	Cotton, Chemical Fiber, Dyeing, Printing and Processing	754689.0	233284.2	596931.8
毛纺织和染整精加工	Wool Textile, Dyeing and Printing	22834.0	455.6	14192.4
纺织服装、鞋、帽制造业	Manufacture of Textile Wearing Apparel,Footware and Caps	12725.6	3257.0	7084.0
皮革、毛皮、羽毛(绒)及其制品业	Leather, Fur, Feather and Related Products Manufacturing	9906.7	2557.6	3993.4
#皮革鞣制加工	Leather Tanning and Processing	6718.0	2422.6	3484.8
皮革制品制造	Manufacture of Leather Products	1335.3		208.6
木材加工及木、竹、藤、棕、草制品业	Processing of Timber, Wood, Bamboo, Cane, Grass Products	40790.7	11288.8	39658.4
家具制造业	Manufacture of Furniture	34583.8	42424.1	272519.8
造纸及纸制品业	Manufacture of Paper and Paper Products	149163.9	51958.6	106014.3
印刷业和记录媒介的复制	Printing and Copying of Medium for Record	50385.9	10401.0	55616.0
石油加工、炼焦及核燃料加工业	Oil Processing, Coking and Nuclear Fuel Processing	2091382.2	1002835.3	4480509.8
#炼　焦	Coking	467373.0	203834.9	390027.5
化学原料及化学制品制造业	Raw Chemical Material and Chemical Products	2096049.3	1147338.7	3167078.2
#基础化学原料制造	Basic Chemical Material	716788.2	305809.2	1288897.3
肥料制造	Fertilizer Making	324202.1	253795.1	379486.2
医药制造业	Manufacture of Medicine	78878.9	14561.8	94712.9
化学纤维制造业	Manufacture of Chemical Fiber	506949.2	154738.3	343069.2
橡胶制品业	Manufacture of Rubber Products	23352.7	553.9	11673.7
塑料制品业	Manufacture of Plastic Products	321968.7	74884.2	279855.3
非金属矿物制品业	Manufacture of Nonmetal Mineral Products	1362300.2	761207.6	2122082.7
#水泥制造	Manufacture of Cement	733825.5	434378.6	1270226.9
黑色金属冶炼及压延加工业	Smelting and Pressing of Ferrous Metals	1946347.0	148261.5	1474394.5
有色金属冶炼及压延加工业	Smelting and Pressing of Nonferrous Metals	568735.9	68539.3	279309.1
金属制品业	Manufacture of Metal Products	254338.6	25756.5	226784.7
通用设备制造业	Manufacture of General Purpose Machinery	97706.4	5639.3	80283.6
专用设备制造业	Manufacture of Special Purpose Machinery	206513.7	26610.9	57456.8
交通运输设备制造业	Manufacture of Transport Equipment	111341.3	5028.2	31687.8
电气机械及器材制造业	Manufacture of Electric Equipment and Machinery	1740019.2	290740.9	2440421.7
通信设备、计算机及其他电子设备制造业	Telecom Equipment, Computer and Other Electronic Equipment	51014.7	115076.5	218336.7
仪器仪表及文化、办公用机械制造业	Measuring Instruments and Machinery for Cultunal Activify and Office Work	8760.0	1399.1	20900.3
工艺品及其他制造业	Art work and Other Manufacturing Sector	2638.8	815.5	4565.1
电力、热力的生产和供应业	Electricity and Thermal Production and Supply	3272223.2	3726590.2	3551270.2
#电力生产和电力供应	Electricity Production and Supply	2916905.7	3513266.8	3299450.2
燃气生产和供应业	Gas Production and Supply	149942.3	140877.0	148096.3
水的生产和供应业	Water Production and Supply	116555.2	193550.8	282464.5

Continued

(10 000 yuan)

主营业务收入 Revenue from Principal Business	#主营业务成本 Cost of Principal Business	主营业务税金及附加 Taxes and Other Charges on Principal Business	营业利润 Business Profit	利润总额 Total Profit	亏损企业亏损总额 Losses Value of Loss-Suffering Enterprises	利税总额 Total Profits and Taxes	本年应交增值税 Value-added Taxes Payable	全部从业人员年平均人数(人) Annual Average Employed Persons (person)
1414063.0	925300.6	36244.2	170941.9	115863.3	120156.9	275956.5	123849.0	62288
12849615.3	6054783.9	697759.8	4648402.8	4756662.1	147780.4	6561704.8	1107282.9	104407
11885848.9	5013656.2	690729.3	4799347.1	4884928.1		6654207.4	1078550.0	77794
905676.2	568722.0	23233.0	174586.6	185279.7	12354.4	291259.1	82746.4	10726
450426.6	184169.9	6163.3	201404.2	201407.2	3299.1	253902.1	46331.6	9909
133055.7	85587.5	3178.8	13878.4	14130.7	505.5	27467.6	10158.1	3265
25377.4	8837.9	1797.2	3261.8	3357.5		8043.4	2888.7	1193
2273128.7	1938308.8	4050.0	125252.1	137006.6	35297.7	170417.2	29360.6	30683
314287.8	290686.3	390.3	12139.5	13709.0	2811.4	16120.5	2021.2	2802
344298.8	286896.0	416.1	19172.9	21437.5	422.9	25949.7	4096.1	3100
231782.8	163350.1	1407.4	31215.9	32263.8		48541.5	14870.3	6803
995934.4	796039.8	3580.1	30274.2	34293.7	48564.7	66846.5	28972.7	20766
376008.2	306256.1	1107.9	-23646.4	-24921.4	44418.0	-19156.7	4656.8	7613
635594.5	412424.5	42470.2	82551.9	114425.0	6832.4	188292.7	31397.5	11910
404131.9	235546.9	41183.6	54982.5	85939.1	5820.0	153402.0	26279.3	9418
235999.0	88935.0	102779.0	23731.0	23434.0		160237.4	34024.4	885
1259151.4	1077973.0	4395.7	82357.3	109302.4	6867.6	157883.6	44185.5	43341
1146161.7	979908.2	4124.1	79112.1	105547.6	3965.8	150640.6	40968.9	36655
32853.3	30431.4	55.9	-636.6	-579.9	2412.8	1122.7	1646.7	2062
27749.0	24241.6	29.7	1070.9	866.9	547.9	1154.8	258.2	1173
46287.7	41074.6	73.1	4538.6	4701.7	53.9	5618.9	844.1	414
32721.8	27773.4	54.3	4583.4	4739.1		5399.0	605.6	258
730.7	575.5	2.5	-61.3	-53.9	53.9	-19.4	32.0	101
84685.8	74993.9	408.5	6093.1	6749.3	733.3	10160.7	3002.9	2044
103686.7	88219.0	125.4	6352.2	4670.1	30.5	7451.7	2656.2	3009
180667.0	152814.5	1034.4	12238.7	13238.3	3020.8	22212.6	7939.9	6782
65990.8	52237.5	314.5	2590.1	4208.5	217.8	7211.1	2688.1	3293
12786126.6	10057551.0	1553277.8	610214.1	600283.6	80646.6	2567164.7	413603.3	41390
601334.5	491339.9	1473.7	60361.1	61421.0	2691.0	82847.7	19953.0	10423
3037416.0	2292331.5	30419.5	404152.5	431191.7	21871.0	583229.7	121618.5	44548
932507.5	762077.3	4939.7	63601.0	66199.3	17735.5	105434.3	34295.3	16995
414259.7	241295.4	13820.1	79236.2	99370.5	1904.0	134103.3	20912.7	6482
94913.8	60562.5	943.8	7828.1	9985.9	3729.7	17815.8	6886.1	3489
1049285.9	924029.1	2008.1	52572.5	59930.5	16.4	87088.7	25150.1	9051
67636.1	57167.7	971.7	1282.0	1343.7	3.1	4678.3	2362.9	1643
564400.9	482274.3	1685.9	38256.4	38172.5	4301.2	50041.0	10182.6	12548
2023615.7	1574408.9	10111.0	277763.4	306034.6	11399.3	414666.4	98520.8	46029
950871.0	688287.6	6365.1	141199.3	162713.0	4600.3	232365.1	63287.0	24097
5543752.0	5001191.6	8877.4	291951.1	277077.9	7170.7	402370.6	116415.3	30866
670247.5	553721.2	1348.9	71567.4	72567.7	2493.0	88107.4	14190.8	7729
533159.5	480207.5	1967.6	23748.6	22916.1	1911.0	34507.3	9623.6	7870
138354.2	113635.6	1094.9	9578.6	9865.0	274.5	14900.8	3940.9	4349
220776.7	177126.7	682.6	15671.9	16094.4	2168.7	21900.8	5123.8	5476
135442.3	129789.6	202.1	-4861.7	-3322.2	4026.7	-2065.2	1054.9	2727
2524345.7	1781232.4	11827.9	605286.8	609300.7	701.1	692383.5	71254.9	8190
145616.3	105375.0	1123.5	25293.0	28035.2	293.3	31006.8	1848.1	3254
11088.0	7312.5	52.5	2157.4	4409.8	84.2	4784.3	322.0	163
12185.5	10370.5	4.0	1323.5	1323.5	192.9	1943.2	615.7	269
3469963.7	2962309.9	14521.3	273153.1	295945.1	61748.2	460081.2	149614.8	50867
3232066.4	2752915.6	13992.0	271485.6	288730.2	47324.3	448124.4	145402.2	42861
155850.6	92567.8	1881.2	25443.2	25955.4	422.3	31991.3	4154.7	2538
69515.7	55239.9	349.6	-16744.4	-13283.7	14214.5	-10160.1	2774.0	3766

13-6 各地、州、市、县(市)规模以上工业企业主要经济指标

单位: 万元 (2010 年)

地 区	Region	企业单位数(个) Number of Enterprises (unit)	#亏损企业 Loss- Suffering Enterprises	工业总产值(当年价格) Gross Industrial Output Value (At Current Prices)
总 计	**Total**	**2465**	**552**	**53419038.4**
乌鲁木齐市	**Urumqi City**	**463**	**108**	**16747591.7**
天山区	Tianshan District	26	6	1465751.8
沙依巴克区	Shayibak District	36	9	473907.6
新市区	Xinshi District	191	43	5957220.2
水磨沟区	Shui Mogou District	30	7	321069.3
头屯河区	Tou Tunhe District	54	12	4416465.4
达坂城区	Da Bancheng District	10	1	159425.7
米东区	Midong District	107	25	3913629.7
乌鲁木齐县	Urumqi County	9	5	40122.0
克拉玛依市	**Karamay City**	**102**	**15**	**13308538.2**
独山子区	Dushanzi District	15	2	5281812.2
克拉玛依区	Karamay District	68	10	7918267.0
白碱滩区	Bai Jiantan District	17	2	88531.4
乌尔河区	Urhe District	2	1	19927.6
吐鲁番地区	**Turpan Administrative Offices**	**76**	**18**	**1767630.3**
吐鲁番市	Turpan City	29	6	376008.9
鄯善县	Shanshan [Piqan] County	29	5	1109528.2
托克逊县	Toksun County	18	7	282093.2
哈密地区	**Hami [Kumul] Administrative Offices**	**150**	**39**	**1075402.6**
哈密市	Hami [Kumul] City	122	32	947893.4
巴里坤哈萨克自治县	Barkol Kazak Autonomous County	23	6	105626.3
伊吾县	Yiwu [Araturuk] County	5	1	21882.9
昌吉回族自治州	**Changji Hui Autonomous Prefecture**	**412**	**85**	**4032278.1**
昌吉市	Changji City	141	16	1605465.2
阜康市	Fukang City	62	11	800734.3
呼图壁县	Hutubi County	75	12	433828.7
玛纳斯县	Manas County	55	17	716546.5
奇台县	Qitai County	36	12	275136.6
吉木萨尔县	Jimsar County	31	13	163281.5
木垒哈萨克自治县	Mori Kazak Autonomous County	12	4	37285.3
伊犁哈萨克自治州	**Ili Kazak Autonomous Prefecture**	**489**	**117**	**4549161.5**
伊犁州直属县(市)	**Counties (Cities) Direct Under Ili Prefecture**	**269**	**59**	**2356151.1**
伊宁市	Yining [Gulja] City	41	12	284518.8
奎屯市	Kuytun City	48	8	792199.0
伊宁县	Yining [Gulja] County	40	8	306634.5
察布查尔锡伯自治县	Qapqal Xibe Autonomous County	26	6	88638.1
霍城县	Huocheng [Korgas] County	41	11	166753.5
巩留县	Gongliu [Tokkuztara] County	10	4	51753.9
新源县	Xinyuan [Kunes] County	23	4	402226.6
昭苏县	Zhaosu [Mongolkure] County	19	3	101013.5
特克斯县	Tekes County	7		30751.8
尼勒克县	Nilka County	14	3	131661.4
塔城地区	**Tacheng [Tarbagatai] Administrative Offices**	**125**	**32**	**1361348.9**
塔城市	Tacheng [Qoqek] City	13	5	96217.9
乌苏市	Usu City	17	4	406839.4
额敏县	Emin [Dorbiljin] County	15	6	137891.1

Main Economic Indicators of Industrial Enterprises above Designated Size by Prefecture, Autonomous Prefecture, City and County

(10 000 yuan)

增加值 Value-added	工业销售产值(当年价) Sales Value of Industry Products (At Current Prices)	出口交货值 Delivery Value of Industry Export	实收资本 Total Capital Hold	资产合计 Total Assets	流动资产合计 Total Working Capitals	#产成品 Finished Product	固定资产原价 Original Value of Fixed Assets
21201273.9	**52266596.1**	**541927.5**	**25400781.3**	**79119654.3**	**25406382.4**	**2704622.8**	**61112837.7**
5022815.2	**16503268.8**	**224364.7**	**7179726.6**	**22456848.9**	**7373791.9**	**558340.3**	**15571638.8**
420347.1	1460965.3	31283.4	356075.1	3475499.1	654190.7	41001.3	3136696.3
144122.6	454305.2	56384.8	415860.6	2397888.2	560846.4	11647.4	739460.6
2920699.4	5765652.6	97499.3	3339562.9	9226833.4	3827812.8	164671.7	5667164.8
91772.7	314431.5		290152.8	584008.6	178275.1	17099.9	507901.7
512825.3	4415377.7	28078.5	839064.9	2442212.2	885929.0	168982.3	2038584.5
108353.8	156987.6		126282.9	350811.9	87011.5	5040.1	232602.5
795867.3	3895480.2	11118.7	1755527.0	3732144.2	1146601.4	148271.7	3039481.3
28827.1	40068.7		57200.4	247451.3	33125.0	1625.9	209747.1
6422967.6	**13336130.9**	**9624.0**	**7016749.0**	**15712156.3**	**3884819.3**	**152744.0**	**17158096.0**
1509908.5	5294908.4	9607.0	90898.9	4362154.9	818972.8	113472.3	4395594.6
4884537.3	7933999.1	17.0	6910409.5	11215866.6	2974394.5	33288.5	12716889.0
21926.8	87926.9		14180.6	116809.0	81403.5	5119.4	37756.3
6595.1	19296.5		1260.0	17325.8	10048.5	863.8	7856.1
907449.5	**1708324.3**	**3547.8**	**760528.7**	**3758894.5**	**1109111.7**	**126974.6**	**3838266.0**
127786.6	378709.8	3547.8	112862.8	623128.8	318414.6	28380.1	310528.3
641077.0	1084691.4		440802.9	2467143.5	555527.4	72987.1	3191538.6
138586.0	244923.1		206863.0	668622.2	235169.7	25607.4	336199.1
429127.5	**1079730.4**	**2891.0**	**742777.2**	**2667606.3**	**928772.7**	**89117.7**	**1110873.7**
364547.0	956694.3	2891.0	500700.4	1829434.6	797166.3	79057.4	956473.2
53186.0	102158.5		44067.9	217316.4	59559.1	9260.0	134681.2
11394.5	20877.6		198008.9	620855.3	72047.3	800.3	19719.3
1075270.2	**3704933.0**	**64616.1**	**1190790.0**	**6110762.1**	**2672550.7**	**338619.5**	**2496132.5**
429582.3	1552255.5	38730.9	477310.6	2876635.8	1353495.4	118382.1	855394.8
229257.2	736874.1		315079.3	1247835.6	403974.7	34615.5	635411.5
112342.6	414683.4	2646.8	70088.4	374494.0	140379.4	34438.6	181187.0
177406.0	623499.3	9771.9	209045.5	1033908.6	521048.9	55352.1	584814.0
74165.5	216564.2		66383.0	291785.8	145664.3	54998.1	133564.6
43639.0	136474.1	13466.5	46480.2	239562.9	85410.7	35296.0	81885.1
8877.6	24582.4		6403.0	46539.4	22577.3	5537.1	23875.5
1990918.3	**4274104.8**	**56955.6**	**1687184.0**	**7524831.2**	**2734764.5**	**426400.8**	**4510282.8**
969628.8	**2267756.3**	**24773.8**	**1103200.2**	**4551565.1**	**1671455.8**	**223591.3**	**2766583.5**
113610.5	276063.8	2021.5	85987.7	440225.6	128909.9	11983.4	378570.1
316662.3	778587.4	8167.8	176428.7	1101782.2	494206.4	75998.1	647165.6
107352.7	290224.8		135004.2	490224.6	187907.0	28652.2	286372.8
28182.2	88352.3		16074.0	112274.6	50726.6	8042.9	69701.2
48095.2	163495.8	13115.0	69834.2	230630.3	119168.7	33322.0	142127.6
26618.5	48611.7		300179.8	730508.9	108151.2	5111.2	436921.3
203883.9	382841.4	1469.5	210459.9	765872.0	437061.1	38311.3	318886.5
32564.4	83780.2		19878.0	101750.7	73617.1	16865.8	27870.2
12240.4	28608.2		7794.2	30302.9	11899.7	1622.4	18289.7
80418.7	127190.7		81559.5	547993.3	59808.1	3682.0	440678.5
570176.0	**1229217.7**	**32181.8**	**353037.4**	**1439850.0**	**616640.9**	**149421.4**	**875970.1**
30259.0	88428.2	1331.5	25455.6	121857.3	24753.3	3047.9	122153.8
240274.0	358693.3	28697.8	64803.3	358472.2	154078.2	52261.5	190693.3
49623.7	129070.9		42923.7	140276.9	77321.1	33752.2	104381.2

13-6 续表 1

单位: 万元

地　　区	Region	企业单位数（个） Number of Enterprises (unit)	#亏损企业 Loss- Suffering Enterprises	工业总产值（当年价格） Gross Industrial Output Value (At Current Prices)
沙湾县	Shawan County	52	8	416929.7
托里县	Toli County	9	3	160521.6
裕民县	Yumin [Qagantokay] County	2	1	1711.0
和布克赛尔蒙古自治县	Hoboksar Mongol Autonomous County	17	5	141238.2
阿勒泰地区	**Altay Administrative Offices**	**95**	**26**	**831661.5**
阿勒泰市	Altay City	20	8	103465.7
布尔津县	Burqin County	9	2	39344.0
富蕴县	Fuyun [Koktokay] County	20	7	334757.1
福海县	Fuhai [Burultokay] County	16	2	48698.2
哈巴河县	Habahe [Kaba] County	10	3	247058.9
青河县	Qinghe [Qinggil] County	15	1	54474.6
吉木乃县	Jeminay County	5	3	3863.0
博尔塔拉蒙古自治州	**Bortala Mongol Autonomous Prefecture**	**58**	**10**	**332217.7**
博乐市	Bole [Bortala] City	44	8	266457.5
精河县	Jinghe [Jing] County	10	1	61233.6
温泉县	Wenquan [Araxang] County	4	1	4526.6
巴音郭楞蒙古自治州	**Bayangol Mongol Autonomous Prefecture**	**188**	**47**	**5523752.5**
库尔勒市	Korla City	91	19	4423329.2
轮台县	Luntai [Bugur] County	15	2	231443.3
尉犁县	Yuli [Lopnur] County	4	2	6435.1
若羌县	Ruoqiang [Qarkilik] County	7	3	230728.9
且末县	Qiemo [Qarqan] County	2	1	2560.4
焉耆回族自治县	Yanqi Hui Autonomous County	12	3	61954.4
和静县	Hejing County	36	10	494256.3
和硕县	Hoxud County	11	3	34715.9
博湖县	Bohu [Bagrax] County	10	4	38329.0
阿克苏地区	**Aksu Administrative Offices**	**201**	**34**	**2504916.6**
阿克苏市	Aksu City	64	13	607805.6
温宿县	Wensu [Onsu] County	29	2	78657.3
库车县	Kuqa County	42	9	1388099.0
沙雅县	Xayar County	15		103373.6
新和县	Xinhe [Toksu] County	13	1	43335.9
拜城县	Baicheng [Bay] County	23	5	237568.4
乌什县	Wushi [Uxturpan] County	4	1	11942.2

Continued

(10 000 yuan)

增加值 Value-added	工业销售产值(当年价) Sales Value of Industry Products (At Current Prices)	出口交货值 Delivery Value of Industry Export	实收资本 Total Capital Hold	资产合计 Total Assets	流动资产合计 Total Working Capitals	#产成品 Finished Product	固定资产原价 Original Value of Fixed Assets
103208.3	388850.6	2152.5	96727.3	388033.6	197988.8	35493.1	213168.1
84558.9	170361.6		77495.0	242591.4	102257.0	17617.5	105849.1
534.0	1711.0		618.0	1446.0	64.7		958.0
61718.2	92102.1		45014.5	187172.6	60177.8	7249.2	138766.6
451113.5	**777130.8**		**230946.4**	**1533416.1**	**446667.8**	**53388.1**	**867729.2**
38558.9	100587.9		47409.4	222612.8	72624.2	2835.0	180489.4
16675.9	38621.2		26035.2	234821.6	26521.8	2496.9	204976.4
180931.8	295178.6		66774.5	651263.2	203014.4	31082.9	250407.4
16447.2	45801.5		25897.2	79967.0	40697.3	5672.5	58177.4
178040.6	243943.1		51693.5	293060.1	80090.7	9759.2	141789.7
19787.7	49321.1		11844.8	47295.1	22111.2	1245.6	27267.5
671.4	3677.4		1291.8	4396.3	1608.2	296.0	4621.4
108741.7	**322368.7**	**3154.9**	**110766.5**	**593494.6**	**259277.6**	**64573.0**	**387382.8**
92249.0	260276.9	3154.9	92505.5	502205.5	196143.4	54316.2	362792.0
15378.4	55263.7		16897.0	83732.4	58508.3	9895.6	21370.2
1114.3	6828.1		1364.0	7556.7	4625.9	361.2	3220.6
3574503.3	**5434894.5**	**57019.9**	**3954967.9**	**9618213.7**	**2363418.6**	**391095.2**	**9815435.6**
3216637.0	4408665.6	15857.4	3643442.4	7669704.8	1656591.0	260902.8	8567124.6
46934.2	208905.3		52718.7	305483.6	148713.0	19223.1	161771.7
1446.1	3793.3		3934.0	7493.4	3378.8	1253.0	3806.9
136139.0	210090.2		62918.9	589947.0	158097.2	12174.9	434542.2
1103.5	2560.4		2682.7	5958.8	1069.7		8877.9
17716.3	58412.5	13062.2	14251.8	112314.8	64851.2	20717.2	67692.4
141562.7	481832.7	3490.5	147544.3	807136.3	273142.9	48653.6	498432.1
5363.2	29471.7	8076.3	10699.3	62460.8	26794.0	14545.1	27527.8
7601.5	31162.8	16533.5	16775.8	57714.2	30780.8	13625.5	45660.0
744190.1	**2403694.0**	**5873.5**	**873055.5**	**3557601.6**	**1314471.9**	**183340.6**	**2077114.0**
160546.1	588938.4	597.8	226423.4	1292479.9	528296.3	81511.0	686423.1
30870.7	76849.9		32727.0	147616.7	53644.8	5248.4	87975.3
401122.6	1358017.2	1075.7	461916.7	1311324.2	340405.1	44086.3	895857.6
21391.0	70819.4		27263.8	114076.7	74139.9	12373.4	42122.3
12159.0	33682.0		11589.0	64375.4	33924.8	7700.8	22924.8
106379.1	236039.7		95106.8	530204.3	229798.8	21605.4	293616.2
3920.1	8164.2	4200.0	6666.8	26581.6	16484.0	5148.0	11516.5

13-6 续表 2

单位：万元

地　　区	Region	企业单位数（个）Number of Enterprises (unit)	#亏损企业 Loss- Suffering Enterprises	工业总产值（当年价格）Gross Industrial Output Value (At Current Prices)
阿瓦提县	Awat County	10	3	30939.2
柯坪县	Kalpin County	1		3195.4
克孜勒苏柯尔克孜自治州	**Kizilsu Kirgiz Autonomous Prefecture**	**18**	**8**	**104702.4**
阿图什市	Artux City	8	3	47261.2
阿克陶县	Akto County	6	3	31407.2
阿合奇县	Akqi County			
乌恰县	Wuqia [Ulugqat] County	4	2	26034.0
喀什地区	**Kashgar [Kaxgar] Administrative Offices**	**76**	**28**	**502745.5**
喀什市	Kashgar [Kaxgar] City	24	9	292361.5
疏附县	Shufu County	2		4939.3
疏勒县	Shule County	16	5	40347.0
英吉沙县	Yengisar County	4	4	6040.4
泽普县	Zepu [Poskam] County	4	1	13849.3
莎车县	Shache [Yarkant] County	8	6	17719.2
叶城县	Yecheng [Kagilik] County	3	1	32697.3
麦盖提县	Makit County	3		18773.2
岳普湖县	Yopurga County	3		9196.1
伽师县	Jiashi [Payzawat] County	4		43657.6
巴楚县	Bachu [Maralbexi] County	4	2	19514.8
塔什库尔干塔吉克自治县	Taxkorgan Tajik Autonomous County	1		3649.8
和田地区	**Hotan Administrative Offices**	**29**	**9**	**122952.9**
和田市	Hotan City	14	6	62305.2
和田县	Hotan County	6	2	24808.8
墨玉县	Moyu [Karakax] County	4		19280.4
皮山县	Pishan [Guma] County	2		6489.7
洛浦县	Lop County	3	1	10068.8
策勒县	Qira County			
于田县	Yutian [Keriya] County			
民丰县	Minfeng [Niya] County			
自治区直辖县级市	**Municpality Country-LevelCity directly under the Central Government**	**203**	**34**	**2847148.4**
石河子市	Shihezi City	108	27	2002302.1
阿拉尔市	Aral City	46	1	337605.6
图木舒克市	Tumxuk City	13		68879.3
五家渠市	Wujiaqu City	36	6	438361.4

Continued

(10 000 yuan)

增加值 Value-added	工业销售产值(当年价) Sales Value of Industry Products (At Current Prices)	出口交货值 Delivery Value of Industry Export	实收资本 Total Capital Hold	资产合计 Total Assets	流动资产合计 Total Working Capitals	#产成品 Finished Product	固定资产原价 Original Value of Fixed Assets
7571.6	29943.3		10762.0	66490.2	34306.8	4249.2	35553.3
230.0	1239.9		600.0	4452.6	3471.4	1418.1	1124.9
40124.6	**95500.4**		**109677.3**	**265656.0**	**99856.7**	**17152.4**	**132020.3**
11938.7	44808.0		65351.3	146525.2	40375.1	5862.6	95659.4
11893.0	35401.4		43936.0	93069.7	40940.4	11225.4	27128.8
16292.9	15291.0		390.0	26061.1	18541.2	64.4	9232.1
133371.4	**521347.5**	**2446.1**	**146124.1**	**930897.3**	**347569.2**	**27067.9**	**721964.0**
80735.6	308637.6	2266.1	86138.1	562749.0	153089.1	7222.2	572441.1
1630.2	4692.1		2170.6	5686.7	2109.7	152.4	6642.5
6295.9	39925.9		11094.8	42963.2	21667.4	6069.0	19974.7
1133.1	5755.9		1669.9	10797.6	4750.8	1660.3	9923.1
3233.5	13968.5	180.0	3397.0	18533.0	10001.5	2224.2	9304.2
1614.4	18500.3		13389.8	57165.0	33001.9	2181.1	22731.2
5053.1	30786.2		2584.3	27208.3	16721.7	3206.6	13448.3
3194.0	18633.0		7663.6	52828.8	45298.8	826.2	8213.6
827.3	9046.1		1295.0	13345.6	10771.6	1555.8	2769.9
26401.8	45405.2		4251.0	93030.9	37029.1	262.0	30235.4
2275.5	23272.5		12350.0	32097.2	10093.5	1353.9	24144.9
977.1	2724.2		120.0	14492.0	3034.1	354.2	2135.1
50984.8	**119767.3**		**196968.1**	**394412.8**	**87484.4**	**5619.4**	**380462.2**
22933.5	61984.5		36336.0	133760.3	19675.0	2594.6	157155.5
15316.1	23205.8		137137.4	177147.3	35847.5	392.5	163400.5
5584.4	18194.0		17037.0	47129.8	14574.9	1154.9	37407.6
2535.6	6194.0		2030.7	18221.1	6874.3	166.7	12993.2
4615.2	10189.0		4427.0	18154.3	10512.7	1310.7	9505.4
700809.6	**2762531.5**	**111433.9**	**1431466.4**	**5528279.0**	**2230493.2**	**323577.4**	**2913169.0**
528851.7	1999737.2	89429.7	798935.5	3939456.9	1487831.4	147930.0	2175488.8
80034.3	327062.6		105053.3	526553.6	209861.4	39772.7	311855.1
18437.9	62059.1		28841.2	175540.0	73283.9	23323.7	98224.1
73485.7	373672.6	22004.2	498636.4	886728.5	459516.5	112551.0	327601.0

13-6 续表 3

单位：万元

地　　区	Region	流动负债合计 Total Working Liabilities	长期负债合计 Long-term Liabilities	所有者权益合计 Total Owners' Equities
总　计	**Total**	**24836841.6**	**14749769.5**	**38884012.0**
乌鲁木齐市	**Urumqi City**	**6858084.9**	**3135193.8**	**12323431.9**
天山区	Tianshan District	1370097.1	995810.9	1106487.9
沙依巴克区	Shayibak District	562414.9	366895.9	1468452.8
新市区	Xinshi District	2202568.8	936687.6	6057714.5
水磨沟区	Shui Mogou District	150646.2	68301.3	365057.8
头屯河区	Tou Tunhe District	1156286.9	117358.1	1164681.4
达坂城区	Da Bancheng District	78264.7	3109.2	239802.2
米东区	Midong District	1224438.7	636264.4	1860612.6
乌鲁木齐县	Urumqi County	113367.6	10766.4	60622.7
克拉玛依市	**Karamay City**	**2998964.1**	**3207279.7**	**9489274.7**
独山子区	Dushanzi District	971572.2	750926.9	2639108.0
克拉玛依区	Karamay District	1937475.0	2454895.8	6807482.6
白碱滩区	Bai Jiantan District	81023.4	1457.0	34251.8
乌尔河区	Urhe District	8893.5		8432.3
吐鲁番地区	**Turpan Administrative Offices**	**1057668.9**	**868434.4**	**1816698.7**
吐鲁番市	Turpan City	281151.8	77559.0	252398.1
鄯善县	Shanshan [Piqan] County	627291.7	567323.3	1268455.9
托克逊县	Toksun County	149225.4	223552.1	295844.7
哈密地区	**Hami [Kumul] Administrative Offices**	**874662.7**	**693177.4**	**1094400.3**
哈密市	Hami [Kumul] City	667123.4	358195.5	801641.9
巴里坤哈萨克自治县	Barkol Kazak Autonomous County	101270.3	47623.4	65530.7
伊吾县	Yiwu [Araturuk] County	106269.0	287358.5	227227.7
昌吉回族自治州	**Changji Hui Autonomous Prefecture**	**2556471.5**	**762071.5**	**2519542.7**
昌吉市	Changji City	1208702.4	297119.6	1363344.6
阜康市	Fukang City	484609.5	155978.5	523544.7
呼图壁县	Hutubi County	158034.4	39307.9	170403.3
玛纳斯县	Manas County	391281.7	222275.9	257757.3
奇台县	Qitai County	149784.2	28762.9	109258.4
吉木萨尔县	Jimsar County	137420.0	17416.6	84040.8
木垒哈萨克自治县	Mori Kazak Autonomous County	26639.3	1210.1	11193.6
伊犁哈萨克自治州	**Ili Kazak Autonomous Prefecture**	**3155674.4**	**1454093.5**	**2849528.6**
伊犁州直属县(市)	**Counties (Cities) Direct Under Ili Prefecture**	**1726656.7**	**1101234.2**	**1694285.4**
伊宁市	Yining [Gulja] City	179079.3	115314.3	142781.5
奎屯市	Kuytun City	431472.4	298922.6	370253.3
伊宁县	Yining [Gulja] County	203213.3	88547.8	197602.9
察布查尔锡伯自治县	Qapqal Xibe Autonomous County	61152.6	9780.6	40105.3
霍城县	Huocheng [Korgas] County	101875.3	21671.5	100126.2
巩留县	Gongliu [Tokkuztara] County	50846.0	383054.1	296594.1
新源县	Xinyuan [Kunes] County	344413.4	35339.7	375019.2
昭苏县	Zhaosu [Mongolkure] County	69306.5	2743.4	27363.5
特克斯县	Tekes County	12652.0	5292.1	9705.0
尼勒克县	Nilka County	272645.9	140568.1	134734.4
塔城地区	**Tacheng [Tarbagatai] Administrative Offices**	**742065.7**	**96401.8**	**567670.6**
塔城市	Tacheng [Qoqek] City	62412.7	18083.9	38828.5
乌苏市	Usu City	195211.6	20597.8	141874.8
额敏县	Emin [Dorbiljin] County	80756.2	3258.4	54241.9

Continued

(10 000 yuan)

主营业务收入 Revenue from Principal Business	#主营业务成本 Cost of Principal Business	主营业务税金及附加 Taxes and Other Charges on Principal Business	营业利润 Business Profit	利润总额 Total Profit	亏损企业亏损总额 Losses Value of Loss-Suffering Enterprises	利税总额 Total Profits and Taxes	本年应交增值税 Value-added Taxes Payable	全部从业人员年平均人数(人) Annual Average Employed Persons (person)
54926143.4	**39489633.0**	**2569233.6**	**8305982.5**	**8524251.8**	**604203.6**	**13708719.9**	**2615234.5**	**601818**
16789327.5	**12862914.3**	**792742.6**	**1981017.6**	**1978773.0**	**240246.3**	**3297837.5**	**526321.9**	**134080**
1456466.3	1308000.2	4760.3	65593.5	70342.0	39561.0	103999.4	28897.1	16289
483638.1	376024.8	4320.6	81437.1	94986.1	12972.3	120019.1	20712.4	10482
5851781.9	3395649.5	304836.2	1595664.6	1612637.0	21518.2	2221014.8	303541.6	46227
319252.5	266541.7	942.3	18603.5	22380.0	1057.6	31300.1	7977.8	5870
4479039.7	4056854.7	6452.6	216258.3	199280.5	2598.6	300623.6	94890.5	16706
156481.4	97241.8	1694.5	37874.5	39134.3	213.4	55277.8	14449.0	6534
4004087.2	3345927.4	469643.9	-47736.7	-77521.4	161716.7	443974.9	51852.4	31561
38580.4	16674.2	92.2	13322.8	17534.5	608.5	21627.8	4001.1	411
14240541.0	**9987416.3**	**1129284.6**	**2176362.3**	**2300544.0**	**155034.1**	**4332792.4**	**902963.8**	**109753**
5422134.4	4288097.0	566365.5	292939.8	310998.2	3691.8	1113771.2	236407.5	19071
8705044.4	5600622.6	560616.7	1879236.0	1984075.8	151043.4	3207018.2	662325.7	87740
95013.4	83002.8	775.2	4224.9	5508.4	71.1	9606.6	3323.0	2766
18348.8	15693.9	1527.2	-38.4	-38.4	227.8	2396.4	907.6	176
2229284.8	**1593122.9**	**51384.2**	**344192.3**	**328785.2**	**8155.4**	**489513.3**	**109343.9**	**24196**
369772.2	269758.2	1895.9	62474.3	62665.2	1503.3	82788.2	18227.1	7228
1624195.7	1198436.8	45601.0	224305.9	232584.2	2960.6	355414.1	77228.9	10728
235316.9	124927.9	3887.3	57412.1	33535.8	3691.5	51311.0	13887.9	6240
1136484.2	**882124.8**	**15296.8**	**117700.6**	**106944.9**	**32730.9**	**190874.2**	**68632.5**	**32587**
1012608.4	807923.8	13141.0	94885.0	84854.2	30388.9	153990.6	55995.4	26592
103775.5	63214.6	1514.1	18923.5	18554.6	1503.9	30372.4	10303.7	3601
20100.3	10986.4	641.7	3892.1	3536.1	838.1	6511.2	2333.4	2394
3857308.4	**3074743.9**	**24481.2**	**439447.5**	**477934.1**	**34873.2**	**623079.2**	**120663.9**	**57125**
1678266.0	1298933.0	8440.2	262881.6	263576.1	5193.1	318691.7	46675.4	20206
742063.1	593849.6	2855.9	87372.9	85877.0	11297.4	116093.4	27360.5	13230
409616.2	334618.3	1655.5	46544.5	46964.4	9116.5	56802.3	8182.4	6309
675959.2	575236.8	6155.0	21189.5	58963.1	2752.0	89103.4	23985.3	8888
215108.0	158980.1	3525.2	21699.5	22365.4	1109.6	34731.3	8840.7	3089
113060.7	95176.3	1315.5	-1581.2	-1128.0	4784.6	4035.9	3848.4	5003
23235.2	17949.8	533.9	1340.7	1316.1	620.0	3621.2	1771.2	400
4327400.7	**3089513.3**	**155954.6**	**587176.9**	**595801.8**	**37715.0**	**979765.2**	**228008.8**	**83143**
2306178.8	**1676584.3**	**132391.5**	**280965.4**	**283689.7**	**17375.4**	**534682.3**	**118601.1**	**45532**
283462.5	237115.0	2798.8	27356.8	27965.5	9452.0	44339.3	13575.0	7214
783910.7	544092.6	104676.6	62060.3	61115.9	2711.4	216041.2	50248.7	9095
296120.5	228027.6	1489.7	31040.2	33759.6	2189.4	47000.7	11751.4	7726
92650.5	75970.3	650.0	12406.1	12636.5	678.2	17282.1	3995.6	1996
169478.8	132769.0	1349.0	23294.4	22709.0	1086.3	27767.9	3709.9	3874
48069.7	32904.5	139.0	6178.9	5187.1	594.6	6909.7	1583.6	1227
392981.0	264581.7	19690.5	68902.6	70371.9	220.8	110465.1	20402.7	10377
85966.4	71158.2	234.6	11627.2	11606.2	121.1	12831.9	991.1	1522
27880.6	15767.5	53.4	7462.9	7546.7		8263.9	663.8	426
125658.1	74197.9	1309.9	30636.0	30791.3	321.6	43780.5	11679.3	2075
1225674.4	**990006.1**	**7907.5**	**75639.2**	**80785.4**	**13410.0**	**128582.1**	**39889.2**	**24777**
75118.6	71606.5	630.2	-520.3	-404.0	2021.8	1362.1	1135.9	1595
398544.7	294414.1	2806.4	21117.6	19995.5	526.6	36416.7	13614.8	5540
104771.5	87693.2	344.0	3796.0	4828.2	3423.0	9258.3	4086.1	2425

13-6 续表 4

单位：万元

地　　区	Region	流动负债合计 Total Working Liabilities	长期负债合计 Long-term Liabilities	所有者权益合计 Total Owners' Equities
沙湾县	Shawan County	213068.9	12310.6	145549.2
托里县	Toli County	108692.8	19231.8	111245.7
裕民县	Yumin [Qagantokay] County	633.9		426.2
和布克赛尔蒙古自治县	Hoboksar Mongol Autonomous County	81289.6	22919.3	75504.3
阿勒泰地区	**Altay Administrative Offices**	**686952.0**	**256457.5**	**587572.6**
阿勒泰市	Altay City	82216.4	86188.2	53804.3
布尔津县	Burqin County	149084.2	56765.1	28914.7
富蕴县	Fuyun [Koktokay] County	315728.5	63333.8	272200.9
福海县	Fuhai [Burultokay] County	28561.6	19587.5	30907.2
哈巴河县	Habahe [Kaba] County	72471.3	27734.8	191902.5
青河县	Qinghe [Qinggil] County	36516.5	1847.6	8820.7
吉木乃县	Jeminay County	2373.5	1000.5	1022.3
博尔塔拉蒙古自治州	**Bortala Mongol Autonomous Prefecture**	**299371.2**	**135948.4**	**157998.5**
博乐市	Bole [Bortala] City	242203.2	131328.5	128497.3
精河县	Jinghe [Jing] County	54380.4	4537.9	24814.1
温泉县	Wenquan [Araxang] County	2787.6	82.0	4687.1
巴音郭楞蒙古自治州	**Bayangol Mongol Autonomous Prefecture**	**2608318.3**	**2403699.1**	**4578372.9**
库尔勒市	Korla City	1717174.1	1982072.0	3966397.1
轮台县	Luntai [Bugur] County	111105.7	21233.1	151017.8
尉犁县	Yuli [Lopnur] County	3584.7	297.5	3611.2
若羌县	Ruoqiang [Qarkilik] County	225901.0	234840.5	129204.7
且末县	Qiemo [Qarqan] County	1975.7	273.2	3133.7
焉耆回族自治县	Yanqi Hui Autonomous County	61845.7	4901.4	45518.1
和静县	Hejing County	424044.1	145896.5	236188.1
和硕县	Hoxud County	26088.5	9172.0	27200.0
博湖县	Bohu [Bagrax] County	36598.8	5012.9	16102.2
阿克苏地区	**Aksu Administrative Offices**	**1484680.3**	**445986.7**	**1584114.2**
阿克苏市	Aksu City	542298.2	196107.7	530049.3
温宿县	Wensu [Onsu] County	104748.9	7617.8	34316.2
库车县	Kuqa County	431329.7	116435.1	758810.9
沙雅县	Xayar County	67642.5	6628.1	39802.9
新和县	Xinhe [Toksu] County	37416.7	2033.9	23240.3
拜城县	Baicheng [Bay] County	236995.4	116232.4	175551.2
乌什县	Wushi [Uxturpan] County	15459.4	645.0	10477.0

Continued

(10 000 yuan)

主营业务收入 Revenue from Principal Business	#主营业务成本 Cost of Principal Business	主营业务税金及附加 Taxes and Other Charges on Principal Business	营业利润 Business Profit	利润总额 Total Profit	亏损企业亏损总额 Losses Value of Loss-Suffering Enterprises	利税总额 Total Profits and Taxes	本年应交增值税 Value-added Taxes Payable	全部从业人员年平均人数(人) Annual Average Employed Persons (person)
383129.0	336227.3	992.2	32369.0	35284.1	614.3	47134.9	10858.6	6633
175201.0	138216.1	655.0	13548.2	14358.0	2488.5	18072.9	3059.9	4052
1711.0	1711.0	8.4	3.9	3.9	0.2	13.7	1.4	109
87198.6	60137.9	2471.3	5324.8	6719.7	4335.6	16323.5	7132.5	4423
795547.5	**422922.9**	**15655.6**	**230572.3**	**231326.7**	**6929.6**	**316500.8**	**69518.5**	**12834**
104458.8	84455.7	450.7	3730.7	4682.9	1798.4	10980.7	5847.1	2583
37310.8	21411.0	132.6	7146.2	7003.7	271.0	7961.6	825.3	666
305118.2	148083.6	8735.8	79329.9	80611.2	1869.8	123225.5	33878.5	4711
45953.6	35097.0	440.3	7151.2	7196.5	755.2	9263.7	1626.9	1021
245435.0	93119.4	3235.0	127534.0	126160.4	1920.2	154481.7	25086.3	2118
53784.8	37606.5	2642.2	5945.2	5963.4	2.1	10710.1	2104.5	1467
3486.3	3149.7	19.0	-264.9	-291.4	312.9	-122.5	149.9	268
356569.3	**296511.1**	**1907.2**	**35221.1**	**38402.9**	**5796.8**	**51002.9**	**10692.8**	**8566**
288611.8	239267.6	1747.0	27969.8	31027.5	5768.2	42232.5	9458.0	7348
61127.9	51192.9	129.5	6748.6	6762.1	2.0	8090.4	1198.8	1147
6829.6	6050.6	30.7	502.7	613.3	26.6	680.0	36.0	71
5915852.9	**2809832.2**	**219168.3**	**2141494.9**	**2161347.3**	**8799.1**	**2801460.4**	**420944.8**	**45258**
4878816.9	2060803.4	195168.6	2015969.9	2015476.8	4611.3	2585119.2	374473.8	30635
222075.1	185783.1	7363.0	16826.0	17295.1	879.1	28437.3	3779.2	2248
4596.7	3384.3	3.7	871.7	879.7	89.2	929.9	46.5	170
205706.7	95114.6	13125.0	41870.1	59647.5	815.6	90677.0	17904.5	3086
2439.3	2203.8	10.3	-76.9	-9.7	41.7	91.5	90.9	176
57144.7	38828.9	626.9	7767.8	8462.4	234.8	11721.8	2632.5	1157
485970.8	373902.6	2675.1	57516.7	57530.9	932.3	79743.1	19537.1	6194
29690.5	25020.1	142.9	689.3	1848.7	424.2	2774.8	783.2	875
29412.2	24791.4	52.8	60.3	215.9	770.9	1965.8	1697.1	717
2449173.2	**1915308.2**	**156495.2**	**215042.1**	**223810.7**	**23833.3**	**470508.5**	**90202.6**	**33573**
626164.3	522891.4	2936.3	46914.8	52077.9	13099.1	74990.2	19976.0	13648
82263.7	62176.0	1078.2	8593.3	8884.6	554.1	13934.4	3971.6	2841
1372385.5	1047104.5	148179.5	109764.6	111364.6	4445.6	303269.9	43725.8	6990
62253.1	55485.9	89.3	6829.7	9668.9		11858.8	2100.6	1591
31237.6	28067.8	75.0	8235.9	7285.9	9.7	7903.5	542.6	1034
232469.4	163227.7	3325.1	33636.9	32973.5	5291.4	55168.5	18869.9	5870
11358.7	7992.5	583.2	536.0	541.2	74.2	1526.3	401.9	400

13-6 续表 5

单位: 万元

地　区	Region	流动负债合计 Total Working Liabilities	长期负债合计 Long-term Liabilities	所有者权益合计 Total Owners' Equities
阿瓦提县	Awat County	44934.5	286.7	11268.8
柯坪县	Kalpin County	3855.0		597.6
克孜勒苏柯尔克孜自治州	**Kizilsu Kirgiz Autonomous Prefecture**	**136241.5**	**14066.0**	**113927.1**
阿图什市	Artux City	66182.9	13711.1	66169.4
阿克陶县	Akto County	41458.1		50652.0
阿合奇县	Akqi County			
乌恰县	Wuqia [Ulugqat] County	28600.5	354.9	-2894.3
喀什地区	**Kashgar [Kaxgar] Administrative Offices**	**431979.1**	**297104.2**	**200384.7**
喀什市	Kashgar [Kaxgar] City	208466.6	263161.5	90159.7
疏附县	Shufu County	3721.3	1732.6	157.1
疏勒县	Shule County	15861.8	1775.0	25325.8
英吉沙县	Yengisar County	10172.4	319.5	305.7
泽普县	Zepu [Poskam] County	6453.1	5889.4	6190.5
莎车县	Shache [Yarkant] County	31410.6	13121.8	12632.5
叶城县	Yecheng [Kagilik] County	24868.1	-7.4	2296.7
麦盖提县	Makit County	40531.1	592.2	11705.4
岳普湖县	Yopurga County	8974.5	90.0	4281.1
伽师县	Jiashi [Payzawat] County	55713.4	44.6	37212.8
巴楚县	Bachu [Maralbexi] County	10994.3	10000.0	11062.8
塔什库尔干塔吉克自治县	Taxkorgan Tajik Autonomous County	14811.9	385.0	-945.4
和田地区	**Hotan Administrative Offices**	**94993.8**	**74251.5**	**224717.6**
和田市	Hotan City	49073.1	61542.4	22705.1
和田县	Hotan County	19478.9	8023.3	149644.9
墨玉县	Moyu [Karakax] County	8420.6	790.8	37918.4
皮山县	Pishan [Guma] County	9481.1	3895.0	4835.0
洛浦县	Lop County	8540.1		9614.2
策勒县	Qira County			
于田县	Yutian [Keriya] County			
民丰县	Minfeng [Niya] County			
自治区直辖县级市	**Municpality Country-LevelCity directly under the Central Government**	**2279730.9**	**1258463.3**	**1931620.1**
石河子市	Shihezi City	1495359.6	916074.3	1489587.4
阿拉尔市	Aral City	253099.2	122941.8	135400.0
图木舒克市	Tumxuk City	68020.7	72397.7	33502.1
五家渠市	Wujiaqu City	463251.4	147049.5	273130.6

Continued

(10 000 yuan)

主营业务收入 Revenue from Principal Business	#主营业务成本 Cost of Principal Business	主营业务税金及附加 Taxes and Other Charges on Principal Business	营业利润 Business Profit	利润总额 Total Profit	亏损企业亏损总额 Losses Value of Loss-Suffering Enterprises	利税总额 Total Profits and Taxes	本年应交增值税 Value-added Taxes Payable	全部从业人员年平均人数(人) Annual Average Employed Persons (person)
26720.1	24124.6	228.6	482.8	966.0	359.2	1808.8	614.2	1163
4320.8	4237.8		48.1	48.1		48.1		36
107382.1	**85998.1**	**2003.9**	**2276.3**	**1872.6**	**1831.1**	**13394.9**	**9518.4**	**2409**
47340.4	39414.8	311.0	234.0	72.0	1361.6	3123.3	2740.3	1130
35401.4	29610	1107.0	863.6	1056.0	317.8	5645.5	3482.5	844
24640.3	16973.3	585.9	1178.7	744.6	151.7	4626.1	3295.6	435
573964.4	**500460.7**	**2529.3**	**17138.7**	**15891.0**	**23399.4**	**42968.4**	**24548.1**	**13711**
319287.9	290375.6	1607.5	-417.9	-3853.5	18147.2	13333.8	15579.8	6919
4292.2	3439.7	22.8	210.7	251.6		537.2	262.8	341
40159.2	35804.7	236.7	78.6	262.1	851.2	1384.2	885.4	780
5113.0	4790.7	38.5	-1171.2	-1139.4	1139.4	-676.9	424.0	375
13490.8	11745.7	49.6	921.6	944.2	17.6	1480.4	486.6	863
18316.2	17136.1	48.3	-1767.4	-1543.0	1744.6	-1196.8	297.9	971
30008.3	25244.5	88.0	718.1	748.4	303.0	2056.2	1219.8	1009
54346.6	51533.4	1.5	1835.6	2465.0		2529.7	63.2	435
7289.8	6721.5	10.4	140.2	787.3		912.9	115.2	175
61827.8	36264.0	405.1	17543.9	17775.7		22863.9	4683.1	1402
17108.4	16339.3	6.0	-1011.7	-901.5	1196.4	-657.3	238.2	336
2724.2	1065.5	14.9	58.2	94.1		401.1	292.1	105
119091.4	**105777.2**	**781.2**	**-720.4**	**8536.0**	**3046.2**	**17811.7**	**8494.5**	**4380**
60620.6	60192.5	292.2	-5108.2	2102.6	1393.2	5640.1	3245.3	2094
23246.2	17920.3	260.0	1731.3	2067.2	1593.1	5004.1	2676.9	645
17957.2	15152.7	105.8	796.8	1976.0		3484.9	1403.1	332
7309.1	5984.4	70.7	348.1	379.6		945.9	495.6	553
9958.3	6527.3	52.5	1511.6	2010.6	59.9	2736.7	673.6	756
2823763.5	**2285910.0**	**17204.5**	**249632.6**	**285608.3**	**28742.8**	**397711.3**	**94898.5**	**53037**
2073287.6	1653090.1	14348.2	203739.6	237524.9	23979.4	323930.6	72057.5	39647
333276.0	279624.2	1630.3	28985.0	29024.9	1042.4	40587.6	9932.4	4957
55155.7	49410.0	145.1	4691.2	4714.2		6153.7	1294.4	1551
362044.2	303785.7	1080.9	12216.8	14344.3	3721.0	27039.4	11614.2	6882

13-7 规模以上工业企业主要经济效益指标

单位: % (2010 年)

项　　目	Item	产值利税率 Ratio of Profits and Taxes to Industrial Output Value
总　　计	**Total**	**25.7**
按登记注册类型分	**Grouped by Registry Type**	
内资企业	Domestic Funded Enterprises	25.9
国有企业	State-owned Enterprises	7.7
#中央企业	Central Enterprises	6.2
地方企业	Local Enterprises	12.3
#自治区属企业	Autonomous	13.7
地区(州、市)属企业	Prefecture or City	-5.7
县(市)属企业	County or City	9.7
集体企业	Collective-owned Enterprises	10.2
#自治区属企业	Autonomous	8.7
地区(州、市)属企业	Prefecture or City	8.7
县(市)属企业	County or City	23.0
镇属企业	Town	45.0
股份合作企业	Share-holding Cooperative Enterprises	13.1
联营企业	Joint Ownership Enterprises	20.5
#国有联营企业	State Joint Ownership Enterprises	28.6
国有与集体联营企业	Joint State-collective Enterprises	6.0
其他联营企业	Other Joint Ownership Enterprises	14.7
有限责任公司	Limited Liability Corporations	16.0
#国有独资公司	State Sole funded Corporations	21.5
其他有限责任公司	Other Limited Liability Corporations	14.9
股份有限公司	Share-holding Corporations Ltd.	37.4
私营企业	Private Enterprises	16.2
#私营独资企业	Private-funded Enterprises	18.4
私营合伙企业	Private Partnership Enterprises	10.2
私营有限责任公司	Private Limited Liability Corporations	12.0
私营股份有限公司	Private Share-holding Corporations Ltd.	24.4
港、澳、台商投资企业	Enterprises with Funds from Hong Kong, Macao and Taiwan	11.6
外商投资企业	Foreign Funded Enterprises	15.5
在总计中: 国有控股企业	Of the Total: State-owned and State-holding Enterprises	29.7
在总计中: 农村工业	Of the Total: Rural Industry	15.3
按轻、重工业分	**Grouped by Light & Heavy Industry**	
轻工业	Light Industry	12.4
以农产品为原料	Using Farm Produces as Raw Materials	12.7
以非农产品为原料	Using Non-Farm Produces as Raw Materials	6.0
重工业	Heavy Industry	27.8
采掘工业	Mining and Quarrying	51.3
原料工业	Raw Materials Industry	16.2
加工工业	Manufacturing Industry	20.5
按企业规模分	**Grouped by Size of Enterprises**	
大型企业	Large Enterprises	33.1
中型企业	Medium-sized Enterprises	19.1
小型企业	Small Enterprises	13.4

Main Indicators on Economic Efficiency of Industrial Enterprises above Designated Size

(%)

总资产贡献率 Ratio of Total Assets to Industrial Output Value	资本保值增值率 Ratio of Capital-hold and Rise	资产负债率 Assets Liability Ratio	流动资产周转次数(次/年) Number of Times of Annual TurnoverWorking Capitals (times/year)	成本费用利润率 Ratio of Profits to Industrial Cost	全员劳动生产率 Overall Labour Productivity
18.2	**131.6**	**50.8**	**2.2**	**19.3**	**35.2**
18.3	131.9	50.6	2.2	19.5	35.7
4.9	108.9	63.8	1.8	0.8	21.4
4.7	99.4	65.1	2.2	-1.3	19.6
5.5	130.8	61.0	1.2	7.7	18.1
4.7	138.5	54.4	1.3	8.4	19.5
-1.3	129.7	82.1	1.0	-7.7	10.0
4.5	107.7	69.3	1.2	6.1	11.4
17.6	125.7	55.4	2.5	5.1	12.7
16.3	106.6	57.5	2.4	3.7	17.4
13.5	108.3	25.9	1.8	4.6	6.9
23.1	113.4	38.4	1.7	15.5	16.3
104.8	117.3	64.0	3.5	34.2	31.8
13.6	369.9	63.1	1.5	13.6	13.3
12.0	140.1	81.4	1.5	10.8	11.2
13.7	147.5	75.0	1.1	20.8	18.6
1.7	41.0	96.6	1.7	-7.4	11.9
17.1	200.7	85.2	2.1	5.9	7.1
11.3	131.4	61.5	1.7	11.4	19.5
13.7	132.2	55.5	2.3	11.8	22.9
10.7	131.2	62.8	1.6	11.4	18.8
27.3	131.1	39.1	3.3	30.0	79.2
13.5	158.3	55.2	1.4	14.7	16.7
17.9	177.0	59.9	2.0	17.6	14.5
16.4	130.8	48.6	2.5	7.7	12.3
11.3	125.1	60.8	1.7	9.5	12.0
16.5	222.9	46.4	1.0	26.9	53.5
8.6	146.8	58.2	1.3	9.0	13.5
13.5	104.7	58.7	1.7	11.4	22.9
20.8	126.6	48.1	2.9	21.9	48.2
11.3	125.7	50.7	1.3	11.8	11.2
10.1	129.5	62.3	1.4	7.8	12.3
10.7	132.6	63.1	1.4	8.1	12.6
3.0	107.4	53.0	1.1	1.7	9.3
19.4	131.9	49.1	2.4	21.3	42.4
26.8	129.0	41.5	2.5	55.7	58.8
14.8	129.7	55.1	3.2	7.5	34.5
13.0	150.5	52.0	1.1	19.8	21.1
24.7	125.7	42.4	3.4	25.8	64.6
13.1	163.5	57.2	1.5	13.8	21.6
9.5	120.1	62.4	1.5	10.4	15.2

13-8 分行业规模以上工业企业主要经济效益指标

单位: % (2010 年)

行　　业	Sector	产值利税率 Ratio of Profits and Taxes to Industrial Output Value
煤炭开采和洗选业	Mining and Washing of Coal	18.3
石油和天然气开采业	Extraction of Petroleum and Natural Gas	57.3
#天然原油和天然气开采	Extraction of Ores Crude Oil and Natural Gas Extraction	63.9
黑色金属矿采选业	Mining and Processing of Ferrous Metals Ores	33.2
有色金属矿采选业	Mining and Processing of Nonferrous Metals Ores	55.2
非金属矿采选业	Mining and Processing of Nonmetal Ores	19.2
#采　盐	Extraction of Salt	24.6
农副食品加工业	Processing of Food from Agricultural Products	7.2
#谷物磨制	Grain Grinding	5.1
饲料加工	Fodder Processing	7.5
制　糖	Sugar Making	19.9
食品制造业	Manufacture of Food	6.1
#罐头制造	Manufacture of can	-4.0
饮料制造业	Manufacture of Beverage	29.1
#酒的制造	Manufacture of Wine	35.5
烟草制品业	Manufacture of Tobacco	67.8
纺织业	Manufacture of Textile	13.1
#棉、化纤纺织及印染精加工	Cotton, Chemical Fiber, Dyeing, Printing and Processing	13.9
毛纺织和染整精加工	Wool Textile, Dyeing and Printing	3.5
纺织服装、鞋、帽制造业	Manufacture of Textile Wearing Apparel,Footware and Caps	8.3
皮革、毛皮、羽毛(绒)及其制品业	Leather, Fur, Feather and Related Products Manufacturing	11.7
#皮革鞣制加工	Leather Tanning and Processing	15.7
皮革制品制造	Manufacture of Leather Products	-2.6
木材加工及木、竹、藤、棕、草制品业	Processing of Timber, Wood, Bamboo, Cane, Grass Products	10.8
家具制造业	Manufacture of Furniture	7.9
造纸及纸制品业	Manufacture of Paper and Paper Products	11.4
印刷业和记录媒介的复制	Printing and Copying of Medium for Record	11.1
石油加工、炼焦及核燃料加工业	Oil Processing, Coking and Nuclear Fuel Processing	20.6
#炼　焦	Coking	11.6
化学原料及化学制品制造业	Raw Chemical Material and Chemical Products	18.4
#基础化学原料制造	Basic Chemical Material	14.5
肥料制造	Fertilizer Making	28.8
医药制造业	Manufacture of Medicine	15.7
化学纤维制造业	Manufacture of Chemical Fiber	9.2
橡胶制品业	Manufacture of Rubber Products	7.0
塑料制品业	Manufacture of Plastic Products	8.8
非金属矿物制品业	Manufacture of Nonmetal Mineral Products	20.2
#水泥制造	Manufacture of Cement	24.2
黑色金属冶炼及压延加工业	Smelting and Pressing of Ferrous Metals	7.3
有色金属冶炼及压延加工业	Smelting and Pressing of Nonferrous Metals	12.7
金属制品业	Manufacture of Metal Products	7.1
通用设备制造业	Manufacture of General Purpose Machinery	11.7
专用设备制造业	Manufacture of Special Purpose Machinery	10.5
交通运输设备制造业	Manufacture of Transport Equipment	-2.2
电气机械及器材制造业	Manufacture of Electric Equipment and Machinery	26.6
通信设备、计算机及其他电子设备制造业	Telecom Equipment, Computer and Other Electronic Equipment	19.8
仪器仪表及文化、办公用机械制造业	Measuring Instruments and Machinery for Cultunal Activify and OfficeWork	42.3
工艺品及其他制造业	Art work and Other Manufacturing Sector	14.3
电力、热力的生产和供应业	Electricity and Thermal Production and Supply	13.6
#电力生产和电力供应	Electricity Production and Supply	14.2
燃气生产和供应业	Gas Production and Supply	21.4
水的生产和供应业	Water Production and Supply	-15.3

Main Indicators on Economic Efficiency of Industrial Enterprises above Designated Size by Sectors

(%)

总资产贡献率 Ratio of Total Assets to Industrial Output Value	资本保值增值率 Ratio of Capital-hold and Rise	资产负债率 Assets Liability Ratio	流动资产周转次数(次/年) Number of Times of Annual TurnoverWorking Capitals (times/year)	成本费用利润率 Ratio of Profits to Industrial Cost	全员劳动生产率 Overall Labour Productivity
7.4	115.0	62.0	1.3	9.7	13.7
31.2	130.3	35.9	3.1	66.0	91.4
33.5	129.9	34.3	3.4	80.1	118.2
20.3	133.4	60.5	1.2	26.1	37.7
22.8	129.0	45.7	1.4	81.6	34.8
25.7	128.1	52.3	2.3	12.0	16.7
29.9	145.5	36.7	1.7	16.4	14.2
7.4	149.1	65.9	1.3	6.3	13.0
7.5	146.5	51.1	2.9	4.5	14.0
10.3	142.7	49.5	2.1	6.6	16.4
15.7	126.1	59.5	1.3	15.9	13.1
5.2	97.6	68.2	1.1	3.6	10.4
0.0	83.1	76.1	0.6	-6.5	7.6
22.0	142.0	64.4	1.3	22.6	19.8
22.8	164.1	67.4	1.0	28.4	19.1
73.6	106.9	45.1	1.8	21.4	212.6
9.8	138.3	62.0	1.3	9.3	6.9
10.6	142.2	62.3	1.3	9.9	7.3
2.9	99.2	62.5	1.5	-1.7	3.7
5.8	114.0	69.3	1.8	3.3	5.1
33.5	112.1	76.2	4.0	11.3	20.2
42.8	167.4	72.4	3.8	16.9	26.4
-1.3	79.5	86.5	0.6	-6.8	2.6
12.1	155.1	56.8	1.8	8.5	9.4
2.8	181.2	22.0	1.4	4.7	8.9
8.1	144.6	66.1	1.2	7.7	7.9
6.8	110.4	52.2	1.2	6.6	7.8
34.1	110.0	41.0	6.5	5.7	79.0
9.2	125.3	63.5	1.4	11.2	15.9
10.5	160.5	50.8	1.6	16.1	21.6
5.6	166.4	45.0	1.4	7.2	12.3
15.8	124.0	60.3	1.3	30.6	34.4
10.5	132.5	49.7	0.9	11.2	10.1
10.4	138.4	65.9	2.3	5.9	21.6
14.3	-30.0	67.2	2.1	2.1	7.4
8.1	130.9	59.1	1.4	7.2	9.7
10.8	159.3	50.6	1.3	16.7	13.6
10.5	179.5	48.6	1.2	19.5	15.0
12.5	113.1	58.7	3.5	5.3	24.6
10.1	140.5	69.9	1.4	12.1	21.2
7.5	132.9	55.5	1.8	4.5	9.1
8.4	120.1	56.3	1.1	7.6	8.4
8.0	126.1	80.2	1.1	7.8	8.9
-0.7	150.7	78.6	1.6	-2.3	3.5
15.8	237.0	45.4	0.8	30.6	81.8
8.4	112.7	43.2	0.8	23.5	16.5
15.6	117.6	32.7	0.5	47.4	20.7
23.4	79.3	40.8	2.8	12.2	11.2
6.1	130.9	66.8	2.1	8.9	27.1
6.5	132.7	66.5	2.4	9.4	30.2
8.8	127.1	66.6	1.0	19.6	23.3
-0.9	103.5	52.9	0.6	-15.8	8.7

13-9 各地、州、市、县(市)规模以上工业企业主要经济效益指标

单位: %　　(2010 年)

地　　区	Region	产值利税率 Ratio of Profits and Taxes to Industrial Output Value
总　计	**Total**	**25.7**
乌鲁木齐市	**Urumqi City**	**19.7**
天山区	Tianshan District	7.1
沙依巴克区	Shayibak District	25.3
新市区	Xinshi District	37.3
水磨沟区	Shui Mogou District	9.8
头屯河区	Tou Tunhe District	6.8
达坂城区	Da Bancheng District	34.7
米东区	Midong District	11.3
乌鲁木齐县	Urumqi County	53.9
克拉玛依市	**Karamay City**	**32.6**
独山子区	Dushanzi District	21.1
克拉玛依区	Karamay District	40.5
白碱滩区	Bai Jiantan District	10.9
乌尔河区	Urhe District	12.0
吐鲁番地区	**Turpan Administrative Offices**	**27.7**
吐鲁番市	Turpan City	22.0
鄯善县	Shanshan [Piqan] County	32.0
托克逊县	Toksun County	18.2
哈密地区	**Hami [Kumul] Administrative Offices**	**17.8**
哈密市	Hami [Kumul] City	16.3
巴里坤哈萨克自治县	Barkol Kazak Autonomous County	28.8
伊吾县	Yiwu [Araturuk] County	29.8
昌吉回族自治州	**Changji Hui Autonomous Prefecture**	**15.5**
昌吉市	Changji City	19.9
阜康市	Fukang City	14.5
呼图壁县	Hutubi County	13.1
玛纳斯县	Manas County	12.4
奇台县	Qitai County	12.6
吉木萨尔县	Jimsar County	2.5
木垒哈萨克自治县	Mori Kazak Autonomous County	9.7
伊犁哈萨克自治州	**Ili Kazak Autonomous Prefecture**	**21.5**
伊犁州直属县(市)	**Counties (Cities) Direct Under Ili Prefecture**	**22.7**
伊宁市	Yining [Gulja] City	15.6
奎屯市	Kuytun City	27.3
伊宁县	Yining [Gulja] County	15.3
察布查尔锡伯自治县	Qapqal Xibe Autonomous County	19.5
霍城县	Huocheng [Korgas] County	16.7
巩留县	Gongliu [Tokkuztara] County	13.4
新源县	Xinyuan [Kunes] County	27.5
昭苏县	Zhaosu [Mongolkure] County	12.7
特克斯县	Tekes County	26.9
尼勒克县	Nilka County	33.3
塔城地区	**Tacheng [Tarbagatai] Administrative Offices**	**9.5**
塔城市	Tacheng [Qoqek] City	1.4
乌苏市	Usu City	9.0
额敏县	Emin [Dorbiljin] County	6.7

Main Indicators on Economic Benefit of Industrial Enterprises above Designated Size by Prefecture, Autonomous Prefecture, City and County

(%)

总资产贡献率 Ratio of Total Assets to Industrial Output Value	资本保值增值率 Ratio of Capital-hold and Rise	资产负债率 Assets Liability Ratio	流动资产周转次数(次/年) Number of Times of Annual TurnoverWorking Capitals (times/year)	成本费用利润率 Ratio of Profits to Industrial Cost	全员劳动生产率 Overall Labour Productivity
18.2	**131.6**	**50.8**	**2.2**	**19.3**	**35.2**
15.6	**143.3**	**45.1**	**2.3**	**13.9**	**37.5**
4.6	118.6	68.2	2.2	5.0	25.8
5.7	180.2	38.8	0.9	19.3	13.7
24.8	172.0	34.3	1.5	39.9	63.2
7.7	111.7	37.5	1.8	7.5	15.6
13.8	111.0	52.3	5.1	4.7	30.7
15.8	137.6	31.6	1.8	33.9	16.6
12.2	138.6	50.1	3.5	-2.2	25.2
11.7	122.9	75.5	1.2	69.2	70.1
27.9	**111.2**	**39.6**	**3.7**	**21.3**	**58.5**
25.9	101.6	39.5	6.6	6.8	79.2
28.9	115.3	39.3	2.9	32.5	55.7
9.0	148.5	70.7	1.2	6.0	7.9
14.0	118.5	51.3	1.8	-0.2	37.5
13.8	**175.1**	**51.6**	**2.0**	**17.6**	**37.5**
14.8	138.3	59.5	1.2	19.9	17.7
14.8	196.3	48.5	2.9	16.9	59.8
9.2	141.7	55.8	1.0	19.3	22.2
8.0	**132.1**	**59.0**	**1.2**	**10.4**	**13.2**
9.6	141.1	56.2	1.3	9.2	13.7
14.9	202.2	69.8	1.7	22.2	14.8
1.0	99.7	63.4	0.3	21.6	4.8
11.3	**164.9**	**58.7**	**1.4**	**13.8**	**18.8**
11.8	176.6	52.6	1.2	17.9	21.3
10.5	157.5	58.0	1.8	13.2	17.3
16.5	151.0	53.6	2.9	12.9	17.8
10.6	127.0	75.0	1.3	9.1	20.0
12.8	161.5	61.9	1.5	11.9	24.0
2.6	303.9	64.9	1.3	-1.0	8.7
7.9	93.7	76.0	1.0	5.2	22.2
14.2	**130.4**	**61.9**	**1.6**	**16.5**	**23.9**
12.9	**126.1**	**62.8**	**1.4**	**14.7**	**21.3**
11.6	163.6	67.6	2.2	10.3	15.7
21.1	125.2	66.4	1.6	9.8	34.8
10.7	131.1	59.7	1.6	12.6	13.9
16.4	183.1	64.3	1.8	15.5	14.1
13.0	120.9	56.6	1.4	15.4	12.4
1.5	118.8	59.4	0.4	11.9	21.7
14.8	115.6	51.0	0.9	23.1	19.6
14.5	116.6	73.1	1.2	15.2	21.4
29.6	123.3	67.0	2.3	40.7	28.7
9.8	135.7	75.4	2.1	32.4	38.8
10.1	**160.6**	**59.6**	**2.0**	**7.2**	**23.0**
2.3	163.3	66.7	3.0	-0.5	19.0
11.3	279.6	60.4	2.6	6.3	43.4
7.0	96.4	61.0	1.4	4.8	20.5

13-9 续表 1

单位: %

地区	Region	产值利税率 Ratio of Profits and Taxes to Industrial Output Value
沙湾县	Shawan County	11.3
托里县	Toli County	11.3
裕民县	Yumin [Qagantokay] County	0.8
和布克赛尔蒙古自治县	Hoboksar Mongol Autonomous County	11.6
阿勒泰地区	**Altay Administrative Offices**	**38.1**
阿勒泰市	Altay City	10.6
布尔津县	Burqin County	20.2
富蕴县	Fuyun [Koktokay] County	36.8
福海县	Fuhai [Burultokay] County	19.0
哈巴河县	Habahe [Kaba] County	62.5
青河县	Qinghe [Qinggil] County	19.7
吉木乃县	Jeminay County	-3.2
博尔塔拉蒙古自治州	**Bortala Mongol Autonomous Prefecture**	**15.4**
博乐市	Bole [Bortala] City	15.9
精河县	Jinghe [Jing] County	13.2
温泉县	Wenquan [Araxang] County	15.0
巴音郭楞蒙古自治州	**Bayangol Mongol Autonomous Prefecture**	**50.7**
库尔勒市	Korla City	58.4
轮台县	Luntai [Bugur] County	12.3
尉犁县	Yuli [Lopnur] County	14.5
若羌县	Ruoqiang [Qarkilik] County	39.3
且末县	Qiemo [Qarqan] County	3.6
焉耆回族自治县	Yanqi Hui Autonomous County	18.9
和静县	Hejing County	16.1
和硕县	Hoxud County	8.0
博湖县	Bohu [Bagrax] County	5.1
阿克苏地区	**Aksu Administrative Offices**	**18.8**
阿克苏市	Aksu City	12.3
温宿县	Wensu [Onsu] County	17.7
库车县	Kuqa County	21.9
沙雅县	Xayar County	11.5
新和县	Xinhe [Toksu] County	18.2
拜城县	Baicheng [Bay] County	23.2
乌什县	Wushi [Uxturpan] County	12.8

Continued

(%)

总资产贡献率 Ratio of Total Assets to Industrial Output Value	资本保值增值率 Ratio of Capital-hold and Rise	资产负债率 Assets Liability Ratio	流动资产周转次数(次/年) Number of Times of Annual TurnoverWorking Capitals (times/year)	成本费用利润率 Ratio of Profits to Industrial Cost	全员劳动生产率 Overall Labour Productivity
13.5	172.1	59.7	1.9	9.1	15.6
8.4	134.8	54.1	1.7	9.0	20.9
1.0	115.2	70.5	26.5	0.2	4.9
10.0	136.5	59.4	1.5	8.4	14.0
21.8	**120.2**	**61.7**	**1.8**	**41.8**	**35.1**
6.0	128.4	75.8	1.4	4.7	14.9
5.6	359.8	87.7	1.4	22.4	25.0
19.9	98.4	58.2	1.5	37.0	38.4
12.2	127.0	61.3	1.1	18.4	16.1
53.5	145.2	34.5	3.1	109.8	84.1
23.8	215.9	81.4	2.4	12.8	13.5
-1.2	69.9	76.8	2.2	-7.7	2.5
10.0	**151.7**	**73.4**	**1.4**	**11.8**	**12.7**
9.8	167.5	74.4	1.5	11.8	12.6
11.4	107.2	70.4	1.0	12.2	13.4
9.8	109.3	38.0	1.5	9.7	15.7
29.8	**122.5**	**52.4**	**2.5**	**62.7**	**79.0**
34.2	122.7	48.3	3.0	78.9	105.0
10.3	127.6	50.0	1.5	8.6	20.9
13.3	9.2	51.8	1.4	23.2	8.5
17.7	130.6	78.1	1.3	39.4	44.1
1.9	216.7	47.4	2.3	-0.4	6.3
11.3	139.6	59.5	0.9	17.2	15.3
11.3	126.3	70.7	1.8	13.4	22.9
5.2	191.3	56.5	1.1	6.4	6.1
4.5	143.3	72.1	1.0	0.7	10.6
14.4	**145.3**	**55.4**	**1.9**	**10.6**	**22.2**
7.0	167.3	59.0	1.2	8.8	11.8
11.3	183.4	76.8	1.5	11.8	10.9
24.1	138.8	42.0	4.0	10.0	57.4
12.0	128.2	65.1	0.8	15.9	13.4
13.2	138.3	61.3	0.9	23.9	11.8
11.8	122.3	66.8	1.0	16.6	18.1
6.8	140.0	60.6	0.7	5.2	9.8

13-9 续表 2

单位: %

地　区	Region	产值利税率 Ratio of Profits and Taxes to Industrial Output Value
阿瓦提县	Awat County	5.9
柯坪县	Kalpin County	1.5
克孜勒苏柯尔克孜自治州	**Kizilsu Kirgiz Autonomous Prefecture**	**12.8**
阿图什市	Artux City	6.6
阿克陶县	Akto County	18.0
阿合奇县	Akqi County	
乌恰县	Wuqia [Ulugqat] County	17.8
喀什地区	**Kashgar [Kaxgar] Administrative Offices**	**8.6**
喀什市	Kashgar [Kaxgar] City	4.6
疏附县	Shufu County	10.9
疏勒县	Shule County	3.4
英吉沙县	Yengisar County	-11.2
泽普县	Zepu [Poskam] County	10.7
莎车县	Shache [Yarkant] County	-6.8
叶城县	Yecheng [Kagilik] County	6.3
麦盖提县	Makit County	13.5
岳普湖县	Yopurga County	9.9
伽师县	Jiashi [Payzawat] County	52.4
巴楚县	Bachu [Maralbexi] County	-3.4
塔什库尔干塔吉克自治县	Taxkorgan Tajik Autonomous County	11.0
和田地区	**Hotan Administrative Offices**	**14.5**
和田市	Hotan City	9.1
和田县	Hotan County	20.2
墨玉县	Moyu [Karakax] County	18.1
皮山县	Pishan [Guma] County	14.6
洛浦县	Lop County	27.2
策勒县	Qira County	
于田县	Yutian [Keriya] County	
民丰县	Minfeng [Niya] County	
自治区直辖县级市	**Municpality Country-LevelCity directly under the Central Government**	**14.0**
石河子市	Shihezi City	16.2
阿拉尔市	Aral City	12.0
图木舒克市	Tumxuk City	8.9
五家渠市	Wujiaqu City	6.2

Continued

(%)

总资产贡献率 Ratio of Total Assets to Industrial Output Value	资本保值增值率 Ratio of Capital-hold and Rise	资产负债率 Assets Liability Ratio	流动资产周转次数(次/年) Number of Times of Annual TurnoverWorking Capitals (times/year)	成本费用利润率 Ratio of Profits to Industrial Cost	全员劳动生产率 Overall Labour Productivity
4.7	137.4	83.1	0.8	3.4	6.5
2.9	109.8	86.6	1.2	1.1	6.4
5.9	**158.7**	**56.6**	**1.1**	**1.8**	**16.7**
3.3	165.5	54.6	1.2	0.2	10.6
6.6	154.1	44.6	0.9	3.1	14.1
17.9	—	111.1	1.3	3.3	37.5
6.5	**121.6**	**78.4**	**1.7**	**2.9**	**9.7**
4.8	130.7	83.8	2.1	-1.2	11.7
11.1	—	97.2	2.0	6.2	4.8
4.1	177.4	41.1	1.9	0.7	8.1
-5.1	21.6	97.2	1.1	-18.4	3.0
8.4	195.7	66.6	1.4	7.4	3.7
-1.0	92.1	77.9	0.6	-7.7	1.7
10.6	17.1	91.6	1.8	2.6	5.0
5.4	136.8	77.8	1.2	4.7	7.3
7.4	147.4	67.9	0.7	11.0	4.7
25.0	114.0	60.0	1.7	42.3	18.8
0.6	180.5	65.5	1.7	-4.7	6.8
2.8	—	106.5	0.9	3.5	9.3
5.3	**127.1**	**43.0**	**1.4**	**7.2**	**11.6**
6.1	127.2	83.0	3.1	3.2	11.0
2.9	125.6	15.5	0.7	9.7	23.7
8.2	120.5	19.5	1.2	11.6	16.8
5.5	244.5	73.5	1.1	5.2	4.6
15.1	151.7	47.0	1.0	23.9	6.1
8.8	**130.2**	**64.8**	**1.3**	**11.2**	**13.2**
9.9	125.8	61.9	1.4	12.8	13.3
9.7	146.0	73.9	1.6	9.4	16.1
4.4	245.4	80.9	0.8	8.8	11.9
4.1	141.2	68.9	0.8	4.2	10.7

13-10 国有控股工业企业主要经济指标

单位: 万元 (2010 年)

项 目	Item	企业单位数(个) Number of Enterprises (unit)	#亏损企业 Loss- Suffering Enterprises	工业总产值(当年价格) Gross Industrial Output Value (At Current Prices)
总 计	**Total**	**574**	**132**	**37703302.8**
按登记注册类型分	**Grouped by Registry Type**			
内资企业	DomesticFunded Enterprises	570	132	37645836.0
国有企业	State-owned Enterprises	170	54	3669961.0
#中央企业	Central Enterprises	68	15	2737465.8
地方企业	Local Enterprises	102	39	932495.2
#自治区属企业	Autonomous	33	11	434810.3
地区(州、市)属企业	Prefecture or City	15	6	147865.3
县(市)属企业	County or City	46	21	156436.0
股份合作企业	Share-holding Cooperative Enterprises	4		26928.3
联营企业	Joint Ownership Enterprises	6	3	20419.7
#国有联营企业	State Joint Enterprises Ownership	5	2	16844.2
国有与集体联营企业	Joint State-collective OwnershipEnterprises	1	1	3575.5
有限责任公司	Limited Liability Corporations	329	63	9039711.6
#国有独资公司	Sole State-funded Corporations	59	14	2493764.6
其他有限责任公司	Other Limited Liability Corporations	270	49	6545947.0
股份有限公司	Share-holding Corporations Ltd.	61	12	24888815.4
外商投资企业	Foreign Funded Enterprises	4		57466.8
在总计中: 国有控股企业	Of the Total : State-owned and State-holding Enterprises	574	132	37703302.8
按轻、重工业分	**Grouped by Light & Heavy Industry**			
轻工业	Light Industry	205	48	2289903.3
以农产品为原料	Using Farm Produces as Raw Materials	171	35	2185796.5
以非农产品为原料	Using Non-Farm Produces as Raw Materials	34	13	104106.8
重工业	Heavy Industry	369	84	35413399.5
采掘工业	Mining and Quarrying	81	17	12760879.6
原料工业	Raw Material Industry	188	45	21239354.4
加工工业	Manufacturing Industry	100	22	1413165.5
按企业规模分	**Grouped by Size of Enterprises**			
大型企业	Large Enterprises	26	5	28180319.7
中型企业	Medium-sized Enterprises	147	28	6784459.3
小型企业	Small Enterprises	401	99	2738523.8

Main Economic Indicators Efficiency of State-holding Industrial Enterprises

(10 000 yuan)

增加值 Value-added	工业销售产值(当年价) Sales Value of Industry Products (At Current Prices)	出口交货值 Delivery Value of Industry Export	实收资本 Total Capital Hold	资产合计 Total Assets	流动资产合计 Total Working Capitals	#产成品 Finished Product	固定资产原价 Original Value of Fixed Assets
17060539.5	**37555639.7**	**328738.3**	**20311592.9**	**55947597.5**	**13677842.2**	**1497921.3**	**52854625.2**
17020766.2	37499524.4	328485.5	20227869.9	55746157.6	13646918.0	1496498.8	52709303.3
1489206.6	3643076.4	20866.0	1999491.6	7788652.6	1992375.2	113793.0	6178091.3
972833.7	2750054.1	11259.0	1257124.1	5167485.5	1235398.0	55948.4	4273911.0
362414.0	893022.3	9607.0	742367.5	2621167.1	756977.2	57844.6	1904180.3
197109.3	427768.9		540902.4	1559182.3	331376.7	14823.6	1192992.4
24408.4	141078.0		68716.0	284154.3	144701.1	11728.6	238592.5
66798.3	146688.7		94175.7	440407.8	109729.0	5154.4	359381.0
7431.4	23950.2		11142.5	34819.9	18640.8	2596.8	27224.5
9924.4	20342.0		11770.0	49128.6	17297.0	974.4	19618.7
7551.2	16895.6		11070.0	36767.9	15213.2	974.4	18725.1
2373.2	3446.4		700.0	12360.7	2083.8		893.6
2831415.3	8911958.9	147330.7	4249342.9	14688540.1	4463406.0	584908.1	10567956.2
954839.1	2464115.2	765.0	1250510.3	4284174.5	1095682.5	86014.5	3374605.1
1876576.3	6447843.7	146565.7	2998832.6	10404365.6	3367723.5	498893.6	7193351.1
12836747.4	24900196.9	160288.8	13956122.9	33185016.4	7155199.0	794226.5	35916412.6
39773.3	56115.3	252.8	83723.0	201439.9	30924.2	1422.5	145321.9
17060539.5	37555639.7	328738.3	20311592.9	55947597.5	13677842.2	1497921.3	52854625.2
720108.1	2179398.8	177323.9	1131826.4	4079499.2	2038245.3	515844.2	2335573.3
677272.1	2077845.9	177230.5	872153.9	3502941.9	1874890.9	505755.5	1881955.5
42836.0	101552.9	93.4	259672.5	576557.3	163354.4	10088.7	453617.8
16340431.4	35376240.9	151414.4	19179766.5	51868098.3	11639596.9	982077.1	50519051.9
10366072.7	12723573.5	40.8	13436806.5	24755831.8	5185408.2	397301.1	27928752.9
5543284.8	21259619.0	138152.7	5187185.7	24559169.9	5226966.7	458798.9	21315086.8
431073.9	1393048.4	13220.9	555774.3	2553096.6	1227222.0	125977.1	1275212.2
13721076.9	28196996.3	24474.3	15471481.3	36971308.5	7734978.2	624933.5	40538814.4
2427761.0	6709305.6	218691.4	2857961.8	12101822.5	3922480.1	522982.4	7505388.8
911701.6	2649337.8	85572.6	1982149.8	6874466.5	2020383.9	350005.4	4810422.0

13-10 续表

单位: 万元

项　　目	Item	流动负债合计 Total Working Liabilities	长期负债合计 Long-term Liabilities	所有者权益合计 Total Owners' Equities
总　　计	**Total**	**14661123.4**	**12003455.7**	**29007782.3**
按登记注册类型分	**Grouped by Registry Type**			
内资企业	DomesticFunded Enterprises	14577991.2	12000292.1	28897947.1
国有企业	State-owned Enterprises	2516488.0	2350695.7	2817308.2
#中央企业	Central Enterprises	1936498.1	1345801.1	1799217.7
地方企业	Local Enterprises	579989.9	1004894.6	1018090.5
#自治区属企业	Autonomous	235832.0	607869.5	710512.8
地区(州、市)属企业	Prefecture or City	133804.9	97840.0	50950.3
县(市)属企业	County or City	115605.9	180714.4	133623.1
股份合作企业	Share-holding Cooperative Enterprises	20435.2		14384.7
联营企业	Joint Ownership Enterprises	28287.8	7277.1	9605.4
#国有联营企业	State Joint Enterprises Ownership	21712.5	1914.1	9183.0
国有与集体联营企业	Joint State-collective OwnershipEnterprises	6575.3	5363.0	422.4
有限责任公司	Limited Liability Corporations	5638517.0	3103272.2	5813747.1
#国有独资公司	Sole State-funded Corporations	1475483.5	806651.9	1907143.2
其他有限责任公司	Other Limited Liability Corporations	4163033.5	2296620.3	3906603.9
股份有限公司	Share-holding Corporations Ltd.	6374263.2	6539047.1	20242901.7
外商投资企业	Foreign Funded Enterprises	83132.2	3163.6	109835.2
在总计中: 国有控股企业	Of the Total : State-owned and State-holding Enterprises	14661123.4	12003455.7	29007782.3
按轻、重工业分	**Grouped by Light & Heavy Industry**			
轻工业	Light Industry	1998658.6	409580.8	1615933.7
以农产品为原料	Using Farm Produces as Raw Materials	1875112.9	255953.1	1325676.8
以非农产品为原料	Using Non-Farm Produces as Raw Materials	123545.7	153627.7	290256.9
重工业	Heavy Industry	12662464.8	11593874.9	27391848.6
采掘工业	Mining and Quarrying	4056932.4	5552667.4	15104956.3
原料工业	Raw Material Industry	7626142.2	5457441.6	11300816.9
加工工业	Manufacturing Industry	979390.2	583765.9	986075.4
按企业规模分	**Grouped by Size of Enterprises**			
大型企业	Large Enterprises	7517652.4	8027891.6	21385514.9
中型企业	Medium-sized Enterprises	4378365.3	2487212.3	5165527.8
小型企业	Small Enterprises	2765105.7	1488351.8	2456739.6

Continued

(10 000 yuan)

主营业务收入 Revenue from Principal Business	#主营业务成本 Cost of Principal Business	主营业务税金及附加 Taxes and Other Charges on Principal Business	营业利润 Business Profit	利润总额 Total Profit	亏损企业亏损总额 Losses Value of Loss-Suffering Enterprises	利税总额 Total Profits and Taxes	本年应交增值税 Value-added Taxes Payable	全部从业人员年平均人数（人） Annual Average Employed Persons (person)
39430339.9	**27244253.3**	**2436861.0**	**6500190.6**	**6647661.5**	**478264.9**	**11186422.4**	**2101899.9**	**353759**
39373537.4	27207989.5	2436769.8	6483918.1	6630584.6	478264.9	11163284.1	2095929.7	353006
3598326.2	3214155.8	119965.2	12900.3	29425.0	201629.7	283622.1	134231.9	69555
2722197.8	2532158.7	112663.0	-53715.5	-34077.4	164727.4	169071.2	90485.6	49525
876128.4	681997.1	7302.2	66615.8	63502.4	36902.3	114550.9	43746.3	20030
421441.3	325778.0	2617.6	32846.1	33555.7	10691.8	59359.2	23185.9	10104
144064.5	137983.2	245.9	-5903.0	-11587.4	21518.1	-8436.4	2905.1	2443
131034.8	99642.7	1730.4	6569.9	7763.3	4415.9	15176.2	5682.5	5850
23927.5	16211.6	160.8	4018.5	4358.0		5051.4	532.6	437
20688.6	13660.9	518.7	2576.0	2758.2	346.4	5035.8	1758.9	607
17122.0	11352.4	445.2	2839.6	3035.8	68.8	4819.6	1338.6	407
3566.6	2308.5	73.5	-263.6	-277.6	277.6	216.2	420.3	200
8868590.5	7097080.6	206086.9	839353.8	906461.4	109359.5	1494892.6	382344.3	128617
2554674.8	1962854.9	161177.5	227278.8	257252.0	22977.4	535071.3	116641.8	41715
6313915.7	5134225.7	44909.4	612075.0	649209.4	86382.1	959821.3	265702.5	86902
26862004.6	16866880.6	2110038.2	5625069.5	5687582.0	166929.3	9374682.2	1577062.0	153790
56802.5	36263.8	91.2	16272.5	17076.9		23138.3	5970.2	753
39430339.9	27244253.3	2436861.0	6500190.6	6647661.5	478264.9	11186422.4	2101899.9	353759
2203458.4	1640128.3	132304.2	105278.1	126147.0	74437.7	370202.8	111751.6	52721
2099328.2	1562174.3	131343.6	116678.2	133959.9	61196.7	371226.9	105923.4	47249
104130.2	77954.0	960.6	-11400.1	-7812.9	13241.0	-1024.1	5828.2	5472
37226881.5	25604125.0	2304556.8	6394912.5	6521514.5	403827.2	10816219.6	1990148.3	301038
14180839.4	6834825.8	730601.0	4919937.5	5010302.5	249404.9	6983594.9	1242691.4	147148
21562551.5	17621942.8	1556036.1	1323532.6	1336108.2	149044.3	3591443.5	699299.2	128299
1483490.6	1147356.4	17919.7	151442.4	175103.8	5378.0	241181.2	48157.7	25591
29811594.3	19809677.6	2129903.8	5597507.5	5675295.8	320673.5	9465193.0	1659993.4	194587
6899004.6	5299772.9	287008.2	614976.2	662652.2	102567.4	1274197.4	324537.0	111750
2719741.0	2134802.8	19949.0	287706.9	309713.5	55024.0	447032.0	117369.5	47422

13-11 分行业国有控股工业企业主要经济指标

单位: 万元 (2010 年)

行业	Sector	企业单位数(个) Number of Enterprises (unit)	#亏损企业 Loss- Suffering Enterprises	工业总产值(当年价格) Gross Industrial Output Value (At Current Prices)
煤炭开采和洗选业	Mining and Washing of Coal	36	10	736736.2
石油和天然气开采业	Extraction of Petroleum and Natural Gas	7	1	11172924.9
#天然原油和天然气开采	Extraction of Ores Crude Oil and Natural Gas Extraction	5		10365232.9
黑色金属矿采选业	Mining and Processing of Ferrous Metals Ores	13	2	457000.3
有色金属矿采选业	Mining and Processing of Nonferrous Metals Ores	16	4	331526.4
非金属矿采选业	Mining and Processing of Nonmetal Ores	9		62691.8
#采 盐	Extraction of Salt	4		32728.4
农副食品加工业	Processing of Food from Agricultural Products	66	11	663557.7
#谷物磨制	Grain Grinding	15	3	68233.8
饲料加工	Fodder Processing	7	1	135170.0
制 糖	Sugar Making	11		210643.8
食品制造业	Manufacture of Food	43	13	438680.9
#罐头制造	Manufacture of can	20	8	246135.9
饮料制造业	Manufacture of Beverage	17	5	178074.7
#酒的制造	Manufacture of Wine	15	4	175163.1
烟草制品业	Manufacture of Tobacco	1		236475.5
纺织业	Manufacture of Textile	15	2	316972.2
#棉、化纤纺织及印染精加工	Cotton, Chemical Fiber, Dyeing, Printing and Processing	11		269043.7
毛纺织和染整精加工	Wool Textile, Dyeing and Printing	1	1	2841.7
纺织服装、鞋、帽制造业	Manufacture of Textile Wearing Apparel,Footware and Caps	3	1	11017.7
木材加工及木、竹、藤、棕、草制品业	Processing of Timber, Wood, Bamboo, Cane, Grass Products	2	1	2667.7
家具制造业	Manufacture of Furniture	1		630.0
造纸及纸制品业	Manufacture of Paper and Paper Products	7	2	76196.3
印刷业和记录媒介的复制	Printing and Copying of Medium for Record	13	2	32273.9
石油加工、炼焦及核燃料加工业	Oil Processing, Coking and Nuclear Fuel Processing	11	2	11156626.0
#炼 焦	Coking	2		53519.0
化学原料及化学制品制造业	Raw Chemical Material and Chemical Products	36	5	2226152.2
#基础化学原料制造	Basic Chemical Material	10	4	411426.6
肥料制造	Fertilizer Making	10		356691.6
医药制造业	Manufacture of Medicine	8		64954.4
化学纤维制造业	Manufacture of Chemical Fiber	3		198863.0
橡胶制品业	Manufacture of Rubber Products	2		62369.0
塑料制品业	Manufacture of Plastic Products	27	6	185495.0
非金属矿物制品业	Manufacture of Nonmetal Mineral Products	57	3	952128.3
#水泥制造	Manufacture of Cement	31		620361.0
黑色金属冶炼及压延加工业	Smelting and Pressing of Ferrous Metals	7	1	4237137.2
有色金属冶炼及压延加工业	Smelting and Pressing of Nonferrous Metals	9	1	298072.4
金属制品业	Manufacture of Metal Products	6	1	172972.2
通用设备制造业	Manufacture of General Purpose Machinery	2	1	3282.2
专用设备制造业	Manufacture of Special Purpose Machinery	8	2	63263.2
交通运输设备制造业	Manufacture of Transport Equipment	6	4	73163.4
电气机械及器材制造业	Manufacture of Electric Equipment and Machinery	5	1	24417.8
仪器仪表及文化、办公用机械制造业	Manufacture of Measuring Instruments and Machinery for Cultural Activity and Office Work	1	1	4831.3
电力、热力的生产和供应业	Electric Power and Thermal Production and Supply	109	34	3119712.8
#电力生产和电力供应	Electric Power Production and Supply	77	26	2988372.7
燃气生产和供应业	Gas Production and Supply	3	1	81315.5
水的生产和供应业	Water Production and Supply	24	15	54188.1

Main Economic Indicators of State-holding Industrial Enterprises by Sectors

(10 000 yuan)

增加值 Value-added	工业销售产值(当年价) Sales Value of Industry Products (At Current Prices)	出口交货值 Delivery Value of Industry Export	实收资本 Total Capital Hold	资产合计 Total Assets	流动资产合计 Total Working Capitals	#产成品 Finished Product	固定资产原价 Net Value of Fixed Assets
436942.9	714833.3		577902.4	2218459.4	605239.0	52101.1	970086.1
9441322.7	11158818.4	17.0	12562417.3	20909083.3	3954841.8	266817.2	26417538.8
9164293.8	10351126.4	17.0	11787259.8	19923348.0	3521950.2	266817.2	25697689.6
199299.3	473951.3		137102.5	791655.4	403876.1	47704.1	258881.8
260830.7	326294.5		150918.4	777330.7	189214.7	23709.0	255506.9
27677.3	49676.0	23.8	8465.9	59303.0	32236.6	6969.7	26739.3
16925.2	26471.0	23.8	3977.3	27458.6	14682.1	4017.4	12669.0
150835.7	616204.4	19582.1	262549.7	1014630.0	595614.8	218015.6	467264.0
10531.9	67594.6		12129.6	56187.1	26126.3	1630.5	24338.5
27583.9	138477.1		27227.6	192299.3	96276.9	2405.9	46262.2
78642.0	206217.2	854.6	65720.9	276733.4	154622.6	88195.1	203860.5
74526.6	395129.4	139218.8	188253.0	978161.5	481001.4	173941.3	525000.5
9210.6	207476.0	127657.0	116265.0	727154.0	407787.4	163882.4	352539.9
89074.8	180988.6		114038.6	293207.9	154491.2	14494.8	114711.6
88315.7	177045.0		108837.6	287017.8	153018.4	14195.7	110227.2
188122.6	235999.5		18741.7	217131.0	131090.0		127180.0
83470.4	319845.1	16907.4	160309.3	456249.0	259959.3	45797.3	305902.2
72073.9	284672.8	2264.0	113223.0	349138.8	191386.1	36401.1	257429.8
517.6	3845.7	619.2	5310.4	16480.0	6063.0	289.0	7447.6
4965.5	9360.7	671.6	2412.9	18742.7	12498.9	132.6	5643.8
543.5	2845.4		777.1	5202.1	2947.0	192.7	5656.9
197.2	630.0		180.0	956.4	630.6	177.0	802.2
24823.3	73543.1		31308.1	157076.3	75774.8	7866.0	120751.8
15614.1	32544.7		17183.4	73009.7	34337.0	1897.5	58882.7
3011240.7	11221747.0	5697.0	955651.7	6344888.0	1379713.5	176934.3	6798641.4
17699.6	57817.5	5697.0	32332.8	243143.0	73011.9	8845.1	82978.4
707158.7	2185487.5	111620.1	1159740.2	5099073.0	1332268.2	90392.1	2827265.7
96448.3	406533.3	51984.0	300902.1	1659680.8	397138.2	16586.0	382188.3
195692.6	344090.7		124980.1	817253.0	255546.3	12844.9	640774.4
19275.3	53074.4	944.0	32744.0	104934.7	63209.3	17255.6	47698.3
37001.4	191041.5		63800.0	255730.3	102633.2	32080.5	139925.4
10801.7	62726.0	2923.7	912.8	30058.2	28355.2	3844.5	2279.4
35669.0	189819.4		106919.0	315281.3	188751.2	46394.9	117646.0
320720.2	952697.4	9607.0	416817.4	2289720.9	821731.6	36933.3	1057011.0
236434.5	620926.2		317119.1	1710038.3	479211.3	14764.4	842675.5
496388.7	4224609.6	20835.6	820395.8	2309454.6	821191.5	170171.0	2030219.8
75458.9	299067.7		45794.5	268775.5	120522.1	19854.2	125738.5
14380.7	178531.8		61455.9	108663.6	48693.0	4334.9	30134.9
988.2	4418.3		1055.9	6812.3	5656.9	3026.0	3414.0
17403.3	63207.5	447.9	35098.0	152059.5	105508.7	16317.1	47290.5
6105.8	71725.4	242.3	29416.3	110835.4	67345.0	11752.4	37926.8
5968.7	25209.6		12064.2	56351.5	47937.9	4751.7	17657.7
250.3	4831.3		1500.0	8732.7	8676.1	1706.3	155.8
1247065.0	3113071.9		2041323.8	9717111.5	1377913.4	2058.1	9345702.1
1196742.7	2981984.7		1938182.7	9244964.4	1183169.7	1567.7	8919743.1
23334.2	63316.8		35638.0	231679.7	96771.1	298.5	99388.5
28119.3	53459.6		253705.1	535292.1	115669.0		456524.8

13-11 续表

单位: 万元

行　　业	Sector	流动负债合计 Total Working Liabilities	长期负债合计 Long-term Liabilities	所有者权益合计 Total Owners' Equities
煤炭开采和洗选业	Mining and Washing of Coal	763595.0	628294.2	790797.7
石油和天然气开采业	Extraction of Petroleum and Natural Gas	2638324.9	4757597.4	13513160.9
#天然原油和天然气开采	Extraction of Ores Crude Oil and Natural Gas Extraction	2211047.4	4598652.4	13113648.2
黑色金属矿采选业	Mining and Processing of Ferrous Metals Ores	368076.9	100062.0	323513.3
有色金属矿采选业	Mining and Processing of Nonferrous Metals Ores	258386.6	64221.1	449544.0
非金属矿采选业	Mining and Processing of Nonmetal Ores	28549.0	2492.7	27940.4
#采　盐	Extraction of Salt	7581.6	2492.7	17384.3
农副食品加工业	Processing of Food from Agricultural Products	550117.8	61497.7	400141.2
#谷物磨制	Grain Grinding	25291.9	6793.9	24101.2
饲料加工	Fodder Processing	68699.8	19593.5	102883.5
制　糖	Sugar Making	161487.7	2062.3	111447.2
食品制造业	Manufacture of Food	634784.9	84132.0	256747.0
#罐头制造	Manufacture of can	501726.2	72246.2	152863.7
饮料制造业	Manufacture of Beverage	105448.9	1601.2	166752.0
#酒的制造	Manufacture of Wine	110554.7	1573.5	155483.8
烟草制品业	Manufacture of Tobacco	97962.0		119169.0
纺织业	Manufacture of Textile	231101.6	28054.0	187305.4
#棉、化纤纺织及印染精加工	Cotton, Chemical Fiber, Dyeing, Printing and Processing	190394.4	16685.7	138978.7
毛纺织和染整精加工	Wool Textile, Dyeing and Printing	3408.2		9467.0
纺织服装、鞋、帽制造业	Manufacture of Textile Wearing Apparel,Footware and Caps	10202.9	3257.0	5282.7
木材加工及木、竹、藤、棕、草制品业	Processing of Timber, Wood, Bamboo, Cane, Grass Products	4484.7	3702.8	-2985.4
造纸及纸制品业	Manufacture of Paper and Paper Products			777.0
家具制造业	Manufacture of Furniture	78405.2	11556.3	67114.7
印刷业和记录媒介的复制	Printing and Copying of Medium for Record	33613.9	5217.0	34178.8
石油加工、炼焦及核燃料加工业	Oil Processing, Coking and Nuclear Fuel Processing	1574544.8	886765.7	3883577.1
#炼　焦	Coking	107812.9	94831.5	40498.5
化学原料及化学制品制造业	Raw Chemical Material and Chemical Products	1551119.7	937901.2	2578161.5
#基础化学原料制造	Basic Chemical Material	490010.6	139176.7	999427.8
肥料制造	Fertilizer Making	249533.1	248726.2	318992.9
医药制造业	Manufacture of Medicine	47674.1	4329.1	52931.5
化学纤维制造业	Manufacture of Chemical Fiber	107429.0	60836.3	75525.7
橡胶制品业	Manufacture of Rubber Products	20476.9	164.6	9416.7
塑料制品业	Manufacture of Plastic Products	138284.8	39071.2	133538.3
非金属矿物制品业	Manufacture of Nonmetal Mineral Products	612996.6	473210.5	1187684.0
#水泥制造	Manufacture of Cement	462322.3	341472.5	893439.7
黑色金属冶炼及压延加工业	Smelting and Pressing of Ferrous Metals	1120045.7	84345.0	1105063.9
有色金属冶炼及压延加工业	Smelting and Pressing of Nonferrous Metals	172043.0	17271.3	79161.1
金属制品业	Manufacture of Metal Products	49739.3	1368.6	57133.2
通用设备制造业	Manufacture of General Purpose Machinery	5251.1		1561.2
专用设备制造业	Manufacture of Special Purpose Machinery	142117.1	15725.5	-5821.2
交通运输设备制造业	Manufacture of Transport Equipment	92881.5	3928.2	14025.7
电气机械及器材制造业	Manufacture of Electric Equipment and Machinery	24841.0	20375	11135.3
仪器仪表及文化、办公用机械制造	Manufacture of Measuring Instruments and Machinery for Cultural Activity and Office Work	6535.8		2196.9
电力、热力的生产和供应业	Electric Power and Thermal Production and Supply	3008585.1	3445231.3	3133437.9
#电力生产和电力供应	Electric Power Production and Supply	2829587.7	3297749.4	2996067.8
燃气生产和供应业	Gas Production and Supply	82817.3	74754.4	74108.0
水的生产和供应业	Water Production and Supply	92599.7	170743.9	267397.6

Continued

(10 000 yuan)

主营业务收入 Revenue from Principal Business	#主营业务成本 Cost of Principal Business	主营业务税金及附加 Taxes and Other Charges on Principal Business	营业利润 Business Profit	利润总额 Total Profit	亏损企业亏损总额 Losses Value of Loss-Suffering Enterprises	利税总额 Total Profits and Taxes	本年应交增值税 Value-added Taxes Payable	全部从业人员年平均人数(人) Ann Employed Persons (person)
746004.2	522355.8	22283.1	33171.0	4677.9	94862.2	97422.2	70461.2	36354
12569960.2	5842604.3	693274.7	4613367.8	4718754.3	147613.2	6509358.7	1097329.7	98237
11829685.7	4979322.1	690450.7	4780428.6	4866015.5		6631673.2	1075207.0	77639
493464.7	327601.5	8472.2	106417.4	119580.6	5514.2	167142.9	39090.1	4058
326880.0	121686.8	4327.3	162056.5	161994.8	1415.3	198078.1	31756.0	6274
44530.3	20577.4	2243.7	4924.8	5294.9		11593.0	4054.4	2225
25377.4	8837.9	1797.2	3261.8	3357.5		8043.4	2888.7	1193
651916.0	525603.3	1984.6	42297.5	46912.3	11873.1	65953.8	17056.9	11649
69746.8	63695.8	79.9	2665.9	3044.2	1627.9	3710.5	586.4	1010
141758.5	106875.7	408.6	10756.7	12506.9	29.5	15320.7	2405.2	1162
206988.9	144304.4	1208.5	29448.7	29403.2		43566.9	12955.2	5658
378632.2	299495.2	2047.7	-8329.1	-5630.6	41106.4	9184.4	12767.3	7848
189264.7	155767.5	711.4	-35175.3	-34727.6	40496.3	-30269.9	3746.3	3919
167303.7	82162.2	21675.4	28377.0	32211.8	5602.4	65658.5	11771.3	4370
163419.7	78966.4	21645.2	28660.5	32472.8	5240.6	65727.9	11609.9	4205
235999.0	88935.0	102779.0	23731.0	23434.0		160237.4	34024.4	885
319710.7	274029.3	1397.4	11475.6	14964.7	255.5	30940.3	14578.2	13696
280841.3	242782.4	1252.2	10448.1	13655.8		28551.2	13643.2	11043
4188.0	3754.0	8.0	-218.5	-254.0	254.0	-117.0	129.0	218
24974.9	21782.2	16.1	1026.2	822.9	547.9	1036.2	197.2	940
2847.9	2473.6	13.6	-354.1	-255.9	410.5	-113.7	128.6	197
613.5	488.0	5.4	70.6	70.6		90.1	14.1	25
71351.9	58945.9	592.0	4165.5	4994.7	1734.5	11037.4	5450.7	3350
33531.5	26162.1	155.7	1395.3	2698.9	198.8	3975.0	1120.4	1982
11480201.3	8943737.1	1524423.9	513894.4	502956.5	75398.3	2408011.7	380631.3	29457
54116.3	42971.4	204.2	1555.2	2072.2		5212.6	2936.2	2034
2117324.9	1577949.3	23088.1	320930.1	344553.0	13465.8	446149.4	78508.3	29301
610280.5	536799.4	2693.6	29339.7	31011.3	13449.3	44440.3	10735.4	10529
344729.0	185501.5	12925.1	73712.8	92668.7		125353.0	19759.2	4659
50299.0	33507.0	524.6	4746.1	5914.3		10050.6	3611.7	1906
192409.7	167163.3	657.9	9066.3	9430.7		17780.4	7691.8	1954
62959.7	53292.8	934.0	1207.4	1222.7		4269.7	2113.0	1373
200836.6	179382.8	369.8	7069.1	8334.2	874.3	12509.9	3805.9	5366
975397.7	746531.3	5230.5	126395.9	149293.0	911.2	208813.3	54289.8	19514
616296.5	446390.2	4264.6	95563.2	115789.0		164464.9	44411.3	13764
4258490.3	3875884.7	5200.8	207694.3	191788.1	44.6	283757.1	86768.2	14168
297248.4	251648.4	151.9	28462.0	28287.2	1520.1	30648.8	2209.7	3523
192589.9	182396.2	461.6	5907.5	5882.0	51.7	8520.9	2177.3	1081
4712.7	4124.7	45.5	-27.3	-15.5	50.4	142.1	112.1	220
78880.6	64003.5	295.3	3454.7	3397.9	218.1	6068.0	2374.8	2759
81025.1	78200.9	85.2	-4244.4	-2989.3	3520.5	-2195.1	709.0	1936
25364.8	20444.7	109.3	534.0	575.2	129.5	1816.5	1132.0	789
4831.3	4073.1	9.0	-82.7	-84.2	84.2	3.9	79.1	50
3199238.0	2747615.4	12527.5	254352.7	268425.6	57562.0	413260.1	132307.0	43727
3056676.7	2624016.1	12231.0	251385.2	265984.7	45315.4	408538.3	130322.6	39713
76673.3	51229.4	1125.1	8622.3	8539.7	0.2	10443.8	779.0	1069
57203.3	45985.7	342.3	-15776.5	-12521.1	13300.0	-9477.6	2701.2	3442

13-12 各地、州、市、县(市)国有控股工业企业主要经济指标

单位: 万元 (2010 年)

地 区	Region	企业单位数(个) Number of Enterprises (unit)	#亏损企业 Loss- Suffering Enterprises	工业总产值(当年价格) Gross Industrial Output Value (At Current Prices)
总 计	**Total**	**574**	**132**	**37703302.8**
乌鲁木齐市	**Urumqi City**	**132**	**28**	**12466851.5**
天山区	Tianshan District	18	4	1449496.9
沙依巴克区	Shayibak District	19	3	421346.7
新市区	Xinshi District	52	15	2831107.2
水磨沟区	Shui Mogou District	7		248269.9
头屯河区	Tou Tunhe District	13		4148664.8
达坂城区	Da Bancheng District	4		143902.5
米东区	Midong District	16	5	3187849.8
乌鲁木齐县	Urumqi County	3	1	36213.7
克拉玛依市	**Karamay City**	**16**	**4**	**12688939.6**
独山子区	Dushanzi District	8	2	5265797.0
克拉玛依区	Karamay District	8	2	7423142.6
白碱滩区	Bai Jiantan District			
乌尔河区	Urhe District			
吐鲁番地区	**Turpan Administrative Offices**	**18**	**4**	**937883.3**
吐鲁番市	Turpan City	6	2	39047.7
鄯善县	Shanshan [Piqan] County	6	1	819933.3
托克逊县	Toksun County	6	1	78902.3
哈密地区	**Hami [Kumul] Administrative Offices**	**48**	**8**	**749051.6**
哈密市	Hami [Kumul] City	39	8	676186.9
巴里坤哈萨克自治县	Barkol Kazak Autonomous County	6		53486.8
伊吾县	Yiwu [Araturuk] County	3		19377.9
昌吉回族自治州	**Changji Hui Autonomous Prefecture**	**26**	**5**	**440522.3**
昌吉市	Changji City	6		43825.2
阜康市	Fukang City	5	2	210382.8
呼图壁县	Hutubi County	4		34313.5
玛纳斯县	Manas County	7	2	107651.4
奇台县	Qitai County	1		18342.4
吉木萨尔县	Jimsar County	3	1	26007.0
木垒哈萨克自治县	Mori Kazak Autonomous County			
伊犁哈萨克自治州	**Ili Kazak Autonomous Prefecture**	**143**	**32**	**2486398.1**
伊犁州直属县(市)	**Counties (Cities) Direct Under Ili Prefecture**	**78**	**16**	**1336309.5**
伊宁市	Yining [Gulja] City	9	5	170843.4
奎屯市	Kuytun City	20	5	553889.4
伊宁县	Yining [Gulja] County	14	1	170290.4
察布查尔锡伯自治县	Qapqal Xibe Autonomous County	6	2	17908.3
霍城县	Huocheng [Korgas] County	7		83261.9
巩留县	Gongliu [Tokkuztara] County	2		27594.8
新源县	Xinyuan [Kunes] County	9	3	232699.7
昭苏县	Zhaosu [Mongolkure] County	6		17678.0
特克斯县	Tekes County	1		918.0
尼勒克县	Nilka County	4		61225.6
塔城地区	**Tacheng [Tarbagatai] Administrative Offices**	**33**	**7**	**641831.1**
塔城市	Tacheng [Qoqek] City	5	3	62933.2
乌苏市	Usu City	5		272326.8
额敏县	Emin [Dorbiljin] County	3	1	41990.2

Main Economic Indicators of State-holding Industrial Enterprises by Prefecture, Autonomous Prefecture, City and County

(10 000 yuan)

增加值 Value-added	工业销售产值(当年价) Sales Value of Industry Products (At Current Prices)	出口交货值 Delivery Value of Industry Export	实收资本 Total Capital Hold	资产合计 Total Assets	流动资产合计 Total Working Capitals	#产成品 Finished Product	固定资产原价 Net Value of Fixed Assets
17060539.5	**37555639.7**	**328738.3**	**20311592.9**	**55947597.5**	**13677842.2**	**1497921.3**	**52854625.2**
4054398.0	**12422946.2**	**112838.7**	**5999833.5**	**16318246.5**	**3783261.1**	**414979.3**	**14177422.1**
415695.3	1444409.8	31283.4	351576.8	3453899.8	642265.6	40773.4	3124978.1
132807.6	401681.7	47127.8	395819.9	2323999.2	522997.0	9449.5	687245.7
2112055.0	2806492.9	12264.0	2444669.1	4094533.3	840930.6	99329.0	4710359.3
80099.8	242922.1		250586.2	469583.3	125521.8	10971.9	444028.0
473056.7	4147115.4	20929.0	795029.5	2249109.8	751682.1	156288.8	1970415.6
101841.1	142154.7		122163.9	331012.6	76636.7	2493.9	218102.7
710661.1	3202530.9	1234.5	1585216.5	3162004.8	794940.6	95305.9	2817468.5
28181.5	35638.7		54771.6	234103.7	28286.7	366.9	204824.2
6246824.3	**12728052.6**	**9624.0**	**6877098.1**	**15063410.7**	**3495508.8**	**127592.2**	**16880511.4**
1504377.4	5278596.9	9607.0	84338.6	4337235.6	798676.9	111744.9	4387087.3
4742447.0	7449455.7	17.0	6792759.5	10726175.1	2696831.9	15847.3	12493424.1
624323.0	**928931.8**		**472125.1**	**2587275.5**	**500593.1**	**57875.3**	**3400786.2**
19957.4	39970.2		28532.4	139568.4	18867.6	299.6	138246.6
563820.7	812796.1		366479.1	2120467.9	413474.2	56543.6	3027189.3
40545.0	76165.5		77113.6	327239.2	68251.3	1032.1	235350.3
316294.3	**757565.6**		**398809.6**	**1513572.7**	**594921.9**	**52723.6**	**861139.8**
276637.1	688161.6		376293.8	1337032.8	535320.1	46526.8	771346.4
30109.6	51031.4		22256.9	150273.0	36535.2	5468.5	85979.4
9547.6	18372.6		258.9	26266.9	23066.6	728.3	3814.0
141617.9	**422403.1**	**27331.4**	**126584.6**	**828918.4**	**191207.7**	**46582.8**	**602203.2**
17799.1	38154.9	4093.0	10733.5	54818.2	28405.2	6022.9	25846.7
55870.3	211942.1		73554.7	408809.4	92799.9	8460.4	247821.9
7156.0	34824		1778.4	18234.9	6305.9	864.4	14662.2
45901.5	90862.4	9771.9	33148.0	264813.6	33045.1	12347.7	265513.3
6482.7	17557.3		1000.0	31009.8	11462.6	8058.3	23548.3
8408.2	29062.4	13466.5	6370.0	51232.5	19189.0	10829.1	24810.8
1296596.1	**2437071.6**	**30508.1**	**1154035.7**	**4961002.2**	**1468472.5**	**231319.5**	**3285765.3**
649702.2	**1320007.8**	**3280.9**	**830349.8**	**3178809.9**	**949527.3**	**124261.3**	**2147859.3**
82536.9	169269.5		50918.9	299203.2	56711.0	3951.2	316831.9
260982.3	547824.7	3280.9	136934.8	861133.4	361313.9	53075.1	542901.8
70355.2	165851.0		84743.9	324262.5	114519.6	13630.9	195857.5
7743.6	18141.5		1222.5	27757.4	9469.7	1383.5	30583.9
27481.1	85903.1		30107.7	135979.9	73796.4	22426.6	85272.5
20832.9	27890.1		294061.8	702123.8	90213.6	274.8	423109.3
128018.9	226240.8		153273.5	398631.3	208122.1	24941.5	195708.3
6416.8	18190.6		6018.0	15794.9	10240.7	3705.1	6003.0
456.8	918.0		129.2	2901.5	377.9		1706.3
44877.9	59778.5		72939.5	411022.0	24762.4	872.6	349884.8
343770.1	**628879.1**	**27227.2**	**181090.1**	**717368.8**	**266459.8**	**68757.9**	**501190.1**
20864.8	61707.6		22775.9	95932.3	14619.8	152.9	107054.8
184241.9	271470.9	25074.7	14724.8	173230.4	61268.2	29224.9	92323.2
13209.9	47824.6		32100.4	66627.0	37823.6	14247.8	48330.8

13-12 续表 1

单位: 万元

地　区	Region	企业单位数(个) Number of Enterprises (unit)	#亏损企业 Loss- Suffering Enterprises	工业总产值(当年价格) Gross Industrial Output Value (At Current Prices)
沙湾县	Shawan County	8		92467.8
托里县	Toli County	4	1	93395.8
裕民县	Yumin [Qagantokay] County	1	1	611.0
和布克赛尔蒙古自治县	Hoboksar Mongol Autonomous County	7	1	78106.3
阿勒泰地区	**Altay Administrative Offices**	**32**	**9**	**508257.5**
阿勒泰市	Altay City	9	5	76200.1
布尔津县	Burqin County	6	1	29744.3
富蕴县	Fuyun [Koktokay] County	6	1	159504.7
福海县	Fuhai [Burultokay] County	4	1	11789.0
哈巴河县	Habahe [Kaba] County	5	1	229381.3
青河县	Qinghe [Qinggil] County	1		1023.3
吉木乃县	Jeminay County	1		614.8
博尔塔拉蒙古自治州	**Bortala Mongol Autonomous Prefecture**	**16**	**2**	**136672.7**
博乐市	Bole [Bortala] City	13	2	127692.5
精河县	Jinghe [Jing] County	2		8498.1
温泉县	Wenquan [Araxang] County	1		482.1
巴音郭楞蒙古自治州	**Bayangol Mongol Autonomous Prefecture**	**49**	**16**	**4185536.3**
库尔勒市	Korla City	28	9	3797511.2
轮台县	Luntai [Bugur] County			
尉犁县	Yuli [Lopnur] County			
若羌县	Ruoqiang [Qarkilik] County	4	1	216159.4
且末县	Qiemo [Qarqan] County	2	1	2560.4
焉耆回族自治县	Yanqi Hui Autonomous County	4	1	32746.4
和静县	Hejing County	7	2	106424.0
和硕县	Hoxud County	1		5090.8
博湖县	Bohu [Bagrax] County	3	2	25044.1
阿克苏地区	**Aksu Administrative Offices**	**38**	**5**	**1585621.8**
阿克苏市	Aksu City	11		278330.4
温宿县	Wensu [Onsu] County	7	2	25722.5
库车县	Kuqa County	11	2	1212161.4
沙雅县	Xayar County			
新和县	Xinhe [Toksu] County			
拜城县	Baicheng [Bay] County	6	1	54143.4
乌什县	Wushi [Uxturpan] County	2		7273.0

Continued

(10 000 yuan)

增加值 Value-added	工业销售产值(当年价) Sales Value of Industry Products (At Current Prices)	出口交货值 Delivery Value of Industry Export	实收资本 Total Capital Hold	资产合计 Total Assets	流动资产合计 Total Working Capitals	#产成品 Finished Product	固定资产原价 Net Value of Fixed Assets
27821.9	85936.4	2152.5	21233.4	97111.9	46490.4	13003.7	87705.4
54807.0	96937.6		55000.0	166541.5	70154.4	6735.9	78572.1
211.7	611.0		228.0	1056.0	64.7		568.0
42612.9	64391.0		35027.6	116869.7	36038.7	5392.7	86635.8
303123.8	**488184.7**		**142595.8**	**1064823.5**	**252485.4**	**38300.3**	**636715.9**
28348.1	75286.6		33164.0	170755.4	41284.0	723.9	165359.8
11465.8	29311.8		14285.2	189721.9	17000.3	924.1	171794.2
86517.9	141396.5		37454.7	422713.7	114616.8	26134.1	140898.3
5271.5	11473.3		17424.1	33109.6	14543.3	1057.7	35105.1
171104.8	228988.7		39480.0	244699.4	64033.1	9380.5	120726.6
363.9	1023.3		727.8	3427.2	783.5		2637.7
51.8	704.5		60.0	396.3	224.4	80.0	194.2
52809.3	**142346.9**		**54340.0**	**356332.3**	**118253.2**	**32937.1**	**296548.4**
49602.3	131497.3		51614.0	338239.4	108558.1	32193.2	290640.9
3083.3	7794.8		1726.0	13405.7	6467.8	533.7	4380.0
123.7	3054.8		1000.0	4687.2	3227.3	210.2	1527.5
3276866.4	**4159263.4**	**41170.9**	**3578402.3**	**7741486.5**	**1553232.7**	**277225.4**	**8827941.5**
3072615.7	3795286.0	14137.7	3431069.3	6651856.0	1246343.1	217235.1	8038527.2
134202.5	198813.9		58108.9	557974.0	151910.9	11513.4	429442.3
1103.5	2560.4		2682.7	5958.8	1069.7		8877.9
9459.6	31698.9	10062.2	2050.0	54310.1	29394.1	19628.6	38680.4
54103.7	106410.2		70674.1	425062.4	96521.2	13230.2	272236.3
637.3	4054.8	1646.7	1450.0	7527.4	5161.0	4387.5	4995.9
4744.0	20439.2	15324.3	12367.3	38797.8	22832.7	11230.6	35181.5
495754.5	**1555420.7**	**4797.8**	**517714.5**	**1883655.5**	**403481.2**	**44795.7**	**1416449.9**
96358.1	273766.7	597.8	112521.8	634650.4	142592.0	8878.8	447799.0
15483.6	24676.6		15550.3	92036.7	22778.5	567.0	61189.8
340982.8	1188624.1		373785.8	1007501.2	192643.4	24331.0	781363.8
39192.1	56118.3		10856.6	115267.3	26641.9	7238.0	109413.0
2546.8	6143.7	4200.0	4000.0	16921.3	8168.3	3780.9	9895.6

13-12 续表 2

单位: 万元

地　　区	Region	企业单位数(个) Number of Enterprises (unit)	#亏损企业 Loss- Suffering Enterprises	工业总产值(当年价格) Gross Industrial Output Value (At Current Prices)
阿瓦提县	Awat County	1		7991.1
柯坪县	Kalpin County			
克孜勒苏柯尔克孜自治州	**Kizilsu Kirgiz Autonomous Prefecture**	**3**	**1**	**13706.6**
阿图什市	Artux City	3	1	13706.6
阿克陶县	Akto County			
阿合奇县	Akqi County			
乌恰县	Wuqia [Ulugqat] County			
喀什地区	**Kashgar [Kaxgar] Administrative Offices**	**11**	**5**	**186977.1**
喀什市	Kashgar [Kaxgar] City	5	2	178848.4
疏附县	Shufu County	2		4939.3
疏勒县	Shule County	1	1	385.2
英吉沙县	Yengisar County	2	2	2195.1
泽普县	Zepu [Poskam] County			
莎车县	Shache [Yarkant] County	1		609.1
叶城县	Yecheng [Kagilik] County			
麦盖提县	Makit County			
岳普湖县	Yopurga County			
伽师县	Jiashi [Payzawat] County			
巴楚县	Bachu [Maralbexi] County			
塔什库尔干塔吉克自治县	Taxkorgan Tajik Autonomous County			
和田地区	**Hotan Administrative Offices**	**11**	**4**	**74196.7**
和田市	Hotan City	6	3	44312.6
和田县	Hotan County	3	1	12548.6
墨玉县	Moyu [Karakax] County	1		15873.9
皮山县	Pishan [Guma] County	1		1461.6
洛浦县	Lop County			
策勒县	Qira County			
于田县	Yutian [Keriya] County			
民丰县	Minfeng [Niya] County			
自治区直辖县级市	**Municpality Country-LevelCity directly under the Central Government**	**63**	**18**	**1750945.2**
石河子市	Shihezi City	40	14	1383058.5
阿拉尔市	Aral City	7	1	212442.2
图木舒克市	Tumxuk City	7		52704.7
五家渠市	Wujiaqu City	9	3	102739.8

Continued

(10 000 yuan)

增加值 Value-added	工业销售产值(当年价) Sales Value of Industry Products (At Current Prices)	出口交货值 Delivery Value of Industry Export	实收资本 Total Capital Hold	资产合计 Total Assets	流动资产合计 Total Working Capitals	#产成品 Finished Product	固定资产原价 Net Value of Fixed Assets
1191.1	6091.3		1000.0	17278.6	10657.1		6788.7
4473.6	**14513.6**		**31111.5**	**46068.7**	**5632.1**	**418.1**	**42848.5**
4473.6	14513.6		31111.5	46068.7	5632.1	418.1	42848.5
48430.1	**189770.2**		**58252.3**	**329838.4**	**45880.1**	**2882.3**	**454285.1**
46112.7	180995.2		49812.8	306824.0	40715.7	897.2	432086.5
1630.2	4692.1		2170.6	5686.7	2109.7	152.4	6642.5
52.5	1563.2		5000.0	4944.8	713.1	234.7	3879.7
246.0	1910.6		1069.9	7293.7	2079.4	1598.0	7776.7
388.7	609.1		199.0	5089.2	262.2		3899.7
36079.2	**72588.7**		**174214.6**	**306495.8**	**48954.9**	**1005.0**	**331285.5**
19355.2	44296.8		26940.5	111543.3	11849.7	568.1	144173.3
11230.0	11697.7		131537.1	153182.7	27968.4		149940.7
4864.4	15538.7		15237.0	37638.4	8595.6	428.7	33721.4
629.6	1055.5		500.0	4131.4	541.2	8.2	3450.1
466073.0	**1724765.3**	**102467.4**	**869071.1**	**4011294.3**	**1468442.9**	**207585.0**	**2277438.3**
390525.5	1383181.3	82242.9	620295.3	3089546.4	1121649.1	106405.7	1782305.7
41902.5	203598.4		80964.5	349719.9	108664.3	31966.9	235152.8
13302.5	43884.6		27579.2	157439.1	64392.8	21247.7	89014.3
20342.6	94101.0	20224.5	140232.1	414588.9	173736.7	47964.7	170965.5

13-12 续表 3

单位: 万元

地　　区	Region	流动负债合计 Total Working Liabilities	长期负债合计 Long-term Liabilities	所有者权益合计 Total Owners' Equities
总　计	**Total**	**14661123.4**	**12003455.7**	**29007782.3**
乌鲁木齐市	**Urumqi City**	**4564602.0**	**2420066.0**	**9225989.0**
天山区	Tianshan District	1355444.1	994893.1	1100459.4
沙依巴克区	Shayibak District	522332.8	360447.0	1441219.4
新市区	Xinshi District	419195.0	322661.7	3343432.4
水磨沟区	Shui Mogou District	101576.9	44805.4	323201.0
头屯河区	Tou Tunhe District	1051467.8	103919.6	1093722.2
达坂城区	Da Bancheng District	70787.3	2489.2	228100.3
米东区	Midong District	939763.6	582120.9	1637200.9
乌鲁木齐县	Urumqi County	104034.5	8729.1	58653.4
克拉玛依市	**Karamay City**	**2698166.5**	**3196405.0**	**9168838.9**
独山子区	Dushanzi District	961596.7	750950.0	2624688.7
克拉玛依区	Karamay District	1736569.8	2445455.0	6544150.2
白碱滩区	Bai Jiantan District			
乌尔河区	Urhe District			
吐鲁番地区	**Turpan Administrative Offices**	**525773.0**	**756499.7**	**1291338.3**
吐鲁番市	Turpan City	39275.3	54996.1	34064.4
鄯善县	Shanshan [Piqan] County	450336.5	516718.8	1150980.7
托克逊县	Toksun County	36161.2	184784.8	106293.2
哈密地区	**Hami [Kumul] Administrative Offices**	**511867.4**	**348746.5**	**651707.2**
哈密市	Hami [Kumul] City	441856.9	302320.6	591918.7
巴里坤哈萨克自治县	Barkol Kazak Autonomous County	63960.6	46337.4	39660.1
伊吾县	Yiwu [Araturuk] County	6049.9	88.5	20128.4
昌吉回族自治州	**Changji Hui Autonomous Prefecture**	**407885.1**	**167926.3**	**171291.6**
昌吉市	Changji City	27563.2	10462.3	16481.2
阜康市	Fukang City	198982.7	16839.6	112683.9
呼图壁县	Hutubi County	12432.9	668.5	3933.0
玛纳斯县	Manas County	95230.5	139934.6	29648.4
奇台县	Qitai County	29638.1		1371.6
吉木萨尔县	Jimsar County	44037.7	21.3	7173.5
木垒哈萨克自治县	Mori Kazak Autonomous County			
伊犁哈萨克自治州	**Ili Kazak Autonomous Prefecture**	**1790343.9**	**1234354.7**	**1902375.0**
伊犁州直属县(市)	**Counties (Cities) Direct Under Ili Prefecture**	**1006901.6**	**984745.6**	**1163187.0**
伊宁市	Yining [Gulja] City	108208.3	103936.0	86958.5
奎屯市	Kuytun City	318740.7	260869.9	280722.3
伊宁县	Yining [Gulja] County	129767.9	71564.3	122069.7
察布查尔锡伯自治县	Qapqal Xibe Autonomous County	22888.2	2899.4	1818.6
霍城县	Huocheng [Korgas] County	52595.1	19205.5	57267.4
巩留县	Gongliu [Tokkuztara] County	34342.7	382656.9	285124.2
新源县	Xinyuan [Kunes] County	147192.9	8665.3	232354.6
昭苏县	Zhaosu [Mongolkure] County	7889.6		5570.4
特克斯县	Tekes County	310.4		238.3
尼勒克县	Nilka County	184965.8	134948.3	91063.0
塔城地区	**Tacheng [Tarbagatai] Administrative Offices**	**327755.0**	**67875.3**	**313679.8**
塔城市	Tacheng [Qoqek] City	47367.6	15301.3	31580.2
乌苏市	Usu City	85316.8	14728.8	72517.0
额敏县	Emin [Dorbiljin] County	34133.5	2802.8	29690.6

Continued

(10 000 yuan)

主营业务收入 Revenue from Principal Business	#主营业务成本 Cost of Principal Business	主营业务税金及附加 Taxes and Other Charges on Principal Business	营业利润 Business Profit	利润总额 Total Profit	亏损企业亏损总额 Losses Value of Loss-Suffering Enterprises	利税总额 Total Profits and Taxes	本年应交增值税 Value-added Taxes Payable	全部从业人员年平均人数(人) Annual Average Employed Persons (person)
39430339.9	**27244253.3**	**2436861**	**6500190.6**	**6647661.5**	**478264.9**	**11186422.4**	**2101899.9**	**353759**
12560521.4	**9583294.2**	**772516.1**	**1348737.5**	**1339474.0**	**220083.3**	**2519989.3**	**407999.2**	**89658**
1438551.7	1292795.6	4642.7	65390.4	69496.9	39456.0	101973.9	27834.3	15567
428588.9	326702.5	4050.0	81101.7	90603.1	12529.3	113080.5	18427.4	9134
2855060.4	1234813.2	288799.2	993021.5	1009218.5	11236.8	1507855.5	209837.8	21244
245766.4	199086.9	753.5	19134.9	22319.4		29411.4	6338.5	4127
4187438.0	3794338.6	5504.2	210278.8	193275.7		287077.7	88297.8	12896
141642.1	87351.8	1515.2	35117.8	36237.7		51099.8	13346.9	5995
3229408.3	2635779.1	467170.3	-69042.8	-99650.4	156815.5	407633.7	40113.8	20590
34065.6	12426.5	81.0	13735.2	17973.1	45.7	21856.8	3802.7	105
13542185.1	**9400887.8**	**1102089.9**	**2139582.1**	**2255529.7**	**151360.0**	**4237879.5**	**880259.9**	**97730**
5404933.8	4274709.2	566271.1	290852.0	308663.3	3691.8	1110500.1	235565.7	18562
8137251.3	5126178.6	535818.8	1848730.1	1946866.4	147668.2	3127379.4	644694.2	79168
1372768.3	**959627.7**	**43827.4**	**206972.3**	**215712.7**	**494.6**	**333051.7**	**73511.6**	**9611**
40191.2	28732.5	389.5	2769.4	3563.6	385.8	6754.4	2801.3	1117
1257312.9	880261.8	42170.6	194845.2	202558.7	64.0	310541.1	65811.8	6942
75264.2	50633.4	1267.3	9357.7	9590.4	44.8	15756.2	4898.5	1552
804947.6	**625267.8**	**11348.4**	**86243.1**	**75134.4**	**20765.2**	**136419.0**	**49936.2**	**21389**
735399.9	588144.6	9807.6	67190.0	56321.9	20765.2	107719.8	41590.3	19888
51249.8	27731.7	1048.0	14572.2	14557.1		21620.6	6015.5	1213
18297.9	9391.5	492.8	4480.9	4255.4		7078.6	2330.4	288
428098.5	**348118.9**	**2099.3**	**30678.1**	**30410.1**	**11876.2**	**50239.5**	**17730.1**	**9240**
55897.3	44109.3	272.3	5233.8	5304.5		7522.6	1945.8	2001
210194.2	181012.3	606.6	13400.2	12898.3	9685.1	19791.5	6286.6	3994
30843.4	26538.5	19.5	1528.8	1593.4		1897.0	284.1	279
90987.4	65611.4	860.3	8957.4	8992.4	793.1	17181.5	7328.8	1434
17504.0	12201.6	110.9	2179.3	2370.3		3794.8	1313.6	426
22672.2	18645.8	229.7	-621.4	-748.8	1398.0	52.1	571.2	1106
2410288.1	**1603567.8**	**134534.7**	**363192.5**	**372864.9**	**20895.1**	**659844.2**	**152444.6**	**43232**
1300592.3	**875468.5**	**124797.2**	**158775.1**	**164885.5**	**11769.0**	**376217.6**	**86534.9**	**23490**
171217.3	145069.0	1117.2	16689.0	18150.4	8678.8	29542.6	10275.0	3920
539261.2	346914.6	103957.2	34988.8	35731.3	2127.7	184141.6	44453.1	5608
163455.1	112903.6	1020.9	24743.7	27332.2	223.4	35774.6	7421.5	4117
18586.6	16243.3	329.7	1050.0	1091.4	525.9	2939.5	1518.4	509
85647.2	62373.8	947.1	14704.6	14893.0		18101.7	2261.6	1898
26478.2	14091.1	112.6	4250.8	4060.0		5458.2	1285.6	474
223358.5	141151.1	16686.9	39362.2	40451.9	213.2	69473.7	12334.9	5945
13712.3	8877.6	80.0	4627.0	4626.4		4836.5	130.1	347
918.4	692.0	6.1	109.7	146.3		194.5	42.1	65
57957.5	27152.4	539.5	18249.3	18402.6		25754.7	6812.6	607
621750.8	**478199.2**	**3587.1**	**37418.3**	**40520.0**	**4852.3**	**66295.0**	**22187.9**	**12385**
56659.6	56390.2	118.9	-1943.1	-1858.7	1983.2	-707.0	1032.8	1307
273368.0	204217.1	122.4	4802.1	5646.4		13209.9	7441.1	1832
48265.4	41940.6	183.2	3804.8	4604.5	207.2	7107.7	2320.0	923

13-12 续表 4

单位: 万元

地　区	Region	流动负债合计 Total Working Liabilities	长期负债合计 Long-term Liabilities	所有者权益合计 Total Owners' Equities
沙湾县	Shawan County	60403.4	1908.5	33710.0
托里县	Toli County	57202.2	19122.4	88571.2
裕民县	Yumin [Qagantokay] County	633.9		422.1
和布克赛尔蒙古自治县	Hoboksar Mongol Autonomous County	42697.6	14011.5	57188.7
阿勒泰地区	**Altay Administrative Offices**	**455687.3**	**181733.8**	**425508.2**
阿勒泰市	Altay City	62310.8	79856.8	28587.8
布尔津县	Burqin County	131997.6	40414.5	17252.2
富蕴县	Fuyun [Koktokay] County	196140.5	37443.4	189129.8
福海县	Fuhai [Burultokay] County	3619.7	14384.3	14220.3
哈巴河县	Habahe [Kaba] County	58841.6	9634.8	175271.7
青河县	Qinghe [Qinggil] County	2472.8		954.4
吉木乃县	Jeminay County	304.3		92.0
博尔塔拉蒙古自治州	**Bortala Mongol Autonomous Prefecture**	**149131.2**	**117559.8**	**89589.1**
博乐市	Bole [Bortala] City	143089.2	115314.5	79783.5
精河县	Jinghe [Jing] County	5172.7	2175.7	6057.3
温泉县	Wenquan [Araxang] County	869.3	69.6	3748.3
巴音郭楞蒙古自治州	**Bayangol Mongol Autonomous Prefecture**	**1720701.9**	**2165683.4**	**3850539.9**
库尔勒市	Korla City	1266564.1	1790829.2	3590528.1
轮台县	Luntai [Bugur] County			
尉犁县	Yuli [Lopnur] County			
若羌县	Ruoqiang [Qarkilik] County	195759.8	234840.5	127372.9
且末县	Qiemo [Qarqan] County	1975.7	273.2	3133.7
焉耆回族自治县	Yanqi Hui Autonomous County	36291.3		17969.3
和静县	Hejing County	188394.4	135780.4	100887.6
和硕县	Hoxud County	4489.7		3037.6
博湖县	Bohu [Bagrax] County	27226.9	3960.1	7610.7
阿克苏地区	**Aksu Administrative Offices**	**594027.9**	**293044.3**	**992579.4**
阿克苏市	Aksu City	132807.5	177206.3	324636.3
温宿县	Wensu [Onsu] County	71281.3	6621.1	13200.8
库车县	Kuqa County	309246.0	77008.4	618929.3
沙雅县	Xayar County			
新和县	Xinhe [Toksu] County			
拜城县	Baicheng [Bay] County	55645.1	31808.5	27061.1
乌什县	Wushi [Uxturpan] County	8531.3	400.0	7990.0

Continued

(10 000 yuan)

主营业务收入 Revenue from Principal Business	#主营业务成本 Cost of Principal Business	主营业务税金及附加 Taxes and Other Charges on Principal Business	营业利润 Business Profit	利润总额 Total Profit	亏损企业亏损总额 Losses Value of Loss-Suffering Enterprises	利税总额 Total Profits and Taxes	本年应交增值税 Value-added Taxes Payable	全部从业人员年平均人数（人） Annual Average Employed Persons (person)
85775.7	70937.1	388.2	9699.3	10316.4		14547.7	3843.1	1529
96961.7	68055.8	480.4	14003.4	13899.3	2431.7	15759.8	1380.1	3272
611.0	611.0		-0.2	-0.2	0.2	-0.2		95
60109.4	36047.4	2294.0	7052.0	7912.3	230.0	16377.1	6170.8	3427
487945.0	**249900.1**	**6150.4**	**166999.1**	**167459.4**	**4273.8**	**217331.6**	**43721.8**	**7357**
76735.1	65497.9	370.6	-1285.7	-401.5	1583.7	4085.1	4116.0	1978
27992.9	16683.6	72.8	4109.0	3874.2	44.6	4681.3	734.3	484
142042.7	74298.3	2562.1	38459.8	39889.0	123.5	56776.1	14325.0	2976
10598.7	8282.2	21.1	1607.4	1534.4	726.9	1921.5	366.0	211
228847.7	83541.6	3118.9	124065.0	122514.4	1795.1	149805.2	24171.9	1648
1023.3	965.2	3.6	24.5	29.8		41.0	7.6	43
704.6	631.3	1.3	19.1	19.1		21.4	1.0	17
171322.3	**148672.9**	**747.9**	**9552.4**	**11174.9**	**5238.8**	**18354.0**	**6431.2**	**4633**
161187.5	140341.9	666.7	8854.9	10345.0	5238.8	17220.9	6209.2	4331
7076.5	5275.9	77.3	783.0	786.6		1085.9	222.0	288
3058.3	3055.1	3.9	-85.5	43.3		47.2		14
4548953.4	**1691108.5**	**206124.5**	**2035099.6**	**2045286.9**	**2279.5**	**2630681.0**	**379269.6**	**27210**
4191490.6	1499049.2	191690.1	1969053.7	1962020.5	1096.6	2503966.4	350255.8	21336
194084.6	85302.2	12770.2	42307.7	60023.4	221.0	89747.8	16954.2	2899
2439.3	2203.8	10.3	-76.9	-9.7	41.7	91.5	90.9	176
30521.7	20779.6	114.6	4476.5	4550.2	78.7	5895.9	1231.1	622
108528.9	66171.9	1500.8	19331.8	18789.9	140.0	29427.8	9137.1	1637
4054.7	3106.9	2.7	43.0	158.8		205.0	43.5	122
17833.6	14494.9	35.8	-36.2	-246.2	701.5	1346.6	1557.0	418
1545587.1	**1194492.7**	**151194.3**	**132342.0**	**137909.4**	**2705.1**	**345129.6**	**56025.9**	**13800**
254587.0	216246.8	1649.7	28524.7	32144.0		46908.8	13115.1	6456
24676.0	13772.0	267.9	3870.4	3859.2	554.1	6049.5	1922.4	966
1196632.8	917848.4	147126.8	88158.2	90150.1	237.3	271585.8	34308.9	4208
55293.4	35884.9	1448.1	10847.6	10808.1	1913.7	18360.2	6104.0	1862
8222.6	5594.9	551.8	561.1	568.0		1339.3	219.5	180

13-12 续表 5

单位：万元

地　　区	Region	流动负债合计 Total Working Liabilities	长期负债合计 Long-term Liabilities	所有者权益合计 Total Owners' Equities
阿瓦提县	Awat County	16516.7		761.9
柯坪县	Kalpin County			
克孜勒苏柯尔克孜自治州	**Kizilsu Kirgiz Autonomous Prefecture**	**11127.5**	**3053.0**	**31426.4**
阿图什市	Artux City	11127.5	3053.0	31426.4
阿克陶县	Akto County			
阿合奇县	Akqi County			
乌恰县	Wuqia [Ulugqat] County			
喀什地区	**Kashgar [Kaxgar] Administrative Offices**	**98973.2**	**183386.6**	**47402.9**
喀什市	Kashgar [Kaxgar] City	93087.8	180992.5	32743.7
疏附县	Shufu County	3721.3	1732.6	157.1
疏勒县	Shule County	-5788.4	27.7	10705.5
英吉沙县	Yengisar County	6821.9	12.0	459.8
泽普县	Zepu [Poskam] County			
莎车县	Shache [Yarkant] County	1130.6	621.8	3336.8
叶城县	Yecheng [Kagilik] County			
麦盖提县	Makit County			
岳普湖县	Yopurga County			
伽师县	Jiashi [Payzawat] County			
巴楚县	Bachu [Maralbexi] County			
塔什库尔干塔吉克自治县	Taxkorgan Tajik Autonomous County			
和田地区	**Hotan Administrative Offices**	**53544.0**	**67135.6**	**185386.8**
和田市	Hotan City	35344.1	61542.4	14227.5
和田县	Hotan County	11411.0	5202.4	136569.2
墨玉县	Moyu [Karakax] County	3113.8	390.8	34133.8
皮山县	Pishan [Guma] County	3675.1		456.3
洛浦县	Lop County			
策勒县	Qira County			
于田县	Yutian [Keriya] County			
民丰县	Minfeng [Niya] County			
自治区直辖县级市	**Municpality Country-LevelCity directly under the Central Government**	**1534979.8**	**1049594.8**	**1399317.8**
石河子市	Shihezi City	1197422.6	739467.6	1138713.2
阿拉尔市	Aral City	137789.7	112898.0	87092.9
图木舒克市	Tumxuk City	58490.6	72397.7	25031.3
五家渠市	Wujiaqu City	141276.9	124831.5	148480.4

Continued

(10 000 yuan)

主营业务收入 Revenue from Principal Business	#主营业务成本 Cost of Principal Business	主营业务税金及附加 Taxes and Other Charges on Principal Business	营业利润 Business Profit	利润总额 Total Profit	亏损企业亏损总额 Losses Value of Loss-Suffering Enterprises	利税总额 Total Profits and Taxes	本年应交增值税 Value-added Taxes Payable	全部从业人员年平均人数(人) Annual Average Employed Persons (person)
6175.3	5145.7	150.0	380.0	380.0		886.0	356.0	128
14459.0	**12354.3**	**49.3**	**559.5**	**83.1**	**58.4**	**357.2**	**224.8**	**440**
14459.0	12354.3	49.3	559.5	83.1	58.4	357.2	224.8	440
183207.6	**182807.5**	**427.3**	**-11846.9**	**-16909.7**	**17219.7**	**-7461.8**	**9020.6**	**4175**
175294.4	175824.7	383.4	-10861.2	-16001.0	16038.7	-6932.3	8685.3	3514
4292.2	3439.7	22.8	210.7	251.6		537.2	262.8	341
1563.2	1665.7	13.9	-387.3	-361.8	361.8	-345.1	2.8	71
1448.7	1549.9	4.1	-835.9	-819.2	819.2	-781.0	34.1	159
609.1	327.5	3.1	26.8	20.7		59.4	35.6	90
74614.7	**70784.9**	**550.5**	**-4637.0**	**3296.2**	**2582.1**	**9722.0**	**5875.3**	**2183**
43952.8	45804.4	244.2	-5356.2	1702.3	994.8	4581.1	2634.6	1405
13053.7	10043.5	204.6	157.0	-151.6	1587.3	1730.0	1677.0	444
15113.2	13160.3	101.7	439.9	1619.1		3077.7	1356.9	234
2495.0	1776.7		122.3	126.4		333.2	206.8	100
1773386.8	**1423268.3**	**11351.4**	**163715.4**	**177694.9**	**22706.9**	**252217.2**	**63170.9**	**30458**
1437514.2	1129667.5	10534.0	157269.4	170249.1	18001.1	231815.3	51032.2	24445
208539.8	184772.6	764.0	6138.1	6123.1	1042.4	15603.9	8716.8	2414
38342.6	34766.5	24.6	2821.5	2829.6		3854.6	1000.4	955
88990.2	74061.7	28.8	-2513.6	-1506.9	3663.4	943.4	2421.5	2644

13-13 国有控股工业企业主要经济效益指标

单位: % (2010 年)

项　　目	Item	产　值利税率 Ratio of Profits and Taxes to Industrial Output Value
总　　计	**Total**	**29.7**
按登记注册类型分	**By Status of Registration**	
内资企业	Domestic Funded Enterprises	29.7
国有企业	State-owned Enterprises	7.7
#中央企业	Central Enterprises	6.2
地方企业	Local Enterprises	12.3
#自治区属企业	Autonomous	13.7
地区(州、市)属企业	Prefecture or City	-5.7
县(市)属企业	County or City	9.7
股份合作企业	Share-holding Cooperative Enterprises	18.8
联营企业	Joint Ownership Enterprises	24.7
#国有联营企业	State Joint Enterprises Ownership	28.6
国有与集体联营企业	Joint State-collectiue Enterprises	6.0
有限责任公司	Limited Liability Corporations	16.5
#国有独资公司	Sole State-funded Corporations	21.5
其他有限责任公司	Other Limited Liability Corporations	14.7
股份有限公司	Share-holding Corporations Ltd.	37.7
外商投资企业	Foreign Funded Enterprises	40.3
在总计中: 国有控股企业	Of the Total : State-owned and State-holding Enterprises	29.7
按轻、重工业分	**Grouped by Light & Heavy Industry**	
轻工业	Light Industry	16.2
以农产品为原料	Using Farm Produces as Raw Materials	17.0
以非农产品为原料	Using Non-Farm Produces as Raw Materials	-1.0
重工业	Heavy Industry	30.5
采掘工业	Mining and Quarrying	54.7
原料工业	Raw Materials Industry	16.9
加工工业	Manufacturing Industry	17.1
按企业规模分	**Grouped by Size of Enterprises**	
大型企业	Large Enterprises	33.6
中型企业	Medium-sized Enterprises	18.8
小型企业	Small Enterprises	16.3

Main Indicators on Economic Efficiency of State-holding Industrial Enterprises

(%)

总资产贡献率 Ratio of Total Assets to Industrial Output Value	资本保值增值率 Ratio of Capital-hold and Rise	资产负债率 Assets Liability Ratio	流动资产周转次数(次/年) Number of Times of Annual TurnoverWorking Capitals (times/year)	成本费用利润率 Ratio of Profits to Industrial Cost	全员劳动生产率 Overall Labour Productivity
20.8	**126.6**	**48.1**	**2.9**	**21.9**	**48.2**
20.9	126.7	48.1	2.9	21.9	48.2
4.9	108.9	63.8	1.8	0.8	21.4
4.7	99.4	65.1	2.2	-1.3	19.6
5.5	130.8	61.0	1.2	7.7	18.1
4.7	138.5	54.4	1.3	8.4	19.5
-1.3	129.7	82.1	1.0	-7.7	10.0
4.5	107.7	69.3	1.2	6.1	11.4
17.2	221.4	58.7	1.3	22.0	17.0
10.7	132.4	80.4	1.2	15.1	16.3
13.7	147.5	75.0	1.1	20.9	18.6
1.7	41.0	96.6	1.7	-7.4	11.9
11.6	131.6	60.4	2.0	11.5	22.0
13.7	132.2	55.5	2.3	11.8	22.9
10.8	131.3	62.4	1.9	11.5	21.6
28.7	128.2	39.0	3.8	30.1	83.5
13.0	116.2	45.5	1.8	40.4	52.8
20.8	126.6	48.1	2.9	21.9	48.2
10.3	116.0	60.2	1.1	6.4	13.7
11.9	120.0	62.0	1.1	7.2	14.3
0.4	100.7	49.4	0.6	-6.9	7.8
21.7	127.3	47.2	3.2	22.9	54.3
28.6	130.9	39.0	2.7	61.0	70.4
15.9	128.3	54.0	4.1	7.1	43.2
10.6	84.5	61.4	1.2	13.2	16.8
26.2	122.2	42.2	3.9	26.0	70.5
11.8	155.7	57.3	1.8	11.0	21.7
8.0	117.9	64.2	1.3	12.4	19.2

13-14 分行业国有控股工业企业主要经济效益指标

单位: %　　(2010 年)

行　　业	Sector	产值利税率 Ratio of Profits and Taxes to Industrial Output Value
煤炭开采和洗选业	Mining and Washing of Coal	13.2
石油和天然气开采业	Extraction of Petroleum and Natural Gas	58.3
#天然原油和天然气开采	Extraction of Ores Crude Oil and Natural Gas Extraction	64.0
黑色金属矿采选业	Mining and Processing of Ferrous Metals Ores	36.6
有色金属矿采选业	Mining and Processing of Nonferrous Metals Ores	59.8
非金属矿采选业	Mining and Processing of Nonmetal Ores	18.5
#采　盐	Extraction of Salt	24.6
农副食品加工业	Processing of Food from Agricultural Products	9.9
#谷物磨制	Grain Grinding	5.4
饲料加工	Fodder Processing	11.3
制　糖	Sugar Making	20.7
食品制造业	Manufacture of Food	2.1
#罐头制造	Manufacture of can	-12.3
饮料制造业	Manufacture of Beverage	36.9
#酒的制造	Manufacture of Wine	37.5
烟草制品业	Manufacture of Tobacco	67.8
纺织业	Manufacture of Textile	9.8
#棉、化纤纺织及印染精加工	Cotton, Chemical Fiber, Dyeing, Printing and Processing	10.6
毛纺织和染整精加工	Wool Textile, Dyeing and Printing	-4.1
纺织服装、鞋、帽制造业	Manufacture of Textile Wearing Apparel, Footware and Caps	9.4
木材加工及木、竹、藤、棕、草制品业	Processing of Timber, Wood, Bamboo, Cane, Grass Products	-4.3
家具制造业	Manufacture of Furniture	14.3
造纸及纸制品业	Manufacture of Paper and Paper Products	14.5
印刷业和记录媒介的复制	Printing and Copying of Medium for Record	12.3
石油加工、炼焦及核燃料加工业	Oil Processing, Coking and Nuclear Fuel Processing	21.6
#炼　焦	Coking	9.7
化学原料及化学制品制造业	Raw Chemical Material and Chemical Products	20.0
#基础化学原料制造	Basic Chemical Material	10.8
肥料制造	Fertilizer Making	35.1
医药制造业	Manufacture of Medicine	15.5
化学纤维制造业	Manufacture of Chemical Fiber	8.9
橡胶制品业	Manufacture of Rubber Products	6.9
塑料制品业	Manufacture of Plastic Products	6.7
非金属矿物制品业	Manufacture of Nonmetal Mineral Products	21.9
#水泥制造	Manufacture of Cement	26.5
黑色金属冶炼及压延加工业	Smelting and Pressing of Ferrous Metals	6.7
有色金属冶炼及压延加工业	Smelting and Pressing of Nonferrous Metals	10.3
金属制品业	Manufacture of Metal Products	4.9
通用设备制造业	Manufacture of General Purpose Machinery	4.3
专用设备制造业	Manufacture of Special Purpose Machinery	9.6
交通运输设备制造业	Manufacture of Transport Equipment	-3.0
电气机械及器材制造业	Manufacture of Electric Equipment and Machinery	7.4
仪器仪表及文化、办公用机械制造业	Manufacture of Measuring Instruments and Machinery for Cultural Activity and Office Work	0.1
电力、热力的生产和供应业	Electricity and Thermal Production and Supply	13.3
#电力生产和电力供应	Electricity Production and Supply	13.7
燃气生产和供应业	Gas Production and Supply	12.8
水的生产和供应业	Water Production and Supply	-17.5

Main Indicators on Economic Efficiency of State-holding Industrial Enterprises by Sectors

(%)

总资产贡献率 Ratio of Total Assets to Industrial Output Value	资本保值增值率 Ratio of Capital-hold and Rise	资产负债率 Assets Liability Ratio	流动资产周转次数(次/年) Number of Times of Annual TurnoverWorking Capitals (times/year)	成本费用利润率 Ratio of Profits to Industrial Cost	全员劳动生产率 Overall Labour Productivity
5.1	120.6	64.3	1.2	0.7	12.0
31.5	130.4	35.4	3.2	67.8	96.1
33.5	130.0	34.2	3.4	80.3	118.0
22.0	152.1	59.1	1.2	31.4	49.1
25.8	147.3	42.2	1.7	99.2	41.6
20.5	112.7	52.9	1.4	14.0	12.4
29.9	145.5	36.7	1.7	16.4	14.2
7.7	170.2	60.5	1.1	7.5	12.9
7.5	91.3	57.1	2.7	4.5	10.4
9.7	152.0	45.9	1.5	9.6	23.7
16.5	127.5	59.7	1.3	16.5	13.9
2.7	85.2	73.6	0.8	-1.5	9.5
-2.2	59.5	79.0	0.5	-16.8	2.4
23.3	133.1	43.1	1.1	29.7	20.4
23.8	134.7	45.8	1.1	31.1	21.0
73.6	106.9	45.1	1.8	21.4	212.6
8.0	119.8	58.4	1.2	4.9	6.1
9.5	134.6	59.4	1.5	5.1	6.5
-0.6	73.4	42.6	0.7	-5.6	2.4
6.5	107.3	71.8	2.0	3.5	5.3
0.9	—	157.4	1.0	-8.0	2.8
9.4			1.0	13.1	7.9
8.3	103.8	57.3	0.9	7.2	7.4
5.7	103.9	53.2	1.0	8.1	7.9
38.2	107.1	38.8	8.3	5.3	102.2
3.8	110.2	83.3	0.7	4.0	8.7
10.2	167.6	49.4	1.6	18.8	24.1
3.3	186.9	39.8	1.5	4.9	9.2
17.2	110.1	61.0	1.4	35.8	42.0
10.3	151.5	49.6	0.8	13.0	10.1
9.6	131.1	70.5	1.9	5.1	18.9
13.9	—	68.7	2.2	2.0	7.9
4.7	112.2	57.6	1.1	4.3	6.6
10.2	168.9	48.1	1.2	17.1	16.4
10.8	180.4	47.7	1.3	21.3	17.2
13.7	108.1	52.2	5.2	4.7	35.0
11.7	142.2	70.5	2.5	10.5	21.4
8.1	111.8	47.1	4.0	3.1	13.3
3.1	102.9	77.1	0.8	-0.3	4.5
4.5	212.1	103.8	0.8	4.5	6.3
-1.2	108.1	87.4	1.2	-3.4	3.2
3.9	71.0	80.2	0.5	2.3	7.6
	63.6	74.8	0.6	-1.7	5.0
6.1	130.3	67.7	2.3	8.8	28.5
6.3	131.8	67.6	2.6	9.1	30.1
5.5	113.6	68.0	0.8	12.3	21.8
-1.2	103.7	49.7	0.5	-17.6	8.2

13-15 各地、州、市、县(市)国有控股工业企业主要经济效益指标

单位: %　　(2010 年)

地　　区	Region	产　值利税率 Ratio of Profits and Taxes to Industrial Output Value
总　计	**Total**	**29.7**
乌鲁木齐市	**Urumqi City**	**20.2**
天山区	Tianshan District	7.0
沙依巴克区	Shayibak District	26.8
新市区	Xinshi District	53.3
水磨沟区	Shui Mogou District	11.9
头屯河区	Tou Tunhe District	6.9
达坂城区	Da Bancheng District	35.5
米东区	Midong District	12.8
乌鲁木齐县	Urumqi County	60.4
克拉玛依市	**Karamay City**	**33.4**
独山子区	Dushanzi District	21.1
克拉玛依区	Karamay District	42.1
白碱滩区	Bai Jiantan District	
乌尔河区	Urhe District	
吐鲁番地区	**Turpan Administrative Offices**	**35.5**
吐鲁番市	Turpan City	17.3
鄯善县	Shanshan [Piqan] County	37.9
托克逊县	Toksun County	20.0
哈密地区	**Hami [Kumul] Administrative Offices**	**18.2**
哈密市	Hami [Kumul] City	15.9
巴里坤哈萨克自治县	Barkol Kazak Autonomous County	40.4
伊吾县	Yiwu [Araturuk] County	36.5
昌吉回族自治州	**Changji Hui Autonomous Prefecture**	**11.4**
昌吉市	Changji City	17.2
阜康市	Fukang City	9.4
呼图壁县	Hutubi County	5.5
玛纳斯县	Manas County	16.0
奇台县	Qitai County	20.7
吉木萨尔县	Jimsar County	0.2
木垒哈萨克自治县	Mori Kazak Autonomous County	
伊犁哈萨克自治州	**Ili Kazak Autonomous Prefecture**	**26.5**
伊犁州直属县(市)	**Counties (Cities) Direct Under Ili Prefecture**	**28.2**
伊宁市	Yining [Gulja] City	17.3
奎屯市	Kuytun City	33.3
伊宁县	Yining [Gulja] County	21.0
察布查尔锡伯自治县	Qapqal Xibe Autonomous County	16.4
霍城县	Huocheng [Korgas] County	21.7
巩留县	Gongliu [Tokkuztara] County	19.8
新源县	Xinyuan [Kunes] County	29.9
昭苏县	Zhaosu [Mongolkure] County	27.4
特克斯县	Tekes County	21.2
尼勒克县	Nilka County	42.1
塔城地区	**Tacheng [Tarbagatai] Administrative Offices**	**10.3**
塔城市	Tacheng [Qoqek] City	-1.1
乌苏市	Usu City	4.9
额敏县	Emin [Dorbiljin] County	16.9

Main Indicators on Economic Efficiency of State-holding Industrial Enterprises by Prefecture, Autonomous Prefecture, City and County

(%)

总资产贡献率 Ratio of Total Assets to Industrial Output Value	资本保值增值率 Ratio of Capital-hold and Rise	资产负债率 Assets Liability Ratio	流动资产周转次数(次/年) Number of Times of Annual TurnoverWorking Capitals (times/year)	成本费用利润率 Ratio of Profits to Industrial Cost	全员劳动生产率 Overall Labour Productivity
20.9	**126.6**	**48.1**	**2.9**	**21.9**	**48.2**
16.5	**136.6**	**43.5**	**3.3**	**12.7**	**45.2**
4.6	118.7	68.1	2.2	5.0	26.7
5.6	181.9	38.0	0.8	20.8	14.5
37.7	166.2	18.3	3.4	63.8	99.4
9.1	113.3	31.2	2.0	9.9	19.4
14.3	110.6	51.4	5.6	4.9	36.7
15.5	139.1	31.1	1.9	35.0	17.0
13.1	142.0	48.2	4.1	-3.5	34.5
12.5	124.9	75.0	1.2	88.8	268.4
28.5	**110.8**	**39.1**	**3.9**	**22.3**	**63.9**
26.0		39.5	6.8	6.8	81.0
29.5		39.0	3.0	34.9	59.9
13.6	**201.9**	**50.1**	**2.7**	**18.9**	**65.0**
8.1	114.3	75.6	2.1	8.5	17.9
15.0	201.9	45.7	3.0	19.6	81.2
7.2	267.8	67.5	1.1	14.8	26.1
10.2	**154.5**	**56.9**	**1.4**	**10.4**	**14.8**
9.3	151.8	55.7	1.4	8.4	13.9
15.2	335.3	73.6	1.4	40.6	24.8
26.9	101.2	23.4	0.8	31.9	33.2
8.0	**138.8**	**79.2**	**2.2**	**7.7**	15.3
15.0	146.1	69.9	2.0	10.5	8.9
5.8	151.8	72.4	2.3	6.6	14.0
14.0	146.3	71.9	4.9	5.5	25.6
10.3	101.0	88.8	2.8	10.9	32.0
13.2	—	95.6	1.5	15.9	15.2
0.8	94.8	86.0	1.2	-3.3	7.6
14.4	**137.9**	**61.6**	**1.6**	**19.8**	**30.0**
13.0	**129.8**	**63.4**	**1.4**	**15.9**	**27.7**
11.6	288.1	70.9	3.0	10.8	21.1
23.0	119.6	67.4	1.5	8.8	46.5
12.0	155.3	62.4	1.4	19.6	17.1
11.1	1818.6	93.5	2.0	6.5	15.2
14.2	126.2	57.9	1.2	21.0	14.5
1.2	120.2	59.4	0.3	18.1	44.0
18.0	113.4	41.7	1.1	24.9	21.5
30.7		64.7	1.3	49.7	18.5
6.8		91.8	2.4	15.5	7.0
8.1	140.0	77.8	2.3	46.2	73.9
10.3	**179.8**	**56.0**	**2.3**	**7.5**	**27.8**
0.6	200.5	65.3	3.9	-3.2	16.0
9.2	1032.2	58.1	4.5	2.7	100.6
10.7	98.3	55.4	1.3	10.0	14.3

13-15 续表 1

单位: %

地　　区	Region	产值利税率 Ratio of Profits and Taxes to Industrial Output Value
沙湾县	Shawan County	15.7
托里县	Toli County	16.9
裕民县	Yumin [Qagantokay] County	
和布克赛尔蒙古自治县	Hoboksar Mongol Autonomous County	21.0
阿勒泰地区	**Altay Administrative Offices**	**42.8**
阿勒泰市	Altay City	5.4
布尔津县	Burqin County	15.7
富蕴县	Fuyun [Koktokay] County	35.6
福海县	Fuhai [Burultokay] County	16.3
哈巴河县	Habahe [Kaba] County	65.3
青河县	Qinghe [Qinggil] County	4.0
吉木乃县	Jeminay County	3.5
博尔塔拉蒙古自治州	**Bortala Mongol Autonomous Prefecture**	**13.4**
博乐市	Bole [Bortala] City	13.5
精河县	Jinghe [Jing] County	12.8
温泉县	Wenquan [Araxang] County	9.8
巴音郭楞蒙古自治州	**Bayangol Mongol Autonomous Prefecture**	**62.9**
库尔勒市	Korla City	65.9
轮台县	Luntai [Bugur] County	
尉犁县	Yuli [Lopnur] County	
若羌县	Ruoqiang [Qarkilik] County	41.5
且末县	Qiemo [Qarqan] County	3.6
焉耆回族自治县	Yanqi Hui Autonomous County	18.0
和静县	Hejing County	27.7
和硕县	Hoxud County	4.0
博湖县	Bohu [Bagrax] County	5.4
阿克苏地区	**Aksu Administrative Offices**	**21.8**
阿克苏市	Aksu City	16.9
温宿县	Wensu [Onsu] County	23.5
库车县	Kuqa County	22.4
沙雅县	Xayar County	
新和县	Xinhe [Toksu] County	
拜城县	Baicheng [Bay] County	33.9
乌什县	Wushi [Uxturpan] County	18.4

Continued

(%)

总资产贡献率 Ratio of Total Assets to Industrial Output Value	资本保值增值率 Ratio of Capital-hold and Rise	资产负债率 Assets Liability Ratio	流动资产周转次数(次/年) Number of Times of Annual TurnoverWorking Capitals (times/year)	成本费用利润率 Ratio of Profits to Industrial Cost	全员劳动生产率 Overall Labour Productivity
16.3	163.3	65.3	1.9	12.1	18.2
10.3	170.9	46.7	1.4	16.8	16.8
		60.0	9.4		2.2
15.0	116.8	51.1	1.7	15.6	12.4
21.3	**137.7**	**60.0**	**1.9**	**53.0**	**41.2**
3.6	168.7	83.3	1.9	-0.5	14.3
4.4	260.3	90.9	1.7	16.6	23.7
14.0	126.1	55.3	1.2	39.1	29.1
6.0	112.3	57.1	0.7	17.2	25.0
61.7	144.1	28.4	3.6	120.3	103.8
1.2	93.7	72.2	1.3	2.7	8.5
5.5	38.0	76.8	3.1	2.8	3.0
6.8	**179.5**	**74.9**	**1.5**	**6.8**	**11.4**
6.7	191.9	76.4	1.5	6.7	11.5
10.4	114.3	54.8	1.1	12.1	10.7
1.2	123.1	20.0	1.0	1.4	8.8
34.5	**120.7**	**50.3**	**2.9**	**93.2**	**120.4**
37.9	120.1	46.0	3.4	102.4	144.0
18.5	130.2	77.2	1.3	43.1	46.3
1.9	216.7	47.4	2.3	-0.4	6.3
11.7	172.9	66.9	1.0	17.2	15.2
8.5	121.2	76.3	1.1	21.3	33.1
3.5	102.8	59.6	0.8	4.0	5.2
4.6	206.9	80.4	0.8	-1.4	11.3
19.5	**148.2**	**47.2**	**3.8**	**10.7**	**35.9**
8.7	150.1	48.9	1.8	13.4	14.9
9.2	175.8	85.7	1.1	18.3	16.0
27.8	151.1	38.4	6.2	9.3	81.0
17.2	94.1	75.9	2.1	23.9	21.0
9.2	106.8	52.8	1.0	7.6	14.1

13-15 续表 2

单位: %

地　　区	Region	产值利税率 Ratio of Profits and Taxes to Industrial Output Value
阿瓦提县	Awat County	11.1
柯坪县	Kalpin County	
克孜勒苏柯尔克孜自治州	**Kizilsu Kirgiz Autonomous Prefecture**	**2.6**
阿图什市	Artux City	2.6
阿克陶县	Akto County	
阿合奇县	Akqi County	
乌恰县	Wuqia [Ulugqat] County	
喀什地区	**Kashgar [Kaxgar] Administrative Offices**	**-4.0**
喀什市	Kashgar [Kaxgar] City	-3.9
疏附县	Shufu County	10.9
疏勒县	Shule County	-89.6
英吉沙县	Yengisar County	-35.6
泽普县	Zepu [Poskam] County	
莎车县	Shache [Yarkant] County	9.8
叶城县	Yecheng [Kagilik] County	
麦盖提县	Makit County	
岳普湖县	Yopurga County	
伽师县	Jiashi [Payzawat] County	
巴楚县	Bachu [Maralbexi] County	
塔什库尔干塔吉克自治县	Taxkorgan Tajik Autonomous County	
和田地区	**Hotan Administrative Offices**	**13.1**
和田市	Hotan City	10.3
和田县	Hotan County	13.8
墨玉县	Moyu [Karakax] County	19.4
皮山县	Pishan [Guma] County	22.8
洛浦县	Lop County	
策勒县	Qira County	
于田县	Yutian [Keriya] County	
民丰县	Minfeng [Niya] County	
自治区直辖县级市	**Municpality Country-LevelCity directly under the Central Government**	**14.4**
石河子市	Shihezi City	16.8
阿拉尔市	Aral City	7.4
图木舒克市	Tumxuk City	7.3
五家渠市	Wujiaqu City	0.9

Continued

(%)

总资产贡献率 Ratio of Total Assets to Industrial Output Value	资本保值增值率 Ratio of Capital-hold and Rise	资产负债率 Assets Liability Ratio	流动资产周转次数(次/年) Number of Times of Annual TurnoverWorking Capitals (times/year)	成本费用利润率 Ratio of Profits to Industrial Cost	全员劳动生产率 Overall Labour Productivity
7.8		95.6	0.6	6.7	9.3
1.2	**180.5**	**30.9**	**2.6**	**0.6**	**10.2**
1.2	180.5	30.9	2.6	0.6	10.2
0.4	**158.9**	**85.6**	**4.0**	**-8.6**	**11.6**
0.6	199.8	89.3	4.3	-8.5	13.1
11.1	—	97.2	2.0	6.2	4.8
-7.0	115.3	-116.5	2.2	-18.1	0.7
-10.7	35.6	93.7	0.7	-36.6	1.5
1.3	103.8	34.4	2.3	3.3	4.3
4.0	**125.8**	**39.5**	**1.5**	**4.2**	**16.5**
6.2	135.7	87.3	3.7	3.4	13.8
1.1	126.3	10.9	0.5	-1.2	25.3
8.5	118.4	9.3	1.8	11.1	20.8
8.7		89.0	4.6	5.3	6.3
8.1	**115.6**	**65.0**	**1.2**	**11.1**	**15.3**
9.3	117.2	63.0	1.3	13.4	16.0
7.0	121.1	75.1	1.9	3.0	17.4
3.4	201.0	84.1	0.6	7.4	13.9
1.8	96.3	64.2	0.5	-1.6	7.7

13-16 分行业大中型工业企业主要经济指标

单位: 万元 (2010 年)

行业	Sector	企业单位数(个) Number of Enterprises (unit)	#亏损企业 Loss- Suffering Enterprises	工业总产值(当年价格) Gross Industrial Output Value (At Current Prices)
煤炭开采和洗选业	Mining and Washing of Coal	33	9	956594.6
石油和天然气开采业	Extraction of Petroleum and Natural Gas	14	1	11325013.8
#天然原油和天然气开采	Extraction of Ores Crude Oil and Natural Gas Extraction	5		10365232.9
黑色金属矿采选业	Mining and Processing of Ferrous Metals Ores	8	1	419921.5
有色金属矿采选业	Mining and Processing of Nonferrous Metals Ores	8	1	316031.0
非金属矿采选业	Mining and Processing of Nonmetal Ores	3		34733.1
#采　盐	Extraction of Salt	2		21930.1
农副食品加工业	Processing of Food from Agricultural Products	21	3	487000.9
饲料加工	Fodder Processing	1		94470.3
制　糖	Sugar Making	13		238678.0
食品制造业	Manufacture of Food	15	3	379830.8
#罐头制造	Manufacture of can	5	2	148304.8
饮料制造业	Manufacture of Beverage	8	2	278883.4
#酒的制造	Manufacture of Wine	6	1	225822.5
烟草制品业	Manufacture of Tobacco	1		236475.5
纺织业	Manufacture of Textile	40	6	875512.1
#棉、化纤纺织及印染精加工	Cotton, Chemical Fiber, Dyeing, Printing and Processing	34	3	807160.9
毛纺织和染整精加工	Wool Textile, Dyeing and Printing	2	2	11026.1
纺织服装、鞋、帽制造业	Manufacture of Textile Wearing Apparel,Footware and Caps	1		8785.8
家具制造业	Manufacture of Furniture	1		58424.8
造纸及纸制品业	Manufacture of Paper and Paper Products	3	2	53136.8
印刷业和记录媒介的复制	Printing and Copying of Medium for Record	1		6445.6
石油加工、炼焦及核燃料加工业	Oil Processing, Coking and Nuclear Fuel Processing	18	3	11563129.0
#炼　焦	Coking	11	2	358993.4
化学原料及化学制品制造业	Raw Chemical Material and Chemical Products	30	3	2424805.9
#基础化学原料制造	Basic Chemical Material	15	3	594656.0
肥料制造	Fertilizer Making	3		334104.5
医药制造业	Manufacture of Medicine	3		32601.3
化学纤维制造业	Manufacture of Chemical Fiber	10		857958.7
橡胶制品业	Manufacture of Rubber Products	1		60269.0
塑料制品业	Manufacture of Plastic Products	3		106473.0
非金属矿物制品业	Manufacture of Nonmetal Mineral Products	33	3	1017563.1
#水泥制造	Manufacture of Cement	21	3	646424.1
黑色金属冶炼及压延加工业	Smelting and Pressing of Ferrous Metals	15	1	5049821.8
有色金属冶炼及压延加工业	Smelting and Pressing of Nonferrous Metals	9		493398.6
金属制品业	Manufacture of Metal Products	4		58296.5
通用设备制造业	Manufacture of General Purpose Machinery	1		13299.7
专用设备制造业	Manufacture of Special Purpose Machinery	3	1	50429.6
交通运输设备制造业	Manufacture of Transport Equipment	2	2	49254.8
电气机械及器材制造业	Manufacture of Electric Equipment and Machinery	5		2470473.0
通信设备、计算机及其他电子设备制造业	Telecom Equipment, Computer and Other Electronic Equipment	1		151751.3
电力、热力的生产和供应业	Electricity and Thermal Production and Supply	33	12	2581525.3
#电力生产和电力供应	Electricity Production and Supply	29	11	2520089.8
燃气生产和供应业	Gas Production and Supply	1		77794.6
水的生产和供应业	Water Production and Supply	1	1	14984.1

Main Indicators of Large-scale and Medium-scale Industrial Enterprises by Sectors

(10 000 yuan)

增加值 Value-added	工业销售产值(当年价) Sales Value of Industry Products (At Current Prices)	出口交货值 Delivery Value of Industry Export	实收资本 Total Capital Hold	资产合计 Total Assets	流动资产合计 Total Working Capitals	#产成品 Finished Product	固定资产原价 Original Value of Fixed Assets
556610.0	886853.0		702198.3	2541594.0	697965.5	69292.6	1168823.5
9499988.4	11310907.3	17.0	12596634.1	21138994.2	4081118.2	271747.3	26526251.6
9164293.8	10351126.4	17.0	11787259.8	19923348.0	3521950.2	266817.2	25697689.6
223821.3	427007.8		112353.7	704581.4	348946.4	29974.8	293481.9
260823.3	322601.1		65893.4	589480.8	148778.5	17930.1	207918.1
15624.3	26321.5	23.8	5170.2	25319.4	15465.0	4924.7	15102.5
12914.1	16841.6	23.8	2170.3	17143.4	10583.6	3700.3	9425.5
137117.0	458923.7	16199.8	229325.1	851680.0	485383.0	160155.2	398096.4
23082.2	96486.6		22673.7	177183.9	86139.8		39609.8
87890.7	231842.8	854.6	68280.9	316207.2	174372.5	97507.2	235041.4
64171.5	343078.9	75637.7	125443.6	719386.6	334920.9	84015.9	396565.1
-7266.3	109946.4	64051.9	59824.6	462185.8	257763.5	72008.6	215281.6
132969.6	267917.4		121196.3	495867.6	293096.8	9473.8	199115.9
117588.7	223497.0		110373.5	446768.5	273400.4	4829.1	157563.1
188122.6	235999.5		18741.7	217131.0	131090.0		127180.0
230984.4	886144.7	29752.0	339298.3	1368732.8	696586.1	87678.9	733356.9
216391.5	830169.9	15011.4	282798.3	1228320.1	623645.9	76235.1	658612.4
1914.2	13235.9	716.4	4607.0	10961.7	6113.5	2022.7	4821.1
3974.1	7143.2	671.6	2025.0	16004.2	10170.4	9.4	5143.4
18475.0	55644.3		63268.0	298805.2	57592.7		40512.8
19596.9	54332.8		24295.2	131078.7	68847.6	5059.0	94003.5
4135.1	6556.0		5727.4	22716.2	6250.1	1166.6	25167.0
3097841.5	11608585.3	5697.0	1111484.2	6903084.5	1569712.7	203283.2	7045287.8
92863.6	348972.2	5697.0	174018.4	763548.5	271675.4	31133.5	303675.3
799610.4	2386090.9	111740.6	1242406.4	5641462.2	1566205.5	99472.0	3105241.3
171842.0	592355.3	51984.0	385646.3	2160979.5	601277.1	27737.3	641470.5
193155.1	320643.2		118649.7	798736.6	243208.0	11531.1	634063.5
9918.7	31327.1	93.4	12960.6	55142.2	31866.2	4790.7	25021.4
165225.3	827008.0	840.5	191148.0	929999.5	417780.8	68324.6	468101.0
10391.1	60901.0	2923.7	800.0	28245.7	27002.6	3759.5	1122.0
19933.4	107132.9		68302.0	174565.8	103347.3	28468.3	59930.5
347128.6	985763.1	9607.0	432324.0	2404633.0	897810.6	49705.6	1033559.5
249826.1	636257.5		338865.1	1889881.3	605899.3	22042.4	832626.8
698994.4	5003385.2	20835.6	943174.2	3224559.7	1355313.3	231235.6	2398980.8
116255.2	450668.9		422131.7	774193.8	376248.0	54496.9	334359.1
13033.1	61342.4		15740.0	92893.0	54758.0	1667.5	21810.7
5952.2	13299.7		900.5	16910.0	13083.4	2.1	4493.5
13758.1	45546.5	447.9	30469.2	108977.6	71505.5	7824.8	43763.0
1561.0	48662.3	242.3	10015.8	69940.0	43336.1	9435.6	27636.4
645760.5	2320738.8	5198.8	493904.2	4281917.8	2880753.8	44442.9	217224.1
53071.8	152069.4	29349.1	35205.9	376882.1	172789.5	7814.0	147234.3
964520.2	2579767.5		1129005.2	6650022.6	1118199.9	2027.5	6476009.8
944487.8	2518332.0		1081274.5	6416538.7	991403.2	1477.4	6280545.3
22125.5	59797.8		35380.0	229716.9	96374.8	298.5	98565.0
5885.2	14984.1		151700.0	276583.7	74036.0		214500.2

13-16 续表

单位：万元

行　业	Sector	流动负债合计 Total Working Liabilities	长期负债合计 Long-term Liabilities
煤炭开采和洗选业	Mining and Washing of Coal	886053.8	664575.8
石油和天然气开采业	Extraction of Petroleum and Natural Gas	2736071.2	4790027.1
＃天然原油和天然气开采	Extraction of Ores Crude Oil and Natural Gas Extraction	2211047.4	4598652.4
黑色金属矿采选业	Mining and Processing of Ferrous Metals Ores	361800.1	71441.5
有色金属矿采选业	Mining and Processing of Nonferrous Metals Ores	187415.7	23279.4
非金属矿采选业	Mining and Processing of Nonmetal Ores	13050.7	317.0
＃采　盐	Extraction of Salt	5647.2	317.0
农副食品加工业	Processing of Food from Agricultural Products	384807.3	64220.4
＃谷物磨制	Grain Grinding		
制　糖	Sugar Making	182713.6	3062.3
食品制造业	Manufacture of Food	440176.6	73498.8
＃罐头制造	Manufacture of can	309987.3	61862.1
饮料制造业	Manufacture of Beverage	167916.6	16756.1
＃酒的制造	Manufacture of Wine	142546.9	16207.2
烟草制品业	Manufacture of Tobacco	97962.0	
纺织业	Manufacture of Textile	562837.1	234441.8
＃棉、化纤纺织及印染精加工	Cotton, Chemical Fiber, Dyeing, Printing and Processing	503473.0	221186.7
毛纺织和染整精加工	Wool Textile, Dyeing and Printing	6565.8	
纺织服装、鞋、帽制造业	Manufacture of Textile Wearing Apparel,Footware and Caps	8238.9	3087.4
家具制造业	Manufacture of Furniture	25860.9	24358.1
造纸及纸制品业	Manufacture of Paper and Paper Products	67922.8	11556.3
印刷业和记录媒介的复制	Printing and Copying of Medium for Record	7092.2	4423.5
石油加工、炼焦及核燃料加工业	Oil Processing, Coking and Nuclear Fuel Processing	1790204.9	969256.3
＃炼　焦	Coking	327426.4	178010.3
化学原料及化学制品制造业	Raw Chemical Material and Chemical Products	1721624.3	1067341.2
＃基础化学原料制造	Basic Chemical Material	652278.6	262021.7
肥料制造	Fertilizer Making	240617.4	248316.2
医药制造业	Manufacture of Medicine	15985.0	3338.5
化学纤维制造业	Manufacture of Chemical Fiber	462844.1	137756.0
橡胶制品业	Manufacture of Rubber Products	20351.9	
塑料制品业	Manufacture of Plastic Products	54637.9	31441.0
非金属矿物制品业	Manufacture of Nonmetal Mineral Products	628456.2	521975.1
＃水泥制造	Manufacture of Cement	491568.5	396289.0
黑色金属冶炼及压延加工业	Smelting and Pressing of Ferrous Metals	1717674.8	128168.8
有色金属冶炼及压延加工业	Smelting and Pressing of Nonferrous Metals	482027.8	56316.7
金属制品业	Manufacture of Metal Products	53687.7	5000.0
通用设备制造业	Manufacture of General Purpose Machinery	11415.3	
专用设备制造业	Manufacture of Special Purpose Machinery	110234.4	9767.1
交通运输设备制造业	Manufacture of Transport Equipment	66827.2	653.2
电气机械及器材制造业	Manufacture of Electric Equipment and Machinery	1639375.7	268087.6
通信设备、计算机及其他电子设备制造业	Telecom Equipment, Computer and Other Electronic Equipment	49248.7	115076.5
电力、热力的生产和供应业	Electricity and Thermal Production and Supply	1922939.2	2504279.8
＃电力生产和电力供应	Electricity Production and Supply	1828884.8	2431981.0
燃气生产和供应业	Gas Production and Supply	81806.4	74754.4
水的生产和供应业	Water Production and Supply	60558.0	76833.2

Continued

(10 000 yuan)

所有者权益合计 Total Owners' Equities	主营业务收入 Revenue from Principal Business	#主营业务成本 Cost of Principal Business	主营业务税金及附加 Taxes and Other Charges on Principal Business	营业利润 Business Profit	利润总额 Total Profit	亏损企业亏损总额 Losses Value of Loss-Suffering Enterprises	利税总额 Total Profits and Taxes	本年应交增值税 Value-added Taxes Payable	全部从业人员年平均人数(人) Ann Employed Persons (person)
954967.3	914233.0	617883.5	25060.3	64329.9	25053.8	104222.4	131681.9	81567.8	43857
13595707.4	12725735.4	5964325.4	695659.3	4627520.9	4735202.0	147613.2	6533156.9	1102295.6	102578
13113648.2	11829685.7	4979322.1	690450.7	4780428.6	4866015.5		6631673.2	1075207.0	77639
271334.7	458524.2	273277.1	10634.6	114360.3	125845.1	1054.9	178435.1	41955.4	4630
376328.8	322327.3	112239.3	3992.8	168067.6	167935.4	123.5	206419.6	34491.4	6204
11951.7	21095.1	9529.0	1238.7	2238.7	2389.1		5912.5	2284.7	1482
11179.2	16467.5	5799.6	1187.9	2276.3	2387.1		5660.2	2085.2	962
400421.7	470370.1	351173.6	1728.8	43164.7	46104.7	6404.3	66216.7	18383.2	10586
95334.1	100415.4	69856.3	250.7	8177.5	9838.7		12490.9	2401.5	861
128215.1	228816.3	161128.6	1397.7	31046.6	32069.7		48267.4	14800.0	6573
204476.4	364157.8	281563.0	1493.0	-5034.2	-3681.9	39191.4	12127.5	14316.4	8015
90336.4	121924.6	105941.1	524.0	-34882.2	-36899.0	38518.5	-35052.0	1323.0	2840
157036.1	282493.3	155557.5	26805.6	43556.2	69199.3	3020.0	116754.9	20750.0	5968
133855.8	216370.4	107168.4	26805.6	38716.7	63555.4	2963.5	109141.6	18780.6	5219
119169.0	235999.0	88935.0	102779.0	23731.0	23434.0		160237.4	34024.4	885
560159.3	921663.8	781341.2	3894.4	59544.8	81462.8	4002.5	123452.2	38095.0	34313
497154.7	862605.7	728819.7	3704.7	60328.0	81827.3	1832.0	121567.4	36035.4	29613
2786.7	13236.7	13999.9	26.2	-2183.9	-2156.1	2156.1	-1246.8	883.1	1423
4677.9	22722.2	19771.8		1329.0	1361.3		1445.9	84.6	836
248586.2	65842.6	55511.2	56.9	2822.6	2735.8		4946.8	2154.1	2345
51599.5	54128.9	44987.7	508.8	1950.3	3163.2	1734.5	8492.6	4820.6	2973
11200.5	6556.0	5335.2	58.3	-741.9	188.6		470.8	223.9	569
4143436.1	11870367.2	9276590.7	1525991.1	548224.9	537652.7	72466.1	2456162.1	392518.3	34649
257924.9	323697.1	263407	1065.3	27585.5	28796.1	707.9	43403.3	13541.9	6086
2818231.3	2334071.5	1717960.7	25835.3	348997.7	373111.7	13444.8	496472.1	97525.1	34203
1213156.6	806328.7	665965.7	4336.8	54212.3	56676.9	13444.8	89270.2	28256.5	13966
309802.2	322143.1	165348.2	12909.0	72943.1	91465.0		123784.9	19410.9	4349
35818.7	28612.9	15842.9	240.0	1505.6	2053.5		4738.0	2444.5	1097
312453.0	976455.2	858595.9	1823.4	44502.9	51632.5		76678.9	23223.0	8298
7893.8	61533.7	52169.3	931.2	1184.9	1200.2		4234.9	2103.5	1283
88486.8	104738.4	93991.6	150.8	4510.5	4757.4		6401.6	1493.4	3085
1221788.4	1007889.9	753350.3	5734.0	132669.6	152082.2	2891.7	214083.2	56267.0	23001
976310.8	635139.7	452931.2	4858.5	94844.9	112341.4	2891.7	163043.7	45843.8	16962
1378665.3	5065280.5	4561533.7	8072.5	275934.6	261516.5	1985.2	379762.9	110173.9	25548
223839.1	475043.5	382630.1	980.2	56653.5	56538.2		69530.4	12012.0	5522
33534.0	51992.8	44775.0	409.3	3670.1	4527.5		7391.7	2454.9	2073
5494.7	14635.7	13531.9	90.1	165.4	181.9		1121.1	849.1	373
-11023.9	52647.5	41409.9	260.7	1847.8	1523.0	203.7	3837.6	2053.9	2067
2459.6	57899.6	57687.7	6.7	-4112.3	-3083.0	3083.0	-3032.7	43.6	1132
2374454.5	2393241.6	1670092.7	11377.0	599718.6	603751.7		682866.8	67738.1	5513
212556.8	138036.9	98269.9	1123.5	25457.8	28207.8		31146.3	1815.0	3163
2214875.7	2682718.7	2383632.6	11130.1	141220.0	152295.4	33751.9	263799.2	100373.7	36586
2149191.4	2617837.5	2329057.6	11069.5	139003.6	144347.7	33122.8	255248.6	99831.4	35078
73156.1	73486.5	49072.6	1119.1	7785.8	7707.4		9582.0	755.5	959
139192.5	21782.8	20338.0	107.8	-14163.3	-11201.8	11201.8	-10076.2	1017.8	791

13-17 分行业大中型工业企业主要经济效益指标

单位: % (2010 年)

行业	Sector	产值利税率 Ratio of Profits and Taxes to Industrial Output Value
煤炭开采和洗选业	Mining and Washing of Coal	13.8
石油和天然气开采业	Extraction of Petroleum and Natural Gas	57.7
#天然原油和天然气开采	Extraction of Ores Crude Oil and Natural Gas Extraction	64.0
黑色金属矿采选业	Mining and Processing of Ferrous Metals Ores	42.5
有色金属矿采选业	Mining and Processing of Nonferrous Metals Ores	65.3
非金属矿采选业	Mining and Processing of Nonmetal Ores	17.0
#采 盐	Extraction of Salt	25.8
农副食品加工业	Processing of Food from Agricultural Products	13.6
饲料加工	Fodder Processing	13.2
制 糖	Sugar Making	20.2
食品制造业	Manufacture of Food	3.2
#罐头制造	Manufacture of can	-23.6
饮料制造业	Manufacture of Beverage	41.9
#酒的制造	Manufacture of Wine	48.3
烟草制品业	Manufacture of Tobacco	67.8
纺织业	Manufacture of Textile	14.1
#棉、化纤纺织及印染精加工	Cotton, Chemical Fiber, Dyeing, Printing and Processing	15.1
毛纺织和染整精加工	Wool Textile, Dyeing and Printing	-11.3
纺织服装、鞋、帽制造业	Manufacture of Textile Wearing Apparel,Footware and Caps	16.5
家具制造业	Manufacture of Furniture	8.5
造纸及纸制品业	Manufacture of Paper and Paper Products	16.0
印刷业和记录媒介的复制	Printing and Copying of Medium for Record	7.3
石油加工、炼焦及核燃料加工业	Oil Processing, Coking and Nuclear Fuel Processing	21.2
#炼 焦	Coking	12.1
化学原料及化学制品制造业	Raw Chemical Material and Chemical Products	20.5
#基础化学原料制造	Basic Chemical Material	15.0
肥料制造	Fertilizer Making	37.1
医药制造业	Manufacture of Medicine	14.5
化学纤维制造业	Manufacture of Chemical Fiber	8.9
橡胶制品业	Manufacture of Rubber Products	7.0
塑料制品业	Manufacture of Plastic Products	6.0
非金属矿物制品业	Manufacture of Nonmetal Mineral Products	21.0
#水泥制造	Manufacture of Cement	25.2
黑色金属冶炼及压延加工业	Smelting and Pressing of Ferrous Metals	7.5
有色金属冶炼及压延加工业	Smelting and Pressing of Nonferrous Metals	14.1
金属制品业	Manufacture of Metal Products	12.7
通用设备制造业	Manufacture of General Purpose Machinery	8.4
专用设备制造业	Manufacture of Special Purpose Machinery	7.6
交通运输设备制造业	Manufacture of Transport Equipment	-6.2
电气机械及器材制造业	Manufacture of Electric Equipment and Machinery	27.6
通信设备、计算机及其他电子设备制造业	Telecom Equipment, Computer and Other Electronic Equipment	20.5
电力、热力的生产和供应业	Electricity and Thermal Production and Supply	10.2
#电力生产和电力供应	Electricity Production and Supply	10.1
燃气生产和供应业	Gas Production and Supply	12.3
水的生产和供应业	Water Production and Supply	-67.3

Main Indicators on Economic Efficiency of Large-scale and Medium-scale Industrial Enterprises by Sectors

(%)

总资产贡献率 Ratio of Total Assets to ndustrial Output Value	资本保值增值率 Ratio of Capital-hold and Rise	资产负债率 Assets Liability Ratio	流动资产周转次数(次/年) Number of Times of Annual TurnoverWorking Capitals (times/year)	成本费用利润率 Ratio of Profits to Industrial Cost	全员劳动生产率 Overall Labour Productivity
6.0	117.9	62.3	1.3	3.1	12.7
31.2	130.5	35.7	3.1	66.7	92.6
33.5	130.0	34.2	3.4	80.3	118.0
26.4	133.9	61.5	1.3	37.5	48.3
35.3	154.1	36.2	2.2	111.4	42.0
24.0	141.7	52.8	1.4	13.4	10.5
33.4	132.6	34.8	1.6	18.4	13.4
9.0	181.8	53.0	1.0	10.7	13.0
8.8	145.1	46.2	1.2	10.8	26.8
16.0	126.7	59.5	1.3	16.1	13.4
3.5	69.5	71.5	1.1	-1.0	8.0
-5.1	43.3	80.5	0.5	-26.7	-2.6
24.7	138.5	68.3	1.0	33.0	22.3
25.7	141.3	70.0	0.8	43.2	22.5
73.6	106.9	45.1	1.8	21.4	212.6
10.2	139.7	58.8	1.3	9.5	6.7
11.2	143.7	59.3	1.4	10.2	7.3
-11.2	52.9	59.9	2.2	-14.1	1.3
10.1	117.9	70.8	2.2	6.4	4.8
2.1	172.0	16.8	1.1	4.3	7.9
8.0	103.0	60.6	0.8	5.8	6.6
2.8	99.3	50.7	1.1	2.4	7.3
35.9	108.4	40.0	7.6	5.5	89.4
7.4	136.3	66.2	1.2	9.7	15.3
10.3	165.5	50.0	1.5	18.5	23.4
5.2	180.3	43.9	1.3	7.1	12.3
17.4	106.9	61.2	1.3	38.6	44.4
9.0	224.6	35.0	0.9	7.8	9.0
10.3	140.4	65.9	2.3	5.5	19.9
14.6	—	72.1	2.3	2.0	8.1
4.3	102.5	49.3	1.0	4.7	6.5
10.0	180.7	49.2	1.1	17.0	15.1
9.8	202.0	48.3	1.1	20.0	14.7
13.0	110.5	57.2	3.7	5.5	27.4
9.6	659.9	71.1	1.3	13.6	21.1
9.1	141.1	63.9	1.0	8.7	6.3
7.2	213.8	67.5	1.1	1.2	16.0
4.0	—	110.1	0.7	3.0	6.7
-3.2	—	96.5	1.3	-4.9	1.4
16.2	243.2	44.6	0.8	32.3	117.1
8.6	113.2	43.6	0.8	25.3	16.8
5.7	152.9	66.7	2.4	5.9	26.4
5.8	151.8	66.5	2.6	5.7	26.9
5.2	112.4	68.2	0.8	11.5	23.1
-3.3		49.7	0.3	-33.3	7.4

13-18 主要工业产品产量
Output of Major Industrial Products

产品名称	Item	2009	2010
原煤(吨)	Raw Coal (ton)	88125500	99267283
天然原油(吨)	Crude Oil (ton)	25128604	25581585
天然气(万立方米)	Natural Gas (10 000 cu.m)	2453887	2499096
铁矿石原矿量(吨)	Crudeiron Ore (ton)	21908869	26914436
铜选矿含铜量(吨)	Cuproaurite (ton)	84212	123250
硫铁矿(折含 S 35%)(吨)	Pyritel with Content of (S35%)(ton)	241189	166310
原盐(吨)	Salt (ton)	1293553	1746712
发电量(万千瓦小时)	Electricity (10 000 kwh)	5713129	6793226
#火 电	Thermalpower	4695120	5509050
水 电	Hydropower	798370	970725
供热量(万吉焦)	Heat Supply (10 000 gigajoules)	21802	25078
大米(吨)	Rice (ton)	173988	188694
小麦粉(万吨)	Wheate Flour (10 000 tons)	274	274
精制食用植物油(吨)	Refined Edible Oil (ton)	1200581	1151673
成品糖(吨)	Sugar (ton)	407710	450976
饲料(吨)	Forage (ton)	1649500	1802771
糖果(吨)	Candy (ton)	3161	3336
乳制品(吨)	Dairy Products (ton)	279708	321158
罐头(吨)	Canned Food (ton)	1203370	1106348
#番茄酱	Tomato Jam	1124852	1049068
味精(吨)	Mono Sodium Glutamate (ton)	16534	21552
酱油(吨)	Soy (ton)	22961	24222
方便面(吨)	Instant Noodles(ton)	36507	37228
发酵酒精(千升)	Zymolytic Alcohol (kilo-liter)	39731	52110
饮料酒(千升)	Alcohol Beverage(kilo-liter)	484936	565041
#白 酒	Liquor	63912	72553
啤 酒	Beer	375352	440895
葡萄酒	Grape Wine	36442	48472
软饮料(吨)	Soft Drink (ton)	1099933	1137518
#碳酸饮料	Carbonic Drink	57856	65868
果汁和蔬菜汁饮料	Fruit Juice and Vegetable Juice Drink	239257	320695
包装饮用水	Bottled Water	649117	524400
冷冻饮品(吨)	Ice Beverage (ton)	44307	46653
卷烟(万支)	Cigarettes (10 000 pieces)	1350000	1500000
纱(吨)	Yarn (ton)	386085	415783
布(万米)	Cloth (10 000 m)	15148	15069
#棉 布	Pure Cotton Cloth	14921	14919
绒线(毛线)(吨)	Knitting Wool (ton)	533	741

注：钢材里包括钢材生产中消耗的外购国内钢。
Note: Rolled steel contain that manufacture of steel consumed outsourcing of internal steel.

13-18 续表 1 Continued

产品名称	Item	2009	2010
呢绒(万米)	Woolen Cloth Goods (10 000 m)	376	326
服装(万件)	Garments (10 000 units)	1591	1451
轻革(平方米)	Light Leather (sq.m)	1586451	3302302
皮鞋(万双)	Leather Shoes (10 000 pairs)	170	148
人造板(立方米)	Artificial Board (cu.m)	982384	1301944
#胶合板	Plywood	284395	341805
纤维板	Fiberboard	403203	653259
刨花板	Chip Board	258379	254031
家具(件)	Furniture (unit)	3329662	3115339
#木制家具	WoodenFurniture	2847026	2675416
金属家具	Steal Furniture	290899	294196
纸浆(吨)	Paper Pulp (ton)	311466	312302
纸制品(吨)	Paper produces (ton)	293272	310529
#瓦楞纸箱(纸箱)	Corrugaled Case	237699	259086
机制纸及纸板(吨)	Machine-made Paper and Paperboard (ton)	355762	371032
本册(万本)	Copy (10 000 copies)	14910	1365
原油加工量(吨)	Processed Crude Oil (ton)	18646034	21903701
汽油(吨)	Gasoline (ton)	2745776	2681492
溶剂油(吨)	Megilp (ton)	200829	155930
煤油(吨)	Kerosene (ton)	308604	456263
柴油(吨)	Diesel Oil (ton)	8357836	9761180
润滑油(吨)	Lubricating Oil (ton)	660250	762322
燃料油(吨)	Fuel Oil (ton)	295459	195176
石油沥青(吨)	Petroleum Bitumen (ton)	1541489	1507775
液化石油气(吨)	Liquefied Petroleum Gas (ton)	584068	514246
焦炭(吨)	Coke (ton)	8994536	11878348
#机械化焦炉生产的焦炭	Coke Turned out by Mechanized Coke Oven	5628686	8296973
煤气(万立方米)	Coal Gas (10 000 cu.m)	965945	1240215
硫酸(折 100%)(吨)	Sulfuric Acid (ton)	300423	326112
盐酸(含量 31%以上)(吨)	Hydrochloric Acid (With Content of 31%) (ton)	224799	281656
氢氧化钠(烧碱)(折 100%)(吨)	Caustic Soda (ton)	814393	916205
碳酸钠(纯碱)(吨)	Soda Ash (ton)	113460	130803
碳化钙(电石)(折 300 升/千克)(吨)	Calcium Carbide (ton)	1560762	1845104
合成氨(吨)	Synthetic Ammonia (ton)	1407674	1484103
农用氮、磷、钾化学肥料(折纯)(吨)	Chemical Fertilizers (ton)	1591027	1591043
#氮肥(折含 N 100%)	Nitrogen Fertilizers	1179874	1146900
#尿 素	Carbamide	1103121	1120660
磷肥(折合 P_2O_5 100%)	Phosphate Fertilizers	11179	7911

13-18 续表 2 Continued

产品名称	Item	2009	2010
乙烯(吨)	Ethylene(ton)	491519	1193261
涂料(吨)	Paint (ton)	91172	107849
合成洗涤剂(吨)	Synthetic Detergents (ton)	49164	46155
化学原料药(吨)	Chemical Medicine (ton)	21	47
中成药(吨)	Traditional Chinese Medicine (ton)	4900	6957
轮胎外胎(条)	Outer Tyres (unit)	997295	921296
塑料制品(吨)	Plastic Produces (ton)	697269	830651
#塑料薄膜	Plastic Film	133619	157471
#农用薄膜	Farm Plastic Sheet	123956	143888
塑料型材(含板片材)	Plastic Moulding Material	37537	33660
塑料制管子及其附件(吨)	Plastic Pipe and Accessory (ton)	278233	330431
塑料编织袋(吨)	Woven Plastic Bag (ton)	82509	93428
泡沫塑料(吨)	Foamed Plastics (ton)	14466	16986
塑料包装箱及容器(吨)	Plastic Packing Case and Container (ton)	32810	46881
日用塑料制品(吨)	Household Plastic Products (ton)	20384	27588
水泥熟料(万吨)	Cement Chamotte (10 000 ton)	1548	1879
窑外分解窑熟料(预分解窑熟料)(万吨)	Clinker Cement (10 000 tons)	947	1314
水泥(万吨)	Cement (10 000 tons)	2050	2401
水泥电杆(根)	Cement Electric Pole Piece (unit)	307755	278519
建筑涂料(吨)	Architectural Coating (ton)	26581	3329
商品混凝土(立方米)	Commercial Concrete (cu.m)	10328515	15872581
预应力混凝土桩 (米)	Prestressed Concrete Piles (m)	1563350	2592414
砖(折标准砖)(万块)	Brick (Standard Brick) (10 000 pieces)	1327698	1252827
瓦(万片)	Tile (10 000 pieces)	5050	7071
大理石板材(平方米)	Marble Slab (sq.m)	190480	328249
花岗石板材(平方米)	Granite Sheet (sq.m)	7369702	9729097
石膏板(万平方米)	Plasterboard (sq.m)	1010	672
平板玻璃(重量箱)	Plate Glass (weight case)	2273361	3420192
沥青和改性沥青防水卷材(平方米)	Bitumen and Rolled Waterproof Material (sq.m)	3926234	3264350
中空玻璃(平方米)	Insulating Glass (sq.m)	67991	91863
钢化玻璃(平方米)	Toughened Glass (sq.m)	129949	118035
夹层玻璃(平方米)	Laminated Glass (sq.m)	55239	31847
日用玻璃制品(吨)	Household Glass Products (ton)	62632	112092
玻璃保温容器(万个)	Glass Attemperator (10 000 units)	1258	919

13-18 续表 3 Continued

产品名称	Item	2009	2010
陶质砖(平方米)	Carbonic Bricks (sq.m)	34633135	32415720
耐火材料制品(吨)	Fire Proof Material (ton)	72832	136074
石墨及碳素制品(吨)	Graphite and Carbon Products (ton)	180203	146398
玻璃纤维增强塑料制品(吨)	Glass Fibre Reinforced Plastices Products (ton)	35890	37368
生铁(吨)	Pig Iron (ton)	7646152	9411248
粗钢(吨)	Crude Steel (ton)	6533199	8255449
钢材(吨)	Rolled Steel (ton)	6908057	8916980
中小型型钢	Medium and Small Fasioned Steel	126694	266809
钢　筋	Concrete Iron	1931022	2403164
盘　条(线材)	Wire Rod	1754362	1964219
铁合金(吨)	Ferroalloy (ton)	79491	149759
铜(吨)	Copper (ton)	5032	6461
镍(吨)	Nickel (ton)	5078	5936
铝(吨)	Aluminium (ton)	54349	65954
铝材(吨)	Aluminium Material (ton)	39990	45174
工业锅炉(蒸发量吨)	Industrial Boiler (evaporating quantity ton)	586	729
泵(台)	Pump (unit)	9051	9033
风机(台)	Fan (unit)	7553	5605
轴承(万套)	Bearing (10 000 sets)	475	443
铸钢件(吨)	Steel Casting (ton)	19525	17094
铸铁件(吨)	Iron Casting (ton)	37499	43436
小型拖拉机(台)	Small-Size Tractor (unit)	2923	1517
农作物收获机械(台)	Grop Harvesting Machinery (unit)	2094	3371
汽车(辆)	Motor Vehicles(unit)	702	1763
#载货汽车	Trucks	702	1763
改装汽车(辆)	Modified Truck (unit)	1894	2236
发电设备(千瓦)	Power Generating Equipment (kw)	2673000	5023500
变压器(千伏安)	Transformer (kva)	26121982	35829383
电力电缆(公里)	Electric Cable (km)	46624	35800

13-19 各地、州、市主要工业产品产量

年份 Year	地区 Region	纱(吨) Yarn (ton)	布(万米) Cloth (10 000 m)	绒线(吨) Knitting Wool (ton)	呢绒(万米) Woolen Piece Goods (10 000 m)
	1978	28008	15616	1239	189.37
	1980	31272	16931	1614	240.08
	1985	39130	21150	2396	680.00
	1990	101941	30017	2179	1230.00
	1995	244689	30460	2286	1262.00
	1996	208526	27186	2202	1361.00
	1997	247143	29862	2393	1227.00
	1998	220332	26719	1361	979.00
	1999	294378	27450	1349	798.00
	2000	334307	28060	1184	754.00
	2001	302654	25380	843	399.00
	2002	316095	20679	811	264.58
	2003	292713	15239	744	205.58
	2004	291386	13989	980	205.92
	2005	340864	14047	1118	283.68
	2006	357324	15415	799	326.67
	2007	408870	16000	637	367.51
	2008	397417	15302	578	412.00
	2009	386085	15148	533	375.76
	2010	415783	15069	741	326.00
乌鲁木齐市	Urumqi City	58938	2064	359	
克拉玛依市	Karamay City				
吐鲁番地区	Turpan Administrative Offices	5356			
哈密地区	Hami [Kumul] Administrative Offices	15669			
昌吉回族自治州	Changji Hui Autonomous Prefecture	26696	1964	53	154.00
伊犁哈萨克自治州	Ili Kazak Autonomous Prefecture	41744	2841	328	
伊犁州直属县(市)	Counties (Cities) Direct Under Ili Prefecture	23549	2556	2	
塔城地区	Tacheng [Tarbagatai] Administrative Offices	18195	285	326	
阿勒泰地区	Altay Administrative Offices				
博尔塔拉蒙古自治州	Bortala Mongol Autonomous Prefecture	18417	125		
巴音郭楞蒙古自治州	Bayangol Mongol Autonomous Prefecture	33497	932		
阿克苏地区	Aksu Administrative Offices	39318	660		
克孜勒苏柯尔克孜自治州	Kizilsu Kirgiz Autonomous Prefecture				
喀什地区	Kashgar [Kaxgar] Administrative Offices	33525	2130		
和田地区	Hotan Administrative Offices	2015			
自治区直辖县级市	Municpality Country-LevelCity directly under the Central Government				
石河子市	Shihezi City	120319	4233	1	172.00
阿拉尔市	Aral City	11120	120		
图木舒克市	Tumxuk City	2774			
五家渠市	Wujiaqu City	6396			

Output of Major Industrial Products by Prefecture, Autonomous Prefecture and City

机制纸及纸板(吨) Machine-made Paper and Paperboard (ton)	原 盐(万吨) Salt (10 000 tons)	成品糖(万吨) Sugar (10 000 tons)	饮料酒(千升) Alcohol Beverage (kilo-liter)	卷 烟(亿支) Cigarettes (100 million pieces)	原 煤(万吨) Coal (10 000 tons)	原 油(万吨) Crude Oil (10 000 tons)	天然气(万立方米) Natural gas (10 000 cu.m)	发电量(亿千瓦时) Electricity (100 million kwh)	#水 电 Hydropower
19851	51.71	2.08	9336	15.05	1079.01	353.05	25100	21.17	4.64
23838	38.18	4.43	17082	15.55	1136.84	390.58	35298	23.58	5.25
41521	35.09	7.18	74809	40.20	1600.22	499.00	54556	38.11	8.64
90857	159.00	16.84	118585	61.70	2100.00	695.00	50161	69.79	14.25
180440	25.98	30.18	249481	68.05	2720.74	1267.83	114821	120.43	22.82
169789	36.54	36.34	219961	67.80	2986.00	1457.10	140609	136.03	24.49
161659	39.85	42.28	259015	66.05	3021.37	1629.25	213006	150.58	26.97
168799	27.53	47.59	271056	60.20	2926.91	1628.38	237826	157.76	28.23
180138	36.14	46.36	269453	55.00	2778.16	1739.65	310600	169.30	30.06
176477	31.78	30.76	269761	52.50	2798.90	1848.43	353930	182.98	30.53
193389	46.02	41.98	296187	55.20	2819.61	1946.95	417429	197.62	34.10
226950	50.75	51.84	307167	60.00	3098.67	2036.19	485237	212.24	34.67
233365	52.71	45.43	317260	62.50	3482.86	2141.39	502942	234.62	36.20
263066	87.32	37.26	345770	70.00	3749.40	2253.02	574805	266.30	37.08
289318	85.35	42.92	355275	70.00	3898.81	2408.32	1066437	306.92	43.27
295338	153.21	53.79	401771	85.00	4518.52	2474.74	1642099	357.15	53.43
252329	111.53	64.94	438502	100.00	5018.64	2604.31	2103348	416.87	58.78
301606	153.06	53.78	486007	120.00	6763.41	2715.13	2358941	489.17	73.84
355762	129.36	40.77	484936	135.00	8812.55	2512.86	2453887	571.31	79.84
371032	174.67	45.10	565041	150.00	9935.73	2558.16	2499096	679.33	97.07
151428	13.22		156019		2424.20	700.02	158010	181.19	3.19
	0.17		59			1089.01	380043	44.77	
	60.09		5930		1113.80	163.03	125100	23.15	
2426	3.90		26022		1213.01			21.37	0.03
64064		5.15	47365		2794.77			105.65	0.68
4960	81.63	25.73	148532	150.00	1064.95	52.00		89.24	48.69
180		17.06	68965	150.00	467.70			65.67	37.70
4200	81.63	7.89	79141		592.84	52.00		12.25	2.76
580		0.78	426		4.41			11.32	8.24
	6.03	2.39	1333		288.80			3.85	1.05
69209	4.07	9.11	29260		942.47	554.10	1835943	45.82	16.87
	2.64	2.31	30704		5.21			37.84	10.01
	2.92				12.44			0.30	0.10
13162		0.40	24017		58.08			20.69	6.56
			163					5.87	5.27
29799			93423					92.84	4.61
			3					6.76	
35985			2110						

13-19 续表

年 份 Year	地 区 Region	生 铁 (万吨) Pig Iron (10 000 tons)	粗钢 (万吨) Crude Steel (10 000 tons)	大理石板 材 (平方米) Marble Plate (sq.m.)	钢 材 (万吨) Steel Rolled (10 000 tons)
	1978	17.52	8.46		6.83
	1980	15.81	10.74		8.59
	1985	22.87	19.79		16.73
	1990	40.57	36.49	9589	28.48
	1995	69.53	70.59	34169	66.55
	1996	85.64	87.47	6420	86.70
	1997	93.82	97.21	53588	99.89
	1998	100.40	107.67	9197	116.19
	1999	101.30	105.60	7807	117.30
	2000	106.42	109.70	6294	131.26
	2001	111.73	131.83	22786	134.42
	2002	122.78	175.45	34185	173.07
	2003	144.86	204.12	117306	203.10
	2004	193.89	249.13	109663	238.52
	2005	258.66	306.54	78577	326.96
	2006	324.08	394.19	176025	411.45
	2007	394.97	447.24	119926	470.94
	2008	505.70	536.60	160011	576.62
	2009	764.62	653.32	190480	690.81
	2010	941.12	825.54	328249	892.04
乌鲁木齐市	Urumqi City	603.94	685.03	10518	753.68
克拉玛依市	Karamay City				0.02
吐鲁番地区	Turpan Administrative Offices	98.71	0.13	17483	
哈密地区	Hami [Kumul] Administrative Offices	8.67		20000	
昌吉回族自治州	Changji Hui Autonomous Prefecture	22.27		32156	0.01
伊犁哈萨克自治州	Ili Kazak Autonomous Prefecture	89.01	52.44	143808	48.27
伊犁州直属县(市)	Counties (Cities) Direct Under Ili Prefecture	81.64	27.15	124971	26.77
塔城地区	Tacheng [Tarbagatai] Administrative Offices		25.28		21.46
阿勒泰地区	Altay Administrative Offices	7.37		18837	0.04
博尔塔拉蒙古自治州	Bortala Mongol Autonomous Prefecture	12.21		98885	
巴音郭楞蒙古自治州	Bayangol Mongol Autonomous Prefecture	87.64	87.95	5400	84.92
阿克苏地区	Aksu Administrative Offices	5.25			0.89
克孜勒苏柯尔克孜自治州	Kizilsu Kirgiz Autonomous Prefecture				
喀什地区	Kashgar [Kaxgar] Administrative Offices	13.43			1.19
和田地区	Hotan Administrative Offices				
自治区直辖县级市	Municpality Country-LevelCity directly under the Central Government				
石河子市	Shihezi City				3.05
阿拉尔市	Aral City				
图木舒克市	Tumxuk City				
五家渠市	Wujiaqu City				

Continued

水 泥(万吨) Cement (10 000 tons)	硫 酸(吨) Sulfuric Acid (ton)	烧 碱(吨) Caustic Soda (ton)	合成氨(吨)(折纯) Synthetic Ammonia (ton)	农用氮、磷、钾化肥(吨) Farm Nitrogen Phophate and Potassium (ton)	碳化钙(电石)(吨) Calcium Crbide (ton)	塑料制品(吨) Plastic Products (ton)	小型拖拉机(台) Small Tractor (unit)
78.15	20262	4164	33155	20276	4895	3194	843
90.89	19153	3542	13762	9207	4486	2051	137
201.05	23921	5045	85728	58080	5989	17974	11117
285.00	47732	15063	397062	287640	15976	40958	17081
489.88	88491	24732	492754	383279	12344	100739	30352
562.87	76413	28008	488337	372056	15901	129059	26671
628.00	77187	35544	581449	428711	28350	143916	14780
728.94	64836	39614	688069	520681	28999	168372	19017
805.83	68169	42161	896632	685587	40216	139497	17048
895.67	71458	51831	947511	754668	51749	197756	13472
981.29	72511	68589	884340	729034	65763	262873	12672
1029.71	70407	93362	956732	766291	73680	230729	4019
1128.98	85322	114110	1082601	854530	82057	314891	
1212.99	114046	174445	1015630	869795	115991	388270	1407
1241.74	126901	295917	1192001	1285346	290591	349151	5171
1334.50	160073	423901	1303586	1290802	501283	412032	
1536.77	183484	485880	1325017	1385279	711277	517069	5408
1672.76	201993	630314	1471312	1609409	910659	653230	4429
2049.60	300423	814393	1407674	1591027	1560762	697269	2923
2400.96	326112	916205	1484103	1591043	1845104	830651	1517
476.16	2524	400186	678271	532697	167266	314732	1517
				760		30205	
78.84	142367			3415	262679	115	
94.63				9408		4348	
203.94	35052	6394		4363	208449	148099	
473.06	55631				191811	121220	
225.50	9710				151974	34098	
172.34	24589				39837	82606	
75.22	21332					4515	
55.34						13941	
207.94		4361	460951	769042		22334	
401.29	54578		344881	271359		22807	
45.32						386	
101.64						26982	
119.98						665	
131.03	35961	505264			1014900	85726	
						9601	
11.79						7416	
						22076	

13-20 国有控股企业主要指标占全区规模以上工业比重

Percentage of Main Indicators in State-holding Enterprises to Enterprises above Designated Size

单位：万元　　(2010 年)　　(10 000 yuan)

指　标	Item	全区规模以上工业企业 Enterprises Above Designated Size	国　有控股企业 State-Holding Enterprises	比 重(%) Percentage (%)
企业单位数(个)	Number of Enterprises(unit)	2465	574	23.3
从业人员(人)	Employed Person (person)	601818	353759	58.8
工业总产值	Gross Industrial Output Value	53419038.4	37703302.8	70.6
工业销售产值	Sales Value of Industry Products	52266596.1	37555639.7	71.9
出口交货值	Delivery Value of Industry Export	541927.5	328738.3	60.7
资产总计	Total Assets	79119654.3	55947597.5	70.7
负债合计	Total Liabilities	40187783.9	2692698.9	6.7
所有者权益	Owner's Right and Interest	38884012.0	29007782.3	74.6
实收资本	Substantial Capital	25400781.3	20311592.9	80.0
主营业务收入	Revenue from Principal Business	54926143.4	39430339.9	71.8
主营业务税金及附加	Taes and Other Charges on Principal Business	2569233.6	2436861.0	94.8
利润总额	Total Profits	8524251.8	6647661.5	78.0
利税总额	Total Profits and Tax	13708719.9	11186422.4	81.6
亏损单位数(个)	Number of Loss-suffering Enterprises (unit)	552	132	23.9
亏损企业亏损额	Losses Value of Loss-suffering	604203.6	478264.9	79.2

13-21 重点行业主要指标占全区规模以上工业比重

Percentage of Main Indicators in Key Industrial Sectors to Xinjiang's Industry above Designated Size

(2010 年)

指 标	Item	合 计 Total	占全区比重 (%) Percentage (%)
从业人员(人)	**Employed Person (person)**	**601818**	
石油和天然气开采业	Extraction of Petroleum and Natural Gas	104407	17.3
石油加工、炼焦及核燃料加工业	Petroleum Processing,Coking and Nuclear Fuel Processing	41390	6.9
黑色金属冶炼及压延加工业	Smelting and Pressing of Ferrous Metal	30866	5.1
电力、热力的生产和供应业	Electric Power, Thermal Power Production and Supply	50867	8.5
化学原料及化学制品制造业	Raw Chemical Material and Chemical Products	44548	7.4
纺织业	Textile Industry	43341	7.2
农副食品加工业	Processing of Food from Agricultural Products	30683	5.1
工业总产值(万元)	**Gross Industrial Output Value (10 000 yuan)**	**53419038.4**	
石油和天然气开采业	Extraction of Petroleum and Natural Gas	11442905.6	21.4
石油加工、炼焦及核燃料加工业	Petroleum Processing,Coking and Nuclear Fuel Processing	12450842.0	23.3
黑色金属冶炼及压延加工业	Smelting and Pressing of Ferrous Metal	5531476.4	10.5
电力、热力的生产和供应业	Electric Power, Thermal Power Production and Supply	3385869.0	6.3
化学原料及化学制品制造业	Raw Chemical Material and Chemical Products	3166536.6	5.9
纺织业	Textile Industry	1204723.9	2.3
农副食品加工业	Processing of Food from Agricultural Products	2371733.4	4.4
工业销售产值(万元)	**Sales Value of Industry Products (10 000 yuan)**	**52266596.1**	
石油和天然气开采业	Extraction of Petroleum and Natural Gas	11429360.4	21.9
石油加工、炼焦及核燃料加工业	Petroleum Processing,Coking and Nuclear Fuel Processing	12392198.0	23.7
黑色金属冶炼及压延加工业	Smelting and Pressing of Ferrous Metal	5455418.7	10.4
电力、热力的生产和供应业	Electric Power, Thermal Power Production and Supply	3378539.6	6.5
化学原料及化学制品制造业	Raw Chemical Material and Chemical Products	3076593.7	5.9
纺织业	Textile Industry	1195560.1	2.3
农副食品加工业	Processing of Food from Agricultural Products	2183155.4	4.2

注：所列行业为工业总产值百亿元以上行业。
Note: Listed sector of gross industrial output value were above ten billion sector.

13-21 续表 Continued

指　标	Item	合　计 Total	占全区比重(%) Percentage(%)
资产总计(万元)	**Total of Assets (10 000 yuan)**	**79119654.3**	
石油和天然气开采业	Extraction of Petroleum and Natural Gas	21293199.4	26.9
石油加工、炼焦及核燃料加工业	Petroleum Processing,Coking and Nuclear Fuel Processing	7603188.0	9.6
黑色金属冶炼及压延加工业	Smelting and Pressing of Ferrous Metal	3570922.6	4.5
电力、热力的生产和供应业	Electric Power, Thermal Power Production and Supply	10695433.3	13.5
化学原料及化学制品制造业	Raw Chemical Material and Chemical Products	6450479.6	8.2
纺织业	Textile Industry	1810392.1	2.3
农副食品加工业	Processing of Food from Agricultural Products	2811592.7	3.6
利润总额(万元)	**Total Profits (10 000 yuan)**	**8524251.8**	
石油和天然气开采业	Extraction of Petroleum and Natural Gas	4756662.1	55.8
石油加工、炼焦及核燃料加工业	Petroleum Processing,Coking and Nuclear Fuel Processing	600283.6	7.0
黑色金属冶炼及压延加工业	Smelting and Pressing of Ferrous Metal	277077.9	3.3
电力、热力的生产和供应业	Electric Power, Thermal Power Production and Supply	295945.1	3.5
化学原料及化学制品制造业	Raw Chemical Material and Chemical Products	431191.7	5.1
纺织业	Textile Industry	109302.4	1.3
农副食品加工业	Processing of Food from Agricultural Products	137006.6	1.6
利税总额(万元)	**Total Profitsand Tax (10 000 yuan)**	**13708719.9**	
石油和天然气开采业	Extraction of Petroleum and Natural Gas	6561704.8	47.9
石油加工、炼焦及核燃料加工业	Petroleum Processing,Coking and Nuclear Fuel Processing	2567164.7	18.7
黑色金属冶炼及压延加工业	Smelting and Pressing of Ferrous Metal	402370.6	2.9
电力、热力的生产和供应业	Electric Power, Thermal Power Production and Supply	460081.2	3.4
化学原料及化学制品制造业	Raw Chemical Material and Chemical Products	583229.7	4.3
纺织业	Textile Industry	157883.6	1.2
农副食品加工业	Processing of Food from Agricultural Products	170417.2	1.2
主营业务收入(万元)	**Revenue from Principal Business (10 000 yuan)**	**54926143.4**	
石油和天然气开采业	Extraction of Petroleum and Natural Gas	12849615.3	23.4
石油加工、炼焦及核燃料加工业	Petroleum Processing,Coking and Nuclear Fuel Processing	12786126.6	23.3
黑色金属冶炼及压延加工业	Smelting and Pressing of Ferrous Metal	5543752.0	10.1
化学原料及化学制品制造业	Raw Chemical Material and Chemical Products	3037416.0	5.5
电力、热力的生产和供应业	Electric Power, Thermal Power Production and Supply	3469963.7	6.3
纺织业	Textile Industry	1259151.4	2.3
农副食品加工业	Processing of Food from Agricultural Products	2273128.7	4.1

13-22 规模以上工业主要产品生产能力

Production Capacity of Major Industrial Products above Designated Size

产品名称	Item	2009	2010
原煤(吨)	Raw Coal (ton)	90480981	107270000
天然原油(吨)	Crude Oil (ton)	26622500	27314200
发电设备容量(万千瓦)	Generating Capacity (10 000 kw)	1213	1380
卷烟(万支)	Cigarettes (10 000 pieces)	1500000	1500000
化学纤维(吨)	Chemical Fiber (ton)	413500	374000
棉纺锭(环锭纺)(锭)	Cotton Hasp (unit)	3362068	3870986
气流纺锭(转杯纺)(头)	Airflow Hasp (unit)	70790	90394
棉布织机(台)	Calico Spinning Machine (set)	6085	6532
焦炭(吨)	Coke (ton)	18679000	24228000
炭化钙(电石)(折 300 升/千克)(吨)	Calcium Carbide (ton)	1935000	2240000
农用氮、磷、钾化学肥料(折纯)(吨)	Chemical Fertilizers (ton)	1943069	2307509
水泥熟料(吨)	Cement Chamotte (ton)	21707500	26726000
#窑外分解窑熟料	Decompose Cellar Chamotte	12973000	20195000
水泥(吨)	Cement (ton)	29040000	35680000
平板玻璃(重量箱)	Plate Glass (weight case)	2368000	4200000
平拉玻璃(重量箱)	Plate Drawing Glass (weight case)	768000	2000000
生铁(吨)	Pig Iron (ton)	9561000	12282000
粗钢(吨)	Crude Steel (ton)	9300000	10350000
钢材(吨)	Rolled Steel (ton)	10132000	12149500
铁合金(吨)	Ferroalloy (ton)	205100	251600
原铝(电解铝)(吨)	Aluminium (ton)	56200	261200
汽车(辆)	Motor Vehicles(unit)	5000	5000

主要统计指标解释

工业 指从事自然资源的开采，对采掘品和农产品进行加工和再加工的物质生产部门。具体包括：(1)对自然资源的开采，如采矿、晒盐等(但不包括禽兽捕猎和水产捕捞)；(2)对农副产品的加工、再加工，如粮油加工、食品加工、缫丝、纺织、制革等；(3)对采掘品的加工、再加工，如炼铁、炼钢、化工生产、石油加工、机器制造、木材加工等，以及电力、自来水、煤气的生产和供应等；(4)对工业品的修理、翻新，如机器设备的修理、交通运输工具(包括小卧车)的修理等。

工业统计调查单位为独立核算法人工业企业。

独立核算法人工业企业指从事工业生产经营活动的单位。独立核算法人工业企业应同时具备以下条件：①依法成立，有自己的名称、组织机构和场所，能够承担民事责任；②独立拥有和使用资产，承担负债，有权与其他单位签订合同；③独立核算盈亏，并能够编制资产负债表。

本年鉴中涉及的企业登记注册类型：

国有及国有控股企业 指国有企业加上国有控股企业。国有企业(即原全民所有制工业或国营工业)指企业全部资产归国家所有，并按《中华人民共和国企业法人登记管理条例》规定登记注册的非公司制的经济组织。包括国有企业、国有独资公司和国有联营企业。1957年以前的公私合营和私营工业，后均改造为国营工业，1992年改为国有工业，这部分工业的资料不单独分列时，均包括在国有企业内。国有控股企业是对混合所有制经济的企业进行的"国有控股"分类。它是指这些企业的全部资产中国有资产(股份)相对其他所有者中的任何一个所有者占资(股)最多的企业。该分组反映了国有经济控股情况。

集体企业 指企业资产归集体所有，并按《中华人民共和国企业法人登记管理条例》规定登记注册的经济组织。是社会主义公有制经济的组成部分。包括城乡所有使用集体投资举办的企业，以及部分个人通过集资自愿放弃所有权并依法经工商行政管理机关认定为集体所有制的企业。

股份合作企业 指以合作制为基础，由企业职工共同出资入股，吸收一定比例的社会资产投资组建，实行自主经营，自负盈亏，共同劳动，民主管理，按劳分配与按股分红相结合的一种集体经济组织。

联营企业 指两个及两个以上相同或不同所有制性质的企业法人或事业单位法人，按自愿、平等、互利的原则，共同投资组成的经济组织。联营企业包括：

国有联营企业指国有企业与国有企业间的联营；

集体联营企业指集体企业与集体企业间的联营；

国有与集体联营企业指国有企业与集体企业间的联营。

有限责任公司 指根据《中华人民共和国公司登记管理条例》规定登记注册，由两个以上，五十个以下的股东共同出资，每个股东以其所认缴的出资额对公司承担有限责任，公司以其全部资产对其债务承担责任的经济组织。

有限责任公司包括国有独资公司以及其他有限责任公司。

股份有限公司 指根据《中华人民共和国企业法人登记管理条例》规定登记注册，其全部注册资本由等额股份构成并通过发行股票筹集资本，股东以其认购的股份对公司承担有限责任，公司以其全部资产对其债务承担责任的经济组织。

私营企业 指由自然人投资设立或由自然人控股，以雇佣劳动为基础的营利性经济组织。包括按照《公司法》、《合伙企业法》、《私营企业暂行条例》规定登记注册的私营有限责任公司、私营股份有限公司、私营合伙企业和私营独资企业。

港、澳、台商投资企业 指企业注册登记类型中的港、澳、台资合资、合作、独资经营企业和股份有限公司之和。

外商投资企业 指企业注册登记类型中的中外合资、合作经营企业、外资企业和外商投资股份有限公司之和。

轻工业 指主要提供生活消费品和制作手工工具的工业。按其所使用的原料不同，可分为两大类：(1)以农产品为原料的轻工业，是指直接或间接以农产品为基本原料的轻工业。主要包括食品制造、饮料制造、烟草加工、纺织、缝纫、皮革和毛皮制作、造纸以及印刷等工业；(2)以非农产品为原料的轻工业，是指以工业品为原料的轻工业。主要包括文教体育用品、化学药品制造、合成纤维制造、日用化学制品、日用玻璃制品、日用金属制品、手工工具制造、医疗器械制造、文化和办公用机械制造等工业。

重工业 指为国民经济各部门提供物质技术基础的主要生产资料的工业。按其生产性质和产品用途，可以分为下列三类：(1)采掘(伐)工业，是指对自然资源的开采，包括石油开采、煤炭开采、金属矿开采、非金属矿开采等工业；(2)原材料工业，指向国民经济各部门提供基本材料、动力和燃料的工业。包括金属冶炼及加工、炼焦及焦炭、化学、化工原料、水泥、人造板以及电力、石油和煤炭加工等工业；(3)加工工业，是指对工业原材料进行再加工制造的工业。包括装备国民经济各部门的机械设备制造工业、金属结构、水泥制品等工业，以及为农业提供的生产资料如化肥、农药等工业。

根据上述划分原则，修理业中以重工业产品为修理作业对象的划为重工业，反之划为轻工业。

工业总产值

(1)定义：工业总产值是以货币形式表现的，工业企业在一定时期内生产的工业最终产品或提供工业性劳务活动的总价值量。它反映一定时间内工业生产的总规模和总水平。

(2)计算原则：

工业生产的原则，即凡是企业在报告期生产的经检验合格的产品，不管是否在报告期销售，均包括在内。

最终产品的原则，即凡是计入工业总产值的产品，必须是本企业生产的经检验合格的，不需要再进行任何加工的最终产品。如果企业有中间产品(半成品)对外销售，则对外销售的中间产品应视为企业的最终产品。

工厂法原则，即工业总产值是以工业企业作为基本计算(核算)单位，即按企业的最终产品计算工业总产值。按这种方法计算的工业总产值，不允许同一产品价值在企业内部重复计算，不能把企业内部各个车间(分厂)生产的成果相加，但允许企业间的重复计算。

(3)内容及计算方法：

1995年全国工业普查对工业总产值(原规定)的内容及计算原则和方法做了某些修订，修订后的工业总产值(新规定)包括三项内容：即本期生产成品价值、对外加工费收入、在制品半成品期末期初差额价值三部分。

本期生产成品价值：指企业本期生产，并在报告期内不再进行加工，经检验、包装入库的全部工业成品(半产品)价值合计，包括企业生产的自制设备及提供给本企业在建工程、其他非工业部门和福利部门等单位使用的成品价值。本期生产成品价值为按自备原材料生产的产品的数量乘以本期不含增值税(销项税额)的产品实际销售平均单价计算；会计核算中按成本价格转帐的自制设备和自产自用的成品，按成本价格计算生产成品价值。生产成品价值中不包括用定货者来料加工的成品(半产品)价值。

对外加工费收入：指企业在报告期内完成的对外承接的工业品加工(包括用定货者来料加工产品)的加工费收入和对外工业修理作业所取得的加工费收入。对外加工费收入按不含增值税(销项税额)的价格计算，可根据会计“产品销售收入”科目的有关资料取得。

对于本企业对内非工业部门提供的加工修理、设备安装的劳务收入，如果企业会计核算基础较好，能取得这部分资料，而且这部分价值所占比重较大，应包括在对外加工费收入中。

自制半成品在制品期末期初差额价值：指企业报告期在制品期末减期初的差额价值，本指标一般可以从会计核算资料中取得。如果会计产品成本核算中不计算半成品、在制品的成本，则总产值中也不包括这部分价值，反之则包括。

(4)工业总产值统计范围变化和计算方法修订情况：

1984年以前工业总产值不包括村办工业，村办工业总产值划归农业。1984年以后工业总产值包括村办工业。

1995年工业普查对工业总产值计算方法做了修订，即从1995年始按新修订(新规定)方法计算工业总产值。新规定与原规定的区别如下：

全价与加工费的计算原则不同：新规定为凡自备原材料，不论其生产繁简程度如何，一律按全价计算工业总产值；凡来料加工，允许按加工费计算工业总产值。原规定则视生产加工的繁简程度不同，规定哪些行业按全价，哪些行业按加工费计算工业总产值。

自制半成品、在产品期末期初差额价值的计算原则不同：新规定要求，凡会计产品成本核算时计算了成本的差额价值，总产值中就应包括，否则可不包括；原规定则按生产周期六个月的界限区分，凡生产周期六个月以上的企业，总产值计算中应包括这部分差额价值，否则可不包括。

计算价格不同：新规定按不含增值税(销项税额)的价格计算；原规定则按含增值税(销项税额)的价格计算。

工业增加值　指工业企业在报告期内以货币表现的工业生产活动的最终成果。

工业增加值有两种计算方法：一是生产法，即工业总产出减去工业中间投入加上应交增值税；二是收入法，即从收入的角度出发，根据生产要素在生产过程中应得到的收入份额计算，具体构成项目有固定资产折旧、劳动者报酬、生产税净额、营业盈余，这种方法也称要素分配法。本年鉴中的工业增加值是以生产法计算的。

生产法工业增加值的计算方法为：

工业增加值=工业总产出-工业中间投入+应交增值税

(1)工业总产出：指工业企业在一定时期内工业生产活动的总成果。工业总产出包括：成品生产价值，对外加工费收入，自制半成品、在产品期末期初差额价值。1995年后用新规定计算的工业总产值代替。

(2)工业中间投入：指工业企业在工业生产活动中消耗的外购物质产品和对外支付的服务费用。服务费用包括支付给物质生产部门(工业、农业、批发零售贸易业、建筑业、运输邮电业)的服务费用和支付给非物质生产部门(如保险、金融、文化教育、科学研究、医疗卫生、行政管理等)的服务费用。工业中间投入的确定须遵循以下原则：必须从外部购入的，并已计入工业总产出的产品和服务价值；必须是本期投入生产，并一次性消耗掉(包括本期摊销的低值易耗品等)的产品和服务价值。

工业中间投入包括直接材料费用、制造费用中的工业中间投入、管理费用中的工业中间投入、销售费用中的工业中间投入和利息支出五部分。

资产总计　指企业拥有或控制的能以货币计量的经济资源，包括各种财产、债权和其他权利。资产按流动性分为流动资产、长期投资、固定资产、无形资产、递延资产和其他资产。该指标根据企业会计“资产负债表”中“资产总计”项目的期末数增列。

流动资产平均余额　指企业在报告期内全部流动资产的平均余额。

固定资产净值年平均余额　指固定资产净值在报告期内余额的平均数。计算公式为：

固定资产净值年平均余额=1至12月各月月初、月末固定资产净值之和/24

该指标根据“资产负债表”中“固定资产原价”、“累计折旧”指标的期初、期末数计算填列。

固定资产净值指固定资产原价减去历年已提折旧额后的净额。计算公式为：

固定资产净值=固定资产原价-累计折旧

负债合计　指企业所承担的能以货币计量，将以资产或劳务偿付的债务，偿还形式包括货币、资产或提供劳务。负债一般按偿还期长短分为流动负债和长期负债。根据会计“资产负债表”中“负债合计”的年末数填列。

所有者权益　指企业投资人对企业净资产的所有权。企业净资产等于企业全部资产减去全部负债后的余额，包括企业投资人对企业的最初投入的实际到位的资产及资本公积金、盈余公积金和未分配利润。所有者权益合计数小于零，表示企业资不抵债。

主营业务收入　指会计“利润表”中对应指标的本年累计数。未执行2001年《企业会计制度》的企业，用“产品销售收入”的本期累计数代替。

主营业务成本　指会计“利润表”中对应指标的本年累计数。未执行2001年《企业会计制度》的企业，用“产品销售成本”的本期累计数代替。

主营业务税金及附加　指会计“利润表”中对应指标的本年累计数。未执行2001年《企业会计制度》的企业，用“产品销售税金及附加”的本期累计数代替。

利润总额　指企业生产经营活动的最终成果，是企业在一定时期内实现的盈亏相抵后的利润总额(亏损以“-”号表示)，它等于营业利润加上补贴收入加上投资收益加上营业外净收入再加上以前年度损益调整。

本年应交增值税　指企业在报告期内应交纳的增值税额。它等于本年销项税额加上出口退税加上进项税额转出数减去本年进项税额。小规模纳税企业直接按全年计税销售额乘以征收率计算取得。

从业人员平均人数　是指报告期内每天拥有的从业人员人数。其计算公式为：

月平均人数=报告月内每天实有人数之和/报告月日历日数

季平均人数=季内各月平均人数之和/3

年平均人数=年内各月平均人数之和/12

工业经济效益综合指数　是指现行综合评价工业经济效益总体水平及工业经济运行质量的指数。它是以若干项代表性经济效益指标，分别除以各项指标的标准值，再乘以各自的权数，加总后除以总权数求得。其计算公式为：

工业经济效益综合指数=(某项经济效益指标报告期数值/该项指标标准值×权数)÷总权数

上式总权数为100。

总资产贡献率　反映企业全部资产的获利能力，是企业经营业绩和管理水平的集中体现，是评价和考核企业盈利能力的核心指标。计算公式为：

总资产贡献率（%）=利润总额+税金总额+利息支出/平均资金总额×100%

公式中：税金总额为产品销售税金及附加与应交增值税之和；平均资产总额为期初期末资产之和的算术平均值。

资产负债率　该指标既反映企业经营风险的大小，也反映企业利用债权人提供的资金从事经营活动的能力。计算公式为：

资产负债率（%）=负债总额/资产总额×100%

资产与负债均为报告期期末数。

流动资产周转次数　指一定时期内流动资产完成的周转次数，反映投入工业企业流动资金的周转速度。计算公式为：

流动资产周转次数=产品销售收入/全部流动资产平均余额

公式中：全部流动资产平均余额为期初和期末的流动资产之和的算术平均值。

成本费用利润率　反映企业投入的生产成本及费用的经济效益，同时也反映企业降低成本所取得的经济效益。计算公式为：

成本费用利润率（%）=利润总额/成本费用总额×100%

公式中：成本费用总额为产品销售成本、销售费用、管理费用、财务费用之和。

产品销售率　该指标反映工业产品已实现销售的程度，是分析工业产销衔接情况，研究工业产品满足社会需求的指标。计算公式为：

$$\text{产品销售率（\%）}=\frac{\text{工业销售产值}}{\text{工业总产值（现价）}}\times 100\%$$

Explanatory Notes on Main Statistical Indicators

Industry refers to the material production sector which is engaged in the extraction of natural resources and processing and reprocessing of minerals and agricultural products, including (1) extraction of natural resources, such as mining, salt production (but not including hunting and fishing); (2) processing and reprocessing of farm and sideline produces, such as rice husking, flour milling, wine making, oil pressing, silk reeling, spinning and weaving, and leather making; (3) manufacture of industrial products, such as steel making, iron smelting, chemicals manufacturing, petroleum processing, machine building, timber processing; water and gas production and electricity generation and supply; (4)repairing of industrial products such as the repairing of machinery and means of transport (including cars).

In industrial statistics surveys, the units of enquiry are corporate industrial enterprises with independent accounting systems.

Corporate industrial enterprises with independent accounting systems refer to enterprises engaging in industrial production activities, which meet the following requirements: (1) They are established legally, having their own names, organizations, location and able to take civil liability; (2) They possess and use their assets independently, assume liabilities and are entitled to sign contracts with other units; (3) They are financially independent and compile their own balance sheets.

Enterprises covered in the industrial statistics in the Yearbook include the following categories by their registration:

State-owned and State-holding Enterprises refer to state-owned enterprises plus State-holding enterprises. State-owned enterprises (originally known as State-run enterprises with ownership by the whole society) are non-corporate economic entities registered in accordance with the Regulation of the People's Republic of China on the Management of Registration of Legal Enterprises, where all assets are owned by the State. Included in this category are State-owned enterprises, State-funded corporations and State-owned joint-operation enterprises. Joint State-private industries and private industries, which existed before 1957, were transformed into state-run industries since 1957, and into State-owned industries after 1992. Statistics on those enterprises are included in the State-owned industries instead of being grouped them separately. State-holding enterprises are a sub-classification of enterprises with mixed ownership, referring to enterprises where the percentage of State assets (or shares by the State) is larger than any other single share holder of the same enterprise. This sub-classification illustrates the control of the State over a particular industry.

Collective-owned Enterprises refer to economic entities registered in accordance with the Regulation of the People's Republic of China on the Management of Registration of Legal Enterprises, where assets are owned collectively. Collective enterprises constitute an integral part of the socialist economy with public ownership. They include urban and rural enterprises invested collectively, and some enterprises registered in industrial and commercial administration agency as collective units where funds are pooled together by individuals who voluntarily give up their right of ownership.

Cooperative Enterprises refer to economic units set up on a cooperative basis, with funding partly from employees of the enterprise and partly from outside investment, where the operation and management is decided by all the members who also participate in the production, and the distribution of income is based both on work (labour input) and on shares (capital input).

Joint Ownership Enterprises refer to economic units that are established by joint investment by two or more corporate enterprises or institutions of the same or different types of ownership on voluntary, equal and mutual-beneficial basis. They include:

a) State-owned joint-operation enterprises (joint operation between State-owned enterprises);

b) Collective joint-operation enterprises (joint operation between collective enterprises; and

c) State-collective joint-operation enterprises (joint operation between state and collective enterprises).

Limited Liability Corporations refer to economic units registered in accordance with the Regulation of the People's Republic of China on the Management of Registration of Corporations, with capital from 2 to 49 investors, each investor bears limited liability to the corporation depending on his/her holding of shares, and the corporation bears liability to its debt to the maximum of its total assets.

Limited liability corporations include state sole funded corporations and other limited liability corporations.

Share-holding Corporations Ltd. refer to economic units registered in accordance with the Regulation of the People's Republic of China on the Management of Registration of Corporate Enterprises, with total registered capital divided into equal shares and raised through issuing stocks. Each investor bears limited liability to the corporation depending on the holding of shares, and the corporation bears liability to its debt to the maximum of its total assets.

Private Enterprises refer to economic units invested or controlled (by holding the majority of the shares) by natural persons who hire labours for profit-making activities. Included in this category are private limited liability corporations, private share-holding corporations Ltd., private partnership enterprises and private sole investment enterprises registered in accordance with the Corporation Law, Partnership Enterprise Law and Tentative Regulation on Private Enterprises.

Enterprises with Funds from Hong Kong, Macao and Taiwan refers to all industrial enterprises registered as the joint-venture, cooperative, sole (exclusive) investment industrial enterprises and limited liability corporations with funds from Hong Kong, Macao and Taiwan.

Foreign Funded Enterprises refer to all industrial enterprises registered as the joint-venture, cooperative, sole (exclusive) investment industrial enterprises and limited liability corporations with foreign funds.

Light Industry refers to the industry that produces consumer goods and hand tools. It consists of two categories, depending on the materials used:

(1) Industries using farm products as raw materials. These are the branches of light industry which directly or indirectly use farm products as basic raw materials, including the manufacture of food and beverages, tobacco processing, textile, clothing, fur and leather manufacturing, paper making, printing, etc.

(2) Industries using non-farm products as raw materials. These are the branches of light industry which use manufactured goods as raw materials, including the manufacture of cultural, educational articles and sports goods, chemicals, synthetic fibre, chemical products for daily use, glass products for daily use, metal products for daily use, hand tools, medical apparatus and instruments, and the manufacture of cultural and office machinery.

Heavy Industry refers to the industry which produces capital goods, and provides various sectors of the national economy with necessary material and technical basis for production. It consists of the following three branches according to the purpose of production or the use of products:

(1) Mining, quarrying and logging industry, which refers to the industry that extracts natural resources, including extraction of petroleum, coal, metal and non-metal ores.

(2) Raw materials industry refers to the industry that provides various sectors of the national economy with raw materials, fuels and power. It includes smelting and processing of metals, coking and coke chemistry, chemical materials and building materials such as cement, plywood, and power, petroleum refining and coal dressing.

(3) Manufacturing industry which refers to the industry that processes raw materials. It includes machine-building industries which equip sectors of the national economy; industries producing metal structure and cement products; and industries producing means of agricultural production, such as chemical fertilizers and pesticides.

In accordance with the above principles of classification, the repairing trades, which are engaged primarily in repairing products of heavy industry, are classified as heavy industry while those which are engaged in repairing products of light industry are classified as light industry.

Gross Industrial Output Value

(1) Definition: Gross industrial output value is the total volume of final industrial products produced and industrial services provided during a given period. It reflects the total achievements and overall scale of industrial production during a given period.

(2) Principles for calculation:

Statistics on industrial production follow the principle that all products produced by the enterprises and accepted through quality check during the reference period are to be included no matter whether they are sold or not during the reference period.

Determination of final products follows the principle that all products that are included in the calculation of gross industrial output value are the final products of the enterprise which have been accepted through quality check and require no further processing. If an enterprise has intermediate (semi-finished) products to sell, these intermediate products are considered as the final products of the enterprise.

Gross industrial output value is calculated following the principle of factory approach, i.e. industrial enterprise is used as the basic accounting unit in calculating the gross industrial output value. By this approach, value of the same product is not to be double-counted, and the output value of different workshops (branch factories) within the enterprise should not be added. However, this approach allows the possibility of double counting between enterprises.

(3) Content and method of calculation: The old definition of gross industrial output value was modified during the 1995 National Industrial Census. The revised (new) definition of gross industrial output value consists of 3 components: value of the finished products during the reference period, income from processing for external parties, and value of change in semi-finished products between the end and the beginning of the reference period.

Value of finished products during the reference period: refers to the value of all finished (semi-finished) industrial products that are produced during the reference period without the need for further processing, checked for acceptance, packed and put into the warehouse of the enterprise, including the value of own-produced equipment and the value of products provided to the projects under construction of the enterprise, and to other non-industrial or welfare units. Value of finished products during the reference period is calculated by the quantity of products produced using own materials multiplied by the average unit prices at which products are sold (excluding value-added tax). Own-produced equipment and products produced for own use are valued at cost prices as in the case of enterprise accounting. Value of finished products does not include the value of finished products (semi-finished products) that are produced using the materials from the clients who place the orders.

Income from external processing: refers to income from contracted external processing of industrial products (including processing of industrial products using materials from the clients), and the income from industrial repairing work provided to other parties. Income from external processing is calculated using information from the item “products sales income” in the enterprise accounting at the prices with value-added tax excluded.

For income from services such as processing, repairing and installation of equipment provided to non-industrial units within the enterprise, if the accounting work of the enterprise is good enough to separate it from other records, and the share of such services is significant, it should also be included in the income from external processing.

Value of change in semi-finished products between the end and the beginning of the reference period: refers to the value of change in semi-finished products between the end and the beginning of the reference period, which generally can be obtained from accounting records of enterprises. If the enterprise accounting excludes the cost of semi-finished products, then it should not be included in the gross industrial output value, and the reverse if otherwise.

(4) Changes in the scope and method of calculation of the gross industrial output value

Prior to 1984, the value of rural industry run by villages was classified into agriculture instead of industry. Since 1984, it has been included in the gross industrial output value. Method of calculation for the gross industrial output value was modified in the industrial census in 1995. The difference in the new method as compared with the old one is outlined below:

Principle in using full value vs. processing fee: The new method stipulates that all products produced using own materials are to be calculated with full value in reporting the gross industrial output value irrespective of the complexity of production, and for external processing, it allows calculation using processing fee. In the old method, however, the use of full value or processing fee was determined by the degree of complexity of production in different branches of industries.

Principle in determining the value of change in semi-finished products: The new method requires that value of change in semi-finished products should be included in the gross industrial output value if it is included in the accounting record of the enterprise, otherwise it should not be included. In the old method, it is determined by the type of enterprises in terms of production cycle. If the production cycle is over 6 months, the value of change in semi-finished products is included in the gross industrial output value, otherwise it is not.

Difference in prices: The new method uses prices excluding value-added tax in the calculation of gross industrial output value, while the old method used prices including value-added tax.

Value-added of Industry refers to the final results of industrial production of industrial enterprises in money terms during the reference period.

Industrial value-added can be calculated by two approaches: the production approach, i.e. gross industrial output value minus intermediate input plus value-added tax, and the income approach, i.e. income for various factors used in the course of production, including depreciation of fixed assets, remuneration of labourers, net of production tax, and operating surplus. Value-added of industry in the Yearbook is calculated by the production approach as follows:

Value-added of industry = gross industrial output - industrial intermediate input + value-added tax

(1) Gross industrial output: refers to the total achievements of industrial production activities during a given period. Gross industrial output includes value of finished products, income from external processing, and value of change in semi-finished products between the end and the beginning of the reference period. Since 1995, the gross industrial output value obtained by the new method is used in the calculation.

(2) Industrial intermediate input: refers to purchased goods and paid services consumed during the industrial production of enterprises. Fees paid for services include fees paid for the services provided by material production sectors (industry, agriculture, wholesale and retail trade, construction, transport, post and telecommunications) and by non-material production sectors (insurance, banking, culture, education, scientific research, health and medical care, public administration, etc.). The determination of industrial intermediate input follows the principle that the goods and services must be purchased from outside and included in the gross industrial output, and that the goods and services are inputted into production and consumed (include low-value consumables) during the reference period.

Industrial intermediate input includes 5 components, namely direct consumption of materials, industrial intermediate input in manufacturing cost, industrial intermediate input in management cost, industrial intermediate input in marketing cost and expenditure on interest.

Total Assets refer to all economic resources, in monetary term, these are owned or controlled by enterprises, including properties, creditor's equity and other economic rights of all forms. Classified by the degree of liquidity, total assets include working capitals, long-term investment, fixed assets, intangible assets, deferred assets and other assets. Data on this indicator can be obtained by the year-end figures of total assets in the Assets and Liability Table of accounting records of enterprises.

Annual Average Value of Working Capital refers to the average value of all working capital of the enterprise during the reference period.

Annual Average of Net Value of Fixed Assets refers to the average of the net value of fixed assets during the reference period, calculated with the following formula:

$$\text{Annual Average of Net Value of Fixed Assets} = \frac{\text{sum of net value of fixed assets at the beginning and at the end of each month from January to December}}{24}$$

Information on this indicator can be obtained from the beginning and ending figures of the original value of fixed assets and cumulative depreciation from the Assets and Liability Table of enterprises.

Net value of fixed assets refers to the original value of fixed assets minus depreciation over the years, i.e.:

Net value of fixed assets = original value of fixed assets - cumulative depreciation

Total Liabilities refer to payable liabilities of enterprises that have to be repaid in terms of money, assets or labour services. In terms of payment, it can be divided into liquid liabilities and long-term liabilities. Data on this item is obtained from the ending figures on total liabilities from the Assets and Liability Table from the enterprises.

Owner's Equity refers to the ownership of net assets of enterprise by its investors. Net assets equal total assets minus total liabilities of the enterprise, including the actual assets invested into the enterprise by investors, accumulation of capital and operating surplus and non-distributed profits. The enterprise's assets are less than its liabilities if the sum of owner's equity is smaller than zero.

Revenue from Principal Business refers to the annual accumulation of the corresponding item in the "profit table" of the accountant. For enterprises that do not follow the 2001 Enterprise Accounting Standards, the year-end accumulation of revenue from the sales of products is used as a substitute.

Cost of Principal Business refers to the annual accumulation of the corresponding item in the "profit table" of the accountant. For enterprises that do not follow the 2001 Enterprise Accounting Standards, the year-end accumulation of cost for the sales of products is used as a substitute.

Tax and Extra Charges from Principal Business refer to the annual accumulation of the corresponding item in the "profit table" of the accountant. For enterprises that do not follow the 2001 Enterprise Accounting Standards, the year-end accumulation of tax and extra charges from the sales of products is used as a substitute.

Total Profits refer to the final achievement of production and operation activities of the enterprises, represented by total profits after deducting losses (loss is expressed by the negative figure). It is the sum of profits from operation, income from subsidies, investment earnings, net income from activities other than operation, and adjustment of profits and losses of previous years.

Value-added Tax Payable in the Current Year refers to the amount of the value-added tax which should be paid by the enterprises during the reference period. It is the sum of tax on sales, export rebate, and transferred tax on purchases of the current year, minus the tax on purchases of the current year. Value-added tax payable of small-size enterprises is determined by the taxable sales of the year multiplied by the tax rate.

Average Annual Number of Employed Persons Employed persons refer to all those who are employed in enterprises and receive remunerations there from, including currently working employees, retirees who are re-employed, teachers of local-run schools, as well as foreigners, staff from Hong Kong, Macao and Taiwan, part-time employees and persons with second job who are employed by the enterprise, and employees of other units temporarily working in the enterprises, but excluding former employees who left the enterprise with their employment records still being kept by the enterprises.

Average number of employed persons refers to the number of employee everyday during the reference period, calculated with the following formula:

$$\text{Monthly average number} = \frac{\text{sum of actual employees everyday in reference month}}{\text{number of calendar dates in reference month}}$$

$$\text{Annual average number} = \frac{\text{sum of monthly average number in reference year}}{12}$$

$$\text{Quarterly average number} = \frac{\text{sum of monthly average number in reference quarter}}{3}$$

Ratio of Profits, Taxes and Interests to Average Assets reflects the profit-making capability of all assets of the enterprise and is a key indicator manifesting the performance and management and evaluating the profit-making potential of the enterprise. It is calculated as follows:

$$\text{Ratio of Profits, Taxes and Interests to Average Assets (\%)} = \frac{\text{total profits} + \text{total taxes} + \text{interest payment}}{\text{average assets}} \times 100\%$$

In the above formula, total taxes is the sum of tax and extra charges on the sales of products and value-added tax payable; and average assets is the arithmetic mean of the sum of beginning assets and ending assets.

Ratio of Debts to Assets reflects both the operation risk and the capability of the enterprise in making use of the capital from the creditors. It is calculated as follows:

$$\text{Ratio of Debts to Assets (\%)} = \frac{\text{total debts}}{\text{total assets}} \times 100\%$$

Both assets and debts are figures at the end of the reference period.

Turnover of Working Capital refers to the number of times of turnover of working capital in a given period of time, which reflects the speed of the turnover of working capital of industrial enterprises, and is calculated as follows:

$$\text{Turnover of Working Capital} = \frac{\text{sales revenue of products}}{\text{average balance of total working capital}}$$

In the above formula, average balance of total working capital refers to the arithmetic mean of the sum of working capital at the beginning and at the end of the reference period.

Ratio of Profits to Total Industrial Costs refers to the ratio of profits realized in a given period to the total costs in the same period, which reflects the economic efficiency of input cost and is calculated as follows:

$$\text{Ratio of Profits to Total Industrial Cost (\%)} = \frac{\text{total profits}}{\text{total costs}} \times 100\%$$

Total costs in the above formula are the sum of cost of products sold, marketing cost, management cost and financial cost.

Sales Ratio of Products is an indicator reflecting the actual sale of industrial products, analyzing the production-selling and supply-demand relations. It is calculated as:

$$\text{Sales Ratio of Products (\%)} = \frac{\text{value of industrial sales}}{\text{gross industrial output value (current prices)}} \times 100\%$$

第十四篇 建筑业

CHAPTER 14 Construction

简要说明
Brief Introduction

本篇资料的主要内容及来源

本篇资料反映在新疆维吾尔自治区注册的建筑法人企业概况及发展情况，包括建筑业企业基本情况和生产经营情况。主要指标有企业个数、从业人员和建筑企业签定合同情况、承包工程完成情况及总产值、增加值、企业技术装备情况、房屋建筑面积、利润、税金、劳动生产率等。

根据建筑业发展的实际情况，建筑业统计范围从 2002 年起，由原具有建筑业资质等级四级及四级以上的独立核算的建筑业企业调整为具有施工总承包、专业承包和劳务分包的法人建筑业企业。

本篇建筑业企业统计数据是根据国家统计局制定的《建筑业统计报表制度》整理汇总的。建筑业统计数据采取全面调查的方法。资料由新疆维吾尔自治区统计局固定资产投资统计处提供。

Main content and source of data

Data in this chapter show the general situation and the development of the construction in Xinjiang Uygur Autonomous Region. They cover the situation of production and management of the enterprises on construction, including the number of enterprises, number of employed persons, complemet and gross output value of construction industry, value added floor space of the buildings, profits and taxes of enterprises and labor productivity, etc.

According to the development of construction industry, starting from 2002,the coverage of construction statistics has been adjusted to include all the construction enterprises of various types of ownership with qualification certificates and with independent accounting system ,instead of the original criteria that required construction enterprises of various types of ownership to have qualification certificates at or above Class 4 with independent accounting system.

Data on construction enterprises are collected in accordance with the Reporting System of Construction Statistics stipulated by the National Bureau of Statistics. Data on the construction industry are collected through comprehensive reporting system and provided by the Department of Investment in Fixed Assets Statistics, Xinjiang Bureau of Statistics.

14-1 建筑企业概况
Main Indicators on Construction Enterprises

年 份 Year	地 区 Region	企业个数(个) Number of Enterprises (unit)				从业人员(万人) Number of Persons Employed (10 000 persons)			
		合 计 Total	国 有 State-owned	集 体 Collec-tive-owned	其 他 Others	合 计 Total	国 有 State-owned	集 体 Collec-tive-owned	其 他 Others
	1985	275	117	158		25.85	19.21	6.64	
	1990	353	183	170		22.86	18.36	4.50	
	1995	928	481	432	15	35.33	26.33	8.72	0.28
	1996	886	478	386	22	24.97	18.53	6.09	0.35
	1997	650	313	312	25	30.75	20.39	8.56	1.80
	1998	682	269	348	65	22.14	14.83	6.42	0.89
	1999	711	272	344	95	19.35	13.00	4.94	1.41
	2000	690	226	293	171	26.16	17.69	4.25	4.22
	2001	594	175	152	267	25.27	14.77	2.68	7.82
	2002	730	146	109	475	23.57	8.64	1.89	13.04
	2003	776	112	77	587	20.81	6.16	1.12	13.53
	2004	932	105	51	776	33.22	7.21	0.84	25.17
	2005	881	107	43	731	34.37	8.70	0.90	24.77
	2006	914	102	39	773	33.84	8.81	0.84	24.19
	2007	967	103	35	829	37.02	9.63	0.92	26.47
	2008	998	99	32	867	42.37	11.28	0.48	30.61
	2009	993	90	28	875	48.18	12.01	0.52	35.65
	2010	1004	81	28	895	56.48	12.66	0.52	43.30
乌鲁木齐市	Urumqi City	485	47	15	423	22.71	7.17	0.20	15.35
克拉玛依市	Karamay City	53	2	2	49	2.83	0.15	0.09	2.58
吐鲁番地区	Turpan Administrative Offices	14	2		12	0.52	0.01		0.51
哈密地区	Hami [Kumul] Administrative Offices	38	3		35	0.97	0.27		0.70
昌吉回族自治州	Changji Hui Autonomous Prefecture	72	2	1	69	3.47	0.30	0.07	3.11
伊犁哈萨克自治州	Ili Kazak Autonomous Prefecture	104	9	7	88	6.25	1.66	0.06	4.53
伊犁州直属县(市)	Counties (Cities) Direct Under Ili Prefecture	64	6	4	54	3.31	1.35	0.03	1.93
塔城地区	Tacheng [Tarbagatai] Administrative Offices	22	2	3	17	2.03	0.10	0.03	1.90
阿勒泰地区	Altay Administrative Offices	18	1		17	0.91	0.21		0.70
博尔塔拉蒙古自治州	Bortala Mongol Autonomous Prefecture	21	2	1	18	0.90	0.01	0.06	0.84
巴音郭楞蒙古自治州	Bayangol Mongol Autonomous Prefecture	46	3	1	42	4.62	0.50		4.12
阿克苏地区	Aksu Administrative Offices	56	2		54	2.80	0.07		2.73
克孜勒苏柯尔克孜自治州	Kizilsu Kirgiz Autonomous Prefecture	13			13	0.62			0.62
喀什地区	Kashgar [Kaxgar] Administrative Offices	41	2	1	38	2.73	0.03	0.04	2.65
和田地区	Hotan Administrative Offices	20			20	0.81			0.81
石河子市	Shihezi City	27	5		22	5.48	2.21		3.27
阿拉尔市	Aral City	6	1		5	0.90	0.26		0.64
图木舒克市	Tumxuk City	3			3	0.29			0.29
五家渠市	Wujiaqu City	5	1		4	0.57	0.02		0.55

注：1.2000 年至 2002 年建筑业所有指标数据均包括克拉玛依石油管理局工业部分，2003 年起将此部分扣除(以下同)。
2.2004 年建筑业所有数据为经济普查数，企业个数及其他指标包括没有工作量或者停业企业，往年未包括(以下同)。
3.根据我区建筑特点，建筑业从业人员为年平均人数。

Note: a) All the quota indices in building sector from 2000 to 2002 include the industrial part of Karamay Oil Administration. From 2003, this part was omitted. (the same as in the following) . b) All the data in architectural sector are the statistics of economic census, enterprise numbers and other quota exclude work volume or closed enterprises except for previous years. (the same as in the following) . c)In view of the features of the construction, the number of employed persons refers to the annual average.

14-2 按登记注册类型分建筑企业总产值

Total Output Value of Construction Enterprises by Registration Status

单位：万元 (10 000 yuan)

年 份 Year	地 区 Region	合 计 Total	国有经济 State-owned Units	集体经济 Collective -owned Units	其他经济 Others Units
	1985	175165	138138	37027	
	1990	273893	220574	53319	
	1995	1070085	816396	238387	15302
	1996	1284669	977358	283776	23535
	1997	1141318	828482	288081	24755
	1998	1434787	1002235	378956	53596
	1999	1569486	1085080	365588	118818
	2000	2349506	1436653	362649	550204
	2001	2742800	1394099	252076	1096625
	2002	3136257	1270601	170319	1695337
	2003	3221502	739953	147256	2334293
	2004	3439968	910264	89189	2440515
	2005	3615674	1138005	102580	2375089
	2006	3856223	1269722	88474	2498027
	2007	4541026	1548285	97418	2895323
	2008	6292562	1879497	86431	4326634
	2009	7913768	2245048	119717	5549003
	2010	9694741	2486878	119917	7087946
乌鲁木齐市	Urumqi City	4131004	1649523	38895	2442587
克拉玛依市	Karamay City	754470	19147	31788	703535
吐鲁番地区	Turpan Administrative Offices	147832	7160		140672
哈密地区	Hami [Kumul] Administrative Offices	185834	59664		126170
昌吉回族自治州	Changji Hui Autonomous Prefecture	520564	40110	14514	465940
伊犁哈萨克自治州	Ili Kazak Autonomous Prefecture	993040	289505	16820	686715
伊犁州直属县(市)	Counties (Cities) Direct Under Ili Prefecture	601833	256262	12807	332764
塔城地区	Tacheng [Tarbagatai] Administrative Offices	248357	14515	4013	229829
阿勒泰地区	Altay Administrative Offices	142850	18728		124122
博尔塔拉蒙古自治州	Bortala Mongol Autonomous Prefecture	137505	776	7500	129229
巴音郭楞蒙古自治州	Bayangol Mongol Autonomous Prefecture	821362	115483	248	705631
阿克苏地区	Aksu Administrative Offices	488056	14811		473245
克孜勒苏柯尔克孜自治州	Kizilsu Kirgiz Autonomous Prefecture	84534			84534
喀什地区	Kashgar [Kaxgar] Administrative Offices	458428	2493	10152	445783
和田地区	Hotan Administrative Offices	145366			145366
石河子市	Shihezi City	536331	244447		291884
阿拉尔市	Aral City	162471	41371		121100
图木舒克市	Tumxuk City	55098			55098
五家渠市	Wujiaqu City	72846	2388		70458

14-3 按构成分建筑企业总产值

Total Output Value of Construction Enterprises by Composition

单位：万元 (10 000 yuan)

年 份 Year	地 区 Region	总产值 Total Output Value	建筑工程 Output Value of Construction Projects	安装工程 Output Value of Installation Projects	其 他 Others
	1985	175165	154496	18042	2627
	1990	273893	241574	28211	4108
	1995	1070085	942158	106744	21183
	1996	1284669	1124271	132079	28319
	1997	1141318	1009082	105891	26345
	1998	1434787	1270483	139104	25200
	1999	1569486	1398179	146154	25153
	2000	2349506	2073166	214425	61915
	2001	2742800	2403688	279909	59203
	2002	3136257	2637362	405115	93780
	2003	3221502	2708269	336535	176698
	2004	3439968	2836668	396509	206791
	2005	3615674	2981373	487239	147062
	2006	3856223	3209192	510770	136261
	2007	4541026	3822922	564228	153876
	2008	6292562	5359129	804719	128714
	2009	7913768	6924156	867812	121800
	2010	9694741	8450628	1107006	137107
乌鲁木齐市	Urumqi City	4131004	3677190	418278	35536
克拉玛依市	Karamay City	754470	339081	380432	34957
吐鲁番地区	Turpan Administrative Offices	147833	59960	83773	4100
哈密地区	Hami [Kumul] Administrative Offices	185833	183578	2224	31
昌吉回族自治州	Changji Hui Autonomous Prefecture	520564	472648	43616	4300
伊犁哈萨克自治州	Ili Kazak Autonomous Prefecture	993040	933304	36569	23167
伊犁州直属县(市)	Counties (Cities) Direct Under Ili Prefecture	601833	564712	19947	17174
塔城地区	Tacheng [Tarbagatai] Administrative Offices	248357	235825	12079	453
阿勒泰地区	Altay Administrative Offices	142850	132767	4543	5540
博尔塔拉蒙古自治州	Bortala Mongol Autonomous Prefecture	137505	137482	23	
巴音郭楞蒙古自治州	Bayangol Mongol Autonomous Prefecture	821362	777491	25776	18095
阿克苏地区	Aksu Administrative Offices	488056	457463	28737	1856
克孜勒苏柯尔克孜自治州	Kizilsu Kirgiz Autonomous Prefecture	84534	78870	1102	4562
喀什地区	Kashgar [Kaxgar] Administrative Offices	458428	408817	43739	5872
和田地区	Hotan Administrative Offices	145366	141142	3123	1101
石河子市	Shihezi City	536331	493244	39584	3503
阿拉尔市	Aral City	162471	162441	30	
图木舒克市	Tumxuk City	55098	55098		
五家渠市	Wujiaqu City	72846	72819		27

14-4 按行业和登记注册类型分建筑企业总产值

Total Output Value of Construction Enterprises by Registration Status and Sectors

单位：万元 (10 000 yuan)

项目	Item	2009	2010
总计	**Total**	**7913768**	**9694741**
#一、二级企业	First Grade and Second Grade Enterprises	6377939	8103645
#国有及国有控股	State-owned and State-holding	3717043	4665988
按登记注册类型分组	**Grouped by Registration Status**		
内资企业	Domestic Funded	7913577	9694418
国有企业	State-owned Enterprises	1543160	1647361
集体企业	Collective-owned Enterprises	119717	119917
股份合作企业	Share-holding Cooperative	35024	52066
联营企业	Joint Ownership Enterprises		
有限责任公司	Limited Liability Corporations	4232153	5334128
国有独资公司	Sole State -funded Company	701889	839517
其他有限责任公司	Other Limited Liability Companies	3530264	4494611
股份有限公司	Share-holding Corporations Ltd	488113	659566
私营企业	Private Enterprises	1493400	1881380
#私营有限责任公司	Private Limited Liability Companies	1437755	1811565
私营股份有限公司	Private Stock Limited Companies	52625	67808
其他企业	Others	2010	
港、澳、台及外商企业	Enterprises With Funds from Hong Kong, Macao , Taiwan and Foreign	191	323
#合资经营企业(港或澳、台资)	Joint-Venture	191	220
按国民经济行业分组	**Grouped by National Economic Sectors**		
房屋和土木工程建筑业	Buildings and Civil Engineering Construction	7072481	8710794
房屋工程建筑	Building Construction	4782579	5886052
土木工程建筑	Civil Engineering Construction	2289902	2824742
铁路、道路、隧道和桥梁	Railways, Roads, Tunnels and Bridges	1586419	2044836
水利和港口建筑	Water Conservancy and Seaport Construction	325903	466486
工矿工程建筑	Mine Project	60696	43662
架线和管道工程建筑	Cabling and Piping Project	278829	221548
其他土木工程建筑	Other Civil Engineering	38055	48210
建筑安装业	Construction and Installation	731193	869919
建筑装饰业	Building Decoration	54079	60979
其他建筑业	Others	56015	53050
按隶属关系分组	**Grouped by Subordination**		
中央	Central Government	2235013	2994670
地方	Local	5678755	6700071
按企业资质等级分组	**Grouped by Enterprise's Qualification**		
施工总承包	Undertaking Porjects	7258850	8924733
特级	Special Grade	149073	148694
一级	First Grade	3238903	4185541
二级	Second Grade	2601828	3287718
三级及以下	Third Grade and Below	7258850	1302780
专业承包	Specialized Undertaking	607091	712456
一级	First Grade	172687	195129
二级	Second Grade	186097	249612
三级及以下	Third Grade and Below	599562	267715
劳务分包	Work Subcontractors	47827	57552
三级及以下	Third Grade and Below	47827	57552

14-5 建筑企业增加值
Value-added of Construction Enterprises

单位：万元 (10 000 yuan)

年份 Year	地区 Region	合计 Total	按注册类型分 Grouped by Ownership: 国有企业 State-owned Enterprise	集体企业 Collective-owned Enterprises	其他企业 Others	按隶属关系分 By Administrative Relationship: 中央企业 Central Enterprises	地方企业 Local Enterprises
	1985	60152	52022	8130			
	1990	109923	91983	17940			
	1995	283882	207212	72598	4072	92259	191623
	1996	303370	218532	78973	5865	96996	206374
	1997	380806	284938	87437	8431	133287	247519
	1998	296444	182903	89375	24166	84239	212205
	1999	323714	198463	87477	37774	92459	213255
	2000	587341	386475	84268	116598	274836	312505
	2001	637472	340470	49298	247704	260784	376688
	2002	621430	223509	37383	360538	211988	409442
	2003	672531	143473	29333	499725	161523	511008
	2004	693070	158801	18938	515331	157382	535688
	2005	716063	199645	18265	498153	176697	539366
	2006	790466	230867	20948	538651	215766	574700
	2007	947319	304278	19234	623807	278640	668679
	2008	1349429	375318	18888	955223	427287	922142
	2009	1627342	417474	19541	1190327	492321	1135021
	2010	2053556	451108	21823	1580625	658449	1395107
乌鲁木齐市	Urumqi City	807880	241199	10409	556271	297084	510796
克拉玛依市	Karamay City	155544	5071	3920	146553	38940	116604
吐鲁番地区	Turpan Administrative Offices	26367	2225		24142		26367
哈密地区	Hami [Kumul] Administrative Offices	35510	13458		22052	10987	24523
昌吉回族自治州	Changji Hui Autonomous Prefecture	122304	10232	2539	109533	3752	118552
伊犁哈萨克自治州	Ili Kazak Autonomous Prefecture	208210	73709	2332	132169	98917	109293
伊犁州直属县(市)	Counties (Cities) Direct Under Ili Prefecture	131746	67495	1443	62808	73513	58233
塔城地区	Tacheng [Tarbagatai] Administrative Offices	46953	1855	889	44209	21045	25908
阿勒泰地区	Altay Administrative Offices	29511	4359		25152	4359	25152
博尔塔拉蒙古自治州	Bortala Mongol Autonomous Prefecture	25475	137	2064	23274	3864	21611
巴音郭楞蒙古自治州	Bayangol Mongol Autonomous Prefecture	179877	17621	88	162168	13539	166338
阿克苏地区	Aksu Administrative Offices	130019	2945		127074	14507	115512
克孜勒苏柯尔克孜自治州	Kizilsu Kirgiz Autonomous Prefecture	16675			16675		16675
喀什地区	Kashgar [Kaxgar] Administrative Offices	87437	819	471	86148	9329	78108
和田地区	Hotan Administrative Offices	38707			38707	6541	32166
石河子市	Shihezi City	154152	71314		82838	138891	15262
阿拉尔市	Aral City	36287	11809		24478	13771	22516
图木舒克市	Tumxuk City	13417			13417	7759	5658
五家渠市	Wujiaqu City	15695	569		15126	569	15126

14-6 建筑企业利税总额

Total Pre-tax Profits of Construction Enterprises

单位：万元 (10 000 yuan)

年份 Year	地区 Region	利税总额合计 Total Pre-tax Profits	利润总额 Total Profits	工程结算税金及附加 Taxes and Extra Charges on Project Settlement Accounts	管理费用中的税金 Taxes in Management Expenses	产值利税率(%) Ratio of Pre-tax Profits to Output Value (%)	资金利税率(%) Ratio of Pre-tax Profits to Assets (%)
	1994	28199	5535	20195	2469	3.81	4.11
	1995	30156	2974	24916	2266	3.44	3.46
	1996	20752	-8625	26816	2561	1.97	-0.93
	1997	31970	-4347	33360	2957	2.80	2.51
	1998	37596	-5875	41162	2309	2.62	2.41
	1999	64777	13359	48995	2423	4.13	3.72
	2000	19274	-48005	64614	2665	0.82	0.63
	2001	28688	-47485	74206	1967	1.05	0.84
	2002	84833	-11089	92484	3438	2.70	2.18
	2003	169594	67146	96888	5560	5.26	5.51
	2004	174255	65037	102990	6228	5.07	5.65
	2005	165236	46909	112565	5762	4.57	4.91
	2006	177102	54570	116426	6106	4.59	4.83
	2007	221117	67796	145119	8202	4.87	5.40
	2008	328484	120146	198718	9620	5.22	6.67
	2009	422062	156541	252547	12974	5.33	7.08
	2010	536197	208372	317056	10769	5.53	7.54
乌鲁木齐市	Urumqi City	231507	93954	132633	4920	5.60	6.58
克拉玛依市	Karamay City	43821	16287	26514	1020	5.81	4.83
吐鲁番地区	Turpan Administrative Offices	6742	2999	3637	106	4.56	5.76
哈密地区	Hami [Kumul] Administrative Offices	8768	3359	5306	103	4.72	5.94
昌吉回族自治州	Changji Hui Autonomous Prefecture	29323	10144	18785	394	5.63	9.47
伊犁哈萨克自治州	Ili Kazak Autonomous Prefecture	43775	8360	34689	727	4.41	9.28
伊犁州直属县(市)	Counties (Cities) Direct Under Ili Prefecture	24851	4587	19713	552	4.13	8.25
塔城地区	Tacheng [Tarbagatai] Administrative Offices	13683	4063	9540	80	5.51	13.38
阿勒泰地区	Altay Administrative Offices	5241	-290	5436	95	3.67	7.68
博尔塔拉蒙古自治州	Bortala Mongol Autonomous Prefecture	6618	669	5912	37	4.81	12.18
巴音郭楞蒙古自治州	Bayangol Mongol Autonomous Prefecture	51683	25868	24954	861	6.29	15.38
阿克苏地区	Aksu Administrative Offices	32053	15728	15204	1121	6.57	8.52
克孜勒苏柯尔克孜自治州	Kizilsu Kirgiz Autonomous Prefecture	3815	471	3234	110	4.51	5.68
喀什地区	Kashgar [Kaxgar] Administrative Offices	31793	14191	16756	846	6.94	10.45
和田地区	Hotan Administrative Offices	6954	82	6652	219	4.78	9.24
石河子市	Shihezi City	21729	7129	14392	208	4.05	8.10
阿拉尔市	Aral City	8757	4368	4374	16	5.39	10.95
图木舒克市	Tumxuk City	4935	3156	1745	34	8.96	12.02
五家渠市	Wujiaqu City	3926	1609	2271	47	5.39	9.30

14-7 建筑企业劳动生产率

Labor Productivity of Construction Enterprises

单位：元/人 (yuan/person)

年 份 Year	地 区 Region	按总产值计算的劳动生产率 Overall Labor Productivity in Terms of Total Output Value	#国有经济 State-owned Enterprises	#集体经济 Collective-owned Enterprises	按增加值计算的劳动生产率 Overall Labor Productivity in Terms of Added-Value	#国有经济 State-owned Enterprises	#集体经济 Collective-owned Enterprises
	1994	29871	32616	23023	9499	10546	7186
	1995	34668	38483	26617	11238	12505	8673
	1996	32606	36557	25291	10648	12286	7719
	1997	38808	40629	33658	12948	13973	10215
	1998	47698	51465	40819	9855	10044	9627
	1999	55593	61196	44235	11466	11766	10584
	2000	74994	87999	48767	25208	32781	14138
	2001	84666	94344	62458	19678	23041	12215
	2002	86302	108857	66231	17100	19149	14537
	2003	94165	98095	86190	19659	19020	17169
	2004	107150	112145	107185	21588	22365	22759
	2005	112214	137966	127587	22223	23971	22718
	2006	121506	149550	118932	24907	27794	28159
	2007	126303	134275	139988	26349	26389	27640
	2008	152795	182536	168023	32767	36451	36718
	2009	173714	204170	233869	35721	37966	38174
	2010	176404	200435	231859	37366	36358	42194
乌鲁木齐市	Urumqi City	186149	231479	196044	36404	33848	52466
克拉玛依市	Karamay City	274173	126298	374863	56524	33444	46232
吐鲁番地区	Turpan Administrative Offices	296912	526493		52956	163597	
哈密地区	Hami [Kumul] Administrative Offices	198520	241947		37934	54573	
昌吉回族自治州	Changji Hui Autonomous Prefecture	156302	134960	216306	36722	34426	37841
伊犁哈萨克自治州	Ili Kazak Autonomous Prefecture	164503	191231	259975	34491	48688	36034
伊犁州直属县(市)	Counties (Cities) Direct Under Ili Prefecture	190586	202354	413158	41721	53297	46516
塔城地区	Tacheng [Tarbagatai] Administrative Offices	125566	323996	119065	23739	41408	26392
阿勒泰地区	Altay Administrative Offices	158564	92393		32757	21503	
博尔塔拉蒙古自治州	Bortala Mongol Autonomous Prefecture	152007	88193	125000	28161	15511	34401
巴音郭楞蒙古自治州	Bayangol Mongol Autonomous Prefecture	179458	243841	206333	39301	37207	72925
阿克苏地区	Aksu Administrative Offices	183190	215905		48802	42931	
克孜勒苏柯尔克孜自治州	Kizilsu Kirgiz Autonomous Prefecture	136964			27018		
喀什地区	Kashgar [Kaxgar] Administrative Offices	181764	85096	247602	34668	27951	11478
和田地区	Hotan Administrative Offices	179975			47923		
石河子市	Shihezi City	97917	110649		28143	32281	
阿拉尔市	Aral City	183666	168790		41021	48179	
图木舒克市	Tumxuk City	201897			49166		
五家渠市	Wujiaqu City	150105	99916		32342	23812	

14-8 建筑企业技术装备情况

Number and Power of Machinery and Equipment Owned by Construction Enterprises

年 份 Year	地 区 Region	自有机械设备总台数(台) Number of Machinery and Equipment Owned (set)	自有机械设备总功率(万千瓦) Total Power of Equipment and Machinery Owned (10 000 kw)	自有机械设备净值(万元) Net Value of Machinery and Equipment Owned (10 000 yuan)	技术装备率(元/人) Value of Machines Per Laborer (yuan/ person)	动力装备率(千瓦/人) Power of Machines Per Laborer (kw/person)
	1985	30307	105	29308	1332	6
	1990	34806	91	46098	2511	5
	1995	55455	138	106383	4211	5
	1996	60567	129	127572	4478	5
	1997	64252	149	139617	4747	5
	1998	72606	148	164157	7415	7
	1999	73735	155	184559	9543	8
	2000	77975	182	224485	8582	7
	2001	85981	177	238142	9425	7
	2002	96116	207	442787	18996	9
	2003	100913	207	395865	11866	6
	2004	98541	239	358397	11389	8
	2005	99324	190	326360	10372	6
	2006	96674	197	348344	11187	6
	2007	103431	203	374396	10650	6
	2008	102266	230	392371	9692	6
	2009	103285	235	407809	9136	5
	2010	97562	238	383196	7145	4
乌鲁木齐市	Urumqi City	25864	85	149325	7119	4
克拉玛依市	Karamay City	6371	25	44165	16399	9
吐鲁番地区	Turpan Administrative Offices	1857	6	11205	22709	11
哈密地区	Hami [Kumul] Administrative Offices	3462	9	6358	6937	10
昌吉回族自治州	Changji Hui Autonomous Prefecture	10202	14	24326	7320	4
伊犁哈萨克自治州	Ili Kazak Autonomous Prefecture	16357	26	30637	5090	4
伊犁州直属县(市)	Counties (Cities) Direct Under Ili Prefecture	8605	9	15500	4918	3
塔城地区	Tacheng [Tarbagatai] Administrative Offices	3736	11	5791	2945	6
阿勒泰地区	Altay Administrative Offices	4016	6	9346	10374	6
博尔塔拉蒙古自治州	Bortala Mongol Autonomous Prefecture	3618	5	11635	12861	6
巴音郭楞蒙古自治州	Bayangol Mongol Autonomous Prefecture	9361	26	36123	7893	6
阿克苏地区	Aksu Administrative Offices	5477	15	16000	6005	6
克孜勒苏柯尔克孜自治州	Kizilsu Kirgiz Autonomous Prefecture	937	2	3034	4915	3
喀什地区	Kashgar [Kaxgar] Administrative Offices	6325	10	16795	6659	4
和田地区	Hotan Administrative Offices	2684	3	4624	5725	4
石河子市	Shihezi City	2961	8	14754	2694	1
阿拉尔市	Aral City	1142	3	10833	12246	3
图木舒克市	Tumxuk City	507	2	2558	9372	7
五家渠市	Wujiaqu City	437	1	828	1706	1

14-9 按登记注册类型分建筑企业技术装备情况

Number and Power of Machinery and Equipment Owned by Registration Status

(2010 年)

项　　目	Item	自有机械设备年末总台数(台) Number of Machinery and Equipment Owned Year-end (set)	自有机械设备年末总功率(千瓦) Total Power of Machinery and Equipment Owned Year-end (kw)	自有机械设备年末净值(万元) Net Value of Machinery and Equipment Owned Year-end (10 000 yuan)
总　计	**Total**	**97562**	**2381071**	**383196**
#一、二级企业	First, Second Enterprises	78836	2058203	325606
#国有及国有控股	State-owned and State-holding	34125	1171567	194889
按登记注册类型分组	**Grouped by Registration Status**			
内资企业	Domestic Funede	97562	2381071	383196
国有企业	State-owned Enterprises	13264	381153	68021
集体企业	Collective-owned Enterprises	898	29255	3692
有限责任公司	Limited Liability Corporations	52520	1302924	189098
国有独资公司	Sole State -funded Company	4106	146910	18711
其他有限责任公司	Other Limited Liability Companies	48414	1156014	170387
股份有限公司	Share-holding Corporations Ltd.	2049	155697	35505
私营企业	Private Enterprises	28831	512042	86880
#私营有限责任公司	Private Limited Liability Companies	27878	495828	84176
私营股份有限公司	Private Stock Limited Companies	939	16079	2683
按国民经济行业分组	**Grouped by National Economic Sectors**			
房屋和土木工程建筑业	Buildings and Givil Engineering	86693	2110091	331823
房屋工程建筑	Building	71642	1373535	186272
土木工程建筑	Civil Engineering	15051	736556	145551
铁路、道路、隧道和桥梁	Railways, Roads, Tunnels and Bridges	7638	554493	100821
水利和港口建筑	Water Conservancy and Seaport	3201	88807	17930
工矿工程建筑	Mining Project	1057	19206	8672
架线和管道工程建筑	Cabling and Piping Project	2698	61974	15907
其他土木工程建筑	Other Civil Engineering	457	12076	2222
建筑安装业	Construction and Installation	9458	242890	41453
建筑装饰业	Building Decoration	944	11493	4139
其他建筑业	Others	467	16597	5782
按隶属关系分组	**Grouped by Subordination**			
中 央	Central Government	18965	759178	133673
地 方	Local	78597	1621893	249523
按企业资质等级分组	**Grouped by Enterprise's Qualification**			
施工总承包	Undertaking Porjects	90526	2224685	347413
特　级	Special Grade	937	28874	1321
一　级	First Grade	26754	962740	156667
二　级	Second Grade	46372	959545	142272
三　级	Third Grade	16463	273526	47154
专业承包	Specialized Undertaking	7036	156386	35783
一　级	First Grade	2364	49173	17066
二　级	Second Grade	2409	57871	8282
三　级	Third Grade	2222	48664	10328

14-10 建筑企业签订合同情况
Contracts Signed by Construction Enterprises

单位：万元 (10 000 yuan)

年份 Year	地区 Region	合同总额 Total Value Of Contracts	上年结转合同 Value from Contracts Signed In 2009	本年新签合同 Value from New Contracts Signed In 2010
	2002	3962086	988485	2973601
	2003	4312515	1236887	3075628
	2004	4725501	1351086	3374415
	2005	4857604	1557300	3300304
	2006	5692120	1483664	4208455
	2007	7220300	1986086	5234214
	2008	9907859	2906991	7000868
	2009	12473691	3859836	8613855
	2010	15883584	5459941	10423643
乌鲁木齐市	Urumqi City	7679039	3336582	4342457
克拉玛依市	Karamay City	1185876	468966	716910
吐鲁番地区	Turpan Administrative Offices	175948	18116	157833
哈密地区	Hami [Kumul] Administrative Offices	277167	70420	206747
昌吉回族自治州	Changji Hui Autonomous Prefecture	754241	131680	622561
伊犁哈萨克自治州	Ili Kazak Autonomous Prefecture	1464008	332956	1131052
伊犁州直属县(市)	Counties (Cities) Direct Under Ili Prefecture	869889	201120	668769
塔城地区	Tacheng [Tarbagatai] Administrative Offices	409682	106295	303387
阿勒泰地区	Altay Administrative Offices	184437	25541	158896
博尔塔拉蒙古自治州	Bortala Mongol Autonomous Prefecture	189129	39137	149992
巴音郭楞蒙古自治州	Bayangol Mongol Autonomous Prefecture	1091975	294253	797722
阿克苏地区	Aksu Administrative Offices	742353	165230	577123
克孜勒苏柯尔克孜自治州	Kizilsu Kirgiz Autonomous Prefecture	114397	20812	93585
喀什地区	Kashgar [Kaxgar] Administrative Offices	654226	180785	473441
和田地区	Hotan Administrative Offices	280542	44208	236334
石河子市	Shihezi City	844792	254242	590550
阿拉尔市	Aral City	228589	63388	165201
图木舒克市	Tumxuk City	73862	15291	58571
五家渠市	Wujiaqu City	127442	23876	103567

注：14-10、14-11 表口径为总承包和专业承包企业。
Note:The data of the table 14-10&14-11 refer to all general construction contractors and professional contractors.

14-11 建筑企业承包工程完成情况

Completion of Contracted Projects by Construction Enterprises

单位：万元 (10 000 yuan)

年 份 Year	地 区 Region	直接从建设单位承揽工程完成产值 Completed Output Value of Projects Contracted Directly from Investors	自行完成施工产值 Own-Completed Output Value	分包出去工程产值 Output Value Of Out-Sourced Projects	从建设单位以外承揽工程产值 Completed Output Value of Projects Contracted From Non-investors
	2002	3141928	3048086	93842	88171
	2003	3238170	3135725	102445	85777
	2004	3443802	3377532	66270	62436
	2005	3634746	3563947	70799	51727
	2006	3856300	3775975	80325	80248
	2007	4534324	4420958	113366	120068
	2008	6309803	6128312	181492	164251
	2009	7993048	7805261	187787	108507
	2010	9723428	9503630	219798	191111
乌鲁木齐市	Urumqi City	4143051	4006677	136374	124327
克拉玛依市	Karamay City	810859	741410	69450	13060
吐鲁番地区	Turpan Administrative Offices	147833	147833		
哈密地区	Hami [Kumul] Administrative Offices	185834	185834		
昌吉回族自治州	Changji Hui Autonomous Prefecture	520564	520564		
伊犁哈萨克自治州	Ili Kazak Autonomous Prefecture	987019	987019		6021
伊犁州直属县(市)	Counties (Cities) Direct Under Ili Prefecture	596747	596747		5086
塔城地区	Tacheng [Tarbagatai] Administrative Offices	248357	248357		
阿勒泰地区	Altay Administrative Offices	141915	141915		935
博尔塔拉蒙古自治州	Bortala Mongol Autonomous Prefecture	137505	137505		
巴音郭楞蒙古自治州	Bayangol Mongol Autonomous Prefecture	823688	821362	2326	
阿克苏地区	Aksu Administrative Offices	472073	472073		15983
克孜勒苏柯尔克孜自治州	Kizilsu Kirgiz Autonomous Prefecture	84534	84534		
喀什地区	Kashgar [Kaxgar] Administrative Offices	457267	447115	10152	11313
和田地区	Hotan Administrative Offices	145366	145366		
石河子市	Shihezi City	515925	515925		20407
阿拉尔市	Aral City	162471	162471		
图木舒克市	Tumxuk City	55098	55098		
五家渠市	Wujiaqu City	74342	72846	1496	

14-12 建筑企业资产及资本金

Assets and Capital Principal of Construction Enterprises

单位：万元 (10 000 yuan)

年份 Year	地区 Region	资产合计 Total Assets	流动资产合计 Circulating Funds	固定资产合计 Total of Fixed Assets	固定资产净值 Net Value of Fixed Assets	本年折旧 Deprecia-tion in the Year	无形及递延资产 Intangible and Deferred Assets	资本金合计 Total of Principal Value	#国家资本金 National Principal
1995		939205	647608	240076	225084	18463	3132	221212	110987
2000		3256421	1855185	1215525	1106384	65383	35063	892851	208214
2001		3740312	2187385	1243161	1048023	82884	138976	1055531	227457
2002		4244587	2527414	1364782	1179599	95565	184827	1327186	227601
2003		3375330	2292828	787690	675947	61335	165349	835618	219826
2004		3810825	2632242	825567	722019	62725	163384	929293	225884
2005		3818087	2665404	826376	700835	72103	150802	936389	184447
2006		4115800	2952267	796558	712740	69191	149062	985436	202670
2007		4611598	3387459	804007	706591	76979	157776	1095997	222967
2008		5527993	4040796	958379	862286	91915	224382	1408249	429579
2009		6565349	4966204	1080129	960338	103188	219640	1528701	396188
2010		7906943	6141713	1078910	939519	99050	222795	1585475	412634
	乌鲁木齐市 Urumqi City	3894890	3106974	424147	380366	47481	146392	664320	237823
	克拉玛依市 Karamay City	1007186	765567	144688	140622	11678	11201	149303	36165
	吐鲁番地区 Turpan Administrative Offices	124216	97276	20577	19663	2595	3753	23180	6959
	哈密地区 Hami [Kumul] Administrative Offices	153475	128711	18974	18062	2084	1451	30019	14275
	昌吉回族自治州 Changji Hui Autonomous Prefecture	362074	268272	42281	40141	3495	10867	98988	4904
	伊犁哈萨克自治州 Ili Kazak Autonomous Prefecture	517741	372178	107120	98343	9306	5601	162459	39774
	伊犁州直属县(市) Counties (Cities) Direct Under Ili Prefecture	336821	237344	67050	62729	5602	4607	101636	28769
	塔城地区 Tacheng [Tarbagatai] Administrative Offices	106575	85893	18814	16307	1523	221	27685	10056
	阿勒泰地区 Altay Administrative Offices	74345	48941	21256	19307	2181	773	33138	949
	博尔塔拉蒙古自治州 Bortala Mongol Autonomous Prefecture	62141	38141	21403	16207	953	709	32186	1518
	巴音郭楞蒙古自治州 Bayangol Mongol Autonomous Prefecture	392994	260571	101333	75536	7016	13502	120262	16994
	阿克苏地区 Aksu Administrative Offices	417768	333129	69011	43165	4513	4674	106889	4102
	克孜勒苏柯尔克孜自治州 Kizilsu Kirgiz Autonomous Prefecture	79145	55077	16252	12043	634	3620	19159	
	喀什地区 Kashgar [Kaxgar] Administrative Offices	353064	271876	44050	32435	2413	12727	74686	3709
	和田地区 Hotan Administrative Offices	81205	59316	17239	15938	1351	2985	30141	1285
	石河子市 Shihezi City	282642	242691	28813	25696	2856	4816	47239	38453
	阿拉尔市 Aral City	85845	63002	17410	16986	1990	48	12689	3758
	图木舒克市 Tumxuk City	42932	37733	4198	3318	456	353	4857	1856
	五家渠市 Wujiaqu City	49625	41199	1414	998	229	96	9098	1059

14-13 建筑企业负债及所有者权益
Liabilities and Owner's Equity of Construction Enterprises

单位：万元 (10 000 yuan)

年 份 Year	地 区 Region	负债合计 Total Liabilities	流动负债 Liquid Liabilities	长期负债 Long-term Liabilities	所有者权益 Owners' Equity
	1994	540403	467895	72508	192618
	1995	699997	614110	84378	239208
	1996	815330	714429	98342	324051
	1997	1018007	901138	115032	350659
	1998	1175839	1044115	131724	385913
	1999	1325825	1205880	119945	415026
	2000	2068439	1941268	127171	1187982
	2001	2300621	2168441	132180	1439690
	2002	2717728	2585374	132354	1526859
	2003	2327382	2206412	120970	1047948
	2004	2631252	2517755	105621	1174864
	2005	2651255	2555028	96227	1159206
	2006	2886203	2797525	88678	1220298
	2007	3240248	3139697	100551	1359137
	2008	3806899	3669521	137378	1707855
	2009	4553885	4380062	173823	1996439
	2010	5798936	5466110	332826	2089888
乌鲁木齐市	Urumqi City	3035099	2772148	262951	844582
克拉玛依市	Karamay City	769075	767556	1519	237668
吐鲁番地区	Turpan Administrative Offices	98110	98074	36	26056
哈密地区	Hami [Kumul] Administrative Offices	119487	119234	253	33628
昌吉回族自治州	Changji Hui Autonomous Prefecture	239148	230032	9116	122057
伊犁哈萨克自治州	Ili Kazak Autonomous Prefecture	322600	297920	24680	194024
伊犁州直属县(市)	Counties (Cities) Direct Under Ili Prefecture	215756	211451	4305	120076
塔城地区	Tacheng [Tarbagatai] Administrative Offices	66079	47286	18793	40368
阿勒泰地区	Altay Administrative Offices	40765	39183	1582	33580
博尔塔拉蒙古自治州	Bortala Mongol Autonomous Prefecture	30445	28083	2362	31696
巴音郭楞蒙古自治州	Bayangol Mongol Autonomous Prefecture	192089	183220	8870	200837
阿克苏地区	Aksu Administrative Offices	271574	265365	6209	146194
克孜勒苏柯尔克孜自治州	Kizilsu Kirgiz Autonomous Prefecture	55800	54489	1311	23345
喀什地区	Kashgar [Kaxgar] Administrative Offices	253860	247831	6029	99204
和田地区	Hotan Administrative Offices	47490	46190	1300	33714
石河子市	Shihezi City	227205	226279	925	55438
阿拉尔市	Aral City	62471	57842	4629	23374
图木舒克市	Tumxuk City	36102	33465	2636	6830
五家渠市	Wujiaqu City	38382	38382		11243

14-14 建筑企业总收入

Total Income of Construction Enterprises

单位：万元　(10 000 yuan)

年份 Year	地区 Region	企业总收入 Total Income of Enterprises	工程结算收入 Revenue of Project Settlement Accounts	#工程结算成本 Costs of Project Settlement Accounts	#工程结算利润 Profits of Project Settlement Accounts	其他业务收入 Revenue from Other Business	#其他业务利润 Profits from Other Business
	1994	813369	714469	627830	66444	98900	9332
	1995	898810	821713	713940	82858	77097	9445
	1996	983170	904800	799183	78801	78370	8765
	1997	1210813	1081666	950091	98216	129147	17368
	1998	1454758	1346748	1193276	112310	108010	19146
	1999	1595986	1500818	1320898	130925	95167	14882
	2000	2659696	2514011	2252154	197243	145686	30012
	2001	2961754	2807549	2521902	211441	154205	34532
	2002	3360613	3199880	2854350	254428	160733	30853
	2003	3221521	3090768	2716009	254015	130753	21692
	2004	3395793	3276421	2900842	253783	119372	21601
	2005	3685197	3566042	3202712	238351	119155	23629
	2006	3766819	3643783	3255171	252876	123036	20730
	2007	4584374	4431221	3983622	285041	153154	22186
	2008	6382510	6225083	5635311	368605	157427	33187
	2009	7958865	7788105	7074708	440109	170760	39289
	2010	9849630	9610000	8752747	510265	239630	46564
乌鲁木齐市	Urumqi City	4273757	4126703	3730313	254265	147054	23832
克拉玛依市	Karamay City	957610	926021	847805	48229	31589	6334
吐鲁番地区	Turpan Administrative Offices	130967	130644	120190	6697	323	286
哈密地区	Hami [Kumul] Administrative Offices	175946	173283	156911	9081	2663	1008
昌吉回族自治州	Changji Hui Autonomous Prefecture	565125	561775	515623	25943	3350	1805
伊犁哈萨克自治州	Ili Kazak Autonomous Prefecture	1026875	1008286	938644	32924	18589	3996
伊犁州直属县(市)	Counties (Cities) Direct Under Ili Prefecture	631175	623567	584552	17309	7608	3498
塔城地区	Tacheng [Tarbagatai] Administrative Offices	255279	252876	232532	11052	2403	417
阿勒泰地区	Altay Administrative Offices	140421	131843	121560	4563	8578	81
博尔塔拉蒙古自治州	Bortala Mongol Autonomous Prefecture	144478	139175	129698	3101	5303	557
巴音郭楞蒙古自治州	Bayangol Mongol Autonomous Prefecture	685378	680696	612861	42026	4682	1007
阿克苏地区	Aksu Administrative Offices	418941	409907	364635	29403	9034	541
克孜勒苏柯尔克孜自治州	Kizilsu Kirgiz Autonomous Prefecture	92825	92763	86744	2679	62	40
喀什地区	Kashgar [Kaxgar] Administrative Offices	451279	449789	402284	21524	1490	1214
和田地区	Hotan Administrative Offices	186651	185584	176037	2894	1067	889
石河子市	Shihezi City	473508	467501	435502	17609	6007	2086
阿拉尔市	Aral City	145590	139940	129294	6181	5650	2848
图木舒克市	Tumxuk City	52741	51003	45003	4255	1738	205
五家渠市	Wujiaqu City	67959	66930	61205	3455	1029	-84

14-15 建筑企业亏损额及从业人数

Losses and Employed Persons of Construction Enterprises

(2010 年)

项目	Item	企业数(个) Number of Enterprises (unit)	#亏损企业个数 Number of loss-Suffering Enterprises	亏损企业亏损额(万元) Amount of Total loss (10 000 yuan)	计算劳动生产率的平均人数(人) Average Number of Staff for Calculation of Labour Productivity (person)	期末从业人数(人) Employees at year-end (person)	#工程技术人员 Engineers and Technicians
总计	**Total**	**1004**	**281**	**24197**	**549577**	**228618**	**50895**
#一、二级企业	First, Second Enterprises	441	106	15339	451371	186120	41063
#国有及国有控股	State-owned and State-holding	150	26	11191	252940	106461	20604
按登记注册类型分组	**Grouped by Registration Status**						
内资企业	Domestic Funede	1000	280	24181	549533	228579	50885
国有企业	State-owned Enterprises	58	10	3305	85655	36882	6510
集体企业	Collective-owned Enterprises	28	8	587	5172	2474	777
股份合作企业	Share-holding Cooperative	1			2083	524	42
有限责任公司	Limited Liability Corporations	346	73	13479	301686	128314	27662
国有独资公司	Sole State -funded Company	23	4	1191	38419	20158	4374
其他有限责任公司	Other Limited Liability Companies	323	69	12289	263267	108156	23288
股份有限公司	Share-holding Corporations Ltd	8	1	7	26268	8362	2765
私营企业	Private Enterprises	559	188	6803	128669	52023	13129
#私营有限责任公司	Private Limited Liability Companies	549	186	6758	124540	49855	12850
私营股份有限公司	Private Stock Limited Companies	7	2	46	3918	2084	259
港、澳、台及外商企业	Enterprises With Funds from Hong Kong, Macao , Taiwan and Foreign	4	1	17	44	39	10
按国民经济行业分组	**Grouped by National Economic Sectors**						
房屋和土木工程建筑业	Buildings and Givil Engineering	599	132	15893	497343	201935	43820
房屋工程建筑	Building	390	83	11952	369875	144467	30648
土木工程建筑	Civil Engineering	209	49	3941	127468	57468	13172
铁路、道路、隧道和桥梁	Railways, Roads, Tunnels and Bridges	71	16	1476	85295	38582	7651
水利和港口建筑	Water Conservancy and Seaport	39	6	405	24450	9311	2547
工矿工程建筑	Mining Project	8	3	667	3556	2221	363
架线和管道工程建筑	Cabling and Piping Project	33	9	869	10996	6086	2256
其他土木工程建筑	Other Civil Engineering	58	15	524	3171	1268	355
建筑安装业	Construction and Installation	215	64	6862	40119	21910	5864
建筑装饰业	Building Decoration	123	54	874	5350	2604	690
其他建筑业	Others	67	31	569	6765	2169	521
按隶属关系分组	**Grouped by Subordination**						
中央	Central Government	59	9	9279	172463	71036	10732
地方	Local	945	272	14918	377114	157582	40163
按企业资质等级分组	**Grouped by Enterprise's Qualification**						
施工总承包	Undertaking Porjects	530	108	18331	491435	205736	43665
特级	Special Grade	1			5974	2169	802
一级	First Grade	62	7	6180	211627	85102	17067
二级	Second Grade	212	28	6629	192731	85508	18536
三级及以下	Third Grade	255	73	5523	81103	32957	7260
专业承包	Specialized Undertaking	352	117	5422	44908	20385	6869
一级	First Grade	21	8	631	10918	4432	1921
二级	Second Grade	88	32	1690	18072	7074	2499
三级及以下	Third Grade	243	77	3101	15918	8879	2449
劳务分包	Work Subcontractors	122	56	444	13234	2497	361
三级及以下	Third Grade	122	56	444	13234	2497	361

14-16 建筑企业工程施工情况

Condition of Building Works by Construction Enterprise

单位：万平方米 (10 000 sq.m)

年 份 Year	地 区 Region	房屋建筑施工面积 Under Floor Space of Buildings Constructing	#本年新开工面积 New-opened Works for This Year	施工面积中实行投标承包面积 Space of Building and Contracting	#本年新开工面积 New-opened Works for This Year	房屋建筑竣工面积 Floor Space of Buildings Completed
	1995	1212.45	657.34	214.65	148.22	609.84
	1996	1207.45	673.17	397.83	272.22	645.89
	1997	1400.28	778.14	653.90	400.75	747.24
	1998	1662.36	1032.15	1023.88	678.42	879.67
	1999	1943.05	1068.05	1210.90	807.87	1042.51
	2000	2241.48	1448.34	1666.87	1110.04	1261.42
	2001	2659.69	1679.41	2056.30	1380.07	1467.54
	2002	2572.62	1489.38	2133.56	1274.07	1469.59
	2003	2719.22	1735.19	2411.27	1527.79	1450.80
	2004	2812.30	1791.50	2426.79	1613.19	1483.35
	2005	2767.64	1639.80	2512.79	1517.41	1429.36
	2006	2889.64	1854.91	2687.63	1751.99	1645.02
	2007	3552.36	2421.17	3299.73	2277.87	1849.64
	2008	4234.71	2862.31	3982.24	2784.92	2155.98
	2009	5151.60	3560.54	4812.84	3378.63	2517.79
	2010	6620.14	4449.78	6119.70	4235.58	2891.45
乌鲁木齐市	Urumqi City	1764.63	991.41	1667.54	983.71	667.08
克拉玛依市	Karamay City	106.87	54.35	103.25	53.79	25.40
吐鲁番地区	Turpan Administrative Offices	67.18	58.22	67.18	58.22	32.77
哈密地区	Hami [Kumul] Administrative Offices	178.52	156.69	172.27	156.25	76.80
昌吉回族自治州	Changji Hui Autonomous Prefecture	473.62	379.91	453.41	373.73	223.49
伊犁哈萨克自治州	Ili Kazak Autonomous Prefecture	998.14	754.88	875.32	677.42	438.87
伊犁州直属县(市)	Counties (Cities) Direct Under Ili Prefecture	478.02	361.28	390.16	297.41	222.17
塔城地区	Tacheng [Tarbagatai] Administrative Offices	381.18	283.06	350.11	270.98	141.49
阿勒泰地区	Altay Administrative Offices	138.94	110.54	135.05	109.03	75.21
博尔塔拉蒙古自治州	Bortala Mongol Autonomous Prefecture	118.35	83.43	110.80	83.43	65.77
巴音郭楞蒙古自治州	Bayangol Mongol Autonomous Prefecture	718.99	475.83	623.99	445.06	307.57
阿克苏地区	Aksu Administrative Offices	487.95	367.79	414.62	319.81	253.98
克孜勒苏柯尔克孜自治州	Kizilsu Kirgiz Autonomous Prefecture	104.28	79.08	90.22	69.47	54.51
喀什地区	Kashgar [Kaxgar] Administrative Offices	675.00	389.91	644.64	371.15	292.01
和田地区	Hotan Administrative Offices	187.14	136.49	186.96	136.49	82.50
石河子市	Shihezi City	507.86	336.30	488.33	321.56	260.17
阿拉尔市	Aral City	161.28	126.31	150.84	126.31	71.05
图木舒克市	Tumxuk City	23.54	22.66	23.54	22.66	18.54
五家渠市	Wujiaqu City	46.79	36.52	46.79	36.52	20.94

注：该表口径为总承包和专业承包企业，以下同。
Note: The data of the table refer to all general construction contractors and professional contractors. (the same as in the following)

14-17 按登记注册类型分建筑企业工程施工情况

Condition of Building Works by Construction Enterprise by Registration Status

单位：万平方米 (2010 年) (10 000 sq.m)

项目	Item	房屋建筑施工面积 Floor Space of Buildings Constructing	#本年新开工面积 New-opened Works for This Year	施工面积中实行投标承包面积 Space of Buildings and Contracting	#本年新开工面积 New-opened Works for This Year	房屋建筑竣工面积 Floor Space of Buildings Completed
总计	**Total**	**6620.14**	**4449.76**	**6119.71**	**4235.58**	**2891.44**
#一、二级企业	First, Second Enterprises	5350.70	3496.98	5041.30	3365.34	2196.41
#国有及国有控股	State-owned and State-holding	2257.56	1417.50	2182.89	1381.14	935.17
按登记注册类型分组	**Grouped by Registration Status**					
内资企业	Domestic Funede	6620.14	4449.76	6119.71	4235.58	2891.44
国有企业	State-owned Enterprises	487.78	312.94	435.99	281.66	191.80
集体企业	Collective-owned Enterprises	34.78	19.23	22.27	19.07	16.30
股份合作企业	Share-holding Cooperative	61.18	48.90	61.18	48.90	41.41
有限责任公司	Limited Liability Corporations	4399.76	2946.91	4096.78	2834.33	1905.10
国有独资公司	Sole State -funded Company	413.50	220.51	405.06	216.81	192.88
其他有限责任公司	Other Limited Liability Companies	3986.26	2726.40	3691.72	2617.52	1712.22
股份有限公司	Share-holding Corporations Ltd	139.86	64.57	139.86	64.57	45.70
私营企业	Private Enterprises	1496.79	1057.21	1363.62	987.05	691.13
#私营有限责任公司	Private Limited Liability Companies	1420.39	999.16	1303.75	945.41	656.04
私营股份有限公司	Private Stock Limited Companies	75.23	56.99	58.96	40.72	34.04
按国民经济行业分组	**Grouped by National Economic Sectors**					
房屋和土木工程建筑业	Buildings and Givil Engineering	6549.99	4394.09	6066.71	4185.53	2845.57
房屋工程建筑	Building	6326.51	4237.38	5907.06	4063.62	2756.85
土木工程建筑	Civil Engineering	223.48	156.71	159.65	121.92	88.72
铁路、道路、隧道和桥梁	Railways, Roads, Tunnels and Bridges	119.70	86.05	69.56	51.25	43.04
水利和港口建筑	Water Conservancy and Seaport	91.93	67.04	78.24	67.05	39.98
工矿工程建筑	Mine Project	11.75	3.52	11.75	3.52	5.60
建筑安装业	Construction and Installation	66.67	52.20	52.30	49.35	43.10
其他建筑业	Others	3.48	3.48	0.70	0.70	2.78
按隶属关系分组	**Grouped by Subordination**					
中央	Central Government	1253.92	796.64	1211.04	776.81	578.07
地方	Local	5366.22	3653.13	4908.66	3458.78	2313.38
按企业资质等级分组	**Grouped by Enterprise's Qualification**					
施工总承包	Undertaking Porjects	6497.56	4370.64	6011.95	4168.04	2830.60
特级	Special Grade	191.22	82.94	191.22	82.94	93.48
一级	First Grade	2111.37	1172.47	2001.22	1132.75	816.96
二级	Second Grade	2940.40	2174.12	2743.97	2084.96	1237.78
三级及以下	Third Grade	1254.57	941.11	1075.54	867.38	682.39
专业承包	Specialized Undertaking	122.58	79.13	107.76	67.54	60.84
一级	First Grade	28.02	19.23	28.02	19.23	21.24
二级	Second Grade	79.69	48.23	76.87	45.46	26.96
三级及以下	Third Grade	14.87	11.67	2.86	2.86	12.65

14-18 建筑企业竣工房屋建筑面积

Floor Space of Completed Building of Construction Enterprises

单位：万平方米 (10 000 sq.m)

时期(年份)	Period (Year)	合计 Total	厂房 Workshop	住宅 Residential Building	办公用房 Office Occupancy
"五五"时期	**Fifth Five-year Plan Period**	**527.31**	**58.53**	**274.62**	**39.81**
"六五"时期	**Sixth Five-year Plan Period**	**1297.63**	**271.01**	**127.61**	**184.40**
"七五"时期	**Seventh Five-year Plan Period**	**2120.30**	**324.20**	**925.20**	**193.90**
"八五"时期	**Eighth Five-year Plan Period**	**2914.41**	**321.35**	**1448.92**	**285.54**
"九五"时期	**Ninth Five-year Plan Period**	**4576.72**	**262.63**	**2891.37**	**405.71**
	2000	1261.42	55.62	851.49	109.59
"十五"时期	**Tenth Five-year Plan Period**	**7300.66**	**376.84**	**4380.93**	**637.48**
	2001	1467.54	60.86	1012.33	110.98
	2002	1469.60	60.98	945.33	103.85
	2003	1450.81	70.48	740.17	159.71
	2004	1483.35	97.37	833.23	136.68
	2005	1429.36	87.15	849.87	126.26
"十一五"时期	**Eleventh Five-year Plan Period**	**11059.87**	**803.01**	**6740.98**	**995.78**
	2006	1645.02	93.82	879.52	181.69
	2007	1849.64	145.11	1096.02	216.88
	2008	2155.98	157.19	1424.29	175.62
	2009	2517.79	159.84	1485.15	193.70
	2010	2891.44	247.05	1856.00	227.89

时期(年份)	Period (Year)	商业、居民服务业用房 House for Commerce and Residential Services	文化教育业用房 House for Culture and Education	医疗用房 House for Medical Care	科研用房 House for Scientific Research	其他 Others
"五五"时期	**Fifth Five-year Plan Period**	**22.94**	**56.85**	**11.07**	**4.80**	**58.69**
"六五"时期	**Sixth Five-year Plan Period**	**106.09**	**263.23**	**51.22**	**22.14**	**271.93**
"七五"时期	**Seventh Five-year Plan Period**	**140.40**	**258.10**	**51.20**	**24.80**	**202.50**
"八五"时期	**Eighth Five-year Plan Period**	**261.87**	**246.55**	**60.55**	**12.28**	**277.35**
"九五"时期	**Ninth Five-year Plan Period**	**351.83**	**287.12**	**63.43**	**13.31**	**301.32**
	2000	86.81	79.86	16.61	3.03	58.42
"十五"时期	**Tenth Five-year Plan Period**	**832.97**	**565.63**	**122.23**	**12.83**	**371.75**
	2001	121.21	76.50	13.29	1.63	70.74
	2002	160.63	98.16	21.29	2.73	76.63
	2003	217.96	132.84	31.22	3.10	95.33
	2004	192.48	113.95	31.11	3.39	75.14
	2005	140.69	144.18	25.32	1.98	53.91
"十一五"时期	**Eleventh Five-year Plan Period**	**604.44**	**1168.61**	**264.14**	**21.92**	**461.00**
	2006	149.41	207.08	44.60	0.97	87.93
	2007	113.16	157.21	44.85	0.92	75.49
	2008	111.44	160.46	32.03	10.87	84.08
	2009	138.38	361.84	69.01	5.69	104.19
	2010	92.05	282.02	73.65	3.47	109.31

主要统计指标解释

建筑业统计单位 指从事房屋、构筑物建造和设备安装活动的法人企业。建筑业法人企业应具有建筑业资质并能够独立核算，同时其应具备以下条件：①依法成立，有自己的名称、组织机构和场所，能够承担民事责任；②独立拥有和使用资产，承担负债，有权与其他单位签订合同；③独立核算盈亏，能够编制资产负债表。

建筑业总产值 是以货币表现的建筑安装企业在一定时期内生产的建筑业产品和提供的服务的总和。建筑业总产值包括：

(1)建筑工程产值：指列入建筑工程预算内的各种工程价值。

(2)安装工程产值：指设备安装工程价值，不包括被安装设备本身价值。

(3)其他产值：建筑业总产值中除建筑工程、安装工程以外的产值。包括房屋构筑物修理产值、非标准设备制造产值、总包企业向分包企业收取的管理费以及不能明确划分的施工活动所完成的产值。

a.房屋构筑物修理产值：指房屋和构筑物修理所完成的产值，但不包括被修理房屋、构筑物本身价值和生产设备的修理价值。

b.非标准设备制造产值：指加工制造没有定型的非标准生产设备的加工费和原材料价值(如化工厂、炼油厂用的各种罐、槽，矿井生产统一使用的各种漏斗、三角槽、阀门等)以及附属加工厂为本企业承建工程制作的非标准设备的价值。

建筑业增加值 指建筑业企业在报告期内以货币表现的建筑业生产经营活动的最终成果。

从2004年第一次全国经济普查开始，建筑业现价增加值按生产法和分配法(收入法)两种方法计算，以收入法的计算结果为准，即从收入的角度出发，根据生产要素在生产过程中应得的收入份额计算。具体计算方法：经济普查年度建筑业增加值按照《经济普查年度GDP核算方案》计算，非经济普查年度建筑业增加值按照《非经济普查年度GDP核算方案》计算

房屋建筑施工面积 指在报告期内施工的全部房屋建筑面积，包括本期新开工的房屋面积、上期施工跨入本期继续施工的房屋面积、上期停缓建在本期恢复施工的房屋面积、本期竣工的房屋面积及本期施工后又停缓建的房屋面积。

房屋建筑竣工面积 指在报告期内房屋建筑按照设计要求全部完工，达到了使用条件，经验收鉴定合格，正式移交使用单位的房屋建筑面积。

自有机械设备年末总台数 指归本企业所有，属于本企业固定资产的生产性机械设备年末总台数。包括施工机械、生产设备、运输设备以及其他设备。

自有机械设备年末总功率 指本企业自有施工机械、生产设备、运输设备以及其他设备等列为在册固定资产的生产性机械设备年末总功率，按设定能力或查定能力计算。包括机械本身的动力和为该机械服务的单独动力设备，如电动机等。计算单位用千瓦，动力换算可按1马力＝0.735千瓦折合成千瓦数。电焊机、变压器、锅炉不计算动力。

工程结算收入 指企业承包工程实现的工程价款结算收入，以及向发包单位收取的除工程价款以外的按规定列作营业收入的各种款项，如临时设施费、劳动保险费、施工机械调迁费等以及向发包单位收取的各种索赔款。

工程结算利润 指已结算工程实现的利润，如亏损以“—”号表示。计算公式为：

工程结算利润＝工程结算收入－工程结算成本－工程结算税金及附加

企业总收入 指与企业生产经营直接有关的各项收入，包括工程结算收入和其他业务收入。计算公式为：

企业总收入＝工程结算收入＋其他业务收入

Explanatory Notes on Main Statistical Indicators

Statistical Unit in the Construction Industry refers to a corporate enterprise engaged in the construction of buildings and structures and in the installation of equipment. A corporate construction enterprise should have qualification certificates with independent accounting system, and should meet the following 3 requirements: a) being set up in line with relevant legal basis, having its full name, organization and location, and capable of taking civil liabilities; b) independently possessing and using its assets and assuming its liabilities, and entitled to sign contracts with other institutions; and c) making independent accounts of its profits and losses, and capable of compiling its own balance sheet.

Gross Output Value of Construction refers to total of construction products and services, expressed in money terms, produced or rendered by construction and installation enterprises during a given period of time. It includes:

(1) Output value of construction projects: the value of projects covered by the project budgets;

(2) Output value of installation projects: the value of the installation of equipment, (excluding the value of the equipment to be installed);

(3) Other output values: the output value of construction industry apart from that of construction projects and installation projects. It includes: output value of repair of buildings and structures; output value of non-standard equipment manufacture-ing; overhead expenses received by contracted enterprises from the sub-contracted enterprises and the completed output value of construction activities for which there is no clear definition.

a. Output value of repair of buildings and structures: the value created through the repairs of buildings or structures. It does not include the value of buildings or structures being repaired and the value of the repair of production equipment;

b. Output value of manufactured non-standard equipment: the value of non-standard production equipment, including raw materials and manufacturing cost, made for the construction project (i.e., chemical plant; kettles or tanks used by refineries; various fillers, triangle tanks, valves used by mines). It also includes the output value of equipment manufactured by subsidiary workshops.

Value-added of Construction refers to the final result of the activities of production and operation of enterprises of the construction industry in monetary terms during the reference period.

Starting from the 2004 economic census, value-added of construction is calculated by both production approach and income approach, with the figures from the income approach as the final figures., Under the income approach,, calculation starts from the perspective of income and is based on the share of income derived from the production process by the relevant factors of production.. Specifically, value-added of construction for the Census years is calculated in accordance with the Programme of Compilation of GDP and National Accounts for the Year of Economic Census, and value-added of construction for other years is calculated in accordance with the Programme of Compilation of GDP and National Accounts for the Non Economic Census Years.

Floor Space of Buildings Under Construction refers to floor space of buildings under construction during the reference period, including the floor space of buildings for which construction has newly started; buildings for which construction has started earlier and is continuing during the reference period; and buildings for which construction has been suspended earlier but has restarted during the reference period; buildings completed during the reference period; and buildings under construction but construction has subsequently been during the reference period.

Floor Space of Buildings Completed refers to the floor space of buildings that are completed in the reference period in accordance with the requirements of the design, up to the standard for being put into use, and having been checked and accepted by departments concerned as qualified ones.

Total Number of Machinery and Equipment Owned by the End of Year refers to the number of machines and equipment owned by the enterprises, and listed as the fixed assets of the enterprises by the end of the year, including machinery and equipment for construction, production and transportation.

Total Power of Machinery and Equipment Owned by the End of Year refers to the total power of machinery and equipment owned by the enterprises,and listed as the fixed assets of the enterprises by the end of the year, including machinery and equipment for construction,production and transportation.The power of the machinery is calculated on basis of the designed or verified capacity,covering the power of the machinery/equipment and the separate power equipment serving the machinery/equipment (such as electric motors), but excluding welders, transformers and boilers.The unit used for the calculation of power is kilowatt, with horsepower converted to kilowatt by 1 horsepower=0.735 kilowatt.

Income from Settlement of Projects refers to the income received by the construction enterprise from the contracted project through settlement procedures, and other charges to the contractoree as operational costs in addition to the value of the project, such as temporary facility fee,labour insurance premium,moving cost of construction equipment,as well as various types of claims to the contractee.

Profit from Settlement of Projects refers to profit realized through settled projects. It is calculated with the following formula:

Profit from Settlement of Projects=Income from Settlement of Projects−Settled Cost−Settled Taxes and Other Cost

Total Revenue of Enterprises refers to the sum of income from production and operation of enterprises, including income from settlement of projects and other operational income, namely:

Total Revenue of Enterprises=Income from Settlement of Projects+Other Operational Incom

第十五篇 运输和邮电

CHAPTER 15 Transport, Postal and Telecommunication Services

新疆统计年鉴
XINJIANG STATISTICAL YEARBOOK 2011

简要说明
Brief Introduction

本篇资料的主要内容及来源

本篇资料反映新疆维吾尔自治区交通运输业和邮政、电信业发展的基本状况。

运输业资料主要包括:铁路、公路、民航、管道四种运输方式的线路条数、里程、总运量及周转量、货物运输平均运距、铁路运输主要技术经济指标;民用机动车辆情况。

邮政、电信业资料主要包括:邮电业务完成情况,邮电业务发展水平等资料。

铁路资料来自乌鲁木齐铁路局;公路资料来自新疆维吾尔自治区公路局;民航运输数据资料来自中国南方航空股份有限公司新疆分公司;电信资料来自新疆维吾尔自治区通信管理局;邮政数据来自新疆维吾尔自治区邮政公司。

本篇资料由新疆维吾尔自治区统计局工业交通统计处收集整理。

Main content and source of data

Data in this chapter cover mainly the basic condition of the development of transportation, post and telecommunications in Xinjiang Uygur Autonomous Region. Data on transport cover mainly the length of the routes of four means of railway, highways, civil aviation and pipeline. total fright traffic, total freight ton-kilometers, average transport distance of fright, principal economic and technical indicators of railway transport, possession of civil vehicles.

Data on post and telecommunication cover mainly the complete business volume of post and telecommunication services, and the development of the post and telecommunication service, ect.

Data on railways transportation come from the Urumqi Bureau of the Railway. Data on the highways come from the Bureau of Transportation. Data on the civil aviation transport come from the China Southwest Airlines, Xinjiang Branch. Data on telecommunication services come from telecommunication Bureau. Data on post are provided by the Post Bureau.

Data in this chapter are collected and compiled by the Division of Industry and Transport Statistics, Xinjiang Bureau of Statistics.

15-1 主要年份运输业基本情况
Basic Conditions of Transport in Main Years

指　标	Item	1995	2000	2010
运输线路长度(公里)	**Length of Transport Routes (km)**			
铁路营业里程	Railways in Operation	2038	3010	4393
公路里程	Highways	30298	80875	152843
民用航线里程	Total Civil Aviation Routes	69789	152941	176992
管道输油（气）里程	Petroleum and Gas Pipelines	875	2696	11464
客运量(万人)	**Total Passenger Traffic (10 000 persons)**	**17533**	**23191**	**46346**
铁　路	Railways	672	1147	1523
公　路	Highways	16739	21877	44333
民用航空	Civil Aviation	122	167	490
旅客周转量(亿人公里)	**Total Passenger-Kilometers (100 million passenger-km)**	**204.89**	**292.80**	**670.75**
铁　路	Railways	58.04	97.40	170.10
公　路	Highways	117.17	158.20	404.00
民用航空	Civil Aviation	29.68	37.20	96.65
货运量(万吨)	**Total Freight Traffic (10 000 tons)**	**25406.0**	**33090.5**	**64596.7**
铁　路	Railways	2733	4199	6853
公　路	Highways	21754	27048	50448
民用航空	Civil Aviation	2.0	3.5	3.7
输油(气)管道	Petroleum and Gas Pipelines	917	1840	7292
货物周转量(亿吨公里)	**Total Freight Ton-kilometers (100 million ton-km)**	**474.39**	**660.88**	**2053.82**
铁　路	Railways	240.88	355.00	814.03
公　路	Highways	219.72	272.90	767.14
民用航空	Civil Aviation	0.57	0.98	0.98
输油(气)管道	Petroleum and Gas Pipelines	13.22	32.00	471.67
民用汽车拥有量(万辆)	**Possession of Civil Motor Vehicles (10 000 units)**	**24.7**	**37.0**	**135.9**
＃载客汽车辆数	Buses and Cars	9.4	18.0	87.6
载货汽车辆数	Trucks	14.3	17.5	37.0
＃私人汽车拥有量	Privat Vehicles	5.6	13.9	85.8

注：1.2000 年以后公路里程包括兵团数据。2.2006 年起新疆公路通车里程包含村道里程(以下同)。
Note: a) Since 2000 the highway mileage cover the data of XJPCC. b) Length of highways include lenth of backroad since 2006.(the same as in the following table)

15-2 主要年份运输线路长度
Length of Transport Routes in Main Years

单位:公里 (km)

年 份 Year	铁路营业里程 Length of Railways in Operation	#新疆境内 Inside Xinjiang	公 路 Length of Highways	#高级次高级公路 High Grade & Seond High Grade Highways	民用航空 Length of the Civil Aviation	#新疆境内 Inside Xinjiang	管道输油(气)里程 Petrolurn and Gas Pipelines
1978	1031	796	23818	5810	4783	4783	443
1980	1103	868	21148	6390	4412	4412	443
1985	1579	1344	22232	8369	4527	4527	473
1990	1578	1343	25425	12566	36465	5159	740
1995	2038	1803	30298	19013	69789	6693	875
1996	2038	1803	31609	20461	122089	9183	928
1997	2038	1803	32053	21495	123664	9717	1373
1998	2038	1803	32762	22485	150473	9717	1955
1999	3008	2780	33484	23214	141872	9719	2496
2000	3010	2775	80875	31059	152941	9719	2696
2001	3010	2774	80947	31635	161814	9719	2965
2002	3010	2775	82929	32541	132483	9898	3153
2003	3009	2775	83633	33891	141456	9898	3008
2004	2999	2763	86824	40679	111768	8664	3003
2005	2925	2761	89531	43803	119481	8664	3003
2006	2925	2761	143736	50119	138564	9064	4631
2007	2925	2761	145219	55080	160354	11363	6793
2008	2925	2925	146652	60233	147753	10560	9455
2009	3837	3673	150683	67684	152392	10754	11235
2010	4393	4228	152843	72887	176992	9939	11464

15-3 主要年份运输线路质量
Quality of Transport Routes in Main Years

单位：公里 (km)

指 标	Item	1995	2000	2009	2010
铁路营业里程	Length of National Railways in Operation	2038	3010	3673	4393
#复线里程	Double-Tracking Length		986	1135	1324
#自动闭塞里程	Automatic Blocking Length	273	685	1150	1408
公路线路里程	Length of Highways	30298	80875	150683	152843
#水泥沥青路面	Lenth of bituminous Pavement	27982	33035	67684	72887

注：铁路上述里程是新疆境内里程。
Note: Length of railways refers to length of railway inside in Xinjiang.

15-4 主要年份客运量及周转量

Passenger Traffic and Passenger kilometers in Main Years

年份 Year	客运量(万人) Passenger Traffic (10 000 persons)				旅客周转量(亿人公里) Passenger-Kilometers (100 million passenger-km)			
	总计 Total	铁路 Railways	公路 Highways	民用航空 Civil Aviation	总计 Total	铁路 Railways	公路 Highways	民用航空 Civil Aviation
1978	941	148	786	7	25.23	13.72	10.96	0.55
1980	1356	193	1152	10	30.49	18.83	10.83	0.83
1985	3728	320	3399	9	63.16	33.16	29.13	0.87
1986	4058	362	3674	22	73.87	36.40	34.00	3.74
1987	4439	377	4327	34	83.67	37.14	39.44	7.09
1988	5205	459	4698	48	99.17	42.86	46.35	9.96
1989	8740	453	8240	47	120.69	44.52	66.37	9.80
1990	9602	388	9161	53	103.80	37.96	55.11	10.73
1991	14582	383	14142	56	122.08	41.94	68.05	12.09
1992	14997	425	14490	82	138.24	44.48	75.38	18.38
1993	16352	513	15749	90	174.23	50.04	103.51	20.73
1994	17181	670	16405	106	195.58	58.08	112.50	25.00
1995	17533	672	16739	122	204.89	58.00	117.17	29.68
1996	18858	610	18110	138	218.79	57.80	128.58	32.20
1997	20237	748	19360	129	233.39	64.70	139.00	29.69
1998	21747	878	20735	134	256.90	76.90	149.60	30.40
1999	22763	1000	21618	145	270.74	81.90	157.05	31.79
2000	23191	1147	21877	167	292.80	97.40	158.20	37.20
2001	24344	932	23255	157	309.70	104.10	170.30	35.30
2002	26016	950	24883	183	330.80	106.00	185.60	39.20
2003	26972	879	25878	215	342.00	106.10	195.00	40.90
2004	29782	1023	28473	286	423.80	121.90	249.00	52.90
2005	33220	1134	31747	339	457.42	125.20	271.20	61.02
2006	34471	1272	32835	364	498.30	138.90	292.10	67.30
2007	38434	1873	36159	402	548.10	144.46	326.70	76.94
2008	42111	1311	40392	408	594.60	149.89	363.60	81.11
2009	43410	1371	41604	435	614.66	152.90	376.30	85.46
2010	46346	1523	44333	490	670.75	170.10	404.00	96.65

注：2010 年民航旅客吞吐量为 1169.89 万人。
Note: Air passenger handling capacity is 11.699 million persons in 2010.

15-5 主要年份货运量及货物周转量

Freight Traffic and Ton-kilometers in Main Years

年 份 Year	货运量(万吨) Freight Traffic (10 000 tons)				
	总 计 Total	铁 路 Railways	公 路 Highways	民用航空 Civil Aviation	输油(气)管道 Petroleum and Gas Pipelines
1978	6064.12	923	4843	0.12	298
1980	8422.16	884	7209	0.16	329
1985	10681.11	1278	8847	0.11	556
1990	13919.87	1691	11551	0.87	677
1995	25406.00	2733	21754	2.00	917
1996	26676.00	2951	22505	2.00	1218
1997	28790.00	3190	24125	3.00	1472
1998	30484.00	3324	25573	3.00	1584
1999	32076.17	3777	26596	3.17	1700
2000	33090.50	4199	27048	3.50	1840
2001	33589.00	3904	27751	2.00	1932
2002	34966.70	4121	28861	2.70	1982
2003	37485.20	4602	30881	2.20	2000
2004	38885.50	5083	31700	2.50	2100
2005	40600.20	5397	33000	3.20	2200
2006	43096.40	6001	34835	3.40	2256
2007	49009.62	7430	38427	3.62	3149
2008	57187.80	6120	44987	3.80	6077
2009	60162.80	6413	46787	3.80	6959
2010	64596.70	6853	50448	3.70	7292

年 份 Year	货物周转量(亿吨公里) Freight Ton-kilometers (100 million ton-km)				
	总 计 Total	铁 路 Railways	公 路 Highways	民用航空(万吨公里) Civil Aviation (10 000 ton-km)	输油(气)管道 Petroleum and Gas Pipelines
1978	106.96	67.76	32.06	98.10	7.13
1980	121.14	67.27	45.89	137.80	7.97
1985	174.75	102.03	61.26	104.00	11.45
1990	262.29	141.16	108.09	2048.00	12.84
1995	474.39	240.88	219.72	5744.00	13.22
1996	507.15	260.96	229.55	6475.00	16.00
1997	541.40	269.70	247.00	7000.00	24.00
1998	553.60	264.20	262.80	7000.00	25.90
1999	602.94	303.60	270.46	8800.00	28.00
2000	660.88	355.00	272.90	9776.00	32.00
2001	714.43	403.90	275.90	6300.00	34.00
2002	759.62	425.30	298.00	8238.00	35.50
2003	837.04	475.00	325.00	6400.00	36.40
2004	947.24	548.50	361.00	7400.00	37.00
2005	1032.75	586.90	405.00	8500.00	40.00
2006	1143.31	647.10	425.68	8921.00	69.64
2007	1264.31	678.53	468.80	9085.78	116.07
2008	1656.88	758.74	672.30	9285.43	224.91
2009	1815.81	751.09	705.90	9700.00	357.85
2010	2053.82	814.03	767.14	9837.00	471.67

15-6 主要年份货物运输平均运距
Average Transport Distance of Freight in Main Years

单位：公里 (km)

年 份 Year	合 计 Total	铁 路 Railways	公 路 Highways	民用航空 Civil Aviation	输油(气)管道 Petroleum and Gas Pipelines
1978	168	565	66	818	239
1980	139	566	64	861	242
1985	158	624	69	945	206
1990	188	835	94	2354	190
1995	187	881	101	2872	144
2000	200	845	101	2857	174
2001	211	1023	99	3150	176
2002	217	1032	103	3051	179
2003	224	865	105	2909	182
2004	244	904	114	2960	176
2005	254	901	122	2656	182
2006	265	894	122	2598	308
2007	257	913	122	2528	368
2008	289	926	149	2456	370
2009	301	873	151	2552	518
2010	317	934	152	2637	514

15-7 主要年份铁路运输主要财务指标
Main Financial Indicators of Railway Transport in Main Years

单位：万元 (10 000 yuan)

指 标	Item	1990	1995	2000	2009	2010
运输总收入	**Total Transport Revenue**	**86686**	**192555**	**509480**	**1666119**	**1926749**
#客运收入	Revenue from Passenger Traffic	18763	33560	82121	200467	234979
货运收入	Revenue from Freight Traffic	62516	142168	318485	1022934	1197619
运输清算收入	**Transportation Claring Revenue**	**59765**		**467142**	**1209674**	**1311275**
运输总支出	**Toatl Transport Expenditure**	**51875**	**193693**	**418497**	**1372005**	**1552877**
#工 资	Wages and Salaries	11163	38429	98293	211400	238570
材 料	Materials	6702	23183	36210	69211	79181
燃 料	Fuel	9308	32996	74487	272701	340960
电 力	Electricity	666	2433	4701	4588	8022
折 旧	Depreciation	17174	13137	60859	108826	127368
营业外收支净额	**Non-operating Net Revenue or Expenditure**	**6886**	**14503**	**23236**	**-34192**	**-21947**
实现利润	**Profits**	**6291**	**-12591**	**34130**	**-160656**	**-273121**
#运输利润	Transport Profits	5501	-11649	33195	-167936	-266910

注：运输总收入、旅客票价收入、货物运费收入是运送到全国范围的客、货运输收入。
Note: Revenue from transport,passenger traffic and freight traffic refer to revenue from transport to allover China.

15-8 铁路运输技术经济主要指标
Main Technical and Economic Indicators of Railway Transport

指　　标	Item	2009	2010
货运机车日产量(万吨公里)	Average Daily Ton-kilometers of Freight Locomotives (10 000 ton-km)	112.0	114.3
#内燃机车	Diesel Locomotives	112.0	114.6
货运列车平均总重(吨)	Average Total Tonnage of Freight Locomotives (ton)	2716	2724
#内燃机车	Diesel Locomotives	2716	2729
货运机车日车公里(公里)	Daily Distance per Freight Locomotive (km)	640	637
客运机车日车公里(公里)	Daily Distance per Passenger Locomotive (km)	640	638
内燃机车每万吨公里耗油(公斤)	Oil Consumption of Diesel Locomotives (kg/10 000 ton-km)	27.0	27.7
货物列车出发正点率(%)	Punctuality Rate of Freight Trains at Departure (%)	98.2	99.3
货物列车运行正点率(%)	Punctuality Rate of Freight Trains in Running (%)	98.2	96.3
旅客列车出发正点率(%)	Punctuality Rate of Passenger Trains at Departure (%)	98.9	98.6
旅客列车运行正点率(%)	Punctuality Rate of Passenger Trains in Running (%)	97.7	98.7
旅客列车技术速度(公里/小时)	Technical Speed of Passenger Trains (km/hr)	74.0	73.6
旅客列车旅行速度(公里/小时)	Travelling Speed of Passenger Trains (km/hr)	65.3	64.6
客运密度(万人公里/公里)	Density of Passenger Transport (10 000 passenger-km/km)	541.7	561.0
货物列车技术速度(公里/小时)	Technical Speed of Freight Trains (km/hr)	48.0	47.8
货物列车旅行速度(公里/小时)	Running Speed of Freight Trains (km/hr)	38.5	39.4
货运密度(万吨公里/公里)	Density of Freight Transport (10 000 ton-km/km)	2581.1	2114.0
货车周转时间(天)	Turning Around Time of Freight Cars (day)	4.1	4.2
一次货物作业时间(小时)	Handling Time of Freight (hour)	24.7	18.8
货车中转停留时间(小时)	Transfer Waiting Time per Car (hour)	4.3	3.3
货车静载重(准轨)(吨)	Static Load of Freight Cars (Standard Gauge) (ton)	56.9	56.8

15-9 民用车辆拥有量
Number of Civil Vehicles

单位：辆 (unit)

指　标	Item	2009		2010	
		总　计 Total	#私　人 Private	总　计 Total	#私　人 Private
民用汽车	**Civil Vehicles**	**1106534**	**651963**	**1358466**	**857663**
载客汽车	Passenger Vehicles	677890	470980	875648	649793
#大　型	Large	26117	1098	27373	1212
中　型	Medium	25712	7661	28019	8360
小　型	Small	597708	440444	789887	615131
微　型	Minicar	28353	21777	30369	25090
载货汽车	Trucks	313788	107061	369625	138638
#重　型	Large	96742	11657	113464	12518
中　型	Medium	47798	11367	49361	12162
轻　型	Light	161203	78845	201295	110185
微　型	Mini	8045	5192	5505	3773
其它汽车	Others	114856	73922	113193	69232

15-10 主要年份邮电事业情况

Basic Conditions of Postal and Telecommunication Services in Main Years

指　　标	Item	2000	2009	2010
邮政局营业网点(处)	**Number of Post Offices (unit)**		**1877**	**1276**
邮路长度(单程)(公里)	**Length of Postal Routes (km)**	**134109**	**126662**	**75571**
#农 村	Rural	55852	12023	18238
邮电业务总量(万元)	**Business Volume of Post and Telecommunication Services (10 000 yuan)**	**473000**	**4796535**	**5820459**
函件(万件)	Number of Letters (10 000 pieces)	7148	2800	2926
包件(万件)	Number of Parcels (10 000 pieces)	163	188	174
特快专递(万件)	Pieces of Express Mail Services (10 000 pieces)	124	412	487
报刊期发数(万份)	Number of Newspapers and Magazines Circulation (10 000 copies)	535	296	307
长途电话(万分钟)	Number of Long-distance Calls (10 000 minutes)	34712	48816	105001
固定电话年末用户(万户)	Local Telephone Subscribers at Year-end (10 000 subscribers)	191.0	573.1	547.5
#城市电话年末数	Urban Telephone Subscribers at Year-end	136.3	409.6	395.8
乡村电话年末数	Number of Rural Telephones Subscribers at Year-end	54.7	140.8	132.1
#住宅电话年末数	Residential Telephone Subscribers	149.3	351.8	346.6
移动电话年末用户(万户)	Number of Mobile Telephones Subscribers at Year-end (10 000 subscribers)	78.0	1119.6	1359.8
长途电信线路	**Telecommunication Lines**			
光缆线路长度(公里)	Length of Long Distance Optical Cable Lines (km)	10828	198445	259307
邮电通信设备	**Telecommunication Facilities**			
固定长途交换机容量(路端)	Capacity of long-distance Telephone Exchanges (circuit)	102540	258153	315982
本地电话局用交换机容量(万门)	Capacity of Local Office Telephone Exchange (10 000 line)	241.7	930.0	928.2
邮电通信水平	**Level of Postal and Telecommunication Services**			
平均每百人每年发函件数(件)	Annual Arerage Number of Letters Mailed Per 100 persons (piece)	387.0	135.0	122.0
平均每百人每年订报刊数(份)	Annual Arerage Number of Newspaper Subscribed Per 100 Persons (piece)	28.9	14.2	12.6
平均每百人拥有电话机数(固定)(部)	Number of Telephone Sets Owned per 100 Persons(stable) (set)	15.0	26.9	25.4
平均每百人拥有电话机数(移动)(部)	Number of Telephone Sets Owned per 100 Persons (mobile) (set)		52.6	63.0
农村邮电通信水平	**Rural Level**			
通电话的乡(镇)比重(%)	Percentage of Townships with Telephone Communication (%)	100	100	100
进入长话自动网的乡(镇)比重(%)	Percentage of Townships with Access to Auto-exchange Net of Long Distance Call (%)	100	100	100

15-11 主要年份邮电业务情况

Conditions of Postal and Telecommunication Services in Main Years

年 份 Year	邮电业务总量(万元) Business Volume of Postal and Telecommunication Services (10 000 yuan)	邮政业务总量 Business Volume of Postal Services	电信业务总量 Business Volume of Telecommunication Services	函件(万件) Number of Letters (10 000 pieces)
1978	2122			4842.7
1980	2332			5890.8
1985	4709			7032.6
1990	17372	8203	8312	7380.5
1995	90226	17322	71220	9041.8
2000	473000	59370	413630	7148.0
2001	634338	62265	572073	5601.0
2002	947000	68032	878968	6814.0
2003	1144838	72007	1072831	5987.0
2004	1531835	74835	1457000	4756.7
2005	1723759	80500	1643259	4450.0
2006	2289188	94188	2195000	4129.8
2007	3036498	100498	2936000	3177.0
2008	3787511	113802	3673709	2900.0
2009	4796535	133535	4663000	2800.0
2010	5820459	165794	5654665	2926.0

年 份 Year	特快专递(万件) Pieces of Express Mail Services (10 000 pieces)	报刊期发数(万份) Issue of Newspapers and Magazines (10 000 copies)	集邮业务(万枚) Stamps for Collection (10 000 pieces)	长途电话(万分钟) Length of Long-distance Calls (10 000 minutes)
1978		223.8		258.8
1980		329.6		276.5
1985		578.9		425.1
1990	…	805.7	1034.5	762.5
1995	93.6	478.1	3086.6	11705.9
2000	124.0	534.5	5766.0	34712.0
2001	147.0	358.0	5491.0	89844.0
2002	163.0	399.0	4620.0	45769.0
2003	199.0	587.3	3112.8	35554.2
2004	238.1	283.0	3141.3	62526.0
2005	266.0	293.0	2072.0	52482.0
2006	291.0	341.7	2205.1	46478.0
2007	324.0	305.0	2134.0	67660.0
2008	362.0	296.0	2335.0	42550.0
2009	412.0	296.0	2520.0	48816.0
2010	487.0	307.0	2672.0	105001.0

注：从 1997 年起，市内电话户数统计口径有了较大调整，故农村电话户数增幅较大。

Note: From 1997, greater readjustment has been made on the Statistic Method about the number of telephone Subscribers and the number of rural Subscribers has gone up by a bigger margin.

15-11 续表 Continued

年 份 Year	移动电话用户(万户) Number of Mobile Telephone Subscribers (10 000 subscribers)	国际互联网络用户(万户) Number of Subscribers of Internet Services (10 000 subscribers)	固定电话年末用户(万户) Number of Subscribers of Local Telephone at Year-end (10 000 subscribers)	#城市电话用户 Number of Urban Telephone Subscribers
1978			2.9	1.9
1980			3.2	2.1
1985			4.7	3.7
1990			8.9	7.9
1995	2.7		44.6	42.0
2000	78.0		191.0	136.3
2001	180.9	12.8	262.6	196.1
2002	297.0	17.3	337.5	238.3
2003	421.2	60.8	431.0	293.9
2004	489.7	78.0	516.7	387.0
2005	531.3	105.8	612.2	457.5
2006	671.1	123.7	706.9	533.6
2007	808.3	157.8	678.1	520.6
2008	1051.3	142.8	634.9	462.2
2009	1119.6	133.7	573.1	409.6
2010	1359.8	161.1	547.5	395.8

年 份 Year	#住宅电话 Household Fixed Telephone Subscribers	#乡村电话用户 Rural Fixed Telephone Subscribers	#住宅电话 Household Fixed Telephone Subscribers	公用电话(户) Public Telephone (subscriber)
1978		1.1		
1980		1.0		
1985		1.0		
1990	1.2	1.1		257
1995	26.0	2.6	1.2	5612
2000	101.1	54.7	48.2	70753
2001	124.3	66.5	57.8	84309
2002	179.9	79.5	73.4	166000
2003	180.0	93.5	88.6	281632
2004	194.0	108.2	103.4	432000
2005	318.9	135.2	115.4	570047
2006	369.9	154.5	131.7	668335
2007	359.6	157.5	136.1	675309
2008	310.6	150.0	126.3	597000
2009	234.6	140.8	117.2	570982
2010	237.4	132.1	109.2	529322

主要统计指标解释

铁路营业里程 又称营业长度(包括正式营业和临时营业里程)，指办理客货运输业务的铁路正线总长度。凡是全线或部分建成双线及以上的线路，以第一线的实际长度计算复线、站线、段管线、岔线和特殊用途线以及不计算运费的联络线都不计算营业里程。该指标可以反映铁路运输业基础设施的发展水平，也是计算客货周转量、运输密度和机车车辆运用效率等指标的基础资料。

铁路自动、半自动闭塞里程 为保证列车安全运行，在一个区间、同一时间内，一般只允许一列列车运行，这种保证列车在这个区间安全间隔运行的技术方法称为"闭塞"。自动和半自动闭塞里程指装有列车自动或人工完成闭塞状态的铁路设备里程。

公路里程 指在一定时期内实际达到《公路工程［WTBZ］技术标准JTJ01-88》规定的等级公路，并经公路主管部门正式验收交付使用的公路里程数。包括大中城市的郊区公路以及通过小城镇街道部分的公路里程和桥梁、渡口的长度，不包括大中城市的街道、厂矿、林区生产用道和农业生产用道的里程。两条或多条公路共同经由同一路段，只计算一次，不得重复计算里程长度。该指标可以反映公路建设的发展规模，也是计算运输网密度等指标的基础资料。

民用航空航线里程 指统计期间内全部民用航空航线的航线总长度。航线长度指民用航空航线的计费距离。计算航线里程可按重复和不重复两种方法，前者是指各航线长度相加的总和；后者则要扣除各航线之间相同航段重复计算的部分。

输油(气)管道长度 也称输油(气)里程，指油品(或天然气)的实际输送距离，一般按输油(气)管道的单线长度计算。若包括复线和备用线长度则称为输油(气)管道延展长度，是指管道铺设的实际长度。我们通常使用的是不包括复线的"输油(气)管道里程"，该指标可以反映管道运输的发展规模和水平。

货(客)运量 指在一定时期内，各种运输工具实际运送的货物(旅客)数量。该指标是反映运输业为国民经济和人民生活服务的数量指标，也是制定和检查运输生产计划、研究运输发展规模和速度的重要指标。货运按吨计算，客运按人计算。货物不论运输距离长短、货物类别，均按实际重量统计。旅客不论行程远近或票价多少，均按一人一次客运量统计；半价票、小孩票也按一人统计。

货物(旅客)周转量 指在一定时期内，由各种运输工具运送的货物(旅客)数量与其相应运输距离的乘积之总和。该指标可以反映运输业生产的总成果，也是编制和检查运输生产计划，计算运输效率、劳动生产率以及核算运输单位成本的主要基础资料。计算货物周转量通常按发出站与到达站之间的最短距离，也就是计费距离计算。计算公式为：

货物(旅客)周转量=∑（货物（旅客）运输量×运输距离）

铁路货车平均静载重 指铁路货车在始发站静止状态下平均每车装载的货物重量，用以分析货车完成装车时车辆载重力的利用情况。计算公式为：

货车平均静载重=货物发送吨数/装车数

静载重的多少取决于运送货物的性质、种类、车辆的类型和装载技术的高低。根据货车的平均标记载重与静载重进行对比，可以反映货车载重能力的利用程度。计算公式为：

货车载重力利用率(%)=货车平均静载重/货车平均标记载重×100%

铁路货运机车日产量 指在一定时期内，平均每台货运机车在一昼夜内所完成的总重吨公里数，包括载运货物的重量和车辆本身的自重。该指标从时间和牵引能力两方面反映了机车运用效率。计算公式为：

货运机车平均日产量=货运总重吨公里数/货运机车台日数

民用汽车拥有量 指报告期末，在公安交通管理部门按照《机动车注册登记工作规范》，已注册登记领有民用车辆牌照的全部汽车数量。汽车拥有量统计的主要分类：根据汽车结构分为载客汽车、载货汽车及其他汽车；根据汽车所有者不同分为个人(私人)汽车、单位汽车；根据汽车的使用性质分为营运汽车、非营运汽车和特种汽车；根据汽车大小规格不同载客汽车分为大型、中型、小型和微型，载货汽车分为重型、中型、轻型和微型。

邮电业务总量 指以货币形式表示的邮电企业为社会提供各类邮电服务的总数量，是用于观察邮电业务发展变化总趋势的综合性总量指标。分别按邮政业务总量和电信业务总量统计。邮电业务总量是以各类业务的实物量分别乘以相应的不变单价，得出各类业务的货币量再加总求得。

移动电话用户 指在电信运营企业营业网点办理开户登记手续，通过移动电话交换机进入移动电话网，占用移动电话号码的各类电话用户。包括GSM数字移动电话用户、CDMA数字移动电话用户和电信运营企业发行的报告期末已激活充值的能异地漫游的各种智能卡用户。

互联网上网人数 指平均每周使用互联网至少1小时的6周岁以上中国公民人数。

固定电话用户 指在电信运营企业营业网点办理开户登记手续并已接入固定电话网上的全部电话用户。包括普通电话用户、公用电话用户、窄带综合业务数字网（N—ISDN）用户、智能网专用接入终端用户等。按行政区划分为城市电话用户和农村电话用户。

住宅电话用户 指安装在居民住宅或农民家里并按照住宅电话用户登记注册和收费的各类电话用户。包括私人付费、单位付费和按规定免费安装的住宅电话用户。

长途电话交换机容量 指用于接入长途电话网的电话交换机的设备额定容量，包括国际电话交换机容量。

局用交换机容量 指安装在电信运营企业内用于接续本地固定电话的电话交换机容量，有倍增设备按倍增后的数量计数。包括现用和备用的人工或自动交换机的全部容量。不包括用户交换机容量。

Explanatory Notes on Main Statistical Indicators

Length of Railways in Operation refers to the total length of the trunk line for passenger and freight transportation (including both full operation and temporary operation). The calculation is based on the actual length of the first line if this line has a full or partial double (or more). Not included are double tracks, station sidings, tracks under the charge of stations, branch lines, special-purpose lines and non-payable connecting lines. The length of railways in operation is an important indicator to show the development of the infrastructure of railway transport. It is also essential data to calculate volume of passenger freight transport, traffic density and utilization efficiency of locomotives and carriages.

Length of Automatic-blocking and Semi-automatic-blocking Railways Blocking is a spacing technique by which a section of the railway only allows one train to pass at a time with the aim of ensuring traffic safety. Length of automatic-blocking and semi-automatic-blocking railways refers to length of railways installed with equipment to perform automatic or manual blocking of trains.

Length of Highways refers to the length of highways which are built in conformity with the grades specified by the highway engineering standard [Highways WTBZ-Technical Standard JTJ01-88] formulated by the Ministry of Transport, and have been formally checked and accepted by the departments of highways and put into use. The length of highways includes that of the suburb highways at large and medium-sized cities, highways passing through streets at small cities and towns, and also the length of bridges and ferry piers. It does not include the length of streets in big and medium-sized cities and highways built for the production purpose at factories, mines, forest areas and agricultural areas. If two or more highways go the same section of the way, the length of the section is only calculated for once and no duplication is allowed. The length of highways is an indicator to show the development of the scale of highway construction and to provide essential information to calculate the transport network density.

Length of Civil Aviation Routes refers to the length of all routes for civil aviation flights, which is used to account the freight, during the period of statistics.. There are usually two ways to calculate the route length: duplicated calculation and non-duplicated calculateion, the former is the sum of length of all civil aviation routes, and the latter should deduct the duplication length of same route among all routes.

Length of Oil (Gas) Pipelines is used as an indicator to show the development, scale and level of the pipeline transportation. It refers to the actual transport distance of oil (or gas) products, and is in general calculated according to the length of single pipeline. If the length of the double pipelines and alternate pipeline are included, it is called the extension length of the oil (gas) pipelines, which indicates the actual length of the pipelines built. The commonly used indicator, the "length of "oil (gas)" pipelines, does not include the double pipelines. It can reflect the extent and level of development of pipeline transport.

Freight (Passenger) Traffic refers to the volume of freight (passenger) transported with various means within a specific period of time. This indicator reflects the service of the transport industry towards the national economy and people's living conditions, as well as an important indicator used in formulating and monitoring transport production plans and research into the scale and pace of transport development. Freight transport is calculated in tons and passenger traffic is calculated in terms of number of persons. Freight transport is calculated in terms of the actual weight of the goods and takes no account of the type of freight and distance of travel. Passenger traffic is calculated by the principle that one person can be counted only once in one trip and takes no account of the travelling distance and ticket price. The passengers who travel with a half price ticket or a child's ticket is also calculated as one person.

Freight Ton-kilometres (Passenger-kilometres) refers to the sum of the product of the volume of transported cargo (passengers) multiplied by the transport distance. It is an important indicator to reflect the achievement of the transportation industry. This is an important indicator to show the total results of the transport industry; to prepare and examine the transport plan; and to serve as the main basic data for calculating the efficiency, labour productivity and unit cost of transport. Normally, the shortest distance between the departure station and the destination station (i.e., the payable distance) is the basis in calculating the freight ton-kilometres. The formula is as follows:

$$\begin{matrix}\text{Freight ton-kilometres}\\ \text{(passenger-kilometres)}\end{matrix} = \sum \begin{matrix}\text{freight}\\ \text{(passenger)traffic}\end{matrix} \times \begin{matrix}\text{distance of}\\ \text{transportation}\end{matrix}$$

Average Static Load of Freight Cars refers to the average cargo weight as loaded by each freight car under the static condition at the departure station. It is used to show the utilization extent of the loading capacity of the freight cars. The formula is:

$$\begin{matrix}\text{Static load (ton)}\\ \text{of freight car}\end{matrix} = \frac{\text{tonnage of goods dispatched}}{\text{number of freight cars loaded}}$$

The static load of freight cars is determined by the nature and type of goods loaded the type of vehicles, and the technique of loading. Comparison of the average marked load with the static load of freight cars provides indication on the degree of utilization of loading capacity of freight cars. For its calculation the following formula is applied:

$$\begin{matrix}\text{Utilization rate of}\\ \text{capacity of freight cars (\%)}\end{matrix} = \frac{\text{Average static load}}{\text{Average marked load}} \times 100\%$$

Average Daily Haul of Freight Locomotives refers to the average total ton-kilometres accomplished by each freight transport locomotive over one day and night during a given period of time. It includes both the weight of the goods carried and the dead weight of the train itself. It is a comprehensive indicator reflecting the locomotive efficiency in terms of both time and the pulling force.

$$\text{Average daily haul of freight transport locomotive (ton − kilometre)} = \frac{\text{Total ton − kilometres of freight}}{\text{Daily number of freight transport locomotive}}$$

Possession of Civil Motor Vehicles refer to the total numbers of vehicles that are registered and received vehicles license tags according to the Work Standard for Motor Vehicles Registration formulated by the Transport Management Office under the department of public security at the end of the reference period. They are divided into categories. According to the structure of motor vehicles, they are divided into passenger vehicles, trucks and others; according to ownership into private vehicles and vehicles for the unit's use; according to kind of usage into working vehicles and non-working vehicles; and according to size of vehicles into large passenger vehicles, medium-sized passenger vehicles, small passenger vehicles and mini passenger vehicles, heavy trucks, light-heavy trucks, light trucks and mini-trucks.

Business Volume of Post and Telecommunications refers to the total amount of postal and telecommunication services, expressed in value terms, provided by the post and telecommunications departments for society. This indicator reflects the overall results of development of postal and telecommunication services. It can be classificated as postal services and and telecommunication services. Business volume of post and telecommunications is the sum of all services in kind multiplying with the unit price (constant price) to get the total business value.

Mobile Telephone Subscribers refer to persons who have gone through registration procedures in the operation points of enterprises engaged in telecommunications and are hence connected with the mobile telephone communication network through the mobile telephone switchboards and occupy mobile phone numbers. Included are GSM digital mobile phone subscribers, CDMA digital mobile phone subscribers and subscribers to intelligent phone cards with roaming facility issued by telecommunications enterprises and which have been subscribed to and activated at the end of the reference period.

Internet Users refer to the number of Chinese citizens aged 6 and over who use the Internet at least for one hour each week.

Local Telephone Subscribers refer to all subscribers who have gone through registration procedures in the operation points of enterprises engaged in telecommunications and are hence connected to the local telecommunications service provider through fixed line network. Included are general subscribers, public telephones subscribers, N-ISDN subscribers and intelligent network terminal subscribers. They are also classified in terms of administrative districts as urban telephone subscribers and rural telephone subscribers according to location.

Household Telephone Subscribers refer to telephone sets installed in the dwelling units of urban or rural residents, and registered as residence subscribers for payment, including three types of payment for the service: private payment, public payment and free service in accordance with relevant regulations.

Capacity of Long Distance Telephone Exchanges refers to the rated capacity of telephone exchanges to connect long distance telephone network, including capacity of international telephone exchanges.

Capacity of Office Telephone Exchanges refers to the capacity (measured in gate) of telephone exchanges installed in the offices of telecommunication service providers for communication between fixed telephones. It includes the capacity of both manual and automatic exchanges in use and for stand-by purpose. The capacity of subscriber exchanges is not included.

第十六篇
批发和零售、住宿和餐饮

CHAPTER 16
Wholesale & Retail Trades, Hotels and Catering Services

简要说明
Brief Introduction

本篇资料的主要内容及来源

本篇资料反映新疆维吾尔自治区商品流通市场发展及批发和零售业、住宿和餐饮业经营情况。主要内容有社会消费品零售额;限额以上批发和零售业、住宿和餐饮业情况;限额以上批发和零售业商品销售及商品分类销售情况;限额以上批发和零售贸易企业及住宿和餐饮企业主要财务情况等。

限额以上批发和零售业、住宿和餐饮业统计限额标准：批发业年销售额 2000 万元及以上;零售业年销售额 500 万元及以上;餐饮业年营业额 200 万元及以上;住宿业为年主营业务收入 200 万元以上企业。

本篇资料由新疆维吾尔自治区统计局贸易外经统计处提供。

Main content and source of data of education

Data in this chapter reflect the development of Xinjiang´s circulation of domestic market and the management situation of wholesale and retail & hotels and catering services, etc.Main contents include the total retail sales,conditon of wholesales & retail trades and hotels and catering services above designated size;condition of sale value of enterprises above designated size of wholesales and retail trade and sale value of trade by category of main commodites.

Criteria for wholesale and retail sale trades, hotels and catering services above designated size is defined as follows: wholesale trade has annual sales over 20 million yuan; retail sale trade have annual sale over 5 million yuan; catering services have annual income over 2 million yuan. Enterprise above designated size in accommodation refers to star-rated unit.

Data in this chapter are provided by the Division of Trade Statistics, the Xinjiang Bureau of Statistics.

16-1 主要年份国内贸易基本情况

Basic Conditions of Domestic Trade in Main Years

指　　标	Item	2000	2005	2009	2010
法人企业(个)	**Number of Corporation Enterprises (unit)**	**394**	**1097**	**1345**	**1449**
批发和零售业	Wholesale and Retail Trades	370	800	1085	1175
住宿和餐饮业	Hotels and Catering Servicess	24	297	260	274
#餐饮业	Catering Services	24	65	56	53
产业活动单位(个)	**Number of Establishments (unit)**	**431**	**2396**	**4387**	**4563**
批发和零售业	Wholesale and Retail Trades	382	1998	4008	4137
住宿和餐饮业	Hotels and Catering Services	49	398	379	426
#餐饮业	Catering Services	49	96	104	122
批发和零售业	**Wholesale and Retail Trades**				
商品销售总额（亿元）	Total Sales (100 million yuan)	478.3	1182.0	4124.4	4230.9
社会消费品零售总额(亿元)	**Total Retail Sales of Consumer Goods (100 million yuan)**	**374.5**	**640.2**	**1177.5**	**1324.5**
按销售单位所在地分	By Location of Establishments				
城　镇	City	233.7	443.9	834.4	1181.3
#城　区	County	65.2	95.6	171.8	945.0
乡　村	Under County Level	75.6	100.7	171.3	143.2
按行业分	By Sector				
批发和零售业	Wholesale and Retail Trades	242.3	509.3	956.6	1156.6
住宿和餐饮业	Hotels and Catering Services	38.2	92.8	177.2	167.9
其他行业	Others	94.0	38.1	43.7	

注：1、法人企业、产业活动单位统计范围为限额以上企业(单位)。2、商品销售总额、社会消费品零售总额为全口径数据。3、2008 年限额以上住宿业数据为年主营业务收入 200 万元以上企业。4、从 2010 年开始,按销售单位所在地分组由市、县、县以下调整为城镇、城区、乡村。5、从 2010 年开始,按行业分组取消其他行业。

Note:a)Scope of corporation enterprises,industrial activity units covers enterprises(units)above designated size.b)Data of total sales and total retail sales of consumer goods are those of full coverage.c)Data of hotels and catering services above designated size in 2008 are figures from enterprises of annual income over 2 million yuan. d) Since 2010,By the sales units of the group was adjusted,from city,county and under county level to town,city and country.e) Since 2010,by the sector of the group canceled oter sectors.

16-2 主要年份社会消费品零售总额

Total Retail Sales of Consumer Goods in Main Years

单位：亿元 (100 million yuan)

年 份 Year	社会消费品零售总额 Total Retail Sales of Consumer Goods	按销售单位所在地分 By Location		
		城 镇 City	#城 区 County	乡 村 Under County Level
1978	21.89	7.44	4.80	9.65
1980	29.36	11.06	6.05	12.25
1985	57.38	24.55	10.70	22.13
1990	104.30	57.17	24.27	22.86
1995	253.65	145.74	50.03	57.88
1996	295.36	171.51	55.38	68.47
1997	310.42	186.37	57.54	66.51
1998	327.52	197.89	59.89	69.74
1999	347.40	213.96	61.51	71.93
2000	374.50	233.66	65.15	75.69
2001	406.35	256.58	69.73	80.04
2002	442.88	284.74	74.32	83.82
2003	421.16	311.33	49.20	60.63
2004	563.41	385.81	85.79	91.81
2005	640.20	443.95	95.60	100.65
2006	733.20	513.12	107.68	112.40
2007	857.50	606.74	123.64	127.12
2008	1041.50	740.85	150.78	149.87
2009	1177.53	834.42	171.76	171.35
2010	1324.48	1181.27	945.03	143.21

年 份 Year	按行业分 By Sector		
	批发和零售业 Wholesale and Retail Trades	住宿和餐饮业 Hotels and Catering Services	其他行业 Others
1978	17.34	0.57	3.98
1980	22.95	0.94	5.47
1985	40.83	2.51	14.04
1990	72.68	6.06	25.56
1995	169.16	17.27	67.22
1996	191.14	19.44	84.78
1997	198.73	22.22	89.47
1998	206.92	27.84	92.76
1999	222.57	32.76	92.07
2000	242.29	38.21	94.00
2001	266.38	44.57	95.40
2002	296.13	53.04	93.71
2003	341.90	60.64	18.62
2004	450.65	76.22	36.54
2005	509.25	92.82	38.13
2006	582.28	111.55	39.37
2007	685.94	130.51	41.05
2008	841.65	156.49	43.36
2009	956.64	177.21	43.68
2010	1156.62	167.86	

16-3 分类型、分地区限额以上批发和零售业、住宿和餐饮业基本情况

Basic Conditions of Enterprises above Designated Size in Wholesale and Retail Trades, Hotels and Catering Services by Category and Region

(2010 年)

指　标	Item	法人企业数(个) Number of Corporation Enterprises (unit)	产业活动单位数(个) Number of Establishments (unit)	从业人员数(人) Engaged Persons (person)
总　计	**Total**	**1449**	**4563**	**139247**
批发业	**Wholesale Trades**	**713**	**2461**	**58156**
内资企业	Domestic Funded Enterprises	708	2446	55125
国有企业	State-owned Enterprises	118	628	19776
集体企业	Collective-owned Enterprises	26	403	2143
联营企业	Joint Ownership Enterprises	1	8	270
国有联营企业	State Joint Ownership Enterprises	1	8	270
有限责任公司	Limited Liability Corporations	205	621	14428
国有独资公司	State Sole Funded Corporations	24	77	2922
其他有限责任公司	Other Limited Liability Corporations	181	544	11506
股份有限公司	Share-holding Corporations Ltd.	24	376	6879
私营企业	Private Enterprises	332	405	11581
私营独资企业	Private-funded Enterprises	4	7	168
私营合伙企业	Private Partnership Enterprises	1	1	17
私营有限责任公司	Private Limited Liability Corporations	321	390	11117
私营股份有限公司	Private Share-holding Corporation Ltd.	6	7	279
其他企业	Other Enterprises	2	5	48
港、澳、台商投资企业	Enterprises With Funds from Hong Kong, Macao and Taiwan	2	6	2473
合资经营企业（港或澳、台资）	Joint-venture Enterprises	1	4	2411
港、澳、台商独资经营企业	Enterprises with Sole Funds from Hong Kong, Macao and Taiwan	1	2	62
外商投资企业	Foreign Funded Enterprises	3	9	558
中外合资经营企业	Enterprises with Foreign Investment	3	6	324
外资企业	Enterprises with Sole Fund		3	234
零售业	**Retail Trades**	**462**	**1676**	**40910**
内资企业	Domestic Funded Enterprises	446	1656	38562
国有企业	State-owned Enterprises	43	440	5590
集体企业	Collective-owned Enterprises	2	3	116
股份合作企业	Share-holding Cooperative Enterprises	1	1	105
有限责任公司	Limited Liability Corporations	98	355	10298
国有独资公司	State Sole Funded Enterprises	7	13	688
其他有限责任公司	Other Limited Liability Corporations	91	342	9610
股份有限公司	Share-holding Corporations Ltd.	4	12	2730
私营企业	Private Enterprises	298	845	19723
私营独资企业	Private-funded Enterprises	9	10	493
私营合伙企业	Private Partnership Enterprises	4	4	97
私营有限责任公司	Private Limited Liability Corporations	279	814	19068
私营股份有限公司	Private Share-holding Corporation Ltd.	6	17	65
港、澳、台商投资企业	Enterprises With Funds from Hong Kong, Macao and Taiwan	4	4	467
港、澳、台商独资经营企业	Enterprises With Sole Funds from Hong Kong, Macao and Taiwan	4	4	467
外商投资企业	Foreign Funded Enterprises	12	16	1881
中外合资经营企业	Enterprises with Foreign Investment	11	11	1278
外资企业	Enterprises with Sole Fund	1	5	603
住宿业	**Hotels**	**221**	**304**	**32883**
内资企业	Domestic-funded Enterprises	217	299	31584
国有企业	State-owned Enterprises	90	123	12990

16-3 续表 Continued

指　　标	Item	法人企业数(个) Number of Corporate Enterprises (unit)	产业活动单位数(个) Number of Economic Active Unit (unit)	从业人员数(人) Engaged Persons (person)
集体企业	Collective-owned Enterprises	4	5	784
股份合作企业	Cooperative Enterprises		1	60
联营企业	Joint Ownership Enterprises	1	1	70
国有联营企业	State Joint Ownership Enterprises	1	1	70
有限责任公司	Limited Liability Corporations	57	80	8513
国有独资公司	State Sole Funded Corporations	3	3	446
其他有限责任公司	Other Limited Liability Corporations	54	77	8067
股份有限公司	Share-holding Corporations Ltd.	4	6	804
私营企业	Private Enterprises	59	80	7843
私营独资企业	Private-funded Enterprises	12	18	856
私营合伙企业	Private Partnership Enterprises	1	1	162
私营有限责任公司	Private Limited Liability Corporations	45	59	6405
私营股份有限公司	Private Share-holding Corporation Ltd.	1	2	420
其他企业	Other Enterprises	2	3	520
港、澳、台商投资企业	Enterprises With Funds from Hong Kong, Macao and Taiwan	4	4	801
合资经营企业（港或澳、台资）	Joint-venture Enterprises (Funds from Hong Kong, Macao and Taiwan)	4	4	801
外商投资企业	Foreign Funded Enterprises		1	498
中外合资经营企业	Enterprises with Foreign Investment		1	498
四、餐饮业	**Catering Services**	**53**	**122**	**7298**
内资企业	Domestic Funded Enterprises	51	101	6139
国有企业	State-owned Enterprises	5	11	662
集体企业	Collective-owned Enterprises	1	1	55
有限责任公司	Limited Liability Corporations	5	8	625
其他有限责任公司	Other Limited Liability Corporations	5	8	625
私营企业	Private Enterprises	40	81	4797
私营独资企业	Private-funded Enterprises	8	8	740
私营合伙企业	Private Partnership Enterprises	1	1	65
私营有限责任公司	Private Limited Liability Corporations	31	72	3992
外商投资企业	Enterprises with Foreign Investment	2	21	1159
中外合资经营企业	Joint-venture Enterprises	1	1	84
外资企业	Enterprises with Sole Fund	1	20	1075
按地区分	**By Region**			
乌鲁木齐市	Urumqi City	519	1425	63771
克拉玛依市	Karamay City	65	127	6520
吐鲁番地区	Turpan Administrative Offices	22	64	1876
哈密地区	Hami [Kumul] Administrative Offices	67	152	4225
昌吉回族自治州	Changji Hui Autonomous Prefecture	80	268	6645
伊犁哈萨克自治州	Ili Kazak Autonomous Prefecture	196	419	12242
伊犁州直属县(市)	Counties (Cities) Direct Under Ili Prefecture	132	211	8124
塔城地区	Tacheng [Tarbagatai] Administrative Offices	43	118	2436
阿勒泰地区	Altay Administrative Offices	21	90	1682
博尔塔拉蒙古自治州	Bortala Mongol Autonomous Prefecture	21	59	1264
巴音郭楞蒙古自治州	Bayangol Mongol Autonomous Prefecture	117	274	8722
阿克苏地区	Aksu Administrative Offices	104	743	7653
克孜勒苏柯尔克孜自治州	Kizilsu Kirgiz Autonomous Prefecture	12	12	792
喀什地区	Kashgar [Kaxgar] Administrative Offices	63	193	7103
和田地区	Hotan Administrative Offices	17	167	1458
生产建设兵团	Xinjiang Production and Construction Corps	166	660	16976

16-4 分行业、分地区限额以上批发零售业商品销售额

Total Sales Values of Enterprises above Designated Size of Wholesale and Retail Trades by Sector and Region

单位：万元 (2010 年) (10 000 yuan)

指 标	Item	销售总额 Total Sales Value	批 发 Wholesale Value	零 售 Retail Value
总 计	**Total**	**40795348**	**34761151**	**6034197**
批发业	**Wholesale Trade**	**35451172**	**34389696**	**1061476**
农畜产品批发业	Wholesale of Farm Produce and Livestock Products	4692887	4690101	2786
谷物、豆及薯类批发业	Wholesale of Grain,Bean and Potato	383223	381264	1959
种子、饲料批发业	Wholesale of Seed and Fodder	176990	176986	4
棉、麻批发业	Wholesale of Cotton and Liner	4100431	4100408	23
其他农畜产品批发业	Wholesale of Other Farm Produce and Livestock Products	32243	31443	800
食品、饮料及烟草制品批发业	Wholesale of Food,Beverages and Tobaccos	1375885	1361531	14354
米、面制品及食用油批发业	Wholesale of Rice, Flour and Edible Oil	153720	152675	1045
糕点、糖果及糖批发业	Wholesale of Pastry,Candy and Sugar	30194	26991	3203
果品、蔬菜批发业	Wholesale of Fruit and Vegetable	121314	121229	85
肉、禽、蛋及水产品批发业	Wholesale of Meat,Birds and Equatic Products	4322	4322	
盐及调味品批发业	Wholesale of Salt and Condiment Flavoring Material	32402	31734	668
饮料及茶叶批发业	Wholesale of Soft Drink and Tea Leaf	56227	55079	1148
烟草制品批发业	Wholesale of Tobaccos	950142	942600	7542
其他食品批发业	Wholesale of Other Food	27564	26901	663
纺织、服装及日用品批发业	Wholesale of Textitle, Garments and Daily Consumer Articles	202894	202497	397
纺织品、针织品及原料批发	Wholesale of Textile,Hosiery and Raw Material	62124	62124	
服装批发业	Wholesale of Garment	74897	74897	
化妆品及卫生用品批发业	Wholesale of Cosmetics and Health Aids	24038	24038	
其他日用品批发业	Wholesale of Other Covenience Goods	41835	41438	397
文化、体育用品及器材批发业	Wholesale of Culture, Sports Appliances and Equipments	158858	144819	14039
图书批发业	Wholesale of Books	117564	110365	7199
其他文化用品批发业	Wholesale of Other Culture Products	41294	34454	6840
医药及医疗器械批发业	Wholesale of Medicines and Medical Appliances	258739	253718	5021
西药批发业	Wholesale of Western Medicine	225739	221216	4523
中药材及中成药批发业	Wholesale of Chinese Medicinal Plant and Chinese Patent Medicine	33000	32502	498
矿产品、建材及化工产品批发业	Wholesale of Mineral Products, Building Material and Chemical Products	26457493	25494167	963326
煤炭及制品批发业	Wholesale of Coal and Related Products	878186	878186	
石油及制品批发业	Wholesale of Petroleum and Related Products	20222927	19275746	947181
金属及金属矿批发业	Wholesale of Metal and Metal Materials	3203640	3203640	
建材批发业	Wholesale of Building Materials	384018	384018	
化肥批发业	Wholesale of Chemical Fertilizer	1272129	1266302	5827

16-4 续表 1 Continued

单位：万元 (10 000 yuan)

指 标	Item	销售总额 Total Sales Value	批 发 Wholesale Value	零 售 Retail Value
农药批发业	Wholesale of Pesticides	5921	5921	
农用薄膜批发业	Wholesale of Agriculture Film	2437	2437	
其他化工产品批发业	Wholesale of Other Chemical Product	488235	477917	10318
机械设备、五金交电及电子产品批发业	Wholesale of Machinery, Hardware and Electronic Equipments	1930040	1868522	61518
农业机械批发业	Wholesale of Agriculture Machinery	115147	115006	141
汽车、摩托车及零配件批发业	Wholesale of Motor Vehicles, Motorcycles and Parts	625215	603815	21400
五金、交电批发业	Wholesale of Hardware and Electronic Equipment	389912	387039	2873
家用电器批发业	Wholesale of Household Electrical Appliances	137980	122272	15708
计算机、软件及辅助设备批发业	Wholesale of Computer, Software and Assistant Appliances	137946	116550	21396
通讯及广播电视设备批发业	Wholesale of Communicating and Broadcasting Television Device	26570	26570	
其他机械设备及电子产品批发业	Wholesale of Other Mechanical Equipment and Electronic Products	497270	497270	
贸易经纪与代理	Trades Broker and Agency	59019	59019	
其他批发业	Wholesales of Others	315357	315322	35
再生物资回收与批发业	Recovery and Wholesale of Regeneration Material	264466	264431	35
其他未列明的批发业	Wholesale of Un-listed	50891	50891	
零售业	**Retail Trades**	**5344176**	**371455**	**4972721**
综合零售业	Integrated Retail	979898	4346	975552
百货零售业	Retail of General Merchandise	697822	4232	693590
超级市场零售业	Retail of Supermarkets	279416		279416
其他综合零售业	Retail of Other Integrate	2660	114	2546
食品、饮料及烟草制品专门零售业	Monopoly Retail of Foods, Beverages and Tobacco	13509	443	13066
粮油零售业	Retail of Grain and Oil	5409		5409
糕点、面包零售业	Retail of Pastry and Bread	166		166
饮料及茶叶零售业	Retail of Soft Drink and Tea Leaf	2842	443	2399
烟草制品零售业	Retail of Tobaccos	4644		4644
其他食品零售	Retail of Other Food	448		448
纺织、服装及日用品专门零售业	Monopoly Retail of Textile, Garments and Daily Consumer Articles	197096	5592	191504
服装零售业	Retail of Garment	160985	5468	155517
钟表、眼镜零售业	Retail of Timelceeper and Spectacle	1314		1314
化妆品及卫生用品零售业	Retail of Cosmetics and Health Aids	33459		33459
其他日用品零售业	Retail of Other Covenience Goods	1338	124	1214
文化、体育用品及器材专门零售业	Monopoly Retail of Cultural, Sports Goods And Apparatus	152255	6947	145308
文具用品零售业	Retail of Stationery and Office Supplies	1186		1186
图书零售业	Retail of Books	125986	4074	121912
珠宝首饰零售业	Retail of Jewelry	21954	2873	19081
照相器材零售业	Retail of Photographic Materials	3129		3129

16-4 续表 2 Continued

单位：万元 (10 000 yuan)

指　　标	Item	销售总额 Total Sales Value	批　发 Wholesale Value	零　售 Retail Value
医药及医疗器材专门零售	Monopoly Retail of Medicine and Medical-care Apparatus	727203	65584	661619
药品零售业	Retail of Medcine	723808	65584	658224
医疗用品及器材零售	Wholesale of Medical Treatment and Equipment	3395		3395
汽车、摩托车、燃料及零配件专门零售业	Monopoly Retail of Car, Motor, Fuel and Parts as Well as Components	2697675	259447	2438228
汽车零售业	Retail of Automobiles	1744775	96612	1648163
汽车零配件零售业	Retail of Automobiles' Parts	6702		6702
摩托车及零配件零售业	Retail of Motorcycle and Fittings	13067	702	12365
机动车燃料零售业	Retail of Auto Fuel	933131	162133	770998
家用电器及电子产品专门零售业	Monopoly Retail of House Hold Electric Appliancesound Electronic Products	352097	22485	329612
家用电器零售业	Retail of Electric Appliances	236170	5987	230183
计算机、软件及辅助设备零售业	Retail of Cumputers,Software and Office Appliances	79631	9579	70052
通讯设备零售业	Retail of Telecommunication Equipments	33247	6919	26328
其他电子产品零售	Retail of other Electric Products	3049		3049
五金、家具及室内装修材料专门零售业	Monopoly Retail of Hardware, Furniture and Indoor Decorating Material	191890	2680	189210
五金零售业	Retail of Hardware	16397		16397
家具零售业	Retail of Living Equipment	172285		172285
其他室内装修材料零售业	Retail of Other Indoor Hardware Fitting	3208	2680	528
无店铺及其他零售业	Retail of Storeless and Others	32553	3931	28622
生活用燃料零售业	Retail of Life Fuels	23791	3931	19860
其他未列明的零售业	Retail of Un-listed	8762		8762
按地区分	**By Region**			
乌鲁木齐市	Urumqi City	25958638	22095945	3862693
克拉玛依市	Karamay City	794503	648574	145929
吐鲁番地区	Turpan Administrative Offices	312422	247921	64501
哈密地区	Hami [Kumul] Administrative Offices	640431	454586	185845
昌吉回族自治州	Changji Hui Autonomous Prefecture	849111	636155	212956
伊犁哈萨克自治州	Ili Kazak Autonomous Prefecture	3346248	3093501	252747
伊犁州直属县(市)	Counties (Cities) Direct Under Ili Prefecture	2434285	2255962	178323
塔城地区	Tacheng [Tarbagatai] Administrative Offices	688621	644569	44052
阿勒泰地区	Altay Administrative Offices	223342	192970	30372
博尔塔拉蒙古自治州	Bortala Mongol Autonomous Prefecture	546047	520859	25188
巴音郭楞蒙古自治州	Bayangol Mongol Autonomous Prefecture	1120151	892903	227248
阿克苏地区	Aksu Administrative Offices	1314728	1026557	288171
克孜勒苏柯尔克孜自治州	Kizilsu Kirgiz Autonomous Prefecture	38656	34450	4206
喀什地区	Kashgar [Kaxgar] Administrative Offices	980645	760186	220459
和田地区	Hotan Administrative Offices	169353	121250	48103
生产建设兵团	Xinjiang Production and Construction Group	4724415	4228264	496151

16-5 限额以上餐饮企业经营情况

Operations of Enterprises above Designated Size of Catering Services

单位：万元　　(2010 年)　　(10 000 yuan)

项　目	Item	法人企业数(个) Number of Corporation Enterprises (unit)	产业活动单位数(个) Number of Establishments (unit)	营业额 Business Revenue	#商品零售额 Retail Sales of Commodities
总 计	**Total**	**53**	**122**	**92130**	**85804**
正餐服务	Dinner	49	70	62472	56707
快餐服务	Snack	4	52	29658	29096
按地区分	**By Region**				
乌鲁木齐市	Urumqi City	25	78	64636	62375
克拉玛依市	Karamay City	2	11	5797	4803
吐鲁番地区	Turpan Administrative Offices	1	1	418	271
哈密地区	Hami [Kumul] Administrative Offices	1	1	282	282
昌吉回族自治州	Changji Hui Autonomous Prefecture	4	6	4164	3336
伊犁哈萨克自治州	Ili Kazak Autonomous Prefecture	3	4	1910	1606
伊犁州直属县(市)	Counties (Cities) Direct Under Ili Prefecture	3	3	1707	1471
塔城地区	Tacheng [Tarbagatai] Administrative Offices		1	203	135
巴音郭楞蒙古自治州	Bayangol Mongol Autonomous Prefecture	13	13	10505	9818
阿克苏地区	Aksu Administrative Offices	1	2	658	267
喀什地区	Kashgar [Kaxgar] Administrative Offices	1	1	1627	1013
生产建设兵团	Xinjiang Production and Construction Group	2	5	2133	2033

16-6 限额以上住宿企业经营情况

Operation of Enterprises above Designated Size in Hotels Services

单位：万元 (2010 年) (10 000 yuan)

项　　目	Item	营业额 Business Revenue	客房收入 From Hotel Rooms	餐费收入 From Meals
总　计	**Total**	**379991**	**171418**	**168155**
按星级分	**By Stars**			
五 星	Five-Star	88906	30817	40514
四 星	Four-Star	98829	42333	47983
三 星	Three-Star	128310	62946	56075
二 星	Two-Star	30614	17412	11062
一 星	One-Star	10442	4247	4681
其 他	Others	22890	13663	7840
按地区分	**By Region**			
乌鲁木齐市	Urumqi City	218465	95047	93708
克拉玛依市	Karamay City	15418	5761	8735
吐鲁番地区	Turpan Administrative Offices	4186	2081	2071
哈密地区	Hami [Kumul] Administrative Offices	14480	7066	6812
昌吉回族自治州	Changji Hui Autonomous Prefecture	8503	3899	3772
伊犁哈萨克自治州	Ili Kazak Autonomous Prefecture	42504	18972	21368
伊犁州直属县(市)	Counties (Cities) Direct Under Ili Prefecture	27767	11950	14362
塔城地区	Tacheng [Tarbagatai] Administrative Offices	5735	2507	2930
阿勒泰地区	Altay Administrative Offices	9002	4515	4076
博尔塔拉蒙古自治州	Bortala Mongol Autonomous Prefecture	2202	959	1126
巴音郭楞蒙古自治州	Bayangol Mongol Autonomous Prefecture	21343	8503	10693
阿克苏地区	Aksu Administrative Offices	5007	2614	2084
克孜勒苏柯尔克孜自治州	Kizilsu Kirgiz Autonomous Prefecture	1348	710	577
喀什地区	Kashgar [Kaxgar] Administrative Offices	6698	3572	2392
和田地区	Hotan Administrative Offices	3444	2109	1235
生产建设兵团	Xinjiang Production and Construction Group	36393	20125	13582

16-6 续表 Continued

单位：万元 (10 000 yuan)

项　　目	Item	商品销售收入 From Commodities	其他收入 Others	床位数（张） Number of beds (unit)
总　计	**Total**	**13142**	**27276**	**70572**
按星级分	**Classified by Star**			
五 星	Five-Star	6806	10769	4871
四 星	Four-Star	3329	5184	18877
三 星	Three-Star	2376	6913	32509
二 星	Two-Star	305	1835	7083
一 星	One-Star	205	1309	1237
其 他	Others	121	1266	5995
按地区分	**By Region**			
乌鲁木齐市	Urumqi City	9542	20168	26599
克拉玛依市	Karamay City	101	821	2460
吐鲁番地区	Turpan Administrative Offices	8	26	1237
哈密地区	Hami [Kumul] Administrative Offices	292	310	2569
昌吉回族自治州	Changji Hui Autonomous Prefecture	250	582	2526
伊犁哈萨克自治州	Ili Kazak Autonomous Prefecture	947	1217	11842
伊犁州直属县(市)	Counties (Cities) Direct Under Ili Prefecture	400	1055	6822
塔城地区	Tacheng [Tarbagatai] Administrative Offices	251	47	1473
阿勒泰地区	Altay Administrative Offices	296	115	3547
博尔塔拉蒙古自治州	Bortala Mongol Autonomous Prefecture	117		553
巴音郭楞蒙古自治州	Bayangol Mongol Autonomous Prefecture	1370	777	4681
阿克苏地区	Aksu Administrative Offices	115	194	1695
克孜勒苏柯尔克孜自治州	Kizilsu Kirgiz Autonomous Prefecture		61	581
喀什地区	Kashgar [Kaxgar] Administrative Offices	179	555	2738
和田地区	Hotan Administrative Offices	58	42	1092
生产建设兵团	Xinjiang Production and Construction Group	163	2523	11999

16-7 各地、州、市、县(市)社会消费品零售总额

Total Retail Sales of Consumer Goods by Prefecture, Autonomous Prefecture, City and County

单位：万元 (2010 年) (10 000 yuan)

地 区	Region	社会消费品零售总额 Total Retail Sales of Consumer Goods	城 镇 City	#城 区 County	乡 村 Under County Level
总 计	**Total**	**13244775**	**11812670**	**9450293**	**1432105**
乌鲁木齐市	**Urumqi City**	**5142359**	**5138853**	**5138853**	**3506**
#乌鲁木齐县	Urumqi County	72498	69947	69947	2551
克拉玛依市	**Karamay City**	**347872**	**346686**	**239163**	**1186**
吐鲁番地区	**TurpanAdministrative Offices**	**284873**	**206007**	**83853**	**78866**
吐鲁番市	Turpan City	148335	115422	83853	32913
鄯善县	Shanshan [piqan]County	100084	67217		32867
托克逊县	Toksun County	36454	23368		13086
哈密地区	**Hami [kumul]Administrative Offices**	**386696**	**364232**	**326124**	**22464**
哈密市	Hami [kumul]City	346704	334185	326124	12519
巴里坤哈萨克自治县	Barkol KazakAutonomous County	30117	20889		9228
伊吾县	Yiwu [Araturuk]County	9875	9158		717
昌吉回族自治州	**Changji Hui Autonomous Prefecture**	**1127924**	**964728**	**523288**	**163196**
昌吉市	Changji City	468594	442095	376780	26499
阜康市	Fukang City	155691	123184	84646	32507
呼图壁县	Hutubi County	132359	106796	3412	25563
玛纳斯县	Manas County	145512	115457	3652	30055
奇台县	Qitai County	127319	102558	6010	24761
吉木萨尔县	Jimsar County	61152	46768	27547	14384
木垒哈萨克自治县	Mori Kazak Autonomous County	37297	27870	21241	9427
伊犁哈萨克自治州	**Ili Kazak Autonomous Prefecture**	**1726672**	**1347924**	**793991**	**378748**
伊犁州直属县(市)	**Counties (Cities) Direct Under Ili Prefecture**	**995658**	**773773**	**604588**	**221885**
伊宁市	Yining [Gulja]City	364339	355849	355849	8490
奎屯市	Kuytun City	135857	135857	135857	
伊宁县	Yining [Gulja]County	77837	30677	7483	47160
察布查尔锡伯自治县	Qapqal Xibe Autonomous County	16374	11044	3854	5330
霍城县	Huocheng [korgas]County	109911	72235	29245	37676
巩留县	Gongliu [Tokkuzlara]County	33468	21009	4033	12459
新源县	Xinyuan [kunes]County	133976	66942	34510	67034
昭苏县	Zhaosu [mongolkure]County	29518	17151	6820	12367
特克斯县	Tekes County	52457	30503	8406	21954
尼勒克县	Nilka County	41921	32506	18531	9415
塔城地区	**Tacheng [Tarbagatai] Administrative Offices**	**407014**	**286446**	**114574**	**120568**
塔城市	Tacheng [Qoqek] City	91809	59010	56097	32799
乌苏市	Usu City	86907	71093	41892	15814
额敏县	Emin [Dorbiljin] County	78756	46162	5637	32594
沙湾县	Shawan County	94341	70321	1442	24020
裕民县	Yumin [Qagantokay] County	15297	10738	1784	4559
和布克赛尔蒙古自治县	Hoboksar Mongol Autonomous County	17137	12118	3409	5019
托里县	Toli County	22767	17004	4313	5763
阿勒泰地区	**Altay Administrative Offices**	**324000**	**287705**	**74829**	**36295**
阿勒泰市	Altay City	113004	103485	74829	9519
布尔津县	Burqin County	70972	62754		8218
富蕴县	Fuyun [Koktokay] County	45023	38845		6178
福海县	Fuhai [Burultokay] County	37064	33019		4045
哈巴河县	Habahe [Kaba] County	30002	26417		3585
青河县	Qinghe [Qinggil] County	20226	17227		2999
吉木乃县	Jeminay County	7709	5958		1751

16-7 续表 Continued

单位：万元 (10 000 yuan)

地区	Region	社会消费品零售总额 Total Retail Sales of Consumer Goods	城镇 City	#城区 County	乡村 Under County Level
博尔塔拉蒙古自治州	**Bortala Mongol Autonomous Prefecture**	**183147**	**152389**	**93473**	**30758**
博乐市	Bole [Bortala] City	134811	125154	93416	9657
精河县	Jinghe [Jing] County	33087	19283	57	13804
温泉县	Wenquan [Araxang] County	15249	7952		7297
巴音郭楞蒙古自治州	**Bayangol Mongol Autonomous Prefecture**	**561339**	**478155**	**298783**	**83184**
库尔勒市	Korla City	425335	363580	298783	61755
轮台县	Luntai [Bugur] County	25982	20752		5230
尉犁县	Yuli [Lopnur] County	12298	10045		2253
若羌县	Ruoqiang [Qarkilik] County	4711	3895		816
且末县	Qiemo [Qarqan] County	5883	5024		859
焉耆回族自治县	Yanqi Hui Autonomous County	38836	35082		3754
和静县	Hejing County	20139	15673		4466
和硕县	Hoxud County	11342	9472		1870
博湖县	Bohu [Bagrax] County	16813	14632		2181
阿克苏地区	**Aksu Administrative Offices**	**602922**	**451952**	**270540**	**150970**
阿克苏市	Aksu City	328201	262873	255902	65328
温宿县	Wensu [Onsu] County	28260	16836		11424
库车县	Kuqa County	94518	71576	5338	22942
沙雅县	Xayar County	51500	40410	6302	11090
新和县	Xinhe [Toksu] County	21196	14154		7042
拜城县	Baicheng [Bay] County	40212	22462	2998	17750
乌什县	Wushi [Uxturpan] County	9910	3740		6170
阿瓦提县	Awat County	26395	18952		7443
柯坪县	Kalpin County	2730	949		1781
克孜勒苏柯尔克孜自治州	**Kizilsu Kirgiz Autonomous Prefecture**	**83272**	**75694**	**71313**	**7578**
阿图什市	Artux City	55554	53314	52490	2240
阿克陶县	Akto County	14774	11163	10068	3611
阿合奇县	Akqi County	5712	5378	3649	334
乌恰县	Wuqia [Ulugqat] County	7232	5839	5106	1393
喀什地区	**Kashgar [Kaxgar] Administrative Offices**	**734408**	**503013**	**215898**	**231395**
喀什市	Kashgar [Kaxgar] City	345560	243099	195868	102461
疏附县	Shufu County	8266	4505	843	3761
疏勒县	Shule County	34669	21781	19149	12888
英吉沙县	Yengisar County	22965	13991		8974
泽普县	Zepu [Poskam] County	24501	16426		8075
莎车县	Shache [Yarkant] County	73191	50097		23094
叶城县	Yecheng [Kagilik] County	59554	40142	38	19412
麦盖提县	Makit County	46558	31836		14722
岳普湖县	Yopurga County	19404	13138		6266
伽师县	Jiashi [Payzawat] County	27166	17043		10123
巴楚县	Bachu [Maralbexi] County	63960	44505		19455
塔什库尔干塔吉克自治县	Taxkorgan Tajik Autonomous County	8614	6450		2164
和田地区	**Hotan Administrative Offices**	**203444**	**146356**	**110145**	**57088**
和田市	Hotan City	99934	83247	88197	16687
和田县	Hotan County	12760	232		12528
墨玉县	Moyu [Karakax] County	25788	17633	8997	8155
皮山县	Pishan [Guma] County	13263	8186		5077
洛浦县	Lop County	14743	10767	5588	3976
策勒县	Qira County	14429	9282		5147
于田县	Yutian [Keriya] County	16200	11880	7363	4320
民丰县	Minfeng [Niya] County	6327	5129		1198
生产建设兵团	**Xinjiang Production andConstruction Group**	**2001146**	**1752970**	**1123735**	**248176**

16-8 各地、州、市、县(市)社会消费品零售总额(按行业分)

Total Retail Sales of Consumer Goods by Sector and Prefecture, Autonomous Prefecture, City and County

单位：万元 (2010 年) (10 000 yuan)

地 区	Region	社会消费品零售总额 Total Retail Sales of Consumer Goods	批发和零售业 Wholesale And Retail Sale Trades	住宿和餐饮业 Hotels and Catering Services
总 计	**Total**	**13244775**	**11566244**	**1678531**
乌鲁木齐市	**Urumqi City**	**5142359**	**4576808**	**565551**
#乌鲁木齐县	Urumqi County	72498	54518	17980
克拉玛依市	**Karamay City**	**347872**	**297974**	**49898**
吐鲁番地区	**TurpanAdministrative Offices**	**284873**	**246263**	**38610**
吐鲁番市	Turpan City	148335	126201	22134
鄯善县	Shanshan [piqan]County	100084	88178	11906
托克逊县	Toksun County	36454	31884	4570
哈密地区	**Hami [kumul]Administrative Offices**	**386696**	**311611**	75085
哈密市	Hami [kumul]City	346704	282789	63915
巴里坤哈萨克自治县	Barkol KazakAutonomous County	30117	22461	7656
伊吾县	Yiwu [Araturuk]County	9875	6361	3514
昌吉回族自治州	**Changji Hui Autonomous Prefecture**	**1127924**	**950245**	**177679**
昌吉市	Changji City	468594	391602	76992
阜康市	Fukang City	155691	128811	26880
呼图壁县	Hutubi County	132359	110838	21521
玛纳斯县	Manas County	145512	126547	18965
奇台县	Qitai County	127319	107736	19583
吉木萨尔县	Jimsar County	61152	52202	8950
木垒哈萨克自治县	Mori Kazak Autonomous County	37297	32509	4788
伊犁哈萨克自治州	**Ili Kazak Autonomous Prefecture**	**1726672**	**1470776**	**255896**
伊犁州直属县(市)	**Counties (Cities) Direct Under Ili Prefecture**	**995658**	**852722**	**142936**
伊宁市	Yining [Gulja]City	364339	315113	49226
奎屯市	Kuytun City	135857	121940	13917
伊宁县	Yining [Gulja]County	77837	71230	6607
察布查尔锡伯自治县	Qapqal Xibe Autonomous County	16374	13907	2467
霍城县	Huocheng [korgas]County	109911	88444	21467
巩留县	Gongliu [Tokkuzlara]County	33468	28081	5387
新源县	Xinyuan [kunes]County	133976	111605	22371
昭苏县	Zhaosu [mongolkure]County	29518	26271	3247
特克斯县	Tekes County	52457	47073	5384
尼勒克县	Nilka County	41921	29058	12863
塔城地区	**Tacheng [Tarbagatai] Administrative Offices**	**407014**	**345606**	**61408**
塔城市	Tacheng [Qoqek] City	91809	76606	15203
乌苏市	Usu City	86907	71669	15238
额敏县	Emin [Dorbiljin] County	78756	72033	6723
沙湾县	Shawan County	94341	79384	14957
裕民县	Yumin [Qagantokay] County	15297	12713	2584
和布克赛尔蒙古自治县	Hoboksar Mongol Autonomous County	17137	13491	3646
托里县	Toli County	22767	19710	3057
阿勒泰地区	**Altay Administrative Offices**	**324000**	**272448**	**51552**
阿勒泰市	Altay City	113004	91967	21037
布尔津县	Burqin County	70972	50625	20347
富蕴县	Fuyun [Koktokay] County	45023	40657	4366
福海县	Fuhai [Burultokay] County	37064	34114	2950
哈巴河县	Habahe [Kaba] County	30002	27712	2290
青河县	Qinghe [Qinggil] County	20226	19765	461
吉木乃县	Jeminay County	7709	7608	101

16-8 续表 Continued

单位：万元 (10 000 yuan)

地区	Region	社会消费品零售总额 Total Retail Sales of Consumer Goods	批发和零售业 Wholesale And Retail Sale Trades	住宿和餐饮业 Hotels and Catering Services
博尔塔拉蒙古自治州	**Bortala Mongol Autonomous Prefecture**	**183147**	**156587**	**26560**
博乐市	Bole [Bortala] City	134811	120331	14480
精河县	Jinghe [Jing] County	33087	23309	9778
温泉县	Wenquan [Araxang] County	15249	12947	2302
巴音郭楞蒙古自治州	**Bayangol Mongol Autonomous Prefecture**	**561339**	**498629**	**62710**
库尔勒市	Korla City	425335	388725	36610
轮台县	Luntai [Bugur] County	25982	20300	5682
尉犁县	Yuli [Lopnur] County	12298	9612	2686
若羌县	Ruoqiang [Qarkilik] County	4711	3372	1339
且末县	Qiemo [Qarqan] County	5883	4186	1697
焉耆回族自治县	Yanqi Hui Autonomous County	38836	34226	4610
和静县	Hejing County	20139	16783	3356
和硕县	Hoxud County	11342	7256	4086
博湖县	Bohu [Bagrax] County	16813	14169	2644
阿克苏地区	**Aksu Administrative Offices**	**602922**	**544044**	**58878**
阿克苏市	Aksu City	328201	315242	12959
温宿县	Wensu [Onsu] County	28260	24848	3412
库车县	Kuqa County	94518	78288	16230
沙雅县	Xayar County	51500	40741	10759
新和县	Xinhe [Toksu] County	21196	17827	3369
拜城县	Baicheng [Bay] County	40212	35701	4511
乌什县	Wushi [Uxturpan] County	9910	8458	1452
阿瓦提县	Awat County	26395	20621	5774
柯坪县	Kalpin County	2730	2318	412
克孜勒苏柯尔克孜自治州	**Kizilsu Kirgiz Autonomous Prefecture**	**83272**	**73492**	**9780**
阿图什市	Artux City	55554	50982	4572
阿克陶县	Akto County	14774	12279	2495
阿合奇县	Akqi County	5712	4972	740
乌恰县	Wuqia [Ulugqat] County	7232	5259	1973
喀什地区	**Kashgar [Kaxgar] Administrative Offices**	**734408**	**635862**	**98546**
喀什市	Kashgar [Kaxgar] City	345560	329308	16252
疏附县	Shufu County	8266	6790	1476
疏勒县	Shule County	34669	24057	10612
英吉沙县	Yengisar County	22965	17523	5442
泽普县	Zepu [Poskam] County	24501	21213	3288
莎车县	Shache [Yarkant] County	73191	62082	11109
叶城县	Yecheng [Kagilik] County	59554	43414	16140
麦盖提县	Makit County	46558	38395	8163
岳普湖县	Yopurga County	19404	13385	6019
伽师县	Jiashi [Payzawat] County	27166	21763	5403
巴楚县	Bachu [Maralbexi] County	63960	49444	14516
塔什库尔干塔吉克自治县	Taxkorgan Tajik Autonomous County	8614	8488	126
和田地区	**Hotan Administrative Offices**	**203444**	**176619**	**26825**
和田市	Hotan City	99934	88699	11235
和田县	Hotan County	12760	9622	3138
墨玉县	Moyu [Karakax] County	25788	23540	2248
皮山县	Pishan [Guma] County	13263	12420	843
洛浦县	Lop County	14743	12401	2342
策勒县	Qira County	14429	11461	2968
于田县	Yutian [Keriya] County	16200	13107	3093
民丰县	Minfeng [Niya] County	6327	5369	958
生产建设兵团	**Xinjiang Production and Construction Group**	**2001146**	**1690107**	**311039**

16-9 限额以上批发企业资产及负债情况

Assets and Liabilities of Enterprises above Designated Size of Wholesale Trades

单位：万元　　(2010 年)　　(10 000 yuan)

指　标	Item	资产合计 Total Assets	#流动资产 Working Capitals	#固定资产 Fixed Assets	负债合计 Total Liabilities
总　计	**Total**	**11803779**	**9143172**	**1207454**	**9375224**
按登记注册类型分	**By Type of Registration**				
内资企业	Domestic Funded Enterprises	11203635	8911476	1161609	9326980
国有企业	State-owned Enterprises	4220637	3349983	488627	3679315
集体企业	Collective-owned Enterprises	358099	304368	39560	317711
联营企业	Joint Ownership Enterprises	58672	53643	4203	52378
国有联营企业	State Joint Ownership Enterprises	58672	53643	4203	52378
有限责任公司	Limited Liability Corporations	3501471	2842065	296521	2718860
国有独资公司	State Sole Funded Corporations	426945	348674	51141	322274
其他有限责任公司	Other Limited Liability Corporations	3074526	2493391	245380	2396586
股份有限公司	Share-holding Corporations Ltd.	1092548	742988	137981	1092542
私营企业	Private Enterprises	1945745	1607442	186891	1450717
私营独资企业	Private-funded Enterprises	6145	5096	836	4842
私营合伙企业	Private Partnership Enterprises	1130	711	88	816
私营有限责任公司	Private Limited Liability Corporations	1877044	1554430	179270	1403676
私营股份有限公司	Private Share-holding Corporation Ltd.	61426	47205	6697	41383
其他企业	Other Enterprises	26463	10987	7826	15457
港、澳、台商投资企业	Enterprises With Funds from Hong Kong, Macao and Taiwan	572821	207419	43871	31410
合资经营企业（港或澳、台资）	Joint-Venture Enterprises	564549	200385	42668	26869
港、澳、台商独资经营企业	Enterprises with Sole Funds from Hong Kong, Macao and Taiwan	8272	7034	1203	4541
外商投资企业	Foreign Funded Enterprises	27323	24277	1974	16834
中外合资经营企业	Enterprises with Foreign Investment	27323	24277	1974	16834
按批发行业小类分组	**By Sector of Wholesale**				
农畜产品批发业	Wholesale of Farm Produce and Livestock Products	4954340	4220825	427058	4268396
谷物、豆及薯类批发业	Wholesale of Grain,Bean and Potato	611029	530331	50201	583345
种子、饲料批发业	Wholesale of Seed and Fodder	313416	202831	46651	168893
棉、麻批发业	Wholesale of Cotton and Liner	3991354	3454570	326398	3481138
其他农畜产品批发业	Wholesale of Other Farm Produce and Livestoclc Products	38541	33093	3808	35020
食品、饮料及烟草制品批发业	Wholesale of Food,Beverages and Tobaccos	672903	478659	114064	462458
米、面制品及食用油批发业	Wholesale of Rice, Flour and Edible Oil	254308	217811	22912	225749
糕点、糖果及糖批发业	Wholesale of Pastry,Candy and Sugar	4782	2304	302	3300
果品、蔬菜批发业	Wholesale of Fruit and Vegetable	185475	114923	40294	138138
肉、禽、蛋及水产品批发业	Wholesale of Meat,Birds and Equatic Products	1083	1052	30	771
盐及调味品批发业	Wholesale of Salt and Condiment Flavoring Material	41981	14407	3992	17192
饮料及茶叶批发业	Wholesale of Soft Drink and Tea Leaf	6678	5865	534	4520
烟草制品批发业	Wholesale of Tobaccos	127297	81656	37191	35141
其他食品批发业	Wholesale of Other Food	51299	40641	8809	37647
纺织、服装及日用品批发业	Wholesale of Textitle, Garments and Daily Consumer Articles	71018	65920	2560	57281
纺织品、针织品及原料批发业	Wholesale of Textile,Hosiery and Raw Material	11524	11106	417	8433
服装批发业	Wholesale of Garment	32969	30881	849	27476
化妆品及卫生用品批发业	Wholesale of Cosmetics and Health Aids	7720	7418	199	6473
其他日用品批发业	Wholesale of Other Covenience Goods	18805	16515	1095	14899

16-9 续表 Continued

单位：万元 (10 000 yuan)

指标	Item	资产合计 Total Assets	#流动资产 Working Capitals	#固定资产 Fixed Assets	负债合计 Total Liabilities
文化、体育用品及器材批发业	Wholesale of Culture, Sports Goods and Apparatus	94971	65411	21898	58166
图书批发业	Wholesale of Books	70571	44464	19815	36623
其他文化用品批发业	Wholesale of Other Culture Products	24400	20947	2083	21543
医药及医疗器械批发业	Wholesale of Medicines and Medical Appliances	183509	152111	15395	105903
西药批发业	Wholesale of Western Medicine	165904	135809	14164	91117
中药材及中成药批发业	Wholesale of Chinese Medicinal Plant and Chinese Patent Medicine	17605	16302	1231	14786
矿产品、建材及化工产品批发业	Wholesale of Mineral Products, Building Material and Chemical Products	4790070	3284973	547377	3654026
煤炭及制品批发业	Wholesale of Coal and Related Products	326012	236154	16739	121862
石油及制品批发业	Wholesale of Petroleum and Related Products	1876319	1102784	395543	1874192
金属及金属矿批发业	Wholesale of Metal and Metal Materials	1388175	909056	67435	664616
建材批发业	Wholesale of Building Materials	139981	115274	10450	102863
化肥批发业	Wholesale of Fertilizer	892718	775262	48690	761223
农药批发业	Wholesale of Pesticides	4828	4232	193	4540
农用薄膜批发业	Wholesale of Film Agriculture	775	718	21	352
其他化工产品批发业	Wholesale of Other Chemical Product	161262	141493	8306	124378
机械设备、五金交电及电子产品批发业	Wholesale of Machinery, Hardware and Electronic Equipments	913565	783668	65300	683827
农业机械批发业	Wholesale of Agriculture Machinery	103347	73955	19822	66972
汽车、摩托车及零配件批发业	Wholesale of Motor Vehicles, Motorcycles and Parts	261765	230405	18260	201305
五金、交电批发业	Wholesale of Hardware and Electromic Equipment	200581	188768	8218	188079
家用电器批发业	Wholesale of Household Electrical Appliances	19868	18649	706	18996
计算机、软件及辅助设备批发业	Wholesale of Computer, Software and Accessory Equipment	28143	25095	1367	20935
通讯及广播电视设备批发业	Wholesale of Communicating and Broadcasting Television Device	6461	4499	1934	1188
其他机械设备及电子产品批发业	Wholesale of Other Mechanical Equipment and Electronic Products	293400	242297	14993	186352
贸易经纪与代理	Trades Broker and Agent	24284	18227	4016	15545
其他批发业	Wholesales of Others	99119	73378	9786	69622
再生物资回收与批发业	Recovery and Wholesale of Regeneration Material	69164	54639	6241	54843
其他未列明的批发业	Wholesale of Un-listed	29955	18739	3545	14779
按地区分	**By Region**				
乌鲁木齐市	Urumqi City	4567798	3416133	373454	3006389
克拉玛依市	Karamay City	179350	91125	58177	168126
吐鲁番地区	Turpan Administrative Offices	120623	101009	11101	95747
哈密地区	Hami [Kumul] Administrative Offices	141470	102925	25783	181238
昌吉回族自治州	Changji Hui Autonomous Prefecture	461925	355856	56520	437816
伊犁哈萨克自治州	Ili Kazak Autonomous Prefecture	1053826	875263	68775	1036374
伊犁州直属县(市)	Counties (Cities) Direct Under Ili Prefecture	580936	501227	41841	577899
塔城地区	Tacheng [Tarbagatai] Administrative Offices	428196	342378	15540	372601
阿勒泰地区	Altay Administrative Offices	44694	31658	11394	85874
博尔塔拉蒙古自治州	Bortala Mongol Autonomous Prefecture	208771	175715	14555	136869
巴音郭楞蒙古自治州	Bayangol Mongol Autonomous Prefecture	408821	276147	107597	322816
阿克苏地区	Aksu Administrative Offices	796278	659536	106841	727443
克孜勒苏柯尔克孜自治州	Kizilsu Kirgiz Autonomous Prefecture	19605	15978	3087	13131
喀什地区	Kashgar [Kaxgar] Administrative Offices	513330	283498	91049	424914
和田地区	Hotan Administrative Offices	72052	15772	15463	64096
生产建设兵团	Xinjiang Production and Construction Group	3259930	2774215	275052	2760265

16-10 限额以上零售企业资产及负债情况

Assets and Liabilities of Enterprises above Designated Size of Retail Trades

单位：万元　　(2010 年)　　(10 000 yuan)

指　标	Item	资产合计 Total Asset	#流动资产 Working Capitals	#固定资产 Fixed Asset	负债合计 Total Liabilities
总　计	**Total**	**2298449**	**1622404**	**371998**	**1639605**
按登记注册类型分	**By Status of Registration**				
内资企业	Domesticfunded Enterprises	2093259	1474806	339755	1501381
国有企业	State-owned Enterprises	426772	274276	88369	369574
集体企业	Collective-owned Enterprises	1842	1300	21	1522
股份合作企业	Share-holding Cooperative Enterprises	1973	1141	689	1233
有限责任公司	Limited Liability Corporations	486286	364804	65405	298059
国有独资公司	State Sole Funded Corporations	18161	12040	3433	16676
其他有限责任公司	Other Limited Liability Corporations	468125	352764	61972	281383
股份有限公司	Share-holding Corporations Ltd.	289304	148794	68319	168416
私营企业	Private Enterprises	887082	684491	116952	662577
私营独资企业	Private-funded Enterprises	14513	13284	937	12619
私营合伙企业	Private Partnership Enterprises	1245	1174	71	1103
私营有限责任公司	Private Limited Liability Corporations	867348	669010	114552	646293
私营股份有限公司	Private Share-holding Corporation Ltd.	3976	1023	1392	2562
港、澳、台投资企业	Enterprises With Funds from Hong Kong, Macao and Taiwan	39750	29542	8034	28853
港、澳、台商独资经营企业	Enterprises with Sole Funds from Hong Kong, Macao and Taiwan	39750	29542	8034	28853
外商投资企业	Foreign Funded Enterprises	165440	118056	24209	109371
中外合资经营企业	Enterprises with Foreign Investment	142703	99092	20829	96746
外资企业	Enterprises with Sole Fund	22737	18964	3380	12625
按零售行业小类分组	**By Sector of Retail**				
综合零售业	Integrated Retail	570275	344060	127786	394419
百货零售业	Retail of Merchandile	441152	253546	102971	298528
超级市场零售业	Retail of Supermarket	126466	89007	24415	93827
其他综合零售业	Retail of other integrate	2657	1507	400	2064
食品、饮料及烟草制品专门零售业	Monopoly Retail of Foods, Beverages and Tobacco	13750	9655	1966	12278
粮油零售业	Retail of Grain and Oil	7521	6395	1117	8655
饮料及茶叶零售业	Retail of Soft Drink and Tea Leaf	2053	1337	296	1960
烟草制品零售业	Retail of Tobauos	4176	1923	553	1663
纺织、服装及日用品专门零售业	Monopoly Retail of Textile, Garments and Daily Consumer Articles	106771	75752	17597	91948
服装零售业	Garment Retail	103940	72999	17521	89354
钟表、眼镜零售业	Retail of Timekeeper and Spectacle	1179	1173	6	1153
化妆品及卫生用品零售	Retail of Cosmetics and Washing Articles	183	183		220
其他日用品零售业	Retail of Other Covenience Goods	1469	1397	70	1221
文化、体育用品及器材专门零售业	Monopoly Retail of Cultural, Sports Appliances And Equipments	148697	90139	36529	68348
文具用品零售业	Retail of Stationery and Office Supplies	647	626	23	141
图书零售业	Retail of Books	120876	63361	36157	58585

16-10 续表 Continued

单位：万元 (10 000 yuan)

指　　标	Item	资产合计 Total Assets	#流动资产 Working Capitals	#固定资产 Fixed Assets	负债合计 Total Liabilities
珠宝首饰零售业	Retail of Jewelry	26424	25433	346	9134
照相器材零售业	Retail of Photographic Materials	750	719	3	488
医药及医疗器材专门零售业	Monopoly Retail of Medicine and Medical-care Apparatus	322811	280901	19231	227277
药品零售业	Retail of Medcine	320897	279166	19052	225934
医疗用品及器材零售	Wholesale of Medical Treatment and Equipment	1914	1735	179	1343
汽车、摩托车、燃料及零配件专门零售业	Monopoly Retail of Car, Motor, Fuel and Parts as Well as Components	759120	509385	135193	649347
汽车零售业	Retail of Car	609680	450238	82331	431828
汽车零配件零售业	Retail of Automobiles' Accessories	3194	1522	550	2147
摩托车及零配件零售业	Retail of Motorcycle and Fittings	5641	4889	519	4540
机动车燃料零售业	Retail of Auto Fuel	140605	52736	51793	210832
家用电器及电子产品专门零售业	Monopoly Retail of House hold Electric Appliancesound Electronic Products	163717	151200	5053	107427
家用电器零售业	Retail of Electric Appliances	96142	89505	2066	68580
计算机、软件及辅助设备零售业	Retail of Cumputers,Software and Office Appliances	55510	51349	2662	32347
通讯设备零售业	Retail of Telecommunication Equipments	8958	7283	282	4386
其他电子产品零售	Retail of other Electric Products	3107	3063	43	2114
五金、家具及室内装修材料专门零售业	Monopoly Retail of Hardware, Furniture and Indoor Decorating Material	182458	146622	14418	73707
五金零售业	Retail of Hardware	7175	7127	49	6535
家具零售业	Retail of Living equipment	174427	138722	14287	66581
其他室内装修材料零售业	Retail of Other Indoor Hardware Fitting	856	773	82	591
无店铺及其他零售业	Retail of Storeless and others	30850	14690	14225	14854
生活用燃料零售业	Retail of Life Fuels	24767	11314	12859	9900
其他未列明的零售业	Retail of Un-listed	6083	3376	1366	4954
按地区分	**By Region**				
乌鲁木齐市	Urumqi City	1669379	1205403	239617	1230845
克拉玛依市	Karamay City	55594	43348	7956	41932
吐鲁番地区	Turpan Administrative Offices	14584	5735	5922	9545
哈密地区	Hami [Kumul] Administrative Offices	54582	35693	9045	36346
昌吉回族自治州	Changji Hui Autonomous Prefecture	62392	40411	14277	50462
伊犁哈萨克自治州	Ili Kazak Autonomous Prefecture	114168	77309	16468	69937
伊犁州直属县(市)	Counties (Cities) Direct Under Ili Prefecture	95732	65830	10901	60253
塔城地区	Tacheng [Tarbagatai] Administrative Offices	13900	8997	4322	7166
阿勒泰地区	Altay Administrative Offices	4536	2482	1245	2518
博尔塔拉蒙古自治州	Bortala Mongol Autonomous Prefecture	4532	2844	1068	2000
巴音郭楞蒙古自治州	Bayangol Mongol Autonomous Prefecture	65052	47024	14848	48085
阿克苏地区	Aksu Administrative Offices	68594	48507	10850	48967
克孜勒苏柯尔克孜自治州	Kizilsu Kirgiz Autonomous Prefecture	3168	1964	848	1392
喀什地区	Kashgar [Kaxgar] Administrative Offices	72449	49156	17427	56519
和田地区	Hotan Administrative Offices	15569	10981	2522	10455
生产建设兵团	Xinjiang Production and Construction Group	98386	54029	31150	33120

16-11 限额以上餐饮企业资产及负债情况
Assets and Liabilities of Enterprises above Designated Size of Catering Services

单位：万元　　(2010 年)　　(10 000 yuan)

指　标	Item	资产合计 Total Asset	#流动资产 Working Capitals	#固定资产 Fixed Asset	负债合计 Total Liabilities
总　计	**Total**	**64064**	**30309**	**26661**	**43248**
按登记注册类型分	**By Status of Registration**				
内资企业	Domestic-funded Enterprises	58048	28599	25060	40265
国有企业	State – owned Enterprises	9286	548	8737	361
集体企业	Collective – owned Enterprises	82	72	10	66
有限责任公司	Limited Liability Corporations	7348	4777	2128	4431
其他有限责任公司	Other Limited Liability Corporations	7348	4777	2128	4431
私营企业	Private Enterprises	41332	23202	14185	35407
私营独资企业	Private-funded Enterprises	2807	1340	1424	2003
私营合伙企业	Private Partnership Enterprises	2773	1815	256	49
私营有限责任公司	Private Limited Liability Corporations	35752	20047	12505	33355
外商投资企业	Foreign Funded Enterprises	6016	1710	1601	2983
中外合资经营企业	Enterprises with Foreign Investment	174	122	30	330
外资企业	Enterprises with Sole Fund	5842	1588	1571	2653
按餐饮行业小类分组	**By Sector of Catering**				
正餐服务	Dinner	50055	23662	22722	37946
快餐服务	Snack	14009	6647	3939	5302
按地区分	**By Region**				
乌鲁木齐市	Urumqi City	48269	22826	19092	32260
克拉玛依市	Karamay City	521	499	21	244
吐鲁番地区	Turpan Administrative Offices	82	72	10	66
哈密地区	Hami [Kumul] Administrative Offices	1481	248	1232	2017
昌吉回族自治州	Changji Hui Autonomous Prefecture	3165	514	2651	623
伊犁哈萨克自治州	Ili Kazak Autonomous Prefecture	1717	473	1244	407
伊犁州直属县(市)	Counties (Cities) Direct Under Ili Prefecture	1717	473	1244	407
巴音郭楞蒙古自治州	Bayangol Mongol Autonomous Prefecture	7526	4623	2187	6745
阿克苏地区	Aksu Administrative Offices	125	100	25	106
喀什地区	Kashgar [Kaxgar] Administrative Offices	540	409	132	380
生产建设兵团	Xinjiang Production and Construction Group	638	545	67	400

16-12 限额以上住宿企业资产及负债情况

Assets and Liabilities of Enterprises above Designated Size of Accommodation Services

单位：万元　　(2010 年)　　(10 000 yuan)

指　标	Item	资产合计 Total Assets	#流动资产 Working Capitals	#固定资产 Fixed Assets	负债合计 Total Liabilities
总　计	**Total**	**838981**	**200489**	**567556**	**499207**
按登记注册类型分	**By Status of Registration**				
内资企业	Domestic-funded Enterprises	783773	185048	530264	436381
国有企业	State-owned Enterprises	345994	71824	253581	146073
集体企业	Collective-owned Enterprises	9171	2027	7104	14199
联营企业	Joint Ounership Enterprises	3548	1391	1115	1042
国有联营企业	State Ounership Enterprises	3548	1391	1115	1042
有限责任公司	Limited Liability Corporations	249665	65484	165897	141259
国有独资公司	State Sole Funded Corporations	8200	3308	4768	5078
其他有限责任公司	Other Limited Liability Corporations	241465	62176	161129	136181
股份有限公司	Share-holding Corporations Ltd.	18757	3821	10051	12690
私营企业	Private Enterprises	152773	39814	89338	119931
私营独资企业	Private-funded Enterprises	12757	3498	7265	9405
私营合伙企业	Private Partnership Enterprises	3739	234	3428	4006
私营有限责任公司	Private Limited Liability Corporations	135882	35979	78357	105928
私营股份有限公司	Private Share-holding Corporations Ltd	395	103	288	592
其他企业	Other Enterprises	3865	687	3178	1187
港、澳、台商投资企业	Enterprises With Funds from Hong Kong, Macao and Taiwan	55208	15441	37292	62826
合资经营企业（港或澳、台资）	Joint-venture Enterprises (Funds from Hong Kong, Macao and Taiwan)	55208	15441	37292	62826
按住宿行业分组	**By Sector of**				
旅游饭店	Tourist Hotel	795682	190442	538201	473574
一般旅馆	Ordinary Hotel	43299	10047	29355	25633
按星级等级分	**Classified by Stars**				
五　星	Five-Star	237059	48936	175899	149701
四　星	Four-Star	197585	39522	145553	113604
三　星	Three-Star	265373	78108	155347	155962
二　星	Two-Star	47313	14307	28356	20683
一　星	One-Star	36343	10495	23670	40046
其　他	Other	55308	9121	38731	19211
按地区分	**By Region**				
乌鲁木齐市	Urumqi City	406410	115823	265284	225449
克拉玛依市	Karamay City	51278	2496	47582	50196
吐鲁番地区	Turpan Administrative Offices	9784	3008	3817	8455
哈密地区	Hami [Kumul] Administrative Offices	33079	7409	17287	20390
昌吉回族自治州	Changji Hui Autonomous Prefecture	19254	3086	13565	18287
伊犁哈萨克自治州	Ili Kazak Autonomous Prefecture	116796	27006	77124	58513
伊犁州直属县(市)	Counties (Cities) Direct Under Ili Prefecture	81956	18155	53925	41352
塔城地区	Tacheng [Tarbagatai] Administrative Offices	12248	3719	7359	8300
阿勒泰地区	Altay Administrative Offices	22592	5132	15840	8861
博尔塔拉蒙古自治州	Bortala Mongol Autonomous Prefecture	2510	1109	903	2004
巴音郭楞蒙古自治州	Bayangol Mongol Autonomous Prefecture	66948	10400	51461	55958
阿克苏地区	Aksu Administrative Offices	17121	4552	12390	6300
克孜勒苏柯尔克孜自治州	Kizilsu Kirgiz Autonomous Prefecture	7341	628	6415	4035
喀什地区	Kashgar [Kaxgar] Administrative Offices	24583	4653	19247	12441
和田地区	Hotan Administrative Offices	10541	2722	7414	3375
生产建设兵团	Xinjiang Production and Construction Group	73336	17597	45067	33804

16-13 限额以上批发企业主要财务指标
Main Financial Indicators of Wholesale Enterprises above Designated Size

单位：万元　　(2010 年)　　(10 000 yuan)

指　　标	Item	商品销售收　入 Revenue of Product Sales	商品销售成　本 Cost of Product Sales	商品销售税金及附加 Sales Tax and Extra Changes	商品销售利　润 Profits of Product Sales
总　计	**Total**	**30389900**	**28945933**	**66158**	**1258586**
按登记注册类型分	**By Status of Registration**				
内资企业	Domesticfunded Enterprises	30229364	28825243	66126	1218772
国有企业	State-owned Enterprises	6908629	6499986	36880	281742
集体企业	Collective-owned Enterprises	349601	331990	247	15316
联营企业	Joint Ownership Enterprises	30634	29118	1	1377
国有联营企业	State Joint Ownership Enterprises	30634	29118	1	1377
有限责任公司	Limited Liability Corporations	10689071	10358402	17050	298528
国有独资公司	State Sole Funded Corporations	972941	909658	12246	50345
其他有限责任公司	Other Limited Liability Corporations	9716130	9448744	4804	248183
股份有限公司	Share-holding Corporations Ltd.	8271453	7880816	8037	391071
私营企业	Private Enterprises	3964278	3709701	3905	230277
私营独资企业	Private-funded Enterprises	22230	20750	21	1378
私营合伙企业	Private Partnership Enterprises	2287	2131	1	155
私营有限责任公司	Private Limited Liability Corporations	3839398	3593150	3856	222078
私营股份有限公司	Private Share-holding Corporation Ltd.	100363	93670	27	6666
其他企业	Other Enterprises	15698	15230	6	461
港、澳、台商投资企业	Enterprises With Funds from Hong Kong, Macao and Taiwan	120222	84468	12	35742
合资经营企业（港或澳、台资）	Joint-Venture Enterprises	109967	75426	12	34529
港、澳、台商独资经营企业	Enterprises with Sole Funds from Hong Kong, Macao and Taiwan	10255	9042		1213
外商投资企业	Foreign funded Enterprises	40314	36222	20	4072
中外合资经营企业	Enterprises with Foreign Investment	40314	36222	20	4072
按批发行业小类分组	**By Sector of Wholesale**				
农畜产品批发业	Wholesale of Farm Produce and Livestock Products	4418796	4110089	1557	292044
谷物、豆及薯类批发业	Wholesale of Grain,Bean and Potato	372268	345280	85	25796
种子、饲料批发业	Wholesale of Seed and Fodder	177773	146689	67	31237
棉、麻批发业	Wholesale of Cotton and Lliner	3843850	3596614	1403	233072
其他农畜产品批发业	Wholesale of Other Farm Produce and Livestoclc Products	24905	21506	2	1939
食品、饮料及烟草制品批发业	Wholesale of Food,Beverages and Tobaccos	1228288	1066369	44049	106173
米、面制品及食用油批发业	Wholesale of Rice, Flour and Edible Oil	147047	141797	44	8538
糕点、糖果及糖批发业	Wholesale of Pastry,Candy and Sugar	16476	15178	21	780
果品、蔬菜批发业	Wholesale of Fruit and Vegetable	115513	104265	83	10258
肉、禽、蛋及水产品批发业	Wholesale of Meat,Birds and Equatic Products	3780	3418	6	355
盐及调味品批发业	Wholesale of Salt and Condiment Flavoring Material	29367	24178	73	5102
饮料及茶叶批发业	Wholesale of Soft Drink and Tea Leaf	48073	44151	69	3690
烟草制品批发业业	Wholesale of Tobaccos	837691	706334	43703	74244
其他食品批发业	Wholesale of Other Food	30341	27048	50	3206
纺织、服装及日用品批发业	Wholesale of Textitle, Garments and Daily Consumer Articles	183383	168506	162	11097
纺织品、针织品及原料批发业	Wholesale of Textile,Hosiery and Raw Material	59997	58236	11	1470
服装批发业	Wholesale of Garment	65452	57124	88	6062
化妆品及卫生用品批发业	Wholesale of Cosmetics and Health Aids	20545	19438	17	642
其他日用品批发业	Wholesale of Other Covenience Goods	37389	33708	46	2923

16-13 续表 Continued

单位：万元 (10 000 yuan)

指　　标	Item	商品销售收入 Revenue of Product Sales	商品销售成本 Cost of Product Sales	商品销售税金及附加 Sales Tax and Extra Changes	商品销售利润 Product Sales Profits
文化、体育用品及器材批发业	Wholesale of Culture, Sports Goods and Apparatus	114549	103206	216	10540
图书批发业	Wholesale of Books	78980	69457	197	9326
其他文化用品批发业	Wholesale of Other Culture Products	35569	33749	19	1214
医药及医疗器械批发业	Wholesale of Medicines and Medical Appliances	232930	213707	392	16842
西药批发业	Wholesale of Western Medicine	202576	187080	358	14720
中药材及中成药批发业	Wholesale of Chinese Medicinal Plant and Chinese Patent Medicine	30354	26627	34	2122
矿产品、建材及化工产品批发业	Wholesale of Mineral Products, Building Material and Chemical Products	22324145	21501274	16622	724863
煤炭及制品批发业	Wholesale of Coal and Related Products	131996	112820	2875	16892
石油及制品批发业	Wholesale of Petroleum and Related Products	17458097	16870466	11174	535815
金属及金属矿批发业	Wholesale of Metal and Metal Materials	2808544	2696856	1649	107401
建材批发业	Wholesale of Building Materials	361874	352570	109	7957
化肥批发业	Wholesale of Fertilizer	1146114	1085386	314	32704
农药批发业	Wholesale of Pesticides	5921	5658	4	259
农用薄膜批发业	Wholesale of Film Agriculture	2083	2056	3	
其他化工产品批发业	Wholesale of Other Chemical Product	409516	375462	494	23835
机械设备、五金交电及电子产品批发业	Wholesale of Machinery, Hardware and Electronic Equipments	1556348	1468819	1869	81628
农业机械批发业	Wholesale of Agriculture Machinery	111169	105622	53	5494
汽车、摩托车及零配件批发业	Wholesale of Motor Vehicles, Motorcycles and Parts	526802	491809	578	33895
五金、交电批发业	Wholesale of Hardware and Electromic Equipment	334302	331334	483	2109
家用电器批发业	Wholesale of Household Electrical Appliances	60339	56071	60	3810
计算机、软件及辅助设备批发业	Wholesale of Computer, Software and Accessory Equipment	88334	84092	199	3984
通讯及广播电视设备批发业	Wholesale of Communicating and Broadcasting Television Device	23298	22490	18	316
其他机械设备及电子产品批发业	Wholesale of Other Mechanical Equipment and Electromic Products	412104	377401	478	32020
贸易经纪与代理	Trades Broker and Agent	49451	46341	34	3076
其他批发业	Wholesales of Others	282010	267622	1257	12323
再生物资回收与批发业	Recovery and Wholesale of Regeneration Material	234435	228827	1173	4384
其他未列明的批发业	Wholesale of Un-listed	47575	38795	84	7939
按地区分	**By Region**				
乌鲁木齐市	Urumqi City	18370478	17693319	28060	616423
克拉玛依市	Karamay City	581347	524003	2896	54448
吐鲁番地区	Turpan Administrative Offices	264835	249428	1705	13702
哈密地区	Hami [Kumul] Administrative Offices	448553	421543	2480	22201
昌吉回族自治州	Changji Hui Autonomous Prefecture	631713	592130	4294	39157
伊犁哈萨克自治州	Ili Kazak Autonomous Prefecture	2813099	2724561	9350	74390
伊犁州直属县(市)	Counties (Cities) Direct Under Ili Prefecture	2020171	1974059	4375	38516
塔城地区	Tacheng [Tarbagatai] Administrative Offices	603478	573174	3316	25411
阿勒泰地区	Altay Administrative Offices	189450	177328	1659	10463
博尔塔拉蒙古自治州	Bortala Mongol Autonomous Prefecture	499354	465801	1523	31979
巴音郭楞蒙古自治州	Bayangol Mongol Autonomous Prefecture	821429	760346	5212	55872
阿克苏地区	Aksu Administrative Offices	1128960	1053351	1929	65614
克孜勒苏柯尔克孜自治州	Kizilsu Kirgiz Autonomous Prefecture	32846	28536	25	4284
喀什地区	Kashgar [Kaxgar] Administrative Offices	859251	736626	3905	67586
和田地区	Hotan Administrative Offices	149783	139867	1386	8504
生产建设兵团	Xinjiang Production and Construction Group	3788252	3556422	3393	204426

16-14 限额以上零售企业主要财务指标

Main Financial Indicators of Retail Enterprises above Designated Size

单位：万元 (2010 年) (10 000 yuan)

指　　标	Item	商品销售收入 Revenue of Product Sales	商品销售成本 Cost of Product Sales	商品销售税金及附加 Sales Tax and Extra Changes	商品销售利润 Product Sales Profits
总　计	**Total**	**4538859**	**4059924**	**16894**	**458369**
按登记注册类型分	**By Status of Registration**				
内资企业	Domestic Funded Enterprises	4044914	3624359	13958	402925
国有企业	State-owned Enterprises	1132425	1045697	1697	83535
集体企业	Collective-owned Enterprises	4513	4044	19	550
股份合作企业	Share-holding Cooperative Enterprises	2037	1794	3	241
有限责任公司	Limited Liability Corporations	764908	637919	2891	114892
国有独资公司	State Sole Funded Corporations	46791	40437	261	6058
其他有限责任公司	Other Limited Liability Corporations	718117	597482	2630	108834
股份有限公司	Share-holding Corporations Ltd.	273137	222370	3468	52702
私营企业	Private Enterprises	1867894	1712535	5880	151005
私营独资企业	Private-funded Enterprises	30996	28269	79	1749
私营合伙企业	Private Partnership Enterprises	5274	5039	6	135
私营有限责任公司	Private Limited Liability Corporations	1822226	1660121	5770	147743
私营股份有限公司	Private Share-holding Corporation Ltd.	9398	19106	25	1378
港、澳、台投资企业	Enterprises With Funds from Hong Kong, Macao and Taiwan	103634	89982	241	13411
港、澳、台商独资经营企业	Enterprises with Sole Funds from Hong Kong, Macao and Taiwan	103634	89982	241	13411
外商投资企业	Foreign funded Enterprises	390311	345583	2695	42033
中外合资经营企业	Enterprises with Foreign Investment	344661	307336	2695	34630
外资企业	Enterprises with Sole Fund	45650	38247		7403
按零售行业小类分组	**By Sector of Retail**				
综合零售业	Integrated Retail	799323	669301	6762	113464
百货零售业	Retail of General Merchandise	550552	457648	5591	84085
超级市场零售业	Retail of Supermarket	246124	209307	1170	29055
其他综合零售业	Retail of Other Integrate	2647	2346	1	324
食品、饮料及烟草制品专门零售业	Monopoly Retail of Foods, Beverages and Tobacco	12148	10956	15	1148
粮油零售业	Retail of Grain and Oil	5409	4954		454
饮料及茶叶零售业	Retail of Soft Drink and Tea Leaf	2594	2314	10	270
烟草制品零售业	Retail of Tobaccos	4145	3688	5	424
纺织、服装及日用品专门零售业	Monopoly Retail of Textile, Garments and Daily Consumer Articles	138224	111485	949	23728
服装零售业	Garment Retail	135878	109401	945	23509
钟表、眼镜零售业	Retail of Timelceeper and Spectacle	1130	967	2	162
化妆品及卫生用品零售	Retail of Cosmetics and Washing Articles	11	5		6
其他日用品零售业	Retail of other Covenience Goods	1205	1112	2	51
文化、体育用品及器材专门零售业	Monopoly Retail of Cultural, Sports Goods And Apparatus	137805	98204	766	38050
文具用品零售业	Retail of Stationery and Office Supplies	1013	949	2	63
图书零售业	Retail of Books	115369	87842	218	26889
珠宝首饰零售业	Retail of Bijouterie	18764	6914	542	10996
照相器材零售业	Retail of Photographic Materials	2659	2499	4	102

16-14 续表 Continued

单位：万元 (10 000 yuan)

指 标	Item	商品销售收入 Revenue of Product Sales	商品销售成本 Cost of Product Sales	商品销售税金及附加 Sales Taxes and Extra Changes	商品销售利润 Product Sales Profits
医药及医疗器材专门零售业	Monopoly Retail of Medicine and Medical-care Apparatus	623784	566003	1634	55869
药品零售业	Retail of Medcine	620748	563756	1624	55089
医疗用品及器材零售	Wholesale of Medical Treatment and Equipment	3036	2247	10	780
汽车、摩托车、燃料及零配件专门零售业	Monopoly Retail of Car, Motor, Fuel and Parts as Well as Components	2365751	2233942	5229	136952
汽车零售业	Retail of Automobiles	1572067	1477654	4478	103200
汽车零配件零售业	Retail of Automobiles' Parts	6681	6048	4	595
摩托车及零配件零售业	Retail of Motorcycle and Fittings	12016	10860	7	819
机动车燃料零售业	Retail of Auto Fuel	774987	739380	740	32338
家用电器及电子产品专门零售业	Monopoly Retail of House hold Electric Appliancesound Electronic Products	310307	280666	631	27483
家用电器零售业	Retail of Electric Appliances	207478	187082	350	18675
计算机、软件及辅助设备零售业	Retail of Cumputers,Software and Office Appliances	68334	62987	204	4942
通讯设备零售业	Retail of Telecommunication Equipments	31446	27841	72	3567
其他电子产品零售	Retail of Electric Products	3049	2756	5	299
五金、家具及室内装修材料专门零售业	Monopoly Retail of Hardware, Furniture and Indoor Decorating Material	126329	69688	721	56564
五金零售业	Retail of Hardware	8903	8636	4	199
家具零售业	Retail of Living Equipment	114295	58057	713	56237
其他室内装修材料零售业	Retail of Other Indoor Hardware Fitting	3131	2995	4	128
无店铺及其他零售业	Retail of Storeless and Others	85188	19679	187	5111
生活用燃料零售业	Retail of Life Fuels	17656	13603	166	3676
其他未列明的零售业	Retail of Un-listed	7532	6076	21	1435
按地区分	**By Region**				
乌鲁木齐市	Urumqi City	3218455	2847532	13088	350937
克拉玛依市	Karamay City	122504	112272	284	9949
吐鲁番地区	Turpan Administrative Offices	11695	10106	11	1578
哈密地区	Hami [Kumul] Administrative Offices	103560	96014	183	6817
昌吉回族自治州	Changji Hui Autonomous Prefecture	116230	115209	166	10671
伊犁哈萨克自治州	Ili Kazak Autonomous Prefecture	142505	125106	341	14787
伊犁州直属县(市)	Counties (Cities) Direct Under Ili Prefecture	110461	96889	242	11288
塔城地区	Tacheng [Tarbagatai] Administrative Offices	24685	21824	23	2608
阿勒泰地区	Altay Administrative Offices	7359	6393	76	891
博尔塔拉蒙古自治州	Bortala Mongol Autonomous Prefecture	9913	8702	11	1200
巴音郭楞蒙古自治州	Bayangol Mongol Autonomous Prefecture	154707	141104	374	13229
阿克苏地区	Aksu Administrative Offices	115482	104489	95	13398
克孜勒苏柯尔克孜自治州	Kizilsu Kirgiz Autonomous Prefecture	3868	3214	3	651
喀什地区	Kashgar [Kaxgar] Administrative Offices	111984	95786	1804	8885
和田地区	Hotan Administrative Offices	19570	17325	94	2151
生产建设兵团	Xinjiang Production and Construction Group	408386	383065	440	24116

16-15 限额以上餐饮企业主要财务指标

Main Financial Indicators of Catering Enterprises above Designated Size

单位：万元 (2010 年) (10 000 yuan)

指标	Item	主营业务收入 Revenue from Principal Business	主营业务成本 Cost of Principal Business	主营业务税金及附加 Tax and Addition of Major Business	主营业务利润 Profit From Principal Business
总计	**Total**	**78900**	**39746**	**4884**	**32297**
按登记注册类型分	**By Status of Registration**				
内资企业	Domestic-funded Enterprises	58834	32688	3868	20305
国有企业	State – owned Enterprises	3337	2071	221	1045
集体企业	Collective – owned Enterprises	404	222	40	142
有限责任公司	Limited Liability Corporations	6479	3295	350	2334
其他有限责任公司	Other Limited Liability Corporations	6479	3295	350	2334
私营企业	Private Enterprises	48614	27100	3257	16784
私营独资企业	Private-funded Enterprises	6299	4074	750	1477
私营合伙企业	Private Partnership Enterprises	864	428	47	388
私营有限责任公司	Private Limited Liability Corporations	41451	22598	2460	14919
外商投资企业	Foreign Funded Enterprises	20066	7058	1016	11992
中外合资经营企业	Enterprises with Foreign Investment	1019	546	52	422
外资企业	Enterprises with Sole Fund	19047	6512	964	11570
按餐饮行业小类分组	**By Sector of Catering**				
正餐服务	Dinner	52463	30259	3503	16727
快餐服务	Snack	26437	9487	1381	15570
按地区分	**By Region**				
乌鲁木齐市	Urumqi City	56441	25929	3051	25986
克拉玛依市	Karamay City	4115	2917	269	929
吐鲁番地区	Turpan Administrative Offices	404	222	40	142
哈密地区	Hami [Kumul] Administrative Offices	277	207	19	52
昌吉回族自治州	Changji Hui Autonomous Prefecture	1852	958	120	274
伊犁哈萨克自治州	Ili Kazak Autonomous Prefecture	1707	973	122	612
伊犁州直属县(市)	Counties (Cities) Direct Under Ili Prefecture	1707	973	122	612
巴音郭楞蒙古自治州	Bayangol Mongol Autonomous Prefecture	10441	6393	784	3264
阿克苏地区	Aksu Administrative Offices	658	371	37	250
喀什地区	Kashgar [Kaxgan] Administratine Offices	1627	983	387	258
生产建设兵团	Xinjiang Production and Construction Group	1378	793	55	530

16-16 限额以上住宿企业主要财务指标

Main Financial Indicators of Hotels Enterprises above Designated

单位：万元 (2010 年) (10 000 yuan)

指　标	Item	主营业务收入 Revenue from Principal Business	主营业务成本 Cost of Principal Business	主营业务税金及附加 Tax and Addition of Major Business	主营业务利润 Profit From Principal Business
总　计	**Total**	**304628**	**136643**	**17146**	**139564**
按登记注册类型分	**By Status of Registration**				
内资企业	Domestic-funded Enterprises	293632	133913	16596	131848
国有企业	State-owned Enterprises	115687	50099	6179	55214
集体企业	Collective-owned Enterprises	6248	1757	308	4183
联营企业	Joint Ownership Enterprises	304	29	17	258
国有联营企业	State Joint Ownership Enterprises	304	29	17	258
有限责任公司	Limited Liability Corporations	94927	53754	5846	33015
国有独资公司	State Sole Funded Corporations	4198	1220	235	2745
其他有限责任公司	Other Limited Liability Corporations	90729	52534	5611	30270
股份有限公司	Share-holding Corporations Ltd.	4832	2210	216	1527
私营企业	Private Enterprises	68776	23419	4012	37456
私营独资企业	Private-funded Enterprises	10521	2913	539	7043
私营合伙企业	Private Partnership Enterprises	910	311	51	549
私营有限责任公司	Private Limited Liability Corporation	57008	20190	3403	29550
私营股份有限公司	Private Share-holding Corporation Ltd	337	5	19	314
其他企业	Other Enterprises	2858	2645	18	195
港、澳、台商投资企业	Enterprises With Funds from Hong Kong, Macao and Taiwan	10996	2730	550	7716
合资经营企业（港或澳、台资）	Joint-venture Enterprises (Funds from Hong Kong, Macao and Taiwan)	10996	2730	550	7716
按住宿行业分组	**By Sector of National Economic**				
旅游饭店	Tourist Hotel	286510	130493	15934	131016
一般旅馆	Ordinary Hotel	18118	6150	1212	8548
按星级等级分	**Classified by Stars**				
五 星	Five-Star	71065	41144	4330	25592
四 星	Four-Star	79402	34118	4127	38115
三 星	Three-Star	104180	45302	6071	47446
二 星	Two-Star	22767	8142	1109	12976
一 星	One-Star	9410	2332	482	6596
其 他	Other	17804	5605	1027	8839
按地区分	**By Region**				
乌鲁木齐市	Urumqi City	172961	77008	10274	80671
克拉玛依市	Karamay City	7718	8263	422	-967
吐鲁番地区	Turpan Administrative Offices	4183	2013	139	2030
哈密地区	Hami [Kumul] Administrative Offices	14481	6822	516	6640
昌吉回族自治州	Changji Hui Autonomous Prefecture	5686	1726	276	2911
伊犁哈萨克自治州	Ili Kazak Autonomous Prefecture	38560	17260	2195	18744
伊犁州直属县(市)	Counties (Cities) Direct Under Ili Prefecture	26768	10742	1493	14308
塔城地区	Tacheng [Tarbagatai] Administrative Offices	5111	3448	330	1197
阿勒泰地区	Altay Administrative Offices	6681	3070	372	3239
博尔塔拉蒙古自治州	Bortala Mongol Autonomous Prefecture	2203	641	159	1403
巴音郭楞蒙古自治州	Bayangol Mongol Autonomous Prefecture	16212	6564	940	8708
阿克苏地区	Aksu Administrative Offices	4490	1086	193	2089
克孜勒苏柯尔克孜自治州	Kizilsu Kirgiz Autonomous Prefecture	1348	439	130	777
喀什地区	Kashgar [Kaxgar] Administrative Offices	6630	2526	223	2391
和田地区	Hotan Administrative Offices	3423	1589	162	1505
生产建设兵团	Xinjiang Production and Construction Group	26733	10706	1517	12662

16-17 限额以上批发和零售业商品销售类值

Total Sales of Enterprises above Designated Size in Wholesale and Retail Trades by Category of Commodities

单位：万元 (10 000 yuan)

项 目	Item	销售总额 Value		批 发 Wholesale Trades		零 售 Retail Trades	
		2009	2010	2009	2010	2009	2010
总 计	**Total**	**28498927**	**39909349**	**24446306**	**34674711**	**4052621**	**5234638**
食品、饮料、烟酒类	Foods, Beverages, Tobacco and Liquor	2455443	2952397	2177726	2589202	277717	363195
服装、鞋帽类、针纺织品类	Garments, Shoes and Hats, Knitted Goods and Textiles	446414	594526	78160	101594	368254	492932
化妆品类	Cosmetics	82557	102757	17031	25162	65526	77595
金银珠宝类	Gold and Silver Jewelry	70088	109579		2921	70088	106658
日用品类	Commodity Categories	110963	157096	26055	35105	84908	121991
五金、电料类	Hardwares, Electrical Materials	32233	20675	27651	14116	4582	6559
体育、娱乐用品类	Sports and Recreational Articles	10702	22845	56	3170	10646	19675
书报杂志类	Books and Newspapers	193057	245418	83142	116152	109915	129266
电子出版物及音像制品类	E-journal and Video Products	2790	2797	1415	741	1375	2056
家用电器及音像器材类	Household Appliances and Video Equipments	321681	311083	123936	86616	197745	224467
中西药品类	Chinese Traditional Medicine and Western Medicines	745997	920952	302132	351821	443865	569131
文化办公用品类	Office Articles	214088	233395	140438	142555	73650	90840
家具类	Furnitures	11939	120761	8003	577	3936	120184
通讯器材类	Communication Appliances	93279	100169	35579	44624	57700	55545
煤炭及制品类	Coal and Related Products	101746	139307	95842	131293	5904	8014
木材及制品类	Wood and Wooden Products	552		552			
石油及制品类	Petroleum and Related Products	13064995	21392892	12122893	20189641	942102	1203251
化工材料及制品类	Raw Chemical Materials and Related Products	1563369	1434494	1563369	1434494		
金属材料类	Metal Materials	1986950	2959212	1986950	2959212		
建筑装潢材料类	Building and Decoration Materials	207836	126953	205940	115370	1896	11583
机电产品及设备类	Mechanical and Electrical Products and Accessories	872202	1001030	863167	987138	9035	13892
汽车类	Automobile	1759349	2196787	475858	616475	1283491	1580312
种子饲料类	Seed and Fddestuff	133444	147463	133444	147463		
棉麻类	Cotton and Hemp	3708421	4139974	3708421	4137739		2235
其他类	Others	308832	476787	268546	441730	40286	35057

主要统计指标解释

社会消费品零售总额 指批发和零售业、餐饮业、新闻出版业、邮政业和其他服务业等，售予城乡居民用于生活消费的商品和社会集团用于公共消费的商品之总量。社会消费品零售总额包括：

一、批发和零售业企业（单位）售予城乡居民用于生活消费和社会集团用于公共消费的商品。包括：

1.售予城乡居民的各种生活消费品；

2.售予入境旅游的外国人、华侨、港澳台同胞的各类商品；

3.售予行政事业单位、社会团体、军队和武警等机构的商品，以及以零售方式售予各类企业的商品。具体包括：用于非生产和社会交往的办公用品，如通讯设备、计算器具和设备、电讯网络设备、文印设备、音像视听器材和设备、纸张、本册、文具及装订文印材料、家具、日用电器、针纺织品、清洁卫生用品、文体用品、奖品、纪念品、礼品等；供内部人员乘坐的交通工具和燃料；用于办公设施修缮的各类配件、材料、工具等；用于取暖和防暑降温的设备、燃料、材料及食品等；专用于教学的用品和设备；非营利医疗机构的中、西药品、中药材和医疗设备器材；非专用的劳动保护用品；不对外营业的内部食堂用的餐具、炊具、设备、清洁卫生工具和食品、燃料等；军队、武警用于其人员生活的衣着品和个人用品；其他各类非生产性设备和用品。

二、餐饮业出售的主食、菜肴、烟酒饮料和其他商品。

三、新闻出版业、邮政业售予城乡居民、企事业单位、军队和武警等机构的书报杂志、音像制品、邮品等。

四、其他服务业出售的食品、烟酒饮料、服装鞋帽、日常生活用品、医药保健用品、艺术品、工艺美术品、玩具、殡葬用品以及其他消费品。

批发零售贸易业商品购、销、存总额 指各种登记注册类型的批发和零售业企业(单位)以本企业(单位)为总体的，从国内、国外市场购进的商品总量，销售和出口的商品总量、库存商品总量等情况。该指标可以反映商品流转过程中商品的购进、销售、库存之间的比例关系和存在的问题。

购进总额 指从本企业(单位)以外的单位和个人购进(包括从境外直接进口)作为转卖或加工后转卖的商品总额。它反映批发和零售贸易业从国内、国外市场上购进商品的总量。商品购进包括：(1)从工农业生产者购进的商品；(2)从出版社、报社的出版发行部门购进的图书、杂志和报纸;(3)从各种登记注册类型的批发零售贸易企业(单位)购进的商品;(4)从其他单位购进的商品，如从机关、团体、企业等单位购进的剩余物资，从餐饮业、服务业购进的商品，从海关、市场管理部门购进的缉私和没收的商品，从居民手中收购的废旧商品等；(5)从国(境)外直接进口的商品。不包括企业(单位)为自身经营用和未通过买卖行为而收入的商品以及销售退回、商品升溢等。

销售总额 指对本企业(单位)以外的单位和个人出售(包括对境外直接出口)的商品总额。它反映批发和零售贸易业在国内市场上销售商品以及出口商品的总量。商品销售包括：(1)售给城乡居民和社会集团消费用的商品；(2)售给工业、农业、建筑业、运输邮电业、批发零售贸易业、餐饮业、服务业等作为生产、经营使用的商品；(3)售给批发零售贸易业作为转卖或加工后转卖的商品；(4)对国(境)外直接出口的商品。不包括出售本企业(单位)自用的废旧包装用品；未通过买卖行为付出的商品；经本单位介绍，由买卖双方直接结算，本单位只收取手续费的业务；购货退出的商品以及商品损耗和损失等。

库存总额 指报告期末各种登记注册类型的批发零售贸易企业(单位)已取得所有权的商品。它反映批发和零售贸易企业(单位)的商品库存情况和对市场商品供应的保证程度。商品库存包括：(1)存放在批发和零售业经营单位(如门市部、批发站、经营处)仓库、货场、货柜和货架中的商品；(2)挑选、整理、包装中的商品；(3)已记入购进而尚未运到本单位的商品，即发货单或银行承兑凭证已到而货未到的部分；(4)寄放他处的商品，如因购货方拒绝承付而暂时存放在购货方的商品和已办完加工成品收回手续而未提回的商品；(5)委托其他单位代销(未作销售或调出)尚未售出的商品；(6)代其他单位购进尚未交付的商品。不包括所有权不属于本单位的商品、拨付除批发零售贸易业以外的其他行业所属独立核算加工厂等加工生产尚未收回成品的商品、代国家物资储备部门保管的商品等。

住宿和餐饮业营业额 指住宿和餐饮业法人企业（单位）在经营活动中因提供服务或销售商品等取得的收入。包括：客房收入、餐费收入、商品销售额和其他收入。客房收入指住宿和餐饮业法人企业（单位）在经营活动中因提供住宿服务取得的收入。餐费收入指住宿和餐饮业法人企业、（单位）因为顾客提供就餐服务取得的收入，包括经烹饪、调制加工后出售的各种食品，如主食、炒菜、凉拌菜等的收入。商品销售额指住宿和餐饮业法人企业（单位）伴随服务而出售商品所取得的收入（含增值税）。其他收入指营业收入中除客房收入、餐费收入、商品销售额以外的其他收入，包括娱乐、健身和商务服务等。

Explanatory Notes on Main Statistical Indicators

Total Retail Sales of Consumer Goods refer to the sum of retail sales of commodities sold by wholesale and retail trades, catering services, publishing, post and telecommunications and other service industries to urban and rural households for household consumption and to social institutions for public consumption. Retail sales of consumer goods include:

1) Sales sold by wholesale and retail trades to urban and rural households for household consumption and to social institutions for public consumption.

a) of commodities to urban and rural households;

b) of commodities to foreigners, overseas Chinese and Chinese compatriots from Hong Kong, Macao and Taiwan visiting China;

c) of commodities to government agencies, institutions, social organizations, military and armed police units, and commodities to enterprises in the form of retail sales. More specifically, they include: office facilities and articles for non-production purposes such as communications equipment, computing equipment and instruments, TV and network equipment, printing and copying equipment, audio-visual equipment and instruments, paper, notebooks, stationeries, furniture, electric appliances, knitwear, sanitation and cleaning articles, cultural and sport articles, articles for prizes, souvenirs, etc.; transport vehicles and fuels for employees; materials, spare parts and tools for the maintenance of office facilities; equipment, fuels, materials and food for winter heating or summer cooling purposes; articles and equipment for teaching purpose; Chinese and western medicines and medical equipment and facilities purchased by non profit-making medical institutes; non-specialized work safety articles; cooking utensils, tableware, equipment, cleaning articles, food and fuels purchased by in-house cafeterias; clothes and personal articles purchased by military or armed police units for their officials and soldiers; and other equipment and articles for non-production purposes.

2) Sales of stable food, cooked dishes, beverages, tobaccos and other articles by catering units.

3) Sales of books, newspapers, magazines, audio-visual products and post products by publishing, post and telecommunications departments to urban and rural households and to enterprises, institutions, military and armed police units.

4) Sales of food, beverages, tobaccos, clothing, hats, footwear, articles for daily use, medicines, medical and health articles, work of art, handicrafts, toys, funeral articles and other articles by other service industries.

Purchase, Sales and Stock of Commodities by Wholesale and Retail Trades refer to the total volume of commodities purchased, total volume of sales and exports, and the stock of commodities by wholesale and retail enterprises (establishments) of different status of registration from domestic and overseas markets. This indicator reflects the relationship among purchase, sales and stock of commodities in the circulation of goods and reveals the existing problems.

Total Purchases of Commodities refer to the total value of purchases of commodities by enterprises (establishments) from other establishments or individuals (including direct import from abroad) for the purpose of re-selling, either with or without further processing of the commodities purchased. This indicator is used to show the total value of purchases of commodities by wholesale and retail establishments from domestic and overseas markets. The purchases include: (1) agricultural and industrial products purchased from producers; (2) books, magazines and newspapers purchased from distribution departments of the publishers; (3) commodities purchased from wholesale and retail establishments of different status of registration; (4) commodities purchased from other units, such as surplus materials purchased from government agencies, enterprises or institutions, commodities purchased from hotels and catering services establishments, confiscated goods purchased from customs authorities or market management agencies, second-hand goods and wastes purchased from residents; and (5) commodities directly imported from abroad. Excluded are commodities purchased by enterprises (establishments) for use in their own business operation, commodities obtained without buying or selling procedures, rejected commodities, etc.

Total Sales of Commodities refer to value of commodities sold by the establishments to other establishments and individuals (including direct export to abroad). This indicator is used to show the total value of sales of commodities at domestic markets and export. The sales include: (1) commodities sold to urban and rural residents and social groups for their consumption; (2) commodities sold to establishments in industry, agriculture, construction, transportation, post and telecommunications, wholesale and retail trades, hotels and catering services, and public utility for their production and operation; (3) commodities sold to wholesale and retail establishments for re-selling, with or without further processing; and (4) commodities for direct export to abroad. Excluded are selling of waste packaging materials used by the establishments (units) themselves, commodities transferred without buying or selling procedures, commission income from brokerage in transactions for which settlement is directly handled by buyers and sellers, rejected commodities in the purchase, loss in commodities, etc.

Total Stock of Commodities refers to total commodities possessed by wholesale and retail enterprises (units) of various types of registration status at the end of the reference period, reflecting the commodity stock level of various wholesale and retail enterprises and the potential for market supply. It includes: (1) commodities located in storage, garages, counters, and shelves of operating units (such as sale stores, wholesale centres, and operating offices) of wholesale and retail enterprises; (2) commodities in the process of being selected, sorted, and packed; (3) commodities not arrived but recorded as purchase in the account, i.e. commodities not arrived but payment receipts for the commodities from the sellers or the banks arrived; (4) commodities deposited in other places rather than places mentioned above, for instance: commodities in the hold of purchasers temporarily due to the refusal of payment and commodities not taken back after going through the formalities; (5) commodities entrusted to other units to sell but not sold yet; (6) commodities purchased for other units but not delivered yet. Commodities not included as stock are those not owned by the enterprises (units), commodities on commission for processing but not yet delivered, imported commodities of agency of foreign trade enterprise but not yet delivered to ordering units and finally those put in stock on behalf of the state material reserves units.

Business Revenue of Hotels and Catering Services refers to revenue received from providing services or selling commodities by corporate enterprises and establishments engaged in hotels and catering services, including income from hotels, from catering services, from selling of commodities and from other services. Income from hotels refers to income of corporate enterprises and establishments engaged in hotels and catering services by providing lodging services. Income from catering services refers to income of corporate enterprises and establishments engaged in hotels and catering services by providing catering services, including selling of cooked or prepared foods such as staple food, cooked dishes or cold dishes. Income from selling of commodities refers to income of corporate enterprises and establishments engaged in hotels and catering services by selling commodities (including value-added tax) that accompany the services they provide. Income from other activities refers to income received other than income from hotels, catering services or selling of commodities, such as income from providing recreation, fitness or business services.

第十七篇 教育、科技和文化

CHAPTER 17 Education, Science & Technology and Culture

简要说明
Brief Introduction

本篇资料的主要内容及来源

教育统计资料包括研究生教育(高等学校研究生教育、科研机构研究生教育);普通高等学校本专科教育;普通中等教育(中等专业教育、技工学校、普通中学、职业高中、工读学校);初等教育(小学)、学前教育、特殊教育(盲聋哑和弱智儿童学校等)以及教育经费等资料。

教育部分资料由新疆维吾尔自治区教育厅依据年报资料整理提供。

科技统计资料包括科技活动基本情况、县级以上政府部门属研究与开发机构及科技信息与文献机构人员数、重大科学技术研究成果及奖励、专利申请和批准情况、高等学校科技活动情况、企事业单位专业技术人员情况、大中型工业企业科技活动情况、各类技术合同鉴定及执行情况、技术经济合同成交情况、技术流向地域情况等。

科技统计范围包括新疆地区有科技活动的企事业单位,具体涵盖规模以上工业企业(标准见工业篇)、各级各部门所属国有独立核算的科学研究与技术开发机构及科技情报与文献机构、普通高等学校等。

科技部分资料由新疆维吾尔自治区统计局社会科技统计处根据科技年报和新疆维吾尔自治区科技厅提供资料整理。

文化部分主要包括艺术表演团体、艺术表演场所、公共图书馆、博物馆、文化馆、档案馆、文化站、广播、电影、电视以及文物等文化单位的机构、人员、经费和业务活动情况。

文化部分资料是由新疆维吾尔自治区统计局社会科技统计处根据部门统计报表制度加工整理而成。艺术事业、图书馆事业、群众文化事业的资料主要来自新疆维吾尔自治区文化厅;档案馆资料来新疆维吾尔自治区档案局;文物资料来自新疆维吾尔自治区文物局;广播、电影、电视资料来自新疆维吾尔自治区广播电视局。

Main content and source of data of education

The data on education cover the situation on postgraduate (regular institutions of higher education,research institutions), regular institution of higher education (universities and colleges), regular secondary education, (professional secondary schools,technical schools,regular secondary school,vocational senior secondary schools, schools for juvenile delinquents);primary education (primary schools), preschool education, special education(schools for the blind, deaf-mutes and the retarded) and expenditure on education.

Statistical data on education compiled by the Statistics Bureau of Xinjiang in accordance with the data from the Bureau of Education.

Data on technology mainly include: condition of scientific and technological activities, state-owned research and development institutions and information and literature institutions at and above county level and persons engaged; the situation of science and technological achievements & prizes and patent applications, basic statistics on scientific and technological activities of high education, condition of professional scientific and technological personnel of enterprises and institutions, statistics on signing and implementing technical contracts, statistics on transaction in technical and economic contract, statistics on location of technical contract.

Statistical scope on technology include scientific and technical activities in enterprises and institution, they are mainly: industrial enterprises above designated size, state -owned research and development institutions and information and literature institutions at and above county level and persons engaged, regular institutions of high .

Data on technology compiled by the Statistics Bureau of Xinjiang in accordance with the data from the Bureau of Science &Technology.

Data on culture cover mainly the situations on institutions, personal and business activities of arts (performing groups and venues), libraries, museums, cultural centers, archives, cultural stations, broadcasting, films, televisions, news and publication.

Data on culture are collected and tabulated in accordance with the statistical reporting schemes stipulated by the Statistical Bureau of Xinjiang. Data on the causes of arts, libraries, mass culture are provided by the Xinjiang Bureau of Culture; Data on archives are from Xinjiang Bureau of Archives; Data on broadcasting, film and television are mainly from Xinjiang Bureau of Broadcasting.

17-1 主要年份各级各类学校数

Number of Schools by Level and Type in Main Years

单位：所 (unit)

年份 Year	普通高等学校 Regular Institutions of Higher Education	中等学校 Secondary Schools	普通中等专业学校 Specialized Secondary Schools	普通中学 Regular Secondary Schools	#高中 Senior Secondary Schools	职业高中 Vocational Secondary Schools	技工学校 Technical Schools	小学 Primary Schools	特殊教育学校 Special Schools
1978	10	2078	78	1997	673		10	9891	1
1980	12	2197	96	2032	720	21	48	9006	2
1985	14	2360	97	2147	794	65	51	8104	3
1990	21	2274	112	1958	766	134	70	7247	6
1995	21	2121	115	1792	554	145	69	7086	6
2000	20	2000	112	1711	484	112	65	6718	7
2001	21	2179	99	1929	472	89	62	6221	7
2002	24	2173	87	1945	507	83	58	6043	7
2003	26	2154	78	1932	500	86	58	5832	8
2004	28	2186	78	1965	498	84	59	5451	8
2005	31	2185	79	1961	503	87	58	5209	10
2006	31	2101	67	1891	486	84	59	4815	9
2007	32	2040	74	1830	454	75	61	4589	9
2008	32	1973	75	1759	444	82	57	4159	10
2009	32	1832	80	1610	413	82	60	3651	10
2010	32	1772	81	1545	385	83	63	3598	13

注：从 2006 年起，职业初中并入普通中学统计。（以下同）
Note:Number of regular secondary schools include the number of junion vocational secondary schools from 2006.(The same follows)

17-2 主要年份各级各类学校教师数

Number of Teachers by Level and Type of School in Main Years

单位：人 (person)

年份 Year	普通高等学校 Regular Institutions of Higher Education	中等学校 Secondary Schools	普通中等专业学校 Specialized Secondary Schools	普通中学 Regular Secondary Schools	#高中 Senior Secondary Schools	职业高中 Vocational Secondary Schools	技工学校 Technical Schools	小学 Primary Schools	特殊教育学校 Special Schools
1978	2458	44417	2543	41661	8064		213	82616	28
1980	3149	50056	3459	45232	9292	77	1288	98027	54
1985	5473	69185	4554	60942	15059	1567	2122	98294	67
1990	7002	78596	6158	65814	19318	3117	3507	95060	139
1995	7687	76584	6540	62934	14434	3494	3616	106001	162
2000	7924	89211	6786	75895	16069	3104	3426	131259	183
2001	9123	93126	6842	79419	17025	2546	4319	132137	187
2002	10369	96469	6031	84714	19031	2399	3325	132435	200
2003	11237	103156	5157	89332	20976	2440	6227	132284	237
2004	12239	106839	5494	94381	22809	3079	3885	134915	257
2005	12733	112941	4993	102168	25153	1696	4084	134768	262
2006	13783	120777	4339	106975	26815	2832	6631	134718	286
2007	15096	123246	5553	108232	27970	2295	7166	133626	298
2008	15755	121898	5381	108729	28735	2586	5202	132797	313
2009	16234	125152	6086	110842	29402	2464	5760	134263	319
2010	16506	128306	6232	113990	30231	2708	5706	133963	347

17-3 主要年份各级各类学校在校学生数
Number of Students Enrollment by Level and Type of School in Main Years

单位：人 (person)

年份 Year	普通高等学校 Regular Institutions of Higher Education	中等学校 Secondary Schools	普通中等专业学校 Specialized Secondary Schools	普通中学 Regular Secondary Schools	#高中 Senior Secondary Schools	职业高中 Vocational Secondary Schools	技工学校 Technical Schools	小学 Primary Schools	特殊教育学校 Special Schools
1978	10229	838560	23696	806386	128376		8478	2028771	270
1980	14308	886740	42362	823161	147446	1416	19801	2055513	371
1985	26500	1054293	33251	955356	223405	41825	23861	1966306	706
1990	31271	1015214	45985	863118	251067	65862	40249	1857246	610
1995	44918	912597	68586	749788	141330	54122	40101	2301274	643
2000	74063	1311845	105255	1132912	198639	51270	22408	2477413	674
2001	109815	1390360	97321	1228566	225411	47673	16800	2435667	922
2002	134831	1493580	83902	1338836	272381	50787	20055	2359788	3876
2003	151256	1584700	71499	1448531	315178	45330	19340	2289066	1863
2004	168247	1676971	71324	1517948	359147	61502	26197	2218109	2549
2005	188752	1717403	86744	1587850	387763	63158	26219	2143833	4961
2006	207672	1739422	108131	1572502	402321	23488	35301	2097975	4843
2007	226012	1742947	141162	1529092	413452	31741	40952	2058884	6396
2008	241288	1722667	150715	1483550	418701	41611	46791	2012004	5574
2009	253272	1695984	147439	1444836	417139	54777	48932	1973890	5991
2010	263835	1684027	152227	1422419	419141	59593	49788	1935798	5974

注：1.17-3、17-4、17-5 表中高等学校含研究生数。2.特殊教育学校 2002 年新增随班就读。(以下同)

Note: a) Institntions of higher education include the number of postgraduates with table 17-3,17-4,17-5.

b) In Special Schools for the blind,deaf, mute, new comers may follow the classes accordingly from the year 2002 (The same as follows).

17-4 主要年份各级各类学校招生数
Number of New Students Enrollment by Level and Type of School in Main Years

单位：人 (person)

年份 Year	普通高等学校 Regular Institutions of Higher Education	中等学校 Secondary Schools	普通中等专业学校 Specialized Secondary Schools	普通中学 Regular Secondary Schools	#高中 Senior Secondary Schools	职业高中 Vocational Secondary Schools	技工学校 Technical Schools	小学 Primary Schools	特殊教育学校 Special Schools
1980	3767	336402	14688	310931	73959	792	10531	433089	90
1985	9298	386074	13919	341123	93692	20429	10603	374643	91
1990	8034	356615	15586	297641	84567	27968	15420	335552	103
1995	12307	356814	25260	286318	58203	25643	19593	419717	165
2000	30689	486763	38866	418790	76744	20027	9080	364193	175
2001	42253	510469	26763	459878	93519	16621	7207	352975	135
2002	42808	551353	22241	501824	113366	16746	10442	346386	874
2003	44733	583033	24016	532987	126163	15378	10652	347619	369
2004	53204	606666	27990	536405	138315	27585	14686	347364	390
2005	58653	602335	34882	539922	145044	12416	15115	338539	847
2006	62395	599748	45536	522425	142853	13017	18770	337994	780
2007	68999	619218	65290	510080	146449	19201	24647	340108	1158
2008	74670	603352	62098	497579	147914	21610	22065	328647	840
2009	73904	593290	53692	489838	148869	28243	21517	318488	869
2010	79216	597621	60418	489356	153238	28767	19080	311861	1204

17-5 主要年份各级各类学校毕业生数

Number of Graduates by Level and Type of School in Main Years

单位：人 (person)

年 份 Year	普通高等学校 Regular Institutions of Higher Education	中等学校 Secondary Schools	普通中等专业学校 Specialized Secondary Schools	普通中学 Regular Secondary Schools	#高 中 Senior Secondary Schools	职业高中 Vocational Secondary Schools	技工学校 Technical Schools	小 学 Primary Schools	特殊教育学校 Special Schools
1978	1509	205862	8801	195542	53970		1519	388359	195
1980	814	264626	11946	246382	60370	341	5957	292515	37
1981	779	280171	17039	257478	67114	367	5287	397524	37
1982	4108	269927	17201	244853	69504	385	7488	310025	32
1983	4823	283120	11584	260906	77546	1144	9486	317227	27
1984	3426	275788	8130	257833	72191	2764	7061	295993	48
1985	3511	290077	8097	267302	68096	7424	7254	289045	73
1986	4797	296360	11551	268402	58585	8543	7864	307047	52
1987	8001	321981	10623	289556	73947	12280	9522	317820	101
1988	7792	346072	12026	311224	85718	12758	10064	288594	68
1989	6900	347719	12441	308467	86489	14650	12161	249888	57
1990	8603	343313	14260	297235	81062	17938	13880	259301	98
1991	7919	324031	15571	274913	79664	17505	16042	183350	159
1992	8402	310076	14950	260953	84518	18999	15174	268074	157
1993	7741	312284	16760	261502	78675	18558	15464	259468	104
1994	7734	250909	16206	198839	57090	18100	17764	262215	55
1995	10505	271992	18981	215756	44589	16490	20765	271227	57
1996	12272	271267	21701	215295	43478	15424	18847	279866	39
1997	10908	284580	21936	228287	37966	17181	17176	294420	71
1998	11401	313807	23090	259910	49702	18038	12769	321044	100
1999	11886	341434	25118	282486	52403	18826	15004	357801	84
2000	11220	363503	25879	308225	54985	17341	12058	371758	70
2001	16121	380946	26403	329801	59251	13881	10861	395010	104
2002	16380	410299	31598	356203	61932	15087	7411	411626	848
2003	25785	434523	31304	379269	70824	15685	8265	421443	264
2004	31013	468849	24758	420583	84418	15475	8033	417588	382
2005	37920	520798	19559	474621	103928	19492	7126	397592	714
2006	45810	541729	22515	501697	115422	5510	12007	373862	684
2007	48372	557512	25735	515494	127129	5943	10340	361921	716
2008	57076	557655	32537	507098	135240	6454	11566	349300	859
2009	60092	554905	41866	492259	137290	8883	11897	339836	935
2010	66903	547288	44478	473216	135706	14442	15152	334362	923

17-6 主要年份研究生数

Number of Postgraduates in Main Years

单位：人 (person)

年份 Year	招生数 New Enrollment	在校学生数 Total Enrollment	攻读博士学位 Working for Doctor's Degree	攻读硕士学位 Working for Master's Degree	毕业生数 Graduates	攻读博士学位 Working for Doctor's Degree	攻读硕士学位 Working for Master's Degree
1978	16	16		16			
1980	15	66		66			
1985	120	179		174	21		21
1990	73	256	3	253	112		112
1995	180	509	14	295	91		91
2000	544	1196	48	1148	235	5	230
2001	827	1749	80	1669	277	8	269
2002	1104	2495	112	2383	355	11	344
2003	1664	3629	186	3443	521	18	503
2004	2336	5120	283	4837	832	30	802
2005	2902	6938	415	6523	1066	35	1031
2006	3147	8421	489	7932	1628	90	1538
2007	3491	9623	549	9074	2244	110	2134
2008	3523	10317	595	9722	2786	132	2654
2009	4189	11635	653	10982	3021	121	2900
2010	4595	12675	713	11962	3360	158	3202

17-7 高等学校基本情况

Basic Statistics on Institutions of Higher Education by Type

单位：人 (2010 年) (person)

项目	Item	学校数(所) Schools (unit)	毕业生数 Graduates	招生数 New Enrollment	在校学生数 Total Enrollment	教职工数 Staff and Teachers	#专任教师 Full-time Teachers
总计	**Total**		**63543**	**74621**	**251160**	**32233**	**19724**
普通高等学校	Regular Institutionsof Higher Education	32	62038	73082	246959	26770	16506
综合大学	Multiversity	6	16914	18800	67016	8311	4794
理工院校	Science Engineering	11	14934	20642	53990	5117	3493
农业院校	Agriculture	4	9653	11746	41501	3773	2387
医药院校	Medicine	3	5029	4784	20081	2437	1480
师范院校	Normal Institutions	4	9986	10988	41563	4324	2712
财经学院	Economics and Finance	1	3232	3849	14956	1680	1035
政法院校	Politics & Law	2	1506	1487	4555	692	360
艺术院校	Art	1	784	786	3297	436	245
总计中：高职学院	In total: Vocational Training	16	22054	27151	72326	7227	4898
成人高等学校	Ordinary Class for Adult Higher Education		1505	1539	4201	5463	3218

17-8 中等专业学校基本情况

Basic Statistics on Specialized Secondary Schools by Type

单位: 人 (2010 年) (person)

项　目	Item	毕业生数 Graduates	招生数 New Student Enrollment	在校学生数 Student Enrollment	专业课教师 Teachers of Various Subjects
总　计	**Total**	**66383**	**98894**	**233319**	**5766**
农林牧渔类	Agriculture	8685	20187	35026	644
资源环境类	Resource and Environment	224	832	2317	81
能源与新能源类	Energy	1749	2601	6757	163
土木水利类	Civil and Hydraulic Engineering	2829	5640	12297	143
加工制造类	Processing and Manufacturing	7989	9222	23993	425
石油化工类	Petroleum and Chemical	5082	3725	10748	122
轻纺食品类	Textile and Food	2194	4366	9735	90
交通运输类	Transportation and Communication	3303	6355	13754	190
信息技术类	Information Technologies	5101	5254	14402	371
医药卫生类	Medcine and Health	9950	12638	38485	565
休闲保健类	Recreation and Health Care	492	1144	2373	29
财经商贸类	Economics and Finance	4241	4363	11137	464
旅游服务类	Trades and Tourism	2406	3992	9186	227
文化艺术类	Culture Arts and Physical Education	5478	8385	18754	499
体育与健身类	Sports and Fitness	1004	1683	4335	210
教育类	Teacher Training	3429	6686	15877	1072
司法服务类	Justice and Services	1319	748	1939	62
公共管理与服务类	Scoial and Public Affairs	425	487	1222	47
其　他	Others	483	586	982	362

17-9 普通中学和其他学校基本情况

Basic Statistics on Regular Secondary Schools and Other Schools by Type

单位: 人 (2010 年) (person)

项　目	Item	学校数(所) Schools (unit)	毕业生数 Graduates	招生数 New Enrollment	在校学生数 Total Enrollment	教职工数 Staff and Teachers	#专任教师 Full-time Teachers
普通中学	Regular Secondary Schools	1545	473216	489356	1422419	130627	113990
高　中	Senior Secondary Schools	385	135706	153238	419141		30231
初　中	Junior Secondary Schools	1160	337510	336118	1003278		83759
职业高中	Vocational Secondary Schools	83	14442	28767	59593	3911	2708
技工学校	Technical Shools	63	15152	19080	49788	8529	5706
小　学	Primary Schools	3598	334362	311861	1935798	148863	133963
特殊教育学校	Special Schools	13	923	1204	5974	461	347

17-10 各类成人教育情况

Basic Statistics on Adult Education by Type

单位: 人 (2010 年) (person)

项 目	Item	学校数(所) Schools (unit)	毕业生数 Graduates	在校学生数 Total Enrollment	教职工数 Staff and Teachers	#专任教师 Full-time Teachers
成人高等教育	Adult Education Schools	8	16522	52829	5463	3218
广播电视大学	Radio and TV Universities	2	645	2521	3674	2055
职工大学	Schools of Higher Education for Staff Workers	1	31	209	103	78
教育学院	Pedagogical Colleges	5	809	2774	1686	1085
普通高校办的成人班	Adult Classes run by Ordinary Colleges and Universities		15037	47325		
成人中等教育	Secondary Schools for Adults	22	7463	21499	1445	1144
成人中学	Secondary Schools for Adults	10	619	2168	185	49
成人技术培训学校	Technical adult college	1749	1498103	1783835	3693	1261
成人初等学校	Primary Schools for Adults	372	22907	41080	1742	371
#扫盲班	Literacy Courses		10118	20911	1250	265

17-11 主要年份教育发展水平

Development Level of Education in Main Years

年份 Year	各类学校在校生占全区人口比重(%) Students as Percentage of Total Population (%)	平均每万人口中(人) Number of Students per 10 000 Population (person)			大中小学生各占普通学校学生总数的比重(%) Students of Different Level as Percentage of Total Students(%)		
		大学生 University and College Students	中学生 Secondary School students	小学生 Primary School Students	大学生 University and College Students	中学生 Secondary School Students	小学生 Primary School Students
1978	23.34	8.30	654.00	1645.38	0.36	28.02	70.50
1980	23.04	11.15	641.47	1601.82	0.48	27.80	69.52
1985	22.39	19.47	701.88	1444.60	0.87	31.35	64.52
1990	18.99	20.45	564.44	1208.01	1.08	29.72	63.94
1995	19.61	26.84	453.23	1330.61	1.38	23.00	70.60
2000	22.84	41.05	638.26	1395.72	1.82	27.93	61.09
2001	20.98	58.53	654.84	1298.22	2.79	31.21	61.87
2002	23.14	70.04	702.72	1238.61	3.21	31.87	56.18
2003	22.53	76.33	749.00	1183.62	3.39	33.25	52.54
2004	21.91	83.09	773.23	1129.89	4.18	38.92	56.90
2005	21.96	90.44	766.67	1066.40	4.70	39.86	55.44
2006	21.78	97.20	767.07	1023.40	5.10	40.64	54.26
2007	21.21	103.20	729.77	982.65	5.69	40.19	54.12
2008	20.68	108.44	696.24	911.60	6.20	39.81	54.00
2009	20.57	111.94	669.33	914.42	6.60	39.47	53.93
2010	20.62	115.14	652.09	887.44	6.96	39.41	53.63

17-12 主要年份各级学校教师负担学生数

Student-teacher Ratio by Level of School in Main Years

单位：人 (person)

年 份 Year	高等学校 University and College		普通中学 Secondary Schools		小 学 Primary Schools	
	教师数 Number of Teachers	平均每个教师负担学生数 Student-Teacher Ratio	教师数 Number of Teachers	平均每个教师负担学生数 Student-Teacher Ratio	教师数 Number of Teachers	平均每个教师负担学生数 Student-Teacher Ratio
1978	2458	4.16	41661	19.36	82616	24.56
1980	3149	4.54	45232	18.20	89027	23.09
1985	5473	4.84	60942	15.68	98294	20.00
1990	7002	4.47	65814	13.12	95060	19.54
1995	7687	5.78	62934	11.91	106001	20.77
2000	7924	9.34	75895	14.92	131259	18.87
2001	9123	12.04	79419	15.47	132137	18.43
2002	10369	13.00	84714	15.80	132435	17.82
2003	11237	13.46	89332	16.22	132284	17.30
2004	12239	13.74	94381	16.08	134915	16.44
2005	12733	14.82	101701	15.16	134768	15.91
2006	13783	15.07	106975	14.70	134718	15.57
2007	15096	14.33	108232	14.13	133626	15.41
2008	15755	14.66	108729	13.64	132797	15.15
2009	16234	14.88	110842	13.04	134263	14.70
2010	16506	15.22	113990	12.48	133963	14.45

17-13 主要年份各级学校女学生和女教师数

Number of Female Students and Teachers by Level of School in Main Years

单位：人 (person)

项 目	Item	1995	2000	2010
女学生	**Number of Female Students**	**1553655**	**1889552**	**1911185**
高等学校	Institutions of Higher Education	21268	38419	136071
中等专业学校	Specialized Secondary Schools	35927	49892	82554
普通中学	Regular Secondary Schools	379171	568060	718438
职业高中	Vocational Secondary Schools	28495	23670	26234
技工学校	Technical Shools	12191	8740	13228
小 学	Primary Schools	1076333	1200513	932296
特殊教育学校	Special Schools for the Blind, Mute and Deaf	270	258	2364
女学生占学生总数的比重(%)	**Percentage of Female Students to Total Students (%)**	**49.2**	**48.9**	**49.3**
女教师	**Number of Female Teachers**	**106877**	**134563**	**178259**
高等学校	Institutions of Higher Education	2857	3192	8362
中等专业学校	Specialized Secondary Schools	3079	3408	3421
普通中学	Regular Secondary Schools	30508	40030	67901
职业高中	Vocational Secondary Schools	1613	1601	1458
技工学校	Technical Schools	1085	1264	3937
小 学	Primary Schools	67617	84944	92917
特殊教育学校	Special Schools for the Blind, Mute and Deaf	118	124	263
女教师占教师总数的比重(%)	**Percentage of Female Teachers to Total Teachers (%)**	**56.5**	**58.9**	**63.1**

17-14 主要年份初中毕业生和小学生升学率及小学学龄儿童入学率

Percentage of Graduates of Junior Secondary Schools and Primary Schools Entering Higher Level Schools, Enrollment Rate of School-age Children in Main Years

单位：人、%　(person,%)

年份 Year	初中毕业生升高中情况 Student of Graduates of Junior Secondary Schools Entering Senior Secondary Schools			小学毕业生升初中情况 Student of Graduates of Primary Schools Entering Junior Secondary Schools			小学学龄儿童入学情况 Student of School-Age Children Enrolled		
	初中毕业生数 Graduates of Junior Secondary Schools	高中招生数 Students Entering Senior Secondary Schools	升学率 Percentage of Graduates of Primary Schools Entering Junior Secondary Schools	小学毕业生数 Graduates of Primary Schools	初中招生数 Students Entering Junior Secondary Schools	升学率 Percentage of Graduates of Primary Schools Entering Junior Secondary Schools	学龄儿童数 School-Age Children	已入学学龄儿童数 School-Age Children Enrolled in Schools	入学率 Enrollment Rate
1978	141572	68261	48.22	788359	255687	88.67	1541148	1480400	96.00
1980	186012	73989	39.76	292515	236432	80.83	1637610	1548653	94.57
1985	199206	93692	47.03	289045	247431	85.60	1645055	1569328	95.40
1990	216173	84567	39.12	259301	213074	82.17	1502163	1465325	97.50
1995	171167	58203	34.00	271227	228115	84.10	2036541	1976120	97.03
2000	253240	76744	30.30	371758	342046	92.01	2313890	2245190	97.03
2001	270550	93519	34.56	395010	366359	92.75	2257795	2212477	97.41
2002	294271	113366	38.52	411626	388558	94.39	2184260	2136643	97.82
2003	308445	126163	40.90	421443	406824	96.53	2122900	2087775	98.34
2004	336165	138315	41.14	417588	398090	95.33	2063210	2038258	97.79
2005	370693	145044	39.13	397592	394878	99.33	2007742	1981569	98.70
2006	386275	142853	36.98	373862	379572	101.53	1957604	1941068	99.15
2007	388365	146449	37.71	361921	363631	100.47	1930074	1916265	99.28
2008	371858	147914	39.78	349300	349665	100.10	1865105	1856800	99.55
2009	354969	148869	41.94	339836	340969	100.33	1839775	1829016	99.41
2010	337510	153238	45.40	334362	336118	100.53	1801872	1797853	99.78

17-15 主要年份各级各类学校少数民族在校学生数

Number of Students Enrollment of Minority Nationalities by Level and Type of School in Main Years

单位：人　(person)

年份 Year	高等学校 Institutions of Higher Education	中等学校 Secondary Schools	中等专业学校 Specialized Secondary Schools	职业高中 Vocational Secondary Schools	技工学校 Technical Schools	普通中学 Regular Secondary Schools	#高中 Senior Secondary Schools	#初中 Junior Secondary Schools	小学(万人) Primary Schools (10 000 persons)
1978	7890	310987	10807			300180	38837	261343	106.58
1980	6455	311213	22263	592	4514	283844	50340	233504	101.73
1985	13996	346833	17888	4915	7649	316381	71199	245182	116.43
1990	17542	439140	23897	13577	13685	387981	94579	293402	126.78
1995	24125	477379	33264	20013	16040	408012	52570	355492	157.84
2000	31989	834390	62572	34992	12260	724566	91843	632723	171.44
2001	47689	867582	58971	37013	9191	762407	103658	658749	165.83
2002	61610	913720	51204	40938	10971	810607	121523	689084	158.25
2003	65394	950853	38025	34863	9898	868067	137714	730353	151.52
2004	70340	985148	31566	49693	13407	890482	148398	742084	143.62
2005	75744	993338	32698	54773	13371	892501	152244	740257	136.94
2006	77627	975346	36393	13216	18002	907735	149963	757772	132.94
2007	81978	958643	55224	19181	20476	863762	156478	707284	131.32
2008	85942	935350	62337	28387	23396	821230	160238	660992	130.44
2009	91243	927939	66502	41666	24466	795305	160720	634585	130.31
2010	94708	933338	75924	49388	24894	783132	162687	620445	129.37

17-16 各地、州、市各级各类学校数

Number of Schools by Level, Type and by Prefecture, Autonomous Prefecture and City

单位：所　　(2010 年)　　(unit)

地　区	Region	普通高等学校 Regular Institutions of Higher Education	中等职业学校 Specialized Secondary Schools	#中等师范学校 Teacher Training Secondary Schools
总　计	**Total**	**32**	**186**	**13**
乌鲁木齐市	Urumqi City	18	43	2
克拉玛依市	Karamay City	1	3	1
石河子市	Shihezi City	1	11	1
吐鲁番地区	Turpan Administrative Offices		3	1
哈密地区	Hami [Kumul] Administrative Offices		5	
昌吉回族自治州	Changji Hui Autonomous Prefecture	2	8	
伊犁哈萨克自治州	Ili Kazak Autonomous Prefecture	2	43	3
伊犁州直属县(市)	Counties (Cities) Direct Under Ili Prefecture	2	21	1
塔城地区	Tacheng [Tarbagatai] Administrative Offices		11	1
阿勒泰地区	Altay Administrative Offices		11	1
博尔塔拉蒙古自治州	Bortala Mongol Autonomous Prefecture		5	1
巴音郭楞蒙古自治州	Bayangol Mongol Autonomous Prefecture	1	9	1
阿克苏地区	Aksu Administrative Offices	1	10	
克孜勒苏柯尔克孜自治州	Kizilsu Kirgiz Autonomous Prefecture		8	1
喀什地区	Kashgar [Kaxgar] Administrative Offices	1	27	1
和田地区	Hotan Administrative Offices	2	11	1
生产建设兵团	Production and Construction Group	3		

地　区	Region	普通中学 Regular Secondary Schools	#高　中 Senior Secondary Schools	小　学 Primary Schools	特殊教育学　校 Special Schools
总　计	**Total**	**1545**	**385**	**3598**	**13**
乌鲁木齐市	Urumqi City	133	54	140	3
克拉玛依市	Karamay City	13	14	5	1
石河子市	Shihezi City	18	3	31	
吐鲁番地区	Turpan Administrative Offices	53	17	91	1
哈密地区	Hami [Kumul] Administrative Offices	47	15	60	1
昌吉回族自治州	Changji Hui Autonomous Prefecture	50	19	94	1
伊犁哈萨克自治州	Ili Kazak Autonomous Prefecture	338	73	535	3
伊犁州直属县(市)	Counties (Cities) Direct Under Ili Prefecture	185	36	360	2
塔城地区	Tacheng [Tarbagatai] Administrative Offices	77	22	109	1
阿勒泰地区	Altay Administrative Offices	76	15	66	
博尔塔拉蒙古自治州	Bortala Mongol Autonomous Prefecture	32	9	39	
巴音郭楞蒙古自治州	Bayangol Mongol Autonomous Prefecture	64	22	97	1
阿克苏地区	Aksu Administrative Offices	152	41	589	1
克孜勒苏柯尔克孜自治州	Kizilsu Kirgiz Autonomous Prefecture	35	10	161	
喀什地区	Kashgar [Kaxgar] Administrative Offices	212	42	1001	1
和田地区	Hotan Administrative Offices	147	15	670	
生产建设兵团	Production and Construction Group	251	51	85	

17-17 各地、州、市各级各类学校教职工数

Number of Teachers and Staff by Level and Type of School and by Prefecture, Autonomous Prefecture and City

单位：人 (2010 年) (person)

地 区	Region	普通高等学校 Regular Institutions of Higher Education	中等职业学校 Specialized Secondary Schools
总 计	**Total**	**26770**	**14988**
乌鲁木齐市	Urumqi City	16660	5449
克拉玛依市	Karamay City	514	633
石河子市	Shihezi City	336	850
吐鲁番地区	Turpan Administrative Offices		301
哈密地区	Hami [Kumul] Administrative Offices		579
昌吉回族自治州	Changji Hui Autonomous Prefecture	1082	720
伊犁哈萨克自治州	Ili Kazak Autonomous Prefecture	1758	2241
伊犁州直属县(市)	Counties (Cities) Direct Under Ili Prefecture	1758	1162
塔城地区	Tacheng [Tarbagatai] Administrative Offices		483
阿勒泰地区	Altay Administrative Offices		596
博尔塔拉蒙古自治州	Bortala Mongol Autonomous Prefecture		274
巴音郭楞蒙古自治州	Bayangol Mongol Autonomous Prefecture	539	819
阿克苏地区	Aksu Administrative Offices	417	441
克孜勒苏柯尔克孜自治州	Kizilsu Kirgiz Autonomous Prefecture		462
喀什地区	Kashgar [Kaxgar] Administrative Offices	946	1567
和田地区	Hotan Administrative Offices	653	652
生产建设兵团	Production and Construction Group	3865	

地 区	Region	普通中学 Regular Secondary Schools	小 学 Primary Schools	特殊教育学 校 Special Schools
总 计	**Total**	**130627**	**148863**	**461**
乌鲁木齐市	Urumqi City	12363	10295	194
克拉玛依市	Karamay City	2577	2250	15
石河子市	Shihezi City	1314	628	
吐鲁番地区	Turpan Administrative Offices	3806	4678	14
哈密地区	Hami [Kumul] Administrative Offices	3059	3418	37
昌吉回族自治州	Changji Hui Autonomous Prefecture	7549	7883	33
伊犁哈萨克自治州	Ili Kazak Autonomous Prefecture	24184	32364	43
伊犁州直属县(市)	Counties (Cities) Direct Under Ili Prefecture	13641	19200	12
塔城地区	Tacheng [Tarbagatai] Administrative Offices	6331	7865	31
阿勒泰地区	Altay Administrative Offices	4212	5299	
博尔塔拉蒙古自治州	Bortala Mongol Autonomous Prefecture	2544	3230	
巴音郭楞蒙古自治州	Bayangol Mongol Autonomous Prefecture	7133	9300	45
阿克苏地区	Aksu Administrative Offices	11513	13776	22
克孜勒苏柯尔克孜自治州	Kizilsu Kirgiz Autonomous Prefecture	3941	5546	
喀什地区	Kashgar [Kaxgar] Administrative Offices	22448	27180	58
和田地区	Hotan Administrative Offices	10607	12747	
生产建设兵团	Production and Construction Group	17589	15568	

17-18 各地、州、市各级各类学校教师数

Number of Teachers by Level and Type of School and by Prefecture, Autonomous Prefecture and City

单位：人 (2010 年) (person)

地区	Region	普通高等学校 Regular Institutions of Higher Education	中等职业学校 Specialized Secondary Schools
总计	**Total**	**16506**	**10084**
乌鲁木齐市	Urumqi City	9819	3250
克拉玛依市	Karamay City	276	296
石河子市	Shihezi City	257	540
吐鲁番地区	Turpan Administrative Offices		236
哈密地区	Hami [Kumul] Administrative Offices		416
昌吉回族自治州	Changji Hui Autonomous Prefecture	713	565
伊犁哈萨克自治州	Ili Kazak Autonomous Prefecture	1053	1547
伊犁州直属县(市)	Counties (Cities) Direct Under Ili Prefecture	1053	818
塔城地区	Tacheng [Tarbagatai] Administrative Offices		312
阿勒泰地区	Altay Administrative Offices		417
博尔塔拉蒙古自治州	Bortala Mongol Autonomous Prefecture		155
巴音郭楞蒙古自治州	Bayangol Mongol Autonomous Prefecture	496	637
阿克苏地区	Aksu Administrative Offices	314	374
克孜勒苏柯尔克孜自治州	Kizilsu Kirgiz Autonomous Prefecture		354
喀什地区	Kashgar [Kaxgar] Administrative Offices	711	1190
和田地区	Hotan Administrative Offices	383	524
生产建设兵团	Production and Construction Group	2484	

地区	Region	普通中学 Regular Secondary Schools	#高中 Senior Secondary Schools	小学 Primary Schools	特殊教育学校 Special Schools
总计	**Total**	**113990**	**30231**	**133963**	**347**
乌鲁木齐市	Urumqi City	9998	3660	9393	139
克拉玛依市	Karamay City	2123	828	1956	12
石河子市	Shihezi City	1147	542	565	
吐鲁番地区	Turpan Administrative Offices	3395	1059	4392	8
哈密地区	Hami [Kumul] Administrative Offices	2666	1035	3072	23
昌吉回族自治州	Changji Hui Autonomous Prefecture	6424	2409	7493	28
伊犁哈萨克自治州	Ili Kazak Autonomous Prefecture	21098	6137	28705	37
伊犁州直属县(市)	Counties (Cities) Direct Under Ili Prefecture	11919	3094	17026	7
塔城地区	Tacheng [Tarbagatai] Administrative Offices	5497	1928	6942	30
阿勒泰地区	Altay Administrative Offices	3682	1115	4737	
博尔塔拉蒙古自治州	Bortala Mongol Autonomous Prefecture	2151	648	2813	
巴音郭楞蒙古自治州	Bayangol Mongol Autonomous Prefecture	6141	2203	8253	38
阿克苏地区	Aksu Administrative Offices	10305	2459	12591	17
克孜勒苏柯尔克孜自治州	Kizilsu Kirgiz Autonomous Prefecture	3652	947	4979	
喀什地区	Kashgar [Kaxgar] Administrative Offices	20646	3135	24684	45
和田地区	Hotan Administrative Offices	9703	902	11486	
生产建设兵团	Production and Construction Group	14541	4267	13581	

17-19 各地、州、市各级各类学校在校学生数

Number of Students Enrollment by Level and Type of School and by Prefecture, Autonomous Prefecture and City

单位：人 (2010 年) (person)

地区	Region	普通高等学校 Regular Institutions of Higher Education	中等职业学校 Specialized Secondary Schools
总计	**Total**	**251160**	**233319**
乌鲁木齐市	Urumqi City	154797	87823
克拉玛依市	Karamay City	3732	1064
石河子市	Shihezi City	5149	20077
吐鲁番地区	Turpan Administrative Offices		3316
哈密地区	Hami [Kumul] Administrative Offices		2334
昌吉回族自治州	Changji Hui Autonomous Prefecture	12398	12358
伊犁哈萨克自治州	Ili Kazak Autonomous Prefecture	13102	23633
伊犁州直属县(市)	Counties (Cities) Direct Under Ili Prefecture	13102	14329
塔城地区	Tacheng [Tarbagatai] Administrative Offices		3005
阿勒泰地区	Altay Administrative Offices		6299
博尔塔拉蒙古自治州	Bortala Mongol Autonomous Prefecture		1872
巴音郭楞蒙古自治州	Bayangol Mongol Autonomous Prefecture	3125	16101
阿克苏地区	Aksu Administrative Offices	3007	15213
克孜勒苏柯尔克孜自治州	Kizilsu Kirgiz Autonomous Prefecture		1687
喀什地区	Kashgar [Kaxgar] Administrative Offices	11419	26807
和田地区	Hotan Administrative Offices	5280	21034
生产建设兵团	Production and Construction Group	39151	

地区	Region	普通中学 Regular Secondary Schools	#高中 Senior Secondary Schools	小学 Primary Schools	特殊教育学校 Special Schools
总计	**Total**	**1422419**	**419141**	**1935798**	**5974**
乌鲁木齐市	Urumqi City	148720	57475	178206	640
克拉玛依市	Karamay City	25175	9229	24256	56
石河子市	Shihezi City	18996	9832	11288	10
吐鲁番地区	Turpan Administrative Offices	33404	10227	51025	150
哈密地区	Hami [Kumul] Administrative Offices	31284	12570	32932	186
昌吉回族自治州	Changji Hui Autonomous Prefecture	80414	31827	81005	1153
伊犁哈萨克自治州	Ili Kazak Autonomous Prefecture	250337	86479	335835	754
伊犁州直属县(市)	Counties (Cities) Direct Under Ili Prefecture	152674	48221	219149	510
塔城地区	Tacheng [Tarbagatai] Administrative Offices	64563	25526	72126	194
阿勒泰地区	Altay Administrative Offices	33100	12732	44560	50
博尔塔拉蒙古自治州	Bortala Mongol Autonomous Prefecture	24236	10586	27228	74
巴音郭楞蒙古自治州	Bayangol Mongol Autonomous Prefecture	70386	26747	90118	195
阿克苏地区	Aksu Administrative Offices	138913	34353	217163	409
克孜勒苏柯尔克孜自治州	Kizilsu Kirgiz Autonomous Prefecture	33900	10397	53404	10
喀什地区	Kashgar [Kaxgar] Administrative Offices	260940	47286	416262	966
和田地区	Hotan Administrative Offices	115352	12177	199476	1048
生产建设兵团	Production and Construction Group	190362	59956	217600	323

17-20 各地、州、市各级各类学校招生数

Number of New Students Enrollment by Level and Type of School and by Prefecture, Autonomous Prefecture and City

单位：人　　(2010 年)　　(person)

地　区	Region	普通高等学校 Regular Institutions of Higher Education	中等职业学校 Specialized Secondary Schools
总　计	**Total**	**74621**	**98894**
乌鲁木齐市	Urumqi City	45872	34706
克拉玛依市	Karamay City	1386	400
石河子市	Shihezi City	2109	6778
吐鲁番地区	Turpan Administrative Offices		872
哈密地区	Hami [Kumul] Administrative Offices		1186
昌吉回族自治州	Changji Hui Autonomous Prefecture	4002	4370
伊犁哈萨克自治州	Ili Kazak Autonomous Prefecture	3775	11229
伊犁州直属县(市)	Counties (Cities) Direct Under Ili Prefecture	3775	7087
塔城地区	Tacheng [Tarbagatai] Administrative Offices		1362
阿勒泰地区	Altay Administrative Offices		2780
博尔塔拉蒙古自治州	Bortala Mongol Autonomous Prefecture		739
巴音郭楞蒙古自治州	Bayangol Mongol Autonomous Prefecture	1448	6104
阿克苏地区	Aksu Administrative Offices	1158	8937
克孜勒苏柯尔克孜自治州	Kizilsu Kirgiz Autonomous Prefecture		918
喀什地区	Kashgar [Kaxgar] Administrative Offices	2796	12271
和田地区	Hotan Administrative Offices	1765	10384
生产建设兵团	Production and Construction Group	10310	

地　区	Region	普通中学 Regular Secondary Schools	#高中 Senior Secondary Schools	小学 Primary Schools	特殊教育学校 Special Schools
总　计	**Total**	**489356**	**153238**	**311861**	**1204**
乌鲁木齐市	Urumqi City	50955	19483	29170	141
克拉玛依市	Karamay City	8770	3202	3680	2
石河子市	Shihezi City	6631	3519	1714	2
吐鲁番地区	Turpan Administrative Offices	11339	3646	8405	90
哈密地区	Hami [Kumul] Administrative Offices	10787	4519	5211	31
昌吉回族自治州	Changji Hui Autonomous Prefecture	26895	10555	12184	181
伊犁哈萨克自治州	IliKazak Autonomous Prefecture	87146	32085	58792	249
伊犁州直属县(市)	Counties (Cities) Direct Under Ili Prefecture	53494	18064	38413	222
塔城地区	Tacheng [Tarbagatai] Administrative Offices	22576	9541	12022	18
阿勒泰地区	Altay Administrative Offices	11076	4480	8357	9
博尔塔拉蒙古自治州	Bortala Mongol Autonomous Prefecture	8355	3687	4579	8
巴音郭楞蒙古自治州	Bayangol Mongol Autonomous Prefecture	24862	10101	15175	46
阿克苏地区	Aksu Administrative Offices	49268	14012	34530	42
克孜勒苏柯尔克孜自治州	Kizilsu Kirgiz Autonomous Prefecture	11546	3513	9572	1
喀什地区	Kashgar [Kaxgar] Administrative Offices	89569	19267	65837	177
和田地区	Hotan Administrative Offices	39804	4728	29757	208
生产建设兵团	Production and Construction Group	63429	20921	33255	26

17-21 各地、州、市各级各类学校毕业生数

Number of Graduates by Level and Type of School and by Prefecture, Autonomous Prefecture and City

单位：人　　(2010 年)　　(person)

地　区	Region	普通高等学校 Regular Institutions of Higher Education	中等职业学校 Specialized Secondary Schools
总　计	**Total**	**63543**	**66383**
乌鲁木齐市	Urumqi City	39375	30499
克拉玛依市	Karamay City	1528	346
石河子市	Shihezi City	807	6621
吐鲁番地区	Turpan Administrative Offices		718
哈密地区	Hami [Kumul] Administrative Offices		622
昌吉回族自治州	Changji Hui Autonomous Prefecture	3386	3768
伊犁哈萨克自治州	Ili Kazak Autonomous Prefecture		6540
伊犁州直属县(市)	Counties (Cities) Direct Under Ili Prefecture	3259	4587
塔城地区	Tacheng [Tarbagatai] Administrative Offices		667
阿勒泰地区	Altay Administrative Offices		1286
博尔塔拉蒙古自治州	Bortala Mongol Autonomous Prefecture		657
巴音郭楞蒙古自治州	Bayangol Mongol Autonomous Prefecture	703	3989
阿克苏地区	Aksu Administrative Offices	1770	2673
克孜勒苏柯尔克孜自治州	Kizilsu Kirgiz Autonomous Prefecture		242
喀什地区	Kashgar [Kaxgar] Administrative Offices	2633	6958
和田地区	Hotan Administrative Offices	1310	2750
生产建设兵团	Production and Construction Group	8772	

地　区	Region	普通中学 Regular Secondary Schools	#高中 Senior Secondary Schools	小学 Primary Schools	特殊教育学校 Special Schools
总　计	**Total**	**473216**	**135706**	**334362**	**923**
乌鲁木齐市	Urumqi City	46154	18143	29891	123
克拉玛依市	Karamay City	7882	2803	4705	1
石河子市	Shihezi City	6291	3173	2174	2
吐鲁番地区	Turpan Administrative Offices	11513	3638	8325	7
哈密地区	Hami [Kumul] Administrative Offices	10028	3984	5998	1
昌吉回族自治州	Changji Hui Autonomous Prefecture	25757	10953	15674	232
伊犁哈萨克自治州	Ili Kazak Autonomous Prefecture	80461	27013	55651	37
伊犁州直属县(市)	Counties (Cities) Direct Under Ili Prefecture	48492	14403	35874	24
塔城地区	Tacheng [Tarbagatai] Administrative Offices	20571	8012	12778	11
阿勒泰地区	Altay Administrative Offices	11398	4598	6999	2
博尔塔拉蒙古自治州	Bortala Mongol Autonomous Prefecture	7495	3139	4820	12
巴音郭楞蒙古自治州	Bayangol Mongol Autonomous Prefecture	24378	9632	15508	14
阿克苏地区	Aksu Administrative Offices	45004	10598	35928	53
克孜勒苏柯尔克孜自治州	Kizilsu Kirgiz Autonomous Prefecture	12007	3810	8429	
喀什地区	Kashgar [Kaxgar] Administrative Offices	93861	15616	70450	161
和田地区	Hotan Administrative Offices	39975	2836	36623	217
生产建设兵团	Production and Construction Group	62410	20368	40186	63

17-22 各类学校教育经费情况
Educational Funds in Various Schools

单位：万元 (2010 年) (10 000 yuan)

指标	Item	合计 Total	国家财政性教育经费 Government Appropriation for Education	#预算内教育经费 Budgetary Education Expense	民办学校中举办者投入 Investor Derotion	社会捐资 Donations	事业收入 Income from Undertakings	其他 Others
总计	**Total**	**3690363.2**	**3283310.2**	**3093729.1**	**2265.6**	**14744.8**	**319795.3**	**70247.3**
高等学校	**Institutions of Higher Education**	**596071.6**	**417998.8**	**399597.3**		**10043.7**	**142391.9**	**25637.2**
普通高等学校	Regular Institutions of Higher Education	560892.4	397439.0	379338.7		10033.7	128759.1	24660.6
成人高等学校	Institutions of Higher Education for Adults	35179.2	20559.8	20258.6		10.0	13632.8	976.6
中等职业学校	**Technical Schools**	**219980.8**	**165713.0**	**153062**	**8.7**	**52.0**	**42308.0**	**11899.1**
中等专业学校	Specialized Secondary Schools	129389.6	96086.4	93090.2	8.7	32.0	28656.3	4606.2
职业高中	Professional Senior High School	41524.5	36883.2	31503.3			3397.0	1244.3
技工学校	Technical Schools	38753.0	24428.9	20523.3		20.0	8629.8	5674.3
成人中专学校	Specialized Secondary Schools for Adults	10313.7	8314.5	7945.2			1624.9	374.3
中学	**Secondary Schools**	**1193841.4**	**1097961.1**	**1030887.0**	**109.4**	**1784.8**	**79763.8**	**14222.3**
普通中学	Regular Secondary Schools	1193586.2	1097732.0	1030657.9	109.4	1784.8	79737.7	14222.3
高中	Senior high school	378556.2	301142.0	279971.9	34.7	796.5	68057.9	8525.1
#农村	Rural Areas	14600.6	14078.4	13574.8		153.7	281.3	87.2
初中	Junior high school	815030.0	796590.0	750686.0	74.7	988.3	11679.8	5697.2
#农村	Rural Areas	425943.3	422089.4	406947.5	11.7	479.8	2014.7	1347.7
小学	**Primary Schools**	**1168427.7**	**1151089.8**	**1099516.1**	**96.0**	**926.8**	**8585.9**	**7729.2**
普通小学	Regular Primary Schools	1168426.7	1151088.8	1099515.1	96.0	926.8	8585.9	7729.2
#农村	Rural Areas	706390.9	700687.1	684496.8	48.3	622.0	1990.6	3042.9
特殊教育	**Special Education Schools**	**10363.7**	**9794.2**	**8957.7**		**21.2**	**160.9**	**387.4**
幼儿园	**Kindergartens**	**255411.2**	**223489.9**	**221386.2**	**2051.5**	**896.5**	**27114.3**	**1859.0**
教育行政单位	**Education administrative unit**	**117160.9**	**106427.6**	**87845.4**		**268.9**	**5351.0**	**5113.4**
教育事业单位	**Education institution**	**88027.0**	**74123.3**	**56771.5**		**750.8**	**10559.0**	**2593.9**
其他	**Others**	**41078.9**	**36712.5**	**35705.9**		**0.1**	**3560.5**	**805.8**

17-23 科技活动基本情况
Basic Statistics on Scientific and Technological Activities

指 标	Item	2008	2009
研究与试验发展人员折合全时当量(人·年)	**Full-time Equivalent of Rearch and Development Personnel (person.year)**	**8810**	**12655**
研究与试验发展经费支出(万元)	**Funding for Scientific and Technological Activities (10 000 yuan)**	**160113**	**218043**
按活动类型分	Government Funds		
#基础研究	Self-raised Funds by Enterprises	16433	10470
应用研究	Bank Loans	46416	77596
试验发展	Experimental Development	94772	129976
按支出用途分	Service Fees		
日常性支出	Purchases or Construction of Fixed Assets	157622	176974
#劳务费	Expenditure on Research and Development	41754	67607
资产性支出	Basic Research	34884	41069
#仪器和设备	Applied Research	32575	36372
研究与试验发展经费支出占新疆生产总值比重(%)	**Proportion of Expenditure on Research and Development to GDP of Xinjiang (%)**	**0.38**	**0.52**

说明：从 2009 年开始该表指标口径有所调整。
Note:Since 2009 Statistial coverage in this table have adjusted

17-24 县级以上政府部门属研究与开发机构及科技信息与文献机构数、人员数
State-owned Research and Development Institutions and Information and Literature Institutions at and above County Level and Persons Engaged

(2010 年)

指 标	Item	合 计 Total	自然科学技术领域 Field of Natural Sciences and Technology	社会、人文科学技术领域 Field of Social Sciences and Humanities	科技信息和文献机构 Scientific-technical Information and Document Institutions
机构数(个)	**Institutions (unit)**	**106**	**92**	**6**	**8**
科技活动人员(人)	**Personal Engaged in Scientific and Technological Activities (person)**	**6084**	**5466**	**379**	**239**
#大学本科及以上学历	University Graduate or above	3718	3292	299	127
研究与试验发展全时人员(人·年)	**Full-time Equivalent of Rearch and Development Personnel (person.year)**	**2883**	**2543**	**297**	**43**
科技活动收入(万元)	**Sources of Funds for S&T(10 000 yuan)**	**109923.6**	**101226.1**	**4695.5**	**4002.0**
#政府拨款	Government Funds	87250.4	79367.8	4464.3	3418.3
科技经费内部支出额(万元)	**Internal Expenditures on Scientific and Technological Activities (10 000 yuan)**	**99971.6**	**91872.2**	**4451.0**	**3648.4**
#劳务费	Service Fees	36281.6	33251.3	1556.8	1473.5
固定资产购建费	Purchases or Construction of Fixed Assets	16581.0	15579.8	463.5	537.7
#研究与发展经费支出	Expenditure on Research and Development	44056.4	41181.3	1974.1	901.0
基础研究	Basic Research	7347.3	6026.0	1321.3	
应用研究	Applied Research	17914.5	16516.7	496.8	901.0
试验发展	Experimental Development	18794.6	18638.6	156.0	

17-25 重大科学技术研究成果及奖励数

Number of Major Achievements in Scientific and Technological Research and Awarded Prizes

单位：项 (item)

年 份 Year	自治区级重大科技成果 Number of Major Achievements in Science and Technology of Autonomous Region	奖励情况 Awarded Prizes					
		国家级 National	自治区级 Autonomous Regional	一等奖 Frist Class Awards	二等奖 Second Class Awards	三等奖 Third Class Awards	四等奖 Fourth Class Awards
1978 年以前	1551	88	610				
1980-1985	1173	16	356	5	31	102	218
1990	444	3	129		18	56	55
1995	218	3	137	4	26	53	54
2000	250	2	90	5	18	67	
2001	285	6	92	4	23	65	
2002	207	5	99	5	30	64	
2003	232	3	111	8	34	69	
2004	218	4	108	4	33	71	
2005	225	3	101	6	27	68	
2006	212	3	107	8	37	62	
2007	220	8	118	10	42	66	
2008	69	8	108	9	40	59	
2009	166	12					
2010	229	9	130	15	47	68	

17-26 专利申请和批准数

Number of Patent Applications Examined and Approved

单位：件 (case)

年 份 Year	申 请 数 Number of Patent Applications Examined				批 准 数 Number of Patent Applications Granted				代理机构（个） Agency (unit)
	合 计 Total	发 明 Inventions	实用新型 Utility Models	外观设计 Designs	合 计 Total	发 明 Inventions	实用新型 Utility Models	外观设计 Designs	
1990	250	38	203	9	139	3	135	1	5
1995	609	92	467	50	312	11	285	16	6
2000	1088	179	699	210	717	66	475	176	7
2001	1088	189	683	216	755	90	522	143	5
2002	1239	216	779	244	627	61	407	159	4
2003	1472	253	940	279	751	75	520	156	5
2004	1492	272	870	350	792	75	530	187	5
2005	1851	320	1117	414	921	88	537	296	5
2006	2256	381	1166	709	1187	107	805	275	5
2007	2270	476	1255	539	1534	90	1035	409	5
2008	2412	482	1408	522	1493	82	1100	311	6
2009	2872	662	1865	345	1867	120	1261	486	6
2010	3560	914	2272	374	2562	189	2012	361	6

17-27 高等学校科技活动情况

Basic Statistics on Higher Education for Science and Technology Activities

指　标	Item	2009	2010
科技活动人员(人)	**Personnel Engaged in Scientific and Technological Activities (person)**	**11821**	**12894**
#科学家与工程师	Scientists and Engineers	11111	9063
研究与发展机构(个)	**Agencies of Research and Development (unit)**	**20**	**24**
研究与发展人员全时当量(人·年)	**Full-time Equivalent of R&D Personnel (person.year)**	**1773**	**1765**
#科学家与工程师	Scientists and Engineers	1741	1534
#基础研究	Basic Research	652	646
应用研究	Applied Research	938	942
试验发展	Experimental Development	99	106
科技经费筹集额(万元)	**Funding for Scientific and Development Activities(10 000 yuan)**	**16697**	**23628**
#政府拨款	Government Funds	7111	18411
科技经费内部支出额(万元)	**Internal Expenditure on Scientific and Technological Activities (10 000 yuan)**	**10131**	**19202**
#劳务费	Service Fees	2605	4412
固定资产购建费	Purchases or Construction of Fixed Assets	3557	3687
#研究与发展经费支出	Expenditure on Research and Development	8666	15644
基础研究	Basic Research	2530	3990
应用研究	Applied Research	5098	9063
试验发展	Experimental Development	1038	1504

17-28 主要年份企事业单位主要专业技术人员数

Number of Main Scientific and Technical Personnel in Enterprises and Institutions in Main Years

单位：人 (person)

年 份 Year	合 计 Total	工程技术人员 Engineering	农业技术人员 Agriculture	卫生技术人员 Health Care	科学研究人员 Scientific Researcn	教学人员 Teaching
1978. 6 月末	85063	22198	13141	31741	3042	14941
1985	158709	51636	20730	57559	3416	25368
1990	241524	92383	25089	71906	4326	47820
1995	437209	109463	28096	79014	4825	215811
2000	368262	58576	27764	62338	2409	217175
2001	385129	59913	30043	65585	2492	227096
2002	387726	58011	31867	65364	2337	230147
2003	385705	57506	30808	65622	2236	229533
2004	398318	55421	32831	68604	2928	238534
2005	402404	51915	32744	67945	2451	247349
2006	412977	52702	34131	68231	2460	255453
2007	411590	50680	33859	69101	2453	255497
2008	414277	49175	31799	71104	2261	259938
2009	411628	47525	30126	72827	2518	258632
2010	407651	47734	28433	77357	2071	252056

注: 1.1991 年起专业技术人员包括企事业单位(不含行政机关)人员数,教学人员包括社会和自然科技领域及小学教师人数。
2.1996 年后数据不包括中央单位的专业技术人员数，故人员减少较多。

Note: a) The Specialezed and technical personnel include those who work in enterprises and institutions (excluding administrative organs), teaching Staff, those work in social and nature scientific fields as well as elementary school teachers since 1991.
b) After 1996, the data exclude the figure of professionals with national establishments stationed to Xinjiang and thus the number of staff is reduced a lot.

17-29 主要年份企事业单位主要专业技术人员比重

Proportion of Scientific and Technical Personnel in Enterprises and Institutions in Main Years

单位：% (%)

年 份 Year	合 计 Total	工程技术 Engineering	农业技术 Agriculture	卫生技术 Health Care	科学研究 Scientific Research	教 学 Teaching
1978. 6 月末	100	26.10	15.45	37.31	3.58	17.56
1985	100	32.54	13.06	36.27	2.15	15.98
1990	100	38.25	10.39	29.77	1.79	19.80
1995	100	25.04	6.43	18.07	1.10	49.36
2000	100	15.91	7.54	16.93	0.65	58.97
2001	100	15.55	7.80	17.03	0.65	58.97
2002	100	14.96	8.22	16.86	0.60	59.36
2003	100	14.91	7.99	17.01	0.58	59.51
2004	100	13.91	8.24	17.22	0.74	59.89
2005	100	12.90	8.14	16.89	0.61	61.46
2006	100	12.76	8.26	16.52	0.60	61.86
2007	100	12.31	8.22	16.79	0.60	62.08
2008	100	11.87	7.68	17.16	0.55	62.74
2009	100	11.55	7.32	17.69	0.61	62.83
2010	100	11.71	6.97	18.98	0.51	61.83

17-30 大中型工业企业科技活动情况

(2009 年)

项 目	Item	企业数 (个) Nnmber of Industrial Enterprises (unit)	#有研究与试验发展活动的企业数 Number of Enterprises Having R & D Activities	科技机构 (个) Number of Scientific Technological Agencies (unit)	研究与试验发展人员数 (人) Number of R & D Persons	研究人员 Research personal
总 计	**Total**	**286**	**59**	**80**	**6745**	**4578**
按登记注册类型分	**Grouped by Ownership**					
内资企业	Domestic-funded Enterprises	270	58	78	6720	4569
国有企业	State-owned	32	6	8	952	676
集体企业	Collective-owned Enterprises	2				
有限责任公司	Limited Liability Corporations	155	24	34	892	280
国有独资公司	Sole State-funded Corporations	23	1	3	4	2
其他有限责任公司	Limited Liability Corporations	132	23	31	888	278
股份有限责任公司	Share-holding Corporations Ltd	42	24	31	4734	3543
私营企业	Private Enterprises	39	4	5	142	70
私营独资企业	Private-funded Enterprises	2				
私营有限责任公司	Private Limited Liability Corporations	32	2	3	72	42
私营股份有限公司	Private Stock Ltd. Co.	5	2	2	70	28
港澳台商投资企业	Enterprises With Funds from Hong Kong, Macao and Taiwan	8	1	2	25	9
#合资经营企业(港或澳、台资)	Joint-ventures Enterprises	3	1	1	25	9
港、澳、台商独资经营企业	Enterprises with Funds from Hong Kong, Macao and Taiwan	4		1		
外商投资企业	Foreign Funded Enterprises	8				
#中外合资经营企业	Joint-venture Enterprises	6				
按工业行业大类分	**Grouped by Sector**					
采矿业	Mining and Quarrying	53	10	22	4514	3430
煤炭开采和洗选业	Coal Extracting and Dressing	27	1	4	49	29
石油和天然气开采业	Petroleum and Natural Gas Extraction	11	6	14	4313	3343
黑色金属矿采选业	Processing of Ferrous Metals Ores	6				
有色金属矿采选业	Processing of Nonferrous Metals Ores	7	2	3	42	36
非金属矿采选业	Processing of Nonmetal Ores	2	1	1	110	22
制造业	Manufacturing	200	47	56	2044	974
农副食品加工业	Processing of Food from Agricultural Products	20	3	3	48	16
食品制造业	Food Manufacturing	12	2	3	158	31
饮料制造业	Beverage Manufacturing	8	1	2	72	12
烟草制品业	Tobacco Manufacturing	1				
纺织业	Textile Industry	34	4	8	117	39
纺织服装、鞋、帽制造业	Leather, Fur, Feather and Related Products Manufacturing	1				
家具制造业	Furniture Manufacturing	2				
造纸及纸制品业	Paper and Paper Products Manufacturing	4	2		16	5

Statistics on Technical Activities of Large and Medium-sized Industrial Enterprises

(2009 年)

研究与试验发展人员折合全时当量(人.年) Full-time Equivalent of R & D personnel	研究人员 Research personal	研究与试验发展经费(万元) Expenditure on R & D	其中 Of which 基础研究 Basic Research	应用研究 Applied Research	试验发展 Experimental Development	其中 Of which 政府资金 Government Appropriation Funds	企业资金 Self-raised Funds by Enterprises	研究与试验发展项目数(项) Projects to R & D	新产品开发项目数(项) Number of New Produots
4527	**3087**	**129772**	**441**	**41816**	**87516**	**2626**	**121155**	**686**	**388**
4517	3083	129686	441	41730	87516	2626	121069	683	388
777	543	12685	441	96	12149	61	12624	95	44
582	170	20846			20846	792	19543	143	150
		11			11		11	3	3
582	170	20834			20834	792	19532	140	147
3049	2314	87043		41634	45408	1773	79789	436	189
108	56	9113			9113		9113	9	5
54	35	1059			1059		1059	3	2
55	21	8054			8054		8054	6	3
10	4	86		86			86	3	
10	4	86		86			86	3	
2943	2297	76143	441	41436	34267	438	70359	404	57
42	25	329			329	29	300	3	4
2757	2221	74119		41436	32684	408	68364	380	50
34	29	1245	441		804		1245	19	1
110	22	450			450		450	2	2
1509	722	49395		285	49110	1685	47065	263	321
16	6	1082			1082	17	555	3	5
78	17	1241			1241	20	1221	5	2
48	8	536			536		536	2	10
75	36	2062			2062	135	1927	7	13
13	4	411			411	85	326	6	5

17-30 续表

(2009 年)

项 目	Item	企业数 (个) Nnmber of Industrial Enterprises (unit)	#有研究与试验发展活动的企业数 Number of Enterprises Having R & D Activities	科技机构 (个) Number of Scientific Technological Agencies (unit)	研究与试验发展人员数 (人) Number of R & D Persons	研究人员 Research personal
印刷业和记录媒介的复制	Printing and Copying of Medium for Record	1				
石油加工、炼焦及核燃料加工业	Oil Processing, Coking and Nuclear Fuel Processing	15	6	3	384	284
化学原料及化学制品制造业	Raw Chemical Material and Chemical Products	28	9	11	372	74
医药制造业	Medicine Manufacturing	2	1	1	6	7
化学纤维制造业	Chemical Fiber Manufacturing	8	1	1	29	15
橡胶制品业	Rubber Products Manufacturing	1	1		13	3
塑料制品业	Plastic Products Manufacturing	3	3	3	164	53
非金属矿物制品业	Nonmetal Mineral Products Manufacturing	27	3	8	132	76
黑色金属冶炼及压延加工业	Smelting and Pressing of Ferrous Metals	13	3	3	180	104
有色金属冶炼及压延加工业	Smelting and Pressing of Nonferrous Metals	4				
金属制品业	Metal Products Manufacturing	5		3		
通用设备制造业	General Purpose Machinery Manufacturing	1				
专用设备制造业	Special Purpose Machinery Manufacturing	2	2	2	93	112
交通运输设备制造业	Transport Equipment Manufacturing	1	1	1	57	37
电气机械及器材制造业	Electric Equipment and Machinery Manufacturing	6	4	3	170	82
通信设备、计算机及其他电子设备制造业	Telecom Equipment, Computer and Other Electronic Equipment	1	1	1	33	24
电力、燃气及水的生产和供应业	Production and Suppoly of Electric Power,Gas and Water	33	2	2	187	174
电力、热力的生产和供应业	Electric Power and Thermal Production and Supply	31	2	2	187	174
燃气生产和供应业	Gas Production and Supply	1				
水的生产和供应业	Water Production and Supply	1				
按企业所在地区划分	**Grouped by Region**					
乌鲁木齐市	Urumqi City	63	21	25	1031	648
克拉玛依市	Karamay City	21	9	16	3335	2504
吐鲁番地区	Turpan Administrative Offices	14	3	3	815	504
哈密地区	Hami [Kumul] Administrative Offices	12		2		
昌吉回族自治州	Changji Hui Autonomous Prefecture	34	2	6	112	55
伊犁州直属县(市)	Counties (Cities) Direct Under Ili Prefecture	24	2	8	91	26
塔城地区	Tacheng [Tarbagatai] Administrative Offices	18	4	2	168	56
阿勒泰地区	Altay Administrative Offices	7	1	2	22	20
博尔塔拉蒙古自治州	Bortala Mongol Autonomous Prefecture	9	1	2	9	5
巴音郭楞蒙古自治州	Bayangol Mongol Autonomous Prefecture	18	6	5	719	528
阿克苏地区	Aksu Administrative Offices	22	3	2	66	14
克孜勒苏柯尔克孜自治州	Kizilsu Kirgiz Autonomous Prefecture	1				
喀什地区	Kashgar [Kaxgar] Administrative Offices	6		1		
和田地区	Hotan Administrative Offices	3				
自治区直辖行政单位	Administrative unite of municipality directly under the central government	34	7	6	377	218

Statistics on Technical Activities of Large and Medium-sized Industrial Enterprises

(2009 年)

研究与试验发展人员折合全时当量 (人.年) Full-time Equivalent of R & D personnel	研究人员 Research personal	研究与试验发展经费 (万元) Expenditure on R & D	其中 Of which 基础研究 Basic Research	应用研究 Applied Research	试验发展 Experimental Development	其中 Of which 政府资金 Government Appropriation Funds	企业资金 Self-raised Funds by Enterprises	研究与试验发展项目数 (项) Projects to R & D	新产品开发项目数 (项) Number of New Produots
289	203	6886		199	6687	398	6488	55	45
321	61	4575		86	4489	293	4282	34	23
6	7	63			63	14	49	2	3
12	6	123			123		123	1	2
10	2	548			548	57	492	2	6
150	47	4584			4584	342	4107	21	22
127	75	6714			6714	13	6702	8	8
104	65	10992			10992	36	10956	51	41
									2
									1
71	83	446			446	24	422	6	10
23	15	1388			1388		1388	39	39
147	72	6348			6348	215	6134	13	39
20	14	1398			1398	40	1359	8	45
75	67	4234		96	4139	504	3731	19	10
75	67	4234		96	4139	504	3731	19	10
602	410	17631		381	17251	549	17082	160	179
2936	2246	52037		37008	15030	713	46836	321	89
174	108	15534		4428	11106		15534	109	7
									3
110	54	5238			5238	46	5192	11	34
67	22	1026			1026	13	1013	5	12
139	41	2698	441		2257		2188	6	4
18	16	140			140		140	17	1
6	4	30			30	12	18	1	1
129	40	20761			20761	100	20662	22	15
50	9	5810			5810		5810	8	11
									4
297	136	8009			8009	1194	6680	26	

17-31 各类技术合同签定及执行情况

Statistics on Signing and Implementing Technical Contracts by Type

单位：项、万元 (item,10 000 yuan)

项目	Item	合同数 Number of Contracts 2008	2009	合同金额 Contract Amount 2008	2009	#技术交易额 Transaction Value in Technical Market 2008	2009
总计	**Total**	**2536**	**1701**	**73963.18**	**46417.70**	**68015.41**	**43145.85**
技术开发合同	Technology Development	423	276	22649.74	14606.23	21285.56	14144.36
技术转让合同	Technology Transfer	94	107	2444.92	4949.42	1758.62	4100.13
技术咨询合同	Technology Consultation	1449	812	22805.65	7762.90	22751.57	7729.30
技术服务合同	Technology Service	570	506	26062.87	19099.15	22219.66	17172.06

17-32 各级技术计划项目进入技术市场情况

Statistics on Projects for Technical Plan Entering Technical Market by Level

单位：项、万元 (2009 年) (item,10 000 yuan)

项目	Item	合计 Total		国家计划 National Plans		部门计划 Department Plans	
		项数 Number of Items	金额 Values	项数 Number of Items	金额 Values	项数 Number of Items	金额 Values
总计	**Total**	**1701**	**46417.70**	**5**	**409.70**	**64**	**1771.45**
机关法人	Government Agency Legal Person						
事业法人	Institntion Legal Person	932	11439.44	1	17.00	25	672.33
社团法人	Corporation Aggregate	17	146.85			1	3.36
企业法人	Business Entity	751	34723.67	4	392.70	38	1095.76
自然人	Person	1	107.74				

项目	Item	省、自治区计划 单列市计划 Provinces, Municipality Plans		地、市、县计划 Area City and County Plans		计划外 Out of Plan	
		项数 Number of Items	金额 Values	项数 Number of Items	金额 Values	项数 Number of Items	金额 Values
总计	**Total**	**19**	**1008.46**	**85**	**1421.24**	**1528**	**41806.85**
机关法人	Government Agency Legal Person						
事业法人	Institntion Legal Person	12	454.00	71	1031.34	823	9264.78
社团法人	Corporation Aggregate					16	143.49
企业法人	Business Entity	7	554.46	14	389.90	688	32290.85
自然人	Person					1	107.74

17-33 技术流向地域情况
Statistics on Location of Technical Contract

单位：项、万元 (2009 年) (item, 10 000 yuan)

地区 Region	合同类别合计 Contracts of Classification Total		技术开发 Technology Development		技术转让 Technology Transfer		技术咨询 Technology Consultation		技术服务 Technology Service	
	项数 Number of Items	金额 Values	项数 Number of Items	金额 Values	项数 Number of Items	金额 Values	项数 Number of Items	金额 Values	项数 Number of Items	金额 Values
总计 Total	**1701**	**46417.70**	**276**	**14606.23**	**107**	**4949.42**	**812**	**7762.90**	**506**	**19099.15**
北京 Beijing	16	537.50	3	55.00	3	40.00	4	190.00	6	252.50
天津 Tianjing	1	16.00			1	16.00				
河北 Hebei	4	97.50	1	75.00	3	22.50				
山西 Shanxi	3	125.00					2	120.00	1	5.00
内蒙古 Inner Mongolia	11	684.98			1	4.98	10	680.00		
黑龙江 Heilongjiang	1	10.00					1	10.00		
上海市 Shanghai	2	74.00	1	70.00	1	4.00				
江苏 Jiangsu	5	71.00	1	16.00	1	4.80	1	0.70	2	49.50
浙江 Zhejiang	2	4.65			1	4.50			1	0.15
安徽 Aanhui	1	20.00	1	20.00						
福建 Fujian	1	3.60			1	3.60				
山东 Shandong	2	104.00	1	90.00					1	14.00
河南	1	50.00	1	50.00						
湖北 Hubei	2	13.60	1	7.60					1	6.00
湖南 Hunan	1	7.00	1	7.00						
广东 Guangdong	2	122.00			2	122.00				
重庆 Chongqing	1	19.45					1	19.45		
四川 Sichuan	3	46.10	2	45.10					1	1.00
云南 Yunnan	1	9.60			1	9.60				
西藏 Tibet	2	28.60					2	28.60		
陕西 Shaanxi	2	3.70					2	3.70		
甘肃 Gansu	4	27.50					4	27.50		
青海 Qinghai	1	6.71							1	6.71
宁夏 Ningxia	2	30.00	1	10.00			1	20.00		
新疆 Xinjiang	1630	44305.20	262	14160.53	92	4717.44	784	6662.95	492	18764.28

17-34 技术经济合同成交情况
Statistics on Transaction in Technical and Economic Contract

单位：项、万元 (2009 年) (item, 10 000 yuan)

卖方类别 Classification of Sellers / 买方类别 Classification of Buyers		合计 Total		#事业法人 Institntion Legal Person		#社团法人 Corporation Aggregate		#企业法人 Business Entity		#自然人 Person	
		项数 Number of Items	金额 Values	项数 Number of Items	金额 Values	项数 Number of Items	金额 Values	项数 Number of Items	金额 Values	项数 Number of Items	金额 Values
总 计	**Total**	**1701**	**46417.70**	**932**	**11439.40**	**17**	**146.85**	**751**	**34723.70**	**1**	**107.74**
机关法人	Government Agency Legal Person	250	7411.67	153	2024.42			97	5387.26		
事业法人	Institntion Legal Person	241	4068.60	135	1842.36			106	2226.24		
社团法人	Corporation Aggregate	4	18.30	2	8.00			2	10.30		
企业法人	Business Entity	1198	33716.20	637	6365.91	17	146.85	543	27095.70	1	107.74
自然人	Person	2	3.20					2	3.20		
其他组织	Others	6	1199.75	5	1198.75			1	1		

17-35 主要年份文化产业基本情况
Basic Statistics on Culture in Main Years

项 目	Item	2000	2005	2010
文化产业机构数(个)	**Number of Culture Institutions (unit)**	**7848**	**11777**	**9430**
文化部门	Culture Departments	1055	2404	1826
其他部门	Other Departments	6793	9373	7604
文化产业人员数(人)	**Number of Person in Culture (person)**	**26621**	**34001**	**37711**
文化部门	Culture Departments	9801	11515	13310
其他部门	Other Departments	16820	22486	24401
各类文化艺术事业单位数(个)	**Number of Institutions on Various Culture and Art (unit)**			
文化馆、艺术馆	Cultural Centers, Art Centers	108	110	112
公共图书馆	Public Libraries	80	94	103
博物馆	Museums	23	28	71
艺术表演场所	Art Performance Places	23	47	15
艺术表演团体	Art Performance Troupes	88	89	132

17-36 文化艺术、文物事业机构和人员情况

Number of Institutions and Personnel in Culture, Art and Cultural Relics

(2010 年)

项 目	Item	机构数（个）Number of Institutions (unit)	从业人员数（人）Number of Persons Engaged (person)
艺术事业	**Art Institutions**	**148**	**5180**
艺术表演团体	Art Performance Troupes	132	4843
#话剧、儿童剧、滑稽剧团	Drama, Children Plays and Comedy Troupes	2	140
歌剧、舞剧、歌舞剧团	Opera, Ballet and Dance Troupes	6	369
歌舞团、轻音乐团	Song and Dance Troupe, Light Music Troupe	65	2207
文工团、文宣队、乌兰牧骑	Cultural and Performance Troupes and Ulanmuchi (equestrain art troupes)	43	1301
戏曲剧团	Local Opera Troupes	8	412
#京 剧	Local Beijing Opera Troupes	1	92
曲艺、杂技、木偶、皮影团	Recitation and Ballad Troupes, Acrobatics and Circus Troupes, Puppet Show Troupes and Shadow Play Troupes	3	135
艺术表演场所	Art Centers	15	317
剧场、影剧院	Theaters and Music Halls	13	269
艺术创作机构	Art Creation Institutions	1	20
图书馆事业	**Libraries**	**103**	**978**
群众文化事业	**Mass Culture**	**1209**	**3596**
群众艺术馆	Mass Art Centers	15	328
文化馆	Cultural Centers	97	1014
文化站	Cultural Stations	1097	2254
#乡镇文化站	Township Cultural Stations	977	2024
艺术教育事业	**Culture and Education**	**2**	**106**
艺术科研机构	**Art Research Institutions**	**2**	**54**
文化市场经营单位	**Entertainment Operators**	**7577**	**24061**
文化娱乐业	Entertainment Operators	2182	11943
文化市场其他经营单位	Cultural Market Operators	5395	12118
其他文化事业	**Other Cultural Units**	**218**	**2110**
文物事业合计	**Cultural Relics**	**171**	**1626**
文物机构	Historical Relics Agency	99	993
文物保护管理机构	Agency of Historical Relics Preservation	96	605
文物科研机构	Scientific and Research Historical Relics Agency	2	96
其他文物机构	Other Historical Relics Agency	1	292
博物馆	Museums	71	599
#历史类	History Museum	30	234
文物商店	Cultural Relics Store	1	34

17-37 电影、电视、广播事业基本情况
Basic Statistics on Feature Film, Television and Broadcasting

项目	Item	2009	2010
电影制片厂(个)	**Number of Film Studios (unit)**	**1**	**1**
广播电台(座)	**Number of Broadcasting Stations (unit)**	**6**	**6**
中短波发射台及转播台(座)	Transmission and Relaying Stations of MW&SW (unit)	47	54
中短波广播发射功率(千瓦)	Power of MW & SW Transmitters (kw)	2711	2820
调频发射台及转播台(座)	FM Transmission and Relaying Stations (unit)	1001	984
调频发射功率(千瓦)	Power of FM Transmitters (kw)	330.95	476.29
节目(套)	Program (set)	154	155
制作广播节目(小时)	Production of Broadcasting (hour)	249449	260510
#新闻资讯类节目	News Programs	51046	52594
专题服务类节目	Feature Programs	64695	79677
综艺类节目	Variety Show	89197	85358
广播剧类节目	Radio Play	9356	6016
广告类节目	Advertisement Programs	14414	15221
其他类节目	Other Programs	20741	21644
广播人口覆盖率((%)	Listener Rate (%)	94.40	94.90
电视台(座)	**Number of Television Stations (unit)**	**8**	**8**
广播电视台(座)	**Radio and TV Stations (unit)**	**83**	**88**
#县级广播电视台(座)	Radio and TV Station at County-Level (unit)	75	80
电视发射台及转播台(座)	TV Transmission Stations and Relaying Stations (unit)	937	914
电视发射机功率(千瓦)	Power of TV Transmitters (kw)	782.301	903.729
节目(套)	Program (set)	188	196
制作电视节目(小时)	Production of TV Programs (hour)	66321	76467
#新闻资讯类节目	News Programs	24387	28256
专题服务类节目	Feature Programs	13536	18599
综艺类节目	Variety Show	7561	8811
影视剧类节目	Film and TV Play Programs	724	2151
广告类节目	Advertisement Programs	13452	12740
其他类节目	Other Programs	6661	5910
电视人口覆盖率(%)	Viewer Rate (%)	94.78	95.28
有线电视用户(万户)	Numbe of Users of CATV (10 000 households)	180.99	192.00
#数字电视用户	Number of users Digital TV	102.88	131.00
卫星地球站(座)	Eearth Satellite Station (unit)	1	1
卫星收转站(座)	Satellite Receiving Stations (unit)	66982	189902

注：影视剧类节目不包括译制节目。
Note:Number of film and television programs exclude film dubbing program .

主要统计指标解释

普通高等学校　指按照国家规定的设置标准和审批程序批准举办的，通过全国普通高等学校统一招生考试，招收高中毕业生为主要培养对象，实施高等教育的全日制大学、独立设置的学院和高等专科学校、高等职业学校和其他机构(独立学院和分校、大专班)。

大学、独立设置的学院主要实施本科层次以上教育。高等专科学校、高等职业学校实施专科层次教育。其他机构是承担国家普通招生计划任务不计校数的机构，包括独立学院、普通高等学校分校、大专班和批准筹建的普通高等学校等。独立学院指由普通本科高校按新机制、新模式举办的本科层次的二级学院，一些普通本科高校按公办机制和模式建立的二级学院,"分校"或其他类似的二级办学机构不属此范畴。

小学学龄儿童净入学率　指调查范围内已入小学学习的学龄儿童占校内外学龄儿童总数(包括弱智儿童，不包括盲聋哑儿童)的比重。计算公式为：

小学学龄儿童净入学率=已入学的小学学龄儿童数/校内外小学学龄儿童总数*100%

科技活动　指在自然科学、农业科学、医药科学、工程与技术科学、人文与社会科学领域(简称科学技术领域)中，与科技知识的产生、发展、传播和应用密切相关的有组织的活动。可分为研究与试验发展(R&D)、研究与试验发展成果应用及相关的科技服务三类活动。该定义是联合国教科文组织考虑成员国特别是发展中国家开展科技统计工作的需要，而对科技活动所作的统计界定。

科技活动人员　指直接从事科技活动、以及专门从事科技活动管理和为科技活动提供直接服务，累计的实际工作时间占全年制度工作时间10%及以上的人员。(1)直接从事科技活动的人员包括：在独立核算的科学研究与技术开发机构、高等学校、各类企业及其他事业单位内设的研究室、实验室、技术开发中心及中试车间(基地)等机构中从事科技活动的研究人员、工程技术人员、技术工人及其它人员；虽不在上述机构工作，但编入科技活动项目(课题)组的人员；科技信息与文献机构中的专业技术人员；从事论文设计的研究生等。(2)专门从事科技活动管理和为科技活动提供直接服务的人员，包括：独立核算的科学研究与技术开发机构、科技信息与文献机构、高等学校、各类企业及其他事业单位主管科技工作的负责人，专门从事科技活动的计划、行政、人事、财务、物资供应、设备维护、图书资料管理等工作的各类人员，但不包括保卫、医疗保健人员、司机、食堂人员、茶炉工、水暖工、清洁工等为科技活动提供间接服务的人员。该指标用来反映投入科技活动人力的规模。

科学家与工程师　指科技活动人员中具有高、中级技术职称(职务)的人员和不具有高、中级技术职称(职务)的大学本科及以上学历人员。该指标用来反映投入科技活动人力的素质。

研究与试验发展(R&D)　指在科学技术领域，为增加知识总量、以及运用这些知识去创造新的应用进行的系统的创造性的活动，包括基础研究、应用研究、试验发展三类活动。国际上通常采用R&D 活动的规模和强度指标反映一国的科技实力和核心竞争力。

基础研究　指为了获得关于现象和可观察事实的基本原理的新知识(揭示客观事物的本质、运动规律，获得新发现、新学说)而进行的实验性或理论性研究，它不以任何专门或特定的应用或使用为目的。其成果以科学论文和科学著作为主要形式。用来反映知识的原始创新能力。

应用研究　指为获得新知识而进行的创造性研究，主要针对某一特定的目的或目标。应用研究是为了确定基础研究成果可能的用途，或是为达到预定的目标探索应采取的新方法(原理性)或新途径。其成果形式以科学论文、专著、原理性模型或发明专利为主。用来反映对基础研究成果应用途径的探索。

研究与试验发展人员　指参与研究与试验发展项目研究、管理和辅助工作的人员，包括项目(课题)组人员，企业科技行政管理人员和直接为项目(课题)活动提供服务的辅助人员。反映投入从事拥有自主知识产权的研究开发活动的人力规模。

研究与试验发展人员全时当量　指全时人员数加非全时人员按工作量折算为全时人员数的总和。例如：有两个全时人员和三个非全时人员(工作时间分别为20%、30% 和70%)，则全时当量为2+0.2+0.3+0.7=3.2 人年。为国际上比较科技人力投入而制定的可比指标。

专业技术人员　指从事专业技术工作和专业技术管理工作的人员，即企事业单位中已经聘任专业技术职务从事专业技术工作和专业技术管理工作的人员，以及未聘任专业技术职务，现在专业技术岗位上工作的人员。包括工程技术人员，农业技术人员，科学研究人员，卫生技术人员，教学人× 100%员，经济人员，会计人员，统计人员，翻译人员，图书资料、档案、文博人员，新闻出版人员，律师、公证人员，广播电视播音人员，工艺美术人员，体育人员，艺术人员及企业政治思想工作人员，共十七个专业技术职务类别。用来反映科技人力资源情况。

科技活动经费筹集　指从各种渠道筹集到的计划用于科技活动的经费，包括政府资金、企业资金、事业单位资金、金融机构贷款、国外资金和其他资金等。反映各社会经济主体对促进科技进步所做的努力。

政府资金　指从各级政府部门获得的计划用于科技活动的经费，包括科学事业费、科技三项费、科研基建费、科学基金、教育等部门事业费中计划用于科技活动的经费以及政府部门预算外资金中计划用于科技活动的经费等。

企业资金 指从自有资金中提取或接受其他企业委托的、科研院所和高校等事业单位接受企业委托获得的，计划用于科研和技术开发的经费。不包括来自政府、金融机构及国外的计划用于科技活动的资金。

科技活动经费内部支出 指报告年内用于科技活动的实际支出，包括劳务费、科研业务费、科研管理费，非基建投资购建的固定资产、科研基建支出以及其他用于科技活动的支出。不包括生产性活动支出、归还贷款支出及转拨外单位支出。反映科技投入实际完成情况。

劳务费 指以货币或实物形式直接或间接支付给从事科技活动人员的劳动报酬及各种费用。包括各种形式的工资、津贴、奖金、福利、离退休人员费用、人民助学金等。反映改善科技人员待遇情况。

固定资产购建费 指报告年内使用非基建投资购建的固定资产和用于科研基建投资的实际支出额，即固定资产实际支出和科研基建投资实际完成额之和。固定资产是指长期使用而不改变原有实物形态的主要物资设备、图书资料、实验材料和标本以及其他设备和家具、房屋、建筑物。反映用于改善科研条件和科研手段方面的投入情况。

新产品 指采用新技术原理、新设计构思研制、生产的全新产品，或在结构、材质、工艺等某一方面比原有产品有明显改进，从而显著提高了产品性能或扩大了使用功能的产品。既包括政府有关部门认定并在有效期内的新产品，也包括企业自行研制开发，未经政府有关部门认定，从投产之日起一年之内的新产品。用来反映科技产出及对经济增长的直接贡献。

专利 是专利权的简称，是对发明人的发明创造经审查合格后，由专利局依据专利法授予发明人和设计人对该项发明创造享有的专有权。包括发明、实用新型和外观设计。反映拥有自主知识产权的科技和设计成果情况。

发明(专利) 指对产品、方法或者其改进所提出的新的技术方案。是国际通行的反映拥有自主知识产权技术的核心指标。

实用新型(专利) 指对产品的形状、构造或者其结合所提出的适于实用的新的技术方案。反映具有一定技术含量的技术成果情况。

外观设计(专利) 指对产品的形状、图案、色彩或者其结合所作出的富有美感并适于工业上应用的新设计。反映拥有自主知识产权的外观设计成果情况。

文化及相关产业 指为社会公众提供文化、娱乐产品和服务的活动以及与这些活动有关联的活动的集合。根据提供文化、娱乐产品和服务活动的属性特点，划分为公益性文化活动和经营性文化活动两大类。

文化及相关产业是第三产业的重要组成部分。是在我国《国民经济行业分类》基础上的派生分类，有文化服务和相关文化服务两大类：

文化服务 主要指新闻服务，出版发行和版权服务，广播、电视、电影服务，文化艺术服务，网络文化服务，文化休闲娱乐服务，其他文化服务。

艺术表演团体 由文化部门主办或实行行业管理（经文化市场行政部门审批或已申报登记并领取相关许可证），专门从事表演艺术等活动的各类专业艺术表演团体，含民间职业剧团。如话剧团、方言话剧团、滑稽剧团、儿童剧团、歌剧团、木偶团、皮影团等以及由若干剧种组成的综合性专业艺术表演团体。不包括半工半艺、半农半艺的剧团。

艺术表演场馆 指由文化部门主办或实行行业管理（经文化市场行政部门审批或已申报登记并领取相关许可证），有观众席、舞台、灯光设备，公开售票、专供文艺团体演出的文化活动场所。包括剧院（场）、音乐厅、歌剧院（场）、舞剧院（场）、话剧院(场)、戏院、马戏场、影剧院等进行文艺表演的场所。不包括电影院、礼堂、体育场馆、美术馆及绘画、雕塑等艺术馆。

文化市场经营机构 经文化市场行政部门审批或已申报登记并领取相关许可证的、从事文化经营和文化服务活动的机构。

广播节目综合人口覆盖率 指根据国家广电总局制定的《广播电视人口覆盖率统计技术标准和方法》进行统计调查的，在对象区内采用无线、有线、卫星等技术手段能够收听到包括中央、省、地市、县广播节目其中任意一套的人口数占全国总人口数的百分比。

电视节目综合人口覆盖率 指根据国家广电总局制定的《广播电视人口覆盖率统计技术标准和方法》进行统计调查的，在对象区内采用无线、有线、卫星等技术手段能够看到包括中央、省、地市、县级电视节目中任意一套的人口数占全国总人口数的百分比。

Explanatory Notes on Main Statistical Indicators

Regular Institutions of Higher Education refer to educational establishments set up according to the government evaluation and approval procedures, recruiting graduates from senior secondary schools as the main target by National Matriculation TEST. They include full-time universities, colleges, institutions of higher professional education, institutions of higher vocational education, institutions of higher vocational education and others (non-university tertiary, branch schools and undergraduate classes).

Universities and colleges primarily provide undergraduate courses; institutions of higher professional education and institutions of higher vocational education primarily provide professional trainings; and others refer to educational establishments, which are responsible for enrolling higher education students under the State Plan but not enumerated in the total number of schools, including: branch schools of universities and colleges, and universities and colleges that have been approved and under plan for construction. Non-university tertiary refers to the regular undergraduate branch college which is running in new mechanism and mode, excluding the branch schools and other similar branches of educational institutions.

Net Enrolment Ratio of Primary Schools refers to the proportion of school age children enrolled at schools to the total number of school age children both in and outside schools (including retarded children, but excluding blind, deaf and mute children). The formula is:

$$\text{Net Enrolment Ratio of Primary Schools} = \frac{\text{Total Primary School} - \text{age Children at Schools}}{\text{Total Primary School} - \text{age Children Whether or Not Attending School}} \times 100\ \%$$

Scientific and Technological Activities (S&T Activities) refer to organized activities which are closely related with the creation, development, dissemination and application of the scientific and technical knowledge in the fields of natural sciences, agricultural science, medical science, engineering and technological science, humanities and social sciences (referred to as scientific and technological fields). S&T activities can be classified into 3 categories: research and development (R&D) activities, application of R&D results, and related S&T services. This statistical definition is made by UNICHIEF for scientific and technological activities to meet the need of carrying out statistical work in this field for its member countries particularly the developing countries.

Personnel Engaged in S&T Activities refer to personnel directly engaged in S&T activities, in the management of S&T activities, and in providing direct service to S&T activities, with over 10% of the total working hours in a year spent on S&T activities. (1) Personnel directly engaged in S&T activities include researchers, engineers, technicians and other related personnel engaged in S&T activities in independent-accounting R&D institutions, institutions of higher learning, and in research institutes, laboratories, technology development centres and central experiment workshops under enterprises and institutions. Also included are people working in S&T research project teams, professional and technical personnel working in S&T information archiving institutes, and graduate students working on the design of their thesis. (2) Personnel engaged in the management of S&T activities and in providing direct service to S&T activities include senior management people responsible for S&T activities in independent-accounting R&D institutions, S&T information archiving institutes, institutions of higher learning and in enterprises and institutions where S&T activities are undertaken. Also included are people responsible for the planning, administration, personnel management, financial management, logistics supply, equipment maintenance, information and library management that are related with S&T activities. People providing indirect services are excluded, such as security, medical service, drivers, plumbers, cleaners and those providing catering and related service. This indicator reflects the size of personnel engaged in S&T activities.

Scientists and Engineers refer to persons engaged in S&T activities either having obtained titles of senior and middle level professional positions, or those without such positions but have completed university or higher education. This indicator reflects the quality of personnel engaged in S&T activities.

Research and Development (R&D) refers to systematic and creative activities in the field of science and technology aiming at increasing the knowledge and using the knowledge for new application. R&D includes 3 categories of activities: basic research, applied research and experimentation for development. The scale and intensity of R&D are widely used internationally to reflect the strength of S&T and the core competitiveness of a country in the world.

Basic Research refers to empirical or theoretical research aiming at obtaining new knowledge on the fundamental principles regarding phenomena or observable facts to reveal the intrinsic nature and underlying laws and to acquire new discoveries or new theories. Basic research takes no specific or designated application as the aim of the research. Results of basic research are mainly released or disseminated in the form of scientific papers or monographs. This indicator reflects the innovation capacity for original knowledge.

Applied Research refers to creative research aiming at obtaining new knowledge on a specific objective or target. Purpose of the applied research is to identify the possible uses of results from basic research, or to explore new (fundamental) methods or new approaches. Results of applied research are expressed in the form of scientific papers, monographs, fundamental models or invention patents. This indicator reflects the exploration of ways to apply the results of basic research.

R&D Personnel refer to persons engaged in research, management and supporting activities of R&D, including persons in the project teams, persons engaged in the management of S&T activities of enterprises and supporting staff providing direct service to the research projects. This indicator reflects the size of personnel engaged in R&D activities with independent intellectual property.

Full-time Equivalent of R&D Personnel refers to the sum of the full-time persons and the full-time equivalent of part-time persons converted by workload. For instance, if there are 2 full-time persons and 3 part-time workers (20%, 30% and 70% of working hours respectively on R&D activities), the full-time equivalent are 2+0.2+0.3+0.7=3.2 person-years. This is an internationally comparable indicator of S&T manpower input.

Professional and Technical Personnel refer to persons engaged in professional and technical work or in the management of professional and technical activities, i.e., people with professional or technical positions who are engaged in professional and technical work or in the management of professional and technical activities, and people without professional or technical positions but are working on professional or technical posts. They include professionals and technicians working in 17 categories of technical occupations including engineering, agriculture, scientific researches, medical service, teaching, economic research and application, accounting, statistics, translation, libraries, archives, cultural and museum service, journalism and publication, lawyers, notarization service, radio and television broadcasting, handicraft and fine arts, sports, performing art, and political workers in enterprises. This indicator reflects the condition of human resources in S&T.

Funding for S&T Activities refers to funds obtained from various sources for S&T activities, including government funds, self-raised funds by enterprises, self-raised funds by institutions, loans from financial institutions, foreign funds and other funds. This indicator reflects the efforts made by various social economic entities in promoting the development of S&T.

Government Funds refer to funds obtained from government agencies at all levels to be used for S&T activities, including fund for scientific undertakings, 3 kinds of fund for S&T activities, fund for capital construction for scientific researches, science fund, funds from education expenditures by education departments for S&T activities, and extra-budget fund from government agencies for S&T activities.

Funds of Enterprises refers to funds of enterprises from their own budget; funds from other enterprises; or funds received by universities or research institutions from enterprises for scientific research or technical development projects. Excluded from this category are funds from government agencies, financial institutions or from foreign institutions.

Internal Expenditure on S&T activities refer to the actual expenditure on S&T activities during the reference year, including service fees, expenditure on research activities, expenditure on research management, purchase or construction of fixed assets not included in the investment for capital construction, expenditure on capital construction for scientific researches, and other expenditure on S&T activities. Not included are expenditure on production activities, repayment of loans and transfer expenditure. This indicator reflects the net investment in S&T more accurately.

Service Fees refer to direct or indirect payment, in cash or in kind, made to personnel engaged in S&T activities as remuneration and other fees. They include, in various forms, salaries, subsidies, bonus, benefits, retirement pension, stipend, etc. This indicator reflects the improvement of the remuneration package for S&T personnel.

Purchase or Construction of Fixed Assets refers to the fixed assets purchased or constructed using funds other than the investment in capital construction, and the actual expenditure on capital construction for scientific researches. In other words, it is the sum of the actual expenditure on fixed assets and the accomplished investment in capital construction for scientific researches. Fixed assets refer to main materials and equipment, literatures and documents in libraries, materials for experiments, specimen, instruments, furniture, buildings and constructions that can be used for a long time without changing the form and shape of those articles or constructions. This indicator reflects the input in improving the condition of S&T and the means of scientific research.

New Products refer to brand new products produced with new technology and new design, or products that represent noticeable improvement in terms of structure, material, or production process for improving significantly the character or function of the older versions. They include new products certified by relevant government agencies within the period of certification, as well as new products designed and produced by enterprises within a year without certification by government agencies. This indicator reflects the direct contribution of S&T output to economic growth.

Patent is an abbreviation for the patent right and refers to the exclusive right of ownership by the inventors or designers for the creation or inventions, given from the patent offices after due process of assessment and approval in accordance with the Patent Law. Patents are granted for inventions, utility models and designs. This indicator reflects the achievements of S&T and design with independent intellectual property.

Patented Inventions refer to new technical proposals to the products or methods or their modifications. This is universal core indicator reflecting the technologies with independent intellectual property.

Patented Utility Models refer to the practical and new technical proposals on the shape and structure of the product or the combination of both. This indicator reflects the condition of technological results with certain technical content.

Designs refer to the aesthetics and industrially applicable new designs for the shape, pattern and colour of the product, or their combinations. This indicator reflects the appearance design achievements with independent intellectual property.

Culture and Related Industries refer to the aggregate of activities, providing the mass with culture goods, amusement goods and services. According to the characteristics of culture goods, amusement goods and services, they can be classified into two categories, or nonprofit cultural activities and profit cultural activities.

Culture and related industries is the important component of the tertiary industry. These are the derivative sector from the Industrial Classification of the National Economy and are composed of two categories of culture services and related cultural services.

Culture services mainly include news services, publishing and copyright services, radio, television, film, arts, network, recreation, and other cultural services

Arts Performance Troupes refer to the various professional performing arts groups, which sponsored by the cultural sectors or guided by the cultural society (approved by the cultural market administration, or registered and permitted with the relative certificate), including non-governmental troupes, such as drama troupes, dialect troupes, comedy troupes, children troupes, Opera troupes, puppetry troupes, Shadowgraph troupes, etc., comprehensive professional arts performance troupes. The semi-working and semi-farming arts troupes are not included.

Arts Performance Places refer to the various sites for cultural activities, which sponsored by the cultural sectors or guided by the cultural society (approved by the cultural market administration, or registered and permitted with the relative certificate), with the facility of auditorium, stage, and lighting, and selling tickets in public, specially performed by arts troupes, including theatre, concert halls, opera halls, dance halls, drama halls, cinemas, circus fields, and other showplaces for the performing arts. The cinemas, auditoriums, stadiums, and arts museums, such as art galleries, painting houses, sculpture houses, are not included.

Cultural Market Operating Units refer to the units dealing in culture and cultural services, which registered and permitted with the relative certificate by cultural market administration.

Radio Coverage of Population refers to the percentage of population, which can listen to one of central, provincial, city, prefecture, and county radio programs by wireless, cable, satellite and other technical means, in the surveying area, to national total population, according to Statistical Standard and Method on Television and Radio Coverage of Population established by the State Administration of Broadcasting, Film and Television.

Television Coverage of Population refers to the percentage of population, which can watch one of central, provincial, city, prefecture, and county television programs by wireless, cable, satellite and other technical means, in the surveying area, to national total population, according to Statistical Standard and Method on Television and Radio Coverage of Population established by the State Administration of Broadcasting, Film and Television.

第十八篇 体育、卫生及其他

CHAPTER 18 Sports, Public Health and Others

简要说明
Brief Introduction

本篇资料的主要内容及来源

本篇资料主要包括卫生事业、体育事业、民政事业、公安机关案件受理处治情况、安全生产情况、道路交通事故和火灾事故等内容，除卫生、体育事业外其他部门数据由新疆维吾尔自治区统计局社会科技处与综合处根据有关部门资料整理。

卫生部门资料是由新疆维吾尔自治区卫生厅依据年报资料整理提供。体育资料是由新疆维吾尔自治区体育局提供。民政部分资料由新疆维吾尔自治区民政厅提供，治安、刑事案件资料由新疆维吾尔自治区公安厅提供，安全生产情况来自新疆维吾尔自治区安全生产监督管理局，道路交通事故和火灾事故分别由新疆维吾尔自治区公安交通管理局和新疆维吾尔自治区消防总队提供。

Main content and source of data

Data in this chapter mainly include the development of public health, sports, civil affairs, labor and society protection, offense cases against public order handled by public Security organs, traffic accidents and fires. These statistics are provided by Department of Population and Social Science &Technology in Statistics Bureau of Xinjiang according to the data from the related Department of Statistics Bureau.

Data on public health are from the Bureau of Public Health,these statistics are according to the data of yearly statistics; Data on sports are from the Bureau of Sports; Data on civil affairs and labor protection are provided respectively by the Bureau of Civil Affairs and the Bureau of Labor and Social Security. Data on public security, statistics on procuratorial, legal and judicial affairs are provided by the Bureau of Public Security. Data on production safety are come from Xinjiang Administration of Work Safety. Data on traffic accident and fire are respectively provided by the Xinjiang Traffic Management Bureau and the Xinjiang Fire Department.

18-1 体育局系统从业人员情况
Statistics on Staff and Workers in Physical Education System

单位：人 (2010 年) (person)

项　目	Item	合　计 Total	公务员 Civil Servants	教练员 Coaches	运动员 Athletes	科研人员 Scientific and Technical Personnel
总　计	**Total**	**3069**	**418**	**636**	**595**	**19**
体育行政机关	Administrative of Physical Culture and Sports	659	418	31	21	
运动项目管理部门	Sports Events Mangement	713		72	448	1
体育运动学校	Physical Education and Sports Schools	572		134		4
业余体校	Spare-time Sports Schools	814		393	125	
体育场馆	Stadium and Gymnasium	174				
体育科研机构	Sport Scientific Research Institutions	20				14
其　他	Others	117		6	1	

项　目	Item	医务人员 Medical Personnel	文化教师 Culture Teachers	管理人员 Administrative Personnel	工勤人员 Logistics Workers	其他人员 Others
总　计	**Total**	**29**	**309**	**447**	**392**	**224**
体育行政机关	Administrative of Physical Culture and Sports			73	77	39
运动项目管理部门	Sports Events Mangement	19		93	63	17
体育运动学校	Physical Education and Sports Schools	7	257	74	56	40
业余体校	Spare-time Sports Schools		51	81	67	97
体育场馆	Stadium and Gymnasium	3	1	63	96	11
体育科研机构	Sport Scientific Research Institutions			4	2	
其　他	Others			59	31	20

18-2 按项目分等级裁判员发展人数
Number of Referees in Levels by Type of Sports

单位：人 (2010 年) (person)

项目	Item	合计 Total	一级裁判员 First Level Referee 小计 Sub-total	男 Male	女 Female	二级裁判员 Second Level Referee 小计 Sub-total	男 Male	女 Female
总 计	**Total**	**955**	**51**	**41**	**10**	**904**	**802**	**102**
田 径	Track and Field	149				149	124	25
拳 击	Boxing	7				7	7	
国际式摔跤	InternationalWrestling	13				13	13	
跆拳道	Taekwondo	14				14	14	
射 箭	Shooting	2				2	2	
足 球	Football	55				55	54	1
篮 球	Basketball	230				230	219	11
乒乓球	Table Tennis	81				81	51	30
网 球	Tennis	60				60	60	
速度滑冰	Speed Skating	13				13	8	5
高山滑雪	Alping Skiing	17				17	12	5
单板滑雪	Snowboarding	7				7	4	3
国际象棋	Chess	39	39	30	9			
中国象棋	Chinese Chess	1				1	1	
武 术	Martial Art	2				2	2	
台 球	Billiards	4				4	4	
门 球	Croquet	78				78	64	14
轮 滑	Inline Skate	35				35	27	8
信 鸽	Carrier Pigeon	135				135	135	
钓 鱼	Angling	13	12	11	1	1	1	

18-3 按项目分等级运动员发展人数
Number of Athletes at Levels by Type of Sports

单位：人 (2010 年) (person)

项目	Item	合计 Total	国际、国家级运动健将 International and National Level		一级运动员 First Grade		二级运动员 Second Grade	
			小计 Sub-total	#男 Male	小计 Sub-total	#男 Male	小计 Sub-total	#男 Male
总 计	**Total**	**622**	**18**	**13**	**167**	**97**	**437**	**281**
田 径	Track and Field	89	1	1	13	9	75	46
游 泳	Swimming	6			2	2	4	3
拳 击	Boxing	53			31	23	22	13
举 重	Weightlifting	8			1	1	7	5
国际式摔跤	InternationalWrestling	24					24	17
中国式摔跤	Chinese-style Wrestling	2					2	2
柔 道	Judo	40			29	14	11	10
跆拳道	Taekwondo	62	1	1	29	15	32	20
射 击	Shooting	28			19	6	9	6
射 箭	Archery	31	3	3	12	6	16	10
足 球	Football	50			11	7	39	21
篮 球	Basketball	85			9	5	76	53
排 球	Volleyball	15	6	6			9	5
沙滩排球	Beach Volleyball	9			4	4	5	3
乒乓球	Table Tennis	50	1				49	27
手 球	Handball	4	2		2			
速度滑冰	Speed Skating	34	2		3	3	29	16
登 山	Mountaineering	2	2	2				
武 术	Martial Art	20			1	1	19	15
围 棋	Weiqi	8					8	8
航空模型	Aviation Model	2			1	1	1	1

18-4 各地、州、市体育局系统机构数

Number of Institutions in Sports Committees by Prefecture,Autonomous Prefecture and City

单位：个 (2010 年) (unit)

地 区	Region	合 计 Total	行政机关 Administrative Agencies	运动项目管理部门 Sports Events Mangement	体育运动学校 Physical Education and Sports Schools
总 计	**Total**	**217**	**110**	**8**	**5**
自治区直属	Under Autonomous Region	17	1	6	1
乌鲁木齐市	Urumqi City	19	9		1
克拉玛依市	Karamay City	6	5		
石河子市	Shihezi City	2	1		
吐鲁番地区	Turpan Administrative Offices	8	4		
哈密地区	Hami [Kumul] Administrative Offices	10	4		
昌吉回族自治州	Changji Hui Autonomous Prefecture	10	8		
伊犁哈萨克自治州	Ili Kazak Autonomous Prefecture	46	27	2	1
伊犁州直属县(市)	Counties (Cities) Direct Under Ili Prefecture	18	11	1	1
塔城地区	Tacheng [Tarbagatai] Administrative Offices	11	8		
阿勒泰地区	Altay Administrative Offices	17	8	1	
博尔塔拉蒙古自治州	Bortala Mongol Autonomous Prefecture	8	4		
巴音郭楞蒙古自治州	Bayangol Mongol Autonomous Prefecture	16	10		
阿克苏地区	Aksu Administrative Offices	22	10		1
克孜勒苏柯尔克孜自治州	Kizilsu Kirgiz Autonomous Prefecture	12	5		
喀什地区	Kashgar [Kaxgar] Administrative Offices	23	13		1
和田地区	Hotan Administrative Offices	18	9		

地 区	Region	业余体校 Spare-time Sports Schools	体育场馆 Stadium and Gymnasium	体育科研机构 Sport Scientific Research Institutions	其 他 Others
总 计	**Total**	**67**	**13**	**2**	**12**
自治区直属	Under Autonomous Region		1	1	7
乌鲁木齐市	Urumqi City	5	2	1	1
克拉玛依市	Karamay City	1			
石河子市	Shihezi City	1			
吐鲁番地区	Turpan Administrative Offices	4			
哈密地区	Hami [Kumul] Administrative Offices	3	1		2
昌吉回族自治州	Changji Hui Autonomous Prefecture	1	1		
伊犁哈萨克自治州	Ili Kazak Autonomous Prefecture	12	3		1
伊犁州直属县(市)	Counties (Cities) Direct Under Ili Prefecture	4	1		
塔城地区	Tacheng [Tarbagatai] Administrative Offices	1	1		1
阿勒泰地区	Altay Administrative Offices	7	1		
博尔塔拉蒙古自治州	Bortala Mongol Autonomous Prefecture	4			
巴音郭楞蒙古自治州	Bayangol Mongol Autonomous Prefecture	5	1		
阿克苏地区	Aksu Administrative Offices	9	2		
克孜勒苏柯尔克孜自治州	Kizilsu Kirgiz Autonomous Prefecture	5	1		1
喀什地区	Kashgar [Kaxgar] Administrative Offices	8	1		
和田地区	Hotan Administrative Offices	9			

18-5 各地、州、市体育局系统机构从业人员数
Number of Staff and Workers in Sports Bureau by Region

单位：人 (2010 年) (person)

地区	Region	合计 Total	行政机关 Administrative Agencies	运动项目管理部门 Sports Events Mangement	体育运动学校 Physical Education and Sports Schools
总计	**Total**	**3069**	**659**	**713**	**572**
自治区直属	Under Autonomous Region	1016	46	684	151
乌鲁木齐市	Urumqi City	456	36		227
克拉玛依市	Karamay City	42	36		
石河子市	Shihezi City	31	5		
吐鲁番地区	Turpan Administrative Offices	59	24		
哈密地区	Hami [Kumul] Administrative Offices	100	40		
昌吉回族自治州	Changji Hui Autonomous Prefecture	43	32		
伊犁哈萨克自治州	Ili Kazak Autonomous Prefecture	438	165	29	79
伊犁州直属县(市)	Counties (Cities) Direct Under Ili Prefecture	247	92	11	79
塔城地区	Tacheng [Tarbagatai] Administrative Offices	73	50		
阿勒泰地区	Altay Administrative Offices	118	23	18	
博尔塔拉蒙古自治州	Bortala Mongol Autonomous Prefecture	74	42		
巴音郭楞蒙古自治州	Bayangol Mongol Autonomous Prefecture	99	42		
阿克苏地区	Aksu Administrative Offices	183	73		53
克孜勒苏柯尔克孜自治州	Kizilsu Kirgiz Autonomous Prefecture	83	28		
喀什地区	Kashgar [Kaxgar] Administrative Offices	406	70		62
和田地区	Hotan Administrative Offices	39	20		

地区	Region	业余体校 Spare-time Sports Schools	体育场馆 Stadium and Gymnasium	体育科研机构 Sport Scientific Research Institutions	其他 Others
总计	**Total**	**814**	**174**	**20**	**117**
自治区直属	Under Autonomous Region		25	13	97
乌鲁木齐市	Urumqi City	113	68	7	5
克拉玛依市	Karamay City	6			
石河子市	Shihezi City	26			
吐鲁番地区	Turpan Administrative Offices	35			
哈密地区	Hami [Kumul] Administrative Offices	51			9
昌吉回族自治州	Changji Hui Autonomous Prefecture	9			
伊犁哈萨克自治州	Ili Kazak Autonomous Prefecture	131	34		
伊犁州直属县(市)	Counties (Cities) Direct Under Ili Prefecture	54	11		
塔城地区	Tacheng [Tarbagatai] Administrative Offices	23			
阿勒泰地区	Altay Administrative Offices	54	23		
博尔塔拉蒙古自治州	Bortala Mongol Autonomous Prefecture	32			
巴音郭楞蒙古自治州	Bayangol Mongol Autonomous Prefecture	44	13		
阿克苏地区	Aksu Administrative Offices	47	10		
克孜勒苏柯尔克孜自治州	Kizilsu Kirgiz Autonomous Prefecture	37	12		6
喀什地区	Kashgar [Kaxgar] Administrative Offices	264	10		
和田地区	Hotan Administrative Offices	19			

18-6 卫生机构、床位、人员数

(2010 年)

项 目	Item	机构数(个) Number of Institutions (unit)	床位数(张) Beds (unit)	卫生人员合计(人) Total Number of Medical Personnel (person)	卫生技术人员 Medical Technical Personnel
总 计	**Total**	**7650**	**116230**	**149069**	**122860**
按市县分	**By City and County**				
市	City	4415	69059	97764	80066
县	County	3235	47171	51305	42794
按经济类型分	**By Economic Sectors**				
国 有	State-owned	2805	100443	121792	99579
集 体	Collective-owned	296	2680	4364	3708
联 营	Joint Operation	22	88	173	145
私 营	Private-owned	4340	10503	19330	16700
其 他	Others	187	2516	3410	2728
按设置主办单位分	**By sponsors**				
政府办	Government sponsored	2463	96993	116132	95083
社会办	Society sponsored	720	8172	12573	10221
个人办	Individual sponsored	4467	11065	20364	17556
按机构分	**By Organizations**				
医院合计	Total Number of Hospitals	802	89871	96777	78206
市	City	479	61157	70748	56706
县	County	323	28714	26029	21500
综合医院	Comprehensive Hospitals	624	69525	79959	64978
中医医院	Hospitals of Traditional Chinese Medicine	43	5254	5248	4287
中西医综合医院	TCM and Western Medicine Hospital	4	569	556	485
民族医院	Hospitals for Nationalities	45	5123	3964	3209
专科医院	Specialist Hospitals	86	9400	7050	5247
口腔医院	Nonnasality Hospitals	4	42	271	223
眼科医院	Ophthalmology Hospitals	5	120	126	95
耳鼻喉科医院	Otolaryngology Hospitals	2	70	191	139
肿瘤医院	Tumour Hospital	2	2104	1618	1260
心血管病医院	Cardiovascular Hospitals	1	293	518	349
胸科医院	Chest Hospital	1	451	416	332
妇产(科)医院	Hospitals for Gynaecology and Obsterics	16	445	540	414
儿童医院	Children Hospital	1	30	28	21
精神病医院	Mental Hospitals	13	3778	1523	997
传染病医院	Infectous Diseases Hospitals	4	516	411	301
结核病医院	Tubercuiosis Hospitals	1	300	173	150
骨科医院	Hospital of Orthopedics	5	275	261	224
康复医院	Recovery Hospitals	3	119	88	63
整形外科医院	Plastic surgical holpital	2	60	69	50
其他专科医院	Other Specialist Hospitals	26	797	817	629
疗养院	Sanitarium	4	463	283	143
社区卫生服务中心(站)	Community Health Service Center	641	3588	7314	6238
社区卫生服务中心	Community Health Service Center	139	2483	4241	3547
社区卫生服务站	Community Health Service Station	502	1105	3073	2691
卫生院合计	Total Number of Public Health Center	910	19980	20015	16881
街道卫生院	Public Health Center in Neighbourhood	9	94	224	183
乡、镇卫生院	Public Health Center in Township and Towns	901	19886	19791	16698
中心卫生院	Public Health Center in Rural Area	135	4213	3802	3217
乡卫生院	Public Health Center in Township	766	15673	15989	13481
门诊部	Outpatients Department	259	500	1955	1626
诊所、卫生所、医务室	Clinics, Health Centers	4555	5	9964	9752
急救中心(站)	First-Aid-Stations(Center)	4	50	167	133
采供血机构	Blood Collection & Supply Organs	21		483	333
妇幼保健院(所、站)	Hospitals for Maternity and Child Care	90	1733	3613	3004
专科疾病防治院(所、站)	Specialized Stations	4	40	85	37
疾病预防控制中心(防疫站)	Diseases Preventing & Controlling Center (Epidemic Prevention Station)	221		6418	4967
卫生监督所	Sanitation Superintendence Office	133		1906	1490
卫生监督检验(监测、检测)	Sanitation Superintendence & Examining(monitoring,testing)office(station)	1		9	9
其它卫生事业机构	Other Health Institutions	5		80	41

Number of Health Institutions, Beds and Persons Engaged by Type of Institutons

执业医师 Lecensed Doctors	执业助理医师 Lecensed Assistant Doctor	注册护士 Registered Nurses	药剂人员 Pharmacist	技师(士) Technician (artificer)	检验人员 Laboratory Technicians	其他 Others	其他技术人员 Other Technicians	管理人员 Administrative Personnel	工勤人员 Logistics Workers
39301	**8865**	**44238**	**6364**	**7742**	**5301**	**16350**	**6979**	**7089**	**12141**
28374	3787	30724	4178	4985	3475	8018	4752	4972	7974
10927	5078	13514	2186	2757	1826	8332	2227	2117	4167
30128	7303	36557	5131	6511	4550	13949	6031	5828	10354
1261	284	1373	231	216	138	343	183	220	253
47	6	61	9	7	5	15	7	10	11
6943	1109	5225	820	838	496	1765	610	804	1216
922	163	1022	173	170	112	278	148	227	307
28222	7259	34816	4860	6204	4328	13722	5827	5464	9758
3770	437	3916	647	656	450	795	466	792	1094
7309	1169	5506	857	882	523	1833	686	833	1289
24777	3813	31814	4631	5040	3159	8131	4973	5055	8543
18880	2073	23777	3278	3543	2290	5155	3828	3871	6343
5897	1740	8037	1353	1497	869	2976	1145	1184	2200
20544	3051	26901	3511	4178	2646	6793	3992	4235	6754
1611	179	1476	372	297	183	352	325	238	398
110	23	180	24	20	14	128	27	38	6
908	381	884	482	173	114	381	244	121	390
1604	179	2373	242	372	202	477	385	423	995
122	16	60	4	4	1	17	8	15	25
26	5	42	7	4	4	11	8	13	10
56	4	58	9	5	5	7	20	3	29
350	3	677	31	108	26	91	53	119	186
94	8	186	25	13	10	23	6	40	123
107	0	140	17	14	13	54	35	4	45
106	37	151	24	48	29	48	25	45	56
5	4	6	3	3	2	0	0	3	4
256	27	565	33	43	27	73	161	59	306
109	13	104	16	22	16	37	15	26	69
57	6	67	6	11	9	3	8	7	8
57	13	74	20	25	10	35	1	15	21
36	1	18	2	2	1	4	9	6	10
20	7	18	1	4	3	0	5	11	3
203	35	207	44	66	46	74	31	57	100
46	6	54	10	16	8	11	6	39	95
2251	392	2316	406	367	249	506	265	390	421
1176	213	1313	259	229	146	357	168	243	283
1075	179	1003	147	138	103	149	97	147	138
2943	2974	4921	777	917	647	4349	950	536	1648
48	24	48	19	15	11	29	16	12	13
2895	2950	4873	758	902	636	4320	934	524	1635
569	594	929	155	197	136	773	151	94	340
2326	2356	3944	603	705	500	3547	783	430	1295
704	117	425	130	136	87	114	113	135	81
5233	580	3187	232	55	45	465			212
59	2	60	1	2	1	9	10	3	21
51	12	96	7	130	129	37	45	37	68
1119	306	917	100	233	183	329	170	187	252
17	8	7	2	3	1		2	43	3
2082	651	431	65	836	786	902	340	465	646
						1490	85	187	144
1	2	2		4	3				
18	2	8	3	3	3	7	20	12	7

18-7 主要年份卫生机构数
Number of Health Institutions in Main Years

单位：个 (unit)

年 份 Year	合 计 Total	医院、卫生院 Hospitals And Township Hospitals	#医院 Hospitals	疗养院 Sanit-arium	门诊部 Clinics	专科防治所、站 Specialized Prevention & Treatment Centers or Stations	疾病防控中心 Sanitation and Antiepide-mic Agencies	妇幼保健所、站 Maternity and Child Care Centers	社区卫生服务中心 Health Service Center for Community	医学科学研究机构 Research Institutes of Medical Science	其他卫生机构 Other Institutions	诊所、医务保健室、医务室 Clinics Health Care Room Infirmary	#私营、个体机构 Institutions of Privately Owned & Individual
1978	2581	806		2	1609	1	104	12		1	46		
1980	2818	884		4	1756	4	102	12		1	55		
1985	3320	947		5	2125	2	139	27		2	73		
1990	3945	1049		6	2536	13	191	59		3	88		
1995	3932	1292		8	2247	16	216	69		6	78		
2000	7314	1352	522	8	154	16	210	74		7	89	5404	3653
2005	8087	1516	685	6	224	8	197	88	46	3	140	5859	4183
2006	8175	1560	699	6	220	7	211	92	62	3	129	5885	4227
2007	7465	1629	756	7	240	7	214	87	250	3	139	4889	4093
2008	6739	1629	741	4	217	6	213	89	264		152	4165	3756
2009	7288	1669	763	5	221	5	214	90	405		158	4521	3678
2010	7650	1712	802	4	259	4	221	90	641		164	4555	3796

注：1.2002 年起卫生部新制度规定持有"医疗执业许可证"所有卫生机构算为一个机构,兵团连队卫生室统计到卫生所中,所以卫生机构总数增加。2. 从 2007 年开始卫生部门实行网络直报。

Note: a)From 2002, in line with new regulations of ministry of public health,all the health institutions that have medical service permit shall be counted as one and health care rooms shall be counted in health clinics,therefore the total number of health institutions increased.
b)Since 2007, health care institution have carried out direct network report.

18-8 主要年份卫生人员数
Number of Persons Engaged in Health Institutions in Main Years

单位：人 (person)

年 份 Year	合 计 Total	#卫生技术人员 Medical Technical Personnel	#医 生 Doctors	执业医师 Lecensed Doctors	执业助理医 师 Lecensed Assistant Doctor	#注 册 护 士 Registered Nurses	平均每万人医生数 Number of Doctors per 10 000 Population	在合计中私人个体开业人员 Persons of Privately Owned & Individual
1978	66252	51050	16898	7368	9530	10765	13.70	
1980	74627	57949	20614	10092	10522	12077	16.06	
1985	88460	68961	25721	13330	12391	17136	18.90	188
1990	102053	79853	33683	24967	8716	23386	22.03	2034
1995	116856	92028	39636	30038	9598	26350	23.86	4252
2000	122064	98093	45402	34892	10510	30850	24.55	5835
2005	117165	96266	41426	32563	8863	30657	20.61	13562
2006	121400	99839	42775	33988	8787	32119	20.87	13256
2007	127621	104671	43551	34838	8713	34662	20.79	14689
2008	130174	106853	43456	35320	8136	36084	20.39	14560
2009	138344	114521	45616	37223	8393	40425	21.13	16616
2010	149069	122860	48166	39301	8865	44238	22.25	19330

注：2002 年以前执业医师为中医师、西医师、中西医结合医师，执业助理医师为中医士、西医士、中西医结合医士，注册护士为护师、护士。(以下同)

Note: Prior to 2002,doctors with license were doctors trained in western medicine,assistant doctors are practioners with secondary western medical education,and registered nurses are master nurses and nurses (The following is the same as below) .

18-9 主要年份卫生机构床位数
Number of Sick-Beds in Health Institutions in Main Years

单位：张 (unit)

年份 Year	合计 Total	医院卫生院 Hospitals And Health Centers	#医院 Hospitals	疗养院 Sanitarium	其他卫生机构 Other Health Institutions	每万人医院、卫生院床位数 Number of Hospital Beds per 10 000 Population
1978	57647	39179		108	18360	31.78
1980	61075	47236		682	13157	36.81
1985	60930	55298		870	4762	40.63
1990	67414	60707	47924	1010	5697	39.70
1995	72955	66696	53336	1233	5026	40.15
2000	70542	65916	52438	1301	3325	35.64
2005	79753	76002	63013	830	2921	37.81
2006	83722	80090	65589	860	2772	39.07
2007	90329	87131	71496	793	2405	41.59
2008	96852	93253	76321	443	3156	43.76
2009	107193	102620	83776	613	3960	47.54
2010	116230	109851	89871	463	5916	50.36

18-10 医疗机构病床使用情况
Utilization of Beds in Medical Institutions

(2010 年)

项目	Item	实际开放总床日数(日) Beds Open to Patients (day)	平均开放病床(张) Average Beds Open to Patients (unit)	病床周转次数(次) Turnover of Beds (times)	病床工作日(日) Number of Days per Bed in Use in a Year (day)	病床使用率(%) Utilization Rate of Beds (%)	出院者平均住院日(日) Average Stay Days in Hospital (day)
总计	**Total**	**40772035**	**111704**	**31.2**	**305.9**	**83.81**	**9.1**
#医院	Total Number of Hospitals	31973217	87598	30.2	325.5	89.19	10.3
疗养院	Sanitarium	95995	263	2.8	74.7	20.48	20.5
社区卫生服务中心	Health Service Center for Community	1119135	3066	20.6	209.0	57.26	8.8
卫生院	Total Number of Public Health Center	6816359	18675	38.0	247.0	67.67	5.3
门诊部	Out-patients Department	155883	427	6.6	46.2	12.66	7.3
诊所.卫生所.医务室	Clinic	1825	5				
妇幼保健院(所、站)	Hospitals for Maternity and Child Care	595021	1630	39.9	222.1	60.85	5.1
专科疾病防治院(所、站)	Specialized Disease Prevention & Treatment Institute	14600	40				

18-11 各地、州、市卫生机构、床位和人员数

年 份 Year	地 区 Region	机构数(个) Number of Institutions (unit)	床位数(张) Beds (unit)	卫生人员合计(人) Total Number of Medical Personnel (person)
	2005	8087	79753	117165
	2006	8175	83722	121400
	2007	7465	90329	127621
	2008	6739	96852	130174
	2009	7288	107193	138344
	2010	7650	116230	149069
乌鲁木齐市	Urumqi City	1675	24942	38024
克拉玛依市	Karamay City	93	1830	3517
吐鲁番地区	Turpan Administrative Offices	202	2137	3691
哈密地区	Hami [Kumul] Administrative Offices	299	3055	4997
昌吉回族自治州	Changji Hui Autonomous Prefecture	775	8907	11531
伊犁哈萨克自治州	Ili Kazak Autonomous Prefecture	1541	19719	28090
伊犁州直属县(市)	Counties (Cities) Direct Under Ili Prefecture	905	12472	16832
塔城地区	Tacheng [Tarbagatai] Administrative Offices	371	4401	6672
阿勒泰地区	Altay Administrative Offices	265	2846	4586
博尔塔拉蒙古自治州	Bortala Mongol Autonomous Prefecture	265	2252	3794
巴音郭楞蒙古自治州	Bayangol Mongol Autonomous Prefecture	723	7866	10356
阿克苏地区	Aksu Administrative Offices	323	11072	10049
克孜勒苏柯尔克孜自治州	Kizilsu Kirgiz Autonomous Prefecture	95	2814	3031
喀什地区	Kashgar [Kaxgar] Administrative Offices	917	16446	16747
和田地区	Hotan Administrative Offices	304	10236	8308
自治区直辖县级市	Municpality Country-LevelCity directly under the Central Govern-ment	438	4954	6934
石河子市	Shihezi City	382	4116	5922
阿拉尔市	Aral City	15	604	598
图木舒克市	Tumxuk City	3	69	145
五家渠市	Wujiaqu City	38	165	269

Number of Health Institutions，Beds and Personnel by Prefecture, Autonomous Prefecture and City

卫生技术人员 Medical Technical Personnel	其他技术人员 Other Technicians	管理人员 Administrative Personnel	工勤人员 Logistics Workers	平均每万人床位数(张) Number of Beds per 10 000 Population (unit)
96266	4626	6330	9943	39.71
99839	5168	6258	10135	39.07
104671	5276	7143	10531	43.11
106853	5694	6419	11208	45.45
114521	6111	6453	11259	49.66
122860	6979	7089	12141	53.28
29912	2461	2177	3474	80.19
2759	141	220	397	46.80
3138	117	180	256	34.32
4344	156	220	277	53.37
9709	502	573	747	62.35
23655	1089	1185	2161	45.80
13993	657	759	1423	50.24
5693	241	241	497	36.10
3969	191	185	241	47.17
3148	86	267	293	50.76
9009	378	424	545	61.53
8360	526	414	749	46.70
2604	148	88	191	53.54
14230	586	769	1162	41.33
6189	475	265	1379	50.81
5803	314	307	510	
4944	283	246	449	
507	13	39	39	
122	5	6	12	
230	13	16	10	

18-12 各地、州、市卫生技术人员数

单位:人

年 份 Year	地 区 Region	卫生技术人员合计 Number of Medical Technical Personnel	执业医师 Doctors with Licence	执业助理医 师 Lecensed Assistant Doctor
	2005	96266	32563	8863
	2006	99839	33988	8787
	2007	104671	34838	8713
	2008	106853	35320	8136
	2009	114521	37223	8393
	2010	122860	39301	8865
乌鲁木齐市	Urumqi City	29912	11353	674
克拉玛依市	Karamay City	2759	1019	72
吐鲁番地区	Turpan Administrative Offices	3138	979	275
哈密地区	Hami [Kumul] Administrative Offices	4344	1499	285
昌吉回族自治州	Changji Hui Autonomous Prefecture	9709	3231	659
伊犁哈萨克自治州	Ili Kazak Autonomous Prefecture	23655	7602	2160
伊犁州直属县(市)	Counties (Cities) Direct Under Ili Prefecture	13993	4488	1130
塔城地区	Tacheng [Tarbagatai] Administrative Offices	5693	1703	673
阿勒泰地区	Altay Administrative Offices	3969	1411	357
博尔塔拉蒙古自治州	Bortala Mongol Autonomous Prefecture	3148	1065	233
巴音郭楞蒙古自治州	Bayangol Mongol Autonomous Prefecture	9009	2888	731
阿克苏地区	Aksu Administrative Offices	8360	2048	1002
克孜勒苏柯尔克孜自治州	Kizilsu Kirgiz Autonomous Prefecture	2604	625	255
喀什地区	Kashgar [Kaxgar] Administrative Offices	14230	3521	1434
和田地区	Hotan Administrative Offices	6189	1505	695
自治区直辖县级市	Municpality Country-LevelCity directly under the Central Govern-ment	5803	1966	390
石河子市	Shihezi City	4944	1773	315
阿拉尔市	Aral City	507	94	45
图木舒克市	Tumxuk City	122	16	13
五家渠市	Wujiaqu City	230	83	17

Number of Medical Technical Personnel by Prefecture, Autonomous Prefecture and City

(person)

注册护士 Registered Nurses	药剂人员 Pharmacist	技师(士) Technician (artificer)	检验人员 Laboratory Technicians	其他 Others	平均每万人医生数 Number of Doctors per 10 000 Population
30657	5848	4773		13562	20.61
32119	5948	4980		14017	20.87
34662	5647	6701	4746	14110	20.79
36084	5721	6876	4803	14716	20.39
40425	5989	7164	4977	15327	21.13
44238	6364	7742	5301	16350	22.25
11729	1467	1690	1154	2999	38.67
1190	193	187	128	98	27.90
1097	171	237	161	379	20.14
1709	228	199	164	424	31.17
3553	584	625	400	1057	27.23
8137	1107	1705	1194	2944	22.68
4860	716	1068	770	1731	22.63
1903	235	410	253	769	19.49
1374	156	227	171	444	29.31
1120	198	217	160	315	29.25
3242	461	566	385	1121	28.31
2985	363	510	335	1452	12.86
864	122	135	87	603	16.74
4581	758	940	638	2996	12.45
1794	434	377	234	1384	10.92
2237	278	354	261	578	
1875	236	286	212	459	
234	26	42	28	66	
52	4	10	7	27	
76	12	16	14	26	

18-13 医疗机构、诊疗人次及入院出院人数

Number of Visits and Inpatients in Medical Institutions

(2010 年)

项 目	Item	机构数(个) Number of Institutions (unit)	诊疗人次(万人次) Total Number of Patients Treated (10 000 patient-times)	#门、急诊人次 Out-patients and Emergency Patients	#急诊人次 Emergency Patients
总 计	**Total**	**7269**	**66416185**	**63850353**	**2423022**
#医 院	Total Number of Hospitals	802	34160068	32858071	2113077
疗养院	Sanitarium	4	25190	22665	
社区卫生服务中心	Health Service Center for Community	641	6542465	6159063	87241
卫生院	Total Number of Public Health Center	910	11017059	10583898	149957
门诊部	Outpatients Department	259	1286121	1279961	9883
诊所.卫生所.医务室	Clinic	4555	11037526	10726797	2
急救中心(站)	Urgent Care Center	4	49098	49098	49098
妇幼保健院(所、站)	Hospitals for Maternity and Child Care	90	2288999	2161141	13764
专科疾病防治院(所、站)	Specialized Stations	4	9659	9659	

项 目	Item	门、急诊诊次占总诊次的比重(%) Percentage of Clinic Case and Emergence Case Among the Total Cases (%)	入院人数(万人) Hospital Admissions (10 000 patients)	出院人数(万人) Patients Discharged (10 000 patients)	治愈率(%) Cure Rate (%)
总 计	**Total**	**96.14**	**3529634**	**3486447**	**57.11**
#医 院	Total Number of Hospitals	96.19	2672364	2644559	53.80
疗养院	Sanitarium	89.98	751	724	35.77
社区卫生服务中心	Health Service Center for Community	94.14	63541	63091	65.67
卫生院	Total Number of Public Health Center	96.07	724366	710195	65.48
门诊部	Outpatients Department	99.52	2865	2818	66.15
诊所.卫生所.医务室	Clinic	97.18			
急救中心(站)	Urgent Care Center	100.00			
妇幼保健院(所、站)	Hospitals for Maternity and Child Care	94.41	65747	65060	91.92
专科疾病防治院(所、站)	Specialized Stations	100.00			

18-14 2000-2010 年历年分市县医院床位和专业卫生技术人员数
Hospital Beds and Medical Technical Personnel by City and County Areas(2000-2010)

年 份 Year	医院床位(张) Number of Hospital Beds (unit)		专业卫生技术人员(人) Number of Medical Technical Personnel (person)		#执业医师、执业助理医师 Lecensed Doctors & Assistant Doctors		#注册护士 Registered Nurses	
	市 City	县 County	市 City	县 County	市 City	县 County	市 City	县 County
2000	38398	27518	44115	31138	18408	13225	16805	9918
2001	38323	27685	44113	31055	18811	13271	16714	10105
2002	38700	26178	41850	27932	16689	10578	15965	8840
2003	42880	26915	44678	28228	17883	10916	17015	9087
2004	46300	27722	46956	28552	19207	10583	17185	9054
2005	50238	29515	54188	31132	23191	12323	18240	9289
2006	52275	31125	56701	32178	24033	13049	19365	9538
2007	54595	32536	68546	36125	28896	14655	24174	10488
2008	57242	36011	69292	37561	28215	15241	24976	11108
2009	58373	25403	54356	19490	20044	7242	22453	6979
2010	61157	28714	56706	21500	20953	7637	23777	8037

18-15 2000-2010 年历年分市县卫生院床位和专业卫生技术人员数
Hospital Beds and Medical Technical Personnel by City and County Areas(2000-2010)

年 份 Year	卫生院床位(张) Number of Hospital Beds (unit)		专业卫生技术人员(人) Number of Medical Technical Personnel (person)		#执业医师、执业助理医师 Lecensed Doctors & Assistant Doctors		#注册护士 Registered Nurses	
	市 City	县 County	市 City	县 County	市 City	县 County	市 City	县 County
2000	2138	11119	3442	13131	1622	6299	1021	3756
2001	2141	11247	3602	13129	1782	6300	1095	3808
2002	2180	9991	4021	11215	1611	4370	970	2829
2003	2471	10147	3645	10901	1364	4227	946	2950
2004	2351	10479	3703	10936	1429	3963	992	2746
2005	5061	11679	10345	13646	5004	5704	2056	3024
2006	4732	13079	10930	14105	5370	6048	2207	3213
2007	2832	12803	18725	18220	9548	8000	4771	4182
2008	3037	13895	17745	19239	8888	8446	4710	4626
2009	3313	15531	3684	12578	1595	4435	1161	3527
2010	3383	16597	3641	13240	1536	4381	1180	3741

18-16 社区卫生服务中心(站)工作量

Medical Services in Health Service Centers for Community

年 份 Year	社区卫生服务中心 Health Service Centers for Community				社区卫生服务站诊疗人次(万人) Health Service Stations for Community (10 000 patients)
	诊疗人次 (万人次) Visits (10 000 patient-times)	入院人数(万人) Inpatients (10 000 patients)	病床使用率(%) Utilization Rate (%)	平均住院日(日) Average Stay Days (day)	
2002	76.84	0.16	53.86	10.16	34.41
2003	88.10	0.60	89.51	16.13	33.75
2004	85.62	0.03	36.42	10.00	82.67
2005	67.04	0.03	16.71	11.08	152.68
2006	107.49	0.35	11.71	6.94	179.32
2007	105.73	0.24	59.77	11.70	109.22
2008	156.05	0.94	51.68	11.30	121.92
2009	232.95	2.36	49.93	9.90	207.23
2010	298.47	4.24	61.07	10.40	355.78

18-17 乡村卫生室基本情况

Basic Conditions of Country Health Room

(2010 年)

项 目	Item	合 计 Total	中 医 Traditional Chinese Medicine	西 医 Western Medicine	中西医结合 Combination Traditional and Western Medicine
机构数(个)	Number of Institutions(unit)	8350	59	7858	433
执业(助理)医师(人)	Lecensed (Assistant) Doctors (person)	890	30	757	103
注册护士(人)	Registered Nurses(person)	305	4	285	16
乡村医生和卫生员(人)	Country Doctor and Assistant Nurse(person)	8653	43	8105	505
乡村医生	Country Doctor	7937	41	7437	459
卫生员	Assistant Nurse	716	2	668	46
诊疗人次数(万人次)	Number of Patients Treated(10 000 patient-times)	795.65	17.13	722.02	56.50
#出 诊	Out-call	45.34	0.62	40.69	4.03

18-18 新型农牧区合作医疗基本情况

Basic Statistics on New Cooperative Health Care in Agricultural and Pastoral Areas

项　　目	Item	2009	2010
开展县(市)数(个)	Number of Counties(citys) to Carry Out(unit)	89	89
覆盖农牧业人口数(万人)	Population Coverage of Agriculture and Animal Husbandry(10 000 persons)	1021.64	1033.70
参合农牧业人口数(万人)	Livestok Population Parameters(10 000 persons)	993.58	1019.03
参合率(%)	Ratio of Participation(%)	97.25	98.58
当年筹集基金(万元)	Paise Funds This Year(10 000 yuan)	114721.59	161270.26
#中央补助	Central Subsidy	41166.00	61140.00
自治区补助	Autonpmous Region Subsidy	35961.60	51245.00
地方补助	Local Subsidy	15736.90	18365.91
个人缴费	Individual Pay	21294.78	29970.99
当年人均筹集资金(元/人·年)	Annual per Capita Raise Funds(yuan/persons.year)	114.90	157.72
当年基金支出(万元)	Expenditure of Fund This Yesr(10 000 yuan)	112097.00	147033.69
当年基金使用率(%)	Ratio of Fund Utilization This Yesr(%)	97.71	91.17
当年补偿受益人次(万人次)	Benefit of Compensation Population this Year(10 000 person-times)	859.40	830.62
住　院	Inpatients	126.98	145.38
门　诊	Out-patient Services	705.80	654.06
体　检	Physical Examination	13.89	30.78
其　他	Others	12.73	0.40
当年总体受益率(%)	Ratio of Total Benefit(%)	86.49	81.51
住院受益率	Benefit Ratio of be in Hospital	12.78	14.27
门诊受益率	Benefit Ratio of out-patient Services	71.04	64.19
当年总补偿比(%)	Total Compensation Ratio(%)	49.22	49.03
#住院平均补偿比	Average Compensation Ratio of be in Hospital	47.64	48.48
新农合管理机构实有人数(人)	Number of Employed Persons in Institution on New Cooperative Health Care of Agriculturial and Pastoral Areas(person)	1086	1146
新农合管理机构经费收入(万元)	Income of Institution on New Cooperative Health Care of Agriculturial and Pastoral Areas(10 000 yuan)	2779.00	3767.45
新农合管理机构经费支出(万元)	Expenditure of Institution on New Cooperative Health Care of Agriculturial and Pastoral Areas(10 000 yuan)	2788.32	3719.78
每实有人员管理参合人数(人)	Number of Participated Persons by per Practical Employed Persons(person)	16300	14800

18-19 法定报告传染病发病及死亡情况
Confirmed Incidence and Death from Infectious Diseases

项　目	Item	发病率 (1/10 万) Disease Incidence (1/100 000)		死亡率 (1/10 万) Death Rate (1/100 000)	
		2009	2010	2009	2010
总　计	**Total**	**792.540**	**682.195**	**2.570**	**2.608**
霍　乱	Cholera		0.014		
病毒性肝炎	Viral Hepatitis	264.891	253.813	0.150	0.093
细菌性和阿米巴性痢疾	Bacterial and Amebic Dysentery	58.448	43.625	0.005	0.009
伤寒副伤寒	Typhoid and Paratyphoid Fever	3.862	3.335	0.005	
艾滋病	AIDS	1.905	2.497	1.197	1.649
淋　病	Gonorrhea	9.626	9.358		
梅　毒	Syphilis	49.573	50.175	0.042	0.019
麻　疹	Measles	1.849	1.427		
百日咳	Pertussis	0.577	0.774		
流行性脑脊髓膜炎	Epidemic Cerebrospinal Meningitis	0.516	0.130	0.047	0.014
猩红热	Scarlet Fever	5.425	4.846		
流行性出血热	Hemorrhage Fever	0.009			
布鲁氏菌病	Brucellosis	2.070	3.692		
炭　疽	Anthrax	0.197	0.255		0.005
流行性乙型脑炎	Encephalitis B	0.009	0.005		
黑热病	Kala-Azar	1.427	0.686		
疟　疾	Malaria	0.028	0.028		
新生儿破伤风	Newborn Baby Tetanus	0.145	0.198	0.009	0.006
肺结核	Pulmonary Tuberculosis	186.353	164.461	0.995	0.783
血吸虫	Schistosomiasis	0.024			
甲型流感	H1N1 Influenza A	24.090	0.561	0.080	

注: 新生儿破伤风死亡率单位为千分率。
Note: The unit of incidence disease rate and death rate of newborn baby tetanus is 1‰.

18-20 城市前十位疾病死亡原因及构成
Death Causes and Percentage of 10 Major Diseases in Urban Areas

(2010 年)

疾病死亡原因	Cause of Death	死亡总人数（人） Total Deaths (person)	占死亡总人数的比重（%） Percentage to Total Deaths (%)
十种死因合计	**Total**	**6829**	**96.90**
循环系统	Circulatory system	2432	35.61
肿　瘤	Malignant Tumour	1725	25.26
呼吸系统	Diseases of the Respiratory System	925	13.55
损伤和中毒外部原因	Trauma and Toxicosis	346	5.07
诊断不明	Diagnosis in nubibus	277	4.06
传染病	Infections Disease	272	3.98
消化系统	Disease of the Digestive System	231	3.38
内分泌	Internal secretion	224	3.28
泌尿生殖系统	Disease of the Genifourinary system	95	1.39
神经系统	Diseases of the Nervous system	90	1.32

注：统计范围包括乌鲁木齐市及辖区资料。
Note: Statistics in data covers Urumqi and its Districts.

18-21 安全生产情况
Basic Statistics on Work Safety

单位：人 (person)

项　目	Item	2009	2010
亿元新疆生产总值生产安全事故死亡人数	Mortality Rate of Work Safety Accident Average 100 Billion Yuan GDP	0.6	0.5
工矿商贸企业就业人员生产安全事故十万人死亡人数	Mortality Rate of Work Safety Accident of Employment in Industrial & Mining and Commercial & Tradal Enterprises Average 100 000 Persons	7.61	8.10
煤矿百万吨死亡人数	Mortality Rate of Coal Procuction Average 1 Million Tons	1.27	1.02
道路交通万车死亡人数	Mortality Rate of Highway Traffic Accident Average 10 000 Vehicles	7.81	7.58

18-22 社会福利事业单位基本情况
Basic Statistics on Social Welfare Institutions

(2010 年)

指 标	Item	院 数 (个) Number of Homes (unit)	工作人员数 (人) Number of Persons Engaged (person)	床位数 (张) Number of Beds (unit)	年末收养人数(人) Number of Persons Housed (person)	#女 性 Female
总 计	**Total**	**546**	**4009**	**36912**	**28964**	**6044**
社会福利院	Social Welfare Homes	46	612	6006	4401	1077
儿童福利院	Children Welfare Homes	43	583	5364	4178	1434
光荣院	Homes for Disabled Veterans	7	480	2027	1956	409
社会福利医院	Psychopathy Welfare Homes	9	60	422	319	57
城镇老年性福利机构	Urban Elderly Welfare Units	61	883	5822	4415	617
农村老年性福利机构	Rural Elderly Welfare Units	379	1355	17191	13686	2450
荣誉军人康复医院	Recuperative Hospital for Soldiers with Honour	1	36	80	9	

18-23 社会福利事业、企业单位数和工作人员数
Number of Social Welfare Institutions and Enterprises and Persons Engaged

(2010 年)

项 目	Item	机构数 (个) Number of Institutions or Enterprises (unit)	工作人员数(人) Number of Persons Engaged (person)
收养性福利事业单位	Adopting Social Welfare Institutions	546	4009
编制部门	Organization Department	373	2889
民政部门	Civil Administration Department	169	1078
社会福利企业	Social Welfare Enterprises	40	430
优抚安置事业单位	Administration Agencies for Martyrs	168	14426
救助类单位	Salvaged Deparement	11	74
殡葬服务事业单位	Funeral and Interment Institutions	40	354
福利彩票发行单位	Welfare Lottery-Ticked Issuance Unit	147	794
社区服务中心	Community Service Institutions	260	1308

18-24 社会救济情况
Basic Statistics on Social Relief Funds

指　标	Item	2010
城镇居民最低生活保障人数(人)	**Number of Persons Receiving Lowest Cost-of-living in Urban Area (person)**	**851268**
老年人	Old Folks	126491
成年人	Adult	442454
在职人员	Full Employed Staff and Workers	10718
灵活就业人员	Flexible Employed Persons	123851
登记失业人员	Registered Employed Persons	134880
未登记失业人员	Unregistered Employed Persons	173005
未成年人	Minors	282323
在校生	Enrollment	172734
其　他	Others	109589
城镇居民最低生活保障家庭数(户)	**Number of Family Receiving Lowest Cost-of-living in Urban Area (household)**	**355115**
农村最低生活保障人数(人)	**Number of Persons Receiving Lowest Cost-of-living in Rural Area (person)**	**1334062**
农村最低生活保障家庭数(户)	**Number of Family Receiving Lowest Cost-of-living in Rural Area (household)**	**509764**

18-25 主要年份工会组织情况
Basic Statistics on Trades Unions in Main Years

年　份 Year	工会基层组织个数(个) Number of Grassroots Unions (unit)	全区已建工会组织的基本单位职工与会员人数(万人) Membership and Number of Staff and Workers in Grassroots Unions (10 000 persons)				专职工会干　部(万人) Number of Full-time Personnel of Unions (10 000 persons)
		职工人数 Number of Staff and Workers	#女 Female	会员人数 Number of Membership	#女 Female	
1980	3255	84.20	30.25	67.13	20.42	0.48
1985	6165	189.48	73.84	151.93	59.03	0.50
1990	10685	231.48	90.64	196.58	76.97	0.79
1995	14457	271.43	114.13	254.49	104.97	1.19
2000	13016	211.73	90.80	200.80	84.93	0.59
2001	18219	234.84	100.71	215.31	91.07	0.73
2002	20806	236.58	99.65	220.85	93.11	0.49
2003	11263	230.24	93.43	220.55	87.05	0.45
2004	11979	224.52	94.49	219.35	90.62	0.48
2005	11721	232.78	97.50	232.03	97.20	0.41
2006	13163	302.05	130.12	263.80	115.64	0.69
2007	15040	323.37	139.45	289.65	124.23	0.60
2008	16880	337.80	147.31	308.81	134.71	0.55
2009	17849	351.69	146.56	326.91	136.48	0.70
2010	19668	371.23	153.55	342.07	147.54	0.60

18-26 残疾人事业基本情况
Basic Information of People with Disabilities

项　目	Item	2009	2010
康　复	**Rehabilitation**		
白内障复明	Sight-restoring of Cataract Surgery		
白内障复明手术(万例)	Sight-restoring of Cataract Surgeries (10 000 cases)	1.23	0.54
低视力配用助视器(人)	Vision-aids Provided for Individuds with Low-vision (person)	601	1722
聋儿康复	Rehabilitation of Children With Hearing Disability		
年收训聋儿(人)	Hearing and Speech Training (person)	231	236
聋儿入普幼普小率(%)	Enrollment Rate to General Infant School or Elementary School (%)	45.5	32.0
培训家长(人)	Parents Trained (person)	391	362
精神病防治康复	Prevention and Treatment of Psychiatric Diseases		
开展精神病防治康复工作市县数(个)	Number of Counties Carried on the Works (unit)	15	39
综合防治康复精神病人数(万人)	Number of Psychosis Sicks Synthetically Prevented, Cured and Rehabilitated (10 000 persons)	1.79	2.50
监护率(%)	Guardianship Rate (%)	75.74	74.18
显好率(%)	Rate of Getting Better (%)	58.19	35.03
社会参与率(%)	Social Participation Rate (%)	41.18	25.99
肇事率(%)	Violent Everds Rate (%)	0.15	0.26
救济贫困患者数(人)	Number of Poor Sufferer Relieved (person)	4648	3220
用品用具供应件数(万件)	Number of Appliances Supplied (10 000 units)	1.01	1.73
康复训练与服务	Rehabilitation Training and Service		
肢体残疾康复训练数(人)	Rehabilitation Training of Body Disabilities (person)	1508	1641
智力残疾儿童康复训练数(人)	Rehabilitation Training of Mental Disabilities Children (person)	306	337
教　育	**Education**		
未入学适龄残疾儿童(万人)	Number of Uneducated Children (10 000 persons)	0.73	0.50
职业教育与培训机构数(个)	Vocational Education and Training Number of Institutions (unit)		
独立建制	Self Help	15	32
依托社会	Supported by Society	95	117
教育与培训人数(万人)	Number of Educated and Trained (10 000 persons)	2.08	1.86

18-26 续表 Continued

项　目	Item	2009	2010
就　业	**Employment**		
城镇残疾人就业状况(万人)	Employment of Urban Handicappeds (10 000 persons)		
当年安排就业	Persons Employed in the Year	0.51	0.54
按比例就业	Employment by Quota Scheme	0.15	0.21
集中就业	Employment at Welfare Enterprises	0.21	0.13
个体就业	Individual Employment	0.15	0.20
未安排就业	Unemployment	2.29	1.88
农村残疾人就业状况(万人)	Employment of Rural Handicapped (10 000 persons)		
就　业	Employed	20.90	17.54
未就业	Unemployed	5.53	4.87
残疾人就业服务机构(个)	Number of Institutions Engaging in Handicappeds Employment (unit)		
省	Provinces	1	1
地	Prefectures	12	12
市(含县级市)	Cities (Cities at County Level)	18	18
县	County	68	68
市辖区	Districts under the Jurisdiction of Cities	11	11
实施分散按比例就业的地区数(个)	Number of Regions Implemented the Policy of the Disperse Employment by Proportion (unit)		
省	Provinces	1	1
地	Prefectures	12	12
市(含县级市)	Cities (Cities at County Level)	18	18
县	County	68	68
市辖区	Districts under the Jurisdiction of Cities	11	11
残联组织建设	**Organization of Association for the Handicapped**		
残疾人工作者(万人)	Number of Workers for the Handicappeds (10 000 persons)	0.22	0.23

18-27 历届全区人民代表大会代表人数

Number of Deputies to all the Previous People's Congresses of Xinjiang

项 目 Item	第一届 (1954) First Congress	第二届 (1959) Second Congress	第三届 (1964) Third Congress	第四届 (1975) Fourth Congress	第五届 (1978) Fifth Congress	第六届 (1983) Sixth Congress	第七届 (1988) Seventh Congress	第八届 (1993) Eighth Congress	第九届 (1998) Ninth Congress	第十届 (2003) Tenth Congress	第十一届 (2008) Eleventh Congress
代表总数(人) Total Number of All Deputies (person)	**376**	**386**	**453**	**809**	**672**	**550**	**550**	**542**	**550**	**550**	**550**
#中国共产党党员 Deputies from the Communist Party of China	178		240			374	357	381	396	396	352
占总数比重(%) Percentage to Total (%)	47.3		53.0			68.0	64.9	70.3	72.0	72.0	64.0
#少数民族 Deputies from National Minorities	331		383	510	430	357	363	355	363	363	363
占总数比重(%) Percentage to Total(%)	88.0		84.5	63.8	64.0	64.9	66.0	65.5	66.0	66.0	66.0
#妇 女 Female Deputies	52	61	89	200	146	17	126	123	135	135	143
占总数比重(%) Percentage to Total(%)	13.8	15.8	19.6	24.7	21.7	21.3	22.9	22.7	24.5	24.5	26.0

18-28 历届全区政治协商会议委员人数

Number of Deputies to all the Previous People's Political Consultative Conferences of Xinjiang

项 目 Item	第一届 (1954) First Congress	第二届 (1959) Second Congress	第三届 (1964) Third Congress	第四届 (1978) Fourth Congress	第五届 (1983) Fifth Congress	第六届 (1988) Sixth Congress	第七届 (1993) Seventh Congress	第八届 (1998) Eighth Congress	第九届 (2003) Ninth Congress	第十届 (2008) Tenth Congress
委员总数(人) Total Number of All Deputies (person)	**141**	**275**	**303**	**407**	**441**	**429**	**416**	**444**	**470**	**515**
#中国共产党党员 Deputies from the Communist Party of China	28	57	65	149	158	157	161	183	196	225
占总数比重(%) Percentage to Total(%)	19.9	20.7	21.5	36.6	35.8	36.6	38.7	41.2	41.7	43.7
#少数民族 Deputies from National Minorities	121	196	205	221	253	245	204	246	246	263
占总数比重(%) Percentage to Total(%)	85.8	71.3	67.7	54.3	57.4	57.0	49.0	55.4	52.3	51.1
#妇 女 Female Deputies	10	28	28	40	49	63	66	82	95	125
占总数比重(%) Percentage to Total(%)	7.1	10.2	9.2	9.8	11.1	14.7	15.9	18.5	20.2	24.3

18-29 主要年份律师、公证、调解工作基本情况
Basic Statistics on Lawyers, Notarization and Mediation in Main Years

项目	Item	1990	1995	2000	2005	2010
律师工作	**Lawyers**					
律师事务所(个)	Number of Law Offices (unit)	130	169	227	243	318
律师(人)	Number of Lawyers (person)	780	1705	2414	2088	2900
#专职律师(人)	Full-time Lawyers (person)	435	1209	1508	1987	2704
兼职和特邀律师(人)	Part-time Lawyers (person)	345	336	418	101	114
聘请担任常年法律顾问的单位(处)	Number of Units with Permanent Legal Advisors (unit)	1748	2560	2613	2663	3858
民事诉讼代理(件)	Agent of Civil Cases (case)	6306	6380	16165	23389	38822
刑事辩护及代理(件)	Defender and Agent of Criminal Cases (case)	6237	5850	5826	7716	8510
非诉讼法律事务(件)	Agent of Non-Litigious Legal Affairs (case)	614	5357	4810	7066	2450
解答法律咨询(万件)	Agent of Legal Advisory Services (10 000 cases)	4.62	4.21	7.45	8.14	10.13
代写法律事务文书(万件)	Agent of Legal Documents Written on Behalf of Clients (10 000 cases)	0.69	1.06	1.94	3.00	2.16
公证工作	**Notarization**					
公证处(个)	Number of Notary Offices (unit)	113	126	131	126	125
公证员(人)	Notaries (person)	173	266	332	457	379
公证员助理(人)	Assistant Notaries (person)	76	49	43	61	144
办理公证文书(万件)	Number of Notarized Document (10 000 cases)	6.79	10.11	18.85	18.05	30.93
人民调解工作	**Number of People's Mediation**					
专职司法助理员(人)	Number of Full-time Judicial Assistants (person)	939	1515	1750	1706	1662
人民调解委员会(个)	Number of People's Mediation Committees (unit)	17422	19045	22294	15852	14157
调解人员(万人)	Number of Mediators (10 000 persons)	7.11	12.04	10.04	7.86	7.62
调解民间纠纷(万件)	Number of Civil Disputes Mediated (10 000 cases)	11.86	9.18	8.09	6.83	17.21

18-30 调解民间纠纷分类
Number of Civil Disputes Mediated by Type

(2010 年)

项　　目	Item	调解纠纷(件) Civil Disputes (case)	各类纠纷所占比重(%) Percentage (%)
总　计	**Total**	**172138**	**100**
婚姻家庭	Marriage and Family	42861	24.9
合　同	Contract	9568	5.56
劳　动	Labor	7820	4.54
村务管理	Village-affair Management	2904	1.69
土　地	Land	13975	8.12
征地拆迁	Requisitioned Land Demolition	1575	0.91
房屋宅基地	Housing and Housing Sites	5231	3.04
计划生育	Family Planning	445	0.26
邻　里	Neighbour	39220	22.78
损害赔偿	Compensation for Damages	13831	8.03
环境保护	Environment Protection	174	0.10
道路交通事故	Road Traffic Accidents	457	0.27
物　业	Property Management	335	0.19
医　疗	Medical Treatment	1218	0.71
生产经营	Production and Operation	2319	1.35
其　他	Others	30205	17.55

18-31 火灾事故发生情况
Basic Statistics on Fire Accidents

(2010 年)

指　　标	Item	合　计 Total	按事故发生程度分 By Serious Dgree of Fires			
			特　大 Extraordinarily Serious	重　大 Serious	较　大 Comparatively Serious	一　般 Ordinary
发生起数(起)	Fires (case)	5209		1	3	5205
死亡(人)	Death (person)	59		12	11	36
受伤(人)	Injuries (person)	44		17		27
损失折款(万元)	Losses Converted into Cash (10 000 yuan)	3040.9		15.5	202.6	2821.9
平均每起事故损失(元)	Average Loss per Fire (yuan)	5837.8		155000.0	675333.3	5421.5

18-32 2008-2010 年历年交通事故发生情况
Basic Statistics on Traffic Accidents(2008-2010)

指　　标	Item	2008	2009	2010
发生起数(起)	Traffic Accidents (case)	5678	5041	4949
死亡(人)	Death (person)	2117	1870	1851
受伤(人)	Injuries (person)	6404	5656	5859
损失折款(万元)	Losses Converted into Cash (10 000 yuan)	1219	897	864
平均每起事故损失(元)	Average Loss per Fire (yuan)	2147	1779	1746

18-33 公安机关受理查处治安案件情况

Offense Cases Against Public Order Handled by Public Security Organs

单位：起 (2010 年) (case)

案件类别	Category of Cases	受理 Number of Cases Accepted to be Treated	查处 Number of Cases Investigated and Treated
总 计	**Total**	**108952**	**101749**
扰乱工作、公共秩序	Disturbing Work or Public Order	2260	2198
扰乱单位秩序	Disturbing Business Orders	459	452
扰乱公共场所秩序	Disturbing the Orders in Public Places	296	290
寻衅滋事	Causing Quarrels and Making Troubles	862	829
其 他	Others	342	337
妨害公共安全	Disorderly Cordnct	628	625
非法携带枪支、弹药、管制刀具	Violation of Firearms Control Regulations	270	269
盗窃、损毁公共设施	Stealing and Damaging Public Facilities	80	81
其 他	Others	224	222
侵犯他人人身权利、财产权利	Offences Against, Citizens'Personal and Property Rights	86157	79143
侮辱、诽谤、诬告陷害	Insult, Slander and Circumvention	665	561
殴打他人	Beating Other Body	60035	56851
故意伤害	Wilfully Injuring Others	2887	2423
盗 窃	Stealing Property	15224	12612
诈 骗	Swindling, Seizing and Extorting Property	786	614
抢 夺	Robbery and Snatch	227	193
敲诈勒索	Extertion and Blackmail	212	189
其 他	Others	1711	1624
妨害社会管理	Disorderly Social Management	19907	19783
阻碍执行职务	Obstructing Government Workers in Performing Their Duties	764	749
违反旅馆业管理	Violating the Hotel Management Regulations	2109	2108
违反房屋出租管理	Violating the Rent Control Regulations	3473	3471
卖淫、嫖娼	Prostitution or Going Whoring	924	921
赌博或为赌博提供条件	Gambling	1232	1215
毒品违法活动	Illegal Drug Related Action	9411	9396
其 他	Others	1473	1373

18-34 2006-2010 年历年刑事案件中青少年犯罪情况

Juvenile Delinquency Among Criminal Cases(2006-2010)

单位：人 (person)

年 份 Year	刑事罪犯总数 Offenders	#青少年罪犯 Young Offenders	不满 18 岁 Less than 18	18 岁至 25 岁 Between 18 to 25	青少年罪犯占刑事罪犯 (%) Percentage to Total (%)
2006	40492	20259	7583	12676	50.00
2007	38878	19838	7142	12696	51.03
2008	37222	18317	5899	12418	49.20
2009	33121	15989	4538	11451	48.27
2010	29257	13299	4012	9287	45.45

主要统计指标解释

等级运动员人数 指经考核正式批准授予等级运动员称号的人数。运动员等级分为国际级运动健将、运动健将、一级运动员、二级运动员、三级运动员、少年级运动员。该指标主要反映运动员队伍的技术质量水平。

等级裁判员人数 指经考核正式批准授予等级裁判员称号的人数。裁判员等级分为国际裁判、国家级裁判、一级裁判、二级裁判、三级裁判。该指标主要反映裁判员队伍的技术质量水平。

体育场 指有400米跑道(中心含足球场),有固定道牙,跑道6条以上,并有固定看台的室外田径场地。体育场按看台容纳观众人数分为:甲级25000人以上,乙级15000-25000人,丙级5000-15000人,丁级5000人以下。该指标主要反映大中型体育场数量水平。

体育馆 指有固定看台,可供篮球、排球、羽毛球、乒乓球、体操等项目训练比赛活动用的室内运动场地。体育馆按看台容纳观众人数分为:甲级6000人以上,乙级4000-6000人,丙级2000-4000人,丁级2000人以下。该指标主要反映大中型体育馆数量水平。

卫生机构 指从卫生行政部门取得《医疗机构执业许可证》,或从民政、工商行政、机构编制管理部门取得法人单位登记证书,为社会提供医疗保健、疾病控制、卫生监督服务或从事医学科研和教育等工作的单位。卫生机构包括医院、疗养院、社区卫生服务中心(站)、卫生院、门诊部、诊所(卫生所、医务室)、急救中心(站)、采供血机构、妇幼保健院(所、站)、专科疾病防治院(所、站)、疾病预防控制中心(防疫站)、卫生监督所、卫生监督检验(监测、检测)机构、医学科研机构、医学在职培训机构、健康教育所(站)等其他卫生机构。

医疗机构 指从卫生行政部门取得《医疗机构执业许可证》的机构,包括医院、疗养院、社区卫生服务中心(站)、卫生院、门诊部、诊所(卫生所、医务室)、妇幼保健院(所、站)、专科疾病防治院(所、站) 、急救中心(站)和临床检验中心。

社区卫生服务中心(站) 指为本社区居民提供预防、医疗、保健、康复、健康教育、计划生育技术服务等的基层卫生机构。包括社区卫生服务中心和社区卫生服务站。

卫生人员 指在医疗、预防保健、医学科研和在职教育等卫生机构工作的职工,包括卫生技术人员、其他技术人员、管理人员和工勤人员。

卫生技术人员 包括执业(助理)医师、注册护士、药剂人员、检验和影像人员等卫生专业人员。不包括从事管理工作的卫生技术人员(一律计入管理人员)。

执业医师 指具有《医师执业证》及其“级别”为“执业医师”且实际从事医疗、预防保健工作的人员,不包括实际从事管理工作的执业医师。执业医师类别分为临床、中医、口腔和公共卫生。

执业助理医师 指具有《医师执业证》及其“级别”为“执业助理医师”且实际从事医疗、预防保健工作的人员,不包括实际从事管理工作的执业助理医师。执业助理医师类别同样分为临床、中医、口腔和公共卫生四类。

每万人口执业(助理)医师 每万人口执业(助理)医师=(执业医师数+执业助理医师数)/人口数×10000。人口数系公安部户籍人口。

每万人口医院、卫生院床位数 每万人口医院卫生院床位数=(医院床位数+卫生院床位数)/人口数×10000。人口数系公安部户籍人口。

每万人口卫生技术人员 每万人口卫生技术人员=卫生技术人员数/人口数×10000。人口数系公安部户籍人口。

法定报告传染病发病率 是指某年某地区每10万人口中甲、乙类法定报告传染病发病情况。即法定报告传染病发病率=甲、乙类法定报告传染病发病数/人口数×100000。

法定报告传染病死亡率 是指某年某地区每10万人口中甲、乙类法定报告传染病死亡情况。即法定报告传染病死亡率=甲、乙类法定报告传染病死亡数/人口数×100000。

法定报告传染病病死率 是指某年某地区甲、乙类法定报告传染病死亡数与发病数之比。即法定报告传染病病死率=甲、乙类法定报告传染病死亡数/发病数×100%。

参加新农合人数 指根据本地新农合实施方案到年内新农合筹资截止时已缴纳新农合资金的人口数。

新农合当年基金支出 指本年度实际从新农合基金帐户中支出用于新农合补偿的资金。

新农合补偿支出受益人次 指年内新农合参合人员因病就医获得补偿的人次数,包括住院、家庭帐户形式、门诊、特殊病种大额门诊、住院正常分娩、体检和其他补偿人次之和。

新农合本年度筹资总额 指为本年度筹集的、实际进入新农合专用帐户的基金数额。包括本年度中央及地方财政配套资金、农民个人交纳资金(含民政部门及其他相关部门代缴的救助资金)、新农合基金本年度产生的全部利息收入及其他渠道实际筹集到的新农合基金额。筹资数额以进入新农合专用帐户的基金数额为准,不含上年结转额资金。

卫生总费用 反映全国当年用于医疗卫生保健服务所消耗的资金总量,用筹资来源法测算。分为政府预算卫生支出、社会卫生支出、个人现金卫生支出三部分。

政府预算卫生支出 指各级政府用于卫生事业的财政拨款。 包括卫生事业费、中医事业费、食品和药品监督管理费、计划生育事业费、医学科研经费、预算内基本建设经费、卫生行政和医疗保险管理费、政府其他部门卫生经费、行政事业单位医疗经费、基本医疗保险基金补助经费。

社会卫生支出 指政府预算外社会各界对卫生事业的资金投入。包括社会基本医疗保险费、社会其他保险医疗卫生费、商业健康保险费、非卫生部门行政事业单位办医支出、企业医疗卫生支出、农村居民医疗保障经费、卫生预算外基本建设支出、私人开业医初始投资、公共卫生机构预算外资金投入等。

个人现金卫生支出 指城乡居民用自己可支配的经济收入，在接受各类医疗卫生服务时的现金支付。包括城镇居民个人现金卫生支出和农村居民个人现金卫生支出。

社会福利事业单位 指集中收养社会孤老、残、幼的机构，包括由民政部门管理的社会福利院、儿童福利院、精神病人福利院和城镇集体举办的福利院及农村集体举办的敬老院以及优抚医院和具有收养能力的社区服务中心等。该指标主要反映我国在社会福利性单位投入的水平。

社会福利事业单位收养人数 包括民政部门管理和城镇、农村集体举办的社会福利事业单位中收养的老人、少年儿童、缺乏生活自理能力的残疾人员和精神病人。该指标主要反映收养性社会福利单位的收养能力。

社会福利企业 指以集中安置有一定劳动能力的残疾人员就业为目（残疾职工占生产人员 10%以上）、带有社会福利性质的企业总称。主要包括福利工厂、假肢厂和其他福利企业。

五保户 指无法定抚养义务人，或者虽有法定抚养义务人，但是抚养人无抚养能力的；无劳动能力的；无生活年人来源的老年人、残疾人和未成年人。

聋儿入普幼普小率 指本年度内经康复训练后进入普通幼儿园、普通小学的聋儿数与在训聋儿数(不含当年新收训聋儿数)之比。

综合防治康复精神病人数 指在开展精神病防治康复工作地区，采取不同形式，接受综合性防治康复措施、开放式管理的精神病人数。该指标主要反映精神病患者接受治疗康复情况。

监护率 指通过监护小组、家庭病床、工疗站、社会就业以及精神卫生机构，接受社会化、综合性、开放式治疗与康复的精神病人占经调查摸底、登记在册的精神病人数的百分比。该指标主要反映对精神病患者落实治疗康复措施的情况。

社会参与率 指生活能自理，并参加生产劳动和社会生活的精神病人数占监护精神病人数的百分比。该指标主要反映精神病人康复状况和参与社会的情况。

未入学学龄残疾儿童少年总人数 指截止到本年度 12 月 31 日，在省级人民政府依照《义务教育法》规定的入学年龄段内的，因各种原因未能入学的各类残疾儿童少年人数。

律师 指依法取得律师执业证书，担任法律顾问，民事(刑事、行政)案件代理人、刑事案件辩护人、办理非诉讼业务，解答法律询问，代写法律事务文书等，为社会提供法律服务的人员。

公证人员 指在公证处工作的人员总称，包括公证处主任、副主任、公证员、公证员助理(助理公证员)和其他从事辅助性工作的人员。

公证文书 指公证处根据当事人申请，依照事实和法律，按照法定程序制作的，具有法律效力的司法证明文书。

调解员 指在人民调解委员会担负调解民间纠纷工作的人员，包括调解委员会的委员和调解小组的调解员。该指标主要反映从事人民调解工作的人员数量。

调解民间纠纷 指调解委员会按照法律规定，根据自愿原则，用说服教育的方法调解民间发生的有关民事权利和义务争执的件数，包括调解成功数和调解未成功数。该指标主要反映人民调解委员会的工作量。

立案 指人民检察院对受理的报案、控告、举报或自首及自行发现的犯罪线索、犯罪嫌疑人进行初步调查后，认为存在职务犯罪事实和应追究刑事责任，并决定作为刑事案件进行侦查的诉讼活动，是追究犯罪的开始。该指标主要反映人民检察院依法将职务犯罪线索作为刑事案件进行侦查的诉讼活动。

大案 指贪污、贿赂案数额在 5 万元以上，挪用公款案数额在 10 万元以上，集体私分、巨额财产来源不明、隐瞒境外存款案数额在 50 万元以上以及按照《人民检察院直接受理的渎职、侵权重、特大案件标准(试行)》认定的案件。该指标主要反映人民检察院立案查办的职务犯罪案件中经济损失大、社会危害严重的案件。

要案 指县、处级以上干部的犯罪案件。该指标主要反映国家工作人员中县、处级以上干部因职务犯罪被人民检察院依法立案侦查的情况。

决定逮捕 指人民检察院对直接受理、自行侦查的案件，认为需要逮捕犯罪嫌疑人时，依据法律做出的逮捕决定。该指标主要反映人民检察院对直接受理的案件行使决定逮捕权的情况。

批准逮捕 指人民检察院对公安机关、国家安全机关、监狱管理机关提出逮捕的犯罪嫌疑人进行审查，根据事实，依法做出逮捕决定。该指标主要反映人民检察院对提请逮捕机关提请逮捕犯罪嫌疑人进行审查后依法做出批准逮捕决定的情况。

决定起诉 指人民检察院对公安机关、国家安全机关、监狱管理机关和检察机关内设机构反贪污贿赂部门等移送起诉的案件进行审查，根据事实，做出提起公诉的案件。该指标主要反映人民检察院对各种刑事案件向人民法院提起公诉的情况。

受理劳动争议案件数 指劳动争议仲裁委员会根据国家有关规定，对劳动争议当事人的申请予以审查，符合受理条件而正式立案、准备处理的劳动争议案件数。

特大交通事故 指一次造成死亡 3 人以上，或者重伤 11 人以上，或者死亡 1 人，同时重伤 8 人以上，或者死亡 2 人，同时重伤 5 人以上，或者财产损失 6 万元以上的交通事故。

重大交通事故 指一次造成死亡 1 至 2 人，或者重伤 3 人以上 10 人以下，或者财产损失 3 万元以上不足 6 万元的交通事故。

特大火灾 指造成 30 人以上死亡，或者 100 人以上重伤，或者 1 亿元以上直接财产损失的火灾。

重大火灾 指造成 10 人以上 30 人以下死亡，或者 50 人以上 100 人以下重伤，或者 5000 万元以上 1 亿元以下直接财产损失的火灾。

较大火灾 指造成 3 人以上 10 人以下死亡，或者 10 人以上 50 人以下重伤，或者 1000 万元以上 5000 万元以下直接财产损失的火灾。

一般火灾 指造成 3 人以下死亡，或者 10 人以下重伤，或者 1000 万元以下直接财产损失的火灾。

Explanatory Notes on Main Statistical Indicators

Number of Athletes in Grades refers to the number of athletes who have been given titles through examination. The titles of athletes include international masters of sports, masters of sports, first-grade, second- grade and third-grade sportsmen and young athletes. This indicator reflects skill of the athletes.

Number of Referees in Grades refers to the number of referees who have been given titles after examination. They are classified as international referees, national referees and referees of the first, second and third grades. This indicator reflects the skill of referees.

Stadiums refer to stadiums for track and field events with six lane 400-meter tracks around soccer fields, permanent track marks and permanent bleachers. Stadiums are classified according to seating capacity. They include: Class A stadiums have the capaCity of seating 25000 people each. Class B stadiums have the capaCity of seating 15000 to 25000 people each. Class C stadiums have the capaCity of s eating 5000 to 15000 people each, and Class D stadiums have the capaCity of seating fewer than 5000 people. This indicator reflects numbers of large and medium-sized stadiums.

Gymnasiums refer to indoor sports grounds with permanent seats in which basketball, volleyball. Badminton, table tennis and gymnastics competitions can be held. Gymnasiums are classified according to seating capaCity. They include: Class Agymnasiums with seating over 6000 people. Class B gymnasiums with seating 4000 to 6000 people. Class Cgymnasiums with seating 2000 to 4000 people, and Class D gymnasiums with eating fewer than 2000 people. This indicator reflects the total number of large and medium-sized gymnasiums Health Care Institutions include: medical institutions, disease prevent ion and control centers (epidemic prevention stations), blood gathering and supplying institutions, health supervision and inspection (checkup) institutions, medicinal scientific research and on-job training institutions, health education and son on.

Health Care Institutions include: medical institutions, disease prevention and control centers(epidemic prevention stations),blood gathering and supplying Institutions,health supervision and inspection(check up)institutions,medical scientific research and on-job training institutions,health education and so on.

Medical Organizations refer to the institutions which have been qualified the Certification of Health Care Institution by the administration of public health, including: hospitals, sanatoriums, community health service centers (stations), health centers, clinics (health stations and infirmaries), women and children care agencies (centres and stations), special disease prevention and curing agencies (centres and stations), first-aid centres (stations) and clinic inspection centers.

Community Health Service Centres (stations) refer to the primary units that provide the health care for community residents, such as disease prevention and control, medical treatment, health care, rehabilitation, health education, family planning technical services, including community health service centres and community health service stations.

Health Care Employee refer to all employee engaged in the health care institutions, such as medical organizations, disease prevention and control centres, health care agencies, medicinal scientific research and on-job training institutions, including medical technical personnel, other technical personnel, manager and labour.

Medical Technical Personnel refer to the professional staff engaged in health care, including licensed (assistant) doctors, registered nurse, pharmacists, laboratory technician, and imaging staff, excluding the medical technical personnel engaged in management job (included as the management staff).

Licensed Doctors refer to the medical workers who have obtained the licenses of qualified doctors and are employed in medical treatment, disease prevention or healthcare institutions, excluding the licensed doctors engaged in management job. The classification of licensed doctors is clinician, Chinese medicine, dentist and public health.

Licensed Assistant Doctors refer to the medical workers who have obtained the licenses of qualified assistant doctors and are employed in medical treatment, disease prevention or healthcare institutions, excluding the licensed assistant doctors engaged in management job. The classification of licensed assistant doctors is clinician, Chinese medicine, dentist and public health.

Number of Licensed (Assistant) Doctors per 10000 Population the formula is:

Number of Licensed Doctors per 10000 Population = (Number of Licensed Doctors + Number of Licensed Assistant Doctors) / Population × 10000

The population is the figure of household registration from the Ministry of Public Security.

Number of Beds of Hospitals and Health Care per 10000 Population the formula is:

Number of Beds of Hospitals and Health Care per 10000 Population = Number of Beds of Hospitals + Number of Beds of Health Care) / Population × 10000

The population is the figure of household registration from the Ministry of Public Security.

Number of Medical Technical Personnel per 10000 Population the formula is:

Number of Medical Technical Personnel per 10000 Population = Number of Medical Technical Personnel / Population × 10000

The population is the figure of household registration from the Ministry of Public Security.

Incidence Rate of Notifiable Infectious Diseases refer to the incidence cases notifiable class A and class B infectious diseases per 100 thousand population in the reference region in the reference year. The formula is:

Incidence Rate of Notifiable Infectious Diseases = Incidence Cases Notifiable Class A and Class B Infectious Diseases / Population × 10000

Death Rate of Notifiable Infectious Diseases refer to the death cases notifiable class A and class B infectious diseases per 100 thousand population in the reference region in the reference year. The formula is:

Death Rate of Notifiable Infectious Diseases = Death Cases Notifiable Class A and Class B Infectious Diseases / Population × 10000

Number of Persons Participated in the New Rural Cooperative Medical System refers to the number of persons who have given payment to the new cooperative medical system by the deadline of fundraising during the year according to the implementation plan of the new system.

Expenditure of Funds for the New Rural Cooperative Medical System This Year refers to expenditures on compensation funds for the new rural cooperative medical system from the fund account of new cooperative medical system this year.

Persons Benefited from the Compensation Expenditure of New Rural Cooperative Medical System refers to the number of persons participated in the new system who have been compensated for medical treatment in the year, including hospitalization, family account form, out-patient, large special diseases out-patient, normal childbirth in hospital, medical examination and other compensations

Funds Raised for the New Rural Cooperative Medical System this Year refers to the amount of funds raised this year and put into the special new rural cooperative medical account, including the matching funds of central and local governments, paid money by farmers (including relief funds paid by the civil affairs department and other relevant departments), all the interest income generated this year of the funds and funds actually raised from other channels this year. The amount of funding equals to the funds entering into the special new rural cooperative medical account, excluding the carry-over funds from the previous year.

Total Expenditure on Health reflects the total expenditure on medical and health care services of a country in a year, estimated using funding source method. It includes government expenditure, social expenditure and individual cash expenditure.

Government Budgetary Expenditure for Public Health refers to budgetary allocation for health undertakings by governments at all levels, including health expenditure, Chinese medicine practitioners' operating expenses, food and drug supervision and management fees, operating expenses of family planning, medical research funding, budget for capital construction funding, health administration and health insurance management fees, health costs of other government departments, medical expenses of administrative departments and institutions, subsidies for basic medical insurance fund.

Social Expenditure for Public Health refers to non-government budgetary capital input, mainly referring to social basic medical care insurance, other social medical care insurance, commercial health insurance, expenditure of non-health-department administrations for health care, expenditure of enterprises for health care, rural household expense on health care, extra-budgetary expenditure for health care in capital investment, private investment on practicing of health care, and extra-budgetary funds of public health institutions, etc.

Individual Cash Expenditure for Public Health refers to cash expenditure for various health services by rural and urban household paid from the disposable income, including urban individual cash expenditure for public health and rural individual cash expenditure for public health.

Social Welfare Institutions refer to institutions taking care of old pople without children, handicapped people and orphans. They include social welfare institutions run by civil affairs departments, children welfare institutions, social welfare institutions for mental patients, collective-owned old peoples homes in rural areas, convalescent homes and community service centers with the capaCity of receiving those people. This indicator reflects the input in social welfare institutions.

Number of People Taken in by Social Welfare Institutions refers to the number of old people, children, totally dependent handicapped people and mental patients taken in by social welfare institutions run by civil affairs departments and those run by collective units in urban and rural areas. This indicator reflects the cap a City of social welfare institutions.

Social Welfare Enterprises are collective owned enterprises which employ the blind, deaf-mute, and other handicapped people who are able to work in cities and towns and enjoy exemption from state taxes, including welfare plants, welfare commercial services, artificial limb plants and farms, etc. This indicator reflects the preferential policies toward disabled persons.

Rural Households with Livelihood Guaranteed in Five Aspects refer to the households in which there are old people without child, orphans and handicapped people who are unable to work and without financial resources in rural areas. They are taken care of by the collective units and their food, clothing, housing, medical care, funeral expenses (or schooling for orphans) are guaranteed to be provided for. This indicator reflects the total number of disadvantageous groups of rural population.

Proportion of Deaf Children Enrolled in Ordinary Preschool and Primary Education refers to the proportion of deaf children who are enrolled in ordinary kindergartens or primary schools during the year in the total number of deaf children under rehabilitation programs (not including new comers into the rehabilitation programs during the year). This indicator mainly reflects number of rehabilitated deaf children entering ordinary kindergartens or primary schools.

Number of Mental Patients under Integrated Prevention and Rehabilitation Program refers to mental disease patients receiving integrated prevention and rehabilitation treatment of various forms under open environment in areas with mental disease rehabilitation programs. This indicator reflects the condition of metal patients receiving rehabilitation treatment.

Supervision Rate refers to the percentage of patients among the total number of registered mental disease patients, who participate in social integrated and open treatment and rehabilitation programs through various forms such as supervision groups, family treatment, employment or guidance from psychiatric institutions. This indicator reflects the implementation of various measures aimed at rehabilitating those metal patients.

Social Participation Rate of Mental Patients refers to proportion of mental disease patients who are able to manage their daily life and participate in economic activities to the total number of mental disease patients under supervision. This indicator reflects the condition of recovery of those metal patient sand their participation in social activities.

School-age Disabled Children not in Schools refer to children with disability in sight, listening, speaking, mentality, limbs or multi-disability who are obliged to compulsory education by law but have not been enrolled in schools due to various reasons. The definition of school age for disabled children is decided by the definition of school age as specified by provincial governments in line wit h the local laws on compulsory education. This indicator reflects the annual change of school-age disable children not entering schools by various reasons. It will provide foundation for the formulation of development plans of compulsory education for those disable children, and for related principles, policies and measures as well. It is also t he base for the job of funding t hose disabled children back to schools across the countries.

Lawyers are certified legal workers according to law, and who are employed by legal counseling firms to act as legal advisers, agents in criminal or civil lawsuits, or defenders in criminal lawsuits, or to handle non-litigious legal affairs, to advise on matters of law or t o write legal papers for others, and provide service to the public.

Notary Personnel refers to people working for notary offices including: directors, deputy direct or, notaries, assistant notaries, and other people providing assistance.

Notary Documents refer to the judicatory notary documents drawn up by the request of the party and are in accordance with facts and laws and following certain legal proceedings. According to usage and locality, the notary documents are divided into following 4 types: domestic notary documents, domestic economic notary documents, foreign-related civil notary documents and foreign-related economic notary documents.

Mediators refer to workers on peoples mediation committees responsible for mediating in civil disputes and cases of slight infraction of the law. They include members of the mediation committees and mediators of mediation groups. This indicator reflects the number of people engaged in meditation.

Mediation of Civil Disputes refers to number of cases made by mediation committees in mediating in civil disputes concerning civil rights and duties through persuasion and education in accordance witht he provisions of lawona voluntary basis, so as to solve disputes by helping the parties involved come to an agreement and understanding, including those unsuccessful ones. This indicator reflects the workload of the mediation committees.

Acceptance of Case refers t o t he decision made by the people's procurator ate office on reported cases, prosecution, impeachment, surrender, self-found criminal clues or suspects after initial investigation to confirm t he act of crime and to start legal proceedings of the case as criminal case.

Large Case refers to the case involves a corruption or bribery of over 50,000 yuan, or a misappropriation of over 100,000 yuan. Cases of collectively illegal possess ion of public funds, unstated sources of large properties, or disguised overseas savings deposits involving 500,000 yuan, or a case that has been defined by the "Standard on Serious and Large Cases of Misconduct and Tortious that Directly Accepted by People's Procurators Office (try out)". This indicator mainly reflects number of accepted cases of job-related criminals that caused serious economic losses or extremely harmful to the society.

Key Case refers to a case committed by government office -als with a ranking of division director or county administrator. This indicator mainly reflects the recorded and spied on cases by the people's procurators offices toward government official with a ranking of division director or county administrator.

Decision on Arrest refers to decision made by people's procurators office, in accordance with laws, to arrest the suspect (s) in the cases that are accepted and to be investigated by procurators office. This indicator mainly reflects the implementation of the decision on arrest by people's procurators office.

Approval for Arrest refers to the decision made by people's procurators office, in accordance with laws and relevant facts, to approve t he arrest of the suspect(s) that is propos ed by the public security departments, state security departments or authority of prisons. This indicator reflects approved arrests made by people's procurators office that are proposed by related departments.

Decision on Prosecution refers to the decision made by people's procurators office, in accordance with laws and relevant facts, to institute proceedings to the people's court against the suspect (s) of criminal cases handed over by the public security departments, state security departments or authority of prisons, or by t he anti-corruption department s within the procurators office. This indicator reflects t he condition of the prosecutions made by people's procurators office toward the people's court.

Number of Labor Dispute Cases Accepted refers to the number of cases of labor dispute submitted that, after being reviewed by the labor dispute arbitration committees in line with the relevant stat e regulations, are accepted and registered or treatment.

Extraordinarily Serious Traffic Accident refers to an accident which has caused three or more deaths; or over 11 serious injuries; or one death and over 8 serious injuries; or two deaths and over 5 serious injuries; or a loss over 60 thousand yuan.

Serious Traffic Accident refers to an accident which has caused one or two deaths; or three to ten serious injuries; or a loss over 30 thousand yuan to 60 thousand yuan.

Extraordinarily Serious Fire Case refers to a case which has caused over 30 deaths; or over 100 serious injuries; or a direct property loss over 100 million yuan.

Serious Fire Case refers to a case which has caused over 10 to 30 deaths; or over 50 to 100 serious injuries; or a direct property loss over 50 million to 100 million yuan.

Comparatively Serious Fire Case refers to a case which has caused over three to ten deaths; or over 10 to 50 serious injuries; or a direct property loss over 10 million to 50 million yuan.

Ordinary Fire Case refers to a case which has caused less than three deaths; or less than 10 serious injuries; or a direct property loss less than 10 million yuan.

第十九篇 各地州市主要经济指标排序

CHAPTER 19 Ranking of Main Economic Indicators by Region of Xinjiang

简要说明
Brief Introduction

本篇资料的主要内容及来源

本篇反映 2010 年新疆各地州(市)主要经济指标排序情况。

本篇资料由新疆维吾尔自治区统计局国民经济综合统计处根据新疆维吾尔自治区统计局各相关专业处提供资料整理。

Main content and Source of Data

Data in this chapter mainly include main social economic statistics by prefecture, autonomous prefecture, city and county in 2010.

Data on this chapter are compiled by the Department of Comprehensive Statistic, XBS according to the data provided by the related department of Statistics Bureau of Xinjiang Uygur Autonomous Region.

19-1 各地、州、市生产总值

Gross Domestic Product by Prefecture, Autonomous Prefecture and City

单位：万元　　(2010 年)　　(10 000 yuan)

地　区	Region	地区生产总值 Gross Domestic Product	位次 Rank	第一产业增加值 Primary Industry	位次 Rank
乌鲁木齐市	Urumqi city	13385172	1	199424	12
克拉玛依市	Karamay city	7113532	2	35171	15
石河子市	Shihezi city	1349995	11	91825	13
吐鲁番地区	Turpan Administrative Offices	1827866	9	244123	10
哈密地区	Hami [Kumul] Administrative Offices	1673848	10	240308	11
昌吉回族自治州	Changji Hui Autonomous Prefecture	5579917	4	1662667	1
伊犁哈萨克自治州	Ili Kazak Autonomous Prefecture	8850339		2546132	
伊犁州直属县(市)	Counties (Cities) Direct Under Ili Prefecture	4082648	5	986517	6
塔城地区	Tacheng [Tarbagatai] Administrative Offices	3419047	8	1263861	4
阿勒泰地区	Altay Administrative Offices	1348644	12	295754	9
博尔塔拉蒙古自治州	Bortala Mongol Autonomous Prefecture	1314500	13	494741	7
巴音郭楞蒙古自治州	Bayangol Mongol Autonomous Prefecture	6401378	3	1081543	5
阿克苏地区	Aksu Administrative Offices	3961175	6	1380325	3
克孜勒苏柯尔克孜自治州	Kizilsu Kirgiz Autonomous Prefecture	388757	15	78022	14
喀什地区	Kashgar [Kaxgar] Administrative Offices	3599718	7	1517509	2
和田地区	Hotan Administrative Offices	1034972	14	363132	8

地　区	Region	第二产业增加值 Secondary Industry	位次 Rank	第三产业增加值 Tertiary Industry	位次 Rank	人均地区生产总值（元） Per-capital GDP (yuan)	位次 Rank
乌鲁木齐市	Urumqi city	6004066	2	7181682	1	43039	3
克拉玛依市	Karamay city	6384205	1	694156	8	121387	1
石河子市	Shihezi city	686175	10	571995	10	42816	4
吐鲁番地区	Turpan Administrative Offices	1161343	8	422400	14	29828	6
哈密地区	Hami [Kumul] Administrative Offices	750045	9	683495	9	29375	7
昌吉回族自治州	Changji Hui Autonomous Prefecture	2341420	4	1575830	3	35554	5
伊犁哈萨克自治州	Ili Kazak Autonomous Prefecture	3226720		3077487		19479	
伊犁州直属县(市)	Counties (Cities) Direct Under Ili Prefecture	1460472	5	1635659	2	15633	12
塔城地区	Tacheng [Tarbagatai] Administrative Offices	1180363	7	974823	7	23562	9
阿勒泰地区	Altay Administrative Offices	585885	12	467005	13	22406	10
博尔塔拉蒙古自治州	Bortala Mongol Autonomous Prefecture	257796	13	561963	11	27374	8
巴音郭楞蒙古自治州	Bayangol Mongol Autonomous Prefecture	4131707	3	1188128	6	46955	2
阿克苏地区	Aksu Administrative Offices	1222787	6	1358063	5	15872	11
克孜勒苏柯尔克孜自治州	Kizilsu Kirgiz Autonomous Prefecture	91153	15	219582	15	7202	14
喀什地区	Kashgar [Kaxgar] Administrative Offices	650210	11	1431999	4	8748	13
和田地区	Hotan Administrative Offices	175493	14	496347	12	5181	15

19-2 各地、州、市全社会固定资产投资

Total Investmment in Fixed Assets by Prefecture, Autonomous Prefecture and City

单位：万元 (2010 年) (10 000 yuan)

地 区	Region	合 计 Total	位 次 Rank	国家预算内资金 State Budget Funds	位 次 Rank
乌鲁木齐市	Urumqi City	6900569	1	208352	9
克拉玛依市	Karamay City	1934056	6	313716	5
石河子市	Shihezi City	1023823	11	30840	15
吐鲁番地区	Turpan Administrative Offices	943186	12	60021	14
哈密地区	Hami [Kumul] Administrative Offices	1492069	9	162971	12
昌吉回族自治州	Changji Hui Autonomous Prefecture	2988210	5	465991	2
伊犁哈萨克自治州	Ili Kazak Autonomous Prefecture	6020137		906849	
伊犁州直属县(市)	Counties (Cities) Direct Under Ili Prefecture	3018184	3	433536	3
塔城地区	Tacheng [Tarbagatai] Administrative Offices	1878818	7	287534	7
阿勒泰地区	Altay Administrative Offices	1123135	10	185779	11
博尔塔拉蒙古自治州	Bortala Mongol Autonomous Prefecture	679162	14	192445	10
巴音郭楞蒙古自治州	Bayangol Mongol Autonomous Prefecture	3102994	2	259753	8
阿克苏地区	Aksu Administrative Offices	1816968	8	292560	6
克孜勒苏柯尔克孜自治州	Kizilsu Kirgiz Autonomous Prefecture	318417	15	115193	13
喀什地区	Kashgar [Kaxgar] Administrative Offices	3017657	4	1106341	1
和田地区	Hotan Administrative Offices	843432	13	385677	4

地 区	Region	国内贷款 Domestic Loans	位 次 Rank	利用外资 Foreign Investment	位 次 Rank	自筹及其他资金 Self-raising And Other Funds	位 次 Rank
乌鲁木齐市	Urumqi City	1553494	1	2635	9	5136088	1
克拉玛依市	Karamay City	50558	12			1569782	6
石河子市	Shi Hezi City	453368	2	3933	8	535682	11
吐鲁番地区	Turpan Administrative Offices	349994	4	14496	2	518675	12
哈密地区	Hami [Kumul] Administrative Offices	252282	6	2100	10	1074716	9
昌吉回族自治州	Changji Hui Autonomous Prefecture	312720	5	11848	3	2197651	4
伊犁哈萨克自治州	Ili Kazak Autonomous Prefecture	643955		35520		4433813	
伊犁州直属县(市)	Counties (Cities) Direct Under Ili Prefecture	357051	3	7990	4	2219607	3
塔城地区	Tacheng [Tarbagatai] Administrative Offices	79415	10	23375	1	1488494	7
阿勒泰地区	Altay Administrative Offices	207489	7	4155	7	725712	10
博尔塔拉蒙古自治州	Bortala Mongol Autonomous Prefecture	48579	13	7537	5	430601	14
巴音郭楞蒙古自治州	Bayangol Mongol Autonomous Prefecture	171275	9			2671966	2
阿克苏地区	Aksu Administrative Offices	180991	8	300	11	1343117	8
克孜勒苏柯尔克孜自治州	Kizilsu Kirgiz Autonomous Prefecture	55970	11	5750	6	141504	15
喀什地区	Kashgar [Kaxgar] Administrative Offices	22930	14	238	12	1888148	5
和田地区	Hotan Administrative Offices	4495	15			453260	13

19-3 各地、州、市农林牧渔业总产值

Gross Output Value of Farming, Forestry, Animal Husbandry and Fishery by Prefecture, Autonomous Prefecture and City

单位：万元 (2010 年) (10 000 yuan)

地区	Region	农林牧渔业总产值 Total	位次 Rank	农业 Farming	位次 Rank	林业 Forestry	位次 Rank
乌鲁木齐市	Urumqi City	273161	12	130416	12	2904	14
克拉玛依市	Karamay City	80604	14	27222	14	13399	7
吐鲁番地区	Turpan Administrative Offices	402992	10	318108	9	4642	12
哈密地区	Hami [Kumul] Administrative Offices	292973	11	152001	11	7936	10
昌吉回族自治州	Changji Hui Autonomous Prefecture	2103836	2	971332	4	22587	5
伊犁哈萨克自治州	Ili Kazak Autonomous Prefecture	3163395		1859698		47015	
伊犁州直属县(市)	Counties (Cities) Direct Under Ili Prefecture	1347896	6	715951	6	24409	4
塔城地区	Tacheng [Tarbagatai] Administrative Offices	1348595	5	922117	5	11200	9
阿勒泰地区	Altay Administrative Offices	466904	9	221630	10	11406	8
博尔塔拉蒙古自治州	Bortala Mongol Autonomous Prefecture	544307	8	425549	8	6294	11
巴音郭楞蒙古自治州	Bayangol Mongol Autonomous Prefecture	1610513	4	1279383	2	20617	6
阿克苏地区	Aksu Administrative Offices	1634693	3	1208014	3	109616	3
克孜勒苏柯尔克孜自治州	Kizilsu Kirgiz Autonomous Prefecture	159098	13	88036	13	2936	13
喀什地区	Kashgar [Kaxgar] Administrative Offices	2599047	1	1535469	1	265036	1
和田地区	Hotan Administrative Offices	764515	7	461789	7	110129	2

地区	Region	牧业 Animal Husbandry	位次 Rank	渔业 Fishery	位次 Rank	农林牧渔服务业 Farming, Forestry, Animal Husbandary and Fishery	位次 Rank
乌鲁木齐市	Urumqi City	130230	9	5801	6	3810	13
克拉玛依市	Karamay City	26772	14	625	11	12586	8
吐鲁番地区	Turpan Administrative Offices	72471	12	418	12	7353	12
哈密地区	Hami [Kumul] Administrative Offices	127898	10	1410	10	3728	14
昌吉回族自治州	Changji Hui Autonomous Prefecture	1072622	1	14644	1	22651	5
伊犁哈萨克自治州	Ili Kazak Autonomous Prefecture	1192553		16848		47281	
伊犁州直属县(市)	Counties (Cities) Direct Under Ili Prefecture	575235	3	9344	4	22957	4
塔城地区	Tacheng [Tarbagatai] Administrative Offices	397610	4	2774	8	14894	7
阿勒泰地区	Altay Administrative Offices	219708	7	4730	7	9430	11
博尔塔拉蒙古自治州	Bortala Mongol Autonomous Prefecture	91197	11	256	13	21011	6
巴音郭楞蒙古自治州	Bayangol Mongol Autonomous Prefecture	252865	5	10204	3	47444	3
阿克苏地区	Aksu Administrative Offices	244288	6	7580	5	65195	1
克孜勒苏柯尔克孜自治州	Kizilsu Kirgiz Autonomous Prefecture	57198	13	198	14	10730	10
喀什地区	Kashgar [Kaxgar] Administrative Offices	722990	2	10398	2	65154	2
和田地区	Hotan Administrative Offices	177697	8	2354	9	12546	9

注：本表按当年价格计算。
Notes：The number in this form is computed by current price.

19-4 各地、州、市主要农产品产量

Yield of Major Farm Crops by Prefecture, Autonomous Prefecture and City

单位：吨 (2010 年) (ton)

地 区	Region	粮 食 Grain	位 次 Rank	棉 花 Cotton	位 次 Rank
乌鲁木齐市	Urumqi City	176082	11	1095	13
克拉玛依市	Karamay City	5463	14	11128	11
吐鲁番地区	Turpan Administrative Offices	22223	13	23372	9
哈密地区	Hami [Kumul] Administrative Offices	122211	12	24504	8
昌吉回族自治州	Changji Hui Autonomous Prefecture	2018999	3	138940	5
伊犁哈萨克自治州	Ili Kazak Autonomous Prefecture	4227384		169395	
伊犁州直属县(市)	Counties (Cities) Direct Under Ili Prefecture	2257043	2	11380	10
塔城地区	Tacheng [Tarbagatai] Administrative Offices	1669036	4	158015	4
阿勒泰地区	Altay Administrative Offices	301305	9		
博尔塔拉蒙古自治州	Bortala Mongol Autonomous Prefecture	536533	7	94400	6
巴音郭楞蒙古自治州	Bayangol Mongol Autonomous Prefecture	387528	8	300680	3
阿克苏地区	Aksu Administrative Offices	1502129	5	455186	1
克孜勒苏柯尔克孜自治州	Kizilsu Kirgiz Autonomous Prefecture	236789	10	9100	12
喀什地区	Kashgar [Kaxgar] Administrative Offices	2699781	1	314240	2
和田地区	Hotan Administrative Offices	1069697	6	46465	7

地 区	Region	油 料 Oil Bearing Crops	位 次 Rank	甜 菜 Beetroots	位 次 Rank
乌鲁木齐市	Urumqi City	8503	10	1107	8
克拉玛依市	Karamay City	394	14	100	9
吐鲁番地区	Turpan Administrative Offices	2165	12		
哈密地区	Hami [Kumul] Administrative Offices	2704	11		
昌吉回族自治州	Changji Hui Autonomous Prefecture	56912	4	414271	2
伊犁哈萨克自治州	Ili Kazak Autonomous Prefecture	335095		1730069	
伊犁州直属县(市)	Counties (Cities) Direct Under Ili Prefecture	131621	1	1419040	1
塔城地区	Tacheng [Tarbagatai] Administrative Offices	92471	3	285052	5
阿勒泰地区	Altay Administrative Offices	111003	2	25977	7
博尔塔拉蒙古自治州	Bortala Mongol Autonomous Prefecture	27177	5	187111	6
巴音郭楞蒙古自治州	Bayangol Mongol Autonomous Prefecture	10056	9	346549	4
阿克苏地区	Aksu Administrative Offices	10505	8	373256	3
克孜勒苏柯尔克孜自治州	Kizilsu Kirgiz Autonomous Prefecture	936	13		
喀什地区	Kashgar [Kaxgar] Administrative Offices	14122	6		
和田地区	Hotan Administrative Offices	11434	7		

19-5 各地、州、市规模以上工业企业主要经济指标

Main Indicators on Economic of Industrial Enterprises above Designated Size by Prefecture, Autonomous Prefecture and City

单位：% (2010 年) (%)

地区	Region	工业总产值(万元) Gross Industrial Output Value (10 000 yuan)	位次 Rank	工业销售产值(当年价)(万元) Sales Value of Industry Products (At Current Prices) (10 000 yuan)	位次 Rank
乌鲁木齐市	Urumqi City	16747592	1	16503269	1
克拉玛依市	Karamay City	13308538	2	13336131	2
石河子市	Shihezi City	2002302	7	1999737	7
吐鲁番地区	Turpan Administrative Offices	1767630	8	1708324	8
哈密地区	Hami [Kumul] Administrative Offices	1075403	10	1079730	10
昌吉回族自治州	Changji Hui Autonomous Prefecture	4032278	4	3704933	4
伊犁哈萨克自治州	Ili Kazak Autonomous Prefecture	4549162		4274105	
伊犁州直属县(市)	Counties (Cities) Direct Under Ili Prefecture	2356151	6	2267756	6
塔城地区	Tacheng [Tarbagatai] Administrative Offices	1361349	9	1229218	9
阿勒泰地区	Altay Administrative Offices	831662	11	777131	11
博尔塔拉蒙古自治州	Bortala Mongol Autonomous Prefecture	332218	13	322369	13
巴音郭楞蒙古自治州	Bayangol Mongol Autonomous Prefecture	5523753	3	5434895	3
阿克苏地区	Aksu Administrative Offices	2504917	5	2403694	5
克孜勒苏柯尔克孜自治州	Kizilsu Kirgiz Autonomous Prefecture	104702	15	95500	15
喀什地区	Kashgar [Kaxgar] Administrative Offices	502746	12	521348	12
和田地区	Hotan Administrative Offices	122953	14	119767	14

地区	Region	总资产贡献率 Ratio of Total Assets To Industrial OutputValue	位次 Rank	资本保值增值率 Ratio of Capital Holding And Rise	位次 Rank
乌鲁木齐市	Urumqi City	15.6	4	143.3	7
克拉玛依市	Karamay City	27.9	2	111.2	15
石河子市	Shihezi City	9.9	11	125.8	11
吐鲁番地区	Turpan Administrative Offices	13.8	6	175.1	1
哈密地区	Hami [Kumul] Administrative Offices	8.0	12	132.1	8
昌吉回族自治州	Changji Hui Autonomous Prefecture	11.3	8	164.9	2
伊犁哈萨克自治州	Ili Kazak Autonomous Prefecture	14.2		130.4	
伊犁州直属县(市)	Counties (Cities) Direct Under Ili Prefecture	12.9	7	126.1	10
塔城地区	Tacheng [Tarbagatai] Administrative Offices	10.1	9	160.6	3
阿勒泰地区	Altay Administrative Offices	21.8	3	120.2	14
博尔塔拉蒙古自治州	Bortala Mongol Autonomous Prefecture	10.0	10	151.7	5
巴音郭楞蒙古自治州	Bayangol Mongol Autonomous Prefecture	29.8	1	122.5	12
阿克苏地区	Aksu Administrative Offices	14.4	5	145.3	6
克孜勒苏柯尔克孜自治州	Kizilsu Kirgiz Autonomous Prefecture	5.9	14	158.7	4
喀什地区	Kashgar [Kaxgar] Administrative Offices	6.5	13	121.6	13
和田地区	Hotan Administrative Offices	5.3	15	127.1	9

19-5 续表 Continued

单位：% (%)

地 区	Region	资产负债率 Assets Liability Ratio	位次 Rank	成本费用利润率 Ratio of Profits to Industrial Cost	位次 Rank
乌鲁木齐市	Urumqi City	45.1	13	13.9	6
克拉玛依市	Karamay City	39.6	15	21.3	3
石河子市	Shihezi City	61.9	4	12.8	8
吐鲁番地区	Turpan Administrative Offices	51.6	12	17.6	4
哈密地区	Hami [Kumul] Administrative Offices	59.0	7	10.4	11
昌吉回族自治州	Changji Hui Autonomous Prefecture	58.7	8	13.8	7
伊犁哈萨克自治州	Ili Kazak Autonomous Prefecture	61.9		16.5	
伊犁州直属县(市)	Counties (Cities) Direct Under Ili Prefecture	62.8	3	14.7	5
塔城地区	Tacheng [Tarbagatai] Administrative Offices	59.6	6	7.2	12
阿勒泰地区	Altay Administrative Offices	61.7	5	41.8	2
博尔塔拉蒙古自治州	Bortala Mongol Autonomous Prefecture	73.4	2	11.8	9
巴音郭楞蒙古自治州	Bayangol Mongol Autonomous Prefecture	52.4	11	62.7	1
阿克苏地区	Aksu Administrative Offices	55.4	10	10.6	10
克孜勒苏柯尔克孜自治州	Kizilsu Kirgiz Autonomous Prefecture	56.6	9	1.8	15
喀什地区	Kashgar [Kaxgar] Administrative Offices	78.4	1	2.9	14
和田地区	Hotan Administrative Offices	43.0	14	7.2	13

地 区	Region	产值利税率 Ratio of Profits and Taxes to Industrial Output Value	位次 Rank	流动资产周转次数(次/年) Number of Times of Annual TurnoverWorking Capitals (times/year)	位次 Rank
乌鲁木齐市	Urumqi City	19.7	6	2.3	3
克拉玛依市	Karamay City	32.6	3	3.7	1
石河子市	Shihezi City	16.2	9	1.4	9
吐鲁番地区	Turpan Administrative Offices	27.7	4	2.0	4
哈密地区	Hami [Kumul] Administrative Offices	17.8	8	1.2	14
昌吉回族自治州	Changji Hui Autonomous Prefecture	15.5	10	1.4	9
伊犁哈萨克自治州	Ili Kazak Autonomous Prefecture	21.5		1.6	
伊犁州直属县(市)	Counties (Cities) Direct Under Ili Prefecture	22.7	5	1.4	9
塔城地区	Tacheng [Tarbagatai] Administrative Offices	9.5	14	2.0	4
阿勒泰地区	Altay Administrative Offices	38.1	2	1.8	7
博尔塔拉蒙古自治州	Bortala Mongol Autonomous Prefecture	15.4	11	1.4	9
巴音郭楞蒙古自治州	Bayangol Mongol Autonomous Prefecture	50.7	1	2.5	2
阿克苏地区	Aksu Administrative Offices	18.8	7	1.9	6
克孜勒苏柯尔克孜自治州	Kizilsu Kirgiz Autonomous Prefecture	12.8	13	1.1	15
喀什地区	Kashgar [Kaxgar] Administrative Offices	8.6	15	1.7	8
和田地区	Hotan Administrative Offices	14.5	12	1.4	9

19-6 各地、州、市主要工业产品产量

Output of Major Industrial Products by Prefecture, Autonomous Prefecture and City

(2010 年)

地 区	Region	纱 (吨) Yarn (ton)	位次 Rank	布 (万米) Cloth (10 000 m)	位次 Rank	呢绒 (万米) Woolen Piece Goods (10 000 m)	位次 Rank
乌鲁木齐市	Urumqi City	58938	2	2064	4		
克拉玛依市	Karamay City						
石河子市	Shihezi City	120319	1	4233	1	172	1
吐鲁番地区	Turpan Administrative Offices	5356	11				
哈密地区	Hami [Kumul] Administrative Offices	15669	10				
昌吉回族自治州	Changji Hui Autonomous Prefecture	26696	6	1964	5	154	2
伊犁哈萨克自治州	Ili Kazak Autonomous Prefecture	41744		2841			
伊犁州直属县(市)	Counties (Cities) Direct Under Ili Prefecture	23549	7	2556	2		
塔城地区	Tacheng [Tarbagatai] Administrative Offices	18195	9	285	8		
阿勒泰地区	Altay Administrative Offices						
博尔塔拉蒙古自治州	Bortala Mongol Autonomous Prefecture	18417	8	125	9		
巴音郭楞蒙古自治州	Bayangol Mongol Autonomous Prefecture	33497	5	932	6		
阿克苏地区	Aksu Administrative Offices	39318	3	660	7		
克孜勒苏柯尔克孜自治州	Kizilsu Kirgiz Autonomous Prefecture						
喀什地区	Kashgar [Kaxgar] Administrative Offices	33525	4	2130	3		
和田地区	Hotan Administrative Offices	2015	12				

地 区	Region	成品糖 (万吨) Sugar (10 000 tons)	位次 Rank	饮料酒 (千升) Alcohol Beverage (kilo-liter)	位次 Rank	塑料制品 (吨) Plastic Products (ton)	位次 Rank
乌鲁木齐市	Urumqi City			156019	1	30205	5
克拉玛依市	Karamay City			59	14	115	14
石河子市	Shihezi City			93423	2	85726	3
吐鲁番地区	Turpan Administrative Offices			5930	10	4348	11
哈密地区	Hami [Kumul] Administrative Offices			26022	8	148099	1
昌吉回族自治州	Changji Hui Autonomous Prefecture	5.15	4	47365	5	121220	2
伊犁哈萨克自治州	Ili Kazak Autonomous Prefecture	25.73		148532		34098	
伊犁州直属县(市)	Counties (Cities) Direct Under Ili Prefecture	17.06	1	68965	4	82606	4
塔城地区	Tacheng [Tarbagatai] Administrative Offices	7.89	3	79141	3	4515	10
阿勒泰地区	Altay Administrative Offices	0.78	7	426	12	13941	9
博尔塔拉蒙古自治州	Bortala Mongol Autonomous Prefecture	2.39	5	1333	11	22334	8
巴音郭楞蒙古自治州	Bayangol Mongol Autonomous Prefecture	9.11	2	29260	7	22807	7
阿克苏地区	Aksu Administrative Offices	2.31	6	30704	6	386	13
克孜勒苏柯尔克孜自治州	Kizilsu Kirgiz Autonomous Prefecture					26982	6
喀什地区	Kashgar [Kaxgar] Administrative Offices	0.40	8	24017	9	665	12
和田地区	Hotan Administrative Offices			163	13		

19-6 续表 Continued

地　区	Region	机制纸及纸板(吨) Machine-made Paper and Paper board (ton)	位次 Rank	原煤(万吨) Coal (10 000 tons)	位次 Rank	原油(万吨) Crude Oil (10 000 tons)	位次 Rank
乌鲁木齐市	Urumqi City	151428	1	2424.20	2	700.02	2
克拉玛依市	Karamay City					1089.01	1
石河子市	Shihezi City	29799	4				
吐鲁番地区	Turpan Administrative Offices			1113.80	4	163.03	4
哈密地区	Hami [Kumul] Administrative Offices	2426	7	1213.01	3		
昌吉回族自治州	Changji Hui Autonomous Prefecture	64064	3	2794.77	1		
伊犁哈萨克自治州	Ili Kazak Autonomous Prefecture	4960		1064.95		52.00	
伊犁州直属县(市)	Counties (Cities) Direct Under Ili Prefecture	180	9	467.70	7		
塔城地区	Tacheng [Tarbagatai] Administrative Offices	4200	6	592.84	6	52.00	5
阿勒泰地区	Altay Administrative Offices	580	8	4.41	12		
博尔塔拉蒙古自治州	Bortala Mongol Autonomous Prefecture			288.80	8		
巴音郭楞蒙古自治州	Bayangol Mongol Autonomous Prefecture	69209	2	942.47	5	554.10	3
阿克苏地区	Aksu Administrative Offices			5.21	11		
克孜勒苏柯尔克孜自治州	Kizilsu Kirgiz Autonomous Prefecture			12.44	10		
喀什地区	Kashgar [Kaxgar] Administrative Offices	13162	5	58.08	9		
和田地区	Hotan Administrative Offices						

地　区	Region	水泥(万吨) Cement (10 000 tons)	位次 Rank	发电量(亿千瓦小时) Electricity (100 million kwh)	位次 Rank	农用化肥(吨) Chemical Fertilizers (ton)	位次 Rank
乌鲁木齐市	Urumqi City			181.19	1	760	6
克拉玛依市	Karamay City	78.84	10	44.77	6	3415	5
石河子市	Shihezi City	131.03	6	92.84	3		
吐鲁番地区	Turpan Administrative Offices	94.63	9	23.15	8	9408	3
哈密地区	Hami [Kumul] Administrative Offices	203.94	4	21.37	9	4363	4
昌吉回族自治州	Changji Hui Autonomous Prefecture	473.06	1	105.65	2		
伊犁哈萨克自治州	Ili Kazak Autonomous Prefecture	225.50		89.24			
伊犁州直属县(市)	Counties (Cities) Direct Under Ili Prefecture	172.34	5	65.67	4		
塔城地区	Tacheng [Tarbagatai] Administrative Offices	75.22	11	12.25	11		
阿勒泰地区	Altay Administrative Offices	55.34	12	11.32	12		
博尔塔拉蒙古自治州	Bortala Mongol Autonomous Prefecture	207.94	3	3.85	14	769042	1
巴音郭楞蒙古自治州	Bayangol Mongol Autonomous Prefecture	401.29	2	45.82	5	271359	2
阿克苏地区	Aksu Administrative Offices	45.32	13	37.84	7		
克孜勒苏柯尔克孜自治州	Kizilsu Kirgiz Autonomous Prefecture	101.64	8	0.30	15		
喀什地区	Kashgar [Kaxgar] Administrative Offices	119.98	7	20.69	10		
和田地区	Hotan Administrative Offices			5.87	13		

19-7 各地、州、市社会消费品零售总额

Total Retail Sales of Consumer Goods by Prefecture, Autonomous Prefecture and City

单位：万元 (2010 年) (10 000 yuan)

地区	Region	社会消费品零售总额 Total Retail Sales of Consumer Goods	位次 Rank	城镇 City	位次 Rank
乌鲁木齐市	Urumqi City	5142359	1	5138853	1
克拉玛依市	Karamay City	347872	9	346686	8
吐鲁番地区	Turpan Administrative Offices	284873	11	206007	11
哈密地区	Hami [Kumul] Administrative Offices	386696	8	364232	7
昌吉回族自治州	Changji Hui Autonomous Prefecture	1127924	2	964728	2
伊犁哈萨克自治州	Ili Kazak Autonomous Prefecture	1726672		1347924	
伊犁州直属县(市)	Counties (Cities) Direct Under Ili Prefecture	995658	3	773773	3
塔城地区	Tacheng [Tarbagatai] Administrative Offices	407014	7	286446	10
阿勒泰地区	Altay Administrative Offices	324000	10	287705	9
博尔塔拉蒙古自治州	Bortala Mongol Autonomous Prefecture	183147	13	152389	12
巴音郭楞蒙古自治州	Bayangol Mongol Autonomous Prefecture	561339	6	478155	5
阿克苏地区	Aksu Administrative Offices	602922	5	451952	6
克孜勒苏柯尔克孜自治州	Kizilsu Kirgiz Autonomous Prefecture	83272	14	75694	14
喀什地区	Kashgar [Kaxgar] Administrative Offices	734408	4	503013	4
和田地区	Hotan Administrative Offices	203444	12	146356	13

地区	Region	#城区 County	位次 Rank	乡村 Under County Level	位次 Rank
乌鲁木齐市	Urumqi City	5138853	1	3506	13
克拉玛依市	Karamay City	239163	7	1186	14
吐鲁番地区	Turpan Administrative Offices	83853	12	78866	7
哈密地区	Hami [Kumul] Administrative Offices	326124	4	22464	11
昌吉回族自治州	Changji Hui Autonomous Prefecture	523288	3	163196	3
伊犁哈萨克自治州	Ili Kazak Autonomous Prefecture	793991		378748	
伊犁州直属县(市)	Counties (Cities) Direct Under Ili Prefecture	604588	2	221885	2
塔城地区	Tacheng [Tarbagatai] Administrative Offices	114574	9	120568	5
阿勒泰地区	Altay Administrative Offices	74829	13	36295	9
博尔塔拉蒙古自治州	Bortala Mongol Autonomous Prefecture	93473	11	30758	10
巴音郭楞蒙古自治州	Bayangol Mongol Autonomous Prefecture	298783	5	83184	6
阿克苏地区	Aksu Administrative Offices	270540	6	150970	4
克孜勒苏柯尔克孜自治州	Kizilsu Kirgiz Autonomous Prefecture	71313	14	7578	12
喀什地区	Kashgar [Kaxgar] Administrative Offices	215898	8	231395	1
和田地区	Hotan Administrative Offices	110145	10	57088	8

19-8 各地、州、市海关进出口总额

Total Value of Imports and Exports by Prefecture, Autonomous Prefecture and City

单位：万美元 (2010 年) (USD 10 000)

地 区	Region	进出口总额 Total Imports and Exports	位 次 Rank	出口额 Exports	位 次 Rank	进口额 Lmports	位 次 Rank
乌鲁木齐市	Urumqi City	598533	1	443695	1	154838	2
克拉玛依市	Karamay City	28008	9	25504	10	2504	8
石河子市	Shihezi City	53666	8	43972	7	9694	6
吐鲁番地区	Turpan Administrative Offices	931	14	652	15	279	13
哈密地区	Hami [Kumul] Administrative Offices	2157	13	1770	13	387	12
昌吉回族自治州	Changji Hui Autonomous Prefecture	207620	3	191685	3	15935	4
伊犁哈萨克自治州	Ili Administrative Offices	622142		421685		200457	
伊犁州直属县(市)	Counties (Cities) Direct Under Ili Prefecture	488391	2	300538	2	187853	1
塔城地区	Tacheng [Tarbagatai] Administrative Offices	65155	6	53125	6	12030	5
阿勒泰地区	Altay Administrative Offices	68596	5	68022	5	574	10
博尔塔拉蒙古自治州	Bortala Mongol Autonomous Prefecture	61045	7	36103	8	24942	3
巴音郭楞蒙古自治州	Bayangol Mongol Autonomous Prefecture	12078	11	10814	11	1264	9
阿克苏地区	Aksu Administrative Offices	26215	10	25707	9	508	11
克孜勒苏柯尔克孜自治州	Kizilsu Kirgiz Autonomous Prefecture	10277	12	5443	12	4834	7
喀什地区	Kashgar [Kaxgar] Administrative Offices	89446	4	89248	4	198	14
和田地区	Hotan Administrative Offices	716	15	703	14	13	15

19-9 各地、州、市在岗职工工资总额和平均工资

Total Wages of Employed Staff and Workers and Average Wage by Prefecture, Autonomous Prefecture and City

(2010 年)

地 区	Region	在岗职工工资总额(万元) Total Wages of Statt and Workers (10 000 yuan)	位 次 Rank	在岗职工平均货币工资(元) Average On-the-Job Wage (yuan)	位 次 Rank
乌鲁木齐市	Urumqi City	2113978	1	41529	2
克拉玛依市	Karamay City	632192	4	42767	1
石河子市	Shihezi City	363814	9	32221	5
吐鲁番地区	Turpan Administrative Offices	269723	12	37757	3
哈密地区	Hami [Kumul] Administrative Offices	260785	13	33040	4
昌吉回族自治州	Changji Hui Autonomous Prefecture	660406	3	32196	6
伊犁哈萨克自治州	Ili Kazak Autonomous Prefecture	1495426		24935	
伊犁州直属县(市)	Counties (Cities) Direct Under Ili Prefecture	709634	2	26438	12
塔城地区	Tacheng [Tarbagatai] Administrative Offices	512321	8	23583	15
阿勒泰地区	Altay Administrative Offices	273471	11	23976	14
博尔塔拉蒙古自治州	Bortala Mongol Autonomous Prefecture	224261	14	25157	13
巴音郭楞蒙古自治州	Bayangol Mongol Autonomous Prefecture	575670	5	31468	8
阿克苏地区	Aksu Administrative Offices	515495	7	28421	11
克孜勒苏柯尔克孜自治州	Kizilsu Kirgiz Autonomous Prefecture	113158	15	30957	10
喀什地区	Kashgar [Kaxgar] Administrative Offices	551953	6	31108	9
和田地区	Hotan Administrative Offices	277426	10	31743	7

19-10 各地、州、市地方财政一般预算收支

The General Budgetary Revenue and Expenditures of Local Finance by Prefecture, Autonomous Prefecture and City

单位：万元 (2010 年) (10 000 yuan)

地区	Region	地方财政一般预算收入 Local Financial Revenue	位次 Rank	地方财政一般预算支出 Local Financial Expenditure	位次 Rank
乌昌地区	Urumqi and Changji Administrative Offices	1807175	1	2474779	1
克拉玛依市	Karamay City	424303	3	547711	9
石河子市	Shihezi City	137555	11	172440	14
吐鲁番地区	Turpan Administrative Offices	145963	10	332106	12
哈密地区	Hami [Kumul] Administrative Offices	150435	9	386270	11
伊犁哈萨克自治州	Ili Kazak Autonomous Prefecture	648482		2646054	
伊犁州直属县(市)	Counties (Cities) Direct Under Ili Prefecture	312194	5	1282002	3
塔城地区	Tacheng [Tarbagatai] Administrative Offices	183366	7	685169	7
阿勒泰地区	Altay Administrative Offices	152922	8	678883	8
博尔塔拉蒙古自治州	Bortala Mongol Autonomous Prefecture	63038	13	315170	13
巴音郭楞蒙古自治州	Bayangol Mongol Autonomous Prefecture	351807	4	880084	6
阿克苏地区	Aksu Administrative Offices	427314	2	1143958	4
克孜勒苏柯尔克孜自治州	Kizilsu Kirgiz Autonomous Prefecture	32581	14	419683	10
喀什地区	Kashgar [Kaxgar] Administrative Offices	196421	6	1880404	2
和田地区	Hotan Administrative Offices	63142	12	976442	5

19-11 分城镇居民消费价格指数和商品零售价格指数

General Retail Price and Consumer Price Index by City/County

(上年=100) (2010 年)(抽样调查) (Sampled Survey) (preceding year=100)

地区	Region	商品零售价格指数 General Retail Price Index	位次 Rank	居民消费价格指数 General Consumer Price Index	位次 Rank
乌鲁木齐市	Urumqi City	103.4	20	102.7	20
喀什市	Kashgar [Kaxgar] City	105.1	9	104.8	9
伊宁市	Yining [Gulja] City	106.5	2	106.2	2
和田市	Hotan City	105.2	8	104.4	15
克拉玛依市	Karamay City	104.2	15	104.5	13
哈密市	Hami [Kumul] City	105.1	9	105.0	8
昌吉市	Changji City	104.0	16	103.6	18
库尔勒市	Korla City	104.5	14	104.5	13
阿克苏市	Aksu City	106.2	3	106.1	3
焉耆回族自治县	Yanqi Hui Autonomous County	104.7	13	104.7	10
塔城市	Tacheng [Qoqek] City	105.7	5	105.2	6
阿勒泰市	Altay City	106.1	4	104.6	11
乌苏市	Usu City	104.9	12	105.5	5
博乐市	Bole [Bortala] City	105.7	5	105.7	4
吐鲁番市	Turpan City	105.5	7	104.6	11
库车县	Kuqa County	103.7	19	105.2	6
阿图什市	Artux City	105.1	9	104.3	16
莎车县	Shache [Yarkant] County	107.9	1	107.3	1
奎屯市	Kuytun City	103.8	18	103.3	19
石河子市	Shihezi City	103.9	17	103.7	17

19-12 各地、州、市各类学校在校学生数

Number of Students Enrollment by Type of School and by Prefecture, Autonomous Prefecture and City

单位：人 (2010 年) (person)

地 区	Region	普通高等学校 Regular Institutions of Higher Education	位次 Rank	中等职业学校 Specialized Secondary Schools	位次 Rank
乌鲁木齐市	Urumqi City	154797	1	87823	1
克拉玛依市	Karamay City	3732	7	1064	15
石河子市	Shihezi City	5149	6	20077	4
吐鲁番地区	Turpan Administrative Offices			3316	10
哈密地区	Hami [Kumul] Administrative Offices			2334	12
昌吉回族自治州	Changji Hui Autonomous Prefecture	12398	3	12358	8
伊犁哈萨克自治州	Ili Kazak Autonomous Prefecture	13102		23633	
伊犁州直属县(市)	Counties (Cities) Direct Under Ili Prefecture	13102	2	14329	7
塔城地区	Tacheng [Tarbagatai] Administrative Offices			3005	11
阿勒泰地区	Altay Administrative Offices			6299	9
博尔塔拉蒙古自治州	Bortala Mongol Autonomous Prefecture			1872	13
巴音郭楞蒙古自治州	Bayangol Mongol Autonomous Prefecture	3125	8	16101	5
阿克苏地区	Aksu Administrative Offices	3007	9	15213	6
克孜勒苏柯尔克孜自治州	Kizilsu Kirgiz Autonomous Prefecture			1687	14
喀什地区	Kashgar [Kaxgar] Administrative Offices	11419	4	26807	2
和田地区	Hotan Administrative Offices	5280	5	21034	3

地 区	Region	普通中学 Regular Secondary Schools	位次 Rank	小学 Primary Schools	位次 Rank
乌鲁木齐市	Urumqi City	148720	3	178206	5
克拉玛依市	Karamay City	25175	13	24256	14
石河子市	Shihezi City	18996	15	11288	15
吐鲁番地区	Turpan Administrative Offices	33404	10	51025	10
哈密地区	Hami [Kumul] Administrative Offices	31284	12	32932	12
昌吉回族自治州	Changji Hui Autonomous Prefecture	80414	6	81005	7
伊犁哈萨克自治州	Ili Kazak Autonomous Prefecture	250337		335835	
伊犁州直属县(市)	Counties (Cities) Direct Under Ili Prefecture	152674	2	219149	2
塔城地区	Tacheng [Tarbagatai] Administrative Offices	64563	8	72126	8
阿勒泰地区	Altay Administrative Offices	33100	11	44560	11
博尔塔拉蒙古自治州	Bortala Mongol Autonomous Prefecture	24236	14	27228	13
巴音郭楞蒙古自治州	Bayangol Mongol Autonomous Prefecture	70386	7	90118	6
阿克苏地区	Aksu Administrative Offices	138913	4	217163	3
克孜勒苏柯尔克孜自治州	Kizilsu Kirgiz Autonomous Prefecture	33900	9	53404	9
喀什地区	Kashgar [Kaxgar] Administrative Offices	260940	1	416262	1
和田地区	Hotan Administrative Offices	115352	5	199476	4

19-13 各地、州、市每万人口医院床位数和医生数

Number of Doctors and Hospital Beds Per 10 000 Population by Prefecture, Autonomous Prefecture and City

(2010 年)

地　区	Region	每万人床位数(张) Number of Beds per 10 000 Population (unit)	位次 Rank	平均每万人医生数(人) Number of Doctors Per 10 000 Population (person)	位次 Rank
乌鲁木齐市	Urumqi City	80.19	1	38.67	1
克拉玛依市	Karamay City	46.80	10	27.90	6
石河子市	Shihezi City				
吐鲁番地区	Turpan Administrative Offices	34.32	14	20.14	9
哈密地区	Hami [Kumul] Administrative Offices	53.37	5	31.17	2
昌吉回族自治州	Changji Hui Autonomous Prefecture	62.35	2	27.23	7
伊犁哈萨克自治州	Ili Kazak Autonomous Prefecture	45.80		22.68	
伊犁州直属县(市)	Counties (Cities) Direct Under Ili Prefecture	50.24	8	22.63	8
塔城地区	Tacheng [Tarbagatai] Administrative Offices	36.10	13	19.49	10
阿勒泰地区	Altay Administrative Offices	47.17	9	29.31	3
博尔塔拉蒙古自治州	Bortala Mongol Autonomous Prefecture	50.76	7	29.25	4
巴音郭楞蒙古自治州	Bayangol Mongol Autonomous Prefecture	61.53	3	28.31	5
阿克苏地区	Aksu Administrative Offices	46.70	11	12.86	12
克孜勒苏柯尔克孜自治州	Kizilsu Kirgiz Autonomous Prefecture	53.54	4	16.74	11
喀什地区	Kashgar [Kaxgar] Administrative Offices	41.33	12	12.45	13
和田地区	Hotan Administrative Offices	50.81	6	10.92	14

19-14 各地、州、市卫生技术人员和医生数

Medical Technical Personnel and Doctors by Prefecture, Autonomous Prefecture and City

单位：人 (2010 年) (person)

地区	Region	卫生技术人员 Medical Technical Personnel	位次 Rank	执业医师 Doctors with Licence	位次 Rank	执业助理医师 Assistant Doctors with Licence	位次 Rank
乌鲁木齐市	Urumqi City	29912	1	11353	1	674	6
克拉玛依市	Karamay City	2759	14	1019	13	72	15
石河子市	Shihezi City	4944	9	1773	7	315	10
吐鲁番地区	Turpan Administrative Offices	3138	13	979	14	275	12
哈密地区	Hami [Kumul] Administrative Offices	4344	10	1499	10	285	11
昌吉回族自治州	Changji Hui Autonomous Prefecture	9709	4	3231	4	659	8
伊犁哈萨克自治州	Ili Kazak Autonomous Prefecture	23655		7602		2160	
伊犁州直属县(市)	Counties (Cities) Direct Under Ili Prefecture	13993	3	4488	2	1130	2
塔城地区	Tacheng [Tarbagatai] Administrative Offices	5693	8	1703	8	673	7
阿勒泰地区	Altay Administrative Offices	3969	11	1411	11	357	9
博尔塔拉蒙古自治州	Bortala Mongol Autonomous Prefecture	3148	12	1065	12	233	14
巴音郭楞蒙古自治州	Bayangol Mongol Autonomous Prefecture	9009	5	2888	5	731	4
阿克苏地区	Aksu Administrative Offices	8360	6	2048	6	1002	3
克孜勒苏柯尔克孜自治州	Kizilsu Kirgiz Autonomous Prefecture	2604	15	625	15	255	13
喀什地区	Kashgar [Kaxgar] Administrative Offices	14230	2	3521	3	1434	1
和田地区	Hotan Administrative Offices	6189	7	1505	9	695	5

附录：各省市区主要经济指标排序

APPENDIX: Ranking of Main Economic Indicators by Region

新疆统计年鉴

XINJIANG STATISTICAL YEARBOOK 2011

各省市区主要经济指标排序
Ranking of Main Economic Indicators by Region

(2010 年)

省市区	Region	地区生产总值(亿元) Region Gross Product (100 million yuan)	位次 Rank	地区生产总值比上年增长(%) Increase Rate of Gross Region Production over the previous year(%)	位次 Rank
全 国	**China**	**397983.3**		**10.3**	
北 京	Beijing	13777.9	13	10.2	30
天 津	Tianjin	9108.8	20	17.4	1
河 北	Hebei	20197.1	6	12.2	24
山 西	Shanxi	9088.1	21	13.9	14
内蒙古	Inner Mongolia	11655.0	15	14.9	6
辽 宁	Liaoning	18278.3	7	14.1	12
吉 林	Jilin	8577.1	22	13.7	16
黑龙江	Heilongjiang	10235.0	16	12.6	19
上 海	Shanghai	16872.4	9	9.9	31
江 苏	Jiangsu	40903.3	2	12.6	20
浙 江	Zhejiang	27226.8	4	11.8	27
安 徽	Anhui	12263.4	14	14.5	8
福 建	Fujian	14357.1	12	13.8	15
江 西	Jiangxi	9435.0	19	14.0	13
山 东	Shandong	39416.2	3	12.5	21
河 南	Henan	22942.7	5	12.2	24
湖 北	Hubei	15806.1	11	14.8	7
湖 南	Hunan	15902.1	10	14.5	8
广 东	Guangdong	45472.8	1	12.2	24
广 西	Guangxi	9502.4	18	14.2	11
海 南	Hainan	2052.1	28	15.8	3
重 庆	Chongqing	7894.2	23	17.1	2
四 川	Sichuan	16898.6	8	15.1	5
贵 州	Guizhou	4594.0	26	12.8	18
云 南	Yunnan	7220.1	24	12.3	22
西 藏	Tibet	507.5	31	12.3	22
陕 西	Shaanxi	10021.5	17	14.5	8
甘 肃	Gansu	4119.5	27	11.7	28
青 海	Qinghai	1350.4	30	15.3	4
宁 夏	Ningxia	1643.4	29	13.4	17
新 疆	Xinjiang	5437.5	25	10.6	29

续表 1

省市区	Region	第一产业增加值(亿元) Value Added of the Primary Industry (100 million yuan)	位次 Rank	第二产业增加值(亿元) Value Added of the Secondary Industry (100 million yuan)	位次 Rank	第三产业增加值(亿元) Value Added of the Tertiary Industry (100 million yuan)	位次 Rank
全　国	**China**	**40497.0**		**186480.9**		**171005.4**	
北　京	Beijing	124.4	29	3323.1	23	10330.5	5
天　津	Tianjin	149.5	27	4837.6	19	4121.8	16
河　北	Hebei	2562.8	3	10705.7	6	6928.6	7
山　西	Shanxi	563.5	24	5161.2	17	3363.4	19
内蒙古	Inner Mongolia	1101.4	17	6365.8	14	4187.8	14
辽　宁	Liaoning	1631.1	11	9872.3	7	6774.9	8
吉　林	Jilin	1050.2	19	4417.4	21	3109.5	21
黑龙江	Heilongjiang	1302.3	14	5100.1	18	3832.6	17
上　海	Shanghai	114.2	30	7140.0	12	9618.3	6
江　苏	Jiangsu	2539.6	4	21753.9	2	16609.8	2
浙　江	Zhejiang	1360.7	13	14121.3	4	11744.8	4
安　徽	Anhui	1729.0	9	6391.0	13	4143.3	15
福　建	Fujian	1363.7	12	7365.5	10	5628.0	13
江　西	Jiangxi	1205.9	15	5194.7	16	3034.4	22
山　东	Shandong	3588.3	1	21398.9	3	14429.0	3
河　南	Henan	3263.2	2	13226.8	5	6452.6	9
湖　北	Hubei	2147.0	8	7764.7	9	5894.4	11
湖　南	Hunan	2339.4	6	7313.6	11	6249.1	10
广　东	Guangdong	2286.9	7	22918.1	1	20267.9	1
广　西	Guangxi	1670.4	10	4510.8	20	3321.2	20
海　南	Hainan	539.3	25	566.6	30	946.3	28
重　庆	Chongqing	685.4	21	4356.4	22	2852.4	24
四　川	Sichuan	2483.0	5	8565.2	8	5850.4	12
贵　州	Guizhou	630.3	22	1800.1	27	2163.6	25
云　南	Yunnan	1105.8	16	3223.9	24	2890.4	23
西　藏	Tibet	68.1	31	163.9	31	275.4	31
陕　西	Shaanxi	988.5	20	5403.5	15	3629.6	18
甘　肃	Gansu	599.0	23	1985.0	26	1535.5	27
青　海	Qinghai	134.9	28	744.6	29	470.9	30
宁　夏	Ningxia	160.3	26	833.2	28	650.0	29
新　疆	Xinjiang	1078.6	18	2592.2	25	1766.7	26

Continued

第一产业占GDP比重(%) Composition of Primary Industry Product to GDP(%)	位次 Rank	第二产业占GDP比重(%) Composition of Secondary Industry Product to GDP(%)	位次 Rank	第三产业占GDP比重(%) Composition of Tertiary Industrial Product to GDP(%)	位次 Rank
10.2		**46.8**		**43.0**	
0.9	30	24.1	31	75.0	1
1.6	29	53.1	11	45.3	6
12.7	14	53.0	12	34.3	27
6.2	25	56.8	2	37.0	18
9.4	21	54.6	6	35.9	23
8.9	23	54.0	8	37.1	17
12.2	16	51.5	15	36.3	20
12.7	14	49.8	20	37.4	14
0.7	31	42.3	27	57.0	2
6.2	25	53.2	10	40.6	9
5.0	27	51.9	14	43.1	8
14.1	9	52.1	13	33.8	28
9.5	20	51.3	16	39.2	13
12.8	13	55.1	4	32.2	30
9.1	22	54.3	7	36.6	19
14.2	8	57.7	1	28.1	31
13.6	11	49.1	21	37.3	15
14.7	5	46.0	25	39.3	12
5.0	27	50.4	19	44.6	7
17.6	3	47.5	24	35.0	24
26.3	1	27.6	30	46.1	5
8.7	24	55.2	3	36.1	22
14.7	5	50.7	17	34.6	26
13.7	10	39.2	28	47.1	4
15.3	4	44.7	26	40.0	10
13.4	12	32.3	29	54.3	3
9.9	18	53.9	9	36.2	21
14.5	7	48.2	22	37.3	15
10.0	17	55.1	4	34.9	25
9.8	19	50.7	17	39.6	11
19.8	2	47.7	23	32.5	29

续表 2

省市区	Region	总人口 (万人) Total Population (10 000 persons)	位 次 Rank	全社会固定资产投资（亿元） Total Investment in Fixed Assets in the Whole Country (100 million yuan)	位 次 Rank
全　国	**China**	**133972.5**		**278139.8**	
北　京	Beijing	1961.2	26	5403.0	23
天　津	Tianjin	1293.8	27	6278.6	20
河　北	Hebei	7185.4	6	15082.5	6
山　西	Shanxi	3571.2	18	6063.2	21
内蒙古	Inner Mongolia	2470.6	23	8929.9	12
辽　宁	Liaoning	4374.6	14	16043.0	4
吉　林	Jilin	2746.2	21	7870.4	16
黑龙江	Heilongjiang	3831.2	15	6812.6	18
上　海	Shanghai	2301.9	24	5108.9	24
江　苏	Jiangsu	7866.0	5	23186.8	2
浙　江	Zhejiang	5442.7	10	12488.1	8
安　徽	Anhui	5950.1	8	11543.4	9
福　建	Fujian	3689.4	17	8198.5	14
江　西	Jiangxi	4456.7	13	8775.5	13
山　东	Shandong	9579.3	2	23282.9	1
河　南	Henan	9402.4	3	16585.9	3
湖　北	Hubei	5723.8	9	10262.7	10
湖　南	Hunan	6568.4	7	9663.8	11
广　东	Guangdong	10430.3	1	15624.0	5
广　西	Guangxi	4602.7	11	7057.6	17
海　南	Hainan	867.2	28	1317.0	29
重　庆	Chongqing	2884.6	20	6692.4	19
四　川	Sichuan	8041.8	4	13119.5	7
贵　州	Guizhou	3474.6	19	3104.9	27
云　南	Yunnan	4596.6	12	5528.7	22
西　藏	Tibet	300.2	31	463.3	31
陕　西	Shaanxi	3732.7	16	7964.4	15
甘　肃	Gansu	2557.5	22	3158.3	26
青　海	Qinghai	562.7	30	1018.7	30
宁　夏	Ningxia	630.1	29	1444.2	28
新　疆	Xinjiang	2181.3	25	3539.7	25

Continued

居民消费价格指数 Consumer Price Index	位次 Rank	城镇居民人均可支配收入(元) Per Capita Annual Disposable Income of Urban households (yuan)	位次 Rank	城镇居民人均消费性支出(元) Per Capita Annual Living Expenditures for Consumption (yuan)	位次 Rank
103.3		**19109.4**		**13471.5**	
102.4	30	29072.9	2	19934.5	2
103.5	12	24292.6	4	16561.8	5
103.1	18	16263.4	14	10318.3	25
103.0	23	15647.7	20	9792.7	29
103.2	14	17698.2	10	13994.6	8
103.0	23	17712.6	9	13280.0	10
103.7	10	15411.5	24	11679.0	15
103.9	7	13856.5	28	10683.9	23
103.1	18	31838.1	1	23200.4	1
103.8	8	22944.3	6	14357.5	7
103.8	8	27359.0	3	17858.2	4
103.1	18	15788.2	18	11512.6	16
103.2	14	21781.3	7	14750.0	6
103.0	23	15481.1	22	10618.7	24
102.9	27	19945.8	8	13118.2	11
103.5	12	15930.3	17	10838.5	22
102.9	27	16058.4	16	11451.0	18
103.1	18	16565.7	13	11825.3	13
103.1	18	23897.8	5	18489.5	3
103.0	23	17063.9	12	11490.1	17
104.8	2	15581.1	21	10926.7	21
103.2	14	17532.4	11	13335.0	9
103.2	14	15461.2	23	12105.1	12
102.9	27	14142.7	27	10058.3	27
103.7	10	16064.5	15	11074.1	20
102.2	31	14980.5	26	9685.5	30
104.0	6	15695.2	19	11821.9	14
104.1	4	13188.6	31	9895.4	28
105.4	1	13855.0	29	9613.8	31
104.1	4	15344.5	25	11334.4	19
104.3	3	13643.8	30	10197.1	26

续表 3

省市区	Region	农民人均纯收入(元) Annual Per Capita Disposable Income of Rural Households (yuan)	位次 Rank	农民人均现金收入(元) Annual Per Capita Cash Income of Rural Households (yuan)	位次 Rank	农民人均生活消费支出(元) Annual Per Capita Living Expenditure of Rural Households (yuan)	位次 Rank
全　国	**China**	**5919.0**		**7088.8**		**4381.8**	
北　京	Beijing	13262.3	2	14793.8	2	9254.8	2
天　津	Tianjin	10074.9	4	12509.0	4	4936.7	7
河　北	Hebei	5958.0	12	7248.6	14	3844.9	19
山　西	Shanxi	4736.3	22	5667.4	22	3663.9	23
内蒙古	Inner Mongolia	5529.6	16	7718.2	12	4460.8	10
辽　宁	Liaoning	6907.9	9	9907.7	7	4489.5	9
吉　林	Jilin	6237.4	10	8386.0	10	4147.4	13
黑龙江	Heilongjiang	6210.7	11	10431.0	5	4391.2	11
上　海	Shanghai	13978.0	1	14603.8	3	10210.5	1
江　苏	Jiangsu	9118.2	5	10230.8	6	6542.9	4
浙　江	Zhejiang	11302.6	3	15042.9	1	8928.9	3
安　徽	Anhui	5285.2	18	5959.8	19	4013.3	15
福　建	Fujian	7426.9	7	8270.2	11	5498.3	6
江　西	Jiangxi	5788.6	14	6462.1	16	3911.6	17
山　东	Shandong	6990.3	8	9093.7	8	4807.2	8
河　南	Henan	5523.7	17	5900.0	20	3682.2	22
湖　北	Hubei	5832.3	13	6664.4	15	4090.8	14
湖　南	Hunan	5622.0	15	6433.0	17	4310.4	12
广　东	Guangdong	7890.3	6	8638.6	9	5515.6	5
广　西	Guangxi	4543.4	25	5151.6	25	3455.3	26
海　南	Hainan	5275.4	20	6118.3	18	3446.2	27
重　庆	Chongqing	5276.7	19	5312.9	24	3624.6	24
四　川	Sichuan	5086.9	21	5626.2	23	3897.5	18
贵　州	Guizhou	3471.9	30	3448.3	31	2852.5	30
云　南	Yunnan	3952.0	28	4565.2	27	3398.3	28
西　藏	Tibet	4138.7	26	3652.4	30	2666.9	31
陕　西	Shaanxi	4105.0	27	5032.7	26	3793.8	20
甘　肃	Gansu	3424.7	31	3856.0	29	2942.0	29
青　海	Qinghai	3862.7	29	4096.3	28	3774.5	21
宁　夏	Ningxia	4674.9	23	5879.2	21	4013.2	16
新　疆	Xinjiang	4642.7	24	7517.2	13	3458.1	25

注：现金收支为不含储蓄借贷后的现金收支。
Note: The cash income and expenditure refer to the one abscent of deposit loan.

Continued

农林牧渔业总产值(亿元) Gross Output Value of Farming, Forestry, Animal Husbandry and Fishery (100 million yuan)	位次 Rank	农林牧渔业总产值比上年增长(%) Output Value Increase Rate in 2009 over 2008 of Farming,Forestry, Animal Husbandry and Fishery(%)	位次 Rank	粮食产量(万吨) Grain (10 000 tons)	位次 Rank	棉花产量(万吨) Cotton (10 000 tons)	位次 Rank	油料产量(万吨) Oil bearing Crops (10 000 tons)	位次 Rank
69319.8		**4.4**		**54647.7**		**596.1**		**3230.1**	
328.0	26	-1.7	30	115.7	29	0.05	22	1.6	30
317.3	27	3.5	25	159.7	27	6.3	13	0.6	31
4309.4	3	3.5	25	2975.9	7	57.0	3	140.3	8
1047.8	22	6.2	3	1085.1	21	6.9	11	17.6	26
1843.6	18	6.2	3	2158.2	11	0.1	19	128.1	9
3106.5	9	5.8	7	1765.4	13	0.1	19	99.6	11
1850.3	16	3.6	23	2842.5	9	0.5	16	70.4	13
2536.3	12	5.8	7	5012.8	2			27.5	23
287.0	29	-5.1	31	118.4	28	0.4	17	2.3	29
4297.1	4	4.4	19	3235.1	4	26.1	7	152.0	7
2172.9	14	2.9	29	770.7	23	2.9	14	39.5	20
2955.4	10	4.5	16	3080.5	6	31.6	6	227.6	5
2307.1	13	3.5	25	661.9	24	0.01	24	26.6	24
1900.6	15	4.0	22	1954.7	12	13.1	9	107.6	10
6650.9	1	3.6	23	4335.7	3	72.4	2	342.2	2
5734.2	2	4.6	15	5437.1	1	44.7	5	540.7	1
3502.0	8	4.5	16	2315.8	10	47.2	4	311.8	3
3787.5	6	4.3	20	2847.5	8	22.7	8	195.3	6
3754.9	7	4.3	20	1316.5	16			88.2	12
2721.0	11	4.7	13	1412.3	15	0.2	18	45.8	18
821.3	25	6.1	5	180.4	26			9.5	27
1021.1	23	5.9	6	1156.1	18	0.01	24	44.4	19
4081.8	5	4.5	16	3222.9	5	1.4	15	268.5	4
997.8	24	5.2	11	1112.3	20	0.1	19	60.3	16
1810.5	19	4.7	13	1531.0	14	0.04	23	34.2	22
100.8	31	3.5	25	91.2	31			5.9	28
1666.1	20	5.8	7	1164.9	17	6.9	11	56.1	17
1057.0	21	5.7	10	958.3	22	7.6	10	64.1	15
201.3	30	6.7	2	102.0	30			34.4	21
305.9	28	7.8	1	356.5	25			20.8	25
1846.2	17	4.9	12	1150.2	19	247.9	1	66.6	14

续表 4

省市区	Region	工业增加值(亿元) Value-added of Industry (100 million yuan)	位次 Rank	天然气(亿立方米) Raw Coal (10 000 tons)	位次 Rank	原油(万吨) Crude Oil (10 000 tons)	位次 Rank
全　国	**China**	**160029.6**		**967.6**		**20301.4**	
北　京	Beijing	2701.6	23				
天　津	Tianjin	4410.7	18	17.2	7	3332.7	2
河　北	Hebei	9554.0	6	12.7	9	599.0	9
山　西	Shanxi	4586.4	15				
内蒙古	Inner Mongolia	5618.4	13				
辽　宁	Liaoning	8684.7	7	8.0	10	950.0	7
吉　林	Jilin	3833.5	21	13.7	8	702.3	8
黑龙江	Heilongjiang	4505.0	17	30.0	6	4004.9	1
上　海	Shanghai	6456.8	10	3.3	13	8.3	17
江　苏	Jiangsu	19266.9	2	0.6	17	186.0	12
浙　江	Zhejiang	12488.6	4				
安　徽	Anhui	5364.5	14				
福　建	Fujian	6242.3	12				
江　西	Jiangxi	4359.2	19				
山　东	Shandong	19026.1	3	5.3	12	2786.0	4
河　南	Henan	11950.8	5	6.7	11	497.9	10
湖　北	Hubei	6726.5	9	2.0	14	86.5	13
湖　南	Hunan	6275.1	11				
广　东	Guangdong	21374.8	1	78.4	4	1287.1	6
广　西	Guangxi	3860.5	20			2.7	19
海　南	Hainan	380.8	30	1.8	15	20.0	15
重　庆	Chongqing	3697.8	22	1.2	16		
四　川	Sichuan	7326.4	8	234.2	2	15.1	16
贵　州	Guizhou	1516.9	27				
云　南	Yunnan	2606.0	24				
西　藏	Tibet	39.7	31				
陕　西	Shaanxi	4516.4	16	223.5	3	3017.3	3
甘　肃	Gansu	1602.9	26	0.2	18	58.2	14
青　海	Qinghai	613.7	29	56.1	5	186.1	11
宁　夏	Ningxia	648.5	28			3.1	18
新　疆	Xinjiang	2161.4	25	249.9	1	2558.2	5

Continued

社会消费品零售总额(亿元) Total Retail Sales of Consumer Goods (100 million yuan)	位次 Rank	社会消费品零售总额比上年增长(%) Increase Rate in 2009over 2008of Total Retail Sales of Consumer Goods(%)	位次 Rank	进出口总额(亿美元) Total Value of Imports and Exports (USD 100 million)	位次 Rank	#出口总额(亿美元) Total Exports (USD 100 million)	位次 Rank
156998.4		**18.3**		**29727.6**		**15779.3**	
6229.3	10	17.3	27	3014.8	4	554.6	7
2902.6	23	19.4	2	822.0	8	375.2	9
6821.8	8	18.3	20	419.3	10	225.7	10
3318.2	18	18.1	25	125.8	22	47.1	23
3384.0	17	18.5	13	87.2	25	33.3	25
6887.6	7	18.5	13	806.7	9	431.2	8
3504.9	16	18.5	13	168.5	19	44.8	24
4039.2	15	18.7	10	255.0	13	162.8	12
6070.5	11	17.3	27	3688.9	3	1807.2	3
13606.8	3	18.5	13	4657.9	2	2705.5	2
10245.4	4	18.8	8	2534.7	5	1804.8	4
4197.7	14	19.0	3	242.8	14	124.2	16
5310.0	13	18.5	13	1087.8	7	715.0	6
2956.2	21	19.0	3	214.7	15	134.2	14
14620.3	2	18.3	20	1889.5	6	1042.5	5
8004.2	5	18.6	12	177.9	16	105.3	17
7013.9	6	18.3	20	259.1	12	144.4	13
5839.5	12	18.8	8	146.7	20	79.6	19
17458.4	1	17.2	29	7846.6	1	4532.0	1
3312.0	19	18.7	10	177.0	17	96.0	18
639.3	28	18.9	6	86.3	26	23.2	26
2938.6	22	18.5	13	124.3	23	74.9	21
6810.1	9	18.3	20	327.8	11	188.5	11
1482.7	25	18.9	6	31.4	28	19.2	27
2500.1	24	21.9	1	133.7	21	76.1	20
185.3	31	18.3	20	8.4	30	7.7	30
3195.7	20	18.4	19	120.8	24	62.1	22
1394.5	26	17.9	26	73.3	27	16.4	28
350.8	30	16.8	30	7.9	31	4.7	31
403.6	29	19.0	3	19.6	29	11.7	29
1324.5	27	12.5	31	171.3	18	129.7	15

续表 5 Continued

省市区	Region	国际旅游人数(万人) Total Number of Overseas Visitor Arrivals (10 000 persons)	位次 Rank	#外国人 Foreigners	位次 Rank	旅游外汇收入(亿美元) Earnings from International Tourism (USD 100 million)	位次 Rank
全　国	**China**	**13376.2**		**2612.7**		**458.1**	
北　京	Beijing	490.1	5	421.6	5	50.45	3
天　津	Tianjin	166.1	16	153.0	11	14.20	9
河　北	Hebei	97.7	24	85.3	21	3.51	23
山　西	Shanxi	130.3	20	82.1	22	4.65	20
内蒙古	Inner Mongolia	142.8	18	140.0	13	6.02	18
辽　宁	Liaoning	361.8	8	307.0	6	22.59	7
吉　林	Jilin	82.0	25	72.2	24	3.05	26
黑龙江	Heilongjiang	172.4	15	164.8	9	7.63	14
上　海	Shanghai	733.7	2	593.1	2	63.41	2
江　苏	Jiangsu	653.5	4	473.5	3	47.83	4
浙　江	Zhejiang	684.7	3	447.4	4	39.30	5
安　徽	Anhui	198.4	12	117.4	15	7.09	16
福　建	Fujian	368.1	6	115.3	16	29.78	6
江　西	Jiangxi	114.0	21	39.9	26	3.46	24
山　东	Shandong	366.8	7	277.9	7	21.55	8
河　南	Henan	146.8	17	96.1	20	4.99	19
湖　北	Hubei	181.7	14	138.5	14	7.51	15
湖　南	Hunan	189.9	13	103.3	18	9.06	12
广　东	Guangdong	3140.9	1	733.3	1	123.83	1
广　西	Guangxi	250.2	10	141.4	12	8.06	13
海　南	Hainan	66.3	26	47.4	25	3.22	25
重　庆	Chongqing	137.0	19	104.0	17	7.03	17
四　川	Sichuan	104.9	23	75.0	23	3.54	22
贵　州	Guizhou	50.0	27	18.6	28	1.30	27
云　南	Yunnan	329.2	9	231.2	8	13.24	10
西　藏	Tibet	22.8	28	21.4	27	1.04	28
陕　西	Shaanxi	212.2	11	155.2	10	10.16	11
甘　肃	Gansu	7.0	29	5.0	29	0.15	30
青　海	Qinghai	4.7	30	3.4	30	0.20	29
宁　夏	Ningxia	1.8	31	1.3	31	0.06	31
新　疆	Xinjiang	106.5	22	101.0	19	3.68	21

中国统计出版社最新图书简目

(仅供参考,以最后出书为准)

统计资料

中国统计年鉴-2011
2011 中国发展报告
中国劳动统计年鉴-2011
中国建筑业统计年鉴-2011
中国商品交易市场统计年鉴-2011
中国民政统计年鉴-2011
中国科技统计年鉴-2011
中国高技术产业统计年鉴-2011
全国农产品成本收益资料汇编-2011
大中型批发零售和住宿餐饮企业统计年鉴-2011
中国县（市）社会经济统计年鉴-2011
第二次全国 R&D 资源清查资料汇编－综合卷

中国统计摘要-2011
中国第三产业统计年鉴-2011
中国社会统计年鉴-2011
中国人口和就业统计年鉴-2011
中国房地产统计年鉴-2011
中国贸易外经统计年鉴-2011
中国农村统计年鉴-2011
中国教育经费统计年鉴-2010
中国科学技术协会统计年鉴-2011
中国农村住户调查年鉴-2011(中、英文)
第二次全国 R&D 资源清查资料汇编－工业企业卷
国际统计年鉴-2011

中国区域经济统计年鉴-2011
中国城市统计年鉴-2009
中国工业经济统计年鉴-2011
中国能源统计年鉴-2011
2011 中国地区经济监测报告
中国农产品价格调查年鉴-2011
中国农村贫困监测报告-2011
工业企业科技活动资料-2011
中国城市(镇)生活与价格年鉴-2011
中国农村全面建设小康监测报告-2011
中国零售和餐饮连锁企业统计年鉴-2011
2010 年中国第六次人口普查公报

2011 年省级综合统计年鉴系列

北京 天津 河北 山西 内蒙古
河南 湖北 湖南 广东 广西
新疆 新疆生产建设兵团
辽宁 吉林 黑龙江 上海 江苏
海南 重庆 四川 贵州 云南
浙江 安徽 福建 江西 山东
西藏 陕西 甘肃 青海 宁夏

2011 年市(县)级综合统计年鉴系列

天津滨海新区
运城 忻州 临汾 呼和浩特
上海浦东新区
杭州 宁波 绍兴 台州 温州
厦门经济特区 南昌 上饶
十堰 荆州 咸宁 长沙 广州
贵阳 昆明 庆阳 西安
石家庄 唐山 邯郸 太原 大同
包头 沈阳 大连 长春 吉林
苏州 无锡 常州 徐州 南通
金华 嘉兴 衢州
济南 青岛 潍坊 郑州
东莞 惠州 深圳 桂林 南宁
兰州 银川 乌鲁木齐
长治 阳泉 晋城 朔州 晋中
四平 哈尔滨 黑龙江垦区
盐城 镇江 江阴 丹阳
福州 福州经济技术开发区
洛阳 三门峡 南阳 武汉 宜昌
柳州 来宾 河池 海口 成都 绵阳

“十一五”规划教材

非参数统计 医学统计学
多元统计分析 经济计量学教程
统计数据处理概论
企业经营管理统计
统计学:从数据到结论
概率论与数理统计 统计学
应用时间序列分析
质量管理统计方法 社会统计学
市场调查与预测
国民经济核算教程(国民经济统计学)
现代金融投资统计分析
统计指数理论及应用
多元统计分析实验
统计学原理（非统计专业使用）
概率论与数理统计(经济、管理类专业使用)

重点图书

挑大学选专业 2011—高考志愿填报指南 挑大学选专业 2011—考研择校指南

欲购以上图书请与中国统计出版社发行部联系。电话:（010）63376907，63376908 同榍行书店电话: 68783171,68783172
通讯地址: 北京市西城区三里河月坛南街 57 号 邮政编码: 100826

New Published Statistical Yearbook by China Statistics Press

Statisticses Data

China Statistical Yearbook -2011
China Development Report in 2011
China Labor Statistical Yearbook-2011
China Construction Statistical Yearbook-2011
China Statistical Yearbook-2011 of Commodities Market
China Civil Affair's Statistical Yearbook -2011
China Science and Technology Statistics Yearbook- 2011
China Statistics Yearbook on High Technology Industry-2011
China Agricultural Production Cost and 2011 Data
China Statistical Yearbook of Retail and Catering Service Corporation in Chain- 2011
China County(City) Social and Economic Statistical Yearbook-2010
China Statistical Abstract-2011
China Tertiary Industry Statistical Yearbook-2011
China Society Statistical Yearbook-2011
China Population and Employment Statistical Yearbook-2011
China Real Estate Statistical Yearbook-2011
China Foreign Economic Statistical Yearbook-2011
China Rural Statistical Yearbook-2011
China Education Finance Statistical Yearbook-2011
China Statistics on Science and Technology Activities of Industry Enterprises-2011
International Statistical Yearbook-2011
China Region Economic StatisticalYearbook-2011
China City Statistical Yearbook-2011
China Industrial Economic Statistical Yearbook-2011
China Energy Statistical Yearbook-2011
Poverty Monitoring Report of Rural China-2011
China Data Industrial Enterprises Activities-2011
China Country(Town) Life and Price Statistical Yearbook-2011
China Monitoring Report on Xiaokang-2011
China Chain Store and Catering Services Statistical Yearbook-2011
China No.6 Population Survey Report-2010

Series of Provinces Comprehensive Statistical Yearbook-2011

Beijing Tianjin Hebei Shanxi Inner Mongolia
Liaoning Jilin Heilongjiang Shanghai Jiangsu
Zhejiang Anhui Fujian Jiangxi Shandong
Henan Hubei Hunan Guangdong Guangxi
Hainan Chongqing Sichuan Guizhou
Yunnan Tibet Shaanxi Gansu Qinghai
Ningxia Xinjiang
Xinjiang Production & Construction Group

Series of City(Country) Comprehensive Statistical Yearbook-2011

Binhai New Region of Tianjing
Yuncheng Xinzhou Linfen Hohhot
Shanghai Pudong New Area
Hangzhou Ningbo Shaoxing Taizhou
Nanchang Shangrao Shiyan Jingzhou
Xianning Changsha Guangzhou
Guiyang Kunmin Qingyang Xi'an
Shijiazhuang Tangshan Handan
Taiyuan Datong Baotou Shenyang Dalian
Changchun Jilin Suzhou Wuxi Changzhou Xuzhou
Nantong Jinhua Jiaxing Quzhou
Jinan Qingdao Weifang Zhengzhou
Dongguan Huizhou Guiling Nanning
Lanzhou Yingchuan Urumqi
Changzhi Yangquan Jincheng Shuozhou Jinzhong
Siping Harbin Heilongjiang Assarting District
Yancheng Zhenjiang Jiangyin Danyang
Fuzhou Economic & Technical Development District
Luoyang Sanmenxia Nanyang Wuhan
Yichang Liuzhou
Laibin Hechi Haikou Chengdu Mianyang

Planning program of the Eleventh five-year

Nonparametric Statistics Medical Statistcs
Mutiple Statistical Analysis
Economic Measure Learning Course
Statistical Data Processing Overview
Enterprise Management Statistics
Probability Theory and Math Statistics Statistics
Application Time Sequence of Analysis
Quality Management Statistical Methods
Society Statistics
Market Research and Forecasts
Modern Financial Investment Statistical Analysis
Multiple statistical analysis experiment Statistical Indicators Theory and Application
Statistical Principles
Statistics (From Practice to Theory)
National Accounts Tutorial
Probability Theory and Math Statistics Statistics (Economic and Management)

Emphases Books

For University Entrance Exam for Professional 2011
---- the Reporting Guidelines
For Postgraduate Entrance Exam for Professional 2011
---- the Reporting Guidelines

Tongjihang Bookstore: (010) 63376907 63376908 68783171 68783172
Address: No 57 Yuetan Nanjie, Sanlihe, Beijing P. R. China Statistics Press Zip code:100826

新疆维吾尔自治区人民检察院

党组书记　杨肇季

检察长　哈斯木·马木提

2011年是"十二五"时期开局之年，是推进新疆跨越式发展和长治久安的关键一年，也是中国共产党建党90周年。今年以来，全疆检察机关在自治区党委和高检院的坚强领导下，在各级人大的监督和各级人民政府、政协的关心支持下，全面贯彻落实科学发展观，深入实践"强化法律监督，维护公平正义"的工作主题，紧紧围绕服务新疆跨越式发展和长治久安，以深入推进四项重点工作为载体，着力强化法律监督、强化自身监督、强化队伍建设，各项检察工作取得了新的成效。

全疆检察机关和广大检察人员着力深化四项重点工作，更好维护社会和谐稳定；着力服务发展第一要务，更好推进经济跨越式发展；着力化民怨解民难，更好维护人民群众权益；着力加大查办和预防职务犯罪工作力度，更好促进反腐倡廉建设；着力强化对诉讼活动的法律监督，更好维护司法公正廉洁；着力抓好检察改革，更好推进检察工作科学发展；紧紧围绕公正廉洁执法，全面加强党的建设和队伍建设。

站在新疆加快发展的新起点上，我们要更加紧密地团结在以胡锦涛同志为总书记的党中央周围，肩负起历史使命和政治责任，坚持党的事业至上、人民利益至上、宪法法律至上，振奋精神，团结一致，锐意进取，扎实工作，努力开创新疆检察工作新局面，为推进新疆跨越式发展和长治久安作出新的更大贡献，以优异成绩迎接中国共产党成立90周年！

全疆基层检查院建设工作会议

第二届自治区检察院机关法庭论辨赛

自治区经济和信息化委员会

（自治区国防科学技术工业办公室）

自治区政协副主席、经济和信息化委员会党组书记、主任　王永明

自治区经济和信息化委员会（自治区国防科学技术工业办公室）由原自治区经济贸易委员会（除内贸以外）与原自治区信息产业厅组建而成，为自治区人民政府组成部门。主要负责产业发展、园区建设、经济运行、企业发展、技术进步、工业节能减排、国防科工、信息化与信息产业、无线电管理等职能，是我区推进新型工业化与信息化的主要机构。

近年来，自治区经信委坚持以邓小平理论和“三个代表”重要思想为指导，深入贯彻落实科学发展观，始终坚持“有为才有位、有思路才有出路”的工作理念，立足新疆实际，全力推动新型工业化建设加快发展，不断创新发展思路，努力提高工作质量，经济与信息化工作不断取得新的成绩。“十一五”期间，我区支柱产业发展取得新进展，企业发展保持较好势头，技术进步明显加快，园区建设取得重大突破，“两化”融合步伐不断加快，经济运行调控能力明显增强，节能减排积极推进，较好地完成了“十一五”规划确定的主要目标任务，为促进新疆经济平稳较快发展做出了突出贡献。

“十二五”时期，自治区经信委将积极贯彻落实中央新疆工作座谈会精神，按照自治区党委、人民政府的决策部署，坚持以科学发展为主题，以加快转变经济发展方式为主线，以信息化带动工业化，以工业化促进信息化，坚持资源开发可持续、生态环境可持续，构建具有新疆特色的现代产业体系，推动新疆跨越式发展和长治久安。

自治区党委常委宋爱荣、自治区党委常委、自治区副主席库热西·买合苏提、自治区政协副主席、经济和信息化委员会主任王永明出席2010年自治区经信工作会议，并共同启动自治区经信委新网站

自治区经信委系统2010年总结表彰大会

自治区政协副主席、经信委主任王永明深入企业调研

新疆维吾尔自治区文化厅

大型杂技剧《你好！阿凡提》荣获国家文华大奖

全国文物系统对口支援新疆工作会议

北京市文化援助和田捐赠仪式

2010年是不平凡的一年，也是新疆各项事业发展具有里程碑意义的一年。刘云山、李长春、张春贤、努尔·白克力、蔡武、欧阳坚等中央、文化部、国家文物局和自治区领导，先后到文化文物系统调研，解决了一大批影响新疆文化发展的大问题，为新疆文化事业跨越式发展奠定了良好的基础。配合国家文化部制定了文化发展规划，率先召开了全国文化文物工作对口援疆会议。紧紧围绕中央和自治区的重大战略决策，规划的“春雨工程”、“文化遗产保护工程”、“新疆文化市场监管能力建设工程”、“新疆文艺译制中心项目”已写入中央新疆工作座谈会会议文件当中，是新疆今后五到十年文化建设的主攻方向和中心工作。截至目前，“春雨工程” 已落实项目10个，资金达27.86亿元。

专业艺术和重大活动主题鲜明，有影响、有声势，推动全社会形成良好的文化环境。在“春满天山”文艺调演、世博演出；赴北京、香港、土耳其、印度尼西亚、利比亚以及赴内地演出的重大艺术活动中表现优异，受到国家部委和自治区的表彰奖励。《大巴扎》的成功创作和演出，受到自治区党政主要领导的好评和重奖；《你好，阿凡提》的定点常态演出，在“九艺节”和香港演出取得佳绩，令人自豪。

公共文化服务体系建设和组织举办大型公益文化活动再上台阶。指导各地、县编制了对口援疆文化规划，19省市对口援疆启动了一批文化项目和文化活动。全疆乡镇文化站建设项目全面扫尾；南疆三地州的村文化室和城市社区文化中心建设全面展开。木卡姆团场所、老艺术家楼、话剧团剧场维修、艺术学校教学楼、文化系统集资建房等建设项目进展顺利。全疆文化站、社区文化中心设备配备，流动舞台车配备，地县“两馆一团”设备配备有序跟进。

自治区党委书记张春贤考察国土资源工作

自治区党委副书记、自治区主席努尔·白克力考察国土资源工作

新疆维吾尔自治区国土资源厅

十一五期间，在自治区党委、自治区人民政府和国土资源部的正确领导下，新疆国土资源厅坚持以邓小平理论和“三个代表”重要思想为指导，深入贯彻落实科学发展观，全面贯彻执行党中央、国务院和自治区党委、自治区人民政府的重大决策部署，紧紧围绕自治区改革发展与稳定的大局，以西部大开发为契机，在服从和服务于自治区优势资源转换战略、大企业大集团战略和新型工业化建设发展中，积极主动服务，严格规范管理，把合理开发利用资源，培育和发展特色产业，促进经济社会发展，造福新疆各族人民摆在突出位置。

目前，新疆经济社会已经进入新的发展时期，特别是中央新疆工作座谈会的召开，为新疆今后的发展指明了方向，做出了部署，新疆将迎来大建设、大开放、大发展的新时期。希望全区广大国土资源工作者，在新的形势下和新的历史起点上，坚持改革开放的正确方向，站在战略和全局的高度，抓住难得的历史发展机遇，树立新型的资源观和资源管理观，切实把国家和自治区关于保护资源、保障发展的方针政策转化为促进新疆经济社会发展的新思路、新举措，不断开创国土资源事业改革发展的新局面，为新疆经济社会实现跨越式发展和长治久安做出新的更大贡献。

国土资源厅领导班子研究工作

自治区矿产资源总体规划院士专家座谈会

国土资源厅学法懂法，坚持依法行政

新疆维吾尔自治区交通运输厅

自治区党委书记张春贤看望红其拉甫养路职工

自治区党委副书记、自治区主席努尔·白克力慰问果子沟交通一线职工

自治区党委常委、常务副主席黄卫在施工现场指导

自治区党委常委宋爱荣在施工现场调研指导

新疆交通运输厅成立于 1950 年 1 月 1 日。60 年来，在自治区党委、自治区人民政府和国家交通运输部的亲切关怀和正确领导下，自治区交通运输厅始终以服从和服务于自治区经济社会发展为己任，以造福新疆各族人民、推动新疆经济社会又好又快发展为宗旨，认真贯彻落实科学发展观，在艰苦奋斗中创业、在顽强拼搏中前进、在开拓进取中发展，新疆交通运输事业发生了巨大的变化，尤其是近年来，交通建设投资规模之大、发展速度之快、质量效益之好、对自治区经济社会影响之深前所未有。“十一五”期间，新疆交通运输系统超额完成了各项目标任务，五年间，累计完成全社会交通固定资产投资 830 亿元（兵团和社会完成投资 158 亿元），全区公路总里程已由 1949 年的 3361 公里达到 15.2 万公里（含兵团），其中高速公路 1137 公里，农村公路 10.3 万公里，改善了 305 个乡镇和 3454 个建制村的通行条件；国省干线好路率达到 89.2%，公路技术等级、通行能力和安全性能及路网整体服务水平明显提高。全区机动车保有量达 307.3 万辆，开通客运班线 3656 条，国际道路运输线路达 107 条。五年全区累计完成国内道路旅客运输量 78.2 亿人次、货运量 17.2 亿吨，国际道路旅客运输量 363.33 万人次、货运量 1014.33 万吨，较“十五”期间分别增长 51.08%、61.9%、420%、80%。全区基本形成了以乌鲁木齐为中心，以 8 条国道干线为主骨架，环绕两大盆地、穿越两大沙漠．横贯天山、连接南北疆，辐射各地县乡，东联甘肃、青海、南接西藏，西出中亚、西亚各国，四通八达的干支线公路运输网络；道路运输逐步向快捷、舒适、安全、高效转变，成为各种运输方式的排头兵和主力军，为自治区经济发展、社会稳定和全方位对外开放等多方面做出了重要贡献。

“十二五”期间，新疆交通运输发展围绕自治区提出的“以打造面向国内、面向周边国家和疆内的交通大通道为重点，加快构建快捷、高效的综合交通运输体系”的目标要求，大力推进构筑“五横”、“七纵”高速公路网，建设七大国家级公路运输枢纽，完善十二条东联内地和西出国际的大通道“57712”和农村公路实现网络化、黑色化为主的农村“畅通富民”两大工程。五年完成交通固定资产投资 1500~2000 亿元（含兵团），建设总里程 7.6 万公里。到 2015 年底，全区高速公路达到 5000 公里，高等级公路（一、二级）超过 15000 公里，农村公路达到 11 万公里，基本实现连接 14 个地州市及兵团师部的公路高速化，各县市和团场通二级及以上公路，具备条件的乡镇全部通沥青路，90%的建制村通沥青路。建设乌鲁木齐、伊宁（霍尔果斯）、喀什、哈密、库尔勒、石河子、奎屯七大国家级公路运输枢纽。国内客货运输量年均分别增长 8.7%、7%，国际客货运输量年均分别增长 8%、7%。乡镇客运班车通车率 100%，建制村客运班车通车率 98%。高速、干线公路好路率分别达到 98%和 71%以上。力争到 2015 年实现交通基础设施网络化、公众出行便捷化、货物运输便利化、公共服务均等化、应急保障信息化，交通运输综合指标名列西部前茅。

自治区人民政府与交通运输部签署会谈纪要

新疆维吾尔自治区主席助理 国土资源厅党组书记 田建荣

自治区国土资源厅长　马敖·赛依提哈木扎

国土资源部援疆工作座谈会暨新疆“358”项目汇报会

参加“迎奥运”活动

丰富多彩的职工文化活动

保障重点建设项目用地

耕地保护——万顷良田遍布天山南北

新疆维吾尔自治区民族事务委员会
新疆维吾尔自治区宗教事务局

自治区领导会见自治区第六次民族团结进步表彰大会模范集体和个人

自治区民族工作会议暨第六次民族团结进步表彰大会会场

自治区民委(宗教局)党组书记　刘振强

自治区民委(宗教局)主任　吐尔干·皮达

新疆是多民族、多宗教地区。有13个世居民族,55个民族成分,各民族在区域分布上"大杂居,小聚居,相互交错杂处"。2010年,全区总人口2181.33万人,其中少数民族人口达到1306.72万人,占59.9%。新疆目前有伊斯兰教、佛教(藏传、汉传)、基督教、天主教、东正教、道教6种宗教,宗教教职人员29000多人,宗教活动场所24400多座,各级爱国宗教团体98个。自治区民委(宗教局)是主管自治区民族、宗教事务工作的政府组成部门。

自治区党委、人民政府历来高度重视民族宗教工作,始终把民族宗教工作作为维护稳定、促进发展的一项重要的基础性工作来抓,坚持以邓小平理论和"三个代表"重要思想为指导,全面贯彻落实科学发展观,紧紧围绕"共同团结奋斗、共同繁荣发展"的主题,认真贯彻落实《民族区域自治法》,推动了民族团结进步事业及民族地区经济社会各项事业发展。坚持全面贯彻党的宗教信仰自由政策、依法加强宗教事务管理,坚持独立自主自办的原则,积极引导宗教与社会主义社会相适应,开创了新疆经济发展、社会稳定、民族团结、宗教和睦、各族人民安居乐业的大好局面。

第三届全国少数民族文艺汇演

自治区第七届民运会摔跤比赛

自治区伊斯兰教中青年爱国宗教人士第六期培训班学员赴内地参观

新疆维吾尔自治区信息中心
新疆维吾尔自治区电子政务外网管理中心

自治区电子政务外网一期工程启动仪式

自治区电子政务外网十二五规划研讨会

自治区电子政务外网建设工程网络技术培训班

自治区信息中心（自治区电子政务外网管理中心）成立于1988年，是隶属于自治区发展和改革委员会管理的副厅级事业单位，核定事业编制85名，专业技术人员占75%，其中高级、中级专业技术人才占50%以上。其主要职责是承担全区经济信息资源开发利用的规划和管理，为自治区党委、人民政府及经济综合管理部门宏观经济决策提供信息服务；承担全区电子政务外网规划、建设、运行、维护及相关管理工作；为党政机关、事业单位提供信息化技术支持与服务。

近年来，在自治区党委、人民政府和自治区发改委党组的正确领导下，自治区信息中心紧紧围绕“一个中心、两大任务、三大建设”的工作方针，以电子政务外网建设为主线、以实现信息化建设和信息服务两翼齐飞为目标，坚持科学、全面、可持续的发展观，强化管理、探索创新、突出重点、狠抓落实，各项工作取得突破性进展，连续三年被评为自治区文明机关，2010年又被自治区文明委授予“自治区级文明单位”荣誉称号。

自治区电子政务外网是我国电子政务重要基础设施的国家电子政务外网组成部分。其建设目标是整合现有网络资源，建成横向连接各级政务部门，纵向链接国家政务外网网络，支持跨部门、跨地区信息交换、资源共享和业务系统的互联互通，满足各级政务部门社会管理和公共服务的需要，促进政府监管能力和服务水平的提高。按照自治区人民政府的要求，2011年将完成区、地、县三级骨干网和区级城域网建设任务。

在新的历史起点上，自治区信息中心将不断开拓创新，全面提升综合服务能力和水平，为推动自治区跨越式发展和长治久安做出新贡献。

精神文明创建动员大会

自治区电子政务外网主机房

团结奋进的干部队伍

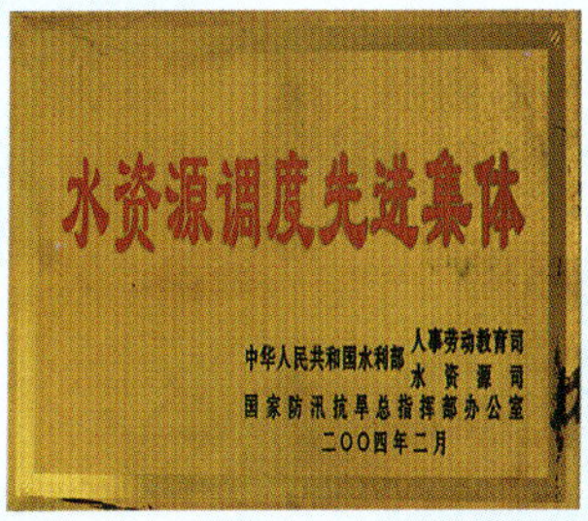

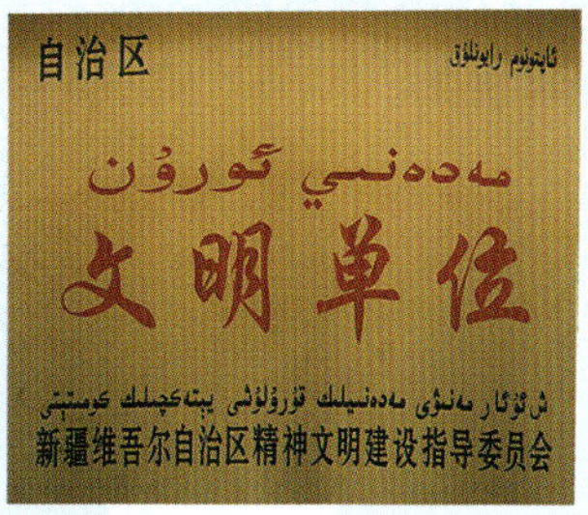

新疆维吾尔自治区塔里木河流域和田管理局

自治区水利厅副厅长、塔管局局长覃新闻和和田行署副专员帕尔哈提·肉孜为塔里木河流域和田管理局揭牌

局长　阿地里江·奴尔买买提

和田河，位于中国新疆维吾尔自治区塔里木盆地西南部，是昆仑山北坡最大的河流。旧称和阗河。有玉龙喀什河与喀拉喀什河两源。主流玉龙喀什河出昆仑山北麓；喀拉喀什河出喀喇昆仑山北麓，汇合后始称和田河。和田河多年平均径流 43.67 亿立方米，多年平均向塔河输送水量 9 亿立方米。和田河流域肩负着和田地区洛浦县灌区、和田县玛牙克灌区、和田县苏巴灌区、和田市灌区、墨玉县灌区、兵团农十四师 47 团、皮墨垦区灌区、皮山县皮亚勒玛乡灌区和皮亚勒玛开发区灌区 50 个乡镇、881 个行政村的 20.53 万公顷农业和 11.33 万公顷生态林草灌溉用水，并严格按塔里木河流域水利委员的统一安排，负责完成和田河流域的引水限额和调水工作。

新疆维吾尔自治区塔里木河流域和田管理局（原名：和田河流域管理局）位于和田市乌鲁木齐南路 29 号，副县级自收自支的事业单位，在职员工 101 人，其中男职工 65 名、女职工 36 名。局下设 11 个职能科室、站，其中局内设 4 个职能科室（分别为：行政办公室、计划财务科、灌溉科、工程科）7 个下属机构科室（塔里木河调水执行办公室、水政水资源监察大队、玉龙喀什河渠首管理站、喀拉喀什河渠首管理站、喀拉喀什河渠首爱国主义教育基地管理处、加玛达水管站、阿克栏杆水管站）具体负责和田河流域水资源统一管理与调度灌区的灌溉管理、防洪抗旱、调水、水利工程管理、水利法律法规的宣传和水政执法，塔河项目执行，喀河渠首爱国主义教育基地——王蔚事迹陈列馆的管理的等工作任务。

根据自治区人民政府第 19 次常务会议和自治区塔河流域主要源流管理体制改革情况通报会议精神，及自治区《关于印发塔里木河流域主要源流管理机构移交塔管局实施方案的通知》和塔管局《关于成立“四源流”管理机构移交工作组的通知》精神，2010 年 3 月 13 日，和田河流域管理局正式移交塔里木河流域管理局，单位更名为：新疆维吾尔自治区塔里木河流域和田管理局。

展望未来，我们信心百倍，全局将齐心协力，在自治区党委、塔河流域管理局正确领导和和田地委行署的关心、支持下，通过全局职工的共同努力，大力弘扬“和谐、求实、创新、奋进”的塔河精神，开创流域水资源管理和供水服务的新局面。

伊犁哈萨克自治州

自治区党委副书记、主席努尔·白克力前来我州检查工作

州党委书记　李湘林

州长　毛肯·赛提哈木扎

伊犁哈萨克自治州，位于新疆西部天山北麓，东北与俄罗斯、蒙古国接壤，西与哈萨克斯坦共和国交界，总面积35万平方公里，相当于全国总面积的三十分之一，幅员十分辽阔，是新疆乃至中国通向中亚与西欧的国际大通道。

自治州成立于1954年11月，辖塔城、阿勒泰两个地区和10个直属县市，全州共有24个县市，是全国唯一的既辖地区又辖县市的自治州。全州总人口444.37万人，有哈萨克、汉、维吾尔、回、蒙古、锡伯等13个世居民族，其中，哈萨克族占26%，汉族占44.45%，维吾尔族占15.87%，回族占8.38%，蒙古族占1.69%，其他少数民族占2.82%。伊犁州直面积为5.67万平方公里，人口281.5万人。自治州境内驻有新疆生产建设兵团五个农业师。

伊犁是新疆富饶美丽的一块宝地，亚欧大陆干旱地区中的一块“湿岛”。幅员辽阔，土地肥沃，水源充沛，资源十分丰富，素有“塞外江南”、“西垂宝地”之美称，是国家实施西部大开发战略的重点地区之一，2008年又获得“中国十大新天府”殊荣。

水土光热资源丰富，伊犁河谷气候温和湿润，属于温带大陆性气候，是新疆最湿润的地区。全州境内地表水年径流量363亿立方米，水能蕴藏量1248万千瓦，占新疆的37%。拥有天然草场2000多万多公顷，森林面积105万公顷。有可耕地200万公顷，已开垦利用90多万公顷。其中，伊犁州直有可耕地120万公顷，已开垦利用53余万公顷。伊犁河谷有广阔的逆温带，农畜产品丰富，是新疆重要的粮、油、棉、糖、烟草和亚麻生产基地，盛产苹果、杏、桃、西瓜、葡萄等，是全国最大的红地球葡萄、薰衣草(香料)和香料烟种植基地，新疆褐牛和细毛羊培育基地，也是全国三大养鹿基地之一。

矿产资源极具开发潜力。目前，已发现矿种9大类86种，其中镀、白云母、钾长石储量居全国之首，黄金、煤炭、铜、铁、锰等23种矿产储量居新疆首位，新源铁矿矿石品位高达60，阿舍勒铜矿是全国规模最大的铜矿之一，境内还有新疆最大的阿希金矿，其探明储量占新疆的三分之二。伊犁州直煤炭远景储量约为6000亿吨，已探明储量1200亿吨，是全国煤炭储量最大的自治州之一。

良好的生态环境，为野生动植物的生长繁育创造了条件。伊犁有近1万公顷野果林，是中国最大的野果林分布地。有60多种野生皮毛兽和数十种珍禽，3000多种植物，700多种野生药材，是野生动植物种基因库。野核桃、野

江苏玉龙钢管股份有限公司投资 6.46 亿元在霍城县建设一条年产 25 万吨的油、气等长距离输送管道生产线

番茄酱加工企业

巴旦杏远近闻名;天山马鹿、雪豹、四爪陆龟、伊犁鼠兔等十分珍贵;裸腹鲟、鲤、鲃、罗鲑、梭鲈等数十种鱼类,驰名中外。现已建立雪岭云杉、野核桃、野巴旦杏、伊犁黑蜂、四爪陆龟、那拉提高山草原等一批自然保护区。

地缘优势突出。自治州边境线长达 2000 多公里,与哈萨克斯坦、俄罗斯、蒙古国接壤,占全国陆地边境线的十分之一,是新疆和全国向西开放的重要商埠和国际大通道。沿边有霍尔果斯、都拉塔、巴克图、吉木乃等 8 个国家一类口岸,其中都拉塔口岸是我国沿边口岸中与哈萨克斯坦国原首都阿拉木图市路程最近的口岸;霍尔果斯口岸是西北地区最大的公路口岸,具有年进出口货物 200 万吨,出入境人员 300 万人次的通关能力。目前,正在建设的中哈霍尔果斯国际边境合作中心是中国唯一的跨国经济合作区。

旅游资源独特。丰富的自然景观。悠久的历史文化、浓郁的民俗风情,构筑了伊犁独特的旅游资源。气势雄伟的冰川雪岭,星罗棋布的高山湖泊,万木葱郁的茫茫林海,水草丰茂的辽阔草原无不闪烁着神奇而迷人的色彩。伊犁有 5A 级景区 1 个,4A 级景区 4 家,60 家星级宾馆遍及县市。草原风情游、水域沙滩游、民俗休闲游、文物古迹游、跨国边境游和各种特色旅游会满足您不同的需要。

"不到新疆不知中国之大,不到伊犁不知新疆之美",伊犁各族人民热情欢迎您的到来!

第二届新疆伊犁天马之乡国际旅游节

伊宁县杏花节

追花夺蜜

大棚种植

丰收的薰衣草

月庆华煤矿循环经济工业园施工

伊犁河谷璀璨明珠——伊宁市

伊犁州党委常委、伊宁市委书记　李宁平

伊宁市委副书记、市长　赛福丁·依木热木则

伊宁市位于伊犁河谷中部，是伊犁哈萨克自治州的首府，也是伊犁河谷的政治、经济、文化、交通中心。全市总面积644平方公里，市辖8乡、1镇、1场、8个街道办事处。截至2010年底，辖区总人口47万余人，有维吾尔、汉、哈萨克、回、蒙古、锡伯、乌兹别克、俄罗斯等37个民族，其中维吾尔族占49.42%，汉族占34.90%，回族占7.44%，哈萨克族占4.54%。

伊宁市是东西陆路交通的要冲，地缘优势突出，对外开放的条件优越，是新疆和全国向西开放的重要商埠，是伊犁河谷的物资交流中心和商品集散地，是连接霍尔果斯口岸、都拉塔口岸、木扎尔特口岸的中心城市，是祖国西部最大的沿边开放城市。伊宁市北倚天山雪峰，南临悠然西去的伊犁河，以及遍布周围的雪岭冰川、高山湖泊、森林公园、草原毡房。市内既有宽敞大道和现代建筑群，又有小巷深处绿荫流水的少数民族人家，是旅游观光、度假休闲的好去处。

2010年，在州党委、政府的正确领导，坚持以科学发展观为指导，团结带领全市各族人民，围绕“保增长、保民生、保稳定”的主题，抢抓机遇，开拓进取，全市呈现经济较快发展、民生持续改善、社会和谐稳定、各项工作统筹推进的良好态势。全年实现生产总值94亿元，财政一般预算收入9.46亿元，地方固定资产投资56.6亿元，社会消费品零售总额36.7亿元，城镇居民人均可支配收入12520元，农牧民人均纯收入7657元。

对外贸易

市领导检查物价工作

2011年，是“十二五”的开局之年，也是深入贯彻落实中央新疆工作座谈会精神的关键之年，我们将认真贯彻党的十七届五中全会、中央新疆工作座谈会和自治区七届十次全委（扩大）会议精神，按照州党委、政府工作部署，一手抓改革发展、一手抓团结稳定，遵循“两个可持续”的原则，坚持产业富市，推进经济发展，以招商引资为抓手，全力推进新型工业化进程，年内力争完成招商引资到位资金30亿元、工业增加值达到19.4亿元。依托伊犁河谷中心城市优势，加快发展以商贸、旅游为重点的第三产业；瞄准城市高端，加快城市化进程，重点围绕“一带、三轴、九组团”，抓好城市建设，力争完成城市建设政府投资6亿元、融资4亿元，争取带动社会投资50亿元以上；加快教育、卫生、科技、就业等社会各项事业发展，努力在保障和改善民生实现新突破，推进为民办十件实事工程，增加城镇居民和农牧民收入，年内使城镇居民人均可支配收入达到14200元、农牧民人均纯收入达到8821元。2011年，伊宁市将以新思路谋求新发展，以新举措赢得新突破，使伊宁市综合经济实力显著提高、发展方式进一步优化、区域竞争力和可持续发展能力明显提升。

双语学习

社区便民活动

伊宁市安琪酵母厂区

设施农业

喀赞其民俗旅游区

民生廉租住房小区

蓬勃发展的霍城县

伊犁州党委书记李湘林（中）、州党委常委、县委书记王进健（右一）与企业家亲切交谈

州党委常委、县委书记　王进健

县长　扎克·左尔东

县委副书记程政看望聋哑儿童

霍城县地处伊犁河谷西北部的开阔地带，北依天山与博尔塔拉蒙古自治州温泉县为邻，南与察布查尔县隔河相望，东与伊宁市接壤，西以霍尔果斯与哈萨克斯坦国为界，国道312线、218线以及精—伊—霍铁路和清—伊、赛—果、果—霍高速公路贯穿全境，边界线长183公里，是祖国的西大门，是伊犁的门户，也是通往中西亚等国的"咽喉"。全县总人口39.65万人（含兵团10万人），聚居着维吾尔、汉、回、哈萨克等30个民族，少数民族人口占54%。霍城县历史悠久、物产丰富，交通便利，人文荟萃，经济发展，社会稳定，素有"塞外明珠城"、"塞外小江南"之美誉。

十分优越的自然条件。全县地势平坦、草原辽阔、河流纵横、田原平整、土地肥沃，有着良好的水、土、光、热、农林矿产和旅游等资源。境内可供开发利用的土地达53余万公顷，四季草场26.67万公顷，森林资源2.51万公顷；有大小河流23条，年径流量12.74亿立方米，地下水储量为0.7–1亿立方米；全县矿产资源丰富，有煤、铁、铜、铅、金、银、磷、石灰石、大理石等33种，尤其是煤的地质储量预计达300亿吨以上；野生动物资源主要有马鹿、四爪陆龟、黄羊、野猪、狐狸、熊、狼、野兔、旱獭、野鸡、天鹅等，野生植物资源主要有野苹果、野樱桃李、野杏、野山楂、核桃等，其中四爪陆龟是世界珍奇动物，野生樱桃李属世界稀有树种。

不断扩大的对外开放。霍城是我国和中亚、西亚等46个国家和地区的商品集散地和中转站，是新疆各地区和祖国各地进入伊犁河谷和霍尔果斯口岸的必经之路。1989年国务院批准霍城县为对外开放县，1992年国务院有关部门先后批准霍城县享有边贸权、建立霍尔果斯边民互市、设置清水河经济技术开发区；2010年国家确定了霍尔果斯为特殊经济区，对全面带动伊犁河谷外向型经济快速发展，实现向西开放的新突破起到了积极的作用。

发展迅速的现代农业。霍城县以富民增收为前提，加快培育粮食、特色种植、优质林果、设施农业、现代畜牧等五大基地，引进了农夫果业、昌泰蔬菜、玛利酵母、德利发食品、恒辉淀粉、杰宇番茄等一大批龙头企业；集中连片建设设施农业，经济效益明显，拉动农牧民人均增收200元以上。

2010年，全县实现生产总值50.24亿元，比上年增长13%；完成固定资产投资12.8亿元，增长39.8%；完成工业增加值2.08亿元，增长21.6%；实现财政一般预算收入1.74亿元，增长6%；农牧民人均增收1211元，达到6743元。

县委十一届六次全委（扩大）会议

霍城县重大产业项目开工奠基仪式

天堑变通途

特克斯县

自治区党委书记张春贤陪同国务委员刘延东在特克斯县调研

自治区党委副书记、主席努尔白克力来特克斯县调研

县委书记　王康虎

县长　克孜尔开勒迪·阿布迪腊合曼

特克斯县位于天山北麓西部特昭盆地东端，隶属于伊犁哈萨克自治州。全县总面积8352平方公里，下辖六乡二镇，总人口16万，境内居住有哈萨克、汉、维吾尔、回、蒙古、锡伯、柯尔克孜等33个民族。

特克斯县城是世界唯一建筑正规、保存完整的八卦城，以其独特的"八卦"城建布局荣膺上海大世界基尼斯之最，2007年，被国务院命名为"国家历史文化名城"，2010年，喀拉达拉乡琼库什台村被国务院命名为"国家历史文化名村"。整个县城根据《周易》八卦"后天图"方位设计建成，县城街道纵横交错，形如一个八卦勘盆，它的奇妙之处在于把64卦386爻易经数完整地设计成一座城整个城区，具有路路相通，街街相连，神奇迷宫般的街道布局，堪称是一部凝固的《周易》、有形的《周易》。

特克斯县资源丰富，可利用天然草原50.53万公顷，耕地2万公顷，水资源年径流量80亿立方米，可供开发的水利资源约150万千瓦；矿产资源有铜、镍、金、铁、铅、锌、钨、白云岩、石英岩、花岗岩、煤等23种；野生动植物有马鹿、雪豹、雪莲、野蔷薇果等。到2010年底,牲畜存栏达65万头（只），拥有10万头良种奶牛基地、50万只细毛羊基地、500万余只鸭鹅基地，畜牧养殖业极具发展潜力；种植业结构得到进一步优化，设施农业发展迅速，拥有无公害全日光高效节能温室大棚3200座733公顷；林果业发展初具规模，拥有优质果品基地7867公顷。

特克斯已成为能源充足、通讯便捷、交通便利、基础设施完善、投资环境良好的名副其实的草原八卦明珠。期待发展和富强的特克斯人民将以更加优惠的政策、良好的环境、优质的服务迎接八方来客。竭诚欢迎国内外朋友来八卦名城旅游观光、投资合作，共同开发创造特克斯美好明天！

秋季丰收的果园

按毛色分群改良的伊犁哈萨克羊

实行冷配后生产的新疆褐牛犊

自治区党委书记张春贤陪同国务委员刘延东在昭苏县调研

自治区党委书记张春贤在昭苏县调研

天马之乡 昭苏县

县委书记　谭培斌

县委副书记、县长　叶力夏提·吐尔逊拜

康尤美油脂公司厂景

昭苏县地处伊犁哈萨克自治州西南，位于北纬42° 38′ ~43° 15′、东经80° 10′ ~80° 30′之间，东邻特克斯县，北依察布查尔锡伯自治县，南扼南疆阿克苏地区的拜城县、温宿县，西与哈萨克斯坦国接壤，为中亚内陆腹地一个群山环抱的高位山间盆地，属大陆性温带山区半干旱半湿润冷凉气候类型，特别是冬长夏短，没有四季之分，年均气温2.9℃，年最高温度33.5℃，最低温度-31℃，全年无霜期平均为98天，年均降雨量达511.8毫米，为全疆之冠，年均日照数为2699小时。总面积1.12万平方千米，海拔2018米，总人口18万人，辖9乡1镇，境内驻有新疆生产建设兵团农四师七十四团、七十五团、七十六团、七十七团，伊犁州昭苏种马场、伊犁州昭苏马场、天西林业局昭苏林场、驻昭某部等单位。居住着哈萨克、汉、维吾尔、蒙古、柯尔克孜、回、塔塔尔等21个民族，是一个以牧为主，农牧结合的边境县。全县拥有耕地面积8.7万公顷，草场面积54.2万公顷，林地面积14万公顷。昭苏县物资富庶，农作物主要有小麦、油菜、马铃薯、六瓣红大蒜、大豆等；畜牧业主要以马、牛、羊为主。境内有大小河流24条，河水年均总流量为110.60立方米/秒，可利用的水资源年径流量为40.73亿立方米。矿产资源品位高、种类多，主要有煤、铜、锰、铅、铁、金、云母、石膏等。动植物资源十分丰富，牧草有5类、37科、125属、183种，纯天然草物植被中伴生有众多野生药材，主要有雪莲、贝母、冬花、大黄、车药子、秦艽等；野生珍稀动物有马鹿、熊、雪豹、旱獭、雪鸡、大头羊等。巴勒克苏草原、阿合牙孜草原、达乎甫尔草原、夏特草原连成一片，形成了千里沃野、气势磅礴的昭苏大草原，加之夏特古道、夏特古城、萨尔阔布水帘洞、洪纳海草原石人、圣佑庙、格登山记功牌等历史文化遗迹，蕴藏着极大的开发利用前景。

昭苏——"天马的故乡"，源于因出产"腾昆仑、历西极"的天马，也因汉朝时著名的"乌孙国"而闻名于世。昭苏历史悠久，可追溯到1万年前远古时期的新石器时代，那时就已有人类在这片土地上繁衍生息，越春秋战国至汉，草原游牧部落兴，在此建立乌孙国，汉朝解忧公主、细君公主嫁乌孙王，到唐代设立西域都护府，清朝设伊犁将军府、夏塔驿站。1938年置特克斯昭苏设置局，1949年9月26日新疆和平解放后，昭苏县归伊犁地区行署管辖，今隶属伊犁哈萨克自治州。

天马之乡

伊犁河谷一颗璀璨的明珠

察布查尔锡伯自治县

自治区党委书记张春贤陪同中央政治局常委李长春一行在察县考察

自治区党委书记张春贤在风情园考察

县党委书记王奕文在干部大会上发言

察布查尔锡伯自治县位于新疆西天山支脉乌孙山北麓，伊犁河以南辽阔的河谷盆地。是全国惟一的以锡伯族为主体的多民族聚居的自治县，隶属于伊犁哈萨克自治州。同时，还是边境县、对外开放县，与哈萨克斯坦国边境线长72公里，有国家批准开放的一类陆路口岸—都拉塔口岸。县内交通十分便利，县城距州首府伊宁市仅十五公里。

“察布查尔”在锡伯语中是“粮仓”的意思。200多年前，由勤劳勇敢的锡伯族人民历经7年开挖的察布查尔渠横贯县境，人们热情歌颂她，比作自己的母亲。因此，1954年3月17日成立自治县时，就将具有历史意义的“察布查尔”作为县名。自治县辖13个乡镇、1个国营农场、1个农村经济管理中心，县内驻有兵团农四师67团、68团、69团等单位。2009年末，全县总人口19.40万人，其中地方人口16.87万人，有锡伯、汉、维吾尔、哈萨克、柯尔克孜、回、俄罗斯等25个民族。全县东西长约90公里，南北宽约70公里，总面积4485平方公里。

伊犁素有“塞外江南”之美称，而察布查尔又是伊犁河谷一颗璀璨的明珠。乌孙山气势如虹，其主峰—白石峰，海拔3475米，犹如巨柱擎天，高耸入云。乌孙山下的琼博拉森林公园集林海、草场、高峡、奇峰、雪原、垂岩、小溪于一园，既与华山竞险，又同黄山争奇。万亩河谷次生林环绕伊犁河绵延数十里，冬季冰雪覆盖，银装素裹，夏季林密树茂，郁郁葱葱。此外，这里还有AAAA级景区——锡伯民俗风情园、伊犁九大名寺——靖远寺及图公祠、乌孙古墓群、海努克古城、银顶寺遗址等名胜古迹，令人心驰神往，流连忘返。

全县共有各类旅游景区(点)69家，其中国家4A级景区1家，3A级景区2家；三星级宾馆2家；五星级农家乐1家，四星级农家乐1家，三星级、二星级农家乐各2家；旅游从业人员近千人。目前以一山(乌孙山白石峰景区)、一边(口岸边境旅游)、一园(锡伯族民俗风情园)、一水(伊犁河清水湾风景区)为依托的一主(以孙扎齐牛录乡锡伯民俗文化旅游名村)、四片(东部以米粮泉乡为重点的特色农家美食区、南部以白石峰为重点的森林生态休闲区、西部以都拉塔口岸为重点的边境旅游区、北部以伊犁河谷风光为重点的次生林风景区)的旅游发展大格局已经形成。

今日的察布查尔潜力无穷、商机无限。开放、文明、诚信的察布查尔热诚欢迎各界朋友和有识之士前来观光考察，投资发展，成就伟业。

县委书记王奕文(右三)在深入乡村了解设施农业发展情况

设施农业

江格尔的故乡 和布克赛尔

自治区人大常委会主任艾力更·依明巴海(右二)一行到县慈善医院实地调研

自治区党委常委尔肯江·吐拉洪(左一)一行到县城关小学调研双语教育

塔城地委书记彭家瑞(左四)到和布克赛尔县调研经济社会发展情况

塔城地委副书记、行署专员马宁(左一)在和布克赛尔县调研越冬饲草料储备情况

和布克赛尔,西部边陲的一颗草原明珠,是全疆唯一的蒙古族自治县,辖2镇、5乡、4个牧场,总面积3.06万平方公里,总人口6.3万人,由蒙古、汉、哈萨克等19个民族组成。富集的资源,独特的文化,便利的交通,突显出自治县科学跨越后发赶超的比较优势,天赐宝地正积蓄着巨大的发展潜力。

和布克赛尔,交通区位优势明显,地处塔城、克拉玛依、阿勒泰三地中心,与哈萨克斯坦共和国接壤,距吉木乃口岸100公里,巴克图口岸280公里,阿拉山口口岸400公里;217国道、318省道及开工建设中的乌尔禾–福海渔场高速公路穿越县境。离克拉玛依机场150公里,奎北铁路在县境预留站点8个,已建成并投入使用客货运转站3个,优越的区位优势和便利的交通条件,为区域经济跨越式发展插上了腾飞的翅膀。

和布克赛尔,天赐物华天宝之地,大自然赋予了我们富集的矿藏,已探明矿产资源30多种。石油、天然气、煤、膨润土、盐、石英砂、芒硝、石灰石等10余种矿产蕴藏量达亿吨,品质均属上乘。氧化铍矿储量4万吨,膨润土储量23亿吨,位居亚洲第一;煤、盐、石英砂、石油、天然气、油页岩等资源位居全国前列;铜、金、铁、高岭土、油砂等金属非金属资源储量可观,开发前景广阔。

和布克赛尔,天然有机农牧基地,有优质无污染天然草场130多万公顷。获得国家认证有机农畜产品生产基地6个,认证面积79.47万公顷。察和特生态农业综合开发区有原始宜农荒地20万公顷,现已开发土地1万公顷,将建成全国最大的有机棉基地。

县委十届八次全委(扩大)会议

阿克苏地区

地区领导、国电新疆公司领导察看国电新疆库玛拉克河小石峡水电站工程截流

地委书记黄三平，地委副书记、行署专员穆铁礼甫·哈斯木参加乌什县秋格尔渠首一级水电站开工仪式

地委书记黄三平，地委副书记、行署专员穆铁礼甫·哈斯木为前往浙江培训的阿克苏地区学员送行

阿克苏市街景

地委书记黄三平，地委副书记、行署专员穆铁礼甫·哈斯木参加新疆立天纺织股份有限公司10万锭家纺项目奠基仪式

阿克苏位于新疆天山南麓、塔里木盆地北缘，总面积13.13万平方公里，东南西分别与巴音郭楞蒙古自治州、和田地区、喀什地区为邻，北以天山为分水岭同伊犁哈萨克自治州交界，西北与吉尔吉斯斯坦和哈萨克斯坦接壤，边境线长235公里，辖8县1市、84个乡镇、56个农林牧场。总人口251.73万（含农一师29.2万），由36个民族组成，是一个以维吾尔族为主体的多民族聚居地区。

阿克苏地区气候宜人，水草丰茂，农牧业发达，是我国重要长绒棉和优质商品棉生产基地，是全疆最大的绒山羊基地和品质最好的细毛羊基地，也是“中国白杏之乡”、“中国红富士之乡”和新疆薄皮核桃、红枣及香梨等优质特色果品的主产区。石油天然气资源十分丰富，是塔里木盆地油气勘探开发的主战场和“西气东输”工程的主要气源地，已探明石油储量超过10亿吨，凝析油储量7169万吨，天然气储量9741亿立方米，溶解气储量483.5亿立方，占塔里木盆地已探明

旅游风光图集

塔河日落

库车克孜尔尕哈风燧

新疆油田公司社会保险管理中心

主任　张建国

团结奋进的领导班子

科学发展观辅导

新疆油田公司社会保险管理中心成立于1998年12月。2001年,自治区劳动保障厅增挂“新疆维吾尔自治区劳动保障厅新疆石油管理局社会保险管理中心”牌子,各项社保业务接受自治区领导,行使地州级社保机构职能。主要负责新疆油田企业、独山子石化、克拉玛依石化、润滑油厂、西部钻探、地调处、CPE新疆油建、设计院以及改制多经等390余家企业在职职工、离退休(退职)人员、市场化用工(就业职工子女)以及有偿解除劳动合同接续保险人员等近15万人的养老、医疗、失业、工伤、生育等保险的管理和业务经办。还担负着3万多名油田退岗职工家属、遗属、遗孀生活补贴、医疗费、供养直系亲属抚恤金的支付和离退休(退职)人员护理费的审批发放等工作;养老金实行社会化发放。每年基金和统筹外资金收支近90个亿。中心现有员工150多名,女职工90人,员工平均年龄43周岁;机关12个科室,除五个险种科室以外,还设有基金,信息,社保档案、家属医疗费报销,征费、综合和财务管理等7个科室;下属10个保险事务所实行窗口式服务,分布于克拉玛依、独山子、准东、乌鲁木齐等地。中心建立党的总支委员会,下设机关、市区、外滩区和乌市明园四个党支部,党员81名。

经过13年的发展,社会保险业务不断扩展。1998年底将分散在油田各厂处单位的基本养老、医疗、失业、工伤保险经办工作集中办理;2000年,将有偿解除劳动合同人员纳入社会保险接续范围;2001年,开展企业补充养老保险基金征缴和管理业务;2004年,启动油田企业生育保险工作;2005年,增加退岗职工家属医疗费报销和大病救助基金管理业务,增加农民工进城务工期间的工伤保险和住院医疗保险业务;2007年,启动新疆油田企业补充医疗保险;2010年,将退岗职工家属纳入基本养老保险统筹范围。

目前,新疆油田社会保险管理中心基本形成了五个险种齐全、信息网络系统健全、经办服务体系完善、社会保障职能全面的社会保险体系,成为向新疆油田石油、石化及改制多经企业提供经办服务的综合性社会保险机构。为维护社会稳定、企业发展发挥了积极作用。

耐心细致的服务

社保中心成立十周年十佳服务明星表彰

社保员工服装秀

朝气蓬勃的团队

县委书记　薛俊强

县委副书记、县长　拉格瓦·才布格加甫

和布克赛尔，文化底蕴丰厚，被首批列入国家级非物质文化遗产名录的英雄史诗《江格尔》由此发源。近年来，以江格尔、阿肯阿依特斯为代表的各民族优秀文化竞相发展，一派繁荣。县境内岩画、古墓、王爷府旧址及古城遗址等古迹历史悠久。哈尔尕图、龙脊谷、魔鬼城等自然景观鬼斧神工，风光独特。

近年来，和布克赛尔县紧紧围绕“科学跨越、后发赶超、富民强县、构建和谐和布克赛尔”的目标，加大招商引资，积极引进大企业、大集团，大力实施优势资源转换战略，加快推进新型工业化进程，着力打造“‘克—和’煤电煤化工、全国重要的盐产品及盐化工、全国最大的铍产品开发加工以及全国最大的膨润土深加工”四大基地，县域经济呈现出速度加快、质量提高、后劲增强的良好发展态势，文化建设以及民生等各项社会事业取得长足发展。2010 年，全县完成生产总值 16.41 亿元，同比增长 25.4%。工业总产值(现价)14.6 亿元，增长 30.4%。地方财政一般预算收入 5.72 亿元，增长 60%。固定资产投资 22 亿元，增长 62.1%。农牧民人均纯收入 5857 元，增加 936 元，招商引资累计到位资金 15.46 亿元，实现社会消费品零售总额 1.7 亿元。

县委书记薛俊强(中)一行在夏孜盖乡调研

县委书记薛俊强(左二)，县委副书记、县长才布格加甫(左三)一行到牧区了解越冬情况

《永恒的故乡·永恒的爱》——叶尔达民族交响乐作品音乐会现场

乌洽会上与辽宁杰事杰新材料有限公司签约仪式现场

再生原盐盐池场景

和布克赛尔县龙脊谷

油田作业区

跨越发展 丝路新城
精河

县委书记　陈洪

县委副书记、县长　艾斯尔江·阿依提哈孜

湖北省党政代表团来精河考察

精河县位于新疆西北部，准噶尔盆地西南边缘，天山支脉婆罗科努山北麓，隶属博尔塔拉蒙古自治州。县境东邻乌苏市，南邻伊宁县和尼勒克县，西邻博乐市，北邻塔城地区的托里县。东西长约166公里，南北宽约134公里，总面积11280平方公里。是古"丝绸之路"北道重镇。它以"精河河"得名，是一个多民族聚居的地区，主要由维吾尔、汉、蒙古、哈萨克、回等26个民族组成，现有人口14万人(含兵团)，现辖两镇、三乡、两场，境内驻有新疆生产建设兵团农五师所属三个团场。精河经济以农为主，农牧结合，工业门类齐全，地处北疆交通要冲，312国道和第二亚欧大陆桥穿境而过，且处在两个国家一类口岸——阿拉山口口岸和霍尔果斯口岸的交汇处，精河县至阿拉山口95公里，精河县至霍尔果斯口岸280公里。奎赛高等级公路、精伊霍铁路和乌西——精河铁路复线，使精河县成为东联西出、西引东进的黄金枢纽。

精河县具有北温带大陆性气候的显著特点，光照充足，干燥少雨。年均无霜期171天，日照2710小时；境内主要河流有4条，多年平均径流总量为7.87亿立方米。全县已建成水库1座、正在开工建设的水库一座，引水渠首4座、干支斗渠1019公里、机电井556眼，已形成较完善的供水工程体系。全县有四季草场71.73万公顷，耕地4.40万公顷。

精河县矿藏丰富，已发现的矿产有32种，矿产地有71处，盐矿以艾比湖为主，盐储量达1.25亿吨，氯化钾200万吨，芒硝9700万吨，硫酸镁1.07亿吨，硼6万吨，溴2万吨，碘400万吨；磷矿1176万吨，钼矿矿脉共15条，长10.06万米，地质储量达9800万吨，钼金属量256吨，储量占新疆总储量的90%，开发前景可观；石灰石矿远景储量达16亿吨，磁铁矿储量33.98万吨，石英砂矿储量达112万吨，驰名中外的"伊力特"等新疆三大名酒的酒瓶的主要原料全部选用精河县的石英砂矿制作。同时，西气东输二线工程现已完工，管线已设在精河县境内开口解决当地用气问题。

精河县是"全国优质棉基地县"和自治区"优质出口棉基地县"，棉花是精河县农业的主导产业。2010年，棉花种植面积达40.4万亩，单产皮棉142.6公斤，皮棉总产达5.76万吨，市场竞争力显著增强。精河枸杞素有"红玛瑙"之称，干果具有果实鲜红、粒大饱满、皮薄肉厚、含糖丰富和药用价值高等显著特点，远销日本、欧美、东南亚等国和港、澳、台地区，赢得了"精河枸杞甲天下"的美誉。2010年，全县枸杞种植面积达10.34万亩，干果总产达1.3万吨。精河枸杞保持种植面积、品质、总产量、出口量、有效营养成份含量的全国第一，1998年被国家农业部命名为"中国枸杞之乡"，2002年，"精河枸杞" 被国家工商局认定并核发了原产地证明商标。

旅游资源：精河境内的艾比湖是新疆第一大咸水湖，水面面积为800平方公里，海拔189米，是准噶尔盆地最低点。每年鸟类繁殖和迁徙的季节，艾比湖聚集的天鹅，大雁，野鸭等水鸟多达几十万只，湖面荡漾，水鸟啼鸣，风吹芦苇，花飘万里，令人心怡神往。艾比湖东畔有广阔的野生林区，丛生的白梭梭、红柳、白杨、勿忘我、紫罗兰等植物和四周的茫茫戈壁形成鲜明的对比，堪称"准噶尔沙漠中的明珠"。

2011年，我们将以邓小平理论和"三个代表"重要思想为指导，深入贯彻落实科学发展观，紧紧抓住中央新疆工作座谈会和全国对口支援新疆加快发展的历史机遇，按照自治区党委七届九次、十次全委(扩大)会议、自治州党委十届十五次、县委十二届十五次全委(扩大)会议的总体部署，坚持资源开发可持续、生态环境可持续的原则，大力推进"城镇化带动"、"口岸强县"和"民生优先"战略，以新型城镇化为载体，以新型工业化和农牧业现代化为产业支撑，全面协调推进经济建设、政治建设、文化建设、社会建设和生态文明建设，努力实现经济社会跨越式发展和长治久安，为实现"十二五"规划各项目标任务开好头、起好步。精河已经步入经济社会发展的战略机遇期，面对新的形势、新的要求，全县各族干部群众，将深入贯彻科学发展观，进一步打牢全县各族人民的思想基础，凝聚全县各族人民的智慧力量，同心同德，团结奋进，努力把精河打造成为天山北坡经济带上一颗璀璨的明珠！

精河生态园景色

第五届环赛里木湖自行车赛精河首发式

原产地枸杞及其产品

神山圣水 西域泉都

温泉县

休闲之旅——圣泉

神韵七彩湖

察哈尔纪念塔

新疆北鲵

温泉县地处祖国西北部，准噶尔盆地西缘，距自治区首府乌鲁木齐市630公里，距亚欧大陆桥西桥头堡阿拉山口口岸169公里，伊犁霍尔果斯口岸170公里。东连博乐市、南邻伊犁霍城县，西北与哈萨克斯坦共和国接壤，边境线长276公里。全县总面积5881平方公里，辖2镇，4乡，2场，境内驻有兵团农五师所属87、88团。居住着汉、蒙古、哈萨克、维吾尔等24个民族，总人口7.48万(其中地方人口6.42万、兵团人口1.06万)，少数民族人口占41.4%。全县属大陆性半干旱温凉气候，冬暖夏凉，年平均气温3.6摄氏度，光热资源丰富，昼夜温差较大。有可耕地3.27万公亩，草场41.23万公顷，森林3.67万公顷。拥有丰富的农牧业、矿产和旅游资源，是自治区的22个畜牧业县和41个粮食生产县之一，为自治州的农业区、生态区和旅游区。农业资源相对富集。在传统的小麦、玉米、油料、甜菜和肉牛肉羊、细毛羊、生猪、禽类等种养业的基础上，积极打造无公害、绿色、有机农牧产品品牌，大力发展西瓜、打瓜、酱用番茄、沙棘、甜糯玉米、花卉、獭兔、冷水鱼等一批特色产业。已拥有“赛湖”牌有机冷水鱼、“阿尔祥”牌有机牦牛肉、“猛进”牌马铃薯、“双劲福”牌绿色面粉等一批疆内外知名品牌。“猛进”牌马铃薯荣获昆明世博会铜奖，“赛湖”牌高白鲑成为新疆首获国家农业部认证的鱼类有机食品，并远销北欧的芬兰等国。矿产资源较为丰富。目前已探明稀有金属、贵金属、黑色金属、有色金属及非金属矿产27种，发现矿床、矿点70余处，钨矿资源占全疆已探明钨资源储量的56%。已开采铜、铁、石灰石、石英石等矿产品，正在勘探钨、锡、钼、铅、锌等矿产资源，待勘探的有钽铌、石墨、煤等矿产资源。旅游资源丰富多样，是全国唯一以地热资源“温泉”命名的县，为“中国新疆北鲵的故乡”、“西迁戍边察哈尔人的故乡”，距国家级自然风景名胜保护区赛里木湖仅70公里，拥有分别被誉为“圣泉”、“天泉”和“仙泉”的博格达尔温泉、鄂托克赛尔温泉、阿尔夏提温泉，还有在全球仅分布在我县和哈萨克斯坦共和国交界处、与恐龙同处一个发展年代、距今约3.5亿年的活化石——新疆北鲵。温泉山水壮美雄奇，草原风光独特，气候冬暖夏凉，文物古迹众多，民俗风情浓郁，已成为全疆理想的旅游、观光、疗养、避暑胜地，2009年成功创建为自治区“旅游强县”。

2010年，全县地方生产总值达到9.5亿元，“十一五”年均增长16.2%；人均生产总值13526元，增长16%。固定资产投资达4.5亿元，增长60%。实现地方财政收入3591万元，增长24.6%。农牧民人均纯收入5295元。

LUNTAIX

轮台县

县委书记　张正荣

县委副书记、县长　吐逊·肉孜

中宣部副部长、国务院新闻办主任王晨（左六），在自治区副主席铁力瓦尔地（左四）、巴州州委副书记刘进喜（左三）、县委书记张正荣（右二）等陪同下对我县考察。

县委书记张正荣（左一）、县长吐逊·肉孜（右一）在第二十五个教师节之际慰问全国优秀教师

AN

① ①轮台县党政综合办公楼
② ②新疆凯涟捷石化有限公司
③ ③西气东输首站
④ ④新疆天源化工有限公司
⑤ ⑤轮台县拉依苏工业园区

轮台县地处天山南麓，塔里木盆地北缘，总面积14184平方公里，辖7乡4镇2个农牧场65个行政村，总人口11.4万人，居住着维吾尔、汉、回等13个民族。是闻名中外的塔里木石油开发主战场，举世瞩目的“西气东输”工程首发站。

过去五年，是轮台日新月异奔小康的5年。已建成1.33万公顷白杏基地，是国家林业局命名的“中国白杏之乡”。5年累计投入农村基础建设资金5.68亿元，实施了“五一”水库、塔里木河综合治理等一大批水利骨干工程，新建（改造）乡村道路328公里，在全国率先实现“村村通公交”目标，小城镇建设初具规模。以园区为平台、项目为龙头，石油石化、农副产品加工、矿业开发“三足鼎立”的工业发展格局不断巩固。2009年1月轮台工业园区被自治区人民政府批准为“自治区级工业园区”，并被列为自治区工业经济领域第二批循环经济试点园区。目前入园企业达102家，累计完成工业总产值100亿元，工业增加值37亿元。“十一五”时期，轮台县地方固定资产投资总额突破60亿元，相当于“十五”时期的2.8倍，5年累计完成70余项民生工程建设，新建（改造）城市道路10条22公里，形成“六纵五横”的城市道路骨架，城市发展框架全面拉开，县城建成区面积由6.5平方公里扩大到20平方公里。轮台塔中机场完成选址，新火车站主体工程完工，县域供电实现双回路。5年累计新建经济适用房、廉租房2829套，建成城乡抗震安居房13413套、残疾人抗震安居房311套。启动实施了500户棚户区改造工程，850户城镇低保户享受了住房补贴。2010年，轮台县城镇居民人均可支配收入达到13896元，“十一五”时期年均增长13.8%；农牧民人均纯收入突破8000元，达到8456元，年均增长15.7%。城乡居民收入及增速均高于全疆平均水平。轮台县在自治区率先启动并顺利实施了新型农村社会养老保险试点工作，参保率达95.6%，6282名60岁以上农村老人享受到了养老保险待遇；符合参保条件的“五七工”、“家属工”全部纳入了养老统筹。新型农牧区合作医疗参合率达97.5%。轮台县先后被评为全国人口与计划生育优质服务工作先进县、全国平原绿化工作先进集体、全国残疾人社区康复示范县、自治区文明县，自治区双拥模范县、自治区民族团结进步模范县，自治区平安县等荣誉称号。

轮台县是西部大开发的焦点，创业者的乐园，这是一片令人瞩目的投资热土。轮台人民正伸开双臂热情地欢迎四海宾朋来这里观光旅游、投资办厂，同商发展大计，共创千秋伟业，迎接灿烂辉煌的美好明天。

冬季魔鬼城

雨后乌尔禾

首届民俗文化旅游节隆重开幕

乌尔禾的胡杨林是我国西北地区最大的自然林区之一

丰富的石油资源

克拉玛依市
乌尔禾区

克拉玛依市乌尔禾区位于新疆准噶尔盆地西北边缘，总面积 2250 平方公里，人口 1 万余人，有汉、蒙古、哈萨克、维吾尔等多个民族。2010 年全区共生产原油 162.22 万吨，实现地区生产总值 48.61 亿元，财政收入 9752 万元，农牧民人均纯收入达到 10043 元。217 国道、奎北铁路横穿乌尔禾全境，具有南去克拉玛依、奎屯，北去阿勒泰、布尔津，西接塔城的交通要道优势。乌尔禾境内旅游资源丰富，有白杨河、艾里克湖、白杨河水库、黄羊泉水库和风城高库等水利资源景区景点，有魔鬼城雅丹、油砂山地质构造和白杨河大峡谷等地质风貌景观，有东归土尔扈特蒙古民俗旅游资源，有壮美的胡杨林、广袤的荒漠草原等极具特色的生态旅游资源。乌尔禾区委、区人民政府把旅游植入新农村建设中，将乌尔禾乡整体打造成 3A 级景区，推进了旅游服务业和特色养殖的发展，建成了别具特色的乡村农家乐旅游区。

作为克拉玛依油田的“后花园”和油气开发的生活基地，乌尔禾区已经具备了大发展的潜力，一个新的生态旅游新城正在形成，乌尔禾正以崭新的姿态期待着您的到来。

白杨河大峡谷

石油储量的80%、天然气储量的90%以上。煤炭储量358.7亿吨，占南疆已探明储量的83%以上。水能资源蕴藏量379.3万千瓦，可开发水能资源为220.3万千瓦。探明储量的矿产46种，矿产资源潜在价值1.75亿元。旅游资源得天独厚，拥有全国8个主类中的7个，旅游资源主类占87.5%，有国家A级景区20个，其中4A级景区3个，3A级景区7个，以历史文化遗址、自然风光、民俗风情、龟兹和多浪文化为特色，是古"丝绸之路"北道政治、经济、文化和佛教中心，古印度、希腊、波斯和中原文化四大文明在此交汇，是新疆旅游资源的富集区。地理位置优越，地处南疆中部，是新疆南北要冲和东西贯通的关节点，是我国向西开放的桥头堡，随着乌什口岸开放顺利推进，阿克苏机场改扩建、库车机场迁建、南疆铁路复线、库(尔勒)–阿(克苏)高速公路等一批民航、铁路和公路项目的实施，地区作为南北疆交通枢纽的地位将更加突出。2010年，全地区生产总值606.3亿元(含一师和石油开采作业区)，比上年增长9.2%。一、二、三产业比重为29：32：39。地方财政一般预算收入42.7亿元，增长44.3%。完成地方固定资产投资170.3亿元，增长27.8%。农牧民人均纯收入5931元、增加1098元，城镇居民人均可支配收入13676元，增加1534元。实现地方社会消费品零售总额60.3亿元，增长16.3%。

当前，中央集全党之智、举全国之力推进新疆跨越式发展和长治久安，出台了一系列含金量高、指导性强、措施有力、支持空前的惠疆政策，自治区党委七届九次、十次全委(扩大)会议，对新疆跨越式发展和长治久安各项工作进行了全面部署，阿克苏地区基于对区情的再认识，再深化，提出了"64122"工程发展战略(即：培植做强石油石化、煤电能源、煤化工盐化工、钢铁冶炼和矿产开发、棉纺织、农林产品精深加工"六大支柱产业"，着力建设特色林果、优质商品棉、商品粮、畜禽产品生产"四大基地"，努力把阿克苏建成充满生机活力和吸引力的旅游及商贸物流集散地，进一步提升阿克苏市、库车县两座"龙头城市"功能，着力彰显龟兹、多浪"两大文化品牌"影响力，努力把阿克苏打造成为新疆经济发展的重要增长极和宜居宜业的南疆中心城市，加快实现"两个率先"目标任务)。到2015年，地方生产总值突破千亿元，达到1100亿元以上，人均生产总值超过4万元，达到全国平均水平；城镇居民人均可支配收入、农民人均纯收入翻一番，分别达到26510元和11862元，公共服务能力达到西部省区平均水平的奋斗目标，任务艰巨繁重，需要付出艰辛努力，阿克苏地区各族人民将在自治区党委、人民政府的坚强领导下，紧紧抓住国家对新疆加大投入和浙江对口支援的大好机遇，勇担跨越发展历史使命，抢抓机遇乘势而上，攻坚克难打开新局，以黄牛精神加袋鼠步伐，加快推进"两个率先"，奋力在阿克苏大地创造新的人间奇迹，为努力把阿克苏打造成为新疆经济发展的重要增长极和宜居宜业的南疆中心城市做出应有贡献。

千载机遇，百业宏开。今天的阿克苏，政通人和，百业俱兴，各民族团结和睦、休戚与共，我们真诚地欢迎更多的有识之士来阿克苏观光旅游，投资兴业，共同打造繁荣富裕文明和谐的阿克苏。

塔河岸边的胡杨

沙漠胡杨

魅力伊吾

县委书记　王跃斌

县委副书记、县长　艾尼瓦尔·阿不列孜

伊吾位于新疆东北部，天山北麓东段。边境线长274公里，总面积19519平方公里，辖五乡两镇，居有15个民族，总人口22440人，其中维吾尔族占41.7%，汉族占36.9%，哈萨克族占17.5%，其他民族占3.9%。

伊吾资源丰富。探明矿产有铁、铜、金、煤、芒硝、花岗岩等28种，开发的淖毛湖大型整装煤田、高品位铁矿、石油、金矿、铜矿是煤电煤化工基地、有色黑色金属开采加工基地的资源后盾。现有国家4A级景区1处，为淖毛湖胡杨林生态景区；国家3A级景区2处，为太阳历广场和伊水园景区；还有中国四大鸣沙山之一的伊吾鸣沙山，亚洲第一大平顶冰川喀尔里克冰川，以及乃愣格尔草原、蝴蝶谷、幻彩湖、胜利峰等胜景，是休闲度假、生态旅游胜地。县域内55.31万公顷天然草场，234.5公顷哈密瓜，200公顷野山杏，2.5万平方米野蘑菇等均通过有机认证，注册的“淖毛湖”牌晚熟哈密瓜和“途阔”牌哈密盐池羊肉享誉区内外。

胡杨赞歌

伊吾是西部大开发新疆十座区域经济增长最快县市之一、全疆第一个有机食品生产示范县和全疆四个循环经济试点县之一，先后荣获“国家科技进步先进县”、国家级“环境优美乡镇”、自治区文明县城、旅游强县、平安县、双拥模范县、文化建设先进县、民族团结进步先进县、计划生育优质服务先进县和婚育新风进万家先进县、抗震安居工程建设先进县等荣誉。

今天的伊吾正勇往直前，紧紧围绕“五个率先”（在哈密地区率先完成脱贫、率先建设社会主义新农村、率先实现新型工业化、率先实现城镇化、率先实现小康），实施“六大战略”（生态立县、工业富县、科教强县、旅游旺县、品牌促县、和谐兴县），培育“八大产业”（煤炭、石油天然气、现代物流、黑色有色金属加工、旅游、有机农副产品加工、新能源、建材），为把伊吾建设成新疆东联西出的东疆重镇、门户强县、环东天山经济圈重要的经济增长极而努力奋斗。

巴里坤哈萨克自治县

县委书记陈毅士（左二）在大河镇防洪设施建设调研

县长叶尔江·胡斯满（右一）督查海子沿乡安居富民工程

巴里坤古称蒲类，是古丝绸之路北新道进入新疆的第一重镇。巴里坤哈萨克自治县位于东疆北部，全县总面积3.84万平方公里，与蒙古人民共和国接壤，县城西距乌鲁木齐市570公里，为全国三个哈萨克族自治县之一。2010年，县辖4镇8乡2区1场，年末总人口102564人（少数民族人口38058人），农村人口55493人，人口出生率12.87‰，自然增长率2.25‰。耕地面积2.44万公顷，草场面积191.07万公顷，主要农牧产品有小麦、马铃薯、大麦、晚熟哈密瓜、牛羊肉、驼奶等，其中“力坤”牌牛羊肉、马铃薯获得国家“绿色食品”认证。矿产资源主要有煤炭、芒硝、石油、天然气、金、铜、油页岩、膨润土等，其中煤炭远景储量预测资源量1012亿吨、探明储量45亿吨。主要旅游景点有古城景区（国家4A级旅游景区）、巴里坤大草原、地藏寺、仙姑庙、哈萨克文化展馆、兰州湾子古遗址、大河唐城、怪石山、王氏古民宅、月牙湾、马圈沟等，为自治区级旅游强县。地形特征为三山夹两盆，有“新疆缩影”之称；属温带大陆性冷凉干旱气候区。国家保护动物有蒙古野驴、雪豹、北山羊、鸨、天山马鹿、盘羊、雪鸡、鹅喉羚等。野生植物有雪莲、益母草、黄芪、党参、当归、大黄、麻黄、锁阳、手掌参等。

种植膜下饲用玉米

2010年，巴里坤县域综合实力大幅提升，全县完成生产总值21.89亿元，同比增长25.4%，比“十五”末增长1.83倍，其中：第一产业增加值6.22亿元，比“十五”末增长90.4%；第二产业增加值9.17亿元，比“十五”末增长3.84倍；第三产业增加埴6.50亿元，比“十五”末增长1.45倍。

全社会固定资产投资17.4亿元。完成邮政业务总量778万元，电信业务总量1203万元。年末固定电话用户9345户，移动电话用户39751户，计算机互联网用户3620户。社会消费品零售总额30117.4万元。接待旅游者28.4万人次，旅游收入5878.8万元。地方财政收入12088万元，比“十五”末增长4.57倍；地方财政支出71952万元，比“十五”末增长2.56倍。年末城乡居民储蓄存款余额65345万元。

巴里坤县农牧兴达奶牛养殖基地

兰州湾子古遗址岩画

草原歌舞

传统哈萨克节目马上拾银

华能三塘湖风力发电场一期工程

麦盖提县

县委书记王胜平陪同山东省委书记姜异康、自治区党委副书记、自治区主席努尔·白克力参加山东援建麦盖提县刀郎中学奠基仪式

县委书记王胜平检查农业生产

县委副书记、县长阿布都艾尼·居买在县人代会上做政府工作报告

麦盖提地名一是传说古代“刀郎”部落首领米盖提带领游牧民在这里定居，以米盖提之名为地名，后转音为麦盖提。二是传说很早以前在今巴楚一带居住着很多游牧部落，因沙漠的侵蚀，迫使集镇唐王城中心地带的人迁来这里，故称“麦尔盖孜”，意为从中心地带搬迁来的人，后逐渐演变为麦盖提。三是传说在过去的莎车王属下，有一位名叫木哈特的部落首领，残酷剥削百姓，人们推举米格提为首领推翻了木哈特的统治，米格提当了首领。这时正值伊斯兰教传入新疆的时期，米格提部下有7人信奉伊斯兰教，后7个信徒逃出居住地来到叶尔羌河东岸的原始森林以打猎为生，使用部落首领米格提的名字命名这片荒野地区，后转音为麦盖提。

麦盖提县位于新疆维吾尔自治区西南部，地处塔克拉玛干沙漠西南边缘、喀喇昆仑山北麓，位于塔里木盆地西部，叶尔羌河中下游和提孜那甫河下游。地理位置为东经77° 28' – 79° 05'，北纬38° 25' – 39° 22'，东部隔塔克拉玛干沙漠与和田地区皮山县相连，东北与阿克苏地区阿瓦提县相邻，南与莎车县相邻，西与岳普湖县相邻，北与巴楚县相邻，总面积1.52万平方公里，县城距乌鲁木齐市公路里程1410千米。辖1镇、9乡、3个农林场，有行政村（社区）139个。境内还驻有新疆生产建设兵团农三师的4个团场和南疆军区的1个部队农场。全县共有维吾尔、汉、回、哈萨克等13个民族，年末总人口25.38万余人，其中：地方人口21.98万人，少数民族人口占总人口的89.6%，人口出生率21.36‰，自然增长率12.57‰。耕地面积6.13万公顷，粮食播种面积2.44万公顷，经济作物播种面积3.4万公顷。

麦盖提县是“刀郎”文化的发祥地，是国家的优质棉基地。盛产粮、棉、红枣、核桃、杏、茴香、西瓜、甜瓜等农作物，重要自然资源有被誉为沙漠黑珍珠的“胡杨蘑菇”、甘草、红花、肉苁蓉、沙棘、枸杞等。属温带大陆性气候。

近年来，在喀什地委、行署的正确领导下，县委、县人民政府坚持把改善民生作为一切工作的出发点和落脚点，以产业结构调整为主线，以红枣和核桃产业为突破口，团结带领全县各级党政组织和各族干部群众攻坚克难、奋力拼搏、抢抓机遇、狠抓落实，主要工作取得了新的突破和可喜进展，实现了县域经济又好又快发展。2010年，全县实现生产总值19.39亿元、比上年增长7.41%，其中：第一产业8.85亿元，第二产业5.91亿元，第三产业4.63亿元；招商引资竣工投产项目投资额2.65亿元；完成全社会固定资产投资14.03亿元；社会消费品零售总额4.66亿元；实现地方财政一般预算收入9216万元；农民人均纯收入达到4951元，比上年增收631元。

麦盖提县刀郎木卡姆组合亮相中央电视台

喀什地区发展和改革委员会

地区发改委主任　李阳

地区发改委主任陪同上级领导调研

团结务实的领导班子成员

喀什地区发展和改革委员会内设1个二级局、17个职能科室，为喀什地区行署工作部门，是综合研究拟定地区国民经济和社会发展战略、发展规划和政策，进行总量平衡、结构调整、行使价格管理与监督、指导地区总体经济体制改革工作，主管固定资产投资的宏观调控部门。

2010年，地区发改委领导班子紧紧围绕地委、行署的中心工作，集中精力抓改革、谋发展、促和谐，全力以赴编制地区"十二五"规划纲要，深入推进重大项目建设，切实抓好市场价格监管，认真做好体制改革工作，成绩斐然，为保持地区经济社会平稳较快发展做出了积极的贡献。一是服务能力不断提高。密切关注经济运行态势，深入开展调查研究，积极主动地为各级党委、政府当好参谋助手。二是规划编制取得突破。认真编制"十二五"规划，深入调查研究、理清发展思路，使规划成为喀什地区"十二五"时期实现科学跨越、后发赶超的强大引擎。三是争取资金成效显著。抢抓历史机遇，积极争取国家、自治区项目资金。全年共争取国家、自治区投资项目2455个，到位资金45.8亿元，比上年增长40%。四是固定资产投资增势强劲。全年完成固定资产投资270.6亿元，比上年增长30%。涉及水利、交通、能源、电力、产业发展以及保障和改善民生的一大批重大项目建设取得新进展。五是社会事业全面进步。坚持把保障和改善民生作为经济发展的首要任务，关系民生的一大批建设项目明显加快。六是价格监管措施有力。充分发挥价格调控、监管、监测和成本监审服务职能，价格管理和执法检查工作取得明显成效。

2010年，全委干部职工始终发扬优良传统，进一步弘扬敬业、奉献、求实、自律的良好风气，领导干部以身作则、率先垂范，机关的凝聚力、战斗力、创新力进一步增强，为促进经济快速发展做出了积极贡献。连续四年被评为喀什地区先进单位。

地区发改系统到叶河中游渠首调研

慰问老干部

慰问驻地官兵

喀什南部中心城市 莎车县

中共喀什地委委员、莎车县委书记何利民调研面粉加工企业工作

县委副书记、县长艾海提沙依提指导巴旦姆夏季修剪工作

莎车县十二木卡姆故乡园

莎车县位于新疆西南边陲，昆仑山北麓，帕米尔高原南缘，塔克拉玛干大沙漠和布古里沙漠之间的叶尔羌河冲积扇平原中上游。总面积8955.65平方公里，是一个以农业为主的人口大县，也是国家级扶贫开发工作重点县。全县耕地面积11.53万公顷，辖29个乡镇、491个行政村、25个社区，有维吾尔、汉、塔吉克、回、乌孜别克、柯尔克孜等二十多个民族，总人口80.41万，农村人口68.5万，少数民族人口约占总人口的96.3%。

莎车距今已有3000多年的历史，是古"丝绸之路"的要冲，军事驻守重地，东西方文明荟萃之地，人类口头和非物质文化遗产——十二木卡姆的故乡。莎车县农副土特产、矿藏、旅游资源丰富，是巴旦姆之乡，是"叶尔羌"牌优质棉生产基地，有被列为国家重点文物保护单位的叶尔羌汗国王陵等众多文物保护遗址。

近年来，莎车县通过大力实施人才强县和打造喀什南部中心城市战略，推动了县域经济社会快速发展。2010年，实现生产总值40.72亿元，比上年增长9.6%。固定资产投资24.9亿元，增长20.8%。地方财政一般预算收入1.76亿元，增长20.7%。社会消费品零售总额7.32亿元，增长7.6%。农民人均纯收入3426元。

"十二五"期间，莎车县委、县人民政府将紧紧围绕"稳疆兴疆、富民固边"的总体战略，按照"一轴三带"、"三区三园"、"九大基地"(清真食品加工基地、棉花生产加工基地、果蔬生产加工基地、肉类生产加工基地、冶炼化工基地、建材工业基地、商贸物流基地、组装加工基地、南疆乃至全疆旅游胜地)产业布局，抢抓上海市对口援建的历史机遇，紧扣跨越式发展和长治久安两大主题，主动融入喀什经济大开发，以现代文化为引领，以科技、教育为支撑，继续加快喀什南部中心城市建设，加速新型工业化、农业现代化、新型城镇化进程，深入实施"农业稳县、工业强县、商贸富县、旅游活县、科教兴县、文化塑县"战略，坚定不移加快发展"世界少有、中国唯一"的巴旦姆产业，力争到2015年，全县生产总值达到136亿元，比2010年翻一番半，年均增长24.42%，其中：一产54亿元、二产50亿元、三产32亿元。工业增加值30亿元，年均增长40.15%；地方财政一般预算收入5.31亿元，年均增长25%；全社会固定资产投资92亿元，年均增长30%；进出口总额1.43亿美元，年均增长32.8%；农民人均纯收入达到6000元以上。

巴旦姆丰产园

设施农业

恒昌冶炼有限公司

职业技术学校

疆南农副产品批发市场

阿勒屯历史文化广场

五载风雨拼搏　今朝春华秋实

伽师县开拓创新谋发展

县委书记　朱雪冰

今天的伽师，正处于两个五年规划的交替点："十一五"规划胜利完成，"十二五"规划即将展开；正处于重要战略机遇期的关节点：西部大开发、援疆大旗已全面拉开，借助外力，增强自我发展能力，向"十二五"目标阔步前进。

5 年来，伽师县坚定不移地实施优势资源转换和大企业大集团战略，紧抓广东佛山援建机遇，深入实施"工业强县"战略，工业经济增势强劲。

伽师县以自治区级工业园区为平台，加大园区水、电、路、气、通讯和污水处理等基础设施配套建设，园区承载能力不断提升，目前入园企业达 34 家，大企业、大集团达 5 家，其中上市公司 3 家，并申报国家经济技术开发区。

新型工业化进程，促进了县域经济发展。从 2005 年到 2010 年，生产总值从 11.16 亿元增加到 31.09 亿元，五年平均增长 22.7%，人均生产总值从 3374 元增加到 8295 元，年均增长 19.7%。国民经济三次产业结构由 65.8：8.2：26 调整为 51：26：23；二产增加值从 0.91 亿元增加到 8.12 亿元，年均增长 54.9%，其中实现工业增加值 4.9 亿元，年均增长 86%；地方财政一般性预算收入从 0.17 亿元增加到 1.2 亿元，年均增长 47.8%。

县长尼亚孜·阿西木接受新疆电视台采访

伽师县领导挑选伽师瓜发往内地

佛山市政协调研组一行 10 人赴伽师考察调研，伽师县委书记朱雪冰在伽师县鑫慧铜业有限公司生产出的第一块铜锭前介绍伽师县经济产业发展情况。

中国·新疆首届伽师瓜文化旅游节开幕式

广东支援伽师项目援建启动

金果玉叶 铜铁之城

XINJIANGYECHENG

县委书记　李国平

县长　司马义·阿不都色力木

石榴园喜获丰收

叶城县位于新疆维吾尔自治区西南部，距首府乌鲁木齐1700多公里，地处两区三地（两区：新疆、西藏；三地：阿里、和田、喀什）交汇处，是通往喀什、和田、西藏阿里的交通要冲。全县国土总面积3万余平方公里，耕地面积7.53万公顷。县辖20个乡镇、5个农林牧场、1个管理区，户籍人口44.56万人。叶城是一个以农业为主、农牧结合的农业县、边境县，有着得天独厚的水土、光热等自然资源，是南疆地区最大的绿色和无公害蔬菜生产销售基地，薄皮核桃、大籽石榴、黑叶杏等果品享誉疆内外。铁、铜、铅锌、玉石、煤炭、石油、天然气、金、大理石、皂石、垤石、石英石、花岗岩、滑石、冰洲石、石墨等矿产资源，储量丰富。

2010年，全年完成地方生产总值32.29亿元(其中一产16.57亿元，二产6.44亿元，三产9.28亿元)，较2005年翻了一番半，年均增长25.2%。全社会固定资产投资完成21.39亿元。地方财政一般性预算收入达到1.61亿元，比2005年翻了近两番。

现代农业蓬勃发展。一是粮食种植总面积83.28万亩，总产39.72万吨，种植棉花0.67万公顷，总产9300吨；设施农业年产各类瓜菜35.59万吨，总产值达1.25亿元，形成了以粮、棉、瓜菜为主的种植生产体系。二是林果总面积5.63万公顷，结果面积4.56万公顷，林果总产量19.73万吨(仅核桃产量就达5.57万吨)，产值9.99亿元，以核桃、杏、石榴为支撑的特色林果产业初步形成。三是年末牲畜存栏119.65万头(只)、出栏90.29万头(只)，出栏家禽1139万只，实现肉产量4.95万吨、奶产量3.19万吨、蛋产量4780吨；实现畜牧业总收入9.08亿元，比上年增长11.44%。四是转移农村富余劳动力7.31万人(次)，比上年增长2.96%，实现劳务创收1.87亿元，增长12.65%。五是外向型农业成效显著。全县获得认证的有机农产品种植面积达24万亩，无公害农产品种植面积0.39万公顷，落实订单农业0.67万公顷以上，签订各类订单20余份，价值近1.5亿元。2010年，全县共销售各类农产品69.25万吨，实现销售金额25.63亿元，分别增长14%和15%。

对口支援工作进展顺利。制定了《叶城县对口支援总体方案》和《专项方案》。积极做好援疆干部各项服务和保障工作，新建的援疆干部(人才)楼正在建设中。"十二五"期间上海市确定援建项目共六类39个，援助资金为21.43亿元。2011年纳入对口援助建设项目共13个，援助资金3.81亿元。维吾尔医医院、富民安居工程、工业园区标准厂房和设施农业育苗中心等4个试点项目全部开工建设，进展顺利。

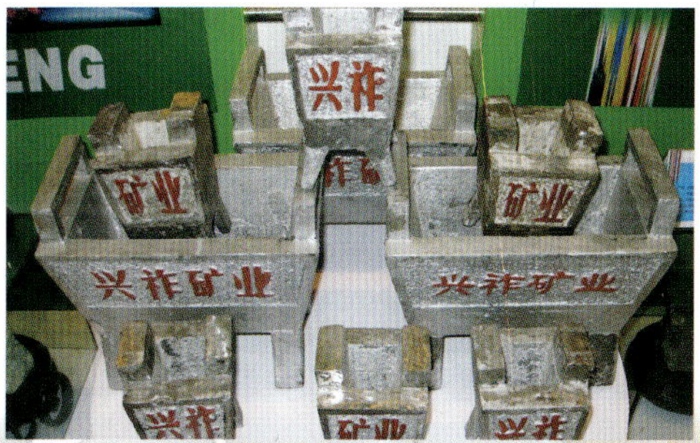

叶城县兴祚矿业有限责任公司生产的铁锭

薄皮核桃

玉石雕刻件

伽师瓜产业成为富民强县的支柱产业。通过良种繁育、提纯复壮和建立质量安全追溯体系，伽师瓜产业形成了规模化生产、产业化经营、区域化种植、科学化管理的生产模式和经营格局，确保每年种植伽师瓜 1 万公顷，其中标准化生产 0.13 万公顷，总产达 38 万吨，并成功打入北京奥运会、广州亚运会。

林果总面积达 4.33 万公顷，人均 2 亩林，林果业效益显现。加大直播、嫁接、补植力度，加强水肥管理和病虫害防治，加快发展以红枣、西梅为主的特色林果业，红枣总面积达 2.33 万公顷，实现人均一亩枣园；西梅总面积 0.67 万公顷，建成精品示范园 0.23 万公顷。

设施农业实现提质增效。县育苗中心实现集中育苗、统一配送，县财政年年补贴资金，用于自动卷帘机、棚膜、棉被等配套设施建设，大棚种植率明显提高，种植春提早、秋延迟和越冬茬蔬菜 19602 座次，实现均衡上市。

畜牧业稳步发展，牲畜存栏达 100.5 万头只，出栏 90.5 万头只，家禽出栏 870 万只羽。新建畜禽养殖小区 22 个，家禽规模化、标准化、专业小区养殖呈现良好发展势头，实现重大动物疫情零发生。

以伽师瓜、林果业、设施农业、畜牧业及劳务输出“五大产业”为主体的现代农业体系，拓宽了农民增收途径，农民人均纯收入由 2005 年的 1710 元增加到 2010 年的 3910 元，全县 15520 户 77600 人摆脱了贫困。

5 年来，该县以更加明确的“民生”指向，导引社会领域的创新举措，赢得了社会建设的各项突破，全社会固定资产投资从 2005 年的 2.25 亿元增加到 2010 年的 21.08 亿元，年均增长 56.43%。

“十二五”期间，该县将围绕建设“富民幸福和谐”美好伽师的目标，全面推进经济建设、文化建设、社会建设和生态文明建设，在 2010 年的基础上，实现“三个翻番”：生产总值翻两番，使经济社会得到又好又快全面发展，基础设施和基础产业建设取得突破性进展，具有竞争优势的特色经济和特色产业基本形成；城乡居民收入翻一番，使城乡居民生活水平和质量明显提高，实现城乡统筹协调发展，基本公共服务水平接近或达到西部平均水平；地方财政一般预算收入翻两番。自我发展能力明显提高，民族团结明显加强，社会稳定明显巩固，基本公共服务水平接近自治区平均水平。

为此，该县将以党的十七届五中全会、中央新疆工作座谈会、自治区七届九次全委（扩大）会议和喀什地委（扩大）会议精神为指导，以先进文化为引领，以科技、教育为支撑，以提高各族人民福祉和幸福感为目标，继续向既定的目标而奋斗——打造“四大示范园区”：加快城市生活、新城镇建设、现代农业和新型工业四大示范园区。

实施“六大战略”：大力实施工业强县、瓜枣富民、商贸活县、城建带县、科教兴县、文化塑县六大战略。

建设“六大基地”：建设铜业、棉纺、农副产品精深加工、机电机械组装加工、小商品小五金小家电出口加工、新型建材六大基地。

打造“瓜乡铜城”，把伽师建设成为南疆的优势资源转换重要基地；

实现安居富民兴县，率先推进大喀什现代产业体系；

将伽师建成喀什、广东（佛山）经济园区产业转移的分园；

把伽师打造成喀什旅游“后花园”。

“两基”国检组在伽师检查验收“两基”工作

伽师县双语小学民汉教职工相互拥抱在一起

《中国 1978–2008》摄制组专程赴伽师县拍摄双语教育

广东佛山援疆伽师三个试点项目全部交付使用

名扬中外的伽师瓜

全国人大副委员长司马义·铁力瓦尔地(左三)视察阿图什市保障性住房

自治区党委书记张春贤书记视察哈拉峻乡双语幼儿园

快速发展的阿图什市

克州党委副书记、阿图什市委书记　刘军海

市长　库尔班江·艾山

南疆果蔬批发市场奠基仪式

沈阳援疆工作队捐资助学

阿图什市位于新疆维吾尔自治区西南部,天山南麓,塔里木盆地西缘,西与吉尔吉斯坦共和国交界,边境线长 120 多公里。市境东西长 241 公里,南北宽 136 公里,全市总面积约 1.55 万平方公里。市区规划面积 9.6 平方公里,现建成面积 8.3 平方公里。

阿图什市于 1986 年经国务院批准撤县设市,辖 7 乡 2 个街道办事处,是克孜勒苏柯尔克孜自治州的首府,为全州政治、经济、文化中心。全市总人口 24.45 万人,有维吾尔、柯尔克孜、汉等 11 个常住民族。其中维吾尔族 19.31 万人,占 78.99%;柯尔克孜族 2.86 万人,占 11.71%,汉族 2.20 万人,占 9.0%。

阿图什成矿条件好,矿藏资源十分丰富,已探明钒、钛、铜、锰、铁、铅、锌、磷、大理石、石灰石、冰洲石等 32 种矿产。已经探明的有皮羌钒钛磁铁矿、霍什布拉克铅锌矿、奇吉尔布拉克铜锌矿、艾西曼铜矿、塞斯布拉克金矿 5 大金属矿,此外还有皮羌含磷砂矿、销尔库勒与吐孜苏盖提湖盐矿、峡口石灰岩矿和皮羌大理石矿 4 大非金属矿。野生动植物分布区广,种类繁多,共有 60 余种列入国家重点保护,有棕熊、仙鹤、猞俐、雪豹、长尾雉、天鹅、青羊、盘羊等十多种动物。还有党参、掌参、独活、阿魏、野红花等珍贵的药用植物。

境内旅游资源丰富,人文景观独具特色,阿图什市辖区内有阿图什大峡谷、摩尔佛塔、哈拉峻巴格苏盖提古柳林、哈拉峻乡盐湖、阿图什天门、赛福鼎·艾则孜故居等等。2010 年,预计完成地区生产总值 17.2 亿元,比 2005 年增长 54.23%,年均增长 9.1%;完成固定资产投资 36.74 亿元,比 2005 年增长 175%,年均增长 22.4%;地方财政收入首次突破亿元大关,达到 1.06 亿元,比 2005 年增长 125.7%,年均增长 17.69%。其中:一般预算收入达到 9961 万元,比 2005 年增长 178.01 %,年均增长 22.69%;招商引资累计到位资金 21.35 亿元, 比 2005 年增长 312%, 年均增长 51%; 农牧民人均纯收入达到 2096 元,比 2005 年增长 25.3%,年均增长 4.6%。

阿图什市是一片希望的热土,是一块尚待开发的宝地。随着西部大开发战略的全面实施和第三条亚欧大陆桥的即将开通,阿图什市以得天独厚的口岸、资源优势日益显示出广阔的发展前景。市委、市人民政府将以最优惠的政策、最优质的服务、最宽松的环境,热忱欢迎国内外各界有识之士来阿图什市大展宏图,创立伟业,共同开发、建设阿图什市。

金奖木纳格葡萄

阿图什市大峡谷景区

在前进中腾飞的乌什县

县委书记　申海涛

县长　吐尔洪·阿不拉

乌什县位于塔里木盆地西北边缘的天山南麓，总面积9082平方公里，边境线长153公里。全县辖八乡一镇、107个行政村，总人口20.8万人，其中农业人口17.26万人。县内居住有维吾尔、汉、回、柯尔克孜等19个民族，其中维吾尔族占94.1%，汉族占5.9%，是全疆32个少数民族边境县之一。

“十一五”期间，县委、政府按照“特色农业和劳务输出富民、矿业开发强县、生态旅游及口岸开发兴边”总体思路，明确目标、抓住关键、重点突破，努力走出了一条符合乌什县实际的发展道路。2010年，全县完成地方生产总值12.47亿元，比2005年翻一番，年均增长14.9%，三次产业结构由“十五”末的49∶9∶42调整为41∶11∶48；财政一般预算收入达到4106万元，年均增长28.3%；全社会固定资产投资五年累计完成17.8亿元，年均增长26%；社会消费品零售总额0.99亿元，年均增长6.3%。农牧民人均纯收入3501.1元，年均增长14.4%；城镇居民可支配收入10415元，年均增长18%。核桃面积达到1.67万公顷，粮食种植面积2.13万公顷，产肉1.4万吨。五年累计签约招商引资项目30个，落实到位资金4.5亿元，促成了铅、锌、磷、钒、金等一批矿产开发项目落地投产；有序推动了秋格尔渠梯级电站、大小石峡电站、亚曼苏电站和乌依布拉克电站的开发利用；依托优质特色农产品优势，发展番茄、核桃、杏、沙棘、鹰嘴豆等农产品深加工，促使全县产业结构更加优化、经济实力显著增强、人民生活不断改善，各项社会事业蓬勃发展。

在今后的工作中，乌什县委、政府将紧紧抓住中央加大支持力度和浙江省衢州市对口支援的历史机遇，围绕“2020年全面实现建设小康社会”这个总目标，大力实施“优势资源转换和新型工业化”两大战略，加快发展“矿业、水电开发和农副产品加工”三大主导产业，积极培育“旅游、物流、商贸流通”三大新兴服务业，力争在农牧业现代化、新型工业化、新型城镇化建设方面实现重大突破，为2020年与全国同步实现全面小康社会目标奠定坚实基础。

核桃

杏子

丰收的番茄

乌什全景

国投公司援建的国庆中学办公楼

洛浦县加快科学发展步伐

洛浦县位于塔里木盆地南缘，喀喇昆仑山北麓，东接策勒县，南接和田县，西与和田市、和田县、墨玉县相邻，北入塔克拉玛干沙漠与阿拉尔市、阿瓦提县接壤。县人民政府驻地洛浦镇，全县总面积 14272.6 平方公里，其中山地占 10.4 %，绿洲占 5.6 %，沙漠占 84 %，耕地面积 2.25 万公顷。现辖 1 镇 8 乡，一个街道办事处，207 个村委会，8 个社区，全县 62097 户、总人口 235785 人，有维吾尔、汉、回、满、哈萨克、蒙古、锡伯、藏族、羌族、瑶族、彝族、土家族等 12 个民族，其中维吾尔族占 98%。

2010 年洛浦县委、县人民政府在中央、自治区党委、人民政府和地委、行署的坚强正确领导下，在全县各族干部群众的共同努力下，以科学发展观为统领，认真贯彻落实中央新疆工作座谈会和自治区党委七届九次、十次全委、地委(扩大)会议精神，解放思想，凝聚力量，抢抓机遇，扎实工作，综合经济实力迈上新台阶，发展质量进一步提升，民生得到持续改善，各项社会事业全面进步。

2010 年，全县实现生产总值 10.98 亿元，按不变价计算，比上年增长 8.0%。其中，第一产业增加值 3.92 亿元，增长 2.1%；第二产业增加值 1.55 亿元，下降 0.1%；第三产业增加值 5.5 亿元，增长 11.5%。三次产业比例为 35.76：14.15：50.09.人均生产总值 4656.78 元。固定资产投资 7.0 亿元，增长 24.21%。财政一般预算收入 4685 万元，增长 15.62%。农牧民人均纯收入 3118.25 元，增长 16.44%。年末畜牧存栏头数 50.10 万头(只)，增长 2.06%. 社会消费品零售总额 1.25 亿元，同比增长 21.38%。

自治区党委书记张春贤在洛浦县农户家座谈

县委书记　杨渭锋

县委副书记、县长　阿力甫·阿不都力米提

设施农业

特色养殖

皮山县

县委书记　何成钢

县长　艾斯喀尔·卡斯木

皮山县位于新疆维吾尔自治区的最南端，是一个以维吾尔族为主体，汉族、塔吉克族、柯尔克孜族等12个民族聚居的边境县，与印控克什米尔交界，是和田地区的西大门，距离首府乌鲁木齐1800公里。境内有全军最高的哨所——神仙湾哨卡(海拔5380米)。全县总面积3.98万平方公里，辖9个山区乡镇(三个边境乡镇)、7个平原乡镇、1个农业综合开发区和1个良种场、1个国营牧场。皮山县乡村非常分散，全县169个行政村分布在54块绿洲上。2010年底全县总人口23.83万人，少数民族占98.4%。

经济发展明显加快。2010年，全县生产总值达到10.52亿元(现价)，比上年增长13.7%。完成固定资产投资6.6亿元，增长0.2%。实现地方财政一般预算收入6803万元，增长62.4%。粮食播种面积27.4万亩，总产12.9万吨，增加0.3万吨。农牧民人均增收510元，农民人均纯收入突破3000元大关、达到3076元。招商引资项目共4个，总投资金额7800万元，实际到位资金5660万元，增长23.9%。

各项社会事业全面进步。县城公共服务和基础设施进一步完善，市政建设和管理水平进一步提高，人居环境进一步改善，生态和环境保护进一步加强，为可持续发展奠定了良好的基础。社会消费品零售总额达到9976.6万元，比上年增长12.3%；实现就业再就业1838人，城镇登记失业率控制在3.2%。社会保障水平进一步提高，全县有1.07万城镇居民和3.88万农村居民享受了最低生活保障政策，全县参加新型农牧区合作医疗的农牧民达18.4万人，参合率达98%；城镇居民参加医疗保险达22825人，参保率达90%。已建农村富民安居房43649户，约17.5万人入住新居。为城镇低保对象发放低保2084万元，为农村低保对象发放2640万元低保资金。2011年12月31日，皮山县三峡工业园区经自治区批准为自治区级工业园区，并依托新建的火车站启动了皮山县安徽省综合经济开发区和三峡工业园区(自治区级)的规划，目前已有20家企业入驻皮山。

核桃王

皮亚曼石榴

墙体大棚

党委书记　武琳琳

党委副书记、场长　王天昊

幸福城农场

唱响和谐文化艺术活动

丰收的喜悦

幸福城农场隶属于新疆塔里木农业综合开发股份有限公司，2004年9月成立。位于阿克苏市东南155公里处，距阿拉尔市26公里。全场耕地面积5478公顷，总人口6836人，职工2113人，离退休人员1224多人，农业单位9个，非农业单位4个，场领导5名，干部172人，党员367人，党支部14个。

2010年，全场种植棉花3478公顷，总产籽棉2246万公斤，平均单产448公斤，林果面积2133公顷，果品总产16000余吨。实现生产总值4.64亿元，职均收入8.9万元，实现利润1838万元。

近年来，在自治区、兵团、师党委正确领导下，坚持以十七届五中全会精神为指导，以科学发展观统领经济社会发展全局，大力调整产业结构，以农业产业化、新型工业化为抓手，以改善民生、促进农场文明和谐为核心，各项事业取得了骄人瞩目的成绩。2009年，幸福城农场荣获师市劳动模范先进集体、一连、九连被兵团授予文明生态小康连队，一连、十三连党支部被兵团授予"五个好"党支部；农场被兵团授予文明团场，被新疆维吾尔自治区授予劳动关系和谐企业，2010年，幸福城农场被兵团授予兵团新闻网先进通讯站，兵团"五五"普法先进单位、兵团法治单位、兵团工会系统"五五"普法先进单位，农场生产科被兵团授予《新疆农垦科技》发行工作先进集体等荣誉称号。

2011年农场将以推进小城镇建设为主题，以职工持续增收为核心，以推进农业产业化为主线，着力提升基地建设、科技支撑、加工转化、市场开拓等能力；依托农业资源，发展优势农产品加工业；做大养殖示范小区，带动畜牧养殖业的发展，提高畜牧业在产业结构中的比重；加强产业筛选和整合，以市场为导向，精选产业化项目，切实保障农产品质量和生态环境安全；大力发展以城镇商贸为龙头的第三产业；力争把幸福城农场逐步建设成城镇化示范区、现代农业的展示区。

农场红枣获得国家银奖

养殖业蓬勃发展

机械化采棉

政委　张世全

场长　艾尼瓦尔·依力牙孜

农十三师黄田农场

兵团农十三师黄田农场，位于哈密市以东二十公里，临近兰新铁路，连霍高速公路和312国道横穿团场中心，距离哈密飞机场10公里，团场地势平坦，交通十分便利。

黄田农场于1958年建场，总面积为650平方公里，现有耕地面积1867公顷，生态林1467公顷，园林面积2017公顷。团场总人口10458人。2001年，黄田农场被兵团列为38个城镇化建设团场之一，通过几年的建设，黄田镇建设已初具规模。2010年，黄田农场党委坚持以人为本，牢固树立科学发展发展观，把发展作为第一要务，进一步深化改革、强化管理，以农业产业结构调整为主，大力发展高效(节水)农业；以大办工业和实施大企业、大集团战略为主，大力发展团场工业；以小城镇建设和旅游开发为主，大力发展商贸流通和旅游业，全力促进黄田农场经济社会又好又快的发展。2010年，实现生产总值2.71亿元，比上年增长24%。其中:第一产业完成1.09亿元，增长14%;第二产业完成0.92亿元，增长36%;第三产业完成0.70亿元，增长21%;团场一、二、三产业比例为

城镇一角

40:34:26。人均生产总值达到了25880元。全场职均收入达到2.74万元,团场实现二三产业分红1502万元,实现利润807万元。

黄田农场以拥有八大石和庙尔沟两处旅游胜景而名冠西北,又以发现湘女巨石而名扬国内外,这里盛产的"木卡姆"品牌葡萄、红枣、核桃誉满全国。

黄田农场拥有丰富的矿产资源,有金、银、铜、铁、钼、花岗岩、石灰石等,还有丰富的旅游资源,热忱欢迎有识之士来黄田农场观光考察投资合作,互惠互利,共谋发展,共创伟业。

庙尔沟古烽火台

万亩红枣

庙尔沟春景

铁粉加工

庙尔沟夏景

支农产业

庙尔沟秋景

塔里木大学

教育部领导与我校和对口支援高校团队领导合影

省部共建重点实验室揭牌仪式

塔里木大学于1958年创建，是国务院学位委员会、教育部批准的首批具有学士学位授予权的本科院校，2003年获得硕士学位授予权，2004年5月更名为塔里木大学。

学校校园面积2570亩，校舍建筑面积40万平方米。现有10个学院，4个一级硕士学位点，19个二级专业硕士学位点，1个专业硕士学位点，40个本科专业。学校图书馆藏书112万册，另有电子图书17万种，各类期刊1500多种。11门省级精品课程，3个教育部特色专业建设点，5个省级重点学科、1个省级重点实验室、1个省部共建国家重点实验室培育基地，设有兵团南疆干部培训中心、生物技术研究开发中心、新疆南疆区域科技创新基地（平台）、塔里木陆地油气资源勘探研究院、非传统安全与边疆民族发展研究中心、西域文化研究所等研究机构。

学校专任教师640人（其中教授、副教授186人，具有硕士、博士学位的教师422人）。学校面向全国招生，现有各类学生12000多人。自建校以来，已为国家培养各类毕业生3万多名，毕业生一次性就业率连续九年排在自治区高校的前列。

学校进一步加强与国内外高校、科研院所在科学研究、人才培养等多方面的合作和学术交流，与国内外20多所高等院校和科研院所签订了合作办学协议。中央新疆工作座谈会的召开，学校被列为新疆重点支持的高校之一，教育部落实中央新疆工作座谈会精神，确定中国农业大学、浙江大学、华中农业大学、北京化工大学、东华大学等五所大学团队式对口支援塔里木大学。

在新的历史时期，按照“做塔里木文章、创区域性优势”的发展思路，立足南疆，面向兵团、服务新疆、辐射西部，努力把学校建设成为整体办学水平较高，优势学科处于国内先进水平，特色学科国际有影响的综合性大学。

2007年9月，学校在教育部本科教学水平评估中获得优秀等级。

海峡两岸西域文化交流学术研讨会

兵团红枣产业发展科技论坛在学校召开

新疆伊斯兰教经学院

院党委书记 吾甫尔·热西提

院党委书记吾甫尔·热西提从北京参加全国民族团结进步表彰大会归来

体育运动会

新疆伊斯兰教经学院是自治区唯一的一所宗教高等院校，培养较高级的年轻爱国宗教教职人员的伊斯兰高等学府，也是全国唯一用本地少数民族语言(维吾尔语)授课的伊斯兰教经学院。学院1987年6月建成，是自治区民委(宗教局)下辖的二级局事业单位。

学院占地总面积43亩、建筑总面积17800平方米，分教学区和家属区。学院图书馆现藏书3万余册，有汉文、维吾尔文、阿拉伯文、波斯文、英文、俄文、乌尔都文等语种，还有一些珍贵的阿拉伯文古兰经抄本。学院的每个建筑采用的建筑技术是新疆各族人民的建筑艺术风格的体现和伊斯兰教的象征。

通过培养教育，造就一支热爱祖国，坚持走社会主义道路，积极引导宗教与社会主义社会相适应，维护祖国统一和民族团结，具有较高文化水平和宗教学识(知识)，并能联系广大信教群众的年轻一代爱国宗教教职人员队伍。学院严格按照“三七开”的比例设置文化课和宗教课。文化课占30%，宗教课占70%。

建院以来，学院共开办本科班十四批，招收学生769名，有十一批毕业生安置在全疆各县(市)、乡、(镇)聚礼清真寺担任伊玛目、哈提甫，或从事伊斯兰教事务及教学、研究等工作。学院已有35名应届毕业生先后被派往埃及等国留学深造。

举办政策法规、宗教专业知识短训班、研讨班十余期，培训教育了区内有影响的在职中青年宗教教职人员707名。协助自治区民委(宗教局)和自治区伊协，对上万名朝觐人员进行了出国前的宗教专业知识培训，为提高朝觐人员的整体素质，确保顺利开展和完成有组织朝觐奠定了良好的基础。

根据自治区外办和自治区民委(宗教局)的安排，学院担任着经常对国外访问参观团和国内的学习参观团的接待任务。在接待中，根据来宾的不同情况，向来宾介绍学院工作中取得的成绩，宣传党的宗教信仰自由政策，突出了经学院这个自治区宗教工作宣传窗口的地位和作用。

2009年9月被授予国务院第五次全国民族团结进步模范集体荣誉称号；2004年以来，一直保持着“文明机关”荣誉称号；几年来先后被评为“天山区综合治理模范单位”、乌鲁木齐市“综合治理模范单位”、“计划生育目标管理达标优秀单位”、“花园式单位”、“绿化合格单位”等荣誉称号。

新疆幼儿师范学校

团结奋进的领导班子

新疆幼儿师范学校暨新疆特殊教育培训中心经自治区人民政府1985年批准筹建，1991年9月开始正式招收首届学生，是自治区唯一一所面向全疆招生，培养幼儿教育师资、学前"双语"师资以及特教师资的民汉合校的中等师范学校。同时是自治区幼儿园园长岗位培训、骨干教师培训、学前"双语"教师培训等基地。2009年成立的"新疆幼儿教师培训中心"在我校挂牌。

经过20年的努力发展，学校在校生规模由建校初的800名发展为目前4500余名，开设有学前教育和学前"双语"教育两个专业，共有初中起点三年制中专、五年一贯制大专和高中起点大专三种类型、五种办学模式。其中学前"双语"教育专业和活动设计课程分别为国家精品专业和精品课程。建校以来为社会输送各类合格幼教师资近20000名。

学校目前与新疆师范大学、北京海淀艺术职业学校、北京黄庄职业高中、青岛艺术学校、喀什师范学校、兵团民族师范学校等学校开展联合办学。2008年9月，学校在西安陆军学院乌鲁木齐边防干部训练大队和新疆人民武装学校设立了办学点。2010年，学校与天津师范大学结成对口支援单位。

学校现已经具备了优质的教育资源和完善的办学条件。20年来，学校在教学与科研方面取得了丰硕果实，参编各类正式出版发行书籍和教材18套，自编校内用教材6套，学校开展国家级、省级科研课题研究8项。校体操队、舞蹈队、女子合唱团在全国和省级的各类比赛中频频获得各类奖项，女子合唱团曾经在两届世界合唱比赛中荣获银奖。

学校为自治区级文明单位，2007年荣获全国教育系统先进单位称号。

四海多风雅 九州竞芬芳

巴音郭楞蒙古自治州第二中学

教育部领导袁贵仁(前排中)一行来校视察

重新布局校园后建设的新校门

甘霖,阳光;滋养,灵动。公元20世纪中叶,深睡中的西部荒原醒了过来。

自此,塔克拉玛干大漠北沿生长了绿洲城市,生长了绿洲城市学校。其间,巴音郭楞蒙古自治州首府库尔勒市巴音东路37号门牌的巴州二中,也一步步生长,壮大。

献力学校生长壮大的一代代巴州二中学人,能不自豪?能不把汗血泼洒?学校成立办学至今,老师们汗血“接力”,已传递半百春秋。

栉风沐雨,桃硕李丰。巴州二中铸成新疆名校。

建校以来,学校培养经世致用人才46届,为高等院校输送合格新生10300人。高考优秀生中,排名巴州“前十”有101人,排名新疆“前十”有12人。考入北京大学、清华大学、中国人民大学、中国科学技术大学、复旦大学等“985工程”“211工程”高校2127人。

名苑出嘉木,栋梁撑华堂。巴州各行各业、新疆科技教育等系统,直至中央国家机关都有巴州二中学子的担当。学子们无不彰示着源自母校的精魂,用爱、用智慧、用创新书写淳朴动人的、向善发展的瑰丽人生。

耕耘,流淌着给予,流淌着期盼,流淌着成就。

芽,抖动露珠。茎,牵住阳光。叶子,跳跃出团团葱笼。花卉,争先恐后,尽呈姹紫嫣红……

巴州二中学人,经春夏、历秋冬。寒暑易节,一轮轮地犁耙,一茬茬地浇灌。播了收,收了播,种子增多,而且呈几何级数地增多。

带着巴州二中的风猷气调,无数种子撒天山南北,落华夏各地,漂向五洲四海。

这风气还在加浓。20世纪70年代,巴州二中先后有6名毕业生留学美国、德国。随后迄今,分布于亚洲、欧洲、美洲、大洋洲的留学生已达189人。

桑梓寄意,海外传真。看,东京地铁、莱茵河畔、华尔街头、昆士兰黄金海岸,都活跃着巴州二中游子的身影……

高中毕业生留学美国、德国

校运会

艺术节

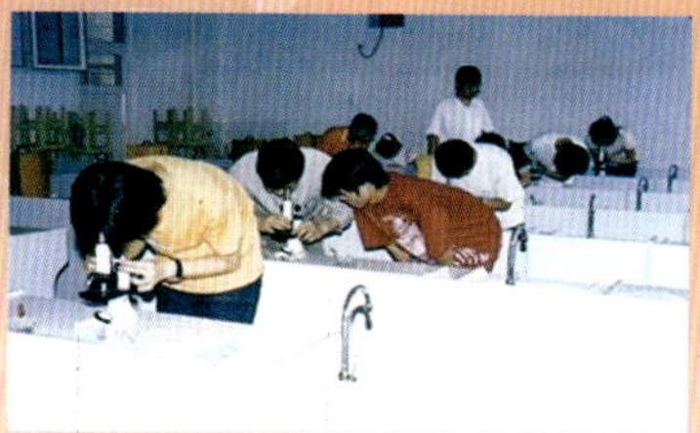

生物兴趣小组

校园一角

运动场

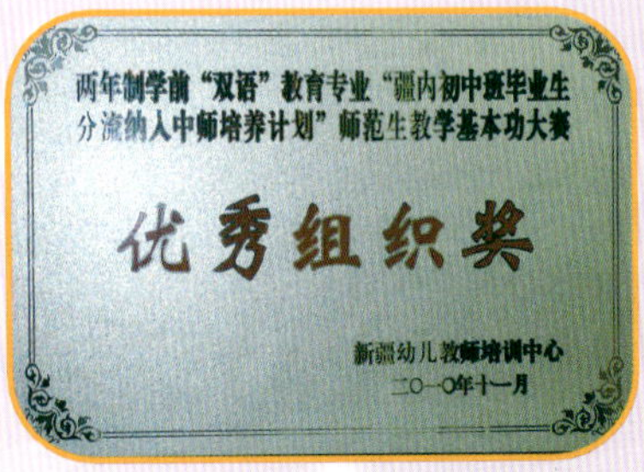

实习支教

实习支教

实习支教

校园的微笑

学生童话剧

阿克苏地区一中

校党委书记、副校长　曹尔慧

校党委副书记、校长　阿布都克热木·伊迪热斯

自治区副主席靳诺等自治区及地区领导来校视察工作

阿克苏地区第一中学建立于1944年，已具有67年的历史。是一所实施高中学历教育的自治区重点中学和自治区示范性高级中学之一。现有在职教职工192人，其中专任教师154人，教辅、总务、后勤30人，工勤8人。中学高级教师40名（含自治区特级教师2名），中学一级教师61名，中学二级及以下人员83名。现有教学班级53个，其中双语班24个，占教学班级总数的45.3%，普通班29个。在校学生数2740名，其中寄宿生1880名，占学生总数的68.6%，双语班学生1221名，占学生总数的44.56%。校园面积4.73公顷，校舍建筑面积27543平方米，具有450亩劳动教育技术基地。

阿克苏地区一中以加强民族团结、维护社会稳定大局为保证，坚持把德育工作放在全校工作的首要位置，培养学生成为德、智、体、美全面发展的“四有新人”，坚持把思想政治工作和德育工作贯穿在教育教学过程的始终，深入开展“热爱伟大祖国、建设美好家园”主题教育活动。明确维护祖国统一，维护民族团结，反对民族分裂和非法宗教活动的极端重要性，增强了有效抵制民族分裂和非法宗教活动的自觉性和坚定性。

阿克苏地区一中为继续办好人民满意教育，坚持“教书育人、管理育人、服务育人、环境育人”的办学理念，本着以双语教学为突破口，以理科教学为重点的教学思想，使整体教学水平有了明显的提高。尤其是把双语教学放在学校整体教学工作的中心位置，在原来的双语教学工作的基础上，不断进行探索，使双语教学工作有了新的进展，取得了较为突出的成绩。2010年高考录取率达到了92%，双语班上线率达到了98.8%；同时加强对教学常规的管理，加大对教师教学工作的检查力度，建立和完善教学管理制度，对教学工作中存在的问题进行针对性的分析和研究，加强对薄弱环节的管理和指导，不断提高学校的教学水平。

原地委书记朱昌杰、行署副专员李更生等地委、行署和地区教育局领导对学校工作进行调研

被自治区教育厅授予自治区级示范性高级中学称号

荣获全国教育系统先进集体称号

新疆博乐五师医院

五师医院地处新疆博乐市中心，是集医疗、教学、科研、预防、康复为一体的综合性二级甲等医院。医院占地46913.7平方米，建筑面积约35000平方米，其中：内科综合楼建筑面积11000多平方米，外科楼建筑面积9000多平方米，13000平方米的医技、住院综合楼2010年破土动工。医院设床位数320张，实际开放400张，在职人员420人，全院现有高级职称50人、中级职称150人。

五师医院下设临床科12个。外科系统有：普外、胸外、泌尿、颅脑、骨科、烧伤整形等专业；内科系统有：心血管、神经、消化、内分泌、肾脏、血液、呼吸等专业；还设有急诊、妇科、产科、五官、小儿、传染、肿瘤等专业科室。

2010年全年，五师医院门诊量20万人次、住院1万多人次。全院固定资产1亿多元。大型医疗设备有：飞利浦MX8000DUAL双层螺旋CT扫描仪，美国惠普240高尖端超声影像、德国狼牌wolf腹腔镜与前列腺电切镜、美国戴安XEP--1型膝关节镜、美国产血透机、意大利产CR等200台(件)医疗设备。

近年来，我院先后开展了人工关节置换、食管及贲门癌根治、脑胶质瘤切除、脑膜瘤摘除术、肝叶切除、晚期食道癌支架置入术、食道球囊扩张术、输卵管介入再通术、肝动脉栓塞术、腹腔镜下子宫摘除、腹腔镜下胆囊甲状腺叶切除和疝气修补术，镜下肺大泡切除、血液透析、阴式子宫切除、宫腔镜下的治疗、宫颈癌及子宫内膜癌根治术等，内科多专业在本地区处领先水平。

我院坚持科技兴院和以病人为中心的方针，始终树立"从严治院，以人为本，内引外联，知识更新"的发展思路，以一流的管理水平，高尚的医德医风，精湛的技术和先进的设备享誉博州，打造出了自己的品牌，创造了多项第一。我们真诚地欢迎各位同学来我院工作，施展才华。

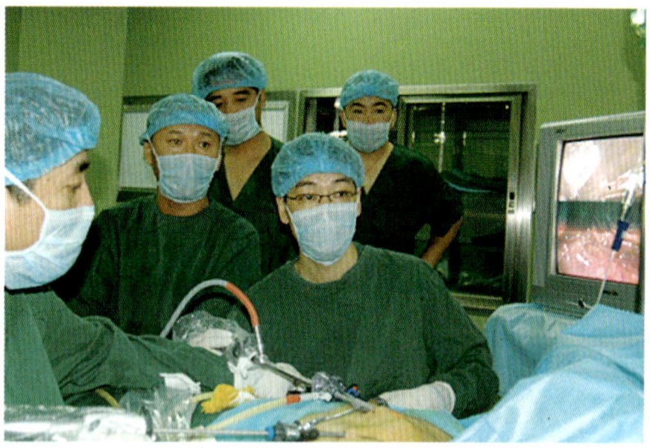
与上海医院视频手术

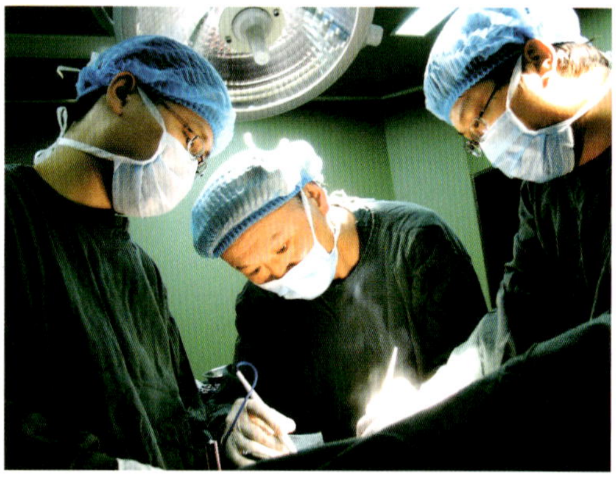
生命之光

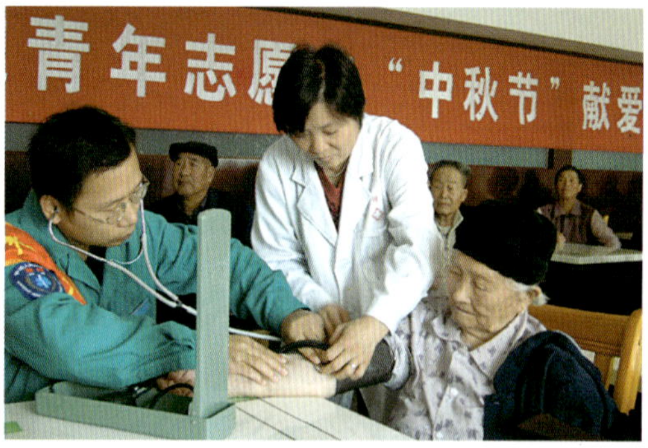

献爱心活动

运动会

舞蹈《塔塔尔舞》

中国石油独山子石化公司

独山子石化千万吨炼油百万吨乙烯

独山子是我国石油工业发祥地之一，是我国西部重要的石化基地，是我国西部油气引进、加工、储备的重要枢纽。

独山子石化具备1000万吨/年原油加工能力、122万吨/年乙烯生产能力和500万方原油储备能力。企业资产总额400亿元。73套炼化装置，可生产燃料油、聚烯烃、橡胶、芳烃等26大类600多种产品。2009年9月全面建成投产的西部大开发标志性工程、新中国成立60周年百项重大经典工程——独山子石化千万吨炼油百万吨乙烯连续安全稳定运行。2010年，公司加工原油873万吨，生产乙烯120万吨，销售收入超过500亿元，利税突破100亿元。

以指标领先为标志的核心竞争力全面提升。瞄准行业先进，深化对标管理，主要经济技术指标持续向好，炼油加工损失率、综合商品率保持股份公司领先，22万吨乙烯能耗一直名列全国第一。2010年29项主要指标，21项进入中国石油前三名，11项名列第一。

与石化基地匹配的运营模式初步确立。全面优化制度流程，内控体系有效覆盖，业绩考核约束有度。巡检值班、岗位责任制不断强化。深化班组核算，成本费用有效控制。杜邦理念与HSE体系有机结合。采用联合车间模式，掌控国际规模装置，实现集中控制、集约管理。

实施人才开发战略。强化管理、科技、操作"三支队伍"建设，一批管理、技术和技能人才快速成长。公司1.3万多名员工中，61.5%为大专以上学历。有硕士158人，博士10人，两级专家和学科带头人91名，全国及省部级技术能手47人。

独山子石化两次获得"全国文明单位"、"全国五一劳动奖状"，四次获得"全国质量效益型企业"，是首批"国家环境友好企业"。

1000万吨常减压装置

员工精心操作

独山子石化百万吨乙烯裂解炉

中国银联新疆分公司

中国银联是经国务院同意，中国人民银行批准设立的中国银行卡联合组织，成立于2002年3月，总部设于上海。目前已拥有近400家境内外成员机构。

中国银联处于我国银行卡产业的核心和枢纽地位，对我国银行卡产业发展发挥着基础性作用，各银行通过银联跨行交易清算系统，实现了系统间的互联互通，使银行卡得以跨银行、跨地区和跨境使用。中国银联的成立标志着“规则联合制定、业务联合推广、市场联合拓展、秩序联合规范、风险联合防范”的产业发展新体制正式形成，标志着我国银行卡产业开始向集约化、规模化发展，进入了全面、快速发展的新阶段。中国已成为全球银行卡产业发展最快、最具潜力的国家之一。

2003年8月，中国银联正式推出了具有自主知识产权，符合统一业务规范和技术标准的高品质、国际化的自主品牌银行卡——银联卡。

在中国银联与各家商业银行共同努力下，我国银行卡的联网通用不断深化，日益普及。截至2010年末，我国累计发行银行卡24亿张，受理商户218万户、POS机333万台、ATM机26万台。银联卡受理网络延伸至境外104个国家和地区。按照跨行交易额计算，“银联”已成为全球第三大银行卡品牌。

围绕多元化用卡需求，中国银联大力推进各类基于银行卡的创新支付业务。人民群众不仅可以在ATM自动取款机、商户POS刷卡终端等使用银行卡，还可以通过网上银联、手机、固定电话、自助终端、数字电视机顶盒等各类新兴渠道实现公用事业缴费、机票、火车票和酒店预订、信用卡还款、自助转账等多种支付。在中国银联和商业银行等相关机构的共同努力下，一个范围更广、领域更多、渠道更丰富的银行卡受理环境正在快速形成。

中国银联新疆分公司是中国银联在新疆维吾尔自治区设立的分支机构，于2009年3月18日正式挂牌成立。主要职责是：负责新疆地区银行卡网络运营、业务规范及技术标准的落实，银行卡跨行通用及业务的联合发展，银行卡受理市场完善，银联卡推广普及，银联品牌维护，银行卡风险防范等工作，推动新疆银行卡产业的健康、快速发展。分公司总经理苏长雄，分公司内设三个部门：综合部（办公室）、市场部、业务技术部。

中国银联新疆分公司成立以来，认真履行卡组织职责，秉承支持地方经济建设、服务民生的理念，恪尽职守、诚挚服务，全力推动和促进新疆银行卡产业健康发展。在深化联网通用，规范银行卡受理市场，打造便民服务，支持农村金融服务，推广创新支付产品，促进消费等方面进行了不懈的努力和探索，使新疆银行卡产业在短短两年的时间内，市场化进程快速推进，发展水平迅速提高。

至2010年末，全区发行银行卡3400余万张，联网特约商户5.1万户，联网机具7万台；2010年全区银行卡跨行交易金额932亿元。

今后，中国银联新疆分公司将在自治区政府的领导和人民银行的科学指导下，联合产业各方，充分发挥卡组织职能作用，努力做好银行卡市场培育和规范，进一步加强银行卡安全防范，同时，通过运营世界领先的第二代银联清算系统，加快网上银联、金融IC卡、手机支付、ATM跨行转账、柜面通、“福农卡”等创新产品的推广应用，着力打造银联便民服务，推动自治区银行卡产业持续、健康、快速发展。

银联随行 世界随心

UnionPay, with you.

UnionPay 银联

总经理　苏长雄

中国银联新疆分公司正式成立

“同创品牌 共享成长”—2011 年新疆银行卡同业年会

鼓励岗位创先争优，积极推进收银员职业化进程——新疆地区第四届“银联杯”商业服务业收银员大赛

构建安全、便利的银行卡支付环境——“安全用卡、放心支付”宣传、“刷卡无障碍”优秀商户、街区、风景区(点)评选活动

全力打造银联便民服务——满足多元化支付需求，为各族群众提供更多的银行卡创新支付产品

不断提升银行卡服务水平——为各商业银行、收单机构开展银行卡业务培训

认真履行社会职责，积极投身慈善公益活动——“银联励志助学基金”资助新疆大学优秀贫困生

加快推动自治区银行卡产业发展——2010 年新疆银行卡受理市场竞赛先进单位

中国移动通信 CHINA MOBILE

移 动 信 息 专 家

做优秀企业公民　为和谐社会尽力

十一年，一路热血激荡，风雨前行。

十一年，一路披荆斩棘，高歌猛进。

十一年，新疆移动写下了由小到大、由弱及强的豪迈壮歌。

2010 年春节大年初一，自治区党委副书记、自治区主席努尔一行到新疆移动慰问

巍巍天山石、悠悠塔河水见证着她的成长，见证着他作为优秀企业公民走出的每一步。1999 年 8 月 16 日，新疆移动通信公司挂牌成立，他如初生婴儿蹒跚起步；5 年后的 2004 年 6 月，新疆与内蒙古、甘肃等 10 省区移动公司在香港注资上市，公司更名为中国移动新疆通信有限责任公司；2006 年 7 月再次更名为中国移动通信集团新疆有限公司；如今，作为新疆通信业的骨干企业，他用遍及天山南北的移动基站让“顺风耳”的梦想在每个角落实现；他用“兼济天下，善尽责任”诠释着“厚民之生”的郑重承诺。

新疆移动成立以来，以“立足新疆、服务新疆”的宗旨，秉承“做优秀企业公民”的理念，致力于消除“数字鸿沟”，积极配合地方经济发展规划，为构建和谐新疆开展了大量工作。历经十二年磨砺，新疆移动各项生产经营指标都有了大跨度的提高。公司网络容量、客户数、通信基站、光缆线路等均比公司成立之初增长 40 多倍以上，实现了持续稳定发展的良好态势。2009 年 1 月 8 日，新疆移动正式开通具有我国自主核心知识产权的第三代移动通信技术 TD-SCDMA 网络，标志着新疆正式进入丰富多彩的 3G 时代。

新疆移动积极服务于地方经济发展，大力推进政务信息化、企业信息化、农村信息化和行业信息化进程，重点开展了信息化扶贫、应急通信体系建设、信息服务产业链等信息工程，为自治区重点建设、旅游开发、石油开采、特色农业等事业提供优质的通信服务。在自治区重大活动和抗击各类自然灾害等突发事件中提供了可靠的通信保障。公司在教育、助残、扶贫、救灾等各个领域以自身的业务专长和可持续的公益参与，用一个“优秀企业公民”的爱心，为构建公平正义的和谐社会贡献着自己的力量。

展望未来，新疆移动将继往开来、不懈创新，继续围绕自治区跨越式发展和长治久安大局，以科学发展观为统领，以改革创新为动力，致力于通信行业建设，做优秀企业公民，积极承担社会责任，为创造和谐稳定的社会环境、促进国民经济持续发展和改善各族人民生活，为建设和谐社会做出更加积极的贡献。

不畏艰难险阻，大力开展通信建设

正德厚生　臻于至善

“MM 百万青年创业计划”，给广大青年一个实现创业梦想的舞台。

积极开展校企合作，为大学生提供实习就业平台。

参加自治区企业信息化年会的代表正在参观“无线克拉玛依”建设成果。

不断提升个人素质，将更加优质的服务提供给各族百姓。

扎实做好应急通信保障工作

叶城县棋盘乡民生桥落成剪彩仪式上，当地少数民族群众跳起了欢快的舞蹈。

电子渠道为各族客户提供了更加便捷的服务新方式。

WWW.10086.CN
客服热线 10086

新疆维吾尔自治区党委书记张春贤(中)在新兴新疆金特视察指导工作

河北省委书记张云川(左一)与新疆维吾尔自治区党委副书记、自治区主席努尔·白克力在新兴新疆金特视察指导工作

新疆金特钢铁股份有限公司

团强奋进的领导班子

新兴新疆金特钢铁股份有限公司前身是“新疆和静钢铁厂”(简称和钢),是国务院1969年国发电(69)43号文批准设立的三线军工项目,时称“7011工程”,该厂于1998年全面停产、2002年破产。2003年12月金特建材收购成立新疆金特和钢钢铁有限公司。2007年4月,新兴际华集团出资控股重组成立新兴新疆金特钢铁股份有限公司。

新兴新疆金特钢铁股份有限公司现有员工4500人,其中少数民族员工1260人(占总数的29%)。目前,主要生产工序包括矿山开采、选矿、烧结、球团、焦化、制氧、炼铁、炼钢、轧钢等。主要产品有低碳钢热轧圆盘条、热轧带肋钢筋、热轧光圆钢筋、冷轧带肋钢筋、盘螺等,在新疆各地州,北京、成都、重庆、兰州、拉萨等20多个疆内外城市建立销售网点,部分产品远销中亚市场。技术改造项目先后通过自治区经信委核准(新经贸技改函【2009】272号),整体环评也经自治区环保厅批准(新环评函【2009】30号),符合国家钢铁产业政策。相继通过了中国质量认证中心的评审认证以及钢筋产品许可证的评审认证,同时荣获“中国2009年质量守信企业”、“中国20家质量信得过产品”和“中国质量战略联盟单位”、“自治区符合标准信用产品标志”、“2009年新疆名牌产品” 以及 “团中央青年就业创业见习基地”、“新疆维吾尔自治区再就业示范基地”、“新疆银行业2008-2009年度信贷诚信企业客户”等荣誉称号。2010年被新兴际华集团表彰为“发展进步特别奖”、“企业文化建设先进单位”、被新疆自治区评为“跨越式发展最具成长力企业”。

自2007年4月,新兴际华集团重组金特钢铁以后,以将新兴新疆金特建成我国西部精品企业为目标,先后分两期累计投入32.8亿元进行大规模技术改造,使新兴新疆金特已具备年产150-180万吨钢的产能。为进一步加快推进新兴新疆金特改造升级,调整优化产品结构,增强市场竞争力,提高产品附加值,新兴际华集团将核心技术大口径热模法离心球墨铸管项目落户和静铁尔曼工业园区,20万吨铸管项目投产后,新兴新疆金特年产钢能力将达到200万吨。

2010年7月21日,新疆维吾尔自治区党委主要领导视察时,高度评价新兴新疆金特现场管理很有序,工艺流程比较合理,技术上比较先进;虽然主要设备都是国产的,但能生产出一流的产品;在节能减排方面也是非常突出的,主要指标也是很先进的,在老企业改造及“老三线”企业改造方面都是成功的典范。并明确要求新疆维吾尔自治区各部门把支持新兴际华集团作为一项任务,在政策、项目等方面给予倾斜扶持。要求新兴际华集团思想再解放一些,目标再远大一些。鼓励支持新兴际华集团依托巴州、和静县的铁矿资源和新疆煤炭资源优势,做大做强,为新疆经济建设做出更大贡献。

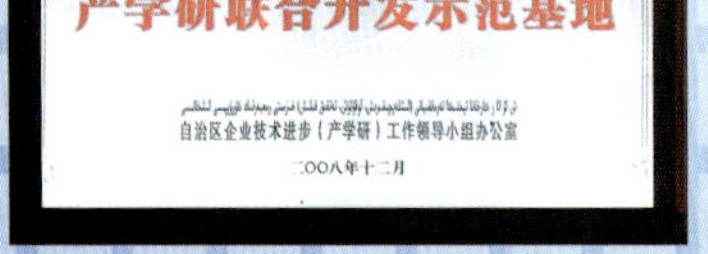

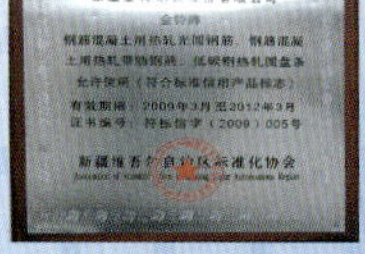

炼钢连铸

四机四流

炼铁高炉

轧钢高线

新疆大明矿业集团股份有限公司
XINJIANG DAMING MINING GROUP CO.,LTD

锐意进取 开拓创新 推动行业进步

董事长 许明

新疆大明矿业集团股份有限公司由许明先生始创立于1997年。公司主要从事铁、铜、锌、金等金属矿的开采、选冶及其产品的生产、加工、销售业务，注册资本15000万元。截止至2010年12月31日，公司员工总数为519人，总资产50144.99万元，净资产32594.64万元。

公司目前拥有一座国内较大的单体磁铁矿矿山，已探明矿石储量3200万吨，可开采年限53年。目前，公司已形成70万吨/年的铁矿石开采和35万吨/年的铁精粉生产能力，已跨入国内中型矿山企业之列。

在创业的历程中大明矿业始终秉承“企业存在的唯一理由是为客户创造价值和服务”的经营理念和价值观，牢固树立客户意识、目标意识、责任意识。成功开发以资源价值转化为评价依据的surpac技术软件与企业创建的ERP实施系统软件，实现了公司发展的战略转型，同时也得到了社会各界广泛的认同，获得自治区及中国管理科学研究院等单位授予的“安全生产先进单位”、“纳税先进企业”、“诚信纳税户”、“诚信企业”、“AAA”级诚信单位、“第一批两化融合示范单位”、“节水型企业”、“诚信中国示范单位”、“环境保护优秀企业”、“推动行业进步贡献企业”、“全国质量、服务、信用AAA级企业”、“中国优秀创新企业”等荣誉称号。董事长许明先生获得“时代楷模 共和国经济建设杰出贡献人物”、“2010年度影响力人物十大创新企业家”等荣誉称号，并于2010年获得美国国际领袖基金会(ILF)在白宫由赵小兰部长亲自颁发并授予“国际杰出领袖楷模奖”荣誉职称。同时成为安全标准化、信息化建设方面新疆行业的标杆企业；

大明矿业决策层以天湖铁矿的运营安全性、收益目的性为出发点，专注于技术能力的培育，近年公司在矿山生产组织模式，机械化、信息化的应用，采矿理论应用等方面进行了大量的投入，并且在地下矿山安全管理、矿山生产机械化信息化应用、采矿生产效率等方面已取得了重大的突破。对行业传统的理论认知与经验主义主导的地下矿山生产安全与效率现状进行了系统全面的变革，以“技术突破，引发地下矿山下一代效率、安全、投资革命的探索者”为使命的战略简述，建立全新的信息化条件下的生产运营模型，成功改变了安全生产保障、部门边界障碍、内部控制方法缺失、与资本市场语言不通、信息对称难等公司治理与发展的问题。

公司前台

视频会议室

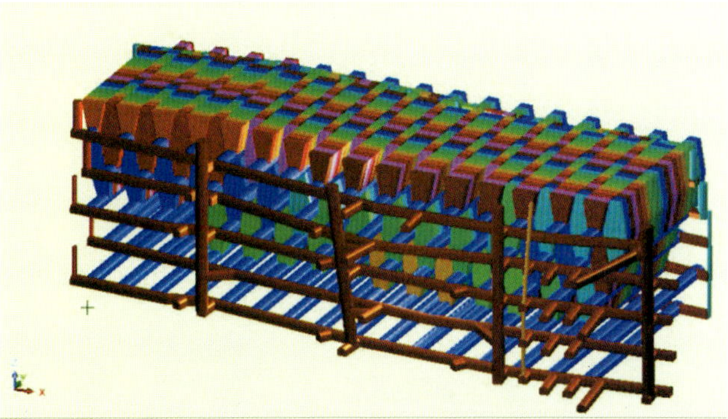

数字化矿山建设成果：利用采矿软件设计出的矿块开采顺序模型

数字模拟控制的 JKMD-3.5*4 (I)E 型 3.5 米多绳摩擦式深井开采提升机，使天湖的采掘触角深入到了 600 米以下的矿脉

XYWJD-1 型和 2 型电动铲运机作业现场

丰富多彩的职工生活

AT1500 型天井钻机作业现场

天湖铁矿主井

好家乡超市有限公司

国家工商总局党组书记、局长周伯华在好家乡视察食品安全工作

公司董事长许平陪同自治区副主席胡伟(左一)、自治区工商局党组书记王新怀(左二)在好家乡检查奶制品安全工作

“好家乡”创立于1998年8月,属民营商业零售企业,专业从事超级市场连锁经营。现设四川省好家乡商业有限公司、新疆好家乡超市有限公司和新疆地州连锁超级市场,年销售额已逾10亿元。“好家乡”商标是中国国家工商行政管理总局商标局注册商标。

好家乡始终本着“好日子,好家乡”的经营宗旨,凭着“诚实、专注、合作、进取、责任”的核心价值观,不断学习国内外先进的零售经营模式,创造了同行业中较好的经营业绩。

好家乡曾先后荣获“AAA级信用企业、纳税先进企业、国家定点重点商品价格调查单位、新疆知名商贸企业”等荣誉。同时,“好家乡”商标被评为“乌鲁木齐名牌商标”,“好家乡”被评为“新疆知名商贸品牌”。2004年9月26日,国务院总理温家宝来到好家乡,与员工、顾客亲切交流,了解超市经营和节日商品供需情况。2006年9月,国家工商行政管理总局党组书记、局长周伯华考察好家乡超市,对好家乡食品质量安全工作给予了充分的肯定。

好家乡十分重视经营管理的投入和人力资源的提升,引进美国JDA和IBM公司的商业软硬件系统提升信息管理技术;引进品类管理技术和商战模拟等全球领先的零售业经营技术提升经营管理水平;引进国际知名的品牌咨询公司和AC尼尔森公司进行品牌定位及形象设计。2009年起,品类管理在好家乡推行。

好家乡公司计划在未来的十年,全力打造一个更具专业化的零售业管理团队,吸引更专业的零售业人才,更高效地为消费者提供满意的商品和服务。力争2018年,实现年销售额100亿元的规模,成为西部领先的零售企业。

我们相信,在更多合作伙伴的支持下,在更多人的帮助下,好家乡一定能成为中国最具竞争力的零售企业,成为中国零售业的前三强。

新疆酱香型白酒的开创者

伊犁肖尔布拉克酒业有限责任公司

董事长王天兵陪同领导参观

总经理杨奕现场指导酱香型酿造工艺

伊犁肖尔布拉克酒业有限责任公司坐落于著名的新疆酒乡——伊犁新源县肖尔布拉克镇。公司占地面积300多亩，建筑面积18万平方米，有固定资产7800万元，流动资产4800万元，总资产达2亿元。公司现拥有两个白酒生产基地，年产优质白酒1万吨。在兰州、西安、杭州、天津等地设有销售公司，在全国多个省设有办事处，产品远销内地十多个省市，2001年通过“ISO9001国际质量体系”认证，2010年8月通过国家AAA级标准化管理体系认证。目前已初步形成了品牌价值达亿元的集白酒生产、销售、生态工业旅游为一体的集团公司。

从2003年起，肖尔布拉克酒业把生产开发“有机、绿色、生态、健康”的高端产品，作为企业的研究课题和发展方向。并于2004年引进贵州茅台酒酿造技术，投资上千万元，建成一座年产量200吨的酱香型白酒酿造车间。被中国酿酒工业协会白酒分会技术委员会认定为“新疆酱香第一坊”。产品经过五年的贮存，于2010年9月1日在乌洽会展出亮相，受到了社会各界的高度关注。肖尔布拉克酱香型白酒的成功研制，填补了新疆无酱香型白酒生产的历史空白。创造了新疆白酒工业史上第一个酿造酱香型白酒的企业，从此，新疆有了第一款能代表新疆酿酒新水平的高品质酱香型白酒。

企业在快速发展的过程中，对国家和社会做出了突出的贡献，历年来，累计向国家上缴利税3亿多元，出资数百万元用于扶贫帮教的社会公益事业，造福了一方百姓、繁荣了一方经济，成为伊犁地区拉动区域经济，带动相关产业发展，增加农牧民收入的龙头企业之一。面对激烈的市场竞争，肖尔布拉克酒业将立足酒业、开拓创新，抢抓机遇，为繁荣伊犁经济、新疆经济做出应有的贡献，把伊犁酒、新疆酒做强、做大。

庄严宏伟的西域酒文化博物馆

酒海坛林一角

古色斑斓的西域第一泉

精英俱乐部北方游

党支部活动

新疆维吾尔自治区社情民意调查中心

新疆维吾尔自治区社情民意调查中心是2006年由自治区人民政府批准成立的，区内唯一一家拥有“社情民意”调查研究资格的专业机构。

中心在新疆首次引进目前世界上广泛采用的先进的计算机辅助电话调查访问系统CATI，同时依托全区统计系统这个平台，凭借翔实权威的社会、经济统计信息资源，得天独厚的调查技术、调查网络和数据处理方法，先进的调查设备，优良的办公环境，专业的调查队伍，科学的研究方法，严谨的工作流程，丰富的调查经验，圆满完成了几十个项目的民意调查。得到了国家、自治区及有关部门的充分肯定和一致好评。

职能定位：承办国家统计局和自治区党委、政府及有关部门委托的社情民意调查任务，为管理和决策部门提供及时、准确、有效的社情民意信息；密切关注、及时反映人民群众对社会热点、难点和焦点问题以及突发事件的态度与看法，为社会公众与党和政府之间架设起沟通的桥梁，使来自人民群众的主流声音成为党和政府科学决策的依据；对社会公共服务部门服务质量和服务水平进行测评，对政风行风进行评议检查，反映人民群众对政府部门在公众中的形象和施政成效的评价与看法。

工作方针：团结、敬业、创新、发展八字方针。

工作目标：深入了解民情、充分反映民意；把准发展脉搏，架设沟通桥梁；提升服务水平，提供决策依据。

服务宗旨：让政府了解百姓，让百姓理解政府；让公众了解市场，让市场贴近公众。

服务理念：追求高效优质、关注细节创新、崇尚正直坦诚。

服务热线：12340是国家统计局社情民意调查中心于2008年9月向工业和信息化部申请的，可在全国范围内使用社情民意调查热线电话号码。它主要用于社情民意调查及咨询等服务，具体内容是开展社情民意调查，包括安全感、群众满意度、绩效评估、民主评议和行风调查等关系国计民生的诸多领域；接受社情民意调查咨询，为党政部门等利用现代科学调查方法了解本部门及社会民众意愿、需求等提供服务和支持；主动收集国家、社会和群众关心的社情民意信息，经科学分析，通过规范渠道及时报送相关管理和决策部门，为党和政府科学决策提供参考。

新起点，新征程，新疆维吾尔自治区社情民意调查中心将以服务党政领导为主线，以市场服务为辅线，围绕既定目标，以专业级的水准，学术般的严谨，全方位开展社情民意调查和市场调查工作，在百姓和政府之间、公众和市场之间架起一座沟通的桥梁，为在我区营造一个倾听百姓心声、自觉参与经济建设、全面构建和谐新疆的良好氛围而贡献力量！

地　　址：新疆·乌鲁木齐市解放北路339号
（酒花大厦13楼、21楼）
电　　话：0991-8878697 2844866 2843599
传　　真：0991-8874855
电子邮箱：zyx_xj@xj.stats.cn

全国人大副委员长热地授予董事长杨光玉荣誉证书

全国政协副主席阿不来提·阿不都热西提亲切与董事长杨光玉交谈

喀什冠维房地产开发有限公司

董事长　杨光玉

经过一年多的市场调研，2004 年 11 月份，通过乌洽会，重庆璧山鹏飞集团公司入驻喀什。成立了喀什冠维房地产开发有限公司（以下简称冠维公司），注册资金 2000 万元。

公司经过几年的经营和发展，至 2008 年底资产合计 9170 多万元，上缴国家税金由 2006 的几百万元陆续上升到千余万元。为喀什房地产业和当地的财政税收做出了积极的贡献，受到了当地政府领导的认可和好评。

冠维公司投资 8000 万在喀什市区最中心的位置建成了渝都大厦，总建筑面积近五万平方米，是喀什首座高档商住楼。位于喀什大十字五一剧院位置六万余平方米中南亚大厦，高 22 层，是喀什市区的一座标志性建筑。目前正在建设的疏勒县民俗风情街，街长 1.2 公里，总建筑面积达 15 万余平方米，生态游乐园建筑面积 24000 平方米，总投资高达 2 亿元。此项目是疏勒县政府大力支持的重点项目。

下一个阶段将在疏勒县开发打造"天泉国际旅游度假村"，总占地面积 180 多万平方米，总建筑面积达 41 万平方米，规划总投资 606 亿元。

冠维公司 2008 年荣获了"新疆电视台法制频道推荐诚信企业"的称号，2009 年至 2011 年连续被喀什市工商行政管理局评选为"守合同 重信用企业"，成为了喀什房地产业的领军企业，2011 年又被授予"中国最具社会责任民营企业家"，被中国经济研究科学院、中国商务部评选为"2011 中国 AAA 级诚信经营示范单位"。

疏勒县民俗风情街鸟瞰图

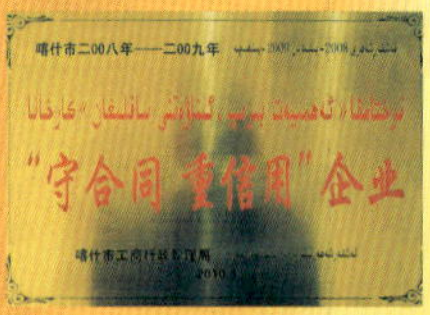

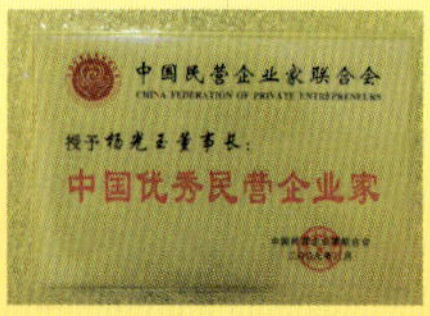

新疆
统计年鉴

XINJIANG
STATISTICAL YEARBOOK

2011

五彩城　　　黄永中 摄影